MW00339870

English Drama from *Everyman* to 1660: Performance and Print

Frederick Kiefer

ARIZONA CENTER FOR MEDIEVAL

ACMRS

AND RENAISSANCE STUDIES

Tempe, Arizona
2015

THE ARIZONA CENTER FOR

MEDIEVAL &
RENAISSANCE
STUDIES

Published by ACMRS (Arizona Center for Medieval and Renaissance Studies)
Tempe, Arizona
© 2015 Arizona Board of Regents for Arizona State University.
All Rights Reserved.

Library of Congress Cataloging-in-Publication Data

Kiefer, Frederick, 1945-
  English drama from Everyman to 1660 : performance and print / Frederick
Kiefer.
      pages cm. -- (Medieval and Renaissance texts and studies ; volume 447)
  Includes bibliographical references.
  ISBN 978-0-86698-494-2 (alk. paper)
1. English drama--Bibliography 2. English drama--Early modern and Eliza-
bethan, 1500-1600--Chronology. 3. English drama--17th century--
Chronology. 4. Theater--England--History--16th century--Chronology.
5. Theater--England--History--17th century--Chronology. 6. Renaissance--
England--Chronology. I. Title.
  Z2014.D7 K44
  [PR635.54]
  016.822--dc23

                                                                    2014026836

Front Cover:
Johann Wilhelm Baur, 146.i.10/9
© The British Library Board

∞

This book is made to last. It is set in Adobe Caslon Pro,
smyth-sewn and printed on acid-free paper to library specifications.
Printed in the United States of America

for

Michelle Morrison Kiefer

TABLE OF CONTENTS

ACKNOWLEDGMENTS

During the preparation of his book, I have often sought the advice of my colleague Carl T. Berkhout. With considerable generosity, he has placed at my disposal his knowledge of manuscripts and the history of printed books. His helpfulness has proved invaluable. I also wish to thank other friends who have assisted me at need, especially A. R. Braunmuller, Russ McDonald, and Stanley Stewart. And I want to acknowledge my late colleague Richard Hosley, who for many years served as a mentor and who first envisaged this project. Finally, I am grateful for the kindness of countless librarians, especially those at The Huntington Library, The Folger Shakespeare Library, The Bodleian Library, and The British Library.

INTRODUCTION

In 1661 the London publisher Francis Kirkman prefaced a new book with this remark: "I have been (as we term it) a gatherer of plays for some years, and I am confident I have more of several sorts than any man in England, book-seller or other." Diligent in tracking down extant plays, Kirkman reported, "I can at any time show 700 in number, which is within a small matter all that were ever printed,"[1] and he specified their titles. As it happens, there survive today, in the period from the middle of the sixteenth century to the closing of the theaters in 1642, approximately the number of plays collected by Kirkman. Since his time additional plays have been discovered in manuscript, but the number he gave has proved accurate over all.[2]

When Kirkman made his claim, offering the plays to buyers, the theaters of England had been closed for eighteen years, following the parliamentary order forbidding playing in 1642 and through the subsequent Civil War and Inter-regnum. He recognized a business opportunity, of course, a potential market for plays produced during the previous hundred years and more. What seems to have motivated him, however, was not only the desire for profit but also his sense that

---

[1] Francis Kirkman, stationer's address to the reader of *A Cure for a Cuckold* by John Webster, William Rowley, [and Thomas Heywood] (London, 1661), sig. A2r. "There is no good reason to doubt that in 1661 Kirkman possessed, or had possessed, copies of the sixteenth- and seventeenth-century English plays he lists, or that his catalogue of those that had reached print was very nearly comprehensive" (*The Works of John Webster*, ed. David Gunby, David Carnegie, and MacDonald P. Jackson [Cambridge: Cambridge University Press, 2003], 2: 388). At the end of *The Spanish Gypsy*, printed in 1661, Kirkman offers the reader a list of "all the playes that were ever yet printed" (sig. K2v). Kirkman appends his list to *Tom Tyler and His Wife* (1661). Kirkman attaches an enlarged list (806 titles) to his printing of Corneille's *Nicomède* in 1671; along with the plays he adds the titles of Ben Jonson's masques and entertainments. Of the lists published in the 1650s and 1660s, Kirkman's is considered the most reliable.

[2] According to Tiffany Stern, "Of the roughly 50350 printed books published between 1580 and 1660, about 700 are plays." See her "Re-patching the Play," in *From Script to Stage in Early Modern England*, ed. Peter Holland and Stephen Orgel (London and New York: Palgrave Macmillan, 2004), 151–77, here 153. Other such lists were prepared by Richard Rogers and William Ley in 1656, appended to Thomas Goffe's *The Careless Shepherdess*, and by Edward Archer in his edition of *The Old Law* (1656). In addition, Humphrey Moseley in 1656 listed 246 titles in an advertisement.

an era had vanished and that its plays were in danger of disappearing as well.[3] Unless they survived in printed form, the plays would be lost to posterity, no matter how successful they might once have been onstage. Hence Kirkman published some plays that had been printed in the previous century and were becoming extremely scarce and others that had never found their way into print at all.[4]

At the time Kirkman compiled his list, most actors of the Renaissance stage were dead as were most of the playwrights. Theaters that had provided venues for Shakespeare and Jonson, Marlowe and Webster, were long gone, and the playwrights' legacy was at risk. With the restoration of the monarchy in 1660, the theatrical scene was altogether different. A new generation of playwrights was active; playgoers had fresh expectations; staging practices had changed; and most of the theaters themselves were new as well.[5] The sense of one era having ended and another having begun was palpable, as evident not only in Kirkman's retrospective compilation but also in the similar lists of Richard Rogers and William Ley in 1656[6] and of Edward Archer the same year.[7] Whether we describe Shakespeare's time with the rubric "Renaissance" or "Early Modern,"

---

[3] Kirkman's prefaces to the books he published contain a wealth of material about his interests and work; they have been edited by Strickland Gibson, *A Bibliography of Francis Kirkman, with His Prefaces, Dedications, and Commendations (1652–80)*, Oxford Bibliographical Publications n.s. 1, fasc. 2 (Oxford: Oxford University Press, 1947).

[4] Kirkman published *Gammer Gurton's Needle* by Mr. S. and the anonymous *Tom Tyler and His Wife*, which had apparently been previously published; the title-page of the 1661 quarto of *Tom Tyler* says, "printed and acted about a hundred years ago." He also published *A Cure for a Cuckold, The Birth of Merlin*, and *The Thracian Wonder* (1661), which would otherwise have been lost.

[5] Martin Butler, in "The Conditions of the Theatres in 1642," in *The Cambridge History of British Theatre*, vol. 1: *Origins to 1660*, ed. Jane Milling and Peter Thomson (Cambridge: Cambridge University Press, 2004), 439–57, observes, "The arrival of actresses and the introduction of changeable scenery into the public theatres were only the most conspicuous signs that the plays that would be seen on the stages of 1660 would take forms radically different from those they had possessed before" (440).

[6] W. W. Greg, in *A Bibliography of the English Printed Drama to the Restoration*, 4 vols. (London: Oxford University Press for the Bibliographical Society, 1939–1959), points to the inadequacy of the Rogers and Ley list: "the titles seem to have been jotted down, perhaps from dictation, and sent to press with little or no revision" (3: 1321). According to S. Schoenbaum, the "Rogers and Ley list is a very casual performance, with authors cited for only a third of the plays." See his *Internal Evidence and Elizabethan Dramatic Authorship: An Essay in Literary History and Method* (Evanston, IL: Northwestern University Press, 1966), 157.

[7] Archer's list, as noted above, was appended to *The Old Law* (1656) by Thomas Middleton, William Rowley, and Thomas Heywood. David J. Lake, in *The Canon of Thomas Middleton's Plays* (Cambridge: Cambridge University Press, 1975), remarks that Archer's list is "not an authority entirely independent of Rogers and Ley, for it repeats some of the earlier list's more elementary errors" (29). Nevertheless, "Archer's catalogue

we share the feeling of Kirkman, Rogers and Ley, and Archer that English plays of the sixteenth and early seventeenth centuries represent a literary and theatrical resource of unmatched achievement.

Today students and scholars of the theater find it helpful to have at hand basic information about the plays collected by Kirkman. When were they first performed? What companies of actors staged the plays? In what theaters were the plays produced? When were they first published? To answer such questions, Alfred Harbage in 1940 published *Annals of English Drama, 975–1700*, revised by Samuel Schoenbaum in 1964 and revised again by Sylvia Stoler Wagonheim in 1989.[8] *Annals* remains so useful that virtually every scholar in the field either owns a copy or has ready access to one. Despite having first been published seventy years ago, Harbage's book, especially in its revised form, is still regularly cited by scholars needing to establish auspices of production. The compilation is, however, not without shortcomings, for it provides information only about each play's first production; evidence of further staging is missing. Also, *Annals* gives only the year of initial publication; any subsequent publishing history is a blank. To remedy some of these omissions, Yoshiko Kawachi in 1986 published her *Calendar of English Renaissance Drama, 1558–1642*, which seeks to record all performances from the accession of Queen Elizabeth to the closing of the theaters.[9] Despite its value Kawachi's work has its own limitations, for, as Harbage had done, she presents information in the form of year-by-year tables. In order to trace the stage history of a play, one needs to find the title in the index and then move through the tables year by year. To trace the performances of Marlowe's *Doctor Faustus*, for instance, one needs to search through the entries on no fewer than twenty pages, and the entries are not alphabetized by title. Although Kawachi does note multiple issues of a first edition, she, like Harbage, provides the year of publication only for that one edition.

In order to ensure easy access to the performance and printing history of the drama, information about each play needs to be presented in a single entry, and the entries need to appear not in difficult-to-use tables but alphabetically in paragraph form. Thus the organization of this book. It seeks to offer as full a stage history of each play as our knowledge allows, as well as a printing history. Chronologically the compilation begins with the morality play *Everyman*,

---

improves upon 'Rogers and Ley,' from which it derives. Archer finds authors for many more plays than did his predecessor" (Schoenbaum, *Internal Evidence*, 157).

  [8] Alfred Harbage, *Annals of English Drama, 975–1700* (Philadelphia: University of Pennsylvania Press, 1940); revised by S. Schoenbaum and published in London by Methuen, 1964; further revised by Sylvia Stoler Wagonheim and published in London and New York by Routledge, 1989. Anne Lancashire's review of the third edition, in *Shakespeare Quarterly* 42.2 (1991): 225–30, voices reservations about the revision.

  [9] Yoshiko Kawachi, *Calendar of English Renaissance Drama, 1558–1642* (New York: Garland, 1986).

generally considered the first printed play in English, and continues to 1660 rather than 1642. The reasons for extending the range covered by Kawachi are twofold.

First, we know that not all theatrical activity ceased with the closing of the theaters. Plays continued to be written and performed in the homes of the nobility; James Wright reports of Cromwell that "in Oliver's time, they [the actors] used to act privately, three or four miles, or more, out of town, now here, now there, sometimes in noblemens houses."[10] In addition, drolls, short adaptations of formerly popular plays, were staged in market squares and other venues, including fairs, halls, taverns, and "mountebancks stages at Charing Cross, Lincolns-Inn-Fields, and other places."[11] In his 1673 edition of these entertainments Kirkman defends their importance: "as meanly as you may now think of these drols, they were then acted by the best comedians then and now in being"; many were performed at the Red Bull, which had an exceptionally long history as a site for drama. By performing drolls, "acting companies reverted to their vagabond heritage,"[12] and the "pieces of plays," as Kirkman calls them, became critical to the livelihood of actors, whose profession had been essentially outlawed in 1642: "these small things were as profitable, and as great get-pennies to the actors as any of our late famed plays." Actors were further drawn to the drolls because they required only a minimum outlay for costumes and props: "they were the fittest for the actors to represent, there being little cost in cloaths, which often were in great danger to be seiz'd by the then souldiers,"[13] who raided theaters when they had news of a performance. Drolls, moreover, "could be readily performed

---

[10] James Wright, *Historia Histrionica: An Historical Account of the English Stage* (London, 1699), 5.

[11] The venues are named on the title-page of *2 The Wits, or, Sport upon Sport* (London, 1673). Neither Harbage nor Kawachi records the performance of these entertainments. The drolls included here are *The Black Man, Bottom the Weaver, The Bouncing Knight, The Bubble, Bumpkin, The Cheater Cheated, The Club Men, Diphilo and Granida, The Doctors of Dullhead College, An Equal Match, The Encounter, The False Heir, Forced Valor, The Gravemakers, Hobbinal, The Imperick, Invisible Smirk, Jenkin's Love-Course, John Swabber, King Ahasuerus, King Solomon's Wisdom, The Lame Commonwealth, The Landlady, The Loyal Citizens, Monsieur The French Dancing Master, Oenone, Philetis and Constantia, A Prince in Conceit, The Sexton, Simpleton, Singing Simpkin, The Stallion, The Surprise, The Testy Lord, The Three Merry Boys, Venus and Adonis,* and *Wiltshire Tom.*

[12] Gary Taylor, "Shakespeare Plays on Renaissance Stages," in *The Cambridge Companion to Shakespeare on Stage*, ed. Stanley Wells and Sarah Stanton (Cambridge: Cambridge University Press, 2002), 1–20, here 19.

[13] Kirkman's remarks, cited in this paragraph, are to be found in his preface to *2 The Wits* (London, 1673), sig. A2r and A3v.

by amateurs."[14] Finally, "the brevity of these pieces made them relatively easy to perform surreptitiously."[15]

Second, just before the closing of the theaters and during the eighteen years following the ban on playing, writers produced short plays on controversial topics of the day. Some of these fascinating works, in which the categories of genuine drama and political pamphlet overlap, may have been performed.[16] Janet Clare observes, "Many of the playlets show clear signs of having been conceived with performance in mind. The theatrical nature of the texts—notably in their detailed, often comic or farcical, stage directions, visual comedy and some quick-fire dialogue—makes it very probable that they were designed for impromptu acting."[17] Kirkman's language describing the shenanigans of Parliamentary leaders points to a conflation of the political and the theatrical: "We have had the private stage for some years clouded, and under a tyrannical command, though the publick stage of England has produc'd many monstrous villains, some of which have deservedly made their *exit*."[18] Nor was Kirkman alone in imagining a confluence of stage and realpolitik: "This was a society accustomed to treating the theater and the world of politics as somehow interchangeable."[19] The play-pamphlets demonstrate, at the very least, the continuity of a theatrical impulse. As Joad Raymond observes, "Play-pamphlets were to some extent a continuation of pre-war theatre, rechannelled when the theatres were closed."[20] "The playlets can only be," notes Peter Holland, "social gestures towards the forms and practices of the theatre from which they were derived but which were now closed."[21]

---

[14] Dale B. J. Randall, *Winter Fruit: English Drama 1642–1660* (Lexington: University Press of Kentucky, 1995), 148.

[15] Lois Potter, "The Plays and the Playwrights: 1642–60," in *The Revels History of Drama in English*, vol. 4: *1613–1660*, ed. Philip Edwards, Gerald Eades Bentley, Kathleen McLuskie, and eadem (London and New York: Methuen, 1981), 261–304, here 281.

[16] "The appeal of these pretend-plays must have been considerable" (Randall, *Winter Fruit*, 52).

[17] Janet Clare, "Theatre and Commonwealth," in *The Cambridge History of British Theatre*, vol. 1: *Origins to 1660*, ed. Jane Milling and Peter Thomson (Cambridge: Cambridge University Press, 2004), 458–76, here 465.

[18] Kirkman, preface to *The Thracian Wonder*, sig. A2r. In this preface Kirkman claims to possess 700 plays, "and most of them several times over, and I intend to increase my store as I sell; and I hope you will by your frequent buying, encourage." These are the same words that Kirkman uses in his preface to *A Cure for a Cuckold*, published in 1661.

[19] F. J. Levy, "Staging the News," in *Print, Manuscript, & Performance: The Changing Relations of the Media in Early Modern England*, ed. Arthur F. Marotti and Michael D. Bristol (Columbus: Ohio State University Press, 2000), 252–78, here 263.

[20] Joad Raymond, *The Invention of the Newspaper: English Newsbooks, 1641–1649* (Oxford: Clarendon Press, 1996), 206.

[21] Peter Holland, "Shakespeare Abbreviated," in *The Cambridge Companion to Shakespeare and Popular Culture*, ed. Robert Shaughnessy (Cambridge: Cambridge

The writers' "choice of this form was a protest against the increasingly severe anti-theatre legislation passed by Parliament in 1647 and 1648."[22] The theaters, then, in effect took revenge on their tormentors through the creation of a new literary genre that perpetuated the format of printed drama: although "suppression of the public playhouses crushed the old drama out of existence, the printing presses in the 1640s worked with a freedom and range unknown before."[23] For royalists especially, drama became "a means of cultural resistance."[24] A representative selection of the play-pamphlets that issued from English presses, drawn from the *Thomason Tracts* in the British Library, is included here. My choice has been guided by the precedent of other scholars, especially W. W. Greg, Margot Heinemann, Lois Potter, Diane Purkiss, Barbara Ravelhofer, Sophie Tomlinson, and William P. Williams, who have singled out certain of the play-pamphlets for their combination of ideological and theatrical significance.

Entries are arranged as follows. Each begins with the name of the play (usually in its first printed form), the name of the author, the date of first production (when known) or an estimate of that date, the name of the acting company, and the name of the theater. In cases of multiple stagings, each is recorded. Where documentary evidence is lacking, an estimate of date and auspices is given along with a scholarly source.

In addition to auspices of production and printing history (including the date recorded in the Stationers' Register), each entry addresses basic questions about the formal properties of the play, questions beyond the purview of Harbage and Kawachi. Does the title of the play change from one edition to another? Does the title in the Stationers' Register differ significantly from the printed title-page? Does the printed play name the author? Is there an "argument," that is, a précis of the dramatic action? Is there a list of characters? Do the names of the actors appear? Does the play contain a prologue, an epilogue, or both? (These features frequently contain valuable information about authorial purpose, reception of the play onstage, and change in theatrical taste.) Are there any special or unusual theatrical effects, either visual or auditory, indicated in the stage directions or dialogue?[25] Does the play contain a carefully described dumb show, the kind of staging that would be especially important in the theater as opposed to

University Press, 2007), 26–45, here 34.

[22] Potter, "The Plays and the Playwrights: 1642–60," 284.

[23] Margot Heinemann, *Puritanism and Theatre: Thomas Middleton and Opposition Drama under the Early Stuarts* (Cambridge: Cambridge University Press, 1980), 237.

[24] Hero Chalmers, *Royalist Women Writers 1650–1689* (Oxford: Clarendon Press, 2004), 145.

[25] By auditory effects I designate what the audience hears, whether the sound is produced offstage or on. I exclude the commonplace directions for horns, trumpets, drums, oboes, and lutes.

the study?[26] Does the play feature a chorus, a convention found especially in drama shaped by classical precedent?[27] How is the play organized? Is it divided into a succession of scenes or, more commonly after 1609, divided into acts (with implications for breaks in performance)? In what format (folio, quarto, octavo, duodecimo) is the play printed? Does the play exist in more than one edition before 1660? If so, are later editions significantly different? And do they contain information about authorship or auspices of production absent in earlier editions? Does the printed play contain illustrations? If so, does it show the play in production? Does the play survive in manuscript? If so, what information about auspices of production and staging does it contain, and where is that manuscript located? When was the manuscript first edited and by whom?

In some instances the only information we have about performance appears on the title-page of a printed play. Where the entry here has been based on such a page, this fact is noted and the actual words are quoted. Admittedly, we need to be cautious about claims in printed editions concerning theatrical reception. We may be told, for instance, that a given play "was greatly applauded" when performed in a particular theater by a particular company of actors. In many cases we have no corroborating evidence. Nevertheless, it seems wise to present the information provided by title-pages, however formulaic, for in some instances it is all we have and may well be accurate. As long as the reader knows that a claim about production originates in a title-page, the reader has a context for evaluating the claim. In those instances where information about performance has been drawn from Philip Henslowe's *Diary*, that invaluable account book maintained in the years corresponding roughly to the first half of Shakespeare's career, this fact is noted. In some instances I cite stage properties recorded by Henslowe.

---

[26] In the surviving eyewitness account of *Gorboduc* in performance, the writer chooses "to dwell on the dumbshows" rather than on some other aspect of performance. See Norman Jones and Paul Whitfield White, "*Gorboduc* and Royal Marriage Politics: An Elizabethan Playgoer's Report of the Premiere Performance," *English Literary Renaissance* 26.1 (1996): 3–16, here 5. Although we cannot say with certainty why the dumb shows loom so large in the account, Jones and White observe that "these sequences of elaborate visual spectacle and movement were the most engaging and therefore most memorable parts of the play" (5). Charles Edelman observes of dumb shows in general that they "were the big 'production numbers' of the time and must have appealed to spectators then as a Broadway musical does today" (Introduction to *The Stukeley Plays*, ed. idem, Revels Plays Companion Library [Manchester and New York: Manchester University Press, 2005], 29). Gabriel Egan, in "Hearing or Seeing a Play?: Evidence of Early Modern Theatrical Terminology," *Ben Jonson Journal* 8 (2001): 327–47, notes that "plays were much more commonly thought of as visual rather than aural experiences in the literary and dramatic writing of the period" (332).

[27] "*Chorus* appears in English only with the first translations from Seneca in the 1560s" (Helen Cooper, *Shakespeare and the Medieval World*, Arden Shakespeare [London: Black, 2010], 74).

The reader should understand that his original list no longer exists, only the copy made by Edmond Malone and reproduced in modern editions of the *Diary*.[28]

As for format, generally the first paragraph in each entry lists known theatrical productions; the second treats the printing history; and the third offers context, which may take several forms: 1) pertinent material from prologues, epilogues, prefatory poems, and addresses to readers; 2) observations by scholars that situate plays in the culture of their time, especially in matters of politics or gender; 3) similarities with other plays in subject or treatment; 4) what might be termed "milestones" of English drama, such as earliest surviving manuscript playbook of the Elizabethan era, earliest surviving tragedy, first vernacular prose comedy, first complete and wholly secular interlude, first English history play to be performed on the popular stage, first play designated a comedy on its title-page, first printed play to represent farce as a dramatic form, first single play printed with an engraved title-page, first English love tragedy, first original pastoral comedy by a woman, first printed play to divide by gender a list of characters, first play explicitly called a tragicomedy, first appearance of *dramatis personae* in a printed play, first play written specifically for women, first play to feature a woman actor on the public stage, first original play written by a woman, first play professionally acted in public with changeable scenery, first known instance of flat revolving wings, first documented use of flying apparatus at a professional playhouse, first staging to adopt a proscenium arch, and so forth.

Necessarily some entries are longer than others; where less is known about a play and its staging, the entry is shorter. So, for example, entries for *Apollo Shroving* or *The Fatal Marriage* are less substantial than those for *The Spanish Tragedy* or *The Jew of Malta*. Plays little read in the modern era on account of critical fashion (e.g., *Tancred and Gismund*, *The Misfortunes of Arthur*) have attracted less notice than they otherwise might have. Yet even neglected plays merit attention, especially to their stagecraft, for staging reveals the playwrights' sensitivity to the dynamics of theater.

Titles of plays have been modernized, but other information on title-pages and quotations of the plays themselves have not.[29] Citations of the Stationers' Register reproduce the original spelling. Dates of first performance in most instances represent estimates; therefore the designation "*c.*" should be understood. Dates quoted directly from title-pages assume that the year begins on 25

---

[28] See *Henslowe's Diary*, ed. R. A. Foakes, 2nd ed. (Cambridge: Cambridge University Press, 2002), 316–25.

[29] However, in quoting from early books and modern original-spelling editions, I have made minor changes: *i/j, u/v,* and long *s* appear as they would in a modern text. Printers' abbreviations have been silently expanded and random capitalizations eliminated.

March; other dates are modern, assuming that the year begins on 1 January.[30]
In quotations, random capital letters and italics have been normalized in accord
with modern typography. I have used the locution "Paul's Boys" rather than
"Children of Paul's" to identify the boy actors of that company. I refer to the
Cockpit in Drury Lane as the Phoenix, its name after rebuilding in 1617. For
plays performed by the King's Men after 1610, when the company began to use
the Blackfriars, I specify either the Blackfriars or the Globe as the venue of production where there exists evidence to associate a play with one theater or the
other. Of course, the company may have performed the same plays in both of
their theaters: the Globe presumably in the summer months, the Blackfriars in
winter, as James Wright indicates in *Historia Histrionica* (1699).[31]

Where a manuscript or printed edition uses the words *dramatis personae*, that
fact is noted; where the Latin term is not used, I refer to a "list of characters."[32]
For the name "Johan," I have preferred the modern "John." The words "according to the title-page" refer to information *preceding* this phrase. The word "Prologue," capitalized, refers to the character/speaker of a prologue. Features enu-
merated in the first edition of a play also apply in subsequent editions unless
otherwise indicated. When a scholarly work is cited more than once in an entry,
the date of publication is usually given only in the first citation, though the date
is sometimes given again to ensure clarity. In some instances, scholarly works
listed in the Abbreviations do not appear within the entries themselves. Usually this means that a more recent scholarly work has superseded an earlier one.
Because the earlier scholar contributed to a consensus and because scholars rou-
tinely build upon the work of others, it has seemed best to preserve the earlier
name and title.

I have used the following abbreviations throughout: TP for title-page, RT
for running title, HT for head title, SD for stage direction, SR for Stationers'
Register, BL for British Library, V&A for Victoria & Albert Museum, F for
Folio, Q for Quarto, O for octavo, D for duodecimo, MS for manuscript, and
ND for no date. SR information is drawn from the texts edited by Edward Arber
for the years 1554–1640 and from the subsequent volumes for 1640–1708, edited

---

[30] According to Carol Chillington Rutter, in *Documents of the Rose Playhouse*, Revels
Plays Companion Library (Manchester: Manchester University Press, 1984), "The
Elizabethan civil calendar dated the new year from 1 January. The older ecclesiastical
calendar began the new year on Lady Day—the Feast of the Annunciation—25 March.
Civil documents could be dated by either convention; Henslowe used both, never
systematically" (30).

[31] Wright, *Historia Histrionica*, 5.

[32] See Bernard Beckerman, "The Persons Personated: Character Lists in English
Renaissance Play Texts," in *Poetry and Drama in the English Renaissance*, ed. Koshi
Nakanori and Yasuo Tamaizumi (Tokyo: Kinokuniya, 1980), 61–69.

by Eyre and Rivington.[33] Where W. W. Greg's *Bibliography of the English Printed Drama* records a different date, the difference is noted.

———

Although this book contains some 800 entries, it does not include all the titles previously recorded by Harbage and Kawachi. Excluded are mystery plays, quasi-theatrical shows, mummings, disguisings, civic pageants, masques, triumphs, entertainments for weddings, and plays written in Latin, as well as performances abroad. Also excluded are plays that seem to have been exercises in translation and intended for readers only: e.g., *An Interlude of Minds, Abraham's Sacrifice, The Tragedy of Antonie, Christ's Passion, Cornelia, Free Will, Iphigenia at Aulis, The Mandrake,* and *The Spanish Bawd*. As a general rule, original plays are excluded when they seem never to have been intended for performance: for example, Fulke Greville's *Alaham* and *Mustapha*, Samuel Brandon's *Virtuous Octavia*, and the drama of William Alexander. More problematic are works that were possibly written with performance in mind. Where evidence of production is scanty or altogether lacking, I comment briefly on the adequacy of stage directions for performance: e.g., "ample stage directions."

Where a play has been lost, leaving only a title without a text, the title is omitted unless a useful account of the dramatic action survives. Fragments are likewise excluded, and so, for example, the reader will not find here *Temperance and Humility*, which survives in a single leaf; *Somebody and Others*, which survives in two leaves; *The Four Cardinal Virtues*, which survives in four; or *The Cruel Debtor*, which also survives in four. Medieval plays earlier than *Everyman* are beyond my scope. Although manuscripts of plays are included, fragmentary manuscripts are not unless they are substantial. I have not included manuscripts whose existence and whereabouts are unknown; for a full list, see Wagonheim's revision of *Annals of English Drama*.[34]

The Records of Early English Drama, a series published by the University of Toronto, has proved less useful for my purposes than initially anticipated, for the information, culled from local records throughout England, does not in most cases name the plays performed at given venues. And so the REED volumes, although indispensable for enhancing our understanding of traveling companies and their reach throughout the countryside, rarely yield much useful

---

[33] Edward Arber, ed., *A Transcript of the Registers of the Company of Stationers of London, 1554–1640*, 5 vols. (London: privately printed, 1875–1894) ; George Edward Briscoe Eyre, Charles Robert Rivington, and Henry Robert Plomer, eds., *A Transcript of the Registers of the Worshipful Company of Stationers from 1640–1708 A.D.*, 3 vols. (London: privately printed, 1913–1914; repr. New York: Peter Smith, 1967).

[34] Sylvia Wagonheim, "List of Extant Play Manuscripts, 975–1700: Their Locations and Catalogue Numbers," in *Annals of English Drama*, 358–75.

information about particular plays and their staging. In the volume on Devon, for example, we find payments recorded to "my Lorde Admiralles plaiers" and "my Lord of Leicesters plaiers," as well as "the Quenes players" and "my lord of Wusterdes players," but none of these entries supplies a title, much less particulars of staging.[35] Occasionally, records contain the names of plays we recognize. For example, a play of "Kinge Lere" and *Pericles* were performed by Sir Richard Cholmeley's players at the home of Sir John Yorke, Gowthwaite Hall in Yorkshire, Christmas season 1609–1610.[36] But such specificity is rare. When the REED volumes report particular performances, they usually name plays that ceased to exist four centuries ago. The volume for Bristol records, among other plays, "Harry of Cornwall," "The Queen of Ethiopia," and "Myngo,"[37] and in the records for Chester we find "the storey of Kinge Ebrauk with all his sonne."[38] Such titles remind us that the majority of plays written between *Everyman* and 1660 are lost.[39] There seems no compelling reason to deploy their names here.

In the last twenty years scholars have explored a number of topics that in one way or another touch upon the contents of this work: the organization and history of repertory companies, the circulation of manuscripts, the relationship of manuscripts to printed plays, the malleability of playbooks during rehearsal and production, the agency and choice of persons who oversaw the transition of playbooks into printed artifacts, procedures of the printing houses, market trends for printed materials in general, the emergence of a market for printed plays along

---

[35] *Devon*, ed. John M. Wasson, REED (Toronto, Buffalo, and London: University of Toronto Press, 1986), 251, 252, 254.

[36] Charles J. Sisson, "Shakespeare Quartos as Prompt-Copies, with Some Account of Cholmeley's Players and a New Shakespeare Allusion," *Review of English Studies* 18 (1942): 129–43, suggests that "Lere" was Shakespeare's *King Lear*. But Gabriel Egan, "'As it was, is, or will be played': Title-pages and the Theatre Industry to 1610," in *From Performance to Print in Shakespeare's England*, ed. Peter Holland and Stephen Orgel (Basingstoke, UK, and New York: Macmillan, 2006), 92–110, maintains that the play "equally might have been" the performance of the anonymous *King Leir*, staged earlier in London (*c.* 1594), perhaps revived later, and the principal source of Shakespeare's play (93). Douglas H. Arrell, in *"King Leir* at Gowthwaite Hall," *Medieval and Renaissance Drama in England* 25 (2012): 83–93, argues convincingly that the play performed in Yorkshire was, as Egan surmised, the anonymous *King Leir*. See also John L. Murphy, *Darkness and Devils: Exorcism and "King Lear"* (Athens, OH: Ohio University Press, 1984).

[37] *Bristol*, ed. Mark C. Pilkinton, REED (Toronto, Buffalo, and London: University of Toronto Press, 1997), 144, 116, 115.

[38] *Chester*, ed. Lawrence M. Clopper, REED (Toronto and Buffalo: University of Toronto Press, 1979), 156.

[39] According to Neil Carson, in *A Companion to Henslowe's Diary* (Cambridge: Cambridge University Press, 1988), "90 percent of the works [named in the *Diary*] have perished" (68).

with the waxing and waning of that market, the profitability of plays in printed form, the infiltration of language concerning printing and literacy in sixteenth- and seventeenth-century England, and the very nature of books. Readers interested in pursuing these issues may wish to consult articles and books by, among others, Melissa Aaron, Peter Blayney, Karen Britland, Alan Farmer and Zachary Lesser, Andrew Gurr, Grace Ioppolo, Roslyn Knutson, William Long, Laurie Maguire, Jeffrey Masten, Scott McMillin and Sally-Beth MacLean, Lucy Munro, Stephen Orgel, Julie Stone Peters, Eric Rasmussen, James Saeger and Christopher Fassler, Marta Straznicky, and Tiffany Stern. All of these names appear in the pages that follow. My purpose, however, is not to rehearse the conclusions of scholars whose work is readily available and whose conclusions are well established. Instead, I have cited the work of these and other scholars when it enhances an understanding of particular productions and printings. In summary, this book assembles documentation about individual plays, the vast majority of which were prepared for production. The selection of scholarship is not driven by theoretical imperative; rather, it is informed by personal judgment.

Abbreviations

BL	British Library
B&F	Beaumont and Fletcher
D	duodecimo
F	folio
HT	head title
MS	manuscript
ND	no date
O	octavo
Q	quarto
RT	running title
SD	stage direction
SR	Stationers' Register
TP	title-page
V&A	Victoria & Albert Museum

A

Adrasta, or The Woman's Spleen and Love's Conquest, A Tragicomedy. John Jones.
Written before 1635, probably by a university man (*JCS*). The author's dedication
indicates that the play was intended for "the stage, and to bring it into that noble
nursery of action, where dramatick poëms usually and rightly take their degrees
of applause from them that can best judge, the spectators." But Jones explains
that "the players, upon a slight and halfe view of it, refus'd to doe it that right."
Although the play was not performed, Jones states in his dedicatory address that
he "fitted it for the stage." Francis Kirkman includes *Adrasta* in his 1661 catalogue of plays.

　　SR none. Q 1635 no author named on the TP but Jones signs the dedication;
"never acted"; list of characters; induction "in the form of a dialogue, between
a Gentleman and the Prologist, which concludes with the short verse prologue"
(Schneider 2011); epilogue; divided into five acts. Extensive SDs: three spirits,
conjured by a witch, "*riseth from under the stage*" through a trap door; the trap is
also used to stage a burial: "*They take her up and bury her.*" Staging calls for Althea
to descend from above to the floor of the stage on a rope ladder: "*she drawes up a
ladder of cords*"; then "*Shee fastens the hookes above, he [Lucillo] below: and then coming downe he receives her.*"

　　The theatricality of the play is suggested by its unusual beginning. When
Prologue enters, he "promptly falls over a gentleman seated on stage. The professional playing troupe clearly found sharing a stage space in the playhouses with
self-aggrandising gallants or self-righteous citizens less of a delight" (Milling
2004). The seated figure complains of the vogue for satirical drama: "an audience desires not to glut their eares with others infamie, nor ever wish'd their
mirth should feed upon the ranke distemperature of other mens vices; but come
to behold a scene merry and harmelesse, as free from sower invectives as fulsome
bawdery." The actor playing Prologue replies, "Sir in our authors name I thanke
you: and would you but please to speake with him your selfe."

The Admiral of France. See *Chabot, Admiral of France.*

Aglaura. John Suckling. Licensed for acting 26 January 1638 (Bawcutt 1996).
Acted by the King's Men at the [second] Blackfriars, according to the O TPs.
"Suckling arranged performances" of his play "at the Blackfriars theatre at his
own expense" (Steggle 2004b). Performed also at court, possibly earlier than the
Blackfriars production (Richards 1968), with changeable scenery, Christmas revels, 1637–38 (cited in letter of George Garrard, 7 February 1638); and at Whitehall Cockpit, before the king and queen, 3 April 1638 (Adams 1917). *Aglaura*
is "the first English play to be professionally acted in public with changeable
scenery," borrowed from the queen's masque *Luminalia* (Freehafer 1968, 1971),

though Star 1972 doubts a connection with *Luminalia* and doubts the use of per-spective scenery in *Aglaura*. "[N]one of the action requires scenic effects beyond the resources of the Blackfriars stage" (McLuskie 1981). Whether or not scenery was used, "Suckling bought costumes of legendary richness" (Edwards 1981). He "did not intend to write a play tailored to the likes and dislikes of the queen's circle. So powerful was her influence at the Blackfriars, however, that Suckling ended in revising his play to suit her and the Blackfriars audience" (Aaron 2005). The tragedy became a tragicomedy.

(1) London, BL, Royal MS 18.C.XXV, fols. 2–26; no TP; no author named; list of characters; prologues for Blackfriars, court, and king; epilogues for Black-friars and court; contains original tragic ending; extensive SDs; five acts. MS "is almost certainly a copy prepared for presentation to the King on the occasion of the original performance at Court" in 1638 (Greg 1931). (2) BL, Harley MS 3889, fols. 28–31; no author named; list of characters; prologue; contains first act and part of second. SR 18 April 1638; transferred 22 February 1648. F 1638 no author named; list of characters; prologues for Blackfriars, court, and king; epi-logues for Blackfriars and court. "Suckling may have subvented the printing" of this "elegant presentation folio" (Corns 2007). In addition to the tragic ending, F contains a new version of act 5, with a tragicomic ending. The alternate last act is accompanied by two alternate prologues and an alternate epilogue. "An im-portant group of corrections in speech headings or additional stage directions in the tragic-comic fifth act are preserved in the Bodleian, Selden copy of *Aglaura*, 1638" (Beaurline 1971). O1 1646 *Fragmenta Aurea* (with *Brennoralt*; *The Goblins*); "printed by his owne copies," according to the general TP ("a false claim with respect to *Aglaura*" [Clayton 1971]); contains both tragic and tragicomic end-ings. O2 1648 *Fragmenta Aurea*; an additional TP indicates that the tragicomic version was performed at court; list of characters. O3 1658–59 *Fragmenta Au-rea*; published in two parts; Part 2 entitled *The Last Remains of Sir John Suckling* (1659); "the third edition, with some new additionals"; separate TP dated 1658; list of characters; prologues for Blackfriars, court, and king; epilogue.

The F epilogue, adopting a judicial metaphor, notes the varied respons-es of playgoers to a play: "first there sits / A grave grand jurie on it of towne-wits; / And they give up their verdict; then agin / The other jurie of the court comes in / (And that's of life and death) for each man sees / That oft condemnes what th'other jurie frees: / Some three dayes hence, the ladies of the towne / Will come to have a judgement of their owne: / And after them, their servants; then the Citie, / For that is modest, and is still last wittie."

Alarum for London. See *A Larum for London.*

Albertus Wallenstein, Late Duke of Friedland. Henry Glapthorne. Licensed for acting as *Walstein, Duke of Fredland*, 1639 (Bawcutt 1996). "Acted with good allowance" by the King's Men at the [second] Globe, according to the TP, "*c.* 1635?" (Butler 1983). "The fact that the *Wallenstein* title-page . . . mentions only the Globe and not the more attractive Blackfriars . . . indicates that the play was acted only at the Globe and therefore in the summer" (*JCS*). This is one of "[o]nly seven non-Shakespearean plays . . . advertised on title pages as exclusively Globe productions" (Straznicky 2006b).

SR 23 September 1639 (Greg 1939 gives 22 September). Q 1639–40 two issues; *The Tragedy of Albertus Wallenstein, Late Duke of Friedland and General to the Emperor Ferdinand the Second*; list of characters; five acts and separate scenes. Few SDs beyond the listing of characters at the beginning of scenes.

This "is an old-fashioned popular play, often distantly echoing Shakespeare and Marlowe" (Butler). The play "appealed to the protestant sympathies of the audience for it depicted, in tragicomic mode, the violent downfall of the Catholic general Wallenstein, who was one of the leaders of the imperial armies in the Thirty Years' War" (Sanders 2004b).

Albovine, King of the Lombards. William Davenant. "Completed in 1627" (Cauthen 1987b); "probably written shortly after Henrietta Maria's arrival in England" (Sharpe 1987). SDs are detailed, the play evidently having been prepared with staging in mind, though there is no record of performance.

SR no original; 27 July 1639 (Greg 1939); transferred 3 May 1651; 7 March 1653; 19 August 1667. Q 1629 *The Tragedy of Albovine, King of the Lombards*; RT *The Tragedy of Albovine, King of Lombardy*; list of characters; in blank verse; five acts and first scenes. Detailed and subtle SDs: "Why should you thinke that I would bruise / Your fingers with my touch — *Sports with her hand.*" Staging calls for a discovery scene: "*A canopy is drawne, the King is discover'd sleeping over papers.*" An unusual frisson is created by this SD: "*Enter Cunymond with a skull, made into a drinking-bowle.*" F 1673 *The Works*; "now published out of the authors original copies," according to general TP; a revised version, in prose, of Q.

Davenant's play illustrates "how Caroline writers located political disorder not in the homoeroticism of favoritism but in the favorite's self-serving manipulation of homoerotic and heteroerotic alliances" (DiGangi 2006). "The monstrous favorite . . . is not the king's minion, who represents the residual type of the Ganymede, but the queen's minion, who violently dislocates political and sexual alliances in his bid for power" (DiGangi 2011).

Albumazar, A Comedy. Thomas Tomkis. "Presented" [the night of] 9 March 1615 by the students of Trinity College, Cambridge, before King James I, according to the Q1 TP, in the college hall; the play "was commissioned for the visit of James" (Ellerbeck 2009). This "adaptation of della Porta's *L'astrologo* . . . was the sole English-language play (out of four, one of the others being *Ignoramus*) performed before James I at Cambridge in 1615" (Braden 2010). The performance space must have been impressive. "At Trinity College, Cambridge, the old hall was superseded in the early seventeenth century by the magnificent new hall built by Master Thomas Nevile (completed 1608). The hall—modelled upon that at Middle Temple (one of the London Inns of Court)—was nearly twice the size of the earlier hall, measuring 103 feet by 40 feet and 50 feet in height. At its upper end was a new dais and at the lower end a richly decorated screen that can still be seen" (Keenan 2002). "A substantial area behind the upper-end wall was reserved from the beginning for a theatrical tiring chamber; . . . a trap-door associated with the fabric of the hall served as a supplementary entrance when the hall was used for plays" (Nelson 1994). Staging may have involved the construction of stage "houses" (Dick 1944). "[W]hen performed [the play] was a failure" (Lesser 1999). John Chamberlain's account of the king's visit to Cambridge, contained in a letter to Dudley Carleton, reports of the play, "there was no great matter in yt more then one goode clowns part."

The SR entry for 28 April 1615 reports that *Albumazar* was performed 10 March but the date on the Q1 TP "appears to be correct" (Greg 1939); transferred 2 August 1630. Q1 1615 no author named on the TP; dramatis personae; prologue and epilogue (by Trincalo); five acts and separate scenes. The prologue "directly addresses women in the audience and states that they are the reason that the play is composed in English" (Ellerbeck). "[R]emarkably few" SDs (Mills 1959). Tomkis indicates awareness of the London theatrical scene: the clown "is ridiculed for wooing a lady in language drawn from Red Bull (and Fortune, in this case) plays" (Straznicky 2006b). "Most of Tomkis's alterations [to *L'astrologo*] make the play more concise and quick-moving, and where he does expand, his dramatic intuition seems sound" (Braden 2010). Q2 1615. Q3 1634 "newly revised and corrected by a speciall hand." Q4 dated 1634 but perhaps printed *c.* 1640 (*STC*) or 1650s (Dick). Although John Dryden wrote a prologue for the revival of 2 February 1668 at the Duke of York's theater, Lincoln's Inn Fields, asserting that this play inspired *The Alchemist*, the claim is rejected today.

"The title character is named for the famous ninth-century Persian astrologer" (McJannet 1999a). "The satire is based on the idiocies of astrology"; "King James was known to be interested in astrology, so there was some adventurousness in presenting such a play before him" (Gurr 2009b).

The Alchemist. Ben Jonson. Performed by King's Men in the City of Oxford, ?4 September 1610 (Elliott et al.), according to a letter by Henry Jackson of Corpus Christi College, but he does not say exactly where performance took place; the venue may have been an inn or a college hall (Keenan 2002). Possibly premiered in the provinces in the later part of 1610 when the public theaters were closed on account of plague (Cook 1991). Or acted before the middle of July 1610, when theaters were similarly closed (Mares 1967). Acted by the King's Men, according to the F and F2 TPs, at the second Blackfriars (a character in the opening scene speaks of being "here, in the *Friers*") in 1610 (Sullivan 2002); "through internal references the action can be . . . precisely dated to 1 November 1610" (Donaldson 2004). Performed at court, Christmas season, 1612–13, before the king (payment to John Heminges dated 20 May 1613). Principal actors were Richard Burbage, John Heminges, John Lowin, William Ostler, Henry Condell, John Underwood, Alexander Cooke, Nicholas Tooley, Robert Armin, and William Eccleston (who belonged to the company in 1610–11 and 1613 or 1614 [Riddell 1969]), according to F1. Armin played Drugger (Butler 2004a); Burbage played Subtle; Field (who joined the company in 1615 or 1616), Face; Underwood (who joined the company in 1608), Dapper; Lowin, Epicure Mammon (*Historia Histrionica*); Condell, Surly; Tooley, Ananias; Eccleston, Kastril, according to notes "almost certainly in a seventeenth-century hand" in a copy of F (Riddell). Joseph Taylor, having joined the company in 1619, played Face (*Historia Histrionica*). Richard [?a mistake for George] Birch probably played Dol Common after 1616; Robert Benfield, (who joined the company *c*. 1614–16 [Riddell], took over the role of Lovewit (Gurr 2004c). Revived at Whitehall, the evening of 1 January 1623 (Adams 1917). Revived 1 December 1631, a benefit for Henry Herbert (H&S). Also by John Ogilby's Men at the Werburgh Street theater, Dublin, 1637–38 (Clark 1955); Shirley wrote a new prologue for the occasion. Revived by an unnamed company in London, January 1639 (*Domestic State Papers*), and ·again on 18 May 1639 (*JCS*). Leonard Digges, in a work published in 1640, compliments "the Fox and subtill Alchemist" (Chambers 1930).

SR 3 October 1610; transferred 3 July 1630; 4 July 1635; 4 March 1939. Q 1612 list of characters; argument; prologue; last speeches of Lovewit and Face may be construed as an epilogue; scanty SDs; five acts and separate scenes. Jonson dedicates the play to Mary Wroth: "Jonson's dedication of an amphitheater play to a woman is, as far as we know, unique for the early modern period" (Straznicky 2006a). The first scene "is one of the most explosive openings in early modern drama. Face bursts onto the stage with a sword in his hand; Subtle follows, clutching a phial and throwing insults. Dol vainly attempts to mediate, before opting for the more successful strategy of matching their violence with her own" (Loxley 2002). These three proceed "to bilk a series of gulls with their razzle-dazzle" (Bevington 2000b). F1 1616 *The Works*; *The Alchemist, A Comedy*; "first acted in the yeere 1610." F1 adds many SDs. F2 1640 vol. 1. Before the Restoration, parts of the play were adapted for a droll entitled *The Imperick*, later published in *1 The Wits, or Sport upon Sport* (O 1662 [two issues] and 1672).

"Jonson develops in *The Alchemist* a potent satire on Puritanism in his picture of Tribulation, a pastor of Amsterdam, and Ananias, his deacon" (Corns 2007); they are both Anabaptists, "an extreme wing of Puritanism" (Sanders 1998b). The Q prologue justifies the satire: "when the wholsome remedies are sweet, / And, in their working, gaine and profit meete, / He hopes to finde no spirit so much diseas'd, / But will, with such fayre correctives, be pleas'd."

Alexander, Campaspe, and Diogenes. See *Campaspe*.

Alexander VI. See *The Devil's Charter.*

Alfonso. See *Alphonsus, Emperor of Germany.*

Alfred, or Right Reinthroned, A Tragicomedy. The translation by R. K. [Robert Knightley] of William Drury's *Aluredus sive Alfredus* (1619). The date 1659 is inscribed on the last page, though the translation may not have been completed till the following year. The author "appears to have been a member of that most threatened of Royalist minorities, the Roman Catholics"; he has created "a lively piece of reading entertainment which probably could, unlike so many other Commonwealth closet dramas, be staged successfully" (Aggeler 1978).

Oxford, Bodleian, MS Rawlinson, poet. 80, fols. 1–61, ed. Tricomi 1993; no author named on the TP but the dedication is signed "R. K."; list of characters; prologue and epilogue (by St. Cuthbert); five acts and separate scenes. Adequate SDs: *"Puts on ye habit of a common soldier . . . lay's his robes in a pit."* The pit may have been represented by the space beneath the trap. The play "abounds with calls for stage props" (Tricomi). First edited by Tricomi, who identified the translator.

Drury's play "is the first dramatic treatment of King Alfred's reign, and Robert Knightley's translation the first English dramatization of his reign" (Tricomi). *Alfred* "appears to be a history-and-legend-based wish-fulfillment that enabled him to write not only about what might have been in King Alfred's time but also about the nightmares of his own time" (Randall 1995). The play "seems to suggest what might have been if King Charles had been wiser and his counselors more just" (Aggeler).

All Fools, A Comedy. George Chapman. If Henslowe's entries for 21 June and 2 July 1599 ("Boocke called the world Rones a whelles & now all foolles but the foolle") refer to Chapman's play, then it was probably acted by the Lord Admiral's Men at the Rose in 1599 (Evans 1970). But Wiggins 2000 doubts that the two titles represent the same play. Possibly revised and subsequently performed at Henslowe's new theater following its opening in autumn 1600. The play, concerned with Fortune, "seems part of an advertising campaign for the Admiral's Men new 'usual house,'" the Fortune theater (Dutton 2000): the prologue begins, "The fortune of a stage (like Fortune's selfe) / Amazeth greatest judgements." Although *All Fools* was "first commissioned, conceived, and (presumably) performed as an outdoor play for the Lord Admiral's Men, it was later acquired and performed by the children's company at the Blackfriars" (Cathcart 2012). "Presented" at the [second] Blackfriars, according to the TP, by the Children of the Queen's Chapel, *c.* 1601 (Munro 2005); Chapman may have revised the play for the Blackfriars "sometime between the opening of the theatres in April 1604 and 1 January 1605" (McIntosh 2009), though Q may not contain the revisions (Manley 1968). Performed "lately" before King James, according to the TP, in the Great Hall at Whitehall, 1 January 1605 (Burnett 2004); the Children of the Queen's Revels acted the play in 1604–05 (Munro).

SR none. Q 1605 two issues; list of characters; prologue ("probably a revision" [Edelman 2012]) and epilogue; five acts. As in many other comedies, SDs describe domestic details: *"A drawer or two, setting a table"*; *"Enter drawer with wine and a cupp."* Also issued in *Comedies, Tragi-Comedies, & Tragedies* (1652), a made-up book no longer extant.

Epilogue, acknowledging the diversity of playgoers, employs a favorite metaphor of playwrights: "Sometimes feastes please the cookes, and not the guestes, / Sometimes the guestes, and curious cookes contemne them. / Our dishes we intirely dedicate / To our kinde guestes, but since yee differ so, / Some to like onely mirth without taxations, / Some to count such workes trifles, and such like, / We can but bring you meate, and set you stooles, / And to our best cheere say, you all are welcome."

All for Money. Thomas Lupton. Acted 1559–77 (Grantley 2007) at undetermined venue. Probably performed by a professional company of men (White 1993b); "its thirty-two characters could be easily shared among half-a-dozen energetic players" (Craik 1958); may be performed by four actors (Mann 1991).

SR 25 November 1577. Q 1578 *A Moral and Pitiful Comedy Entitled All for Money*; "compiled by T. Lupton"; list of characters on the TP; prologue; not divided. Staging seems to call for three uses of a trap, but "a real trap door was probably lacking" (Bevington 1962). "The costume directions are unusually detailed. All are emblematic: Theology wears 'a long ancient garment, like a Prophet'" (Twycross & Carpenter 2002). Satan is "'as deformedly dressed as may be,' . . . his body covered in leather skins, or in a hairy pelt, or in feathers" (Craik 1958); Satan's sons, Gluttony and Pride, are *"dressed in devils apparel."* Damnation *"shal have a terrible vysard on his face, & his garment shalbe painted with flames of fire."* Money wears the most elaborate costume: *"Money commeth in, having the one halfe of his gowne yellow, and the other white, having the coyne of silver and golde painted upon it, & there must be a chayre for him to sit in, and under it or neere the same there must be some hollowe place for one to come up in."* This chair figures in the most interesting staging of the play: *"Here Money shal make as though he would vomit, and with some fine conveyance Pleasure shal appeare from beneath, and lie there apparelled."* That is, "Sin, the vice of the play, is brought physically to birth on the stage, being vomited up by his father Pleasure" (Craik). Brown 1999 calls this "a very difficult scene to stage."

As the moral interludes developed, controversial plays "dealt necessarily with the policies of real men, as well as with dogma" (Thompson 1910). According to the TP, the play represents "the ma[n]ners of men, and fashion of the world noweadayes." In its treatment of the contemporary scene, this and other plays seem "written largely for working and mercantile audiences in a period when . . . some fortunate Londoners were able to achieve prosperity"; the plays "breathe an optimism in the very acerbity to their tirades against abuses of the system" (Bevington 1968).

All Is True. See *Henry VIII*.

All's Lost by Lust. William Rowley. Acted late 1618 or 1619 (Taylor 2002a). Probably originally performed by Prince Charles's Men (*AED 3*), the predecessor of Lady Elizabeth's Men, "who played at the Phoenix from the departure of Queen Anne's company, the original occupants, in 1619" (*JCS*). "Divers times acted by" Lady Elizabeth's Men and, later, "with great applause," by Queen Henrietta Maria's Men (*JCS*) at the Phoenix, according to the TP. "Lady Elizabeth's Men amalgamated with the Children of the Queen's Revels in 1613, and . . . [i]n 1614–15 Prince Charles's Men joined forces for a while with the expanded Lady Elizabeth's company" (Taylor 1993a). In the dramatis personae "Rowley identifies himself as the actor who created the role of Jaques" (Bentley 1971). In playlist of Beeston's Boys 10 August 1639.

SR 27 September 1632. Q 1633 *A Tragedy Called All's Lost by Lust*; dramatis personae; argument (i.e., summary); prologue (nearly the same as that published in Dekker's *Wonder of a Kingdom* [1636]); the "prologue is not particularly applicable to either play" (*JCS*); five acts. Special effects: "*Thunder and lightning*," a sign in other plays of divine disapproval. "In outdoor playhouses . . . in addition to 'tempestuous' drums, a 'bullet,' i.e., a cannonball, was 'rolled' along a sheet of metal or a wooden trough [to simulate thunder]" (White 2007). The play's title "refers to the loss of the Spanish throne to the Moorish king Mulymumen, as well as the loss of life occasioned by Spanish lust, or misdirected love"; "in both the main plot and the subplot lust proves the ruin of Spaniards high and low" (D'Amico 1991). The play "depicts a bawd's seductive powers in unabashedly corporeal, and homoerotic, terms" (DiGangi 2011).

Prologue adopts a defensive tone against "the over-curious criticke": "Tis not a gay sute, or distorted face, / Can beate his merit off, which has wonne grace / In the full theater, nor can now feare / The teeth of any snakie whisperer: / But to the white, and sweet unclouded brow, / (The heaven where true worth moves) our poet does bow; / Patrons of arts, and pilots to the stage, / Who guide it (through all tempests) from the rage / Of envious whirle windes."

All's Well That Ends Well. William Shakespeare. Acted 1602–03 (Evans 1997), or *c*. 1603 (Leggatt 2003), or 1604–05 (Snyder 1993), or mid-1606 (Jackson 2001d) by the Lord Chamberlain's/King's Men at the first Globe. Speech-prefixes in F1 record the letters E and G, "perhaps for the actors William Eccleston and Robert Goughe" (King 1992a). "Most critics have agreed that Lavatch belongs to the series of clown roles which Shakespeare created for Robert Armin, who joined the company *c*. 1600, after the departure of William Kempe" (Wells & Taylor 1987); but Sutcliffe 1996 suggests: "It is entirely possible that Armin's arrival predated Kempe's departure and that, for a short time, both played in the Lord Chamberlain's simultaneously."

SR 8 November 1623; transferred ?4 August 1626 Paviers right in Shakes-peres *plaies*; ?19 June 1627 widow of Isaac Jaggard . . . her parte in Shackspheere *playes*; 16 November 1630; 1 July 1637 Shakespeares *workes* their Part; 6 August 1674; 21 August 1683. F1 1623 *William Shakespeare's Comedies, Histories & Trag-edies*; three issues; "published according to the true originall copies"; epilogue (by King); five acts. This division into acts "was presumably done by the company in anticipation of a revival or of the Folio printing" (Snyder 1993). F2 1632 "the sec-ond impression"; three issues. F3 1663 "the third impression"; reissued 1664 with seven additional plays. F4 1685 "the fourth edition"; two issues.

Boas 1896 first termed *All's Well* a "problem play," a status it shares with *Troilus and Cressida* and *Measure for Measure*, "plays of social and psychological malaise": these plays "pose intricate ethical issues which require unorthodox so-lutions" (Snyder). Dowden 1875 had first suggested the grouping.

The Almanac. See *No Wit, No Help, Like a Woman's.*

Alphonsus, Emperor of Germany. Anonymous. Original acted ?before 1604; re-vised version acted ?1630–31 (*JCS*) at undetermined venue. Performed by the King's Men, possibly in a revised version, at Hampton Court, 3 October 1630; and, under the title *Alfonso*, at the second Blackfriars before Queen Henrietta Maria and the Elector Palatine, 5 May 1636 (Adams 1917); "the 1636 reviv-al coincided with the joint diplomatic missions to Vienna and Paris. *Alphonsus*, with its attack on the 'viperous blood-thirsty Spaniard' . . . and its depiction of aggressive English leadership in Germany, exactly matched the needs of the French lobby at a crucial juncture" (Butler 1983). "Very often acted (with great applause)" by the King's Men at the [second] Blackfriars, according to the Q TP. In playlist of the King's Men 7 August 1641 as "Alphonso, Emper^{or} of Germany." Publication in 1654 suggests a relevance to present events: "I will be King, and Tyrant if I please," says Alphonsus, "For what is Empire but a Tyrannie?" "The driving force of the work . . . is strongly political and largely dependent on the canny machinations of the tyrant" (Randall 1995).

SR 9 September 1653 ascribes the play to "John Peele." Q 1654 *The Tragedy of Alphonsus, Emperor of Germany*; the TP erroneously credits the play to George Chapman; dramatis personae; five acts. SDs describe the characters' appearance: "*Enter* Alphonsus *the Emperour in his night-gown, and his shirt, and a torch in his hand.*" Spectacular staging includes the entry of Hedewick, the Duke of Saxon's daughter, "*apparelled like Fortune, drawn on a globe, with a cup in her hand, wherein are bay leaves, whereupon are written the lots. A train of ladies following with musick.*" "What the visual globe and lottery cup suggest about Fortune—her fickleness, her instability, her indifference—also extend to the situation of Hedewick who is ruled by fortune and, metaphorically as well as literally, on an instable globe" (Diehl 1986). Alphonsus dispatches the King of Bohemia by putting "*poyson into the beaker.*" The Emperor resorts to cruelty against his wife: "Alphonsus *trayls the*

Empress by the hair." In this crescendo of violence the Duke of Saxony kills Hedewick's child: "*He dashes out the childs brains.*"

⸱The address to the Q reader, referring to performance "with all the elegance of life and action on the Black-Friers stage," suggests a connection between theatrical success and readers' delight: "if it be a stranger to thee, give me leave to prepare thy acceptation, by telling thee, it was receiv'd with general applause, and thy judgement (I doubt not) will be satisfied in the reading." "The comment . . . is typical of [Humphrey] Moseley's particular kind of propaganda: it appeals to nostalgia for a pre-war England which was also a Stuart England; it assumes a shared set of values on the part of his readers; and it whets their appetites for finding hidden meanings in polite literature" (Potter 1989).

Alphonsus, King of Aragon. Robert Greene. "Sundrie times acted," according to the TP, winter 1587–88 (Chambers 1923). Possibly first performed by the Queen's Men, at undetermined venue, perhaps an inn-yard (Lawrence 1927), "but it is not absolutely certain" that the play belonged to the Queen's Men (Schoone-Jongen 2008), and in any event "when actors performed at inns they usually occupied a large room rather than a yard and performed by candlelight" (Orrell 1997). Henslowe's "Mahomet," performed by the Lord Admiral's Men 14 and 27 August 1594, may designate this play.

SR none. Q 1599 *The Comical History of Alphonsus, King of Aragon*; author's initials on the TP; at the beginning of each act Venus gives a choral speech; five acts. Staging involves the descent of Venus, probably by machinery, and later a chair lowered to the stage for her ascent: "*Exit Venus. Or if you can conveniently, let a chaire come downe from the top of the stage, and draw her up.*" "'The top of the stage' is clearly the trapdoor in the heavens" (Ichikawa 2002). This represents the "first documented use of flying apparatus at a professional playhouse" (Graves 1999). Yet "the staging of flying effects in plays, masques, and shows was as well known and understood in 1576 as it was twenty years later" (Astington 1985). Greene "hopes for a spectacular visual beginning and end to his play, but is quite prepared to accept a strictly pedestrian conclusion if no machinery for an ascent to heaven exists" (Wickham 1979). Special effects include "*a brazen head set in the middle of the place behind the stage, out of the which, cast flames of fire, drums rumble within.*" "Here, as in previous tradition, the head is a source of secret information that turns out to be dangerous" (LaGrandeur 1999). Staging also involves the entry from below of a ghost "*in a white cirples and a cardinal's myter.*" "Stage ghosts seem to have worn the clothes they wore when they were alive; Henslowe's inventory of properties owned by the Admiral's Men in 1598 lists 'j gostes sewt'" (Thompson 2010). A portable canopy figures in staging when Alphonsus enters "*with a canapie carried over him by three lords.*" George Buc purchased a copy of Q and wrote Greene's name on the TP (Shapiro 2005).

Greene's play was inspired by the success of Marlowe's *Tamburlaine*, performed 1587; *Alphonsus* "almost parodies Marlowe" (Newcomb 2004). But *Alphonsus* "was a failure when it first appeared on the stage" (Morris 1987).

Amarath the Turk. See *The Courageous Turk.*

Amends for Ladies, A Comedy. Nathan Field. Acted *c.* 1611 by the Children of the Queen's Revels at the Whitefriars (Munro 2005). Performed also by the combined Lady Elizabeth's and Prince Charles's Men, according to the Q1 TPs, at Rosseter's Blackfriars/Porter's Hall playhouse, winter of 1616–17 (Peery 1950). "A title-page would hardly allow two companies to lay separate claims to [the play], so it must indicate either a joint performance or a series of performances that started under the Lady Elizabeth's name and then took the name of Prince Charles's after the merger" (Gurr 1996). "On 3 June 1615 Philip Rosseter was authorized to build a new theatre in which the Children of the Revels, Lady Elizabeth's Men and Prince Charles's Men were to play"; this indicates "some sort of agreement by which the company of the Lady Elizabeth was no longer completely distinct" (Bentley 1981). "Since Lady Elizabeth's Men merged with Prince Charles's Men in or around 1614, the [1618] title page presumably describes an original Lady Elizabeth's play coming into Prince Charles's repertory after the merger" (Nicol 2006a). The title-page claim that the play was staged at the Blackfriars by the Prince's Men and Lady Elizabeth's is "a somewhat deceptive description since 'at the Blackfriars' implies not the brief tenancy of these second-string companies at the short-lived Porter's Hall Theatre, but the prestigious King's Men with whom Field was by then acting" (MacIntyre 1996).

SR none. Q1 1618 two issues, one entitled *Amends for Ladies, A Comedy*; the other, *Amends for Ladies, with the Humour of Roaring, A Comedy*; five acts. The subtitle alludes "to a subplot in which a cowardly gentleman gets drunk and learns to brawl like a 'roaring boy'" (Panek 2011). "The 1618 quarto represents the script of Whitefriars" (MacIntyre). "Q1 contains a "cameo performance of Moll Cutpurse, a central figure in the Prince's Men's *The Roaring Girl* (*c.* 1610)" (Munro 2005). A temporary structure may be suggested by these SDs: "*Enter* Seldome *his* Wife *working as in their shop*"; "Seldome *having fetch[ed] a candle, walk's off at the other end of the shop.*" MacIntyre believes that the shop was located in the discovery space. But the actors may have "brought 'the shop' with them onto the main stage" (Dessen 1996). The SDs offer much domestic detail: "*Enter* Maid *like an Irish foot-boy, and gloves in her pocket, and a handkercher.*" Q2 1639 *Amends for Ladies, with the Merry Pranks of Moll Cut-Purse, or, The Humor of Roaring, A Comedy Full of Honest Mirth and Wit*; "acted at the Blacke-Fryers, both by the princes servants, and the Lady Elizabeths." The Q2 title "suggests that Moll in 1639 was a popular enough figure for a publisher to hope that advertising her 'merry pranks' might help bring new readers to an old play" (Panek).

"Field wrote *Amends for Ladies* in response to female audience members' criticisms as reflected by his Mrs. Seldome: 'Oh men! What are you? Why is our poore sexe Still made the disgrac't subjects, in these plaies?'" (Whitney 2006).

The Amorous Phantasm, A Tragicomedy. William Lower. No evidence of production; possibly not performed (Gates 1932). Dedicated to Elizabeth, Queen of Bohemia and daughter of King James I, "indicating Lower's close connection with the exiled royal family" (Kathman 2004b).

D 1660 published in The Hague but "it appears that copies were actually available in London before the end of 1659" (Greg 1939); list of characters; prologue and epilogue to court; five acts and separate scenes. SDs sufficient for performance: "*The curtaine is drawne, and he sees upon a bed a murthered body*"; "*a noise under the stage*"; "Fabritio *comming out [of] the mine.*" Opposite the TP an engraving depicts two women in the company of a richly dressed man wearing a sword; in the background, seen through an arch, two soldiers, armed with spears, stand over a man who lies on his back; seen through another window a woman talks with a king. D, with a new TP, was reissued in London in 1661. Also issued in a made-up book, *Three New Plays* (with *The Enchanted Lovers* and *The Noble Ingratitude*); two issues; both general and separate TPs dated 1661; each play has separate register and pagination. "[A]s with his other translations of contemporary French drama, [Lower] neither specifies his French source, Philippe Quinault's *Le Fantôme amoureux*, nor identifies his work as a translation" (Braden 2010).

Prologue contrasts popular theater with drama in a courtly setting, leaving no doubt which is preferable: "[the play is] in my judgment fit / But for the publick stage, not to appear / Within the verge of this illustrious sphere, / Where nothing but the quintescence of wit / Should dare to enter." Similarly, the epilogue anticipates courtly production: "Faire queen of this night, / Not Cynthia, but a goddesse far more bright, / To you I kneel."

The Amorous War, A Tragicomedy. Jasper Mayne. ?Acted 1628–48 (*AED 3*) at undetermined venue, possibly a university.

SR none. Q1 1648 no author named on the TP; list of characters; five acts and separate scenes. Highly detailed SDs and descriptions of costume: "*Here six Moores dance after the ancient Ætheopian manner. Erect arrowes stucke round their heads, in their curled haire, instead of quivers. Their bowes in their hands, their upper parts naked; their neather from the wast, to their knees cover'd with bases of blew satin, edged with a deepe silver fringe. Their legs also naked, incircled with rings of gold; the like their armes. Great pendants of pearle at their eares. At every close, expressing a cheerefull adoration of their gods.*" Reissued 1658 both separately and in *Two Plays* (with *The City Match*); author's identity indicated by initials on the general TP; "long since written"; separate TP in *Two Plays,* a made-up book, "printed in the yeare 1648." Reissued 1659: "This issue was evidently prepared to replace the edition of 1648 . . . in *Two Plays,* originally issued in 1658, when the former stock was exhausted" (Greg 1939); despite the 1659 date on the TP, this edition, which has the author's initials on the TP, "was certainly later than 1659" (Greg), perhaps 1662. Also reissued in 1659 in octavo format.

The women of the play are "forbidden by their menfolk to accompany them to battle [and so] disguise themselves as Amazons and offer military assistance"; the play represents a "celebration of female heroism" (Chalmers 2004).

Amphrisa, or The Forsaken Shepherdess. Thomas Heywood. A short dramatic entertainment possibly intended for private performance. The address to the reader calls this work "stage-poetry." Fleay 1891 speculates that *Amphrisa* was part of *"Five Plays in One*, acted at the Rose 1597," though Bentley finds it "Caroline in tone" (*JCS*) as does Clark 1931. *Amphrisa* "may very well have formed with four other similar pieces, such a play as the present title [*Five Plays in One*] implies" (Greg 1904–08); other plays in the group may include *Apollo and Daphne* and *Jupiter and Io*.

SR 29 August 1635. O 1637 *Pleasant Dialogues and Dramas*; separate TP entitled *A Pastoral Drama called Amphrisa, or The Forsaken Shepherdess*; RT *Pelopœa and Alope*; "never before published," according to the address to the reader; argument; not divided. Some SDs: "*She presents a wreath of willow*"; "*Musicke sounds, and they dance the measure.*" In addition to the SDs, *Amphrisa* uses speech headings (Johnson 2003).

Amphrisa is "clearly designed as a showcase for the female participants' singing, discoursing, and dancing," and within the work "a queen asserts to a group of innocent shepherdesses that these accomplishments 'may become a theatre of eyes, / Yet wrest no blushes from you'" (Tomlinson 1992b). The acting by Queen Henrietta Maria and her ladies in *The Shepherd's Paradise* (1633) may have inspired Heywood's entertainment.

Amurath. See *The Courageous Turk*.

Amyntas, or The Impossible Dowry, A Pastoral. Thomas Randolph. Licensed for acting 26 November 1630 (Kelliher 2004b). Possibly written originally for an audience at Cambridge University (Levenson 1987). Later acted by the King's Revels Children at Salisbury Court (Burner 1988). Possibly, like *The Muses' Looking Glass*, performed earlier by that company on tour during the plague closing of April-November 1630. The O1 separate TP records performance at Whitehall before the king and queen, "probably in 1631" (Kelliher).

SR 5 April 1642. O1 1638 *Poems* (with *The Muses' Looking Glass*); dramatis personae; prologue and epilogue (by Pilumnus); chorus of swains; five acts and separate scenes; continuous register but page numbers begin anew with this play. In the "Prologus" a Nymph and Shepherd argue about who should deliver the prologue: the Shepherd maintains that "Men are more eloquent then women made," while the Nymph responds, "But women are more powerfull to perswade." The Shepherd and Nymph amicably decide to divide the lines of the prologue. Sound effects include birdsong: a character says, "What aire is that? The voice of—turtles billing." A SD indicates a different sound effect: "*A crow cawes*." Another such direction has: "*Dorilas with a quaile-pipe*." Yet another kind of auditory effect is heard at the close: "There is an echo scene at the very end of the play in which Echo brings about the final resolution" (Herrick 1955). O2 1640 "the 2^d edition much enlarged," according to the engraved TP; author's initials on the separate TP; continuous register with *Muses* but new pagination for this play. O3 1643 *Poems* (with *The Muses' Looking Glass*, *The Jealous Lovers*); "the third edition inlarged"; general TP dated 1643; each play has separately dated TP; *Amyntas* dated 1640. O3 reissued 1646. O4 1652 *Poems* (with *The Jealous Lovers*, *The Muses' Looking Glass*, *Aristippus*); two issues; "the fourth edition inlarged." O5 1664 *Poems* (with *Aristippus*, *The Conceited Peddler*, *The Jealous Lovers*, *The Muses' Looking Glass*); "the fifth edition, with several additions, corrected and amended"; separate TP dated 1662.

In this, "the most entertaining" of English pastoral tragicomedies (Herrick 1955), Randolph has "retained almost unaltered the dramatic construction of Guarini and his school, though evincing a tendency towards greater complexity in the arrangement of characters; but he sought at the same time to bring the whole into accordance with English taste by the addition, very skillfully managed, of a comic underplot" (Greg 1905). Randolph's treatment of love resembles that of French pastoral, "which [Queen] Henrietta helped introduce in the twenties and whose popularity continued into the thirties" (Veevers 1989).

Andromana, or The Merchant's Wife. J. S. Probably written in 1642 (Bowers 1940, Randall 1995). Because the theaters closed in September, it was probably not performed.

SR 19 May 1660 *The Tragedy of Andromana, or the fatall & deserved end of disloyalty & ambition*, by Jam: Shirley [almost certainly a mistaken attribution]. Q 1660 author's initials on the TP; HT same as that given in the SR; list of characters; five acts and separate scenes. Ample SDs: "*Enter to him* Andromana *in mourning, with a hood over her face, which she throws up when she sees the king*." A murder seems inspired by the killing of Polonius in *Hamlet*: "Plangus *stirs behinde the hangings.* Rinatus *draws and runs at him. They fetch him out*."

"The title *Andromana* accurately indicates that the primary focus is on a woman. We may assume that Andromana's multifaced heinousness is supposed to be magnified by the fact that she is—as advertised in the subtitle—a 'Merchant's Wife'"; "the story of the havoc that may be wrought by an insatiate, unscrupulous, merchant-class woman is laid out for us plainly in the drama's second and suspiciously timely subtitle . . . printed on the first page of the 1660 text: '*The Fatal and Deserved End of Disloyalty and Ambition*'" (Randall 1995).

Andronicus, A Tragedy: Impiety's Long Success, or Heaven's Late Revenge. Thomas Fuller. "[A]ppears to have been written in the 1640s" (Potter 1981); written 1643 (Wood 1954). The address to the reader, signed by "Philanax," reports of the play: "It was born some eighteen years since in Oxford, thence carried by a casualty to York. The author thereof, conceiving this, (the only copy) utterly lost, found it beyond his expectation in London some moneths since. Thus weary with long wandring, it hopeth at last to finde quiet repose, and candid reception, reader, with thee." This comment suggests performance by students at Oxford.

    SR none. O 1661 no author named; dramatis personae; "chorus consisting of two companies"; five acts and separate scenes. A colloquy closes the play: "A chorus consisting of two parts *Grecian* and *Persian*, one gown-men, the other sword-men." Some detailed SDs: "*Enter* Menander, *and six of his servants in mourning, bringing* Artemia's *corps in a black coffin under a velvet herse; and advance it in the midst of the roome.*" Detailed auditory effects: "*Enter* Monobius *a great noise and busling within. One swears and curses aloud above all the rest.*" Staging requires a scaffold for the execution of Lapardus, which is not carried out; instead, the man is blinded: "[the executioner] *binds him, bores out his eyes, the surgeon claps plaisters on them.*" Lepardus then "*holds his eyes in his hand.*"

    The play is not an early draft by John Wilson of his *Andronicus Comnenius* (1664): "Wilson's play is based upon Fuller's prose account [of Andronicus], which in turn often follows quite closely the play that underlies it" (Wood).

Antigone, the Theban Princess. Thomas May. ?Acted 1627–31 (*JCS*) at undetermined venue. Although performance is uncertain, the play "registers some deep anxieties about the trend in Caroline politics at the dawn of the 1630s, juxtaposing notions of tyrannical rule against an ideal of leadership based upon monarchical responsibility and dialogue with the people" (Britland 2006a).

    SR none. O 1631 *The Tragedy of Antigone, the Theban Princess*; author's initials on the TP and May signs the dedication; "a short argument of this tragedy"; chorus; five acts and separate scenes. SDs, though minimal, anticipate production: "*Menaetes and Argia with the dead body*"; "*Antigone with a torch*"; "*Two haggs passe over the stage.*"

    The author's dedication discusses reasons for the pleasure afforded by tragedy on the stage: "All the spectatours are either wretched or fortunate; the wretched in sad storyes are in some sort eased by fellowship in woe, or delighted with tragicall expressions, as being somewhat of kindred with their owne thoughts; those that are fortunate, are affected, in such showes, either with delight, or wholsome sorrow; if they be delighted, it is in the tast of their own prosperity, which appeares greater, set off by an object of such contrariety; & this delight is not out of malice (as pleased with the woes of others) but acknowledgement to those high powers which made the difference; if they be sorrowfull, their sorrow is wholsome; for as in melancholly diseases merry tales are used to assist nature: so in too great a joy, & wantonnes of the soule, such sad representations are as a good allay, depressing the levity of their thoughts to such a meane, as is fit to entertaine the best contemplations."

The Antipodes, A Comedy. Richard Brome. Written 1636 (Clark 1992) and intended for Beeston's Boys at the Phoenix, but "a complex and protracted dispute requiring arbitration from the Master of the Revels" ensued; there is no evidence that the play, composed "half illicitly, in exchange for a loan" was ever performed at the Phoenix (Steggle 2004b). Instead, it was "acted in the yeare 1638" by Queen Henrietta Maria's Men at the Salisbury Court playhouse, according to the TP; the Queen's Men acted at this theater from 1637 "until the closing of the theatres" (Parr 1995). The Selbourne copy of Q contains a handwritten cast list next to the printed names of the characters (McEvilla 2012).

SR 19 March 1640; transferred 17 February 1648. Q 1640 list of characters; prologue printed between commendatory poems; a prologue (by Quailpipe) also precedes a play-within-the-play which is not actually presented; epilogue by Doctor and Peregrine; description of dumb shows; five acts and separate scenes. SDs specify domestic detail and costumes: "*Hoboyes. A service as for dinner, passe over the stage, borne by many servitors richly apparreld*"; "*Enter in sea-gownes and caps, Doctor and Peregrine brought in a chaire by 2 sailors: cloaks and hats brought on.*" The most unusual staging involves the play-within-the-play: "In order to cure Peregrine of his [Sir John] Mandeville-inspired melancholy, Dr. Hughball and Lord Letoy stage a play to persuade the young man that he has travelled to the Antipodean lands described in Mandeville's text—a world of Amazons, and one-footed peoples, of woolly hens, and women with stings in their hymens who would slay their husbands on their wedding nights were other men not hired" (Sanders 1999b). (Doctor Hughball is "the first practicing psychiatrist to appear on the English stage" [Kaufmann 1961].) "The antipodean 'byplay,' presenting to Peregrine the things he imagined he most wished to see, forces him to see them not as desirable but as repugnant, driving him steadily back to normality" (Donaldson 1970). This entails consummating his marriage with Martha, who in her frustration would find companionship with Barbara: "I'll lie with you and practise, if you please. Pray take me for a night or two." "Peregrine's obsession with travel and his lack of attention to his wife have driven her out of her wits" (Jowitt 2002). Martha's sexual history includes "casual sex with an unnamed woman; marriage utterly devoid of sex; request to a female acquaintance for erotic instruction; marital consummation with an unfaithful husband" (Traub 2009). "The play ends with two masques. An antimasque, in which Discord and her henchmen—Folly, Jealousy, Melancholy, and Madness—the breeders of common strife, take over, is followed by the main masque in which Harmony leads Mercury, Cupid, Bacchus, and Apollo—the maintainers of a commonwealth" (Haaker 1966).

Brome objected to the trend for court plays, staged with expensive costumes and represented by Suckling's *Aglaura*, a play characterized by "sterile formalism"

(Neill 1978). Prologue distinguishes "between 'the old way of plays' (now, he claims, 'the weakest branch o'th' stage') from the current fashion for empty high-sounding spectacle" (Parr 1995). In a postscript the playwright explains that the acted and printed forms of his play are different, that he had intended *Antipodes* for Beeston's Boys but was forced by his contract with Salisbury Court to have it performed there: "You shal[l] find in this booke more then was presented upon the stage, and left out of the presentation, for superfluous length (as some of the players pretended). I tho[u]ght good al[l] should be inserted according to the al-lowed original; and as it was, at first, intended for the Cock-pit stage, in the right of my most deserving friend Mr. William Beeston, unto whom it properly apper-tained; and so I leave it to thy perusal, as it was generally applauded, and well act-ed at Salisbury Court." "The confusion about companies in this note derives from Brome's troubles over his playwright's contract with the Salisbury Court players, and the slight animosity in the phrase 'as some of the players pretended' reflects his irritation at what he thought was his ill-usage" (Bentley 1971). However, "the players' sense of theatre was more acute than Brome's" (McLuskie 1981).

Antipoe. Francis Verney. ?Acted 1603–08 (*AED 3*) at undetermined venue, pos-sibly Trinity College, Oxford, by students.

Oxford, Bodleian, MS Eng. Poet. e.5; *The Tragedy of Antipoe*; no author named on the TP but Verney signs the dedication and address to the reader; list of characters; prologue ("You brave assembly that doe here attend"); five acts and separate scenes. Ample SDs: *"Drupon takes his rapier to runne Macros through, and plucks his hatt in his eyes, fearing to looke on his face."* Spectacular staging includes: *"Enter a crue of blacke divells running to Macros to strangle him"; "Enter the Ghost of Dramurgon"*; Antipoe calls the Ghost "monster of hell." Possible use of descent machinery: *"Enter an Angell hoveringe over their heads."*

Nicolas Leatt, apparently the scribe, records the date June 1622 in the MS; this notation appears in a different hand from that of the play and was added to the MS after its composition.

The Antiquary, A Comedy. Shackerley Marmion. Acted winter season of 1634–35; no acting license extant (Green 1987). By Queen Henrietta Maria's Men at the Phoenix, according to the TP.

SR 11 March 1640. Q 1641 list of characters; five acts. A character alludes to descent machinery: "I will have all these descend from the top of my roof, in a throne, as you see Cupid or Mercury in a play."

Marmion's comedy "incorporates an actual historical event, the closure in 1629 of an antiquarian library, presumed to be that of Sir Robert Cotton" (Drakakis 2004).

Antonio and Mellida. John Marston. Acted October 1599 (Gair 1982), or 1599/1600 (Cathcart 2001a), or 1601 (Neill & Jackson 1998). "Sundry times acted by" Paul's Boys, according to the Q TP, at Paul's playhouse. Paul's Boys "possibly opened their new playhouse in 1599" with this play (White 1998), which is "strikingly self-conscious about its venue and its presentation, as if it was their first overt venture into the openly commercial playing world of the adult groups" (Gurr 2009d). A Q SD preserves the names of Robert Coles and John Norwood, members of the company. Marston "generally framed his plays for eighteen characters. That is the precise number in each of the two parts of *Antonio and Mellida*" (Lawrence 1927).

SR 24 October 1601; transferred 10 April 1627; 30 May 1627; 6 November 1628; 6 December 1630; 22 July 1644. Q 1602 *The History of Antonio and Mellida, The First Part*; author's initials on the TP; induction, "which flatters the 'elect' audience and introduces the new company" (Gair 2000); prologue and epilogue (by Andrugio); in act 1 two groups of characters appear, one on main stage and one above, and the former "performs a kind of mime" (Mehl 1965); five acts. The epilogue is spoken by an actor wearing a distinctive costume as "armed" (Stern 2004b). In keeping with the small dimensions of Paul's playhouse, "the *Antonio* plays create a constant sense that characters and situations are miniaturized within an encircling frame of actors" (Gair 2000). Unusual staging includes a chance meeting of the lovers, who have become separated and are in disguise: "Antonio shifts from English to Italian to vent his sorrow over Mellida, and finds Mellida responding to him on her own sorrow also in the new tongue. Thus, the recognition takes place entirely in Italian" (Hoenselaars 1992b). Staging includes the use of portraits as props when a painter carries them onstage as evidence of his talent: "*Enter* Balurdo, *a painter with two pictures.*" One portrait may be Marston's, the other that of William Stanley (Gair 1978b). In a *coup de théâtre* a coffin is carried onto stage and Antonio rises from it, astonishing Andrugio, who thought his son dead. O 1633 *The Works of Mr. John Marston, Being Tragedies and Comedies, Collected into One Volume* (with *Antonio's Revenge, The Dutch Courtesan, Parasitaster, What You Will, The Wonder of Women*); two issues; separate TPs bear a 1633 date and Marston's name. The reissue, *Tragedies and Comedies Collected into One Volume*, removes Marston's name from general and separate TPs; William Sheares had published the collection without Marston's consent. Also issued in a made-up Q entitled *Comedies, Tragi-Comedies, & Tragedies* (1652), no longer extant.

Q Prologue salutes "this faire troope: / Select, and most respected auditours" at Paul's, a so-called private playhouse, which attracted more socially distinguished playgoers than those at public theaters. The induction alludes to the custom of playing instrumental music before performance at private theaters: "Come, sirs, come: the musique will sounde straight for entrance." Music also figures in many SDs, including the first: "*The cornets sound a battle within*"; "*Enter Matzagente, Piero meetes him, embraceth; at which the cornets sound a florish.*" By the play's attention to music and dance, "Marston is consciously and deliberately using the special talents of his chorister-actors to extend the dramatic context with a musical dimension: a first tentative and hesitant step towards a pseudo-operatic form" (Gair 1982).

Antonio in the induction anticipates a sequel: "[the characters] should receive more exact accomplishment in a second part: which, if this obtain gratious acceptance, meanes to try his fortune."

Antonio's Revenge. John Marston. Acted 1599–1600 (Mann 2012) or 1600–01 (Gair 1978a). "Sundry times acted by" Paul's Boys, according to the Q TP, at Paul's playhouse. Prologue indicates performance in winter: "The rawish dank of clumszie winter ramps / The fluent summers vaine: and drizling sleete / Chilleth the wan bleak cheek of the numd earth, / Whilst snarling gusts nibble the juyceles leaves, / From the nak't shuddring branch." Striking similarities between this play and Shakespeare's *Hamlet* have led to the supposition that one depends on the other (Frost 1968); the likelihood is that *Hamlet* precedes *Antonio's Revenge* (Jenkins 1982, Cathcart 2001a), though both plays may be independently indebted to Thomas Kyd's lost *Hamlet*. "[R]equires at least twenty players" (Knutson 2001b).

SR 24 October 1601. Q 1602 *Antonio's Revenge, the Second Part*; author's initials on the TP; HT *The Second Part of the History of Antonio and Mellida*; RT *The Second Part of Antonio and Mellida*; prologue; detailed descriptions of three dumb shows; five acts and separate scenes. "A profusion of stage directions, especially those for music, and they are unusually long and descriptive" (Jewkes 1958). The play "exploits at every turn the musical potential of the young performers for pathos, humour, contrast, surprise, as well as the more conventional functions of royal entries, vocal accompaniment, dumb shows, masquing, and dances" (Mann 2012). The play opens "with a startling theatrical effect" (Lever 1971b), which may be termed "an emblematic" SD (Geckle 1980): "*Enter* Piero, *unbrac't, his armes bare, smear'd in blood, a poniard in one hand bloodie and a torch in the other,* Strotzo *following him with a corde.*" "No other Elizabethan play begins with anything like the announcement of the savage nature of its world that Marston makes here" (Ayres 1972). This entry "is reminiscent . . . of Hieronimo's entry with a dagger in one hand and a rope in the other to commit suicide in *The Spanish Tragedy*" (Ingram 1978). Later, "*Enter* Antonio, *his arms bloody, a torch [in one hand] and a poniard [in the other].*" "The visual link between Piero in act 1 and Antonio in act 3 is firm and obvious and raises questions about the stature of our hero-revenger when for a striking moment he stands before us as a duplication or reincarnation of his bloody antagonist" (Dessen 1977). "Antonio is a grotesque inflation of the traditional revenger" (Ayres). Grotesque staging includes "the carved-up limbs of a child [Piero's son Julio] on a platter and the severing of a tongue"; "[d]ismemberment so pervades the play as to infiltrate its very structure" (Owens 2005). "An ample bladder of blood, capable of producing a visible fountain, may have been required for the moment when Antonio addresses" the body parts of the dead child (Owens). Piero himself is tortured and stabbed: "*the conspirators bind* Piero, *pluck out his tongue and tryumph over him*"; then "*They all run at* Piero *with their rapiers.*" "Marston exploits the surprise effect of the sudden drawing of curtains: the "*body of* Feliche, *stabbed thick with wounds*"; later "the curtains of a bed are drawn to display to Maria the '*Ghost of* Andrugio'" (Gair 1978b). "At the instigation of the Ghost, who groans encouragingly beneath the stage, Antonio takes his revenge on Piero by stabbing his little boy to death and doing it with a kiss" (Styan 1996); Antonio "allows [Piero's] blood to drip upon Andrugio's tomb as a sacrificial offering to the god of Vengeance" (Gair 1978b). A dungeon holds Mellida, and Antonio visits her: "*Antonio kisseth Mellida's hand: then Mellida goes from the grate*"; "[t]his scene clearly requires some kind of vent, if not real grating. What is not certain is whether the stage trap represented it, or whether one of the doors in the *frons scenae* included a grating"; later Balurdo's prison "certainly lies below the stage trap, for he speaks several lines '*from under the stage*'" (Ichikawa 2005). Staging culminates in a masque that facilitates revenge: "*Enter Antonio and Alberto, at severall doors, their rapiers drawne, in their masking attyre.*" A SD indicates the existence of not one but two music houses: "*While the measure is dauncing, Andrugios ghost is placed betwixt the music houses.*" "Symbolically Andrugio looks down from heaven upon the hell in which Piero will find himself" (Gair 1978b). Prologue's allusion to "black-visag'd showes" may point to the use of stage hangings appropriate for tragedy. A stage funeral for Andrugio offers "a glimpse of a dramatist mobilizing all the resources of his company to evoke the splendor of the real event" (Neill 1985).

O 1633 *The Works of Mr. John Marston, Being Tragedies and Comedies, Collected into One Volume* (with *Antonio and Mellida, The Dutch Courtesan, Parasitaster, What You Will, The Wonder of Women*); two issues. The reissue, entitled *Tragedies and Comedies Collected into One Volume*, removes Marston's name from the general and separate TPs; William Sheares had published the collection without Marston's consent. Also issued in a made-up Q entitled *Comedies, Tragi-Comedies, & Tragedies* (1652), no longer extant.

RT *The Second Part of Antonio and Mellida*; the play was originally intended as a sequel to *Antonio and Mellida*. However, "*Antonio's Revenge* has little in common with the earlier play except for the reappearance of some of the characters. *Antonio and Mellida* is a romantic comedy" (Lever 1971b); in the sequel "fantastical comedy converts to tragedy" (Butler 2002). "The two parts were never performed at a single sitting" (Hunter 1965).

Antony and Cleopatra. William Shakespeare. Acted 1606-early 1607 (Neill 1994) by the King's Men, "although we have no direct evidence of this" (Bevington 1990). Possibly written for the Blackfriars: "The smaller private theater offered the theatrical advantages of a more 'claustrophobic' atmosphere, appropriate to this play's often satirically framed wars—indoors and also suitable for a stylized presentation of its battle scenes" (Madelaine 1998). Probably performed at Whitehall, Christmas season 1606–07 (Barroll 1991). Richard Burbage "probably" played Antony (Taylor 2002b). John Rice "might be considered a likely first performer of the role of Cleopatra" (Astington 2010). Probably also acted at the first Globe.

SR 20 May 1608; 8 November 1623; transferred ?4 August 1626 Paviers right in Shaksperes *plaies*; ?19 June 1627 widow of Isaac Jaggard . . . her parte in Shackspheere *playes*; 16 November 1630; 1 July 1637 Shakespeares *workes* their Part; 6 August 1674; 21 August 1683. F1 1623 *Comedies, Histories, & Tragedies*; three issues; "published according to the true originall copies"; *The Tragedy of Antony and Cleopatra*; not divided despite the designation of act 1, scene 1. "The act and scene divisions are in the main the contributions of eighteenth-century editors" (Garber 2004). A SD indicates the source of other-worldly music in 4.3 as *"under the stage"* (Bevington 1990); this "is clearly a special effect imposed by the dialogue of that play, which requires mysterious music when the god Hercules leaves Antony" (Hosley 1960); "the very stage has given up on its hero" (Stern 2010b). Such music would have been more effective at the indoor Blackfriars than at the Globe (Madelaine). Before the battle of Actium "Eros enters with a heavy, amorphous, and unwieldy armful of Antony's armour and deposits it on the stage. Cleopatra gathers up the many scattered pieces and, in arming Antony, constructs 'a man of steel'" (Harlan 2008). Sound effects suggest the battle of Actium offstage: they include *"the noise of a sea-fight"*; later a SD reads, *"Alarum afarre off, as at a sea-fight."* After Actium, Cleopatra and her attendants take refuge in "her monument": *"Enter Cleopatra, and her maides aloft."* The monument scene "is unique in the Shakespeare canon in that it seems to have demanded a special structure to stage the first of the play's two tragic deaths," presumably in front of the tiring-house wall (Gurr & Ichikawa 2000); Hodges 1968 similarly suggests such "an impermanent special structure." But Reynolds 1967 observes that "so large a structure—and it must be large enough to allow at least six persons in its upper story—could be moved into place only with difficulty, or if it were imposed on the regular set at the beginning of the play, would be very much in the way." So there may have been no such structure: Cleopatra could simply have been positioned in the gallery, occupying a space akin to one of the boxes, or compartments, *above* in the De Witt sketch of the Swan (Saunders 1968); the mortally wounded Antony could then be hoisted *"aloft to Cleopatra,"* perhaps by means of a chair, rope, and winch (Hosley 1964b), though there is "only one other recorded contemporary theatrical hoisting" (Lamb 1980). Alternatively, Antony may have been hoisted by means of taffeta wrapped around the actor: Daniel's *Cleopatra* describes her drawing "him up in rowles of taffety" (Rees 1953). Another possibility is "that Antony is lifted up to Cleopatra in the gallery [by ropes] but not on to it, and that he is lowered again to the main stage after he dies to be carried out by his men at the end of the scene" (Thomson 1988b). F2 1632 "the second impression"; three issues. F3 1663 "the third impression"; reissued 1664 with seven additional plays. F4 1685 "the fourth edition"; two issues.

Shakespeare's is "the first known rendering of this hitherto recondite love-affair for the public stage" (Barroll 2002); Samuel Daniel's *Cleopatra*, first published in 1594, was "newly altered" by Daniel, who may have been influenced by Shakespeare's play, and published in 1607; Daniel's revision "is probably indebted in a number of details to Shakespeare's play" (Wells & Taylor 1987). Shakespeare, in turn, may have been influenced by Daniel's 1594 *Cleopatra* (Wilders 1995) or Daniel's 1605 edition (Curran 2007); "his reading of Daniel's play impelled him towards . . . the divided catastrophe" (Barton 1973). Shakespeare may also have been influenced by Mary Sidney's *Antonie* (Norland 2009) as well as by *Caesar and Pompey, or Caesar's Revenge* (Ronan 1987). Cleopatra is "one of only three female characters whose names are featured in the titles of Shakespeare's plays, and of those three she is the only one who has a greater role in the dramatic action than the male character with whom her name is paired" (Rackin 2005).

Anything for a Quiet Life, A Comedy. Thomas Middleton and John Webster (Jackson 2006a). Acted 1621 (Lake 1975a). "Formerly acted" at the [second] Blackfriars by the King's Men, according to the TP, but "the play sounds more like Globe than Blackfriars fare" (*JCS*).

SR none. Q 1662 "never before printed"; dramatis personae; prologue and epilogue; five acts. Middleton's name alone appears on the TP, and Kirkman in 1662 wrote that the play was "written by Middleton." But "Webster's hand" in the play "is established beyond reasonable doubt" (Lake). "That both authors are in the extant play can be regarded as highly probable" (Jackson 1979).

With the exception of the prologue and epilogue, the play is written entirely in prose.

The Aphrodisial, or Sea Feast. William Percy. No evidence of production but, according to a note in MSS Huntington HM 4 and Alnwick 509, the author intended that his plays be staged either by Paul's Boys or by the Children of the Revels. Percy's "plays suggest private performance" (Hillebrand 1938). "A version of" this play "could possibly have been played at Paul's in the early phase of their revival (1599–1603)" (Gair 2004). "The occasion for which [the play] was written seems to have been the christening of William Percy's nephew Algernon Percy, the eldest surviving son of the ninth earl of Northumberland," 14 October 1602, at Essex House (Dodds 1931c).

(1) San Marino, CA, Huntington, MS HM 4 [later of the Percy MSS of this play], fols. 120–51; in *Comedies and Pastorals*; the general TP, dated 1647, gives the author's initials; the date "1602" is written under title of this play; entitled *The Aphrodisial or Sea-Feast*; signs of revision; list of characters; list of properties; prologue (by Cupid in disguise as Harpax the fisherman) and epilogue (by Cupid); chorus; five acts and separate scenes. Staging calls for use of trap door, apparently, when Leander, "*naked crownd with blewe seaweedes,*" draws Hero downward: "*He pluckt [her] under water to him.*" Also "*a showre of rose-water and comfits, as was once acted at Christ Church in Oxford, in Dido and Aeneas.*" Careful description of costumes: "*Vulcan, apparreld lyke a lord, aprone and hammer withall, knit*

scull-cap called a night-cap, chuff and oldish. His ordinary suite in the Marinall gold lace wholelye." Elaborate staging and painted scenery and description of stage properties: *"Next Proteus hall. A chaire of state of turves and clowdes, and a long bank of turves and clowdes jumpe even on either syde the chaire representing a verdaunt banck of the sea. The chaire not highly raild and plact in midde under the court. Highest of all on top of the musick tree the title* The Aphrodysial or Sea Feast. *In a corner of the stage the Balenes denne. The stage hong all . . . with clowd cullour, otherwise with arras, or other sea properties befitting, arras best I conceive."* Percy's plays "show a use of locality boards which is nowhere else so completely illustrated in Elizabethan drama; that such signboards existed is adequately proved by considerable other evidence, but Percy's plays furnish a unique statement as to how they were employed" (Reynolds 1914). Percy also makes prominent use of music: "the consort plays for a 'transcension' (perhaps a processional dance) by sailors and tritons, then for a banquet, then for a dance of 'Ceales and of Porpusyes'" (Long 1980). (2) Alnwick, UK, Alnwick Castle, MS 509 [earlier than Huntington MS]; *The Aphrodisial, or Fish-Feast, A Marinal*; "finis 1602"; the general TP dated 1646; author's initials on the TP.

"The most interesting part of the play is the imitation of 'The Merry Wives of Windsor' in the scenes between Vulcan and the two nymphs Arida and Humida. . . . Vulcan sends to each of the nymphs a letter in almost identical terms. . . . The two compare their letters and resolve to be revenged on Vulcan" (Dodds 1931c).

Apius and Virginia. R. B. [?Richard Bower]. Acted 1565 or 1566 (Hedley 1988). "[T]he modesty of the prologue, suggesting a first attempt at playing, the songs for all the cast, and the reference to a 'worshipful' audience, suggest a children's play before a civic or courtly audience" (Walker 1998). However, the character of the Vice, Haphazard, suggests a connection with drama performed by professional companies: "His intimacy with [the audience], his repeated and conventional pickpurse warnings, his colloquialisms and coarse humour, all come from the popular stage" (Hedley).

SR *c.* October 1567 (Grantley 2004). Q 1575 *A New Tragical Comedy of Apius and Virginia, wherein is Lively Expressed a Rare Example of the Virtue of Chastity, by Virginia's Constancy, in Wishing rather to be Slain at her own Father's Hands, than to be Deflowered of the Wicked Judge Appius*; author's initials and list of characters on the TP; prologue and epilogue; during a monologue personified characters enact, if not a dumb show, at least "a kind of allegorical intensification" (Mehl 1965); not divided. Unusual staging includes *"Here let him* [Apius] *make as thogh he went out and let Conscience and Justice come out of him, and let Conscience hold in his hande a lamp burning and let Justice have a sworde and hold it before Apius brest."* "It seems that they [Conscience and Justice] glide out from an entrance at the back of the stage, this entrance being masked by Apius as he turns away from the audience towards it. They are obviously meant to appear to issue from his body" (Craik 1958). "The theatrically emphatic presence of these two figures (with their striking entrance, their emblems, and their gestures) is then linked verbally to Apius's own conscience and sense of justice" (Dessen 1977). The beheading of Virginia occurs in sight of playgoers: *"Here tye a handcarcher aboute hir eyes, and then strike of hir heade."* Later, Virginius gives the severed head to Apius. Staging requires a property tomb following Virginia's execution: "Doctrina *and* Memorie *and* Virginius *bring a tome."* "The tomb serves as a magisterial emblem of the enclosure of the virgin body, a sign not of loss but of triumph, the culmination of the virgin's struggle to fortify her body against sexual penetration" (Owens 2005). The staging dramatizes Virginia's virtuous reputation: *"Here let* Memorie *wright on the tome."*

"The cast includes a large number of women's parts" (Bevington 1962). "This is one of a small number of extant interludes about exemplary sexual virtue and one of relatively few in which women feature to any great extent" (Grantley). The play "represents an attempt to accommodate the spectacle of martyrdom to the post-Reformation stage" (Owens 2005). R. B.'s play "expresses the ideology of militant Protestantism at a time when its goals were to protect the Elizabethan government against attack from Catholicism and, at the same time, to work on developing its infra-structure of a family church" (Goldberg 1986).

Apollo and Daphne. Thomas Heywood. A short dramatic entertainment possibly intended for private performance. The address to the reader calls this work "stage-poetry." Possibly written for inclusion in *The Ages* (Clark 1931).

SR 29 August 1635. O 1637 *Pleasant Dialogues and Dramas,* wherein the table of contents calls it *A second [drama] from Ovid called Apollo and Daphne;* "never before published," according to the address to the reader; argument; concludes with song; not divided. Some SDs: *"Enter* Apollo *with his glittering beames";* "Sudden musicke, and she is turned into a lawrel tree." In addition to the SDs, *Apollo and Daphne* uses speech headings (Johnson 2003).

Fleay 1891 speculates that *Apollo and Daphne* was part of *"Five Plays in One,* acted at the Rose 1597." Heywood's play "may very well have formed with four other similar pieces, such a play as the present title [*Five Plays in One*] implies" (Greg 1904–08); other pieces in the group may include *Amphrisa, The Forsaken Shepherdess,* and *Jupiter and Io.*

Apollo Shroving. William Hawkins; author's identity established by Isaac Reed 1782. Acted 6 February 1627 (Shrove Tuesday) by scholars of the Free School of Hadleigh, Suffolk, according to the TP. "Shrove Tuesday, unlike both Christmas and Easter, is not a religious feast but rather a secular festival, a final opportunity for the household to celebrate before the strict observance of Lent" (Westfall 1990).

SR 8 April 1627 A Comodie called *Apollo Shrovinge.* O 1627 no author named; dramatis personae with names of the student actors; prologue and epilogue; scanty SDs; five acts and separate scenes. The play's title is printed within a pennant on the TP. A prefatory note explains that the author wrote the play as a "by-exercise for his schollars at the last carneval." Performed in a schoolroom (Rhoads 1936).

A "young scholar" speaks the prologue; he is interrupted by a woman play-goer (also an actor). In act 1, scene 1, this female playgoer/actor says: "I'le into the tyreing house, and scramble and rangle for a mans part. Why should not women act men, as well as boyes act women? I will wear the breeches, so I will." "The wearing of breeches would become a fact of the court theatricals of Henrietta Maria" (Sanders 1999a). "[T]his prologue functions as a graphic articulation of assertiveness on the part of the female audience, both as auditors and would-be actors" (Tomlinson 1992b). Within the play a woman complains, "I'd rather spin at home, then hear these barbarians spout Latin." "Presenting a domestic spectator out of control, *Apollo Shroving* burlesques the cultural antagonism between Latin and domesticity" (Wall 2002).

Appius and Virginia, A Tragedy. John Webster and Thomas Heywood (Clark 1931, Boas 1950b, Jackson 1985, 1998). "[W]ritten originally for Henslowe's Red Bull company" (Gurr 1988a). Acted "before 1616, probably around 1608" (Culhane 2004) or 1626 (Gunby & Lees-Jeffries 2002) "for one of Beeston's companies" (Gunby et al. 2003) at the Phoenix. In playlist of Beeston's Boys 10 August 1639.

SR 13 May 1654 *Appeus and Virginia* Tragedy written by John Webster; transferred 11 June 1659. Q 1654 five issues (two dated 1654; the third, 1655; fourth, 1659; fifth, 1679); Webster's name alone appears on the TP; five acts and first scenes.

Although Virginia "has few lines with which to assert herself," neverthe-less "in performance her symbolic importance as an icon of innocence and virtue is humanized, and she can be powerful in her silent awareness and resistance" (Carnegie 2003c). At the climactic moment Virginius usurps the power of an unjust court and kills his own daughter. He is then pursued: *"Enter Virginius with his knife, that and his arms stript up to the elbowes all bloudy; coming into the midst of the souldiers, he makes a stand."* Covered in his daughter's blood, he justifies his actions and wins over the soldiers but subsequently kills himself.

The story "seems to provide a vehicle for criticism of the duke of Buckingham, the deeply unpopular favourite of King Charles I" (Gunby 2004). "An obvious question . . . is whether it is mere coincidence that [Appius's] story was registered for publication in mid-May 1654, a relatively short time after Cromwell had become Lord Protector (December 1653) and dissolved the Parliament of the Saints (January 1654)" (Randall 1995). The play makes the point that "undue reverence for authority, whether through awe, cowardice, cynicism or political naiveté, is destructive of individuals and of the commonweal" (Goldberg 1986).

Arabia Sitiens, or A Dream of a Dry Year, a Tragicomedy. William Percy. No evidence of production but, according to a note in MSS Huntington HM 4 and Alnwick 509, the author intended that his plays be staged either by Paul's Boys or by the Children of the Revels. Percy's "plays suggest private performance" (Hillebrand 1938). "A version of" this play "could possibly have been played at Paul's in the early phase of their revival (1599–1603)" (Gair 2004). "One of the angels may have been played by Solomon Pavy" (Gair 1982), the celebrated child actor who died in July 1602. Perhaps written for a specific occasion (Hillebrand); according to the prologue, "Comoedyes be not for sad dayes, you seye, / Tragoedyes too will not this blissd day fit." "The reference here is to Essex's rebellion in January 1601"; "'this blissd day' is the festival for which the play was written" (Dodds 1933). Possibly intended for reading aloud at Percy's home (Dimmock 2006).

(1) San Marino, CA, Huntington, MS HM 4, fols. 32–61 [latest of Percy MSS of this play]; *Comedies and Pastorals*; author's initials on the general TP, dated 1647; *Arabia Sitiens, or a Dream of a Dry Year*; "finis 1601"; list of characters; list of properties; prologue (by "Mahomet or Woman" ["you may chuse the fitter"]) and epilogue; chorus; signs of revision; five acts and separate scenes. Detailed SDs. Following the epilogue, a direction reads, "if for actors": "*a huge globe of fyre pendaunt from roofe of the howse . . . If for Powles, a full moone onely appearing on face of the stage, thourough the cloth and right over the tribunall, so till the whole companie be departed*." The staging is often intricate: in what he calls a "Logicall fugue," Percy describes "four characters—Mahomet, Gabriel, Metraon, and Adriel—each representing the major premise of a syllogism. They stand each at one of the four points of the compass and each holds a colored ball. The azure ball represents Prudence; the silver ball, Temperance; the gold ball, Justice; and the red ball, Fortitude. As Mahomet sings the major premise, 'All vertues be of equall complexion,' he throws the azure ball to another singer and moves diagonally toward his opposite singer who exchanges places with him. The other singers follow suit, each singing his particular premise, until the syllogisms are completed with a statement of all the major premises" (Long 1980). (2) Alnwick, UK, Alnwick Castle, MS 508 [earliest of the Percy MSS], fols. 30–64; entitled *Mahomet and His Heaven, or Epimenide* [changed from *Epimethea*], *Grand Empress of the Deserts of Arabia, or A Dream of a Dry Summer, or The Weather-Woman, A Tragicomedy*; alternate prologue (by Epimenide as the Weather Woman) and epilogue; "finis 1601"; MS dated 1644 (in *The Fairy Pastoral*). (3) Alnwick MS 509; *Arabia Sitiens, or A Dream of a Dry Year, A Tragicomedy*; "finis 1601"; the general TP, which gives author's initials, is dated 1646. First edited by Dimmock 2006.

"Percy knew a good deal about Islam, and a good deal about the legends which the Christians told of it" (Dodds 1933). "Percy's characters bear the traditional signifiers of the Ottoman Empire—turbans, Qur'an, and crescent moon" (Vaughan 2010). This is "the only early modern play extant to personify Muhammad," and "the only play extant that flaunts its Qur'ānic source" (Dimmock).

The Arcadia. ?James Shirley, or ?John Kirke, or ?Thomas Heywood (Harbage 1938). "[A]pparently performed in 1632" (Herrick 1955). "Acted by" Queen Henrietta Maria's Men at the Phoenix, according to the TP. No license for acting exists.

SR 29 November 1639. Q 1640 *A Pastoral called The Arcadia*; [actually the play is a romance rather than a pastoral (*JCS*)]; the TP names Shirley as author; list of characters; five acts. Some highly detailed SDs: *"Basilius runnes in, a bell rings, Philoclea and Gynecia hide themselves, Pyrocles fights with them, Basilius comes in with a two handed sword, after some skirmish enter Philonax and Calander with a guard, the rebells beaten off."*

Shirley's putative authorship is in doubt. The play is not included in the list of his drama in *Six New Plays* (1653). Moreover, "the publisher of *The Arcadia* was not William Cooke, most frequent purveyor of Shirley's plays, but Francis Eglesfeild, who had previously handled none of them" (Harbage). But Bentley (*JCS*) is inclined to credit Shirley with the play.

Arcadia Reformed. See *The Queen's Arcadia*.

Arden of Faversham. Anonymous; probably "the result of collaboration between two or more dramatists" (Lockwood 2007). Crawford 1906, Sykes 1919, and Schelling 1925 credit the play to Thomas Kyd; Vickers 2008b supports the attribution. But Jackson 2008 is dubious, and Kinney 2009a argues that his computerized analysis of the text gives "no support for the idea that Marlowe or Kyd were collaborators in writing *Arden*." Archer 1656 intended to attribute the play to Shakespeare (Greg 1945); Jacob 1770 supports the attribution as does Swinburne 1880. Boas 1901 disputes Shakespeare's authorship as does Freeman 1967. Jackson 1993 and 2006c, however, argues for Shakespeare's authorship of the quarrel scene between between Alice and her lover Mosby. If the play "is partly by Shakespeare, the 1592 Quarto is the first part-Shakespearian play to appear in print" (Jowett 2007e). Kinney 2009a believes that the play was chiefly written by Shakespeare. But Vickers 2011 says, "Kinney's version of computational stylistics fails to provide any reliable evidence for ascribing five scenes of *Arden of Faversham*, totaling 567 lines, to Shakespeare." And Taylor 2011 doubts the claim for Shakespeare's authorship. Jackson 2010, however, argues: "Shakespeare remains a strong candidate for the authorship of at least a substantial part of *Arden*." Clearly, no consensus about authorship exists.

Arden was written "between 1587/8 and 1591/2" (White 1982) and acted at undetermined venue. Possibly performed by the Earl of Pembroke's Men (Wentersdorf 1977) in the early 90s; likely performed on "a tour in the southern provinces prior to 1592" (Tassi 2005), and later by the Lord Chamberlain's Men (Knutson 1999); ?revived *c.* 1599 (Lockwood).

SR 3 April 1592 The tragedie of *Arden of Feversham and Blackwall*; transferred 29 June 1624. An entry "of 18 December 1592 records Stationers' Court order that copies of an edition printed by Abel Jeffes be confiscated. No copies survive" (Jowett 2007e). Q1 1592 *The Lamentable and True Tragedy of Master Arden of Feversham in Kent, Who Was Most Wickedly Murdered by the Means of His Disloyal and Wanton Wife, Who for the Love She Bare to One Mosby, Hired Two Desperate Ruffians Blackwill and Shakebag, to Kill Him*; no author named; epilogue (by Franklin); unnumbered scenes. Another edition seems to have been published in 1592, but no copy survives (Wine 1973). Division into acts and scenes was made by Henry Tyrrell in 1851 (MacDonald 1940). Staging calls for a shop — "I were best shute up my stall" — and a window: *"Then lettes he downe his window, and it breaks Black Wils head."* This last SD indicates the location of the window on the main stage. Special effects include "a prolonged mist . . . to enable Arden once more to escape from his would-be assassins" (Lawrence 1927): "Fy what a mist is here." Although Dessen & Thomson 1999 call this "fictional rather than linked to a special onstage effect," a mist could be simulated by smoke. Will tells Shakebag, "I can not see my way for smoake." Staging may call for a trap (Lawrence): *"Then Shakebag falles into a ditch."* Alice Arden reveals her pernicious nature when she mutilates a prayerbook to demonstrate her (adulterous) passion for Mosby; "the shock value of Alice Arden's attack on her prayer book is considerable" (Williamson 2009). Arden's wife meets with a painter who offers to produce a portrait of her that will kill the viewer by poison. Arden's murder, however, is more direct: *"Then Will pulles him down with a towell"*; and *"they lay the body in the countinghouse." "Then they beare the body into the fields"* but in vain; the killers' footprints in the snow and the bleeding of the dead body point to the culprits. Q2 1599. Q3 1633. The verso of the Q3 TP features a woodcut depicting the scene of Arden's murder: "The drama represented here consists only of its action, and if we did not know this was an illustration of the play, we would not identify the setting as a stage" (Orgel 2003). The image may have been borrowed from a broadside (Lockwood).

Arden is "usually thought to be the first of the extant domestic tragedies" (Adams 1943); others include *A Woman Killed with Kindness, A Warning for Fair Women, The Witch of Edmonton*, and *A Yorkshire Tragedy*. Like *Arden*, these plays dramatize "three sorts of realism, that of character portrayal, that of the presentation of social milieu, and that of atmospheric of local detail" (Sturgess 1969). In keeping with the genre, the Q1 epilogue announces the author's modest intention: "we hope youle pardon this naked tragedy, / Wherin no filed points are foisted in / To make it gratious to the eare or eye; / For simple trueth is gratious enough, / And needs no other points of glosing stuffe." The play may also be seen, as the TP suggests, as a dramatization of sexual desire, male or female, which is inevitably destructive: *Arden* "laments an idealized Renaissance world foreign to modern sexuality. In sexual and in economic terms, *Arden of Faversham* is securely a text of the homosocial imaginary" (Bach 2007).

Argalus and Parthenia. Henry Glapthorne. Acted 1632–38 (*AED 3*); "probably" 1638 (Greg 1906); 1637–38 (Gurr 2009d). At the Phoenix by Beeston's Boys and at court, before the king and queen, according to the TP. "The exaggerated romantic stances and bursts of Neoplatonism were clearly aimed to meet the fashionable tastes of Queen Henrietta Maria and her courtiers" (Squier 1987).

SR 11 January 1639. Q 1639 list of characters; five acts and separate scenes. SDs are limited chiefly to entrances and exits. Parts of two drolls, published in *2 The Wits or Sport upon Sport* (Q and O 1673) and based on *Argalus*, may suggest the play's continuing popularity.

Aristippus, or The Jovial Philosopher. Thomas Randolph. "Presented in a private shew," according to the Q TPs, at a university (Heinemann 1978). "Prepared in 1625 or 1626 for a Cambridge audience" (Levenson 1987). Probably first performed at Trinity College, Cambridge, in the college hall, autumn 1625–autumn 1626 (Davis 1967); MS (1) describes the scene as Cambridge. Perhaps performed on Shrove Tuesday or Ash Wednesday (Nelson 1989). May have been acted "by the young men in [Lord Deputy] Wentworth's entourage at Dublin Castle" (Dutton 2006). In *Aristippus* Randolph "was in a sense reviving the English Mummers' Play on the university stage" (Walsh 1973). Later performed in London.

(1) London, BL, MS Sloane 2531, fols. 124–40; "preserves what appears to be the original text for student actors and audience" (Levenson); no TP; no author named; list of characters; prologue (by Conjurer, who proceeds to interact with a character named Show, "*whipt by two Furies*"); epilogue by Simplicius; not divided. (2) Washington, Folger, MS V.b.320, fols. 1–19; "A private shewe presented on a fast night to the seniours and fellowes of Trinitie Colledge in Cambridge"; no TP; no author named; prologue (by Conjurer); not divided. (3) London, BL, Additional MS 37425, fols. 54–55; Praeludium (i.e., induction), consisting of "about two hundred lines of dialogue between Histrio and Gentleman, mostly concerned with the trials of the players during the [1630] plague closing" (Bentley 1971). SR 26 March 1630; transferred 1 July 1637. Q1 1630 no author named; praeludium [consisting of Prologue and Show]; epilogue; not divided. Q1 represents "the same comedy [as MSS] revised several years after it was written" (Levenson). Q2 1630 (Bowers 1939). Q3 1630. Q4 1631. Q5 1635. Q6 ND Dublin ?1635. Printed with *The Conceited Peddler* (continuous register). O1 1652 *Poems* (with *Amyntas*, *The Jealous Lovers*, *The Muses' Looking Glass*, *The Peddler*); "the fourth edition inlarged"; continuous register but new pagination; separate TP dated 1652; no author named on this TP; begins with Praeludium: "Enter Prologue in a circle"; not divided. O2 1664 *Poems* (with *Amyntas*, *Conceited Peddler*, *Jealous Lovers*, and *Muses' Looking Glass*); "the fifth edition, with severall additions, corrected and amended"; each play has a separate TP and all are dated 1662.

"*Aristippus* (shown both at Cambridge and later in London), included anti-Spanish and pro-Parliament satirical references, which had to be cut out when it was printed and several times reprinted from 1630 to 1635" (Heinemann 1978).

The Arraignment. Jonson's *Poetaster*, apparently known as *The Arraignment* to his contemporaries, "may well have reminded early audiences of the celebrated trial earlier that year [1601] of Essex and Southampton" (Donaldson 2004).

The Arraignment of Mr. Persecution. Martin Mar-Priest [Richard Overton]. A play-pamphlet possibly acted *c.* 8 April 1645.

SR "not entered into the Stationers monopole," according to the TP. Q1 [8 April] 1645 (Plomer 1904); "printed by Martin Claw Clergie"; list of characters; not divided. Q2 1645 "the second edition, enlarged and corrected by the au-thour." This edition "shows slight alterations and additions, the chief of which are some verses at the end addressed to Martin Mar-Priest by 'Christopher Scale-skie, Mathematician in chief to the Reverend Assembly of Divines' and a note defending the language used in the pamphlet on the ground that the author is deriding fools" (Haller 1934).

"Overton sets out his pamphlet in play form with the members of the 'Court of Assizes' arranged on the page like Dramatis Personae" (Skantze 2003). "This was the first of a series of satirical attacks [by Overton] on the presbyterians" (Gibbons 2004): "Mr. Persecution, defended by Sir Symon Synod and Sir John Presbyter for treason by Mr. Gods-Vengeance before Lord parliament as judge" (Haller). "Apart from their polemical purpose, the Marpriest tracts were also an attempt to refashion the tradition of Puritan writing founded by Martin Mar-prelate, in terms of the more overtly dramatic ridicule of Overton's earlier pam-phlets. Overton clearly saw parallels between his own situation and that of Mar-prelate" (Smith 1987d).

The Arraignment of Paris, A Pastoral. George Peele. Acted 1581-May 1584 (Ben-bow 1970) or 1583–84 (Dillon 2004a). "Presented" by Children of the Queen's Chapel, according to the TP, or by the combined Chapel and Paul's Boys, at the first Blackfriars. *Arraignment* is one of "three plays known to have been per-formed at this theater" (Shapiro 2009). "Probably staged at court" (Butler 2003a), perhaps 6 January or 2 February 1584; the TP reports that the play "was present-ed before the queenes majestie." "The queen's presence is necessary to make the combined dénouement and compliment work, and thus the play as it was pub-lished is a court play like no other, especially designed in the writing to connect the performance with the central member of the audience" (Astington 1999a). In this dramatization of an ancient story, Elizabeth is the "final arbitrator surpass-ing the pagan gods. She receives the apple or ball of gold for which ancient Troy burned, and reconciles the factions of Juno, Venus, and Pallas by subsuming all their immortal qualities into her own godlike persona" (Bevington 1968).

SR none. Q 1584 no author named but the play was ascribed to Peele by Thomas Nashe in 1589 and by *England's Helicon* in 1600; erroneously ascribed to Shakespeare in Archer's 1656 list; prologue (by Ate) and epilogue (by "Omnes simul"); three dumb shows illustrating the power of Venus, Athena, and Diana;

five acts and separate scenes. "The play itself is called into being by the feminine: 'I ende / Till just assemblie of the goddesses / Make me beginne the Tragedie of Troie.' Thus the play's prologue endows what is to follow with a feminine seal of authority" (Schneider 2011). A play of "extravagant spectacle" (Braunmuller 1983a), *Arraignment* "probably incorporated some spectacular entries for its gods and goddesses. Juno's show, if not her entry, requires a descent machine for the tree" (Dillon 2004a), "*laden with diadems & crownes of golde.*" Pluto, seated on a chair, ascends from below. "[A] pageant car is suggested, though not specified, by the stage direction for Helen of Troy's entry" (Dillon): "*Here* Helen *entreth in her braverie, with 4 Cupides attending on her, each having his fan in his hande to fan fresh ayre in her face.*" Pallas's show combines sight and sound: "*Hereuppon did enter 9 knights in armour, treading a warlike Almaine, by drome and fife.*" A golden ball figures in the stage action: "*The storm being past of thunder & lightning, & Ate having trundled the ball into place, crying* Fatum Troie, Juno *taketh the bal up.*" The sound of thunder could be achieved by what Jonson in *Every Man in His Humor* calls "roul'd bullet heard / To say, it thunders"; John Melton in *Astrologaster* (1620) says, "Drummers make thunder in the tyring-house." Sound effects include birdsong (SD specifies "*An artificiall charme of birdes being h[e]arde within*"); this could have been achieved by "a mechanical device" (Lawrence 1927). Paris "*giveth the golden ball to Venus,*" but the gods ask that she surrender it, preparing for its award to Eliza, "a figure of the Queene." The play's ending, "in which the prize golden apple rolls to the queen's feet, demonstrates just how blatant appeals to feminine influence might be" (Westfall 2004). The play's "elaborate and costly stage edifices, schematized color symbolism and bestiary lore, and festive ritual are all designed to the scale of a royal entry" (Bevington 1968).

"This play, though probably staged at court, resembles the entertainments mounted for royal progresses in the country in its combination of pastoral setting, mythological fable, and ethico-political debate" (Butler 2003a).

1 Arviragus and Philicia. Lodowick Carlell. Acted November 1635-February 1636 (*JCS*). By the King's Men at the [second] Blackfriars, according to the D TP, before Queen Henrietta Maria, and at court; priority uncertain; the Queen "took her nephew Prince Charles Louis" (Prince Elector of the Palatine) to the Blackfriars (Butler 2009). The queen's "attendance at the public theater was a high compliment to the dramatist" (Wood 1987b). Performed also at the Whitehall Cockpit, before the king, queen, prince, and prince elector, 18 April 1636 (bill of King's Men for performances at court); and at Hampton Court, the afternoon of 26 December 1636 (Adams 1917). Charles, Prince Palatine, reported that the play was "hugely liked of every one." "Such courtly drama is inherently playful, gratifying its audience with a series of romantic, heroic roles which reflect in a general manner the relationships existing within the court without pursuing them too closely" (Butler 1983).

(1) Oxford, Bodleian, MS Eng. Misc. d.ll, fols. 39–89 and 4–5; *The First Part of Arviragus and Philicia*; "a presentation copy" (Ruoff 1955); no author named on the TP; prologue and epilogue; "contains a prologue to Part II that was omitted from the only printed edition of the play" (Ruoff 1956); five acts. (2) Petworth, UK, Petworth House, Lord Leconfield's library (Ruoff 1955); MS "negligently copied" (Ruoff 1955). SR 26 October 1638. D 1639 no author named; prologue and epilogue; five acts. Numerous sound effects include "*Shout within*"; "*A pistoll shot off within*"; "*An owle shreeks*"; "*A horne blowne.*" A trap may have been used: "*Fire flashes out of the [witch's] cave, and hideous noyse.*" Parts 1 and 2 are published as one book with continuous register.

Epilogue singles out female playgoers: "Our author at the barre of censure standes, / Yet feares no hisse, nor hopes, noe clappe of handes; / The gentler sex that gives life to his muse, / Such rude dislikes, or plaudits never use; / But with a pleas'd, or discontented eye, / Can make a poem live, or poët dye." Such sentiment "reflects the increasing importance of upper-class women as arbiters of taste in the Caroline audiences, largely as a result of the influence of Queen Henrietta Maria and her circle" (Levin 1989b).

The second half of the D prologue anticipates *Part 2*: "If these, and who are theires, in part approve / This our first play, the second then may move / A better liking; for the persons known, / Their griefes, or joyes oft move us, as our owne."

2 *Arviragus and Philicia*. Data as for *Part 1*. Performed at the Whitehall Cockpit, before the king and queen, 16 February 1636; Herbert reports, "with great approbation of k[ing] and queene" (Adams 1917). Performed at the Whitehall Cockpit, before the king, queen, prince, and prince elector, 19 April 1636 (bill of King's Men for performances at court), and at Hampton Court, 27 December 1636 (Adams).

(1) Oxford, Bodleian, MS Eng. Misc. d.1, fols. 6–35; *The Second Part of Arviragus and Philicia*; "a presentation copy" (Ruoff 1955); prologue and epilogue; five acts. MS (2) Petworth, UK, Petworth House, Lord Leconfield's library; MS "negligently copied" (Ruoff). SR 26 October 1638. D 1639 list of characters; epilogue. Printed together with *Part 1*: "*Arviragus and Philicia* is really a ten-act play broken in the middle" (*JCS*). SDs attend to dramatized action: "*silent actions of passions, kisse her hand.*" Staging involves a miniature portrait when a character "*takes a picture out of her bosome.*"

Prologue in MS (1) locates the appeal of this play: "theres some wee knowe will say / that this is a romance, not a play / Proper to read, not fitted for the stage / And if it chance to please they dare ingage / tis onely women, or the vulgar sort / Perhapps some weaker judges of the court / But the towne witts, that cry upp or condemne / It is impossible it should please them: / They must have lines, soe strong, scarce understood / The yongue disciples then will sweare they'r good / Soe drunk with eloquence, one must not say / Good morrow, or farewell, a common way."

As You Like It. William Shakespeare. Perhaps acted Shrove Tuesday, 20 February 1599, by the Lord Chamberlain's Men at Richmond Palace before the queen (Dusinberre 2006). Possibly performed at the Curtain (Potter 2012). Performed at the first Globe when that theater opened later in 1599 (Gossett 2000). "Almost certainly the first play Shakespeare wrote for the Globe" (Gurr 1996); the seven ages of man speech may allude to "what is thought to have been the new playhouse's motto (*Totus mundus agit histrionem*, or 'all the globe's a stage')" (Gurr 2005); but Stern 1997 finds the connection spurious: "the motto can only be traced to a Restoration theatre with no observable connection to the Globe." Possibly performed by the King's Men before King James at Wilton House, seat of the Earl of Pembroke, 2 December 1603; William Cory in the nineteenth century reports seeing a letter from Lady Pembroke recounting the performance (Chambers 1930). "This may have been the King's Men's first performance for their new patron" (Hattaway 2000a). "Unfortunately, for all sorts of reasons this [speculation] is unlikely to have any foundation in fact" (Duncan-Jones 2001). Will Kemp may originally have played Touchstone (Dusinberre), though such a part would not seem in keeping with Kemp's comic gifts, and the name of the character seems to allude to Robert Armin's training as a goldsmith. Armin, who in 1598 or 1599 (Feather 1972) replaced Kemp as chief comic actor of the company, played Touchstone at the Globe (Hornback 2009b), and Touchstone "may have been the first part Shakespeare wrote for Robert Armin" (Potter 2012). But Wells & Taylor 1987 maintain that Armin "seems not to have joined the Chamberlain's Men until early in 1600," and Stern 2010b agrees. In any event with Touchstone, "the old-style Elizabethan clown metamorphosed into a more psychologically layered, self-aware, and wittily ingenious figure" (Butler 2004a). "Shakespeare's clowning changed to suit the more intellectual and musical gifts of the new resident comedian" (Taylor 2002b). "From the musicality of his dramatic roles we can infer that [Armin] was hired for his singing voice, and from what we can surmise about his diminutive physique it seems equally likely he was hired because he was *not* a dancer" (Preiss 2006). Shakespeare may have played Adam (Honan 1998), though this speculation cannot be traced before 1779 (Dobson 2001); Bate 2008 calls the suggestion an "unsubstantiated theatrical tradition." Nicholas Tooley may have played Rosalind (Potter 2012).

SR 4 August 1600 this staying order "means that [the play] must have been ready to be printed in quarto, even though it never was" (Dusinberre); 8 November 1623; transferred ?4 August 1626 Paviers right in Shakesperes *plaies*; ?19 June 1627 widow of Isaac Jaggard . . . her parte in Shackspeere *playes*; 16 November 1630; 1 July 1637 Shakespeares *workes* their Part; 6 August 1674; 21 August 1683. F1 1623 *Comedies, Histories, & Tragedies*; three issues; "published according to the true originall copies"; final speech by the actor playing Rosalind functions as an epilogue though it is not called such; "[t]he only other play in the period in which a woman speaks an epilogue is Lyly's *Galatea*" (Dusinberre); Rosalind's speech may not be the original epilogue; verses discovered by

Ringler & May in 1972 may constitute an earlier version; five acts and separate scenes. The epilogue "could have been used at only one [courtly] performance, and equally possible that a prayer was spoken after that" (Hattaway 2009). Rosalind's epilogue "reminds us that she is a boy, and that the drama has not represented an erotic and heterosexual reality at all. . . . This is the only place in Shakespeare where the heroine undoes her gender in this way" (Orgel 1989). "The epilogue's metadramatic self-reflexiveness might well remind the audience that when Rosalind played a boy, she was perhaps not adding a layer of disguise so much as stripping one away, revealing the homoerotic foundations underpinning the play's marital structure" (DiGangi 1997). In Rosalind and Orlando the audience saw "a man and a boy flirting with abandon and getting away with it" (Smith 1991b). The epilogue and play generate a "simultaneous commitment to homoeroticism and heterosexuality" (Traub 1992). Shakespeare had of course previously used the device of women characters disguising themselves as young men, but now he "explored the idea to something approaching its limits" (Holland 2004a). The epilogue demonstrates "that Shakespeare was aware of women as a distinct component of his audience that he had to please" (Levin 1989b). Immediately before the epilogue, Hymen appears onstage to sanction the various marriages; although contemporary productions often replace this figure with one of the other characters, "the text does nothing to suggest that he is anything other than a god: not Amiens, or another lord, or William, or anyone else, dressed up" (Brissenden 1981). The role "required an impressive special costume" (Taylor 2002b), incuding a white tunic, yellow shoes, socks, and overmantle, a veil over his left arm, flowers in his hair, and a torch in his right (Kiefer 2003). The actor playing the god probably entered through a door: "Although the Globe may have been furnished with a descent machine from the start, Shakespeare did not make this god fly" (Gurr & Ichikawa 2000). But Shapiro 2005 has another view: "There's a possibility that . . . Hymen enters from above, descending in a throne from the cover of the Globe's stage. If so, it shows off for the first time at the Globe the stage technology previously unavailable to Shakespeare's company at the Theatre or Curtain." Hymen's entrance is very different in effect from that of Jupiter in *Cymbeline*: "Hymen's descent is confirmatory and celebratory, not interventionist" (Dillon 2010). The marriage scene "is halfway between the usual marriage allotments that resolve so many comedies, and a Jacobean masque" (Gossett 1988). F2 1632 "the second impression"; three issues. F3 1663 "the third impression"; two issues; reissued 1664 with seven additional plays. F4 1685 "the fourth edition"; two issues.

In the character of Jaques, Shakespeare probably satirizes Ben Jonson, a contribution to the poetomachia, or "war of the theaters." "This 'war,' like the Marprelate controversy, arguably served the theatre business as a whole: it attracted patrons eager to be *au courant* and enjoy another form of topical humour in the wake of the 1599 bishops' ban on printed satire" (Henderson 2004). Jaques is the only character who refuses the Duke's invitation at the close: "Play musicke and

. . . to'th measures fall." This character appears "to glance humorously at the more extreme rhetoric of moral denunciation that Jonson's comical satire had brought into fashion" (Donaldson 2011).

The Asparagus Garden. See ***The Sparagus Garden.***

Astraea, or True Love's Mirror: A Pastoral. Leonard Willan. Written ?1640s. Possibly not acted, though the SDs are extensive. The final SD "clearly invoked traditional masquing technique" (Randall 1995): "*Whereat the theater is opened, and both companies uniting themselves, spend the rest of the night in their accustomed dances.*"

O 1651 list of characters; chorus; five acts and separate scenes. The play is preceded by a description of "*the scene,*" which apparently anticipates the use of painted scenery: "*The frontispiece is a wreath of fresh foliage, much like the entrance into a close alley, the tops whereof interlac'd, represent the perfect figure of an arch; at whose intersection is a kind of knot, whereon is enscribed in letters of gold, FOREST: over which two little* Cupidons *by either hand support a garland little distant from the same.*"

Astraea "compares homoerotic attachments with heterosexual unions in several narrative strands and continually finds the former comparably affecting, sustaining, and fulfilling" (Walen 2005).

The Atheist's Tragedy, or The Honest Man's Revenge. Cyril Tourneur. Acted probably 1610 (Maus 1995) or 1611 (Ribner 1964) at undetermined venue. "In divers places it hath often beene acted," according to the TP, but no other evidence of performance exists (Parfitt 1978). "[I]t is doubtful whether the publisher would have been content with this rather lame inducement to prospective buyers had the play been performed by a prestigious company at a well-known theater" (Jackson 1983), but Smith 2012 speculates that the play may have been performed by the King's Men.

SR 14 September 1611. Q 1611–12 two issues; five acts. Unusual staging involves "the bawd Cataplasma who employs herself and her maid with the embroidering of emblems. The profligate Sebastian joins them and attempts to explain the devices. All the corruption and wickedness of the aristocratic world, as portrayed in this play, seems to be depicted in that emblematic embroidery and its highly ambiguous interpretation" (Mehl 1969). Tourneur "reverses" the role of the traditional vengeful ghost: here the ghost of Charlemont's murdered father enjoins his son *not* to take revenge (Bowers 1940). Ghosts or supposed ghosts populate the stage. "The atheist D'Amville encounters a number of different ghostlike figures and reacts differently to each one" (Diehl 1981). "D'Amville 'counterfeits to take [Charlemont] for a ghost' in order to maintain his lie that Charlemont is dead, thus outfacing Charlemont, as well as others who see the 'real' Charlemont when he returns"; when "Montferrers' ghost appears . . . , Charlemont's reaction is identical to the 'false' reaction of D'Amville, even though

Montferrers is 'truly' a ghost, and D'Amville only feigns to see one" (Cox 2000). At one point "the bodies of five lifeless characters appear on stage, along with the bones of an untold number of skeletons during the graveyard scene" (Nunn 2005); in keeping with the play's dramaturgy, all of these have a symbolic resonance: "human skulls remind Charlemont that man is fragile, life transitory, the flesh subject to decay" (Diehl 1981). Charlemont's rival, D'Amville, schemes with impunity until he accidentally kills himself while attempting to execute Charlemont: "The accidental self-execution by ax of D'Amville" has annoyed readers, but such scenes are symbolic: the ax is a conventional icon "of divine retribution and divine wrath" (Diehl 1980). The play "prominently features emblematic or allegorical moments that assert the correspondence between spiritual and material truths, between heavenly and mundane realms, between God and human beings"; for example, "when thunder sounds after Montferrers's murder, it quite straightforwardly signifies divine displeasure, and D'Amville's attempts to reassure Borachio ring hollow" (Maus).

This is "the only surviving play that is unquestionably the work of Tourneur" (Cantor 1987a).

B

Bajazet. See *The Raging Turk*.

The Ball, A Comedy. James Shirley. Licensed for acting 16 November 1632 (Adams 1917). "Presented by" Queen Henrietta Maria's Men at the Phoenix, according to the TP. On 18 November Henry Herbert witnessed a performance and demanded that Shirley excise parts of the play because "ther were divers personated so naturally, both of lords and others of the court, that I took it ill, and would have forbidden the play, but that Biston [Christopher Beeston] promiste many things which I found faulte withall should be left out" (Bawcutt 1996). "[I]n performance offensive implications had come to light which had not been apparent on the written page" (Dutton 1991), perhaps because the performance involved mimicry of particular people (Bentley 1981). Beeston, manager of the queen's players, assured Herbert that the objectionable material would be cut.

SR 24 October 1638 by James Shirley. Q 1639 TP credits the play to both Chapman and Shirley whose names are bracketed; perhaps the ascription is a publisher's error (Parrott 1910), or perhaps Chapman revised sections found objectionable by Herbert (Burner 1988); list of characters; five acts. The play's alternate title is given in *Six New Plays* [1652–53], a collection of Shirley's work: *The Ball, or French Dancing Master*. "The dancing lesson was a device used at times for bringing in exhibitions of dancing" (Wright 1928). Spectacular staging involves the descent, presumably by machinery, of a golden sphere: "*A golden ball descends, enter Venus and Cupid*"; this action "signaled the beginning of a short masque in which Venus and Diana struggled for control of Cupid" (Howard 2007). The "ball" has two meanings. "It refers both to the event at which the dancing and the masque occur and to the decorative ball that descends to signal the beginning of the festivities" (Howard 2006a). "Unfortunately there is nothing to indicate that Venus and Cupid enter from within the ball" (Stevens 1977).

A character named Jack Freshwater, alluding to theatrical practice in France, says, "the women are the best actors, they play / Their owne parts, a thing much desir'd in England / By some ladies, Innes a Court gentlemen, and others." "Shirley's allusion suggests that female acting was a topic of the moment in fashionable circles" (Tomlinson 1992b).

Band, Cuff, and Ruff (*Exchange Ware*). Anonymous. "Acted in a shew" by students of Cambridge University, according to the Q1 TP, perhaps before King James upon his visit to Cambridge in 1615 (Smith 1908). Acted 24 February 1647 at Oxford, according to MS (4), but this performance "is not confirmed by other evidence and seems doubtful" (Nelson 1989). The entertainment "is short, plays extensively on words, has no female roles, and needs no special equipment for production" (Gossett & Berger 1988). Records from the diocese of Canterbury suggest preparations for performance: "On 4 December [1623] Edward [Dering] purchased six copies of 'Band Ruff and Cuff' . . . no doubt for a proposed future production at Surrenden. Since the title page mentions performance at Cambridge, Sir Edward may have first seen the comedy there, while he was at Magdalene College between January 1614/15 and September 1617" (Gibson 2002). Dering "collected at least 221 'playbooks,' as he called them, between 1619 and 1624, and he may have also had a collection of dramatic manuscripts that were later damaged or dispersed" (Ioppolo 2006). Archer in his 1656 catalogue gives the title as *Band ruffe and cuffe*; Kirkman in his 1661 catalogue gives the title as *Band Ruff & cuff*.

(1) Washington, Folger, MS J.a.2, fol. 25r-v; *Ruff, Band, Cuff*, ed. Gossett and Berger 1988; no separate TP; no author named; epilogue (by Cuff); not divided. This MS follows "closely the second printed edition of 1615" (Bowers 1959). (2) BL Additional MS 23723, fols. 1–3; list of characters; "omits the Introductory Part of the Interlude" (Smith); no prologue or epilogue. (3) Oxford, Bodleian, MS Lyell 37, fols. 124–26 and 139. MS (4) Bradford, UK, West Yorkshire Archive Service, MS Hopkinson 32D86/17. SR 10 February 1615 a Dialogue betwene *Ruffe Cuffe and Band*. Q1 1615 *A Merry Dialogue between Band, Cuff, and Ruff*; no author named; "lately acted in a shew in the famous universitie of Cambridge"; not divided. Q2 1615 *Exchange Ware at the Second Hand, viz. Band, Ruff, and Cuff*; "lately out, and now newly dearned up"; "the second edition"; no author named. "The text [of Q2] appears to be the same, but the second edition adds elaborate preliminaries of a humorous nature" (Greg 1939); it begins

with "Ruff, Cuff, and Bands complaint against the printer." There follow "The owners appeale from M. Printer his false judgement"; "A jurie of seamsters, and their verdi[c]t upon Band, Ruffe, and Cuffe"; "A Merrie Dialogue"; epilogue (by Cuff). Q3 1661 *A Merry Dialogue between Band, Cuff, and Ruff*; list of characters; lacks introductory material of Q2.

Band, Cuff, and Ruff "is a companion to the academic *Work for Cutlers* (1615) . . . and to the anonymous dialogue *Wine, Beere, Ale, and Tobacco*, printed in 1629 and 1630" (Bowers 1959).

The Banished Shepherdess. Cosmo Manuche. Probably written in 1659 or early 1660 (Williams 1980). SDs suggest that the play was prepared for the stage, perhaps at the home of James Compton, third earl of Northampton, to whom MS (1) is dedicated. The plays of Manuche may also have been performed at Northampton's London residence, Canonbury House in Islington (Wolf 1983). No record of production, but "very likely" intended for staging (Nelles 1990). Possibly performed for Henrietta Maria "at her court in exile in France just before the Restoration" (Williams 1992); "Manuche's primary intention was to ingratiate himself with the Court" (Aggeler 1978). The play "recycles moments from the court drama of the 1630s in the new context of the civil wars"; Manuche "positions his work alongside the dramatic products of the queen's own circle in a manner that demonstrates how early Caroline drama became a political tool in the construction of an optimistic royalist identity" (Britland 2007).

(1) London, BL, Additional MS 60273, fols. 2–43; no TP but Manuche signs the dedication to Compton; "presentation copy" (Williams 2004b) in the author's hand; list of characters; prologue and epilogue; five acts. The play contains "over two hundred stage directions" (Nelles): e.g., *Enter Morpheus with a leaden croune: on his head, mead collor'd wand in his hand (unseene by them) waveing the wand over their sleepie heads.* SDs suggest the use of descent machinery: *"An angell descends from above with a goulden croune and sceptor."* Special effects: *"thunder: and lightning"* at the entry of a devil. This MS formerly belonged to the library at Castle Ashby. (2) San Marino, CA, Huntington, MS EL 8395 [or EL 35/C/18]; a "presentation copy" (Williams 2004b) in the author's hand; dedicated to the Queen dowager, Henrietta Maria; this MS was formerly part of the Bridgewater library. Differences between the two MSS represent purposeful changes, and "most, if not all, of these changes may be authorial" (Williams 1980). "Two of the most striking variants are the wholesale reductions in the *dramatis personae* and the omission of an entire scene from the British Library manuscript" (Williams 1992).

Although set in Arcadia and Thessalia, the play "presents idealized pastoral representations of Henrietta Maria and Prince Charles" (Randall 1995). "The banished shepherdess seems to be Henrietta Maria, and her son, Charilaus of Arcadia (England), is Prince Charles" (*JCS*). The MS (1) prologue points to a political meaning: "Part of Arcadia's fflock, sated with ease, / And plenty, surfeits whilst the ranke desease, / Rooted in rebbells blood, to that hight springs / That their proud heades, strikes at the heads of kings." The play's true subject is "the impending restoration of Charles II" (Williams 2004b). The play "has no plot as such, but rather depicts the exiled Stuart courtiers during this brief interval [October 1659 to May 1660] before the Restoration" (Maguire 1992). "Working in one of the most artificial and derivative of all literary modes, [Manuche] gives the impression of putting current events into dramatic form with relatively little indirection" (Randall 1995).

Barnavelt. See *Sir John van Olden Barnavelt.*

Bartholomew Fair, A Comedy. Ben Jonson. Acted 31 October 1614, according to the induction. By Lady Elizabeth's Men, according to the TP, at the Hope, "a multipurpose bear garden and playhouse built by Philip Henslowe" and Jacob Meade (Knutson 2006a). (This company combined "an adult troupe, Lady Elizabeth's Men, and a boy company, the Children of the Queen's Revels, under the management of Philip Henslowe" [Leggatt 2007].) Jonson disdained the Hope, which "newly reopened in 1614 as a combination theater and bull- and bearbaiting arena" (Burt 1993). Performed also before the king at Whitehall, probably in the Banqueting House (Sturgess 1987), the night of 1 November 1614, "the only occasion we know of when a play was transferred so quickly from the public stage to Court" (Dutton 1983). The induction alludes to several contemporary actors who were members of the King's Men: Nathan Field, Joseph Taylor, Richard Burbage, and William Ostler. The book-holder in the induction "may have been the actual book keeper for the Lady Elizabeth's company, but it seems more likely that he was a regular player impersonating the company's book keeper" (Bentley 1984). "With well over thirty speaking parts, an enormous number for a Renaissance comedy, *Bartholomew Fair* is a conspicuously large-cast play" (Barton 1984). Possibly "Lady Elizabeth's Men were enlarged by amalgamating at this time with the theatre-less boys' company the Children of the Queen's Revels for whom Jonson had authored *Epicoene*" (Sanders 1998b). The play is "longer in running time than almost any other play of the early modern theatre" (Donaldson 2011).

SR no original; transferred 1 July 1637. Jonson held back the comedy "from his ground-breaking 1616 Folio, not abandoning it, but hoping to rework it into a better play" (Teague 1985). "By 1631 [Jonson] had prepared and partially supervised what he must have thought of as Volume Two of his *Works*, comprising *Bartholomew Fair*, *The Staple of News* and *The Devil is an Ass*. His quarrel with John Beale, the printer, and John Allot, the bookseller or publisher, caused the suspension of the project even though Jonson may have intended to add other works to it. Though these plays were undoubtedly printed by 1631, they were not released, and they became part of a complex trade dispute" (Happé 2000). *Bartholomew Fair*, *The Devil Is an Ass*, and *The Staple of News* "were meant to be

bound together in a single volume" (Riggs 1989). *Bartholomew Fair*, printed in
1631 for the abortive F, "remained unissued" (Butler 2010) and was later included in "The Second Volume" of F2 1640–41 *The Works*; two issues; "acted in the
yeare 1614"; the separate TP is dated 1631; list of characters; court prologue and
epilogue; the long induction (in prose, involves the Stage-keeper, Bookholder,
and Scrivener) functions "like an elongated prologue" (Stern 2009c); five acts and
separate scenes. The Stage-keeper mentions [John] Adams, a comic actor, and
[Richard] Tarlton, a brilliant Elizabethan comedian. Jonson also mockingly alludes to *The Spanish Tragedy*, *Titus Andronicus*, *The Winter's Tale*, and *The Tempest*;
Jonson sought "to stand apart from the theatrical scene, printed or performed"
(Murray 1983). Jonson's play "depicts a richly textured world in minute material
detail"; the Fair, "an event that took place every August in Smithfield, just outside the city limits, brings together tradespeople, entertainers, prostitutes, gamblers, eager to profit from the appetites of an undiscriminating public greedy for
pleasure, especially in the forms of food and sex" (Clark 2007). Staging calls for
"booths for Ursula and Leatherhead very like actual fair booths" (Waith 1974),
thereby "reviving a mediaeval form of staging in which several locations were
represented in one playing area, with the actors moving from one to another"
(Leggatt 2007). "Rather than employ the convention whereby the booth might
be understood to represent a house, a shop, or a palace, Jonson used the booth to
represent a booth" (Egan 1998). Staging also incorporates a puppet show, "a parody of court taste designed to appeal to the urban populace" (Sanders 1998b).

"The Prologue to the King's Majesty" "took the place of the Induction when
the play was presented before James I at court on 1 November 1614" (Hibbard
2007); it claims that the author does not mean to satirize individuals: "Your
majesty is welcome to a fayre; / Such place, such men, such language & such
ware, / You must expect: with these, the zealous noyse / Of your lands faction,
scandaliz'd at toyes, / As babies, hobby-horses, puppet-playes, / And such like
rage, whereof the petulant wayes / Your selfe have knowne, and have bin vext
with long. / These for your sport, without perticular wrong, / Or just complaint
of any private man, / (Who of himselfe, or shall thinke well or can) / The maker
doth present: and hopes, to night / To give you for a fayring, true delight." "Jonson's pious caveats against politic picklocking have the effect of whetting our curiosity for precisely the activity he warns us against" (Marcus 1986).

A Bartholomew Fairing. Anonymous. A play-pamphlet published 30 August
1649 and possibly acted that year.

Q 1649 prologue and epilogue (by Roger); five short acts. Ample SDs. "Mrs.
Tryall, the wife of a committee man, makes an unconsciously ironic comment on
the suppression of drama: 'Deer was the tyrant's game; but bulls is ours / Bishops
and plays were in a day put down / I well remember'" (Clare 2002).

"As the title suggests, the inspiration is pre-war city comedy, and the style
often recalls Jonson or Middleton" (Potter 1981).

The Bashful Lover, A Tragicomedy. Philip Massinger. Licensed for acting 9 May 1636 (Adams 1917; E&G 1976). "Often acted . . . with great applause" by the King's Men at the [second] Blackfriars, according to the separate TP. The theaters were closed three days after the 9 May 1636 licensing and ramained closed till October, and so the play may not have been performed until October 1637 or later. In playlist of King's Men 7 August 1641.

SR 9 September 1653 *Alexius, the chast gallant, or, The bashfull lover*; "since Alexius is not a character in *The Bashful Lover* the first title must refer to another piece" (Greg 1939); re-entered 29 June 1660 *The Bashfull Lovers*. O 1655 *Three New Plays* (with *The Guardian, A Very Woman*—separate TPs and pagination but continuous register); "never printed before," according to the general TP; dramatis personae; prologue and epilogue; five acts and first scenes. "There are many long descriptive directions, characteristic of an author who seems to have visualized in considerable detail the stage performance of the work on which he was engaged" (E&G): "*Enter soldiers (unarm'd with olive-branches), captains;* Lorenzo, Galeazo, Martino, Matilda *(a wreath of laurel on her head, in her chariot drawn through them)*." The play also "stages a scene in which a quack physician is attacked by the Duke he is attempting to paint with cosmetics"; Massinger "represents makeup as the device that bedevils and associates it with lechery" (Karim-Cooper 2007).

"The play makes a critical tilt at the kind of romantic, factional politicking in which the queen and her circle were engaged" (Butler 1984b).

Bassianus. See *Caracalla.*

The Bastard, A Tragedy. Cosmo Manuche (Williams 2004b); Archer's 1656 catalogue makes the attribution. ?Acted *c*. 1652 at undetermined venue. The play may have been written for performance at the country estate of James Compton, third earl of Northampton, or at Northampton's London residence, Canonbury House, Islington (Wolf 1983).

SR none. Q 1652 no author named; dramatis personae; prologue (spoken in two parts, the second by Gaspar) and epilogue; five acts and separate scenes. Scores of detailed SDs: "*He tries [to frown] and cannot, they smile on each other*"; "*Enter* Catalina *with bottles and glasses*"; "*Enter* Chaves, Roderiquez, *without disguise and swords drawn*." Epilogue alludes to the twofold appeal of the just completed play—to the eyes and ears of playgoers: "Now we have done, 'tis the greatest of our fears, / You'll say, W'ave led you hither by the ears / To see some strange conceit."

Prologue relates the play's content to the temper of the times: "No comick scene shall here salute your eye, . . . The tragick buskin traverses our stage / In bloody fillets, fitter for this age, / Where Treason, Murder, Lust, and ev'ry vice / Grows impudent, and rifles for the dice."

The Battle of Alcazar. George Peele. Original version acted 1587–89 (Edelman 2005). "Sundrie times plaid" by the Lord Admiral's Men, according to the TP, at undetermined venue, possibly an inn-yard (Lawrence 1927), though "when actors performed at inns they usually occupied a large room rather than a yard and performed by candlelight" (Orrell 1997). Revived in a revised version 1598 or 1600 (Kathman 2005). Henslowe does not mention *Alcazar*, at least not by this title; it is, however, possible that *Alcazar* "was the text that Henslowe called 'mahomett,' performed by Admiral's Men in August 1594" (Knutson 1991) at the Rose. Henslowe also records performances of "Muly Mullocco" (possibly the same play) by Lord Strange's Men ("the so-called amalgamated company of Strange's and the Admiral's" [Gurr 2004a]) at the Rose, 20, 29 February, 17, 29 March, 8, 17, 27, 30 April, 17, [22] 31 May, 13 June, 29 December 1592. Also 9, 20 January 1593. "The identification is, however, uncertain" (Greg 1904–08). "Peele's *Battle of Alcazar* was in revival in 1601, if it was the play called 'Mahomet'" (Knutson 2001b); it would have been revived at the first Fortune (Gurr 2009c), which opened autumn 1600; Edward Alleyn played Muly Mahamet (Gurr 2009d); Alleyn thus "impersonated the first speaking black African on London's public stages" (Vaughan 2006). "Ben Jonson's *Poetaster* (1602) offers a rare glimpse of how Alleyn played the part. When a boy actor offers to 'do the Moor,' he borrows a scarf (presumably for his Muslim headgear), then rides in on someone's shoulders while his bearer 'stalks' in an imitation of the tall Alleyn's distinctive walk" (Potter 2012). The play marks "the very first representation of Moors on the English Renaissance stage" (Bartels 2007). "[I]n one brief period prior to the onset of the plague of 1592–94, there were five instances in Henslowe's *Diary* in which a performance of *The Jew of Malta* is noted on the day before or the day after a performance of *Mully Mulloco*, as if performing the two plays in tandem was thought of as a way of profiting from public interest in Ottoman history" (Barroll 2007). Twenty-five actors play forty-two characters (Lawrence). Edward Alleyn played Muly Mahamet, the Moor (Cerasano 1994); Richard Jones, Silva; Edward Juby, Calcepius Bassa and Avero; Richard Juby, Abdula Rais and Tavora; Thomas Kendall, Abdelmenen, Attendant, Ghost, and Hercules; Charles Massey, Zareo and Barcelis; Thomas Parsons, a Fury; Samuel Rowley, an Ambassador; George Somersett, Attendant, Fury, and Vinioso; Robert Tailor, Jonas; Thomas Towne, Stukeley. Antony Jeffes played Young Mahamet "at the Fortune in the early 1600s"; Humphrey Jeffes played Muly Mahamet Xeque (Astington 2010).

SR none. Q 1594 *The Battle of Alcazar, Fought in Barbary between Sebastian King of Portugal and Abdelmelec King of Morocco, with the Death of Captain Stukeley*; no author named; an abridgment of the lost original text, perhaps "a shortened performance script" (Bartels 2008), but Bradley 1992 maintains that Q represents the play more or less as performed at the Rose and other playhouses; the opening speech of the Presenter constitutes a prologue; detailed descriptions of three dumb shows — "[s]ome fragmentary stage directions make it seem probable that originally there were more dumb shows" (Mehl 1965); "the combined evidence of Plot and Quarto reveals that *Alcazar* contains five dumb shows" (Beckerman 1989); the shows commingle human characters with Fates and Furies; divided into five acts by entries of the Presenter; "only 'Actus Secunda' and 'Actus 4' are marked" (Jewkes 1958). The Presenter "combines the function of an interpreter of spectacles (the presenter's role in pageants) with the function of a chorus in a classical play or in the various English plays modeled on Seneca" (Braunmuller 1983a). The play, "as first performed, must have been longer than the published version" (Edelman). In performance *Alcazar* "may have been . . . even more breathtaking than the printed text suggests" (Foakes 2004). Staging calls for a "*blazing starre*," which "consisted either of a firework on a line or flaming material suspended in an iron cage or cresset, and burned for up to a minute" (Holdsworth 1990). The term "is synonymous with 'comet'" (Udall 1991). SDs call for a variety of special effects, including "*Lightning and thunder*," "*streaming comets*," "*Three ghosts crying* Vindicta," "*Fire workes*," the entry of Fame "*like an Angell*," apparently by machinery, the entry of "*the Moore in his chariot*," "a deliberate reminder to the Fortune audiences of *Tamburlaine*'s device" (Gurr 2009c), i.e., his *Part 2* entry onstage in a chariot pulled by four kings. In fact, Peele's play tries "to out-Tamburlaine Tamburlaine" (Ewbank 1975). There are also parallels between *Alcazar* and Marlowe's *Doctor Faustus*; "it is impossible to say who was the borrower" (Smith 2000). Grotesque staging includes "*Enter to the bloudie banket Sebastian, Muly Mahamet, the Duke of Avero, and Stukley. To them enter Death and three Furies, one with blood, one with dead mens heads in dishes, another with dead mens bones*" [reconstructed SD]. This action "not only foreshadows the impending slaughter of the Moor on the battlefield, but also visually embodies the metaphoric feast of death" (Diehl 1980). Much onstage violence: "*they draw the curtains and smoother the yong princes in the bed . . . Which done, in sight of the unkle they strangle him in his chaire*" [reconstructed SD]. "[T]hree characters are disembowelled on stage," requiring "3 violls of blood" (Gurr & Ichikawa 2000). The line "Here is a horse my lord" "seems to point to the bringing of a horse" onstage (Lawrence 1927).

Edmond Malone (*d.* 1812) was the first to suggest Peele's authorship. "His conjecture was announced by Philip Bliss in *The London Magazine* in 1824" (Yoklavich 1961).

The Battle of Alcazar. Fragmentary MS of George Peele's play: London, BL, Additional MS 10449, fol. 3, ed. Greg 1923. A severely damaged playhouse "plat" (plot, or "backstage storyboard" [Bate 2008]); divided by dumb shows into parts corresponding to the acts of Q (but the last act is missing); "no formal act division" (Greg 1931). The plot was "prepared for the later Admiral's company between 1594 and 1603, when they were acting first at the Rose and later at the Fortune" (Greg 1931), which opened autumn 1600; "the plot survives for a revival, in the late 1590s or possibly 1600" (Foakes 2004), or 1600–01 (Edelman

2005), or 1601 at the Fortune (Gurr 2009c). Henslowe does not mention *Alcazar*, at least not by this title; he does record performances of "muly mollocco" by Strange's Men, acted a dozen times in 1592–93. The plot, "despite being prepared from what appears to be a fuller version, is an abstract of the stage requirements as they appeared in the original" (Beckerman 1989). *Battle of Alcazar* is "the only Elizabethan play that survives in both a plot and an early printed text" (King 1992a).

Staging at the Fortune differed from earlier staging at the Rose. At the Fortune Peele added "some gory dumbshows to amplify what Peele's Presenter declares at the outset to each act" (Gurr 2009c).

Twenty-four actors are named: Edward Alleyn played Muly Mahamet; Charles Massey, Zareo, an Ambassador of Spain, and the Duke of Barcelis; Edward Juby, Calcepius Bassa and the Duke of Avero; Robert Shaw, the Irish Bishop and the Governor of Tangier; Richard Jones, Luis de Silva and an Ambassador of Spain; Richard Alleyn, Portinagall-Presenter and Governor of Lisbon [possibly the same role]; James (a boy), Ruben Arches (a female character) and Sebastian's Page. Also in the cast were Thomas Downton, Thomas Towne, Richard Jones, Humphrey Jeffes, Anthony Jeffes (Young Mahamet), William Kendall (Hercules), Richard Juby, Robert Tailor, Thomas Hunt (Moorish Ambassador and Attendant in dumb show), William Cartwright, Samuel Rowley (Pisano), Thomas Drom, Thomas Parsons, William Cartwright (attendant in dumb show), Robert Shaa, George Somersett, and Mr. Towne's boy.

Beaunans Meriasek. See *Saint Meriasek*.

Beauty of Women. See *Calisto and Melebea*.

The Beauties. See *The Bird in a Cage*.

Beggars' Bush. John Fletcher and Philip Massinger; Francis Beaumont may have contributed to an earlier version of this play. "[F]irst performed at Christmas 1622 but possibly written at an earlier date" (McMullan 1994); "it must date in its original form from sometime prior to Beaumont's death in March 1616" (Hoy 1985). By the King's Men at the first Globe (which burned on 29 June 1613), second Blackfriars, or second Globe. Performed also at Whitehall, the evening of 27 December 1622 (John Astley's list of plays performed at Whitehall during the Christmas season); the play may have been "revised for this occasion by Fletcher or by Massinger or by both" (Hoy 1985). A bill of 30 November specifies court performance at Cockpit-in-Court, 1630 (Teague 2009); at Hampton Court, before the king and queen, 19 November 1636 (bill of King's Men for plays acted at court); and at Richmond Palace, probably in the Great Chamber, 1 January 1639 (Astington 1999a). In playlist of King's Men 7 August 1641 as *Beggars*. "In the only copy recorded [of 1661 F at the Folger] a slip of paper has been pasted on at the end of the text recording in manuscript a performance at the Red Bull in 1659–60" (Greg 1939).

Washington, Folger, MS J.b.5; no TP; five acts. MS "may have been commissioned after performance at court" (Erne 2003a). A variety of auditory effects: "*Drum, flourish, peeces discharge, enter sailors*"; numerous songs. Few SDs beyond the entry of characters, although some of these are descriptive: "*Enter Hubert like a huntsman.*" SR 4 September 1646; 30 January 1673. B&F F1 1647 *Comedies and Tragedies*; "never printed before, and now published by the authours originall copies"; HT *Beggars' Bush*, but table of contents has *The Beggars' Bush*; at the end 24 lines are set off "for an epilogue" but they "are not typographically distinguished" (Greg 1939); five acts and separate scenes. Q 1661 *The Beggars' Bush*; ascribed to B&F whose names are bracketed on the TP; dramatis personae; prologue and epilogue. The Q "was copied from the text supplied by the 1647 *Comedies and Tragedies*, but given the prologue and epilogue that had been attached there to *The Captaine*" (Stern 2009c). F 1661 "a facsimile reprint" of the play in 1647 F1 (Greg 1939). B&F F2 1679 *Fifty Comedies and Tragedies*; "the songs to each play being added"; *Beggars' Bush, A Comedy* (but Clark 1993 calls it a "political tragicomedy"); list of characters. There are significant differences between F1 and F2.

Following the closing of the theaters, one scene was adapted for a droll entitled *The Lame Commonwealth*, later published in *1 The Wits, or Sport upon Sport* (O 1662 [two issues] and 1672). The engraved frontispiece of *The Wits* depicts a figure named "Clause," king of the beggars; he is dressed in ragged clothes, has a crippled leg, and supports himself with a T-shaped cane. In *Beggars' Bush* Clause, virtuous king of the beggars, is actually a disguise adopted by the aristocratic Gerrard, in whom the play accommodates "the meritorious with the hereditary" (Clark).

Believe As You List. Philip Massinger. Licensed for acting 6 May 1631, according to the MS. "Though the license itself is dated May 6, probably Herbert did not deliver the play to the actors until the following day, hence the entry in his office-book of May 7" (Adams 1917). Acted by the King's Men. "[I]ntended for performances at the Blackfriars theatre rather than at the Globe" (E&G 1976). Herbert had refused to license the play, 11 January 1631, because "itt did contain dangerous matter, as the deposing of Sebastian king of Portugal, by Philip the [Second]" (Bawcutt 1996); such references "might have compromised delicate Anglo-Spanish negotiations" (Sharpe 1987). Massinger rewrote the play, changing its setting "from the sixteenth-century Iberian peninsula to ancient Carthage" (Worden 1987); the "names and the geography are changed, but in other essentials the story remains the same" (Dutton 1991); the empire of Carthage was "easily identified with that of early modern Spain" (Patterson 1984). Performed 7 May 1631 (*JCS*). "[Edward] Knight's annotations make it possible to reconstruct much of the original cast" (E&G): Joseph Taylor played Antiochus; John Lowin, Flaminius; Thomas Pollard, Berecinthius; Richard Robinson,

Lentulus; John Honeyman, First Merchant; William Penn, the Jailer and Second Merchant; Curtis Greville, Third Merchant; Rowland Dowle, the First Officer, Philoxenus and two other mute roles; Richard Baxter probably played the Carthaginian Carthalo and Titus (King 1992a). Baxter played Marcellus; Nicholas Underhill played "minor parts"; Harry [?Henry] Wilson was a lute player (Gurr 2004c). Other actors in the cast included Thomas Hobbes, who "played Calistus" (Astington 2010), William Patrick (a Captain), William Mago, Francis Balls, Eilert Swanston (Chrysalus), Robert Benfield, Thomas Pollard (King). Alexander Gough played Eurinia (Kathman 2005). "At least forty-four characters are indicated even allowing for only one Roman soldier; players can be assigned for twenty-nine of these roles, thus giving the largest number of cast assignments we have, even though about nineteen roles are unassigned" (Bentley 1984). SDs preserve the names of William Gascoyne, and "Hubert," presumably actors or stage attendants.

London, BL, Egerton MS 2828, fols. 3–29, ed. Sisson 1927; "a newe playe," according to the TP; partly in Massinger's hand; the words "A Tragedy" are written in a different hand; damaged (fol. 5 is almost completely missing); there is a gap at the beginning; some lines missing; numerous corrections/changes in a second hand; prologue and epilogue, "which may not be Massinger's" (Greg 1931); they "are written in later and placed *after* Herbert's hand-written licence" (Stern 2009c); "fully divided into [five] acts and scenes" (Greg). "[S]everal plays provide solid evidence that a trap door could be used to establish a prison or dungeon below," as in *Believe*; "the annotator anticipates the temptation of Antiochus in his dungeon with: *'Gascoigne and Hubert below: ready to open the trap door for Mr. Taylor'* and *'Antiochus ready: under the stage'*" (Dessen 1984). MS is the theatrical copy, "written between 11 January and 6 May 1631" (E&G), and bears Henry Herbert's license and signature. "On the last leaf [fol. 29v] of the manuscript, the book-keeper, Edward Knight, adds a list of six properties with the names of the six actors who need them" (King 1992a). Knight "almost literally left no direction untouched" (Long 1999); he also "deletes all Massinger's act and scene divisions and adds his own" (Long). SR 9 September 1653 *The Judge, or Believe as you list* [this entry apparently designates two plays, one of which is lost]; 29 June 1660 *Believe as you List*, a Tragedy. First edited by Thomas Crofton Croker, assisted by Frederick William Fairholt, for the Percy Society (1849). Croker records that he received the MS from Samuel Beltz, who wrote, "I have reason to believe that the MS was formerly in the hands of David Garrick."

The MS bears a note by James Orchard Halliwell[-Phillipps]: "This is one of the plays said to have been made into pye-bottoms by Warburton's servant, a story in which I have no faith whatever. I gave the present MS. to Mr. Corser, April, 1857, in exchange for a fragment of sixteen leaves of the first edition of Shakespeare's Lucrece."

The play "represents a strikingly modern commentary upon the conflict between political expediency and the basic human values of trust and honor"

(Howard 1985). "The real political importance of the play lies not in immediate reference to contemporary events but in providing a myth for England forsaken by its ancient protector and abandoned to a fierce modernity. The title, *Believe As You List*, reveals the secret of the play's message" (Edwards 1987).

1 Bellamira Her Dream, or The Love of Shadows, A Tragicomedy. Thomas Killigrew. Written 1650–52 (Bulman 1987). Although there is no record of performance, the SDs and costume descriptions anticipate production. Killigrew also envisions painted scenery: "*Enter* Pollidor *from hunting, and some part of the quarry in his hand; the scene must be a fine land-skip, and a* cave *must be in the scene.*"
    SR 24 October 1663. F 1663–64 *Comedies and Tragedies*; two issues; the general TP dated 1664, separate 1663; *The First Part of Bellamira Her Dream, or The Love of Shadows, A Tragicomedy*; "written in Venice"; list of characters; five acts and separate scenes. Extensive SDs: "*She* [Phillora] *levels her bowe at the Satyr, but spying* Leopoldo *gazes upon him, and stands in the posture, and all the company seems amazed, the Satyr creeps out from behinde* Leopoldo, *and looks in the face of one, and then of the other.*" Description of some costumes: e.g., "Arcus *must be in a noble habit, rich, and his person black, being a Moor.*"
    "As Killigrew's annotated copy of his *Comedies and Tragedies* (1664) preserved in the library of Worcester College, Oxford, demonstrates, he was ambitious enough to prepare his own plays for production on the new, scenic [Restoration] stage" (Vander Motten 2004).

2 Bellamira Her Dream, or The Love of Shadows, A Tragicomedy. Thomas Killigrew. Data as for *Part 1*.
    Staging seems to call for painted scenery and the simulation of darkness: "*The scene opens and discovers a prison, where* Pollidor *and* Phillora *appear next the stage chained to a ring fastned to the ground upon the other side of the prison, and in a darker part of the scene lies* Palantus *chained behinde them in the dark*, Bellamira *chained, and afar off in prospective other prisoners and dead carcases.*"

The Benefice, A Comedy. Robert Wild. Perhaps acted 1641 (Kawachi 1986) at undetermined venue. "This seems too late for any college production except perhaps at Trinity. Wild, however, was from St John's, and the last play known at St John's was performed in 1618–19" (Nelson 1989). Greg 1939 doubts performance. "Designed to be played in a barn by children" (Randall 1995). "Perhaps Wild prepared the piece for a zealous schoolmaster" (*JCS*).
    (1) London, BL, Lansdowne MS 807, fols. 78–88; a fragment; part of fol. 85 missing; no TP; author's name given at end; epilogue; five acts; "another hand apparently has added a division into scenes" (Greg 1931). The SDs "are rather scanty" (Greg). (2) Washington, Folger, MS V.a.232, pp. 1–33; dramatis personae; epilogue; author's name on last page; written in pencil, apparently in 1858, are the words "original MSS & otherwise from Hockwold Hall." Q 1689

The Benefice, A Comedy; two issues; author's initials on TP, and he is named in the address to reader; "written in his younger days: now made publick for promoting innocent mirth"; dramatis personae; prologue (by Ceres and inserted following act 1) and two epilogues; act 1 constitutes an induction (Greg 1939); five acts.

Beunans Meriasek. See *Saint Meriasek.*

The Bird in a Cage, A Comedy. James Shirley. Licensed for acting as *The Beauties* 21 January 1633 (Adams 1917). "At some point prior to publication (and possibly performance), Shirley altered the title" (Chalmers et al. 2006). "Presented at the Phoenix," according to the TP, by Queen Henrietta Maria's Men.

SR 19 March 1633 *The Bird in the Cage.* Q 1633 list of characters; five acts. A SD points to the play's most important property: "*A cage discovered.*" A character describes it as "A present . . . from the duke: one of the finest pieces of pageantry that ere you saw: 'tis a cage with variety of birds in it: it mooves on wheeles." The cage is "large enough to hold a man [and] must be drawn on stage through one of the entries" (Stevens 1977).

Confined in a tower, women resort to song, dance, and the performance of a play about Danae and Jupiter, who says, "Let the musique of the spheares, / Captivate these mortall eares; / While *Jove* descends into this tower, / In a golden streaming shower." "The link between sexuality and acting culminates in a near-lesbian encounter between Donella and Eugenia (playing Jupiter and Danae)" (Chalmers 2004). The play's juxtaposition of "successful female actors (actually boy-actors dressed as women dressed as men) with male characters manifestly failing in their female impersonations must have called to mind for contemporary audiences the equally successful performances of Henrietta Maria and her court women" (Sanders 1999a). Shirley dedicates the play, ironically, to William Prynne, who called female actors "notorious whores." "At a time when familiar structures were changing, the play takes up the issue of women's freedom and supports a degree of female autonomy" (Walker 1991b). The women's theatricality in the play may owe something to "the first appearance of actresses on the London stage. A French company including women in the female rôles was allowed three performances" in November and December 1629; the performances may have been allowed because of the queen's influence (Senescu 1980).

The Birth of Hercules. ?Richard Bernard (Nelson 1989). Acted 1600–06 (*AED 3*). "Probably meant for university performance" (Braden 2010). Because the play features elements that are academic, courtly, and popular, it may have been designed for an "audience who embraced all three traditions," gentlemen at the Inns of Court (Smith 1988a). "The apparent author was a member of Christ's College [Cambridge]; but the Records contain no evidence of a play at Christ's after 1567–8" (Nelson).

London, BL, Additional MS 28722, fols. 2–32, ed. Bond & Greg 1911; no separate TP; no author named; evidence of corrections; dramatis personae; two prologues (Prologus Laureatus and Mercurius Prologus); chorus; five acts and separate scenes. The SDs, some in English, most in Latin, are written in the margins. The plot is resolved through a *deus ex machina*: the play "manages the whole thing as a grand theophany: thunder crashes, the music of trumpeters and other instruments begins to sound out of the painted heavens, and Jupiter's voice booms out, apparently in disembodied majesty" (Smith 1988a). First edited by Wallace 1903.

Prologus Laureatus affirms the translator's right to depart from the language of the original (*Amphitruo* by Plautus): "Our poets aucthor himself translated it. / Some for addinge to yt and alteringe yt, / must be offended, wch for yor sake / Our poet did; yet no injustice neither / Unto his aucthor." Wallace 1903 comments of the playwright, "he is much more interested in the elaboration of a comic situation than in the development of the plot, and his successive expansions and curtailings have usually been in accordance with this predilection."

The Birth of Merlin, or The Child Hath Found His Father. William Rowley with unidentified collaborators. Licensed for acting spring 1622 (Bawcutt 1996). "Several times acted with great applause," according to the TP, by Prince Charles's Men at the Curtain, according to Herbert's license. *Merlin* may have "at one time played in conjunction with" *Hengist, King of Kent* (Bald 1938b). William Rowley probably played the Clown (Nicol 2008b).

SR none. Q 1662 TP credits the play to William Rowley and William Shakespeare (a claim not usually accepted today except for Dominik 1985 whose arguments are "wholly unconvincing" [Wells & Taylor 1987]); designated a tragicomedy in Kirkman's list of plays appended to Corneille's *Nicomède* (1671); dramatis personae; three dumb shows—"conjured up and explained by some magicians" (Mehl 1965); five acts and first scenes (of acts 3, 4, 5). SDs of *Merlin* are "full and detailed" and suited for performance at a public theater (Udall 1991). The play "offers spectacularly staged devils and fighting dragons in conjunction with sleight-of-hand magic as equal demonstrations of 'art,' that is, of uncanny effects" (Cox 2000): playgoers witness "*a spirit in flame colours with a torch*" and "*a spirit in black*"; "*[t]hunder and lightning, two Dragons appear, a White and a Red; they fight a while*"; then "*Thunder: the two Dragons fight agen, and the White Dragon drives off the Red*"; entry of the devil "*in mans habit, richly attir'd, his feet and his head horrid*"; entry of personified Death, who "*strikes*" a king "*in armour*"; Lucina, "Queen of the Shades," arises with the three Fates from "Stigian darkness," apparently through a trap; "*Thunder and lightning in the rock . . . The rock incloses him* [the devil]." The rock "has to be large enough to stand on, easy to climb from the outside, capable of 'swallowing' an actor, and also of giving vent to thunder and lightning" (Udall); the stage's trapdoor is "perhaps covered by" the rock (Dessen & Thomson 1999). The dialogue describes special effects following the appearance of a "*blazing star*": the Prince says, "this fiery exalation shoots his frightful horrors on th'amazed world, see, in the beam that 'bout his flaming ring, a dragons head appears, from out whose mouth two flaming flakes of fire, stretch east and west." Edol replies, "And see, from forth the body of the star, seven smaller blazing streams, directly point on this affrighted kingdom." A blazing star "consisted either of a firework on a line or flaming material suspended in an iron cage or cresset, and burned for up to a minute" (Holdsworth 1990).

The Bishop's Potion, or A Dialogue between the Bishop of Canterbury and His Physician. ?Richard Overton (Wolfe 1958). A "playlet with a good claim to performance" (Butler 1984b), probably during the Interregnum.

SR none. Published July 1641. Q 1641 HT *Canterbury's Potion*; no author named; not divided. The TP features two pictures, one of a man striding forward, the other of a man chained.

In the form of a short dialogue, the play features only two characters: Bishop Laud and his doctor. In this mock-dialogue "the Archbishop vomits up the symbols of all his transgressions, including the tobacco patent; the Book of Sports; a parchment with the Star Chamber Order against Prynne, Burton and Bastwick; a bundle of papers presenting livings to dumb-dog clergy and suspending preaching ministers; and finally, after a supreme convulsion, up comes the Mitre" (Heinemann 1980).

The Black Man. Anonymous. A "'jig' or song drama probably older than 1633 and quite possibly dating back to the sixteenth century" (Elson 1932). Performed both before and after the closing of the theaters. According to *2 The Wits*, "Written for six players" (Lawrence 1927). Although the name of Robert Cox has been attached to this drama, he was probably not the originator: "At least two of his drolls, *Singing Simpkin* and *The Black Man*, are nothing but revivals of popular old jigs, now lost, of which translations, earlier in date than his own work, survive in German, Dutch, and Scandinavian versions" (Rollins 1921). Kirkman, on the TP of *2 The Wits*, reports that the drolls were "written I know not when, by several persons, I know not who," but his preface says that Robert Cox "was not only the principal actor, but also the contriver of most of these farces." Kirkman's attribution is "probable" (Holland 2007).

Published in *2 The Wits, or Sport upon Sport* (Q and O 1673), which gives as venues of performance fairs, halls, taverns, and "mountebancks stages at Charing Cross, Lincolns-Inn-Fields, and other places"; list of characters.

The title refers to "the common conception of the devil as black" (Elson). This is "a low farce in which the clownish hero joins forces with the tinker of the title to retrieve his sweetheart from two raffish gentlemen" (Mann 1991).

The Blind Beggar of Alexandria. George Chapman. "Sundry times publickly acted in London" by Lord Admiral Nottingham's Men, according to the TP.

Henslowe's *Diary* lists performances by the Admiral's Men at the Rose in 1596: 12, 16, 19, 22, 26 February; 15, 26 April; 3, 13, 18 May; 3, 25 June; 5 July; 6, 12 November; 2, 10 December. Also in 1597: 15, 25 January; 14 March; 1 April; this represents a number "greater than all but three of the contemporary works cited by Philip Henslowe" (Braden 1987a). "*The Blind Beggar* was the Rose's most profitable play of 1596" (Wiggins 2000). "The remarkable performance records" of *Blind Beggar* "must have owed a lot to [Edward] Alleyn" (Read 1994), who "took on not only the main part but appeared in three disguises, each of them parodying one or other of his famous Marlowe roles" (Gurr 2009d). Henslowe also records expenditures on 2, 5, and 8 May 1601 and June 1601 for a revival at the Fortune, which opened autumn 1600. Edward Alleyn reprised his role when he emerged from retirement in 1600 (Astington 2010).

SR 15 August 1598. Q 1598 *The Blind Beggar of Alexandria, Most Pleasantly Discoursing His Variable Humors in Disguised Shapes Full of Conceit and Pleasure*; not divided. "Full and careful" SDs (Jewkes 1958), "but obvious heavy cuts, especially to the more serious romance sections" (Gurr 2009c). As the word *Humors* in the full title suggests, Chapman's play helped initiate the vogue for comedies of humors. Also issued in *Comedies, Tragi-Comedies, & Tragedies* (1652), a made-up book no longer extant.

In its surviving state the play is much reduced from its theatrical form: "it is impossible to tell from the extant text, printed in 1598 and containing a little more than 1600 lines, what it was like, because the text omits the main plot almost entirely. From the rudimentary remains of that plot we can surmise that it might originally have been a heroic play along the lines of *Tamburlaine*" (Hyland 2005). But perhaps Chapman was initiating the "idea of a plotless comedy written entirely around 'humours'" (Wiggins 2000). "The rather harum-scarum plot is a vehicle for virtuoso quick changes, of costume and personality, or 'variable humours,' by the central performer, who confides in the audience as he rapidly shifts identities to confound his enemies and emerge triumphant as King of Egypt" (Astington 2010).

The Blind Beggar of Bednal [Bethnal] Green. John Day and Henry Chettle. Acted by Lord Admiral Nottingham's Men at the Rose or Fortune, which opened autumn 1600. Henslowe records payment to the playwrights, 26 May 1600; in addition he records payment for (the lost) *Part 2* to William Haughton and John Day, 29 January 1601 and later. Also "divers times publickly acted," by the Prince's Men, according to the TP, *c.* 1631 (Gurr 2009d); the players "are unlikely to be Prince Henry's. It may have survived as a part of the Fortune repertory until the Prince Charles (II) company performed it there in the late 1630s" (Gurr 2009c). A SD mentions Sill Clark, "a printer's misreading of the contraction 'Will Carp,' which stood for William Carpenter," an actor (Lawrence 1927).

SR 14 September 1657 *The pleasant history of the blind beggar of Bednall Greene, declaring his life and death.* Q 1659 *The Blind Beggar of Bednal Green, with the Merry Humor of Tom Strowd the Norfolk Yeoman*; only Day's name appears on the TP, also on last page; dramatis personae; five acts.

The play is apparently the first part of a three-play sequence, the second and third parts of which are lost (Parr 2004a).

The Bloody Banquet, A Tragedy. Thomas Dekker and Thomas Middleton; the play seems to have been chiefly written by Dekker and adapted by Middleton (Taylor 2000). "Rogers and Ley, in their playlist of 1656, and Kirkman in his catalogues of 1661 and 1671, attribute [the play] only to 'T.D.'" (Schoenbaum & Brown 1961). Gurr 2009d attributes the play to Thomas Drue. Acted *c.* 1609 (Taylor 2002a) by an unidentified company, perhaps Queen Anne's Men, at the Red Bull or Phoenix. In playlist of Beeston's Boys 10 August 1639.

SR none. Q 1639 one author's initials on TP—"by T. D."; dramatis personae; five acts and separate scenes. Induction consists of a dumb show, followed by a choral explanation: *"At one doore the old king of* Lydia, Tymethes *his sonne,* Lapyrus *his nephew, and souldiers. At the other the old king of* Lycia, Zantippus *his son,* Eurymone *his daughter, and souldiers. The two kings parley, and change hostages for peace."* Staging calls for the use of a trap (for a pit covered over with boughs and, possibly, for a vault): *"He [Lapirus] falls in the pit."* A subsequent dumb show is also explained by the chorus. Grotesque staging includes "the quarters of a man . . . hung up like a butchered carcass" (Owens 2005), and a bloody banquet: *"Sertorio brings in the flesh with a skull all bloody."* Sertorio forces his wife to eat her lover's flesh, an action that "literalizes—in the most gruesome way possible—the idea of sexual appetite" (Diehl 1980): "The letcher must be swallowed rib by rib." Special effects include thunder, lightning, and *"a blazing starre,"* which "consisted either of a firework on a line or flaming material suspended in an iron cage or cresset, and burned for up to a minute" (Holdsworth 1990).

"The first anthology of memorable passages from English Renaissance drama—John Cotgrave's *English Treasury* (1655)—quotes *The Bloody Banquet* fifteen times; more than any other Middleton play but *The Revenger's Tragedy*, more than any Shakespeare play but *Hamlet*. Nobody quotes a failure" (Gasper 2007). "A tragedy of adultery and cannibalism, popular enough to remain in the repertory for three decades, the play survives only in a posthumously adapted text" (Taylor 2004b). "There is . . . some evidence that the play may have been abridged" (Schoenbaum & Brown).

The Bloody Brother, A Tragedy. John Fletcher and Philip Massinger (Williams 1996); also probably George Chapman (Wells 1928, Jump 1948) or Nathan Field; and perhaps a fourth dramatist as well. Acted by the King's Men ?1617 (Gurr 2009d) or 1619–20 (Taylor & Jowett 1993). Q2 specifies performance at the [second] Blackfriars, 1630. Performed also at Whitehall Cockpit, 7 November 1630 and at the Cockpit during the day, 21 February 1631 (both performances listed in bill of King's Men for performances before the king); at Globe,

23 May 1633 (diary of Humphrey Mildmay); at Hampton Court, 17 January 1637 (bill of King's Men for performances before king and queen). *"Rollo* was one of the most popular plays of the seventeenth century" (Jump). No license for acting extant.

SR 4 October 1639 A Tragedy called *The Bloody Brother,* by J: B:; transferred 8 August 1661 *Rollo, Duke of Normandy* (ascribed to B&F). Q1 1639 *The Bloody Brother, A Tragedy*; author identified by initials — "B. J. F." ("I am tempted to speculate [wildly] that these initials signify a collaborative contraction" of Jonson, Fletcher, and Beaumont [Masten 2002]); dramatis personae; five acts and separate scenes. Grotesque staging includes: *"Enter Latorch [and] Hamond with a head."* Staging seems to call for a blazing star, which "consisted either of a firework on a line or flaming material suspended in an iron cage or cresset, and burned for up to a minute" (Holdsworth 1990). Q2 1640 *The Tragedy of Rollo, Duke of Normandy*; "written by John Fletcher"; list of characters; "act and scene divisions of the second quarto are strange" (Williams). A 1660 advertisement by Humphrey Moseley attributes the play to B&F. B&F F2 1679 *Fifty Comedies and Tragedies*; "published by the authors original copies, the songs to each play being added"; *The Bloody Brother, or Rollo, A Tragedy*; RT *The Bloody Brother*; list of characters. Q3 1686 *Rollo, Duke of Normandy: or, The Bloody Brother, A Tragedy*. Before the Restoration, probably in the 1640s and 50s, parts of the play were adapted for a droll entitled *The Three Merry Boys*, later published in *1 The Wits, or Sport upon Sport* (O 1662 [two issues] and 1672).

In the winter of 1648 a troupe made up of "the scatter'd members of several" companies "ventured to act some plays with as much caution and privacy as cou'd be, at the Cockpit." For several days in *Rollo*, John Lowin played Aubrey; Joseph Taylor, Rollo; Thomas Pollard, the Cook; Nicholas Burt, Latorch; Charles Hart, Otto; but as they performed on 5 February, "a party of foot souldiers beset the house, surprized 'em about the mid[d]le of the play, and carried 'em away in their habits [costumes], not admitting them to shift, to Hatton-house then a prison, where having detain'd them sometime, they plunder'd them of their cloth[e]s and let 'em loose again" (*Historia Histrionica*).

Blurt, Master Constable, or The Spaniard's Night Walk. Thomas Dekker. Acted 1601–02 (Berger 1979). The lists of plays prepared by Rogers and Ley in 1656 and by Archer the same year fail to reveal the author's identity. Kirkman in 1661 attributed the play to Middleton, and this identification was accepted until Oliphant 1926 challenged it and suggested Dekker's authorship. "Objective tests support Oliphant's repudiation of Kirkman's ascription" (Jackson 1979). But Bradbrook 1955 and Ellis-Fermor 1958 revived the ascription to Middleton, as did Holmes 1969. Although today the issue remains unsettled, "Dekker's hand is visible literally from the first to the last sentence of the play" (Lake 1975a). "Sundry times privately acted" by Paul's Boys, according to the TP, 1601–02 (Tassi 2005) at Paul's playhouse. "[A]ppears to demand" twenty-four players (Knutson 2001b).

SR 7 June 1602. Q 1602 no author named; not divided. A "prostitute receives a miniature [portrait] of a gentleman intended for his lover: she refuses to part with it, and declares that she will sleep with it until he comes to replace it" (Rochester 2010): "these small, alluring pictures, frequently set in jewels, drew attention to the smallness and effeminacy of the boy actors"; here Dekker "burlesques the role portrait miniatures played in love" (Tassi 2005); Elizabethan, Jacobean, and Caroline painters raised miniature portraits to the status of high art (Fumerton 1991). Staging calls for a trap that has symbolic value: Lazarillo lies down, proceeds to fall through the trap, and cries, "I am in hell." "There are many directions for music" (Jewkes 1958): "*Musicke for a measure. Whilst* Fontinell *speakes, they dance a straine*"; "*The cornets sound a lavolto which the maskers are to daunce*"; "*The Spanish pavin.*" Sound effects include birdsong: "*Musicke sodainly plaies, and birds sing*"; "a mechanical device" may have produced the birdsong (Lawrence 1927). The principal character, "an incompetent police officer, [was] obviously inspired by Shakespeare's Dogberry [in *Much Ado*]" (Bevington 1968).

"The penchant for putting on the stage scenes depicting the life of brothels extends, in the first half-dozen years of the seventeenth century, from plays as various as Middleton's *Michaelmas Term*, *A Mad World, My Masters*, and *Your Five Gallants* and Marston's *Dutch Courtesan* to Shakespeare's *Measure for Measure* and *Pericles*, Beaumont and Fletcher's *The Woman Hater* and Sharpham's *The Fleer*" (Hoy 1980).

The Bondman, An Ancient Story. Philip Massinger. Licensed for acting as *The Noble Bondman* 3 December 1623 (Adams 1917). "Often acted with good allowance" by Lady Elizabeth's Men [Queen of Bohemia's Men] at the Phoenix, according to the TP; in "1621 or 1622 a revived Lady Elizabeth's company was formed and began playing at the Phoenix under Christopher Beeston" (Bentley 1981). Performed also at Whitehall, 27 December 1623, "the prince only being there" (Adams). "[P]erhaps revised by Massinger in the spring of 1624 prior to being entered in the Stationers' Register" (Jowitt 2006a). In playlist of Beeston's Boys 10 August 1639.

SR 12 March 1624; transferred 28 April 1660. Q1 1624 a Folger copy contains corrections/revisions in Massinger's hand; list of characters; five acts and separate scenes. SDs "are full, and rather 'literary'" (E&G 1976): "*Gracculo leading Asotus [a foolish lover] in an apes habit, with a chaine about his necke. Zanthia [slave to Corsica], in Corsicaes cloathes, she bearing up her traine.*" Before Q1 was printed, "Massinger not only corrected the original version, but also . . . rewrote Act I, significantly changing its meaning"; Massinger altered the play "to create a conspicuous parallel between a parliamentary debate in the created world and a debate in the English Parliament of 1624" (Limon 1986). "About 1633 Massinger had eight of his previously published plays bound together in a single volume. Possibly he was thinking of publishing a collection of his works; possibly he intended the volume as a gift to a patron. He made extensive ink corrections in a number of the plays [including *The Bondman*]" (Edwards 1987). The Folger own the collection. Q2 1638 two issues.

A Q1 prefatory poem by W. B., "the author's friend," characterizes the play by announcing what the reader will *not* find: "Here are no gipsie jigges, no drumming stuffe, / Dances, or other trumpery to delight, / Or take, by common way, the common sight. / The author of this poem, as he dares / To stand th'austerest censure; so he cares, / As little what it is."

The dialogue has clear implications for contemporary politics: "O shame! That we that are a populous nation, / Ingag'd to liberall nature, for all blessings / An island can bring forth; we that have limbs / And able bodies; shipping, armes, and treasure, / The sinnewes of the warre, now we are call'd / To stand upon our guard, cannot produce / One fit to be our generall." "The island in question is Sicily, not England; but at the end of 1623 an English audience would surely decode this as glancing at James's refusal to offer military support for his daughter Elizabeth, forced into exile along with her husband the Elector Palatine by Hapsburg armies in November 1620" (Robinson 2006). "[T]he case for a bold foreign and military policy is directly and powerfully dramatized" (Heinemann 1993a).

The Bonds of Peace. See *Time's Distractions.*

Bonduca. John Fletcher, named by Rogers and Ley, Archer, and Kirkman. Acted 1609–14 (McMullan 1994) or 1611–14 (Gurr 2009d) by the King's Men at the first Globe, second Blackfriars, or second Globe. Principal actors were Richard Burbage, Henry Condell, William Ostler, John Lowin, William Eccleston, Nicholas Tooley, John Underwood, and Richard Robinson, according to F2. In playlist of King's Men 7 August 1641. "*Bonduca* articulates an important cross-section of anxieties and conceptual shifts about women worthies and male homosociality that alludes to the court and reign of James I. The figure of Boadicea as a powerful, warlike, or 'Amazonian' woman identified with British nationalism necessarily constituted a challenge to the official ideology of James's court" (Crawford 1999).

London, BL, Additional MS 36758, fols. 1–25; *Bonduca, Queen of Britain*; written *c.* 1630 (Stern 2009c); "evidently a copy of the play prepared for a private collector" (Greg 1951); copied by Edward Knight, "book-keeper of the King's Company in the later 1620s and the early 30s" (Hoy 1979); no author named; divided "into acts only" and first scenes (Greg 1931). The MS is "unique among early modern dramatic manuscripts for containing within it some account of its origin" (Werstine 1997). MS omits three scenes and part of a fourth; Edward Knight explains: "the occasion why these are wanting here. the booke where by it [the play] was first acted from is lost: and this hath beene transcrib'd from the fowle papers of the authors wch were found." "But the author's foul papers were themselves defective, and the scribe is reduced to summarizing (somewhat incorrectly) the action of the scenes . . . missing from his copy" (Hoy 1979). The term *foul papers* designates "the play more of less as the author intended it to stand, but not . . . clear or tidy enough to serve as a prompt-book" (Greg 1955). However, the "sense in which Greg used *foul papers* appears at odds with the sense in which the terms *foul sheet* or *foul papers* were used in the Jacobean and Caroline documents from which Greg drew these words" (Werstine 1990). That is, "the composition of plays could and did issue from collaboration between playwright and players, rather than from playwright alone"; in short, "there never would have been a manuscript that conformed to Greg's normative conception of 'fowle papers,' that is a manuscript wholly the author's work" (Werstine 1997). Perhaps Fletcher had "only outlined" the scenes "when composing the play and wrote them out more fully by providing dialogue and stage directions in a later copy. Or the foul papers contained more than an outline but not enough coherent text for the scribe to transcribe, so he summarised them instead" (Ioppolo 2006). The most interesting staging calls for an elaborate procession, followed by a sacrifice to the gods on an altar. "[T]he illusion of a mighty struggle" is created in part by sound": "[d]rums and trumpets in severall places afar off, as at a main battell," "loud shout," "Drums loud again, more shouting" (Lawrence 1927). First modern edition by Greg 1951.

SR 4 September 1646 *Bonducca, or, Boadicia*; transferred 30 January 1673. B&F F1 1647 *Comedies and Tragedies*; "never printed before, and now published by the authours originall copies"; *The Tragedy of Bonduca*; five acts and separate scenes. The SDs of F1 "tend to be fuller and more graphic" than those of MS; "[t]hey suggest amplifications by the scribe writing for readers and with recollections of actual performance in mind" (Greg 1931). Differences between MS and F1 suggest that Fletcher revised his play (Ioppolo 1990). Humphrey Moseley's introduction to F1 "mentions copies [of the plays] having been made available by actors to their 'private friends'" (Love 1993). B&F F2 1679 *Fifty Comedies and Tragedies*; "published by the authors originall copies, the songs to each play being added"; *Bonduca, A Tragedy*; list of characters; names of actors.

"That the play is substantially Fletcher's is hardly open to doubt. The early playlists by Rogers and Ley and Archer (1656), Kirkman (1661, 1671), and Langbaine (1680) give him as the author, and so does George Powell in his adaptation of the play published in 1696" (Greg 1951).

The Book of Sir Thomas More. See *Sir Thomas More.*

Boot and Spur. Anonymous. Acted 1611–17 (Gossett & Berger 1988) or 1622–25 (Thomson 1988a). Possibly written at Cambridge University for performance there (Nelson 1989). However, "[n]othing about *Boote & Spurre* would recommend it as an academic play. While it lacks the intellectual verve of most academic plays, it also has neither the dull pedantry of the worst nor the biting satire of the best of the productions of undergraduate thespians"; instead, the play is "self-evidently the kind of material that would recommend it to apprentices" (Thomson).

Washington, Folger, MS J.a.1, fols. 19–23; no separate TP; the title *Boot &* *Spurre* is written in a different hand from that of the text; no author named; list of characters; prologue and epilogue (both by Shoemaker); not divided. "There are few stage directions, and no indications that the manuscript was used for acting" (Gossett & Berger). First edited by Gossett & Berger 1988 and by Thomson 1988.

Bottom the Weaver. A droll based on scenes in Shakespeare's *A Midsummer Night's Dream* and "often publikely acted by some of his majesties comedians, and lately, privately, presented, by several apprentices for their harmless recreation, with great applause," according to the 1661 TP, in the 1640s and 50s. Written *c.* 1646 and "exceedingly popular" (Halliwell[-Phillipps] 1860d). Although Kirkman on the TP of *2 The Wits* says that the drolls were "written I know not when, by several persons, I know not who," his preface reports that Robert Cox "was not only the principal actor, but also the contriver and author of most of these farces." Kirkman's attribution is "probable" (Holland 2007). Cox "was an actor associated with surreptitious performances in fair-grounds and elsewhere during the period of the Civil Wars and Commonwealth, when public theatrical performances were prohibited" (Wells 1970). This droll is "especially interesting because, despite its excessive length and the number of actors it requires (nine, even with the doubling provided for), there is very definite evidence that it was performed" (Elson 1932).

Q 1661 *The Merry Conceited Humors of Bottom the Weaver*; RT *Bottom the Weaver*; list of characters. Ample SDs: "*Fayries first dance*"; "*Enter* Bottome *with an asses head*"; "*Enter Lyon and Moon-shine*." Published also in *2 The Wits, or Sport upon Sport* (Q and O 1673), which gives as venues of performance fairs, halls, taverns, and "mountebancks stages at Charing Cross, Lincolns-Inn-Fields, and other places"; list of characters. *Bottom the weaver* is included in Kirkman's 1661 catalogue of plays.

The stationers' address from Francis Kirkman and Henry Marsh anticipates the restoration of the monarchy and reopening of the theaters: "It hath been the desire of several (who know we have many pieces of this nature in our hands) that we should publish them, and we considering the general mirth that is likely, very suddainly to happen about the kings coronation; and supposing that things of this nature, will be acceptable, have therefore begun with this which we know may be easily acted, and may be now as fit for a private recreation as formerly it hath been for a publike." "Kirkman and Marsh expected the new official tolerance for stage plays to lead to a boom in amateur performances" (Marino 2011). An advertisement is printed on the last page: "If you please to repair to our shops aforementioned, you may be furnished with all plays that were ever yet printed."

The Bouncing Knight, or The Robbers Robbed. A droll based upon several scenes in Shakespeare's *1 Henry IV* and performed in the 1640s and 50s. The droll "is an amalgam of various scenes in *1 Henry IV* in which Falstaff appears. Thus, we move from the tavern scene (3.3), in which Falstaff accuses Mistress Quickly of rifling his pockets, to Falstaff's comic soliloquy about his abuse of recruitment . . ., followed by his preposterous claim to have killed Hotspur" (Clare 2004). "The title is apparently a coinage by the droll-maker" (Elson 1932). "The piece is rather long for a droll"; "six or eight actors are required" (Elson).

Published in *1 The Wits, or Sport upon Sport* (O 1662 [two issues] and 1672); RT *The Humors of the Bouncing Knight*; argument; list of characters. *The Wits* mistakenly attributes the source of the droll to *Edward IV* (Halliwell[-Phillips] 1860c). The frontispiece to *The Wits* depicts both Falstaff and the Hostess, characters in the droll.

The Brazen Age. Thomas Heywood. Acted 1609–11 (Taylor 1993a) or 1610–13 (Gurr 2009d) by Queen Anne's Men at the Red Bull (Harbage 1952).

SR none. Q 1613 *The Brazen Age: The First Act Containing the Death of the Centaur Nessus, the Second, the Tragedy of Meleager, the Third, the Tragedy of Jason and Medea, the Fourth, Vulcan's Net, the Fifth, the Labors and Death of Hercules*; two issues; dramatis personae; detailed descriptions of four dumb shows before the acts, explained by Homer; although the TP announces a five-act play, there are no numbered divisions after act 2. However, the appearances of Homer may be interpreted as initiating each of five acts. The first and last speeches by Homer serve the functions of prologue and epilogue. Heywood dramatizes, in "the confrontation between Hercules and the shape-shifter Achelous," action that is "seemingly impossible" to stage; "[t]he narrative fiction requires that Achelous start in his own shape, shift three times, and reappear in his own guise to confess defeat" (Dessen 2006): in the space of ten lines, Achelous "*is beaten in, and immediately enters in the shape of a dragon*"; then Hercules "*beats away the dragon. Enter a Fury all fire-workes*"; "*When the Fury sinkes, a buls head appears*"; Hercules "*tugs with the bull, and pluckes off one of his hornes.*" Staging calls for Medea, "*with strange fiery-workes,*" to hang "*above in the aire,*" apparently by machinery. "*A shower of raine*" falls in a dumb show. In another scene Hercules enters, "*tearing downe trees*" and killing Omphale "*with a peece of a rocke*"; then "*All the princes breake downe the trees, and make a fire, in which Hercules placeth himselfe.*" Subsequently "*Jupiter above strikes him [Hercules] with a thunder-bolt, his body sinkes, and from the heavens discends a hand in a cloud, that from the place where Hercules was burnt, brings up a starre, and fixeth it in the firmament.*" A SD calls for action above when Vulcan catches Mars and Venus in a net: "*All the gods appear above, and laugh.*" The play contains "the most elaborate" hunting scene in the period, "the hunt for the Caledonian boar" (Dessen). Staging calls for a "violet banke," a stage property on which Venus wants Adonis "to 'tumble,'" and on which he may have been laid to die" (Reynolds 1940).

Heywood's *Ages* plays "demand some of the most spectacular staging ever suggested for the Elizabethan public stage" (Reynolds). In *The Brazen Age*, as in *The Silver Age*, "there were cloud effects and aerial flights rivalling anything of the sort already seen in the court masques" (Lawrence 1927).

Brennoralt, or The Discontented Colonel. John Suckling. Probably acted "summer 1640" (Butler 1984b). "Presented at" the [second] Blackfriars by the King's Men, according to the O TPs. Possibly performed at court. In playlist of the King's Men 7 August 1641 as *The discontented Colonell.*

SR 5 April 1642 *The discontented colonell*; transferred 1 August 1646. Q ND ?1642 *The Discontented Colonel*; list of characters; five acts. Staging may have involved a staircase in the playgoers' view: "This was the entry, these the stairs" (Lawrence 1927). O1 1646 *Fragmenta Aurea* (with *Aglaura*, *The Goblins*); "printed by his owne copies," according to the general TP; entitled *Brennoralt, A Tragedy*; list of characters; the text is "wholly independent of the quarto—with over 600 substantive differences" (Beaurline 1971). O2 1648 *Fragmenta Aurea*; RT *The Tragedy of Brennoralt*. O3 1658–59 *Fragmenta Aurea*; "the third edition, with some new additionals"; printed in two parts; Part 1 dated 1658; Part 2 entitled *The Last Remains of Sir John Suckling* (1659).

"The play's concluding scene begins with Iphigene and Francelia alone in Francelia's bed, apparently having spent the night together"; the scene "seems constructed specifically to pique the audience's prurient sexual imagination, but also romanticizes the couple" (Walen 2005).

The Bride, A Comedy. Thomas Nabbes. "Acted in the yeere 1638" by Beeston's Boys at the Phoenix, according to the Q TP, probably in the summer (Kathman 2004c). The prologue "was spoken while Bartholomew Fair was running 23–25 August, or Southwark Fair, 7–9 September" (*JCS*). The play is "aimed at an audience of merchants and citizens rather than the Cockpit's normal upper-crust clientele" (Kathman).

SR 8 July 1639. Q 1639–40 list of characters; prologue and epilogue (by the Bride); five acts and separate scenes. Also issued in *Plays, Masques, Epigrams, Elegies, and Epithalamiums*, a made-up book containing plays dated from 1637 to 1640; the general TP bears 1639 date, separate 1640.

In the dedication (to gentlemen at the Inns-of-Court) Nabbes alludes to alterations made during production: "She [the play] is here drest according to mine own desire and intention; without aught taken from her that my selfe thought ornament; nor supplyed with any thing which I valued but as rags." Nabbes felt that "the usual theatrical cuts seemed excessive" (Bentley 1971). The prologue notes a fall-off in the number of playgoers: "Vacation still: so little custome comes / To buy our merchandize, and fill our roomes, / It would perswade us but for after hope / Of better takings quite to shut up shop." Prologue goes on to defend the author from imputations of satire directed at individuals: "Perhaps there will be some concluding that / A person or a place is pointed at; / Such make that satire which the pure intent / Of th'author meant but harmelesse merriment; / Who only labours here in what he can / T'expresse a citizen a gentleman."

A Brief Comedy or Interlude concerning the Temptation of Our Lord and Savior, Jesus Christ. See *The Temptation of our Lord.*

A Brief Comedy or Interlude of John Baptist's Preaching in the Wilderness. See *John Baptist's Preaching.*

The Broken Heart, A Tragedy. John Ford. Probably acted late 1629 (Gurr 1988a). By the King's Men at the [second] Blackfriars, according to the TP. Joseph Taylor probably played Orgilus; Robert Benfield, Ithocles; John Lowin, Bassanes; ?John Honeyman, Penthea; ?John Thompson, Calantha (Sturgess 1987).

SR 28 March 1633. Q 1633 no author named on the TP, but Ford's anagram *Fide Honor* follows the title, and Ford signs the dedication; list of characters providing brief descriptions (e.g., "Orgilus, Angry, Sonne to Crotolon"; prologue and epilogue; carefully described dumb show; five acts and separate scenes. The play "focuses on the rituals and ceremonies by which societies, in particular powerful societies, sustain and restrain themselves" (Sanders 1999a): "the extent of ceremonial in the play is extraordinary" (Clark 1992); e.g., "Calantha continues dancing as three messengers deliver her news of the deaths of her father, friend and lover. What her courtiers construe as a lack of 'female pity' is shortly after belied by her self-willed death, a choreographed ritual which is at once a display of extreme self-control and emotional abandon" (Tomlinson 2005). Ford's play is "composed of stage tableaux, of dumbshow, masques, and music that contribute to an air of melancholy and fatalism that is all-pervasive" (Sanders). Within that stylized action, Penthea appears with "*her haire about her eares*"; she "presents a familiar stage icon of feminine madness"; her "performative madness locates her simultaneously as the victim of a powerfully internalized patriarchal culture and as an ambiguous agent of revenge" (Tomlinson 2005). "Discovering that Penthea has starved herself to death through grief, Orgilus obtains possession of her body and places it on stage in a chair. Next to it, he positions another chair, which conceals an unspecified 'engine'" (Hopkins 1995b): "*Ithocles sits downe, and is catcht in the engine.*" "The mechanical device pinioning the victim makes Orgilus's act of revenge look rather more like an execution" (Madelaine 1988). "Orgilus presents a show to Ithocles which is both a funeral for Penthea (with dirge, orations and ceremonial observances) and also a ritual revenge on Ithocles himself" (Sturgess 1987). It is difficult to know how the actors handled the effect created when "Orgilus opens a vein in his arm, and has another opened by Bassanes in the other arm; he is seen to bleed slowly to death, falls, and is carried off" (Lawrence 1927). "Orgilus's bleeding to death . . . uses more gushing blood than any other scene on the English stage since Lavinia's 'three issuing conduits' in *Titus Andronicus*"

(Madelaine). The death scene of a crowned and robed Calantha, in the presence of altar, candles, and music, as well as Ithocles *"on a hea[r]se, or in a chaire,"* achieves "a powerfully sacramental atmosphere, half Christian and half pagan" (Sturgess). Here "religion is represented as a mechanism for defending chastity, and altars are positioned as the bulwarks of virtue" (Williamson 2009). Calantha's death scene "can be read as suggesting that in a world as dark as that of the Sparta of the play, the only solace to be found must come from Catholic religious practice" (Hopkins 1995b). Also issued in *Comedies, Tragicomedies, and Tragedies* (1652), a made-up book.

Prologue defends the genre of tragedy at a time "when comedy was the mode" (Gurr 1988a): "The title lends no expectation here / Of apish laughter, or of some lame jeere / At place or persons; no pretended clause / Of jest's fit for a brothell courts' applause / From vulgar admiration: such low songs, / Tun'd to unchast eares, suit not modest tongues." In short, Ford "seeks the discriminating approval of courtiers and barristers" (Clark 1992). Prologue also refers to the playwright's "best of art," which has been taken to mean that "he is trying to do his best artistically; that is, to be controlling and organising his material in accordance with a preconceived plan, avoiding any excess or superfluity, and aiming at an intensity of appropriate emotional effect" (Spencer 1980). "The only exceptional thing about this prologue is its rather heavy emphasis on the moral value of poetry" (Neill 1978).

The Brothers, A Comedy. James Shirley. A play by Shirley entitled *The Brothers* was licensed for acting 4 November 1626; that play is apparently lost (*JCS*). *The Brothers, A Comedy*, was licensed as *The Politique Father* 26 May 1641 (Adams 1917, Wertheim 1978); for unknown reasons the title was changed. Acted "with great applause" at the [second] Blackfriars, according to the general TP, by the King's Men. In playlist of the King's Men 7 August 1641.

SR 4 September 1646. O 1652–53 *Six New Plays* (with *The Cardinal, The Court Secret, The Doubtful Heir, The Imposture, The Sisters*); the separate TP of *The Brothers* is dated 1652 and indicates "never printed before"; separate register and pagination; list of characters; prologue and epilogue, which had already appeared in Shirley's 1646 *Poems* (Greg 1939); five acts. Shirley's dedication observes that although the reader of the printed page does not experience drama in the way a playgoer does, the play comes to life when the reader enjoys the work: "though it appear not in that naturall dress of the scene, nor so powerfull, as when it had the soul of action, yet your smile upon it now will give it second animation."

According to the prologue, the author "saies the tymes are dangerous, who knowes / What treason may be wrapt in giant prose, / Or swelling verse, at least to sense? nay then / Have at you Mr. Poet, gentlemen, / Though he pretend fair, I dissemble not, / Y'are all betray'd here to a Spanish plot." "Part of the jest . . . is that this playwright who 'pretends fair' refers ambiguously to earlier known Spanish plots, to the current rumor-filled atmosphere of foreign plots, including

Spanish ones, and—perhaps most deftly and directly—to the fact that the play at hand is set in Spain" (Randall 1995).

The Bubble. A droll based upon scenes in *Greene's Tu Quoque* and performed in the 1640s and 50s. "There are two ensemble scenes, one requiring five actors, the other six or seven, with supernumeraries desirable" (Elson 1932).

Published in *1 The Wits, or Sport upon Sport* (O 1662 [two issues] and 1672); RT *The Humors of the Bubble*; argument; list of characters. Bubble is depicted in the frontispiece to *1 The Wits* "as a fool, wearing a hat with a cockscomb" (Foakes 1985); he's "a foolish servant who tries to use an inheritance to turn himself into a fashionable gallant" (Mann 1991). Whoever prepared this droll did so deftly, making changes that enhance the theatricality and coherence of the adaptation.

The Bugbears. ?John Jeffere. Acted 1563–*c.* 1570 (Clark 1979) or 1563–66 (Grantley 2008a) at undetermined venue. "That it is a children's play is shown by the last chorus, in which the actors refer to themselves as 'we boyes'" (Hillebrand 1926). "[P]ossibly performed at Gray's Inn" (Grantley 2004). "Spectacle and entertainment matter more than anything else" (Guinle 1982). "We have no real information about performance, and the work stayed in manuscript until the late nineteenth century" (Braden 2010).

London, BL, Lansdowne MS 807, fols. 57–75; no TP; damaged—one leaf is mostly torn away, another leaf crossed out; written "in at least five hands" (Guinle); "a group of revelers in guise of devils, wearing visards and using squibs, sing a chorus" (Baskervill 1929); five songs are included; five acts and separate scenes. At the end of the MS is written: "Johannus Jeffere scribebat hoc." It is not clear whether this name designates the author or merely the scribe. First edited by Grabau 1897. First edited in English by Bond 1911.

"*The Bugbears* is an interesting example of the adaptation of foreign dramaturgy [*La Spiritata* by Grazzini] to a native English tradition" (Potter 1980).

Bumpkin. A droll probably acted in the 1650s and "ascribed to Robert Cox, but pronounced by Baskervill to be probably of sixteenth-century origin" (Elson 1932). "Acted at the Red Bull," according to the Q2 TP of *Actaeon*. "It is a short pastoral play, bearing some resemblance to a Court masque" (Elson). "Seven actors at most are required" (Elson). Robert Cox probably acted the principal part.

First published in *Actaeon and Diana* (Q1 ?1655, Q2 1656 ["the second edition"]), ascribed to Cox in Kirkman's 1661 catalogue; TP *A Pastoral Story of the Nymph Oenone: Followed by the Several Conceited Humors of Bumpkin the Huntsman, Hobbinal the Shepherd, Singing Simpkin, and John Swabber the Seaman*; address to the reader by Cox. Ample SDs: e.g., "*Enter the Huntsman, with three country wenches, as they come in, they sing this song.*" "The title is misleading" (Greg 1939): Bumpkin is simply a character in *Actaeon and Diana*. But the "humor" of the character was "extracted to form [an] independent" droll (Greg) entitled

The Humor of Bumpkin and published in *1 The Wits, or Sport upon Sport* (O 1662 [two issues] and 1672); RT *The Humors of Bumpkin*; "argument needless, it being a thorow farce, very well known"; list of characters. *Bumpkin* is "a droll abridged from a droll" (Elson).

In the address to the reader of Q1 *Actaeon*, Cox writes of his purpose: "if you ever vouchsafed your presence when it was presented on the stage, I am confident, your (no way erring) judgements will now allow it as it then was intended, which was, rather to provoke a laughter, then occasion a contemplation."

Bussy D'Ambois, A Tragedy. George Chapman. "There is evidence that it was originally written for the Blackfriars but was stolen" (Nicol 2006a). Presumably acted by Paul's Boys in 1604 (Brooke 1964) or *c.* 1605–06 (Munro 2005): "often presented" at Paul's playhouse, according to the Q1 TP. "The Blackfriars Boys probably acquired the play when the Children of Paul's disbanded in 1606" (Nicol). Revised, "reclaimed," and performed by the Children of the Queen's Revels at Whitefriars, *c.* 1611–12 (Munro 2005); the revisions were occasioned "probably because there had been official objections to its French political content" (Burnett 2004). Revived by the King's Men at the Whitehall Cockpit, Easter Monday night, 7 April 1634 (Adams 1917). Performed by the same company, 27 March 1638, before the king and queen at Whitehall Cockpit (Adams). The Q2 prologue names Nathan Field, "whose action first did give it name," and who probably enacted the part of Bussy when he "played as a member of the Queen's Revels" (Lamb 2009); it is uncertain whether Field originated the role or played in a revival. Prologue also alludes to another actor, probably Joseph Taylor (who joined the King's Men by 1619), as having played Bussy; Eilert Swanston was probably the third actor to play the lead (Brooke).

SR 3 June 1607. Q1 1607–08 two issues; no author named; five acts. Staging includes the conjuration of Behemoth, who arises from beneath the stage; Tamyra ascends from a vault; Bussy and the Friar descend and later ascend; the ghost ascends, apparently through a trap. "On the whole, stage ghosts seem to have worn the clothes they wore when they were alive" (Thompson 2010). Staging also requires characters to ascend a staircase in view of the playgoers (Gair 1982). Sound effects include repeated thunder, a sign of divine displeasure. In highly unusual staging Behemoth shows to Bussy and Friar Comolet what is happening elsewhere among Monsieur, the Guise, and Montsurry (i.e., two locales are represented onstage simultaneously) (Kiefer 1996a). "The three characters in the vision speak to each other in order that the audience may thoroughly grasp the situation, but only their dumb show is patent to the anxious lovers" (Lawrence 1927). Chapman stages extraordinary violence: Montsurry pulls *"Tamyra in by the haire"*; he "threatens and then stabs his wife with a knife, then stretches her on the rack"; "it must be a horrible and extended bit of stage business" (Burks 2003). The final dumb show "in which the ghosts of Bussy, Guise, Cardinal Guise, Chatillon and Monsieur circle the dead body of Montsurry . . . completes the marginalization of women" (Findlay 1999). Bussy himself is killed by a "gun fired offstage" (Goldberg 1983). Q2 1641 two issues; "often acted with great applause"; "much corrected and amended by the author before his death"; no author named; prologue "obviously [written] for the play in revival, as it mentions as now dead the actor Nathan Field" (Stern 2009c), and epilogue (also written for a revival [Smith 1987a]). Reissued 1646 and again in 1657 (Chapman's name on the TP). Also issued in *Comedies, Tragicomedies, & Tragedies* (1652), a made-up book no longer extant.

The text appearing in Q2 (and later) had been considerably revised between 1604 and 1614, either solely by Chapman (Ure 1952, Tricomi 1979) or partly by Chapman and partly by a second reviser, perhaps Nathan Field (Brooke 1964, Braunmuller 1979). Chapman possibly "undertook a tailor-made revision of the successful *Bussy* in order to present it at the new Whitefriars Theatre in conjunction with his newly composed *Revenge of Bussy D'Ambois*" (Tricomi 1972). The Whitefriars and Whitehall Cockpit performances were probably of this revised version.

1 and 2 Byron. See *1 and 2 Charles Duke of Byron.*

C

Caesar and Pompey (The Wars of Caesar and Pompey). George Chapman. Written 1604 (Tricomi 1982). The SDs are extensive: "it has all the appearance of being written for the theater" (Soellner 1985); "it was written in the tradition of the commercial theatre and should be visualized on its stage," but the play probably "never touched the stage" (Brown 1954a). The TP of the 1653 reissue claims that the play "was acted at the Black-fryers." But this claim of performance is an "irresponsible statement to promote sales" (Brown 1954a). Between original composition and printing, the play was probably revised, perhaps in 1612 or 1613 (Berger & Donovan 1987). The play "in showing a vacillating Caesar who, with the removal of republicans, finds a supremely imperial position, asks searching questions of political absolutism" (Burnett 2004). The play "may simply have reflected rather too carefully on James's notorious attempts to control parliament and parliamentary elections, as well as buy supporters by giving them titles and favours" (Hadfield 2005).

SR 18 May 1631 *Caesar and Pompey*. Q 1631 *Caesar and Pompey, A Roman Tragedy, Declaring Their Wars*, in one issue; *The Wars of Pompey and Caesar*, in the other (apparently the original title [Jacob 2002]); HT *Only a Just Man is a Free Man*; RT *The Tragedy of Caesar and Pompey*; author's name given in one issue, author's initials in the other; argument but no prologue or epilogue; five acts and first scenes. Abundant SDs describe not only elaborate entrances and ceremony but also arresting action. As a character "*offers to hang himselfe,*" a devil ascends from under the stage: "*Thunder, and the gulfe opens, flames issuing; and Ophioneus ascending, with the face, wings and taile of a dragon; a skin coate all speckled on the throat.*" Staging calls for "some highly bizarre scenes of violence" (Owens 2005): "[Catiline] *thrusts him back, & plucks out his entrals.*" The staging heralds Caesar's victory: "Pompey's loss of power is figured in terms of the 'panick terrors' of his captains, and the 'strange confusion' of his camp where soldiers, instead of keeping to their allotted places and defined tasks, are 'every way routing.' In Pompey's camp, the bustle of the night has degenerated into the 'dismay' of purposeless activity, with soldiers aimlessly picking up weapons and 'hurling' them down again" (Taunton 2000). At the close Pompey's severed head is displayed to a surprised and enraged Caesar. Reissued 1652 with new TP; *Caesar and Pompey, A Roman Tragedy*; "secunda editio." Reissued 1653. "The 1653 republication . . . was patently topical" (Hirst 1990). Chapman's play cannot be the "seser & pompie" mentioned by Henslowe, 8 November 1594.

In his dedication Chapman writes, "Though . . . this martiall history suffer the division of acts and scenes, both for the more perspicuity and height of the celebration, yet never toucht it at the stage; or if it had . . . yet would it, I hope, fall under no exception in your lordships better-judgeing estimation, since scenicall representation is so farre from giving just cause of any least diminution; that the personall and exact life it gives to any history, or other such delineation of humane actions, ad[d]s to them luster, spirit, and apprehension, which the only section of acts and scenes makes mee stand upon thus much, since that only in some precisianismes will require a little prevention." Here Chapman "very specifically applauds theatrical performance—or 'scenical representation'—because it gives 'personal and exact life' to 'all-moving truth'"; in other words, when "the audience sees the 'personal and exact life' provided by specific human actors, they more readily and more pleasurably understand the play's 'delineation of human actions'" (Braunmuller 1992).

Caesar and Pompey, or Caesar's Revenge. Anonymous. Acted mid-1593 (Poole 2002) or *c.* 1596 (Ronan 2005). "Privately acted by the studentes of Trinity Colledge in Oxford," according to the Q2 TP. Despite this claim, "no record can be found of any such performance, and [*Caesar's*] *Revenge* does not look like typical undergraduate fare of the Jacobean period. . . . Instead, *Revenge* exhibits close resemblances to works popular some ten or twenty years earlier, in the late 1580s and early 1590s" (Ronan 1987). And despite the TP statement about academic auspices of production, the play "is written in a style modelled on the revenge plays popular in London" (Keenan 2002). Henslowe records eight performances of "seser & pompie" between November 1594 and June 1595, but it is not clear that he refers to this play.

SR 5 June 1606 *Julius Caesars revenge.* Q1 ND ?1606 (Boas & Greg 1911); ?1607 (Ronan); *The Tragedy of Caesar and Pompey, or Caesar's Revenge*; list of characters; Discord, who appears at the beginning of each act and at the close, functions as chorus; Discord's first speech constitutes a prologue; five acts and separate scenes, but the division "neither follows a consistent principle, nor exhibits a correct numbering" (Boas & Greg). Onstage violence includes the assassination of Caesar. Special effects include the entry of Discord, amid *"alarum then flames of fire,"* probably through a trap, and the entry of *"Caesars Ghost,"* whom Brutus describes as an "ugly f[i]end." The SDs choreograph the violence: *"The fight neerer; and enter, Crassineus, a sword, as thrust through his face; he fal[l]s. To him Pompey and Caesar fighting: Pompey gives way, Caesar follows, and enters at another do[o]re."* Q2 1607.

Shakespeare's knowledge of this anonymous play is evident in *Richard II*, *Julius Caesar*, and *Troilus and Cressida* (Pearson 1981), as well as *Antony and Cleopatra* (Weis 1983). There is a "genetic connection" between *Caesar and Pompey* and Shakespeare's *Julius Caesar* (Poole 2002). "*Caesar's Revenge* was almost certainly written by 1596" and "Shakespeare somehow got to know it and made quite extensive use of it while writing *Julius Caesar*" (Mandel 2012).

Caesar's Revenge. See *Caesar and Pompey* (Anonymous).

Calisto. See *The Escapes of Jupiter.*

Calisto and Melebea. ?John Rastell, who printed the play. Adapted from a Spanish narrative written as a dialogue by Fernando de Rojas and entitled *Celestina*; the play is "the first English version of the Spanish tale that was then taking all Europe by storm" (Wallace 1912); "[a]ny adaptation from the Spanish at this date . . . is remarkable" (Wilson 1969). Acted 1523–25 (*DTRB* 1984); probably intended for a great hall (Walker 1998) before an aristocratic audience. Possibly "written for the entertainment of [Sir Thomas] More's household and . . . acted on the occasion of the marriage of John More and Anne Cresacre in 1529" (Ungerer 1956). "It has a small cast of six characters, and was thus probably for professional players" (Southern 1973). "[C]ould be performed by no more than four actors" (Lancashire 2002).

SR ?5 October 1598 *The tragicke Comedye of Celestina* [a character]; no printing ensued. F ND ?1525–30 unique copy at Bodleian; *A New Comedy in English in Manner of an Interlude Right Elegant and Full of Craft of Rhetoric, Wherein Is Showed and Described as well the Beauty and Good Properties of Women, as Their Vices and Evil Conditions, with a Moral Conclusion and Exhortation to Virtue*; usually called *Calisto and Melibea* "from the chief characters" (Greg 1908); not divided, though the action falls into "three almost equal 'acts' . . . and an epilogue" (Axton 1979).

The first play composed in English to be identified as a "comedy" on its TP (Norland 1995). In *Calisto and Melebea* the "combination of witchcraft and women . . . appears on the English stage for the first time" (Tatzl 2005).

Cambises, King of Persia. Thomas Preston. Acted *c.* 1561 (Johnson 1975). "[T]he use of gittern music, and conspicuous use of the 'make room!' topos suggest an indoor, hall performance. The play between the Vice, Ambidexter, and his brother Cutpurse — assumed to be among the audience — might, however, suggest an outdoor performance" (Walker 1998). Possibly performed at court under the title of *Huff, Snuff, and Ruff*, Christmas 1560–61 (Bevington 1962); performed "at court probably by Sir Robert Dudley's company in 1560–1" (Streitberger 2009). Perhaps performed at a London inn (Bevington 1973). "Intended for performance . . . by a traveling troupe of six men and two boys" (Creeth 1966). *Cambises* "possibly continued to be performed for some time [following publication]. Indeed 'Cambyses vein' was familiar enough to a playhouse audience to be alluded to in Shakespeare's *1 Henry IV* in the late 1590s" (Lunney 2002). Preston's is "the most commercially successful of all early Elizabethan plays" (Wiggins 2000). "The crudeness and 'dramatic ineptitude' perceived in the play may result not from Preston's lack of skill or taste but from adapters' attempts to tailor the play to the tastes of the popular audience and the performance conditions of a touring company" (Norland 1992–93).

SR *c.* September/October 1569. Q1 ND ?1570 *A Lamentable Tragedy Mixed Full of Pleasant Mirth, Containing the Life of Cambises, King of Persia, from the Beginning of His Kingdom unto His Death, His One Good Deed of Execution, after that Many Wicked Deeds and Tyrannous Murders Committed by and through Him, and Last of All His Odious Death by God's Justice Appointed*; RT *The Comedy of King Cambises*; the TP divides the roles for eight players, who enact 38 parts; prologue and epilogue; the "epilogue may not have been written for a court performance, but it would seem particularly appropriate for an academic one" (Norland); not divided. Although the play does not feature a chorus, Common's Cry and Common's Complaint serve a choral function (Dessen 1977); also, Ambidexter, the Vice, has a "choric function of interpreting past action and preparing the audience for future events" (Norland). Detailed SDs: "*Heer let them fight with their staves, not come neer an other by three or foure yardes; the Vice set them on as hard as he can; one of their wives come out, and all to beat the Vice; he run[s] away.*" In contrast to plays shaped by classical precedent, Preston brings "all the important deeds, however violent and bloody, before the eyes of the spectator" (Creeth): "*strike him [Smirdis] in divers places . . . A little bladder of vinegar prickt*"; "*smite him [Sisamnes] in the neck with a swoord to signify his death,*" and then "*Flea him with a false skin.*" "One can only presume that after the stylized smiting of Sisamnes . . . the bloodied false skin was pulled over Sisamnes' head and shown to the audience" (Fishman 1976). Cambises shoots an arrow into the heart of a child; that heart is then cut out and displayed onstage. At the play's close a SD indicates a spectacular entry: "*Enter the king without a gowne, a swoord thrust up into his side bleeding.*" The king's end "offers a sensational example of divine punishment" (Ward 2008b), but "he meets his death through apparent mischance" (Kiefer 1983): "Wounded I am by sodain chaunce." Q2 ND ?1585. Q3 ND ?1588–95 The Bodleian contains a fragment of two leaves (Johnson 1968c).

Cambises is "the earliest surviving tragedy of the Elizabethan age" (Hill 1992); at the same time it descends "from the mystery cycles and the subsequent Biblical plays" (Margeson 1967). "With its delays, surprises, juxtapositions, and reversals, Preston's dramaturgy of chronology keeps meaning open and contingent, darkly mirroring England's religious and political changes in the 1550s and 1560s" (Cartwright 1999).

Campaspe (*Alexander, Campaspe, and Diogenes*). John Lyly. "Possibly composed in 1580" (Erne 2003b). Acted late 1583 (Pincombe 1996). By the combined Children of the Chapel Royal and Paul's Boys, according to the Q TPs, at the first Blackfriars. *Campaspe* is one of three plays "known to have been performed at this theater" (Shapiro 2009). The combined troupe "functioned under the patronage of the Earl of Oxford" (Scragg 2002) and was known as Oxford's Boys, "in reality, apparently, a nonce group composed, as title-pages state, of 'the Children of her Majesty's Chapel and the Boys of [St] Paul's [Cathedral]'" (Hunter 2004). Performed also at court before the queen, the night of 6 January 1584, according to the Q1 TP; performed at court, the night of 1 January 1584, according to the Q2 and Q3 TPs; the altered date "is presumably a correction" (Greg 1933). In all likelihood *Campaspe* was acted on New Year's day, 1584, in the Great Chamber at Whitehall (Hunter 1991). Intended for Elizabeth, the play was "a uniquely elegant entertainment, offering a blend of courtly compliment, classical learning, songs, and witty dialogue" (Hunter 2004). Lyly's plays were "often presented and acted" before Queen Elizabeth, according to the D general TP. "*Campaspe* was evidently not a popular success, judging from the prologue written for the Blackfriars performances of its successor, *Sapho and Phao*" [spelling on the TP] (Gurr 1987b).

SR no original; transferred 12 April 1597; 23 August 1601; 9 January 1628. Q1 1584 *A Most Excellent Comedy of Alexander, Campaspe, and Diogenes*; RT *A Tragical Comedy of Alexander and Campaspe*; Kirkman 1661 calls it *Alexander and Campaspe*; no author named; prologue at Blackfriars and prologue at court; epilogue at Blackfriars and at court; five acts and separate scenes. Stage "houses," made of canvas, must have been used for Diogenes' tub and Apelles' studio (Best 1968b). Another such house may have represented Alexander's palace (Saccio 1969); "whether or not Alexander's palace was visually represented remains unclear" (Scragg 2005). "Despite the first quarto's title, Lyly's play came to be known as *Campaspe*, which reflects the dramatist's and his coterie audience's interest in Campaspe's character and legend": "Campaspe is Alexander the Great's Theban concubine; when Alexander commissions his favorite painter, Apelles, to paint her portrait, the artist falls in love with her" (Tassi 2005). But "the title given to the play in modern editions is a misleading one, in that it foregrounds an aspect of the drama that constitutes only one element of the total design. Remarkably few scenes of the play are directly concerned with the triangular relationship between Alexander, Campaspe and the painter Apelles" (Scragg 1999). "Lyly's vivid evocation of the glory that was Athens is among the first, and certainly one of the most successful attempts ever made on the stage to make the lost world of ancient Greece come alive again" (Truchet 1979). Q2 1584 *Campaspe.* Q3 1584 *Campaspe*; unique copy at V&A. Q4 1591 *Campaspe.* D 1632 *Six Court Comedies* (with *Endymion, Gallathea, Midas, Mother Bombie, Sappho and Phao*); two issues; by "John Lilly"; adds three "songs to the plays where in quarto they had only been indicated by stage directions" (Bevington 1991).

"*Campaspe* debates at length the role of the learned man in a society of courtiers and soldiers. Lyly had himself only recently come down from Oxford, seeking not only to prosper but to justify himself in the world of practical deeds" (Bevington 1968).

Candy Restored (*Candia Restaurata*). Mildmay Fane. Acted 12 February 1641, according to the Huntington and BL MSS. "Presented in a shew at Apethorpe [Northamptonshire] . . . to the Lord [earl of Westmorland] and Lady of that place, by some of their owne children and familie," according to MS (2). The actors included Fane's stepsons, Sir Roger and Horatio Townshend (Harbage 1936); "women's parts are assigned to boys" (Greg 1931). "The staging . . . was unusually elaborate, and one of his sketches [Huntington MS] provides the first known instance of flat revolving wings in England"; there were "three flats on each side which were revolved to change the set, and at the back a traverse which was drawn, concealing an elaborate painted scene" (*JCS*).

(1) San Marino, CA, Huntington, MS HM 771, fols. 1–20, ed. Leech 1938; no author named; corrections and additional SDs in the author's hand; list of characters ("drama personarum") along with brief descriptions and names of the actors who performed the roles; prologue (by a nymph of Diana) and epilogue (by a chorus of sylvans); not divided. *Candy Restored* is "the only one of Fane's plays for which we have two manuscripts: that at the Huntington is certainly the earlier, since many of Fane's corrections in it have been included in the British Museum [i.e., Library] manuscript in the hand of the scribe" (Leech). Very detailed SDs: "*A picture of Diana with a cressant, under which in a scroule written in greate CANDY RESTORED under which in perspective a goodly fabrick or cittie the emblem of Concord Unitie and Peace. Under which a landskipp representinge the springe for the fresh greennesse of itt and those innocent, and usefull delights of huntinge.*" As this description indicates, Fane anticipates the use of painted scenery and locale designations. First edited by Leech. (2) London, BL, Additional MS 34221, fols. 1–18; no author named. The Latin and English titles are on facing pages at the beginning of the BL MS, which also records the names of the actors.

Fane's play, a pastoral, deals with the conflict between king and parliament. "The most remarkable feature of the political content of Fane's play is its optimism. The performance at Apethorpe took place three months after the first meeting of the Long Parliament and little more than a year before the beginning of the Civil War, but Fane's lyrical proclamation of Candy's return to health and prosperity rings true and is in marked contrast to the generally pessimistic treatment of his next play" (Leech 1938). "Somewhat surprisingly, considering that he wrote as late as 1641, Fane apparently thought that Candia might be restored by the wise ministrations of one Dr. Synodarke (Parliament)" (Randall 1995). *Candy Restored* is "the only work in which Fane shows himself to have been a Parliamentarian; his subsequent efforts all reject Parliament and advocate a Royalist position" (Morton 1991).

Canterbury His Change of Diet. Richard Overton (Smith 1987d). "Privately acted neare the palace-yard at Westminster," according to the TP, but this statement "is clearly an indication of the locale of the satiric action, not a record of a dramatic performance" (*JCS*). Although no evidence of production exists, "it is certainly a drama which could have been acted, much in the mode of twentieth-century guerilla theatre" (Williams 1977). The playlet "for its verve and theatricality looks almost certain to have achieved stage realization" (Butler 1984b). This playlet satirizing Archbishop Laud has been called a pamphlet or a closet drama, but "[t]he idiom is obviously that of the live theater with its sharply caricatured character types, its jigs, its snatches of folk-song, and its jesters who mix in serious matters and dare answer back to the king. Indeed it is not impossible that in these crisis years performances of this sort of show went on in private houses or barns" (Heinemann 1980). If Overton is indeed the author of this play-pamphlet, then "he was more aware than the other Leveller authors . . . of the evocative power of dialogue, and of the directness of theatre's appeal to both the intellect and the senses" (Borot 2007).

Q 1641 *A New Play called Canterbury His Change of Diet* [i.e., course of life, way of living or thinking]; no author named; jig as epilogue; four short acts. Ample SDs. This is "the first pamphlet to use an obvious dramatic form" (Potter 1981). The Q contains woodcuts that "crudely portray Archbishop Laud" (Foakes 1985). One depicts Laud and a Jesuit in a cage while a fool laughs at them. "No doubt the Bull or Fortune would have had Bajazet's cage handy after their revivals of *Tamburlaine*" (Butler 1984b). The next woodcut depicts Laud dining with a physician, lawyer, and divine, who "bring a variety of dishes to the Archbishop's table, all of which displease him; he punishes them by cutting off their ears" (Foakes); the playlet's title "is a visual pun; the 'diet' this archbishop convenes is a meal of the ears of his puritan critics" (Butler). The third woodcut depicts a carpenter holding Laud's nose to a grindstone: in the play a carpenter, "asked by Laud for the use of his grindstone to whet his knife, instead ties the Archbishop's nose to it" (Heinemann).

The play "comes to a close with a 'Gig' — a clear reminiscence of such song-and-dance jigs as traditionally followed the performance of real plays" (Randall 1995); this "may have been in form a characteristic stage jig of its period" (Baskervill 1929). This and other playlets "represent a further development of the jig or after piece, that satirical dialogue or song-and-dance by the clowns so popular in the Elizabethan theatre" (Butler 1984b).

Canterbury's Potion. See *The Bishop's Potion.*

Canterbury's Will, with a Serious Conference between His Scrivener and Him. Anonymous. A sequel to *Canterbury His Change of Diet*, this play-pamphlet was perhaps performed shortly before the closing of the theaters.

Q 1641 no author named; not divided. The TP bears a representation of Archbishop Laud, who summons his scrivener to assist with his last will. At the play's close the scrivener tells Laud, "had your grace been in this minde you now are in six yeares since, you never had exchanged Lambeth palace for a Tower lodging," and Laud replies, "Thou sayst too true."

This work belongs to a group of play-pamphlets "in which public figures are brought forward confessing their crimes or making their wills" (Butler 1984a).

The Captain. Francis Beaumont and John Fletcher; "this is largely Fletcher's work" (Clark 1994). Acted 1609–12 (Finkelpearl 2004) by the King's Men at the first Globe/second Blackfriars. (Originally written for company of boys [Gurr 2004c].) Performed at court, Christmas season 1612–13; payment to John Heminges recorded 20 May 1613. Principal actors were Richard Burbage, Henry Condell, William Ostler, and Alexander Cooke, according to B&F F2. In playlist of the King's Men 7 August 1641.

SR 4 September 1646; 30 January 1673. B&F F1 1647 *Comedies and Tragedies*; "never printed before, and now published by the authours originall copies"; prologue and epilogue; five acts and separate scenes. Some detailed SDs: *"Ang[ilo] makes discontented signes . . . Maid lais her finger crosse her mouth to him . . . Stops his ears, shews he is troubled with the musicke."* B&F F2 1679 *Fifty Comedies and Tragedies*; "published by the authors original copies, the songs to each play being added"; *The Captain, A Comedy*; list of characters, "which is faulty" (Beaurline 1966a); actors' names.

The F1 prologue addresses the play's genre: "This is nor comody, nor tragedy, / Nor history, nor any thing that may / (Yet in a weeke) be made a perfect play: / Yet those that love to laugh, and those that thinke / Twelve-pence goes farther this way then in drinke, / Or damsels, if they marke the matter through, / May stumble on a foolish toy, or two / Will make 'em shew their teeth: pray, for my sake / (That likely am your first man) doe not take / A distaste before you feele it: for ye may / When this is hist to ashes, have a play."

Captain Thomas Stukeley. Anonymous; likely a work of collaboration involving Thomas Heywood (Edelman 2005). Acted 11, 14, 29 December 1596. In 1597: 10, 20 January; 10 February; 15 March; 14 April; 18 May; 27 June, according to Henslowe, by the Lord Admiral's Men at the Rose (Levinson & Proudfoot 1970); Henslowe calls the play "stewtley." He also records expenditures for the play, 8 December 1596. Kirkman calls the play *Stukeley's Life and Death*. *Stukeley* may have been revised *c.* 1598–1600 (Yoklavich 1961). Such revision may "commemorate the exploits of [the Earl of] Essex" (Bevington 1968). The play, published in 1605, was "probably revived" around this time at the Fortune theater (Parr 1995); if so, such performances would have capitalized on the writing and performance of *The Travails of the Three English Brothers*.

SR 11 August 1600. Q 1605 *The Famous History of the Life and Death of Captain Thomas Stukeley, with His Marriage to Alderman Curtis His Daughter, and Valiant Ending of His Life at the Battle of Alcazar*; no author named; "as it hath beene acted"; "an awkwardly introduced chorus" (O'Neill 2007) functions to bridge a "gap in the plot" at several points (Mehl 1965); elaborate pantomime involving King Philip of Spain; not divided. Extensive SDs: *"Alarum is sounded, divers excurtions, Stukly pursues, Shane Oneale, and Neale Mackener, and after a good pretty fight his Lieutenant and Auntient rescue Stuklie, and chace the Ireshe out. Then an excurtion betwixt Herbert and O Hanlon, and so a retreat sounded. Enter Harbart, Gainsford, and some souldiors on the walles."* Spectacular staging evoking *Tamburlaine* includes *"Enter muly Mahamet with Calipolis drawne in their chariot."* Special effects include the close of the pantomime: *"with a sudden thunder-clap the sky is on fire and the blazing star appears."* A blazing star "consisted either of a firework on a line or flaming material suspended in an iron cage or cresset, and burned for up to a minute" (Holdsworth 1990). "In outdoor playhouses . . . in addition to 'tempestuous' drums, a 'bullet,' i.e., a cannonball, was 'rolled' along a sheet of metal or a wooden trough [to simulate thunder]" (White 2007). Offstage sound effects include *"a noies within of driving beasts."* "This conveyed that, after defeating the Irish, Stukeley had seized their cattle" (Lawrence 1927). "There is no denying that the Q text contains inconsistencies and oddities almost from the start, and that things seem to get worse towards the end"; some anomalies may be explained by positing a scrambling of the order of scenes near the end of the play (Wiggins 2004).

The play "contains more Gaelic than any other extant play of its period, . . . which suggest[s] first-hand knowledge of Ireland" (Levinson & Proudfoot). "In a few scenes . . . the Irish wars [are] actually brought onto the stage" (Neill 2000a). "In the Irish scenes . . . the text probes the nature and significance of rebellion and treason" (Jowitt 2003). "With the exception of Thomas Heywood's *Four Prentices of London* . . . *Stukeley* is the only Elizabethan play to bring Ireland on stage" (O'Neill).

Captain Underwit. See *The Country Captain*.

The Captive Lady, A Tragicomedy. Anonymous. Acted 1618–1630s (Braunmuller 1982) at undetermined venue.

New Haven, CT, Yale University, Beinecke Library, Osborn collection, fols. 1–30; cropping has caused damage to the text; list of characters; five acts and separate scenes. First edited by Braunmuller.

The play is inspired by Cervantes's "La española inglesa" (1613). "[F]irst Fletcher, then Fletcher collaborating with Massinger or William Rowley, and still later Shirley found Spanish prose fiction and drama as rich a source as their Elizabethan forebears did the Italian *novella* and the French *nouvelle*" (Braunmuller).

The Captives, or The Lost Recovered. Thomas Heywood; author identified by Bullen 1885. Licensed for acting 3 September 1624 (Adams 1917); Herbert's office-book identifies the playwright and gives the title. Acted by Lady Elizabeth's Men at the Phoenix (Merchant 1996), *Captives* "was probably Thomas Heywood's last Jacobean play" (Rowland 2010). "The bookkeeper added the names of minor players on three occasions and a number of notations for clarity and timing" (Long 1999). A marginal note preserves the names of H. Gibson, Taylor, and Jack, presumably actors.

(1) London, BL, Egerton MS 1994, fols. 52–73; no TP; no author named; in Heywood's hand; "a foul-paper text" (Ioppolo 2002b); theatrical provenance (Long 1989), but the MS is "too illegible to have served in the theatre" (Ioppolo 2002a); SDs "in a different and evidently later hand" (Judson 1921); evidence of revision by author; some speeches crossed out; "an original division throughout into [five] acts and scenes" (Greg 1931). The book-keeper "regularly places the word 'clere' at the ends of scenes" (Gurr & Ichikawa 2000). Staging involves the carrying of a body up a ladder. SDs record "*a greate tempestuous storme*," and "*Storme contynewed*." Staging also includes an echo scene: two women sing a song, and "after each couplet there is a one-line reply sung by an invisible character representing the echo" (Ichikawa 2005). Sound effects include: a "*bell ringes to mattens*"; "*a great noyse within*," "*A tumult within and suddein noyse*," "*a noyse, or tumult*"; "*A noyse within. Trampling of horses*." (2) London, BL, Additional MS 60281, fols. 73–77; contains act 2. First edited by Bullen 1885, *A Collection of Old English Plays*, vol. 4, then by Judson 1921, then Brown 1953.

This "is the only play now generally ascribed to Thomas Heywood which is not contained in the standard edition of his dramatic works, published by John Pearson in 1874. Its omission was due to the fact that it had not at that time been discovered" (Judson).

Caracalla (The Reign of the Emperor Caracalla; Bassianus). Probably written "during the 1640s or 1650s" (Williams 1980) by Cosmo Manuche or James Compton (Kelliher 1980). Scanty SDs, but the play may have been intended for performance at the country home of Compton, third earl of Northampton, or at his London residence, Canonbury House, Islington (Wolf 1983).

London, BL, Additional MS 60281, fols. 3–46; no TP; no author named; revised apparently by the author; ending is missing and possibly never written (MS breaks off in the middle of a line); five acts. "The apparent status of the present text as a heavily revised fair-copy implies the existence of an earlier draft that may well have been complete" (Kelliher). The MS formerly belonged to the library at Castle Ashby, home of Northampton. *AED 3* proposes as title *The Reign of the Emperor Caracalla*; Kelliher and Randall propose *Bassianus*. The emperor Bassianus was "historically known as Caracalla" (Randall 1995).

"This play is a nearly complete historical drama in blank verse dealing with the events of Roman history from the death of Septimius Severus to, in all probability, the death of Caracalla. . . . The play seems to be as much influenced by Shakespeare's *Richard III* as by the events of Roman history" (Williams).

Cardenio. See *Double Falsehood.*

The Cardinal, A Tragedy. James Shirley. Licensed for acting 25 November 1641 (Adams 1917, Yearling 1986). Acted "with great applause" by the King's Men at the [second] Blackfriars, according to the general TP. "[T]he only tragedy Shirley wrote expressly for the Blackfriars theatre" (Burner 1988). "The existence of an alternative prologue which, with its allusion to the court's sojourn in York, could not have belonged to the original performance, suggests a revival in 1642" (Yearling). "In the midst of the civil upheavals of 1641–42, *The Cardinal* played to audiences in a metropolis preoccupied with the very issues of monarchy, religion and civil rights that are the play's central concern" (Burks 2003). Charles Hart, who joined the company *c.* 1640, played the Duchess (*Historia Histrionica*).

SR 4 September 1646; 30 January 1673. O 1652–53 *Six New Plays* (with *The Brothers, The Court Secret, The Doubtful Heir, The Imposture, The Sisters*); general TP dated 1653, separate 1652; "never printed before"; separate register and pagination; list of characters; prologue, which "dates, presumably, from performance" (Stern 2009c), and epilogue in the form of a brief dialogue between Thomas Pollard, the actor, and a Servant; five acts. Music for song in the last act was written by William Lawes and published in the second edition of *The Musical Companion* (1673). In Shirley's 1646 *Poems* appear verses headed "Prologue to his Tragedy call'd *the Cardinall*"; the verses (in a different version) appear as the prologue to *The Sisters* in *Six New Plays*. Perhaps this alternative prologue "was originally written for *The Sisters* and revised for a summer production of *The Cardinal*" or perhaps Shirley simply "attached it to his favourite play" (Yearling). SDs "frequently betray that indefiniteness in matters of production which is one of the hallmarks of authorial copy" (Forker 1964). Elaborate staging includes a masque: "*Enter Columbo, and five more in rich habits visarded; between every two a torch bearer: they dance*"; "*Enter Columbo, four masquers, bring in Alvarez dead, in one of their habits, and having laid him down, exeunt.*" Then "*Columbo points to the body, they unvizard it, & find Alvar[ez] bleeding.*" Sensational action crowns the tragedy:

the Cardinal "ushers the duchess into her chamber and dismisses her attendants"; this sexual predator embraces her and then struggles with her "when she resists his advances" (Burks); only the intervention of Hernando prevents her rape; the scene culminates in her murder by poison.

The dedication indicates that Shirley thought this his best play: "[I] make this offering, which as I conceive to be the best of my flock, I knew not a better altar whereon to make it a sacrifice." A prefatory poem by "Hall" (possibly the John Hall who wrote verses for *The Grateful Servant* [1630]) alludes to the closing of the theaters in 1642: "when our English dramma was at hight, / And shin'd, and rul'd with majesty and might, / A sudden whirlwind threw it from its seat, / Deflowr'd the groves, and quench'd the Muses heat."

The Careless Shepherdess, A Tragicomedy. Thomas Goffe (Schoenbaum 1964a, Carnegie 1971); Rogers and Ley make the attribution; but O'Donnell 1954 suggests John Gough; revised by Richard Brome (Bentley 1971). The lost original version was probably acted at Christ Church, Oxford, 1618–29 (Elliott et al.), perhaps in the great hall. That hall, "finished in 1529" and "measuring approximately 115 feet by 40 feet and 50 feet in height," was the largest hall at the university (Keenan 2002). The revised version was acted "with great applause" before the king and queen [at Whitehall] by Queen Henrietta Maria's Men and at the Salisbury Court playhouse, according to the Q TP, *c.* 1638 (*JCS*); the revival included a new induction, the praeludium, according to the Q TP, which was performed by "the remnants of the Queen's Men ejected from the Cockpit in 1636" and angry at their fate (Butler 2004c).

SR 22 October 1655 *The Carelesse Shepheardesse, a pastorall* by Thomas Gough. Q 1656 *The Careless Shepherdess, A Tragicomedy*; author's initials on the TP; list of characters; argument in verse; praeludium "specially written for a revival" (Butler); prologue for original performance, prologue for performance before king and queen, and epilogue ("spoken by the Grand Satyre"); five acts and separate scenes. The epilogue "was probably written by Richard Brome, who was contracted to provide such items at the Salisbury Court, and both the *praeludium* and the prologue refer specifically to the playhouse" (Orrell 1988). Appended to Q, which was printed for Rogers and Ley, is "an exact and perfect catalogue of all playes that are printed."

The praeludium was written after Goffe's death: Steggle 2004b finds that it is "almost certainly" by Richard Brome, but Butler 2006 is doubtful; Levenson 1987 attributes it to Thomas Randolph. This praeludium describes theatrical conditions and the nature of drama through the discussion of four characters "who find themselves seated alongside each other in a private theatre, the Salisbury Court" (Grantley 2000): Spruce, a "court dandy" (Sturgess 1987); Landlord, a country gentleman; Thrift, a citizen; Spark, an Inns-of-Court man. "This Praeludium offers an unusually complex vignette of theatre-goers in the seventeenth century" (McLuskie 2005). The Inns-of-Court man comments approvingly of changes in the nature of comedy: "The poets now have with their heavenly fire / Purg'd their inventions of those grosser follies, / And with sublime conceits enrich'd the stage: / Instead of loose lascivious mirth, they bring / Ingenious raptures, which do please, not tickle, / And rather move us to admire, then laugh. / The motley coat was banish'd with trunk hose, / And since their wits grew sharp, the swords are sheath'd." "The fashion in theater, he attests, has followed the fashion in clothes and the more refined social mores of a new audience for art" (McLuskie 2006). Thrift, for his part, observing that he likes the old-time drama, declares that he will make his way to one of the theaters that still offer what he seeks: "I will hasten to the money box, / And take my shilling out again, for now / I have considered that it is too much; / I'le go to th' Bull, or Fortune, and there see / A play for two pense, with a jig to boot." The Landlord seems equally unsophisticated: "I would have the fool in every act, / Be't comedy, or tragedy, I'ave laugh'd / Untill I cry'd again, to see what faces / The rogue will make."

The Case Is Altered, A Comedy. Ben Jonson. The lost original version may have been performed by the Lord Admiral's Men at the Rose or by the Lord Chamberlain's Men at the Theater, 1597–98, or by Lord Pembroke's Men (Kay 1995). Performed by Pembroke's Men probably in May or June 1597 (Donaldson 2011). "Sundry times acted" by Children of the Blackfriars, [i.e., the Queen's Revels Children], according to the Q TP; this revised version was acted *c.* 1605–08 (Munro 2005). The play "seems to have been performed at Welbeck," a property belonging to the Earl of Newcastle, in the 1630s (Hopkins 1999b).

SR 26 January and 20 July 1609 (revised entry). Q 1609 two issues; one issue entitled *Ben Jonson, His Case is Altered*; the other, *A Pleasant Comedy called The Case is Altered . . . by Ben Jonson*; Jonson's name was added to this issue during printing (H&S); four acts and separate scenes (a division into five acts was almost certainly intended). Numerous SDs are "more lengthy and frequent than is common in other Jonson texts" (Jewkes 1958): *"After a flourish: Juniper a cobler is discovered, sitting at worke in his shoppe and singing"*; *"Enter Jaques with his gold, and a scuttle full of horse-dung."* Jaques fears that "suitors [for his stepdaughter] have smelled his gold . . . and attempts to put them off the scent" with the dung; this is "the most grossly scatological scene in all of Elizabethan drama" (Riggs 1989).

This is "Jonson's earliest known play" (Riggs), "an Elizabethan play with all the Elizabethan clichés freshly touched up" (Knoll 1964); "[v]irtually all of Shakespeare's comedies before 1597 contain situations, characters, themes, phrases, and dramatic effects that have found their way somehow into Jonson's first effort" (McDonald 1988). The characterization of Antony Balladino represents Jonson's "satirical portrait of Marston" (Grantley 2000). Jonson did not authorize the printing of Q and chose to omit this play from his 1616 F.

Catiline His Conspiracy. Ben Jonson. Acted 1611 by the King's Men, according
to the F1 TP, at the first Globe/second Blackfriars; it was performed "some time
before 29 August" (Donaldson 2011). Principal actors were Richard Burbage,
John Heminges, Alexander Cooke, Henry Condell, John Lowin, John Underwood, William Ostler, Nicholas Tooley, Richard Robinson, and William Eccleston, according to F1. Burbage probably played Cicero (Cain 2009), who, by
the play's conclusion, "has gradually replaced Catiline as the principal figure of
a narrative which centres on the conflict between the two men" (Worden 1999).
Revived at court, 9 November 1634 (*JCS*). The Q2 TP suggests that the revival
may have been more successful than the 1611 debacle: "now acted by his majesties servants with great applause." This claim, however, may have been made simply to sell copies of the play.

SR no original; transferred 10 June 1621; 4 July 1635; 4 March 1639. Q1
1611 two issues; "written by Ben Jonson"; list of characters; opening speech by
Sylla's ghost, who rises through a trap; closing speech by Cicero; chorus at end of
each act except last; the chorus, "embodied by a single actor, nonetheless made
use of the first person plural, functioning throughout as the fallible, enquiring
communal consciousness of Rome" (Barton 1984); five acts. The opening is "one
of the most remarkable scenes ever written, the apparition of the past in the form
of Sylla's Ghost, breathing life into Catiline's conspiracy. Quite literally, this evil
spirit invents the play, giving life and mind to its hero" (Goldberg 1983). Spectacle and sound produce eerie effects: "*A darknesse comes over the place*"; then "*A
grone of many people is heard under ground*"; and "*A fiery light appeares*"; a character
comments, "A bloudy arme it is, that holds a pine / Lighted, above the Capitoll."
Later "*It thunders, and lightens violently on the sodaine*," and Cato says, "The gods
grow angry." "In outdoor playhouses . . . in addition to 'tempestuous' drums, a
'bullet,' i.e., a cannonball, was 'rolled' along a sheet of metal or a wooden trough
[to simulate thunder]" (White 2007). Jonson exploits "the sheer size of the Renaissance stage" when Cicero passes over the stage "again and again in the final
act," bringing "death to every house beside whose door his progress is halted.
One by one he visits the homes of the conspirators and on their appearance consigns them to death" (Cave 1999). F1 1616 *The Works*; *Catiline His Conspiracy, A
Tragedy*; despite this appellation, "it is not altogether unreasonable to designate
Catiline as a 'Comœdy' since the play's true protagonist, Cicero, is triumphant at
the end" (De Luna 1967); "acted in the yeere 1611." Many SDs added. Q2 1635
two issues; "a grossly careless reprint" (H&S). F2 1640 vol. 1.

Jonson may have been led to write his second Roman tragedy by the success
of Shakespeare's *Antony and Cleopatra* and *Coriolanus* (Blissett 1991), and Jonson "evidently knew *Julius Caesar* very well" (Donaldson 2000). But like the earlier *Sejanus*, *Catiline* met with a hostile reception, "Cicero's long orations in the
fourth act evidently straining the patience of its audiences" (Donaldson 2004).
Leonard Digges, in a work published in 1640, compares "tedious" *Catiline* unfa-
vorably with Shakespeare's *Julius Caesar* (Chambers 1930), and Edmund Gayton

called the play "of excellent worth, but not of equal applause" (Lesser 1999); however, *Catiline* attracted readers by its evocation of the 1605 Gunpowder Plot (De Luna); the character of Cicero appears to represent Robert Cecil, who "knew about [the Gunpowder Plot] and manipulated it to his own ends" (Dutton 2008). *Catiline*, however, is not necessarily a *pièce à clef*: Jonson is dramatizing an episode "of Roman history in which 'crimes' dominated the state, in order that his contemporaries, some of whom harbour similar 'faults,' may learn the dangers that threaten their comonwealth" (Cain 2009). Long after its failure onstage, the play would appeal to readers: it "may have technically racked up more separate citations between 1600 and 1700 than any other early modern play (primarily because of its political applicability)" (Whitney 2006). "By mid-century, the central themes of Jonson's *Catiline*—conspiracy, rebellion, the imperiling of the commonwealth, the duties of the citizen—were sharply relevant topics of the day" (Donaldson 2010).

Jonson addresses the theatrical failure in his Q1 dedication to the Earl of Pembroke: "In so thicke, and darke an ignorance, as now almost covers the age, I crave leave to stand neare your light: and, by that, to be read. Posterity may pay your benefit the honor, and thanks; when it shall know, that you dare, in these jig-given times, to countenance a legitimate poëme. I must call it so, against all noise of opinion: from whose crude, and ayry reports, I appeale, to that great and singular faculty of judgment in your lordship, able to vindicate truth from error." Jonson seems to feel that the medium of print can compensate for the misfortune of theatrical production.

The Cavaliers' Jubilee, or Long Looked for Come at Last: viz. the General Pardon, in a Pleasant Dialogue between Sir Timothy Turn-coat and Sir Rowland Resolute, Two Cavaliers that Met Accidentally and Were Lately Come over from Beyond Sea. Anonymous. A play-pamphlet "written as Commonwealth propaganda" (Potter 1981).

Q 1652, written on the TP of the Thomason copy in the BL is 8 March; the "2" in the date of this copy has been crossed out and the date changed to 1651; no author named; not divided.

The dialogue "depicts two former royalists in a tavern. They agree that their sufferings for the King have been a waste of time and money" (Potter). As Timothy says of the king, "nor do I care for his pretended preferments and promises made to me, and to others, for I'le trust to them no more than to the man in the moone, one Parliament pardon is worth all his promised pensions, for words are but wind."

The Censure of the Judges. See *Mercurius Britanicus, or The English Intelligencer.*

Chabot, Admiral of France. George Chapman; revised by James Shirley (Parrott 1910, Solve 1928). This play's title is included in a list of plays by Shirley, given in *Six New Plays* (1652–53). The original version, perhaps written by Chapman

1611–12 (Tricomi 1982) "for the Children of the Queen's Revels" (Burnett 2004), may have been first performed 1614, when it evoked "the rise of George Villiers (later Duke of Buckingham) and the threat he posed to Somerset, who was himself one of Chapman's patrons" (Perry 2006b). But "it actually makes more sense to see it in relation to the fall of James's favourite Robert Carr, who was convicted in 1616, along with his wife Frances Howard, of involvement in the murder of Sir Thomas Overbury" (Wymer 2001). The revised play was performed by Lady Elizabeth's Men at the Phoenix, 1621–22 (Evans 1987); "in 1621 or 1622 a revived Lady Elizabeth's company was formed and began playing at the Phoenix under Christopher Beeston" (Bentley 1981). The version revised by Shirley (after Chapman's death) was licensed for acting 29 April 1635 (Adams 1917); "it was presented by" Queen Henrietta Maria's Men at the Phoenix, according to the TP. In playlist of Beeston's Boys 10 August 1639.

SR 24 October 1638. Q 1639 *The Tragedy of Chabot, Admiral of France*; HT *The Tragedy of Philip Chabot, Admiral of France*; RT *The Admiral of France*; the TP ascribes the play to both Chapman and Shirley; list of characters; five acts. As befits a dramatized trial, the SDs describe ceremonial entrances in detail: "*Enter Chabot in his gowne, a guard about him, his father and his wife on each side.*" Unlike "the metaphysical pyrotechnics which usually surround the death of Chapman's heroes," the circumstances of Chabot's death are muted; he dies of a broken heart (Braunmuller 1975).

The play may call to mind the career of Robert Carr, Earl of Somerset, who fell from favor and was arrested in 1615; Chapman, who believed the Earl innocent of wrongdoing, proved "steadfast in his loyalty to the fallen and disgraced" Somerset (Solve). Hillman 2005, however, views Solve's speculation skeptically.

A Challenge for Beauty. Thomas Heywood. Acted 1635 (Gurr 2009d). "Sundry times acted by" the King's Men at the [second] Blackfriars and [second] Globe, according to the TP.

SR 17 June 1636. Q "and octavo quires" (Greg 1939) 1636; dramatis personae; prologue and epilogue; "contains a song [in act 5] first printed in the 1630 Quarto of *The Rape of Lucrece*" (Clark 1931); five acts and first scenes. SDs limited mostly to entrances and exits. Q "seems to have been printed from a stage copy, shortened perhaps for court performance" (Clark), but Bentley wonders why "a court performance would have been ignored on the title-page" (*JCS*).

Prologue complains of the drama currently in fashion: "For where before great patriots, dukes and kings / Presented for some hie facinorious things, / Were the stage-subject; now we strive to flie / In their low pitch, who never could soare hie: / For now the common argument intreats, / Of puling lovers, craftie bawdes or cheates." But Heywood "is clearly trying to adapt himself to the vogue" for tragicomedies (*JCS*); indeed, the play is "an attempt to write in the Cavalier fashion" (Harbage 1936). Prologue also laments changes in styles of acting: "I only wish that they would sometimes bend / To memorise the valours of such men, / Whose very names might dignifie the pen, / And that our (once applauded) Roscian straine, / In acting such might be reviv'd againe: / Which you to countenance, would the stage make proud, / And poets strive to key their strings more loud." Heywood is praising "the great tradition of English drama in contrast to the more immediately local concerns of newer plays"; his "insistence on transcendent themes protected the plays from unwelcome political reading. It also gave an aesthetic value to the commercial promise that a repertory of old plays provided" (McLuskie 2006).

Champions of Christendom. See *The Seven Champions of Christendom.*

The Chances. John Fletcher. Acted *c.* 1617 (*JCS*) by the King's Men at the second Blackfriars/second Globe. "Revised ca. 1627, shortly after Fletcher's death" (Hoy 1987a) and performed in 1627 (Gurr 2004c). Performed also at the Whitehall Cockpit-in-Court, 30 December 1630 (bill of King's Men for plays presented at court). SDs preserve the name "Rowl," who was probably Rowland Dowle (Lawrence 1927, Powell 1941) and who probably played in revivals after 1631 (Gurr 2004c). Revived 22 November 1638 at the Whitehall Cockpit before the king and queen (Adams 1917). The play was "most popular on the stage" (Williams 1979). In playlist of the King's Men 7 August 1641.

SR 4 September 1646; 30 January 1673. B&F F1 1647 *Comedies and Tragedies*; "never printed before, and now published by the authours originall copies"; prologue (written for a revival) and epilogue; five acts and separate scenes "though the scene division is in error in several places" (Williams 1979). Some descriptive SDs: e.g., *"Enter Duke, pursued by Petruchio, Antonio, and that faction . . . Enter Don John . . . "*; *"Du[ke] fal[l]s down, Don Joh[n] bestrides him."* Sound effects include *"A noyse within like horses"*; *"[t]rampling above."* A magician "produces fake demonic effects"; the target "appears to be Puritans"; "the sole purpose of the conjuring scene is to expose the falseness of conjuring" (Cox 2000). B&F F2 1679 *Fifty Comedies and Tragedies*; "published by the authors originall copies, the songs to each play being added"; *The Chances, A Comedy*; list of characters. In the 1640s and 50s parts of the play were adapted for a droll entitled *The Landlady*, later published in *1 The Wits, or Sport upon Sport* (O 1662 [two issues] and 1672).

The F1 prologue, written after Fletcher's death, tells us what *not* to expect: "we doe entreat that you would not / Expect strange turnes, and windings in the plot, / Objects of state, and now and then a rhime, / To gall particular persons, with the time." Instead, the artistry of the play is to be found in its language: "if that sweet expressions, quick conceit, / Familiar language, fashion'd to the weight / Of such as speake it, have the power to raise / Your grace to us, with trophies to his praise: / We may professe, presuming on his skill, / If his *Chances* please not you, our fortune's ill."

The Change. Mildmay Fane. "A showe written in December 1642," according to the MS, while the author was imprisoned in the Tower, a captive of parliamentary forces. Probably intended for performance by friends and family at his home, Apethorpe in Northamptonshire, but possibly not performed. The play consists of "a succession of dialogues, full of elaborate symbolism" (Harbage 1936). Fane "either constructed a theater or (more likely) modified his home, Apethorpe Hall, so that he could indulge in the pleasure of home-grown theatricals that required machinery, including something so newfangled as flat revolving wings" (Randall 1995).

London, BL, Additional MS 34221, fols. 50–68; list of characters; prologue and epilogue (spoken by the author himself "in the role of a prisoner" [Harbage 1934]); some SDs; five scenes.

Fane, second earl of Westmorland, "was a moderate conservative who believed in church and state rather than in the King, and so the ideas expressed in this play seem to veer from one side to the other" (Leech 1938).

Change is No Robbery. See *The Cuckqueans and Cuckolds Errants.*

The Changeling. Thomas Middleton and William Rowley. Licensed for acting 7 May 1622 (Neill 2006a). "Acted (with great applause)" at the Phoenix, according to the TP, by Lady Elizabeth's Men (Howard-Hill 1987a); the playwrights "appealed to Parliamentary opposition to Stuart policy by objecting to James's plans for a Spanish marriage" [of Prince Charles to a Spanish princess] (Malcolmson 1990). Performed by the same company at Whitehall, before the prince, 4 January 1624 (Adams 1917); court records refer to the Queen of Bohemia's company, i.e., the troupe named for Princess Elizabeth, Queen of Bohemia (Williams 1966a). "In 1621 or 1622 a revived Lady Elizabeth's company was formed and began playing at the Phoenix under Christopher Beeston" (Bentley 1981). The Q TP reports that the play was also performed, presumably by Queen Henrietta Maria's Men, at the Salisbury Court playhouse, built in 1629; "the company had been forced to move out of the Phoenix" (*JCS*). The play is known to have been performed in March 1635 (diary of John Greene), though the company and theater are unknown. In playlist of Beeston's Boys 10 August 1639. *The Changeling* is "arguably the finest product of collaboration which the Jacobean theater produced" (Hoy 1976). "It may have been revived in 1659 at the Phoenix Theatre" (Bruzzi 1990).

SR 19 October 1652 a comedie called, *The changeling*, written by Rowley; though now accounted a tragedy, the play "was most often remembered for its comic scenes," which feature Antonio (Taylor 2004b). "A 'changeling' was a child left by fairies as a replacement for one they had stolen (or sometimes the stolen child itself) but, by the time of this play, it had become a broad term for those exhibiting mental anxiety or 'abnormality': thus most critics regard the subplot's Antonio (who pretends to be a 'natural fool') as the changeling of the title"

(Barker & Hinds 2003). Q 1653 two issues; "never printed before"; the TP attributes the play to Middleton and Rowley, whose names are bracketed; dramatis personae; detailed description of a dumb show (this is "one of the last Jacobean plays to include a dumb-show" [Lomax 1987]); epilogue (by Alsemero); five acts. Unusual staging includes the virginity test administered to Beatrice-Joanna, perhaps inspired by the scandal of Frances Howard's marriage to Robert Devereux, Earl of Essex, who claimed that witchcraft prevented him from consummating his marriage; subsequently Frances was examined to establish her virginity (Schafer 1994); "similarities between Beatrice-Joanna and Frances Howard are too striking to ignore" (Malcolmson). The murder of Beatrice-Joanna's fiancé, Alonzo, occurs early, when DeFlores runs him through with a sword and then cuts off a finger adorned with a ring, which he presents to Beatrice-Joanna. Later, in the dumb show, Alonzo's ghost "*startles*" DeFlores, "*shewing him the hand whose finger he had cut off.*" The ghost returns and confronts B-J, who says, "'t has left behind it, / A shivering sweat upon me." When "*a clock strikes*" the hour at one, two, and three, on her wedding night, B-J urgently needs to substitute herself for Diaphanta (a body double) in her husband's bed. DeFlores solves the problem by starting a fire ("*Within*. 'Fire, fire, fire'") and then picks up a gun so that he may "scour the chimney"; "*The piece* [i.e., weapon] *goes off*," killing Diaphanta: "Diaphanta's burnt," reports DeFlores. The play's comedy is restricted chiefly to scenes involving madmen (Kiefer 1987); in some scenes SDs make it seem "very probably that they would have shouted from the upper level of the tiring-house" (Ichikawa 2005): "*Mad-men above, some as birds, others as beasts.*" The "*madmen and fools*" also engage in "elaborate" dancing (Wright 1928). A SD suggests dramatic action occurring during an act-break: "*In the act time Deflores hides a naked rapier.*" Reissued 1668 with a new TP. The frontispiece of *1 The Wits, or Sport upon Sport* (O 1662 [two issues]), a collection of drolls, depicts a theatrical stage filled with various characters, including "Changeling" (i.e., "probably" Antonio [Dutton 1999]), who "wears a fool's cap and has a hornbook dangling from his wrist" (Bruster 2003). It is not clear what connection, if any, exists between the costuming of this figure and the appearance of the actor in the original production. "*The Wits* contains no droll based on *The Changeling*, and possibly one was omitted for some reason" (Foakes 1985). "Although Antonio is identified as 'the' changeling in the *dramatis personae* of the 1653 quarto, this may well have been a later interpolation" (Bruster 2007).

"Rowley is credited with the first and last scenes together with the whole of the sub-plot [the madhouse scenes], and Middleton is agreed to have been responsible for the remainder" (Frost 1968). "It was the comic material [in the subplot] that gave the play its title, and the actors mentioned especially in seventeenth-century performances, William Robbins, Timothy Reade, and Thomas Sheppy, were all comedians" (Bentley 1971). Rowley "played the fat fool Lollio" (Hornback 2009b).

Changes, or Love in a Maze, A Comedy. James Shirley. Licensed for acting 10 January 1632 (Adams 1917). "Presented" by the King's Revels Company at the Salisbury Court playhouse, according to the TP. But the Company of the Revels "had left the Salisbury Court" by January 1632 (Butler 2006). "Why Shirley gave this one play to them instead of his usual customer, Beeston, we do not know" (Gurr 1996). Bentley, following Adams 1917, thinks the TP must be in error, that Prince Charles's Men performed the play at Salisbury Court (*JCS*) after the Company of the Revels moved out. But Collins 2007 accepts the evidence of the TP: "in the context of the patterns of production of his contemporaries, Shirley's deviance from a permanent commitment to only one company is far more representative of playwriting customs than the requirements of [Richard] Heton," manager of the Salisbury Court, who in 1640 brought a legal action against the playwright for failing to provide the scripts he had agreed to write for the theater, then occupied by Queen Henrietta Maria's Men.

SR 9 February 1632. Q 1632 list of characters; prologue and epilogue; five acts. The prologue and epilogue are also printed in Shirley's 1646 *Poems*. The epilogue would later appear in the second issue (1649) of Q2 *Thierry and Theodoret*. A character comments on theatrical taste: "Many gentlemen / Are not, as in the dayes of understanding, / Now satisfied without a jigge, which since / They cannot with their honour, call for, after / The play, they looke to be serv'd up i'th' middle. / Your dance is the best language of some comedies." "Jigs were often more politically daring and topical than the plays they followed; a phenomenon guaranteed to generate interest among audiences, drawing directly on the political and cultural world beyond the theatre experience" (Milling 2004).

In his dedication to Dorothy Shirley, daughter of the earl of Essex and wife of Robert Shirley, the playwright explains his choice of a woman as dedicatee rather than a man: "I doe acknowledge custome, that to men / Such poems are presented; but my pen / Is not engag'd, nor can allow too farre / A *Salick* law in poetry, to barre / Ladies th'inheritance of wit, whose soule / Is active, and as able to controule, / As some usurpe the chaire, which write a stile / To breath the reader better than a mile; / But no such empty titles buy my flame; / Nor will I sinne so much as to shew their name / In print; some servile Muses be their drudge, / That sweat to finde a patron, not a judge." "[B]y 1632 singling out women as dedicatees of drama, if not commonplace, was not uncommon" (Bergeron 2006).

Charlemagne. Anonymous. Acted 1610–22 (Perry 2006a) at undetermined venue. "We know nothing of its stage history or even of its precise date" (Clare 1999).

London, BL, Egerton MS 1994, fols. 119–35; no TP; no author named; theatrical provenance (Long 1989); damaged (top and bottom of some leaves are lost); five acts and first scenes. A MS "subjected to censorship" (Briggs 1998). "A number of passages have been marked for omission, apparently by a stage reviser abridging the play for performance" (Clare). Ample SDs: "They place ye dead bodie in a chayre." SR none. First edited by Bullen 1884, *A Collection of*

Old English Plays, vol. 3. Bullen calls the play *The Distracted Emperor*; Schoell in his 1920 edition calls it *Charlemagne*; Walter & Greg in their 1938 edition call it *Charlemagne, or The Distracted Emperor*. Both Bullen and Schoell attribute the play to George Chapman; Walter & Greg suggest that the author was "an amateur — influenced, possibly, by the work of Chapman."

1 Charles Duke of Byron (The Conspiracy of Charles, Duke of Byron). George Chapman. "Acted lately" at the [second] Blackfriars, according to the Q1 TP, late 1607-March 1608 (Ray 1979), "by an unknown theatrical company" (Burnett 2004), probably the Children of Blackfriars (Margeson 1988), earlier known as the Queen's Revels Children. Because of a complaint from the French ambassador, Antoine Lefèvre de la Boderie, that the French Queen was being mocked, performances were stopped for a time, but the players evidently performed the play "when the King and Court were out of London" (Clare 1999). The French again complained, and the London theaters were temporarily closed and some actors arrested; "the most serious punishment affected the Children of the Blackfriars company," who were ordered "to vacate their indoor theater" (Auchter 2001). Chapman then sought to publish the play but failed immediately to receive a license, resulting in revisions; the fourth act "has been drastically cut" (Bentley 1971); at issue was a scene "representing Queen Marie de Médici and King Henry IV's mistress, Madame D'Entragues, the Marquise de Verneuil" (Lamb 2009); "the offending scene, and others from the first two acts and the fourth act, were deleted from the printed copies" (Burnett). "The surviving play, in which the scene is omitted, does not include an explanation of why Auvergne comes to be arrested despite the king's earlier decision to the contrary" (Loftis 1987). As a result of the trouble, "Chapman appears to have stopped writing for the stage for at least the next five years" (Wickham et al. 2000).

SR 5 June 1608 A booke called The Conspiracy and Tragedie of Charles Duke of Byronn; transferred 9 July 1653. Q1 1608 HT *Byron's Conspiracy*; prologue for both parts of the play; five acts. Published together with *The Tragedy of Charles, Duke of Byron* as *The Conspiracy and Tragedy of Charles, Duke of Byron, Marshal of France*. "That publication should be so immediate upon the controversial stage production is yet another indication of the unpredictability of early Jacobean censorship" (Clare). Q2 1625 "acted lately in two playes, at the Blacke-Friers, and other publique stages." "The re-issue of the play during Chapman's lifetime, the only one of his plays to have been so re-issued, may possibly indicate renewed interest after a revival" (Margeson).

A Q2 copy of the Byron plays in the BL contains marginalia *c.* 1633 by Philip Herbert, Earl of Montgomery, and, later, fourth Earl of Pembroke (Massai 2007). "Pembroke applies Chapman's *sententiae* to the conditions in English court life that he knew best, and . . . his frame of application is to English, not French court life" (Tricomi 1986). "[A]nalogies are specifically drawn between Byron and Essex [in *Part 2*] by the doomed protagonist himself" (Heinemann

2003). Moreover, "the political doctrines that Chapman presents appear in the works that James had published before 1608, and they represent the King's basic political beliefs" (Kennedy 1965). "In the Byron plays, the signs of erotic treachery reveal political treachery; embracing the enemies of his king, Byron commits a sodomitical crime of tragic proportions" (DiGangi 1997).

2 Charles Duke of Byron (The Tragedy of Charles Duke of Byron). Data as for *Part 1.* The two parts were printed as one book with continuous register and entitled *The Conspiracy and Tragedy of Charles, Duke of Byron, Marshal of France.* This play "can stand by itself; it is provided with a separate exposition in which the relevant facts from Part One are summarized; the two parts, however, combine to form a more complete and coherent unit than either part in isolation" (Hunter 1978). "Acted lately in two plays," according to the TP. The printed text of *Part 2* "is heavily cut (the second act is missing) and we do not know what scandalous matter was excised before printing. However, it is certain that this play deliberately reminded the audience of a parallel between Byron's conspiracy and the Essex rebellion" (Heinemann 1980). HT *Byron's Tragedy.*

Staging requires a scaffold for the scene of Byron's death: Byron "ascends the scaffold, blindfolds himself, and finishes a long speech while kneeling at the block by bidding the executioner strike. But he does not strike; and just here the play ends without as much as an 'exeunt' to mark the departure of the characters" (Lawrence 1927). "The impact of this scaffold scene derives not from the hero's exemplary adherence to received values but from the audacity with which he repudiates the pious, submissive formulas that governed real-life executions" (Owens 2005). Byron's final words may have been followed by a simulated beheading (Ray 1979).

"Considered in the broad context of everything else we know about the composition and patronage of political drama in the early Stuart period, Philip Herbert's marginal notations on his personal [Q2] copy of the Byron tragedies give us more reason than ever to speak of a *tradition* of reformist political drama" (Tricomi 1986). The *Byron* plays express "fears and doubt about James's doctrine of the divine right of kings" (Florby 2004).

A Chaste Maid in Cheapside, A Comedy. Thomas Middleton. Acted spring (Taylor 2004b) or June 1613 (Parker 1969). "Often acted at the Swan on the Banke-side," according to the TP, by the combined Lady Elizabeth's Men and Queen's Revels Children (Parker). "This is the only extant play known to have been played" at the Swan (Dutton 1999), "and the Swan in turn happens to be the only theatre of which we possess an eyewitness drawing [by De Witt] and description" (Woodbridge 2007). In 1613 the Queen's Revels Children "amalgamated with the Lady Elizabeth's Men (an adult company) with whom they may have performed" the play at the Swan, "the presence of youths perhaps accounting for the unusually large number of female roles in that play" (White 2004c); the christening scene "has eleven speaking female characters on stage simultaneously" (Taylor 2002b). Despite the TP claim ["often acted"], "there appear to be no contemporary allusions to the play, nor any record of any kind of performance until" 1912 (Brissenden 2002).

SR 8 April 1630 *The Chast Mayd of Cheapside*; transferred 17 February 1648. Q 1630 *A Chaste Maid in Cheapside, A Pleasant Conceited Comedy*; "never before printed"; acted "by the Lady Elizabeth her servants"; list of characters; elaborate pantomime of a mock-funeral; five acts. SDs "are frequent and fairly long and descriptive" (Jewkes 1958). Staging may call for a temporary structure: "*Enter Maudline and Moll, a shop being discovered.*" The most complex SD, describing a double funeral procession, alludes to the "music room," which apparently designates one of the boxes, or compartments, depicted in De Witt's drawing of the Swan (Hosley 1957, 1960): "*Recorders dolefully playing: Enter at one dore the coffin of the gentleman, solemnly deck't, his sword upon it, attended by many in blacke, his brother being the chiefe mourner: at the other doore, the coffin of the virgin, with a garland of flowers, with epitaphs pin'd on't, attended by mayds and women: then set downe one right over-against the other, while all the company seeme to weepe and mourne, there is a sad song in the musicke roome.*" In a *coup de théâtre* the two characters rise from their coffins.

This city comedy "shows economic forces undermining religion, and in turn social institutions"; "the city is shown as a place of indulgence and indiscipline, with a disorderly and indulgent christening scene providing a prime example of dissolution" (Hutchings & Bromham 2008). The play's title is a paradox: "in the commercial world of London's Cheapside, a chaste maid is a fish out of water" (Danson 2000).

The Cheater Cheated. A droll based on scenes in John Marston's *The Dutch Courtesan* and performed in the 1640s and 50s. May be performed by seven actors. "[E]vidently written for some civic entertainment" (Lawrence 1927). Kirkman on TP of *2 The Wits* writes that the adapter's identity is a mystery; the drolls were "written I know not when, by several persons, I know not who"; however, his preface reports that Robert Cox "was not only the principal actor, but also the contriver and author of most of these farces." Kirkman's attribution is "probable" (Holland 2007).

Published in *2 The Wits*, or *Sport upon Sport* (Q and O 1673), which gives as venues of performance fairs, halls, taverns, and "mountebancks stages at Charing Cross, Lincolns-Inn-Fields, and other places"; list of characters. "The piece is entirely distinct from a lengthy jig or song-play by Thomas Jordan, *The Cheaters Cheated*, which was published in 1659, 1664, and 1665" (Elson 1932).

The Chief Promises of God (God's Promises). John Bale. Acted *c.* 1538 (White 1993b) and "aptly suited for parish performance" (White 2008). Probably intended for acting indoors (Craik 1958). Presumably performed by "Bale and his fellows" at St. Stephen's [Hackington], near Canterbury, 8 September 1538; Thomas Cromwell sponsored the production. However, the performance "need not have taken place in the church building" (Gibson 2002). Performed also by Bale's "young men" at the Market Cross in Kilkenny, Ireland, 20 August 1553, the day Mary was proclaimed monarch. In Kilkenny the play was performed "by a local group of players, perhaps [Bale's] cathedral choristers" (White 2004c). The play "may well have been intended primarily for tours of churches" (Bevington 1962). Requires a minimum of four actors in addition to Bale (Fletcher 2000). Performance took place in the morning (Happé 2004).

Q1 ND ?1547 *A Tragedy or Interlude Manifesting the Chief Promises of God unto Man by All Ages in the Old Law, from the Fall of Adam to the Incarnation of the Lord Jesus Christ*; "compyled" by Bale in 1538, according to the TP and colophon ("Bale is notable for the consistency with which he writes of compiling, collecting or gathering his works" [Shrank 2007]); he speaks as Prolocutor at the beginning [prologue] and end [epilogue]; list of characters on the TP; "use of the Chorus to end each Act may . . . be a classical device" (Happé 1985–86); seven short "acts" ("one for each divine promise selected" [Blatt 1968]); "the division into seven reflects the division of the history of the world into seven ages" (Grantley 2004). "The seven ages recapitulate the division of history in *Three Laws*: three ages under the Law of Nature, three under that of Moses, and the seventh age of the Law of Christ" (Taylor 2008). "Bale's use of 'Tragedye' to describe the play can hardly be justified by the optimistic outcome of the promises" (Happé 1985–86). "The impersonation of Christ is treated with great decorum (Luther was uneasy about the appearance of Christ as a character in plays)" (Happé). Q2 1577 "now fyrst imprynted" (a spurious claim "though it is apparently the first [printing] in England" [Happé 1985–86]); Baleus Prolocutor "disappears from" the list of actors' parts (Schneider 2011). Performed together with *John Baptist's Preaching* and *The Temptation of Our Lord*: the three plays form a trilogy (Greg 1930), which adopts "themes, conventions, and devices from the medieval mystery and morality plays to protestant purposes" (King 2004). The "close interlocking" of the plays "suggests that Bale saw them as a version of the mystery cycles" (Happé 1985–86). However, "Bale may have written *God's Promises* originally as a separate piece designed for performance during the Advent season, perhaps at his Thorndon parish in 1536 or earlier" (White 1993b).

"John the Baptist is depicted on the title page of *God's Promises* wearing a cloak, clasped at the right shoulder, billowing in the wind," and the character may have resembled this figure. "However, one must practice caution in applying such woodcut images on play title pages to actual costumes in performance since illustrations were often selected arbitrarily by printers" (White).

***Christ's Burial* and *Christ's Resurrection*.** Anonymous. Acted *c.* 1520 possibly in a Carthusian priory in southern Yorkshire, perhaps Kingston-on-Hull (Baker et al. 1982), though there is no record of production. "[P]erhaps the plays were intended not for the converses [lay brothers] or for the monks but for an out-side audience, of either patrons of the Carthusian community or just interested citizens of Hull" (Groenveld 2009). Other possible sites of performance in Hull are the Carmelite priory church, the Austin friary, and St. Michael's hospital (Groenveld). A notation in the MS "makes suggestions for performing the play in two parts, one on Good Friday, one on Easter morning" (McJannet 1999b). The two parts "are effectively one play" (Grantley 2004).

Oxford, Bodleian, MS e Museo 160, fols. 140–72; a substantial MS consist-ing of four fragments (1321 lines); no separate TP; no author named; prologue (to be omitted when the play is performed); divided into two parts (i.e., "The first dayes playe," "the seconde dayes playe"). This "is the one complete surviv-ing example of vernacular liturgical drama" (Twycross 2008). *Christ's Burial* and *Christ's Resurrection* are titles chosen by modern editors. First edited by Wright and Halliwell[-Phillips] (1843), then by Furnivall, *The Digby Mysteries* (1882), and, more recently, by Baker et al.

A Christian Turned Turk, or The Tragical Lives and Deaths of the Two Famous Pirates, Ward and Dansiker. Robert Daborne. Acted *c.* 1611–12 (Potter 1996). "Publickly acted," according to the TP, by the Children of the Queen's Revels (Munro 2005). "[P]robably written for performance by Rosseter's Queen's Rev-els company at the indoors Whitefriars Hall theater" (Vitkus 2000). "Daborne's play fictionalizes the life of John Ward, a fifty-year-old sailor who, in 1603, led a group of deserters from the English navy to Tunis where he was protected by a privateering agreement with the head of the local Janissaries" (Burton 2005).

SR 1 February 1612. Q 1612 dramatis personae; prologue and epilogue; de-tailed description of two dumb shows, interpreted by the chorus; act 1 is divided into four numbered scenes, but no divisions thereafter except for "scoena ulti-ma." "Daborne's printed text is notoriously hard to follow: the list of characters does not correspond with the names of those who appear in the character calls; speeches are wrongly assigned; scene changes are sometimes indicated but stage directions are irregular" (MacLean 2007). Unusual staging: Daborne simultane-ously uses "the upper and lower stage to represent two different vessels" (Wright 1927b). Staging calls for an ass: "In a dumb show . . . representing the recep-tion of Ward the pirate into the Turkish faith, the apostate rides in on an ass, dismounts for the ceremony, and then departs in the manner in which he came" (Lawrence 1935).

The address to the reader recounts the play's unfortunate reception: "I have . . . procured the publishing this oppressed and much martird tragedy, not that I promise to my selfe any reputation hereby, or affect to see my name in print, ush-erd with new praises, for feare the reader should call in question their judgements that give applause in the action." This address defends the play against "silken gulls and ignorant cittizens."

A Christmas Messe. Anonymous. Acted Christmas season (*JCS*) ?1619 (Russell 1987) by the students of either Oxford or Cambridge University. Probably a Cambridge play "on the grounds that Oxford is not known to have performed such 'shows,' whereas the tradition was firmly established at Cambridge" (Nelson 1989). However, "there seems to be much better reason to assign the play to Oxford than to Cambridge" (Russell). "The play was probably performed in the college hall . . . and the staging was adapted to an after-dinner performance" (Gossett & Berger 1988).

Washington, Folger, MS J.a.1(9), fols. 105–15; no separate TP; no author named; the date 1619 appears on first page; speech by Belly at beginning functions as a prologue but he "specifically denies he is a prologue" (Schneider 2011); speech by Cook at close functions as an epilogue; damaged by ink bleeding through the pages; five short acts and separate scenes. The action "consists of boasting dialogue, debate style, by the various accessories of the feast, and a battle between King Beef, Sir Vinegar, and Sir Pepper on one side, and King Brawn, Lord Sauce, and Mustard on the other" (*JCS*). First edited by Russell.

The Christmas Prince. The title given to a MS containing various entertainments performed by students and recent bachelors at St. John's College, Oxford, in the Christmas revels of 1607–08 (Bevington 1962); the MS "commemorates the most ambitious experiment in dramatics recorded at any of the colleges" (Harbage 1935a). "All the plays were performed between 30 November 1607 (St. Andrew's Day) and 13 February 1608" (Richards 1982). "[T]he individual plays marked the stages of a larger festive occasion, the election, coronation, and reign of a Christmas Prince, or Lord of Misrule, who in this year was a bachelor of arts named Thomas Tucker" (Elliott 1995). By the time these entertainments were enacted, they were "thoroughly provincial and out of date. Although the writers of this collection of Christmas plays show an engaging sense of humour, they were quite unpractised in drama; the charm of their 'game' depends on its being truly improvised and intimate" (Bradbrook 1962b).

(1) Oxford, St. John's College, MS 52, fols. 5–260; no TP; no author named; contains much miscellaneous material relating to entertainments at the college; most are in Latin; three are in English: *Periander, Time's Complaint,* and *The Seven Days of the Week.* First described by Bliss 1816. First edited in full by Boas & Greg 1922. Reproduced in photographic facsimile by Richards 1982. (2) Washington, Folger, MS J.a.1 (9); contains *Periander* only.

The Chronicle History of Henry the Fifth. See *Henry V.*

The Chronicle History of Perkin Warbeck. See *Perkin Warbeck.*

1 Cicilia and Clorinda, or Love in Arms, A Tragicomedy. Thomas Killigrew. Written 1649–50 (Bulman 1987). The SDs anticipate production, and "Killigrew seems to have been planning a production in 1666/7" (*JCS*) but there is no record of performance,.

Washington, Folger, MS V.b.208; "written in Turin"; list of characters; five acts and separate scenes. Detailed SDs: "*Enter Orante and Turnus, Orante is cloath'd in black, with black feathers, black perriwigg, his person is crooked and ugly, with a dagger by his side.*" SR 24 October 1663. F 1663–64 *Comedies and Tragedies*; two issues; the general TP dated 1664, separate 1663; *The First Part of Cicilia and Clorinda.* Ample SDs: "*He gives her* Lucius *challenge to read; she reads the paper, strikes her breast, and throws it away, and goes in.*" "As Killigrew's annotated copy of his *Comedies and Tragedies* (1664) preserved in the library of Worcester College, Oxford, demonstrates, he was ambitious enough to prepare his own plays for production on the new, scenic [Restoration] stage" (Vander Motten 2004).

"The play's plot, its many rhetorical flourishes on the themes of virtue, honesty, war, peace, sexual desire, and love, and its weaving of gendered love and virtue with conflict, corruption, and resolution provide a map for the preoccupations of an exiled class and an exiled court" (Raber 2000).

2 Cicilia and Clorinda, or Love in Arms, A Tragicomedy. Thomas Killigrew. Written 1649–50 (Bulman 1987). SDs anticipate production, and "Killigrew seems to have been planning a production in 1666/7" (*JCS*), but there is no record of performance.

Washington, Folger, MS V.b.209; "written in Florence"; list of characters; five acts and separate scenes. SR 24 October 1663. F 1663–64 *Comedies and Tragedies*; two issues; general TP dated 1664, separate 1663; *The Second Part of Cicilia and Clorinda*; concluding song functions as epilogue; five acts and separate scenes. Very detailed SDs: in the opening scene, "*Enter* Amadeo *and* Lucius, *they stripp and make ready to fight*"; then "*They fight, & the noise of their swords makes* Manlius *come out. Both are wounded. He* [Manlius] *drawes, and runs to part them.*"

At the conclusion we find "The Song in Parts," and following the song is printed a note: "This chorus was written by M. Thomas Carew, cup-bearer to Charles the First; and sung in a masque at White-hall, anno 1633. And I presume to make use of it here, because in the first design, 'twas writ at my request." "Killigrew's use of the song is vigorously justified by his friendship with its author and his part in its creation" (Stern 2009c).

1 The Cid, A Tragicomedy. Joseph Rutter. Acted the last week of February 1637 or between 2 October 1637 and 12 January 1638 (*JCS*). By Beeston's Boys [the King and Queen's Young Company] at the Phoenix, according to the D TPs. Performed also at court, before the king and queen, according to the D TPs, earlier than 12 January 1638 (date of printing license). Performance at the Whitehall Cockpit may have used painted scenery designed by Inigo Jones, but not at the first performance (Freehafer 1971); Star 1972 doubts the use of scenery.

SR 29 January 1638 a Play called *The Cid, a Tragi-comedy*; transferred 3 November 1649 *The Valiant Cid*. D1 1637 *The Cid, A Tragicomedy out of French Made English*; no author named on the TP but Rutter signs the dedication and his name appears in the SR; list of characters; preface to reader in "place of a prologue"; five acts and separate scenes. Scanty SDs. Herbert's license for printing, which calls the play *The Valiant Cid*, is published in D. D2 1650 "the second edition, corrected and amended."

The play is a verse translation of Pierre Corneille's highly successful *Le Cid*, performed in Paris, January 1637. "The success of *Le Cid*, which was produced at the Théâtre du Marais about 4 January 1637, was unprecedented in the history of the French stage" (Freehafer 1971). Rutter's preface to the D reader contrasts the "oeconomy" of language in the translation with fashionable dramatic language: "I know I speak to deafe people, whose eares have been furr'd with so many hyperboles, which is the wit in fashion, though the same in Seneca's dayes, were accounted madnesse. But if they knew how dissenting with a right eare any affected speech is, they would rather trespasse the other way, and not straine nature beyond what we finde it commonly is." The absence of a prologue is noted: "The place of a prologue let this leaf take up; which would gently advise you to suspend your censure of this translation, till you be skilled in both the languages; for from the ignorant in either I may suffer."

2 The Cid, A Tragicomedy. Joseph Rutter. Probably acted 1639 at court together with *1 The Cid* (Freehafer 1971). No record of performance on the TP or elsewhere, but "[t]he obvious appeal of the play to the Queen, and the fact that it was translated on the command of the King, indicate that it was acted at court" (Freehafer). Rutter dedicates this play dealing with "the preferring of dutie, and respects before love" to Lady Theophilia Cooke [Cook]; "Rutter makes an explicit connection between the patron and the play's topic" (Bergeron 2006).

SR 6 April 1639 *The Second part of the valiant Cid*. D 1640 *The Second Part of the Cid*; no author named on the TP but Rutter signs the dedication and his name appears in the SR; list of characters; five acts and separate scenes. Scanty SDs.

2 The Cid is a translation of *La vraye suitte du Cid*, a sequel to Corneille's play written by Nicolas-Marc Desfontaines and published in December 1637. Rutter's "version of Desfontaines' continuation was done at [King] Charles's command" (Butler 1984b).

The City Cozener. See *The Ordinary*.

The City Gallant. See *Greene's Tu Quoque*.

The City Madam, A Comedy. Philip Massinger. Licensed for acting 25 May 1632 (Adams 1917). Acted "with great applause" at the [second] Blackfriars, according to the TP, by the King's Men. "The play remained in the Blackfriars repertoire, and was withheld from publication (often the sign of a theatrical success) until the closing of the theatres in 1642" (Gibson 1978). In playlist of King's Men 7 August 1641. The play's title "is an antonym for 'Court lady'" (Gurr 2009d).

SR none. Q 1658–59 two issues; list of characters; five acts and separate scenes. The copy for Q "was very clearly a manuscript that had been used as a theatrical promptbook" (Hoy 1964). Unusual staging includes Lacy and Plenty, "having been directed to be '*ready behind*' (i.e. behind a curtain . . .), are discovered above as 'statues.'" A character "orders the statues to descend, whereupon they are directed to enter to the stage [below]" (Hosley 1960); the characters/ statues "are reanimated by supposedly magical means" (Wiggins 2000). Another SD has, "*Musicians come down to make ready for the song at ar[r]as*": the musicians may exit their customary location above the tiring-house and descend to stage level, where they proceed to take their places, probably at the center of the arras. But "[s]ince Plenty and Lacy have been directed earlier in the scene to be "*ready behind*' . . ., they should be discovered there behind the arras at the stage level. When they are ordered by Sir John to 'Descend' . . ., Plenty and Lacy would have descended from the statues' plinths and come forth from the discovery space" (Ichikawa 2005). A SD suggests that the stage was made ready between the acts while playgoers listened to music: "*Whil'st the act plays, the footstep, little table, and arras hung up for the musicians.*" The play concludes with "the longest and most complex of all Massinger's inset masques" (Rochester 2010).

Andrew Pennycuicke, in his dedication, combines praise of the play with admiration for drama generally: "In that age when wit and learning were outconquered by injury, and violence; this poem was the object of love and commendations, it being composed by an infallible pen, and censured by an unerring auditory. In this epistle I shall not need to make an apologie: for playes in generall by exhibiting their antiquity and utility, in a word they are mirrors or glasses which none but deformed faces, and fouler consciences fear to look into." He goes on to speak of his effort to preserve the play through the medium of print: "I have redeemed it from the teeth of time, by committing of it to the press."

The City Match, A Comedy. Jasper Mayne. Acted between 30 September 1637 and 3 February 1638 (*JCS*) by the King's Men at Hampton Court. Intended for performance at Christ Church, Oxford, before the king, late August 1636, but not performed there. "Presented" by King's Men at Whitehall, before the king and queen (Flynn 2004) during the Christmas season, and, later, at the [second] Blackfriars, according to the F TP, 1637–38. No license for acting survives.

SR none. F 1639 no author named; list of characters; prologues for king and queen at Whitehall, and for Blackfriars; epilogues for Whitehall and Blackfriars; five acts and separate scenes. Q 1658 *Two Plays, The City Match, a Comedy, and The Amorous War, a Tragicomedy*; some copies of *City Match* sold separately and some sold with *Amorous War*; author's initials on the TP. Also issued 1659 as O. Unusual staging: "[T]wo gallants attempt to have themselves smuggled into a woman's bedchamber disguised as full-length portraits" (Rochester 2010). Mayne's "unfavorable representation of Puritans undoubtedly helped to gain readers among the less saintly, who had long been weary of piety" (Wright 1934). Winstanley 1687 calls the play "ingenious" and judges it "comparable to the best" comedies of its time.

The F note to the reader reports the author's reluctance to seek publication: "As it was meerly out of obedience that he first wrote it, so when it was made, had it not been commanded from him, it had died upon the place, where it took life. Himselfe being so averse from raysing fame from the stage, that at the presentment, he was one of the severest spectators there; nor ever show'd other signe whereby it might be knowne to be his, but his liberty to despise it. Yet he hath at length consented it should passe the presse; not with an ayme to purchase a new reputation, but to keep that which he hath already from growing worse. For understanding that some at London, without his approbation or allowance, were ready to print a false, imperfect coppy, he was loth to be libell'd by his owne worke; or that his play should appeare to the world with more then its own faults." This attitude represents a "fairly characteristic example of the amateur dramatist toward professionalism" (Bentley 1971). The F epilogue written for Whitehall alludes to the vogue for "rules": "The author was deceiv'd, for should the parts, / And play which you have seen, plead rules & arts, / Such as strict criticks write by, who refuse / T'allow the buskin to the comick muse, / Whose region is the people, every straine / Of royalty being tragick, though none slaine: / He'd now, great sir, hold all his rules untrue, / And thinks his best rule is the queen and you."

The City Nightcap, or Crede Quod Habes, & Habes, A Tragicomedy. Robert Davenport. Licensed for acting 14 October 1624 (Adams 1917, Monie 1979). "Acted with great applause" at the Phoenix, according to the TP, by Lady Elizabeth's Men; "in 1621 or 1622 a revived Lady Elizabeth's company was formed and began playing at the Phoenix under Christopher Beeston" (Bentley 1981). Later acted by Queen Henrietta Maria's Men (*JCS*). In playlist of Beeston's Boys 10 August 1639.

SR none. Q 1661 dramatis personae; five acts. Staging features a masque: "*Enter Lodovico, Clown and Masquers: a Stag, a Ram, A Bull, and a Goat.*" Some scenes were later adapted for a droll entitled *The Politic Whore, or The Conceited Cuckold*, performed after the closing of the theaters and subsequently printed in *The Muse of Newmarket* (1680).

The City Wit, or The Woman Wears the Breeches, A Comedy. Richard Brome. Acted sometime between early 1630 and December 1631 (Kaufmann 1961); ?1629–30 (Butler 2004b). By the King's Revels Company at the Salisbury Court playhouse; "[t]he unusually large number of characters who are boys or women—eight—and the importance of their roles suggest that the comedy was written for a boy company" (*JCS*). Probably revised 1637–39 and performed by

Queen Henrietta Maria's Men at Salisbury Court, 1637–39 (Shaw 1980). According to the prologue, "The author sayes [the play] has past with good applause / In former times."

SR no original; transferred 11 June 1659. O 1653–54 *Five New Plays* (with *The Court Beggar*, *The Damoiselle*, *The Mad Couple Well Matched*, *The Novella*); register begins anew with this play; two issues; separate TP dated 1653; dramatis personae; prologue and epilogue; five acts and separate scenes. Many details of staging: e.g., "*A table set forth with empty mon[e]y-bags, bills, bonds, & bookes of accompts, &c.*"

The prologue, written for a revival, addresses the gap between performance and publication: "it was written, when / It bore just judgement, and the seal of Ben. / Some in this round may have both seen't, and heard, / Ere I, that beare its title, wore a beard." "George Powell's *A Very Good Wife* (1693) is a plagiarized combination of earlier plays including *The City Wit* and *The Court Beggar*" (Steggle 2004b).

Claracilla, A Tragicomedy. Thomas Killigrew. Probably written 1636 (Harbage 1930); performed *c.* 1636–38 (Reich 1980); Shirley refers to *Claracilla* in *Rosania* (acted 1 June 1638). "Allowed" 1639, according to Herbert's office-book. "Presented" by Queen Henrietta Maria's Men at the Phoenix, according to the D TP. Apparently a performance was interrupted in March 1653 at Charles Gibbons's Tennis Court near Lincoln's Inn Fields: "The poor comoedians, (whose sad condition ought to be look'd upon with a pittying eye, as being debarr'd of that livelyhood to which they were bred up) adventuring not long since to act a play called *Claracilla* at one Mr. Gibbions his tennis court; an ill Beest [?Will Beeston], or rather [?Theophilus] Bird (because the rest denyed him a share of their profts) be-t his own nest, causing the poor actors to be routed by the souldiery" (*Mercurius Democritus*, 2–9 March 1653). Acted by "the Kings Companie at Red Bull and the new house in Gibbon's Tennis Court near Clare Market," according to Herbert's list of plays dated 1 December 1660.

Cambridge, MA, Harvard University, Houghton Library Theater Collection, fMS Thr 7, fols. 1–41; June 1639 appears on the TP; corrections and additions; five acts and separate scenes. SR 4 August 1640. D 1640–41 *The Prisoners and Claracilla, Two Tragicomedies*; general TP dated 1641; list of characters; five acts. F 1663–64 *Comedies and Tragedies*; two issues; general TP dated 1664, separate 1663 in some copies, 1664 in others; "written . . . in Rome"; spelling changes from Claracilla to Claricilla; list of characters. Although the play was originally printed in blank verse, the F version appears in prose. Extensive SDs: "*As they go singing off the stage, enter* Timillus *with a rope to make his escape, hears them sing, and thence understands 'tis all joy and peace.*" *Claracilla* dramatizes the intersection of sex and politics in Caroline drama: the king "inadvertently provoke[s] disorder by obstructing the marital (and hence political) ambitions" of the royal favorite, who is "immoderately" loved and rewarded (DiGangi 2006).

"At the Restoration *Claricilla* was listed among the stock plays of the Red Bull company, and it was probably among the plays earliest revived at the period" (Harbage 1930). "As Killigrew's annotated copy of his *Comedies and Tragedies* (1664) preserved in the library of Worcester College, Oxford, demonstrates, he was ambitious enough to prepare his own plays for production on the new, scenic [Restoration] stage" (Vander Motten 2004).

Claudius Tiberius Nero, Rome's Greatest Tyrant. Anonymous. Acted 1607 (Findlay 1994) or possibly earlier (Hopkins 2008b) at undetermined venue. Written by a young university man (Brooke 1967). Francis Burton's dedication calls the author "[t]his young scholler," adding, "by his speech it should seeme that his father was an academian." The playwright's identity is otherwise unknown. It was probably politic for the author to remain anonymous since the tragedy implicitly comments on the king's authoritarian views of kingship: "while James I was vehemently opposing Neo-Stoic Taciteanism, the same teachings were highly influential in plays that perceived Jacobean absolutism as nothing less than tyranny" (Cetin 2009–10).

SR 10 April 1607 *the tragicall Life and Death of Claudius Tiberius Nero*. Archer lists the title as *Nero's life and death* and so does Kirkman. Q 1607 two issues, one entitled *The Stately Tragedy of Claudius Tiberius Nero, Rome's Greatest Tyrant*; the other, *The Tragedy of Claudius Tiberius Nero, Rome's Greatest Tyrant*; no author named; "truly represented out of the purest records of those [ancient] times"; in lieu of a prologue the playwright explains his dedication to historical truth: "I use no sceane suppos'd as many doe, / But make the truth my sceane, and actors too. / For / Of Romes great tyrant I the storie tell, / And what unto that state in Neroes raigne befell"; "ceremonious processions and entries" but "[n]o proper dumb shows" (Mehl 1965); not divided. Staging calls for use of a trap: Livia "*leapeth in*" a well and, at another point, Tiberius and Sejanus enter "*out of the cave,*" perhaps represented by the trap or by an opening in the tiring-house wall. Unusual (and anachronistic) staging includes "*Enter Caligula with a racket and tennis-ball in his hand.*" Detailed SDs describe not only elaborate entries but also considerable violence: e.g., "*Germanicus and Piso scale the walles, Germanicus is repulst the first assault, Piso winneth the wall first, but is in danger by Vonones and his sonne: Germanicus rescueth Piso, Vonones and his sonne flie.*" Scaling the walls would presumably involve the façade of the tiring house and the compartments above, corresponding to those in the De Witt drawing of the Swan (Hosley 1957). Unusual SD "requires the two imprisoned and hungry characters, Nero and Drusus, to perform the following actions: 'They eate each others armes.' Presumably, false arms are used to fulfil the requirement and presented in such a way as to disguise the substitution" (Butterworth 2005). The play dramatizes an astonishing number of killings, including that of Celsus, who "*puts the chain about his necke and strangles himself.*" Perhaps the most spectacular moment occurs when Tiberius "*sets the burning crowne upon*" Sejanus' head, thereby killing him. This play contains the "only full-scale dismemberment that is visually represented in a history play" (Owens 2005) when a mob pursues Piso: *"[t]hey drag him in, and enter againe with his lim[b]s in their hands."*

The protagonist is named "Tiberius Claudius Nero Caesar, and it is therefore desirable that it should be known as the *Tragedy of Tiberius* to distinguish it from the *Tragedy of Nero*, which deals with Nero Claudius Caesar Drusus Germanicus" (Greg 1914b).

Cleander. See *The Lovers' Progress.*

Cleodora. See *The Queen of Aragon.*

Cleopatra. Samuel Daniel. Written *c.* 1594 and revised 1599 (Harner 1987). Possibly intended for private performance (Hadfield 2005). Whether or not performed, the play has a significant connection with Shakespeare's *Antony and Cleopatra*. "Almost certainly, Shakespeare knew and was influenced by [Daniel's] play" (Barton 1973). Daniel, in turn, revised his own play, making it more theatrical, apparently after seeing a performance of Shakespeare's *Antony and Cleopatra*, 1606–07 (Norman 1959). "Daniel so completely revised *Cleopatra* that it became in effect a new work" (Harner). In the revision of 1607, Daniel substitutes dialogue for long soliloquies and "dramatic action for narrative" (Seronsy 1967); "the major purpose of the revision appears to have been to prepare the play for performance" (Norland 2009). Daniel's 1607 edition contains a speech about hoisting the dying Antony at the monument that may "be a reminiscence by Daniel of an actual production of *Antony and Cleopatra*" (Rees 1953); the description "is remarkably vivid and . . . cannot be accounted for by any known source"; Daniel writes that Antony "is drawn up 'in rowles of taffaty'" (Rees 1964). Daniel also "recanted his previous representation of Cleopatra as a lying seductress" (Sanders 1998a). Indeed, Daniel "caught at something new in English, at least among the Elizabethan writers, the grace and pathos of a great woman who was suffering" (Pitcher 2004).

SR 19 October 1593; transferred 19 August 1635. The publication history is exceedingly complicated. D 1594 *Delia and Rosamond Augmented*; *The Tragedy of Cleopatra*; "the format of the volume is not quite certain. It might possibly be a 16° of unusual shape, or it might be a 12° in which one third of each sheet was cut off before printing and the rest imposed as an 8°" (Greg 1939); argument; list of characters; chorus at close of each act; five acts and separate scenes. Reprinted 1595 as D and O and reissued 1598. Q1 1599 *The Poetical Essays of Samuel Daniel*; two issues; "newly corrected and augmented." "Each of the pieces in it has its own title-page and printer's signature, and could be sold separately (and they were: there are surviving copies of each in original vellum covers)" (Pitcher 2005). F 1601–02 *The Works*; two issues; "newly augmented"; *Cleopatra* has been revised. O 1605 *Certain Small Poems Lately Printed* (with *Philotas*). O 1607 *Certain Small*

Works (with *Philotas*, *The Queen's Arcadia*); two issues; "newly altered." D 1607 [no general TP]. Reissued 1611 (O and D); *Certain Small Works* (with *Philotas*, *The Queen's Arcadia*); two issues; "corrected and augmented." Q 1623 *The Whole Works* (with *Hymen's Triumph*, *Philotas*, *The Queen's Arcadia*). 1623 *Works* adopts "the 1599 version rather than the more dramatic 1607 version" (Norland). In 1635 "some copies of this drama portion of the *Whole Works* were reissued, with a new title page, as a set of 'Dramaticke poems'" (Pitcher 2005).

Daniel's Q1 dedication acknowledges the example of *Antonius*, published in 1592; "published in revised form" (Purkiss 1998) as *The Tragedy of Antony* (1595, 1600, 1606, 1607), the translation by Mary Herbert, Countess of Pembroke, of *Marc Antoine*, a play by Robert Garnier: "thy well grac'd *Antony*, / . . . Requir'd his *Cleopatras* company." But Daniel "set out to recast Sidney's *Antonius* completely" (Sanders). Mary Herbert's patronage was responsible for the translation of a number of French plays, none of which, apparently, was ever performed in England.

Cleopatra, Queen of Egypt. Thomas May. "Acted 1626," according to the MS and D TPs. "The learned character of the play suggests a college or an Inns of Court performance" (*JCS*). "Acted in an unknown venue" (Norbrook 2004).

London, BL, Royal MS 18.C.VII, fols. 3–34, ed. Smith 1979; evidence of revision; no author named on the TP, which lists the characters; five acts. MS first edited by Smith. SR 26 October 1638; transferred 20 November 1658. D 1639 *The Tragedy of Cleopatra, Queen of Egypt*; author's initials on the TP; "acted 1626"; list of characters follows the text; divided into five acts. *Cleopatra* and *Agrippina* "were intended to be issued together as well as separately" (Greg 1939). Dialogue possibly preserves the staging of a scene in Shakespeare's *Antony and Cleopatra*: when one character asks of Antony, "Where did he die?" another answers, "In Cleopatraes arms / By her with ropes let up into the tombe." The tomb is clearly above; a character reports, "We came and call'd at Cleopatraes tombe, / Who from above made answer." Another issue of May's play with a new TP appeared 1654; some copies were issued separately, some bound with May's *Julia Agrippina* and entitled *Two Tragedies*; author's name on the separate TP.

May "clearly shows his dependence on Shakespeare's *Antony and Cleopatra*" (Smith 1979). *Cleopatra, Queen of Egypt* represents a response to Fletcher and Massinger's earlier "pro-Cleopatra play," *The False One*, which was acted in 1620 (Sanders 1998a).

Club Law. Anonymous. Acted 1599–1600 (Smith 1907a, Cathcart 2003a) by students of Clare College, Cambridge, in the college hall. "Thomas Fuller reports that *Club Law* was performed . . . before town dignitaries who were themselves the target of the play's satire" (Nelson 1994). "The immediate context of the play was a long running dispute between the university and the town, in which the central government and members of the royal family were called in as arbitrators from time to time" (Grantley 2000). The characters and episodes correspond "fairly closely to specific town leaders and events of the late 1590s"; the play "may be the most richly topical play about provincial town life in Elizabethan England, even if it views that life within the deeply biased and distorted perspective of the university" (White 2008). The play "was allegedly written in English so that the uneducated citizens of the town would understand it. Such social prejudice was an integral part of the outlook of Cambridge students" (Gurr 2009b).

Cambridge, St. John's College, MS S.62; no TP; no author named; lacks four or five leaves at beginning, and another leaf in act 4; epilogue (by Cricket, an undergraduate); five acts and separate scenes. Staging calls for two stage "houses" (Boas 1914). First edited by Smith.

"The term 'club law' ('the use of the club to enforce obedience, physical force as contrasted with argument,' etc.) seems not to be found before the date of this play" (Smith).

The Club Men. A droll adapted from a scene in B&F's *Philaster* and performed in the 1640s and 50s. "The dialogue requires five Citizens, though the list of characters prescribes only 'three or four.' Five would bring the total number of actors to eight, but six could act the piece" (Elson 1932). The term "Club men" refers to "such physical citizen force as might be raised from time to time" (Randall 1995); such men were associated with mischief and violence. In the mid-1640s *Clubmen* became a term associated with politically neutral men who "made tactical alliances with other groups to fend off armies"; "the Clubmen movement briefly created influential and historically significant opposition to the war and the two contesting sides" (Skerpan 1992).

Printed in *1 The Wits, or Sport upon Sport* (O 1662 [two issues] and 1672), which mistakenly identifies the source as *Cupid's Revenge*; RT *The Humors of the Club Men*; argument; list of characters.

Clyomon and Clamydes (*Sir Clyomon and Sir Clamydes*). Possibly written by the author of *Common Conditions* (Greg 1913a). Acted 1576–83 (Littleton 1968) at undetermined venue. "Sundry times acted" by the Queen's Men, according to the TP, after 1583; perhaps revived 1583–94 (Chambers 1923). Continued to be staged in the late 1590s (McMillin & MacLean 1998). "The total number of actors on stage at one time is nine" (Bevington 1962).

SR none. Q 1599 *The History of the Two Valiant Knights, Sir Clyomon, Knight of the Golden Shield, Son to the King of Denmark: and Clamydes, the White Knight, Son to the King of Swavia*; no author named; prologue; not divided. Some detailed SDs: "*Here let him slip unto the stage backwards, as though he had puld his leg out of the mire, one boote off, and rise up to run in againe.*" "Only two *domus* are needed, a palace . . . in the Isle, and Bryan Sans Foy's Castle in the Forest. This is a prison, with a practicable door and a window, from which Clamydes speaks" (Chambers 1923). The descent of Providence from the heavens "suggests elaborate 'descent' machinery, but in fact Providence can descend a flight of stairs if that is what is available" (McMillin & MacLean). Moreover, since the play was performed in the 1570s and not printed until 1599, it is possible that this SD "was added to the prompt copy after 1595," when Henslowe altered the Rose theater to allow "a mechanically operated throne" (Wickham 1979). A copy of Q was purchased by George Buc, who wrote George Peele's name on the TP (Shapiro 2005).

This play "initiates a genre of romances that were to become the rage in the 1570s and 1580s" (Bevington 2002a). "It has been estimated that of the sixty-five plays performed at court between 1570 and 1585, a third to one half of them were romances" (Cartwright 1998). "One of the earliest plays to present the homoerotic potential of the cross-dressed female heroine" (Walen 2005), *Clyomon* is "the earliest extant play to have a woman disguise herself as a man" (Hyland 2011).

The Cobbler's Prophecy. Robert Wilson. Acted 1590–94 (Grantley 2000) at undetermined venue, possibly an inn-yard (Lawrence 1927), though "when actors performed at inns they usually occupied a large room rather than a yard and performed by candlelight" (Orrell 1997). Perhaps performed by the Queen's Men (McMillin & MacLean 1998), "but it is not absolutely certain" that the play belonged to this company (Schoone-Jongen 2008). "The allusion to an audience who 'sit and see' and the stage direction for Ceres to '*Cast comfets*' argue private production" (Saccio 1969); perhaps "a Chapel or Paul's play" (Chambers 1923). Possibly performed at court 6 January 1588 (Dutton 1991).

SR 8 June 1594. Q 1594 dumb show and "[s]everal pantomimic stage directions" (Mehl 1965); not divided. "[O]ne side of the stage must represent a wood in which a duke will go riding, while the other side remains bare and serves for a varied succession of places" (Smith 1977). Staging calls for "spectacular pyrotechnical effects" (Manley 2001); a SD records the use of smoke when gods are propitiated: "*from one part [of the stage] let a smoke arise*"; then after the characters kneel, they "*all rise and cast incense into the fire.*" Although the play mentions various "houses," "there is no reason to believe that they were realistically represented" (Craik 1958).

"[T]he play is a survey of the state of society, with much interesting detail" (Cameron 1982): "*Enter* Souldier, Raph, Mars *his lame Porter in rustie armour, and broken bill, the* Herrald *with a pensill and colours.*" "The kingdom is sick owing to the primacy of Contempt, and Mars has been reduced to the state of a Porter" (Harlan 2008). *Cobbler's Prophecy* "is remarkable for the emotional power with which it represents a national *disunity* that almost allows foreign invasion to succeed" (Heinemann 2003). Along with *The Tide Tarrieth No Man* and *A Looking Glass for London and England*, *The Cobbler's Prophecy* may be termed an "estates morality" (Lunney 2002). "[T]he emphasis is on promoting interclass harmony rather than inciting class war or workers' rebellion" (Kermode 1999).

Cockledemoy. See *The Dutch Courtesan.*

Cola's Fury, or Lirenda's Misery. Henry Burkhead. Probably written "between June 1645 and very early 1646" (Coughlan 1990). No evidence of production but "it is entirely possible that it was staged, at least privately [in 1646]"; one speech suggests that a performance was intended for New Year's day (Morash 2002). "Burkhead may have been drawing on the Kilkenny theatre traditions of an annual civic miracle play and some drama at the 1642 Jesuit college" (Coughlan 2004). "The frequent stage directions calling for music and dancing would . . . seem redundant in a play not intended for the stage. Torture scenes and supernatural apparitions closely similar to those in Burkhead's script were in fact staged in many Stuart plays, within a flourishing popular-theatre culture in which realism was not the norm" (Coughlan 2009). "The possibility that such a play was meant to be played on a stage as well as read . . is hinted by [the playwright's] request in the epilogue that his 'Noble, worthy audience / . . . clap hands'" (Randall 1995).

SR none. Q 1646 *A Tragedy of Cola's Fury, or Lirenda's Misery*; "printed at Kilkenny [Ireland], 1645"; unique copy at BL; list of characters with handwritten (and fragmentary) names of actors; prologue and epilogue; five acts. "'Lirenda' is an anagram for 'Ireland,' and the invading 'Angoleans' are the New English of Cromwell's army"; "the villainous 'Angolean Governors of Lirenda' Pitho and Berosus are, appropriately enough, Sir William Parsons and Sir John Borlase, the men who ordered the closing of the Werburgh Street Theatre" (Morash). "Cola, the chief villain of the play, is [based upon] Sir Charles Coote; the name 'Cola' must derive from Collooney in Connaught where this cruel English colonist held lands" (Harbage 1936). At one point Cola orders, "kill, kill, spare neither man, woman, child / regard not age or sex."

Horrific violence fills the play: "*Enter men, women and children . . . They are kild*"; "*The souldi[e]rs fetch in the racke . . . Cephalon is layde on the racke and drawne*"; "*Here she [Barbazella] is drawne aloft, with burning matches between each finger.*" SDs call for a variety of special effects: "*Flashes of fire, with a horrid noise is h[e]ard, then enter Revenge with a sword in one hand, and a flaming torch in the other followed by three spirits in sheets.*" Revenge tells Cola, "This bloodie sword, and flaming torch are the / true emblems of thy furious stratageme / invented chiefely to depopulate / distroy, consume, and wast the regall state / of this brave kingdome." The play's treatment of a raging Cola is "one among many elements of the play which may indicate that it draws upon popular theatre of the 1630s" (Coughlan 2009). "On the night of his death, Cola is visited, like Shakespeare's Richard III the night before the Battle of Bosworth, by the ghosts of those he has killed" (Kerrigan 2008).

A prefatory poem by Daniel Breede employs an unusual artistic metaphor to describe the playwright's talent: "Had *Rubens* and *Vandike* liv'd and at strife / Who should pourtray best, *Cola* to the life, / Their curious art, the way could never find / To paint his body, as thy Muse, his minde; / Thou hast so lively him exprest that I / Reading was rapt into an extasie, / But straight againe perplext with so great feare / As if that cruell *Cola* present were."

The Colonel. See *The Siege* (Davenant).

The Combat of Lingua. See *Lingua.*

The Combat of Love and Friendship, A Comedy. Robert Mead. Acted 1634–38 (Brayne 2004); *c.* 1634–42 (Elliott 1997). "Formerly . . . presented by the gentlemen" students of Christ Church, Oxford, according to the TP, probably in the great hall. The author studied at this college "from 1634 until at least 1639, and [the play] was probably written during the early years of his academic career" (Marlow 2009). The stationer's address to the reader mentions the dramatist's youth when he wrote the play.

SR none. Q 1654 list of characters; five acts and separate scenes. Sparse SDs: "*She walks melancholy*"; "*He walks by.*"

A dejected stationer laments the closing of the theaters: "The scene is vanish'd, and with it, all encouragement to this musical part of humane learning. I murmur not against any that sit at the helm, though policy of state have formerly allow'd the exercise of these recreations in time of troubles, as a means to divert tumultuary and turbulent spirits, whose otherwise uncorrected heat would be employ'd to the distraction of the most considerable affaires, and persons of the common wealth."

Come See a Wonder. See *The Wonder of a Kingdom.*

A Comedy concerning Three Laws of Nature, Moses, and Christ. See *Three Laws.*

The Comedy of Errors. William Shakespeare. Acted *c.* 1590 (Dorsch & King 2004). Possibly first performed by Lord Strange's Men; "it may have had a Bankside debut, if it is Henslowe's 'the gelyous comodey' (or *Jealous Comedy*), staged at the Rose during a break in the plague in January 1593" (Honan 1998). Performed "presumably" by the Lord Chamberlain's Men at Gray's Inn (Nelson 2009a), the evening of 28 December 1594 (Holy Innocents' Day) "before a crowded and tumultuous assembly" (Duncan-Jones 2001); possibly at Greenwich on the same day; and by the King's Men in the Great Hall at Whitehall, the night of 28 December 1604 (Chambers 1930). Praised by Francis Meres in *Palladis Tamia* (SR 7 September 1598). A document called *Gesta Grayorum*, published anonymously in 1688, "is clearly an account written by someone who had taken part in the 1594 festivities" at Gray's Inn; the report indicates that Shakespeare's play was enacted on a stage "erected directly in front of the dais" (Knapp & Kobialka 1984). "*Gesta Grayorum* gives us an account of what must have been an especially sumptuous period of revels: preparations began in early December 1594, and various costly events and ceremonies took place until Shrovetide in early March" (Leonidas 2008). "Plays and masques were written and performed by members [of the Inns of Court], often before the court, but with the production of Shakespeare's

Comedy of Errors in 1594 the emphasis shifted to the commissioning of special performances by professional players" (Whitney 2006). Shakespeare may later have revised the play: "What the law students and their guests saw may have been a much simpler work than the one in the Folio" (Potter 2012).

SR 8 November 1623; transferred ?4 August 1626 Paviers right in Shakspperes *plaies*; ?19 June 1627 widow of Isaac Jaggard . . . her parte in Shackspheere *playes*; 16 November 1630; 1 July 1637 Shakespeares *workes* their Part; 6 August 1674; 21 August 1683. F1 1623 *Comedies, Histories, & Tragedies*; three issues; "published according to the true originall copies"; five acts. "Only one other play of the canon shows as much rapidity of movement on and off the stage," which "may well reflect a 'private' dramatic provenance" (Farley-Hills 2002). F2 1632 "the second impression"; three issues. F3 1663 "the third impression"; reissued 1664 with seven additional plays. F4 1685 "the fourth edition"; two issues.

"This unusually learned farce was the only play that Shakespeare modeled entirely, though probably with the help of a translation, on a classical original, Plautus's *Menaechmi*" (Duncan-Jones), "a play Shakespeare might well have read at school" (Holland 2004a). "The play is unique among his early comedies for its sustained allusion to Roman comedy . . . and for its sensitivity to classical conventions" (Beecher 1999). *Comedy of Errors* is also Shakespeare's "first tragicomedy" (Dorsch & King) and "the shortest" of his plays (Berger 2007). *The Comedy* "is exceptional among Shakespeare's plays in that it seems to make use of the conventionalized arcade setting of academic drama" (Ichikawa 2002).

The Comedy of Hieronimo. See *1 Hieronimo*.

The Comedy of Humors. See *An Humorous Day's Mirth*.

The Comedy of King Cambises. See *Cambises*.

The Comedy of Susanna. See *Susanna*.

The Comedy of the Most Virtuous and Godly Susanna. See *Susanna*.

The Comedy of Timon. See *Timon* (Anonymous).

A Comedy or Interlude entitled Enough is as Good as a Feast. See *Enough is as Good as a Feast*.

A Comical History called The Wasp. See *The Wasp*.

The Comical History of Alphonsus, King of Aragon. See *Alphonsus, King of Aragon*.

The Comical History of the Merchant of Venice. See *The Merchant of Venice*.

1 *The Committeeman Curried, A Comedy*. Samuel Sheppard. ?Acted *c.* July 1647 (Randall 1995) at undetermined venue. This play-pamphlet appeared "on the very day—16 July 1647—that the House of Commons drew up a new order for the suppression of stage-plays" (Potter 1981). The play and its sequel "offer in miniature most of the standard situations of pre-war drama, with its hard-up cavalier, hypocritical Puritan and rowdy soldier, further enlivened by borrowings from Suckling and Webster" (Potter). The title is included in Kirkman's 1661 catalogue of plays.

SR none. Q 1647 the subtitle gives the political program: *A piece Discovering the Corruption of Committee-men, and Excise-men; the Unjust Sufferings of the Royal Party, the Devilish Hypocrisy of Some Roundheads, the Revolt for Gain of Some Ministers*; "written by S. Sheppard"; dramatis personae; prologue; five acts and separate scenes. Ample SDs: "*A curtaine drawn,* Common-Curse, Suck-Dry, *discovered sitting in a taverne taking tobacco, wine before them,* Sneake and Shallow *steale off.*"

The prologue "advertised itself as a near alternative to the theatre" (Raymond 1996): "Since it is held a crime, that on the stage / Wit should present it selfe (since that the age) / Degenerates so farre, that nothing may / Be countenanc'd, that shew but like a play; / How shall these sceanes scape free (ye wiser few) / That are not retrograded with the crew / O'the reforming ones, since 'tis enacted / That nought but fiery faction shall be acted; / And since the prudent now have ordered so, / Fooles onely speake *cum privilegio*." This play-pamphlet "ridicules committeemen in particular and the Puritan party in general" (Wright 1934).

2 *The Committeeman Curried*. Samuel Sheppard. ?Acted *c.* August 1647 at undetermined venue (Randall 1995). This play-pamphlet appeared 14 August, a month after *Part 1* (Potter 1981).

SR none. Q 1647 author's initials on the TP; list of characters not present in *Part 1*; argument and prologue; five acts and separate scenes. Ample SDs: "*Recorders: Enter* Sleep *and* Death, *bearing a young man betwixt them naked, they lay him down, dance about him. Enter* Poverty, *she bewailes over him, and danceth with the rest.* Death *and* Sleep *seem to strive for the body,* Sleep *prevaileth. Enter* Mammon, *and placing two bags of gold under either arme, he reviveth, danceth with* Sleep *and* Poverty." "In the manner of the old morality plays, [this play] has among its characters certain personified abstractions: Rebellion, Loyalty, Poverty, Sleep, and Death" (Wright 1934).

Prologue evokes theatrical conditions before the closing of the theaters: "you might consider, that the age / Allowes not wit to enter on the stage / As formerly, the sweat of *Johnsons* braine, / Nor yet the comick *Fletchers* easier straine, / Which once a hackney coach convey'd you to, / Where you sate scorning all the raine could doe, / And for your twelvepences apeece could sit / As sterne-brow'd judges of all fresher wit."

Common Conditions. Possibly written by Richard Edwardes (Cope 1984), but the play "lacks several distinctive features of Edwardes's style" (Barker 2004). Listed in the Rogers and Ley catalogue of 1656 and in Archer's the same year, as well as in Kirkman's catalogues of 1661 and 1671. Acted before July 1576 (SR date) at undetermined venue. The language of the prologue "suggests staging in the 'place' of a Tudor great hall, the performance site for which the vast majority of plays printed before 1580 were probably designed" (Barker). Possibly performed by the Chapel Children (Cope). But "the broad comedy, the songs, the professional Vice, the limited cast, and the extensive doubling all point to an adult company with perhaps two trained boys" (Bevington 1962). The Q1 TP indicates that "six may play this comedie," but the doubling is not explained and the penultimate scene "involves as many as seven characters" (Barker).

SR 26 July 1576 A newe and pleasant comedie or plaie after the maner of common condycons. Q1 ND ?1576 *An Excellent and Pleasant Comedy, Termed after the Name of the Vice, Common Conditions, Drawn out of the Most Famous History of Galiarbus, Duke of Arabia, and of the Good and Evil Success of Him and His Two Children, Sedmond His Son, and Clarisia His Daughter*; unique copy at Yale; no author named; list of characters on the TP; prologue and epilogue; not divided. The TP announces, "set foorth with delectable mirth, and pleasant shewes." "[M]arginal [stage] directions . . . suggest revision with a reading rather than playing public in mind" (Walker 1998). Sound effects include "the carolling of birds, notably of the nightingale" (Lawrence 1927): "You see the chirpping birds beginnes you mellody to make." Most SDs are limited to entrances and exits, and even these are incomplete. Q2 ND ?1576 unique copy at Huntington; no TP; damaged.

This play is one of "only three such dramatic romances" to have survived from the period; the others are *Clyomon and Clamydes* and *The Rare Triumphs of Love and Fortune* (Butler 2005).

The Concealed Fancies. Jane Cavendish and Elizabeth Brackley. "Written sometime between 1642 and 1649" (Ballaster 1996), perhaps 1645 (Whitney 2006), by "two daughters of [William Cavendish, the Earl of] Newcastle's first marriage" (Potter 1981). Although there is no evidence of production, "the Cavendish sisters . . . may have acted in a performance at the family home of Welbeck Abbey [Nottinghamshire] before it was surrendered to parliamentary forces in November 1645" (Clare 2004). "There seems to be a reference to the elaborate decorative schemes characteristic of Cavendish houses when Luceny says that 'Each chamber ceiling doth create true sad, / Yet tempered so as I am quiet, glad'" (Hopkins 1999b). Or the sisters may have written the play "in late 1644 or early 1645," after Welbeck and Bolsover Castle were captured by parliamentary forces (Findlay 2006). Welbeck "is represented in the drama by Bellamo [Castle]" (Wynne-Davies 1998). In any event "the play was obviously intended for presentation, not merely a reading aloud of parts," and scene directions "suggest that the authors had considered the use of stage machinery" (Cerasano & Wynne-Davies 1996). The SDs demonstrate "an awareness of staging as well as writing" (Wynne-Davies 2000). "Through its constant use of metatheatrical effects, *The Concealed Fancies* ingeniously blurs the lines between role play on and off-stage, both of which happen in the same place" (Findlay 1998). "The spectacular scene in Act 5 where the heroes appear as gods gives striking evidence that its authors were writing for a production, either real or imagined. This masque-like interlude within the play is designed to assault the audience's senses from all sides" (Findlay et al. 1999). But the authors "were unable to construct a coherent plot" (Cotton 1980). "The absence of William Cavendish [in exile on the Continent], who so clearly forms a major part of the intended audience, until after the end of the Civil War may have deterred the sisters from staging it" (Hopkins 1996). "The play registers the new-found status many noblewomen enjoyed as commanders of the little commonwealth in their menfolk's absences" (Findlay 2000); it "offers a view of theatrical self-fashioning that caters to female fantasy, and crucially, pragmatism" (Tomlinson 1999). But Stanton 2007 demurs: the play is not "a mutinous work endeavoring to overturn the gendered hierarchy"; indeed, "rebelling against Parliamentarianism and undermining patriarchalism are mutually exclusive endeavors, neither of which can be unproblematically attributed to Cavendish and Brackley."

Oxford, Bodleian, MS Rawlinson poet. 16, fols. 87–157; in *Poems, Songs, a Pastoral, and a Play*; undated; the words *and a Play* on the general TP look like a later addition (Ezell 1988); "the author of each scene is designated by the initials 'JC' or 'EB' in the upper left-hand corner" (Ezell); three prologues — "to the stage," "second prologue spoken by a woman," "a particular prologue to your lordship"; these three speeches "display robust support for women presenting such framing texts" (Schneider 2011); three epilogues — "by Luceny," "by Tattiney," "to your lordship"; five acts and separate scenes. One page is headed "The Actors," but the names are missing. A SD suggests the use of suspension gear: *"A song sung by 2 gods coming downe out of the skye to the nunns."* "The central hallway of Bolsover Little Castle would have provided an ideal indoor space for such a spectacular descent" (Findlay 2006). Adequate SDs. First edited by Starr 1931; edited by Cerasano and Wynne-Davies 1996 in a modernized version.

The play has "strong autobiographical elements: the Civil War background is vivid, and Lady Tranquillity, who schemes to marry the great lord Calsindow, may represent Margaret Cavendish through the unfriendly eyes of her stepdaughters" (Pearson 1988). "The basic plot of the play is a reversal of *The Taming of the Shrew*" (Ezell). At the same time "this pre-Restoration comedy" seems to anticipate drama after 1660 (Wynne-Davies).

The Conceited Humor of Bumpkin. See *The Humor of Bumpkin.*

The Conceited Humor of Hobbinal. See *Oenone.*

The Conceited Humor of John Swabber. See *John Swabber*.

The Conceited Humor of Singing Simpkin. See *Singing Simpkin*.

The Conceited Humors of Simpleton the Smith. See *Simpleton the Smith*.

The Conceited Peddler. Thomas Randolph. "Performed at Trinity College, Cambridge, on All Saints' Day [1 November] 1627" (Wagner 1931, Levenson 1987), presumably in the college hall.

(1) London, BL, Additional MS 27406, fols. 121–27; no TP; the date 1627 appears on the first folio; dated All Saints' Day; not divided. (2) Edinburgh, Edinburgh University Library, Laing III.493, fols. 49–56; dated 7 August 1629. SR 26 March 1630; transferred 1 July 1637. SR 8 April 1630 entry "A Comedy called *The Pedler* by R: Davenport" may be a mistaken attribution for Randolph's play; transferred 1 July 1637. Q1 1630 "presented in a private show," according to the TP; not divided. Q2 1630. Q3 1630. Q4 1631. Q5 1635. Q6 ND Dublin ?1635. Q1–6 printed together with *Aristippus* (continuous register). O 1652 *Poems* (with *Amyntas*, *Aristippus*, *Jealous Lovers*, *Muses' Looking Glass*); "the fourth edition, inlarged"; "presented in a strange show." O 1664; the separate TPs dated 1662. The play was also known as *The University Peddler* (Nelson 1989). "The publishers seem always to have considered *Aristippus* and *The Conceited Pedlar* as a single item, for [Richard] Marriott was charged a single fee for entering the two together, and in the seventeenth century they were always printed together with a joint title-page" (*JCS*).

"Neither a play nor a show, *The Conceited Pedlar* is a benign satirical monologue in verse and prose delivered by the Pedlar (probably Randolph)" (Levenson 1987).

The Conflict of Conscience. Nathaniel Woodes. Acted 1569–80 (Davis & Wilson 1952a) at undetermined venue. "[M]ay not have been written with the public stage in mind" (Lunney 2002); the play "presents no evidence . . . of having been performed by any professional acting troupe" (Bevington 2009); probably played by amateurs (White 1993b). Probably written when the author was at Cambridge or at Norwich, where he was ordained (Wine 1935), or at South Walsham, Norfolk, where Woodes was rector, and "possibly intended for his congregation there" (White 2008).

SR none. Q 1581 two issues, one entitled *An Excellent New Comedy Entitled The Conflict of Conscience, Containing the Most Lamentable History of the Desperation of Francis Spera, Who Forsook the Truth of God's Gospel for Fear of the Loss of Life and Worldly Goods*; the other issue, *An Excellent New Comedy entitled The Conflict of Conscience, Containing a Most Lamentable Example of the Doleful Desperation of a Miserable Worldling, termed by the Name of Philologus, Who Forsook the Truth of God's Gospel for Fear of the Loss of Life and Worldly Goods*; list of characters, on the TP, arranged for six actors to play eighteen roles "either to shew this comedie in private houses, or otherwise"—"[t]he doubling of roles is functional even if inept" (Bevington 2009); prologue; epilogue "not designated, but last speech given by 'Nuntius'" (Schneider 2011); "notable for being divided into [five] acts and [separate] scenes" (Lawrence 1927). The SDs "are sparse" (Bevington 1962), but "after Philologus has allowed himself to be bullied into accepting Catholicism, the grisly figure of Horror enters to portray in his person the spiritual agony of the hero" (Pineas 1962). Through Philologus the playwright "pointedly asks what may happen when typical English Protestants again have to face a papal inquisition like that afflicting Woodes's protagonist, Philologus. Will they, like him, break under questioning and despairingly renounce the true faith?" (Bevington 1968). The Q first issue has a tragic ending; the second issue has an altered prologue and single additional speech by a Nuntius (with a redemptive ending) constituting "acte sixe, seane last": "Oh joyfull newes."

This is "the only English morality taken from the life of a real person, Francis Spira" (Houle 1972). Spira (or Spiera) was "a convert to Protestantism who subsequently lapsed back into Catholicism and thereafter fell into despair, believing himself damned" (Grantley 2007).

The Conspiracy, A Tragedy (***Pallantus and Eudora***). Henry Killigrew. Acted 8 January 1635 (Kawachi 1986). By unidentified players at York House, before King Charles and Queen Henrietta Maria, celebrating "the nuptialls of the lord Charles Herbert, and the lady [Mary] Villiers [daughter of the duke of Buckingham]," according to the Q TP; with changeable scenery (Freehafer 1971). "It is quite possible that the actors in this production were not professional players, but members of the Earl of Pembroke's own household" (Richards 1968). Performed also by the King's Men at the [second] Blackfriars, 5 or 6 November 1635 (diary of John Greene). A note in F explains of the original production at York House: "This play being design'd for an entertainment . . . [at a wedding] had scenes [i.e., painted set designs] fitted to every passage of it throughout." Also used, apparently, was an overhead curtain: *"At the end of the song the curtain falls, and shuts both the scene and actors from the beholders sight."*

SR 13 March 1638 *The Conspiracy*. Q 1638 *The Conspiracy, A Tragedy*; introduction (a kind of induction) featuring a conversation between Diana, Juno, and Tragedia; prologue (by Tragedia) and epilogue; chorus at end of each act; five acts. Detailed SDs. A flamen enters *"with the images of some of the gods"*; *"Here they all seeme to take an oath by touching of the image."* The *images* must be statues, for a character says, "consider 'tis not gold or marble that wee touch, but a modle of a sensible and living power." Sound is important to the staging of violence: *"Pallantus is heard without, spare no opposition, breake the gates, adde fire unto your force. A noyse is heard as if the gates were broken, and Pallantus, a captaine, and souldiers, rush in with their swords drawne, and seaze upon the ladies; they give a shreeke."* The sequence of auditory effects creates suspense: *"A mutinous noyse is heard"*; *"A greater noyse of muteny is heard"*; *"An uprore is heard at the doore, and Pallantus enters and wounds the king.*" Unusual SD: "*Enter a nimph, persued by a wild beare.*" F 1653 two issues; *Pallantus and Eudora, A Tragedy*; list of characters; lacks introduction, prologue, and epilogue. In F, a revision of Q, we find a play that has been "reworked to make its meanings more obviously political" (Britland 2006b, 2007). "The play abounds in speeches which sound like propaganda urging the restoration of the House of Stuart" (Wright 1934).

The F publisher addresses the reader, explaining the change of title: "the former impression [Q] is no better than a corrupted fragment, or foul draught, of what this play was intended, and differing so much from what it now is, that if the corrections, expungings, and additions be consider'd, it is almost the one half otherwise. This hath made me likewise impose a new name upon it: for it is a creature now wholly at my disposition, and belonging to me, not as to a plagiarie, but a susceptor, or foster-father, that has taken up this child long since ejected by the true parent."

The Conspiracy of Charles Duke of Byron. See *1 Charles Duke of Byron.*

The Constant Maid, A Comedy. James Shirley. Perhaps first performed by Ogilby's Men at the Werburgh Street theater, Dublin (Wertheim 1978). No license for performance in England exists. Acted early 1630s (Riemer 1966). The Q2 TP claims performance by Queen Henrietta Maria's Men at the Phoenix: "acted with great applause." But this claim cannot be verified.

SR 28 April 1640. Q1 1640 list of characters; five acts. Also issued in a made-up book of 1657 entitled *Two Plays* (with *Saint Patrick for Ireland*). Elaborate SDs: "*Enter Playfaire, dancing, with a golden ball in his hand*"; "*Enter Juno, Pallas, Venus*"; "*the goddesses dance, and court Paris for his ball: to Juno enters one like a king: takes his crown and scepter, offers it to Paris, he refuses.*" Q2 1661 *Love Will Find out the Way, An Excellent Comedy*; a revision of Q1; the TP attributes the play to T. B., who also signs the newly printed epilogue; this "possibly refers to the actor Theophilus Bird" (Burner 1988), but the attribution depends on an epilogue that the actor added (Riemer). Q2 is substantially different from Q1: "Q2 must, in some way, represent an earlier version of the play than the one printed in Q1" (Riemer). Reissued 1667 with a new TP, *The Constant Maid, or Love Will Find Out the Way.*

The Contention between Liberality and Prodigality. See *Liberality and Prodigality.*

The Contention betwixt the Two Famous Houses of York and Lancaster. See *2 Henry VI.*

A Contention for Honor and Riches. James Shirley. "Privately performed, 1631" (Grantley 2000). Possibly acted by the Children of the Revels at the Salisbury Court playhouse (Butler 2006).

SR 9 November 1632 *a Dialogue of Riches & honor*; transferred 12 December 1646. Q 1633 author's initials on the TP and Shirley signs the dedication; list of characters; not divided; concludes with dance (the music "excellently composed" by Edward Coleman) and a final couplet by Ingenuity. It "reads much like a moral treatise written by a young schoolmaster for his scholars" (Burner 1988).

Later altered and enlarged as *Honoria and Mammon*.

The Contention of Ajax and Ulysses for the Armor of Achilles. James Shirley. "[N]obly represented by young gentlemen of quality, at a private entertainment of some persons of honour," according to the TP, possibly following the closing of the theaters. "[I]t apparently was an occasional piece," probably "written and presented at the request of a patron such as Thomas Stanley or the Earl of Newcastle" (Burner 1988). "The piece is the sort of thing that might have been presented by schoolboys, who might—in the proper school—have been called 'young Gentlemen of quality'" (*JCS*); it "may have been designed for performance by [Shirley's] Whitefriars schoolboys" (Chalmers et al. 2006).

O ND ?1658; three issues, the last dated 1659 on the general TP; list of characters; not divided. *The Contention* is appended to *Honoria and Mammon*; continuous register and pagination. Ample SDs: *"Enter officers one after another, bearing the pieces of Achilles armour, after them in state, Agamemnon, Nestor, Menelaus, Diomedes, Thersander, &c."*

The Conversion of St. Paul. Anonymous. The names John Parfrey and Myles Blomefield appear in the MS, but the nature of their contributions remains unclear; they may simply have been owners of the MS. Acted ?1500–25 (Baker et al. 1982) at undetermined venue, though "[w]e have no certain record of its performance" (Scoville 2007). The play is "presumably intended to celebrate the festival of the Conversion of St. Paul on January 25," probably outdoors (Bevington 1975), though Coldewey 2008 suggests that "the church itself was included as part of the playing area." *The Conversion* "went through at least two important phases in its life, one probably as a travelling play in Cambridgeshire and East Anglia, and a second probably as a town play in Chelmsford, Essex" (Baker et al.). "Constructed in three self-contained sections, which could be played with a substantial lapse of time between them; alternatively all three could be performed in sequence" (Wickham 1976). "The only extant interlude likely to have had a processional staging (on pageant wagons)" (Grantley 2007), though this contention has been challenged by Pentzell 1973, who, while positing "three separate fixed settings, each with its own ground-level *platea*," and spectators moving from one to another, finds no indication of pageant wagons. Recent opinion sees the audience as moving "from station to station" (Grantley 2008b, Coldewey 1993). Twycross 2008 also argues that this is a "place-and-scaffold" play, "a rather curious case, as it appears to be a genuine promenade performance in our sense of the word." Additions to the MS suggest that the play was performed as late as 1540s-50s. "[M]ay have been revived in Chelmsford in the early years" of Queen Elizabeth's reign (Cooper 2010).

Oxford, Bodleian, MS Digby 133, fols. 37–50; no title but a scribe has written *"finis co[n]vercionis Sancti Pauli"*; speech by Poeta; prologues and epilogues frame each section; divided into three parts. "As a play it is spectacular, even by modern standards" (Wickham). Pyrotechnics accompany Belial and Mercury: *"Here to enter a dyvel wyth thunder and fyre . . . Here thei shal vanyshe away wyth a fyrye flame, and a tempest"* (Palmer 2008). A SD calls for a special effect: *"Here comyth a fervent, with gret tempest, and Saule faulyth down of hys horse."* "The word 'fervent' may well refer to the provision of bright light" (Butterworth 1998). "A 'fervent' (representing lightning) is sent down a wire" (Twycross 1994). "What may have been used are explosive fireworks which appear to have been used elsewhere in the play at the entry of devils" (Grantley 1983). At another point a devil enters *"with thunder and fyre."* The descent of the Holy Spirit upon St. Paul "may well have taken the traditional form of a live white dove" (Tydeman 1986). First edited by Sharp 1835, then by Furnivall 1882; modern edition by Baker et al.

"Though *The Conversion of Paul* uses no abstract characters, it does contain two non-biblical episodes of a popular stamp: in the first . . . Saul's servant exchanges filthy insults with an Ostler, and in the other . . . the devils Belial and Mercury lament Saul's defection with the thunder-claps, flashes of fire, crying and roaring which were standard in scenes of Hell. No doubt, like Belial in *The Castle of Perseverance* a century before, these demons concealed gunpowder in pipes disposed strategically about their persons. The devil-scene was probably added to the play as late as 1530, a concession to unsophisticated taste which foreshadows the Robin and Ralph episode in Marlowe's *Doctor Faustus*" (Jones 1983).

The Converted Courtesan. See *1 The Honest Whore.*

The Converted Robber, A Pastoral. John Speed. Acted 1637 by students of St. John's College, Oxford, according to the MS TP. SDs, *"The sceane is opend and it shews to be like the wonder that is upon that playne of Sarum [Stonehenge],"* "indicate either the exposure of a painted backdrop or an actual edifice of some sort" (Shaw 1979).

London, BL, Additional MS 14047, fols. 44–59; no author named; list of characters; epilogue; not divided into numbered acts or scenes. Possibly entered in SR 29 [December] 1653 as *Salisbury Plaine*, a comedy; Speed's TP identifies the locale as "Salisburye playne." *The Converted Robber* may be the play known as *Stonehenge* (Greg 1906). "No play with the title *Salisbury Plain* is otherwise known, and the title would be appropriate for this comedy with its setting on Salisbury Plain and its several references to Salisbury" (*JCS*).

Coriolanus. William Shakespeare. "*Coriolanus*'s official opening is likely to have been at court, as one of the twelve unnamed plays performed by the King's Men for the 1608–9 Christmas season" (Bliss 2010). Parker 1994 also puts the likely first production in 1608–09, though Ripley 1998 prefers "late in December 1609

or sometime in January 1610." "[A]ppears to be Shakespeare's first play written with the Blackfriars in mind as a possible venue" (Bliss); the leasing of the
Blackfriars on 10 August 1608 and the closing of the theaters for the second half
of 1608 and much of 1609 make plausible the staging of this play at the private
theater. But Barroll 2005 argues that the King's Men did not begin performing
at the Blackfriars until 1610. Richard Burbage "probably created the the role of
Martius" (Ripley), but Taylor 2002b suggests that John Lowin played the part.
The role of Menenius may have been played by the same actor who earlier played
"Polonius (*Hamlet*), Brabanzio (*Othello*), [and] Duncan (*Macbeth*)" (Stern 2010b).

SR 8 November 1623; transferred ?4 August 1626 Paviers right in Shakesperes
plaies; ?19 June 1627 widow of Isaac Jaggard . . . her parte in Shackspheeres *playes*;
16 November 1630; 1 July 1637 Shakespeares *workes* their Part; 6 August 1674; 21
August 1683. F1 1623 *Comedies, Histories, & Tragedies*; three issues; "published according to the true originall copies"; *The Tragedy of Coriolanus*; "composed in terms
of the five-act structure common at the indoor private theatres, where there were
intervals between the acts" (Bliss). Despite "no decisive evidence for a production
in Shakespeare's lifetime, the stage-directions show the play ripe for the theatre"
(Brockbank 1976); the SDs are "relatively full and descriptive" (Wells & Taylor
1987). In the opening scene *"shouts within"* signify that "The other side o'th'city is
risen." "In no other Shakespearean play does the opinion of masses of people have
so constant or important an effect on the course of the action" (Shirley 1961). "The
opening words of *Coriolanus* shape an armed, starving multitude, bent on violence"
(Jones 1995). Despite the political argumentation, such violence is at the center
of the play: in a single act, *"Alarum, the Romans are beat back to their trenches. Enter
Martius cursing"*; then *"Another alarum, and Martius followes them to gates, and is shut
in"*; *"Enter Martius bleeding, assaulted by the enemy"*; *"They fight, and all enter the city.
Enter certain Romanes with spoiles"*; *"They all shout and wave their swords, take him
[Martius] up in their armes, and cast up their caps."* "The graphic depictions of battle . . . echo the spectacular final scenes of [Thomas Heywood's *Rape of*] *Lucrece*"
(Rutter 2009). Martius himself is frequently identified with blood: *"Enter Martius,
bleeding"*; and he is "required to retain his bloody makeup for a lengthy period while
the spectator's attention is relentlessly directed to it" (Ripley). Sound effects include
trumpets calling for a parley; then *"Drumme a farre off,"* and *"Alarum farre off."* SDs
"repeatedly call for cornets, instruments with a mellower tone than trumpets and
associated with the indoor private theatres" (Bliss). When Volumnia and Virgilia
return to Rome after securing mercy from Coriolanus, we hear: *"Trumpets, hoboyes;
drums beate; altogether"*; a messenger adds, "The trumpets, sack-buts, psalteries, and
fifes, / Tabors and symbols [cymbals], and the shouting Romans / Make the sunne
dance." Despite the spectacle and sound, the moment when Coriolanus and Volumnia part is eerily quiet: he *"Holds her by the hand silent"* when he "yields to his
mother's entreaty that he should spare Rome" (David 1978). F2 1632 "the second
impression"; three issues. F3 1663 "the third impression"; reissued 1664 with seven
additional plays. F4 1685 "the fourth edition"; two issues.

"The Rome of *Coriolanus* is a fiercely masculine world. Only four female characters have speaking parts in the play. Of these four, only Volumnia makes any impression whatsoever" (Smith 1991b). The play is also "the most uniformly political tragedy in the [Shakespeare] canon" (Dobson 2001). Jonson's *Sejanus*, which dramatizes political struggle in imperial Rome, "would have been unavoidably in Shakespeare's mind" as he wrote *Coriolanus* (Donaldson 2000). "*Coriolanus* constitutes Shakespeare's most detailed representation of class struggle" (Corns 2007). "A series of riots in Northamptonshire, Leicestershire and Warwickshire, now collectively known as the 1607 Midland Revolt, presumably lies behind Shakespeare's decision to collapse Plutarch's two citizen rebellions . . . into the riot that opens the play" (Bliss).

The Coronation, A Comedy. James Shirley. Licensed for acting 6 February 1635 (Adams 1917) and attributed to Shirley. "Presented by" Queen Henrietta Maria's Men at the Phoenix, according to the Q TP. Performed also by Ogilby's Men at the Werburgh Street theater, Dublin, 1638. In playlist of Beeston's Boys 10 August 1639.

SR 25 April 1639. Q 1640 the TP ascribes the play to John Fletcher; perhaps Shirley revised an earlier work by Fletcher (Dutton 2006); list of characters; prologue and epilogue; five acts. Minimal SDs except for masquelike scene: "*Enter Fortune crown'd, attended with Youth, Health, and Pleasure*; then "*Enter Fame . . . Enter Love [i.e., Cupid], . . . Dance . . . Enter Honour with the crowne upon a mourning cushion.*" In the list of plays appended to *The Cardinal* (1652–53 collection entitled *Six New Plays*), Shirley says that *The Coronation* had been "falsely ascribed to Jo[hn] Fletcher" in the 1640 Q. "On the other hand it was included . . . in a list of 'Plays written by Francis Beaumont and John Fletcher,'" appended to the 1661 edition of *Wit without Money* (Greg 1939). The prologue, with minor changes, is reprinted in Shirley's 1646 *Poems*. B&F F2 1679 *Fifty Comedies and Tragedies*; "published by the authors original copies, the songs to each play being added"; *The Coronation, A Comedy*; list of characters.

The Q prologue, spoken by a woman, addresses female playgoers: "is there not / A blush upon my cheekes that I forgot / The ladies, and a female prologue too? / Your pardon noble gentlewomen, you / Were first within my thoughts, I know you sit / As free, and high commissioners of wit, / Have cleare, and active soules, nay though the men / Were lost in your eyes, they'l be found agen, / You are the bright intelligences move, / And make a harmony this sphere of love, / Be you propitious then, our poet sayes, / Our wreath from you, is worth their grove of bayes." Her words, which refer to the bay garland worn by most actors delivering prologues, emphasize the increasing influence of women among Caroline playgoers. Similarly, the epilogue (also female) says in the same spirit: "If smiles appear within each ladies eye, / Which are the leading stares in the faire skie, / Our solemne day sets glorious."

The Costly Whore, A Comical History. Anonymous. Acted before 1632, perhaps 1619–23 (*JCS*), but Bullen 1885 suggests 1613, a date supported by Werner 1995. "By the Companie of the Revels," according to the TP, at unnamed venue; this "has often been taken as referring to the King's Revels company, which played at the Salisbury Court theatre and elsewhere for several years after 1629"; but "the play seems much too crude for this troupe and more characteristic of the repertory of the Red Bull Revels company of 1619–23" (*JCS*). The troupe's name on the TP may designate either the Red Bull Revels Company (*JCS*) or the King's Revels Company (Stevens 1979). If the latter, the date of performance must be later, 1629–36 (Davidson 1978).

SR 2 November 1632. Q 1633 two issues; no author named; list of characters; epilogue, which refers to a second performance (Stern 2004a): "[E]very labour dyes, / Save such whose second springs comes from your eyes"; five acts. SDs pay close attention to what playgoers see: "*Enter Rainaldo, and Alberto like schollers, grieving before the beare* [i.e., *bier*], *others following them with the bodies of Euphrata, and Constantine covered with blacke*." Staging includes dramatized violence: "*Alarum, fight lustily and drive away the Duke, Fredericke pursues Valentia, over the stage, and takes her, a retreat sounded*."

The Country Captain, A Comedy. William Cavendish and, perhaps, James Shirley. Acted late spring–early summer 1641 (Johnson & Woudhuysen 1999). "Lately presented by" the King's Men at the [second] Blackfriars, according to the D TP. Possibly performed at court. In playlist of King's Men 7 August 1641.

London, BL, Harley MS 7650, fols. 1–79; no TP; no author named; contains extra (large) leaf with an additional passage in act 4; corrections in author's hand; "many passages are marked for omission" (Greg 1931); five acts. The play, which circulated in MS (Butler 1984b), "appears to date from the mid-1640s" (Ioppolo 2006). SR 4 September 1646 by my Lord [duke] of Newcastle; 30 January 1673. D and O 1649 "printed at The Hague in 1649 and reissued in London during the same year" (Johnson & Woudhuysen); published in London with *The Variety* and entitled *Two Comedies* (separate pagination for each); no author named on the separate TP, but the general TP reports, "written by a person of honor"; list of characters; first issue lacks prologue and epilogue but the second issue supplies them on a separate leaf; five acts. "The version of 1649 has been attributed to the Earl of Newcastle [Cavendish]. We may suppose that as a patron and close friend to Shirley he collaborated with the playwright" (Burner 1988). Archer in 1656 and Kirkman in 1661 both assign the play to Cavendish. The MS was first edited by Bullen, *A Collection of Old English Plays*, vol. 2 (1883): "I have followed Halliwell[-Phillipps] (*[A] Dictionary of Old [English] Plays* [1860b]) in adopting the title, *Captain Underwit*." Bullen suggests Shirley as author; he "may have corrected and adapted Newcastle's manuscript for the stage" (Johnson & Woudhuysen). "The most direct evidence of Shirley's part in the play is the appearance of the dicing song at the beginning of Act IV in Shirley's *Poems &c.*, 1646" (*JCS*). Modern edition by Johnson & Woudhuysen.

Although a courtier play, the prologue scorns "new strong lines" and dramatists who present "a glorious painted scene . . . in stead of wit." The "plain and satirical style associates" the author with "the manner of the more popular playwrights" (Butler 1984b). Prologue sets forth the playwright's purpose: "Gallants, I'le tell you what we doe not meane / To shew you here, a glorious painted scene, / With various doores, to stand in stead of wit, / Or richer cloathes with lace, for lines well writ; / Taylors and painters thus, your deare delight; / May prove your poets onely for your sight, / Not understandings, that will plainely see: / To write like wit, and that not prove to be, / It is a great mistake in poetrie. / Nor put you to schoole ith'poetique mines, / Or have a grammar made for new strong lines, / And when with labour constru'd, what they bring / Unto your knowledge prove it just nothing; / So we bring nothing too, as well as they; / If not beleeve me, pray beleeve our play." "The allusion here is undoubtedly to William Habington's tragi-comedy *The Queen of Aragon*, which was first played before the King and Queen at Whitehall," 9 April 1640 (Lawrence 1913b).

The Country Girl, A Comedy. T. B. The initials were "expanded to Thomas Brewer by Archer in his play-list of 1656. Kirkman in his play-lists of 1661 and 1671 credited the play to Anthony Brewer" (*JCS*). Acted ?1632-c. 1633 (Kawachi 1986) at undetermined venue. "Often acted with much applause," according to the TP, probably by the King's Men (Saeger & Fassler 1995).

SR 18 November 1640. Q 1647 "never printed before"; author's initials on TP; list of characters at end; prologue and epilogue (shared by several characters); five acts.

Prologue alludes to several other plays (such as Brome's *Northern Lass* and Heywood's *Fair Maid of the West, or A Girl Worth Gold*) dealing with spirited women: "What can she sing? and, like the Northerne Lasse, / (That brave blithe girle) hope to procure a passe? / Or, can she fight?—If so, so stout, so bold / A brave virago, like the Girle worth Gold. / Or is shee one, that once a countrey maide, / Crack'd in the carriage, is come to trade, / And set up some new leaguer? Or suppose / Our girle, a virtuous copy, and so close / This inquisition of her,—shee is—what? / Her own presentment, best can tell you that, / Which he but pleas'd to grace, with love and favour, / You make the poore girle rich, and crowne our labour."

A Country Tragedy in Vacunium. See *A Forest Tragedy in Vacunium.*

The Courage of Love. See *Love and Honor.*

The Courageous Turk, or Amurath the First, A Tragedy. Thomas Goffe. Acted 24 February 1619, according to the Tabley MS. "Publiquely presented" by students of Christ Church, Oxford, according to the MS, probably in the great hall. Despite the academic auspices of production, "popular drama is surprisingly influential in this play," which "borrows from both Senecan tragedy and the Marlovian rhetoric and staging of Shakespeare's *Richard III*" (Cox 2000). "There is some evidence that [Goffe] may have played the lead" (Larkum 2004).

(1) Chester, UK, Cheshire and Chester Archives, Tabley MS DLT/B 71, fols. 1–25 (Elliott et al.); *The Tragedy of Amurath, Third Tyrant of the Turks*; list of characters; argument, prologue, and epilogue; dumb show; five acts and separate scenes. (2) Cambridge, MA, Harvard University, Houghton Library Theater Collection, MS Thr. 10.1, fols. 57–71; entitled *Amurath*; in Goffe's hand, this is the player's side, or part, for Amurath. SR 7 September 1631 the Play of *Amarath the Turke*; transferred 7 November 1646. Q 1632 *The Courageous Turk, or Amurath the First, A Tragedy*; list of characters; argument and prologue; five acts and separate scenes. There are differences between "the full printed play and the manuscript part" (Palfrey & Stern 2007). Unlike the SDs in MS (2), those in Q indicate that Olympian gods descend from the heavens, apparently by machinery: "*Enter from aloft two torchbearers, then* Jupiter *and* Juno"; SDs refer to Cupid as "*hanging in the ayre*." Violence takes the form of beheading: "Amurath *cuts off* Eumorphes *head, shewes it to the nobles*"; "*Here Schahin calls in his souldiers, and each of them presents to Amurath, the head of a dead Christian*." Special effects include "*The heavens seeme on fire, comets and blazing starres appeare*." Amurath exclaims at the pyrotechnic effect, "Who set the world on fire?" Just then "*a vault opens*," and four fiends "*arise*," presumably through a trap in the stage floor. "Four devils who visit Amurath the Turk on the eve of his defeat imitate the ghosts who appear to Richard III on the eve of Bosworth" (Cox); these devils dance around Amurath "*to a kind of hideous noyse*." O 1656 *Three Excellent Tragedies* (with *Orestes* and *The Raging Turk*); "the second edition"; "carefully corrected by a friend of the authors."

"The play seems to have been known only by the title *Amurath* until its publication as *The Couragious Turke* in 1632" (Carnegie & Davison 1968). The Q title "was probably chosen to link it with Goffe's other Turkish tragedy, *The Raging Turke, or, Bajazet the Second*, which had been published in 1631" (Carnegie 1971).

The Court Beggar, A Comedy. Richard Brome. Acted May 1640 (Butler 1984b). By Beeston's Boys (the King and Queen's Young Company) at the Phoenix, despite the O TP, which erroneously ascribes performance to the King's Men. The players lacked a license for performance and acted "in defiance of a royal command to forbear" (Butler). The play "was banned because 'it had relation to the passages of the King's journey into the Northe'" (McLuskie 1981); Brome's work includes "sharp remarks about Charles's failed military campaign against the Scots" (Butler 2002).

SR no original; transferred 11 June 1659. O 1653–54 *Five New Plays* (with *The City Wit, The Damoiselle, The Mad Couple Well Matched, The Novella*); two issues; separate TP dated 1653; dramatis personae; prologue and epilogue; following the epilogue is a speech by Swaywit, "which may be designated as a second epilogue" (Schneider 2011); five acts and separate scenes. The TP says, apparently erroneously, that the play was acted "Anno 1632." The O prologue distinguishes Brome's play from fashionable fare: "y'are grown, / Deeply in love with a new strayne of wit / Which he condemns, at least disliketh it, / And solemnely protests you are to blame / If at his hands you doe expect the same; / Hee'l tread his usuall way, no gaudy sceane / Shall give instructions, what his plot doth meane; / No handsome love-toy shall your time beguile / Forcing your pitty to a sigh or smile, / But a slight piece of mirth, yet such were writ / By our great masters of the stage and wit / Whom you approv'd: let not your suffrage then / Condemne't in him and prayse't in other men." Brome objected to the lavish staging of drama by Suckling (in *Aglaura*) and others; Brome also "was particularly antagonistic to Davenant's and Suckling's tendency to incorporate the interests of Platonic court ladies and Cavalier mannerisms into the theatre" (Burner 1988). Through the character of Sir Ralph Winterplum, "a self-announced Platonic lover who is in fact a castrated bachelor horrified by every allusion to sex," Brome "lampoon[s] Platonic love as a trivial and empty deceit" (Sharpe 1987). "The prologue and epilogue to *The Court Beggar* express blunt antipathy toward those new 'wits o' Court' who, by subsidizing performances of faddish, ghostwritten fluff and by bribing audiences, were destroying the professional dramatic heritage" (Clark 1992). "Brome attacked Suckling and Davenant because they intended to add to the courtly influences upon the theater that had already threatened Brome's position as a playwright"; the play is also "personally satirical," for it "puts on stage" Suckling in the figure of Ferdinando, "the mad courtier"; the character Court-Wit, a playwright, is "a caricature of Davenant" (Steggle 2004b). In retaliation for the staging, Beeston, manager of the Phoenix, was imprisoned (Freehafer 1968).

Brome's epilogue, spoken by six characters, addresses playgoers at the private theater, who consist largely of "ladyes," "cavaliers," and "generous spirits of the City," the kind of upscale playgoers for whom this playwright wrote. This epilogue, spoken in part by two females, "reflects the increasing importance of upper-class women as arbiters of taste in the Caroline audience, largely as a result of Queen Henrietta Maria and her circle" (Levin 1989b).

The Court Secret, A Tragicomedy. James Shirley. "Never acted, but prepared for the scene at Black-friers," according to the separate TP, autumn 1642 (*JCS*); no license for acting exists. The play, which "was in rehearsal" (Braden 1987b), was not performed because of the parliamentary order forbidding playing. Shirley's dedication explains that the play "happened to receive birth, when the stage was interdicted, and wanted that publique seal which other compositions enjoyed; though it hath been read and honour'd with the allowance of some men, whose opinion was as acceptable to mee, as the vote of a smiling theater." *The Court Secret* was "not played until the Restoration" (Clark 2004).

Oxford, Worcester College, MS 1200, fols. 1–30; no TP; the play circulated in MS (Randall 1995); evidence of revision; induction (Spectator and Prolocutor), possibly added for performance after the Restoration; five acts. SR 10 September 1653. O 1652–53 *Six New Plays* (with *The Brothers, The Cardinal, The Doubtful Heir, The Imposture, The Sisters*); "never printed before"; separate TP dated 1653, other TPs in the collection dated 1652; separate register and pagination; list of characters; no induction. O "has been extensively revised and indeed largely rewritten" (Greg 1931).

"Had it been staged, the Blackfriars spectators could scarcely have missed the resonance between its double vision over royalty and the inner contradictions with which they were increasingly occupied. Simultaneously deferential towards monarchs and mistrustful about the nature of their power, the play struggles to reconcile the contemporary conflict of perceptions, seeking to render the divided experience of 1642 in a historically coherent form" (Butler 2004c).

Covent Garden, A Comedy. Thomas Nabbes. "Acted in the yeare MDCXXXII" [1632] by Queen Henrietta Maria's Men, according to the Q TP, at the Phoenix. But "the usual early modern uncertainty about whether the year changes on 1 January or on 25 March still allows for a first performance possibly as late as March 1633 of the calendar year" (Steggle 2004b). The Q dedication hints at the play's lukewarm reception in the theater: "It is likewise an error in my weaknesse, to put so meane a piece to a second tryall; when in your perusall it will meet with a more piercing judgement, then the stages, that gave it some partiall allowance."

SR 28 May 1638; transferred 4 August 1640. Q 1638–39 *Covent Garden, A Pleasant Comedy*; two issues; list of characters; prologue and epilogue; five acts and separate scenes. Q "is unique in that its entry and exit stage directions repeatedly specify '*by the right scoene,*' '*by the left scoene,*' '*by the middle scoene*'" (Ichikawa 2002). Fitzpatrick 2011, who believes that there were ordinarily only two entrypoints onto the stages, concedes that this play "overtly uses three entrances." If the widely reproduced stage façade by Inigo Jones for an unidentified theater represents the Phoenix, then the 1632 performance of *Covent Garden* "was one of the first productions by an English professional acting company to use a stage façade as a representational setting" (King 1992b). Also issued in *Plays, Masques, Epigrams, Elegies, and Epithalamiums*, a made-up book containing plays published from 1637 to 1640; although the general TP is dated 1639, some separate TPs of *Covent Garden* are dated 1638, others 1639. "For Acts One and Three of *Covent Garden*, the fictional locale is an exterior setting, Covent Garden Piazza, which was being built in 1632 and which was probably designed by Inigo Jones a year or two earlier" (King 1992b).

Prologue tells playgoers what they will *not* find: "Doe not expect th'abuses of a place; / Nor th'ills sprung from a strumpets painted face / To be exprest. Our author doth not meane / With such vile stuffe to clothe his modest scœne. / Nor doth he brand it with a satyres marke; / But makes a justice wiser then his clerke. / His rusticks likewise will pretend to wit: / So all the persons which wee counterfeit. / He justifies that 'tis no borrow'd straine, / From the invention of anothers braine." This prologue "repeatedly alludes to Richard Brome's *The Weeding of Covent Garden*, to which Nabbes's play is a response" (Kathman 2004c), but Steggle 2004b says, "it is possible, at least, that the two plays were developed simultaneously and independently." Both belong to "a small group of plays that exploited the vogue for place-realism in the early thirties" (*JCS*); other such plays containing descriptions of specific locales in London include Marmion's *Holland's Leaguer*, Shirley's *Hyde Park*, Brome's *Sparagus Garden*, Nabbes's *Tottenham Court*, and Brome's *The Weeding of the Covent Garden*.

Covent Garden Weeded. See *The Weeding of the Covent Garden*.

The Coxcomb. John Fletcher, with Francis Beaumont. Acted 1608 (Lamb 2009). By the Children of the Queen's Revels at the Whitefriars, October-November 1612 (Munro 2005). Performed by the same company at court, 2 or 3 November 1612 (Cauthen 1966). "Subsequently performed by Lady Elizabeth's Men" (Nicol 2006a) *c.* 1614 (Gurr 2009d). Later acted by the King's Men at court, before the king, 5 March 1622; and at Hampton Court, 17 November 1636 (Chambers 1923). Principal actors were Nathan Field, Joseph Taylor, Giles Garey, Richard Allen, Robert Benfield, Emmanuel Reade, Hugh Attwell, and William Barksted, according to F2. The name "Rowland" appears in an F1 SD; Rowland Dowle probably played in revivals after 1631 (Gurr 2004c). In playlist of King's Men 7 August 1641.

SR 4 September 1646; 30 January 1673. B&F F1 1647 *Comedies and Tragedies*; "never printed before, and now published by the authours originall copies"; prologue and epilogue (apparently both written for a revival); five acts and first scenes. Descriptive SDs at characters' entries: "*Enter Viola with a key and a little casket*"; "*Enter Wife in night attire*"; "*Enter Justice, and Curio with a paper.*" B&F F2 1679 *Fifty Comedies and Tragedies*; "published by the authors original copies, the songs to each play being added"; *The Coxcomb, A Comedy*; list of characters; actors' names. Division into scenes begins with Weber's 1812 edition.

The F1 prologue refers to the time separating performance from printing: "This comedy long forgot, by some thought dead, / By us preserv'd, once more doth raise her head. / And to your noble censures does present, / Her outward forme, and inward ornament." Prologue goes on to report the original reception of the play and suggests that the reader confronts a revised version: "The worke it selfe too, when it first came forth, / In the opinion of men of worth, / Was well receiv'd, and favour'd, though some rude / And harsh among the ignorant multitude / . . . wanting wit and strength, / Truly to judge, condemn'd it for the length, / That fault's reform'd, and now 'tis to be tri'd, / Before such judges 'twill not be deni'd."

The Cradle of Security. Anonymous. Acted at the Guildhall (White 1993b) in Gloucester during the 1570s (Douglas & Greenfield 1986), by a professional troupe of actors. No printed edition survives; in fact, the play may never have been printed. "[T]he cradle of the title" is "the visual image upon which the whole action was based—an image of sloth and apathy" (Powell 1964). R. Willis in *Mount Tabor, or Private Exercises of a Penitent Sinner* (1639), describes the plot of the play, which he had seen as a child when his father took him to a performance: a prince is misled by three ladies representing pride, covetousness, and luxury; they "drew him from his graver Counsellors," got him to "lye downe in a cradle upon the stage," and "closely conveyed under the cloaths where withal he was covered, a vizard like a swines snout upon his face." Then a "Serjeant at Armes, his mace on his shoulder," struck the cradle "whereat all the Courtiers with the three Ladies and the vizard all vanished" and the man found himself sent to judgment, whereupon he "made a lamentable complaint of his miserable case, and so was carried away by wicked spirits." Willis concludes his account, saying, "This sight tooke such impression in me, that when I came towards mans estate, it was as fresh in my memory, as if I had seen it newly acted. From whence I observe out of mine owne experience, what great care should bee had in the education of children" (Douglas & Greenfield).

The title is mentioned in *Sir Thomas More* (written *c.* 1600) by one of the fictional Lord Cardinal's players, who offer to perform it; this may suggest that *Cradle* had a long stage history. The play "requires a cast of six" (Greenfield 2009).

The plot summary represents one of the very rare eyewitness accounts of plays in performance. For others, see the entries for *Cymbeline, A Game at Chess, Gorboduc, 1 Henry VI, The Late Lancashire Witches, Macbeth, Twelfth Night,* and *The Winter's Tale.*

1 Crafty Cromwell, or Oliver Ordering Our New State, A Tragicomedy. Mercurius Melancholicus [John Crouch]. A play-pamphlet published 10 February 1648 (Potter 1981) and possibly acted around that time, perhaps at an inn or market: "There is little doubt its author intended it to be playable, if not strictly a play"; requires only four actors (Howlett 1978). "The play-pamphlets authored by royalist mercuries were an unstable composite genre, mixing elements of drama, reportage, satire, and prose polemic" (Raymond 1996). The title is included in Kirkman's 1661 catalogue of plays.

Q 1648 dramatis personae; prologue; chorus at end of each act; final chorus functions as epilogue; five short acts. Ample SDs, which "are full and consistent, including sound effects, props, and stage business" (Howlett). Special effects include thunder and the conjuring and appearance of Behemoth, as well as the ghost of Pym. "The ghost draws a curtain to reveal the sleeping Cromwell and the latter, upon awaking, resolves to make himself ruler" (Potter 1987b). "Behind all the melodrama is a close record of contemporary events, as reported in newspapers and pamphlets" (Potter 1981).

Publication of the play coincides "with a new ordinance of 9 February 'for the utter suppression and abolishing of all stage-playes and interludes'" (Potter 1981). Prologue condemns the government's suppression of theatrical performance: "An ordinance from our pretended state, / Sowes up the players mouths, they must not prate / Like parrats what they're taught upon the stage, / Yet we may print the errors of the age: / All their projections cannot hinder so, / But if we write, the presses needs must goe. / That, that alone, heales our dejected sense, / We can divulge our pen'd intelligence." "The perverse irony of the prologue is that the fictions which had once been displayed on the stage in order to expose and hence to criticize the 'Errors of the Age' have been replaced by news reports" (Raymond).

2 Crafty Cromwell, or Oliver in His Glory as King, A Tragicomedy. Mercurius Pragmaticus [Marchamont Nedham, or John Cleveland, or Samuel Sheppard (Randall 1995)]. A play-pamphlet published ?February 1648 and possibly acted around that time, perhaps at an inn or a market. "The play-pamphlets authored by royalist mercuries were an unstable composite genre, mixing elements of drama, reportage, satire, and prose polemic" (Raymond 1996).

Q 1648 *The Second Part of Crafty Cromwell, or Oliver in His Glory as King, A Tragicomedy*; dramatis personae; prologue; chorus at the end of each act; final chorus functions as epilogue; five short acts. Ample SDs: *"Recorders, enter* Cromwell *in state, a canopie borne over his head, by* Harry Martin, Pride, Ireton, *and Joyce, they place him in a throne, and then put a crowne upon his head"*; special effects include a vault opening and three Furies arising. SD, "Rainsborow *drawne in a chariot, six trumpeters sounding before him,*" has a topical source: "Rainsborough was a Leveller who had just been appointed Vice-Admiral of the Navy. *A New Magna Charta*, a pamphlet published in the same week as Part Two of *Crafty Cromwell*, described him on his way to take up the new post, 'in a Coach and four horses, with a trumpeter and some troopers riding before and after it'" (Potter 1988).

The address to the reader captures the playwright's political stance: "Once more I come againe, for 'tis not all / The threats the members use, can me forestall / When mov'd with spleene, I justly on the stage, / Do whip the crimes of this licentious age." Prologue alludes to the illegality of theatrical performance: "Speake not a worde, what er'e you hear or see. / For this auther, bid me to you say, / Heed live, to see this plaid another day." This "address to the reader sustains the idea or the illusion of the play's secret performance" (Clare 2004). "Curiously, the sense of danger here is associated with public display of the author's writing, which his willingness to publish would seem rather to hasten" (Straznicky 1995).

Cromwell. See *Thomas Lord Cromwell.*

Cromwell's Conspiracy, A Tragicomedy, Relating to Our Latter Times, Beginning at the Death of King Charles the First and Ending with the Happy Restoration of King Charles the Second. Anonymous. The title is included in Kirkman's 1661 catalogue of plays. "Written by a person of quality," according to the TP. ?Acted *c.* 1658. This play-pamphlet "borrows a good deal from *The Famous Tragedy [of Charles I]*, with the Colchester siege replaced by royalist martyrdoms of 1658, a death-scene for Cromwell and a tribute to General Monk" (Potter 1981). "In the final scene Cromwell on his death-bed was tormented by demons in the shape of black human figures" (Johnstone 2006).

Q 1660 no author named; dramatis personae; prologue; five acts and separate scenes. "The play-pamphlets authored by royalist mercuries were an unstable composite genre, mixing elements of drama, reportage, satire, and prose polemic" (Raymond 1996). The playlet stages the execution of King Charles.

"Uniting the varied segments of action and the characters who phase in and out of view is the author's powerful animus against Cromwell" (Randall 1995). Prologue remarks of him, "By treachery and guile the crown he gain'd, / And by the blood of loyalists he stain'd / The land." *Cromwell's Conspiracy* is "exceptional in calling both masquers and executioners to the stage and showing the monarch's last moments" (Ravelhofer 2008).

The Cruel Brother, A Tragedy. William Davenant. Licensed for acting 12 January 1627 (Adams 1917, Edmond 1987). "Presented" by the King's Men at the [second] Blackfriars, according to the Q TP. The play "is closely modelled upon *The Duchess of Malfi* but . . . is also very much about the problematic figure of the Duke of Buckingham" (Perry & Walter 2011).

SR 10 January 1630; transferred 31 October 1646; 19 August 1667. Q 1630 no author named on the TP but Davenant signs the dedication; written in verse; list of characters; five acts. SDs specify the music accompanying Corsa's death: first, *"Recorders: sadly"*; then, *"She dies, still musicke above [i.e., in the music room]"*; and finally *"cease rec[orders]."* F 1673 *The Works*; "now published out of the authors originall copies"; a revised version, in prose, of Q. "Extreme liberties have . . . been taken by the editor of the folio edition, with the original text" (Maidment & Logan 1872–74).

The Cruelty of the Spaniards in Peru. William Davenant. Acted July 1658 (Edmond 1987). "Represented daily at the Cockpit in Drury-Lane, at three after noone punctually," according to the Q TP, "and the audience was charged admission" (Bentley 1981). The play "consisted of a series of panoramic backgrounds, one to each entry, accompanied by illustrative songs and dances" (Lawrence 1913b). "[T]he frontispiece is described as 'An Arch . . . rais'd upon stone of Rustick work; upon the top of which is written, in an Antique Shield, PERU . . .'

Beyond the arch was a curtain, drawn up at the beginning of the performance to reveal a scenic stage" (Orrell 1985). "It can be assumed that" the "indistinct generic identity, part debate, part opera, part masque, and part play, enabled" this play and other such works by Davenant "to circumvent the prohibition of 1642, subsequently reinforced, on the presentation of plays" (Clare 1994). This and other plays by Davenant in the late 1650s "made themselves acceptable to the Republic by eschewing the overt Royalism of the pre-1642 masques and embracing a mercantile nationalism that echoed the imperialist ambitions of Cromwell's regime" (Butler 2002). At the same time by writing the plays and "in adapting such nationalist themes as the apocryphal colonisation of Peru and Drake's plundering voyages to South America, Davenant produced a drama which harked back to Elizabethan foreign policy" (Clare 2004).

SR 30 November 1658. Q 1658 *The Cruelty of the Spaniards in Peru, Expressed by Instrumental and Vocal Music, and by Art of Perspective in Scenes, &c.*; no author named; "argument of the whole designe"; divided into five acts by six "entries," "each entry consisting of a monologue declaimed by the Priest of the Sun" (Clare). "Formerly, playhouses had fiercely guarded their scripts. Davenant happily publishes his because the theatrical experience rests so much on staging and music that the mere words can only encourage their readers to seek out the play in performance" (Corns 2007). This Q SD, following the raising of the front curtain, suggests the importance of music and the elaboration of set design: "*The audience are entertain'd by instrumentall musick and a symphany (being a wild ayre sutable to the region) which having prepar'd the scene, a lantdchap of the West-Indies is discern'd; distinguisht from other regions by the parcht and bare tops of distant hills, by sands shining on the shores of rivers, and the natives, in feather'd habits and bonnets, carrying, in Indian baskets, ingots of gold and wedges of silver.*" A music room figures in the action when the Peruvian Priest waves "*his verge, towards the room where the musick are plac'd behind the curtain*"; a song follows. The music room "appears to have been on or close to the stage" (Orrell 1985). F 1673 *The Works*; "now published out of the authors originall copies"; conjoined with *Sir Francis Drake* and entitled *The Playhouse to be Let* (*Cruelty* constitutes the fourth act); prologue and epilogue. In *The Playhouse to be Let*, "first performed in the late summer of 1663, Davenant revived *The Cruelty of the Spaniards in Peru* and *Sir Francis Drake*, but framed them ironically, thus economically recycling his own materials while indicating his awareness of the tastes of the Restoration audience" (Winn 1998).

"The problem of the theatre to the authorities in the 1650s is, in part, how to contain meaning, to deny and circumvent the radical instability of theatrical signs and the multiplicity of potentially subversive meanings generated by direction, acting and the ideological commitments of an audience" (Wiseman 1990).

The Cuckoo's Nest at Westminster, or the Parliament between Two Lady-Birds, Queen Fairfax and Lady Cromwell. Mercurius Melancholicus [?Marchamont Nedham]. Published 15 June 1648 (Raymond 1996). "The play-pamphlets authored by royalist mercuries were an unstable composite genre, mixing elements of drama, reportage, satire, and prose polemic" (Raymond).

Q 1648 not divided. "[A] slanging-match between the wives of Cromwell and Fairfax, ends with a messenger bringing news that both men have been killed in a popular uprising in favour of King Charles" (Potter 1981). "[T]he unruliness of Elizabeth Cromwell signifies the unruliness of the state and in particular the lower orders; just as Cromwell cannot control Elizabeth's tongue, so he is figured as failing to control the nation" (Purkiss 2005).

The Cuckqueans and Cuckolds Errants, or The Bearing Down the Inn, A Comedy. William Percy. No evidence of production but, according to a note in MSS Huntington HM 4 and Alnwick 509, the author intended that his plays be staged either by the Children of the Revels or by Paul's Boys. Percy's "plays suggest private performance" (Hillebrand 1938). Until 1603 John Marston "seems to have been a de facto theatre manager at Paul's, and it is possible that a version of *The Cuck-queanes and Cuckolds Errants* was passed to him in the hope that he would consider it for production" (Kincaid 2001). "[T]here seems a certain amount of probability in the conjecture that [the play] was originally written by Percy to be acted by [Charles] Fitzjeffrey and some of his fellow undergraduates at Broadgates Hall [afterwards Pembroke College, Oxford], soon after 1590" (Dodds 1931a), and the play "concerns the adventures of two Oxford undergraduates" (Gair 2004). Percy, however, would have been sixteen in 1590.

(1) San Marino, CA, Huntington, MS HM 4 [latest of Percy MSS of this play], fols. 7–31, ed. Haslewood 1824; *Comedies and Pastorals*; author's initials on the general TP, which is dated 1647; this play "finis 1601"; list of characters; list of properties; prologue (by the ghost of Richard Tarlton, the comic actor); ends with song; signs of revision; five acts and separate scenes. For this play Percy "provides a prologue that is 'Rather to be omitted if for Powles, and another prologue for [Tarlton's ghost] to be brought in place' — a prologue, presumably, that someone else must write" (Stern 2004b). Detailed SDs: *"Claribel in cullourd velvet, gentleman lyke, as Floradin in cullours. Aruania, Rooke, Janekin. A serving man in blewe coate, Claribel with letter in hand open. They enterd from Harwich all."* "All the stage directions are in the past tense, evidently referring to a particular performance; and this evident reference to a single occasion leads me to suppose that there may have been only *one* performance" (Hillebrand 1926). In a list of properties before the play we read: "Harwich, *in midde of the stage* Colchester *with image of Tarlton, signe and ghirlond under him also.* The Raungers Lodge, Maldon, *a ladder of roapes trussd up neare* Harwich. *Highest and aloft the title* The Cuck-Queanes and Cuckolds Errants. A long fourme." Percy's plays "show a use of locality boards which is nowhere else so completely illustrated in Elizabethan drama; that such signboards existed is adequately proved by considerable other evidence, but Percy's plays furnish a unique statement as to how they were employed" (Reynolds 1914). (2) Alnwick, UK, Alnwick Castle, MS 508 [earliest of Percy MSS of this play],

fols. 2–29; *Change Is No Robbery, or The Bearing Down of the Inn, A Comedy*; MS dated 1644 (in *The Fairy Pastoral*), this play "finis 1601." (3) Alnwick MS 509 *The Cuckqueans and Cuckolds Errants, or The Bearing Down of the Inn*; the general TP dated 1646, this play "finis 1601"; author's initials on the general TP.

First edited by Haslewood and published by the Shakespeare Press for the Roxburghe Club; Haslewood's copy of the MS was purchased by the Huntington (San Marino, CA, Huntington Library, MS HM 4).

The Cunning Lovers, A Comedy. Alexander Brome. Acted 1632–39 (*JCS*). "Acted with great applause" by Beeston's Boys at the Phoenix, according to the TP. In playlist of Beeston's Boys 10 August 1639. Possibly performed after the closing of the theaters: "plays such as *The Cunning Lovers* that had been part of the Phoenix repertory before 1642 may have found their way to other playhouses or been adapted for illegal Commonwealth performances before printing" (King 1965).

SR none. Q 1654 list of characters; detailed description of a dumb show; five acts and first scenes. SDs are straightforward: *"A table with a booke and papers set out"*; *"Enter Montecelso as a ghost."* "On the whole, stage ghosts seem to have worn the clothes they wore when they were alive" (Thompson 2010).

Cupid's Revenge. Francis Beaumont and John Fletcher. Hoy 1958 believes that the play "has been given its final form by Beaumont," but McDonald 2003 says, it "is thought to be originally Beaumont's work touched up by Fletcher"; "the date of this doctoring is unknown: did it occur before production, or after production but before publication in 1615?" (McDonald). "Divers times acted" by the Children of the Queen's Revels, according to the Q1 TP, at the Whitefriars. "Probably first performed in 1607–8" (McMullan 2004). "First recorded performance by the Children of the Queen's Revels in January 1612" (McMullan); this company was "the last vestige of the old Blackfriars boys" (Marino 2009). Performed also by "The Children of Whitefriars" (Chambers 1923) at St. James's Palace before Prince Henry and Princess Elizabeth, 5 January 1612; and, before the king, the night of 1 January 1613; before Prince Charles, 9 January 1613 (Astington 1999a); by Lady Elizabeth's Men [Queen of Bohemia's] at Whitehall, before prince and Duke of Brunswick, the night of 28 December 1624 (Bawcutt 1996). "In 1621 or 1622 a revived Lady Elizabeth's company was formed and began playing at the Phoenix under Christopher Beeston" (Bentley 1981). Revived by Beeston's Boys at St. James's Palace 7 February 1637 (Adams 1917), in the Presence Chamber (Astington 1986). In playlist of Beeston's Boys 10 August 1639. The play proved "phenomenally popular" (Dutton 2003).

SR 24 April 1615; transferred 15 April 1619; 24 October 1633; 28 July 1641; 4 March 1647. Q1 1615 the TP names Fletcher alone; five acts. "The majority of stage directions are unlike those in the other plays of Beaumont and Fletcher. They are infrequent, and very brief" (Jewkes 1958). Staging involves three descents by Cupid, apparently by suspension machinery, an effort "to imitate as closely as possible the newly fashionable scenic effects of the court masques" (Astington 1979). But King 1971 suggests that Cupid may have managed ascent and descent by "a movable staircase set in place for the scenes in which it is required." Cupid's temple is "revealed by discovery" (Astington 1986). Q2 1630 "the second edition"; "often acted (with great applause)"; the TP names B&F; list of characters. Q3 1635 "the third edition." B&F F2 1679 *Fifty Comedies and Tragedies*; "published by the authors original copies, the songs to each play being added"; list of characters. Between the closing of the theaters and the Restoration, part of the play was adapted for a droll entitled *The Loyal Citizens*, later published in *1 The Wits, or Sport upon Sport* (O 1662 [two issues] and 1672) and "identified erroneously as from *Philaster*" (Bowers 1970).

The Q1 printer's note to the reader prizes the response of a theatrical audience: "I once againe dedicate this booke to the juditious, some whereof I have heard commend it to be excellent, who, because they saw it acted, and knew what they spake, are the better to be beleeved."

Cupid's Whirligig. Edward Sharpham. First performed by the Children of the King's Revels in 1607 (*AED 3*). "Sundry times acted" by this company, according to the second issue of the Q1 TP, at the Whitefriars. This "was probably the first play to be performed by the Children of the King's Revels" (Petter 1986); the Children were "tenants of the Whitefriars theater in 1607 and 1608" (Cathcart 2005). Revived at Oxford "by apprentices," 26 December 1631 (Munro 2006d).

SR 29 June 1607 A Comedie called *Cupids Whirleygigge*; transferred 29 January 1630; 7 November 1646. Q1 1607 two issues; no author named on the TP but the initials "E. S." appear at end of the dedicatory epistle (Jones 1812 suggests that the initials belong to Sharpham); list of characters; prologue and epilogue (by Cupid); five acts. Although SDs fail to mention suspension gear, Cupid upon his entry reports that "with winges and bowe come I / Newlie from Joves hye court in skie." Q2 1611. Q3 1616. Q4 1630.

Prologue begins by explaining to playgoers what they will *not* see: "Our authors pen, loves not to swim in blood, / He dips no incke, from out blacke Acheron: / Nor suckes invention, from the depth of hell, / Nor crosseth seas to get a forraine plot." Instead of dramatizing tragic material, Sharpham is interested in exploring "the debate as to the true nature of modern womanhood" (Petter).

The Curates' Conference, or A Discourse betwixt Two Scholars; both of them relating their hard condition, and consulting which way to mend it. Anonymous. A playpamphlet possibly written for performance, April 1641.

Q 1641 no author named; no SDs; not divided.

This dialogue of two scholars, Master Poorest and Master Needham, belongs to the genre of social protest. Master Poorest, for example, relates his experience at Oxford: "I stayd in the Universitie of Oxford till I was forc'd to leave it for want of subsistence. I stood for three or foure severall schollerships, and though I was found upon examination sufficient, yet do I seriously protest, that one time I was prevented by halfe a bucke and some good wine, that was sent up to make the Fellowes merry: and another time a great ladyes letter prevail'd against all ability of parts, and endowments whatsoever." In much the same spirit Master Needham complains, "I thinke wee curates are worse dealt withall by the rich double beneficed men, then the children of Israel were by the Ægyptians."

A Cure for a Cuckold, A Comedy. John Webster, William Rowley, and Thomas Heywood (Jackson 2001c). Written 1624 (Wiggins 1995) and licensed for acting 26 July 1624 (Gunby 2004) as *A Wedding, or A Cure for a Cuckold*; Henry Herbert names Webster as author (Bawcutt 1996). "Several times acted with great applause," according to the TP, by Prince Charles's Men "either at the Phoenix or at the Curtain" (Hammond 1987a). "Webster wrote, it seems, the major scenes in the main plot . . . and Rowley was responsible for the fine comic subplot" (Gunby). Rowley probably wrote the role of Compass for himself, though Rowley had joined the King's Men by 1623; "the explanation may be that Rowley was allowed to separate his acting duties from his writing from the time he left the Prince's company for the King's" (Carnegie 2003b).

   SR none. Q 1661 *A Cure for a Cuckold, A Pleasant Comedy*; two issues; the TP names Webster and Rowley; dramatis personae; five acts and first scenes. In 1661 some copies of Q were issued with *The Thracian Wonder* and entitled *Two New Plays*.

   In his address to the reader, Francis Kirkman writes of the play, "several persons remember the acting of it, and say that it then pleased generally well; and let me tell you, in my judgement it is an excellent old play."

The Custom of the Country. John Fletcher and Philip Massinger. "First performed by the King's Men probably in" 1619 (McMullan 2004) at the second Blackfriars. Revived at Blackfriars, 22 November 1628, a benefit for Henry Herbert (Adams 1917); at Hampton Court 24 October 1630 (bill of the King's Men for plays presented at court); and at the Whitehall Cockpit 27 November 1638 (bill of King's Men). "The play was popular and profitable, facts not inconsistent with the notorious reputation it gained for its scenes set in a male brothel" (Hoy 1987a). "The 'custom' in question is the governor's exercise of his *droit de seigneur* and is treated with splendid indelicacy" (McMullan). "The crisis that frames *Custom* is sexual exploitation, but the opening scene establishes erotic enslavement as a metaphor for intemperate relations based upon various forms of corporal coercion" (Bailey 2011). Principal actors were Joseph Taylor, John Lowin, Nicholas Tooley, John Underwood, Robert Benfield, William Eccleston, Richard Sharp, and Thomas Holcomb, according to F2. In playlist of the King's Men 7 August 1641.

   SR 4 September 1646; 30 January 1673. B&F F1 1647 *Comedies and Tragedies*; "never printed before, and now published by the authours originall copies"; two prologues and two epilogues, "one set for a new play and the second set clearly for a revival" (*JCS*); Hugh Clark, "member of Queen Henrietta's Company in the late 1620s and early 1630s . . . [who] transferred to the King's Company *c.* 1636/7" (Hoy 1992a), spoke the prologue and epilogue for a revival, probably in 1638; five acts and separate scenes. Some descriptive SDs, especially at characters' entries: "*Enter Charino and servants in blackes. Covering the place with blackes*"; "[v]isually this is a shock, especially since it is the marriage bed they cover. No doubt it begins to look like a bier" (Gossett 1988). Then when Clodio comes to bed, awaiting the bride, "*Enter Zenocia with bow and quiver, an arrow bent, Arnoldo and Rutillo after her, arm'd.*" "Against the background of the black-draped bed and the impression made by the black-clothed dancing servants, it is easy to see an emblematic construction here" (Gossett). B&F F2 1679 *Fifty Comedies and Tragedies*; "published by the authors original copies, the songs to each play being added"; list of characters; actors' names. In the 1640s and 50s parts of the play were adapted for a droll entitled *The Stallion*, later published in *1 The Wits, or Sport upon Sport* (O 1662 [two issues] and 1672).

This "is the most dramatically satisfying play that Massinger and Fletcher ever wrote together" (Hoy 1985).

Cutter of Coleman Street. See *The Guardian* (Cowley).

Cymbeline, King of Britain. William Shakespeare. Acted by autumn 1610 (Warren 1998) by the King's Men at the first Globe/second Blackfriars; "it seems likeliest that the first performances came in December 1610" (Butler 2005); perhaps the "first of the King's Men plays to be written specially for the Blackfriars" (Dobson 2001); "Shakespeare seems to have had in mind the resources and audience of the indoor theatre" (Wells & Taylor 1987). The company began using the Blackfriars "after January 1610" (Barroll 2005). Simon Forman witnessed a performance at an unnamed theater between 20 and 30 April 1611 (Oxford, Bodleian, MS Ashmole 208, fol. 206); "the plot is summarized accurately, and no moral is drawn" (Gurr 1987b); but Traister 2001 finds a "jumbled plot summary." Forman recapitulates the plot "as if the invading Roman General, Caius Lucius, the rustic trio of Belarius and his adopted sons, and especially Giacomo, were as important as the central character, Innogen, whose fiancé Posthumous is not mentioned by name at all" (Whitney 2006). The "leading role [however spelled] has been prepared for a boy" (Bentley 1984). (Simon Forman calls the chief female character Innogen, but F1 spells the name Imogen; some recent editions [*Oxford* 1986, *Norton* 1997, Warren 1998, Butler 2005] adopt Forman's spelling, which is also used by Holinshed. "Shakespeare had an Innogen as a mute in *Much Ado about Nothing*" [Chambers 1930]). Possibly performed at court "in the holiday season of 1610–11" (Barroll 1991). Revived at court, the night of 1 January 1634; Herbert reports, "well likte by the kinge" (Adams 1917). The role of Iachimo, "the charismatic villain," may have been played by the same actor who earlier played "Iago (*Othello*) [and] Edmund (*King Lear*)" (Stern 2010b). John Rice may have played Innogen (Astington 2010).

SR 8 November 1623; transferred ?4 August 1626 Paviers right in Shakes-peres *plaies*; ?19 June 1627 widow of Isaac Jaggard . . . her part in Shackspheeres *playes*; 16 November 1630; 1 July 1637 Shakespeares *workes* their Part; 6 August 1674; 21 August 1683. F1 1623 *Comedies, Histories, & Tragedies*; three issues; "published according to the true originall copies"; *The Tragedy of Cymbeline*; grouped with the tragedies in this volume; "*Cymbeline*'s affinities lie more with the Tragedies than the Comedies" (Butler); five acts and separate scenes. *Cymbeline* is "the most overtly theatrical of Shakespeare's plays in the sense that its events and emotions are presented, even paraded, so openly before the audience" (Warren 1998). A property "*trunke*" in which Jachimo hides and gains access to Innogen's bedchamber is specified; when he has seen the sleeping woman, a "*[c] locke strikes.*" Although he "does not actually rape Innogen, the threat coexists, in the tense atmosphere of the scene, with the lyrical beauty" of his tribute to her (Warren 1989b). Following this incident Cloten arranges for musicians to waken Innogen with music and song; "Shakespeare usually associated this form of serenade with male lovers who are more lecherous than loving" (Long 1971). Cloten becomes the focus of a *coup de théâtre* when, later, Innogen awakes to find Cloten's headless corpse. "This is the central scene of the play," and this grotesque incident "is the scene with the greatest impact in performance" (Warren 1989b). Another powerful moment is the entry of Arviragus "*with Imogen dead, bearing her in his arms.*" Although the audience knows that Innogen has taken a drug inducing her condition, "that knowledge is not so much forgotten as suppressed. The audience responds to the pathos of the moment" (Warren 1989b). Staging involves a descent (of Jupiter "*sitting upon an eagle*"), apparently by machinery: "Here and elsewhere, the sounds of thunder would probably have masked the noise of the machinery used for lowering or raising figures or objects" (Thomson 1999). "Stage thunder was created by rolling a cannon ball in a groove above the ceiling" (Butler). The god "*throwes a thunder-bolt*"; "[w]hat he threw was an explosive firecracker" (Gurr & Ichikawa 2000). The descent and ascent "may have been added for later performances at St. James and may not have been part of the original production at the Globe" (Graves 1999). Jupiter is "the first of Shakespeare's gods to fly in" (Gurr 2009d). The ghosts of Posthumus's relatives, who enter to the sound of "*solemne musicke*," may emerge from a trap (Lawrence 1927), though Warren 1998 observes that "they have come from the Elysian fields" and thus would probably not enter from below. The ghosts encircle the sleeping man, whose dead father is "*attyred like a warriour*"; the ghostly brothers of Posthumus appear "*with wounds as they died in the wars*"; "the scene resembles" a dumb show (Lomax 1987). "Even though there is no specific direction that the ghosts dance around the sleeping prisoner it is clearly apparent that they circle him with regular motion, first, because of the music, then because of the pronounced rhythms of the prayer" (Brissenden 1981). "[T]he comic outcome in *Cymbeline* depends on a female character assuming control in the guise of a man, . . . a strange combination of realism and fantasy" (Smith 1991b). F2 1632 "the second impression"; three issues. F3 1663 "the third impression"; reissued 1664 with seven additional plays. F4 1685 "the fourth edition"; two issues.

Cymbeline is one of the very few plays that feature Wales prominently, others being *A Shoemaker, a Gentleman* and *The Valiant Welshman*. "When a site of authentic Britishness was sought, writers looked to the mountainous country which had resisted Rome and kept out the Saxons" (Kerrigan 2006). *Cymbeline* and *The Valiant Welshman* "were staged in the immediate aftermath of the [June] 1610 investiture of Henry Frederick as Prince of Wales, an event that raised the profile of Wales and invited new theatrical explorations of Wales and its relationship to the ancient British past" (Cull 2010). "Wales is both symbolically incorporated into and displaced from the Anglocentric world of Shakespeare's *Cymbeline*" (Sullivan 1998). "The much-mentioned destination of Milford Haven [Wales] turns out to be singularly unimportant in the action, however famous it may have been as the place where Henry Tudor had made landfall in his own invasion of England," leading to his confrontation with Richard III at Bosworth (Cooper 2010).

Cynthia's Revels, or The Fountain of Self-Love. Ben Jonson. Acted between 29 September and 31 December 1600 (Bednarz 2001). "Sundry times privately acted" by the Children of the Queen's Chapel, according to the Q and F1 TPs, at the second Blackfriars. ("[N]o commercial theatre attribution appeared on a title page until the Blackfriars was named on the 1601 *Cynthia's Revels*" [Farmer & Lesser 2000]). The actors of this company "were at that time famous for good action" (*Historia Histrionica*). Also performed at Whitehall, 6 January 1601 (Donaldson 2004). "Elizabeth is figured as the moon-goddess Cynthia who, in a thinly disguised allegory of the disgrace of the Earl of Essex, has punished the impetuous Actaeon for daring to see her naked" (Steggle 2010). The play "was carefully designed with court performance and the repertory of the boy actors in mind" (Kay 1995); Jonson "was seeking court patronage, attempting to extricate himself from the confused literary market of the public theaters and to insert himself into what might be called a neoconservative patronage market" (Loewenstein 1985). However, "Dekker's jibe that 'your plays are misliked at court' (*Satiromastix* . . .) suggests that this early bid for royal favour was not successful" (Dutton 1993). Principal actors were Nathan Field, John Underwood, Salamon Pavy, Robert Baxter, Thomas Day, and John Frost, according to F1.

SR 23 May 1601 *Narcissus the fountaine of self love*; transferred 3 July 1630; 4 July 1635; 4 March 1639. Q 1601 two issues; *The Fountain of Self-Love, or Cynthia's Revels*; RT *Cynthia's Revels*; list of characters; praeludium (i.e., induction [Hosley 1961]) by "three of the children"; prologue and epilogue; five acts and separate scenes. The two halves of the title point in different directions: "Jonson hoped to move from the lowly medium of stage comedy (*The Fountain of Self*

Love) to the more exalted sphere of the court masque (*Cynthia's Revels*)" (Riggs 1989). The characters who enact the two masques (a courtly feature) are carefully described, along with their symbolic costumes and props: "*The first in citron coullour is* naturall Affection, *which given us to procure our good, is sometime* called Storge, ... *Her device is a* perpendicular levell *upon a* cube or square. *The word, SE SUO MODULO: alluding to that true measure of ones selfe, which as every one ought to make, so is it most conspicuous in thy divine example.*" Mercury strikes the ground three times with his caduceus, and Echo rises through a trap; striking the stage floor was the signal for the trap to open (Lawrence 1927). "The performance of music within the tiring-house is alluded to by Jonson in the Induction" (Hosley 1960). The induction also refers to "fresh pictures that use to beautifie the decaied dead arras, in a public theatre"; this "allusion suggests that the 'arras' or heavy tapestry may have been a permanent feature, and that painted cloths were hung over this when desired" (Foakes 2003). In the echo scene, "the character named Echo first repeats the words of Mercury, who is onstage, and then rises from under the stage" (Ichikawa 2005), instead of emerging from a discovery space. F1 1616 *The Works*; *Cynthia's Revels, or The Fountain of Self-Love, A Comical Satire*; "acted in the yeere 1600." The F1 version, much longer than Q, represents "a revision and expansion" of the play (H&S). "The additional folio passages and scenes do contain the play's most trenchant court satire, which may well have been censored by the Master of the Revels when he perused the play in readiness for a Court performance in January 1601" (Clare 1999). Jonson also "reversed the alternative titles . . . , transliterated the hero's name from Latin into Greek, and stressed the importance of Crites's promotion to the office of masque writer" (Riggs). The F1 revision made it "less satisfactory for performance, but fuller and more engaging for the private reader" (Dutton 1996). F2 1640 vol. 1.

Jonson addresses the court, somewhat ironically, in his F1 dedication: "Thou art a bountifull, and brave spring: and waterest all the noble plants of this iland. In thee, the whole kingdome dresseth it selfe, and is ambitious to use thee as her glasse. Beware, then, thou render mens figures truly, and teach them no lesse to hate their deformities, then to love their formes: for, to grace, there should come reverence; and no man can call that lovely, which is not also venerable." Jonson's "words to the court consist of a good deal of moral finger-shaking disguised as advice" (Herendeen 1991). The play contributes to the poetomachia, Jonson's "publicly-staged mud-slinging match with Thomas Dekker and John Marston, which extended over several years and a number of different plays" (Evans 1989). The characters of "Hedon and Anaides are taken to represent Marston and Dekker" (Steggle 1998).

Cynthia's Revenge, or Maenander's Ecstasy. John Stephens. ?Acted 1611–13 (Chambers 1923) at undetermined venue.

SR none. Q 1613 two issues, one of which names the author; list of characters; argument; first and last scenes, in which Cynthia appears alone, are much like "a prologue and epilogue" (Greg 1939), but Schneider 2011 regards them as soliloquies; five acts and separate scenes. Sparse SDs.

The author's epistle to the reader adopts a feisty tone: "I could now descant (like some sage fabulist) upon reall difference betwixt readers, and understanding readers; prescribe a formall limitation who should, with my consent, survey this poem [i.e., play], (which, no doubt, many will terme tedious) or could most humbly beg at the fowle-fisted paw of each pretending asse, each staulking gull, to spare his cheape detraction, or rather unboyled carpes, till the authors next service, and then to choake him with unchewed gobbets of his owne dressing, if each particle in the cookery were not amended."

The Cyprian Conqueror, or The Faithless Relict. Anonymous. Epilogue reports, "Our author is a countryman"; he is otherwise unknown. Acted "in one of the regular playhouses of London" (Adams 1908); Greg 1931 suggests performance *c.* 1640; Harbage 1939 suggests *c.* 1633. "Both prologue and epilogue are intended for performance, but there is no evidence that there ever was one" (*JCS*), though Adams finds in the second prologue evidence that "the play was acted more than once"; Bentley (*JCS*) finds the evidence for this claim "negligible."

London, BL, MS Sloane 3709, fols. 1–51; no author named; lengthy preface; dramatis personae; evidence of correction; prologue and "the other prologue" spoken by an actor dressed like an attorney; epilogue (by Aeneas); five acts and separate scenes. HT follows the preface: *The Faithless Relict or The Cyprian Conqueror.* Numerous SDs written in the margins: "*Enter Petronia, Calista and Dido all in mourning, with other mourners with the corps, goe out, and return, and take their leaves: Petronia, Calista and Dido stay.*" The last folio contains "The song sung in ye first act of Philanthes & Calista"; "The song sung ye next daie b[y] Eneas"; and "The song with ye soft musicke as Cupid descends."

The preface offers a defense of drama at a time when theaters were about to be closed: "by plaies, the rude & barbarouse people, by example, are more civilized, by whose insinuation, the more strong & robust brests, are molified: & the nerves and sinewes of a well modelized & cyvill state, are by them strengthened, by which the whole mind is irritated & pricked on to a noble emulation. Let not then the pretended illuminist, or severe conconformist, carpe at playes, or play abusively with that innocent recreation: but run into admiration, in what is admirable in the actor & action."

D

The Damoiselle, or The New Ordinary, A Comedy. Richard Brome. Acted summer-autumn 1638 (Kaufmann 1961). By Queen Henrietta Maria's Men at the Salisbury Court playhouse (Steggle 2004b).

SR no original; transferred 11 June 1659. O 1653–54 *Five New Plays* (with *The City Wit*, *The Court Beggar*, *The Mad Couple Well Matched*, *The Novella*); two issues; registration begins anew with the last play in the collection; separate TP dated 1653; dramatis personae; prologue and epilogue; five acts and separate scenes.

Prologue announces the playwright's pragmatic intent: "He does not ayme, / So much at praise, as pardon; nor does claime / Lawrell, but money; bayes will buy no sack, / And honour fills no belly, cloaths no back. / And therefore you may see his maine intent / Is his owne welfare, and your merriment." This prologue "snipes away at Davenant" (Butler 2006), whom Brome thought pretentious.

Damon and Pithias. Richard Edwards. Acted 1564 (White 1980) at Whitehall during the Christmas season of 1564–65. By the Children of the Queen's Chapel, according to the Q1 TP: "shewed before the queenes majestie." "Apparently" the play performed at Lincoln's Inn, 2 February 1565 (White 1987, Elliott 2004). Revived at Merton College, Oxford, 1568 (Boas 1914, Elliott). "There is no way of knowing how many other schools, colleges or households took up the invitation of the printed title page to perform it for 'private audience'" (King 2001). Grim the Collier may have been played by an adult actor (Shapiro 1977); Grim would later appear as a character in *Grim the Collier of Croydon*.

SR *c*. 22 July 1567 (Brown & Wilson 1957) *the tragecall comedye of Damonde & pethyas*. Q1 1571 (possibly a reprint) *The Excellent Comedy of Two the Most Faithfullest Friends, Damon and Pithias*; "newly imprinted"; RT *The Tragical Comedy of Damon and Pithias* (this is "the first English play to call itself a 'tragical comedy'" [Pincombe 1996]); list of characters; prologue; no epilogue as such but a song perhaps sung by the entire cast; not divided. Q1 represents the version presented before the queen "except the prologue, that is somewhat altered for the proper use of them that hereafter shall have occasion to plaie it, either in private, or open audience." "The printer is aware that future productions will need to make alterations because of the occasional nature of the original performance. But he knows that part of its sale will depend on the accuracy of its link to a prestigious performance. The text hovers between being a record and a script" (Holland 1979). "Perhaps, for the court performance, Edwards had introduced some topical references, or a compliment to the queen" (Potter 1980). The Q1 TP contains three small woodcuts. SDs "are full and clear" (Brown & Wilson). When "Prologue pointed out Dionysius's palace and the town of Syracuse, he would have been standing in front of scenic representations of those places: wooden frames, perhaps with cut-out outlines made by the 'carvars,' covered with painted canvas" (King 2001). Q2 1582 no woodcuts; unique copy at BL. The subject of male friendship would continue to find dramatic form, as for example in *Edward II*, *The Two Gentlemen of Verona*, *The Old Wives Tale*, *The Coxcomb*, and *The Two Noble Kinsmen* (Stretter 2005).

"Despite the Prologue's insistent disclaimer eschewing any political application, Edwards plainly envisages a viable role in Elizabeth's government for himself and like-minded Protestant humanists" (Bevington 2002a). "The philosopher must be permitted, indeed encouraged, to evaluate the contemporary political situation. He is not, however, to take action or recommend practical reforms" (Bevington 1968).

"The extraordinary Grim-the-Collier scene in *Damon and Pythias* is by far and away the longest in the play. It is also apparently almost completely unconnected to the play's main story — the pair of friends trapped in a tyrannical court. It is, however, a rather more effective defence of the drama than any attempt to take on the polemicists on their own terms, and seems to have inspired a series of plays by other people" (King).

Darius. See *King Darius.*

David and Bethsabe. George Peele. Acted 1593–94 (Blistein 1970). "Divers times plaied on the stage," according to the TP, at undetermined venue, possibly an inn-yard (Lawrence 1927), though "when actors performed at inns they usually occupied a large room rather than a yard and performed by candlelight" (Orrell 1997). "This play seems to have been in the repertoire of one of Henslowe's companies" (O'Connell 2000b). Probably performed by Worcester's Men when they were using the Rose (Gurr 2009c). Edward Alleyn may have played the role of David (Cerasano 2005).

SR 14 May 1594 possibly first printed this year (Greg 1939). Q 1599 *The Love of King David and Fair Bethsabe, with the Tragedy of Absalon*; prologue; chorus (twice); not divided. Prologue, exiting, "*drawes a curtaine, and discovers Bethsabe with her maid bathing over a spring: she sings, and David sits above vewing her*"; the song "creates a landscape of sensuousness" (Ewbank 1975). Staging apparently calls for an onstage structure: "*He goes to his pavilion, and sits close a while.*" "Peele deliberately replicates aspects of stage spectacle from Marlowe's *Tamburlaine*, including scenes of siege warfare with vaunting between characters upon city walls, together with the hanging of characters either from walls or, in the case of Absalon, from a tree" (Connolly 2007). David's men scale the walls of their enemies, climbing "up to the gallery from the main stage" (Rhodes 1976). Absalom "*hangs by the haire*" from an oak tree, an effect whose expense is apparently recorded in Henslowe's *Diary* [3 October 1602]: "pd. for poleyes & worckmanshipp for to hange absolome" (Mcmillin 1992). "'Poleyes' in the plural may indicate more than one pulley" (Butterworth 2005). Henslowe's entry suggests a revival. But "unfortunately there is no further evidence which indicates that the entry refers specifically to Peele's play or to a performance of that play" (Connolly).

David and Bethsabe is "the best surviving late-Elizabethan play on a biblical subject" (Braunmuller 1983a). It "unites the rich pagan pastoralism of the *Arraignment [of Paris]* with the renaissance patriotism and self-awareness of *Edward I*, against a finely apprehended Old Testament background" (Morris 1987). "Peele's play also taps into the political significance of the equivalence between David and Elizabeth as God's anointed servants to underline England's position as a providential nation and to celebrate their role as the underdogs in the war with Spain" (Connolly).

De Pugna Animi. Mildmay Fane. ?Acted 1650. Intended for performance at Fane's estate, Apethorpe, by family and friends, but no record of production exists.

London, BL, Additional MS 34221, fols. 124–47; no TP; no author named; dated 1650; argument; list of characters; prologue and epilogue; three folios are damaged, words missing; five acts and separate scenes. Ample SDs.

Harbage 1936 notes a connection between this play and Nabbes's *Microcosmus*, "concerning as it does the anarchous revolt but final subjugation of the five Senses." "Another play which may well have influenced Fane in the writing of *De Pugna Animi* is *Pathomachia*, which was published in 1630" (Leech 1938). Although Fane called this play a comedy, "it might also be considered a latter-day morality play, a seventeenth-century *Psychomachia* that is more economical, more lively linguistically, and somewhat better built than his other works" (Randall 1995).

"Fane's Royalist posture had matured and his perspective on the events of the English Civil War sobered" (Morton 1991). "Fane analyzes the consequences of a faltering monarch's inability to understand and work with his supporters" (Randall).

The Dead Man's Fortune. Anonymous. Acted *c*. 1590 (Bradley 1992) by the combined Strange's and Admiral's Men at undetermined venue, possibly the Theater and/or Curtain (Bevington 1962). It is possible, however, that the play was performed as early as the mid-1580s (Astington 2010). Unlike other surviving "plots," this one does not provide most of the principal actors' names.

London, BL, Additional MS 10449, fol. 1; a "plot," or "backstage storyboard" (Bate 2008), of a lost play; prologue; "divided into five acts, the divisions being marked by rows of crosses superimposed on or placed above a line drawn across the column"; "we know that there were intervals, and that they were filled with music" (Greg 1931). "[O]ne of the two Plots perfectly preserved" (Greg). It contains a skeletal outline of the play, a list of properties, and the names of some actors, including Richard Burbage, Robert Lee, Richard Darlowe, and "Sam," possibly Samuel Rowley. First edited by Greg 1931.

The Death of Robert, Earl of Huntingdon (2 Robin Hood). Anthony Munday, with additions by Henry Chettle. Acted early 1598 (Meagher 1980) by Lord Admiral Nottingham's Men at the Rose. On 20 February 1598 Henslowe records payment to Munday "upon his seconde parte of the downefall of earlle huntyngton surnamed Roben Hoode"; on 25 February he records payment to Chettle; on 28 February and 8 March he records further expenditures; on 28 March Henslowe records payment "for the licencynge of ii boocke to the m^r of the Revelles called the ii ptes of Robart hoode." Probably performed also at court, Christmas 1598–99: on 18 November 1598 Henslowe records payment to Henry Chettle; another payment to Chettle, 25 November, "for mendinge of Roben hood for the corte." Chettle, "the junior collaborator" with Munday, "probably supplied a prologue and epilogue to compliment the royal audience" (Rutter 1984). As the records suggest, this play and Munday's *Downfall of Robert* dramatize the legend of the folk hero.

SR 1 December 1600; transferred 16 February 1617; 8 March 1620; 4 September 1638. Q 1601 *The Death of Robert, Earl of Huntington, Otherwise Called Robin Hood of Merry Sherwood, with the Lamentable Tragedy of Chaste Matilda, His Fair Maid Marian, Poisoned at Dunmowe by King John*; no author named; description of three dumb shows "revealing three visions of King John and explained by Skelton" (Mehl 1965); Friar Tuck's opening speech serves as prologue; chorus; epilogue; partly divided into numbered scenes at the beginning. Apparently stairs were used for characters to move from the gallery to the main stage: "Bruce descends from the gallery and comes through the door representing the gates to Windsor Castle" (Rhodes 1976). Friar Tuck wins "the approval of the player king, as well as the groundlings who witnessed the play, by a trick dance"; the purpose of the dance is purely entertainment (Wright 1928).

A sequel to *The Downfall of Robert, Earl of Huntingdon*, this play "had compelling topical associations for the English elect: the third Earl of Huntingdon had been, as a candidate for succession to the throne during the 1560s, the hope of many ardent Protestants fearful of Elizabeth's untimely death, and his brothers had served the Puritan cause in Parliament throughout the reign" (Bevington 1968).

Demetrius and Enanthe. See *The Humorous Lieutenant.*

A Description of the Passage of Thomas, Late Earl of Strafford, over the River of Styx, with the Conference betwixt Him, Charon, and William Noy. Richard Overton (Wolfe 1958). A play-pamphlet in the form of a dialogue, published May 1641.

Q 1641 no author named; not divided. "The attack is on the riches of a Church which exploits the poor; the spending of ordinary people's money on 'trinkets' and frivolities of ceremony; the luxurious life-style of bishops, who live like lords and eat like gluttons; above all the persecution not only of Prynne, Burton and Bastwick but of all manner of ordinary men and women" (Heinemann 1980).

"Strafford is presented confessing his own overreaching to the expectantly waiting William Noye, the former Attorney General, who had died in 1634" (Randall 1995). The TP features the woodcut of a man being rowed across the river Styx.

The Deserving Favorite. Lodowick Carlell. Probably acted *c.* 1628 (Kathman 2005). "Lately acted" by the King's Men at Whitehall before King Charles and, later, at the [second] Blackfriars "with great applause," according to the Q TP; "this is a reversal of the usual order" (Bentley 1984). The actors, whose names in Q appear next to the roles they played, were Robert Benfield who played the King; Joseph Taylor, the Duke; John Lowin, Iacomo; Richard Sharp, Lysander; Eilert Swanston, Count Utrante; Richard Robinson, Count Orsinio and the Hermit; Anthony Smith, Gerard; John Honeyman, Clarinda; John Thompson, Cleonarda; Edward Horton, Mariana. Unnamed actors played "Jaspero, Bernardo, Servants, Huntsmen, &c." "This small cast of six or seven sharers . . . and three boys is not enough to produce the play" (Bentley).

SR no original; transferred 7 March 1653. Q 1629 *The Deserving Favorite*; RT *The Favorite*; list of characters; prologue for king and epilogue; five acts. Staging calls for an imagined nighttime setting: "*Enter Clarinda, and Lysander, (as in an arbour) in the night.*" O 1659 *The Deserving Favorite, A Tragicomedy*; dramatis personae. The epilogue would later appear in *Love's Cure*, published in B&F F1 1647 *Comedies and Tragedies*.

The Q dedication suggests that Carlell disdained to write for the theatergoing public: "this play, which know at first was not design'd to travell so farre as the common stage, is now prest for a greater journey, almost without my knowledge." "Huntsman to Charles I, and later Keeper of the Royal Park at Richmond," Carlell was an amateur dramatist, despite the number of plays he wrote (Bentley 1971). He was also "a particular favourite of the Queen" (Veevers 1989). The prologue, spoken before the king, shapes the expectations of playgoers: "Doe not expect strong lines, nor mirth, though they / Justly the towne-wits, and the vulgar sway: / What hope have we then that our play can please / This more judicious presence, wanting these?"

The Device called The World Tossed at Tennis. See *The World Tossed at Tennis.*

The Devil and His Dam. See *Grim the Collier of Croydon.*

The Devil is an Ass, A Comedy. Ben Jonson. Acted November-December 1616 (Happé 1994). By the King's Men, according to the TP, at the second Blackfriars; the prologue's reference to "grandees" designates "gallants customarily occupying stools on stage at the private theatres, including the Blackfriars" (Happé); "the stage sweeper by way of Prologue requires those spectators wealthy enough to sit onstage for the performance not to take up so much room with their fine clothes and antics" (Cave 1999). Richard Robinson "may have played Merecraft, the young hero" (Gurr 2004c); "Jonson singled him out for special praise as a female impersonator in the text" of the play (Bentley 1984). Wittipoll "was originally played by Richard Robinson"; later "Wittipoll/Robinson appears dressed as the Spanish Lady" (White 1998). "Perhaps because [the play] gave offence to someone at Court on its first performance in 1616 it may have been withdrawn or suppressed almost immediately" (Happé).

SR no original; 17 September 1658; 20 November 1658; 19 August 1667. "By 1631 [Jonson] had prepared and partially supervised what he must have thought of as Volume Two of his *Works*, comprising *Bartholomew Fair*, *The Staple of News* and *The Devil is an Ass*. His quarrel with John Beale, the printer, and John Allot, the bookseller or publisher, caused the suspension of the project even though Jonson may have intended to add other works to it. Though these plays were undoubtedly printed by 1631, they were not released, and they became part of a complex trade dispute" (Happé 2000). *The Devil Is an Ass*, *Bartholomew Fair*, and *The Staple of News* "were meant to be bound together in a single volume" (Riggs 1989). Printed 1631 for the abortive Folio but "remained unissued" (Butler 2010) and included as "The Second Volume" of F2 1640–41 *The Works*; two issues; "acted in the yeare, 1616"; list of characters; prologue and epilogue; SDs mostly printed in the margins; five acts and separate scenes. Staging calls for action above "when Wittipol in Act 2 courts Frances Fitzdottrel through the window of his friend Manly's upper chamber which fronts the Fitzdottrel's house across, we are to suppose, a narrow street" (Cave 1999). "Windows specified for the wooing in II.vi and vii could have been an adaptation of the musicians' gallery" (Happé). "[U]nique and probably fictional" SD (Dessen & Thomson 1999), printed as a marginal gloss describing Wittipol and Fitzdottrel's wife: "*He growes more familiar in his court-ship. Plaies with her paps, kisseth her hands, etc.*" "Satan's introduction, or the subsequent entry of the Vice in the first scene, could have used the mid-stage trap" (Happé). The 1669 reissue gives an alternate title: *The Devil is an Ass, or The Cheater Cheated*.

Jonson's play "is a reworking of the Elizabethan devil play" (Donovan 1987), and the F2 prologue alludes to such plays as *The Merry Devil of Edmonton*: "If you'll come / To see new plaies, pray you affoord us roome, / And shew this, but the same face you have done / Your deare delight, the *Divell of Edmunton*. / Or, if, for want of roome it must mis-carry, / 'Twill be but justice, that your censure tarry, / Till you give some. And when six times you ha'seen't, / If this play doe not like, the divell is in't." These last words allude to Dekker's *If This Be Not a Good Play, the Devil Is in It*. "The connection between the devil and the theatre is . . . exploited in *The Devil is an Ass* where we have a feigned possession" (Sanders 1998b). Jonson "shows that people are so bad there is no need for devils: hell is a grammar-school compared to London" (Heinemann 1992). The play's title is proverbial (Hornback 2009b).

The Devil's Charter, A Tragedy Containing the Life and Death of Pope Alexander the Sixth. Barnaby Barnes. "Plaide" by the King's Men at court, before the king, the night of 2 February 1607 (Candlemas), according to the TP. Acted 1606–07 (Pogue 1980) at the first Globe. Probably the original performance took place shortly before the plague closing of July-December 1606.

SR 16 October 1607 *The tragedie of Pope Alexander the Sixt.* Q 1607 two issues; "more exactly rev[i]ewed, corrected, and augmented since [staging] by the author for the more pleasure and profit of the reader"; Barnes is not named on the TP but he signs the dedication, which appears in some copies; HT *The Tragedy of Alexander the Sixth*; prologue; induction with Guicciardini, who explains the dumb show, "closes the play, and appears at the end of each act as commentator" (Gossett 2004b); he *"mooveth the ayre three times"* with a silver rod; this brings onstage Roderigo with two other cardinals, one of whom guides him to a tent *"where a table is furnished with divers bagges of money"*; the other cardinal leads him to a second tent *"where he delivereth him a great quantity of rich plate"*; epilogue; five acts and separate scenes. "An unusual profusion of elaborately descriptive stage directions" (Jewkes 1958): "the seductively evil Lucretia Borgia is sent a poisonous cosmetic lotion by one of her lovers. As she applies it in front of a mirror, she sees and feels the corrosive ointment eat into and disfigure her face. Like a morality figure, she recognizes in her hideously altered face a reflection of her true moral nature" (Twycross & Carpenter 2002). The pope murders two boys when he *"draweth out of his boxes aspiks"*; *"He putteth to either of their brests an aspike."* Special effects include the conjuration of a devil, who appears amid *"exhalations of lightning and sulphurous smoke."* In an elaborate dumb show a devil ascends in the garb of the pope: *"another divill in robes pontificall with a triple crowne on his head, and cross keyes in his hand"*; *"he bringeth the ghost of* Candie *gastly haunted by* Caesar *persuing and stabing it."* SDs indicate various ascents and descents, presumably through a trap: *"Fiery exhalations, lightning thunder ascend a devil like a king, with a red face crowned imperiall riding upon a lyon, or dragon"*; *"The divell descendeth with thunder and lightning and after more exhalations ascends another all in armor"*; at the conclusion devils *"thrust him* [Alexander] *downe"* into hell. Staging requires the use of a "discovery-space six times for different tableaux" (Gurr 2009d).

This play and Dekker's *Whore of Babylon* "are fierce, even bigoted reactions to Gunpowder Plot—with angels on one side, devils on the other, and a clear (if today unacceptable) immediate political conclusion to be drawn by the audience" (Heinemann 2003). "The play is a rabidly anti-papist cross between *Dr Faustus* and *The Revenger's Tragedy*, perhaps calculated to speak to anti-Catholic feeling in the wake of the Gunpowder Plot" (Dutton 2009a). *The Devil's Charter*, a play about magic, also "seem[s] to have been prompted by *Macbeth*" (Orgel 2011).

The Devil's Law Case, or When Women Go to Law, the Devil is Full of Business, A New Tragicomedy. John Webster. Acted *c.* 1618 and "no later than February 1619"

(Gunby et al. 2003). "Approovedly well acted by" Queen Anne's Men, according to the TP, probably at the Phoenix (Gunby 2004), but the play "could also have been performed in any known playhouse of the period" (Carnegie 2003a). Richard Perkins may first have played the role of Romelio (*JCS*).

SR none. Q 1623 "the true and perfect copie from the originall"; list of characters; five acts and first scenes. Detailed SDs: *"A table set forth with two tapers, a deaths head, a booke, Iolenta in mourning, Romelio sits by her"*; *"Enter Leonora with two coffins borne by her servants, and two winding-sheets stucke with flowers, presents one to her sonne, and the other to Julio"*; *"Enter Crispiano like a judge, with another judge, Contilupo, and another lawyer at one barre, Romelio, Ariosto, at another, Leonora with a blacke vaile over her, and Julio."* Staging calls for *"The lists set up."*

In his address to the reader Webster pays tribute to the actors: "A great part of the grace of this (I confesse) lay in action; yet can no action ever be gracious, where the decency of the language, and ingenious structure of the scæne, arrive not to make up a perfect harmony." "Webster's apology for the play's appearance in print reveals a double-edged attitude — neither anti-theatrical nor hostile to print, blind to the virtues of neither medium" (Erne 2003a).

A Dialogue between Policy and Piety. Robert Davenport. A short "religious-political dialogue" about Irish matters, probably written 1634–35 (Tricomi 1991). "Composed neither for publication nor for dramatic performance, it nevertheless displays the features of staging that would be required for theatrical presentation. These include dialogue (albeit rather stiff), directions for entrances and exits, and descriptions of characters and costumes" (Tricomi).

Washington, Folger, MS V.a.315, 3 fols. and two additional half-sheets; no separate TP; in author's hand; author signs dedication; description of both Policy and Piety at the beginning (color of garment, facial expression, demeanor); substantial description of Hibernia upon entrance; not divided. Detailed description in the SDs: *"Hibernia passes by. ffayre is her hayre, / Lively, and comely is her fface. Her hand / white, and of gentile shape. Bigg-breasted, and / of goodly stature. Her Large Mantle, red, / and frindg'd with greene. . . ."* Attention to spectacle and symbol in the manner of a masque. First edited by Tricomi.

A Dialogue on Wit and Folly. See *Witty and Witless*.

A Dialogue or Accidental Discourse betwixt Mr. Alderman Abell and Richard Kilvert, the Two Main Projectors for Wine. Anonymous. A play-pamphlet possibly performed, venue unknown.

SR none. Q 1641 no author named; not divided. The TP woodcut depicts two well-dressed men, one of whom bears a "pattent for wine" in his hand. At the end of *A Dialogue* another woodcut depicts a man riding backward on a horse as part of a procession; men with pikes behold the spectacle.

This belongs to a group of play-pamphlets "in which ecclesiastical officials, lazy priests and monopolists lament the decay of their fortunes" (Butler 1984a).

Dick of Devonshire, A Tragicomedy. Anonymous; "probably by Heywood" (Heinemann 1993a). ?Acted summer 1626 (McManaway 1955) at undetermined venue. SDs suggest that the play "was used in the theater" (Hoenselaars 1992a), but there is no record of performance.

London, BL, Egerton MS 1994, fols. 30–51; *The Play of Dick of Devonshire, A Tragicomedy*; "apparently in the hand of a playhouse scribe" (McManaway); no author named; dramatis personae; five acts and separate scenes. SDs "are fairly frequent and full, but not distinctively theatrical" (Greg 1931). "The chief interest of the play . . . centers in the skill of weapon displayed by Dick Pike, about whose fencing the action of the play is built" (Wright 1968). The appearance of a ravished woman is indicated in a SD: Eleanor enters "*loose haired, and weeping.*" SR none. First edited by Bullen, *A Collection of Old English Plays*, vol. 2 (1883).

Bullen 1883, Clark 1931, Boas 1950b, and *JCS* conjecture Thomas Heywood's authorship. However, McManaway 1955 suggests Robert Davenport.

Dido, Queen of Carthage. Christopher Marlowe and Thomas Nashe (both named in Kirkman's catalogue). "The first part of *Dido* was generally composed by Christopher Marlowe," and the rest of the play was written by Thomas Nashe (Merriam 2000). *Dido* "is generally thought to have been written at Cambridge"; "it is possible *Dido* was some kind of spin-off from a college production" (Nicholl 2004a). Acted 1585–86 (Oliver 1968). "Played by" the Children of the Queen's Chapel, according to the TP, at undetermined venue, perhaps in East Anglia in May 1587 (Nicholl). *Dido* "is recorded as being acted at Norwich and Ipswich" (Hopkins 2005a). "[A]lmost certainly the only play that Marlowe wrote for a boy company" (Gurr 2004a). "*Dido* would presumably have been written especially for performance in a 'private' indoor theatre, such as the first Blackfriars, or at Court" (Oliver). An entry in Henslowe's *Diary* may indicate performance of this play by the Lord Admiral's Men, 8 January 1598; this entry, "lent unto the company when they fyrst played dido at nyght," may designate a nighttime performance (Graves 1999). "The performance at night must indicate a special winter showing, possibly at court" (Gurr 2004a). Henslowe records payment for costuming in "the playe of dido & eneus," 3 January 1598. An inventory of properties belonging to the Admiral's Men, 10 March 1598, includes "Cupedes bowe, & quiver," "Dides robe," and "j tome of Dido," but this last item "would not belong to Marlowe's play" (Gurr). If Henslowe refers to the play by Marlowe and Nashe, then the auspices of production had changed from a boys' company in a private theater to a men's troupe in a public theater. "[Henry] Herbert's office-book records the licensing of a play for the 'Queen's Company' in 1639 called *Dido and Aeneas*, which perhaps can be identified with" Marlowe and Nashe's play (Lloyd 2005); Herbert's notation, however, contains only the title and date (Bawcutt 1996).

SR no original; transferred 9 February 1596; 26 June 1600 (this entry is "presumably the play" [Greg 1939]). Q 1594 *The Tragedy of Dido, Queen of Carthage*; both authors named on the TP, which also gives a list of characters; five acts. "There may have been a second edition, containing an elegy on Marlowe by Nashe, of which no copies now survive" (Hopkins 2005a). "The technique of opening a play with a striking moment that initiates a visual and verbal pattern of thematic significance is a hallmark of Marlowe's stagecraft" (Thomson 2005): "*Here the curtaines draw, there is discovered* Jupiter *dandling* Ganimed *upon his knee, and* Mercury *lying asleepe*"; here "the goddess of Love interrupts mutual homoerotic fondling between Jupiter and Ganymede" (Bowers 2002). Jupiter and Ganymede emerge "as the very types of sexual desire—amusing and seductive, but ultimately pernicious to social duty" (Smith 1991b). "The term 'ganymede' had become the commonest slang term for a young man who was the minion of an older male" (MacDonald 1999). Dido's palace, on one side of the stage, "may well be represented only by the portraits of Dido's suitors, which hang in full view" (Smith 1977). Special effects include "*the storme*"; "[t]here seems no reason to doubt that Marlowe intended an elaborate spectacle" (Smith). During the storm Dido and Aeneas enter and exit a "cave" (possibly by going into and out of a stage "house," made of canvas) or entering a discovery space in the tiring-house opening. Another "mansion" may have represented Olympus, and still another "would represent the gates or, more probably, the walls of the city of Carthage" (Oliver). "Dido instructs her lords to bring her the sails and tackling from his ship, to prevent his breaking his word and obeying the warnings of the god. The confiscated ropes, sails, and oars are brought to her on the stage," and she finds herself tangled in the gear (Powell 1964). Aeneas' desertion of Dido arises out of his quest to found a new Troy: "*Enter Aeneas with a paper in his hand, drawing the platforme of the citie*": "Here will Aeneas build a statelier Troy." A despondent Dido kills herself by jumping into flames, located probably in the trap: "Dido in these flames / Hath burnt her selfe." "[N]ot one but three people [Dido, Iarbus and Anna] cast themselves into a fire" (Hopkins 2008a). A "wall with a functional gate," to signify the wall of Carthage, may bisect the stage; it would run "from the front of the acting area to the back" (Smith 1977).

"The earliest known collaborated play by professional authors" (Lawrence 1927), this is "one of the very few plays of the period to have an eponymous heroine" (Hopkins 2008a). "For an Elizabethan audience, it would have been obvious that the character of Dido could be seen as reflecting on the real-life Elizabeth" (Hopkins).

Ding Dong, or Sir Pitiful Parliament on his Death Bed, His Pulses Felt by Doctor King, and His Water Cast by Doctor Bishop. Mercurius Melancholicus. A royalist play-pamphlet in form of a dialogue.

SR none. Q 1648 induction (prologue) and epitaph (epilogue); not divided. The Last Will and Testament of Sir Pitiful Parliament begins: "In the name of Lucifer, Amen."

"*Ding Dong* depicts Sir Pitifull in bed, wasted 'with a *Scotch* Feaver' and shaken by a '*Welch* Ague' . . . with Sir Ralph Rebellion holding his head. Parliament confesses his wrongs, explains that '*Machiavill* was my master'" (Randall 1995).

Diphilo and Granida. Anonymous. A droll performed in the 1640s and 50s. "This piece has the smallest cast (two characters) and the simplest plot of any of the drolls" (Elson 1932). Kirkman on the TP of *2 The Wits* says that the drolls were "written I know not when, by several persons, I know not who"; however, his preface reports that Robert Cox "was not only the principal actor, but also the contriver and author of most of these farces." Kirkman's attribution is "probable" (Holland 2007).

Published in *2 The Wits, or Sport upon Sport* (Q and O 1673), which gives as venues of performance fairs, halls, taverns, and "mountebancks stages at Charing Cross, Lincolns-Inn-Fields, and other places"; list of characters.

The Discontented Colonel. See *Brennoralt.*

The Discreet Lover. See *The Fool would be a Favorite.*

The Disease of the House, or The State Mountebank, Administering Physic to a Sick Parliament, with the Merry Conceits of John Capon, His Antidotes, Plasters, and Salves to Cure Rebellion. Anonymous. Acted 1640s, possibly at the Red Bull (Clare 2002). "A short prose drama with a verse prologue and epilogue" (Clare 2004).

SR none. Q 1649 "dated by George Thomason August 21" (Rollins 1921); no author named; verse "prologue on the stage" by John Capon ("a generic name like that of Jack Pudding" [Clare 2004]) and epilogue (also by Capon); not divided. A very short entertainment in prose with scanty SDs.

"One of the most remarkable playlets of the period" (Rollins), the drama "presents a French quack who is to administer physic to 'Madame le Parlament' . . . but who at the close admits, 'begar, me have no *Cure* . . . ; this be dying Nation, lost, lost, begar utterly lost'" (Randall 1995). The tone of the royalist polemic is epitomized by the epilogue: "May pox and plague, and Egypts Furyes cease / On all their bodies, and some worse disease / Hunt their red souls, and their high pride fling down, / That murder'd Charles and trampl'd on his crown."

The Disloyal Favorite, or The Tragedy of Metellus. Anonymous. ?Acted at undetermined venue. "[R]eferences to the horrors of civil war and a scene in which quarreling citizens argue about who contributes most to the 'commonwealthe' suggest sometime after 1649" (Aggeler 1978). Although the play is ostensibly set in Egypt, "our minds can hardly help turning to England. An ignorant rabble comes in to shout that the King is guilty of 'perfect arbitrary government' — 'tis very tyrannically done, tyrannically done,' cries one" (Randall 1995).

Oxford, Bodleian, MS Rawlinson D.1361, fols. 285–305; no separate TP; no author named; the first leaf is seriously damaged; five acts. Ample SDs: "*Enter a priest with a bell ringing, sings . . . King Metellus & other attendants passing over the stage, priests bearing some ridiculous creature before them which they call gods.*"

"[T]he author may have been a Presbyterian, perhaps one of those who turned Royalist during the second civil war and who, as a result of this war, were more than ever hostile to the champions of toleration, the Independents" (Aggeler).

The Disobedient Child. Thomas Ingelend; the TP describes the author as "late student in Cambridge." Acted *c.* 1550 (*DTRB* 1984) or 1560s (Potter 2008). "The use of music and the obsessive interest in schooling and punishment suggest a school play" (Walker 1998), "most likely a provincial boarding school" (Potter); the "lesson it would teach is prudence and obedience" (Thompson 1910). Probably performed "by pupils of provincial grammar schools rather than by the London schoolboy and chorister troupes who brought plays to court each Christmas" (Shapiro 1977). "An epilogue (evidently added later) indicates a performance in the presence of Queen Elizabeth, but an allusion earlier in the text to a reigning king suggests that it may have been composed during the reign of Edward VI" (Beadle 2004).

London, BL, Egerton [fragmentary] MS 2623, fols. 35–36, 43 (prologue), and 44 (epilogue). SR 1569–70 (Chambers 1923). Q ND ?early 1560s (Norland 1995); *A Pretty and Merry New Interlude Called the Disobedient Child*; "compiled by" Thomas Ingelend; list of characters; prologue ("first eight lines are also found in the interlude introduced into the play of Sir Thomas More" [Halliwell 1848a]); "the word 'king' is retained in one part of the epilogue so as not to spoil the rhyme scheme, while the last 20 lines are a prayer to Elizabeth" (Schneider 2011); speech by Perorator at the close, verses by each of the players, and a song; not divided. The SDs mostly take the form of entrances and exits. "The last play printed exclusively in black letter" (Howard-Hill 1990a). Edward Dering's collection of playbooks in the early seventeenth century apparently contained a copy of *The Disobedient Child* (Lennam 1965).

The play represents "one of the more carefully considered portrayals of fatherhood in sixteenth-century comedy"; it "rejects the Terentian comic *senex* figure, as it does the humanist ideal of the wise and firm father, portraying instead a figure of pathos, naïveté, and just as prone to the misguided expressions of love for his child more usually attributed to mothers" (Potter 2008).

The Disputation of Nobleness. See *Fulgens and Lucrece.*

The Distracted Emperor. See *Charlemagne.*

The Distracted State, A Tragedy. John Tatham. ?Written and acted 1650 (Wallace 1960) at undetermined venue. Although the TP asserts that the play was written in 1641, there is no evidence to confirm this claim and no evidence that the play was performed before the closing of the theaters. In fact, the play may not have been written much before publication in 1651 (Wiseman 1998a). The 1641 TP date "may well be a ruse to distract attention from the evident contemporary relevance of its royalist story" (Salmon 2004).

SR 23 November 1650. Q 1651 "written in the yeer, 1641"; author's initials on the TP, Tatham signs the dedication, and Winstanley 1687 assigns the play to him, as does Langbaine 1691 and the SR entry; list of characters; five acts and first scenes. Ample SDs: "Mazares *ascends the chaire of state, the Archbishop puts the crown on's head; then, all, but* Agathocles, *cry long live* Mazares *lawfully king of Sicily*"; "*They throw a silk bag over her* [Harmonia], *shee strives with them, they stop her mouth with a glove, and bind her hands and feet.*" Onstage violence fills the play: "*The head of* Philander *is thrown over the wall*"; Mazares "*Throws himself upon his sword.*" Staging calls for use of a trap: "[Adulanter] *Kils* Harmonia, *and runs to the trap door where he fals and breaks his neck.*" Twelve characters are "killed by different means: one is decapitated, some are killed in hand-to-hand combat, the heroine becomes a prey to the assassin, who in turn meets his death by falling through a trap-door. Neither *Hamlet* nor *Tom Thumb* can equal this" (Maidment & Logan 1879).

The play "is transparently designed to carry political implications" (Wallace). "[O]nce it is seen in the context of the debate as to whether royalists could justifiably swear loyalty to the new Commonwealth, the play becomes a satire on the history of the rebellion" (Potter 1981). "That this play could be boldly printed is an indication of the carelessness of the Parliamentary licensers" (Wright 1934).

The Distresses. William Davenant. Licensed for acting as *The Spanish Lovers* 30 November 1639 (Edmond 1987). Edmond Malone speculated *The Spanish Lovers* and *The Distresses* were the same play (Adams 1917). ?Acted by the King's Men at the second Blackfriars. Possibly performed at the Phoenix (Edmond). In playlist of King's Men 7 August 1641.

SR 4 September 1646; 12 February 1658; transferred 14 October 1672; 30 January 1673. F 1673 *The Works*; "now published out of the authors originall copies"; list of characters; five acts and first scenes. *The Distresses* is printed "in the separately paged and signed section at the end of the Davenant folio" (*JCS*).

Davenant's play adopts the vogue for Platonic love, fashionable at court: "none too virtuous men constantly are reformed by women's superior virtue, and . . . there is much discussion of women's wrongs, their steadfastness, and their superiority to male passions" (Veevers 1989). Charles's court was "notable for the emergence of a feminocentric culture associated with his wife, Henrietta Maria, who brought with her from France codes of polite manners, moral renewal and neoplatonic woman-worship" (Butler 2010).

Doctor Dodypoll. See *The Wisdom of Doctor Dodypoll.*

Doctor Faustus. Christopher Marlowe. Acted "sometime between late 1588 and November 1589" (Wootton 2005) at undetermined venue, perhaps the Belsavage playhouse; a ballad about Doctor Faustus, registered 28 February 1589, "was written after Marlowe's play had been staged" (Jackson 1971). *Faustus* "was probably acted by an unknown company before the worsening plague put an end to London playing in January 1593" (Carson 1988). "We can be fairly sure . . . that *Faustus* was staged at the Theatre before it came to the Rose in 1594" (Gurr 2009c). Performed by the Lord Admiral's Men at the Rose, 1594–97; Henslowe records these 1594 performances: 30 September; 9, 21 October; 5, 20 November; 8, 20, 27 December. In 1595: 9, 24 January; 8 February; 30 April/1 May; 5 June; 11, 26 September. In 1596: 13 February; 19 April; 5 May; 12 June; 3 July; 28 October; 4 November; 17 December. And 5 January 1597. Edward Alleyn played the lead (White 1998). Performed by the combined Admiral's and Pembroke's Men at the Rose, 11–19 October 1597, according to Henslowe. Sixteen actors played forty-five parts (Rutter 1984). Henslowe's inventory of properties, dated 10 March 1598 and surviving in Malone's copy, records "j dragon in fostes" and "the sittie of Rome" for *Faustus*; an inventory of uncertain date, ?1602, includes "Faustus Jerkin his clo[a]k." Presumably revived at the first Fortune by Lord Admiral Nottingham's Men *c.* 22 November 1602, when Henslowe paid Samuel Rowley and William Birde for "adicyones in docter fostes"; Birde and Rowley "must have revised rather extensively" (Bentley 1971). "It is difficult to pinpoint precisely what these 'additions' were, though literary historians commonly assume that they were the comic passages in the middle of Marlowe's play which was preserved in the 1616 text" (Cerasano 2004c). "We do not know whether these were the *only* additions made to the play between Marlowe's death and its appearances in print" (Kastan 2005). Edward Alleyn, "who had retired in 1597, returned to the Fortune for several years and reprised many of his famous roles," including Faustus in 1602 (Knutson 2009a). Alleyn wore cross and surplice; Rowland's *Knave of Clubs* (1609) reports: "The gull gets on a surplus, / With a crosse upon his breast, / Like Allen playing Faustus" (Brown 1964b). Revived by Palsgrave's Men, formerly Prince Henry's Men until his death in 1612, at the first Fortune, *c.* 1619; and by Prince Charles's Men at the second Fortune 1640–42. John Melton in his *Astrologaster* of 1620 explains what attracted playgoers to Marlowe's tragedy at the Fortune: "a man may behold shagge-hayr'd devills runne roaring over the stage with squibs in their mouthes, while drummers make thunder in the tyring-house, and the twelve-penny hirelings make artificiall lightning in their heavens." "From a number of contemporary references to the play, we can tell that it was the special effects that sold this show" (King 2008b). "[Thomas] Middleton tells us that the old theatre 'cracked and frighted the audience.' Presumably the cracking refers to the '*Thunder and lightning*' that accompanies the arrival of Lucifer, Mephistopheles, and other devils to claim Faustus's soul in the final scene of the A-text" (Bevington 2010). *Faustus* "was sometimes paired [in performance] with either the lost 'Wise Man of West Chester' or the also lost 'French Doctor' (e.g. 23 and 24 January 1595, 7 and 8 February 1595)" (Knutson 2009a).

SR 7 January 1601 *the plaie of Doctor Faustus*; transferred 13 September 1610 *The tragicall history of the horrible life and Death of Doctor Ffaustus*; 2 March 1618; 23 February 1626; 27 June 1646; 4 April 1655; 18 April 1666. Q1 1604 *The Tragical History of D. Faustus*; unique copy at Bodleian; this "may not have been the first" edition (Nicholl 2004a); acted by the right honorable the Earle of Nottingham his servants"; "written by Ch. Marl."; choral prologue and epilogue; Wagner, who may have spoken the prologue and epilogue (Gill 1990), summarizes offstage action in a choral role during the play; not divided. A "central 'discovery space'" is needed for Faustus's study (Ichikawa 2002). When Faustus conjures the devil, he immediately commands the ugly figure to "returne and chaunge thy shape"; the Q4 TP shows how the devil may have looked upon first appearance. That TP also "shows a magic circle described on the floor"; "this suggests that the circle was painted on a cloth laid on the stage proper instead of the usual rushes" (Hattaway 1982); "in one hand he holds the necromantic book whose spells have raised the demon that rears in front of him, in the other he clasps his magician's staff of power, thrust forward in a gesture of command as though to hold the menacing creature at bay" (Neill 1988). Unusual staging involves Mephistophilis bringing "*a chafer of coles*" onstage in order to melt Faustus' congealed blood and thus allow him to sign the contract with the devil. Spectacle includes the entry of "*divels, giving crownes and rich apparell to Faustus, and daunce*" when he signs the contract and, later, the elaborately costumed Seven Deadly Sins, summoned to distract Faustus. Other spectacle involves the entry of "*a divell drest like a woman with fireworks*," which were often attached to the costumes of devils and clowns in ways designed to make fun of sexual and excretory functions" (Keefer 2007); Mephistophilis arranges for this devil when Faustus requests a wife. Comic action includes Faustus giving the pope "*a boxe of the eare*"; "*Enter the Knight with a paire of hornes on his head.*" The Clown may have been played by John Adams, who "played with Sussex's Men in 1576, and with The Queen's Men in 1583 and 1588" (Gill 1990). SDs call for Mephistophilis and Faustus to "*Beat the friers, and fling fier-workes among them*"; this effect could have been created by "the straightforward act of throwing fireworks such as squibs, serpents or fiz-gigs" (Butterworth 1998). The appearance of Helen, who "*passeth over the stage*," resembles a dumb show; she does not speak. Helen "would wear face-paint to signify both her role as a tempting paramour and her function as a white devil disguising her true ugliness" (Drew-Bear 1994). Special effects include thunder at certain points and "*thunder and lightning*" at the close; devils swarm the stage. Staging involves dismemberment: "Faustus is the victim of an apparent beheading when Benvolio takes revenge for the horns conjured on his head"; "a cozened horse-courser inadvertently pulls off Faustus's leg while trying to wake him" (Owens

2005). Sound effects include the striking of a clock at the play's climax. Q2 1609 *The Tragical History of the Horrible Life and Death of Doctor Faustus*; with this edition "the *D.* was expanded to *Doctor*" (Bland 1998); "written by Ch. Marl." Q3 [octavo-in-fours] 1611 unique copy at Huntington.

Q4 1616 *The Tragical History of the Life and Death of Doctor Faustus*; incorporates "those revisions advertised on the 1619 title page" (Bentley 1971); "magic apparition, conjured up by Faustus (Alexander and Darius)" (Mehl 1965); Pettit 1988 calls this a dumb show. "The exploitation of new stage machinery takes the form of a descent from the 'heavens' [in Q4] of the heavenly throne" (Bevington 2002b): "*Musicke while the throne descends*"; this SD "hints at the slow operation of the lifting machine" (Booth 2007). This staging may "be safely said to have been inserted after Henslowe installed the throne in his heavens at the Rose in 1595" (Wickham 1979); the throne "was almost certainly not scripted by Marlowe" (Dillon 2004a). In the play's final action Lucifer and the other devils "ascend" from hell and "[p]robably they enter above" (Bevington 2007a), "so that they look down upon Faustus and the audience . . . and seem to guide the action" (Styan 1996). "This is an amazing difference in staging from that of the A-text, where, in 5.2, Faustus is alone after the departure of his fellow scholars until the devils arrive right at the end" (Bevington 2007a). When the Good Angel departs for the last time, "*Hell is discovered*," "presumably by the dropping or parting of a curtain that has concealed a 'discovery space' in the tiring house wall" (Bevington 2007a). This evoked the medieval hellmouth; an inventory in Henslowe's *Diary* lists "j Hell mought." Grotesque staging involves the "discovery of Faustus's limbs after he has been carried off by devils" (Owens 2005): "see, here are Faustus limbs, / All torne asunder." Other changes include the deletion of lines, rearrangement of speeches, creation of new scenes out of existing text, and the writing of wholly new scenes (Knutson 1985). Q5 1619 "with new additions"; these words "presumably refer to those which appeared" in 1616 (Greg 1939). Q6 1620. Q7 1624. Q8 1628. Q9 1631. Q10 1633 list of characters. Despite the use of a trap for entrances of Mephistophilis in some modern revivals, "in none of Marlowe's plays do any stage-directions exist authorizing us to assume the existence of a stage-trap at floor level" (Wickham 1964).

Q1–3 represent the so-called A-text, which "derives from provincial performance" (Hattaway 2000b) and "is some 676 lines shorter than the B-text" (King 2008b). Q4–10 represent the B-text, which "derives from performances in a fully equipped London playhouse" (Hattaway). "The B-text makes more spectacular use of the stage than does the A-text" (Bevington & Rasmussen 1993) and is characterized by "greater emphasis on violent spectacle" (Owens 2005). For example, "Faustus is the victim of an apparent beheading when Benvolio takes revenge for the horns conjured on his head" (Owens 1996). The B-text additions "are pretty uniformly in the direction of augmenting the play's notorious scare factor, delighting in 'black magical' stunts" (Bevington 2010). The B-text, which omits several dozen lines that appear in A, was apparently prepared chiefly from a theatrical manuscript, including the revisions presumably made in 1602 by Rowley and Birde, as well as numerous further playhouse alterations before 1616; it "contains extensions to the satirical anti-catholic material" and "a greatly expanded version of the incident in which Faustus places horns on the head of a knight at the court of the Holy Roman Emperor" (King 2008b). "The A-text knows nothing of Bruno the antipope either at the papal or at the imperial court; it knows nothing of the plan of revenge by the injured knight and his friends or of its frustration by Faustus; and it is equally ignorant of the conspiracy by the Horse-courser and his associates and of their humiliation at Vanholt" (Jump 1962). Elements of the A-text present in the 1616 edition indicate the printers' reliance on a 1611 copy of the earlier quarto. "[A]t about a dozen . . . points where the A text implies that Faustus's fate is due to powers beyond his control, the B text makes alterations that put the blame on his own willful perversity, thereby turning a play that in its original version insistently interrogated the Calvinist orthodoxy of Elizabethan England into something at once tamer and more homiletic" (Keefer 2007). "Marlowe was working with a collaborator, perhaps Henry Porter" (Wootton); the comic scenes may be the work of Porter (Rasmussen 1993). But Gill 1990 theorizes that the comic scenes may be owing to improvisations by the actor John Adams, perhaps a member of the Admiral's Men in the early 1590s, though Nungezer 1929 assigns him to Sussex's and the Queen's Men. The Q TPs, beginning in 1616, feature a woodcut of Doctor Faustus in his study; this may represent the character as he appeared onstage. If so, a "window" was represented in the tiring-house wall. Q10 uses a different woodcut.

The Doctors of Dullhead College. A droll based upon scenes in B&F's *Monsieur Thomas* and performed in the 1640s and 50s. "The title presumably puns on the name of Dulwich College, founded by Edward Alleyn, the Elizabethan actor, and seems an imaginative flourish of the droll-maker, for the doctors are not described as attached to any college"; "seven or eight actors are required" (Elson 1932).
　　Published in *1 The Wits, or Sport upon Sport* (O 1662 [two issues] and 1672); argument. *The Wits* erroneously locates the source in *Father's Own Son.*

Don Horatio, or The Spanish Comedy. Possibly the play known as *1 Hieronimo.*

Don Phoebo's Triumph. Mildmay Fane. Written 1645 and probably performed by members of Fane's family and friends at Apethorpe, Northamptonshire (Smith 1988b). "[A]n elaborate masque-like show" (*JCS*).
　　San Marino, CA, Huntington, MS HM 770, fols. 1–9; no separate TP; no author named; in Fane's hand with his corrections; the date 1645 is written at the beginning of the MS but in a different ink; dramatis personae with the names of family and friends who played the roles; the opening song serves as prologue; a song closes the play; five acts. SDs specify use of a front curtain, which closes at the end of each act. Elaborate SDs: "*The first scene—Don Phoebo sitting in a*

chaire hemisphericall stuck full of sises one either side the names of 6 monthes, above
wch scrowle, the names of the 12 signes, wth that perpendiculer & just over his chaire in
wch he is at the time—& over them the windes in an other scrowle — all wch by degrees
is discoverd wth the drawing of a curtaine, wch must be imagined a clowde, the musick
playing softly." The SD "*A rainbow rises & it raynes*" suggests "that his theatre [at
Apethorpe] included a pulley mechanism" (Morton 1991).

"Fane [second earl of Westmoreland] is celebrating the monarchy and point-
ing up his belief that the state could be ordered only when a strong king sat on
the uncontested throne of the realm" (Morton).

Double Falsehood, or The Distressed Lovers. Performed 13 December 1727
and published by Lewis Theobald, who claimed that he had adapted a MS by
Shakespeare: "There is a tradition (which I have from the noble person, who
supply'd me with one of my copies) that it was given by our author, as a present
of value, to a natural daughter of his, for whose sake he wrote it, in the time of
his retirement from the stage" (Theobald 1728). The MS may have been Shakespeare's lost play, *The History of Cardenio*, performed at the Globe and Blackfriars
(McDonald 2003). *Cardenio* was performed before "'the prince,' Lady Elizabeth
and the Elector Palatine" (Hammond 2010) at Greenwich in spring 1613 (payment to John Heminges dated 20 May), and again "in a special presentation for
the benefit of the Duke of Savoy's ambassador on 8 June 1613" (Bate 2008); payment to Heminges 9 July 1613. Entered in the SR as "*The history of Cardenio*, by
Mr Fletcher & Shakespeare," 9 September 1653, but no publication ensued. A
MS of *Cardenio* "was still extant in the 1650s" (Dobson 2001) and possibly even
in the eighteenth century, for "in the preface to the first edition of the play, published early in 1728, Theobald claimed to own three manuscript copies of the
original play by Shakespeare" (Hammond 1984). The plot of *Double Falsehood* "is
a version of the story of Cardenio found in Miguel de Cervantes' *Don Quixote*
(1605) as translated by Thomas Shelton, published in 1612 though in circulation
earlier" (Hammond 2010). Theobald may have worked from a Restoration adaptation of the original play (Freehafer 1969a, Hammond 1984).

Freehafer contends that *Cardenio* "was written by Shakespeare and Fletcher
. . . [then] cut and perhaps altered during the Restoration period, then altered by
Theobald." Metz 1989 assigns Shakespeare a lesser role: "*Double Falsehood* is mainly Theobald, or Theobald and an earlier adapter, with a substantial admixture of
Fletcher and a modicum of Shakespeare." Hope 1994 suggests, "The early parts of
Double Falsehood . . . are those with most evidence for Shakespeare's presence." Pujante sees a broader connection with the later Shakespeare: "*Double Falsehood* develops like a tragicomedy comparable to Shakespeare's last plays, and fits tantalizingly into the pattern of betrayal or disloyalty, spousal contracts, marriage and final
reconciliation that can be found in these works." But Kahan 2007 demurs: "Pujante
wants to define the 'Shakespearean' by his own metaphysical ideal, a completed

and corrected construction that is no more based in objective 'fact' than the supposedly incomplete and incorrect mistaken ideal he criticizes."

Fleissner 1996 questions a Shakespeare connection: "no cogent evidence has yet been summoned, even stylometrically, to substantiate Shakespeare's having had really anything to do with the original drama or Theobald's supposed redaction." Stern 2011 is similarly skeptical: "Whatever Theobald had, he would have overlaid it with his imitations in the style of Shakespeare; these, combined with his native Fletcherisms and his use of [the Cervantes translator Thomas] Shelton, makes designating authorship in the text-behind-the-text more perilous than has been thought—especially as *Cardenio* may not even have been cowritten by Shakespeare."

The Double Marriage. John Fletcher and Philip Massinger (Hoy 1985). Acted ?1621 (E&G 1976) or 1619–23 (Gurr 2009d) by the King's Men at the second Blackfriars/second Globe. Principal actors were Joseph Taylor, Robert Benfield, John Underwood, George Birch, John Lowin, Richard Robinson, Nicholas Tooley, and Richard Sharp, according to F2. In playlist of the King's Men 7 August 1641.

SR 4 September 1646; 30 January 1673. B&F F1 1647 *Comedies and Tragedies*; "never printed before, and now published by the authours originall copies"; five acts and first scenes. "F1's stage-directions are a mixture of specific instruction (especially where off-stage sounds are concerned), descriptive detail, and permissiveness" (Hoy 1994): "*Charge, trumpets, pieces goe off. Enter Master, Boatswaine following.*" Sound creates an odd effect: "*Strange musick within, hoboys . . . Within strange cries, horrid noyse, trumpets.*" This "suggests something eerie and supernatural" (Clark 1994). Staging calls for a torture device: "*Enter Ronvere, guard, executioners with a rack.*" The most unusual staging involves "a ship scene in which the platform [main stage] serves as the main deck, the tarras as the raised quarterdeck, and the music gallery as the main-top or crow's nest" (Smith 1956). B&F F2 1679 *Fifty Comedies and Tragedies*; "published by the authors original copies, the songs to each play being added"; *The Double Marriage, A Tragedy*; list of characters; actors' names.

"In the opening situation" Fletcher and Massinger "depend on *Julius Caesar* for a foreboding mood" (Clark 1992). *The Double Marriage* also "re-presents a series of key moments" from *The Tempest* (McMullan 1994).

The Doubtful Heir, A Tragicomedy. James Shirley. Acted in Ireland as *Rosania, or Love's Victory*, 1 June 1638, by Ogilby's Men at the Werburgh Street theater, Dublin. "[R]ewritten from an earlier play of Shirley, *The Coronation*" (Burner 1988) and licensed for acting in London as *Rosania, or Love's Victory*, 1 June 1640 (Adams 1917). Revised for London production (Gurr 2004c). When Shirley brought the play to England, he intended that performance take place at the Blackfriars, as the TP indicates, but the play was licensed too late in the season and so it was "acted . . . with great applause," according to the general TP of O, by the King's Men at the second Globe in the summer of 1640. The epilogue alludes to Stephen Hammerton, who probably played King Ferdinand. The original title was changed to *The Doubtful Heir* sometime after licensing and before 7 August 1641, when Shirley's drama appeared in the playlist of the King's Men.

SR 4 September 1646; transferred 30 January 1673. O 1652–53 *Six New Plays* (with *The Brothers, The Cardinal, The Court Secret, The Imposture, The Sisters*); "never printed before"; general TP dated 1653, separate 1652; separate register and pagination; list of characters; "new prologue" (Reich 1980) and epilogue by the Captain; five acts. Prologue and epilogue, with changes, had been printed in Shirley's 1646 *Poems*; "same collection contains . . . another prologue 'to his own comedy there [in Ireland] called *Rosania*,'" the alternate title (Greg 1939). Prologue calls attention to the title-board: "the speaker doubtless reversed the title-board, which he had been holding all the time, and showed the sub-title on the other side" (Lawrence 1912b).

The mocking prologue suggests that Shirley meant the play for a more sophisticated audience than would be expected at the Globe: "Our author did not calculate this play / For this meridian; the Banckside, he knows, / Are far more skilfull at the ebbes and flows / Of water, than of wit, he did not mean / For the elevation of your poles [latitudes], this scene. / No shews, no dance, and what you most delight in, / Grave understanders, here's no target fighting / Upon the stage, all work for cutlers barr'd, / No bawdery, nor no ballets; this goes hard; / But language clean; and, what affects you not, / Without impossibilities the plot; / No clown, no squibs, no devill in't; oh now / You squirrels that want nuts, what will you do?" This prologue "could be read as a kind of reverse flattery, assuring the audience of the excellence of their taste in attending a play which offered none of these old-fashioned devices" (McLuskie 1981). The prologue may also be interpreted as "the playwright's willingness to dismiss a substantial swathe of those who had paid to see his play" (Grantley 2000).

The Downfall of Robert, Earl of Huntingdon (*1 Robin Hood*). Anthony Munday, with revisions by Henry Chettle. Licensed for acting 28 March 1598, according to Henslowe, and performed by Lord Admiral Nottingham's Men at the Rose (Meagher 1964). Possibly performed at court, Christmas 1598–99, but "nothing in the text as published in 1601 singles it out as a version performed at court" (Dutton 2009a). Henslowe records payment to Munday, 15 February 1598, "for a playe boocke called the firste parte of Robyne Hoode." On 28 March Henslowe paid "for the licencynge of ii boocke to the m^r of the Revelles called the ii ptes of Robart hoode." On 18 November 1598 Henslowe paid Chettle for "the mendynge of the first pt of Robart hoode." And on 25 November 1598 Henslowe paid Chettle "for mendinge of Roben hood for the corte." Also "acted by" Lord Admiral Nottingham's Men, according to the TP, perhaps at the newly built Fortune theater, 1600–01. Henslowe's 1598 inventory, copied by Malone, lists properties probably for this play: "j green gown for Maryan"; "j hatte for Robin Hoode"; "j shelde, with iij lyones"; "Roben Hoodes sewtte"; and "the fryers trusse in Roben Hoode." As these entries indicate, Munday's play brings Robin Hood to the stage, creating "a historically-oriented biography of a hero whose legend had hitherto been dominated by episodic narratives and folk plays" (Singman 1998).

SR 1 December 1600; transferred 16 February 1617; 8 March 1620; 4 September 1638. Q 1601 *The Downfall of Robert, Earl of Huntington, afterward called Robin Hood of Merry Sherwood, with His Love to Chaste Matilda, the Lord Fitzwater's Daughter, afterwards His Fair Maid Marian*; no author named on TP; elaborate induction involving Sir John Eltham and Skelton (who calls himself the Prologue), along with various players and dumb show "in which the main characters and the action are introduced" (Mehl 1965); epilogue, though not called such, consisting of a colloquy between Eltham and Skelton, "which seems strangely out of place" and may be "intended as induction to the second play [*The Death of Robert*] rather than epilogue for the first" (Shaw 1979); not divided. "There are four particularly problematic sections of the extant text which reveal its incomplete and unfinished nature" (Meagher). Staging calls for considerable use of curtains: characters "*infolde each other, and sit downe within the curteins*"; "*curtaines open, Robin Hoode sleepes on a greene banke, and Marian strewing flowers on him.*" Henslowe's 1598 inventory of properties includes "ij mose banckes." Staging also calls for extensive use of disguise: "seven different characters appear in disguise, some of them in more than one disguise" (Hyland 2011).

In the play's final speech Skelton anticipates a continuation of the story: "Well judging hearers, for a while suspence / Your censures of this plaies unfinisht end: / And Skelton promises for this offence, / The second part shall presently be pend: / There shall you see, as late my friend did note / King Richards revels at earle Roberts bower, / The purpos'd mirth, and the performed mone, / The death of Robin, and his murderers."

The Drinking Academy, or Cheater's Holiday. Thomas Randolph (identified by Day 1928, Bowers 1937–38). "[C]onceivably performed at Cambridge after Randolph's admission to Trinity College on 8 July 1624, but for this there is no evidence" (Nelson 1989); perhaps performed *c.* 1626 (Bowers). Possibly written for performance at Westminster School (Rollins 1924). The play, "at a mere 900 lines, seems unlike any other professionally produced play of the period. It has only seven roles, all male, and shows an absurdly penurious miser, his prodigal son, and foolish servant being rooked by a group of rogues using devices borrowed from Jonsonian comedy. This could come from Randolph's university period, though it might equally well have been devised for the boys" who performed at the Salisbury Court playhouse (Butler 2006). "In June 1660 a play called *The Prodigal Scholar* was entered on the Stationers' Register with an attribution to Randolph; a number of critics think this lost comedy may be identical with *The Drinking Academy*" (Levenson 1987).

San Marino, CA, Huntington, MS HM 91, fols. 2–20; no author named; contains corrections; similarities to *The Jealous Lovers* (Smith 1929); list of characters on the TP; prologue; five acts and separate scenes. Ample SDs: e.g., *"Enter Simple out of the drinking academy with a pipe in on[e] hand and a candle in the other."* Staging may call for use of a trap door: *"Enter Shirke like a ghost with a torch in his hand."*

First edited by Rollins 1924, then by Tannenbaum & Rollins 1930.

The Duchess of Malfi. John Webster. Acted late 1613 or 1614 (Brown 2009). "Presented privatly, at the Blacke-Friers; and publiquely at the Globe" by the King's Men, according to the Q1 TP. "It seems clear that the play was initially given at the Blackfriars theater" (Hammond 1987a). "The new Globe would not have been available until 1614, when it was rebuilt after a fire" (Marcus 2009). In a communiqué dated 7 February 1618, Orazio Busino, a visitor to London, reports having recently seen a play that was probably *The Duchess*. Also performed at the Whitehall Cockpit-in-Court, 26 December 1630 (Brown). "Unique among dramatic quartos of its period," *The Duchess* "gives two partial casts for the play, one for the original production, the other presumably for a revival near the date of publication [1623]" (Hammond). In the first production (before 16 December 1614) John Lowin played Bosola; Richard Burbage, Ferdinand; Henry Condell, the Cardinal; Richard Sharp, the Duchess (but he "could not have played the Duchess in the play's first run, since he did not join the company until 1616" [Marcus]— Richard Robinson, the leading boy-actor of the company, may have originated the role); William Ostler (who died 16 December 1614), Antonio; John Underwood, Delio and a Madman; Nicholas Tooley, Forobosco [a ghost character] and a Madman; Thomas Pollard, Silvio, according to Q1 cast list; the name of Robert Pallant [?the Younger] is bracketed with the roles of the Doctor and Cariola. This may indicate doubling "or the fact that he played Cariola in 1613 (when he was nine years old) and subsequently took over the part of the Doctor at a revival" (Sturgess 1987). (Not all the roles are accounted for; some of the named actors may have played other parts.) Subsequently (i.e., between 13 March 1619 when Burbage died and 1623), John Lowin played Bosola; Joseph Taylor, Ferdinand; Richard Robinson, the Cardinal; Richard Sharp, the Duchess; Robert Benfield, Antonio; John Underwood, Delio and a Madman; Nicholas Tooley, Forobosco [a ghost character] and a Madman; John Rice, Pescara; Thomas Pollard, Silvio; John Thompson, Julia; R[obert] Pallant, Cariola (Kathman 2005), according to the Q1 cast list. "The Q actually brackets Pallant's name with 'The Doctor' and 'Court Officers' as well as Cariola, but since it would have been physically impossible to play all these roles, someone in the printing house probably added the bracket by mistake" (Kathman).

Did the original performance antedate the burning of the Globe on 29 June 1613? If not, as seems likely, then the play was probably first staged at the second

Blackfriars (Carnegie 1995a), a theater especially amenable to Webster's dramaturgy, especially his penchant for scenes set in near darkness.

SR no original; transferred 31 October 1646. Q1 1623 *The Tragedy of The Duchess of Malfi*; "the perfect and exact coppy, with diverse things printed, that the length of the play would not beare in the presentment" (i.e., with the restoration of deletions necessary for performance); during the printing Webster apparently twice corrected the text (Brown); "Q1 exists in one uncorrected and two corrected states (Gibbons 2001); list of characters with the names of the actors; detailed description of a dumb show in which the Cardinal is installed "*in the habit of a soldier*" and the Duchess and her children are banished; five acts and separate scenes. Eerie staging includes the Duchess staring at her face in a mirror while Ferdinand creeps up behind her and gives her a poniard. Bizarre staging includes Bosola's trick to expose the Duchess' pregnancy by a gift of apricots and, later, "the spectacle of Antonio and her children as wax figures, 'appearing as they were dead'" (Zimmerman 2005): "*Here is discover'd, (behind a traverse;) the artificiall figures of* Antonio *and his children*"; the King's Men would have had no need to fashion "waxwork dummies," for "the actors themselves might act them at no cost" (Sturgess 1987). Similarly unsettling is Ferdinand's gift of "*a dead mans hand*" to his sister in the same scene. Even stranger are the dancing madmen who surround the captive Duchess, an incident that emphasizes not "the psychology of her reactions" but rather "the contrast between her solitary stillness and the grotesque caperings which are an image of the tyranny she is 'chain'd to endure'" (Belsey 1980). Horrific staging includes the Duchess being strangled in view of the playgoers. Following her death, Webster stages an echo scene wherein Antonio visits the Duchess' grave and hears his last words repeated; this staging "shows how the Duchess . . . is reduced; the echo is powerless to protect Antonio" (Belsey), who is killed by accident. The Duchess "returns only as admonitory fragments of her husband's speech" (Dolan 2007). But Antonio's words, "on the sudden, a cleare light / Presented me a face folded in sorrow," suggest an unusual lighting effect similar to one "previously used by the King's Men in *The Second Maiden's Tragedy* in 1611 and probably at the Blackfriars" (Brown). (The 1985 National Theatre production brought the Duchess back to the stage as a ghost to repeat Antonio's words though electronically distorted.) Much dramatic action occurs in darkness, and "surprise entrances from secret concealment have become almost the play's trademark, and they are especially associated with Ferdinand" (Gibbons), who succumbs to madness, a victim of lycanthropy. A marginal note next to the song accompanying the dumb show that depicts the Cardinal's arming says, "The author disclaimes this ditty to be his." "Webster, this suggests, entered the printing house while the sheet was being printed, and made the compositors insert his additional note before pulling any more pages" (Stern 2009c). Music for the song sung by a madman in act 4 ("*this song is sung to a dismal kind of musique*") is preserved in (1) New York, New York Public Library, MS Drexel 4175, no. 42; (2) London, BL, Additional MS 29481, fols. 5–6; (3)

New York Public Library, MS Drexel 4041, pt. II, no. 26. The music accompanying the dance of the madmen and the nature of their dance can only be conjectured: *"the daunce, consisting of 8 mad-men, with music answerable thereunto"* (Kiefer 1987). Q2 1640 *The Duchess of Malfi, A Tragedy*; "approvedly well acted" at the Blackfriars; two issues, the second of which features a new TP; this second issue "does not offer a date but must be from some time in the early 1660s" (Marcus), probably 1664 (Hammond & DelVecchio 1995); Q2 was printed "to take advantage of the play's resonance with anti-Laudian and anti-absolutist sentiment" (Marcus). Q3 1678 *The Duchess of Malfi, A Tragedy.*

"[O]nly Webster made a woman/boy actor the ethical and structural centerpiece of a tragedy about sexual obsession" (Zimmerman). Webster's play must have had a special appeal for women, though Middleton's commendatory poem in Q1 asks, "who e're saw this *Dutchesse* live, and dye, / That could get off under a bleeding eye[?]" This would seem to mean that "the entire audience cried" (Levin 1989b). William Rowley's dedicatory poem reports that the Duchess "was lively body'd" in the play; "the apprentice [actor] more than held his own opposite the most prominent shareholders in the company" (Barker 2011). Despite the play's "artistic risks," it is "capable of overwhelming an audience's critical defences" (Wymer 2001).

The Duchess of Suffolk. Thomas Drue, according to Henry Herbert's office-book. Licensed for acting 2 January 1624 (Clare 1999) as *The History of the Duchess of Suffolk.* "Divers and sundry times acted, with good applause," according to the TP, by Palsgrave's Men at the second Fortune (Gurr 2009c), which "probably opened in the spring of 1623" (Bentley 1981), following the fire of December 1621.

SR 13 November 1629. Q 1631 *The Life of the Duchess of Suffolk*; no author named; list of characters; five acts. SDs contain information about hand props: *"Enter Hugh Tiler, and Jenkin going to worke with a tray of tiles and a ladder."* Special effects: *"It snowes, and raines, thunders."* "In outdoor playhouses . . . in addition to 'tempestuous' drums, a 'bullet,' i.e., a cannonball, was 'rolled' along a sheet of metal or a wooden trough [to simulate thunder]" (White 2007).

Herbert records, 2 January 1624, that the play, "being full of dangerous matter was much reformed" (Bawcutt 1996). The play was censored because of its criticism of the Spanish: when Herbert found it "'full of dangerous matter' he briskly set about reforming it and charged twice his usual fee for his pains" (Dutton 1991). Herbert "unmistakably caught the underlying meaning of the play as an open criticism of James I's foreign policy" (Limon 1986). "[D]uring a period when a Catholic alliance had appeared for the first time in seventy years to be a distinct prospect, the play had an obvious topical resonance" (Clare). "The character is based on the historical Duchess of Suffolk, persecuted for her Protestant faith during the reign of Mary Tudor" (Findlay 1999). The Duchess goes "into exile rather than submit to the Catholic restoraton, and [is] shown defending her husband, sword in hand" (Heinemann 2003). Herbert also has a note, 2 July 1624, indicating permission for printing (Bawcutt).

The Duke. See *The Humorous Courtier.*

The Duke of Milan, A Tragedy. Philip Massinger. Acted 1621–22 (E&G 1976). "Often acted by" the King's Men at the [second] Blackfriars, according to the TPs. "No record of the licence for performance has survived" (Gibson 1978).

SR 20 January 1623 *Sforza, Duke of Millaine*; transferred 5 May 1623. Q1 1623 a copy at the Folger and another at the V&A contain corrections/revisions in Massinger's hand (Massai 2007); list of characters; five acts and separate scenes. Massinger takes "the slightly unusual step of dedicating his *Duke of Milan* to a woman [Katherine Stanhope]" (Neill 1978); this dedication would be reprinted in Q2 "even though she had died in 1636" (Bergeron 2006). Staging involves the Duke stabbing his wife in a jealous rage. Her dead body is subsequently painted by the Duke's enemies so that it appears alive. When the Duke kisses the body, he is poisoned (a scene perhaps inspired by *The Revenger's Tragedy*). "By kissing the painted and poisoned face of the woman he has murdered because of jealous lust, the Duke presents a climactic 'speaking shew' of how blind lust destroys" (Drew-Bear 1994). Q2 1638.

"About 1633 Massinger had eight of his previously published plays bound together in a single volume. Possibly he was thinking of publishing a collection of his works; possibly he wanted the volume as a gift to a patron" (Edwards 1987). The Folger owns the collection.

The Duke's Mistress. James Shirley. Licensed for acting 18 January 1636 (Adams 1917). "Presented by" Queen Henrietta Maria's Men at the Phoenix, according to the TP. Performed also at St. James's Palace, 25 February 1636 (Bawcutt 1996), in the Presence Chamber (Astington 1986). Shirley's play dramatizes the Caroline intersection of politics and sex: "a favorite with a blood claim to the throne plots to seize power by exacerbating the political disorder unleashed by his prince's indulgence of heteroerotic desire" (DiGangi 2006).

SR 13 March 1638. Q 1638 three issues; prologue and epilogue (by Horatio); five acts. Fiametta and Horatio kibitz and "enter dancing a coranto: Horatio comments, 'I never met with such a dancing devil.' The dance is followed by a song within" (Wright 1928). An incident recalls the death of Polonius in *Hamlet*: when Valerio "*goes behind the hangings*" to elude detection, Bentivolio enters and "*wounds Valerio behind the hangings.*"

In the prologue Shirley addresses the challenge of appealing to a diverse theatrical audience: "So various are the pallates of our age / That nothing is presented on the stage, / Though nere so square, and apted to the lawes / Of poesy, that can winne full applause. / This likes a story, that a cunning plot, / This wit, that lines, here one, he know's not what. / But after all this looking severall wayes, / We do observe the generall guests to playes, / Meet in opinion of two straines: that please / Satire, and wantonnes, the last of these / Though old, if in new dressing it appeare / Will move a smile from all, but shall not heare. / Our author hath no guilt of scurrile friends. / For satire they do know best what it meanes, / That dare apply, and if a poets pen, / Ayming at generall errors not the men, / 'Tis not his fault, the safest cure is, they / That purge their bosomes, may see any play."

The Dumb Knight, A Historical Comedy. Gervase Markham and Lewis Machin. Performed 1607–July 1608 (Chambers 1923). "Acted sundry times by" the King's Revels Children, according to the Q TP, at the Whitefriars; the Children were "tenants of the Whitefriars theater in 1607 and 1608" (Cathcart 2005). "In 1618 Sir Richard Cholmeley of Brandsby Hall rewarded Lord Wharton's Men for 'one play, the dumb Knight'" (Keenan 2002).

SR 6 October 1608; transferred 19 November 1610. Q1 1608, two reissues the same year, one of which has *A Pleasant Comedy* as the subtitle; Markham is listed as the author in Q1 but not in the cancel title; five acts. Machin signs the address to the reader in which he calls himself "a partner" of the author. Most SDs "are long, descriptive" (Jewkes 1958): "*Enter the Queene, Mariana, and waiting women, Philocles and other lords, the King disguised like one of the guard at the one end of the stage, and the Duke so likewise disguised at the other end of the stage.*" Staging calls for a staircase: "those stairs direct you to his lodging" (Lawrence 1927). Staging also requires a portable scaffold: "*Enter Chyp, Shaveing and others with a scaffold.*" "This dais or scaffold was certainly carried on . . . by stage hands" (Gurr 2009d). Q2 1633.

In an address to the Q1 reader, Machin suggests that the play was severely criticized and that the play in its printed form has the capacity to refute such complaint: "Rumor that Hydra headed monster, with more tongues then eyes: by help of intelligencer envy hath made strange misconstructions on this dumbe knight which then could not answere for himselfe, but now this publication doth unty his tongue, to answer the objections of all sharp critticall sensures which heretofore have undeservedly past upon him."

The Dutch Courtesan. John Marston. Acted late 1604-early 1605 (Jackson & Neill 1986). "Playd" by the Children of the Queen's Revels at the [second] Blackfriars, according to the Q TP. "Staged during the king of Denmark's visit in July and August 1606" (Knowles 2004); "may have been performed at court at Greenwich on 29 July 1606" (Munro 2005). Revived by the combined Lady Elizabeth's Men and Queen's Revels Children at court, 25 February and 12 December 1613, celebrating the marriage of Princess Elizabeth and Frederick, the Elector Palatine (Wine 1965); the two companies merged in March 1613. Possibly performed by Prince Charles's Men *c.* 1619 (Nicol 2006a). The play "may well have been in the repertory in 1622" (Hutchings & Bromham 2008).

SR 26 June 1605; transferred 19 April 1613. Q 1605 argument; dramatis personae; prologue and final address to the audience by Cocledemoy, "a knavishly witty city companion"; five acts and separate scenes. The SDs "are long and descriptive" (Jewkes 1958): "*Enter Master Garnish, and Lionell: Master Mulligrubbe, with a standing cup in his hand, and an obligation in the other, Cockledemoy stands at the other dore disguised like a French pedler, and over-heares them.*" The play's appeal must largely have depended on the resourcefulness of the actor playing the trickster Cockledemoy, "who becomes in turn a barber, a French pedlar, a bellman, a serjeant" (Hunter 1980). Sound effects include birdsong: Malheureux says, "Harke how the free-borne birdes / Caroll their unaffected passions." The accompanying SD reads: "*The nitingalls sing.*" The song may have been produced by "a mechanical device" (Lawrence 1927). In contrast to his plays acted at Paul's playhouse, where he makes considerable use of song, Marston relies "on orchestral performance" at Blackfriars (Gair 2000). O 1633 *The Works of Mr. John Marston, Being Tragedies and Comedies, Collected into One Volume* (with *Antonio and Mellida, Antonio's Revenge, Parasitaster, What You Will, The Wonder of Women*); "divers times presented at the Blacke Fryars"; two issues. The reissue, *Tragedies and Comedies Collected into One Volume,* removes Marston's name from the separate TPs and the general TP; William Sheares had published the collection without Marston's consent. Also issued in *Comedies, Tragicomedies, & Tragedies* (1652), a made-up Q no longer extant. During the Interregnum, the comic underplot was adapted for a droll entitled *The Cheater Cheated*, later published in *2 The Wits, or Sport upon Sport* (Q and O 1673).

"A line of 'brothel plays' was staged at both public and private theatres, including *Measure for Measure* (1604), Dekker's *The Honest Whore* (1604), Marston's *The Dutch Courtesan* (1605), Sharpham's *Cupid's Whirligig* (1606–7) and Heywood's *The Royal King and the Loyal Subject*" (Gossett 2004b).

Dyccon of Bedlam. See *Gammer Gurton's Needle.*

E

Eastward Ho! George Chapman, Ben Jonson, and John Marston; collaboration was such that "we may never be able entirely to reconstruct" the authors' working methods or shares in the play (Gossett 2004a). Acted July–August 1605; "the play was staged, unlicensed, while the court and the lord chamberlain were away from London" (Burnett 2004). "Playd" by the Children of the Queen's Revels at the [second] Blackfriars, according to the Q1–3 TPs. Revived by the combined Lady Elizabeth's Men and Queen's Revels Children at court, before King James, 25 January 1614; the two companies merged "in early 1613" (Munro 2005).

SR 4 September 1605 *A Comedie called Eastward Ho*. Q1 1605 the TP names all three dramatists; prologue and epilogue (by Quicksilver); five acts (and separate scenes in act 3). "Critical consensus assigns Chapman primary responsibility for the subplot of the middle acts"; the conclusion is "probably by Jonson" (Braden 1987a). The play "opens with a triple entrance" (Ichikawa 2002): "*Enter Maister Touch-stone, and Quick-silver at severall dores, Quicksilver with his hat, pumps, short sword and dagger, and a racket trussed up under his cloake. At the middle dore, enter Golding discovering a goldsmiths shoppe.*" Although Fitzpatrick 2011 maintains that there were two entry-points onto the stage, this SD "implies three doors, the central one large enough to conceal a shop" (Gurr 2009d). Epilogue highlights the play's appeal to the visual: "O may you find in this our pageant, here, / The same contentment which you came to seeke; / And as that shew but drawes you once a yeare, / May this attract you, hether, once a week." "The words 'that shew' suggest that plays, too, provide a feast for the eye analogous to the one provided by pageants" (Schneider 2011). Q2 1605. Q3 1605. The play replies to Dekker and Webster's *Westward Ho!*, performed "in the late autumn or early winter of 1604" (Van Fossen 1979). "The watermen of the Thames and the players were closely connected and belonged to the same economic system. The titles of the plays *Eastward Ho!* and *Westward Ho!*, so named after the hailing cries used by passengers, ought to serve as a reminder of just how close that connection was" (Aaron 2005).

"[T]he authors took the reckless step of tying their depiction of London society very closely to immediately contemporary circumstances" (Corns 2007). *Eastward Ho!* "satirized both citizen mores and their literary taste for romance, repentance narratives, and moral dramas, while also not sparing the pretensions to gentility of the impecunious knight, Sir Petronel Flash, and his deluded search for fabulous wealth in Virginia" (Knowles 2004). The play lampoons Scottish followers of King James, who distributed knighthoods in abundance; the satire landed the playwrights in trouble: Chapman and Jonson were jailed; Marston went into hiding. It is not clear whether the authorities were "provoked by an unlicensed performance during the absence of the king and lord chamberlain at Oxford during the summer months or by the preparation of the play for printing in September, when the printers were obliged to cancel a number of offensive passages" (Donaldson 2004). In addition, Queen Anne was "particularly offended by the play and withdrew her sponsorship of the [theatrical] company" (Auchter 2001), which may have "risked putting on an unlicensed production while the court and its Lord Chamberlain were away from London" (Dutton 1991). "The arbitrariness of Jacobean censorship is borne out by the fact that *Eastward Ho* was published and twice reprinted in 1605" (Clare 1999).

Edmond Ironside, or War Hath Made All Friends. Anonymous; possibly written by the author of *Edward III* (Sams 1996), possibly by William Shakespeare (Everitt 1954, Sams). But "it is most unlikely that Shakespeare wrote any substantial part of *Edmond Ironside*" (Palmer 2009a); Taylor 2011 concurs. Acted 1588–89 (Sams 1985a) or early 1590s (Boswell 1927), perhaps May 1593-January 1594 (Martin 1991), or "the late 1590s" (Bate 1995) at undetermined venue. "[D]ated no more precisely than the final decade of the century" (Long 1999). Possibly first performed by the Queen's Men (Ribner 1965, Knutson 2009b). "The actors' names in the manuscript . . . show it to have been revived by either Prince Charles's Men or King's Revels Company at the Salisbury Court playhouse, *c.* 1631–34" (Butler 1984b). A marginal note in the MS preserves name of H[enry] Gradwell, the actor who played a Nobleman's Son and a Herald; also G[eorge] Stutfield, a Nobleman's Son; and E[dward] May, a Bailiff. These actors "likely took part in a late revival" (Greg 1931).

London, BL, Egerton MS 1994, fols. 96–118; no author named; damaged; theatrical provenance (Long 1989); extensive SD/dumb show explained by chorus: since battles' "length will be too tedious, / Then in dumb shows I will explain at large / Their fights"; five acts but "divisions were supplied only by a later hand" (Taylor 1993a). The MS TP calls the play *Edmond Ironside, The English King*, but HT has *A True Chronicle History called War Hath Made All Friends*; *Edmond Ironside* "may have been prefixed on the present title-page by a later hand or hands" (Boas 1923). The MS bears "many marks of revision and the play has been abridged by almost 200 lines by an annotator who appears to have been preparing it for performance" (Clare 1999). MS "appears to have offended the censor because of its analogous theme of Catholic betrayal at court permitting successful invasion of England . . . and its glorification of the military leader who is a friend of the poor and the common soldier" (Bevington 1968). MS shows "signs that scenes or characters have been omitted in transcription or performance" (Carson 1988). "Explicit stage directions require amputations [of hands and noses] to be conducted by Stich on behalf of Canutus. This action is carried out by two 'Pledges' because their 'fathers did abuse theire tongues in perjury'" (Butterworth 2005). The play contains "visual emblems": "the villain Edric crosses the stage with a man's head on his sword's point" (Knutson 2009b).

First edited by Boswell 1927; modern edition by Sams 1985a. *Edmond Ironside* is "the most elaborate extant Elizabethan play on a subject taken from the Anglo-Saxon period" (Boas 1923).

Edward I, surnamed Edward Longshanks. George Peele. The lost original version may have been performed by Lord Strange's Men or the combined Strange's and Admiral's Men, 1590–91 (Davenport 1998). The revised version was acted 1595 (Hook 1961) by the Lord Admiral's Men at the Rose. Henslowe records the following performances of "longshankes" in 1595: 29 August; 10, 30 September; 21 October; 9, 26 November; 10, 29 December. In 1596: 5, 27 February; 21, 28 April; 2 June; 9 July; these entries of 1595–96 "almost certainly" refer to Peele's play (Hook). Ashe 1955 believes that the Admiral's Men acquired *Edward I* and performed it as *Longshanks*; Hook also thinks the two titles represent the same play; Greg 1911b suggests that *Longshanks* was a revision of *Edward I*. It is possible, however, that two plays were written about the reign of Edward I: "During the 1590s, repertory companies frequently produced plays on the same subjects" (Knutson 1985). *Edward I* is "influenced by the Queen's Men's house style" (Knutson 2009b). The play requires an exceptionally large cast: the coronation scene "requires 24 people on stage at once" (Morris 1987). Edward Alleyn probably played the lead (McMillin 1989).

SR 8 October 1593; transferred 13 August 1599; 14 August 1600. Q1 1593 *The Famous Chronicle of King Edward the First, Surnamed Edward Longshanks, with His Return from the Holy Land, also the Life of Lleuellen Rebel in Wales, Lastly the Sinking of Queen Eleanor, Who Sank at Charing Cross and Rose again at Pottershith, now named Queenehith*; author's name in "explicit" but not on the TP; not divided. "Pantomimic" SDs (Mehl 1965). A portable canopy symbolic of status appears with the entry of king and queen *"under a canopie."* Staging calls for a stage tent or perhaps a curtain covering a discovery space: *"the Queenes tent opens"*; *"They close the tent"*; *"the King sits in his tent."* Queen Eleanor enters "in her litter borne by foure Negro Mores." She murders London Maris, nurse to the young prince: Eleanor "orders her waiting maid Katherina to 'binde [Maris] in the chaire,' 'draw forth her brest / And let the Serpent sucke his fill'" (Griffin 2009a); here "the dialogue makes it clear that prosthesis *was* used" (Mann 2008). Later the queen disappears into the earth, apparently through a trap door: "help Jone thy mother sinckes." Subsequently Eleanor, the "queene who suncke this daie on Charing greene," reappears, rising from below. Special effects include *"thunder and lightning when the Queen comes in."* The actor playing the king enters one scene wearing "his sute of glasse"; a 13 March 1598 inventory of props belonging to the Admiral's Men records "longe-shanckes sewte"; it "seems to have been a precious piece of property" of the company (Ewbank 1975). Staging involves the upper stage: *"On the walle: enter Longshankes, Sussex, Mortimor, David the Friar, Meredith holding David by the collar, with a dagger in his hande."* Subsequently, *"Meredith stabs him [David] into the armes and shoulders . . . He shows him hote pincers . . . He cuts his nose."* Staging also calls for the severed head of the rebel Lluellen to be carried *"on a speare."* Peele "seems generally to conceive his scenes as spectacles" (Hook). Q2 1599. A copy of Q2 was purchased by George Buc, who wrote Peele's name on the TP (Shapiro 2005).

"Although Marlowe has a modern reputation for staging violence, *Edward I* exceeds in variety and number the scenes of torture and cruelty shown in Marlowe's plays. . . . The staged violence vividly portrays the dangers of political action, specifically rebellion against legitimate authority" (Braunmuller 1983a). *Edward I*, however, also brings Robin Hood to the stage, "representing what appears to be an escape from the demands of political life" (Davenport).

Edward II. Christopher Marlowe. Acted 1591-early 1592 (Forker 1994). "Sundrie times publiquely acted in the honourable citie of London" by the Earl of

Pembroke's Men, according to the Q1 TP, probably at the Theater (Gurr 2004a). Pembroke's Men "were a mysterious grouping of players, coming to prominence suddenly at the beginning of 1592, and 'breaking' for lack of money, according to a letter from Henslowe to Alleyn, on their travels in the late summer of 1593" (Gurr). Possibly first performed in the provinces. Probably revived in early 1598 by the Lord Chamberlain's Men (Grote 2002). According to Q4, "Publikely act-ed by the late queenes majesties servants [the troupe "now usually called the Red Bull Revels company" (Lloyd 2005)] at the Red Bull, "some time between 1604 and 1606" (Hopkins 2005a). Mortimer the Younger is "the only [role] that would have suited [Edward] Alleyn" (Bradbrook 1991). "We do not . . . know who played the role of King Edward" (Geckle 1988).

SR 6 July 1593; transferred 16 December 1611; 17 April 1617; 4 September 1638. Q1 [octavo-in-fours] 1594 *The Troublesome Reign and Lamentable Death of Edward the Second, King of England, with the Tragical Fall of Proud Mortimer*; unique copy in Zentralbibliothek, Zurich; possibly the reprint of a lost edition or possibly a book whose TP originally gave the date as 1593 and then was re-placed with a newer TP while in press; "written by Chri. Marlow"; not divided. (A five-act division was not introduced until 1818.) Gaveston, the king's favor-ite, is richly dressed, "a traditional morality indication of vanity and worldliness" (Powell 1964). "In a play so centred on the acquisition of power, it is likely that the stage was adorned only with the 'state' or throne" (Hattaway 1982). When Gaveston and Edward part, they exchange portraits, which "apparently consist of miniatures mounted on chains" (Bosonnet 1978); Elizabethan, Jacobean, and Caroline painters raised miniature portraits to a high art (Fumerton 1991). Sym-bolic staging includes the various barons bearing *imprese* on their shields (Kiefer 2011), which the king accurately interprets as signifying a threat. "The barons' emblematic shields may be the most ornate and expensive properties in the play" (Bevington & Shapiro 1988). When Edward's power is broken, he flees to a monastery. "To mark the change in Edward's fortunes, Marlowe has him dis-guised in monkish weeds; he enters to sit and philosophize at the feet of the Abbot and monks of Neath, perhaps before the empty stage throne, now a mute symbol of his former estate" (Hattaway). A Mower, "an invention of Marlowe's" (Bosonnet 1978), advances like personified Death upon the king: "*Enter with Welch hookes, Rice ap Howell, a Mower*," "and we must assume he comes carrying his scythe" (Leech 1959), symbol of time and death. The scene of the king's im-prisonment and degradation in a dungeon may have used a trap in the floor of the stage (Wiggins & Lindsey 1997): "*They wash him with puddle water, and shave his beard away*," "symbolically emasculating and rechristening him as a subject" (DiGangi 1997) and marking "an inversion of the anointing of a king" (Dessen 1984). Or the dungeon may have been represented by an opening in the tiring-house wall, which would allow for the property bed that figures in the murder (Thomson 2005). Stunning violence takes the form of Lightborne murdering the King "with an anally inserted poker"; Mortimer thereby "enacts both regicide

and sodomy" (DiGangi); "the murder of Edward as given in Holinshed was enacted in full view of the audience" (Bray 1990). "Jacobean playwrights could
think of strange ways of torment and murder, but they never tear at our nerves as
Marlowe does in this play" (Leech 1959).

Q2 1598 *The Troublesome Reign . . . and also the Life and Death of Piers
Gaveston, the Great Earl of Cornwall, and Mighty Favorite of King Edward the Second.* Q3 1612 two issues; *Edward II* "remains a Pembroke's play on its printed
title page in 1612 and 1625, long after Pembroke's players . . . had ceased to exist" (Marino 2011). Q4 1622 two issues; the play was "reprinted presumably as
a result of its newfound topicality in the light of James I's liaison with the Duke
of Buckingham" (Hopkins 2005a); "[t]he Red Bull attribution is made on a variant title page, where earlier stage history ('As it was publickely acted by the right
Honourable the Earle of Pembrooke his servants.') is replaced with what W. W.
Greg surmises is more recent information" (Straznicky 2006b).

"[T]he only dramatic instance of a homosexual relationship presented in the
terms in which the culture formally conceived it—as antisocial, seditious, ultimately disastrous—is in Marlowe's *Edward II*" (Orgel 1989). The play's "account
of Edward's homosexual infatuation for Piers Gaveston may contain an under-
tone of comment about James VI of Scotland and the earl of Lennox; the play
thus touches obliquely on the question of the succession, and on the pro-Jacobean
factions already forming in the early 1590s" (Nicholl 2004a).

Edward III. ?William Shakespeare (Muir 1960, Lapides 1980, Hope 1994, Sams
1996) and perhaps others, possibly George Peele (Brooke 1908). The 1656 catalogue by Rogers and Ley attributes the play to Shakespeare, who may have "had
a hand in revising a play already fully worked out" (Tobin 1997); "Shakespeare
wrote the scenes with the Countess, a substantial contribution" (Watt 2009b).
Acted *c.* 1589 (Sams) or late 1592-early 1593 (Melchiori 1998). "Sundrie times
plaied about the Citie of London," according to the Q1 TP, probably by the Earl
of Pembroke's Men (Gurr 2009c) or Strange's Men or both. Possibly performed by
the Lord Admiral's Men (Lapides); the play represents "a natural starring vehicle"
for Edward Alleyn (Sams). Because of the plague, the play may not have been performed at one of the regular London theaters. "*Edward III* would have been playable and persuasive in virtually any space having an upper platform and a rear wall
with doors" (Thomson 2002). Probably revived in 1595 (Grote 2002).

SR 1 December 1595; transferred 16 October 1609; 2 March 1618; 23 February 1626; 4 March 1639. Q1 1596 *The Reign of King Edward the Third*; no author named; not divided. Prince Philip comments on "this sodain fog," perhaps
indicating some kind of theatrical illusion probably effected by smoke. "[S]ounds
are central to the play both structurally and thematically" (Thomson 2002): "*The
battell hard a farre off*," "*Shot*," "*Retreat sounded*," "*A clamor of ravens*." *Clamor* designates "a loud and cacophonous noise produced within" (Dessen & Thomson
1999). The most interesting staging involves four heralds bringing onstage a coat

of armor, helmet, lance, and shield; Edward is invested with the military gear, and its symbolic significance is described. "The 'investment' of the Black Prince before the battle of Crecy dignifies the warrior with a ceremonial ritual, the armor symbolizing matchless fortitude: the helmet, laurel victory; the lance, the pen of bloody stratagems; and the target, paralyzing amazement to befall his enemies" (Armstrong 1965). Later Prince Edward enters "*in triumph, bearing in his hande his shivered launce, and the King of Boheme, borne before, wrapt in the collours.*" Q2 1599. "The 1599 quarto is a better job of printing than the 1596 quarto" (Lapides). Capell's 1760 edition divided the play into acts and scenes.

"Apart from an unreliable reference in a bookseller's catalogue of 1656, the first suggestion of Shakespearian authorship did not occur until 1760, when Edward Capell included *Edward III* in a volume preliminary to his complete edition of Shakespeare (1767–8)" (Warren 2002). Scholarly opinion today favors the attribution. "Of all the non-canonical plays [it] has the strongest claim to inclusion in the Complete Works" (Wells & Taylor 1987), and it is included in the revised *Riverside Shakespeare* 1997 and the revised *Oxford Shakespeare: The Complete Works* 2005. Shakespeare may have outlined the plot and later revised the play (Melchiori). It "seems to have undergone substantial and stratified revision — probably involving Shakespeare for the version of the Countess of Salisbury's story that survives in the extant text" (Forker 2005); this episode is "markedly better than the rest of a mundane play" (Holland 2004a). The Countess and other female characters are "courageous women warriors who are also models of feminine virtue" (Rackin 2006).

1 Edward IV. Thomas Heywood, according to Kirkman's 1661 catalogue; revised by Henry Chettle and John Day, whose names Henslowe records in May 1603 for a play about "shores wife." Thomas Dekker may also have contributed to the play (Rowland 2005a). Payment exists for a performance of "K E[dward] the 4" at Coventry in 1591 (Ingram 1981), but this is probably not Heywood's play. "Probably performed in 1599" (Crupi 1995), likely at the Curtain (Davison 1987). "Divers times . . . publikely played" by the Earl of Derby's Men, according to the Q1–5 TPs; this company was chiefly a touring company before becoming established in London. "In 1599 Derby's Men at the Boar's Head playhouse acquired a two-part play called *Edward IV*" (Knutson 2002a); Robert Browne, who "led a company of players" (Berry 1986), acted the lead (Knutson 2006a). The play "must have been revised with the crisis [Spanish threat] in mind," 1599 (Shapiro 2005). "*Edward IV* did not remain long in Derby Men's possession"; the play was "sold to Worcester's Men," who performed at the Rose and then the Red Bull; there "it met with immense popularity in 1605" (Greenberg 2009).

SR 28 August 1599; transferred 23 February 1600; 30 May 1627 [*Jane Shore*, 2 parts]; 6 November 1628; 6 December 1630; 22 July 1644. Q1 1599 *The First and Second Parts of King Edward the Fourth, Containing His Merry Pastime with the Tanner of Tamworth, as Also His Love to Fair Mistress Shore, Her Great Promotion,*

Fall, and Misery, and Lastly the Lamentable Death of Both Her and Her Husband;
unique copy at Newberry; no author named; not divided but the play "has a tripartite structure" (Rowland 2010). Detailed SDs: *"As he goes forth, Shoare lookes
earnestly, and perceives it is the king, whereat he seemeth greatly discontented"*; *"Enter
Mistris Shoare, lady-like attired, with divers supplications in her hand, she unpin-
ning her mask, and attended on by many sutors."* Staging may involve a freestanding
structure: *"Enter two prentizes preparing the goldsmiths shop with plate."* Staging
involves considerable violence, though the beheading of Falconbridge apparently
occurs offstage: *"Falconbridge bound, the headsman bearing the axe before him."* Q2
1600 [octavo-in-fours]. Q3 1605. Q4 1613 [octavo-in-fours]. Q5 1619. Q6 1626
"the fourth impression," but "this is actually the sixth known edition" (Greg
1939); no company of actors named. The publication history suggests that the
play was "much more popular in [its] own day than in ours" (Bruster 2004).

The two parts of *Edward IV* "are nominally history plays, but half their action concerns Edward's mistress Jane Shore, whose story unfolds like a domestic
tragedy" (Orlin 2002). "Edward meets Jane at the Mayor's house, goes in disguise to the Shores' shop to woo her, and eventually succeeds in inducing her
to come to the palace" (Crupi 1995). "The virtuous Matthew Shore, husband of
the king's mistress, displays a saintly forbearance and undeviating sense of moral
principle peculiar to his class and implicitly critical of Edward's *droit du seigneur*"
(Bevington 1968).

2 Edward IV. Data as for *Part 1. Parts 1* and *2* were printed together as a single
book with continuous register and entitled *The First and Second Parts of King Edward the Fourth.* "The two parts seem to have been planned as a whole, with the
planting of episodes whose significance will appear only in the final unfolding
of the whole plan" (McLuskie 1994). *The Second Part of King Edward the Fourth,
Containing His Journey into France for Obtaining of His Right There: the Treacherous
Falsehood of the Duke of Burgundy, and the Constable of France Used against Him,
and His Return Home Again. Likewise the Prosecution of the History of Master Shore
and His Fair Wife, Concluding with the Lamentable Death of Them Both.* Detailed
SDs: *"As thy march upon the stage, the Lord Scales is strucke downe, and two souldiours
slaine outright, with great shot from the towne."* Equally detailed are SDs for Jane
Shore's repentance: *"Enter the two parators, with mistris Shoare in a white sheete,
bare footed, with her haire about her eares, and in her hand a waxe taper."* She dies
while sitting on one side of an executed man's coffin. Her husband climbs a scaffold to be hanged: *"while the hangman prepares, Shoare at this speech mounts up the
ladder,"* but he is pardoned at the last moment. *Part 2* contains a chorus marking
a change of scene.

"While part 1 of the play details Edward's seduction of Jane Shore, part 2
focuses almost exclusively on her humility. After her lover the king dies, Jane
stages her penance publicly, but she also performs a private display with her
prayer book in her jail cell" (Williamson 2009).

The Elder Brother, A Comedy. John Fletcher, revised by Philip Massinger, but the play may have been "an actual collaboration between the two" (Hoy 1987a). "Massinger wrote the first and last acts, and Fletcher . . . the matter in between" (McLuskie 1981). "[C]omposed 9 January-27 March 1625" (McMullan 1994). Performed also at the Blackfriars "with great applause," according to the Q3 TP, February 1635 (diary of John Greene) and 25 April 1635 (diary of Humphrey Mildmay); at Hampton Court, 5 January 1637 (Henry Herbert's office-book [Gurr 2004c]).

London, BL, Egerton MS 1994, fols. 2–29; no TP but the title appears on fol. 28r; the first leaf is damaged; epilogue; five acts and separate scenes. A "paucity of stage directions" (Greg 1931) apart from entrances and exits. SR 29 March 1637 [Greg 1939 has 24 March]; transferred 31 October 1646. Q1 1637 *The Elder Brother, A Comedy*; "written by John Fletcher"; "printed according to the true copie"; list of characters; prologue and epilogue. Dialogue suggests a sound effect: "What did ye bring to carry her?" "A coach and four horses." This may have been accompanied by the sound of horses or "the rumble of wheels" (Lawrence 1927), or both. Q2 dated 1637 but probably printed later. Q3 1650–51 two issues; "the second edition, corrected and amended"; the TP names B&F. Q4 1661 the TP names Fletcher. Q5 1678 the TP names B&F. B&F F2 1679 *Fifty Comedies and Tragedies*; "published by the authors original copies, the songs to each play being added"; list of characters; prologue (written after Fletcher's death in 1625) and epilogue.

The Q1 prologue, written for a revival, salutes Fletcher: "And if he / That made it, still lives in your memory; / You will expect what we present tonight, / Should be judg'd worthy of your eares and sight. / You shall heare Fletcher in it; his true straine, / And neate expressions; living he did gaine / Your good opinions; but now dead commends / This orphan to the care of noble friends."

The Emperor of the East, A Tragicomedy. Philip Massinger. Licensed for acting 11 March 1631 (Adams 1917). "Divers times acted" by the King's Men at the [second] Blackfriars and [second] Globe, according to the TP.

SR 19 November 1631. Q 1632 *The Emperor of the East, A Tragicomedy, The Scene Constantinople*; list of characters; prologue at Blackfriars and prologue at court; epilogue; five acts and separate scenes. The SDs, "which are full and interesting, are characteristic of Massinger's concern for detail" (E&G 1976). Unusual staging involves characters concealed above by a curtain: "*the curtaines drawne above,* Theodosius, *and his* Eunuches *discover'd.*" Pulcheria arranges that the emperor examine "court portraits" in order to select a wife (Rochester 2010): "*Pictures brought in.*" In Pulcheria emerges "a distinctive kind of Caroline heroine, remarkable for her constancy, courage, and lofty dignity" (Neill 1978). "Massinger surely invokes the memory of Elizabeth in the character of Pulcheria, the wise and good regent of Constantinople" (Barton 1977). "About 1633 Massinger had eight of his previously published plays bound together in a single volume. Possibly he was thinking of publishing a collection of his works; possibly he wanted the volume as a gift to a patron. He made extensive ink corrections in a number of plays [including *The Emperor*]" (Edwards 1987). The Folger owns this collection.

The play "may have been seen at court" (Barton 1984), as the existence of a court prologue may suggest, but Bentley is doubtful: "one wonders if the court prologue was not prepared for an expected court performance which was never given because of the bad public reception of the play" (*JCS*). That reception is indicated in William Singleton's commendatory poem: "what I have read / With an impartiall censure I dare crowne / With a deserv'd applause, how ere cri'd downe / By such whose malice will not let 'em bee / Equall to any peece limnd forth by thee." The court prologue itself concedes an unfavorable reception from playgoers at the Blackfriars: "this poore worke suffer'd by the rage, / And envie of some Catos of the stage: / Yet still hee hopes, this play which then was seene / With sore eyes, and condemn'd out of their spleen, / May bee by you, the supreme judge, set free, / And rais'd above the reach of calumnie." The epilogue explains apologetically that the actor who played the lead was too young to act the part successfully: "The burden was too heavie for his youth / To undergoe."

The Emperor Valentinian. See *Valentinian*.

The Emperor's Favorite. John Newdigate III (Howard-Hill 1988, Inglis & Johnstone 2011). "Prob[ably] dated between 1623 and 1628" (*AED 3*). No record of production, but this and the other MS plays from Arbury Hall "were written by an author attuned to live performance" (Kidnie 2007). "One of the first indications of staging in *The Emperor's Favourite* is to be found in the cast list, which groups the female roles under the subtitle '*Women speakers*'. . . . This phrase points to the tantalizing possibility of spoken delivery and female performance"; SDs "afford more substantial evidence of a concern with the practicalities of performance" (Keenan 2011). "[W]ith doubling *The Emperor's Favourite* could have been performed or read by a cast as small as fifteen, made up perhaps of family, friends, and other household members" (Keenan).

Nuneaton, UK, Arbury Hall, MS A414, fols. 145–94; microfilm in Warwickshire County Record Office, M.I. 351/3, Item 20; title proposed by Howard-Hill; no author named; much evidence of revision; list of characters; prologue; five acts. First edited by Keenan 2010.

The play features a character named Crispinus, "the corrupt favourite of the tyrannical Roman Emperor Nero"; a "subplot focuses on the battle for the Armenian throne between Tiridates . . . and Tigranes" (Keenan 2011). This Roman tragedy is "rife with topical allusions to the role of court favourites in general and to George Villiers, first duke of Buckingham (1592–1628), in particular" (Inglis & Johnstone). Prologue promises a drama of political comeuppance: "You shall see / Tigranes fate twice chang'd, the majestie / Of Tiridates shaken, & reviv'd / Againe by plots crosse layd, & so contriv'd / The deeds disgrace the actors, every man / That is this way a politian [politician] / Shame payes at last; The play will let you know / At large their riseing, & their overthrow."

The Enchanted Lovers, A Pastoral. William Lower. Possibly acted following the closing of the theaters, perhaps at a country house.

D1 1658 published in The Hague; list of characters; five acts and separate scenes. Staging includes the ascent (of Diana), possibly by machinery: a SD reads, *"Seeing the goddess to ascend."* Special effects include *"thunder and lightning."* Preceding the TP an engraving depicts three episodes: in one a prayerful figure kneels over a man lying on the ground; in another a company of men surrounds a woman; in the third a man laments over the body of a woman. D2 1659 published in London with a new TP. Unsold copies of D were bound with *The Amorous Fantasm* and *The Noble Ingratitude* in a volume called *Three New Plays*, 1661 (Gates 1932); two issues. Folger copy contains "about fifteen manuscript corrections, all in Lower's hand" (Kathman 2004b). Copies of *The Enchanted Lovers* in *Three New Plays* have two TPs, one dated 1658 (The Hague) and the other dated 1661 (London); general TP dated 1661; the three plays have separate register and pagination.

The plot "almost certainly was keyed to political events in England" (Wright 1934). In Lower's play and in Cosmo Manuche's *The Banished Shepherdess* (1660), "the pastoral world is . . . emphatically a space of exile, where feelings of deprivation can be vented and plots show lost rulers returning and loyal subjects miraculously rewarded" (Butler 2002).

The Encounter. A droll based upon a scene in B&F's *The Knight of the Burning Pestle* and performed in the 1640s and 50s. "The episode is short but complete, with amusing situations and dialogue and abundant action. It could be performed by seven actors" (Elson 1932).

Published in *1 The Wits, or Sport upon Sport* (O 1662 [two issues] and 1672) which mistakenly locates the source in *The Humorous Lieutenant*; RT *The Humors of The Encounter*; argument; list of characters.

Endymion, The Man in the Moon. John Lyly. Acted early 1588 (Bevington 1996) probably by Paul's Boys at Paul's playhouse and by the Blackfriars Boys at the Blackfriars (Montrose 1996). Performed also by same company at Greenwich, before the queen, on Candlemas (2 February) night, [1588], according to the Q TP. It is likely that the roles of "Sir Tophas and the members of the watch were played by adults" (Bevington). Lyly's plays were "often presented and acted" before Queen Elizabeth, according to the D general TP. "The play contains a sustained note of adoration for Cynthia, the moon goddess, Queen of the Heavens, and a well-established type of Elizabeth" (Parry 1997). *Endymion* "looks innocent enough in its fable of a man in love with the moon; but by reversing the emphasis of the received legend (in which the moon falls in love with a mortal)

to stress instead the love of Endymion for Queen Cynthia, Lyly clearly points to
the Queen of England (commonly identified with Cynthia and Diana) and invites titillating speculation as to who is meant by Endymion" (Bevington 2002a).
"Endymion may represent Lyly's employer the Earl of Oxford, one of a group of
courtiers suspected of open or assumed Catholicism" (Gossett 2000).

SR 4 October 1591; transferred 23 August 1601; 9 January 1628. Q 1591
no author named; prologue and epilogue (addressed to the queen); five acts and
separate scenes. Staging calls for two "houses" (a castle and a lunary bank where
Endymion sleeps); also a well (Best 1968b). "Lyly gives Cynthia only one short
scene . . . before her closing displays of power"; "[t]his careful restriction of Cynthia's on-stage role greatly influences her effect upon us" (Saccio 1975). Special
effects include the transformation of Bagoa into an aspen tree and subsequently
the transformation of the tree back into the form of a woman (Scragg 2005). D
1632 *Six Court Comedies* (with *Campaspe, Gallathea, Midas, Mother Bombie, Sappho and Phao*); two issues; by "John Lilly"; songs omitted from Q are added to
this edition "in order to make his play seem more literary" (Massai 2007); detailed description of dumb show representing the dream of Endymion (possibly
not part of the original production). If the pantomime "really was part of the
first version of the play it would be the earliest example of the representation of
dreams and visions by means of pantomimes, a favourite device in later Elizabethan and Stuart drama" (Mehl 1965).

The Q printer explains that the script, which became available following
the suppression of the acting company, may be faulty: "Since the plaies in Paules
were dissolved, there are certaine commedies come to my handes by chaunce,
which were presented before her majestie at severall [i.e., different] times by the
children of Paules. This is the first, and if in any place it shall dysplease, I will
take more pains to perfect the next. . . . And if this may passe with thy good lyk-
ing, I will then goe forwarde to publish the rest." "Most scholars believe that the
troupe was silenced as a result of its participation in the Marprelate controversy,
although there is no evidence as to what was deemed offensive" (Shapiro 2002).

The English Moor, or the Mock Marriage, A Comedy. Richard Brome. Acted October–December 1637 (Steen 1983). "Often acted with general applause" by Queen
Henrietta Maria's Men, according to the O separate TP. "Written for the reformed Queen Henrietta's Men, *The English Moor* may have been among the first
plays performed for the new Salisbury Court Theater in the fall of 1637" (Stevens 2009).

Lichfield, UK, Lichfield Cathedral Library, MS 68, ed. Steen; a "presentation" MS (Steggle 2004b); prologue and short epilogue "that are simply different from the prologue and epilogue in the printed text" (Stern 2009c); five acts.
The play circulated in manuscript (Butler 1984b) and was presented to William
Seymour, its dedicatee. MS "differs in many respects from that printed in 1659";
those differences may represent revisions by the author (Steggle 2004b). The play

was "disseminated only in manuscript until long after the closure of the theatres" (Peters 2000). SR 4 August 1640. O 1658–59 *Five New Plays* (with *The Love-sick Court*, *The New Academy*, *The Queen and Concubine*, *The Weeding of the Covent Garden*); two issues; separate TP is dated 1658 in some copies, 1659 in others; separately paginated; no author named on 1658 separate TP; author named on TP of 1659 issue; dramatis personae; prologue and epilogue; five acts and separate scenes. The play's first expansive stage action consists of what may be called a "Masque of Cuckolds" (Shaw 1979), featuring dancers as stag, ram, goat, and ox, together with a courtier, captain, scholar, and butcher. A later masque involves an elaborate hoax in which participants think they are gulling someone else: "*Florish enter* Inductor *like a* Moor *leading* Phillis *black and gorgeously deck't with jewels*"; then "*Enter the rest of the Moors. They dance an antique in which they use action of mockery and derision to the three gentlemen.*" The most unusual staging involves the protagonist painting his wife in order to prevent her from cuckolding him: "Quicksands paints Millicent black . . . to make her ugly and undesirable, forgetting that black women were also considered prone to venery" (Hall 1995). Millicent "is automatically interpreted as someone offering sexual favours. Her husband's lustful friends start groping her in corners and cracking jokes about her barbary buttocks. Black skin denoted both access and entitlement" (Korhonen 2005). Brome "supercharges the convention of racial disguise. He openly shows the application of blackface makeup, scripts not one but two racial transformations, and then fills the space of the stage with yet a further complement of dancing Moors" (Stevens 2009). And because "the devil, the Saracens, and other enemies of Christianity were represented as black" (Loomba 2002), black paint served "as a threatening signal of the pervasiveness and infectiousness of foreigners, their culture, religion, and sexual behaviour" (Karim-Cooper 2007).

Epilogue asks the audience to "judge but by the antient comick lawes. / Not by their course who in this latter age / Have sown such pleasing errors on the stage, / Which he no more will chuse to imitate / Then they to fly from truth, and run the state." The note to the reader of this collection of plays alludes to the gap separating performance from print: *The English Moor* "is older than our troubles."

The English Traveler. Thomas Heywood. Acted *c.* 1624 (Merchant 1996), probably "in the late spring or early summer" (Wiggins 2008), or 1626–27 (Rowland 2010). "Publikely acted . . . by her majesties servants," according to the TP; this probably means Lady Elizabeth's Men at the the Phoenix (Wiggins); the play "later passed into the repertory of the company's successors, Queen Henrietta's Men" (Wiggins), a "troupe apparently assembled during the long plague closing of 1625" (Bentley 1981). Richard Perkins may have played young Geraldine; Andrew Cane may have played Reignald, a "parasiticall serving-man" (Merchant).

SR 15 July 1633 a Comedy called *the Traveller*; 30 June 1673. Heywood's play, called a "Tragi-Comedy" in his address to the reader, is "concerned with the instability of generic conventions, and yet it is also one which confidently insists on its capacity to amuse and disturb in the same breath" (Rowland). Q 1633 dramatis personae; prologue; five acts and separate scenes. The TP features a small woodcut depicting a soldier in classical garb, armed with shield and spear, the blazing sun above. The picture was not designed for this book. "It was presumably part of [Robert] Raworth's old stock" (Merchant). Although Fitzpatrick 2011 argues that there were only two entry-points onto the stage, SDs seem to call for a triple entrance: *"Enter at one doore an* Usurer *and his* Man, *at the other,* Old Lionell *with his servant: in the midst* Reignald."

In his address to the reader Heywood contrasts his attitude toward publication with Ben Jonson's: "True it is, that my playes are not exposed unto the world in volumes, to beare the title of *Workes,* (as others): one reason is, that many of them by shifting and change of companies, have beene negligently lost, others of them are still retained in the hands of some actors, who thinke it against their peculiar profit to have them come in print, and a third, that it never was any great ambition in me, to bee in this kind voluminously read." However, in *2 Iron Age* (1632) Heywood intimates that he in fact planned to publish his collected *Ages* plays: "If the three former *Ages* (now out of print), bee added to these (as I am promised) to make up an handsome volume; I purpose (*Deo Assistente,*) to illustrate the whole Worke, with an explanation of all the difficulties, an historical comment of every hard name, which may appear obscure or intricate to such as are not frequent in poetry."

Englishmen for My Money, or A Woman Will Have Her Will. William Haughton. Entries by Henslowe, 18 February and [unspecified day] May 1598, establish authorship. Acted "during the spring of 1598" by the Lord Admiral's Men at the Rose (Wiggins 2000). "Divers times acted with great applause," according to the Q2 TP.

SR 3 August 1601 A comedy of *A woman Will have her Will.* Q1 1616 *Englishman for My Money, or, A Pleasant Comedy Called A Woman Will Have Her Will*; the subtitle was probably Haughton's choice for the main title (Kermode 2009b); no author named; list of characters; not divided. The Q1 TP woodcut depicts a richly dressed woman in Elizabethan costume, which "seems to have no specific connection with the play, apart from the general reference to the title *A Woman Will Have Her Will*" (Foakes 1985). Staging calls for action above and a staircase: "the staires are bad." "Two columns seem to figure in two night scenes": "two foolish men stumble around in the dark and on both occasions run into both of the columns, again referred to in the dialogue as posts" (Rhodes 1976). The most unusual staging involves "a corpulent elderly Dutchman named Vandalle [who] is paying unwelcome court to a girl named Laurentia. Hoping to cool his ardor, she persuades him to climb into a basket and be hauled up to her window in the expectation of being admitted, by way of the window, to her chamber. He gets into the basket, and Laurentia and her two sisters hoist him up; but instead of permitting him to enter, they leave him dangling outside the window all night long" (Smith 1956). Staging also includes the ringing of a bell: "First, it represented the Exchange Bell, and by its ringing conveyed that it was noon and dinner-time; later on it stood for Bow-bell" (Lawrence 1935). Q2 1626 the woodcut in the previous edition disappears. Q3 1631 the words *Englishmen for My Money* are dropped from the TP, but they appear in the HT and, from B4v onward, in the RT. "Englishmen for my money" was "a proverbial saying" (Lawrence 1935).

"The first of the London citizen comedies" (Smallwood & Wells 1979), the play "includes a bustling scene in the city's trade centre, the Exchange, and a farcical nocturnal sequence which depends on the familiar layout of its streets" (Wiggins 2000). "Haughton deviates from earlier plays in his representation of London's extant topography as *enacted* space: the characters putatively interact with each other in a geographically specific London coeval with that of its original audience" (Bartolovich 2008). Haughton's play presents "the first dramatic pastiche of everyday conversation in a familiar urban setting" (Butler 2002), and that conversation has a linguistically nationalistic quality: the plot involves "a Portuguese merchant-userer Pisaro, and the three daughters he has begot with an Englishwoman now deceased. The father wishes them to marry three broken-English speaking foreign merchants because of their wealth. The daughters, however, prefer three Englishmen. In this patriotic comedy, the English girls eventually have their will, but only after an involved battle of languages" (Hoenselaars 1992b). Haughton creates a "new kind of London play, what I call the London chronicle comedy" (Howard 2007). "Haughton may well have written the play in response to *The Merchant of Venice*, for the play triples the motif of the elopement of the usurer's daughter" (Shapiro 1994).

Enough Is as Good as a Feast. W. [?William] Wager. Acted *c.* 1568 (*DTRB* 1984) probably in a great hall (Walker 1998). Wager may also be the author of *The Trial of Treasure* (Happé 2008). "Seven may easely play this enterlude," according to the TP, which explains the doubling, dividing the eighteen roles for actors.

SR none. Q ND ?1565–70 (Walker) *A Comedy or Interlude entitled Enough Is as Good as a Feast*; unique copy (which came to light in 1919 at the Mostyn Hall sale [De Ricci 1920b]) at the Huntington; list of characters on the TP; prologue in which "the Prologist refers twice to the whole of his introductory speech as a 'preface'" (Schneider 2011); ends with a speech calling on God to preserve the queen; not divided. SDs "are graphic and plentiful" (Bevington 1962). Worldly Man's apparel "grows rich while his soul grows mean" (Craik 1958). Covetous represents the Vice, "a demonic force of evil" (Margeson 1967), who wields a dagger, common hand prop of a Vice (Dessen 1977). Staging includes the devil exiting "with the Vice on his back at the end of the play, a stage device anticipated by Bale in *King Johan*, when he has Usurped Power carry Sedition in the same manner" (Cox 2000). Later God's Plague, armed with a sword, affirms justice (Dessen).

"As in most moral plays, debate counts for more than action, and moral attitudes are more important than emotion" (Margeson). The play "demonstrates vividly how the formula of the morality play could be adapted in the sixteenth century to the polemical purposes of the English Reformation" (Bevington 2007). "This is a Protestant morality with a Calvinist message about predestination, which is clearly stated towards the end of the play. It has, however, strong social and economic dimensions and refers to several abuses in the realm that were also the subject of contemporary pamphleteers" (Grantley 2004): namely, "rent gouging, the influx of immigrant labour, and economic hard times for the poor" (Bevington).

The Entertainment. See *The Muses' Looking Glass.*

The Entertainment at Rutland House. See *The First Day's Entertainment at Rutland House.*

Epicene, or The Silent Woman. Ben Jonson. "[F]irst performed either late in 1609 or early in 1610," probably between 4 January and 8 February 1610 (Dutton 2003). "First acted in the yeere 1609" by the Children of the Queen's Revels, according to the F TP, at the Whitefriars theater (Munro 2005); *Epicene* "is the earliest play we can date . . . specifically written for the Children of the Whitefriars" (Dutton 2002). "The Children of the Queen's Revels did not technically act under that title until 4 January 1610, which was when they acquired a patent that invested them with their new name" (Butler 2003b); previously they were known as the Blackfriars Boys (Dobson 2001). "It is not impossible that the first performance of the play was at court" (Dutton); "it seems likely that *Epicene* was one of the five plays" the Queen's Revels Children "took to court that Christmas" (Butler). The papers of the Venetian ambassador (8 February 1610) suggest that the play was suppressed for a time because of a complaint from Lady Arbella Stuart, cousin of the king, that the play alluded to her, especially "rumours that she had been engaged to the adventurer Stephano Janiculo, who was passing himself off as Bogdan, prince of the Romanian province of Moldavia" (Dutton 2003). "Jonson strenuously denied that he had revised the piece to include any reference to contemporary events" (Donaldson 2004). Also performed at the Blackfriars, where it "was acted in perfection" (*Historia Histrionica*) by the King's Men (Gurr 2004c): principal actors were Nathan Field (who joined the company in 1615 or 1616), William Barksted, Giles Carey, William Penn, Hugh Attwell, Richard Allen, John Smith, and John Blaney, according to F1. Attwell played Sir Amorous La Foole; Barksted, Morose, according to notes "almost certainly in a seventeenth-century hand" written in a copy of F (Riddell 1969). "[T]he most likely role for Field in *Epicene* is Truewit" (Munro 2010c). Revived 1619–20 at court (Dutton). John Lowin, having joined the King's Men, played Morose; Joseph Taylor, having joined King's Men in 1619, played Truewit (*Historia Histrionica*). Performed by King's Men at St. James's Palace, 18 February 1636 (Adams 1917), in the Presence Chamber (Astington 1986); and at Whitehall Cockpit, before king and queen, 21 April 1636 (Dutton).

SR 20 September 1610; transferred 28 September 1612; [10 June 1621]; 17 February 1623 [entry crossed out]; 3 July 1630; 4 July 1635; 4 March 1639. As the first two records in the SR suggest, the play "was apparently printed" in 1610 and 1612, but "no copies of these editions are extant" (Ioppolo 2006). F1 1616 *The Works*; *Epicene, or The Silent Woman, A Comedy*; RT *The Silent Woman*; list of characters; two prologues—one "occasion'd by some persons impertinent exception"—and "apparently written after the early performances at Whitefriars" (Clare 1999); no speech labeled epilogue but Truewit makes a conventional bid for applause at the end; five acts and separate scenes. "Jonson seems to have rewritten some parts" of *Epicene* before publication in F1 (MacIntyre 1996). The play participates in the vogue for humors comedy in which characters have "some bizarre, fanatical fixation like Morose . . . whose manic desire for silence causes him to sound-proof his house with mattresses" (Wiggins 2000). Although the play culminates in marriage, it is "devoid of erotic love"; Jonson "focuses his satire on social mobility, the scramble for position, power, status, and prestige" (Rose 1988). The play's *coup de théâtre* involves a boy impersonating a woman: Epicene, "the 'silent woman' of Jonson's subtitle, is simply a pretty boy in female disguise" (Rackin 1987). At the close "we are as astonished as everyone else to discover that Morose has married a boy. Even Clerimont and Truewit, the stage-manager figures who have guided us through the play's maze of fools . . . are totally taken by surprise" (Smith 1991b). Q 1620 two issues; the TP of the second issue gives the title as *The Silent Woman*. F2 1640 vol. 1.

In the F1 dedication Jonson writes, "There is not a line, or syllable in it changed from the simplicity of the first copy." Jonson had been criticized for his satirical bite. The second F prologue says, "If any, yet, will (with particular slight / Of application) wrest what he doth write; / And that he meant or him or her, will say: / They make a libell, which he made a play." This remark reflects a less than happy reception in the theater: "The play's cold brilliance accounts for its varied reception, and the distaste that some of the original audience seem to have felt" (Munro). Moreover, "by 1619 the play must inevitably have become identified with the Essex divorce of 1613, which involved both the Earl's public admission of impotence with his wife and the examination of Lady Frances by twelve matrons (who pronounced her to be a virgin)" (Dutton).

Epicene is "saturated with the fear of women who have moved or might move from their proper place of subordination, and it points to some of the changing social conditions that made such movement a possibility and a threat" (Howard 1988). "The play attacks 'hermaphroditical' talking women, women who transgress the culturally constructed codes of behavior believed appropriate to them in early modern England" (Newman 1991). "[H]eterosexual love is never actually experienced in *Epicoene*; instead, it is regarded by all the characters, particularly the males, with subtle but distinct aversion" (Rose).

An Equal Match. A droll based on several scenes in B&F's *Rule a Wife and Have a Wife* and performed in the 1640s and 50s. "Only three actors are necessary" (Elson 1932).

Published in *1 The Wits, or Sport upon Sport* (O 1662 two issues] and 1672); RT *The Humors of An Equal Match*; argument; list of characters.

The Escapes of Jupiter. Thomas Heywood (identified by Bullen 1885). Written 1620–23 (Janzen 1993). The SDs indicate preparation for performance, perhaps by Prince Charles's Men at the Phoenix (Bawcutt 1996). "[C]omposed of a number of scenes extracted from *The Golden Age* (1611) and *The Silver Age* (1613) and revised to form a new play dealing exclusively with Jupiter's affairs with Calisto, Danae, Semele, and Alcmena" (Janzen 1976); "New links are written for Homer, and there is some revision, especially in the first three acts" (Davison 1987). "The play is not merely an adapted or pasted-together version of the two old plays but a thorough revision of them into a new creative work" (Ioppolo 2006).

London, BL, Egerton MS 1994, fols. 74–95; no TP; no author named; in Heywood's hand; "The Escapes of Jupiter" is written on the last page (probably in a later hand [Greg 1931]); preceding act 1 is the title *Calisto*, "which refers only to the action of the first act" (Janzen 1976); "act-scene breaks, signalled by a ruled line" (Ioppolo 2006) but "no formal division into scenes" (Greg). The MS has been considered a draft, but the play was, in some form, staged. Herbert's entry of 26 August 1623 notes that it was "taken from the Cockpitt upon the remove of some of the sharers & because they had payde their parts thogh itt hath byn acted in the Kings house I have allowed of itt" (Bawcutt 1996). Bawcutt comments: "Possibly the sharers mentioned belonged to Prince Charles's company, which moved to the Cockpit or Phoenix theatre in 1619, but left it early in 1622 to go to the Curtain, when a totally new Lady Elizabeth's company was formed to play at the Phoenix." Very detailed SDs: the entry of Juno and Iris "*in a clowde above*" suggests the use of machinery; special effects include thunder and lightning and the descent of Jupiter with "*his thonder-bolt burning in his hande.*" "In outdoor playhouses . . . in addition to 'tempestuous' drums, a 'bullet,' i.e., a cannonball, was 'rolled' along a sheet of metal or a wooden trough [to simulate thunder]" (White 2007). One SD offers the acting company a choice: "*Eather strykes him with a staffe, or casts a stone.*"

SR none. First edited in its entirety by Janzen 1976; Bullen in an appendix to vol. 2 of *A Collection of Old English Plays* (1883) prints two songs from the play; Greg 1925 prints extracts.

The Eunuch. See *The Fatal Contract.*

Everyman (The Summoning of Everyman). Anonymous. Acted *c.* 1495 (Bevington 1975) at undetermined venue. "The use of Latin tags and quotations suggests a school or college play" (Walker 1998). *Everyman* represents a translation from the Dutch *Elckerlijc*, written by Peter van Diest *c.* 1470 and printed *c.* 1495 (Cooper & Wortham 1980). This continental origin helps explain a distinctive feature of the play: "Despite its well-deserved reputation as the most successfully timeless of morality plays, *Everyman* is designed for a crisis. The play is related to a particular continental reform movement of the fifteenth century, just as its atypical text appears to have affinities with drama of the Low Countries" (Bevington 1968). *Everyman* may have been "brought to England in the repertory of one of the groups of English players who are known to have toured in the Low Countries" (Mills 1995). "[T]he play in English may be as late as the first quarter of the sixteenth century" (King 2008a). Details mentioned in the text suggest that "the envisaged theatre of the English play is the Tudor hall" (Mills 1996). "[A]t least seven actors are required to play on a set which includes multiple locations, and multiple levels, and which demands iconographically intelligible visual spectacle" (King). The sixteen roles would have required more actors than the early companies (consisting of four men and a boy) could have supplied.

Because the quartos are undated, we cannot know with certainty the order in which they were printed. Q1 ND *c.* 1518–19 (Bruster & Rasmussen 2009); imperfect copy at Bodleian; first 682 lines missing; printed by Richard Pynson, named in colophon; two fragments survive: four leaves owned by the Bodleian (Douce fragment) plus another two in a private collection (Bandinel fragment). Q2 ND *c.* 1525–28; printed by Pynson; imperfect copy at BL; fragment of ten leaves; first 304 lines missing. Q3 ND *c.* 1522–29 (Cooper & Wortham); printed by John Skot, named in colophon; formerly in the Library of Lincoln Cathedral, then Britwell Library, now at the Huntington; *Here beginneth a treatise how the high father of heaven sendeth Death to summon every creature to come and give a count of their lives in this world and is in manner of a moral play*; ed. Greg 1904; the TP features woodcuts of a well-dressed Everyman (with a blank identifying label in a scroll above) and the skeletal figure of Death, who holds a coffin lid in his hand; both figures come from earlier French woodblocks (Davidson 1991); "ends with a short sermon from . . . a Doctor of Divinity, who points up the moral" (Walker 2000); not divided. "The text gives no guidance about Death's appearance, alluding only to his spear; but the woodcut prefacing the printed editions shows a wholly traditional skeletal Death, suggesting that this was how he was envisaged by readers, and most probably also audiences of the play" (Twycross & Carpenter 2002). "*Everyman* depends heavily on its iconography—its representation of persons, things and ideas through visual images" (Bruster & Rasmussen). Q4 ND *c.* 1529–31; printed by Skot; formerly in the possession of Henry Huth, now at the BL and catalogued as Huth 32; ed. Davidson et al. 2007; same TP woodcuts as Q3; verso of the TP is illustrated with five additional woodcuts, which depict six characters: Fellowship, Everyman, Beauty, Discretion, and (in a single woodcut) Strength and Kindred; labels in scrolls identify each.

Everyman "is an intensely solemn play which recalls the earliest period of moral drama: it is wholly an effectively dramatized sermon" (Jones 1983). "[T]he first printed play text in English" (Clopper 2001). "The only printed play to come out of the Middle Ages" (Coldewey 2004). "This is the only fully fledged 'coming of death' play in the English repertoire" (Grantley 2007). But because it represents a translation or adaptation of a Dutch play, "[i]t is hard to see [*Everyman*] as being a typical example of the English morality play" (Davidson et al. 2007); "it is part of a theatrical tradition significantly different from the English one" exemplified by *Wisdom, Mankind*, and the plays in the Digby MS (Coldewey 1993).

Every Man In His Humour. Ben Jonson. "Completed in the summer of 1598" (Riggs 1989); acted September 1598 (Miola 2000). "Sundry times publickly acted by" the Lord Chamberlain's Men, according to the Q TP, at the Curtain (Stern 2009b). Because of these TP words, Riggs concludes that "the production must have been at least moderately successful, although probably no more than that." As the title indicates, Jonson follows "a new trend by building his plot around a display of humor characters" (Potter 2012). He "hoped to capitalize on the phenomenal popularity" of Chapman's *An Humorous Day's Mirth* (Riggs). A complimentary reference to Falstaff (a humors character) by Macilente in *Every Man Out* indicates Jonson's awareness of Shakespeare's *1 Henry IV*. It is also possible that *The Merry Wives of Windsor*, a comedy of humors, "functioned as something of a dramatic model" for Jonson's play (Tiffany 1995). *Every Man In*, "wittily exploiting the fashionable notion of 'humours,' clearly established Jonson as the coming dramatist of the 1590s" (Donaldson 2004). Jonson "tailored his script to a cast of 16"; he later revised the play "for a slightly larger cast" (Ringler 1968). At the performance on 20 September "a foreign visitor lost three hundred crowns to a pickpocket at the Curtain" (Kay 1995). Praised by Francis Meres in *Palladis Tamia* (SR 7 September 1598). Performed also by the King's Men at Whitehall, 2 February 1605 (Chambers 1930), "possibly in the revised (1616 folio) version" (Dutton 1996). Principal actors were William Shakespeare, Richard Burbage, Augustine Phillips, Henry Condell, Thomas Pope, William Sly, Christopher Beeston, Will Kemp, John Heminges, and John Duke, according to F1. We do not know which role Shakespeare played, but this comedy "brought together in creative conjunction for the first time Shakespeare and Jonson, the two great dramatic geniuses of the English theatre" (Donaldson 2011). In the original production Kemp played the role of Cob (Butler 2004d). "[I]t is reasonable to suppose a revival some time in 1609–12" (Knutson 1999). Revived at Cockpit-in-Court 17 February 1631 (Teague 2009). Performed at the Blackfriars, 18 February 1631 (Dutton 1996), a benefit for Henry Herbert.

SR 4 August 1600 to be staied; 14 August 1600; transferred 16 October 1609; 2 March 1618; [10 June 1621]; 23 February 1626; 4 July 1635; 4 March 1639. Q 1601 "written by Ben. Johnson"; list of characters; five acts and separate scenes (in acts 1–3). F1 1616 *The Works*; *Every Man In His Humor, A Comedy*; "acted in the yeere 1598"; prologue, "written specifically for the revised version of the play" (Dutton 1996). The play "had been extensively rewritten at some point between 1604 and 1612" (Riggs 1989). Q has an Italian setting and names; F1, substantially revised probably near the time that F1 was published (Riddell 1997), has an English setting and anglicized names. The revision "involves a shift in focus towards more detailed social texturing of the action" (Grantley 2008a). The "King's Men's move to the Blackfriars may help explain why Jonson revised *Every Man in His Humour*, written for the Curtain, from its generalized Florentine setting to a carefully imagined London" (Cohen 2009). "Q has more explicit stage directions, including entrances and exits" (Miola). F2 1640 vol. 1; although no speech is labeled epilogue, Clement makes a conventional bid for applause at close.

The (new) F1 prologue, distinguishing this play from others, speaks disparagingly of typical staging practice at public playhouses: "you will be pleas'd to see / One such, to day, as other playes should be; / Where neither chorus wafts you ore the seas; / Nor creaking throne comes downe, the boyes to please; / Nor nimble squibbe is seene, to make afear'd / The gentlewomen; nor roul'd bullet heard / To say, it thunders; nor tempestuous drumme / Rumbles, to tell you when the storme doth come; / But deedes, and language, such as men doe use: / And persons, such as comœdie would chuse, / When she would shew an image of the times, / And sport with humane follies, not with crimes." Here Jonson "rejects the stage's established subject matter, notably including Shakespeare's civil war plays of *Henry VI*, as contemptuously as Marlowe did the 'rhyming mother wits' of the early 1580s in his prologue to *Tamburlaine the Great*; he also dismisses the kind of characters created by Marlowe and [Edward] Alleyn" (Wiggins 2000). "Jonson was echoing Sidney in his contempt not for realism in itself but for a too literal-minded use of mechanical devices and for the simple-minded belief that illusion can successfully become delusion" (Gurr 2009d).

Every Man Out of His Humour. Ben Jonson. Acted between 15 November and 20 December 1599 (Ostovich 2001). By the Lord Chamberlain's Men, according to the F1 TP, at the first Globe; the revised epilogue refers to "The happier spirits in this faire-fild Globe"; this was Jonson's "first work for the Globe theatre" (Donaldson 2011). Performed also by the Chamberlain's Men at Whitehall, between 26 December 1599 and Twelfth Night 1600. "In the revised ending written for court performance, the envious figure Macilente declares himself to be wholly redeemed by the sudden appearance of the queen herself: a hopeful, if implausible conclusion" (Donaldson 2004). (In Q1, F1, and F2 Macilente's address is printed as an appendix.) "[P]ossibly performed at Middle Temple during the 1599/1600 Christmas season" (Clare 2005), "especially in light of the play's connexions with the Middle Temple revels" (Gras 1989). Revived by the King's Men in the Great Hall at Whitehall, 8 January 1605 (Chambers 1930). Principal actors were Richard Burbage, John Heminges, Augustine Phillips, Henry Condell, William Sly, and Thomas Pope, according to F1. The absence of Shakespeare's name from the cast list "is rather striking" (Duncan-Jones 2001). Will Kemp is also "a conspicuous absentee from the cast" (Butler 2004d). "Jonson wrote the part of the bitter-witted Carlo Buffone" for Robert Armin (Hornback 2009b), whose "principal physical traits were ugliness and dwarfishness" (Wiles 1987).

SR 8 April 1600; transferred 28 April 1638; 4 March 1639. Q1 1600 [octavo-in-fours] *The Comical Satire of Every Man Out of His Humor*; "as it was first composed by the author B. J."; "contrary to normal practice" the TP "omits any reference either to the acting company or to stage performances" (Riggs 1989); the TP "proclaims the writer with an emphasis such that his presence is felt as the very hand behind the usually neutral and anonymous wording" (Jowett 1993); the first play Jonson published in Q; list of characters with a paragraph of description for each (a "daring" innovation [H&S]); the "lengthy descriptions provide for the reader a mass of information that was not available on stage" (Holland 1979); substantial induction including Prologue, who declines to speak a prologue; alternative ending with Macilente and *Grex*, which serves function of chorus; five acts and separate scenes. "[T]he only real point of resemblance" between this play and its predecessor "is their titles" (McDonald 1988). The differences "are greater than the likenesses. The characters in the second play are more highly individualized, less personifications of type, and more definitely in the traditions of contemporary satire"; Jonson seeks to create a "recognizable dramatic equivalent of formal satire" (Campbell 1938). By coining the term "comical satire," Jonson "was positing a new departure in English comedy. The term 'comical satire' draws attention to the mixture of linguistic and stylistic registers demonstrable in the play, while the alignment with comedy of the sub-species of satire also evokes the verse satire as practised by John Marston and Joseph Hall" (Clare 1998). The genre would be "developed further in the two subsequent 'comical satires,'" *Cynthia's Revels* and *Poetaster* (Steggle 2010). As the title indicates, *Every Man Out* also participates in the vogue for humors comedy; humors "characterization is always to some degree satirical, because it assumes a critical distance between character and spectator" (Wiggins 2000). Character in Jonson's play, "as is innate in the concept of the humour character, is a given, a premise from which the action emerges" (Holland).

Q TPs report that the printed versions contain "more than hath been publickely spoken or acted" ("the declaration is somewhat superfluous since the text in its entirety is unstageworthy" [Clare 2005]); the TP "clearly publicizes Jonson's own text, not its performance" (Murray 1983). "[T]he gambit of offering a *non*-theatrical text had not been tried before" (Jowett 1991a). Jonson "is thinking of the play now as a reading experience rather than a theatrical experience" (Barish 1981). At the close of Q1 Jonson tells us: "It had another catastrophe or conclusion, at the first playing: which . . . many seem'd not to rellish it; and therefore 'twas since alter'd: yet that a right-eyd and solide reader may perceive it was not so great a part of the heaven awry, as they would make it; we request him but to looke downe upon these following reasons." "Given that Jonson did not restore the original version when he printed the play, we may suspect that it was official intervention rather than popular opinion that forced the change on him" (Dutton 1993).

Q2 1600. Q3 1600. "The printed version was a best-seller, going through a remarkable three editions in eight months" (Shapiro 2005), "a feat unequaled by any play since John Lyly's *Campaspe* in 1584" (Riggs 1989). F1 1616 *The Works*; *Every Man Out of His Humor, A Comical Satire*; "acted in the yeere 1599." The alternative ending of F1, called "The epilogue at the presentation before Queene Elizabeth, by Macilente" in F2, suffered "censorship following a Globe performance, because it had dared to represent the Queen on the stage" (Clare 1999). "The suppressed address to the Queen remains as an addition to the Folio version of the play, but it is stripped of Jonson's justification for its inclusion and hence his elaborate praise of the Queen" (Clare 1998). F1 also presents "changes in act/scene division and stage directions in accordance with the neoclassical system of massed entries" (Donovan 1999). F1 offers both "a considerably revised ending, as well as persistent changes in spelling, punctuation, wording, scene-division, and stage directions" (Ostovich). F2 1640 vol. 1.

Jonson's play contains his "first recorded reactions to Shakespeare": "there may be some degree of homage to Shakespeare in the dog which accompanies the foolish knight Sir Puntarvolo on his travels—perhaps played by the same animal that made a hit as Crab in *Two Gentlemen of Verona*—and in the play's last line, where Macilente/Asper, the author-surrogate, asks the audience for applause which 'may, in time, make lean Macilente as fat as Sir John Falstaff'"; "there is also a personal sneer at the coat of arms Shakespeare had acquired for his father in 1596" (Clark 2007).

In F Jonson dedicates the play to the Inns of Court: "I understand you, gentlemen, not your houses: and a worthy succession of you, to all time, as being borne the judges of these studies. When I wrote this poeme [i.e., play], I had friendship with divers in your societies; who, as they were great names in learning, so they were no lesse examples of living. Of them, and then (that I say no more) it was not despis'd. Now that the printer, by a doubled charge, thinkes it worthy a longer life, then commonly the ayre of such things doth promise; I am carefull to put it a servant to their pleasures, who are the inheriters of the first favour borne it." "Jonson seems to say that Inns of Court gentlemen prominently attended the earliest performances of the play, apparently in 1599" (Nelson 2009b). The play contributes to the poetomachia; Jonson attacks Marston in the characters of Clove and Orange (Knowles 2004): these characters speak "fustian—meaningless pretentious vocabulary of the sort affected by Marston and including incidentally some of the words given to Chrisoganus by Marston" (Steggle 1998). "Marston responded with lampoons in *Jack Drum's Entertainment* (1600) and *What You Will*" (Rutter 1984).

Every Woman In Her Humour. ?Lewis Machin (Adams 1913). Acted November 1599-*c*. 1603 (Tyson 1980) at undetermined venue. Possibly acted by the Children of the King's Revels (Cathcart 2008).

SR none. Q 1609 no author named; prologue (by Flavia); not divided. The play "is an imitation in part of Jonson's two early comedies of humor; and it is frankly indebted for the suggestion of several of its characters and some of its plot to *Every Man Out of His Humour*" (Adams 1913). The SDs "are hopelessly brief" (Jewkes 1958). A song, however, indicates offstage sound effects: "Chaunt birds in everie bush / The blackbird and the thrush / The chirping nightingale. / The mavis and wagtaile, / The linnet and the larke / Oh how they begin, harke, harke!" A "contemporary musical setting" has been discovered for "Philautus' 'Here's none but only I'—the one snatch which is quoted twice in the play" (Cutts 1965). "Prosecutors of vice, Acutus and Graccus satirize the analogous female and male makeup scenes of the bawd Getica's makeup and of Philautus's (self-love's) cosmetic rites"; "[t]he bawd Getica and the vain foolish courtier Philautus are linked by their mutual face-paint" (Drew-Bear 1994). The play concludes with a "trick dance": "let pipers strike up, ile daunce my cinquepace [galliard], cut aloft my brave capers, whirle about my toe, doe my tricks above ground" (Wright 1928).

Contrary to usual practice, the speaker of the prologue is female, in keeping with the play's title: "Gentles of both sexes, and all sortes, I am sent to bid yee welcome; I am but insteade of a prologue: for a she prologue is as rare as an usurers almes." The prologue "offers at least a modicum of authority to the woman as spectator and to the woman as character, and 'feminizes' what is to follow" (Schneider 2011).

The Example. James Shirley. Licensed for acting 24 June 1634 (Adams 1917, Jones 1987). "Presented by" Queen Henrietta Maria's Men at the Phoenix, according to the TP. In playlist of Beeston's Boys 10 August 1639.

SR 18 October 1637. Q 1637 prologue (printed at end) and epilogue; five acts. A song near the close is included in Shirley's 1646 *Poems* and entitled "Melancholy converted."

Prologue targets those who sit on the stage at private theaters and carp about the drama: "hee that in the parish never was / Thought fit to bee o'th jury, has a place / Here, on the bench, for six pence; and dares sit, / And boast himselfe commissioner of wit, / Which though he want, he can condemne with othes, / As much as they that weare the purple clothes, / Robes I should say, or whom i'th Roman state / Some ill-look'd stage-keepers, like lictors waite / With pipes for fasces, while another beares / Three-footed stooles in stead of ivory chaires, / This is a destiny, to which wee bow, / For all are innocent but the poets now, / Who suffer for their guilt of truth, and arts, / And we for only speaking of their parts." Shirley's complaint refers not only to the gallants who sat on the stage but also "to those who prefer only the type of entertainment that pleased the Court taste" (Burner 1988).

An Excellent Conceited Tragedy of Romeo and Juliet. See *Romeo and Juliet.*

An Excellent and Pleasant Comedy, Termed after the Name of the Vice, Common Conditions. See *Common Conditions.*

An Excellent New Comedy entitled The Conflict of Conscience. See *The Conflict of Conscience.*

An Excellent Tragedy of Muleasses the Turk. See *The Turk.*

Exchange Ware. See *Band, Ruff, and Cuff.*

Ezechias. Nicholas Udall. Probably written before 1540 (Aston 1993) or "as late as the mid-1540s" (Hornback 2007) and acted the night of 8 August 1564 (Boas 1914) by students of King's College, Cambridge, in the college chapel, before Queen Elizabeth (White 2004a). "*Ezechias* was quite possibly staged on at least one earlier occasion, before [Thomas] Cromwell in 1538 while its author, Nicholas Udall, was Headmaster of Eton, the sister foundation to King's College" (White). The play "was doubtless revised" for the 1564 performance (Aston).

Although this play about the Old Testament King Hezekiah is lost, a Latin summary by Abraham Hartwell of King's College survives in *Regina Literata* (1565): "The play opened with Hezekiah's destruction of the altars and shrines of the idolaters. The brazen serpent, abused by those who had strayed so far from Moses' law, was struck down; false religion was abolished and true observance set up in its place. The incensed heathen worshippers thereupon rebelled and overthrew (apparently on stage) the altars of Jehovah" (Aston). The play "must have dramatized King Hezekiah's conversion of the Israelites from pagan deities to the worship of Jehova—a timely parallel to Elizabeth's championing of the protestant cause against the Roman church" (Smith 1988a). Udall's play closed with an epilogue (Boas).

"In the biblical episode, Ezechias is the king who destroys idols and images, but his son, once on the throne, surrounded by wicked counsellors, allows idolatry. At the end, Ezechias's grandson comes to the throne and, following the advice of wise counsellors, restores David's laws. Protestants saw in this episode an allegory of their battle against Romanism and its symbols" (Cioni 2008).

F

Fair Em, The Miller's Daughter of Manchester. Possibly written by Thomas Kyd (Vickers 2008b), or Robert Wilson (Mithal 1960), or Anthony Munday (Henning 1980), or William Shakespeare (Sams 1995); "the corrupt text makes authorship attribution by means of internal evidence very difficult" (Erne 2003a). Acted 1589–91 (Henning) at undetermined venue. "Sundrie times publiquely acted in the honourable Citie of London" by Lord Strange's Men, according to the Q1 TP. Possibly performed by Sussex's Men at the Rose under the title *William the Conqueror*, 4 January 1594 (Greg 1927). Possibly performed by the Lord Chamberlain's Men, 1594–96 (Knutson 1999). The play "shows signs of being calculated for performance in Manchester, being highly complimentary to Sir Edmund Trafford. Edward Alleyn may have led Strange's men through Manchester in 1593 on his way from Chester to York" (George 1991).

SR none. Q1 ND ?1591 *A Pleasant Comedy of Fair Em, The Miller's Daughter of Manchester, with the Love of William the Conqueror*; no author named; not divided, despite the designation of act 1, scene 1. "*Fair Em* purports to be about William the Conqueror but confines itself to his imaginary love life" (Potter 2012). A painting figures in the staging when "William the Conqueror is 'overthrown' at the tilt by the portrait of Blanche, Princess of Denmark, painted on his opponent's shield" (Rochester 2010). When William goes to Denmark and actually sees Blanche, "he finds her ugly, and falls instead for Mariana, the Swedish princess held hostage in the Danish court. He wants to free her from the court, but she loves Lubeck, and comes up with the idea of escaping in a mask that will in fact conceal the substitution of Blanche" (Hyland 2011). "[T]he play has been abridged almost to the point of obscuring the action" (Greg). Q2 1631.

Q1 "was catalogued as Shakespeare's in the library of King Charles II" (Dobson 2001).

The Fair Favorite. William Davenant. Licensed for acting 17 November 1638 (Adams 1917, Edmond 1987). Acted by the King's Men at the second Blackfriars. Performed also before the king and queen at Whitehall Cockpit, 20 November and 11 December 1638 (Adams). Royal interest in the play may have arisen out of Davenant's treatment of marriage: his point "is not to devalue marriage, but to praise both 'mistriss' and wife for making virtue and love, not public or political expediency, the proper basis for it" (Veevers 1989). "The play's miracle ending—in which the king belatedly falls in love with his foreign queen—also seems designed to allude to the late blossoming of Charles's own conjugal affections after the death of Buckingham" (Perry 2006a). "The king recovers both his humanity and his kingship *through* his marriage" (Sharpe 1987). In playlist of King's Men 7 August 1641.

SR 4 September 1646; transferred 14 October 1672; 30 January 1673. F 1673 *The Works*; "now published out of the authors originall copies"; list of characters; five acts and first scenes.

Fair Favorite is "perhaps the most explicitly political of Davenant's works" (Sharpe). "The one principle that significantly interrelates the three problematic relationships of the play . . . is an emphasis on government as an agreement involving the *consent* of both ruler and ruled" (Butler 1984b).

The Fair Maid of Bristow. Anonymous. Acted late 1603 (Duncan-Jones 2001) by the Lord Chamberlain's/King's Men at the first Globe. Also "plaide at Hampton [Court]," before the king and queen, according to the TP and the SR, Christmas season 1603–04; this performance took place on 26 December 1603 (Gurr 2004c). *Fair Maid* has "a rather old-fashioned air" (Astington 1999a). Robert Armin may have played the role of Frog (Gurr); "a number of verbal jokes play upon Armin's [diminutive] size" (Wiles 1987).

SR 8 February 1605. Q 1605 no author named; not divided. "The feigned death of Sentloe . . . is determined by an explicit stage direction: 'Heere he stabs his arme, and blodies Sentloes face, and pluckes out Vallingers sword and blodies it, and laies it by him'" (Butterworth 2005). "A platform with three or four steps up to it, which could be used as an executioner's scaffold, is needed" (Gurr 2009d), but at the last moment the condemned person "gains a reprieve" (Owens 2005).

Other "late prodigal plays" include *Eastward Ho*, *The Honest Whore*, *How a Man May Choose a Good Wife*, *If You Know Not Me You Know Nobody*, *If It Be Not a Good Play*, *The London Prodigal*, and *The Wise Woman of Hogsdon* (Skura 2003).

The Fair Maid of the Exchange, with the Pleasant Humors of the Cripple of Fanchurch. "Perhaps written by Thomas Heywood" (Egan 2006a); Kirkman's 1671 list attributes the play to him. "[P]robably first performed in 1607" (Howard 2007) at undetermined venue. Possibly performed by Worcester's Men, who became the Queen's Men upon the accession of James I. Possibly performed at the Red Bull (Reynolds 1940). Possibly performed only on tour in the provinces (Snyder 1980). The twenty-two characters named in the Q1 list are arranged to show how "eleven may easily acte this comedie." However, this claim is "mendacious," for "the table is inoperative" (Lawrence 1927).

SR 24 April 1607; transferred 9 April 1616; 27 February 1636; 22 December 1647. Q1 1607 "very delectable, and full of mirth"; no author named; list of characters; prologue; not divided despite the designation of scene 1. "Frequent marginal" SDs (Jewkes 1958), some of which "suggest that the copy behind the quarto of 1607 may at some time have been used in the theatre" (Brown 1962). Considerable onstage entertainment: "Bowdler capers and sings so frivolously that Ralfe comments: 'Faith sir, me thinkes of late you are very light'" (Wright 1928). Staging apparently requires a drawer's shop: "*Enter Cripple in his shop.*" Q2 [octavo-in-fours] 1625 *The Fair Maid of the Exchange, together with the Merry Humors and Pleasant Passages of the Cripple of Fanchurch*. Q3 1637.

Cripple's "deformity has set him somewhat aside from the stream of life so that he is both observer and participant" (Snyder). "Cripple is the ambiguous genius of the [Royal] Exchange, the spirit of the place, and that spirit is of mixed and vaguely sinister origins" (Howard). The Exchange was built by Thomas Gresham *c.* 1564–70.

The Fair Maid of the Inn. Philip Massinger, John Webster, and John Ford (Sykes 1924); with John Fletcher. Webster wrote "nearly half of the play" (Hoy 1960). "It appears that after plotting *The Fair Maid of the Inn* (perhaps with Massinger) and making a bare beginning of writing it, Fletcher died of the plague, for only a little of his writing survives in two scenes" (Lloyd 2005). Licensed for acting at the [second] Blackfriars, 22 January 1626 (Adams 1917) by the King's Men; the license ascribes the play to Fletcher, who had been buried 29 August 1625.

SR not included in entry of 4 September 1646; 29 June 1660; 30 January 1673. B&F F1 1647 *Comedies and Tragedies*; "never printed before, and now published by the authours originall copies"; *The Fair Maid of the Inn*; prologue; five acts and first scenes. Few SDs apart from entrances and exits. However, "*Foro[bosco] lookes in a booke, strikes with his wand, musick playes. Enter 4 boys shap't like frogs, and dance*"; "*Clown teares off his doublet, making strange faces as if compeld to it, falls into the daunce.*" "The printer's copy seems to have been authorial papers prepared for use as a prompt-book" (Bowers 1996). B&F F2 1679 *Fifty Comedies and Tragedies*; "the songs to each play being added"; *The Fair Maid of the Inn, A Tragicomedy*; list of characters. "Jacobean tragicomedy is famous for the surprising turns its various actions can take, but few plays of the period can outdo" *Fair Maid* (Hoy 1985).

The F1 prologue complains of unappreciative playgoers: "Playes have their fates, not as in their true sence / They're understood, but as the influence / Of idle custome madly workes upon / The drosse of many-tongu'd opinion. / A worthy story, howsoever writ / For language, modest mirth, conceite or witt, / Meetes often times with the sweett commendation / Of *hang't, 'tis scurvy*, when for approbation / A jigg shall be clapt at, and every rime / Prais'd and applauded by a clamorous chime."

1 The Fair Maid of the West, or A Girl Worth Gold. Thomas Heywood. Acted 1597–1603 (Turner 1967) or perhaps the early Jacobean era (Potter 1996). Probably first performed by Worcester's/Queen Anne's Men at the Red Bull. "Lately acted before the king and queen, with approved liking, by the queens majesties comedians," according to the TP. (Both parts of *Fair Maid* may have been performed in the same evening at court [Bentley 1984] as they were by the RSC at Stratford-upon-Avon 1992.) Revived by Queen Henrietta Maria's Men at the Phoenix, *c.* 1630, and at Hampton Court, before the king and queen, between 30

October 1630 and 20 February 1631 (King 1992a). Michael Bowyer played Mr. Spencer; Richard Perkins, Captain Goodlack; Hugh Clark, Bess Bridges; Christopher Goad, Mr. Forset and a Spanish Captain; William Sherlock, Roughman; William Robbins, Clem; Anthony Turner [Q has *Furner*, "a misprint" (Kathman 2005)], Kitchen Maid; Robert Axell, an English Merchant; William Allen, Mullisheg, King of Fez; [William] Wilbraham, Bashaw Alcade, according to dramatis personae. "But many small parts remain undistributed, and many of these must have been doubled" (Lawrence 1927). "The fairly full cast (ten actors) before Part 1 must be that for the revival with Part 2, for the players named are the familiar members of Queen Henrietta's company, a troupe which was not organized until fifteen or more years after Part 1 first appeared" (*JCS*).

SR 16 June 1631. Q 1631 author's initials on the TP and Heywood signs the dedication; dramatis personae; prologue (for Hampton Court) ["one prologue and one epilogue serve for both parts" (*JCS*)]; chorus at end of Act 4 says, "Our stage so lamely can expresse a sea, / That we are forst by Chorus to discourse / What should have beene in action"; the chorus "then acts as an expository prologue to the last act" (Schneider 2011); description of dumb show; five acts and first scenes. Published together with *2 Fair Maid* as one book, though each part has its own TP (Turner). "The prologue and epilogue were reprinted in Heywood's *Pleasant Dialogues and Dramas* (1637)" (Kathman 2005). SDs "provide for [the Earl of] Essex and the Mayor of Plymouth to appear in walk-on dumb-show parts" (Heinemann 1993b). The Q TP features a woodcut, which "is presumably intended to suggest Bess Bridges, the 'fair maid' of the title, and central figure in the two plays" (Foakes 1985). She falls in love with Captain Spencer and, "when he is falsely reported killed in the island voyage to the Azores, she fits out a ship with a legacy he has left her, and goes in quest of his body" (Boas 1950a). A painting expresses the heroine's love: "*Enter Bess with Spencers picture*"; she says, "I vow / Never to marry other." "In essence Bess exists in an all-male world, but she proves absolutely central to that world and to the text's construction of an English national identity" (Howard 1994a). In *Part 1* Bess Bridges "dresses as a man in order to expose the cowardice of the appropriately named Roughman"; "[p]retending to be her brother, she forces Roughman to throw down his sword, tie up her shoe, untruss her points, and lie on the ground while she walks over him" (Crupi 1998).

In his preface Heywood writes, "I hold it no necessity to trouble thee with the Argument of the story, the matter itself lying so plainly before thee in Acts and Scenes, without any deviations, or winding indents." Although the play is "published specifically for 'thy private reading,' [Heywood] is vigorously anti-Argument" (Stern 2009c). In his address to the reader Heywood adopts a characteristic lament: "my plaies have not beene exposed to the publike view of the world in numerous sheets, and a large volume; but singly (as thou seest) with great modesty, and small noise."

2 The Fair Maid of the West, or a Girl Worth Gold. Thomas Heywood. Acted *c.* 1630 (Turner 1967). "Lately acted before the king and queen, with approved liking" by Queen Henrietta Maria's Men, according to the *Part 2* TP, at Hampton Court between 30 October 1630 and 20 February 1631; also performed at the Phoenix. Theophilus Bourne/Bird played Toota, Queen of Fez; Anthony Turner, Bashaw Alcade; Christopher Goad, the Duke of Ferrara; Robert Axell, the Duke of Mantua; John Sumner, the Duke of Florence, according to dramatis personae in *Part 2*, which does not provide the names of the actors who performed the major roles in *Part 1*, perhaps because those roles were performed by the same actors in *Part 2*.

SR 16 June 1631. Q 1631 author's initials on the TP and Heywood signs the dedication; dramatis personae; chorus (describing a plot development); description of dumb show; epilogue at court; five acts and first scenes. "The fact that both title pages boast of a court performance suggests that they were acted together, a suggestion apparently confirmed by the fact that there is no epilogue for Part 1 and no prologue for Part 2, but only a prologue addressed to the court before Part 1 and an epilogue obviously to the court for Part 2" (Bentley 1984). Prologue to *Part 1* and epilogue to *Part 2* appear (in somewhat different form) in Heywood's *Pleasant Dialogues and Dramas*. The SDs call for "*a storme*" and "*a blasing starre*." The latter "consisted either of a firework on a line or flaming material suspended in an iron cage or cresset, and burned for up to a minute" (Holdsworth 1990). Published together with *1 Fair Maid* as one book but with separate pagination. The *Part 2* TP reproduces the woodcut of *Part 1*.

The two parts of the play, written decades apart, "show how prevailing dramatic modes had changed": in place of the "simplicity" of *Part 1*, "the action [of *Part 2*] turns on sexual passion and revenge" (McLuskie 1981). "In the earlier drama, written under Elizabeth, the military and financial competence of Bess was celebrated even though it is clear that Bess's success threatened to undermine the masculinity of her followers. In Part II, by contrast, Bess is represented as potentially fickle, tyrannical and misguided in contrast to the male characters, whose code of honour she is unable to understand" (Jowitt 2003). "Part II, staged at the Caroline court, recasts the characters to confirm a stable social arrangement resting on mythicized monarchy and the self-idealizations of Charles and Henrietta Maria" (Crupi 1998).

A Fair Quarrel. Thomas Middleton and William Rowley. Rowley wrote the "domestic" and clown material, along with "the opening and closing scenes" (Mooney 1986). Acted autumn or winter of 1616–17 (Price 1976a). "[P]robably written for the Red Bull" (Gurr 1988a); "divers times publikely" acted by Prince Charles's Men, according to the Q1 TP. First performances would have occurred "before Prince Charles's Men started performing at the Red Bull . . . but the added roaring scene is evidence of a revival in 1617, and given the abundant evidence for the play's continuing popularity, it is inconceivable that they did not perform it during their approximately two years' tenure at the Red Bull" (Taylor 2002a). Rowley "was a leading member of the company" (Howard-Hill 1987b). Performed by that company at court, "before the king," according to the Q1 TP, probably 28 December 1616 (Nicol 2009); "King James would have been particularly interested in the principal action of the play, with its suggested condemnation of hasty duels" (*JCS*). Records from Office of the Revels "show that this play was considered for performance at Court in 1619 or 1620, and perhaps it was performed" (Price). "Prior to its first publication in 1617 it had already been revised, probably for a stage revival" (Jowett 2007a). In playlist of Beeston's Boys 10 August 1639.

SR no original; transferred 2 September 1621; 3 December 1627; 21 May 1628. Q1 1617 two issues; names of the authors are bracketed on the TP, "a practice that became common in early seventeenth-century English drama" (Peters 2000); five acts and first scenes. Additions in the second issue of Q1 were intended for performance (Price 1949); the TP specifies "new additions of Mr. Chaughs and Tristrams Roaring, and the Bauds Song. Never before printed"; the "new songs are inserted after act 4 in four leaves which were added to this edition" (Bentley 1971). "Since William Rowley was both a collaborator in the original composition of the play and a patented member of Prince Charles's Company, it seems likely that he wrote the new songs for the company" (Bentley). The additional material "forms a single 223-line extension of the fourth act" (Rasmussen 1997). Rowley "likely" played Chough (Hutchings & Bromham 2008, Nicol 2008b). The supplementary scene must have been added for a revival "probably a year or two later than the rest of Q1's text, in 1617" (Holdsworth 1974). Staging includes "a regular fencing match" between two characters whose friends "watch and comment upon" it (Wright 1968). "Middleton and Rowley target habitues of schools of fencing and dueling that inculcated manliness, an indispensable requisite for gentlemanliness in an era when masculinity was being redefined more as serving to govern in peace than as waging war" (Clark 2003). The play's embedded jig "reveals the external code of honor to be no more than a noble and quarrelsome kind of roaring and serves as a fitting completion to the process by which meaningful concepts like *fair* and *honor* are reduced to absurdity through blind adherence to the dueling code" (Mooney 1980). "The play's critique of honor is . . . not restricted to exploding the Christian pretensions of the dueling code; rather, it goes so far as to locate honor's origins in a gender system through which men convert the sexual destinies of their female kin into social prestige and kinship alliances, thereby insuring that men hold sway over a social order comprising a hierarchy of male bonds constructed out of female lives" (Pacheco 1998). Q2 1622 "with new additions [described on the Q1 TP]." The Q1–2 TPs feature a woodcut of two men fighting with swords. "The taller one on the left has a full beard, and may be intended to suggest the Colonel, who has 'a beard' (I.i.84), while the shorter figure may indicate Captain Ager, who is called 'a boy' by the Colonel (I.i.84), a few lines before they draw swords on one another" (Foakes 1985). The woodcut suggests "the popularity of such battles" onstage (Borden 2006).

The Q1 dedication, signed by Rowley, evokes a metaphor popular in late 1590s and early seventeenth-century: "this great world is no more then a stage, where every one must act his part. . . . all have exites and must all be stript in the tyring-house (*viz.*, the grave) for none must carry any thing out of the stocke."

The Fairy Chase. See *The Fairy Pastoral.*

The Fairy Knight, or Oberon the Second. ?Thomas Randolph (Bowers 1942); authorship remains uncertain (Davidson 1978); "the attribution continues to appear extremely questionable" (Levenson 1987). In its original form, possibly acted *c.* 1623–24 for Christmas festivities at Westminster School (Bowers). However, Bentley (*JCS*) doubts both Randolph's authorship and the venue proposed by Bowers; Bentley also finds evidence of a Jacobean date "negligble," preferring *c.* 1631–33. Leishman 1944 judges Bowers' ascription of the play to Randolph "improbable."

Washington, Folger, MS V.a.128, fols. 1–38; a revised and augmented version of the original, transcribed by an unknown writer *c.* 1657–58 (Bowers); list of characters on the TP; prologue and epilogue; five acts and separate scenes. Ample SDs: "*The divil rises out of the ground*"; "*Here is to be exhibited an anticke dance of wiches.*" First edited by Bowers.

This play is to be distinguished from the lost *Fairy Knight* by Ford and Dekker, licensed for acting by Herbert 11 June 1624.

The Fairy Pastoral, or Forest of Elves. William Percy. No evidence of production but, according to a note in MSS Huntington HM 4 and Alnwick 509, the author intended that his plays be staged either by Paul's Boys or by the Children of the Revels. "William Percy wrote the play with the intention that it should be performed before the King, probably on his visit to Syon House [the home of the Earl of Northumberland, William Percy's eldest brother], on 8 June, 1603" (Dodds 1931b). Percy's "plays suggest private performance" (Hillebrand 1938).

(1) San Marino, CA, Huntington, MS HM 4 [latest of Percy MSS of this play], fols. 62–91; *The Fairy Pastoral, or Forest of Elves*; *Comedies and Pastorals*; the general TP, which contains the author's initials, is dated 1647; the date 1603 appears near the end of this play; list of characters; list of properties; prologue ("clearly addressed to a sovereign" [Dodds 1931b]) for the court; epilogue "delivered by a 'Chorus' of three characters" (Schneider 2011); signs of revision; tipped onto fol. 4 of this volume is a song that Percy attributes to Sir Philip Sidney: intended for act 4, scene 3, it is sung "to the tune of Green sleeves"; five acts and separate scenes. Staging calls for a trap door (a character hides in "*a lowe well with roape and pulley*"); "*a hollowe oake with vice of wood to shutt to*"; "*a greene bank being pillowe to the hed.*" Highly detailed SDs: "All the directions sound more like notes taken upon some production than general directions for all performances"

(Hillebrand 1926). The script designates "both title and locality boards" (Lawrence 1912b). Percy's plays "show a use of locality boards which is nowhere else so completely illustrated in Elizabethan drama; that such signboards existed is adequately proved by considerable other evidence, but Percy's plays furnish a unique statement as to how they were employed" (Reynolds 1914): "*Highest, aloft, and on top of the musick tree the title* The Faery Pastorall, *beneath him pind on post of the tree The Scene* Elvida Forrest." Percy makes prominent use of music: "one of the characters remarks, 'Five parts do make a whole consort they say. . . .' The term 'whole consort' usually refers to a band of instruments all of one family, that is, a consort of viols or of recorders" (Long 1980). (2) Alnwick, UK, Alnwick Castle, MS 508 [earliest of Percy MSS], fols. 65–96; *The Fairy Chase, or A Forest of Elves, A Pastoral*; at another point in Alnwick 508 appears "Sir Philip Sidneys Song," written for act 4, scene 3; MS dated 1644, this play "finis 1603." MS (3) Alnwick MS 509; *The Forest Pastoral, or Forest of Elves*; author's initials on the TP; general TP dated 1646, this play "finis 1603."

MS (1) first edited by Joseph Haslewood 1824 and published by the Shakspeare Press for the Roxburghe Club; this MS was later acquired by the Huntington.

The Faithful Friends. ?John Fletcher (Mehl 1962); written "possibly in collaboration with others" (Ioppolo 2006). ?Acted *c.* mid to late 1620s (Pinciss & Proudfoot 1970) at undetermined venue. "The music directions . . . may point towards the facilities of a private, indoor playhouse" (Pinciss & Proudfoot). No record of license for acting.

London, V&A, Dyce, MS 10 (D25.F10), fols. 1–78; the TP ascribes the play to B&F; dramatis personae on the TP; some speeches have been crossed out; damaged by stains; carefully described dumb show "containing a festive procession" (Mehl 1965); fol. 69 has "the plott of a scene of mirth to conclude this fourth acte"; possibly "the scene was originally left to be acted extempore, and . . . it was only later thought desirable to have the text written out" (Greg 1931); five acts, with scenes "marked in Act I only" (Greg). Staging includes *"An altar to be set forth with the image [i.e. statue] of Mars."* "[T]he purpose of this copy of *Faithful Friends* is not entirely clear—it might be for a censor or a printer or for performance" (Stern 2009c). SR 29 June 1660 *The Faithfull Friend*, a Comedy; ascribed to B&F. First edited by Weber 1812, *The Works of Beaumont and Fletcher*, vol. 1, then by Pinciss & Proudfoot.

The Faithful Friends may be identical with *The Noble Friend*, a title recorded by Malone in 1821 (Jackson 1973).

The Faithful Servant. See ***The Grateful Servant.***

The Faithful Shepherdess. John Fletcher. Acted 1607-March 1608 (Gurr 1969) or "around 1608–09" (Perry 1997) by the Children of the Queen's Revels (Munro 2005) at the second Blackfriars; the production was "a drastic failure" (Rose

1988). Later revived by the King's Men in the Presence Chamber at Somerset House, before King Charles and Queen Henrietta Maria, with changeable scenery designed by Inigo Jones, the night of 6 January (Twelfth Night) 1634, according to the Q2 TP; Herbert reports of the costumes, "in the cloathes the queene had given [Joseph] Taylor [lead actor of the King's Men] the year before of her owne pastorall [*The Shepherd's Paradise* by Walter Montagu]" (Adams 1917). In contrast to the original production, this revival "was an unqualified success" (Barton 1984). The play had been "transformed from its paternalistic Jacobean origins into a Caroline production which refines and redefines heroism, not as martial valour, but as self-abnegating devotion, and which validates spiritually strong women as the caretakers of a community's moral health" (Britland 2008). This revival "revealed the Queen's determination to promote her own interests through the theatre" (Bulman 2003). Probably performed at Whitehall Cockpit, the night of 8 April 1634 (Bawcutt 1996).

SR no original; transferred 8 December 1628; 7 November 1646; 17 March 1665. Q1 ND *c.* December 1608-May 1610 (Munro 2005) or 1610 (Erne 2003a); *The Pastoral of the Faithful Shepherdess* in explicit; five acts. SDs "are usually long and descriptive" (Jewkes 1958): "*The curtayne is drawne, Clorin appeares sitting in the cabin, Amoret sitting on the on[e] side of her, Allexis and Cloe on the other, the Satyre standing by*"; "*Enter Clorin the shepheardesse sorting of hearbs, and telling the natures of them.*" This "is the only play of nearly seventy in the Fletcher canon which shows clearly that the author himself was concerned in its publication" (Bentley 1971). Q2 1629 "the second edition, newly corrected"; omits Fletcher's preface to the reader. Q3 1634 "the third edition, with addition"; "acted at Somerset House before the king and queen on Twelfth Night last, 1633. And divers times since with great applause" at Blackfriars; immediately before act 1 we read: "This dialogue [between Priest and Nymph] newly added, was spoken by way of prologue to both their majesties at the first acting of this pastorall at Somerset-house on Twelfe-night 1633"; Davenant wrote this new prologue (Clark 1994). The dialogue "was later printed (with some variants)" in Davenant's 1673 *Dramatic Works* (Greg 1939). Q3 adds a poem by Shackerley Marmion celebrating Joseph Taylor "upon his presentment" of the play at Whitehall in 1633: "Thou brought'st her to the court, and made her be / A fitting spectacle for majestie." Marmion creates "a sense that an audience's new and refined taste made the revival especially appropriate" (McLuskie 2006). The Q3 TP "suggests that the play was a success this time," i.e., in its 1633 revival (Aaron 2005). Q4 1656 "the fourth edition." Q5 1665 "the fifth edition." B&F F2 1679 *Fifty Comedies and Tragedies*; "published by the authors original copies, the songs to each play being added"; no list, no prologue or epilogue, no actors' names.

"Various commendatory verses indicated that the play was a failure in its first production" (Bentley 1971). Jonson's poem in Q2, for example, recounts that "The wise, and many-headed bench . . . before / They saw it halfe, damd thy whole play." Fletcher's preface to the Q1 reader explains the play's initial failure (playgoers, unfamiliar with the genre, had mistaken expectations): "If you be not reasonably assurde of your knowledge in this kinde of poeme, lay downe the booke or read this, which I would wish had bene the prologue. It is a pastorall tragie-comedie, which the people seeing when it was plaid, having ever had a singuler guift in defining, concluded to be a play of country hired shepheards, in gray cloakes, with curtaild dogs in strings, sometimes laughing together, and sometimes killing one another: and missing whitsun ales, creame, wassel & morris-dances, began to be angry." This preface, which provides "the first adequate English definition of tragicomedy" (Foster 2004) and which draws upon the work of Giambattista Guarini, represents "an unusual and important attempt by Fletcher to influence a play-reading public that he did not customarily court" (Cannan 2002). "For Fletcher tragicomedy is not a mechanical combination of the attributes of tragedy and comedy but a subtle fusion in which each loses its identity" (Waith 1952). Beaumont's Q1 commendatory poem calls the printed play a "second publication, which may strike / Their consciences, to see the thing they scornd, / To be with so much will [?wit] and art adornd." The "uncontrolled Jacobean anger" of the first production "makes the play especially fitting for production at the reformed Caroline court, contrasting an earlier uneducated misrecognition with a new Caroline sensibility" (Britland 2006b).

The Faithful Shepherdess "served as a source both for Shakespeare in *The Tempest* and for Milton in *Comus*" (McMullan 2004). "*Philaster* has much in common with Shakespeare's *Cymbeline* . . . but it is not clear which came first" (Dobson 2001).

The Faithful Virgins. Elizabeth Polwhele/Polewheele. Acted *c.* 1670 (*AED 3*) or 1660s (Bodleian cataloguer) but the dramaturgy suggests a much earlier date: "it is a throwback to popular types of the 1620s and 1630s, filled with *précieux* sentiment" (Milhous 2004). According to the MS, "This tragedy apoynted to be acted by the dukes company of actors only leaving out what was cross'd by Henry Herbert." "The play was evidently intended for performance, and more than likely was indeed professionally performed" (Hurley 2009).

Oxford, Bodleian, MS Rawlinson poet. 195, fols. 49–78; no separate TP; no author named; careful description of a dumb show; five acts. Ample SDs describe spectacle: "*Here is discovered with tapers burning round it at the feet of it Merantha in black weeping a little noyse within.*" A witch commands spirits, who arise through a trap: "*two spirits ascende in white like nimphs.*" When the witch stamps her foot, the "*spirits descend.*" The witch conjures "spirits of the ayre": "*Thunder as in the ayre at that ceaseless soft musique and a song, song ended & spirit's in the shape of men and women descend and dance wth being don all vanish.*" Description of a dumb show suggests the possibility of painted scenery: "*a temple discovered, the duke with his lords and attendants on the one side: on the other Isabella and ladies.*"

The Faithless Relict. See *The Cyprian Conqueror*.

Fallacy. See *The Sophister.*

The False Favorite Disgraced, and The Reward of Loyalty, A Tragicomedy. George
Gerbier d'Ouvilly. The SR entry and the TP report, "never acted," but ample
SDs suggest attention to what playgoers might see: "*Enter Vatinius in a wastcoate,
drawers, and night cappe, them, and his face besmutted.*"
    SR 16 June 1657. O 1657 two issues, one of which fails to name the author
and omits the prefatory poems; list of characters; five acts. The prefatory poem by
J. Cole comments on the suppression of drama in his time: "Dramatick poems,
though the zealous age / Will not permit them to adorn the stage / Are without
doubt of greater excellence / Then they suppose, who want both wit and sence."
Cole concludes, offering the printed play in lieu of a performance, "Wee'l read,
and like, and think we see thy play."

The False Heir and Formal Curate. A droll based upon several scenes in B&F's *The
Scornful Lady* and performed in the 1640s and 50s. "Extensive cuts sometimes leave
episodes inconclusive. It is unlikely that the droll could be understood by an audience
unfamiliar with the play" (Elson 1932). Requires seven actors for performance.
    Published in *1 The Wits, or Sport upon Sport* (O 1662 [two issues] and 1672);
RT *The Humors of the False Heir*; argument; list of characters.

The False One, A Tragedy. John Fletcher and Philip Massinger. Acted ?1620
(E&G 1976) or 1619–23 (Gurr 2009d) by the King's Men at the second Black-
friars/second Globe. The play "is a response to the contemporary controversy
surrounding King James's pacifist and Hispanophile foreign policy, echoing the
concerns voiced in the anti-Spanish, anti-Catholic pamphlets of the early 1620s";
the play seems not "to have encountered obstacles from the authorities, as it had
an ancient setting; the transposition of the time frame was usually enough to
make a play acceptable to the censor" (Hila 2007). Principal actors were John
Lowin, John Underwood, Robert Benfield, Richard Sharp, Joseph Taylor, Nicholas Tooley, John Rice, and George Birch, according to F2. Richard Burbage and
Henry Condell may have acted in the original production (Turner 1992); Burbage died in March 1619.
    SR not included in entry of 4 September 1646; 29 June 1660; 30 January
1673 *The Safe One*, "probably a misreading of *The False One*" (*JCS*). B&F F1
1647 *Comedies and Tragedies*; "never printed before, and now published by the
authours originall copies"; prologue and epilogue, both perhaps written for a
revival (Schneider 2011); five acts and separate scenes. Few SDs apart from entrances and exits, but at one point the Roman soldier Septimius, the "false one"
of the play's title, enters "*with a head.*" "The property head, a perfect example of
the horrors classicism kept offstage, fits into the long tradition of emblematic
spectacle found in the dumb shows of Elizabethan plays as in street pageants and
masques" (Waith 1989). Staging also includes a masque-like interlude with Isis

and Nylus; the latter brings "*hidden holy heads.*" "The nine heads of Nile rise up and dance" (Gossett 1988). At the close Caesar and others "enter . . . with the heads" of their enemies. B&F F2 1679 *Fifty Comedies and Tragedies*; "published by the authors original copies, the songs to each play being added"; list of characters; actors' names.

The F1 prologue asserts the value of a fresh treatment of historical figures: "New titles, warrant not a play for new, / The subject being old: and 'tis as true, / Fresh, and neate matter may with ease be fram'd / Out of their stories that have oft been nam'd / With glory on the stage . . . . What wee present and offer to your view, / (Upon their faiths) the stage yet never knew." The King's Men were concerned "that their audience should not think that this new play . . . about Cleopatra was a revision of Daniel's *Tragedy of Cleopatra*, or Brandon's *The Virtuous Octavia*, or Shakespeare's *Antony and Cleopatra*" (Bentley 1971). "The Prologue to *The False One* disingenuously denies any intent to compete with earlier plays (not naming Shakespeare), because it deals with '*Young* Cleopatra' and not 'her fatal love to Antony'" (Clark 2007). *The False One* "is very different in tone from Shakespearian tragedy, nearer to Fletcher's customary tragicomic form" (McMullan 2004). Massinger seems particularly to have favored "strong-willed, active women," especially those "who hold public power" (Clark 1992).

The Family of Love. Lording Barry. Acted *c.* 1606 (Taylor et al. 1999). "By the Children of" the King's Revels, according to the Q TP, at the Whitefriars, 1607 (Lake 1975a); the Children were "tenants of the Whitefriars theater in 1607 and 1608" (Cathcart 2005). But the play was "originally written for the Paul's Boys" (Bly 2000) and possibly staged in 1602 or 1603 (Cathcart 2008). The author of this play shows a close acquaintance with the earlier *Club Law*, performed at Cambridge (Cathcart 2003a). Archer in 1656 ascribed the play to Thomas Middleton; Barry's role may have been that of reviser of a play written by Middleton *c.* 1602 and revised by Dekker *c.* 1605 (Lake). But the prologue refers to a single author, and Taylor, Mulholland, & Jackson argue for Barry's sole authorship. Cathcart believes that Marston was "an original composer of the play."

SR 12 October 1607; transferred 3 December 1627. Q 1608 two issues; no author named; list of characters; prologue (perhaps dates from a staging before that of the King's Revels [Jackson 1979]) and epilogue; five acts and separate scenes.

The address to the reader, possibly by Middleton (Lake), comments on the gap between performance and printing: "Too soone and too late, this work is published: too soone, in that it was in the presse, before I had notice of it, by which meanes some faults may escape in the printing. Too late, for that it was not published when the general voice of the people had seald it for good, and the newnesse of it made it much more desired, then at this time: for plaies in this citie are like wenches new falne to the trade, onelie desired of your neatest gallants, whiles the'are fresh: when they grow stale they must be vented by termers and cuntrie chapmen."

The Famous Chronicle of King Edward the First. See *Edward I.*

The Famous History of Promos and Cassandra. See *Promos and Cassandra.*

The Famous History of Sir Thomas Wyatt. See *Sir Thomas Wyatt.*

The Famous History of the Knight of the Burning Pestle. See *The Knight of the Burning Pestle.*

The Famous History of the Life and Death of Captain Thomas Stukeley. See *Captain Thomas Stukeley.*

The Famous History of the Life of King Henry VIII. See *Henry VIII.*

The Famous History of Troilus and Cressida. See *Troilus and Cressida.*

The Famous Tragedy of King Charles I, Basely Butchered. ?Samuel Sheppard (Smith 1994). A play-pamphlet, "primarily a dramatization of events late in 1648" (Potter 1981) and possibly acted *c.* 1649, it "could only have been staged in private locations, or in inns on an ad hoc basis" (Ravelhofer 2008). The commendatory verse epistle comments, "I wisht thy play had been more largely writ / Or I had ne're seene, or perused it." "Significantly, 'perusal,' the standard term for private reading at this time, is preempted here by its theatrical equivalent, 'seene.' What is registered in this momentary transfer of discourses is the mock-theatrical vividness of the play. At the same time, however, that vividness is not associated with visual experience alone, and here the special resources of closet drama creep back into the description" (Straznicky 1995).

SR none. Q1 1649 no author named; list of characters; "prologue to the gentry" and choral epilogue; chorus; five short acts. Although some readers doubt that the play was intended for performance (Aaron 2005), the SDs are expansive: "*Enter six masquers, habited for Ambition, Treason, Lust, Revenge, Perjury, Sacriledge, musick; they daunce with them, joyne Cromwell and Mistresse Lambert, Peters singing out last, they daunce together by themselves.*" This scene "reverses all the usual conventions: the performers are apparently Members of Parliament, dressed to represent not the virtues normally embodied by courtly masquers but the vices which are really theirs" (Potter 1981). "[T]he fact that the style was old-fashioned may . . . be significant. Supporters of Parliament claimed to be restoring a freedom that had previously existed, rather than introducing new ideas" (Potter 1988). Q2 dated 1649 but not printed until *c.* 1660 (Greg 1939).

The Q1 prologue to the gentry salutes past playwrights while condemning present hostility to the theater: "Though Johnson, Shakespeare, Goffe, and Davenant, / Brave Sucklin[g], Beaumont, Fletcher, Shurley want / The life of action, and their learned lines / Are loathed, by the monsters of the times; / Yet your refined soules, can penetrate / Their depth of merit, and excuse their fate." This prologue "emphatically joins the whole of the national literary tradition with a particular political and social order" (Hirst 1990).

"To a large extent [the play] is a passionate patchwork that gathers up a variety of events and names in the news in order to pass vindictive or vindicating judgment in one of the few ways that remained open to a royalist" (Randall 1995). The dramatist creates "a spectacular revelation of the king's mutilated body in the last scene, a discovery in the tradition of Hieronymo's revelation of his murdered son in *The Spanish Tragedy*" (Barton 1977). The play "staged the martyrdom of Cavalier heroes at the siege of Colchester, depicting Cromwell as a Marlovian machiavel, and ending with a chorus of lament at Charles's execution" (Butler 2002). This "is one of the very few plays concerned with the Rebellion that deals explicitly with current events and personages" (Aggeler 1978). For readers/playgoers *c.* 1649 "the play's characters would have been easily identifiable" (Ravelhofer).

The Famous Tragedy of Osmond the Great Turk. See *Osmond the Great Turk.*

The Famous Tragedy of the Rich Jew of Malta. See *The Jew of Malta.*

The Famous Victories of Henry V. Anonymous. Acted before mid-1587 (McMillin & MacLean 1998) at undetermined venue, possibly an inn-yard (Lawrence 1927), though "when actors performed at inns they usually occupied a large room rather than a yard and performed by candlelight" (Orrell 1997). The play "cannot be dated later than June 1587 because of the jest about Tarlton and Knell playing in it together" (Knutson 2009b). "An anecdote told in *Tarlton's Jests* [*c.* 1594] of [William] Knell and [Richard] Tarlton in the play reveals that it had been given at the Bull [Inn] in Bishopsgate Street" (Lawrence). Tarlton, who "was particularly noted for the physicality of his performances and for his *extempore* genius" (Walsh 2009b) and who died in 1588, played Derick, the rustic carrier turned cobbler. "Plaide by" the Queen's Men, according to the Q1 TP. The play "might have been played by them at the Swan playhouse at its opening in 1595–6" (Knutson 2004). Henslowe records thirteen performances of "harey the v," but it is unlikely that these entries designate *The Famous Victories* (Gurr 2009c): 28 November, 2, 8, 16, and 28 December 1595; 5 and 19 January 1596; 6 February 1596; 23 April 1596; 26 May 1596; 17 June 1596; 10 and 15 July 1596. "At one performance of *The Victories* [Richard Tarlton] played the Justice as well as the Clown, and then made fun of the doubling by alluding humorously, as the Clown, to the box on the ear he had received as the justice" (Mann 1991). "[N]o other Elizabethan actor was so much spoken and written about after his death [in 1588]" (Thomson 2004b). The part of Prince Henry "was originally played by William Knell" (Corbin & Sedge 1991). After the Queen's Men disbanded, the play "continued to be performed by other companies" (Shapiro 2005). *Famous*

Victories "appears to have had stage life after its registration at Stationers' Hall [in 1594]" (Knutson 2001b). The play "has 41 speaking roles, 47 roles in all" (Mc-Millin & MacLean).

SR 14 May 1594 "There was probably a 1594 edition" that is lost (Griffin 2001). Q1 1598 *The Famous Victories of Henry the Fifth, Containing the Honorable Battle of Agincourt*; no author named; not divided. At the play's beginning, actors may have entered riding horses: "An entry on horseback into the yard was probably practical when the play was first performed at the Bull Inn" (Corbin & Sedge). The best known SD of the play involves a gift to the King from the Dauphin: "*He delivereth a tunne of tennis balles.*" The gift is explained: "You are more fitter for a tennis court / Then a field." Shakespeare would incorporate this incident in his *Henry V.* Q1 may have been "condensed from either two plays or a two-part play on the reigns of Henry IV and Henry V" (Hanabusa 2006). Q2 1617 two issues; "acted by the kinges majesties servants."

"[I]t may be the earliest of extant English history plays among the professional companies" (McMillin & MacLean). It "is generally regarded as the first English history play to be performed on the popular stage" (Walsh). "The century's great revolution in subject matter was the emergence of the English history play during the 1580s" (Wiggins 2000). Like the histories of the 1590s, *Famous Victories* "recounts the fifteenth century to explain the sixteenth" (Gossett 2000). "The straightforward expression of feeling, presented in terse, unadorned prose is . . . a characteristic of *The Famous Victories*" (Clemen 1961). "This is a clear instance of a secular conversion play" (Wasson 1986b). But despite its adoption of a traditional moral pattern, the play's "comic buffoonery and pronounced visual effects dilute any serious religious message intended. We need to keep in mind that whenever didacticism enters the commerical domain of the public playhouse its teeth are inevitably blunted by the tacit agreement that paying spectators come to be pleasured, not preached to" (White 2000).

The Fancies, Chaste and Noble. John Ford. Possibly first acted 1631, then revised 1635–36 (McLuskie 1981). "Presented by" Queen Henrietta Maria's Men at the Phoenix, according to the TP.

SR 3 February 1638. Q 1638 two issues; no author named on the TP, but the words "Fide Honor" appear, and these represent "Ford's familiar anagram" (Hart 1985); Ford also signs the dedicatory epistle; prologue and epilogue (shared by four female characters); five acts. Some detailed SDs: e.g., "*Enter Secco with a castingbottle, sprinckling his hatte and face, and a little looking glasse at his girdle, setling his countenance.*" Also issued in *Comedies, Tragicomedies, and Tragedies* (1652), a made-up book no longer extant.

The play gives voice to the "*topos* of the insubordinate woman actor," a *topos* inspired by Queen Henrietta Maria and her ladies, who performed in *The Shepherd's Paradise* (Tomlinson 1992b). The play's title, "though initially referring to three young ladies called 'the Fancies,' becomes at the play's end primarily an ironic reminder to the audience that its own fancies have been anything but chaste and noble" (Anderson 1986).

The Fatal Contract, A French Tragedy. William Heminges. Performed 1633–34 (Morley 2006) or *c.* 1638 (Stevens 2010). "Acted with great applause" by Queen Henrietta Maria's Men, according to the Q1 TP, at the Salisbury Court playhouse (Stevens).

SR 29 [December] 1653 *The Eunuch*, a tragedy; 13 March 1675. Q1 1653–54 "*The Eunuch* was Heminge's working title, surviving in manuscript, but changed to the distinct and tantalizing *Fatal Contract* for performance" (Morley); two issues; "printed by the original copy"; author's name spelled *Hemings* on the TP; list of characters; pantomime/dumb show of a funeral described in considerable detail; five acts and separate scenes. Extensive SDs; the play is "a tour de force of visual and aural effects" (Stevens). Unusual staging involves a vengeful queen who paints a picture depicting a murder she swears to avenge, along with "a representation of the horrible deaths which she hopes will, or which has caused to . . . overtake the murderers" (Bowers 1932); imagining her vengeance, she "*stabs the picture.*" The queen is determined to kill her husband, replace him with her favorite, and avenge the death of her brother; in her schemes she is aided by the Eunuch, ostensibly an Ethiopian, who, unbeknownst to her, is really a white woman named Crotilda, previously raped by Clotaire, the queen's son. "The premise of the victim's disguising herself to revenge her rape is unique to *The Fatal Contract*"; her disguise involves both crossdressing and the adoption of a black persona; "her ravisher being a member of the royal family, there is no redress for her at law" (Morley). She "follows the procedure of the disguised revengers in Chettle and Tourneur": "She has been injured by only one person, Clotaire, but, as with Hoffman and Vindici, she extends her revenge to include the whole family" (Bowers 1940), including the queen. Hence the so-called Eunuch plots against the queen, starting a fire in the royal bedroom: "Look how it flames"; the SD reads, "*The bedchamb[er] on fire.*" In the play's climactic action the Eunuch binds and poisons the Queen and her favorite so that "they may, while dying, witness from behind a curtain the violence about to unfold" (Stevens). Aphelia, "*in her petticoat and hair,*" is dragged in, and Clotair, who earlier attempted to rape her, orders, "bring forth the tortures there; / I'l trie if in these fiery instruments / There lies a tongue, which better can perswade / Confession from thee." A SD reads: "*Ent[er] Man with pan and irons*"; then "*they bind her to the chair, the* Eunuch *much sears her* breast." "Theatrically the scene echoes Tamyra's onstage torture by her husband in Chapman's *Bussy D'Ambois*" (Morley). Crotilda/the Eunuch then "triumphs over Clotaire by recounting the whole course of her intrigue" (Bowers). Q2 1661.

The Q1 dedication to James Compton, earl of Northampton, signed by A. T. (possibly Anthony Turner [Astington 2010]) and A. P. (possibly Andrew Pennycuicke), alludes to the author's death and, implicitly, the gap between performance and print: "having suffered very much by private transcripts, where it past through many hands as a curiosity of wit and language, it is now emergent from darkness, and appears in a publike dress, having shaken off some dust and imperfections that too usually waits upon multipli'd copies." This remark "provides incidental evidence that in at least some quarters a reasonably lively circulation of manuscript drama took place" (Randall 1995).

The playwright "was the son of Shakespeare's fellow sharer and editor John Heminges, and hence the heir to shares in the Globe and Blackfriars" (Randall). It is, then, no coincidence that *The Fatal Contract* "exploits language, character types, and plot elements from at least three Shakespearean tragedies: *Hamlet*, *Othello*, and *King Lear*" (Vaughan 2005). "[I]n the whole scope of the Tudor-Stuart drama, perhaps, there is no such striking case of indebtedness to the great master, for language, imagery, ideas, and even in part for characters and plot" (Adams 1914).

The Fatal Dowry, A Tragedy. Philip Massinger and Nathan Field. Acted 1615–20 (E&G 1976); "first performed 1616 or 1617" (Williams 2004a); "1619 would seem to be a likely date" (Dunn 1969). "Often acted" by the King's Men at the [second] Blackfriars, according to the TP. Revived at the Whitehall Cockpit-in-Court 3 February 1631 (bill of King's Men for plays acted at court). No license for acting exists, at least not under this title. Despite the fifteenth-century French setting, the play takes "some of its intrigue from the notorious economic and political machinations of King James, his favorite Buckingham, the feuding parents Sir Edward Coke and Elizabeth Lady Hatton, and a lover Sir Robert Howard, which enveloped Frances Coke's enforced marriage to the manic John Villiers" (Clark 1993).

SR 30 March 1632; transferred 17 February 1648. Q 1632 the TP identifies the authors by initials — "written by P. M. and N. F."; list of characters; four songs precede the text; festive processions but "[n]o dumb shows proper" (Mehl 1965); five acts and separate scenes. Q contains evidence of theatrical action during the musical interludes between the acts: at the end of act 2, "*Hoboyes. Here a passage over the stage, while the act is playing for the marriage of Charalois with Beaumelle, &c.*" A portait figures in the onstage action when Charalois weeps over "the lively picture of my [dead] father," triggering "the titular marriage of the play" (Rochester 2010).

"About 1633 Massinger had eight of his previously published plays [including *Fatal Dowry*] bound together in a single volume. Possibly he was thinking of publishing a collection of his works; possibly he wanted the volume as a gift to a patron" (Edwards 1987). The Folger owns the collection.

The Fatal Marriage, or a Second Lucretia. Anonymous. ?Acted 1620–30 (Younghughes & Jenkins 1958) at undetermined venue. But Duxfield 2004 argues that the MS "is a revision of a much earlier original, to which a number of topical additions and adjustments have been made, perhaps by another author." And Duxfield 2007 speculates that there may be "a link" between this play and Dekker and Middleton.

London, BL, Egerton MS 1994, fols. 136–60; no separate TP; no author named; slightly damaged; speeches crossed out; not divided. Few SDs except for entrances and exits. "There is no trace of censorship, and no indication of playhouse use" (Greg 1931). SR none. First edited by Younghughes & Jenkins, though Bullen 1883 had given extracts in *A Collection of Old English Plays*, vol. 2.

Father's Own Son. See *Monsieur Thomas.*

The Favorite. See *The Deserving Favorite.*

The Fawn. See *Parasitaster.*

The Feast. Cosmo Manuche. Written "ca. 1663–64" (Randall 1995); "no earlier than January 1665" (Williams 2004b). The play contains "over three hundred" SDs (Nelles 1990), which suggest that the play may have been prepared for the stage, perhaps at the home of James Compton, third earl of Northampton, to whom the play is dedicated. "Very likely" intended for performance (Nelles). The play may have been performed at Northampton's London residence, Canonbury House, Islington (Wolf 1983).

(1) London, BL, Additional MS 60274, fols. 1–41; "presentation copy" in the author's hand (Nelles); no TP; dramatis personae; epilogue; five acts. This MS, formerly part of the library at Castle Ashby, concludes with a note by Manuche to Northampton. (2) Oxford, Worcester College, an incomplete copy; Plays 9.22; written "in several hands" (Williams 1992); "a considerable amount of correction of words, stage directions, and the deletion of words has been done in yet a third hand" (Williams 1980).

"[I]t is conceivable that some of [Manuche's] manuscript plays . . . could have been written before the wars" (*JCS*).

Fedele and Fortunio, The Deceits in Love (Two Italian Gentlemen). Anthony Munday; Collier 1831 first identified the author. Acted *c.* 1579–84; probably first performed by the combined Chapel and Paul's Boys at the first Blackfriars, 1583–84 (Hosley 1981). "Presented before the queens most excellent majestie," according to the TP, probably 6 January or 2 February 1584, by Oxford's Boys under the name of one of their component companies, the Children of the Queen's Chapel.

SR 12 November 1584 *Fedele et Fortuna, The deceiptes in love, Discoursed in a Commedia of ii Italyan gent[lemen].* Q 1585 *Fedele and Fortunio, The Deceits in Love: Excellently Discoursed in a Very Pleasant and Fine Conceited Comedy of Two Italian Gentlemen;* RT *A Pleasant Comedy of Two Italian Gentlemen;* HT *The Pleasant and Fine Conceited Comedy of Two Italian Gentlemen, with the Merry Devises of*

Captain Crack-stone; no author named on the TP but "A. M." signs the dedication in the Huntington copy; prologue before the queen; epilogue at court; five acts and separate scenes. Q "appears to contain additions and alterations made for the court performance mentioned in its title page" (Ichikawa 2005). The SDs "are full and descriptive" (Jewkes 1958): "*Enter* Fortunio *running halfe unreadie; after him,* Ottaviano *the father to Mistress Virginia, [*Virginia,*] and* Medusa *with a spitte in her hande; and to them [later],* Fedele *and* Pedante *with weapons in their handes.*" SDs designate instrumental music at the end of each act: "*the consorte of musique soundeth a pleasant galliard,*"; "*the consort sounds a sollemne dump* [i.e., a mournful or plaintive melody]"; "*the consort soundeth a pleasant allemaigne* [i.e., dance music in slow time]."

In this adaptation of *Il Fedele* by Luigi Pasqualigo, Munday has "created the first model of the genre of romantic comedy that Shakespeare so successfully practiced in the 1590s" (Melchiori 2000). In *Palladis Tamia* Francis Meres calls Munday "our best plotter."

The Female Rebellion, A Tragicomedy. By H. B. [?Henry Birkhead or Burkhead]. "[W]ritten sometime between 1657 and 1659 but never staged" (Walen 2005).

(1) Glasgow, University of Glasgow, Hunterian Museum MS 635; no author named; list of characters; prologue and epilogue; five acts and separate scenes. Ample SDs: "Queen *and* king *sit under a bower,* Tha[lestris] *and* Alc[ymen] *below. Enter Attend. (from the right) and sit by;* Laranda, *an Orpheus with a harp,* Jasius *in a lions skin,* Ericthonius *in a bulls, and* Ilus *in a horses (from the left): they dance an antimasq, then uncover their faces, and bowe low to their majestys, who rise up.*" Staging calls for a trap: "Ant[iopa] *stamps,* Alc[ymen] *below makes a trapdoor sink, & close upon the* Que[en] *struling against it.*" Entry for a ghost suggests the figure's theatrical impact: "*Enter* Sagalus's *ghost (from the right) & frights* Ant[iopa] *about the stage.*" MS (2) Oxford, Bodleian, MS Tanner 466, fols. 174 et seq.; Dr. Henry Birkhead ["formerly fellow of All-Souls College"], anticipating performance, signs the address to the king that precedes the play; some words and speeches crossed out; SDs suggest possible use of painted scenery: "Appearance, a royall palace"; "Appearance, a park"; "Appearance, a dungeon." First edited by Smith 1872, with notes partly by John Payne Collier.

The MS (1) epilogue connects attitudes toward theater with attitudes toward politics: "Since the same fate doth stage & state befall, / That who dislike White fryars hate White-hall; / Wid'ning with calumnys this double breach, / Drawn by the nose thrô which their brethren preach. / That snarl at kings, as th'Attic cur did snub / The mighty Macedon, and from a tub: / Such foes this writer aim'd by a safe stile, / At least to silence if not reconcile; / And so perhaps has forfeited their praise, / Who like the faults both of the times & plays. / For of wits small shot here had been less dearth, / Would he have us'd all the lew'd helps to mirth; / But 'cause sick minds love what feeds their disease, / He thinks he has not writ so ill to please."

Ferrex and Porrex. See *Gorboduc.*

A Fine Companion. Shackerley Marmion. Acted 1632-*c.* August 1633 (Sonnenshein 1979). Acted "sundrie times with great applause" by Prince Charles's Men at the Salisbury Court playhouse, according to the TP, but the acting license is not extant. Performed also at Whitehall, before the king and queen, according to the TP, shortly after commercial-playhouse performance; the "court staging may have been at Christmas 1632–33, undoubtedly in the Cockpit theatre completed in 1630" (Astington 2006). When the company moved to the Red Bull, they "presumably took with them to their new house the successful comedies that had proved themselves in performance, to be played on the Bull stage as part of their operating repertory"; *Fine Companion* "should be thought of belonging to the Bull as much as to Salisbury Court" (Astington).

SR 15 June 1633 *The fyne Companion*; transferred 7 November 1646. Q 1633 *A Fine Companion*; dramatis personae; prologue (a dialogue between the Author, who appears onstage, and the Critic); five acts and separate scenes. In the prefatory dialogue, "the author is cast by the Critic as the object of a popular contempt the source of which is the 'ignorance' of an audience, and whose habitual consolation resides in the dual compensation of the protective power afforded by patronage and the possibility of self-justification afforded by publication" (Drakakis 2007).

The author's dedication affirms the value of poetry (i.e., drama) in the face of detraction: "How such an excellent, and divine part of humanitie should fall under the least contempt, or arme the petulancy of writers to declaime against her, I know not: but I guesse the reason, that having their soules darkned, and rejoycing in their errors, are offended at the lustre of those arts that would enlighten them."

"The play took its title from a well-known dance . . . and appeared in the same year that Charles I reissued James I's declaration of sports, which had been originally formulated in 1618; its emphasis on festivity indicates a degree of sympathy with Charles's championing of such 'sports'" (Drakakis 2004).

The First Day's Entertainment at Rutland House, by Declamations and Music, after the Manner of the Ancients. William Davenant. Acted at Rutland House (Davenant's home) in Charterhouse Square, 23 May 1656; but there may have been "probably furtive private performances" earlier (Sharpe 1987). "This curious hodge-podge of music and of dialogues was a semi-private entertainment to which admission was charged; but only 150 people of the 450 for which preparation was made attended" (Rollins 1921). "It can be assumed that" the "indistinct generic identity, part debate, part opera, part masque, and part play, enabled" this and other such works of Davenant "to circumvent the prohibition of 1642, subsequently reinforced, on the presentation of plays" (Clare 1994). Davenant was "careful to incorporate into his 'Entertainment' anti-French propaganda and songs in praise of Cromwell, the Lord Protector" (Bentley 1981); this drama "was the first piece of theatre permitted by the Protectorate government" (Wiseman 1990), and it "featured women performers" (Crawford 2005).

SR 9 September 1656. D 1657 author's initials on the TP; prologue and epilogue; chorus; divided into five parts by directions for "instrumental musick" and for the raising of a curtain. Music composed by Henry Lawes, Charles Coleman, Henry Cook, and George Hudson. Prologue points to the originality of the play: "Think this your passage, and the narrow way / To our Elisian field, the *Opera*: / Tow'rds which some say we have gone far about, / Because it seems so long since we set out." This marks "the first appearance of the crucial word [opera]" (Edmond 2004b). F 1673 *The Works*; "now published out of the authors originall copies."

This is "essentially a dialogue concerned with the moral status of theatrical performance" (Smith 1994). "In the first dialogue Diogenes voices and possibly anticipates objections to recitative and scenic drama" (Clare 2004). Aristophanes replies to Diogenes, making "sweeping claims about the practical and didactical value of special effects" (Cope 1999). The play "sets the scene for theatre under the Protectorate as radically different from most things which preceded it" (Wiseman 1990). "The entertainment is not an opera "but an introduction to, or argument in favour of, opera" (Edmond 1987). The play "used music as an auxiliary to the words, as had been done by the ancients" (Cauthen 1987b).

The First Part of Arviragus and Philicia. See *1 Arviragus and Philicia.*

The First Part of Bellamira Her Dream. See *1 Bellamira Her Dream.*

The First Part of Cicilia and Clorinda. See *1 Cicilia and Clorinda.*

The First Part of Hieronimo. See *1 Hieronimo.*

The First Part of King Edward the Fourth. See *1 Edward IV.*

The First Part of King Henry the Fourth. See *1 Henry IV.*

The First Part of King Henry the Sixth. See *1 Henry VI.*

The First Part of Selimus. See *1 Selimus.*

The First Part of Sir Francis Drake. See *1 Sir Francis Drake.*

The First Part of Tamburlaine. See *1 Tamburlaine.*

The First Part of the Contention betwixt the Two Famous Houses of York and Lancaster. See *2 Henry VI.*

The First Part of the Reign of King Richard the Second, or Thomas of Woodstock. See *Woodstock.*

The First Part of the Tragical Reign of Selimus. See *1 Selimus.*

The First Part of the Troublesome Reign. See *1 Troublesome Reign.*

The First Part of Thomaso. See *1 Thomaso.*

Five Plays in One. See *Amphrisa; Apollo and Daphne; Jupiter and Io.*

The Fleer. Edward Sharpham. Acted winter 1605–06 (Petter 1986). "Often played" by the Children of the Revels at the [second] Blackfriars, according to the Q1 TP. ("This was . . . the old Children of the Queen's Revels after they had lost their royal patronage" [Leech 1935]). They lost her favor "in the furore over John Day's incendiary play *The Isle of Gulls*" (Munro 2006a). A reference in Anthony Nixon's *A Strange Foot-Post* (London 1613) may indicate a revival "around 1612" (Munro).

SR 13 May 1606 a Comedie called *The fleare*; transferred 21 November 1606. "Sharpham invented 'Fleire' (one who fleers or jeers) to describe the disguise of his hero, Signor Antifront" (Greg 1939). Q1 1607 five acts. In his address to the reader, the printer confesses that although the playwright gave him "an epistle or apological præamble . . . I have lost it, remembring none of the contentes." The BL copy of Q1 contains MS alterations, possibly for use as a playbook; the changes "would seem to point to either a private or a provincial performance" (Leech); Munro 2006d believes "the extensive cuts and revisions" are "one reader's response to the play." Staging may involve a freestanding structure: "*Enter Signior Alunio the apothecarie in his shop with wares about him.*" Q2 1610. Q3 1615. Q4 1631.

The Fleer was "written as a response to or replacement for *The Fawn*, which was taken to Children of Paul's *c.* early 1606" (Munro 2005). Sharpham's comedy "presents a London in which English cultural practices have been superseded by alternative, and specifically Scottish, practices" (Lamb 2009).

"The play is a cynical, thinly veiled satire of King James's court, modeled on John Marston's *The Malcontent* and *The Fawne* with elements of the Gunpowder Plot thrown in" (Kathman 2004e).

The Floating Island, A Tragicomedy. William Strode. Acted the evening of 29 August 1636, according to the Q TP (Elliott & Buttrey 1985). By students of Christ Church, Oxford, before King Charles and Queen Henrietta Maria, in the great hall with changeable scenery; "it would seem that sliding wings, in addition to shutters, were a feature" of the production (Richards 1968). Archbishop Laud had arranged the royal visit; the royal couple would also see *Love's Hospital* and *The Royal Slave* the following day. Inigo Jones probably designed the scenery, perhaps with John Webb (Orrell 1985). Performed again the afternoon of 3 September 1636 (Elliott et al.), with the same scenery, for the university community. Anthony à Wood records a detailed account of the staging: "It was acted on a goodly stage, reaching from the upper end of the Hall almost to the hearth place, and had on it three or four openings on each side thereof, and partitions between them, much resembling the desks or studies in a Library, out of which the Actors issued forth" (*JCS*); this account is derived from that of Brian Twyne, an eyewitness and Oxford's first Keeper of the Archives (Orrell). Despite the huge expense, the production "was a dramatic failure" (Smyth 2006). No license for acting extant.

SR 9 February 1654 *Passions calm'd or the setling of the floating iland*. Q 1655 *The Floating Island, A Tragicomedy*; list of characters; prologues to king and to university; epilogues to king and to university; five acts and separate scenes. The Q TP reports: "The aires and songs set by Mr. Henry Lawes"; the music is contained in Oxford, Bodleian, MS Malone 21. SDs of extraordinary detail: "*Enter in the midst of the song* Amorous *ushering the solemnity*, Irato *bearing the sword*, Malevolo *the scepter; then six others bearing six crowns, two in a rank. First* Andax *on the right hand bearing a crown of gold, and with him poet* Ovidian *a lawrel: then* Desperato *a Turkish turbant, and with him* Timerous *a Persian Cydaris.*" Wood's account of the staging refers to the use of "partitions," which attendants "could draw in and out at their pleasure upon a sudden, and thrust out new in their places according to the nature of the screen, whereon were represented churches, dwelling-houses, palaces, etc."

When the play was finally published, "it was in effect a statement on the potentially imminent return of the royal family with whom the work was so inalterably associated" (Randall 1995). "Written as an allegory of the troubles that beset Charles I, even before the Civil Wars, the play must have undergone some alterations to bring it up-to-date at the time of publication, a suspicion strengthened by a disclaimer with which the publisher equipped it" (Wright 1934): "Before you read so farre as the prologue, be pleased to consider this tragi-comedy was both written and presented above eighteen years since; and if now it seem (in language or plot) to fit these times, it must be by prophesie, the author also himselfe having been long dead. He wrote it at the instance of those who might command him; else he had scarce condescended to a play, his serious thoughts being fill'd with notions of deeper consideration. 'Tis sufficient for its worth that the best lik'd it best; the rest (especially those great ones of the weaker sect [i.e., sex]) should claim no lawful judicature over it, since it was not written for them, though they thought themselves too severely dealt with, which was an injury to the author as well as his poem." The interval between performance and printing changed the play's significance: "what was, in 1636, a predictably Laudian plea [for moderation], becomes in 1655 a much more potent royalist lament for the Civil War" (Smyth).

The Fool Would Be a Favorite, or The Discreet Lover, A Tragicomedy. Lodowick Car-
lell. Acted *c.* 1632-*c.* 1638 (Kawachi 1986) at undetermined venue. The TP of *Two
New Plays* claims performance by "the queen's majesty's servants" (i.e., Queen
Henrietta Maria's Men), but *Osmond the Great Turk*, also published in *Two New
Plays*, belonged to the King's Men. The play "may have been written originally for
a popular audience rather than for Carlell's customary courtly one" (*JCS*).

SR 9 September 1653 *The Discreet Lover, or, The Foole would bee a Favourite.*
O 1657 dramatis personae; five acts. Some copies were bound with *Osmond the
Great Turk* in 1657 and issued as *Two New Plays* (separate register and pagina-
tion); "often acted . . . with great applause" according to the general TP.

Carlell's plays "are solid examples of Caroline courtier drama, their complex
plot lines echoing the 1630s vogue for pastoral and romance" (Sanders 2004a).

Forced Valor. A droll based on scenes in B&F's *The Humorous Lieutenant* and performed in the 1640s and 50s. "This droll presents a well-developed episode possessing considerable humor and action"; it may require as many as "ten or eleven
actors" (Elson 1932).

Published in *1 The Wits, or Sport upon Sport* (O 1662 [two issues] and 1672),
which mistakenly locates the source in *A King and No King*; RT *The Humors of
Forced Valor*; argument; list of characters.

The Forest Pastoral. See *The Fairy Pastoral.*

A Forest Tragedy in Vacunium. William Percy. Written 1602, according to the MSS.
"Percy seems to have written his plays for amateur performance in the household
of his brother the Earl of Northumberland" (Dodds 1945). No evidence of production but, according to notes in MSS Huntington HM 4 and Alnwick 509, the
author intended that his plays be staged either by Paul's Boys or by the Children
of the Revels. Because of the different possible venues, the three presenters en-
visioned at Paul's become nine at another venue. "A version of" this play "could
possibly have been played at Paul's in the early phase of their revival (1599–1603)"
(Gair 2004). Percy's "plays suggest private performance" (Hillebrand 1938).

(1) San Marino, CA, Huntington, MS HM 4 [latest of Percy MSS of this
play], fols. 92–117; *Comedies and Pastorals*; general TP dated 1647, this play "finis
1602"; *A Forest Tragedy in Vacunium*; the original word *Country* in the title has
been changed in the margin to *Forest*; list of characters; list of properties; induction (though not called such); prologue and epilogue (both by presenter); chorus;
signs of revision; five acts and separate scenes. Percy "provides a *parodos* or entering processional song sung to Apollo . . . and an *exodos* or exit song . . . both
songs to be sung by a double-chorus composed of eight great lovers from antiquity" (Long 1980). Elaborate use of stage properties and painted scenery: e.g.,
"Tremellioes Castell, Affranioes Mannour, Sir Clodioes Desmene *over the midde
doore in capitull letters* Cupids Grove, *with a little Cupid erect upon an altar sub dio*,

and deckt with sundry boughes and kinds of fruites. Next Amadours Garden. *A cano-pie with chaire and cushion of state within the canopie, and with a velvet stoole by him without the canopie. A cupborde with faire linen coverd by Amadours Garden. The title aloft and above being both title and scene* A Country Tragoedye in Vacunium or Cupids Sacrifice *one of the two, the first in regard of propertie of scene.*" Percy's plays "show a use of locality boards which is nowhere else so completely illustrated in Elizabethan drama; that such signboards existed is adequately proved by considerable other evidence, but Percy's plays furnish a unique statement as to how they were employed" (Reynolds 1914). (2) Alnwick, UK, Alnwick Castle, MS 508 [earliest of Percy MSS], fols. 97–119; *A Forest Tragedy in Vacunium, or Love's Sacrifice*; incomplete MS breaks off near the beginning of act 5, scene 1; MS dated 1644 (in *Fairy Pastoral*). (3) Alnwick MS 509 *A Forest Tragedy in Vacunium, or Cupid's Sacrifice*; general TP, dated 1646, identifies the author by initials; this play "finis 1602."

"Vacunium is the name of the imaginary country where the action takes place" (Dodds 1945).

Fortune by Land and Sea, A Tragicomedy. Thomas Heywood and William Rowley. "Acted with great applause" by Queen Anne's Men, according to the TP, 1607–09 (Doh 1980) at the Red Bull (Reynolds 1940).

SR 20 June 1655; transferred 16 July 1662. Q 1655 list of characters; five acts and separate scenes. "[O]ffers an example in its naval battle of the presentation of an almost impossible scene with apparently a minimum of scenic equipment" (Reynolds). "There is no evidence that shots are actually fired on stage (although there is considerable talk of guns and gunnery) but there is frenzied activity, much noise, and presentation of '*Sea devices fitting for a fight,*' all appropriate for two ships in battle at sea" (Dessen 2006). "All of the dialogue is intensely dramatic; the progress of the battle is subtly implied; combatants display their fighting equipment and in a few phrases describe the condition of the opposing craft; meanwhile the audience listens to the din of battle and sniffs the powder smoke which drifts in from off stage" (Wright 1927b).

The play may be seen as "an early expression of anxieties about James's leadership and . . . as one which in its championing of buccaneers might have helped create the oppositional climate of the second decade of the king's reign" (Jowitt 2003). The play's attitude toward piracy is ambivalent: "Piracy is not necessarily a threat to the integrity of English commercial expansion. Though Purser and Clinton are punished for their transgressions through hanging at Wapping in the play, nevertheless their nostalgic representation of their ship as a 'parallel state' to England . . . and their elegiac execution speeches, unsettle a triumphalist reading of their deaths. Indeed, their piratical empire has in many ways superseded that of England's as the pirates have been immensely successful in their exploits" (Jowitt 2005).

2 Fortune's Tennis. Anonymous; Thomas Dekker may have worked on the lost play (Greg 1931), acted *c.* 1598 by the Lord Admiral's Men (Bradley 1992) at undetermined venue. Henslowe records a payment to Dekker "for his boocke called the fortewn tenes," 6 September 1600, probably for revisions, "perhaps in connection with a version of the play for the new theater [the Fortune]" (McMillin 1992), which opened autumn 1600. A "play with such a name would have been appropriate now [i.e. at the Fortune]" (Gurr 2009c). Probable date of this plot, or "backstage storyboard" (Bate 2008), is between September 1602 and early 1603 (Foakes 2002). Actors included John Singer, William Cartwright, ?Charles Massey, ?Samuel Rowley, Robert Tailor, ?Richard Juby, ?George Somerset, and William Pavye.

London, BL, Additional MS 10449, fol. 4, ed. Greg; fragmentary and severely damaged; "no trace of any formal division into acts, although there is a hint of structural division in the play itself" (Greg).

The Fountain of Self-Love. See *Cynthia's Revels*.

The Four Elements (*The Nature of the Four Elements*). John Rastell. Acted 1517–20 (*DTRB* 1984) at undetermined venue. "The play is scattered with various references suggesting hall performance" (Dillon 1996), but it "seems a play in part designed (at least in its *c.* 1520 printing) for movement among varying performance sites and for varying theatrical requirements of length and complexity" (Lancashire 2002). "Unabashedly vernacular" (Watkins 1999), the play, "with its undisguised borrowing from popular comic traditions, was probably intended for a stage that Rastell himself designed as a way of bringing humanist issues before select audiences of intellectuals and also a broader public" (Bevington 2002a). *Four Elements* "is really two plays, a 'philosophical work' and an interlude of 'merry conceits,' offered for two audiences, and evidently presented under such auspices — perhaps on Rastell's stage — that the humbler sort might be induced to come of their own volition as to a public play" (Bevington 1962). The first part of the play was designed to be played "at dyner," "which would begin about noon, the second 'in the evynyng about suppere'" (Twycross 2008).

O ND printed "some time between November 1519 and mid-1520" (Clough 2004), or *c.* 1527 (Lennam 1975); HT *A New Interlude and a Merry of the Nature of the Four Elements, Declaring Many Proper Points of Philosophy Natural and of Divers Strange Lands, and of Divers Strange Effects and Causes*; unique BL copy, printed by Rastell, is incomplete ("the end of the play is missing" [Axton 1979]); no separate TP and no colophon (Greg 1930); list of characters; prologue (by Messenger); not divided. "By far the most prominent literary feature in the *mise en page* of Rastell's *Four Elements* is the use of pilcrows, or paragraph signs. These conventional signs, which in other sixteenth-century printed playbooks mark changes of speakers, are also used to highlight rhyming patterns which in turn signal the different social and moral qualities of the characters" (Massai 2007).

The O TP says, "Also, yf ye lyst ye may brynge in a dysgysynge," suggesting that the interlude "might be decorated with music and dancing supplementary to the action" (Craik 1958); following are "detailed instructions on what, alternatively, you can cut—'muche of the sad (*serious*) mater'—if you wish to reduce the running time from one-and-a-half hours to forty-five minutes, a delightfully pragmatic approach to theatrical integrity" (Twycross 2007); this comment suggests that the uncut play could prove tedious in performance. The shorter version may be presented by five actors, but "the full version, designed for household performance, incorporates a disguising, which required dancers, minstrels, and additional costuming" (Westfall 1990). Staging calls for an orrery, a mechanical apparatus showing the positions of the heavenly bodies.

This play "not only was apparently the first English printed work to define the New World as America, but also, in its inclusion of a three-part song, . . . marked the first attempt anywhere in Europe to print a musical score" (Clough 2004). The play is also interesting in its suggestion that "the exhibition of scientific truth is a direct furtherance of religion" (Thompson 1910).

Four Plays, or Moral Representations, in One (The Triumph of Honor, The Triumph of Love, The Triumph of Death, The Triumph of Time). John Fletcher and Nathan Field (Hoy 1959). *The Triumph of Honor, The Triumph of Love,* the Induction, "and the connecting scenes of this entertainment are all by Field" (Williams 2004a). Acted *c.* 1613–15 by Lady Elizabeth's Men, who "amalgamated with the Children of the Queens' Revels" (Taylor 1993a), at, probably, the Fortune theater. *Four Plays* "is an early example of a theatrical trend that would seek at once to accommodate stage spectacles of the sort familiar from plays like those represented by the plot of *The Seven Deadly Sins* to more sophisticated dramatic materials and to accommodate the moral and allegorical personifications of the Court masque to the broader didactic purposes of the public theatre" (Hoy 1992b).

SR not included in entry of 4 September 1646; 29 June 1660; 30 January 1673. B&F F1 1647 *Comedies and Tragedies*; "never printed before, and now published by the authours originall copies"; induction consisting of a "frame" (Greenfield 1969); Frigozo speaks the prologue; a prologue precedes each of four parts; epilogue; detailed description of three pantomimes, the first of which "must be one of the most eventful dumb shows in the history of Elizabethan drama" (Mehl 1965); "the only play without act-divisions" in the B&F canon (Taylor 1993a). The play "eschews five-act structure, and comprises instead four brief playlets or 'Triumphs' which represent the generic range available to the stage: comedy, tragicomedy, tragedy, and masque. The influence of the latter is particularly marked throughout the whole" (McMullan 1994). "[A]mong the most interesting scenically of all seventeenth-century dramas" (Nicoll 1937). Staging, which "aspire[s] more and more to the condition of the Court masque" (Hoy 1992b), involves the descent of various deities (Diana, Cupid, Jupiter, Mercury), apparently by machinery. In *The Triumph of Honor* we find "a magical transformation unlike anything to be found in the whole range of early seventeenth-century drama" (Lawrence 1927): playgoers see "a rocky view near Athens" (Lawrence); then "*Solemn musick, a mist ariseth, the rocks remove.*" *The Triumph of Love* contains two long and elaborate dumb shows, as well as another substantial SD that reads like a pantomime. *The Triumph of Death* culminates in an extraordinary "triumph": "*Enter musicians: next them,* Perolot *with the wound he died with. Then* Gabriella *and* Maria, *with their wounds: after them four Furies with bannerets inscrib'd* Revenge, Murder, Lust *and* Drunkennesse, *singing. Next them* Lavall *wounded. Then a chariot with* Death, *drawn by the Destinies.*" *The Triumph of Time* displays "an element of allegorical pageantry poised midway between the sophistication of a Stuart Court masque and the exuberant literalism of a contemporary lord mayor's show" (Hoy). "The stage was occupied by a symbolical golden rock, evidently a massive 'property,' which spurted fire when Plutus struck it" (Lawrence); the stage's trapdoor is "perhaps covered by" the rock (Dessen & Thomson 1999). Staging also calls for a trap when a spirit "*sinks . . . to darkness*"; Plutus "*stamps*" (a signal for the trap to open) and "Labour *rises.*" *Four Plays* "may have been acted with scenery" (Freehafer 1973): e.g., in *The Triumph of Time*: "*One half of a cloud drawn. Singers are discovered: then the other half drawn.* Jupiter *seen in glory.*" "Not since the first success of *Tamburlaine* had there been such a profuse employment of chariots as is to be noted in this piece" (Lawrence): e.g., "*a chariot drawn by two* Moors"; "*a chariot drawn by two* Cupids, *and a* Cupid *sitting in it*"; "*a chariot with* Death"; "*a chariot with the person of* Time *sitting in it, drawn by four persons, representing Hours.*" B&F F2 1679 *Fifty Comedies and Tragedies*; "published by the authors original copies, the songs to each play being added"; list of characters.

Four Plays, whose title is not included along with the list of other plays published in F2, is listed with *A Masque of Gray's Inn* at the bottom of the contents page. "This does not mean that its editors thought of it as a masque but rather that they recognized it as somehow different from the fifty-one plays listed above it" (Shaw 1979).

The Four PP. John Heywood. Acted *c.* 1520–28 (Grantley 2008a) or *c.* 1531 (Betteridge 2009) at undetermined venue. The play "is a prime candidate for company hall performance: a verbal farce written by a court entertainer whose plays should certainly have been in the repertory of the King's Players or another such company" (Lancashire 2002). Requires only four adult performers. "All that is needed [for staging] is the space in the centre of a great hall, and the limited number of portable properties that symbolizes each of the characters' vocations" (Walker 2000). "The play could certainly have been performed at court, and is in the tradition of Chaucer's fabliaux, but does not limit itself to patrician surroundings" (Bevington 1973); "it is the most thoroughly Chaucerian piece of work since Chaucer" (Wallace 1912). *The Four PP* is one of the titles named in *Sir Thomas More* (originally written *c.* 1592–93 or *c.* 1600) when a company of actors visits More's home for the purpose of performing a play. "Judging from its mention by the itinerant actors in *The Book of Sir Thomas More*, *The Four PP* had an active stage life for fifty years after its publication in the 1540s" (Cartwright 1999).

SR no original; transferred 15 January 1582. "It is highly likely" that the play was first printed *c.* 1533–34 (Walker). Q1 ND *c.* 1544 ("but this edition may have been a reprint of an earlier play" [Happé 2010]) *The Play called The Four PP: A New and a Very Merry Interlude of A Palmer, A Pardoner, A Poticary, A Peddler*; list of characters on the TP; not divided. Few SDs. Q2 ND *c.* 1555. Q3 1569. The Q1 TP features woodcuts of three figures with spaces for labels over their heads, but none is identified. The Q3 TP features a picture of two death-like figures, one of whom plays bagpipes; the other plays an organ. "None of these figures has anything to do with the occupations of the characters of Heywood's play" (Davidson 1991).

"The *Four PP* . . . is essentially a dramatized debate, a dispute in the humanist tradition between two or more contending individuals over the merits of their respective vocations or conditions" (Walker). "Instead of a radical reasessment of doctrine and practice as threatened by Protestant thinking, there is rather a respect for the church as an institution" (Happé 2007b). "The disguising of serious doctrine in comic entertainment is a remarkable development of techniques found in *Fulgens and Lucrece* and *Magnificence*" (Axton & Happé 1991).

The Four Prentices of London, with the Conquest of Jerusalem. Thomas Heywood. Possibly acted in a version earlier than Q1, *c.* 1592 (Gasior 1980), entitled *Jerusalem or Godfrey of Bulloigne [Boulogne]*, by Lord Strange's Men at the Rose. Probably the *Godfrey of Bullen, Second Part*, performed by the Admiral's Men at the Rose in 1594 according to Henslowe: 19 July; 6, 26 August; 8, 20 September; 6, 30 October. In 1595: 27 April; 17 May. The words *Second Part* may designate a revision by Heywood of an earlier version. *Godfrey* may have been "deliberately paired with the lost play *Mahomet*, so that they might complement one another" (Connolly 2009). *The Four Prentices* "seems to have been Heywood's first" play and thus may have coincided with "the vogue for prose accounts of heroic prentices" in the early 1590s; it may then have been reworked and "revived in 1602" by Worcester's Men (McLuskie 1994). The 1615 Q1 prefatory epistle speaks of the play as having been in fashion "fifteene or sixteene yeares agoe." "However, it seems that the epistle was written for an edition of the play planned in 1610" (Jewkes 1958). "Diverse times acted at the Red Bull" by the Queen's Men, according to the Q1 TP, and acted "with good applause," according to the Q2 TP.

SR 19 June 1594 an enterlude entituled *Godfrey of Bulloigne, with the Conquest of Jerusalem*; transferred 2 August 1630; 30 June 1673. Q1 1615 dramatis personae; prologue divided among three speakers (i.e., an induction [Hosley 1961]), each of whom claims "to have a prologue to present" (Schneider 2011); "a chorus, or presenter"; detailed descriptions of four dumb shows, "showing the fate of the four brothers after their shipwreck" (Mehl 1965); "at the end of each episode the presenter explains what is meant by the action" (Rhodes 1976); not divided despite the designation of act 1, scene 1. The Q1 prologue refers to the play's title as *True and Strange, or The Four Prentices of London*. The play "dramatizes the historical figure of Godfrey of Bouillon who was the leader of the first crusade and the first Latin ruler of Palestine after the capture of Jerusalem in 1099"; Heywood "develops this premise to present the story of Godfrey and his three brothers and their decision to enlist as part of a crusade" (Connolly 2009). The four heroes "march across Europe and Asia performing the incredible feats of knight errantry that were the staple fare of the chivalric romances long popular with the sixteenth-century reading public" (Gurr 2009d). As the TP woodcut leads us to expect, the play dramatizes scenes of considerable violence (using the upper stage) and accompanying pageantry: "*The Christians are repulst. Enter at two severall dores,* Guy *and* Eustace *climbe up the wals, beate the pagans, take away the crownes on their heads, and in the stead hang up the contrary shields, and bring away the ensignes, flourishing them, severall wayes*"; the shields have "distinctive insignia" (Reynolds 1940). "[T]here are seven single combats, all of which furnish extraneous spectacle" (Wright 1968). Some of the staging, however, is quite subtle: "*Enter* Tancred *with* Bella Franca, *richly attired, shee some-what affecting him, though she makes no shew of it.*" Despite the argument by Fitzpatrick 2011 that there were only two entry points onto the stage, SDs here call for three entrances: "*Enter three in blacke clokes, at three doores.*" Q2 1632 "newly revised" (an accurate claim [Brown 1954b]); "Q2 is quite literally strewn with verbal substitutions" (Massai 2007). The TPs of Q1–2 feature a woodcut of four men who wear armor and wield pikes; they are named Eustace, Godfrey, Charles, and Guy: "the costumes, shields, and exercise with the pikes, all relate well to the text of the play" (Foakes 1985).

Heywood's address to the Q1 reader addresses the gap between performance and publication: "this labour, which though written many yeares since, in my infancy of judgement in this kinde of poetry, and my first practise: yet understanding (by what meanes I know not) it was in these more exquisite & refined times to come to the presse, in such a forwardnesse ere it came to my knowledge, that it was past prevention, and then knowing withall, that it comes short of that accuratenesse both in plot and stile, that these more censorious dayes with greater curiosity acquire, I must thus excuse. That as playes were then some fifteene or sixteene yeares agoe it was in the fashion."

The Fox. See *Volpone.*

Frederick and Basilea. Anonymous. The "plot," or "backstage storyboard" (Bate 2008) of a lost play. Acted 3 June 1597 by the Lord Admiral's Men at the Rose, according to Henslowe's *Diary*. The plot "almost certainly belongs to that performance"; it "served as a road map through the production for players who performed different plays, with several doubles, every day of the week and who must have found it necessary to check their stage movements frequently" (Rutter

1984). Performed "four times thereafter, at a time when the company was temporarily depleted by the defection of some of its members to Langley's enterprise at the Swan" (Bradley 1992). "This play demanded huge numbers on stage. The 'plot' even specifies 'gatherers' to do walk-on parts in the most crowded scenes" (Gurr 2009c).

London, BL, Additional MS 10449, fol. 2, ed. Greg 1931; prologue and epilogue; "horizontal lines divide the plot into eighteen scenes" (King 1992a). "[S]ixteen players undertook twenty-seven parts" (Lawrence 1927): Edward Alleyn (the most prominent of the Admiral's Men and Henslowe's son-in-law, played Sebastian), Richard Allen (Prologue and Epilogue, Frederick), Edward Dutton (Philippo), Robert Ledbetter (Pedro, a Lord), Thomas Hunt (a Guard, a Lord, a Servant), Dick [E Dutton his boye] (Basilea), Black Dick (Messenger, Soldier, Guard, Jailor), Charles Massey (a Moor, Thamar), Edward Juby (the King), James Tunstall/Dunstall/Dunstone/Dunstan (Governor, Friar), Martin Slater (Theodore), Samuel Rowley (Heraclius), and Thomas Towne (Myron-Hamec). Other actors are indicated by single or abbreviated names: i.e., Saunder (?Alexander Cooke), R[obert] Go[ugh] (Aspatia), [John] Pigg/Pyk (Andreo), T. Belt (Servant, Panthea), Griffin (Athanasia), Will (Leonora) (Greg 1931, Nungezer 1929).

French Dancing Master. See *The Ball.*

Friar Bacon and Friar Bungay. Robert Greene. Acted 1589–90 (Seltzer 1963). Possibly first performed by the Queen's Men, named on the Q TP, at an inn-yard (Lawrence 1927), though "when actors performed at inns they usually occupied a large room rather than a yard and performed by candlelight" (Orrell 1997). Acted by the combined Queen's and Sussex's Men at the Rose, 1 and 5 April 1594, according to Henslowe's *Diary*. "[I]t appears that Henslowe used 'Friar Bacon' in reference to two separate plays: *John of Bordeaux* for Strange's Men and *Friar Bacon and Friar Bungay* . . . for the Queen's Men" (McMillin & MacLean 1998). The "fryer bacune" listed by Henslowe in 19 February, 25 March, 26 April, and 6 May 1592, as well as 10, 17, 30 January 1593, and performed by Lord Strange's Men, may designate *John of Bordeaux* (McMillin 1992), a sequel or companion play to *Friar Bacon*. Revived at the first Fortune in 1602 (Gurr 2009c). Acted by Nottingham's Men at Whitehall, Christmas 1602–03; for the revival Henslowe records payment to Thomas Middleton, 14 December 1602, for "a prologe & A epelogue for the playe of bacon for the corte"; both are lost. "Conceivably it could be counted as one of the many [plays that Edward] Alleyn had previously been famous for, revived after he returned to the stage in 1600 [following his retirement]" (Gurr 2009c). "Lately plaid by the Prince Palatine [Frederick, Count Palatine of the Rhine] his Servants," successors of the Admiral's Men (renamed Prince Henry's Men after James I's accession), according to the Q2 TP. "[W]e may assume that [the play] was acted occasionally during the reigns of James and Charles I" (Seltzer). The play has "32 speaking roles, 35 roles in all" (McMillin

& MacLean). Greene's play "was popular in performance and much less so in print" (Dillon 2002). *Friar Bacon* "has been claimed as the first successful romantic comedy, but more significantly it is the earliest of the 'double plot' plays" (Morris 1987).

SR 14 May 1594; transferred 29 June 1624; 22 April 1640. Q1 1594 *The Honorable History of Friar Bacon and Friar Bungay*; a conjurer's trick initiates what is in effect a dumb show for the prince: "Only the audience is supposed to hear the speeches" (Mehl 1965); not divided. *Friar Bacon* is "very likely printed from theatrical copy" (Seltzer). "The play employs a new Elizabethan repertoire of spectacular devices and effects, including the prospective glass, Hercules and the Hesperidian golden tree conjured from below, the Brazen Head that talks, and the arm that appears in lightning to smash it with a hammer" (Cartwright 1999). The episode of the Brazen Head is especially intriguing: *"Here the head speakes, and a lightning flasheth forth, and a hand appeares that breaketh downe the head with a hammer."* "Bacon's brass head is an embodiment of the scientist's intellect, together with a harnessed, natural force" (LaGrandeur 1999). Bungay conjures a tree with a *"dragon shooting fire"*; then *"Hercules appeares in his lions skin,"* and he "begins to breake the branches." Finally Bacon orders Hercules to *"[t]ransport the Germane unto Haspurge"*; this SD follows: *"Exit the spirit with Vandermast and the tree."* Unusual staging includes the representation of different locales simultaneously when one set of characters is in Oxford and the other in Fressingfield; "when the two parties are established in two separate areas of the stage, the Oxford party may look in Bacon's magic glass and 'see' the other" (Styan 1996). Q2 1630. Q3 1655.

The Q2–3 TPs feature a woodcut purportedly illustrating "three moments in the play . . . Friar Bacon sitting up to speak, Friar Bacon nodding off at the table, and the moment in which lightning strikes and the inanimate and previously silent 'brazen-head' speaks aloud" (Peters 2000); "the sleeping friar represents negligence and lassitude: his study is trivialised by the musician with pipe and tabor, and by the book, abandoned on the desk, with its alchemical symbols casually displayed" (Williams 2007). "The woodcut does not in fact represent the action in the play, but was made for a chapbook based on it" (Foakes 1985). However, "the figure of Miles in this woodcut bears a striking resemblance to contemporary portrayals of Richard Tarlton, the famous clown, in John Scottowe's drawing, which illustrates an elegy to Tarlton and so was probably made soon after his death in September 1588, and in the woodcut on the title page of *Tarlton's Jests*" (Levin 1999). But Astington 1999b doubts the Tarlton connection: "while the Scottowe drawing was copied from the woodcut, the woodcut itself was copied from a print made in Antwerp twenty-two years before Tarlton's death."

Fuimus Troes, or The True Trojans. Jasper Fisher; identified by Anthony à Wood. Written *"c.* 1611–23" (Elliott 1997). Acted *c.* 1625 (Ronan 2005). "Publikely represented by the gentlemen students of Magdalen Colledge in Oxford," according to the TP.

SR 1 August 1633 a Tragedy called *ffuimus Troes or the true Trojans;* transferred 1 July 1637. Q 1633 *Fuimus Troes, Æneid 2, The True Trojans, Being a Story of the Britains' Valor at the Romans' First Invasion*; no author named; dramatis personae; induction; chorus at close of each act; five acts and separate scenes. The play's title is misleading: "the play's plot, nomenclature, and moral all owe a very great deal more to Geoffrey of Monmouth than to Virgil" (Hopkins 2008b). *Fuimus*, a play about the Roman conquest of Britain, "presents Julius Caesar as a manifest tyrant who is initially humbled by British valour" (Butler 2005). The SDs describe extravagant costumes: "*Two Druids, in long robes, hats like pyramids, branches of mistletoe*"; "*Eulinus, in a nightcap, unbraced . . . playes and sings to the violl.*" When the Britons celebrate a victory: "*A dauncing maske of six enters . . . Androgens and Themantius play at foyles.*" Unusual staging includes Hulacus propitiating the gods: "*The image of the Moone, the shrine opens.*" Offstage sound conveys violence: "*Noyse of ships landing, and the battell within*"; "*They march about, and goe out. The whole battaile with-in.*"

An induction dramatizes the Roman invasion of Britain: "*Mercury, conducting the ghosts of Brennus and Camillus, in compleate armour, and swords drawne*"; together they witness the ensuing action, and at the end Mercury's words conclude the play: "You must be friends at last. The cloze is sweete, / When after tumults, hearts and hands doe meete."

Fulgens and Lucrece. Henry Medwall. Probably acted during the Christmas season of 1497 (Moeslein 1981) in the evening (Walker 1998). Performed at one of Cardinal Morton's seats, probably Lambeth Palace, perhaps before the Flemish and Spanish ambassadors (Boas & Reed 1926); Medwall was Morton's chaplain, according to the Q TP. "A number of connections are readily apparent between the legal aspects of *Fulgens and Lucres* and Chancellor Morton's professional life" (Horner 1993), though Twycross 2008 argues that the play need not have been acted *in* the palace. Possibly not performed until May 1516, at celebrations marking the visit to Greenwich of Margaret, dowager queen of Scotland (Godfrey 1996). *Fulgens* "incorporates many of the features we would expect in court maskings: a song, a wrestling match, a comic joust, and elaborate mumming (a dance accompanied by musical instruments)" (Clopper 2001). Presented in a great hall (Southern 1973): "these folke . . . sitt in the halle." Such a room, with a screens passage at one end, would constitute "the ideal playing-place" (Tydeman 1986). "The spectators are guests at a patrician banquet who have already dined when the first part of the play commences . . . and who expect to feast again between the two halves" (Bevington 1973). The play requires "nothing more than the hall itself as a setting and the furniture of the hall—chairs and stools—as props" (Nelson 1980). "Seemingly performed by professional actors" (Bevington 1962). "Professional actors may have performed the major roles," but "some of the actors were boys" (Nelson). "The performers were probably chapel choristers from the archbishop's household, professionals in their way, highly skilled in singing" (Milling 2004). "[C]ould be acted by five players" (Streitberger 2009).

SR none. Q ND 1510–16 (Walker 2000) *A Godly Interlude of Fulgens, Senator of Rome, Lucrece His Daughter, and Publius Cornelius of the Disputation of Nobleness*; unique copy at Huntington; "compyled" by Henry Medwall; induction, epilogue; divided into "two partyes to be played at two tymes," perhaps "during the course of a feast" (Nelson); not otherwise divided. "What Rastell's title page suggests is that he, and perhaps Medwall too, probably thought of the play as *The Disputation of Nobleness*, a title more in keeping with his source . . . and that the names of the principal characters were provided as supplementary information only" (Walker 2006). The play's subject, the nature of nobility, "had an obvious relevance a dozen years after the Tudors came to the throne and the new dynasty began to bring forth new gentlemen" (Craik 196). Q was "discovered among the Lord Moyston papers at Cambridge" (Kitch 2005) and sold at Sotheby's in 1919; Seymour de Ricci subsequently published a facsimile (1920a). The Q TP features a woodcut depicting a richly dressed man and woman in conversation. "But the illustration . . . does not show an actual production of the play, nor is it even an artist's visualization of the probable staging of a contemporary drama," for it is copied from a woodblock used in an earlier book (Davidson 1991).

"The first complete and wholly secular interlude that has survived" (Wickham 1976), "a form of secular *psychomachia*" (Grantley 2007), Medwall's play "is the first known drama in England to draw on a humanist source text: Buonaccorso da Montemagno's *De Vera Nobilitate*, written in 1428 and translated into English (from the French) by John Tiptoft in the 1470s" (Kitch 2005). "The first English play to reach print" (Howard-Hill 1990a). "The first [English play] for which an author can be identified"; "the first real sub-plot, rather than merely a comic interlude, in English drama" (Walker 2000).

G

The Gallant Cavaliero. See *The Trial of Chivalry.*

Gallathea. John Lyly. Probably acted early 1584 (Lancashire 1969a) by Paul's Boys at the first Blackfriars. Or first performed by that company in late 1587 or early 1588 (Bevington 1996); the Q TP records performance by Paul's Boys at Greenwich before the queen, the evening of 1 January 1588; this production may represent a revised version of the play that Lyly wrote in 1584 (Hunter 2000). Lyly's plays were "often presented and acted" before Queen Elizabeth, according to the D general TP. *Gallathea* contributes "to the cult of the virgin Queen in its celebration of the triumph of Diana (frequently associated with Elizabeth) over Cupid" (Scragg 1997).

SR 1 April 1585 and 4 October 1591; transferred 23 August 1601; 9 January 1628. Q 1592 no author named; prologue (addressed to queen) and epilogue; five acts and separate scenes. A tree functions "initially as a means of shelter from the heat of the sun, and subsequently as the site of the virgin sacrifice which threatens the life of the title figure" (Scragg 2008). SDs provide a few indications of how the actors looked: e.g., "*Cupid alone in Nimphes apparell.*" Rudimentary SDs describe onstage action: "*Enter Fayries dauncing and playing.*" D 1632 *Six Court Comedies* (with *Campaspe, Endymion, Midas, Mother Bombie, Sappho and Phao*); two issues; by "John Lilly"; includes two songs from *Gallathea* not printed in Q.

Gallathea is "Lyly's outstanding achievement in the translation of the euphuistic mode into a dramatic technique" (Scragg 1998). Lyly "had his characters discuss the state of being in love for the first time on a London stage" (Honan 1998). "Lyly gave cross-dressing its theatrical prominence and virtually invented romantic comedy, both major contributions to playhouse drama" (Cartwright 1999). The plot concerns the sacrifice of a virgin to Neptune every five years; to protect their daughters two shepherds disguise their girls as boys. "The two girls fall in love with each other, both at first supposing the other to be a boy, and continue in their love even after they have come to suspect that the other might, in fact, be a girl" (Pincombe 1996). "As confusion becomes the condition—and the camouflage—for transgressive erotic fantasy, it achieves the status of psychological pleasure" (Cartwright 1998). At the close when the girls arrive at church to be married, "Venus turns one of the two girls into a boy by giving her a penis" (Pincombe). "That neither we nor the characters know or care which of Lyly's girls will be transformed demonstrates the arbitrary quality of sexual difference in *Gallathea*" (Rackin 1987). *Gallathea* is the "most striking example of female homoeroticism to emerge in dramatic literature before the end of the sixteenth century" (Walen 2005). "It is more thoroughly and frankly homoerotic in plot, structure, and character than *As You Like It* or *Twelfth Night*" (Traub 2002). "In a remarkably erotic scene, the heroines move through a process of metaphorical undressing to recognition of same-sex passion" (Findlay 2001). "In *Gallathea* the final image is of single-sex marriage" (Gossett 2000).

A Game at Chess. Thomas Middleton. Licensed for acting 12 June 1624, according to a marginal note in a copy of the play (Limon 1986). Acted by the King's Men at the second Globe, "possibly twice a day" (Ioppolo 2006); this is one of "[o]nly seven non-Shakespearean plays . . . advertised on title pages as exclusively Globe productions" (Straznicky 2006b). The gap between licensing and performance is significant: the company "deferred presenting [the play] until August, when the court was away on progress in the Midlands. As a result it was six days before James heard of the play's scandalous success" (Dutton 1991). The Q1 TP records that the play "was acted nine days together." A run of nine consecutive performances, beginning 5 August 1624 and continuing until 14 August (with the exception of Sunday, 8 August), was most unusual, a sign of extraordinary popularity and topicality: "Among pre-Restoration plays that have survived, it is by some way the closest depiction of contemporary political events on the public stage" (Corns 2007). The actors playing the chess pieces "clearly impersonated James (White King), Charles (White Knight), Buckingham (White Duke), Philip IV (Black King)" (Darby 2011). Middleton apparently wrote the play "after the collapse of James's negotiations for a Spanish bride for Prince Charles" (Butler 2002); Prince Charles and the Duke of Buckingham had visited Madrid "in order to negotiate the marriage of the Prince to the Spanish Infanta" (Dutton 1999). The play's appeal was owing to its satire of the Spanish, especially the former Spanish ambassador in London, Count Gondomar, "the most hated man in Shakespeare's England" (Rasmussen 2011) and represented in the play by the Black Knight. The current Spanish Ambassador, Don Carlos de Coloma, complained to King James, and the play was suppressed; a warrant was also issued to have the playwright summoned to the Privy Council. Revels documents report: "Middleton the poet is sought after, and it is supposed shall be clapt in prison, if he doe not cleere him selfe by the M^r. of the Revells, who al[l]owed of it" (Bawcutt 1996). "The players and Middleton himself were admonished and punished, though apparently not severely. Probably the Lords of the Council found the play an amusing expression of opinions that, in the summer of 1624, were not uncongenial to them" (Loftis 1987). The King's Men were forbidden to perform again until licensed by the king, which occurred 27 August 1624. There exists an eyewitness account of a performance of the play (10 August) by John Holles, Baron Haughton, sent to the disgraced Robert Carr, Earl of Somerset, and preserved in the Nottingham University Library MS Newcastle Correspondence 15405 (Braunmuller 1990). A letter from John Chamberlain to Dudley Carleton, 21 August 1624, reports that the play "was frequented by all sorts of people old and young, rich and poor, masters and servants, papists and puritans, wise men, etc., churchmen and statesmen" (Heinemann 2003). The audience has been "estimated in total at about 30,000 people" (Corns). "It is not impossible that nearly 10 percent of the total population of London saw the play" (Levy 2000). William Rowley "probably [played] the Fat Bishop" (Gurr 2004c).

A Game at Chess "survives in more manuscripts than any other play" (Taylor 2004b), though "the text Herbert 'allowed' has not survived" (Dutton 1991). (1) London, BL, Lansdowne MS 690, fols. 2–53; ed. Dutton 1999; "By Tho: Middleton"; dated 1624 on the TP; copied by Ralph Crane; "reflects something close to the final version of the play" (Dutton 2004); induction (Ignatius Loyola and Error); prologue and epilogue; five acts and separate scenes. Staging calls for a property altar *and divers images* [i.e., statues] *about it*"; the statues move to the sound of music. (2) San Marino, CA, Huntington, MS EL 34/B/17; "Bridgewater MS"; "by Tho: Middleton"; partially in Middleton's hand; "a defective manuscript initially divided between two unpracticed copyists and completed with substantial indifference to the integrity of the text by Middleton" (Howard-Hill 1999); induction, prologue, and epilogue; five acts and "scaena ultima." (3) Cambridge, Trinity College, MS 0.2.66, ed. Bald 1929; ed. Howard-Hill 1990b; "by T. M."—the last name is filled out in another hand; entirely in Middleton's writing (Ioppolo 2006); "the playwright's own careless transcript of his revised foul papers" (Howard-Hill 1999); "represents a relatively early version of the play" (Dutton 1999); prologue and epilogue; induction; five acts. Staging calls for "*an altar discovered and statues.*" (4) Oxford, Bodleian, MS Malone 25, fols. v-xii and 1–69; ed. Bawcutt & Duncan-Jones 1993; the TP dated 1624; "by Tho. Middleton"; partly copied by Ralph Crane but the TP is in Middleton's hand; "apparently the only early literary manuscript which contracts the text of a play while preserving its essential action" (Howard-Hill 1993); "drastically abridged" (Bawcutt & Duncan-Jones); no prologue; induction; dumb show; epilogue spoken by White Queen's pawn; five acts and separate scenes. Staging calls for "*An altar discovered with tapers on it: and images about it*"; then "*the images [i.e. statues] move in a dance.*" (5) Washington, Folger, MS V.a.231; "Archdall MS"; no author named on the TP; copied by Ralph Crane; "[i]t is apparently the only instance of a play written for the public theater being copied while the play was being presented on stage" (Howard-Hill 1993); the TP records the date of 13 August 1624 "and was therefore completed on the day before the play's last performance" (Howard-Hill 1999); "derived from an early version of the play which Middleton revised before production" (Bawcutt & Duncan-Jones 1993). This MS "entirely omits the character of the Fat Bishop and a good many lines associated with the intriguing character of the White King's Pawn" (Dutton 1991). (6) Washington, Folger, MS V.a.342, fols. 1–7; "Rosenbach MS"; the MS "is a pretty cursory performance possibly intended for casual sale" (Howard-Hill 1999); "compos'd by Tho: Middleton"; "as it was acted nine dayes together"; copied by amateur scribes; no prologue; induction and epilogue; five acts.

SR none; publication was "surreptitious" (Greg 1931). Q1 ND ?1625 an unauthorized edition printed on the continent; two issues; "the picture [on the TP] plainly explained"; induction, prologue and epilogue (by White Queen's Pawn); dumb show described; five acts. "The first single play printed with engraved title-pages" (Taylor 2004b). The Q1 TP features two engraved scenes: the top one depicts eight figures at a chess-board; the lower one depicts "the leading characters in the main plot, the Fat Bishop (Marco Antonio de Dominis), the Black Knight (Count Gondomar), and the White Knight (Prince Charles)" (Foakes 1985). Staging includes statues on an altar; these "dance to the tune of a song that attributes their motion to the 'joy' felt by their masters" (Williamson 2009). Q2 ND ?1625 printed "in Lydden" [Leiden, The Netherlands]; actually printed in London (Jakacki 2011); two issues, one with an engraved TP and one without. Q3 ?1625 the TP features an engraving that depicts the Fat Bishop and Black Knight, each with a foot on a chess-board.

A Game at Chess "is the most striking manifestation of popular political sentiment to survive from the early English drama" (Howard-Hill 1990b); "[t]he most successful play of the Tudor/Stuart era" (Dutton 2004). "No other play of the entire Jacobean period has provoked so much comment from contemporaries, no other play caused a comparable scandal" (Limon). "The biggest box-office success and most talked-about dramatic work of its era" (Taylor 2004b).

The Gamester. James Shirley. Licensed for acting 11 November 1633 (Adams 1917). "Presented by" Queen Henrietta Maria's Men at the Phoenix, according to the TP. Performed also at Whitehall the night of 6 February 1634, according to Henry Herbert (Nason 1915), who reports that the play was made "out of a plot of the king's, given him by mee; and well likte. The king sayd it was the best play he had seen for seven years" (Adams). Shirley "wrote [the play] specifically for court performance" (Butler 1984b). "Probably there were other court and Phoenix performances which have left no record" (*JCS*).

SR 15 November 1637. Q 1637 five acts. The play "is especially interesting for its realistic pictures of gaming-houses, gamblers, and men about town" (Nason). "Shirley's play and tavern are populated with those who dissipate their lives and livelihoods and men whose names signify their condition: Acre-less, Little Stock and Sell-Away. Even the nobility join in the frivolous squander of their patrimony" (Sharpe 1987). "[T]he scene appears to be a street upon which there are shops," and although there are no explicit SDs to indicate actual shops onstage, "the context of the dialogue suggests that a shop may have been set up within one of the unused doorways" (Stevens 1977).

"Shirley's emphasis in this and other plays on the proper conduct of love and honor corresponds to the Cavalier taste for form and social manner as opposed to impassioned commitment. His restrained, elegant expression fits perfectly with the Caroline liking for decorum and culture, often called 'wit'" (Burner 1988). But Sharpe 1987 argues: "Platonic love is . . . shown to be a front for promiscuity"; the play "not only contrasts with the lofty prose and noble sentiments of [Walter Montagu's] *The Shepherd's Paradise*; it bears no resemblance to [Alfred] Harbage's identikit of the face of cavalier drama."

Gammer Gurton's Needle. Mr. S. (?William Stevenson, fellow of Christ's College [Bradley 1903]). Possibly written or revised by John Bridges: "Two Martin Marprelate tracts of 1588 state in so many words that the playwright of *Gammer Gurton* was John Bridges" (Creeth 1966); Joseph Hunter "first noted the attribution to Bridges" in 1848 (Norland 1995). Acted 1551–54 (*DTRB* 1984). "Played on stage, not longe ago" by the students of Christ's College, Cambridge, according to the Q1 TP, probably on a stage erected in the great hall (Southern 1973). The original staging probably involved "a lath-and-canvas structure showing a street and two houses" (Craik 1958): the play "seems to require two functional stage houses for Gammer Gurton and Dame Chat, with a hole in the latter house through which

Dr. Rat climbs and is beaten for his pains" (Bevington 1973). Probably performed "in the late afternoon and early evening" (Whitworth 1984).

SR entry of 1562–63 for *Dyccon of Bedlam* probably refers to the play "under another name" (Boas 1914). Q1 1575 [colophon] *A Right Pithy, Pleasant and Merry Comedy Entitled Gammer Gurton's Needle*; list of characters; prologue; no epilogue labeled as such but Diccon bids the audience applaud; five acts and separate scenes. Diccon "is an outstanding presence" in the play; "As rootless and disconnected as a Shakespearean fool, Diccon is licensed by his creator to wreak havoc in a tight-knit rural community for no clearer reason than that his community is ripe for exploitation" (Thomson 2007). The Q1 TP reports, "played on stage, not longe ago in Christes Colledge," words that "may have been reprinted from a lost edition of *c.* 1563" (Wilson 1969). Q2 1661 "played on the stage near a hundred years ago in Christs-Colledge in Cambridge"; Q2 "seems to have been printed directly from Q, preserving most of its errors" (Whitworth). The "old-fashioned appeal" of Q2 is "made visually explicit by its black-letter type" (Randall 1995).

This "is the first English play which states definitely of itself that it was played at a university" (Southern). "This is the earliest extant play for which the explicit claim that it was played 'on stage' is made" (Whitworth). In *Historia Histrionica* (1699) one of the speakers says, "The first comedy that I have seen that looks like regular, is *Gammer Gurton's Needle*, writ I think in the reign of King Edward 6. This is composed of five acts, the scenes unbroken, and the unities of time and place duly observed." This comedy is one of "the earliest full-scale, five-act Terentian comedies written in English" (Hornback 2009b). "Critics nominate *Gammer* as a candidate for the 'first English play' because no previous plays followed a Latin precedent in terms of act and scene division, secular subject matter, and respect for unities of time and place. It is provocative, then, that when a playwright chose to introduce the very first English play to undergraduates steeped in Latin, he chose the topic of a housewife's mischances" (Wall 2002). "And it is the unique achievement of *Gammer Gurton's Needle* to generate so much visual theatre out of an invisible property, one that will be scarcely visible even when found" (Thomson 2007).

The Generous Portugal. See *The Island Princess.*

The Gentle Craft. See *The Shoemakers' Holiday.*

The Gentleman of Venice, A Tragicomedy. James Shirley. Possibly first performed by Ogilby's Men at the Werburgh Street theater, Dublin (*JCS*). Licensed for acting in London 30 October 1639 (Adams 1917). Also "presented" by Queen Henrietta Maria's Men at the Salisbury Court playhouse, according to the TP, later in 1639, according to a notation in a Houghton Library copy (Burner 1988).

SR 9 July 1653. O and Q 1655 two issues; list of characters with brief descriptions; "five acts of unequal lengths" (Engel 1976). Publication in O format permits buyers to bind this play with the O 1652–53 collection, *Six New Plays*; "it is not known whether" this play was "ever actually sold singly" (Greg 1939). *Gentleman of Venice* and *The Politician* "were issued at the same time by Humphrey Moseley . . . and the two octavo editions are frequently found bound together" (*JCS*). Unusual staging includes: "*The scene adorn'd with pictures, amongst the rest Claudiana's*" to simulate a gallery; "*The pieces of armour hung upon severall trees.*"

According to the dedication, the staging was successful: "The poem [i.e., the play in printed form] that approacheth to kiss your hand, had once a singular grace and lustre from the scene, when it enjoy'd the life of action; nor did it want the best hands to applaud it in the theater."

The Gentleman Usher. George Chapman. Acted late 1602-early 1603 by the Children of the Chapel at the second Blackfriars (Smith 1970).

SR 26 November 1605 A book called *Vincentio and Margaret* [principal characters]. Q 1606 contains "two fairly elaborate masques" (Ornstein 1970); five acts. The masque "draws attention precisely to the sexual substitution of role-playing male servants for actual women" (DiGangi 1997). Unusual staging: "Margaret, Vincentio's virgin wife, hearing of her husband's supposed death for which she feels responsible, smears her face with a depilatory ointment to deform it in order to destroy the cause of her husband's love"; but Vincentio is not dead and pledges "his love for her despite her loss of beauty. Margaret's beauty is suddenly miraculously restored by a doctor who applies a medical mask to her face" (Drew-Bear 1994). Also issued in *Comedies, Tragicomedies, & Tragedies* (1652), a made-up book no longer extant.

"In performing his duty the usher is seen from *behind*—a perspective from which he is subordinated and potentially eroticized" (DiGangi). The gentleman usher of the title, Bassiolo, "forges a homoerotic bond with Vincentio, lying on the ground with him and creating an image of the collapse of hierarchical distinctions" (Burnett 2004).

Gentleness and Nobility. ?John Heywood (Massai 2007) or ?John Rastell, who printed the play (Watkins 1999). Acted 1527–30 (Grantley 2004) indoors (Southern 1973), probably in a great hall (Walker 1998). The play takes the form of a dialogue among three characters (Merchant, Knight, and Plowman) and so requires three actors; at the close a Philosopher, probably played by a fourth actor, gives a moralistic speech. "The Phylosopher's references to 'soferayns' ('citizens') who are present in the audience suggest that *Gentylnes and Nobylyte* was not a court play, but one performed in the City" (Fox 1989). But Dillon 1996 contends that "Fox's evidence will not stand up to this interpretation," and Craik 1958 suggests that much of the amusement "depends on the play's being performed before an aristocratic audience."

F ND ?1529 (Walker) no author named on the TP, which calls the play *Of Gentleness and Nobility, A Dialogue between the Merchant, the Knight, and the*

Plowman, Disputing Who is a Very Gentleman and Who is a Noble Man and How Men Should Come to Authority; "compilid in man[n]er of an enterlude with divers toys and gestis addyd therto to make mery pastyme and disport"; a philosopher "delivers an epilogue unequivocally approving the Plowman's arguments" (Fox); divided into a first and a second "pars" (i.e., part), "for presentation on two occasions such as dinner and supper on the same day" (Lancashire 2002); not otherwise divided. Sparse SDs: "the only two stage directions in a play primarily in dialogue-form direct the Ploughman to whip the Knight" (Dillon 1996). "The mixture of stage directions (Latin and English) points . . . to collaboration or revision" (Axton 1979). F2 ND ?1535.

"The play was first attributed to John Heywood in the play-catalogue which Francis Kirkman and others appended to their edition of *Tom Tyler and His Wife* (1661)" (Partridge & Wilson 1949). "[T]he epilogue is probably Rastell's chief contribution" (Cameron 1941).

George a Greene, the Pinner of Wakefield. ?Robert Greene; attribution suggested by the actor Edward Juby to George Buc (Gurr 2009c), but "Juby's attribution of the play to Robert Greene may have been nothing more than a shrewd but mistaken inference from the play's title" (Nelson 1998). Murphy 2012a, however, persuasively argues that the play was indeed written by Greene. Acted 1587–93 (Skura 2003) at undetermined venue. "[W]ritten originally for Henslowe's Red Bull company" (Gurr 1988a). "Sundry times acted" by Sussex's Men, according to the TP; Henslowe records five such performances at the Rose: 29 December 1593; 2, 8, 15 and 22 January 1594. This is the only play "attributable solely to Sussex's Men" (McMillin 1991). In playlist of Beeston's Boys 10 August 1639.

SR 1 April 1595 ("no edition bearing an earlier date than 1599 is at present known" [Clarke 1911]); transferred 16 October 1609; 2 March 1618; 23 February 1626; 4 March 1639. Q 1599 *A Pleasant Conceited Comedy of George a Greene, the Pinner of Wakefield*; no author named; not divided. Q represents "an abridged, corrupt version" (Murphy). A SD suggests that "some tradesmen enter with their work rather than being discovered: '*Enter a Shoomaker sitting upon the stage at worke Jenkin to him*'" (Dessen 1996). A gallery above figures in the staging: "James seeks admission at the gates of Sir John a Barley's house, and then, '*Enter Jane a Barley upon the walles*'" (Rhodes 1976). George Buc purchased a copy of Q; this book, now at the Folger, contains inscriptions by Buc (Nelson 2006). Q records the names John Taylour and Will Perkins, perhaps actors. "The printed text of *George a Greene* is only 1341 lines long, quite short for an Elizabethan play, but the many required feats of stage combat would not only have filled the time allotted for performance, but might also have evoked earlier Robin Hood texts" (Shapiro 1998).

This is "[t]he earliest extant professional play that includes a Robin Hood plot" (Davenport 1998). In *George a Greene* "George's victory over Robin is a friendly one but still an assertion of mastery. George refuses a place in Robin's band just as he refuses knighthood and attendance on the king. He is neither courtly hanger-on nor outlaw" (Bevington 1968).

Geronymo. See *Jeronimo.*

Ghismonda (Tancred and Ghismonda, Ghismonda and Guiscardo). John Newdigate III. Perhaps performed in some version *c.* 1623 (Howard-Hill 1988). This play has been thought to be a closet drama. However, the prologue argues for the superiority of a performed play to a narrated story, making clear that a performance is about to begin; the epilogue cites the just-concluded performance in illustration of that argument; and the SDs are clear and generally consistent with others of the period. A possible venue is the hall of a great house, almost certainly Arbury Hall. "The prologue imagines an audience that, like the audience in the professional theatres, is not necessarily bound by the host/guest dynamic and the courtesy it requires" (Scott 2011).

(1) Warwick, UK, Warwickshire County Record Office, MS CR136/B766; entitled *Glausamond and Fidelia* by Howard-Hill; no TP; no author named; "seems to be an early draft of *Ghismonda and Guiscardo*" (Kidnie 2011); "datable to 1618–20" (Inglis & Johnstone 2011); from the library at Arbury Hall, Nuneaton; evidence of revision; prologue and epilogue; five acts ("first four acts are separated by stage-directions calling for music" [Howard-Hill 1980]). (2) Nuneaton, UK, Arbury Hall, MS A414; fols. 77–102; microfilm in Warwickshire County Record Office, M.I. 351/3, Item 20; authorial copy of a "substantially revised" version of *Glausamond* (Polito & Scott 2011); no TP; entitled *Ghismonda and Guiscardo* by Howard-Hill 1988 and by *AED 3*; no author named; "the names of the lovers have been altered from Glausamond and Fidelia to Guiscardo and Ghismonda" (Howard-Hill 1988); prologue and epilogue. (3) London, BL, Additional MS 34312, fols. 139–86, ed. Wright 1944; a new version of MS (1), revised 1623–24 (Howard-Hill 1980); no TP; *Ghismonda* is the title suggested by Wright; no author named; not written in Newdigate's hand; list of characters; prologue and epilogue; five acts. The MS "is an entirely distinct piece from the *Gismund of Salerne* of MSS. Hargrave 205 and Lansdowne 786" (Greg 1931). MS (3) first edited by Wright 1944.

The attibution to John Newdigate was made by Howard-Hill 1988 and supported by Inglis & Johnstone.

The Ghost, or The Woman Wears the Breeches, A Comedy. Anonymous. "Written in the year" 1640, according to the TP, and "conceivably put on surreptitiously after the theaters closed" (Randall 1995) at undetermined venue. The price of admission cited in the epilogue, eighteen pence, cannot "apply to performances at a public theatre" (*JCS*).

SR none. Q 1653 dramatis personae; prologue and epilogue; five acts. Although the Q offers no information about auspices of production, SDs are ample:

"*She gives* Engin *the breeches and he puts them on a pole, and carries them before her*"; "Cunicula *picks* Procus *his pockets.*" Staging creates a frisson when Engin impersonates a ghost: "Eng[in] *from the coffin in a sheet*"; the effect is instantaneous: "*They are all frighted.*"

Epilogue attacks opponents of drama, suggesting that they are motivated by self-interest and hobbled by lack of mental acuity: "What think ye now of plays? Abominable: / Or is't 'cause you want wit to unfold a fable, / Pick out the allegory, drive the sense / Where the plot aims it: that your benevolence / Should clap us, and our mouths up. Confess, confess; / You would be something, and 'gainst plays you press, / To be prickt down as states-men, not because / You do conceive um hurtfull, but will make laws, / To undo the gallants pastime of the land: / Beats down because you cannot understand." The play "goes out of its way to make an issue with the Puritans" (Harbage 1936).

Gigantomachia, or Work for Jupiter. Anonymous. Acted ?1610–19 (Russell 1987) at undetermined venue. Probably performed by students of Cambridge University (Gossett & Berger 1988) during the Christmas season *c.* 1613 (Nelson 1989).

Washington, Folger, MS J.a.1(15), fols. 186–200; no separate TP; no author named; list of characters; the Knave of Clubs "acts as Prologue and emerges occasionally as Chorus" (Russell); epilogue; corrections/additions on separate sheet; ten numbered scenes.

"The original title of this play was 'Worke for Jupiter,' and it is the annotating hand . . . which adds the title 'Gigantomachia'" (Gossett & Berger). The play dramatizes the attempt of the Titans "to overthrow the newly-enthroned gods, only to be quelled after a brief struggle by the wrath and might of Jupiter" (Russell). First edited by Russell.

Giles Goosecap. See *Sir Giles Goosecap.*

A Girl Worth Gold. See *1 The Fair Maid of the West.*

Gismond of Salerne. Rod. Stafford, Henry Noel, G. Al., Christopher Hatton, and Robert Wilmot; the name of the playwright responsible for each act is appended to that act in *Tancred and Gismund*, a "completely reworked" version of *Gismond* (Braunmuller 1984) made by Wilmot in 1591. Probably acted 1566 by the gentlemen of the Inner Temple (Kingsley-Smith 2008) or "in 1567 or early 1568" (Norland 2009) in their hall. Performed also at Greenwich, before the queen, ?1566; a prefatory sonnet refers to this performance, which seems to have had admonitory force: the play's tragedy is "caused by a sovereign who will not allow the heir to the throne to marry an earl worthy to be her husband" (Axton 1977). "The immediate political concerns animating *Gismond of Salern* are the succession and plight of Lady Catherine Grey, a potential claimant to the throne who had been imprisoned for her secret marriage to Edward Seymour. But more generally, the play comments, via a cautionary tale hedged by profuse flattery, upon Elizabeth's peremptory refusal to accept counsel about marriage and succession" (Perry & Walter 2011).

(1) London, BL, Lansdowne MS 786, fols. 1–36, ed. Cunliffe 1912; *Gismond of Salerne in Love* (the last two words in a later hand and different ink); no author named; argument; list of characters; prologue by Cupid; epilogue; chorus; five acts and separate scenes. SDs include a descent of Cupid, who "*cometh downe from heaven*," apparently by machinery (Dillon 2004a); later "*Cupid remounteth to heaven*." At another point Megaera "*ariseth out of hell*," presumably through a trap door. Violence takes the form of Gismond's father Tancred killing her lover and sending his heart to her in a golden cup. Such spectacle helps balance a play "completely dominated by set speeches" (Clemen 1961). Three sonnets "of the Quenes maydes" precede the play, which was written "for a particular audience consisting of the Queen's maids of honour accompanied by their mistress and other sophisticated representatives of her government and judiciary" (Wickham 1981). (2) London, BL, Hargrave MS 205, fols. 9–22; *The Tragedy of Gismond of Salerne*; no author named; argument and list of characters at end; chorus; epilogue; five acts and separate scenes; three sonnets follow the play. The Folger owns a fragment: MS V.a.198, fols. 10–11. SR none. First edited by Cunliffe, though Isaac Reed had earlier (in the 1825 edition of *Dodsley's Old Plays*) published a brief excerpt.

William Webbe's prefatory epistle to *Tancred* states that the gentlemen of the Inner Temple performed *Gismond* "in view of her majesty, by whom it was then as princely accepted, as of the whole honorable audience notably applauded: yea, and of al men generally desired, as a work, either in statelines of shew, depth of conceit, or true ornaments of poeticall arte, inferior to none of the best in that kinde: no were the Roman *Seneca* the censurer."

"This is the first English love tragedy that has survived" (Cunliffe), and "the first English tragedy to be based on an Italian *novella*" (Irish 2009).

The Glass of Government, A Tragical Comedy. George Gascoigne. The author "seems to have written [the play] ten years" before its publication in 1575 (Gaggero 2004). No record of production. However, "[t]hough this is possibly a closet play, it is written very much along the lines of a piece for performance apart from the long speeches, . . . and it exhibits the humanist concerns found in much interlude drama" (Grantley 2004).

Q 1575 *The Glass of Government, A Tragical Comedy, so Entitled Because Therein Are Handled as Well the Rewards for Virtues as Also the Punishment of Vices*; three issues; argument; list of characters; prologue and epilogue; chorus at end of each act except last; five acts and separate scenes. Ample SDs: "*Philosarchus beckneth Eccho, Philomusus and Philotimus go together*"; "*Philosarchus taketh her by the hand to comfort her.*"

Prologue, contrasting the play with ancient Roman drama, announces the author's didactic intent: "Deformed shewes were then esteemed muche, / Reformed speeche doth now become us best, / Mens wordes muste weye and tryed be by touche / Of Gods owne worde, wherein the truth doth rest." Although this must have sounded familiar to contemporary audiences, the play is "advanced in structure and characterization": Gascoigne "drops the allegorical element of the English sacred drama, and, like the Continental humanists, deals altogether with human types. He abandons, too, the imperfectly constructed verse of his contemporaries, and writes in the style of the Elizabethan *littérateur* a prose that contains marks of incipient Euphuism" (Thompson 1910).

***Glausamond and Fidelia.* See *Ghismonda*.**

The Goblins, A Comedy. John Suckling. Acted 1637 (Steggle 2004b). "Presented" by the King's Men at the [second] Blackfriars, according to the O TP. "There is no evidence of court performance, and its satire of courtiers links it more closely with the public stages than with the court" (Butler 1984b). As the epilogue implies, Stephen Hammerton "must have played Orsabrin" (Bentley 1984). In playlist of King's Men 7 August 1641. *The Goblins*, like Brome's *A Jovial Crew* and Shirley's *The Sisters*, belongs to a group of plays in the early 1640s that deploy "an alternative woodland community" as a means of challenging Charles I's policies (Sanders 2002).

SR 24 July 1646. O1 1646 *Fragmenta Aurea* (with *Aglaura, Brennoralt*); "printed by his owne copies," according to the general TP; prologue and epilogue; five acts. "The trick in Suckling's play is that the identity of the 'goblins' is concealed until the very end. They appear and reappear as devils, but they are really noblemen who have been unfairly treated at court and have therefore taken up thievery to survive; they conceal themselves by using devil costumes but reveal their sense of injured justice by acting like Robin Hood" (Cox 2000): "Orsabrin *[f]lyes into the woods severall wayes pursued by theeves in devils habits.*" "The play is so heavily loaded with dancing and singing that it becomes almost a rogue's opera" (Wright 1928). O2 1648 *Fragmenta Aurea*; list of characters; "about eighty alterations in *The Goblins* were made for the second edition of *Fragmenta* in stage directions, wording, and significant punctuation" (Beaurline 1971). O3 1658–59 *Fragmenta Aurea*; "the third edition, with some new additionals"; published in two parts; separate TP in Part 1 dated 1658; Part 2 entitled *The Last Remains of Sir John Suckling* (1659).

The prologue names earlier playwrights: "When Shakespeare, Bea[u]mont, Fletcher rul'd the stage, / There scarce were ten good pallats in the age." The epilogue comments on the varied reactions of playgoers: "One will like all the ill things in a play, / Another, some o'th'good, but the wrong way; / So from one poore play there comes t'arise / At severall tables, severall comedies." The play contains a "drunken poet fond of mythological masques, who is kidnapped and deluded into believing he is in hell"; the character "seems to be a personation of Jonson" (Steggle 1998).

God's Promises. See *The Chief Promises of God.*

Godfrey of Bulloigne [Boulogne]. See *Four Prentices.*

Godly Queen Hester. Anonymous. "Most likely written between 1525–29" (Ephraim 2001); acted ?Christmas season 1529 (Walker 1991a) or 1540–41 (Fox 1989). "Casting requirements are large, and the demand for extras is heavy" (Bevington 1962). During performance "the chappell" sings a hymn, indicating the presence of a choir: the play "bears signs of performance by household chapel personnel in a chapel setting" (McCarthy 2008). Possibly acted "in an abbot's hall before his guests and his leading brethren"; Westminster Abbey is one such site (Walker). "Probably originally performed . . . in the great hall of a palace or manor house, most probably within the court itself" (Walker 2000). "The play may have belonged . . . to the Chapel Children, who did not perform outside the court" (Lancashire 2002). The courtly venue raises a question about the nature of the play's didacticism: "Esther represents an English Queen married to King Assewerus or Henry VIII and threatened by Aman, the King's chief minister. The puzzle lies in identifying which Queen and which chief minister. Is Esther the beleaguered Catherine of Aragon, and Aman, Cardinal Wolsey, who had already begun the dismantling of the monasteries (a clear political subtext here)? Or is Esther the hapless Catherine Howard, and the fall of Cromwell the fall of Aman by which the righteous faction in the state—the Howards and old nobility as the Jews—rises again?" (Sessions 2002).

    SR *c.* January-February 1561 (Greg 1939). Q 1561 *A New Interlude Drawn out of the Holy Scripture of Godly Queen Hester*; "newly made and imprinted"; list of characters on the TP; prologue; not divided. SDs specify a "*traverse*," apparently a curtain furnishing "a means of temporary concealment or retirement from the action" (Southern 1973): "*Here the kynge entryth the travers.*" This designates "(seemingly a curtained structure) into which King Assuerus can retire and hear music played to him without leaving the stage, like Jupiter in *Wether*" (Bevington 1973).

    Godly Queen Hester dramatizes "a humanist defense of the ideally educated woman, as elaborated by More and especially Vives" (Bevington 1968). "The play derives from the More era but participates in the 1560s dialogue about women shared with *Mary Magdalene, Patient Grissell, Susanna*, and *Appius and Virginia*" (Cartwright 1999). "No female character of such secular resolution and initiative was to emerge again on the early modern stage until perhaps Bellimperia in *The Spanish Tragedy*" (Dillon 2007). The play also "create[s] one of the few actively positive representations of Jews in early English drama" (Grantley 2007).

The Golden Age, or The Lives of Jupiter and Saturn, with the Deifying of the Heathen Gods. Thomas Heywood. Acted 1609–11 (Taylor 1993a); "late 1610 or 1611" (Butler 2005). "Sundry times acted" by Queen Anne's Men at the Red Bull, according to the TP.

SR 14 October 1611; transferred 2 August 1630; 30 June 1673. Q 1611 two issues; list of characters; first and last speeches of Homer serve functions of prologue and epilogue; detailed descriptions of five dumb shows, explained by Homer, whose choral speeches divide the play into five acts. Spectacular staging: in first dumb show a king is presented with "*a bleeding heart upon a knives point.*" Staged violence includes a battle between Jupiter's forces and Enceladus's: "*They combat with javelings first, after with swords and targets.*" Grotesque staging includes "*A banquet brought in, with the limbes of a man in the service.*" Another dumb show, in several parts differentiated by speeches of Homer, creates astonishing visual effects: "*Enter the three fatall sisters [the Fates], with a rocke, a threed, and a paire of sheeres, bringing in a gloabe, in which they put three lots. Jupiter drawes heaven: at which* Iris *descends and presents him with his eagle, crowne, and scepter, and his thunder-bolt.* Jupiter *first ascends upon the eagle.*" "In appearance the thunderbolt is essentially a fizzing or flaming streak of fire delivered at rapid speed"; this effect could be accomplished by "the use of rockets or squibs" (Butterworth 1998). Then "Neptune *drawes the sea, is mounted upon a sea-horse, a roabe and trident, with a crowne are given him by the Fates.*" Subsequently, "Pluto *drawes hell: the Fates put upon him a burning roabe, and present him a mace, and burning crowne.*" When Jupiter goes up to Danaë, "it seems likely that he would have used a discovery space . . . from which place stairs leading to the gallery were clearly accessible" (Rhodes 1976). In disguise as a peddler, Jupiter "approaches the castle gates. To gain access [to Danaë], he bids his companion ring the bell, and the clown replies, 'Nay, do you take the rope in hand for luck's sake.' Then, Jupiter rings the bell" (Lawrence 1935).

The address to the Q reader calls the play "the eldest brother of three Ages [Heywood's other *Ages* plays] that have adventured the stage, but the onely yet that hath beene judged to the presse." Acts 2 and 4, the stories of Calisto and Danae, were revised by Heywood as Acts 1 and 2 of *The Escapes of Jupiter, c.* 1625.

A Goodly Interlude of Fulgens. See *Fulgens and Lucrece.*

A Goodly Interlude of Nature. See *Nature.*

Gorboduc (*Ferrex and Porrex*). Thomas Sackville and Thomas Norton. Acted "on an unknown date in January" 1562 (Nelson 2009a); Cauthen 1970 suggests Twelfth Night; Martin 2001 suggests 5 January; by gentlemen of the Inner Temple in their hall. "The audience included members of the Inner Temple, Gray's Inn, and the privy council, as well as courtiers and potentially ladies from the court" (Winston 2005). Performed also in the Great Hall at Whitehall, before the queen, 18 January 1562, according to the O1 TP. A "grett scaffold" was erected for performance; this was "a raised stage" (Bevington 1973). "No doubt its political content kept the original spectators, including Queen Elizabeth, on the edge of their courtly seats" (Danson 2000). An eyewitness report of this production exists in London, BL, Additional MS 48023, fol. 359v (Jones & White 1996); Robert Beale's account suggests that the play was "read by the audience in the specific context of [Robert, Lord] Dudley's suit to marry the Queen" (James & Walker 1995). Sir Philip Sidney in his *Apology for Poetry* (written *c.* 1582, printed 1595) praises *Gorboduc* as "full of stately speeches and well sounding phrases, climbing to the height of Seneca his style." Sidney's knowledge of the play "suggests that it was performed through the 1570s" (Gurr 1987b). Revived at Dublin Castle, 7 September 1601 (Chetwood 1749), before Baron Mountjoy, the Lord Deputy, by the gentlemen of the castle (Morash 2002); Mountjoy "had perhaps chosen the play to define his position in relation to the rebellion by O'Neill, the Earl of Tyrone, and the imminent arrival of an invading Spanish force in Kinsale" (Holland 2006). Twenty-one cast members are required at a minimum (Bevington 1962).

SR *c.* September 1565; no entry for the 1570 edition. O1 1565 *The Tragedy of Gorboduc*; unique copy at Huntington; "three actes were wrytten by Thomas Nortone, and the two laste by Thomas Sackvyle," according to the TP, but this printer's claim "may be an attempt to attribute these Acts' explicit political advice to the more influential of the two" (Ullyot 2008); argument; list of characters; chorus at end of each act except last; carefully described dumb shows precede the acts (this is the first play to introduce "each act with a pantomimic prologue" [Mehl 1965]); five acts and separate scenes. "[T]he visual effect is often spectacular. The dumb-shows between the acts call for elaborate staging and expensive costuming" (Bevington 1973): e.g., SDs before act 4 stipulate the ascent of three elaborately costumed Furies "*from under the stage*": they are "*clad in blacke garments sprinkled with bloud & flames, their bodies girt with snakes, their heds spread with serpents in steade of heare.*" The dumb show before the last act features "'a companie of hargabusiers and of armed men, all in order of battaile,' who discharge their pieces and march three times about the stage to the accompaniment of drums and fifes" (Bevington 1973). Following the dumb shows, O1 presents an explanation of the symbolic action, but "the audience of the original performances would not have been provided with these expository appendices" (Griffin 2001). Typically "the brilliant spectacle of the dumb show gives way to purely verbal display" (Waith 1988); "speech is the life-blood of *Gorboduc*" (Clemen 1961). O2 1570 *The Tragedy of Ferrex and Porrex*; no authors named on the TP; "set forth without addition or alteration but altogether as the same was shewed on stage before the queenes majestie"; this, the "'authorised' version," is "the text used in the royal performance" (Graves 1994). Neither the O1 nor O2 title "seems sufficient to describe the structure or genre of the play, considered from the vantage point of either Senecan or later Elizabethan tragedy. Although Gorboduc himself serves as the center of a 'mirror for magistrates' tragedy, *Gorboduc* contains but is not contained by such a tragedy, as the final act makes clear by continuing the action beyond the death of the royal characters" (Dunn 2003). Q 1590 *The Tragedy of Gorboduc*; appended to *The Serpent of Division* by John Lydgate and perhaps issued separately; the TP of the play names Sackville and Norton.

John Day's note to the O2 reader explains that the play first came to be printed when a man who "lacked a litle money and much discretion" surreptitiously brought the script to a printer; the resulting book was "exceedingly corrupted: even as if by meanes of a broker [pimp] for hire, he should have entised into his house a faire maide and done her villanie, and after all to bescratched her face, torne her apparell, berayed [defiled] and disfigured her, and then thrust her out of dores dishonested." The "publisher's lengthy analogy indelibly inscribes the text as a promiscuous and immoral object" (Wall 1993). But "there is nothing corrupt about [William] Griffith's 1565 text" (Orgel 2006).

We can see from *Gorboduc* "and its successors exactly what classical imports offered to the dramatists of the 70's and 80's, and what they made of them" (Rossiter 1950). "*Gorboduc* doubles as the first extant Senecan tragedy and the first neoclassical history play in the vernacular . . . as well as being the first play in blank verse to be written in English" (Grantley 2000); the play's blank verse was "created to approximate the Latin meters of Seneca" (Bevington 2004). *Gorboduc* has been called "the first tragedy in English aiming at anything like classic 'regularity'" (Farnham 1936). "Yet beneath this [classical] façade it remains stubbornly within the English dramatic tradition received from Bale, Bucer, and Ingelend" (Wickham 1981).

The Gossips' Brawl, or The Women Wear the Breeches, A Mock Comedy. Anonymous. A play-pamphlet "possibly produced" (Harbage 1936) *c.* 1655. The play "must have given grave offense to the Puritans" (Rollins 1921).

SR none. Q 1655 list of characters on the TP; epilogue of two lines; not divided. A "miniature play in prose" (Greg 1939) with adequate SDs.

One of several "misogynistic dramatizations of alehouse quarrels" (Potter 1981), "a scolding match between whores in an ale-house" (*JCS*).

"[T]his is a tongue combat between Jone, Doll, Meg, and Bess (a dunghill raker, a fishwife, a washerwoman, and a hostess)" (Randall 1995).

The Governor, A Tragicomedy. Anonymous. This play may be *The Governor* by Cornelius Fermedo. "However, the number of plays that may have shared the same name and Fermedo's connection with any of them, or the British Library manuscript, are hotly disputed" (Cerasano 2004b). A play called *The Governor* was acted at St. James's palace, 16 February 1637, according to a bill of the King's Men for plays acted before the king and queen (*JCS*); Herbert refers to this performance as taking place 17 February (Adams 1917).

London, BL, Additional MS 10419, fols. 2–48; no author named, but the name Samuel [?author's or ?scribe's first name] is written between the scene designation and the list of characters on the first folio; the TP bears a 1656 date (?date of transcription); evidence of revision; list of characters; prologue and epilogue; five acts. A note appears on a leaf immediately before the text: "This play formerly belonged to John Warburton, Somerset Herald Supposed in Jones's *Biographia Dram.* to be destroyed by the servant."

"'The Governor. By Sʳ Cornelius Formido' appears in a long list of plays entered by Humphrey Mosely in the Stationers' register (9 September 1653)" (Cerasano).

Gown, Hood, and Cap. Anonymous. A very brief entertainment acted at Cambridge University (Gossett & Berger 1988), presumably by students at a college, in the early seventeenth century. "References in the text to a Sophister (usually a Cambridge term) and to football 'ath'leayes' (ie, at the Leys, a field behind Pembroke College) . . . identify this as a Cambridge play" (Nelson 1989). "[T]he play is short, has no female roles, and requires no special machinery for production" (Gossett & Berger).

Washington, Folger, MS J.a.2, fols. 49–50; no author named; conventional bid for applause at close; not divided. First edited by Gossett & Berger.

The Grateful Servant, A Comedy. James Shirley. Licensed for acting as *The Faithful Servant* 3 November 1629 (Adams 1917). "Presented in December of 1629" (Burner 1988). "Lately presented with good applause" by Queen Henrietta Maria's Men at the Phoenix, according to the Q1 TP. The production was "a resounding success" (Burner). In playlist of Beeston's Boys 10 August 1639 as *The Grateful Servant*. The commendatory poems in Q1 hint at criticism of the play, perhaps by "someone who was a dramatist for a rival company" (*JCS*): John Fox urges Shirley to "scorne malicious censures." But Thomas Craford reports that the play, "grac'd with comely action, did appeare / The full delight of every eye and eare."

SR 26 February 1630; transferred 25 September 1637. Q1 1630 list of characters; five acts and first scenes. A masque figures importantly in the plot, and music, "both instrumental and vocal, is chiefly responsible for the air of enchantment surrounding this masque" (Stevens 1977). Q2 1637. Q3 ND ?1662 (Greg 1939).

In his Q1 dedication Shirley salutes Ben Jonson: "When the age declineth from her primitive vertue, and the silken witts of the time, (that I may borrow from our acknowledg'd master, learned *Johnson*) disgracing nature, & harmonious poësie, are transported with many illiterate and prodigious births, it is not safe to appear without protection." A prefatory poem by Massinger, complimenting Shirley's stylistic restraint, explains what the reader will *not* find: "Here are no forc'd expressions, no rack'd phraze / No Babell compositions to amaze / The tortur'd reader, no beleev'd defence / To strengthen the bold atheists insolence, / No obscene sillable, that may compell / A blush from a chast maide."

The Gravemakers. A droll based upon a scene in Shakespeare's *Hamlet* and performed in the 1640s and 50s. "The famous Gravediggers' Scene, up to the entrance of Ophelia's funeral train, at which the adapter is careful to stop, makes a practical droll for three actors" (Elson 1932). "It is significant that this scene had come iconically to stand in for the entire play as early as the 1650s" (Dobson 2001).

Published in *1 The Wits, or Sport upon Sport* (O 1662 [two issues] and 1672); RT *The Humors of the Gravemakers*; argument; list of characters.

The Great Duke of Florence, A Comical History. Philip Massinger. Licensed for acting as *The Great Duke* 5 July 1627 (Adams 1917). "Often presented with good allowance by" Queen Henrietta Maria's Men at the Phoenix, according to the TP. This is "the only play written by Massinger for a company other than the King's men after the death of Fletcher in 1625"; in all likelihood "Massinger had in earlier times undertaken to produce the play for Beeston, had been paid for it, but was very slow in delivering the copy" (E&G 1976). In playlist of Beeston's Boys 10 August 1639.

SR 7 December 1635. Q 1636 list of characters; five acts and separate scenes. "The full stage directions are interesting examples of Massinger's concern to indicate action and gesture" (E&G): "*This spoke as if shee studied an evasion*"; "[Calandrino] *rises and resignes his chaire.*" The most unusual staging involves Sanazarro who, imprisoned, finds a way to communicate: "*Takes off the ring & a pane of glasse*"; "This supplies / The want of penne and ink, this of paper." "The actor must take the glass from somewhere when he says 'and this of paper.' Just before this he '*Lookes backwards*' out of the 'back-part' of his prison . . . making it probable that he seems to take the pane from that fictional window" (Thomson 1991). When the panel of glass is tossed down, Fiorinda says: "What's that? / A pane throwne from the window no winde stirring?"; Fiorinda proceeds to read the inscription. Massinger's "dramatic style is extremely sensitive to non-verbal theatrical effects and his unusually explicit stage directions show a precise awareness of the actor's craft" (McLuskie 1981). Sound effects are suggested by the dialogue: "What noise of horses? / A goodly troope!"

John Ford's prefatory poem anticipates the long life of a printed play: "Action gives many poems right to live, / This piece gave life to action; and will give / For state, and language, in each change of age, / To time, delight; and honour to the stage."

Greene's Tu Quoque, or The City Gallant. John Cooke. Acted 1611 (Berman 1984). "Divers times acted" by Queen Anne's Men, according to the Q1 TP, at the Red Bull (Grantley 2008a). Performed also by that company at court, 9 and 19 November and 27 December 1611, and 2 February 1612; and by Lady Elizabeth's Men [Queen of Bohemia's] at Whitehall, "the prince only there," 6 January 1625 (Adams 1917). Christopher Beeston took the play "belonging to Queen Anne's Players with him from the populist Red Bull Theater to the aspiring Cockpit" (Clark 2003). *Greene's Tu Quoque* "is a straightforward adaptation of Lording

Barry's Whitefriars play, *Ram Alley*"; "Cooke not only adapts the plot; his play is marked by detailed, explicit borrowings" (Bly 1998). Edmund Gayton mentions the play in *Pleasant Notes upon Don Quixot[e]* (1654).

SR no original; transferred 2 September 1621; 3 December 1627; 21 May 1628. Q1 1614 two issues; not divided. Cooke's play was "probably originally called *The City Gallant*" (Bentley 1981). The Q1 TP features a woodcut apparently of Thomas Greene, sharer in Queen Anne's Men, in the role of Bubble, a city gallant; wearing a clown's attire, he says, "Tu quoque. To you sir." Greene "was the distinguished clown who replaced Will Kemp in the Queen Anne's Men Company (formerly Worcester's Men)" (Howard 2007). Staging possibly calls for an onstage structure: "*A mercers shop discovered, Gartred working in it.*" Q2 1622. Q3 ND ?1630. Following the closing of the theaters, parts of the play were adapted for a droll entitled *The Bubble*, later published in *1 The Wits, or Sport upon Sport* (O 1662 [two issues] and 1672). The engraved frontispiece of *The Wits* depicts Bubble, emerging from behind a curtain, costumed "more as a fool [than a gallant], wearing a hat with a cockscomb" (Foakes 1985).

Thomas Heywood's epistle to the reader in the Q1 second issue praises Thomas Greene, who died in 1612: "As for Maister *Greene*, all that I will speake of him (and that without flattery) is this (if I were worthy to censure) there was not an actor of his nature in his time of better ability in performance of what he undertooke; more applaudent by the audience, of greater grace at the court, or of more general love in the Citty." Heywood also reports that he does not know "whether this worke was divulged with his [the author's] consent or no: but howsoever, since it hath past the test of the stage with so generall an applause, pitty it were but it should likewise have the honour of the presse."

Grim the Collier of Croydon, or The Devil and His Dam, with the Devil and Saint Dunstan. William Haughton, who apparently meant the main title to be *The Devil and His Dam* (Kermode 2009b). "Presumably the publisher chose to feature the subplot title . . . because he thought it more likely to catch a buyer's eye" (Baillie 1984). Acted *c.* 1600–06 (Baillie) probably by the Lord Admiral's Men; Henslowe records earnest payment to Haughton, 6 May 1600, for "the devell & his dame." *Grim the Collier* "is presumably a version of Haughton's independently written play of May 1600, *The Devil and his Dam*" (Cathcart 2010). Probably performed first at the Rose and then at the Fortune (Gurr 2009c), when the company changed theaters, autumn 1600. This play "may have been acquired from the Fortune company after 1625 by Beeston for the Cockpit or the Red Bull" (Gurr). In its principal character, the play adopts a figure that had earlier appeared in *Damon and Pythias* by Richard Edwards. There is "the strong possibility of revision by a later writer" (Kermode).

SR none. D 1662 *Gratiae Theatrales, or A Choice Ternary of English Plays*, with *Thorney Abbey, The Marriage Broker* (separate pagination for each play); "never before published," according to the general TP; author identified on TP by initials "I. T." (probably spurious though Cathcart 2010 suggests John Tatham, and Kathman 2004a proposes "perhaps a reviser"); list of characters; prologue probably commissioned by the publisher (Baillie); opening scene constitutes an induction; five acts, with separate scenes in act 1. The SDs "are lengthy" (Jewkes 1958). At the outset Saint Dunstan feels sleepy, "*layeth him down to sleep; lightning and thunder; the curtains drawn, on a sudden* Pluto, Minos, Æacus, Rhadamantus *set in counsell, before them* Malbecco *his ghost guarded with Furies.*" This action initiates a kind of dream vision in which the devils parley. "The main plot centres around Belphegor, a devil sent from hell disguised as a Spaniard to test the shrewishness of earthly women" (Kathman 2004a). This play "seems to have been the first Elizabethan play in which a devil was the central character" (Baillie); other such plays include Dekker's *If It Be Not Good, the Devil is in It* and Jonson's *The Devil Is an Ass*, which "rather more successfully uses the same device of real devils outwitted and literally beaten by City of London merchants and speculators" (King 2001). Robin Goodfellow, called a devil in the list of characters, "integrates neatly the three aspects of the folk tradition: Puck, Goodfellow, and Hobgoblin" (Baillie); he appears onstage "*in a suite of leather close to his body, his face and hands coloured russet-colour, with a flayle.*"

The address to the reader reflects on the ways a play may be enjoyed—by playgoers and readers: "While that queint prologues th'hearer's ears bewitch, / 'Tis, reader, my design, your eyes to catch. / Our aim's in both alike; we to attain / Applause do strive, and get a private gain. / As cunning fencers make at parts below, / When they intend to give the head a blow: / So we do humbly court your ears and eyes, / While 'tis your purse we aim at for our prize. / A play's commended, if the stage be full, / And what book sells well, 's never counted dull. / Thus do the actor's and bookseller's gains / Give the best judgement of the poet's brains. / Then ne're enquire how these plays have took, / But buy them quickly, and commend the book."

Grobiana's Nuptials. ?Charles May (*AED 3*, Elliott et al.) or ?Roger Shipman (*JCS*, Kawachi 1986) and ?William Taylor (names written in the MS). Written and performed ?1637–?41 (*JCS*); ?1638 (*AED 3*). Acted by students of St. John's College, Oxford, 14 January 1637 (Elliott). Performed before an audience of sophisticates, the play pokes fun at bad manners: "'Old Grobian' is the head of an Oxford club of slovens, rusty pedants, and Mohocks [hooligans], sworn enemies of good manners, from among whom he desires to choose a husband for his daughter, Grobiana" (Herford 1886).

Oxford, Bodleian, MS Bodl. 30, fols. 13–25; no separate TP; no author named; prologue and epilogue (both by Grobianus); nine numbered scenes. Ample SDs: e.g., "*Enter Grobiana sicke ungartred holdinge her head.*" First edited by Rühl 1904.

Epilogue, marking the end of performance, makes a conventional plea for applause: "somewhat is left for me that am behinde: / Not to begge applause or desire your handes / To joyne these jolly lovers in new bandes, / But to tell you true, because I begunne, / You may goe away, the play is done."

The Guardian, A Comedy. Abraham Cowley. Acted 12 March 1642 by students of Trinity College, Cambridge, before Prince Charles, according to the Q TP, in the college hall. Performed also "several times after [the original performance] privately during the troubles" [i.e., following the closing of the theaters], according to the preface to *The Cutter of Coleman Street, A Comedy*, a version of the play reworked by Cowley, perfomed in 1661 (Randall 1995) and published in 1663. In his 1656 *Poems* Cowley reported that since the play "was 'rough-drawn onely' when it was rushed into performance for the prince, he had been only too happy to revise the text" (Stern 2004a).

SR none. Q 1650 two issues; list of characters; prologue and epilogue; five acts and separate scenes. Prologue and epilogue, in BL Harley MS 6918, fol.25, and Egerton 2725, fol. 31, and 2623, as well as in the Bodleian, MS Douce 357 and MS Rawlinson poet. 26, fol. 138, published in 1642, "probably the first prologue and epilogue to receive separate publication" (Wiley 1940). The "printed prologue . . . was evidently written or altered after the performance of the play" (Wright 1934).

Prologue to *The Guardian* comments on zealots' hostility toward the stage: "We perish if the Roundheads be about: / For now no ornament the head must wear, / No bays, no mitre, not so much as hair. / How can a play pass safely, when we know, / Cheapside-Cross falls for making but a show? / Our onely hope is this, that it may be / A play may pass too, made *ex tempore*. / Though other arts poor and neglected grow, / They'll admit poetry, which was always so. / Besides, the Muses of late times have bin / Sanctifi'd by the verse of Master Prin."

The Guardian, A Comical History. Philip Massinger. Licensed for acting 31 October 1633 (Adams 1917). "Often acted . . . with great applause" by the King's Men at the [second] Blackfriars, according to the general and separate TPs. Revived at court 12 January 1634; Herbert reports that it was "well likte" (Adams). In playlist of the King's Men 7 August 1641.

SR 9 September 1653 *The citie honest man, or the guardian* (probably "a fraudulent licensing of two plays under one title" [*JCS*]); 29 June 1660 ("probably a mistake for the *City Honest Man* of 1653" [Greg 1939]). O 1655 *Three New Plays* (with *The Bashful Lover, A Very Woman*—separate TPs and pagination but continuous register); "never printed before," according to the general TP; dramatis personae; prologue (possibly written by Davenant for another play and attached to this play [Adler 1987]) and epilogue; five acts and first scenes. The SDs "are detailed and full" (E&G 1976): "Enter *Jolante (with a rich banquet, and tapers) (in a chair, behind a curtain)*." Unusual auditory effects include "*A noise within, as the fall of a horse*"; a character comments, "The horse hath broke his neck." Between the last lines of the play and the epilogue are a song "between Juno and Hymen"

and another entitled "Entertainment of the Forests Queen," which accompanies
the masque that "triggers the play's resolution" (Rochester 2010).

Guiscardo. See *Ghismonda*.

Guy, Earl of Warwick, A Tragedy. B. J. These initials "were probably intended to
imply" that Ben Jonson wrote the play (*JCS*). "[S]eems to have been written, or
perhaps rewritten, in the early 1590s, most likely in 1593–94; it may conceivably
be a rewriting of a play current a decade or more earlier" (Cooper 2006). "Acted
very frequently with great applause by his late majesties servants," according to
the TP, at undetermined venue. John Taylor, the Water Poet, reports that he
saw a play called *The Life and Death of Guy of Warwick* performed by the Earl of
Derby's Men at the Maidenhead Inn, Islington, 14 October 1618 (Cooper). "The
stagecraft of the play suggests that it could originally have been designed with
a traveling company in mind" (Cooper). Possibly performed at the Red Bull *c.*
1620 (Moore 2006).

SR entries for 15 January 1620 (*the life and Death of Guy of Warwicke*) and
13 December 1620 (The Play of *Guy of Warwicke*) perhaps refer to this play, but
the first entry attributes the play to John Day and Thomas Dekker. There may
have been several plays about Guy of Warwick: Q may represent a play written
in the 1590s, the play seen by John Taylor in 1618, or a revision of one of these.
Q 1661 *The Tragical History, Admirable Achievements, and Various Events of Guy,
Earl of Warwick, A Tragedy*; author's initials on the TP (possibly spurious); speech
by Time at the beginning functions as prologue, Time's last speech, an epilogue;
Time appears at the beginning of each act; five acts. To historical adventures the
play adds "fairy lore and spectacle" (Richmond 1996): Guy meets an "Inchanter
or dam'd sorcerer" and becomes a victim of the enchanter's spell. But Oberon
enters, followed by various spirits: *"Enter the faeries with musick, they dance about
him,* Oberon *strikes* Guy *with his wand, he awakes and speakes."* When Guy expresses gratitude to the Fairy King, *"It thunders, lightens."* Guy's cave may be represented by a trap in the stage floor or perhaps by one of the doorways into the
tiring-house: *"Enter* Guy *being in his cave, to him the Angell"*; the Angel then says,
"rise and pray." Or the cave may be a temporary structure, for in act 5 Time says,
"with his own hands he builds himself a cave."

The play's "story of a quest that involves travelling to Jerusalem and violent
encounters with Muslim forces" relates it to such "Turk" plays as *1 and 2 Tamburlaine, The Jew of Malta, The Battle of Alcazar,* and *The Famous History of Thomas
Stukeley,* as well as *The Four Prentices of London, with the Conquest of Jerusalem*
(Connolly 2009).

H

Hamlet, Prince of Denmark. William Shakespeare. Written late 1599 (Cathcart 2001a, Shapiro 2005). "Latelie acted" by the Lord Chamberlain's Men, according to the SR, at the first Globe; "*Hamlet* was specially designed as part of the new theatre's opening season" (Cathcart). The Q1 TP reports that the play had been "diverse times acted . . . in the Cittie of London: as also in the two Universities of Cambridge and Oxford [probably in 1603], and else-where." "The allusion to performances in the universities suggests the play was performed within university colleges and/or the university towns" (Keenan 2002). Possibly performed at Hampton Court, 26 December 1603, but the play's title is not named in the court records (Chambers 1930). In early performances Richard Burbage "certainly" played the lead (Taylor 2002b); an elegy for Burbage singles out his performance in the role: "Oft have I seen him leap into the grave, / Suiting the person which he seemed to have" (Hibbard 1987); these lines, referring to Hamlet's grappling with Laertes at Ophelia's grave, "are evidence of what was done in performance" (Jenkins 1982). Robert Armin "would presumably have played the First Clown" (Astington 2010). Also performed by amateurs aboard the *Red Dragon*, a ship of the East India Company, in the harbor of Freeport, off Sierra Leone, 5 September 1607, according to the journal of Captain William Keeling (Taylor 2001a, Barbour 2009, Dobson 2011, Marino 2011); this represents "the first time Shakespeare was performed outside Europe" (Pechter 2002); "[s]ix months later [31 March 1608] they gave a repeat performance" (Shapiro 2005). Kliman 2011, however, believes that the shipboard performances never took place, that the account represents a forgery, probably by John Payne Collier. Possibly performed by Queen Anne's Men in Oxford, 1607 (Dutton 2000). After the death of Richard Burbage on 13 March 1619, Joseph Taylor, who joined the King's Men the same year, played the lead "incomparably well" (*Historia Histrionica*). Possibly performed by the King's Men at court *c.* 1619 (Chambers 1930), and in the hall at Hampton Court, 24 January 1637 (Chambers). (Thomas Nashe, in his preface to Robert Greene's *Menaphon* [1589], alludes to "whole Hamlets, I should say handfuls, of tragical speeches"; this likely refers to an earlier play by Thomas Kyd. Henslowe also records a performance of *Hamlet*, probably the lost work of Kyd, at Newington Butts, 9 June 1594, when the theater was occupied by the Admiral's and Chamberlain's Men. Thomas Lodge in *Wit's Misery* [1596] alludes to a performance of *Hamlet*, also probably Kyd's play, at the Theater, presumably by the Lord Chamberlain's Men. Francis Meres does not name *Hamlet* in his 1598 list of Shakespeare's plays.)

   SR 26 July 1602 *the Revenge of Hamlett Prince [of] Denmarke*; transferred 19 November 1607; ?4 August 1626 Paviers right in Shakesperes *plaies*; ?19 June 1627 widow of Isaac Jaggard . . . her parte in Shackspheere *playes*; 16 November 1630; 1 July 1637 Shakespeares *workes* their Part; 24 August 1642; 14 September 1642;

6 August 1674; 19 May 1683; 27 July 1683; 21 August 1683. Q1 1603 *The Tragical History of Hamlet, Prince of Denmark*; "by William Shake-speare"; extant (but defective) copies in BL and Huntington (has TP); a dumb show, unusual in that it merely mimes the action to follow (Cooper 2010), initiates the play-within-the-play, which is preceded by a three-line prologue; not divided. The first entry of the Ghost, who appears in armor, and, later, the burial of Ophelia probably involve the use of a trap in the stage floor (Gurr 1997), though Astington 1999a maintains that "the ghost enters and leaves the stage by means of the tiring-house entries," at least when *Hamlet* was performed at Hampton Court. In the closet scene the Ghost probably enters "through the hangings" covering the central discovery space (Gurr & Ichikawa 2000), though Fitzpatrick 2011 argues that there were only two entry-points onto the stage. The play-within-the-play probably "used the central opening" in the tiring-house wall (Gurr & Ichikawa); when the curtains are drawn back to reveal the dumb show, we see *"an arbor,"* probably a theatrical property; Q2, which does not mention an arbor, says the King *"Layes him downe upon a banke of flowers."* SDs unique to Q1 include these: in the closet scene the Ghost enters *"in his night gowne"*; the mad Ophelia enters *"playing on a lute, and her haire downe singing"* (a sign of "feminine distress" [Thompson 2010]); the entry of the king, queen, Laertes, and others *"with a priest after the coffin"*; when Ophelia is buried, *"Hamlet leapes in [the grave] after Laertes"* (presumably into the trap); at the climactic swordfight Hamlet and Laertes *"catch one anothers rapiers and both are wounded"*; Gertrude *"falles downe and dies"* after drinking poison. These details "seem to preserve elements of a very early production" (Irace 1998). A line spoken by the king provides an implicit SD: "see where hee comes poring uppon a booke"; the hand prop is in keeping with Hamlet's meditative nature, his melancholy mood, his status as a student at Wittenberg, a university renowned for theological study, and his incipient role as revenger. The visit of the players to Elsinore is "one of the most famous imaginative accounts of the arrival and performance of a troupe of touring players" (Westfall 1990). When the play-within-the-play is interrupted by the guilty Claudius, confirming Hamlet's suspicions about the king, the world of the court suddenly collapses and the characters disappear, leaving only Hamlet and Horatio to interpret what they have witnessed (Howard 1984). When Hamlet contrasts his father and his uncle in the closet scene, he uses miniature portraits (Tassi 2005), a highly developed art form in Elizabethan, Jacobean, and Caroline England (Fumerton 1991); earlier, Hamlet had spoken of a "picture in little." The graveyard scene, with Hamlet and Horatio in conversation, focuses on Yorick's skull, "the most famous prop in Early Modern drama" (Thompson 2010); Middleton would use a similar prop at the beginning of *The Revenger's Tragedy*. Sound effects may include a clock striking as Hamlet awaits the Ghost; the crowing of a cock when Horatio confronts the Ghost; the sound of trumpets, prompting Hamlet to complain of the king's carousing; the sound of the Ghost *"under the stage"*; *"a noyse within,"* heralding the return of Laertes; the sound of cannon as Horatio explains the preparations

for war. "The cannon used by the theatre companies were the type of cast-iron chambers often fired in salute. They were without long barrels or carriages, and were loaded with blank charges" (Shirley 1961). Cannons "fire more often in *Hamlet* than in any other play of Shakespeare's, and perform such diverse tasks as proclaiming the King's toast, greeting the English ambassadors, and giving the final note of honor to Hamlet's funeral procession" (Shirley). "*Hamlet* has seventeen musical stage directions and at least six songs, of which Ophelia sings the first five and the Gravedigger the sixth" (Thompson & Taylor 2006).

Q2 1604–05 some copies have a 1604 date, others 1605; *The Tragical History of Hamlet, Prince of Denmark*; "by William Shakespeare"; "newly imprinted and enlarged to almost as much againe as it was, according to the true and perfect coppie"; no act or scene divisions. "Clearly the true and perfect copy includes a great deal more than you could see at the theater" (Orgel 2006). Q2, which contains 4,056 lines compared with 2,221 in Q1 (Irace) and which is the longest of his plays (Berger 2007), "gives *Hamlet* at the state of an advanced working draft, the basis of rehearsal and revision" (Jones 1995). Q2 adds sound effects: e.g., repeated use of trumpets in the final scene. Horatio, after Hamlet's death, asks, "Why dooes the drum come hether?" "A drum played to march time was the stage convention to indicate the approach of an army" (Ogilvie 1927). Q2 also gives a detail of staging when Horatio confronts the Ghost: "*It spreads his armes,*" which may signify "the Ghost's reaction to being accosted" (Jenkins 1982). Q3 1611. Q4 ND "between 1621 and 1623" (Rasmussen 2003). F1 1623 *Comedies, Histories, & Tragedies*; three issues; *The Tragedy of Hamlet, Prince of Denmark*; "published according to the true originall copies"; partly divided into acts (first three scenes of act 1 and two scenes of act 2). F1, which "lacks 219 lines present in Q3 and includes 70 lines not found in Q2" (Irace), is "Shakespeare's finished version" (Jones 1995). Q1, Q2, and F1 "are the results of a competitive revision process, reiterated over many years of repertory existence, under the pressure of rival tragedies like *Antonio's Revenge* and *The Spanish Tragedy*" (Marino 2011).

F2 1632 "the second impression"; three issues. Q5 1637. F3 1663 "the third impression"; reissued 1664 with seven additional plays. Q6 1676 divides the play into five acts. Q7 "dated 1676, but possibly printed later with a false date" (Rasmussen 2003). Q8 1683. F4 1685 "the fourth edition"; two issues. Following the closing of the theaters, part of the play was adapted for a droll (employing four actors) entitled *The Gravemakers*, later published in *1 The Wits, or Sport upon Sport* (O 1662 [two issues] and 1672).

"Hamlet is by far the most famous early modern playgoer, and his response to the First Player's speech well exemplifies a shattering experience that leads to self-scrutiny and application to a problem of present life" (Whitney 2006).

Hannibal and Scipio, An Historical Tragedy. Thomas Nabbes. Acted May 1635 (Bawcutt 1996). By Queen Henrietta Maria's Men at the Phoenix, according to the Q TP, which reports, "acted in the yeare 1635." Herbert's office-book indicates that the play was performed at the Salisbury Court playhouse, 12 May 1636, by the Prince's Men (Bawcutt); this was "a one-off performance" (Butler 2006). William Allen played Hannibal; Michael Bowyer, Scipio and Epilogue; William Sherlock, Maharbal and Prusias; John Sumner, Himulco; George Stutfield, a Soldier and Bostar; Robert Axen, Bomilcar and Giscon; Hugh Clark, Syphax and Nuntius; Anthony Turner, Piston; John Page, Lelius; Ezekiel Fenn, Sophonisba; Theophilus Bird/Bourne, Massanissa; Richard Perkins, Hanno, according to "The speaking persons" [i.e., the cast list]. "The play uses a large number of characters, notably four female roles plus 'Ladies' in addition to Ezekiel Fenn's role of Sophonisba" (Bentley 1984). No license for acting extant.

SR 6 August 1636 *the history of Anniball and Scipio.* Q 1637 "To the ghosts of Hannibal and Scipio"; "The ghosts of Hanniball and Scipio to the authour"; names of the actors attached to their roles; prose argument (i.e., summary) precedes each act; prologue "presumably" by Scipio (King 1992a) and epilogue by Scipio; five acts and separate scenes. "*Hannibal and Scipio* stands out from the rest of Nabbes's plays by reason of its considerable use of music, song and dance" (Cutts 1963): e.g., "*To them* Sophonisba, *ladies all in white, and veil'd: who to the musicke of the song, place themselves in a figure for a daunce*"; after a song, "*In the daunce they discover themselves in order,* Sophonisba *last.*" Her dramatic importance is owing to her status as a sexual gift: "When argument fails to convince Syphax that he should form an alliance with Carthage, Hannibal offers him Sophonisba as a bribe, and the effect is to make the king a slave of passion" (Vince 1971). Other pageantry: "*The souldiers led in by their captaines, distinguisht severally by their armes and ensignes, to the musick of the following, put themselves into a figure like a battalia.*" Also issued in *Plays, Masques, Epigrams, Elegies, and Epithalamiums,* a made-up book containing plays published between 1637 and 1640; general TP dated 1639, separate 1637.

Staging may have used "perspective scenery" (Kathman 2004c). Nicoll 1937 and Freehafer 1973 see in the Q prologue an allusion to such scenery: "The places sometimes chang'd too for the scene, / Which is translated as the musick playes / Betwixt the acts." But Gurr 1992 argues that the lines refer to "fictional localities," and King 1965 suggests that "the speaker is probably asking the audience to 'conceive' changes in locale while the music plays between the acts." King 1975 maintains that nothing in Q "suppports the contention that changeable perspective scenery was used in the Phoenix production of *Hannibal and Scipio.*"

Hans Beer-Pot, His Invisible Comedy of See Me and See Me Not. Daubridgcourt Belchier.

Acted before November 1617, date of the dedication, at undetermined venue. Performed "in the Low Countries by an honest company of health-drinkers," according to the TP.

SR 3 June 1618 a poeme called *see me and see me not.* Q 1618 no author named on the TP but Belchier signs the dedicatory epistle; RT *See Me, and See Me Not;*

list of characters; prologue; concludes with a song; not divided. *JCS* calls this "an irregular sort of entertainment evidently intended for a specialized audience."

The author's dedicatory epistle discusses the play's division into acts: "I here present unto your view, nor comedie, nor tragedie, as wanting first the just number of speakers: secondarily, those parts or acts it should have, which should bee at the least five, but a plaine dialogue or conference between so many persons, consisting of three acts, and no more."

The Hector of Germany, or The Palsgrave, Prime Elector, A New Play, An Honorable History. W. [?Wentworth] Smith. Acted 1613–15 (Payne 1906). "Publikely acted" by a "companie of young men of this Citie" at the Red Bull and Curtain, according to the TP, priority uncertain; this is the only play that "acknowledges Curtain performance on its title-page" (Stern 2009b). "If apprentices could mount such high-profile performances, then the culture of guild theatricals must have been thriving" (Marino 2011). The play "was written to celebrate the marriage of Princess Elizabeth to the Elector Palatine, an important event for those committed to specifically Protestant alliances" (McLuskie 1981). However, as the prologue announces, "[t]he author wants to make sure that everyone understands that the Palsgrave of his play is *not* Frederick IV, Count Palatine of the Rhine, who had married James's daughter" (Bentley 1971).

SR 24 April 1615; transferred 15 April 1619; 24 October 1633. Q 1615 two issues; "with new additions"; RT *The Palsgrave*; prologue; not divided. SDs include descriptions of the characters' appearance: "*Enter the Page, drest in one of Floramells gownes, wearing a maske*"; "*Enter King Edward disguised like a private man.*" Staging includes much onstage violence: "*Charge upon them, and the Bastard taken prisoner on the stage, Saxon and the bishops beaten off.*" Staging also includes "the onstage rescue of a man marooned on a rock by means of a ship" (Dessen 2006). A SD reads, "*Sit on the railes*," suggesting that in "some theatres the edge of the stage appears to have been fenced with low rails" (Ichikawa 2002).

The dedication to Lord Mayor John Swinnerton indicates that the play was "made for citizens, who acted it well." The play is unique "in boldly proclaiming itself to be a production of, by and for London citizens" (Werner 1996). Prologue discusses the amateur status of the actors: "If you should aske us, being men of trade, / Wherefore the players facultie we invade? / Our answere is, No ambition to compare / With any, in that qualitie held rare; / Nor with a thought for any grace you give / To our weake action, by their course to live: / But as in camps, and nurseries of art, / Learning and valour have assum'd a part, / In a cathurnall sceane their wits to try, / Such is our purpose in this history."

The Hectors, or The False Challenge, A Comedy. ?Edmund Prestwich; attribution by Winstanley 1687, but Schneider 2011 regards it as unlikely. Possibly acted 1655 at undetermined venue. "The central characters of the play are polite and sober . . . and they reject the excesses of Cavalier and Puritan alike" (Potter 1981).

SR 22 October 1655. Q 1656 no author named; "written in the year" 1655; dramatis personae; an address to the reader in lieu of a prologue; five acts and separate scenes. The SDs are sufficiently detailed for production: "*Enter Lagul and Mrs.* Bud, *Mrs.* Crisis *standing at the other door, beckens to [Mrs.]* Lovewit, *to the end that she should come and hear what they say.*"

An unsigned note to the reader alludes disapprovingly to the closing of the theaters in 1642: "I'll not enquire why this all-knowing age / Hath crop'd the laurell, that adorn'd the stage, / That looking-glasse of morals, whose re-flex / Shew'd most their errors, whom it most did vex."

The Heir, A Comedy. Thomas May. "[M]ay have initially received a college per-formance" (Norbrook 2004). Acted 1620, according to the Q2 TP. "Lately acted by the Company of the [King's] Revels," according to the Q1 TP; this company, successor to Queen Anne's Men, was performing at the Red Bull in 1620.

SR no original; transferred 24 October 1633. Q1 1622 *The Heir, An Excel-lent Comedy*; author's initials on the TP, and Thomas Carew's prefatory poem is addressed to Thomas May; list of characters; prologue and epilogue; five acts. Q2 1633 *The Heir, A Comedy*; two issues, one of which specifies "the second im-pression"; "as it was acted by the Company of the Revels"; prologue and epilogue slightly altered.

Carew's Q1 prefatory poem says that May's drama "was in his tender age / Rockt in the cradle of a private stage, / Where lifted up by many a will-ing hand, / The child doth from the first day fairely stand, / Since, having gath-ered strength, he dares preferre / His steps into the publicke theater / The world: where he dispaires not but to find / A doome from men more able, but lesse kind." "Carew seems to mean that the play had had a performance before the one at the Red Bull" (*JCS*). At the play's beginning a character, speaking of having seen *Jeronimo* (?*The Spanish Tragedy*), comments that the actor (?Richard Burbage) performed the lead so well that "ladyes in the boxes / Kept time with sighes, and teares to his sad accents / As had he truely bin the man he seemd." "We do not know what performance of *The Spanish Tragedy* May is recalling, but it probably took place while Shakespeare was writing for the stage" (Levin 1989b). The "boxes" may refer to seating at the Blackfriars, "but the same ladies frequented the Globe in summer, where the equivalent places were on the bal-cony over the stage" (Gurr 1987b).

Hengist, King of Kent, or The Mayor of Queenborough. Thomas Middleton. "The 'Vortiger' or 'Henges' performed, according to Henslowe, by the Admiral's Men in 1596–7 may possibly have been a yet earlier form of the play" (Greg 1939). "Written between 1616 and 1620, revised by the author sometime before his death in 1627, and revised again by the King's Men before its first printing" (Iop-polo 1996a). Acted *c.* 1619–20 (Ioppolo 2003) at undetermined venue. Possibly written for Prince Charles's Men (Heinemann 1980). "Some early performances may well have been put on by a touring company to audiences in Kent"; "apparently acted by the King's Men at the Blackfriars a number of times before 1640" (Heinemann). Probably performed by Lady Elizabeth's Men (Howard-Hill 1987a). "Often acted with much applause" by the King's Men at the [second] Blackfriars, according to the Q TP. *Hengist* may at some point have been performed as a companion play to *The Birth of Merlin* (Bald 1938b). In playlist of King's Men 7 August 1641 as "The Maior of Quinborow &," "probably denoting that the play had an alternative title" (Ioppolo 2003). Middleton likely composed the play "as *Hengist, King of Kent*, but it later took on the title *The Mayor of Queenborough* when it drew larger audiences for its comic subplot of an eccentric mayor than for its tragic main plot about a ruthless Anglo-Saxon king" (Ioppolo 2006); "the confusion over titles accurately reflects Middleton's challenge to genre" (Taylor 2004b). Kirkman's 1661 catalogue calls it *The Mayor of Queenborough*. The names Robb Briggs, Blackson, and Robert Stratford appear in both MSS; the "names most likely refer to hired actors performing in the dumb shows or in such minor roles as the Gentleman or other court figures" (Ioppolo 2003).

(1) Washington, Folger, MS J.b.6, fols. 1–46, ed. Bald 1938b; dates from 1640s (Ioppolo 2007); no TP but the words "Hengist King of Kent" appear at end of the MS, following "Finis"; list of characters; leaves cropped and so are missing some punctuation, words, and SDs; contains songs omitted from Q; careful description of three dumb shows, explained by Raynulph Higden, who serves as chorus; prologue and epilogue; five acts and some division into separate scenes. "[T]he musical directions in the manuscripts are unusually full and systematic" (Ioppolo 1995). In the first dumb show, "*ffortune is discovered uppon an alter, in her hand a golden round full of lotts.*" The statue, like that of Fortune in Jonson's *Sejanus* (Kiefer 1983), may have been represented by an actor. (2) Nottingham, UK, University of Nottingham, Hallward Library MS Pw.v.20, fols. 1–43; the "Portland MS" named for the Portland Papers formerly at Welbeck Abbey, Nottinghamshire; ed. Ioppolo 2003; entitled *Hengist, King of Kent, or The Mayor of Quinborough*. The two MSS "carefully preserve playbook features such as prompter's notes and deletion marks" (Erne 2003a).

SR 4 September 1646 *Maior of Quinborough* (no author named); 13 February 1661 *A Comedie called The Maior of Quinborough*, By Tho: Middleton. Q 1661 *The Mayor of Queenborough, A Comedy*, "after the protagonist of its comic scenes" (Taylor 2004b); two issues, the second of which calls the play *A Tragedy*; dramatis personae; chorus; detailed description of three dumb shows; no epilogue and no songs; five acts and separate scenes. "What calls itself a prologue . . ., different from that in either printed or manuscript text, had already been separately published in *Wit Restor'd in Severall Select Poems* [1658]" (Stern 2004a). "The stage-directions of Q . . . have in the main been purged of references to the actual details of stage production" (Bald). Special effects include the death of Roxena by fire. By the time it was printed, the play had been revised: Q "represents an inferior and shortened version of the play, with an altered ending" (Lake 1975a); Q "presents a briefer conclusion to the play's final scene, possibly to make it suitable as a companion play to *The Birth of Merlin*" (Ioppolo 2003). Also "Middleton appears to have redrawn the characters of Castiza and Roxena in order to shift dramatic attention away from domestic, female tragedy and towards a martial, male tragedy" (Ioppolo 1995). The Q title "suggests that the play's main character had become Simon the Mayor rather than Hengist the Saxon" (Ioppolo 2007).

The address to the Q reader comments on the connection between production and print: "You have the first flight of him I assure you; this *Mayor of Quinborough* whom you have all heard of, and some of you beheld upon the stage, now begins to walk abroad in print; he has been known sufficiently by the reputation of his wit, which is enough (by the way) to distinguish him from ordinary mayors; but wit you know, has skulk'd in corners for many years past, and he was thought to have most of it that could best hide himself."

1 Henry IV (*Sir John Oldcastle*; *Sir John Falstaff*). William Shakespeare. Acted November 1596–February 1597 (Bevington 1987) by the Lord Chamberlain's/ Hunsdon's Men at the Curtain, Swan, or Theater; "Shakespeare's company may have been in transition among several playhouses" (Weil & Weil 2007). "When Henry Carey died in July 1596, his son George, the second Lord Hunsdon, became their patron, so that for the next few months they were the second Lord Hunsdon's Men" (Gurr 2004c). Praised by Francis Meres in *Palladis Tamia* (SR 7 September 1598), which calls the play a tragedy. Possibly performed as *Sir John Oldcastle* by the Chamberlain's Men at Hunsdon House, 6 March 1600, for the Flemish ambassador (recorded in letter of Rowland Whyte to Robert Sidney), but the title may designate another play featuring Falstaff. Will Kemp may have played Falstaff in early productions (Wiles 1987, Gurr 2004c), but "his age, size, and gentility do not match Kemp's athleticism and plainness" (Butler 2004d). "It may be that there are echoes of [Richard] Tarlton in Shakespeare's Falstaff" (Thomson 2004b). John Lowin, after joining the company in 1603, subsequently played the role (*Historia Histrionica*). Richard Burbage played Prince Hal. Henry Condell probably played Hotspur (Potter 2012). Also performed as *Sir John Falstaff*, probably by the King's Men at court, 1612–13 (payment to John Heminges 20 May 1613); Heminges was also paid for *The Hotspur* on that date; at Whitehall, before the prince, the evening of 1 January 1625, under the title *The First Part of Sir John Falstaff* (Adams 1917); and, probably, at Whitehall Cockpit, 6 January 1631, under the title *Sir John Oldcastle, Part 1*; possibly at Blackfriars, April 1635, under the title *Falstaff*; and, probably, at Cockpit-in-Court, 29 May 1638, under the title *Oldcastle* (Adams). The confusion over the title is related to a personnel change in the Revels office in 1596: "the unexpected appointment of [William Brooke] Lord Cobham as Lord Chamberlain in Henry Carey's place made him a powerful objector to [the play's] ridicule of his Lollard ancestor" (Gurr 1996). As a result, Shakespeare's company changed the name of the character from Oldcastle to Falstaff, but the "cleanup . . . left plenty of fingerprints" (Whitney 2006);

the switch "took place after the composition of *Part One*, but before the composition or performance of *Part Two* or *Merry Wives*" (Taylor 1987). Further confusion is owing to the difficulty of knowing whether a title designates *1 Henry IV*, *1 Sir John Oldcastle*, or *The Merry Wives of Windsor*, all of which feature a character named Falstaff. In a work published in 1640 Leonard Digges cites this character and this play as having had huge appeal: "let but Falstaffe come, / Hall, Poines, the rest you scarce shall have a roome / All is so pester'd" (Chambers 1930). *1 Henry IV* was probably Shakespeare's "most popular" play (Taylor 2002b).

Following the closing of the theaters, parts of the play were adapted for a droll entitled *The Bouncing Knight, or The Robbers Robbed*, written for eight actors and later published in *1 The Wits, or Sport upon Sport* (O 1662 [two issues] and 1672). The engraved frontispiece of *The Wits* depicts Falstaff holding a goblet in one hand and a staff in the other; the picture may be based on the character's appearance onstage. "It is likely that the engraving" depicts John Lowin (Gurr 2004c). The frontispiece pictures the Hostess next to Falstaff.

SR 25 February 1598; transferred 25 June 1603; ?4 August 1626 Paviers right in Shakesperes *plaies*; ?19 June 1627 widow of Isaac Jaggard . . . her parte in Shackspheere *playes*; 16 November 1630; 1 July 1637 Shakespeares *workes* their Part; 6 August 1674; 21 August 1683. Qo [fragment printed in 1598 and now at the Folger]. Q1 1598 *The History of Henry the Fourth, with the Battle of Shrewsbury between the King and Lord Henry Percy, Surnamed Henry Hotspur of the North, with the Humorous Conceits of Sir John Falstaff*; no author named; not divided. The word "*Humorous*" in the title alludes to the popularity of comedies featuring characters dominated by some eccentricity of temperament: "The most remarkable achievement of *1 Henry IV* is its fusion of humors comedy with history" (Potter 2012). At the same time the play draws inspiration from the moral interludes: the development of Hal's character evokes the "morality pattern of spiritual reform" (Weil & Weil), common to many interludes, including *Youth* (Cooper 2010). "Come here is the map," says Glendower as the rebels divide up the kingdom, a parallel to Falstaff's division of the booty after the Gadshill robbery. Action culminates in the battle of Shrewsbury: "*the king enters with his power, alarme to the battle.*" There the prince engages in hand-to-hand combat with Hotspur and kills him: Hal's "transformation is literally one of costume, of helmet and feathers and thigh-armour" (Bevington 1987). Falstaff, who plays dead, rises up and "*takes up Hotspur on his backe*," evoking the Vice of the interludes; at one point Hal calls Falstaff "that reverend Vice," and Falstaff threatens Hal with a dagger of lath, essential equipment for a Vice (Dessen 1977, 1986). The moral danger Falstaff represents is also apparent when in the tavern he impersonates Hal's father: in lieu of a crown Falstaff places a cushion on his head, a symbol of sloth (Steadman 1963). Q2 1599 "newly corrected by W. Shake-speare." Q3 1604. Q4 1608. Q5 1613. Q6 1622. F1 1623 *Comedies, Histories, & Tragedies*; three issues; *The First Part of Henry the Fourth, with the Life and Death of Henry surnamed Hotspur*; "published according to the true originall copies"; five acts and separate scenes. The antiquarian Edward

Dering in February 1623 paid for a MS version of *Parts 1* and *2* [Folger V.b.34]
"for private performances" (Weis 1998), presumably at Surrenden Hall, Kent; it is
a "very adroit adaptation of the two parts of Shakespeare's *Henry IV* into one play"
(Holland 2004b); it is "the earliest extant manuscript of a play by Shakespeare,
albeit a conflation of the two parts of the play with emendations in Sir Edward's
hand" (Yeandle 1986); it "is a highly actable script, which takes matters of theatrical practicability very seriously" (Dobson 2011). "Dering based his conflation on
the 1613 quarto of *I Henry IV* and the 1600 quarto of *II Henry IV*" (Gibson 2002).
The MS was mostly copied by a scribe named Carrington; "Dering added corrections, additions, and deletions to the entire manuscript, reworking the staging
and further condensing the scenes" (Wolfe 2006). Q7 1632. F2 1632 "the second
impression"; three issues. Q8 1639 not divided. F3 1663 "the third impression";
reissued 1664 with seven additional plays. F4 1685 "the fourth edition"; two issues. Following its initial publication in 1598, the play was "reprinted more often,
in the next twenty-five years, than any other Shakespeare play" (Honan 1998). *1
Henry IV* "appears to have been the most popular dramatic text for readers during
Shakespeare's lifetime" (Rasmussen 2008).

The relationship of the two *Henry IV* plays "is that of a diptych, in which
repetition of shape and design focuses attention on what is parallel in the two
parts" (Hunter 1978).

2 Henry IV. William Shakespeare. Acted *c.* March–December 1598 (Melchiori
1989). "Sundrie times publikely acted by" the Lord Chamberlain's Men, according to the Q TP, at the Curtain. Probably performed at court, Christmas season
1598 (Shapiro 2005). "Probably still in production at the newly built Globe in
1599–1600" (Knutson 1997). Will Kemp probably played Falstaff in early productions (Gurr 2004c); Kemp "was the best dancer of Shakespeare's company
and might logically have delivered the epilogue, which is delivered as a lead-in
to a jig" (Walsh 2009b). John Lowin played Falstaff after he joined the company (*Historia Histrionica*) in 1603. Probably performed by the King's Men at
Whitehall, Christmas revels 1612–13, as *Sir John Falstaff* (Melchiori); record of
payment to John Heminges dated 20 May 1613. Possibly performed at court
as *Second Part of Falstaff*, 1619–20 (Chambers 1930). Possibly performed at the
Blackfriars, April 1635, as *Falstaff*. Possibly performed at Cockpit-in-Court under the title *Oldcastle*, 29 May 1638. A scene heading and speech prefixes in Q
preserve the name "Sincklo," which probably designates John Sincler, who "had
several parts specially written for him in the post-1594 plays: Nym, the beadle,
and Slender in *2 Henry IV*, *Henry V*, and *Merry Wives*" (Gurr 2004c).

SR 23 August 1600 (Shakespeare's name appears in this entry); transferred
8 November 1623; ?4 August 1626 Paviers right in Shakesperes *plaies*; ?19 June
1627 widow of Isaac Jaggard . . . her parte in Shackspheere *playes*; 1 July 1637
Shakespeares *workes* their Part; 6 August 1674; 21 August 1683. Q 1600 *The Second Part of Henry the Fourth, Continuing to His Death, and Coronation of Henry*

the Fifth, with the Humors of Sir John Falstaff and Swaggering Pistol; "written by William Shakespeare"; two issues; Rumor, "*painted full of tongues*," speaks the prologue (called "induction" in this Q [Hosley 1961]); epilogue (spoken by Will Kemp [Shapiro 2005]); not divided. "The unusual prose epilogue . . . is divided into three sections written at different times and serving different purposes" (Melchiori). Stern 2010a identifies several possibilities to explain the epilogue: "It could be that we have, in this medley, two alternate public theatre endings: one epilogue leading to a jig, and one leading to a prayer, perhaps representing two options — secular or religious — for performance; or one of the endings is for touring production and one for fixed performance; or one represents a first performance and one a revival; or one provides a censored text and another gives the replacement." Schneider 2011 argues that the epilogue is "thoroughly coherent and very deftly constructed." The epilogue represents "the only time Shakespeare ever shared with his audience what he planned to write next" (Shapiro); he will "continue the storie, with sir John in it." The epilogue also demonstrates "that Shakespeare was aware of women as a distinct component of his audience that he had to please" (Levin 1989b): "All the gentlewomen heere, have forgiven me." "The King's Men made prudent cuts in their *Henry IV, Part 2* before publication in 1600" (Heinemann 2003). The first issue of Q omits the first scene of act 3, where Hal takes the crown from his sleeping father; the second issue restores it. "If the scene already existed when the first issue was printed, it may have been misplaced or withheld by the company or overlooked by the printer. But it is also possible that Shakespeare wrote it during or after the printing of the first issue" (Ioppolo 2006). The king's state of mind is suggested by his appearance onstage "*in his night-gowne*" [i.e., dressing gown]; such garb "signals not only the fact that on stage it is supposed to be night or early morning but also that the character is troubled or disturbed in some way" (Thompson 2010). When Hal visits his dying father and sees the crown on a pillow, he puts the crown on his own head, perhaps recalling Falstaff's placing a cushion on his head when they impersonate King Henry in a tavern scene of *1 Henry IV* (Dillon 2012). In its portrayal of Hal, who is attracted to Falstaff but called to a life of duty, the play evokes the moral interludes, though "the reformation is presented here as political rather than theological" (Cooper 2010). "The most purely theatrical character in the *Henriad*, Falstaff is also the most subversive" (Rackin 1990) and so must finally be rejected by Hal. "Battle scenes were becoming a thing of the past in Shakespeare's history scripts"; if the battles in *Part 1* were "fundamental," *Part 2* "lets the Falstaff attitude toward swordsmanship and combat prevail" (McMillin 2005); confrontations in *Part 2* are chiefly verbal. F1 1623 *Comedies, Histories, & Tragedies*; three issues; "published according to the true originall copies"; *The Second Part of Henry the Fourth, containing His Death, and the Coronation of King Henry the Fifth*; "written by William Shakespeare"; list of characters at end; induction (i.e., Rumor's speech) and epilogue; "irregular division into acts and scenes" (King 1992a). F2 1632 "the second impression"; three issues. F3 1663 "the third impression"; reissued 1664 with seven additional plays. F4 1685 "the fourth edition"; two issues.

"*2 Henry IV* incurred censorship on two accounts: its copious and not unsympathetic exposition of the rebel cause; and the original choice of the name Oldcastle for Falstaff" (Clare 1999); a speech prefix early in the play has "*Old.*" "It is often observed that Sir John in *The Merry Wives of Windsor* and of *2 Henry IV* appears somewhat festively diminished and more calculating by comparison with *1 Henry IV*. Possibly the cold-blooded pleasure Essex took in exploiting the Falstaff-Cobham equation through earlier, unrecorded remarks was a factor influencing the author's own understanding of his creation as he wrote these sequels" (Whitney 2006).

Henry V (anonymous). See *The Famous Victories of Henry V.*

Henry V. William Shakespeare. Acted *c.* March–September 1599 (Craik 1995); late March 1599 (Shapiro 2005); "by July of 1599" (Bednarz 2012). "Sundry times playd by" the Lord Chamberlain's Men, according to the Q1 TP. If the play was written early in 1599, then the prologue's "'wooden O' must have been the Curtain, which Shakespeare's company used while they waited for the Globe to be built" (Stern 2009b). If later in 1599, it "could have been the new Globe" (Gurr 2005). Richard Burbage "probably" played the lead (Taylor 2002b); Shakespeare may have played the chorus (Bate & Rasmussen 2010). "The obvious role for [Robert] Armin in *Henry V* is Nym" (Wiles 1987). Performed also by the King's Men in the Great Hall at Whitehall, before King James, 7 January 1605 (Chambers 1930); this revival "might have had more to do with the martial interests of Prince Henry than with the play's continuing popularity" (Craik). At the close of *2 Henry IV*, the epilogue promises the return of Falstaff. "The disappearance of Falstaff from *Henry V*" has been attributed to Will Kemp's leaving the Lord Chamberlain's Men (Wiles 1987), but Kemp "might have left the company *because* Shakespeare killed off Falstaff" (Taylor 1982). "What is clear is that the role of the clown in adult company plays had diminished markedly in value as plays began to offer more scope for the tragic actors" (Gurr 2009d). The naming of Pistol in the Q title may compensate for the absence of Falstaff (Gurr 2000); the title-page reference is "probably to distinguish this book from *The Famous Victories*" (Potter 2012).

SR 4 August 1600 "to be staied," perhaps because the text "lacked ecclesiastical authorization or the wardens were not present to waive that authorization" (Blayney 1997); transferred 14 August 1600 "among a list of titles being assigned to Thomas Pavier" (Clegg 1999); "possibly transferred 4 August 1626 from widow of [Thomas] Pavier to Edward Brewster and Robert Bird" (Jowett 2007e); ?19 June 1627 widow of Isaac Jaggard . . . her parte in Shackspheere *playes*; 8 November 1630; 1 July 1637 Shakespeares *workes* their Part; 6 August 1674; 21 August 1683. Q1 1600 *The Chronicle History of Henry the Fifth, with His Battle Fought at*

Agincourt in France, together with Ancient Pistol; no author named; no chorus, "the play's most distinctive feature" (Craik); no prologue or epilogue; no dialogue of the four captains; not divided. This is "a remarkably compressed and speeded-up version of the play" that would be printed in the First Folio (Gurr 2009d). The MS "behind the quarto text was based ultimately on the authorial manuscript sold to Shakespeare's playing company . . . in 1599 and later printed as the F text, but was a copy which had been radically revised by the company for performance at the Globe"; in this adaptation "Prologue, Epilogue and all the Choruses disappeared" (Gurr 2000). But Stern 2004a asks: "Were [the prologue, epilogue, and chorus] in fact subsequently written for the play, or had they already been detached from it?" The chorus may not have been added until 1602 (Dutton 2009b), or perhaps the chorus was revised in 1602 (Stern 2009b), or perhaps an extant prologue was suppressed for provincial performance of Q1: "The Quarto is based upon a deliberate adaptation and abridgement of *Henry V*, designed for performance, probably in the provinces, by a cast of eleven" (Taylor 1979). A problem presented by the chorus is that he "seems to be describing a play he has heard about, but which is not the one that actually takes place" (Hammond 1987b). The chorus "operates not as a classical Nuntius but as a Prologue to each act" (Gurr 2005); however, the chorus "might have wandered in from another play" (Honan 1998). The chorus resembles, in some respects, that of *Old Fortunatus*, priority uncertain (Walsh 2009b); Bednarz 2012 believes that "Dekker's imitations of the Chorus of *Henry V* by December of 1599 in *Old Fortunatus* prove that Shakespeare's Chorus had already been staged in a performance by the Lord Chamberlain's Men which Dekker had witnessed and remembered." The chorus also finds "a source and model" in *A Mirror for Magistrates* (Vickers 1997).

Staging includes Henry's confrontation with the governor of Harfleur, who stands on the walls of the city, which "must have been the tiring-house front" (Gurr 2005); this recalls Tamburlaine's confrontation at the gates of Damascus. Oddly, for a play chronicling Henry's victory at Agincourt, "[t]he war is always offstage" (Ornstein 1972); the play "is *about* battles, but it does not stage them" (McMillin 2005). Scaling ladders provided for in F do not appear in Q. Q2 1602 "a line-for-line following of Q1" (Craik). Q3 1619 published by Thomas Pavier and falsely dated 1608; no author named. F1 1623 *Comedies, Histories, & Tragedies*; three issues; "published according to the true originall copies"; *The Life of Henry the Fifth*; choral prologue and choral epilogue (absent from Q versions) and other appearances of chorus (among Shakespeare's histories the play is "anomalous in using a presenter" [Bruster 2003]); entry of chorus marks the beginning of acts, but the "act-divisions are grotesquely inappropriate" (Taylor 1993a). Modern editors customarily divide the play into five numbered acts in accordance with the divisions indicated by the chorus, but the act divisions may have been "added in the printing house" (Taylor 1982). The F1 playbook is "the 'maximal' text, the fullest possible version that would be sent to the Master of the Revels for his approval to become the 'allowed book'" (Gurr 2009d). Auditory effects probably include the sound of cannons when act 2 chorus says, "the nimble gunner / With lynstock now the divellish cannon touches"; a SD reads, *"Alarum, and chambers goe off."* "Chambers were small pieces of ordnance which stood on their breeching, without other support" (Lawrence 1927). The sound of offstage horses seems suggested by the chorus: "Steed threatens steed, in high and boastfull neighs / Piercing the nights dull eare." The version of *Henry V* in F1 dates from 1602 (Dutton 2009b). F2 1632 "the second impression"; three issues. F3 1663 "the third impression"; reissued 1664 with seven additional plays. F4 1685 "the fourth edition"; two issues.

The fifth-act chorus may allude to the Earl of Essex (in Ireland) and anticipates his triumphant return to London. This return, which occurred on 28 September 1599, was a debacle, for Essex had angered Elizabeth by having a private parley with the Irish leader and by failing to suppress the rebellion there. "The censor may well have licensed this most topical of plays on the condition that lines which directly or indirectly promoted such allusions were removed in performance" (Clare 1999). This allusion to Essex, probably written *c.* March 1599 (Wells & Taylor 1987) when the earl departed London, is the "only explicit reference to a contemporary political figure in Shakespeare's plays" (Worden 2006). However, Smith 1954 argues that the passage refers not to Essex but to Charles Blount, Lord Mountjoy, "who succeeded the hapless Essex as commander-in-chief of the forces in Ireland early in 1600, and who returned to London a decisive victor over the rebel Tyrone and his Spanish ally after the death of the Queen, in April, 1603." Dutton 2005 supports Smith's interpretation as does Potter 2012.

1 Henry VI. William Shakespeare and, probably, Thomas Nashe (Hart 1909, Wilson 1952); two other playwrights may also have collaborated (Taylor 1995), including Christopher Marlowe in acts 3 and 5 (Craig 2009). It is not "entirely clear whether Shakespeare was revising their earlier work independently or actively co-writing with them" (Bate 2008). Vickers 2008b argues that Thomas Kyd contributed to the play, but Craig 2009 contests the suggestion. Taylor 1995 believes act 1 the work of Nashe alone; Vincent 2005 sees evidence of revision by another hand. Because of coauthorship and revision, "[i]ncongruities and inconsistencies abound in *1 Henry VI*" (Vickers 2007). *1 Henry VI* was probably written "after both *The First Part of the Contention* [*2 Henry VI*] and *True Tragedy* [*3 Henry VI*]" (Martin 2001). Acted March 1592 (Burns 2000) by Lord Strange's Men at the Rose; the play was "probably written with the Rose's new stage specifically in mind" (Gurr 2009c); Henslowe records performances of "harey the vj" [unspecified part] at the Rose: 3, 7, 11, 16, 28 March; 5, 13, 21 April; 4, 7 [or 9], 14, 19, 25 May; 12, 19 June 1592. Also 16, 31 January 1593. "Edward Alleyn seems the most likely actor to have created the role of Talbot" (Burns), but Bate 2008 suggests that Richard Burbage also "probably" played the role at some point. Nashe's *Pierce Penniless his Supplication to the Devil* (SR 8 August 1592) contains "what seems to be a first-hand description of *1 Henry VI* on stage" (Burns): Nashe "records the powerful effect created by the figure of Talbot—over time, ten thousand spectators wept, Nashe claims, at the hero's stage death" (Howard 2006b). This account constitutes "the earliest description of audiences' responses to a play at least partly by Shakespeare" (Taylor 2002b). Francis Meres in *Palladis Tamia* (SR 7 September 1598) does not mention this play.

SR 8 November 1623 *The third parte of Henry the Sixt* [Because *Parts 1* and *2* were registered in 1602 and already printed as the first and second parts, "it was erroneously assumed that the unprinted part was the third instead of the first" (Greg 1939)]; ?4 August 1626 Paviers right in Shakesperes *plaies*; ?19 June 1627 widow of Isaac Jaggard . . . her parte in Shackspheere *playes*; 16 November 1630; 1 July 1637 Shakespeares *workes* their Part; 6 August 1674; 21 August 1683. F1 1623 *Comedies, Histories, & Tragedies*; three issues; "published according to the true originall copies"; *The First Part of Henry the Sixth*; five acts and "incomplete scene division" (King 1992a) but "[t]he act divisions seem to be literary rather than theatrical in origin" (Wells & Taylor 1987). The Temple Garden scene, in which two factions pick white and red roses, would seem to require "the presence of bushes on the stage" (Rhodes 1976): "Though the red and white roses were historically the badges of Lancaster and York, it was Shakespeare's idea to make them visible as fresh flowers in a garden" (Potter 2012). "The schematic opposition of this scene . . . provides in pageant form the basis for the next two plays, as they play out the Wars of the Roses" (Dillon 2012). Spectacular staging includes "*the funerall of King Henry the Fift,*" accompanied by a "*dead march,*" which "is menacingly prophetic" (Lindley 2006). Sound repeatedly heralds military conflict as for example when Talbot vows vengeance for Salisbury's death: "What stirre is this? what tumult's in the heavens? / Whence commeth this alarum, and the noyse?" The numerous scenes of violence are accompanied by appropriate sound: "*Enter Talbot, Bedford, and Burgundy, with scaling ladders: their drummes beating a dead march*"; the soldiers mount to the gallery above the main stage (Rhodes 1976). Unusual sound effects: SDs "for sennets [in Shakespeare's plays] are relatively few, and a third of them are in the *Henry VI* plays. There they emphasize the contrast between Henry's inability to rule his strifetorn country and his retention of all the formal display of office" (Shirley 1961). The play "makes use in a comparatively large number of scenes of the playing space 'aloft'" (Hattaway 1990): e.g., Salisbury enters "*on the turrets*" and spies on the French "through this grate"; meanwhile a French boy enters "*with a linstock*" and touches off his ordnance: "*Here they shot, and Salisbury falls downe.*" "Siege warfare abounds in the *Henry VI* plays" (Bevington 2002a), and the upper stage provides a site for confrontation: "*Enter Talbot and Burgonie without: within, Pucell, Charles, Bastard, and Reignier on the walls*"; the terms *without* and *within* "refer to outside and inside the city of Rouen, which are represented, respectively, by the outside and inside of the tiring-house" (Ichikawa 2005). Joan la Pucelle is the most formidable female warrior in the *Henry VI* plays: at Rouen "*Enter Pucell on the top, thrusting out a torch burning.*" When French fortunes decline, she consorts with evil spirits: "*Enter fiends*"; "*They hang their heads.*" "Joan's witchcraft is closely related to her appropriation of masculine dress and masculine behavior" (Rackin 1990). Despite the demonic, *1 Henry VI*, compared with *Doctor Faustus*, relegates "stage devils to the margins" (Cox 2000). F2 1632 "the second impression"; three issues. F3 1663 "the third impression"; reissued 1664 with seven additional plays. F4 1685 "the fourth edition"; two issues. Taylor 1995 calls this play a "prequel" to *2* and *3 Henry VI*.

Shakespeare appropriated "the formula of the English history play patented by the Queen's Men for his serial on the Wars of the Roses, beginning with *1 Henry VI*" (Knutson 2006a). "The idea of a two-part play was probably a response to the phenomenal success of Marlowe's *Tamburlaine*, though there were many other two-part plays"; however, "his decision to create a three-part work was an innovation" (Holland 2004a).

2 Henry VI (The First Part of the Contention). William Shakespeare ?and others. Craig 2009 argues that Christopher Marlowe wrote the Jack Cade scenes; "unless Craig's evidence can be discredited Marlowe will be added to the list of Shakespeare collaborators" (Taylor 2011). This has been called the earliest of the *Henry VI* plays (Wells & Taylor 1987) though the issue is unsettled: "Perhaps *The First Part of the Contention* was chosen as a more interesting title and one more likely to attract an audience than '*The Second Part of King Henry VI*'" (Hattaway 1991). It was probably first performed by Lord Strange's Men *c.* 1591 at the Theater or Rose (Knowles 1999), though Hattaway prefers March 1592 (when Henslowe records "harey the vj" [unspecified part] at the Rose), and Born 1974 argues for a date "between March and August 1592." Almost certainly performed by Lord Pembroke's Men (Schoone-Jongsten 2008), 1592–93, in the provinces; the plague closed London theaters from late June 1592 until, apparently, near the end of the year (Hattaway). It is also possible that *2 Henry VI* was "originally written for performance by a touring company in the Midlands" (Potter 2012). A scene heading in F lists John Holland, an actor; also listed is Bevis, possibly "an actor's name, though nobody of that name is definitely traceable in the scanty theatrical records of the 1590s" (Kathman 2009). "After 1594, the part of [Jack] Cade may well have been assumed by Will Kemp, the famous acrobat, dancer, and actor who was a member of the Chamberlain's Men between 1594 and 1599" (Howard 2006b). "The text as reported reflects the full staging facilities of a well equipped London amphitheatre or hall playhouse" (Montgomery 1988).

SR 12 March 1594; transferred 19 April 1602; ?4 August 1626 Paviers right in Shakesperes *plaies*; ?19 June 1627 widow of Isaac Jaggard . . . her parte in Shackspheere *playes*; 8 November 1630; 1 July 1637 Shakespeares *workes* their Part; 6 August 1674 [*Yorke & Lancaster*]; 21 August 1683. Q1 1594 *The First Part of the Contention betwixt the Two Famous Houses of York and Lancaster, with the Death of the Good Duke Humphrey, and the Banishment and Death of the Duke of*

Suffolk, and the Tragical End of the Proud Cardinal of Winchester, with the Notable Rebellion of Jack Cade, and the Duke of York's First Claim unto the Crown; no author named; not divided. "Perhaps the most written-about proof-sheet from the period is to be found in the Bridgewater copy at the Huntington Library": "This shows [Valentine] Simmes's corrector making changes to spelling and punctuation" (Bland 1999). "The play makes a markedly different impact from *1* and *3 Henry VI* in virtue of the fact that the lower orders — 'the commons' — make several important appearances" (Jones 1977). This play "is arguably the only one of the histories that gives a substantial voice to the presence of ordinary people in history and their ability to mobilise themselves in sufficient numbers . . . to disrupt the conventional notion of history as the story of kings and nobles" (Hampton-Reeves & Rutter 2006). The Clerk of Chatham is murdered by the mob; the Staffords are killed, and "Lord Say and his brother-in-law are beheaded"; Jack Cade's peasant rebellion threatens the kingdom; civil war follows (Jones). Unusual staging involves a conflict between an armorer and his apprentice, both equipped with staffs topped by sandbags: "The stage direction scripts their entry in extraordinary detail, as a class-based parody of a chivalric trial by combat" (Dillon 2012). Unusual action includes Simpcox's fake miracle: he claims to have been cured of blindness but remains lame; Gloucester demonstrates that Simpcox (the name combines "simpleton and coxcomb" [Jones]) can leap and run. Staging calls for a conjuration by a witch: "*It thunders and lightens, and then the spirit riseth up.*" The spirit is named Asnath, "a transparent anagram of 'Sathan'" (Cox 2000). Elinor Cobham, apprehended at the conjuration, is required to do penance: "*Enter Dame* Elnor Cobham *bare-foote, and a white sheete about her, with a waxe candle in her hand, and verses written on her backe and pin[ne]d on.*" SDs call for a property bed as a site of murder: "*Duke* Humphrey *is discovered in his bed, and two men lying on his brest and smothering him*"; "the presentation of the action is akin to that of a dumbshow" (Wells 1997). Graphic violence includes the display of "the severed heads of four different characters" (Owens 2005). Auditory effects simulate a naval battle: "*Alarmes within, and the chambers be discharged, like as it were a fight at sea.*" "Chambers were small pieces of ordnance which stood on their breeching, without other support" (Lawrence 1927). Staging seems to require a tent: "*Alarmes againe, and then enter three or foure, bearing the Duke of* Buckingham *wounded to his tent*"; another tent may be pitched for the king. But Dessen & Thomson 1999 believe that the tents are "likely fictional." A "unique stage direction" appears: "*Enter the Duke of Yorke with drum and [Irish] souldiers*"; this represents "the only occasion in Renaissance drama where the Irish are collectively staged" (O'Neill 2007). Francis Meres in *Palladis Tamia* (SR 7 September 1598) does not mention this play. Q2 1600 this printing perhaps signals a recent revival (Knutson 2006a). Q3 1619 "written by William Shakespeare"; published by Thomas Pavier together with *3 Henry VI* (continuous register) as *The Whole Contention between the Two Famous Houses, Lancaster and York*; "newly corrected and enlarged." F1 1623 *Comedies, Histories, & Tragedies*; three issues; "published according to the true originall copies"; *The Second Part of Henry the Sixth, with the Death of the Good Duke Humphrey*; not divided despite the designation of act 1, scene 1. F1 SDs are less full than those of the quartos. F2 1632 "the second impression"; three issues. F3 1663 "the third impression"; reissued 1664 with seven additional plays. F4 1685 "the fourth edition"; two issues.

"There are omissions and variant passages in the folio which can only reasonably be accounted for by censorship of the copy text. The lines in question contain references to the deposition of Henry VI or to the Irish rebellion which York is sent to quell" (Clare 1999).

3 Henry VI (The True Tragedy of Richard Duke of York). William Shakespeare ?and others. Acted 1591 (Martin 2001); Henslowe records a "ne" [presumably "new"] performance of "harey the vj" on 3 March 1592 at the Rose, which was remodeled in 1592. Probably first performed by Lord Strange's Men; the play may have been "originally written for performance by a touring company in the Midlands" (Potter 2012). Also "sundrie times acted" by Lord Pembroke's Men, according to the O TP, 1592–93 (Wentersdorf 1977); Pembroke's Men "were formed between 1591 and 1593 out of Strange's Men by Richard Burbage after he had quarreled with their leader Edward Alleyn"; a reference to Warwick's physical characteristics in 5.3 suggests a connection with Alleyn (Martin). Speech prefixes and scene headings in F1 preserve the names of three actors who were associated with Pembroke's Men in the mid-1590s: Gabriel [Spencer], John Sincklo [or Sincler], and Humphrey [Jeffes], "a leading actor in the Admiral's Men who is mentioned frequently in Henslowe's *Diary*" (King 1992a). "Twenty-one adult and four boy actors were required to play the sixty-seven parts" (Cox & Rasmussen 2001).

SR no original; transferred 19 April 1602; 8 November 1623; ?4 August 1626 Paviers right in Shakesperes *plaies*; ?19 June 1627 widow of Isaac Jaggard . . . her parte in Shackspheere *playes*; 16 November 1630; 1 July 1637 Shakespeares *workes* their Part; 6 August 1674; 21 August 1683. O 1595 (this is the "one exception to the quarto format of all the [other individually published] plays" [Woudhuysen 2004]); *The True Tragedy of Richard Duke of York, and the Death of Good King Henry the Sixth, with the Whole Contention between the Two Houses Lancaster and York*; no author named; unique copy at Bodleian; not divided but "the play falls into two parts" (Jones 1977). *The True Tragedy* is "the second part of a two-part play telling the story of the closing events of Henry VI's reign" (Martin). The play "opens with a striking theatrical image. The Yorkists break down the doors of Parliament and invade the stage" (Hampton-Reeves & Rutter 2006); the scene requires a chair of state "equipped with a canopy . . . which was probably placed on an elevated platform" (Hattaway 1993). The conflict of the Wars of the Roses is symbolized at the outset when Richard, Duke of York, and others enter "*with white roses in their hats*"; then King Henry and others enter "*with red roses in their hats.*" "To an Elizabethan audience it would seem obvious that the only satisfactory outcome was the blending of the red and white roses in the Tudor dynasty" (Jones). The play revels "in gratuitous cruelty and murder" (Riggs 2004). Staging calls for the display of severed heads: young Richard "brandishes the head of Somerset" (Owens 2005). "*Part 3* will always be remembered for its scenes of death: those of the children Rutland and Prince Edward, that of York, those of the arch-enemies Clifford and Warwick the kingmaker, and that, finally, of King Henry" (Hattaway 1993). The play contains "a scene of superb theatricality when York is taunted with a paper crown before being stabbed to death" (Bate 2008). The action "resembles those scenes in the mystery cycles where Christ is taunted and tormented prior to his crucifixion" (Dillon 2012). The scene of York's death "is one of the most violent in all Shakespeare's plays" (Jones), and "the Lancastrian side mounts the Duke of York's head on the gates of his own city," thereby "producing a stage picture remarkably similar to the gruesome spectacle that greeted Elizabethan Londoners whenever they crossed London Bridge" (Owens). Entries signal offstage violence: "*Enter* Clifford *wounded with an arrow in his necke.*" An unusual effect is called for in this SD: "*Three sunnes appeare in the aire,*" "presumably lowered from above" (Hattaway 1991); this refers to the "triple sun" omen reportedly seen at the Battle of Mortimer's Cross in 1461; subsequently the sunburst became a Yorkist badge (Wagner 2001). Francis Meres in *Palladis Tamia* (SR 7 September 1598) does not mention this play. Q2 1600 *The True Tragedy of Richard Duke of York*; no author named. The printing of Q2 perhaps signals a recent revival of the play (Knutson 2006a). Q3 ND 1619 "written by William Shake-speare"; published by Thomas Pavier together with *2 Henry VI* (continuous register) as *The Whole Contention between the Two Famous Houses, Lancaster and York*; "newly corrected and enlarged"; the TP's "claim is demonstrably justifiable" (Cox & Rasmussen). F1 1623 *Comedies, Histories, & Tragedies*; three issues; "published according to the true originall copies"; *The Third Part of Henry the Sixth, with the Death of the Duke of York*; not divided despite the designation of act 1, scene 1. F1 is a thousand lines longer than Q1 and "was probably written sometime between 1594 and 1596" (Martin 2001). Martin believes that *The True Tragedy* "represents an earlier and memorially reported version of *3 Henry VI*"; Cox and Rasmussen doubt this hypothesis, which is based "upon an interpretation of a single variant passage." F2 1632 "the second impression"; three issues. F3 1663 "the third impression"; reissued 1664 with seven additional plays. F4 1685 "the fourth edition"; two issues. Robert Greene parodies a line from *3 Henry VI* in *Greene's Groatsworth of Wit* (SR 20 September 1592); this represents "the earliest surviving notice of Shakespeare in performance" (Rutter 2006).

 "All three parts of *Henry VI*, as well as *King John*, feature women in what are now considered 'untraditional' roles—as generals leading victorious armies on the battlefield and as political actors who exercise significant power in the conduct of state affairs" (Rackin 2006).

Henry VIII, or All is True. William Shakespeare and John Fletcher (Vickers 2002); the play appears in F1 "without acknowledgement of Fletcher's involvement, but authorship analysis suggests that [Fletcher] wrote approximately half" (McMullan 2004). Hickson 1847 and Spedding 1850 suggested the collaboration; Vickers 2008 assigns 1,645 lines to Fletcher. Acted spring 1613 (Margeson 1990) by the King's Men at the first Globe/second Blackfriars; "many scenes seem to be designed more for the bigger Globe stage" (White 2004c). "A late tradition recorded by John Downes has [John Lowin] as Shakespeare's original Henry VIII" (Butler 2004e). The play was possibly prompted by the wedding celebrations of Princess Elizabeth and Prince Frederick, the Elector Palatine, 14 February 1613 (Halio 1999). But there is no record of court payment for such a performance, and Gasper 1993 argues that the subject of the play, divorce, would have made this play inappropriate for a nuptial celebration. During performance in the afternoon of 29 June 1613 (recorded in a letter of Henry Wotton to Edmund Bacon), the Globe burned; this was the third day of the play's run (Gurr 2004c); "the discharge of chambers attending the banquet at which Henry meets Anne Bullen" started the fire (Frye 2004). "The cannon used by the theatre companies were the type of cast-iron chambers often fired in salute. They were without long barrels or carriages, and were loaded with blank charges" (Shirley 1961). George Villiers, Duke of Buckingham, sponsored and attended a performance at the rebuilt Globe; "he stayed till the Duke of Buckingham was beheaded & then departed" (Chambers 1930); the date was 5 August 1628, according to a letter from Robert Gell to Martin Stuteville (Braunmuller 1990). "On 6 May 1632 nine men were apprehended in a Warrington [Lancashire] alehouse for acting a play called *Henry VIII.* There may have been enough actors for a performance, since there were allegedly 'others' besides the nine who were arrested . . ., but they may have been members of an audience. Presumably the nine men were the major offenders. Shakespeare's play of that name required about thirteen actors for an uncut performance"; "the play performed was presumably either Shakespeare's *Henry VIII* . . . or, more likely, Samuel Rowley's *When You See Me, You Know Me: or, the Famous Chronicle Historie of King Henry the Eight*" (George 1991). *Henry VIII* seems to have been known as *All is True* when it was first performed (Wells & Taylor 1987); the alternate title "reflects the play's habit of offering alternative versions of historical truth without resolving incompatibilities" (McMullan 2004).

SR 8 November 1623; transferred ?4 August 1626 Paviers right in Shakesperes *plaies*; ?19 June 1627 widow of Isaac Jaggard . . . her parte in Shackspheere *playes*; 16 November 1630; 1 July 1637 Shakespeares *workes* their Part; 6 August 1674; 21 August 1683. F1 1623 *Comedies, Histories, & Tragedies*; three issues; "published according to the true originall copies"; *The Famous History of the Life of King Henry the Eighth*; prologue and epilogue; "elaborate visual effects" including pantomimes and ceremonial processions (Mehl 1965); the Old Lady, Gentlemen, and Porter and his Man are "choric commentators" (Dillon 2012); five acts and separate scenes. Epilogue, who speaks of "The mercifull construction of good women," demonstrates "that Shakespeare was aware of women as a distinct component of his audience that he had to please" (Levin 1989b). Henry Wotton wrote that the play presented "some principal pieces of the reign of Henry VIII, which was set forth with many extraordinary circumstances of pomp and majesty, even to the matting of the stage; the Knights of the Order with their Georges and garters, the Guards with their embroidered coats, and the like: sufficient in truth within a while to make greatness very familiar, if not ridiculous" (Smith 1907b). *Henry VIII* "shows a concern with pageantry that far outstrips that in previous Shakespearean plays including masques or masque elements" (Aaron 2005). SDs are unusually detailed for a Shakespearean play; *Henry VIII* "is notable for its elaborately staged and costumed scenes, often involving very large numbers of actors" (White 2004c): e.g., *"Enter king and others as maskers, habited like shepheards, usher'd by the Lord Chamberlaine. They passe directly before the Cardinall, and gracefully salute him"*; a moment later King Henry selects Anne Boleyn as his dancing partner. "Queen Anne's coronation procession . . . is set out in one of the most elaborate and eloquent stage directions in early modern theatre" (Fitzpatrick 2011). Later, in what is essentially a dumb show, we see a dreamlike "vision" of future events, *"Enter solemnely tripping one after another, sixe personages, clad in white robes, wearing on their heads garlands of bayes, and golden vizards on their faces, branches of bayes or palme in their hands. They first conge unto her [Queen Katherine], then dance: and at certain changes, the first two hold a spare garland over her head, at which the other foure make reverend curtsies. Then the two that held the garland, deliver the same to the other next two, who observe the same order in their changes, and holding the garland over her head."* "But the two other on-stage figures, Griffith and Patience, have seen nothing, so when Katherine asks: 'Saw ye none enter since I slept?' the answer is 'None, madam'" (Dessen 1984). The dance represents "a vision of the heaven to which she is shortly to ascend" (Lindley 2006). "This is no less than the apotheosis of Queen Katherine. It is quite remarkable for its time and place, in a post-Reformation play that will end by celebrating the future Queen Elizabeth, daughter of Anne Boleyn, the wife for whom Henry VIII casts off Katherine" (Dillon 2012). F2 1632 "the second impression"; three issues. F3 1663 "the third impression"; reissued 1664 with seven additional plays. F4 1685 "the fourth edition"; two issues.

"Inhabiting multiple, conflicting perspectives on controversial uses of consciences and historical interpretations of them, *Henry VIII*'s ambivalence argues for the impossibility of integrating conflicting sources and testimonies into a unified English Reformation history" (Monta 2005). "After his other more fanciful late plays, Shakespeare returns his London audiences to the English tradition in order to demonstrate his works' relevance to their own experience. *Henry VIII* validates his last romances by recapitulating their themes while reverting to recent English history, familiar to all" (Richmond 1994).

Here Beginneth a Proper New Interlude of The World and the Child. See *The World and the Child.*

Here is Contained a Goodly Interlude of Fulgens, Senator of Rome, Lucrece his Daughter. See *Fulgens and Lucrece.*

Herod and Antipater. Gervase Markham and William Sampson. Acted 1619–22 (Gurr 2009d); 1621 (Ross 1979). "Of late, divers times publiquely acted (with great applause)" by the King's Revels Company at the Red Bull, according to the TP. "The play could even have been written for Queen Anne's men and inherited by the Revels company" (*JCS*). "[O]ne of the few collaborations known to have been written by amateurs for the professional acting companies in London" (Bentley 1971).

SR 22 February 1622; transferred 9 May 1633; 3 August 1633; 2 January 1634. Q 1622 *The True Tragedy of Herod and Antipater, with the Death of Fair Mariam, according to Josephus, the Learned and Famous Jew*; two issues; prologue by Truth, probably "a female figure" (Schneider 2011), and epilogue; Josephus serves as chorus; detailed descriptions of four dumb shows, two of which "foreshadow Antipater's crimes in symbolic form" and the other two "summarize parts of the plot" (Mehl 1965); five acts and first scenes. Violence pervades the play: "*They strangle the princes on Herod's order.*" Staging calls for a scaffold on which a character is beheaded; this staging "may reflect the influence of a contemporary execution, namely that of Ralegh in October 1618" (Owens 2005). Staging calls for torture: "*They racke Adda.*" Unusual staging includes the entry of Salumith "*betweene two Furies, waving a torch.*" Herod's own death takes place onstage: "*Here the Executioner strikes, and Herod dies.*" Two trunks are featured in a scene and characters emerge: "*Here they breake open the trunks, and finde Alexandra, and Aristobulus the elder.*" Staging also calls for the unusual representation of "two different locations at the same time. We see at once both Antipater in prison and Herod in the palace" (Ross) during the play's final scene.

The printer's epistle argues for the claims of tragedy over comedy and bewails the taste of book buyers who prefer the latter: "stories (like to this) / Shall lie in darke obscurity, and misse / The printers presse, t'adorne and set them forth / In the true glories of their native worth; / When carrion-comedies (not worth an hayre) / Must be set out with *Excellent* and *Rare*; / Strange underserving titles: but, let these / Merit such liking as their readers please. / Heere I have sent and printed to your view, / A story, which I dare be bold is true." In his dedication of a play dealing with religious and political tyranny, Sampson argues defensively, "if we may give credence to antiquity, it is nothing more then truth as saith Josephus." Markham and Sampson base their play on the history of Josephus, which was also the source of *The Jews' Tragedy.* "[T]he tone and stagecraft of both plays are at times strikingly similar" (Morley 2006). Markham may also have been "inspired to write his play after reading [Elizabeth Cary's] *Mariam*" (Britland 2010).

The Heroic Lover, or The Infanta of Spain. George Cartwright. Written *c.* 1645–*c.* 1655 (*AED 3*). No evidence of production.

O 1661 list of characters with brief descriptions; five acts and separate scenes. Adequate SDs: "*Enter* Prince, *and Princess* Flora, *with the Spanish train, and the rest of the officers of the army.*"

Cartwright "has constructed both the play itself and its introductory matter so as to provide frequent thoughts of historical facts. For example, he observes in the dedication that the play was 'penn'd many years ago [?1640s-50s], but not published till now: the Muses among our sad misfortunes here, suffering an Ecclipse: which I hope Your most Illustrious Rayes will over-power'" (Randall 1995).

Hester. See *Godly Queen Hester.*

Heteroclitanomalonomia. ?Robert Robinson. Acted ?1613 (Russell 1987) at undetermined venue. Possibly presented by itinerant actors at various grammar schools. Probably written at Cambridge University for performance there (Gossett & Berger 1988). "[N]o evidence has been discovered to assign the play with confidence to one or the other university" (Nelson 1989). "At least the chief characters were played by seniors; whether the outlaws were played by freshmen it is impossible to tell" (Gossett & Berger). Indications of music played between the acts.

Washington, Folger, MS J.a.1(10), fols. 119–33; the date 1613 appears just above the title; no author named; prologue and epilogue; chorus; five short acts and separate scenes. "[T]he adequate stage directions suggest that the present manuscript may have been copied from another, either used or intended for performance" (Gossett & Berger). First edited by Russell.

"The earliest extant academic grammar play written in English" (Russell).

Hey for Honesty, Down with Knavery. Thomas Randolph. "Composed circa 1626–1628 possibly for a Cambridge audience" (Levenson 1987), probably at Trinity College in the college hall. "It is not unimaginable that during his period of association with the Salisbury Court playhouse (*c.* 1629–30) this play could have been brought by Randolph to the professional stages, especially since it is now known that the Salisbury Court opened with a company of boys or youths, rather than adult players. *Hey for Honesty*, being more in the way of a show than a play, and with its frequent opportunities for song, broadly humorous caricature, pert satire, and its large cast of characters, would have been an ideal vehicle for displaying the talents of a company of young players, and if that was indeed the case, it is the most precise instance that we have of cross-fertilization between the academic and professional stages in the period" (Butler 1988). "Augmented and published" [?1648–49] by F. J., according to the TP. "Apparently the first

writer to suggest the identification of 'F. J.' with Francis Jaques was W. C. Hazlitt in his edition of [Thomas] Randolph: his only evidence was their having the
same initials" (Leech 1947). But Braden 2010 believes that "the best guess" is
that the initials belong to Jaques. F. J. "introduced certain additions and interpolations in 1649 or 1650" (Day 1926). The revisions provide "Royalist jabs at
Roundhead absurdities" (Smith 1988a). "References to the Roundhead troopers,
to impoverished Cavaliers, to sequestrations and compounding and Goldsmiths'
Hall, come thick upon one another" (Leech). Performed "at Oxford circa 1652"
(Levenson). The play refers to "various parliamentary measures in the 1640s designed first to discourage the traditional celebration of Christmas and then to
outlaw it" (Randall 1995).

SR none. Q 1651 *A Pleasant Comedy entitled Hey for Honesty, Down with
Knavery*; "the argument or subject of this comedy"; list of characters; induction
(the only Elizabethan text wherein "the term *introduction* is used to designate an
induction" [Hosley 1961]); epilogue (added by F. J.); five acts and separate scenes.
This version of the play has been "updated" (Braden 2010). The induction presents a colloquy between the Greek playwright (Aristophanes), the translator, and
the Ghost of Cleon. This comedy is much more than a translation of the Greek
playwright: "There are about a dozen new characters and six and a half new
scenes" (Davis 1967). The play, which marks Randolph's transition from author
of shows to author of comedy (Smith 1927), is not included in the collections of
his work published in the 1640s.

F. J.'s preface to the reader, which refers to the play's origin in Aristophanes'
Ploutos, justifies the satire: "This is a pleasant comedy, though some may judge
it satyrical: 'Tis the more like *Aristophanes* the father: besides, if it be biting, 'tis
a biting age we live in; then biting for biting. Again, Tom Randal, the adopted
sonne of Ben Johnson, being the translator hereof, followed his fathers steps;
they both of them loved sack, and harmlesse mirth, and here they shew it; and I
(that know my self) am not averse from it neither." In the induction the translator
comments disparagingly of other theaters and playgoers: "It might have pleased
the rout, had it been done / In some old rotten barn at Islington; / Where tables
clapt together might have been / A stage well fitting such a worthy scene. / We
meant it but a show; if more it be, / Your kind acceptance christens it comedie."

Hezekiah. See *Ezekias*.

Hick Scorner. Anonymous. Acted mid-1514 (Lancashire 1980). Intended for indoor performance (Walker 1991), "likely . . . at a banquet" (Grantley 2004),
apparently by a four-man company, though the text contains no SDs. Perhaps
performed in a chapel (McCarthy 2008). Possibly performed at Suffolk Place,
the Southwark seat of Charles Brandon, Duke of Suffolk (Lancashire 1980).
"The play supported the king, and might have been available to London companies from Suffolk's players" (Lancashire 2002). Robert Langham [Laneham] in a

letter written at Coventry in 1575 mentions the play's title in a description of the contents of a private library (Ingram 1981, Kuin 1983).

SR no original; transferred 15 January 1582. Q1 ND ?1515 *The Interlude of Hick Scorner*; concluding prayer; not divided. Staging calls for Hick Scorner to threaten Pity "with imprisonment in Newgate, Freewill bringing a pair of gyves for Pity's feet, and Imagination producing a halter with which to bind his hands" (Craik 1958); in the moral interludes virtuous characters are conventionally bound by the forces of vice. "Freewill gives a leaping and springing act, accompanied by a song in which he calls attention to his feats" (Wright 1928); Freewill, a minor vice (Houle 1972), is eventually converted by Perseverance and Contemplation. Although the Q1 TP features an illustration depicting four men at work, along with a king and an old man, it "has absolutely nothing whatever to do with the play, but is merely intended to be decorative" (Davidson 1991). The verso of the Q1 TP depicts six figures, each of whom bears an identifying label, but the pictures are made from earlier woodblocks, probably French in origin. Q2 ND ?1525–29 (Walker); fragment of two leaves at BL. Q2 contains four woodcuts on one page; in the largest, two men converse indoors; two of the woodcuts bear blank labels. Q3 ?1546–53 unique copy at Bodleian.

"[M]orality figures are used to express a generalized complaint about the unreformed state of contemporary England, while the topical identification of the vice figure, 'Hick (alias "Dick," alias the Devil) Scorner,' with the pretender Richard de la Pole, who had amassed an army to invade England in 1514, warns Englishmen against being tempted to seek reform by supporting him" (Fox 1989). This play is "the only extant pre-Reformation morality that is titled for one of the vices" (Norland 1995).

Hieronimo. See *The Spanish Tragedy.*

1 Hieronimo. Anonymous. Possibly by Ben Jonson (Lidh 2010) or Thomas Kyd (Cairncross 1967), but Smith 1998 finds "no internal or external evidence to suggest that this is by Kyd." According to Henslowe's *Diary*, the Lord Admiral's Men performed "Joronymo" on 7 January 1597 and at other dates, but it is not clear what play is designated: it may be *1 Hieronimo*, or *The Comedy of Hieronimo*, or *The Spanish Tragedy*. Henslowe records performances of "spanes comodye donne oracoe," "the comodey of doneoracio," "doneoracio," and "the comodey of Jeronymo"; these titles may designate the same play but the issue remains uncertain: "Henslowe's erratic titling makes it difficult to know how many different plays were represented by these names" (Smith). "[C]learly written after *The Spanish Tragedy*" (Edwards 1959). Acted 1602–03 (Munro 2005) by an unidentified boys' company, probably the Children of the Queen's Revels (Shapiro 1977), at undetermined venue. The play is the purported first part of a two-play sequence of which the second part would be *The Spanish Tragedy*: "As its title advertises, *The First Part of Hieronimo* offers itself as the pre-history of *The Spanish*

Tragedy" (Griffin 2009b). *Hieronimo* features several of the same characters who turn up in *The Spanish Tragedy*, including the Ghost of Andrea, Revenge, Lorenzo, and Bel-Imperia.

It is not clear what relationship *1 Hieronimo* bears to the *Spanish Comedy* (referred to variously as *The Comedy of Don Horatio* or *Comedy of Hieronimo*), played in conjunction with *The Spanish Tragedy* by Lord Strange's Men at the Rose in spring 1592; Henslowe records a performance of *The Spanish Comedy of Don Horatio*, 23 February 1592 ("presumably a spinoff of *The Spanish Tragedy*" [Hopkins 2008a]); also 13, 30 March; 22 April; 21 May; 20 June 1592. *1 Hieronimo* may represent "a revision or rewriting" of the *Comedy* (Brown 1967). "Strange's Men played *The Spanish Comedy* on March 13, 1592, as prelude to the introduction of *The Spanish Tragedy* on the next day" (Knutson 1997). The anonymous *1 Hieronimo* may have an exceedingly complicated genesis: the play "is made up of two textual layers": one is "a textually corrupt version of parts of *Don Horatio*" (a lost original by Kyd), the other is "a mixture of farce, parody, and grotesque" written for a company of boys (Erne 2001a). But Gurr 2009a argues, "I cannot see how the exceptionally short *1 Hieronimo* could come from a doubling-up of an earlier complete play." At some point the Children of the Queen's Revels apparently appropriated either *1 Hieronimo*, or *The Comedy of Hieronimo*, or *The Spanish Tragedy*, and the King's Men retaliated by performing *The Malcontent*, which belonged to the Children of the Chapel Royal/Children of the Queen's Revels.

SR none. Q 1605 *The First Part of Hieronimo, with the Wars of Portugal and the Life and Death of Don Andrea*; no author named; the opening SD in which Hieronimo is installed as marshal constitutes a "brief ceremonial induction" (Greenfield 1969) or dumb show (Mehl 1965); the final speech by Hieronimo may be construed as an epilogue; not divided. SDs, which are "brief" (Jewkes 1958), include: "*a boat, then enter Charon, and the ghost of Andrea.*"

1 Hieronimo "was performed, in almost every case, on the afternoon before *The Spanish Tragedie*, or but a few days earlier" (Boas 1901); this "prequel play" (Smith 1999) was meant to provide "meta-theatrical commentary" on Kyd's great tragedy (Griffin). Or perhaps *1 Hieronimo* "is a full-blown theatrical burlesque of *The Spanish Tragedy*, written for and initially performed by child actors" (Reibetanz 1972). The title is included in Kirkman's 1661 catalogue.

Hieronimo is Mad Again. See *The Spanish Tragedy.*

The History of Antonio and Mellida. See *Antonio and Mellida.*

The History of Cardenio. See *The Double Falsehood.*

The History of Friar Bacon. See *Friar Bacon and Friar Bungay.*

The History of Hannibal and Scipio. See *Hannibal and Scipio.*

The History of Henry the Fourth. See *1 Henry IV.*

The History of Jacob and Esau. See *Jacob and Esau.*

The History of King Lear. See *King Lear.*

History of Love and Fortune. See *The Rare Triumphs of Love and Fortune.*

The History of Orlando Furioso. See *Orlando Furioso.*

The History of Promos and Cassandra. See *Promos and Cassandra.*

The History of Sir Clyomon, Knight of the Golden Shield, Son to the King of Denmark, and Clamydes, the White Knight, Son to the King of Swavia. See *Clyomon and Clamydes.*

The History of Sir Francis Drake. See *Sir Francis Drake.*

The History of Sir John Oldcastle, the Good Lord Cobham. See *1 Sir John Oldcastle.*

The History of the Duchess of Suffolk. See *The Duchess of Suffolk.*

The History of the Life and Death of Thomas Lord Cromwell. See *Thomas Lord Cromwell.*

The History of the Maids of Moreclack. See *The Maids of Moreclack.*

The History of the Trial of Chivalry. See *The Trial of Chivalry.*

The History of the Two Valiant Knights. See *Clyomon and Clamydes.*

The History of Thomas Lord Cromwell. See *Thomas Lord Cromwell.*

The History of Troilus and Cressida. See *Troilus and Cressida.*

Histriomastix, or The Player Whipped. Anonymous. One of the most problematic plays of the period, it was originally written and acted *c.* 1588–91 and perhaps revised later (Knutson 2001a); first performance "between February 1598 and some time late in 1599" (Lake 1981a); "likely to have been updated around 1599" (Shapiro 2005). Possibly written for Paul's Boys, who revived the play 13 November 1599 (Ostovich 2001). However, "none of the men's or boys' companies in London around 1600 could have staged it, even if the most ambitious of doubling schemes were used, because it requires more players than any company would have assembled" (Knutson 2001b). Possibly intended for production at one of the Inns of Court (Finkelpearl 1966, 1969; Mann 1991), perhaps the Middle Temple (Geckle 1987), at the Christmas Revels. "The Hall of the Middle Temple is one of the finest examples of Elizabethan formal interior architecture extant"; "Marston used the whole physical structure of Middle Temple Hall as his playing space" (Gair 2000). "In theory there are some 120 parts in this play so all the Middle Templars who wished to perform could have done so" (Gair).

SR 31 October 1610. Q 1610 no author named; prologue to play-within-the-play; "inexplicably divided into six acts" (Jewkes 1958); the play ends with song (Baskervill 1929). "The tableaux which open each act are quite carefully arranged . . . and differentiated only in the person of their leading figure" (Ingram 1978). The play "briefly stages a devil as part of a play-within-the-play presented by a group of traveling actors. In other words, the devil in *Histriomastix* is explicitly presented as a player disguised as a devil, with the intent to satirize common players" (Cox 2000). Special effects include entry of *"a roaring divell, with the Vice on his back."* Also "Pride *casts a mist*," allowing characters to *"vanish."* This mist would be "[e]ffected by a cloud of smoke emerging from a stage trap" (Lawrence 1912a). "This technique of effecting an exit covered by an artificial fog is a theatrical artifice which suits the enclosed, indoor environment [of an Inn of Court] and is clearly comparable with [Marston's] later exploitation of the indoor context of the children's theatres" (Gair). Butterworth 2005, however, finds the mist "not a literal requirement but a metaphoric one."

John Marston's name was associated with *Histriomastix* in 1878, when Richard Simpson suggested that Peele wrote the play and Marston revised it. Caputi 1961 and others support the theory that Marston revised an earlier play. Bednarz 2002 maintains that "Marston was involved in its composition" between 1599 and 1600. But Kernan 1958 sees the work as Marston's alone. Knutson 2001b demurs: "John Marston did not write any of it; it lacks not only the marks of Marstonian parody and imagery but also the topicality of Marstonian allusions."

Histriomastix is thought to have begun the poetomachia, or personal conflict among the London playwrights: Marston satirizes Jonson. "Jonson appears to have taken the character of Chrisoganus the scholar, perhaps intended as a compliment, as in some respect a personal slight" (Steggle 1998). But Marston borrowed that name from an epigram in Everard Guilpin's *Skialetheia*, which "is the first published parody of Jonson" (Bednarz 1991).

Hobbinal. See *Oenone.*

Hoffman. Henry Chettle or ?Anthony Munday (Braunmuller 2003). Acted 1602 (Gurr 2009d); 1603 (Jenkins 1950). First performed by Lord Admiral's/ Prince Henry's Men or Worcester's/Queen Anne's Men, presumably at the Fortune. Henslowe records payment to Chettle for "A tragedie called Hawghman," 29 December 1602. "Because there is no record of any further payments it was probably not completed till after Henslowe's entries stop in March 1603" (Gurr 2009c); "the incomplete payment must have been followed by others now lost, since the play was certainly staged" (Gurr). *Hoffman* may have been written as a sequel to a lost play, which Henslowe on 7 July 1602 calls "A danyshe tragedy" (Greg 1904–08); the title Henslowe records "is more than coincidentally like *Hamlet*" (Merriam 2012), probably written two years before *Hoffman*. "It seems at least possible that Chettle's two-part structure was . . . inspired by Kyd's [*1 Hieronimo* and *The Spanish Tragedy*]" (Erne 2001a). "Divers times acted with great applause" at the Phoenix, according to the TP, by Queen Henrietta Maria's Men, *c.* 1631 (Butler 2004c). This information "implies a successful revival or series of revivals from 1617 onwards, the year that Christopher Beeston opened the Phoenix" (Farley-Hills 1990). The "revival by the Cockpit company in 1630 goes with [Christopher] Beeston's acquisition of other former Fortune plays such as *The Jew of Malta*" (Gurr 2009c).

SR 26 February 1630 *Hoffman the Revengfull ffather*; transferred 25 September 1637. Q 1631 *The Tragedy of Hoffman, or A Revenge for a Father*; no author named; five acts, but the act divisions are "suspect" and "distort the play's informal five-part structure" (Jowett 1994). The play, written "probably to capitalize on the popularity of revenge plays at the turn of the seventeenth century" (Brucher 1999), begins with a *coup de théâtre*: Hoffman "*strikes ope a curtaine where appeares a body*" [his father's]; this is accompanied by "*thunder and lightning.*" Hoffman has already determined to avenge his father's death: "*Hoffman* produced the first major innovation in Kydian plot construction by creating a revenger of blood as a villain from the start" (Bowers 1940). Grotesque staging includes the "murder of Otho, who is killed by a red-hot crown clamped to his head" (Gibbons 2008); "Hoffman, having stripped the flesh off the bones, hangs the skeleton [of Otho] in chains, by the side of that of his father" (Cunliffe 1893). Hoffman's "hanging of the two articulated skeletons recalls the mounted skeletons decorating the anatomical theatres of Padua, Leiden, and London" (Pesta 2006). Unlike Kyd's Hieronimo, Hoffman "commands no ethical sympathy"; his "sidekick Lorrique, a villainous servant in the mould of Ithamore in *The Jew of Malta* or Aaron in *Titus Andronicus*, who take conscious delight in evil, draws attention to the excessive quality of Hoffman's revenge" (Clark 2007). When he is finally apprehended, Hoffman is "forced to wear a flaming crown similar to the ones that killed his father and Otho" (Pesta). Chettle seems to have based the form of execution on an actual incident in Poland, perhaps known to the playwright from Robert Browne of the Admiral's Men who "did visit Gdansk in 1601" (Browne 2004). Nearly thirty years separate first performance and printing: "Revision there may have been; rewriting there was not" (Jenkins 1934).

In his dedication the publisher Hugh Perry indicates that the play "hath passed the stage already with good applause"; now it "enjoys life as a newly printed text, protected by a kind patron" (Bergeron 2006). Perry takes "the extremely unusual step of dedicating the play to that patron, Richard Kilvert" (Jowett

1991a); such a dedication would normally be made by the author. "Perry's dedication encapsulates two primary functions of printers and publishers: recapture older texts and make them available and find protection and sponsorship for them" (Bergeron).

The Hog Hath Lost His Pearl, A Comedy. Robert Tailor. Acted 21 February 1613 (McKenzie 1967). "Divers times publikely acted by certaine London prentices," according to the TP, at Whitefriars. "It is presumably apprentices with genteel aspirations who hired the private theatre of Whitefriars in order to perform a play which is highly critical of the popular theatre" (Mann 1991). Performance was not authorized. "That the play was performed without permission on a Sunday night in Lent was reason enough for it to have been stopped by the authorities" (Kermode 2009b). The extant prologue was "written presumably for later performances at The Curtain and The Red Bull" (Mann).

SR 23 May 1614. Q 1614 list of characters; prologue and epilogue; five acts (and first scene of act 1). Staging calls for use of a trap: "*A flash of fire and Lightfoote ascends like a spirit*"; another character "*fals into the hole*" and speaks from under the stage. Domestic detail: "*Enter Hogge in his chamber with Rebecka laying downe his bed.*" Unusual staging: a madman holds a dialogue with Echo "and concludes it by dancing a cinque pace" (Wright 1928).

Henry Wotton records in a letter to Edmund Bacon that the original production at Whitefriars, acted by "some sixteen apprentices," was interrupted: "Towards the end of the play, the sheriffs (who by chance had heard of it) came in (as they say) and carried some six or seven of them to perform the last act at Bridewel [a nearby prison]; the rest are fled" (Wickham et al. 2000). It seems that the play satirized John Swinnerton, the Lord Mayor, who "had presented a chain of oriental pearl to James's daughter, Elizabeth, Queen of Bohemia, a week before the apprentices had performed the play" (Clare 1999). But the prologue, which "seems to have been written for subsequent performances and with an eye to publication" (Mann), denies satirical purpose: "And thus much let me tell you, that our swyne / Is not as divers critickes did define, / Grunting at state affaires, or invecting / Much, at our Citty vices; no, nor detecting / The pride, or fraude, in it." It is also possible that the authorities intervened because of "the illicit nature of the performance" (Clare). "It may be that the text . . . has been recast. As it stands the play reads less like a personal satire than general burlesque" (McKenzie).

"Among the numerous metadramatic moments in *Hog* are a number of allusions to Shakespeare" (Kermode). The play "was one of the earliest imitations of *Cymbeline* and other Shakespearean romances" (Shapiro 1994).

Holland's Leaguer, A Comedy. Shackerley Marmion. Licensed for acting December 1631 (Green 1987) and acted "six days successively" in that month according to Herbert's office-book. "The run is one of the longest known in the Elizabethan, Jacobean, or Caroline theatre" (*JCS*). "Lately and often acted with great applause" by Prince Charles's Men at the Salisbury Court playhouse, according to the TP. William Browne played Philautus; Ellis Worth, Ardelio; Andrew Cane, Trimalchio; Matthew Smith, Agurtes; James Sneller, Autolicus; Henry Gradwell, Capritio; Thomas Bond, Miscellanio; Richard Fowler, Snarl; Edward May, Fidelio; Robert Hunt [Huyt], Jeffery; Robert Stratford, Triphoena; Richard Godwin, Faustina; John Wright, Millicent; Richard Fouch, Margery; Arthur Saville, Quartilla; Samuel Mannery, a Bawd, according to the dramatis personae. "Probably the most unusual feature of this cast is the large number of apprentices. One wonders if some of the boys had been held over from the previous tenants of the Salisbury Court theater (the speaker of the prologue says that Prince Charles's company was 'New planted in this soile'). The previous occupants of the theater had been the King's Revels company, a kind of training school to provide apprentices for the King's company" (Bentley 1984). When Prince Charles's Men moved to the Red Bull not long after initial performance, they "presumably took with them to their new house the successful comedies that had proved themselves in performance, to be played occasionally on the Bull stage as part of their operating repertory"; *Holland's Leaguer* "should be thought of belonging to the Bull as much as to Salisbury Court" (Astington 2006).

SR 26 January 1632; transferred 25 September 1637. Henry Herbert censored the play, demanding "certain 'alterations'" (Drakakis 2004). Q 1632 *Holland's Leaguer, An Excellent Comedy*; two issues; dramatis personae; prologue; five acts and separate scenes. Few SDs apart from entrances and exits. The play depicts "a notorious real-life battle between prostitutes and constables at one of the Bankside's most upscale brothels" (Howard 2007), run by "Mrs. Holland," who "was twice summoned before the Court of High Commission" (Miles 1942). The brothel, named Holland's Leaguer and also mentioned in *The Knave in Grain*, "was certainly at the zenith of its fame in 1631–2, which is also when place-realism seems most to have been in vogue as a dramatic technique" (Steggle 2004a).

In his address to the reader Marmion writes defensively of his subject: "If there be any so supercilious to condemne it, before they read it, let them rest content with the title, and not enter into the theater, unless they intend to behold the Florales. However, my Muse has descended to this subject; let men esteeme of her, onely as a reprover, not an interpreter of wickednesse." Despite success onstage Marmion "acknowledges a desire for acceptance beyond the theater — by readers, who will validate the theater's response" (Bergeron 2006).

The Hollander, A Comedy. Henry Glapthorne. Licensed for acting as *Love's Trial, or The Hollander* 12 March 1636 (Bawcutt 1996). Acted at the Phoenix, according to TP, by Queen Henrietta Maria's Men and performed also by Beeston's Boys at court, before the king and queen, according to the TP, 1635–36 (*JCS*).

SR 22 May 1640. Q 1640 "now printed as it was then acted"; "written 1635"; list of characters; five acts and first scenes.

The play implies "that heterosexual relationships are too passionately intense and that love between women, because more rational and more chaste, is a preferable model" (Walen 2005).

The Honest Lawyer. S. S. Acted 1614–15 (*AED 3*). By Queen Anne's Men, according to the TP, at the Red Bull (Reynolds 1940). (The title is oxymoronic [Wiggins 2000].)

SR 14 August 1615; transferred 11 January 1623. Q 1616 author's initials on the TP (speculation that Samuel Sheppard wrote the play cannot be right—he was born *c.* 1624 [Schoenbaum 1966b]); epilogue (by Benjamin); five acts. SD specifies: "*Rob[in] flashes powder*" to simulate entry of a ghost. Staging calls for "a tree, which is climbed" (Reynolds 1940). A character is directed to "stand to the barre," implying a theatrical property.

Epilogue's conventional bid for applause adopts an extended judicial metaphor: "The session now dissolves: each justice rises: / No hurt is done; this is the milde assises. / We have scap'd faire thus farre: yet there remaines / A stronger judgement to passe on our paines. / Too much to hope or doubt we must not dare. / We humbly then stand at your censures barre. / If the worst comes that may be, yet I looke / For this grace, to be saved by my booke. / But if with your applause our merit stands: / Faith then be friends with us, and give's your hands."

The Honest Man's Fortune. Nathan Field, with John Fletcher and Philip Massinger ("the shares of Fletcher and Massinger are comparatively small" [Hoy 1987a]); "possibly co-written by [Robert] Daborne" (Ioppolo 2006). The original version, represented by F1, was "plaide in the yeare 1613," according to the MS TP, by the combined Lady Elizabeth's Men and Queen's Revels Children at the Whitefriars or Swan; the two companies "were amalgamated in March 1613" (Hoy 1992b). The revised version, relicensed for acting by Herbert (who notes in the MS that "the originall [was] lost"), 8 February 1625 (Adams 1917), and represented by MS, was performed by the King's Men at the [second] Blackfriars (Hoy 1959). Principal actors were Nathan Field, Joseph Taylor, Robert Benfield, William Eccleston, Emmanuel Reade, and Thomas Basse, according to F2, "all of whom were at one time with Lady Elizabeth's Men" (King 1992a). The cast also included George Ver[non], who "played a Creditor" (Astington 2010), John Rho[des], and G[eorge] Rick[ner] (King 1988). Vernon and Rhodes belonged to the King's Men in 1624 "and no doubt acted in the revival rather than the original performance" (Greg 1931). In playlist of the King's Men 7 August 1641.

London, V&A, Dyce MS 9 (D25.F9), fols. 1–34, ed. Gerritsen 1952; no author named on the TP; in the hand of Edward Knight, bookkeeper of King's Men; theatrical provenance (Long 1989); contains Herbert's license dated 8 February 1625, which "he seems not to have signed" (Bawcutt 1996); five acts and first scenes. SDs "though fairly frequent are not very elaborate except in a few cases" (Greg). The MS provides extensive evidence of censorship: "A passage which could be interpreted as a satirical gloss on James's foreign policy has been excised. Criticism of the Court and the nobility has been toned down" (Clare 1999). The MS "lacks Act 5, Scene 3, found in the 1647 printed text, and presents a different final scene" (Ioppolo 2006). SR 4 September 1646; 30 January 1673. B&F F1 1647 *Comedies and Tragedies*; "never printed before, and now published by the authours originall copies." The F1 text "often seems maddeningly unprofessional. It is a wretched job of printing" (Hoy 1996). Following the play in F1 and F2 is Fletcher's poem entitled "Upon an Honest Man's Fortune." "The great length of the poem and its slight relevance to the play it follows make it unlikely that it ever served as an epilogue" (Finkelpearl 1990). The verses "do not directly comment on the play or performance," but "the unusual placement of the poem suggests that the Folio editors must have known some tradition linking it with the play" (Potter 1997). B&F F2 1679 *Fifty Comedies and Tragedies*; "published by the authors original copies, the songs to each play being added"; *The Honest Man's Fortune, A Tragicomedy*; list of characters; actors' names.

Sexual ambiguity informs the play: "The page, symbolically named Veramour ('true love') initially in every action conforms to the Beaumont and Fletcher girl-page stereotype"; "Veramour's sexual ambiguity is the subject of bawdy by-play between Veramour and the waiting woman, Charlotte"; the dialogue between these two "creates a moment when stage conventions for representing gender are openly in question" (Clark 1994).

1 The Honest Whore. Thomas Dekker and Thomas Middleton. Henslowe records payment to the playwrights between 1 January and 14 March 1604 for "the patient man and the honest whore" (Hoy 1980). Probably first performed "some time between April . . . and October 1604" (Mulholland 2007) by Prince Henry's Men at the first Fortune (Taylor 2004b); the Admiral's Men were renamed Prince Henry's Men after the accession of James I. Probably revived by Queen Henrietta Maria's Men, as suggested by the Q5 TP, at the Phoenix (Mulholland) *c*. 1635. "The relationship of Middleton and Dekker during Middleton's apprenticeship in the profession was unusually close so that for many works it is difficult to distinguish the contribution of one from the other's" (Howard-Hill 1987a). Middleton probably "wrote the first draft of some scenes and perhaps even of a large portion of the play," but Dekker "was largely responsible for its final form" (Jackson 1979).

SR 9 November 1604 *The humors of the patient man. The longinge wyfe and the honest whore*. Q1 1604 *The Honest Whore, with The Humors of the Patient Man and the Longing Wife*; only Dekker's name appears on the TP: Middleton's name was probably omitted either because "the fact of a collaboration was not duly noted by the printer" or because "his share in the play is not as great as Dekker's" (Hoy 1980); irregularly divided into numbered scenes despite the designation of act 1, scene 1. The SDs "are frequent and full" (Jewkes 1958): Roger lays out the tools of the whore's trade, *"a stoole, cushin, looking-glasse, and chafing dish . . . a violl with white cullor in it. And 2 boxes, one with white, another red painting, he places all things in order & a candle*"; "*Enter* Bellafronte *with a lute, pen, inke, and paper placed before her*"; "*Enter a servant setting out a table, on which he places a scull, a picture, a booke and a taper.*" Staging may call for a temporary structure: "*Enter* Candido *his* wife, George, *and two prentices in the shope.*" Another SD reads, "*Enter Towne like a sweeper,*" apparently designating the actor Thomas Towne (Lawrence 1927, Nungezer 1929). Q2 1604 the title and RT are changed from *The Honest Whore* to *The Converted Courtesan*; Q2 "contains many and important corrections and alterations evidently of an authoritative nature" (Greg 1939). Q3 1605 *The Honest Whore.* Q4 1615 [octavo-in-fours]. Reissued 1616. Q5 1635 "acted by her majesties servants with great applause" (i.e., ?Queen Henrietta Maria's Men).

"The patient man [of the subtitle] is Candido, a linen draper, whose story the play's title subordinates to that of Bellafront"; in his *Diary* Henslowe "highlighted the role of Candido by calling the play *The Patient Man and the Honest Whore*" (Howard 2007).

The play "is nominally set in Milan but the only clear geographical referents in the play are to known London locations transposed to the vaguer Italian context, Bedlam and Bridewell, with a scene set in each" (Grantley 2008a).

2 The Honest Whore, with the Humours of the Patient Man, the Impatient Wife. Thomas Dekker. Acted autumn 1604 or early 1605 (Hoy 1980) by Prince Henry's Men at the first Fortune; the Lord Admiral's Men were renamed Prince Henry's Men after the accession of James I.

SR 29 April 1608 *The second parte of the converted Courtisan or honest Whore*; no author named; 29 June 1630 (ascribes the play to Dekker); transferred 21 May 1639. Despite the 1608 SR entry, there is no evidence of publication before 1630. Q 1630 *The Second Part of the Honest Whore, with the Humors of the Patient Man, the Impatient Wife: the Honest Whore, Persuaded by Strong Arguments to Turn Courtesan Again: Her Brave Refuting Those Arguments, and Lastly the Comical Passages of an Italian Bridewell, Where the Scene Ends*; ascribes the play to Dekker; not divided despite the designation of act 1, scene 1. The SDs "are long and descriptive" (Jewkes 1958): e.g., "*Enter the two Masters, after them the Constable, after him* Penelope Whore-hound, *like a citizens wife, after her two Beadles, one with a blue gowne, another with chalke and a mallet.*" Staging may call for a temporary structure: "Candido *and his wife appeare in the shop.*" This printed version "might reflect later revisions" (McMillin 1989).

Dekker "made an unorthodox choice when he made a whore the sympathetic titular heroine; and in part 2 he self-consciously addressed the double standard and rose to the defense of women by exposing the fallacious logic of sexual disparity on which it is based" (Kreps 2002). Similarities between Dekker's play and Shakespeare's *Measure for Measure* are manifold (Hoy). Other plays featuring prostitutes and "staged soon after 1603, the year of James I's accession," include *The Dutch Courtesan, Westward Ho, Eastward Ho*, and *Northward Ho* (Howard 2002).

The Honorable History of Friar Bacon and Friar Bungay. See *Friar Bacon and Friar Bungay.*

Honoria and Mammon. James Shirley. Acted ?1647–58 (*JCS*). "Represented by young gentlemen of quality at a private entertainment of some persons of honour," according to the TP of one issue. Shirley may have revised his *Contention for Honor and Riches* "for presentation by his students during his career as a schoolmaster" (Wertheim 1978).

O 1658–59 two issues; list of characters; five acts. SDs offer domestic detail: "*Enter Honoria attended, a table set forth, with a cabinet upon it*"; "*She takes a wreath of bayes from the cabinet.*" The 1659 issue reports on the TP: "whereunto is added The Contention of Ajax and Ulisses for the Armour of Achilles"; continuous register and pagination.

The play represents "an elaboration and expansion of the author's *A Contention for Honour and Riches* [SR 9 November 1632; transferred 12 December 1646], published fifteen years before [i.e., 1633]" (*JCS*). The address to the reader alludes to the rewriting of Shirley's earlier work: "A small part of this subject, many years since had drop'd from my pen: but looking at some opportunities upon the argument, I thought some things more considerable might be deduced; and applying my self further, at times of recess, I felt it grow and multiply under my imagination: nor left I it then (the matter being so pregnant in itself) till I form'd it into such limbs and proportions as you now see it. Modesty after this, invited me to cover it, and to cut off many impertinences, and purge some humour, that sate, I confess, unhandsomely upon it."

The play "is not merely a moralized comedy (or a comedic morality) but also a dramatic tract for the times, an obvious but safely general depiction of forces at work in the period" (Randall 1995).

Horestes. John Pickeryng. (The author may have been Sir John Pickering [or Puckering], a student at Lincoln's Inn and later Speaker in the House of Commons [Massey 1998, Winkelman 2005].) "[R]eferences to London, the Lord Mayor and 'this noble citye' suggest auspices in the capital—probably the 'Orestes' played at court in 1567/8" (Walker 1998). "If Pickeryng's play was the same as the play of *Horestes* performed at court in 1567–68, then it was probably performed either by Richard Edwards's Chapel Children, John Taylor's Westminster choirboys, or the Windsor choirboys" (Shapiro 1989). "Indication of a youthful rather than an adult company is the fact that six of the listed parts are female, which in the doubling arrangement proposed would be divided among three actors" (Norland 2000). The Q TP divides 27 roles for six actors, which suggests an adult company, but this may not represent the author's intent; the list may have been put together by the printer (Craik 1958). If the court performance of "Orestes" at the Christmas revels of 1567–68 designates this play, then "the actors must have been Lord Rich's Men rather than Paul's Boys, for the violent action and extensive doubling of roles are entirely unsuited to juvenile players" (Bevington 1973). Even if *Horestes* was acted at court, it "is just the kind of play that must have been shown in the public inns of London—the Red Lion, the Bull, the Cross Keys—which were showing signs of rapidly increasing dramatic activity in the 1560s" (Bevington). Despite its dependence upon the classical story of Orestes' revenge against his mother Clytemnestra for the murder of Agamemnon, *Horestes* may have had an immediate significance for the time of its performance: "It has long been recognised that *Horestes* dramatises the problems raised by the murder of Henry Stuart, King of Scots, and by Mary's precipitous marriage with the Earl of Bothwell" (Axton 1982).

SR none. Q 1567 *A New Interlude of Vice Containing the History of Horestes with the Cruel Revengement of His Father's Death, upon His Own Natural Mother*; list of characters on the TP; roles divided for six actors; "pantomimic stage directions, some of them similar to later dumb shows" (Mehl 1965); not divided. The TP "assigns an actor to the part of the prologue, though no prologue is, in fact, delivered" (Schneider 2011). "The extensive stage directions speak often of drums, trumpets, and marching armies"; the "main action is Horestes' siege of Mycoene, represented by a city wall and gate facing the stage" (Bevington 1973). Staging of violence includes the hanging of Egistus in view of playgoers: *"Fling him of the lader, and then let on bringe in his mother Clytemnestra, but let her loke wher Egistus hangeth."*

Horestes, "usually described as a 'hybrid' play because of its mixture of classical interlude with English morality form" (Dillon 1998), is the "first extant English revenge play" (Grantley 2004); the name of the Vice is, in fact, Revenge, "disguised as a messenger from the gods" (Ward 2008b). "He is the tempter in the mind when Horestes wavers over his unnatural revenge on his mother, and when the story is ending Revenge appears as a rascal out-of-work, sacked, but confident that the vengefulness of women will soon restore him to service" (Rossiter 1950).

The Hotspur. See *1 Henry IV.*

How a Man May Choose a Good Wife from a Bad. Thomas Heywood (Fleay 1891, Swaen 1912). "Sundry times acted by" Worcester's Men, according to the Q1 TP, in 1600–01 (Knutson 2001b) or 1601–02 (Cathcart 2009). "May well have been written for performance at the Boar's Head" (Berry 1986). Possibly performed at the Red Bull (Reynolds 1940). Possibly performed by Worcester's Men on tour during summer 1601.

SR none. Q1 1602 *A Pleasant Conceited Comedy, Wherein Is Showed, How a Man May Choose a Good Wife from a Bad*; no author named; not divided. In the final scene a Justice directs his listener to answer "at the barre," implying a theatrical property. Staging apparently calls for a property tomb: *"Mistris Arthur in the toombe."* "Of course the tomb might have been only the trapdoor, but we must note that Henslowe definitely lists a 'tombe' besides the two more dubious entries 'tombe of Guido' and 'tombe of Dido'" (Reynolds 1940). A SD referring to "*The cushions in the windows neately laid*," probably imagines the windows as located on the main stage (Reynolds). Q2 1605. Q3 1608. Q4 1614. Q5 1621. Q6 1630. Q7 1634. "[I]ts numerous editions suggest its continued popularity" (Reynolds).

How a Man "is conceived as a riposte to *Romeo and Juliet*, complete with feast, sleeping potion, tomb scene and accompanying rhetoric" (Wiles 1987). In this play "young Arthur 'poisons' his chaste Juliet-like wife (actually with a sleeping-potion: she later wakes up in her tomb) in order to marry 'an immodest curtizan'" (Stern 2009b).

The Humor of Bumpkin. See *Bumpkin*.

The Humor of Hobbinal. See *Oenone*.

The Humor of John Swabber. See *John Swabber*.

The Humor of Simpkin/Singing Simpkin. See *Singing Simpkin*.

The Humor of Simpleton. See *Simpleton the Smith*.

Humor out of Breath, A Comedy. John Day; the play's "epistle glancingly alludes to a second hand" (Cathcart 2005). Acted 1607-July 1608 (Chambers 1923). "Divers times latelie acted by the Children of the Kings Revells," according to the TP, at the Whitefriars.

SR 12 April 1608; transferred 3 December 1627; 21 May 1628. Q 1608 conventional appeal for applause at end; five acts. SDs specify two areas for acting: "the upper stage" and "the lower stage."

Instead of dedicating the play to a wealthy patron in the hope of financial reward, Day defies convention, mockingly addressing Signior No-body: "Worthlesse sir, I present you with these my unperfect labours, knowing that what defect in me or neglect in the printer hath left unperfect, judgement in you will winke at, if not thinke absolute. Being to turne a poore friendlesse childe into the world, yet sufficiently featur'd too, had it been all of one mans getting, (woe to the iniquitie of Time the whilest) my desire is to preferre him to your service: in which, as he shall be sure to get nothing, so likewise my hope is, he shall not loose much: for your bountie neither makes straungers love you, nor your followers envie you."

The Humorous Courtier, A Comedy. James Shirley. Licensed for acting as *The Duke* 17 May 1631 (Morillo 1979); "I account his [Frederick Fleay's] identification of *The Duke* and *The Humorous Courtier* wholly probable" (Nason 1915). "Presented with good applause" at the Phoenix, according to the TP, by Queen Henrietta Maria's Men.

SR 29 July 1639. Q 1640 list of characters; five acts. "Shirley's ridiculous courtier is a comment on the singleminded greed for power and status" (Burner 1988). Following the Q TP is a list of Shirley's plays and masques previously published.

An Humorous Day's Mirth. George Chapman. Acted by the Lord Admiral's Men 11 May 1597, according to Henslowe's *Diary*, which records the following performances at the Rose: 11, 19, 24, 31 May; 4, 7, 11, 17, 21 June; 7, 13 July. Additional performances by the combined Admiral's and Pembroke's Men: 11 October; 4 November. Henslowe's *Diary*, which records "an unprecedented average receipt of fifty-three shillings per performance" (Riggs 1989), reveals that the takings for Chapman's play were "comparable with those for Marlowe's plays in their heyday" (Wiggins 2000). "Sundrie times publikely acted" by Lord Admiral Nottingham's Men, according to the TP, at the Rose.

SR none. Q 1599 *A Pleasant Comedy Entitled An Humorous Day's Mirth*; author's initials on the TP; "printed from a theatrical manuscript" (Greg & Smith 1937); not divided. "The original compositors printed the entire play, excepting three couplets and two additional lines, as prose" (Holaday 1970); "most passages can be resolved into good iambic pentameter" (Jowett 2007e). "As with other play-texts, setting verse as prose was a consequence of the manuscript copy lacking clear line divisions" (Gurr 2009c). Also included in *Comedies, Tragi-Comedies, & Tragedies* (1652), a made-up book no longer extant. The play was "originally called *The Comedy of Humours*" (Palfrey & Stern 2007).

Chapman's play "was quite unlike anything which had been seen before: there is no real plot, only a sequence of comic intrigues orchestrated by a courtly prankster"; *Mirth* is "based on the underlying premise that people are in themselves funny enough to sustain a comic action without the need for a conventional story"; the characterizations are based on "specific personal eccentricities or 'humours'" (Wiggins 2000). "By the 1590s 'humour' was commonly used in a[n] . . . extended sense to mean simply a whim, a fancy, a caprice, or a mere affectation" (Donaldson 2011). Chapman has "enlarged the 'humorous' Count Hermes of *The Blind Beggar* into a whole play of humours characters" (Gurr 2009c). In a letter to Dudley Carlton, 11 June 1597, John Chamberlain testifies to the play's success: "we have here a new play of humors in very great request, and I was drawn alonge to yt by the common applause" (Gurr). This play "began the vogue for humours comedy" (Dillon 2000). "One of the few plays [Chapman] wrote for the public theatre" (Grantley 2000).

The Humorous Lieutenant. John Fletcher. "The attribution to Fletcher alone is confirmed by an ascription in the manuscript of the play prepared for Sir Kenelm Digby" (Finkelpearl 1990). Acted 1619 (Oxley 1987) by the King's Men at the second Blackfriars/second Globe; "likely staged between 1618 and 1625"

(Pasupathi 2008). Principal actors were Henry Condell, John Lowin, Richard Sharp, Robert Benfield, Joseph Taylor, William Eccleston, John Underwood, and Thomas Pollard, according to F2. "The longest role in the play was prepared for a boy player" (Bentley 1984). The play "was highly successful" in its day (McMullan 2004). In playlist of the King's Men 7 August 1641.

Aberystwyth, UK, National Library of Wales, Brogyntyn 42, ed. Cook & Wilson 1950; *Demetrius and Enanthe, A Pleasant Comedy*; copied by Ralph Crane for Kenelm Digby and dated 27 November 1625, "although Crane might have copied the text" earlier (Ioppolo 2006); "written by John Fletcher"; five acts and separate scenes. The MS was first edited by Dyce 1830, who notes that it "contains several passages not found in the folio." The MS also preserves some SDs missing from F1: "*Enter a magitian wth a bowle in his hand. He seemes to conjure: sweete musique is heard, and an antick of litle fayeries enter, & dance about ye bowle, and fling in things, & ex^t.*" But the SDs generally "are neither frequent nor full" (Greg 1931), though some describe useful details: "*Enter Leucippe (reading) and two maids at a table, writing.*" Paintings figure onstage when "an usher attempts to seduce a serving-maid by showing her his master's pictures" (Rochester 2010). SR 4 September 1646 *The Noble Enemie, or, the humerous Leiftenant*; transferred 30 January 1673. B&F F1 1647 *Comedies and Tragedies*; "never printed before, and now published by the authours originall copies"; *The Humorous Lieutenant*; prologue and epilogue (by Lieutenant). F "gives a censored and cut text which omits about seventy lines" (Smith 1978). B&F F2 1679 *Fifty Comedies and Tragedies*; "published by the authors original copies, the songs to each play being added"; *The Humorous Lieutenant, A Tragicomedy*; list of characters; actors' names. During the Commonwealth, parts of the play were adapted for a droll entitled *Forced Valor*, performed 1640s and 50s, later published in *1 The Wits, or Sport upon Sport* (O 1662 [two issues] and 1672).

The F1 prologue comments on the conventionality of a play's opening speech: "Would some man would instruct me what to say: / For this same prologue, usuall to a play, / Is tied to such an old forme of petition; / Men must say nothing now beyond commission: / The cloakes we weare, the leggs we make, the place / We stand in, must be one; and one the face. / Nor alter'd, nor exceeded; if it be, / A generall hisse, hangs on our levitie." "This definition of appearance, place on stage, style of text ('petition') and manner of delivery seems to be demanded by the audience" (Schneider 2011).

The Humorous Magistrate. Written by John Newdigate III after 1635 "with the prospect of production" (Howard-Hill 1988); written "in the mid-1630s" (Kidnie 2007); "likely written between 1625 and 1637" (Inglis & Johnstone 2011). This and the other plays from Arbury Hall "were written by an author attuned to live performance"; there is, for example, "careful attention to staging" (Kidnie). "Could the play have been part of an entertainment for friends who gathered . . . to celebrate a marriage at Arbury Hall?" (Scott 2011).

MS (1) Nuneaton, UK, Arbury Hall, A414, fols. 104–43; microfilm in Warwickshire County Record Office, M.I. 351/3, Item 20; no TP; the present title proposed by Howard-Hill; no author named; considerable evidence of revision; prologue and epilogue ("the unexpectedly sombre tone adopted by *The Humorous Magistrate's* epilogue raises the possibility that it was added after the play was first performed" [Scott]); five acts. This MS "not only includes copying errors, but also contains passages of extremely heavily revised dialogue" (Kidnie 2011). MS (2) Calgary, Canada, University of Calgary Library, Osborne Collection 132.27, fols. 1–26; no TP; no author named; list of characters; no prologue or epilogue; revised "in the early 1640s" (Polito & Windle 2009). "The Osborne manuscript, at 18,000 words has been reduced from the Arbury at approximately 29,000" (Polito & Windle). Both MSS "date to around the second quarter of the seventeenth century" (Kidnie).

"Set in an unnamed country shire, the play satirizes the incompetent and corrupt Justice of the Peace, Thrifty"; "[t]hrough its satire, *The Humorous Magistrate* condemns the legal corruption in country jurisdictions in the Caroline period and refers to some strategies, employed by Charles I during his personal rule (1629–1640), aimed at correcting the problem"; the play also "contributes to the revival of the pastoral as a means to dramatize the idealization of the English countryside as commonwealth and fears about its corruption" (Polito & Windle).

Humors Reconciled. See *The Magnetic Lady.*

The Humors of A Prince in Conceit. See *A Prince in Conceit.*

The Humors of An Equal Match. See *An Equal Match.*

The Humors of Bumpkin. See *Bumpkin.*

The Humors of Forced Valor. See *Forced Valor.*

The Humors of Invisible Smirk. See *Invisible Smirk.*

The Humors of Jenkin's Love-Course. See *Jenkin's Love-Course.*

The Humors of John Swabber. See *John Swabber.*

The Humors of Monsieur Galliard. See *Monsieur, The French Dancing Master.*

The Humors of Simpkin. See *Singing Simpkin.*

The Humors of Simpleton. See *Simpleton the Smith.*

The Humors of the Bouncing Knight. See *The Bouncing Knight.*

The Humors of the Bubble. See *The Bubble.*

The Humors of the Club Men. See *The Club Men.*

The Humors of the Encounter. See *The Encounter.*

The Humors of the False Heir. See *The False Heir.*

The Humors of the Gravemakers. See *The Gravemakers.*

The Humors of the Lame Commonwealth. See *The Lame Commonwealth.*

The Humors of the Loyal Citizens. See *The Loyal Citizens.*

The Humors of the Patient Man. See *1 Honest Whore.*

The Humors of the Sexton. See *The Sexton.*

The Humors of the Stallion. See *The Stallion.*

The Humors of the Three Merry Boys. See *Three Merry Boys.*

Hyde Park, A Comedy. James Shirley. Licensed for acting 20 April 1632 (Adams 1917). "Presented by" Queen Henrietta Maria's Men at the Phoenix, according to the TP. The Q dedication refers to "[t]he applause it [the play] once receiv'd in the action." Also performed at the Middle Temple, 1 November 1632 (Nelson 2009b). In playlist of Beeston's Boys 10 August 1639.

SR 13 April 1637. Q 1637 list of characters; five acts. *Hyde Park* is "the first racing play on record" (Lawrence 1927). "In a *coup de théâtre*, a horse race is represented as taking place just off stage, while characters exit to place bets, to watch it, to return with reports and to respond to the result" (Corns 2007). "The horse race was conveyed imaginatively by illusive sounds and shouts" (Lawrence): "*Confused noyse of betting within, after that a shoute.*" Other auditory effects include the sound of birds: "harke the nightingale!"; "*a bagpipe playing*" as a successful jockey enters; the sounds of "musicke and revelles." Shirley creates an outdoor milieu largely through sound: "how the birds / On every tree sing." A song was reprinted in Shirley's 1646 *Poems.*

Audiences at the Phoenix (Drury Lane Cockpit) "had a particular taste for plays that depicted everyday life in their familiar London environments" (Butler 2004c). "By the 1630s Hyde Park had become associated with the conspicuous self-fashioning of London's leisured gentry and nobility. Shirley's targeting of that elite audience is suggested by the probable timing of his play's production to coincide with the park's springtime opening, and by his dedicating the comedy to the park's noble patron, Henry Rich, Earl of Holland" (Tomlinson 2005). Hyde Park was also a place for amorous encounters, and the right to choose one's mate "is asserted by all the women" in the play (Sanders 1999a). "*Hyde Park* becomes a Caroline version of Elizabethan pastoral, a space where values are explored, true selves are found" (Graham 2004).

Hymen's Triumph, A Pastoral Tragicomedy. Samuel Daniel. Acted 3 February 1614 (Pitcher & Woudhuysen 1994). By unidentified young women in the courtyard theater at Denmark (Somerset) House, celebrating the marriage of Lady Jean Drummond to Robert Ker, Lord Roxborough, according to the O TP; "Daniel gave the bride a presentation manuscript copy" of the play (Procter 1984). Attending this performance were King James, Queen Anne, and Prince Charles. It is possible that the Queen originally commissioned the play "to provide a suitable celebration for her new palace" (Pitcher & Woudhuysen); the opening of the palace coincided with the Roxborough wedding. Queen Anne's "expanded activities" had prompted her "to appropriate Somerset House, rename it Denmark House, renovate it extensively, and make this her own winter palace in central London, thereby effecting a physical separation from the ambience of James's monarchic court" (Barroll 2001).

Edinburgh, Edinburgh University Library, MS Drummond, ed. Pitcher & Woudhuysen; represents an earlier version than Q; contains "an addition in Daniel's hand" (Rees 1964); no prologue; three songs. SR 13 January 1615. O 1615 list of characters; prologue (Hymen opposed by Avarice, Envy, and Jealousy, "the disturbers of quiet marriage"); chorus "closes each act with a song" (Herrick 1955); "seven songs interspersed throughout the play" (Rees); five acts and separate scenes. The opening dialogue offers hints of costumes and props: Hymen says that he is "[w]ithout my saffron robe, without my torch, / Or other ensigns of my duty" because he comes to Arcadia "secretly." He says of Avarice, "I know thou art / A hagge"; and Hymen calls Jealousy "vile fury." Q 1623 *The Whole Works* (with *Cleopatra, Philotas, The Queen's Arcadia*).

Daniel "concludes the action not with the traditional promise of marriage, but with the desiring subject's discomfiture and humiliation over her homoerotic inclination" (Walen 2005).

I

If It Be Not Good, the Devil Is in It (If This Be Not a Good Play, the Devil Is in It).
Thomas Dekker. Acted mid-January to late May or early June 1611 (Hoy 1980);
1611–12 (Gurr 2009d). "Lately acted, with great applause," by Queen Anne's Men
at the Red Bull, according to the TP. Intended for Prince Henry's Men at the first
Fortune but not performed there; the Prince's Men apparently rejected the play,
"perhaps because it was too radically anti-court" (Heinemann 1993b). For performance Dekker "wrote a bitter prologue about the Prince's Men" (Gurr 2009c).

SR none. Q 1612 "a new play"; RT *If This Be Not a Good Play, the Devil is
in It*; induction; prologue and epilogue; not divided. The prologue and epilogue
were probably added later in an effort to make the play more politically acceptable (Gasper 1990). Prologue refers to the "author's benefit," his takings from
the second or third performance of his play; this is "the earliest clear contemporary reference to a benefit" (Stern 2004a). Dekker's dedication to the Queen's
Men alludes to the Fortune, their former theater: "When Fortune (in her blinde
pride) set her foote upon this imperfect building, (as scorning the foundation and
workmanship:) you, gently raizd it up (on the same columnes,) the frontispi[e]ce
onely a little more garnished: to you therefore deservedly is the whole frame con-
secrated." The "frontispiece" represents the play's beginning scene in hell, which
was apparently "garnished" for the Red Bull audience: Dekker added "spectacle,
crowd-pleasing noise, and other sensational effects" (Braunmuller 1983b). The
SDs provide specificity: *"A table is set out by young fellewes like merchants men,
bookes of accounts upon it, small deskes to write upon, they sit downe to write tick-
ets."* Staging calls for a wide range of special effects, which become increasingly
spectacular: entry of Fury from below; a *"golden head ascends"* and then descends
through a trap; *"Rayne, thunder and lightning"* accompany the entry of Lucifer
and devils; *"Fireworkes"*; *"Enter . . . some spirit in a frightfull shape"*; an evil spirit
enters *"with a handfull of snakes"*; *"The play ending, as they goe off, from under the
ground in severall places, rise up spirits"* [?suggests multiple traps]; *"Enter a ghoast,
cole-blacke."* A SD reads, *"Enter Shacklesoule with a burning torch, and a long knife."*
"A few lines later, another stage direction states: *'Hand burn't off'"* (Butterworth
2005). Auditory effects include *"hellish musick"* at the entry of Pluto and Charon,
and, later, *"A confused noyse to come pressing in."*

Prologue decries current theatrical fashion: "'tis with poets now, as 'tis
with nations, / Th il-favouredst vices, are the bravest fashions. / A play whose
rudenes, Indians would abhorre, / Ift fill a house with fishwives, *Rare*, they all
roare. / It is not praise is sought for (now) but pence, / Tho dropd, from greasie-
apron audience. / Clapd may he bee with thunder, that plucks bayes, / With such
foule hands, & with squint-eyes does gaze / On Pallas shield; not caring (so hee
gaines,) / A cramd third-day, what filth drops from his braines." This "trenchant-
ly cynical" prologue "makes reference to all the dimensions of the playwright's

problem in having to cater for a broad audience for financial reasons, while his art requires an address to more educated tastes" (Grantley 2000). Heywood "responds to the increasing segregation of audiences by social rank that began with the opening of private theatres in 1599" (Whitney 2006).

If This Be Not a Good Play, the Devil Is in It. See *If It Be Not Good, the Devil Is in It. If It* is the title as it appears on TP; *If This* is the HT.

1 If You Know Not Me, You Know Nobody, or the Troubles of Queen Elizabeth. Thomas Heywood (identified in Kirkman's 1661 catalogue). Written for the Earl of Worcester's Men (Grant 2008). Acted 1604–05 (Doran 1934a) by Queen Anne's Men (successors of Worcester's Men) at the Red Bull (Gurr 1996). But "Heywood was as likely as Rowley to have written for the Fortune as the Red Bull" (Gurr 2009c). In its original form *Part 1* may have contained the defeat of the Armada and the Dr. Parry episode from what is now *Part 2*; then Heywood combined the original *Part 1* and *The Life and Death of Sir Thomas Gresham* ("mentioned in *The Knight of the Burning Pestle*" [Grant, 2003]) into a two-part play (Doran). Revived, possibly with revisions, by Queen Henrietta Maria's Men at the Phoenix *c.* 1632–33 (Doran) or *c.* 1630 (Davison 1987). This play, "in the new political context, was a cultural gesture which explicitly supported those for whom Elizabeth's reign was an exemplar of militant Protestantism and a contrast to the politics of Charles I" (McLuskie 1994). The prologue printed in Q8 reports that the play had been "well receiv'd, as well perform'd at first: / Grac'd, and frequented." In short, the play "was a huge success" (Dillon 2004b).

SR 5 July 1605; transferred 21 May 1639. Q1 1605 Heywood may originally have called his drama "the Play of Queene Elizabeth," his locution in the prologue; no author named; detailed descriptions of three dumb shows (in one an angel puts an English Bible into the hands of Elizabeth, the re-enactment of an incident in her coronation entry into London); not divided. "A late instance of a very popular 'secular saint's play'" (Wasson 1986b). *The Troubles* of the title "are not of Elizabeth as Queen, but as Princess before she came to the throne" (Boas 1950a). The SDs describe extraordinary pageantry: "*Enter 4 trumpetors, after them Sargeant trumpetor with a mace, after him Purse-bearer,* Sussex *with the crown,* Howard *the scepter,* Constable *with the cap of mayntenance,* Shandoyse *with the sword,* Tame *with the coller and a* George, *foure gentlemen bearing the canapy over the* Queene, *two gentle-women bearing up her trayne, six gentle-men* Pensioners, *the* Queene *takes state."* Q2 1606. Q3 1608 two issues. Q4 1610 unique copy at BL. Q5 1613. Q6 1623. Q7 1632. Q8 1639 prologue and epilogue (earlier printed in Heywood's *Pleasant Dialogues and Dramas* [1637]); "several stage-directions of a descriptive character are added" (Doran 1934a); five acts. None of these editions names the author on the TP. "Judging by its large number of reprintings, *If You Know Not Me, You Know Nobody* was one of Stuart England's favorite plays" (Watkins 2002).

TPs of Q1–5 feature a woodcut of a crowned Queen Elizabeth, holding orb and scepter and ensconced on her throne, behind her an elaborately decorated background. Q6–7 contain a cruder woodcut, depicting the queen standing on a checkerboard floor, again with orb and scepter, curtains drawn back at upper left and right. Q8 features yet another woodcut: Elizabeth, with orb and scepter, wears "a long veil or train and a pleated ruff" (Foakes 1985). These images, however, are "not the Elizabeth the play depicts, except in the final scene"; "up to that point she is not a queen, but a queen in waiting, a princess. The character could not, there-fore, be dressed in the crown and robes of state we see in the 1605 woodcut, nor could she carry the orb and scepter before her accession" (Howard 2005).

This play "is interesting as the only extant Elizabethan play which is stated by an authoritative contemporary witness — the author himself — to have been reported by stenography" (Giordano-Orsini 1933). Heywood's Q8 prologue (1639) explains that he resorted to publication to remedy the botched printings of his plays, which resulted from the practice of stealing the texts of those plays by transcribing dialogue during performance: "the cradle age / Did throng the seates, the boxes, and the stage / So much, that some by stenography, drew / The plot: put it in print, scarce one word true: / And in that lamenesse it hath limpt so long. / The author, now to vindicate that wrong, / Hath took the paines, upright upon it's feet, / To teache it walke: so please you sit and see't." "The presence of those mysterious Stenographers suggests that print, with its power to lame a text, is an aspect of audience reception" (Johnson 2003).

2 If You Know Not Me, You Know Nobody. Thomas Heywood. Original version, represented by Q1, acted 1604 at the Red Bull (Grantley 2008a). Revised ver-sion, represented by Q4, acted *c.* 1632 by Queen Henrietta Maria's Men at the Phoenix (Doran 1934b). Heywood dramatizes "the day when Elizabeth I visited Gresham's edifice in January 1571 and gave it the name the Royal Exchange" (Howard 2007).

SR 14 September 1605; transferred 21 May 1639. Q1 1606 two issues, one entitled *The Second Part of If You Know Not Me, You Know Nobody, with the Build-ing of the Royal Exchange and the Famous Victory of Queen Elizabeth in the Year 1588*; the other issue, *The Second Part of Queen Elizabeth's Troubles, Doctor Parry's Treasons, the Building of the Royal Exchange, and the Famous Victory in 1588, with the Humors of Hobson and Tawny-Coat*; no author named; "the chorus makes his only appearance in order to waft the audience across three decades in a few dis-arming lines" (Wiggins 2000); not divided despite the designation of act 1, scene 1. "Though the circumstances of the production of the stage-text and the printed text of the plays are shrouded in mystery, it seems likely that the printed version of Part II does not represent what was first seen on stage" (Grant 2003). "If the Gresham scenes in *2 If You Know Not Me* once made up a play devoted entirely to Gresham, one might conjecture a date [of composition] in the later 1590s, a time of horrifying economic hardship" (Crupi 2004). Despite the words *and the Famous Victory of Queen Elizabeth* in the title, "during two thirds of the play the Queen does not appear, and the central figure is the patriotic merchant, Sir Thomas Gresham" (Boas 1950a).

Staging calls for "*a storme*" and "*a blasing starre*," which "consisted either of a firework on a line or flaming material suspended in an iron cage or cresset, and burned for up to a minute" (Holdsworth 1990). Staging may call for a temporary structure: "*Enter in the shop 2 of Hobsons folkes, and opening the shoppe.*" Hobson says that "a thick myst is here," but "there is no direction to show that the mist was manifested" (Lawrence 1927). The battle with the Armada is suggested by reports from a messenger and "*a peal of chambers*"; *chambers* are "short cannon fired within to produce the sound of a salute or to indicate a battle and to replace or supplement onstage action" (Dessen & Thomson 1999). Q2 1609 *The Second Part of Queen Elizabeth's Troubles, Doctor Parry's Treasons, The Building of the Royal Exchange, and The Famous Victory in Anno 1588.* Q3 1623 *If You Know Not Me, You Know Nobody, The Second Part, With the Building of the Royal Exchange, and The Famous Victory of Queen Elizabeth, Anno 1588.* Q4 1633 with amplified text and variant ending involving the Armada, but the TP fails to advertise the additions (Bentley 1971). The two parts of this play were printed independently.

The second issue of Q1 features the woodcut of a crowned Elizabeth holding orb and scepter and surrounded by roses. The Q2 TP woodcut depicts a seated Elizabeth with orb and scepter; elaborately decorated background; curtains drawn back at upper left and right. Q3–4 TPs depict Elizabeth holding orb and scepter and standing on checkerboard floor; curtains drawn back at upper left and right.

The play represents "a sardonic warning to merchants about the costs of their reputation, in particular their ability to suffer hazard and willingness to act as fathers to the realm" (Sullivan 2002). *Part 2* "bears the conspicuous traces of two different kinds of plays. Its dominant action, Gresham's building of the Royal Exchange, reads like a typical citizen comedy and is based in part on Dekker's commemoration of Simon Eyre and the building of Leadenhall in *The Shoemaker's Holiday*"; "The play's final scenes, however, suggest an Armada pageant like Dekker's *The Whore of Babylon*" (Watkins 2002).

Impatient Poverty. Anonymous. Acted 1553-October 1558 (Tennenhouse 1984) at undetermined venue. The play "is really a patched revision of an even earlier play" (Bevington 1962). "It is quite evident that the closing speech of the play has been revised in order to fit it for the reign of Elizabeth" (McKerrow 1911). Performance takes place in a hall (Southern 1973). Robert Langham [Laneham] in a letter written at Coventry in August 1575 mentions the play's title when he describes the contents of a private library (Ingram 1981, Kuin 1983). *Impatient Poverty* is one of the titles named in *Sir Thomas More* (written *c.* 1593 or *c.* 1600) when a company of actors visits More's home for the purpose of performing a play; the naming of the anonymous interlude may suggest that it had a long stage history. "Foure men may well and easelye playe thys interlude," according to the Q1 TP, which explains the doubling for eight characters.

SR 10 June 1560; transferred 15 January 1582. Q1 1560 *A New Interlude of Impatient Poverty*; unique copy, discovered in 1906, now at BL; no author named; "newlye imprynted"; list of characters on the TP; not divided. Costumes signal a change in material and moral status. When "the hero is raised by Peace from his original poor estate," his name changes from Poverty to Prosperity, "and his 'bare' and 'poore' array to a new 'vesture,' unspecified but presumably including a rich cloak. He is now tempted by Envy and Misrule to gaming and fornication" (Craik 1958). Prosperity threatens Peace with the stocks, the fate of virtuous characters in the interludes. Misrule and Envy "win Prosperity to their company and propose a dance in celebration, a dance in which Prosperity promises to 'bounce above the ground'" (Wright 1928). Q2 ND ?1561. There are numerous differences between Q1 and Q2: "the primary text behind Q2 was a revised version of the play rather than a lost original" (Tennenhouse). Q2 features an illustrated TP, which depicts three figures (with blank labels); these have their origin in earlier books (Davidson 1991).

Interludes "were actually part of a conscious plan to inculcate a firm acceptance for the ideology of social concepts of hierarchy, retention, and ceremony, by using these very things as patterns for dramatic development" (Westfall 1990). This interlude deals not "with man's salvation and his way to God, but with earthly matters and social estates" (Mullini 2007).

The Imperick. A droll based upon several scenes in Jonson's *The Alchemist* and performed in the 1640s and 50s. "Three actors, or at most four, are required"; the deft adaptation is accomplished with "ingenuity and sureness" (Elson 1932).

Published in *1 The Wits, or Sport upon Sport* (O 1662 [two issues] and 1672); argument; list of characters.

The Impostor. See *The Imposture.*

The Imposture, A Tragicomedy. James Shirley. Licensed for acting as *The Impostor* 10 November 1640 (Adams 1917). Acted "with great applause" by the King's Men at the [second] Blackfriars, according to the general TP. In playlist of the King's Men 7 August 1641.

SR 4 September 1646; 30 January 1673. O 1652–53 *Six New Plays* (with *The Brothers, The Cardinal, The Court Secret, The Doubtful Heir, The Sisters*); general TP dated 1653, separate 1652; "never printed before"; list of characters; prologue and epilogue (by Juliana); five acts. Considerable use of song: "*Enter men . . . singing before the Duke*"; "*Nunns discovered singing.*"

Prologue refers to Shirley's absence from England: "He knowes not what to write, fears what to say. / He has been stranger long to th'English scene, / Knowes not the mode, nor how with artfull pen / To charm your airy soules." *The*

Imposture "is the second play that Shirley prepared for the King's company at Blackfriars after his return from Ireland" (*JCS*), and, according to his dedication, Shirley was pleased with the play's reception: "this poem [i.e., play], I may modestly affirm, had a fair reception, when [it] was personated on the stage, and may march in the first rank of my own compositions." The prologue addresses the "ladies" in the audience, an acknowledgment of the increasing influence of women among Caroline playgoers (Levin 1989b). Although Shirley calls the "'gentlemen' of his audience the 'commissioners of wit'," the ladies are "the arbiters of decorum" (Gurr 2009d).

The Inconstant Lady, or Better Late Than Never. Arthur Wilson. Acted 30 September 1630 (Itzoe 1980) by the King's Men at Hampton Court before the king and queen, according to a bill drawn up by the company. Possibly performed in mid-1620s at the London residence of the Countess of Leicester; "presumably originally written for" performance at a great house (Bentley 1971). "Acted at Blackfriars," according to MS (2), presumably the revival in March 1635 (diary of John Greene). No license for acting extant. In playlist of King's Men 7 August 1641.

(1) Washington, Folger, MS J.b.l; no author named; list of characters; revisions by Wilson; some lines crossed out; additions/corrections on separate page inserted into the MS; five acts. The Folger is the earliest of the three MSS (*JCS*). (2) Oxford, Bodleian, MS Rawlinson poet. 9, fols. 1–45, ed. Itzoe; "acted at Blackfriars"; five acts and separate scenes. (3) Oxford, Bodleian, MS Rawlinson poet. 128, fols. 1–39; the word *Tragedy* on the TP has been crossed out and replaced by *A Tragicomedy*; dramatis personae; written in an eighteenth-century hand. Despite the 9 September 1653 SR entry, the play seems not to have been published until 1814, when it was edited by Bliss.

The Induction to The Malcontent. See *The Malcontent, The Induction to.*

The Insatiate Countess, A Tragedy. John Marston; revised by William Barksted and Lewis Machin and possibly another; further revised by Barksted or by some other playwright. Marston's original version, written before June 1608, and possibly as early as 1601 (Cathcart 2008), and now lost, was apparently an unfinished draft. "[I]t appears that Barksted took particular responsibility for the tragic plot and Machin for the comic" (Wiggins 1998). Revised version acted December 1609–13 (Melchiori 1984). "[M]eant originally for the Blackfriars boys" (Dutton 2003). After early performances, the play was probably performed by the Children of the Queen's Revels, who took over the Whitefriars in 1609 (Bly 2000). This revised version was "designed specifically for performance at the Whitefriars" (Munro 2005). A Folger copy of Q1 has a cancel leaf for the original TP, stating that the play was "sundry times acted at the White-Friers, by the Children of the Revels." But the Whitefriars performances may originally have been played by the Children of the King's Revels, who preceded the Children of the Queen's Revels at this theater (Cathcart 2003b).

SR no original; transferred 10 February 1631; 15 September 1634. Q1 1613 the original TP attributes the play to Marston; a cancel leaf of that page attributes the play to Machin and Barksted; one dumb show; five acts. "An abundance of" SDs (Jewkes 1958). Unusual staging includes a masquelike scene wherein dancing characters bear shields with *imprese*, which are read and interpreted: "*They deliver the shields to their severall mistresses*" (Kiefer 2011). Mendosa uses a rope ladder to reach Lady Lentulus: "*He throwes up a ladder of cords, which she makes fast to some part of the window, he ascends, and at top fals.*" Staging calls for a scaffold upon which the countess is beheaded: "*Enter* Isabella, *with her haire hanging downe, a chaplet of flowers on her head, a nosegay in her hand, Executioner before her, and with her a Cardinall*"; she ascends the scaffold and is executed onstage. Auditory effects include "*A trampling of horses heard,*" which Gurr 2009d calls a "trick of realism." A more mysterious special effect is the "effusion of blood from the dead body of [Guido,] Count Massino" (Lawrence 1927). At another point a character says, "The stage of heav'n is hung with solemn black, / A time best fitting to act tragedies"; this reference suggests that acting companies may have varied the stage hangings in order to match the mood of the play. Q2 1616 neither author nor auspices of production named. Q3 1631 the original TP names Marston and the Whitefriars; the alternative TP attributes the play to Barksted and reports, "acted at White-Friers." Also included in a made-up book entitled *Comedies, Tragi-Comedies & Tragedies* (1652), no longer extant. *Countess* is not included in Marston's *Works* (1633).

The revised play may "have been calculated to suit the changing nature of tragedy in the early Jacobean period, increasing its sexual content and incorporating queasily comic effects into tragic structures" (Munro 2005). The word *insatiate*, "especially when applied to great women, extends beyond sexuality and is quickly associated with lust for power and, even from its earliest usages, covetousness" (Tricomi 2001).

An Interlude called Lusty Juventus. See *Lusty Juventus.*

An Interlude entitled Like Will to Like. See *Like Will to Like.*

An Interlude of the Repentance of Mary Magdalene. See *Mary Magdalene* (Wager).

An Interlude of Wealth and Health. See *Wealth and Health.*

The Interlude of Fulgens and Lucres. See *Fulgens and Lucres.*

The Interlude of Hick Scorner. See *Hick Scorner.*

The Interlude of John the Evangelist. See *John the Evangelist.*

The Interlude of King Darius. See *King Darius.*

The Interlude of Nature. See *Nature.*

Interlude of Vice. See *Horestes.*

The Interlude of Youth. See *Youth.*

Invisible Smirk, or the Pen Combatants. A droll based upon a scene in *The Two Merry Milkmaids* and performed in the 1640s and 50s. "The droll shows free retouching of the dialogue by a skilful hand. All the additions are brief but witty, heightening the comedy and showing a thorough understanding of the spirit of the occasion" (Elson 1932). Production requires at least six actors and probably more.

    Published in *1 The Wits, or Sport upon Sport* (O 1662 [two issues] and 1672); RT *The Humors of Invisible Smirk*; argument; list of characters.

1 The Iron Age. Thomas Heywood. Acted 1612–13 (Taylor 1993a) by Queen Anne's Men at the Red Bull (Harbage 1952). Later the play "very likely made the transfer" to the Phoenix (Gurr 1988a). "Frances Wolfreston, an avid playgoer in Caroline London, owned a copy of Heywood's *The Iron Age* in which she wrote a detailed plot summary suggesting that she saw the play performed and purchased the quarto as a commemorative edition" (Straznicky 2006b).

    SR no original; transferred 2 August 1630 ["probably an error for *The Brazen Age*" (Greg 1939)]; 30 June 1673. Q 1631 or 1632 *The Iron Age, Containing the Rape of Helen, the Siege of Troy, the Combat betwixt Hector and Ajax, Hector and Troilus Slain by Achilles, Achilles Slain by Paris, Ajax and Ulysses Contend for the Armor of Achilles, the Death of Ajax, etc.*; two issues; "never till now published," according to the address to reader; dramatis personae; epilogue (by Thersites); five acts and first scenes. Staging involves complicated scenes of violence dramatizing the Trojan war: e.g., between their armies Hector & Ajax engage in single combat: "*Alarum, in this combate both having lost their swords and shields.* Hector *takes up a great peece of a rocke, and casts at* Ajax; *who teares a young tree up by the rootes, and assailes* Hector, *at which they are parted by both armies*"; "*Alarum. Enter* Hector, Paris, Troilus, Æneas, *with burning staves and fire-bals*"; *fireball* is a "graphic but undefined term" (Dessen & Thomson 1999). Later "Achilles *[is] discovered in his tent*," suggesting a temporary structure; "the tent is a feature in the staging of a considerable part of the play" (Reynolds 1940). The action culminates in the division of Achilles' armor and the exchange of corpses (Hector's for Achilles'). One issue of Q features a TP woodcut depicting the combat of Hector and Ajax. The other issue has only a printer's device on the TP.

In his address to the reader, Heywood says that *1* and *2 The Iron Age* were "often (and not with the least applause) publickely acted by two companies [presumably Queen Anne's and King's Men], uppon one stage at once, and have at sundry times thronged three severall theaters [probably the Red Bull, Curtain, and Phoenix], with numerous and mighty auditories." Such collaboration was apparently necessary because of the large number of speaking parts, along with the other roles. Possibly each company assumed "one of the sides [Greeks and Trojans] in the famous conflict" (Hirschfeld 2004).

2 The Iron Age. Acted 1612–13 (Taylor 1993a) by Queen Anne's Men at the Red Bull (Harbage 1952). Subsequently, the play "very likely made the transfer" to the Phoenix (Gurr 1988a). Despite a similar title, *Part 2*, a revenge drama, is quite different from *Part 1*, a chronicle play. *Part 2* may be indebted to Shakespeare's *Troilus and Cressida* (Weiner 1979).

SR 2 August 1630 ["probably an error for *The Brazen Age*" (Greg 1939)]. Q 1632 *The Second Part of The Iron Age, which Containeth the Death of Penthesilea, Paris, Priam, and Hecuba, the Burning of Troy, the Deaths of Agamemnon, Menelaus, Clytemnestra, Helen, Orestes, Egistus, Pillades, King Diomed[es], Pyrrhus, Cethus, Sinon, Thersites, etc.*; HT *The Second Part of the Iron Age, with the Destruction of Troy*; dramatis personae ("new persons not presented in the former part of this history"); Ulysses' final speech constitutes an epilogue; five acts and first scenes, though there are errors in the numbering. When Orestes kills Egistus, and Clytemnestra denies a part in Agamemnon's death, Orestes invokes the heavens for a sign: "*Enter the Ghost of* Agamemnon, *poynting unto his wounds: and then to* Egistus *and the Queene, who were his murderers, which done, he vanisheth*"; Clytemnestra claims not to see the ghost, like Gertrude in the closet scene of *Hamlet*. Staging calls for the Trojan horse: "*The horse is discovered*"; then "*Enter* Agamemnon, Menelaus, Ulisses, *with souldiers in a soft march, without noise.*" Sound amplifies the atmosphere of violence: "*The alarum continued, shreiks and clamours are heard within*"; "*A noyse of uproar within. Enter all the kings with other servants halfe unready, as newly started from their beds.*" Auditory effects include "*a greate thunder crack*" at the death of Agamemnon. "In outdoor playhouses . . . in addition to 'tempestuous' drums, a 'bullet,' i.e., a cannonball, was 'rolled' along a sheet of metal or a wooden trough [to simulate thunder]" (White 2007). The Q TP depicts the Trojan horse and an episode where Sinon and Thersites congratulate each other; "there is nothing that connects these woodcuts with the stage, and they may simply reflect an artist's license" (Foakes 1985).

In his address to the reader, Heywood remarks on the gap between performance and publication and points to a change in theatrical taste: "These *Ages* have beene long since writ, and suited with the time then: I know not how they may bee received in this age, where nothing but *Satirica Dictæria* [satirical sayings], and *Comica Scommata* [comical jibes] are now in request: For mine owne part, I never affected either, when they stretched to the abuse of any person publicke, or private." Heywood also looks forward to combining the *Ages* plays in one book: "If the three former *Ages* (now out of print) bee added to these (as I am promised) to make up an handsome volume; I purpose (*Deo assistente*) to illustrate the whole worke, with an explanation of all the difficulties, and an historicall comment of every hard name, which may appeare obscure or intricate to such as are not frequent in poetry."

The Island Princess. John Fletcher. Acted 1619–21 (*JCS*) by the King's Men at the second Blackfriars/second Globe. Performed also at court, 26 December 1621 (Hoy 1987a). Principal actors were John Lowin, Joseph Taylor, John Underwood, Robert Benfield, William Eccleston, Richard Sharp, George Birch, and Thomas Pollard, according to F2. In playlist of the King's Men 7 August 1641.

   SR 4 September 1646 by m^r Beamont & m^r fflesher; 30 January 1673. B&F F1 1647 *Comedies and Tragedies*; "never printed before, and now published by the authours originall copies"; five acts and first scenes. Auditory effects include an explosion, an alarm bell ("*A bell rings*"), and cries of "Fire, fire," though playgoers do not see the fire: "neither the fire nor the quenching of the fire can be shown directly on the Elizabethan stage. But through a combination of sound effects, vivid reports, exits and entrances, and alternating scenes Fletcher has provided all the excitement of such a fire" (Dessen 1984). "[S]ome visible smoke from the fire is possible but not necessary" (Dessen 2010). Q 1669 *The Island Princess, or The Generous Portugal, A Comedy*; "with the alterations and new additional scenes"; list of characters; prologue and epilogue. B&F F2 1679 *Fifty Comedies and Tragedies*; "published by the authors original copies, the songs to each play being added"; *The Island Princess, A Tragicomedy*; list of characters; actors' names; no prologue or epilogue. This play and *The Sea Voyage* were "evidently designed as companion pieces" (Neill 2000b). "To the threat of disruptive heteroerotic desire commonly found in Fletcher's tragicomedies, *The Island Princess* adds the threat of racial and religious difference" (DiGangi 1997). "The first English play . . . to choose the East of India and the Indies as its setting" (Raman 1995). Although F1 specifies the setting as India, "the play itself refers more specifically to two islands . . . in the Bay of Bengal, which were better known as the Spice Islands" (Jowitt 2006b). The play presents "the first portrayal of an Indonesian woman on the English stage and a gloriously complex portrayal at that" (McMullan 2002). "*The Island Princess* offers a satirical vision of the effect of European occupation and trade competition on the inhabitants of the Moluccas" (McMullan 2004).

   The Q epilogue, borrowed from *The Noble Gentleman* (1647), comments on the gap between performance and publication: "We have done our best for your contents to fit / With new paines this old monument of wit." The Q prologue, also borrowed from *Noble Gentleman*, claims that the playwrights' reputation compensates for the passage of time since first performance: "That which was worn some thirty years ago, / May come in grace again, and we pursue / That custom by presenting to your view, / A play in fashion then, not doubting now / But 'twill appear the same, if you allow / Worth to their noble memory, whose names / Beyond all power of death, live in their fames."

The Isle of Gulls. John Day. Acted mid-February 1606 (Burns 1987). "Often playd" by the Children of the Revels at the [second] Blackfriars, according to the Q1 TP. "Written for the Children of the Queen's Revels," but because of official disapproval "the company had to drop the word 'Queen's' from their title" (Parr 2004a). The Q texts "are obviously censored" (Gurr 2009d).

SR none. Q1 1606 substantial induction in which three gallants question Prologue; not divided except for designation of act 1, scene 1, and act 5, scene 1. In exasperation Prologue expresses hostility toward playgoers who, insecure in their judgments, follow others who leave their seats before the performance ends: "'tis growne into a custome at playes, if any one rise (especially of any fashionable sort) about what serious busines soever, the rest thinking it in dislike of the play, tho he never thinks it, cry *mew, by Jesus vilde*; and leave the poore hartlesse children to speake their epilogue to the emptie seates." "[D]escriptive stage directions" (Jewkes 1958): *"Enter the two captaines, with Aminter & Julio two princes, attyred one like a poore souldior, the other like a poore scholler"*; *"Enter Aminter and Julio, attyred like Satyres"*; *"Enter Lisander like an Amazon."* Sound effects include *"Musicke of bels &c,"* "signifying the arrival of strangers at the fortified island" (Lawrence 1927). Q2 1633 no author named; no designation of acts 3 and 4.

The play's satire, directed against King James, Robert Cecil, and the influx of Scotsmen at court, gave offense: Edward Hoby notes in a letter of 7 March 1606 that "sundry [actors] were committed to Bridewell." In addition, the company of actors was "deprived of the queen's patronage, forbidden thereafter from using her name as part of its official title. As a consequence of this loss of patronage, Samuel Daniel appears to have lost his position as censor of the company" (Tricomi 1989).

J

Jack Drum's Entertainment, or The Comedy of Pasquill and Katherine. John Marston; attributed "on the basis of an ascription in Edward Pudsey's commonplace book" (Finkelpearl 1969). Acted late spring or early summer 1600 (Caputi 1961). "Sundry times plaide by" Paul's Boys, according to the Q TP, at Paul's playhouse. The title "is named after a rustic country dance, and seems to have contained many mini-entertainments" (Bly 2009). Edmund Gayton mentions the play in *Pleasant Notes upon Don Quixot[e]* (1654).

SR 8 September 1600; transferred 23 October 1600; 6 November 1615. Q1 1601 HT *John Drum's Entertainment*; RT *A Pleasant Comedy of Pasquill and*

Katherine; no author named; list of characters (on last page); this is the first such list "to divide characters by gender" (Taylor et al. 2007); induction; five acts. In lieu of a conventional prologue, the play begins with a tire-man, who complains that the author "snatched" the script and "with violence keepes the boyes from comming on the stage." One of Paul's Boys then enters and says that the play-wright "was loth, / Wanting a prologue, & our selves not perfect, / To rush upon your eyes without respect." He also contrasts this play with "mouldy fopperies of stale poetry, / Unpossible drie mustie fictions." Descriptive SDs (Jewkes 1958): e.g., *"Enter Katherin, tearing her haire"*; *"She [Katherine] offers to stabbe her selfe."* A morris dance provides entertainment: "Oh a morice is come, observe our country sport, / 'Tis Whitson-tyde, and we must frolick it" (Wright 1928). Unusual staging: "Mamon poisons Katherine's face with 'oyle of toades' because she refuses his love"; but "'a skilfull beldame with the juice of hearbes' cures her face"; and "she is reunited with her suitor, Pasquil, who had previously fallen into a state of madness caused by his grief at her deformity" (Drew-Bear 1994). Q2 1616 "newly correct-ed." Q3 1618 the TP describes the actors as "12 men and 4 women." The Q3 TP features a woodcut of a man with a pike; he may represent one of the characters.

The play's title is "a colloquial phrase meaning 'a brusque reception'" (Buck-ridge 2000). The play contributes to the poetomachia; Marston satirizes Jonson: "Brabant Senior is generally, although not universally, regarded as a caricature of Jonson" (Steggle 1998). And "it burlesques the naïvely romantic crudities of the public theatres in general" and "is directed specifically at *The Trial of Chivalry*, which had recently been staged by the Earl of Derby's Men" (Andrews 1971).

Jack Juggler. Anonymous. Perhaps written by Nicholas Udall (White 1993b), but the play's "metrical irregularity, humour, facility for wordplay, ability to adapt classical literature to an English domestic situation and numerous instances of its phraseology and choice of rhyme are characteristic of Richard Edwards's known work" (King 2001). Acted *c.* 1550–51 (Hornback 2010) or 1553–58 (*DTRB* 1984), probably in the evening (Walker 1998). Intended for performance by chil-dren, according to the TP, probably indoors during the Christmas season. The full title, *A New Interlude for Children to Play named Jack Juggler*, indicates "that it was intended for schoolboys rather than college students. Since it contains no singing, it seems more suitable for a grammar school than for a choir school" (White). "It appears to be written—or at least printed—so as to be consistent either with presentation in a hall, or with something a little more elaborate if the 'chyldren' happened to be members of a school, or with considerably more elaboration if they were members of one of the royal choirs and summoned to perform at court" (Southern 1973). "[C]ould be played by five" actors (Streit-berger 2009).

    SR *c.* October 1562-July 1563 (Smart & Greg 1933). Q1 ND ?1562 (Wil-liams 1914) or *c.* 1565 (Braden 2010) *A New Interlude for Children to Play entitled Jack Juggler, both Witty, Very Pleasant, and Merry*; "never before imprinted"; no author named; list of characters on the TP; prologue; no speech called "epilogue" but final speech by Jenkin Careaway addresses the audience: "to you that be now here / I praye god graunt, and send many a good newe yere" [this "may be a later addition" (Grantley 2004)]; not divided. The "superfluous epilogue and the prologue" may "come from another hand than that which produced the play" (Craik 1958); the epilogue is "probably an Elizabethan, Protestant addition" (Bruster 1992). The play "is a dramatized practical joke, one of the kind featured in jestbooks" (Thomson 2007). Few SDs. Q2 ND ?1565 "newly imprented." Q3 ND ?1569–70. The text of Q3 has been "largely and sometimes drastically revised" (Evans & Greg 1936a).

The Q1 TP features three figures in woodcuts. The one identified as Jack is "not a likely representation at all" (Davidson 1991). Q2 replaces two of the woodcuts with new ones. The Q3 TP replaces all three with a woodcut that, although depicting "dancers and musicians on a stage in the background, was not designed as an illustration to the interlude, being in fact a representation of the Return of the Prodigal Son" (Greg 1939).

This is "apparently the only surviving play to attack the Roman Catholic doctrine of transubstantiation" (White). The play "is a satire specifically directed against the spearhead of the Counter-Reformation, the newly founded Jesuit order and the casuistry in argument for which its members became a byword in Elizabethan and Jacobean England" (Wickham 1981).

Jack Straw. ?George Peele (Murphy 2012b). Acted *c.* 1590 (Demiralp 2012); 1593 or 1594 (Schillinger 2008) at undetermined venue, possibly an inn-yard (Lawrence 1927), though "when actors performed at inns they usually occupied a large room rather than a yard and performed by candlelight" (Orrell 1997). Dramatizing the Wat Tyler rebellion (Grantley 2008a), the play "was written for the London public stage" (Bevington 1968). "*Jack Straw* can be played by a team of fourteen actors including between one and three boys and a clown. The presence of a clown part indicates that professional performance was probably envisaged" (Longstaffe 2002).

SR 23 October 1593; transferred 14 August 1600; 13 July 1638. Q1 1593–94 TP bears the earlier date, the colophon the later; *The Life and Death of Jack Straw, a Notable Rebel in England, Who Was Killed in Smithfield by the Lord Mayor of London*; no author named; four acts, plus a section entitled "The King's pardon delivered by Sir John Morton to the Rebels," followed by the denouement; divisions are "irregular and confused" (Jewkes 1958). In dramatizing the king's clemency to the rebels, the play glorifies Queen "Elizabeth's merciful handling of both her Catholic enemies and the restive peasantry" (Bevington 1968). "The allegiances of the author of *Jack Straw* are so unambiguously monarchical that he can present the rebels' position in the serene confidence that it will be contemptuously dismissed" (Cohen 1985). Q2 1604 Muir & Wilson 1957 call this quarto "textually worthless," but Schillinger argues that "the multiple editions of the play suggest a level of popularity over and above the median for the period since under half of all plays were fortunate enough to see a second printing," and "it is hard to fathom putting any special emphasis on the 1593 version."

Jack Straw "is the second shortest play of the period (only *The Yorkshire Tragedy* is shorter)" (Jewkes). "[T]here is a strong case for arguing that a censored prompt book underlies the printed text of *Jack Straw*" (Clare 1999).

Jacob and Esau. ?William Hunnis (White 1993a) or ?Nicholas Udall (King 1982). Acted *c.* 1550–52 (Hornback 2010) or *c.* 1557–58 (Butler 2004f). Probably performed "by pupils of provincial grammar schools rather than by the London schoolboy and chorister troupes who brought plays to court each Christmas" (Shapiro 1977). Perhaps performed by the Children of the Chapel Royal (White 1992). "The play's ten listed acting parts . . . seem suitable for the eight children residing at the Chapel in 1553" (White 1993b). Possibly performed in the chapel of a private household (Westfall 2004). Acted during the reign of Edward VI [1547–53] and "possibly revived under Mary and Elizabeth" (White 2004a).

SR *c.* October/November 1557 (Grantley 2004) *an enterlude upon the history of Jacobe and Esawe.* "*Jacob and Esau* was printed for the first time between 1557 and 1558 but came out in a second edition in 1568" (Ephraim 2003); the BL owns a fragment of this edition. Q2 1568 *A New, Merry, and Witty Comedy or Interlude . . . Treating upon the History of Jacob and Esau;* "newely imprinted"; no author named; RT *The History of Jacob and Esau;* list of characters on the TP; prologue, concluding speech by "the poete," and a prayer; five acts and separate scenes. The TP alerts actors to the importance of costume: "The partes and names of the players who are to be considered to be Hebrews and so should be apparailed with attire." SDs specify hand props: *"Ragau entreth with his horn at his back and his huntyng staffe in hys hande, and leadeth iij greyhoundes or one as may be gotten."* There are twenty references to "tents": the structure "must be big enough to conceal five or six people at a time" and "it must have at least two — and preferably three — entrances" (Southern 1973). "The play could in fact be staged without scenery, but I think 'a house' representing 'the tent' . . . is desirable" (Craik 1958).

The play "is as lively a work for the stage as survives from the 1550s and 1560s" (O'Connell 2000b); it addresses "matters specific to the reign of a boy-king reformer" (Westfall 2002).

James IV (The Scottish History of James IV). Robert Greene. "Sundrie times publikely plaide," according to the TP, summer or autumn, 1590 (Sanders 1970), perhaps at an inn-yard (Lawrence 1927), though "when actors performed at inns they usually occupied a large room rather than a yard and performed by candlelight" (Orrell 1997). Although sometimes attributed to the Queen's Men (Walen 2005), "nothing" about the play indicates that it belonged to that company (McMillin & MacLean 1998).

SR 14 May 1594. Q 1598 *The Scottish History of James IV, Slain at Flodden, Intermixed with a Pleasant Comedy Presented by Oberon, King of Fairies*; induction consisting of Oberon, Bohan, and the fairies, "who constitute a chorus, and upon occasion are so labeled—'Chorus'" (Herrick 1955); description of three dumb shows; five acts. "Despite the title, this play is not historical and the audience would probably not have surmised the plot in advance" (Foster 2004). "Anyone who went to see [the play] expecting to learn about his death at the Battle of Flodden would have been startled to find that the confrontation between England and Scotland was caused by the king's attempt to murder his wife and marry another woman, and that it ended, without a battle, through the couple's happy reunion" (Potter 2012). Although "the title sounds like that of a typical—that is, Shakespearean—history play, the content resembles nothing of the sort. The plot derives not from the chronicles but from the Italian romantic novellas of Cinthio" (Crumley 1998). "Greene has set his play within a dramatic framework, consisting principally of the dialogue of Oberon, King of Fairies, and the misanthropic Scot Bohan"; Shakespeare borrows "the juxtaposition of the fairy king and the soured worldling" for *A Midsummer Night's Dream* (Brooke 1911). The SDs "are long and descriptive" (Jewkes 1958): *After a solemne service, enter from the widdowes house a service, musical songs of marriages, or a maske, or what prettie triumph you list.* The play "has songs or dances including a hornpipe and a jig after Acts 1, 2, and 4 to mark pauses in the story" (Gurr 2009d). "Comic dancing is one of the chief entertaining features" of the play; the "induction contains a dancing contest between the clowns, Nano and Slipper, and Oberon's antics" (Wright 1928). Staging calls for a property tomb, *plac'st conveniently on the stage,* around which Oberon and others dance. The play is "particularly striking in its concern for spatial arrangement and movement, with unusual notations like 'aloof,' 'stands aside,' 'spying him,' 'descend down,' 'overhears,' 'approaching,' 'march over'" (Styan 1996).

James IV, "the most important English tragicomedy before 1600" and a play dramatizing "the cult of the feminine" (Herrick), "depicts a woman's infatuation with a female page. As such it is a precursor of *Twelfth Night*, the only one of Shakespeare's disguised heroine plays to explore the relationship between the protagonist and another woman" (Shapiro 1994).

The Jealous Comedy. See *The Comedy of Errors.*

The Jealous Lovers, A Comedy. Thomas Randolph. "One of two plays written for production before King Charles and Queen Henrietta Maria on their visit to Cambridge in March 1632 [the other was *The Rival Friends*]" (Levenson 1987). Hausted's play "competed with *The Jealous Lovers* for the first performance and won"; "a notorious academic quarrel ensued, and evidently as a result the vice-chancellor of Cambridge [Dr. Butts] committed suicide" (Levenson). "[P]repared for [performance] *c* 8 March 1632, but postponed on word of an accident befallen the chancellor, Lord Holland; performed in Trinity College hall by students of the college on 20 March (for royal audience)" (Nelson 1989). "Presented" before King Charles and Queen Henrietta Maria, according to the Q TPs. A Q1 prefatory poem by James Duport reports the play's success onstage: "Thou hadst th'applause of all: king, queen and court / And university, all lik'd thy sport."

SR no original (it was published at Cambridge); transferred 3 June 1645. The comedy, revised between first performance and publication, "draws on his earlier play, 'The drinking academy'" (Kelliher 2004b). Q1 1632 two issues; dramatis personae; epilogue (colloquy of Asotus and Astrologer); five acts and separate scenes. In the play's major *coup de théâtre*, "*Priests and sacrifice, and Hymens statue discovered*"; the priest "*presents Tyndarus and Evadne*," and explains what playgoers see: "Mercy you Gods, the statue turns away" from lovers "whose seemingly irrational jealousies have kept the plot turning" (Veevers 1989). Next the Priest "*presents Pamphil[us] & Techmessa*" to the statue, with these words, "wilt thou please to prove / This other knot? The statue turns again!" Another striking moment occurs when "*Tyndarus and Techmessa rise from the coffins*"; beholders, "affrighted, fall into a swoon." Q2 1634. Printed in 1640 added to O3 *Poems*, which exists in a variety of configurations and includes *The Muses' Looking Glass* and *Amyntas*; the general TP of *Poems* is dated 1643, the separate 1640; "the third edition inlarged"; new register and pagination for *Jealous Lovers*. O3 reissued 1646. O4 1652 *Poems* (with *Amyntas, Aristippus, The Muses' Looking Glass*); "the fourth edition inlarged"; two issues. O5 1664 *Poems* (with *Amyntas, The Conceited Peddler, The Muses' Looking Glass*); "the fifth edition, with several additions, corrected and amended"; separate TP dated 1662.

In his address to the Q1 reader, Randolph announces his agenda: "I confesse no heights here, no strong conceits; I speak the language of the people." He also alludes to the price of a printed play, "I beg thy pardon, if I put thee to the expence of a sixpence, and the losse of an houre. If I could by my own industrie have furnished the desires of my friends, I had not troubled the presse."

Jenkin's Love-Course and Perambulation. A droll based on several scenes in James Shirley's *Love Tricks, or The School of Compliments*, and performed in the 1640s and 50s. Halliwell[-Phillipps] 1861 suggests performance at the Red Bull *c.* 1647. "In the adventures of the braggart Welshman, Jenkin, the droll presents a minor and unessential element of the parent comedy" (Elson 1932).

Published in *1 The Wits, or Sport upon Sport* (O 1662 [two issues] and 1672); RT *The Humors of Jenkin's Love-Course and Perambulation*; argument; list of characters. "There is an unusual amount of revision of the dialogue" (Elson).

1 Jeronimo. See *1 Hieronimo*.

The Jew of Malta. Christopher Marlowe. Acted 1589–90 (Bawcutt 1978) at undetermined venue. Perhaps first performed by the Lord Admiral's Men; "the best of actors" played Barabas, according to the Q prologue, alluding to Edward Al-leyn, named in Heywood's dedicatory epistle. Performed by various companies at the Rose, 1592–93; Henslowe records performances by Lord Strange's Men in 1592: 26 February ("the highest-grossing performance of the week" [Hop-kins 2008a]); 10, 18 March; 4, 18 April; 5, 11, 20, 30 May; 14 June. In 1593: 1, 18, ?26 (Hopkins 2005a) January. Will Kemp "would have acted" in Mar-lowe's play when it was performed by Strange's Men at the Rose (Butler 2004d). Performed by Sussex's Men, "who may have included former members of Lord Strange's Men and of Pembroke's Men" (Hopkins 2005a), 4 February 1594. By the combined Sussex's and Queen's Men, 3, 7 April 1594. By the "re-formed" (Hopkins) Admiral's Men at the Rose, 14 May 1594. At Newington Butts, oc-cupied by the Admiral's and Chamberlain's Men [the two companies "took turns playing their own plays" (Wickham et al. 2000)], 4, 13, 23, and 30 June. Addi-tional performances in 1594: 10, 22 July; 5, 7 August; 2 September; 20 October; 9 December. In 1596: 9, 18, and 29 January; 2 and 17 February; 20 April; 14 May; 21 June. Possibly performed at the Theater (Gurr 2009d). Marlowe's trag-edy "was probably the most popular play of the Elizabethan era" (Siemon 1994); the prologue at court asserts that the play was "writ many yeares agone, / And in that age, thought second unto none." On 19 May 1601 Henslowe records two expenditures, "divers thinges for the Jewe of malta" and "more thinges for the Jewe of malta," apparently for a revival at the first Fortune (Gurr 2009c). The Admiral's Men paid Thomas Dekker for changes: 16 January, 3 November, and 4 December 1601. In making the revisions, Dekker may have collaborated with Thomas Heywood (Lake 1983). Edward Alleyn, "who had retired in 1597, re-turned to the Fortune for several years and reprised many of his famous roles," including Barabas in 1601 (Knutson 2009a). "Playd" by Queen Henrietta Ma-ria's Men at Whitehall, before the king and queen, and at the Phoenix, accord-ing to the Q TP, in or before 1632. The revival spoke to contemporary concerns: "The plague of piracy that [the play] dramatizes, together with the appropriation of a private estate by the Church, the Maltese Christians' opportunistic alliance with the Spanish, the subsequent skewering of the political establishment by someone who borrows wholesale from conventional anti-Catholic polemic — all this had become in the time of Charles more topical than it had ever been under Elizabeth" (Parker 2008). The Q prologue alludes to Richard Perkins, "who doth personate / Our Jew this day" (i.e., when the play was revived *c.* 1632). Barabas "was played — and perceived — as a grotesque with fool or demonic qualities" (Palfrey & Stern 2007).

SR 17 May 1594 *the famouse tragedie of the Riche Jewe of Malta*; no printing ensued so far as is known, but "it is possible that the Caroline edition is actually a reprint of an earlier, now-lost first edition" (Farmer & Lesser 2006); 20 Novem-ber 1632 a Tragedy called *the Jew of Malta*. Q 1633 *The Famous Tragedy of the Rich Jew of Malta*; "written by Christopher Marlo"; prologue at court and prologue "to the stage"; introductory speech by "Machevil" (i.e., Machiavelli), the "infamous name here twisted into 'make evil'" (Riggs 2004); epilogue addressed to the queen and regular epilogue; five acts. Thomas Heywood wrote the prologue and epilogue for performance at the Whitehall Cockpit; he also wrote the prologue and epilogue for revival at the Phoenix; these were written "presumably at the request of the manager of Queen Henrietta's company, his friend Christopher Beeston" (Bentley 1984). Q contains all of them. Heywood may have revised the play, "but the full extent of his revising cannot be ascertained" (Gill 1987). The text "gives no sign that it was at any time rewritten in order to make it more profitable on revival" (Knutson 1985). "*The Jew of Malta* is the only extant sixteenth-century English drama to be first printed in the 1630s" (Lesser 2004).

"The technique of opening a play with a striking moment that initiates a visual and verbal pattern of thematic significance is a hallmark of Marlowe's stagecraft" (Thomson 2005): "Barabas *in his counting-house with heapes of gold before him*"; the counting-house requires "a central 'discovery space'" (Ichikawa 2002). Later Barabas inveigles his daughter to fetch money hidden in their home, which has been confiscated and converted into a nunnery: "*Enter Abigaill above*" and she "*throwes downe bags [of gold]*." Barabas poisons the entire community of nuns. Like the Vice of the moral interludes, Barabas exults in his capacity to bring confusion to his enemies (Spivack 1958); hence the black humor of his arranging for Lodowick and Mathias to kill one another as he observes the incident from "*above*." Ithamore, the Muslim slave, comments, "Why was there ever seene such villany, so neatly / Plotted, and so well perform'd?" Unusual staging includes "the large scaffold" that Barabas builds with hammers and ropes "to catch the Turkish caliph" (Gurr & Ichikawa 2000). In this trickery he overreaches. A trumpet signals: "*A charge [sounded], the cable cut, a caldron discovered*." Instead of killing the Turk, Barabas plunges to his death in a boiling cauldron; Henslowe records "j cauderm for the Jewe" in his 1598 inventory of theatrical properties. Such a plunge would evoke the hellmouth of late medieval drama and art (Diehl 1980).

"The Admiral's Men often scheduled *The Jew of Malta* in proximity to a play Henslowe called 'Mahomett,' which undoubtedly exploited similarly prickly views of Mediterranean otherness" (Knutson 2006a). The play was "produced alongside *Mully Mullocco*, *The Spanish Comedy*, *The Spanish Tragedy*, *Orlando Furioso*, and *Sir John Mandeville*, all plays that center on foreign themes, characters, or interests" (Bartels 1993). Shakespeare's *Merchant of Venice* "at once borrows from *The Jew of Malta* and repudiates its corrosive, merciless irony" (Greenblatt 2004).

The Jew of Venice. See *The Merchant of Venice*.

The Jews' Tragedy, or Their Fatal and Final Overthrow by Vespasian and Titus His Son. William Heminges. Written *c*. 1628–30 (Morley 2006) and possibly acted, venue unknown. "It was clearly published in a form written with professional staging in mind" (Morley). Heminges' father was a co-compiler of Shakespeare's F1.

SR none. Q 1662 "never before published"; list of characters; prologue and epilogue; chorus (summarizes offstage action); detailed description of dumb show; five acts and separate scenes (in act 1). Staging includes the appearance of Persephone "*with the three Furies*," who enter through a trap door; a character is "*put on the rack*": "torture the old ruffin," and "*they beat him down with a stone.*" A SD, "*The Temple is fir'd*," suggests (unnamed) theatrical effects; it "recalls those conflagration scenes so beloved of the Italian Renaissance" (Nicoll 1937). Another SD: "*they enter the cave*"; it is not clear whether this was managed by a trap or by an entrance into the tiring-house; Dessen & Thomson 1999 believe that many SDs about the cave in this play "are fictional." A SD calls for the entry of a "*Ghost in white*"; the actor's face may have been whitened with flour, and he may have worn a sheet. Offstage auditory effects include "*Groan in the cave*"; "*It thunders*"; "*A noise of still musick.*" The upper section of the tiring-house was used for confrontation between Romans and Jews: "*enter* Joseph *and captains upon the wall.*" The SDs give detailed description of onstage battle. Directions for a masque are similarly specific: "*Enter* Time *bearing an escutcheon, six Roman champions crown'd with lawrel follow, each bears an escutcheon:* Jehochanan *and* Simeon *follow guarded:* Time *presents his escutcheon to the general.*" The champions are personified figures whose symbolic costumes are described and explained; the scutcheons, which bear symbolic pictures, are interpreted; cf. *Edward II*, *The Misfortunes of Arthur*, *The Three Lords and Three Ladies of London*, *Pericles* (Kiefer 2011).

The TP claims that the play is "agreeable to the authentick and famous history of Josephus." *Herod and Antipater*, "was the only play of its generation based on the history of Josephus to be performed by professional actors at a public theater" (Morley). Elizabeth Cary's *Tragedy of Mariam* was never staged.

Jocasta, A Tragedy. George Gascoigne and Francis Kinwelmarshe [the spelling in the MS]. Gascoigne was "responsible for the lion's share of *Jocasta*" (Pigman 2000). "Presented" by gentlemen of Gray's Inn, according to the MS and Q TPs, at the Christmas Revels, 1566–67 (Smith 1988a). Although *Jocasta* is essentially the translation of Lodovico Dolce's *Giocasta* (1549), which is itself based on a Latin translation of Euripides' *Phoenissae*, perhaps by R. Winter (Cunliffe 1912, Miola 2002), the English authors add dumb shows for spectacle and for symbolic emphasis at the beginning of each act.

London, BL, Additional MS 34063, fols. 1–38, *Jocasta, A Tragedy*; a presentation copy; argument; list of characters; chorus at close of each act; epilogue; detailed descriptions of dumb shows at beginnings of the acts; five acts and separate scenes. The MS credits acts 1 and 4 to Kinwelmarshe, acts 2, 3, and 5 to Gascoigne; the epilogue to Christopher Yelverton. Q1 1573 [undated but the preface to the reader indicates the date]; *A Hundreth Sundry Flowers*. "Since Gascoigne apparently left England in haste before he was able to see the publication of his works through the press, the printer was free to follow his commercial judgment that dramatic texts should be included in the book because they were much more marketable than lyric poetry" (Marotti 1995). Elaborate SDs of Q1 "allow us to reconstruct the performance in some detail" (Smith). A trap is required for a grave into which coffins are lowered in the second dumb show; in the third dumb show men with baskets of earth seek to fill "*a great gulfe*"; a knight then "*lepte into the gulfe*," which closes. Dumb shows before acts 1 and 5 feature "spectacular chariot entries" (Dillon 2004a): in the first the chariot of Sesostres, representing Ambition, is "*drawne in by foure kinges*"; in the last the "*figure of unstable fortune*" is "*drawen in by iiij noble personages*"; these SDs may have inspired Tamburlaine's entry in a chariot (Kiefer 1983). "Such stage images, puzzling as they must sometimes have been, were no doubt appealing both as spectacles and as challenges to interpreters" (Waith 1988). Auditory effects include "*a greate peale of ordinaunce*" during fourth dumb show, "*a very mournful melody*" during the last. Music is important to the dumb shows: "*before the beginning of the first acte did sounde a dolefull & straunge noyse of violles, cythern, bandurion, and such like*"; "*a very dolefull noise of flutes*"; "*a very dolefull noise of cornettes*"; "*trumpets, drummes and fifes sounded*"; "*the stillpipes sounded a very mournful melody.*" At various points the actors enter and exit through "*the gates called* Electrae" or "*the gates called* Homoloydes"; a note to the reader following the epilogue explains that these were among the principal gates at Thebes. "It is clear that the significance of these gates could not have been rendered to the spectators unless each were inscribed" (Lawrence 1912b). Q2 1575 *The Posies*; two issues; "corrected, perfected, and augmented by the authour," according to the general TP; "prologue or argument." Q3 1587 *The Whole Works* (with *Supposes*), actually an enlarged edition of *A Hundreth Sundry Flowers*; two issues.

    Jocasta represents "the first performance of Greek tragedy in English" (Miola). The playwrights "must be given credit for achieving a play which approximates both in its construction and content to the sprit of classical tragedy more closely than any other play of its time written and performed in English" (Wickham 1981). "*Jocasta* serves as an object lesson of the danger of civil war to a realm plagued by a disputed succession" (Pigman). "Creon's refusal to sacrifice his son for Thebes marks his absolute faith that God will relieve Thebes from Eteocles' tyranny and Polynices' rebellion. Despite the complexities of the political situation, Creon at least, makes the right decision and is rewarded in the end. Throughout the 1560s the orthodox line on resistance theory was repeatedly adjusted but with none of the anxieties resolved" (Ward 2008a).

Johan Baptystes Preachyng. See *John Baptist's Preaching.*

Johan Johan the Husband. See *John John the Husband.*

Johan the Evangelist. See *John the Evangelist.*

John a Kent and John a Cumber. Anthony Munday (Hill 2004). Acted *c.* 1587–89 (Pennell 1980) or 1590 (Hamilton 2005) or 1595 (Jackson 2007a) at undetermined venue. Possibly first performed by the Lord Admiral's Men (Harbage 1952). "[P]robably given at the Rose" (Rhodes 1976). "[P]robably performed by Lord Strange's Company in 1589–1590" (Skura 2003). On 19 September 1601 Henslowe records the purchase of *The Wise Man of West Chester* from Edward Alleyn; Fleay 1891 identifies this play with *John a Kent*, as does Greg 1904–08; Bentley 1971 suggests that *Wise Man*, "bought from Alleyn was probably a revision [of *John a Kent*] which had come into his [Alleyn's] possession"; Gurr 2009c also regards the two titles as designating the same play. But Knutson 1984 argues that *John a Kent* and *The Wise Man* "were separate—perhaps even rival—texts." Speculation that *The Wise Man* is the same as *John a Kent* has "been discounted" (Hamilton 2005). *John a Kent* was "phenomenally popular" (Hyland 2011).

San Marino, CA, Huntington, MS HM 500, fols. 1–12, ed. Byrne 1923; no separate TP but the title appears on the vellum wrapper; in Munday's hand with his signature at the end; "Decembris 1595" apparently inscribed on last leaf, but the play was probably acted before this, and the date is actually 1590 (Shapiro 1955); whatever the date, it is "not in Munday's hand" and "mutilation of the leaf has destroyed the words that presumably preceded it" (Blayney 1972); theatrical provenance (Long 1989); evidence of revision (Ashton 1933); some SDs in a different hand (Byrne); damaged (most of the last leaf is lost); five acts and first scenes. "Act and scene divisions in playbooks arise mostly from the playwrights, and, not surprisingly, are not regularized" (Long 1999). This is "the earliest surviving manuscript playbook from the Elizabethan theater" (Long 1989). The SDs, which "are decidedly full" (Greg 1931), refer to a stage-house, which the actors enter. A "tree" may have been erected onstage: "*The fourth [Antique] out of a tree, if possible it may be*"; possibly the tree was represented by one of the columns "supporting the heavens"; it "seems that [the playwright] is suggesting the use of a prop tree but admitting it might not be worth the trouble" (Rhodes 1976). Various references to a "castle" may indicate that "the company was using something representational as well as functional" (Long). Sound effects include "*the chyme playes*"; "*the chymes agayne.*" Chime is "probably an abbreviation of 'bell chimes'—small bells arranged by size, suspended on a bar, and played with a hammer" (Dessen & Thomson 1999). Unusual staging includes the creation of a "silly mist" by Kent, ensuring his victory over Cumber (Johnson 2006); the mist may have been simulated by smoke. SR none. First edited by Collier 1851.

In *John a Kent* "two ladies plan to 'revendgefully' kill both themselves and their husbands in order to escape an arranged marriage; their plan is forestalled, however, when the magician John a Kent happily spoils the nuptials" (Irish 2009). The play "is a sort of *Midsummer Night's Dream*, but with the rival lovers Lysander and Demetrius each doubled, and with Oberon split into two competing Fairy Kings" (Skura).

John Baptist's Preaching in the Wilderness. John Bale. Acted *c.* 1538 (White 1993b) at undetermined venue. Possibly first performed by "Bale and his fellows" in or near St. Stephen's [Hackington], near Canterbury, 8 September 1538; Thomas Cromwell sponsored the production. However, the performance "need not have taken place in the church building" (Gibson 2002). Performed also by Bale's "young men" at the Market Cross in Kilkenny, Ireland, on 20 August 1553, the day Mary was proclaimed monarch. In Kilkenny the play was performed "by a local group of players, perhaps [Bale's] cathedral choristers" (White 2004a). Performance took place in the afternoon (Happé 2004). Requires a minimum of four actors in addition to Bale (Fletcher 2000). "[P]erhaps initially written for household performance by Bale's company, but rewritten while the author was in exile" (Walker 1998).

The extant reprint (*Harleian Miscellany*, vol. 1 [1744]) preserves the text of a lost quarto, printed *c.* 1538 (Walker 2000); *A Brief Comedy or Interlude of John Baptist's Preaching in the Wilderness, Opening the Crafty Assaults of the Hypocrites, with the Glorious Baptism of the Lord Jesus Christ*; "compyled" by Bale in 1538; list of characters; begins with a speech by Bale as Prolocutor and concludes with a similar speech; not divided, but the play "falls symmetrically into three sections, each highlighting John's evangelical office" (Kendall 1986). Unusual staging calls for the descent of a dove following Christ's baptism: "*Descendit tunc super Christum spiritus sanctus in columbae specie.*"

"Bale was one of the most vigorous advocates of the use of drama for didactic and polemical ends" (Walker). *John Baptist's Preaching* forms a trilogy with *The Chief Promises of God* and *The Temptation of Our Lord* (Greg 1930); the three plays adopt "themes, conventions, and devices from the medieval mystery and morality plays to protestant purposes" (King 2004). At Kilkenny these plays represented "a zealous, but short-lived attempt to counter the city's vigorous Catholic mystery cycle tradition, which continued until at least 1639" (Morash 2002). "Bale is the product of a 'medieval' upbringing, and it is therefore unsurprising that he should turn to didactic genres familiar from his boyhood—such as mystery and morality plays—to instruct his audience in the 'true' religion" (Shrank 2007).

John John the Husband. ?John Heywood; the play "was first attributed to John Heywood by Francis Kirkman in the list of English plays appended to his editions of *Tom Tyler* (1661) and *Nicomède* (1671)" (Proudfoot 1967). Acted *c.* 1526–30 (Betteridge 2009) at undetermined venue. Performed indoors: "the playwright uses what appear to be three different, or 'differentiated,' acting-areas" (Southern 1973). "[T]he fireplace, commonly to be found on one side of a hall, comes directly into the action. But we do not know whose hall or halls were involved" (Happé 2007b). "No special staging requirements" (Lancashire 2002). The play "shares with *Witty and Witless* a cast of only three" (Happé 1999).

F 1533 no separate TP; HT *A Merry Play between John John the Husband, Tyb his Wife, and Sir John the Priest*; no author named; extant copies at Bodleian and

Pepys Library at Magdalene College, Cambridge; not divided. Contains "the sort of directions necessary if the action is to be realized effectively" (Walker 1998).

"[T]he first play printed in England to represent farce as a dramatic form" (Norland 1995); "close in spirit to continental traditions of the farce and the fabliau" (Bevington 1975).

John of Bordeaux, or The Second Part of Friar Bacon. ?Robert Greene (McNeir 1949); addition by Henry Chettle. Acted *c.* 1590–94 (Walsh 2009a) at undetermined venue. Probably first performed by Lord Strange's Men at the Rose (Jenkins 1934). Henslowe records performances of *Friar Bacon*, perhaps this play, in 1592: 19 February; 25 March; 26 April; 6 May. Also 10, 17, ?26 (Hopkins 2005a) January 1593. "It appears that Henslowe used 'Friar Bacon' in reference to two separate plays: *John of Bordeaux* for Strange's Men and *Friar Bacon and Friar Bungay* . . . for the Queen's Men" (McMillin & MacLean 1998). "In plot terms, *John of Bordeaux* picks up where *Friar Bacon and Friar Bungay* ended" (Maguire 1999a); *John* was perhaps "composed as a revival piece for Strange's men" (Greg 1931). Dean 1981 calls *Friar Bacon* and *John of Bordeaux* "a dramatic diptych": "they are constructed less as a continuously developing action than on a pattern of repetition-with-variation; materials are repeated from one part to the next with complementary effect, the two sides of the diptych being festive comedy and homiletic (near-) tragedy." *John of Bordeaux* was almost certainly "performed in a London theater by a London company" (Maguire). Probably revived *c.* 1623–32 (Long 1999).

Alnwick, UK, Alnwick Castle, MS 507, fols. 1–14; no TP but Sir John is "among the leading characters" (Greg); no author named; an abridgment of the lost original text; two scenes are missing; contains addition by Henry Chettle (Jenkins), consisting of "one speech of a dozen lines only" (Ioppolo 2006); edges of folios are damaged; several "shows" but "[n]o pantomimes in the stricter sense" (Mehl 1965); not divided. "Marginal directions by a playhouse reviser, which thrice include the name of John Holland [an actor], make it clear that the manuscript has served as a prompt book" (Greg). SR none. MS first edited by Renwick & Greg 1935, who propose the present title.

John Swabber the Seaman. Attributed to Robert Cox by Francis Kirkman in his preface to *2 The Wits.* A droll performed in the 1650s. "Acted at the Red Bull" according to the Q2 TP. The droll was possibly "taken from a lost stage play" (Elson 1932). Eight actors needed; Robert Cox played Swabber. During performance on 9 June 1653 at the Red Bull, Cox had a most unpleasant experience: "Employed by the rope- and sword-dancers to present the well-known jig, or droll, of *John Swabber*, Cox was betrayed to the soldiers by two jealous rivals: the theatre was raided, the spectators fined five shillings each, and Cox imprisoned" (Rollins 1921). "The attending gentry were compelled to pay five shillings apiece as an exit fee" (Randall 1995). This playlet "is included in Cox's collection, which provides the only sure evidence of the Commonwealth interlude and of which pieces were actually performed" (Clare 2004).

Published in *Actaeon and Diana, with a Pastoral Story of the Nymph Oenone*; Q1 ?1655 and Q2 1656 *The Humor of John Swabber*; list of characters. Some SDs with descriptions of costume and props: "*Enter John Swabber, armed with a sword, a gun, a spit, a pair of tongs, and other ridiculous weapons*"; "*Enter Swabber with a great bowl of batter, and a ladle.*" Later published (in slightly abridged form) in *1 The Wits, or Sport upon Sport* (O 1662 [two issues] and 1672); RT *The Humors of John Swabber*; "argument needless, it being an ancient farce, and generally known"; list of characters.

John the Evangelist. Anonymous. Acted before 1520 at undetermined venue: "the kind of saint play which could conceivably have been associated with a craft guild" (Lancashire 2002). Performed outdoors (Thompson 1910). Requires "three to four actors" (Lancashire).

SR none. Q ND ?1550 *The Interlude of John the Evangelist*; not divided. (There may have been an earlier edition *c.* 1520 [Greg 1907b].) "The text contains virtually no" SDs (Bevington 1962); "several sections of dialogue [are] obviously missing" (Walker 1998). The TP features a woodcut of St. John holding a chalice from which a dragon emerges. "This legend is not part of the drama" (Davidson 1991).

The play represents a "pre-Reformation homily on roistering and the need for rudimentary instruction in the meaning of the Catholic service" (Bevington 1968).

A Jovial Crew, or the Merry Beggars, A Comedy. Richard Brome. Probably first performed in late 1641 or the early months of 1642 (Steggle 2004b); "presented . . . in the yeer 1641" at the Phoenix, according to the TP, by Beeston's Boys (the King and Queen's Young Company). Brome's remark in the dedicatory epistle that the play "had the luck to tumble last of all in the epidemicall ruine of the scene" means "that it was being performed as the theatres closed" (Butler 1984b) in September 1642; it "was perhaps the last play performed before the closing of the theaters" (Cohen 1985). The Q1 prologue, referring to tensions that would soon issue in the closing of the theaters and then in civil war, speaks of "these sad and tragick daies." The play is "regarded as the terminus not just of Brome's career but of early modern drama in general" (Steggle). *A Jovial Crew* "is coloured with a tough political skepticism and a deeply resonant mood of foreboding" (Butler 2002).

SR none. Q1 1652 *A Jovial Crew, or The Merry Beggars, Presented in a Comedy*; list of characters; prologue to the play-within-the-play; Poet serves as Master of Revels/Inductor to entertainment within the play; five acts. The word *crew* "is an established collective noun for a group of beggars" (Steggle). Song and offstage sound create a festive mood that infuses the play: "*A noyse and singing within*"; "*A confused noyse within of laughing and singing, and one crying out*"; "*A great noyse within of rude musick, laughing, singing, &c.*" Sound effects are suggested by a song at the end of act 1: "The spring / (By every bird that can but sing, / Or chirp a note) doth now invite us forth"; at another point a "*Nightingale sings*"; and at still another point, "*Sing Nightingale, Cuckoe &c.*" A discovery space covered by a curtain is used to dramatize the beggars' activity: "*He opens the scene; the* Beggars *are discovered in their postures; then they issue forth*"; "Randal *opens the scene. The Beggars discovered at their feast. After they have scrambled a while at their victuals: this song.*" "One of the remarkable features of *A Jovial Crew* is the rehearsal, on the stage, of a mock-masque presented for the nuptials of two old beggars, a parodic device which looks back to a solid, if somewhat remote, tradition of celebratory entertainments — the betrothal masque in *The Tempest* and, more characteristically, Ben Jonson's archetypal *Hymenaei* of 1606" (Bitot 1995). Q2 1661 "acted by his majesties servants at the New Theatre in Vere-Street, 1661."

"*A Jovial Crew* is a truly national play written at a turning-point in the history of the English stage and the English nation, and Brome is wholly conscious of that fact and of all that is at stake; at a moment when England was embroiled in a political crisis more grave and uncertain than anything within living memory, the play stood as an elegant plea for everything that was valuable, permanent and sanctioned by time in the English way of life" (Butler). This play, along with *The Goblins* and *The Sisters*, dramatizes the beggar "in an emblematic way in order to facilitate the discussion of social and political issues" (Sanders 2002). "At one point the forces of law enter, to put a stop to an illegal performance done by a group of social outsiders, beggars. What they find instead is that it is a group of insiders, genteel young people dressed up as beggars. To make matters worse, two of these insiders — the women — are really trying to be beggars. They are doing this because they feel their lives are stifled and their liberty limited 'in our father's rule and government'; they want for themselves the 'absolute freedom, such as the very beggars have.' So they resolve to become beggars, not as play-acting but for real" (Shepherd & Womack 1996).

"There had been earlier beggar and gipsy plays, such as Fletcher's *Beggars' Bush*, Middleton and Rowley's *Spanish Gipsy*, and Jonson's *Gipsies Metamorphosed*" (*JCS*).

The Jovial Crew, or The Devil Turned Ranter, being a Character of the Roaring Ranters of These Times, Represented in a Comedy. S. S. (The 1656 list of plays compiled by Rogers and Ley identifies the author as Samuel Sheppard; Rollins 1923a concurs.) A play-pamphlet possibly acted *c.* 1651. Thomason's copy at the BL is dated 6 January 1651 (*JCS*).

SR none. Q 1651 author's initials on the TP; prologue; five short acts. Ample SDs. A woodcut opposite the TP depicts Lucifer, "with horns and flaming head-dress, carrying a torch, and seated in a pageant-wagon like those used in masques, drawn by two dragons" (Foakes 1985); this is superimposed on a map of the British Isles. The woodcut "has no reference to the action of the playlet, except in so far as it portrays Lucifer" (Foakes).

"While drawing upon contemporary pamphlets which claimed to expose the Ranters and alleged abominations amongst members of the sect, the play strongly evokes theatrical antecedents" (Clare 2002).

Jugurtha. William Boyle. Fleay 1891 speculates that "Boyle" is "merely a *nom de plume* for [W] Bird." William Bird, who acted for Henslowe at the Rose and Fortune, was also known as William Bourne (Nungezer 1929); "[h]e always signed himself Birde, but was generally called Borne" (Greg 1931). Bird is best known for the additions that he and Samuel Rowley made to *Doctor Faustus* in 1602. Chambers 1923, however, calls Fleay's speculation an "irresponsible guess." *Jugurtha* was presumably acted *c.* February 1600 by the Lord Admiral's Men at the Rose, and subsequently at the first Fortune, which opened autumn 1600; Edward Alleyn probably played Jugurtha (Astington 2006); Henslowe records payment for the play: "lent unto me W birde the 9 of februarye [1600] to paye for a new booke to will: Boyle, cald Jugurth xxx^s w^c if you dislike Ile repaye it back." "Here the allusion must be to Henslowe, and the implication is that he had some say in the choice of scripts" (Carson 1988). "Was it Henslowe who might dislike the new play, or was Bird afraid he would object to the act of purchase, since it was Henslowe himself who normally paid his writers?" (Gurr 2009c). The play was later relicensed for performance (Adams 1917): "On the 3d of May 1624, Henry Herbert states, that he had licensed, without a fee, *Jugurth*, an old play, allowed by Sir George Bucke, and *burnt, with his other books*" (Bawcutt 1996). Herbert refers to playbooks lost when the Fortune theater burned the night of 9 December 1621; *Jugurth* and other plays must have been "recopied from old manuscripts that survived and . . . re-licensed" (Gurr). It seems likely that "the *Jugurth, King of Numidia* which Herbert licensed without fee in 1624 was the same play as Boyle's *Jugurth* of 1599/1600, for Sir George Buc was Deputy Master of the Revels at the time Henslowe paid for the play, and he was active in the office as Deputy or Master until 1622" (*JCS*). By the time of the 1624 revival, *Jugurth* "belonged to the Palsgrave's company at the [second] Fortune" (Astington), which had "probably opened in the spring of 1623" (Bentley 1981); Prince Henry's company had become the Palsgrave's Men after the death of the prince.

Oxford, Bodleian, MS Rawlinson poet. 195, fols. 99–132; *Jugurtha or the Fait[h]less Cosen German, A Tragedy*; no author named; dramatis personae; dumb show; many words and lines crossed out; four acts (no designation of act 5; the MS is incomplete). At certain points the name of the protagonist is given in its Latin form, Jugurtha; at others in its English form, Jugurth. Scholars have usually called *Jugurtha* "lost" (Limon 1986, Kawachi 1986, *AED 3*); others have suggested that the MS is an adaptation of the original play (*JCS*); the MS is "written in a mid-century hand" (Gurr 2009c). But the dialogue and SDs are consistent with a play staged in 1600. An allusion to *Jugurtha* in Edmund Gayton's *Pleasant Notes upon Don Quixot[e]* (1654) may refer to the play; if so, it suggests the continuing popularity of *Jugurtha* in the 1630s, 1640s, and even later: "I have known upon one of these festivals, but especially at Shrove-tide, where the players have been appointed . . . to act what the major part of the company had a mind to, sometimes *Tamerlane*, sometimes *Jugurth*, sometimes the *Jew of Malta*, and sometimes parts of all these."

"'Jugurtha' presumably recounted events in the life of the Numidian king, 160–104 BCE. . . . As classical tragical history, 'Jugurtha' invites comparison with *Julius Caesar* in the Chamberlain's repertory, as well as *Titus Andronicus*, with which there would have been the additional connection of North Africa through the character of Aaron the Moor" (Knutson 2006b).

Julia Agrippina. Thomas May. "Acted 1628," according to a note printed beneath the list of characters in D, at undetermined venue.

SR 26 October 1638; transferred 20 November 1658. D 1639 *The Tragedy of Julia Agrippina, Empress of Rome*; two issues; author's initials on the TP; list of characters; five acts. *Julia Agrippina* and *Cleopatra* "were intended to be issued together as well as separately" (Greg 1939). *Agrippina* begins with what amounts to an induction: the ascent of Megaera from hell, along with Caligula's Ghost (presumably through a trap) and their conversation; sound effects accompany the action: "that thunder, which wee heare / from Acheron." Another issue appeared in 1654, and some copies were bound with May's 1639 *Cleopatra* (separate register) and entitled *Two Tragedies*.

"Given the political sensitivity of the times and the ubiquitous convention of utilizing parallels, and even some of the other play-texts put forth in this same year, 1654, we may hypothesize that the publication of *Julia Agrippina* was inspired by something more than aesthetic and commercial impulses" (Randall 1995). "The political unease, insecurity and fear of absolutism in the later 1620s is expressed" in such "anti-tyrant plays" as *Julia Agrippina* (Heinemann 1993a). May "presents the imperial court as a place of wholesale decay" (Peltonen 1995); he dramatizes "a terrifying world of power, cruelty, and inhumanity" (Butler 1985). The play "sets imperial tyranny against the memory of republican virtue, and so . . . tells a Roman story as the story of institutional degeneration and the loss of liberty" (Perry 2006a).

Julius Caesar. William Shakespeare. Acted June–September 1599 (Humphreys 1984) by the Lord Chamberlain's Men at the first Globe. Thomas Platter, a Swiss visitor, witnessed a performance at the Globe on the afternoon of 11 September 1599; Platter, "who seems to have mistakenly assumed that England was on the Gregorian calendar," records the date as 21 September (Shapiro 2005). Platter says that performance began "about two o'clock"; he also relates that the cast consisted of "some fifteen people." *Julius Caesar* may have been the first play performed at the new Globe, perhaps 12 June (Sohmer 1999); or Platter may have witnessed in September one of the earliest performances (Daniell 1998). Richard Burbage probably played Brutus (Cerasano 2012). Revived by the King's

Men at Whitehall during the marriage festivities of Princess Elizabeth, 1612–13 (payment for "Caesars Tragedye," "presumably *Julius Caesar* in revival" [Knutson 1999], to John Heminges dated 20 May 1613); at St. James's Palace 31 January 1637, in the Presence Chamber (Astington 1986); and at the Whitehall Cockpit, 13 November 1638 (Adams 1917). Leonard Digges, in a poem published in 1640, cites the play as a huge success: "oh how the audience, / Were ravish'd" (Chambers 1930). Digges was especially impressed by the scene in which Brutus and Cassius quarrel. John Weever admired the funeral oration: "The many-headed multitude were drawn / By Brutus' speech that Caesar was ambitious. / When eloquent Mark Antony had shown / His virtues, who but Brutus then was vicious?" (Honigmann 1987). Ben Jonson, whose Roman tragedies may in part have been inspired by the success of Shakespeare's play, complained in *Timber: or Discoveries* of a solecism, "Many times [Shakespeare] fell into those things, could not escape laughter: As when hee said in the person of *Caesar*, one speaking to him; *Caesar, thou dost me wrong*. He replied: *Caesar did never wrong, but with just cause* and such like: which were ridiculous" (Chambers 1930). The words cited here do not appear in F, and it is possible that they represent an alteration of what Shakespeare actually wrote, though Jackson 2001a suggests that the speech Jonson recalls "is probably authentic." Jonson "may have been remembering Shakespeare playing Caesar . . . and being laughed at, either because his line was deliberately self-contradictory or because he had extemporized something absurd" (Potter 2012).

SR 8 November 1623; transferred ?4 August 1626 Paviers right in Shakesperes *plaies*; ?19 June 1627 widow of Isaac Jaggard . . . her parte in Shackspheere *playes*; 16 November 1630; 1 July 1637 Shakespeares *workes* their Part; 6 August 1674; 21 August 1683; 12 January 1684. F1 1623 *Comedies, Histories, & Tragedies*; three issues; "published according to the true originall copies"; *The Tragedy of Julius Caesar*; five acts. In the F1 catalogue of plays (i.e. table of contents), the play is entitled *The Life and Death of Julius Caesar*. F1 "is on the whole well furnished with stage directions" (Wells & Taylor 1987). "How far Shakespeare's actors donned Roman dress is still uncertain," though the Peacham drawing of *Titus Andronicus* "shows elements of classical costume" (Humphreys). Both Caesar and Brutus, in domestic scenes, are said to wear "nightgowns," i.e. dressing gowns; the garb "signals not only the fact that on stage it is supposed to be night or early morning but also that the character is troubled or disturbed in some way" (Thompson 2010). An article of clothing becomes important when Brutus is visited by Caius Ligarius, who wears a "kerchiefe," perhaps a shawl, on account of illness, or a headscarf (Cerasano); the ailing visitor represents metaphorically the sickness of the conspirators' enterprise. A hand prop also has symbolic significance: a sleepless Brutus finds comfort when Lucius plays a lute, symbol of melancholy. Early in the morning Caesar is troubled by his wife's outcries in her sleep and by "*thunder & lightning*," a customary sign of divine displeasure. Other sound effects include the offstage shouting that greets Caesar's refusal of a crown and the onstage shouting following Antony's speech over Caesar's body; in a notable anachronism a "*Clocke strikes*" when the conspirators meet at Brutus' home; ironically, "whenever he faces a decision that requires a deft handling of the time, he makes a calamitous error" (Kiefer 1983). The oration of Brutus after the assassination seems to require a "dais" (Gurr & Ichikawa 2000): "*Enter Brutus and goes into the pulpit.*" This SD may designate a platform built in front of the tiring house (Spevack 1988), or "some kind of rostrum" (Humphreys), or a formal raised seat (Reynolds 1940). "*Alarums*" suggest the battle of Philippi fought offstage. Before Philippi, Brutus says, "in my tent Cassius enlarge your greefes," but the tent "is presumably imaginary" (Meagher 2003). Violence includes the murder of Cinna the Poet by the mob (possibly offstage), the suicide of Brutus, and the stabbing of Cassius by Pindarus, as well as the assassination of Caesar. "*The Ghost of Caesar*" appears to Brutus; ordinarily "stage ghosts seem to have worn the clothes they wore when they were alive" (Thompson 2010), though the actor's "face was doubtless whitened" (Meagher). This ghost, however, is called a "monstrous apparition," and extra makeup may have been applied; it is not clear whether the ghost enters through a trap or through one of the doorways onto the stage. F2 1632 "the second impression"; three issues. F3 1663 "the third impression"; reissued 1664 with seven additional plays. Q ND ?1684. F4 1685 "the fourth edition"; two issues.

A seventeenth-century Folger MS "provides a text that traces back through earlier manuscripts to a copy of the 1632 Shakespeare Second Folio in which the text of *Julius Caesar* had been annotated for performance" (Mowat 1997). The MS SDs "are rather more circumstantial than those of the Folio"; taken together, they indicate "that we are here dealing with an actual stage version and not a closet transcript"; in addition, the MS contains a list of dramatis personae: the entries indicate "a careful consideration of the actual roles involved" (Evans 1942).

Julius Caesar's Revenge. See *Caesar and Pompey, or Caesar's Revenge.*

July and Julian. Anonymous. Acted 1559–71 (Potter 2002b) at undetermined venue. Prologue refers to performance by "children at a time of myrth," apparently before an audience of schoolboys. Performed "probably by a schoolmaster and his boys in or near London . . . perhaps Paul's Boys" (*DTRB* 1984).

Washington, Folger, MS V.a.159; *A New Comedy of July and Julian*; no author named; argument; prologue and epilogue (by Wilkin); some additions/alterations; four acts and separate scenes; a five-act division may have been intended. First edited by Dawson & Brown 1955.

"That the play is in a general way an imitation of Roman comedy is apparent"; "the plot of the clever servant conspiring with his young master to marry a bondwoman is common to several of the comedies of Terence and Plautus" (Dawson & Brown). At the same time the "school dramatist uses his medium to engage with pedagogical debate in general and with gender stereotypes in particular" (Potter 2008).

Juno in Arcadia. See *Time's Distractions*.

Juno's Pastoral. See *Time's Distractions*.

Jupiter and Io. Thomas Heywood. ?Acted 1630s. A short dramatic entertainment possibly intended for private performance. The address to the reader calls this "stage-poetry." Possibly written for inclusion in *The Ages* (Clark 1931).

SR 29 August 1635. O 1637 *Pleasant Dialogues and Dramas*, wherein the table of contents calls it *A Drama from Ovid, called Jupiter and Io*; "never before published," according to the address to the reader; argument; not divided. Some detailed SDs: *"A noise of thunder. Enter* Jupiter *in his glory, his trisull* [epithet of lightning or thunderbolt] *in his hand burning; at sight of whom they stand afrighted."* Special effects include *"a great damp* [i.e., fog] *ariseth,"* presumably by the release of smoke through a trap. In addition to the SDs, *Jupiter and Io* also uses speech headings (Johnson 2003).

Fleay 1891 speculates that *Jupiter and Io* was part of *"Five Plays in One*, acted at the Rose 1597"; other plays in the group may include *Amphrisa, or the Forsaken Shepherdess* and *Apollo and Daphne*; "[i]n the 1598 inventory [of Henslowe] is an Argus' head. Such a property is needed in *Jupiter and Io*, but in no other play I know of." "There is . . . a good deal to be said for Fleay's view of its being a Heywood play"; "as Fleay points out, the Argus' head mentioned in the Admiral's inventories . . . is required for no known play except the short piece of *Jupiter and Io*" (Greg 1904–08). Chambers 1923 seems sympathetic to Fleay and Greg's opinion.

The Just General, A Tragicomedy. Cosmo Manuche. ?Acted late 1651 or early 1652 at undetermined venue. The play has "obvious stageability" (Aggeler 1978). "Manuche's works may well have been performed at Castle Ashby, [third earl of] Northampton's home" (Clare 2002); Manuche dedicates the play to him. "Castle Ashby offers at least two potential theaters: the Great Hall, and the central bays and gallery of the south wall of the courtyard, in front of the screen and inside and above the screen building" (Nelles 1990). Manuche's play may also have been performed at Northampton's London residence, Canonbury House, Islington (Wolf 1983). Like Manuche's other plays, this one supports the royalist cause; the prologue for the stage "concludes with a bold attack upon the Puritans" (Phelps 1979); "there would seem to be implicit parallels with events in England on the very eve of the Rebellion" (Aggeler). In this tragicomedy "we are whisked away to far-off Sicily, but the fact is that Manuche never really allows us to forget the England of his day" (Randall 1995). The title is included in Kirkman's 1661 catalogue.

SR 29 November 1651. Q 1652 prologue for the stage and prologue for the reader; epilogue for stage and epilogue for reader; list of characters; five acts. Scores of detailed SDs: "*The King puts one hand in his pocket as for letters, & with t'other takes off his false beard.*" Another direction suggests that the stage is draped, in keeping with the dramatic action: "*Enter upon a black stage.*"

The prologue for the stage consists of a dialogue between Prologue and Critic, the latter of whom caustically describes those who attend theatrical performances: "The play being done, they on each other look / To read in one another's faces how it took. / None daring (though suppos'd valiant) for to say / It was well acted, or 'tis a good play." The plot probably has relevance for the political and military situation *c.* 1651: "The play may well refer to some episode in the royal army, in which both Manuche and his patron Northumberland served" (Potter 1981).

The Just Italian. William Davenant. Licensed for acting 2 October 1629 (Adams 1917, Edmond 1987). "Lately presented" by the King's Men at the [second] Blackfriars, according to the Q TP. "*The Just Italian* played to bare benches" (Gurr 1988a). (The title is oxymoronic [Wiggins 2000].)

SR 10 January 1630; transferred 31 October 1646; 19 August 1667. Q 1630 no author named on the TP but Davenant signs the dedication; list of characters; five acts and first scenes. F 1673 *The Works*; "now published out of the authors originall copies"; *The Just Italian, A Tragicomedy.*

Davenant's address (in Q and F) to the Earl of Dorset praises him for rescuing a play that had failed onstage: "The uncivill ignorance of the people, had depriv'd this humble worke of life; but that your lordships approbation, stept in, to succour it." Thomas Carew contributes a prefatory poem to Q that decries detractors and notes with disapproval the success of Red Bull plays at the Phoenix: "they'le still slight / All that exceeds Red Bull, and Cockpit flight. / These are the men in crowded heapes that throng / To that adulterate stage, where not a tong / Of th'untun'd kennell, can a line repeat / Of serious sense: but like lips, meet like meat; / Whilst the true brood of actors, that alone / Keepe naturall unstrayn'd action in her throne / Behold their benches [at Blackfriars] bare, though they rehearse / The tearser *Beaumonts* or great *Johnsons* verse." Carew implies that "the dramatic styles of the previous age tended to be regarded as unfashionable and barbarous" (Neill 1978). "This denigration of audience taste was an attempt to claim for Davenant the twin attributes of exclusiveness and modernity" (McLuskie 1981). In a similar vein the prefatory poem by William Hopkins castigates unsophisticated playgoers: "Hence, giddy fooles; run to the noyse they make / At Paris-garden [i.e., the Swan]; or your selves betake / To the new motion, the fine puppet playes, / And there adore." Such prefatory material suggests that the play fared poorly in performance.

K

The Kentish Fair, or The Parliament Sold to Their Best Worth. ?Roger L'Estrange. Written 31 May 1648 and possibly acted shortly thereafter: it "may have been performed [at an inn or market], but if so it was as a crude sort of skit. Certain features of the play, though, are dramatically notable. The inclusion of women among the cast of rebels is of particular interest" (Woodson 1984).

SR none. Published 8 June 1648 (Raymond 1996). O 1648 list of characters; the cryer's opening speech functions as a prologue; his closing speech functions as an epilogue; not divided. Simple SDs: "*Mrs.* Webster *and Mrs.* Maine, *with pistols and swords.*"

The play's "most serious purpose was to galvanize opposition to Parliament's army throughout Kent" (Woodson): e.g., "Then let the rebels, and their *Fairfax* know, / That they must fall, for fate will have it so: / Wee have begun to rout them."

The Killing of the Children. Anonymous; probably written by John Parfre (Baker & Murphy 1967). Acted ?1512 (Baker et al. 1982) at undetermined venue; associated with East Anglia. The play consists of two actions: the Massacre of the Innocents and the presentation of the infant Jesus in the temple. May have been performed on the feast of the Holy Innocents, 28 December, and the feast of the Purification, 2 February. Probably performed by a traveling company. "[C]ould have been performed under almost any circumstances, in a market square, or a broad street, or green" (Baker et al.). An instance of "place-and-scaffold staging" (Grantley 2007, Twycross 2008). "This required a single playing-space, which might be outdoors or indoors. Those outdoors might be fixed gameplaces recurrently used for performances and other entertainments too. East Anglia, which had a lively dramatic tradition of saints' plays and moralities that use this form of staging, had a number" (Cooper 2010). "Whether the theatrical career of *The Killing of the Children* extended into Chelmsford, Essex, during the third quarter of the sixteenth century, as seems to have been the case with the other Digby plays, remains an intriguing possibility" (Coldewey 1993).

Oxford, Bodleian, MS Digby 133, fols. 146–57, ed. Baker et al.; *Candlemas Day and the Killing of the Children of Israel*; "John Parfre [?scribe or author] ded wryte this booke"; the date 1512 is inscribed in a different hand from that of the text; prologue by Poeta, who also speaks the epilogue and who "could possibly be female" (Schneider 2011); dramatis personae; divided into "two relatively separate dramatic sequences" (Grantley 2004). "Dance is called for after" the play (Baskervill 1929): "an elaborate masque of virgins and minstrels who 'shewe some sport and plesure, these people to solas'" (Wright 1928). The play "is the second part of a lost Nativity group in honour of St. Anne" (Twycross). First edited by Hawkins 1773, then Sharp 1835, then Furnivall 1882.

King Ahasuerus and Queen Esther. Anonymous. A droll based on the Book of Esther and performed in the 1640s and 50s. It "may have been used originally in puppet shows" (Harbage 1936), but "[i]t is likelier that the ambitious but ignorant author was here essaying sacred drama, perhaps with a faint recollection of the mystery plays" (Elson 1932). There is no connection with *Godly Queen Hester,* the early sixteenth-century interlude.

Published in *2 The Wits, or Sport upon Sport* (Q and O 1673), which gives as venues of performance fairs, halls, taverns, and "mountebancks stages at Charing Cross, Lincolns-Inn-Fields, and other places"; list of characters. Kirkman, on the TP of *2 The Wits,* says that the drolls were "written I know not when, by several persons, I know not who"; however, his preface reports that Robert Cox "was not only the principal actor, but also the contriver and author of most of these farces." Kirkman's attribution is "probable" (Holland 2007).

A King and No King. Francis Beaumont and John Fletcher. "Most scholars give Beaumont the larger share of the composition" (Finkelpearl 1990). Licensed for acting 1611 (Bliss 2004). Acted by the King's Men at the [first] Globe, according to the Q1 TP; "it is likely that the play was performed at both" the Globe and Blackfriars in its first year (Bliss). Performed at Whitehall, before the king, 26 December 1611 (Revels Account); at court, winter 1612–13 "as part of the celebration of the marriage of Princess Elizabeth and the Elector Palatine" (Lesser 2002); payment to John Heminges dated 20 May 1613. A SD mentions Will Adkinson, "apparently an actor" (Nungezer 1929). Joseph Taylor, having joined the King's Men in 1619 played Arbaces in revivals (Gurr 2004c). Revived at the Blackfriars, according to the Q2 TP, "sometime between 1619 and 1625" (Graves 1978). Revived at the Whitehall Cockpit-in-Court, 10 February 1631 (Teague 2009); and at Hampton Court, probably in the Great Chamber, 10 January 1637 (Adams 1917). An illegal performance was under way on 5 or 6 October 1647 at the Salisbury Court playhouse when it was raided: "The sheriffs of the City of London with their officers went thither, and found a great number of people; some young lords, and other eminent persons; and the men and women with the boxes, (that took monies) fled. The sheriffs brought away Tim Reade the Foole, and the people cryed out for their monies, but slunke away like a company of drowned mice without it" (Henry Walker, *Perfect Occurrences,* [1647–49]).

SR 7 August 1618; transferred 1 March 1628; 29 May 1638; 25 January 1639. Q1 1619 the TP names B&F; five acts and first scenes. This TP features a woodcut depicting a richly dressed man in a landscape; a hand that extends out of a cloud either places a crown on his head or removes it; it is not clear "whether Arbaces has just dropped the royal scepter or is about to pick it up. In leaving the viewer unable to decide whether the king is being anointed or deposed, the woodcut enacts the play's own transformation of Arbaces's sovereignty from absolute to mixed, allegorically embodying the play's final moments" (Lesser). However, "although the woodcut neatly emblematizes the play's central issue, it probably has no relation to the play in performance" (Foakes 1985). Q2 1625 "now the second time printed, according to the true copie"; "acted at the Blacke-Fryars." "Q2 supplies some [SDs] lacking in Q1, and in many instances where both Q1 and Q2 give directions the Q2 version is fuller or more accurately placed" (Turner 1963). Q3 1631 "now the third time printed"; adds "the personated persons," an "indication of [Q3's] constitution as a readerly text" (Masten 2002). Q4 1639 "now the fourth time printed." Q5 1655 "now the fifth time printed." Q6 1661 "now the fourth time [*sic*] printed." Q7 1676. B&F F2 1679 *Fifty Comedies and Tragedies*; "published by the authors original copies, the songs to each play being added"; list of characters. The publication history suggests that the play was "much more popular in [its] own day than in ours" (Bruster 2004).

The play conflates sexuality and politics: "the King's desire for his sister is not identified with the tyrant's conventional lust (she reciprocates his feelings), but instead provides a kind of worst-case scenario for testing that logical corollary of absolutist theory which proposes that for a ruler, desire is its own legitimating principle. Thus power creates legality and exonerates from blame" (Clark 1994).

King Charles I Basely Butchered. See *The Famous Tragedy of King Charles I.*

King Darius. Anonymous. Acted 1565 (*DTRB* 1984) at undetermined venue. Perhaps acted by a nobleman's troupe of actors (White 1993b). "Six persons may easily play it"; twenty-one roles are listed but the doubling is not specified. "At least seven [actors] appear on stage together in one scene" (Bevington 1962).

SR *c.* October 1565. Q 1565 A *Pretty New Interlude, Both Pithy and Pleasant, of the Story of King Darius*; RT *The Story of King Darius*; list of characters on the TP; speech by Prolocutor (a rare term also used in Bale's plays and in "the second version of the Norwich Grocers' play" [Butler 2004f]); Constancy gives the final speech followed by a prayer for Queen Elizabeth; not divided. Q2 1577.

King Darius is "modelled on Bale's anti-Catholic plays" (Craik 1958). The play "seeks to compound a conventional morality with two biblical incidents and thereby to create a drama of anti-Catholic polemic" (Wickham 1981). As in numerous other interludes, biblical characters share the stage with abstractions.

King David and Fair Bethsabe. See *David and Bethsabe.*

King Henry VIII (Shakespeare). See *Henry VIII.*

King Johan. See *King John* (John Bale).

King John, The A-version of. John Bale. "Prepared sometime in mid to late 1537" and "used for a series of performances up to early 1539" (Leininger 2002) "in the middle of the Henrician Reformation" (Womack 1992). Possibly acted *c.* 8 September 1538 when "Bale and his fellows" were paid 40 shillings by Thomas

Cromwell. Probably performed before the Canterbury residence of Archbishop Cranmer, December 1538 (White 1993b); Bale received payment 31 January 1539. "[T]he fact that Bale's company was sponsored by Thomas Cromwell suggests the probability that it may have been taken on tour very deliberately to play to a wider and lower-class audience" (Dillon 2008). Evidence of doubling suggests that Bale worked with professional actors (Happé 1985–86). "[C]ould be acted by five players" (Streitberger 2009).

San Marino, CA, Huntington, MS HM 3, fols. 1–22, ed. Pafford & Greg 1931; ed. Happé 1985–86; "the only one of Bale's extant plays that lacks a prologue" (Pafford & Greg); originally conceived as a two-part play; evidence of revision. "Doubling was necessitated by the small size of itinerant companies, but is sometimes used creatively to suggest connections between characters, most notably in Bale's" play (Grantley 2007). The Vices "assume historical roles: Sedition becomes Stephen Langton, the monks' candidate for the archbishopric of Canterbury; Private Wealth becomes Pandulphus, the papal legate; and Dissimulation assumes the role of John's alleged murderer, the Cistercian monk Simon of Swynsett" (Kendall 1986). The king would have been equipped with "formal accoutrements including crown, spurs and a sword. There is also extensive use of clerical and monastic garb, most of it with polemical intent" (Happé). "[C]hurch and civil ceremonies become the actions through which the vice chracters degrade the King" (Westfall 1990). MS first edited by Collier 1838.

"Bale's mind hovers ambivalently between the personified abstraction of the old allegorical drama and the literal concreteness of history" (Creeth 1966). The play "turns its back on the fanciful historicism of Geoffrey [of Monmouth] and makes its audience *aware* of itself as a morality-play-history hybrid by showing where literature and history intersect" (Kamps 1996). Bale's "innovation was to couch his apology for the Reformation in an historical figure" (Potter 1975); the play "demonstrates the adaptability of the morality to the Reformation" (Cohen 1985). "Cromwell supported a performance of *King Johan* by Bale's players in 1538 because an important source for the text is a passage in Tyndale's 1528 *Obedience of a Christian Man* portraying the medieval King John as a royal martyr to unbridled papal power. Like Tyndale, Bale presented his historical exemplum without ambiguity or irony" (Sessions 2002). *King John* forms "almost a model of the political use of the stage" (Westfall 2004). It is "arguably the first English history play of all" (Womack).

King John, The B-version of. John Bale. "[P]repared after 1558" (Leininger 2002). Acted *c.* 1560–61 (White 1993b) at undetermined venue. Apparently intended for performance before Queen Elizabeth at Ipswich Hall, 5–11 August 1561; possibly performed by a company led by Peter Moone.

San Marino, CA, Huntington, MS HM 3, fols. 23–35, ed. Pafford & Greg 1931; ed. Happé 1985–86; divided into two "actus," also referred to as "playes." The text is a composite of the A-version of 1537–39, revisions of 1547–53, and new writing after 1558. "When Bale revised the play he put his corrections on to A's pages, and added the two separate leaves (pages 23 and 26); but after page 38 his revisions became so extensive that he made a fair copy of the revised ending on quarto leaves with a watermark which has been read as 1558" (Happé). "Bale revised the play extensively several times after 1538 to tailor it to new circumstances" (Fox 1989). For Bale "the Reformation was not the temporary cause of England's misfortunes [as it was in Udall's *Respublica*], but the permanent solution to them" (Potter 1975). Near the end of his life Bale praised Queen "Elizabeth in a revised ending to *King John*" (King 2004).

"The purpose of this revision was complex. [Bale] elaborated the Anti-Catholic material, perhaps as a by-product of his extensive reading for the prose tracts he composed at the time. . . . He also shows interest in elaborating the role of the Vice whose popularity increased between 1538 and 1558" (Happé).

King John. Anonymous. See *The Troublesome Reign of King John*.

King John. William Shakespeare. Acted 1595–96 (Braunmuller 1989). Probably first performed by the Lord Chamberlain's Men at the Theater (Hosley 1979). Praised by Francis Meres in *Palladis Tamia* (SR 7 September 1598), where it is called a tragedy. John Sincler probably played Falconbridge (Gurr 2004c), "the first major non-historical character to appear in a Shakespeare history play, and his story has the suggestiveness of a legend" (Womack 1992). Possibly revived in 1610 (Gurr) and 1621–22 (Taylor 1993b).

SR not entered on 8 November 1623: "It doubtless passed as identical with *The Troublesome Reign of King John*" already in print (Greg 1939); transferred ?4 August 1626 Paviers right in Shakesperes *plaies*; ?19 June 1627 widow of Isaac Jaggard . . . her *parte* in Shackspheere *playes*; 1 July 1637 Shakespeares *workes* their Part; 6 August 1674; 21 August 1683. F1 1623 *Comedies, Histories, & Tragedies*; three issues; "published according to the true originall copies"; *The Life and Death of King John*; five acts and separate scenes but the divisions are "anomalous" (King 1992a). "Today, John's reign is remembered for the Magna Carta and the adventures of Robin Hood. Both concern resistance to royal tyranny, by the aristocracy and the lower class, respectively. Though both stories were available in the 1590s, neither appears in the play. The lords rebel late in the action, but the issue of the balance of power between King and nobility remains secondary" (Cohen 1997). Shakespeare "returns to a diffuse, episodic structure to depict a world where no principle of historical causation can be discovered. Here, as in the Henry VI plays, no one has an undisputed right to the English throne, and no conflict is fully resolved. Battles end in stalemates, alliances are no sooner made than broken, and the conflict between John's power and Arthur's right is never really resolved" (Rackin 1990). F2 1632 "the second impression"; three issues. F3 1663 "the third impression"; reissued 1664 with seven additional plays. F4 1685 "the fourth edition"; two issues.

The play may post-date the anonymous *Troublesome Reign of King John* (Forker 2010): Shakespeare's play was perhaps "the Chamberlain's response to the performance of *The Troublesome Reign of King John* at the Swan" (Knutson 2001b). However, Honigmann 1954, Beaurline 1990, and Boyd 1995 argue that Shakespeare's play was written first. Whichever play preceded the other, Shakespeare avoids a simplistic treatment of the king: "in its lack of clear endorsement of the extreme Protestant vindication of John espoused by Foxe and other writers, it offers instead a balanced, dual view of a complex monarch as both proto-Protestant victim of Rome's machinations and as a weak, selfishly motivated ruler" (Bevington 2002a). "The prevailing fear of foreign invasion and civil unrest would have been only too well understood by an audience of Shakespeare's day" (Cousin 1994).

King John and Matilda, A Tragedy. Robert Davenport. Acted 1628–29 (Davis 1980), *c.* 1630 (Astington 2010), or *c.* 1628–34 (*JCS*). "With great applause by" Queen Henrietta Maria's Men at the Phoenix, according to the Q1 TP. Michael Bowyer played King John; Richard Perkins, "whose action gave grace to the play," Fitzwater; Anthony Turner, Old Lord Bruce; John Sumner, Young Bruce; Mr. Jackson, Chester; Christopher Goad, Oxford; John Young, Leicester; Hugh Clark, Hubert; William Allen, Pandolph; William Sherlock, "who performed excellently well," Brand, according to "The Names of the Persons in the Play, and of the Actors that first acted it on the stage, and often before their Majesties." The cast list "must date from before 1634" (Kathman 2005). "The cast [Andrew] Pennycuicke presents with his edition seems rather careless and one wonders how much to rely upon it" (Bentley 1984). Performed also at court shortly after commercial-playhouse performance. "It past the stage with generall applause," according to the dedication. In playlist of Beeston's Boys 10 August 1639.

SR none. Q1 1655 list of characters; detailed description of two pantomimes/dumb shows; a song concludes the play; five acts. Violence and the threat of violence fill the play: e.g., "*Enter the* Queene, *dragging in* Matilda, *her haire loose, and face bloody.*" Matilda dies when she kisses a "poyson'd glove" given her by Brand. Later "*Enter to the king and lords, the Lady* Abbess, *ushering* Matilda's *herse, born by Virgins, this motto fastned unto it*—To Piety and Chastity." Q2 1662. The play is "in general a fairly close imitation of the tragedy of Matilda as it appears" in *The Death of Robert, Earl of Huntingdon* (Meagher 1965). Davenport's play "is the first English history to give the king's name in the title equal weight with that of the lady he loves" (Barton 1977).

In the dedication Andrew Pennycuicke reports that he was "the last that acted Matilda" [for Beeston's Boys]. "If he did play Matilda, Pennycuicke's statement implies that he did not do so in the original production" (Kathman). He also writes that although the printed play may not appear "in its ancient and full glory," it nevertheless has a claim on the reader: "yet it comes drest; first, with an humble regard to your honour, and then a confidence of its naked worth." "Figuring the printed text as an unclothed body captures the operative difference in all of these plays between the 'full glory' of performance and the embarrassing nakedness of print" (Straznicky 1995).

King Lear and His Three Daughters. William Shakespeare. Acted 1605 (Taylor 1993a) by the King's Men "playing usually" at the [first] Globe, according to the Q1 TP. "Played before" the king at Whitehall on St. Stephen's night, 26 December 1606, according to the SR entry and the Q1 TP. Richard Burbage "almost certainly" played Lear at the Globe (Gurr 2004c). Robert Armin played the Fool (Hornback 2009b): the play's setting allowed Armin "for the first time in the extant repertoire, to don the traditional motley and cockscomb of medieval tradition" (Wiles 1987). Cordelia was played "by one of the three talented boys required to play the three daughters, possibly by the youngest of the group" (Astington 2010). At Christmastide 1609–10 "King Lere" was performed by Sir Richard Cholmeley's players at the home of Sir John Yorke, Gowthwaite Hall in Yorkshire; although Shakespeareans have tended to assume that this record refers to Shakespeare's play (Sisson 1942, Greenfield 2009), it "equally might have been" a performance of *King Leir* (Egan 2006a). "There are strong reasons for believing that the play . . . was the anonymous *King Leir*" (Arrell 2012).

 SR 26 November 1607 William Shakespeare *his "historye of Kinge Lear"*; transferred ?4 August 1626 Paviers right in Shakesperes *plaies*; ?19 June 1627 widow of Isaac Jaggard . . . her parte in Shackspheere *playes*; 1 July 1637 Shakespeares *workes* their Part; 21 May 1639; 6 August 1674; 21 August 1683. Q1 the so-called "Pied Bull" Q; probably printed in December and January of 1607–08 (Blayney 1982); *William Shakespeare: His True Chronicle History of the Life and Death of King Lear and His Three Daughters, with the Unfortunate Life of Edgar, Son and Heir to the Earl of Gloucester, and His Sullen and Assumed Humor of Tom of Bedlam*; RT *The History of King Lear*; not divided. The TP makes it look "very much as if the publisher was anxious to challenge *Leir* by claiming simultaneously that the new play was like the old one, and superior to it" (Foakes 1997).

 The SDs "tend to be descriptive" (Halio 1994a). Lear probably entered "from the central opening," a manifestation of "power and authority" (Ichikawa 2002), though Fitzpatrick 2011 believes that there were only two entry-points onto the stage. "The map there," says Lear as he divides his kingdom in three parts. Staging calls for Kent to be placed in the stocks, the fate of virtuous characters in the moral interludes (Kiefer 2003). The hovel of Poor Tom may have been represented by a central opening in the tiring-house wall (Gurr & Ichikawa 2000). Special effects include the storm on the heath, with appropriate sound. "In outdoor playhouses . . . in addition to 'tempestuous' drums, a 'bullet,' i.e., a cannonball, was 'rolled' along a sheet of metal or a wooden trough [to simulate thunder]" (White 2007). Staged violence includes the horrific blinding of Gloucester and the stabbing of Cornwall's servant in the back by Regan as he tries to prevent that blinding: "*Shee takes a sword and runs at him behind.*" Music helps in healing the king's wits; the Doctor says, "louder the musicke there." The music "must be asumed to be an agent in his recovery" (Lindley 2006). At the close "the challenging and answering trumpets are used with immense effect when Edgar, incognito, comes to avenge his own wrongs and his father's" (Ogilvie 1927). The play's most poignant moment is the final entry of Lear "*with Cordelia in his armes.*" Q2 1619 printed by William Jaggard for Thomas Pavier and falsely dated 1608; "some evidence points to its use in Jaggard's shop during the printing of F *Lear*" (Halio). F1 1623 *Comedies, Histories, & Tragedies*; three issues; "published according to the true originall copies"; *The Tragedy of King Lear*; five acts and separate scenes. "[O]ne entire Q scene (4.3) is missing from F, the crucially important last lines of the play are spoken by Albany in Q and by Edgar in F, and the two plays differ significantly in their titles" (Weis 2010). F1 omits the mock-trial of Q1; differences in the characterizations of Lear, Cordelia, and Gonerill are "discernible and important" (Halio); the Fool changes, too, becoming "a sweetly pathetic figure" (Hornback 2009b). (The texts of Q1, Q2, and F1 are all available in a facsimile edition prepared by Warren 1989a; his edition presents parallel-texts of Q1 and F1; Weis 2010 presents modernized texts of Q1 and F1 on facing pages.) Q1 apparently represents an early draft by Shakespeare, F1 his substantial revision of that draft (Warren 1978), accomplished *c.* 1608–11 (Urkowitz 1980); Q1 represents "an almost final draft," F1 "a practical working script" (Urkowitz 1986). The treatment of Cordelia's army, for example, differs; F omits reference to the invasion of England by the French. "We may suppose that scenes depicting the successful invasion of Britain by a French army in a play which touched directly on matters of current political debate would have been unwelcome to James" (Clare 1999). Shakespeare may well have revised his play: "F is a careful, coherent, consistent revision of Q, and Shakespeare is much the most likely candidate for the changes" (Kinney 2009b). But "the playbook on which F1 is based could have been modified at any time between 1606 and 1623" (Knowles 2008). F2 1632 "the second impression"; three issues. Q3 1655 "the first [text] to bear a woman's name in its imprint, that of Jane Bell" (Murphy 2003). F3 1663 "the third impression"; reissued 1664 with seven additional plays. F4 1685 "the fourth edition"; two issues.

"*King Lear* was the most explicitly loyal of all the plays Shakespeare wrote for the company's royal patron in the Jacobean period, even more than the acknowledgment of James's royal lineage in *Macbeth*. It was designed to uphold, at least on the face of it, James's policy of uniting his kingdoms by its demonstration of the effects of a divided kingdom" (Gurr 2004c). However, the play may be construed as critical of King James: "the flattering, cadging courtiers and upstarts were seen at the time as . . . like James's expensive and much-resented Scottish favourites" (Heinemann 2003).

King Leir and His Three Daughters. Anonymous; "the play does not clearly recall the style of any one particular playwright from the period" (Stern 2002). Possibly staged before 1588 (Knutson 2009b). Performed *c.* 1590 (Halio 2005). Probably the play acted 6 and 8 April 1594 by the combined Queen's and Earl of Sussex's Men, according to Henslowe's *Diary,* at the Rose (Michie 1991). Probably performed by the Queen's Men (McMillin & MacLean 1998). The 1605 TP claims that the play has been "divers and sundry times lately acted," suggesting performance shortly before Shakespeare's *Lear*; this claim "was probably intended to lead the public to suppose that it was none other than Shakespeare's *King Lear,* the recent popularity of which upon the stage no doubt suggested the publication or republication of the earlier work" (Greg 1907a). It is also possible, however, that the TP claim is true, that the play had been performed by a touring company, the re-formed Queen's Men, "which performed until 1603" (Ioppolo 2005). Probably performed by Richard Cholmeley's players at the home of John Yorke, Gowthwaite Hall in Yorkshire, Christmas season 1609–10 (Egan 2006a, Arrell 2012).

SR 14 May 1594 *The moste famous Chronicle historye of Leire kinge of England and his Three Daughters* (if the play was printed at this time, no copy has survived); transferred 8 May 1605 *the Tragecall historie of kinge Leir and his Three Daughters &c. As it was latelie Acted*; 29 June 1624 *Leire and his daughters*; 22 April 1640 *Leire and his 3 daughters*; 4 April 1655 *The tragicall history of King Leire, & his 3 daughters.* Q 1605 *The True Chronicle History of King Leir and His Three Daughters, Gonorill, Ragan, and Cordella*; RT *The History of King Leir and His Three Daughters*; no author named; not formally divided despite the designation "Actus 1," but the scenes "can easily be delineated by the fact that every new scene follows a cleared stage that is consistently marked by '*Exit*' or '*Exeunt*'" (Ioppolo 2005). Thunder and lightning, a sign of divine watchfulness, accompany a man's change of heart: sent to kill Leir, the Messenger acknowledges that Leir's daughters have sent him to murder the king. Similarly, when the good counselor Perillus argues that the perpetrator of crime will surely suffer everlasting torments, a SD reads, "*It thunders,*" and the guilty Messenger "quakes and lets fall the dagger next to Perillus." Dialogue amplifies the SDs: when Ragan receives a letter, "*She reads the letter, frownes and stamps.*" The Messenger says, "See how she knits her brow, and bytes her lips, / And stamps, and makes a dumb shewe of disdayne."

"Shakespeare's *Lear* shows in nearly a hundred significant details a close familiarity with the old play [*King Leir*] as it exists in the 1605 edition" (Knowles 2002). At the same time, "Shakespeare not only introduced a major second plot, inspired by the misadventures of the Paphlagonian King in Sidney's *Arcadia*; he also introduced several new characters and episodes that *King Leir* lacks" (Halio 2005). *King Leir* "belongs to the tradition of a Christianized medieval England," *King Lear* "to the vanished world of pagan antiquity" (Kiefer 2012).

King Solomon's Wisdom. Anonymous. This droll, which "may have been used originally in puppet shows" (Harbage 1936), was performed in the 1640s and 50s. "This is a purely Biblical playlet, taken from the story of Solomon's judgment in *1 Kings*, chap. 3" (Elson 1932).

Published in *2 The Wits, or Sport upon Sport* (Q and O 1673), which gives as venues of performance fairs, halls, taverns, and "mountebancks stages at Charing Cross, Lincolns-Inn-Fields, and other places"; list of characters. Kirkman, on the TP of 2 *The Wits*, reports that the drolls were "written I know not when, by several persons, I know not who." But his preface indicates that Robert Cox "was not only the principal actor, but also the contriver and author of most of these farces." Kirkman's attribution is "probable" (Holland 2007).

A Knack to Know a Knave. Anonymous, but the play exhibits the "fingerprints" of Robert Wilson (Knutson 2009b); Robert Greene may have contributed to the play (Born 1971). Acted 10 June 1592, according to Henslowe's *Diary*, by Lord Strange's Men at the Rose. The play was "probably written with the Rose's new stage specifically in mind" (Gurr 2009c). Henslowe records performances in 1592: 10, 15, 22 June; 31 December. In 1593: 3, 14, 24 January. The Q TP takes the unusual step of singling out performances by two actors: "Newlie set foorth, as it hath sundrie tymes bene played by Ed[ward] Allen and his companie. With [Will] Kemps applauded merrimentes of the men of Goteham, in receiving the king into Goteham"; "the references are clearly to Strange's men" (McMillin 1992). "Kemp's section is completely self-contained" (Wiles 1987); Kemp "likely took the conventional anti-puritan part of Jeffrey the cobbler, who is the misterming mayor of Gotham" (Hornback 2009b). Alleyn played the role of King Edgar (Cerasano 2004a). "Edward Alleyn and William Kempe, two of the most famous actors of the 1590s, here serve to authorize the playtext an anonymous playwright has produced. This ironic reversal finds its modern equivalent in the marketing of spin-off novels based on recent box-office hits which appeal to the potential customer with a picture of the star actor(s) or actress(es) on the front cover" (Erne 2003a). Alleyn "is the only player whose personal name is used to identify an early modern acting company on the title page of a printed play" (Marino 2011). The comedy "can be played by eleven men and one or two boys" (McMillin 1991).

SR 7 January 1594. Q 1594 *A Most Pleasant and Merry New Comedy Entitled A Knack to Know a Knave*; no author named; RT *A Merry Knack to Know a Knave*; not divided. "Dunston calls for Asmoroth to ascend and orders him to 'follow me invisible,'" indicating the use of a special garment; Henslowe "purchased 'a robe for to goo invisible'" (Rhodes 1976). Later Dunston "brings Alfrida and Ethenwald before the king"; a SD, "*here enter Alfrida disguised with the devil,*" indicates "that the devil appears although no mention is made of him"; "presumably Asmoroth was invisible to everyone except the magician and, of course, the audience" (Rhodes). "A number of essential stage directions are missing" (Proudfoot 1963). The play was "published in what appears to be an abridged form" (McMillin).

Despite having been staged in the early 1590s and despite its dependence upon historical materials, the play contains "traces" of the moral interludes: "The

Devil is brought into the action to claim the soul of the dying Bailiff of Hexam, and later to play the part of a human being; and an allegorical character, Honesty, serves as the connecting link between the scenes of the two plots" (Thompson 1910). The play is "an estates comedy featuring the knavery of familiar provincial types: a farmer, a nobleman, and a parish clergyman" (White 2008). The attention of the audience shuttles "back and forward between different social groups"; "our attention continually moves between Cuthbert Cutpurse, Walter the usurious farmer, John the Precise who brings the word of God into disrepute, Philarchus the jumped-up courtier who curries favour with the commons, and King Edgar who seeks to debauch the virtuous Alfrida" (Hunter 1987). In this and the plays of Robert Wilson, "the devilish jollity of figures of supernatural or allegorical evil gave way to the actual wickedness of dishonest tradesmen, grasping landlords, and corrupt usurers, and the eternal torment of hell was supplanted by gruesomely physical punishments in this world" (Wiggins 2000).

A Knack to Know an Honest Man. Anonymous. Acted 22 [possibly an error for 23] October 1594, according to Henslowe, by the Lord Admiral's Men at the Rose; "sundrie times plaied about the Citie of London," according to the TP. The play was "probably written with the Rose's new stage specifically in mind" (Gurr 2009c). Henslowe records the following performances in 1594: 22 [?23], 29 October; 1, 7, 21, 29 November; 13 December. In 1595: 7, 13 January; 6, 26 February; 10 March; 23 April; 5 May; 9, 21 June; 25 August; 18 September. In 1596: 7 January; 16 April; 3 November. "Few plays had either as long or as persistent a run as this" (Vocht 1910). "The remarkable performance records of this comedy . . . must have owed a lot to [Edward] Alleyn" (Read 1994). Dekker and Middleton allude to the play in *The Roaring Girl* (1611), suggesting that *Knack* was known to their playgoers.

SR 26 November 1595 *The most Rare and plesaunt historie of A knack to knowe an honest man.* Q 1596 *A Pleasant Conceited Comedy Called A Knack to Know an Honest Man*; no author named; not divided. "The text of the *Honest Man* is in a terrible state of confusion" (Vocht). Staging includes spectacle: a character says, "This is the feastivall of holy Marke, / Yond come the pompious shew"; the following SD, *"Enter the shew on the stage,"* suggests a "festive procession" (Mehl 1965).

A Knack to Know an Honest Man was "written seemingly in response to the anti-Puritan *A Knack to Know a Knave*" (Bevington 1968).

The Knave in Grain, New Vampt, A Comedy. J. D. [?John Davenport or ?John Day]. Original version acted *c.* 1625; revised version, *c.* 1632 (Bald & Brown 1960). "Acted at the [second] Fortune many dayes together with great applause," according to the TP, by the King's Revels Men; this is one of only two plays "identified on their title pages as having been performed at the Fortune" (Straznicky 2006b). The lost original version was presumably performed by one of the companies whose remnants formed the King's Revels Men in 1629. Possibly intended for performance in London, February 1655 (Rollins 1921): "a company of young Citts that met the last week to act a comedy, called *Knavery in all Trades*, but putting down their half crowns apiece the first meeting for a stock, and to engage each person to the performance of his part, the chief of them who was to act the *Knave in grain*, having his part studied before-hand, having taken about 30 s. of his fellow actors money, made an exit instead of an entrance, and so is gone to Holland" (*Mercurius Fumigosus*, 7–14 February 1655).

SR 18 June 1639 *The Knave in Graine or Jack Cottington*; transferred 22 October 1639 *A knave in graine new vampt*. Q 1640 *The Knave in Grain, New Vampt, A Witty Comedy*; HT *The Knave in Grain, or New Vampt*; author's initials on the TP; list of characters; five acts and first scenes. The absence of the name "Cottington" in the Q title may suggest that the play had been revised before publication, cutting the character: Edmund Gayton in *Pleasant Notes upon Don Quixot[e]* (1654) indicates that "there *was* a play about Cottington or Mull Sack, that it was popular, and, presumably that it included tavern scenes. . . . All this suggests *The Knave in Grain*" (*JCS*). "*Vampt*" means "revised" (*JCS*), but the words "do not mean that the piece had been revised" (Greg 1939).

The Knave in Grain "is generally agreed to be a Frankenstein's monster of a play, containing as it does at least two distinct plots incompletely revised into one whole by the expedient of giving the central character of both the same name"; one of these plots involves Holland's Leaguer, a notorious brothel (Steggle 2004a).

The Knight of Malta. John Fletcher, Philip Massinger, and Nathan Field (Hoy 1959). Acted 1616–18 (E&G 1976) by the King's Men at the second Blackfriars/second Globe. Principal actors were Richard Burbage, Nathan Field, Henry Condell, John Underwood, Richard Sharp, Robert Benfield, John Lowin, and Thomas Holcomb, according to F2. "The longest role in the play was prepared for a boy player" (Bentley 1984). In playlist of the King's Men 7 August 1641.

SR 4 September 1646 *Knights of Malta*; 30 January 1673 *Knights of Maltha*. B&F F1 1647 *Comedies and Tragedies*; "never printed before, and now published by the authours originall copies"; *The Knight of Malta*; five acts and separate scenes. The Knights of Malta were "a chivalrous order of Christian soldiers," but the play "consigns chivalry to the margins, deftly exposing it not only as irrelevant but also absurd" (Rose 1988). Sound effects indicate military conflict: "*A sea fight within, alarum*"; "*low alarmes*"; "*Drums a far off, A low march.*" SDs call for theatrical props: "*The scaffold set out and the staires*," as a character is prepared for execution. The scaffold may also have served, in another scene, to support an altar. The play employs "altars in scenes that highlight the ongoing metamorphosis of English church interiors after the Reformation and point[s] to the social impact of these changes" (Williamson 2009). B&F F2 1679 *Fifty Comedies and Tragedies*; "published by the authors original copies, the songs to each play being added"; list of characters; actors' names.

The Knight of the Burning Pestle. Francis Beaumont (this is "the only play of Beaumont's sole authorship that we have" [Hoy 1987a]). Acted 1607 (Zitner 1984) by the Children of the Queen's Revels at the second Blackfriars, where the company "played intermittently from their reorganization in 1600 until 1608" (Doebler 1967). "There are so many references to holiday festivities in the text that we might even postulate a Shrovetide or possibly Midsummer first performance" (Hattaway 2002). Walter Burre, the publisher, reports in Q1 that, when the play was first staged, the playgoers "for want of judgement, or not understanding the privy marke of ironie about it . . . utterly rejected it." The hostility was possibly occasioned by "an unforeseen number of the citizen class whose tastes were being satirised" (Lomax 1987); the play "shows a citizen Grocer and his wife being fooled by a sophisticated boy company at the Blackfriars into exposing their taste for *Don Quixote*-like feats of improbable valour" (Gurr 2009d). The role of Master Humphrey may have been played by Nathan Field after he joined the company in 1615–16 (Dutton 2003). Revived by Queen Henrietta Maria's Men at the Phoenix in 1635, according to the Q2 TP; and at St. James's Palace, 28 February 1636 (Adams 1917), in the Presence Chamber (Astington 1986). "By the 1630s, the theatrical world had apparently caught up to [Walter] Burre, for *The Knight* seems then to have been a stage success" (Lesser 2004). "[M]ay have been revived at the Cockpit in 1639 by the King and Queen's Young Company under William Beeston" (Hattaway). Performed by an unknown company at Skipton Castle, the West Riding of Yorkshire, seat of Henry Clifford's family, February 1636 (Greenfield 2009); "the hall is 28 feet wide by 50 feet long" (Palmer 2009b). In playlist of Beeston's Boys 10 August 1639.

SR no original; transferred 8 August 1661 *The Knight of the Bur[n]ing Pestle*, a merry comedy [ascribed to B&F]. Q1 1613 HT *The Famous History of the Knight of the Burning Pestle*; no author named; induction; epilogue; five acts and four interludes (though the term "interlude" does not appear in Q1). Q1 begins with an induction: a colloquy involving Prologue, George (a Citizen), his wife Nell, and Rafe. The epilogue consists of a brief colloquy between the Citizen and his Wife. The SDs give a sense of locale—"*Enter Rafe like a grocer in's shop, with two prentices reading Palmerin of England*"—and provide specifics: "*Enter Squire leading a man with a glasse of lotion in his hand, and the Dwarfe leading a woman, with diet-bread and drinke.*" "'[H]ouses' (or stage 'mansions') thrust out upon the stage may have been used for Rafe's shop or at least the locales associated with Venturewel, Merrythought, and Barbaroso" (Hattaway). Staging would probably have used "signs to mark locations, like shop signs on the streets outside the theater" (Thomson 2006). A character disguised as a ghost enters "'*his face mealed*' (presumably meaning whitened with flour)" (Thompson 2010). As well as music played between the acts, "we find inserted pieces of action or 'interludes'" (Hattaway). Q2 1635 "acted by her majesties servants at the private house in Drury Lane, 1635"; the TP names B&F; substitutes an address "To the readers of this comedy" in place of Walter Burre's dedicatory epistle; list of characters;

new prose prologue ("a speech transferred into this text from an earlier play by John Lyly [*Sappho and Phao*], which explains, in the only sentence it alters from its 1584 pre-text, that the 'authors intention' was not to satirize any particular subject" [Masten 1997]). "Whether this text was ever delivered at a performance is not known" (Schneider 2011). "It is unlikely that either Beaumont or Fletcher, who had both died many years before the publication of Q2, were responsible for either the Address or the Prologue" (Doebler 1967). Q3 dated 1635 but probably printed in the 1650s (Hoy 1966); the TP names both Beaumont (spelled Beamount) and Fletcher. B&F F2 1679 *Fifty Comedies and Tragedies*; "published by the authors original copies, the songs to each play being added"; list of characters. Following the closing of the theaters, part of the play was adapted for a droll entitled *The Encounter*, later published in *1 The Wits, or Sport upon Sport* (O 1662 [two issues] and 1672); the table of contents of *The Wits* erroneously claims that the droll derives from *The Humorous Lieutenant*. "The episode is short but complete, with amusing situations and dialogue and abundant action" (Elson 1932).

The play is "a direct parody of Thomas Heywood's *Four Prentices of London*" (Morris 1987), which is specifically cited in the dialogue. In the Q2 address "To the Readers of this Comedie," Beaumont's work is distinguished from that of trendy contemporaries: "the world is so nice [i.e., fastidious] in these our times, that for apparrell, there is no fashion; for musicke, which is a rare art, (though now slighted) no instrument; for diet, none but the French kickshoes that are delicate; and for playes, no invention but that which now runneth an invective way, touching some particular person, or else it is contemned before it is th[o] roughly understood. This is all that I have to say, that the author had no intent to wrong any one in this comedy, but as a merry passage, here and there interlaced it with delight, which hee hopes will please all, and be hurtfull to none." The play "is formally the most innovative play in Jacobean drama. It portrays a battle for possession of the stage between the child players, who had ostensibly been planning a satire on the current vogue of bourgeois success plays, and a grocer and his wife who jumped out of the audience to demand that the children stage a chivalric romance with their apprentice as hero" (Finkelpearl 2004).

A Knot of Fools. Thomas Brewer. A "semi-dramatic satire in dialogue," which "could possibly have had some sort of occasional presentation" (*JCS*), presumably during the 1620s and later. "It is of exactly the same type as the drolls of Robert Cox" (Rollins 1921). "A play called *A Knott of ffooles; or, Come laughe and spare not* was performed at Court in 1613 but it is not clear whether this is Thomas Brewer's work" (Butterworth 2005).

SR 28 August 1623 *A Knott of fooles: or Come laughe and spare not*. Q 1624 *A Knot of Fools, but Fools or Knaves or Both, I Care Not, Here They Are; Come Laugh and Spare Not*; no author named on the TP but the address to the reader is signed "Tho. Brewer"; in this dialogue "a number of fools meet and deliver numbered speeches" (Butterworth). Q2 1658.

L

The Ladies' [?Lady's] Privilege. Henry Glapthorne. Acted 1637–40 (*AED 3*). "Acted with good allowance" by Beeston's Boys at the Phoenix, and performed before the king and queen at Whitehall "twice," according to the TP. The play contains "debates about women and performance that were topical in the period of Henrietta Maria's sponsorship of court theatricals" (Sanders 2004b).

SR 4 April 1640 *The Ladies Priviledge*; transferred 17 February 1648 *The Ladies Priviledge*. Q 1640 list of characters; prologue and epilogue (by Frangipan); five acts.

Like many another prologue, this one shapes the expectations of playgoers by specifying what they are *not* going to experience: "Some in an humorous sque[a]mishnesse will say, / They only come to heare, not see the play, / Others to see it only, there have beene, / And are good store, that come but to be seene: / Not see nor heare the play: how shall we then / Please the so various appetites of men. / It starts our authors confidence, who by me / Tel[l]s you thus much t'excuse the comedy. / You shall not here be feasted with the sight / Of anticke showes; but actions, such as might / And have beene reall, and in such a phrase, / As men should speake in: ladies if you praise, / At least allow his language and his plot, / Your owne just priviledge, his Muse hath got / So full a wreath, that spight of Envies frowne / Shall in his brow sit as a lasting crowne." This prologue compliments "a closed group of *cognoscenti* who came to the playhouse not merely to be entertained but to appreciate and judge the offerings of the poet's fancy" (Neill 1978).

Lady Alimony, or The Alimony Lady, A Comedy. Anonymous; possibly "a joint work of Brome and Newcastle" (Freehafer 1973). ?Acted late 1650s (Randall 1995) at a "theatre unknown but evidently designed for a public theatre" (Hosley 1960). A comedy "duly authorized, daily acted, and frequently followed," according to the TP.

SR none. Q 1659 *Lady Alimony, or The Alimony Lady, an Excellent, Pleasant, New Comedy*; no author named; list of characters; induction, which occupies the first act (Hosley 1961) and which may have been added at a later date (*JCS*); prologue (which appears between the first and second acts) and epilogue; possibly the play "originated in the Caroline period and . . . the Induction was written for a revival" (Schneider 2011); five acts and separate scenes. Elaborate SDs: "*Enter six ladies fantastically habited; in a wanton and pleasant posture: passing over the stage, they are encountred by six amorous complemental servants. Every one singling forth his mistress, for discourse.*" SDs call for a number of auditory effects: "*Trumpets and kettle-drums sounding, with other martial musick usually observed in that countrey*"; moments later "*They march over the stage with trumpets, fifes, drums and colours.*" Also "*Voices of nightingals*"; the birdsong has thematic force: "Hark how that ev'ning quire of nightingals / Warble with shrillest notes, pricks at their brests, / Tereus incestuous crime; as if't had been / A fact inexpiable."

This play "suggests that the dramatists and managers remaining in London during the Protectorate who had worked in more popular theatres were well aware of the threat the élite tradition posed to them. Although technically the theatres had been closed since 1642, a number of citizen playhouses (especially the Red Bull) hosted performances sporadically throughout the period, providing straggling bands of actors and dramatists who had remained in England with occasional employment" (Payne 1993).

The Lady Errant, A Tragicomedy. William Cartwright. Acted *c.* 1633–35 (Evans 1951); mid- to late 1630s (Tomlinson 1992b). Probably prepared for private production at a great house with actresses, possibly for a wedding. The prologue hints "that the play was intended to be performed outdoors in front of a courtly audience" (Tomlinson); SDs make repeated references to a grove and trees, but these could have been represented by painted scenery (Nicoll 1937). Other lines in the prologue ("each sex keeps to it's part" and "Being the female's habit is / Her owne, and the male's his") "seem to indicate definitely that *The Lady-Errant* was acted by both men and women" (Evans). "Notable is the highly abnormal fact that half the characters are women, and that women have far more lines than the men" (*JCS*). "In the female characters' calculated use of poetry and theatre, *The Lady-Errant* both reflects and anticipates a world in which women's literacy functions as a means of cultural and political empowerment" (Tomlinson 2005).

SR 4 May 1648. O 1651 *Comedies, Tragi-Comedies, with Other Poems* (includes *The Ordinary, The Royal Slave, The Siege, or Love's Convert*); list of characters; prologue and epilogue; five acts and separate scenes.

"Cartwright, as an ardent royalist and staunch Anglican who sat on the king's Council of War in Oxford in 1642, participated, through *The Lady-Errant*, in a delicate contest of power between the king and the queen (and their respective factions"; one aspect "that certainly marks this play as political commentary is the presence of the assembly or parliament of women. Behind this element lies, of course, the fact of Charles's personal rule without parliament throughout the 1630s"; "the play is a defense of Charles's policy of peace"; the play counterattacks "the theatrical lobbying of the queen on the question of the European war" (Farnsworth 2002).

The Lady Mother. Henry Glapthorne. Licensed for acting 15 October 1635 (Adams 1917) by William Blagrave, Deputy to the Master of the Revels and a builder of the Salisbury Court theater in 1629. Acted by the King's Revels Company at Salisbury Court (Squier 1987). The MS contains the name of T[homas] Sands, an actor who belonged to an unidentified company, possibly "an amalgamation of the King's Revels and another still unidentified" (Brown 1958).

London, BL, Egerton MS 1994, fols. 186–211; no TP but the license at the end gives the title and permission to act, with "the reformacions observ'd"; no author named; damaged; theatrical provenance (Long 1989); five acts and first scenes. "[E]vidence of extensive revision in some parts of the manuscript" (Brown); some revisions made by Glapthorne, others by censors: e.g., oaths have been deleted. The MS "has been carefully prepared for the stage" (Greg 1931). No evidence of printing in the seventeenth century. Spectacle: Glapthorne "uses a death masque to save Lady Marlove and her son from execution for their supposed murder of Thurston. In this masque, Grimes, dressed as Death, invokes Despair and the Furies; but Timothy, as Hymen, chases Death away" (Spinrad 1987). First edited by Bullen, who conjectures Glapthorne's authorship in *A Collection of Old English Plays*, vol. 2 (1883); modern edition by Brown 1958. "This attribution has never seriously been challenged" (Sanders 2004b).

The play's subplot, "involving a drunken steward who fantasizes about a social and sexual liaison with his mistress, is indebted to *Twelfth Night*" (Sanders).

The Lady of Pleasure, A Comedy. James Shirley. Licensed for acting 15 October 1635 (Adams 1917, Huebert 1986). "Acted by" Queen Henrietta Maria's Men at the Phoenix, according to the TP. Diary entry by John Greene records performance 5 or 6 November 1635 at the Phoenix; the diary of Humphrey Mildmay, who calls it "that rare play" (Sturgess 1987), records a performance 8 December (*JCS*, Thorssen 1980). Richard Perkins probably played Sir Thomas Bornwell; William Sherlock, Littleworth; William Robbins, Sir William Sentlove; John Sumner, Alexander Kickshaw; Ezekiel Fenn, either Celestina or Aretina (Huebert 1981). Shirley's dedication alludes to the play's success, saying that it was "fortunate in the scene [i.e., onstage]." In playlist of Beeston's Boys 10 August 1639.

SR 13 April 1637. Q 1637 list of characters; five acts. As befits a forerunner of Restoration comedy, the play calls for no special effects or unusual staging. A character questions her steward: "What hangings have we here?" and hears a lengthy answer, describing a biblical story: "Shirley seems to have been the Renaissance dramatist most aware of the dramatic possibilities of stage hangings" (Stevens 1977). The world of Shirley's play is distinctively Caroline: his "social world consists only of the peerage and the gentry, to which class a steward, a bawd, a pimp, and a barber somewhat incongruously belong. The play proposes an absolutist ideal that combines praise of the court with a commitment to return to the country, there to reestablish human relations with the peasantry on neofeudal lines" (Cohen 1985).

Shirley "was perhaps the most sympathetic Caroline dramatist in terms of equality of the sexes. Women were major figures in his comedies, women who were witty, who acted as the equals of their men, and who wanted marriage, but not at the price of their freedom. Celestina [one of the female leads] is such a young woman" (Thorssen). At the same time, Shirley criticizes women "who adopt court fashions merely to waste their husbands' revenue in balls, banquets, and plate" (Veevers 1989). Both Shirley's *Lady of Pleasure* and Jonson's *The New Inn* "engage in anti-Platonic satire of a sort, yet both dramatists are openly sympathetic towards the idea of female performance both here and elsewhere in their *oeuvres*" (Sanders 2000).

The Lady's Privilege. See *The Ladies' Privilege.*

The Lady's Tragedy. See *The Second Maiden's Tragedy.* Briggs 2007 adopts as title *The Lady's Tragedy* "since its heroine, like the Duchess of Malfi, has no personal name, and is always referred to as the Lady, or else as Govianus's Lady."

The Lady's Trial. John Ford. Licensed for acting and first performed 3 May 1638 (Adams 1917, Bawcutt 1996). By Beeston's Boys at the Phoenix, according to the TP.

SR 6 November 1638. Q 1639 no author named on the TP but the words "Fide Honor" (author's anagram) follow the title, and Ford signs the dedication; prologue and epilogue, possibly both written by Theophilus Bird (*JCS*); list of characters; five acts. Also issued in *Comedies, Tragicomedies, and Tragedies* (1652), a made-up book no longer extant.

Theophilus Bird, who belonged to "Queen Henrietta's men when they were playing under the management of Christopher Beeston at the Phoenix before the plague of 1636" (Greg 1939), contributes a prologue in rhymed couplets attacking the repertory of the King's Men: "Wit, wit's the word in fashion, that alone / Cryes up the poet, which though neatly showne, / Is rather censur'd often-times than knowne. / He who will venture on a jest, that can / Raile on anothers paine, or idlely scan / Affaires of state, oh, hee's the onely man. / A goodly approbation, which must bring / Fame with contempt, by such a deadly sting, / The Muses chatter, who were wont to sing. / Your favours in what we present to day, / Our fearlesse author boldly bids me say, / He tenders you no satyr, but a play." "[T]he views expressed in the prologue to *The Lady's Trial* could not have been far from Ford's own attitude. They describe an antithesis between wit and chatter on the one side, and the poet who sings on the other, lamenting the fact that the wrong side is in favour at the time" (Gurr 1988a). "Bird's gloss on 'wit' extends its application from verbal and narrative dexterity to cruel personal attack and, most dangerous, idle animadversions on 'affaires of state'" (McLuskie 2006).

The Lame Commonwealth. A droll based upon a scene in B&F's *Beggars' Bush* and performed in the 1640s and 50s; the title may arise from a line in the play: "Have you a king and commonwealth among you?" "The text requires nine actors, a large number for a droll-troupe" (Elson 1932); contains evidence of performance.

Published in *1 The Wits, or Sport upon Sport* (O 1662 [two issues] and 1672); RT *The Humors of the Lame Commonwealth*; argument; list of characters. Clause, one of the characters, is pictured on the frontispiece to *1 Wits*. He is dressed in ragged clothes, has a crippled leg, and supports himself with a T-shaped cane (Foakes 1985).

The Lamentable and True Tragedy of M. Arden of Feversham in Kent. See *Arden of Faversham*.

A Lamentable Tragedy Mixed Full of Pleasant Mirth. See *Cambises*.

The Lamentable Tragedy of Locrine. See *Locrine*.

Landgartha, A Tragicomedy. Henry Burnell. "First acted on S. Patricks Day [17 March] 1639," according to a note printed at the end of Q; this "probably means" 1640 (*JCS*). "Presented in the new theater in Dublin with good applause," according to the TP. This designates the Werburgh Street theater, where Ogilby's Men performed. "Much about the play suggests that it was written to appeal to MPs . . . and, given its sexual politics, and dedicatory address to women, to their wives and daughters" (Kerrigan 2008).

SR none. Q Dublin, 1641; author's initials on the TP and Burnell signs the dedicatory epistle; list of characters; prologue, "delivered by an Amazon with a battle-axe in her hand," and epilogue, by Scania "apparelled as in the last scene, with her sword and belt in her hand"; description of dumb show; five acts. Some highly detailed SDs specify costume: "*Enter Hubba and Marfisa in an Irish gowne tuck'd up to mid-legge, with a broad basket-hilt sword on, hanging in a great belt, broags on her feet, her hayre dishevell'd, and a payre of long-neck'd big rowll'd spurs on her heels.*"

The play "brings to the fore Charles's current and very real troubles in Ireland" (Randall 1995); Charles had sent Thomas Wentworth to Ireland as Lord Deputy, and he proved a most unpopular figure. *Landgartha* was "the first Irish play by an Irish writer" (Morash 2002). "Burnell's infusion into *Landgartha* of local Irish colour was affectionately handled" (Fletcher 2000).

On the last page of Q, Burnell defends the ending by citing the play's genre: "Some (but not of best judgements) were offended at the conclusion of this play, in regard *Landgartha* tooke not then, what she was perswaded to by so many, the kings kind night-imbraces. To which kind of people (that know not what they say) I answer (omitting all other reasons:) that a tragie-comedy sho'd neither end comically or tragically, but betwixt both: which *decorum* I did my best to observe, not to goe against art, to please the over-amorous. To the rest of bablers, I despise any answer." When Burnell wrote these words, tragicomedy had come to dominate the stage. "Clearly there had been objections to the ending, which Burnell answers (just as Jonson would have done) in aesthetic terms: his definition of a tragicomedy . . . allows him to address the nature of his ending without raising any considerations other than dramatic/generic ones" (Dutton 2006).

The Landlady. A droll based upon several scenes in B&F's *The Chances* and performed in the 1640s and 50s. "The episodes included in the droll are full of racy and lively dialogue, but have very little action" (Elson 1932).

Published in *1 The Wits, or Sport upon Sport* (O 1662 [two issues] and 1672); RT *The Landlady*; argument; list of characters.

A Larum for London, or The Siege of Antwerp (*Alarum for London*). Anonymous. Acted "fall 1599 to spring 1600," the first season of the Lord Chamberlain's Men at their new theater, the Globe (Knutson 2002a). Maguire 1986 identifies *The Siege of London*, recorded in Henslowe's *Diary*, with *A Larum for London*, but it is unclear how the Admiral's Men could have acquired a play belonging to the Chamberlain's Men.

SR 29 May 1600. Q 1602 *A Larum for London, or The Siege of Antwerp, with the Ventrous Acts and Valorous Deeds of the Lame Soldier*; no author named; prologue and epilogue (both by Time); not divided. HT *A Larum for London, or the Siege of Antwerp, with the Virtuous Acts and Valorous Deeds of the Lame Soldier*. SDs suggest that portions of the text are missing (Jewkes 1958). The play "dramatizes George Gascoigne's eye-witness account of *The Spoyle of Antwerp*, the so-called Spanish Fury of 1576, when a band of Spanish troops, mutinous for want of pay, massacred 8000 civilians" (Somogyi 1998). Staging dramatizes Spanish atrocities: "*The alarum againe, and* Champaigne *is pursued in by* Romero, Verdugo *and* Van End, *where he is slaine: so is the* Marques Hauurie, *and all engirting Count* Egmont, Alva *steps to defend him, & they strike at him*"; "Champaignes *wife hurried by two rascall soldiers . . . They stand to search her . . . They begin to strip her.*" Later an old man and his daughter are menaced: "*Shootes her with a pistoll*"; "*Stab the olde man.*" Another Spaniard "*Stabs the children,*" who are fleeing the onslaught; an old blind man and his wife are also stabbed despite their pleas. Sound effects accompany the violence: "*The piece discharges*"; "*A great screeke heard within*"; "*a drum sounding a dead march.*" The play "is keenly aware of the impact of noise, especially that of gunpowder weapons" (Cahill 2008). Suspension gear is needed for torture by the strippado ("*Hoise him up*") and for a hanging. Spanish strategy involves a cortege for the Duke of Alva (who is actually alive), "an effective stage device, comparable in theatrics to ruses by the Vice in moral plays" (Knutson); Alva is "*carried upon a horse covered with blacke.*"

"The buying and staging" of the play "was one of the most overt bids for political relevance ever made by the Chamberlain's Men" (Thomson 1980). *A Larum* is "an episodic dramatisation of the Siege of Antwerp by the Spaniards, and it stands as an overt piece of anti-Catholic scaremongering" (Thomson 1992b). The play's title "suggests its didactic purpose. It warns Londoners against the Spaniards and also against the self-indulgence that comes with worldly success" (Howard 2007). The play taps "into the fear among Londoners of a Spanish invasion" (Knutson).

The Last Discourse betwixt Master Abel and Master Richard Kilvert, Interrupted at the First by An Ancient and Angry Gentlewoman. Anonymous. A dialogue that may have been performed, venue unknown.

Q 1641 no author named; not divided. The TP woodcut depicts two men seated at table, a woman between them.

All three characters voice a sense of grievance and dispossession, and they feel no hope of redress. Kilvert ends by saying, "Wee must arme ourselves with Jobs patience, though we cannot with his innocence, and make our sufferings examples unto times to come."

The Late Lancashire Witches, A Comedy. Thomas Heywood and Richard Brome. Acted *c*. 11 August 1634 (Berry 1984). "A well received comedy, lately acted" by the King's Men at the [second] Globe, according to the TP; this is one of "[o]nly seven non-Shakespearean plays . . . advertised on title pages as exclusively Globe productions" (Straznicky 2006b). "On 20 July [1634] the King's Men petitioned the Lord Chamberlain to protect their intended play against competition from the Salisbury Court company, which, they complained, was 'intermingling some passages of witches in old playes'" (Gurr 1996). The Chamberlain intervened with the Master of the Revels to accommodate the King's Men. Nathaniel Tomkyns wrote a letter to a friend in which he describes a performance *c*. 16 August 1634; he says that the play was "acted by reason of the great concourse of people 3 dayes together"; its popularity was occasioned by "a sensational witch case" (Barber 1979a); three women accused of witchcraft had been brought to London; Tomkyns concludes that although the play lacks "any poeticall genius, or art, or language, or judgement to state our tenet of witches," nevertheless "it passeth for a merrie and excellent new play" (Stokes 1996). The play "attracted large numbers of nobility and 'fine folk' when such people were supposed to be out of town [in the summer]" (Wickham et al. 2000). The play "was taken on tour in the provinces by the King's Men in 1635," as a diary entry for 13 July 1635 by Thomas Crosfield of Oxford reveals (White 2008). Q mentions the name of "J. Adson" in a SD, presumably John Adson, "hired man and musician" (Gurr 2004c).

SR 28 October 1634 *The Witches of Lancasheire*; transferred 27 March 1637; 14 June 1642; 22 July 1644. Q 1634 *The Late Lancashire Witches, A Well Received Comedy*; prologue and epilogue; five acts and first scenes. The eyewitness account by Nathaniel Tomkyns contains "useful information such as that Mrs Generous was dressed as a cat in the scene where the miller cuts off her hand, and that birds and cats both fly out of the (presumably different) pies at the wedding feast" (McLuskie 2006). Staging includes *"Enter drum (beating before) a Skimington, and his wife on a horse; divers country rusticks (as they passe) Par[nell] pul[l]s Skimington of[f] the horse: and Law. Skimingtons wife: they beat em. Drum beats alar[um]. horse comes away."* We do not know whether a real horse appeared onstage, but "we have no record of property horses" (Lawrence 1935). Staging also calls for the entry of an *"invisible spirit,"* perhaps indicated by a special robe; Henslowe records having "purchased 'a robe for to goo invisible'" (Rhodes 1976). The dialogue calls for bewitched musicians to annoy wedding guests with their music; a SD reads *"Musitians shew themselves above,"* indicating that they occupy the music room, which corresponds to one of the boxes, or compartments, depicted in De Witt's drawing of the Swan (Hosley 1957, 1960). "The muddled, out-of-tune music that had been the sign of witchcraft in *The Witch of Edmonton* and *The Masque of Queens* is used again at the Seely wedding where the musicians first play *'Selengers Round'*. . .; then *'As they beginne to daunce, they play another tune, then fall into many'*. . .; and finally *'Every one a severall tune'*" (McLuskie 2006). Sound effects accompany the spirit world: *"The witches retire: the spirits come about him [the soldier] with a dreadfull noise: he starts."*

When originally acted, the play was called *The Witches of Lancashire* (RT and SR title); in his 1661 catalogue Kirkman calls the play *Lancaster Witches*. The play, "by depicting a comic version of the witches, emphasizes and exposes the tendentious investments that motivate judicial approaches to witchcraft; it thus renders judgment on the witches impossible" (Hirschfeld 2004).

The Launching of the Mary, or The Seaman's Honest Wife. Walter Mountfort (authorship established by Boas 1923). Written 1632 and licensed for acting 27 June 1633, according to the MS. "The performance may have been commissioned for an invited audience rather than one in the public theatre, perhaps a subsidised performance for the East India company and their friends" (Heinemann 1980). The play "was prepared for some house that in 1633 had the custom of music between the acts" (Walter 1933). Henry Herbert, Master of the Revels, censored the play, demanding a "fairer copy," one without "all oathes, prophaness, & publick ribaldry" (Bawcutt 1996). Herbert may have felt that "the play is an attack on the court (or at least on Henrietta's influence there)" (Dutton 2000). The play "called attention to the politically sensitive topic of privileges granted to the East India Company, and the English government's failure to punish the Dutch for the massacre of English sailors at Amboyna [one of the Spice Islands]" (Auchter 2001). Herbert "crossed out all references to the Amboyna massacres, a total of seventy-five or eighty lines at different places in the play" (Bentley 1971).

London, BL, Egerton MS 1994, fols. 317–49; author's initials on the TP; author's hand; theatrical provenance (Long 1989); annotations by Henry Herbert; numerous speeches crossed out, presumably by Herbert; list of characters; prologue and epilogue; two extensive SDs "which might have assumed the character of dumb shows in performance" (Mehl 1965); "regular division into [five] acts, and a very imperfect one into scenes" (Greg 1931). The SDs "are not differentiated in script, and are, moreover, often mixed up with the text in a rather confusing manner" (Walter 1933). A lengthy SD specifies action *aloft*: *"after the setting of the crabbs, & bendinge of the cables, there must appeare aloft, as many gallants & ladies as the roome canne well hold."* Ordinarily, action aloft involves only a few actors. MS contains "a number of small sheets of paper, pinned over censored passages, which contain the post-licensing additions by the author" (Ioppolo 2006). First edited by Walter 1933.

"Mountfort, an employee of the East India Company for at least twenty years, had written his play, as he notes on his manuscript, during a long voyage from India to England" (Bentley 1971).

The Law Against Lovers. William Davenant. Acted at the Duke's Playhouse, Lincoln's Inn Fields, 15 February 1662 (Edmond 1987).

SR transferred 31 October 1672. F 1673 *The Works*; "now published out of the authors originall copies"; list of characters; five acts.

This is Davenant's "own ill-advised adaptation of *Measure for Measure* into which he imported Beatrice, Benedick . . ., and the singing Balthazar from *Much Ado*" (Edmond). Like his other adaptations of Shakespeare, *Law Against Lovers* changes the original profoundly: "it is clear that by Davenant's time — or at least in Davenant's view — the whole issue [of Isabella's virginity] had ceased to have any living, dynamic interest. Isabella's honour has simply become a convenient piece of dramatic machinery, to be accepted like any other stage convention: a catch phrase which would be understood without enquiry or explanation, but which had not particular reference to the real flesh-and-blood world of the audience" (Harvey 1994).

Law Tricks, or Who Would Have Thought It. John Day; "probably written with George Wilkins" (Parr 2004a). "Divers times acted by the Children of the Revels," according to the TP, *c.* 1604 (Crow 1949). Written "either for the Queen's Revels, who would have performed it in 1606, or for the Whitefriars syndicate, who would have staged the play in 1608" (Bly 2000); Bly believes the latter possibility the more probable.

SR 28 March 1608 *A most wytty and merry conceited comedie called "who would a thought it or Lawetrykes."* Q 1608 list of characters; epilogue; five acts. The SDs provide much domestic detail: "*Enter Polymetes reading and Julio taking tobacco*"; "*Enter Countesse, three or foure young gentlewomen sowing by an houre-glasse.*" SDs call for a hearse: "*Solemnpe musique to a funerall song the herse borne over the stage*"; a property tomb is also required: "*Countesse in the tombe.*" "A husband attempts to poison his virtuous wife, but the poison has been replaced with a sleeping potion, and the wife emerges from her tomb to wonder at her situation before finally forgiving him and appearing at his trial to save him from execution" (Williamson 2009).

The epistle to the reader proclaims the author's benign intent: "I reverence all modest advertisements, and submit my selfe to any judicious censurer, protesting I never held any irregular course, but my inke hath beene alwaies simple, without the juice of worm-wood, and my pen smooth without teeth, and so it shall continue."

The Laws of Candy. William Wells first proposed Ford's authorship, as reported by Oliphant 1927. "The play has been attributed to John Ford, whose career as a dramatist was getting under way in these years, and there is some internal (but no external) evidence for the attribution" (Hoy 1987a). John Fletcher may also have "had some hand in it" (Waith 1952). Acted 1619–23 (*AED 3*) by the King's Men at the second Blackfriars/second Globe. Principal actors were Joseph Taylor, John Lowin, William Eccleston, Nicholas Tooley, Richard Sharp, George Birch, Thomas Pollard, and John Underwood, according to F2. "The longest role in the play was prepared for a boy player" (Bentley 1984).

SR 4 September 1646; 30 January 1673. B&F F1 1647 *Comedies and Tragedies*; "never printed before, and now published by the authours originall copies"; five acts and first scenes. Few SDs apart from entrances and exits. B&F F2 1679 *Fifty Comedies and Tragedies*; "published by the authors original copies, the songs to each play being added"; *The Laws of Candy, A Tragicomedy*; list of characters; actors' names.

Leontius, King of Cyprus. James Compton (Kelliher 1980). Probably written in the 1640s (Williams 1980), perhaps 1649 (Randall 1995). Possibly performed at Compton's home, Castle Ashby, before friends and family, or at his London residence, Canonbury House, Islington (Wolf 1983).

MS BL Additional 60279, fols. 1–32; formerly belonged to the library at Castle Ashby; no TP; no author named; "a scribe probably copied the play for presentation" (Wolf 1980); the beginning of the text is severely damaged (both left and right sides of the leaves have been torn away); the ending is missing; "not only contains three hands, but at least two, and possibly three, inks" (Wolf); five acts. Minimal SDs. "A close acquaintance with Shakespeare is apparent" (Kelliher 2004a). London, BL, Additional MS 60278, fols. 22–23, contains a short section of this drama.

"The play, in blank verse, concerns a rebellion in Cyprus which is aided by forces from Sicily, but the rebellion is eventually overthrown when the Sicilians join forces with King Leontius of Cyprus and destroy the rebels. The events of the play would seem to associate it with events in England during the late 1640s when there was still hope that the Scots would join with King Charles to defeat the Parliament" (Williams).

The Levellers Levelled, or The Independents' Conspiracy to Root Out Monarchy, An Interlude. Mercurius Pragmaticus [Marchamont Nedham]. A play-pamphlet published 3 December 1647 (Potter 1981) and possibly acted in the late 1640s. "The play-pamphlets authored by royalist mercuries were an unstable composite genre, mixing elements of drama, reportage, satire, and prose polemic" (Raymond 1996). "[T]o write in dramatic form was itself an act of defiance, since Parliament's antitheatrical legislation had been renewed in July 1647" (Potter 1988). Included in Kirkman's 1661 catalogue.

SR none. Q 1647 list of characters; prologue by Mercurius Pragmaticus, the pseudonymous author, and epilogue; Pragmaticus, who speaks at the close of each act, functions as chorus (Potter 1981); "five miniature acts" (Greg 1939). Adequate SDs. Prologue claims that, although the printed play is intended for readers, it was staged: "[I] on the stage / Present to view the monsters of the age, / These sonnes of Belial [i.e., the Levellers], you must onely read; / And yet this play was acted once indeed."

The play "aims its strong political attack at the radical political party which sprang up in the New Model Army in the environs of London during the summer of 1647 and came to an end in 1649" (Dust 1980). The play "ends with a piece of news only two weeks old, Charles I's escape to the Isle of Wight" (Potter 1981).

Liberality and Prodigality (The Contention between Liberality and Prodigality). Possibly written by George Gascoigne and Francis Kinwelmarsh (Smith 1987b). "This play, while undoubtedly performed by the Children of Paul's, was later either stolen by the Chapel Children, who performed it in February 1601 when they were hastening to capitalize on the successful revival at Paul's of late 1599, or planned as a revival by Paul's but not produced" (Gair 1982). "Playd before her majestie," according to the TP, 4 February 1601 (Scattergood 1985), by the Children of the Chapel (Greg 1913b): at the end of the play, "*Vertue, Equitie, Liberalitie, Judge, and all come downe before the Queene, and after reverence made, Vertue speaketh* [the epilogue]." Q is possibly a revised version of the lost *Prodigality*, performed by Paul's Boys at Christmas or Shrovetide 1567–68, and revived before Queen Elizabeth, 1574–75 (Hillebrand 1915); Collier 1831 first made the suggestion.

SR none. Q 1602 *A Pleasant Comedy Showing the Contention between Liberality and Prodigality*; list of characters; prologue; epilogue addressed to Queen Elizabeth and spoken by Virtue, "but the lines are more appropriate to Fortune" (Craik 1958); five acts (though there is no indication of act division at the opening) and separate scenes. Staging "requires a substantial 'house.' This is an impressive structure, a palace" (Gair), which "has an upper storey with a 'stately sumptuous throne,' wherein Fortune is ceremonially installed" (Craik). "Adjacent to Fortune's palace, and in vivid contrast to it, is Virtue's 'homely bowre' (not otherwise described)" (Craik). Staging also calls for the entry of "*Fortune in her chariot drawne with kings*" (Kiefer 2000). This may have been part of the original play, and Marlowe seems to recall the staging when Tamburlaine enters in a chariot similarly drawn by kings (Craik). Staging involves a near hanging; death is averted when the rope breaks: "*Here Prod[igality] scaleth. Fortune claps a halter about his neck, he breaketh the halter & falles.*" Symbolic costumes: e.g., "*Enter Vanitie solus, all in feathers.*"

"[T]his late survival of the type [moral interlude] reveals one direction in which the morality spent part of its force. The allegory teaches, instead of spiritual morality, only a single lesson in conduct—prudence and honesty" (Thompson 1910). "The play advocates essentially what John Skelton advocated nearly a century earlier in *Magnificence*: namely, that Fortune's gifts should be handled prudently" (Kiefer 1983).

The Life and Death of Captain Thomas Stukeley. See *Captain Thomas Stukeley.*

The Life and Death of Cavaliero Dick Bowyer. See *The Trial of Chivalry.*

The Life and Death of Henry the Fifth. See *Henry V.*

The Life and Death of Jack Straw. See *Jack Straw.*

The Life and Death of Julius Caesar. See *Julius Caesar.*

The Life and Death of King Henry the Fourth. See *1 Henry IV.*

The Life and Death of King John. See *King John.*

The Life and Death of King Lear. See *King Lear.*

The Life and Death of King Richard the Second. See *Richard II.*

The Life and Death of Richard the Third. See *Richard III.*

The Life and Repentance of Mary Magdalene. See *Mary Magdalene* (Wager).

The Life of Henry the Fifth. See *Henry V.*

The Life of King Henry the Eighth. See *Henry VIII.*

The Life of King Henry the Fifth. See *Henry V.*

The Life of Saint Meriasek. See *Saint Meriasek.*

The Life of Sir John Oldcastle. See *Sir John Oldcastle.*

The Life of the Duchess of Suffolk. See *The Duchess of Suffolk.*

The Life of Timon of Athens. See *Timon of Athens.*

Like Will to Like. Ulpian Fulwell. Acted *c.* 1566 (Happé 1991). "[R]eferences to men and boys 'standing by' and the use of a gittern [musical instrument] suggest an indoor, hall, audience" (Walker 1998). "[P]ossibly played at court as well as by popular troupes" (Kermode 2009a). "On its title-page the play was offered as a piece which could be doubled and played by five actors, and it may be that a professional men's company was seen as a prospective purchaser" (Happé); a chart divides sixteen roles for five actors. However, "the list does not work perfectly for the play" (Bevington 1962). Possibly "originally designed (and perhaps produced) as a boys' play at St Paul's" (Happé).

SR *c.* September 1568; transferred 22 April 1640. Q1 1568 *An Interlude Entitled Like Will to Like, Quoth the Devil to the Collier . . . Wherein Is Declared Not Only What Punishment Followeth Those That Will Rather Follow Licentious Living, Than to Esteem and Follow Good Counsel: and What Great Benefits and Commodities They Receive that Apply Them unto Virtuous Living and Good Exercises*; unique copy at Bodleian; list of characters on the TP; prologue; no epilogue as such but a song is printed at the end; not divided. At the start Lucifer "enters tumbling apparently, for Nichol Newfangle asks if he is 'Tom Tumbler or else some dancing bear'" (Wright 1928); Satan "is so grotesque that he has to be labelled: 'This name Lucifer, must be written on his back and on his brest'" (Craik 1958). "This is one of the very few direct references to the practice of this convention in England" (Southern 1973), "although it is a device illustrated by Brueghel and other artists on the Continent" (Brown 1999). SDs "pay close attention to such details of production as hand-properties, beards, and costuming" (Bevington 1962): "*Heer entreth* Nichol Newfangle *the Vice laughing, and [he] hath a knave of clubs in his hand which as soon as he speakth: he offreth unto one of the men or boyes standing by.*" Costumes have symbolic import: "the direction 'Tom Tospot commeth in with a fether in his Hat' announces him as a debauched prodigal" (Craik). Staging includes the devil exiting "with the Vice on his back at the end of the play, a stage device anticipated by Bale in *King Johan*, when he has Usurped Power carry Sedition in the same manner" (Cox 2000); "[The Vice, Nichol Newfangle] *rideth away on the devils back.*" Shakespeare recalls this precedent in *1 Henry IV* when Falstaff hoists Hotspur's body on his back as he exits the battlefield. The Vice "with his wooden dagger is contrasted to Severity, a figure of justice who carries a sword as his major property" (Dessen 1984). Q2 ND ?1570 unique copy at Folger. Q3 1587.

The Q1 prologue announces the play's didactic nature: "Sith pithie proverbs in our English tung doo abound, / Our author thought good such a one for to chuse: / As may shew good example and mirth may eke be found, / But no lascivious toyes he purposeth to use, / Heerin as it were in a glasse see you may: / the advauncement of vertue and of vice the decay." The play is "a satire written in the form of a traditional morality play" (King 2001); it is "an amalgamation of comedy and sermon" (Hoenselaars 1992a). *Like Will to Like* "takes its title from the proverbial idea that wicked people come in couples and reinforce each others' bad behavior" (Archer 2011).

Lingua, or The Combat of the Tongue and the Five Senses for Superiority, A Comedy. Thomas Tomkis; authorship established by the notebook of John Harington

[London, BL, Additional MS 27632] in 1610 (Carpenter 2002). Probably acted in 1607 "or shortly before" by students of Trinity College, Cambridge (Nelson 1989); *Lingua* "is one of the first Cambridge student comedies written and performed in English" (Carpenter). "*Lingua* is a farcical presentation of a struggle between personifications of the tongue and the five senses, all of which are identified by their Latin names" (Cerasano 2004d). The Q1 epilogue suggests that performance took place at night: "it is so late at night, / I cannot waken hungrie *Appetite*." Possibly revived in 1616 or 1617 (Smith 1908).

SR 23 February 1607 A Commedie called *Lingua*; transferred 19 August 1635; 5 February 1657. Q1 1607 *Lingua, or The Combat of the Tongue and the Five Senses for Superiority, A Pleasant Comedy*; no author named; dramatis personae; prologue and epilogue; five acts and separate scenes. The SDs describe in extraordinary detail the costumes of the personified characters: e.g., "Lingua, *appareled in a crimson satten gowne, a dressing of white roses, a little skeane tyed in a purple skarfe, a paire of red buskins drawne with white ribband, silk garters, gloves, &c.*" Pageantry accompanies each of the Five Senses: "*Auditus leads his showe about the stage, and then goes out*" (Kiefer 2003). The play features "song, dance, and elaborate spectacle" (Wright 1928). Q2 ?1610 (Ellerbeck 2009). Q3 1617. Q4 1622. Q5 1632. O 1657 two issues. "With the exception of Lingua, all of the play's characters are male and most are clearly modeled on academics. Lingua's verbal agility and her role as a female translator establish her as a menace to the play's orderly, patriarchal, and scholarly society: she threatens the academy with language" (Ellerbeck). "*Lingua* was one of the most popular academic plays of its century, at least among readers" (Dick 1944).

"In later years [the play] attracted fresh attention when the story got about that in a performance at the Free School at Huntington, the boy-actor who played Tactus [Touch] was none other than Oliver Cromwell" (Randall 1995); Winstanley 1687 makes the claim. Cerasano 2004d calls this story a "myth."

The Little French Lawyer. John Fletcher and Philip Massinger (Hoy 1959). Acted May 1619-May 1623 (E&G 1976) by the King's Men at the second Blackfriars/second Globe; "most probably written in 1621" (McMullan 2004). Principal actors were Joseph Taylor, John Lowin, John Underwood, Nicholas Tooley, William Eccleston, Richard Sharp, Robert Benfield, and Thomas Holcomb, according to F2. In playlist of the King's Men 7 August 1641.

SR 4 September 1646 *Litle french Lawyer . . .* by mr Beamont & mr fflesher; transferred 30 January 1673. B&F F1 1647 *Comedies and Tragedies*; "never printed before, and now published by the authours originall copies"; *The Little French Lawyer*; prologue and epilogue; five acts and first scenes. Descriptive SDs: "*Enter Nurse and Charloth, pass 'ore the stage with pillowes, night cloaths and such things*"; "*Enter a company of gentlemen, like ruffians.*" Extraordinary range of sound effects: "*Still musick within*"; "*Musick for the dance*"; "*A horrid noise of musique within*"; "*A strange musick. Sackbut & troup musick.*" When a party is captured by thieves, "the imprisoned women are being deliberately terrified by 'frights and noises . . . The villains put on shapes to torture us.' After emotions are heightened by '*strange Musick*,' '*Enter four over the stage with* Beaupre, *and* Verdone, *bound and halters around their necks*.' Lamira exclaims, 'What mask of death is this?'"; the "procession is intentionally theatrical, but it is not a masque; Lamira's word 'mask' is here generic for a show" (Gossett 1974). B&F F2 1679 *Fifty Comedies and Tragedies*; "published by the authors original copies, the songs to each play being added"; *The Little French Lawyer, A Comedy*; list of characters; actors' names.

"The comic design of the play seems essentially Fletcherian" (Hoy 1985).

Locrine, the Eldest Son of King Brutus. Anonymous; "almost certainly the work of one of the University Wits" (Clemen 1961). Possibly first written by Charles Tilney and entitled *Estrild*, then revised by another playwright in the 1590s (Berek 1987). Probably written by Thomas Greene and revised by Thomas Lodge (Murphy 2009). Possibly first performed by the Queen's Men (Berek) before 1586. Comic roles of Strumbo and Trompart "bolster" *Locrine*'s "candidacy as a Queen's Men play" (Knutson 2009b). But "nothing" about the play indicates that it belonged to the Queen's Men (McMillin & MacLean 1998). Acted *c*. 1590-July 1594 (Gooch 1981) at undetermined venue.

SR 20 July 1594. Q 1595 *The Lamentable Tragedy of Locrine, the Eldest Son of King Brutus, Discoursing the Wars of the Britains and Huns, with Their Discomfiture: The Britains' Victory with Their Accidents, and the Death of Albanact*; no author named; "newly set foorth, overseene and corrected, by W. S. [?William Smith]" (Brooke 1908). "A corrected quarto would seem to indicate the existence of an earlier printing that required correction" (Grote 2002). Ate's speech following the first dumb show constitutes a prologue, her last speech, an epilogue; the epilogue "has a considerably later date than the rest of the play" (Stern 2009c); Ate's speeches following the dumb shows at the beginning of each act serve a choral function; "the close relationship between the Elizabethan dumb shows and the popular emblem books is nowhere more evident than in" this play (Mehl 1969); five acts and separate scenes. Initials on the Q TP, "W. S.," "may have been intended to connect the play" with Shakespeare (McKerrow 1908), and "there is no good reason to doubt that he was indeed the 'overseer' of the text" (Duncan-Jones 2001); but the initials may stand for Wentworth Smith. The play begins with a tour de force of staging: "*Enter* Atey *with thunder and lightning all in black, with a burning torch in one hand, and a bloodie swoord in the other hand, and presently let there come foorth a lion running after a beare or any other beast, then come foorth an Archer who must kill the lion in a dumbe show*." "*Locrine* provides a smorgasbord of effects" (Waith 1988). Unusual staging includes an "emblematic tableau" (Sunesen 1954): "*A crocodile sitting on a rivers banke, and a little snake stinging it. Then let both of them fall into the water*"; the river bank was perhaps represented by a property concealing a trap (Lawrence 1927); Dessen & Thomson 1999 call *rivers banke* a "rare fictional term" for the trap. A stunning action is signaled in this

SD: "*Enter* Ate *as before.* Jason *leading* Creons *daughter.* Medea *following, hath a garland in her hand, and putting it on* Creons *daughters head, setteth it on fire, and then killing* Jason *and her, departeth.*" Later a ghost enters, apparently accompanied by "sharpe dartes of flames" and "a mightie noise." Estrild dispatches herself with the same sword that killed Locrine; their daughter would kill herself but "her hands are too too weake, / To penetrate the bullwarke" of her breast, and so "*She drowneth her selfe*" in a stream. Shakespeare F3 1664 second issue; "the third impression. And unto this impression is added seven playes never before printed in folio." Shakespeare F4 1685 "the fourth edition"; two issues.

Locrine is inspired by *Tamburlaine* and closely related to *Selimus* (Brooke 1908). Although most scholars today do not credit the F3 and F4 attribution to Shakespeare, he may have "bombasted up its blank verse for the press" (Duncan-Jones 2001).

Lodovick Sforza, Duke of Milan. Robert Gomersall. ?Acted 1628 (Kawachi 1986) at undetermined venue.

SR 27 February 1628; transferred 3 May 1651; 11 June 1659. O1 1628 *The Tragedy of Lodovick Sforza, Duke of Milan*; RT *The Tragedy of Sforza*; list of characters; lengthy argument; prologue and epilogue; five acts and separate scenes. O2 1633 *Poems of Robert Gomersall*; "the second edition." Both editions conclude with a poem entitled "To the Ambitious." The allegorical frontispiece to O1 and O2 depicts "a wolf sitting in a chair of state holding a scepter, while in front another version of the wolf mauls sheep" (Foakes 1985). A lion seems to place a crown on the wolf's head. According to the accompanying explanation, "It was when Industry did sleepe / The wolfe was tutor to the sheep, / And to amaze a plainer man, / The thiefe was made the guardian. / But can a wolfe forget to prey? / Can night be lightned into day? / Without respect of lawes or blood, / His charge he makes to be his food. / With that triumphant he sits downe, / Opprest, not honour'd with a crowne, / And on the lesser beasts does try / A most authenticke tyranny: / This the French lyon heares, and when / He's thought fast sleeping in his denne, / Vengeance and he at once doe wake, / And on the wolfe their fury slake. / Bad acts may bloome sometimes, but n'ere grow high, / Nor doe they live so sure, as they shall dye."

In his dedicatory epistle Gomersall distances himself from what he sees as prevailing attitudes: "in this age, wherein only heresie or sedition preferre a booke, wherein contradiction is called learning, and zeale wonders that she is become faction, I can expect but a few readers, whose small number shall be no discouragement at all to me, if that your judgement shall counterpoise them."

The London Chanticleers, A Comedy. Anonymous. ?Acted 1640s-50s, possibly in front of "Royalists expelled from London" (Harbage 1936). "Often acted with great applause and never before published," according to the TP. Prologue suggests production somewhere other than London: "You're welcome then to London, which our show / Since you mayn't go to that, has brought to you."

SR 28 January 1659. Q 1659 *The London Chanticleers, A Witty Comedy, Full of Various and Delightful Mirth*; included in Kirkman's 1661 catalogue but without attribution; list of characters; prologue and epilogue (by Host); divided into fourteen numbered scenes. The play "has a cast consisting of cockney street-criers, a ballad-singer, and a tavern-keeper, and seems a cross between jig and ballad opera" (Potter 1981).

The London Prodigal. Anonymous. "[I]t was written and, presumably, performed between the death of Queen Elizabeth I (24 March 1603) and its publication sometime in 1605" (Edmondson 2007). "Plaide by" the King's Men, according to the Q TP, at the first Globe.

SR none. Q 1605 "by William Shakespeare"; ascribed to Shakespeare by Rogers and Ley's 1656 catalogue and by Archer's and Kirkman's; not divided. Shakespeare F3 1664 second issue; "the third impression. And unto this impression is added seven playes, never before printed in folio"; "written by W. Shakespeare." Shakespeare F4 1685 "the fourth edition"; two issues.

The attribution to Shakespeare is not credited today, "but no convincing alternative has been offered" (Wells & Taylor 1987). "We shall never know whether the first publisher thought of the ascription as a mere salesman's ploy or whether he seriously believed that Shakespeare had a hand in the composition" (Mehl 2004).

The Longer Thou Livest, the More Fool Thou Art. W. [?William] Wager. Acted 1559–68 (*AED 3*) at undetermined venue. "Foure may playe it easely" according to the verso of the TP, and the fifteen roles are arranged for doubling: "This arrangement of the parts would suggest that the play was intended for a small company of professional players" (Southern 1973). Although the play requires only four actors, it "appears in most respects to be a children's play" (White 1993b). "[T]he songs and stress upon education as a virtue suggest a school or college play" (Walker 1998). "With its abundant Latin quotations and the humour of beating the intractable fool Moros at the beginning of the play, [Wager's drama] seems particularly apt to schoolboy performance" (Craik 1958). But Bevington 2007b disagrees: the fact that the play "abounds in Latin quotations and the humour of beating the intractable young fool, urged by Craik as evidence of boys' auspices, does not strike me as a wholly persuasive argument: the Latin is all immediately translated in the dialogue, and is found in other popular touring plays like *Mankind*, and the same is true of humorous beatings."

SR *c.* April 1569. Q ND ?1569–80 *A Very Merry and Pithy Comedy Called The Longer Thou Livest, The More Fool Thou Art*, but "it is in fact, both in terms of subject-matter and typographical conventions, a humanist interlude" (Massai 2007); unique copy at BL; "newly compiled by W. Wager"; list of characters;

prologue; "sparse" SDs (Massai); not divided. "A remarkably high percentage of the play's inventive stage directions are intended for the actor playing Moros"; he is "explicitly directed to improvise inane dialogue and gestures" (Bevington). When "Moros is elevated to authority by Fortune," he enters "gaily disguised and with a foolish beard" (Craik 1958). He "acts out his foolishness through his inept use of his weapons" (Dessen 1984); at the denouement God's Judgment wields a sword, symbolic of justice (Dessen 1977); he strikes Moros "with this sword of vengeance." Staging includes the devil exiting "with the Vice on his back at the end of the play, a device anticipated by Bale in *King Johan*, when he has Usurped Power carry Sedition in the same manner" (Cox 2000).

The TP affirms the value of education, appropriate for an audience of students: "A myrour very necessarie for youth and specially for such as are like to come to dignitie and promotion." Prologue also points to the Calvinist nature of that education: "nothing, God except, is so strong of nature, / For neither councell, learninge nor sapience, / Can an evill nature to honest manners allure: / Do we not see at these daies so many past cure, / That nothing can their crokednes rectefie, / Till they have destroied them utterly?" Wager's religious agenda is manifest in how Moros behaves: "when Fortune capriciously gives him power he oppresses the commons and persecutes Protestants" (Craik 1966).

Longshanks. See *Edward I.*

Look About You. Anonymous. Anthony Munday "probably had a hand in" the play (Skura 2003); possibly written by Anthony Wadeson (Greg 1913d). "[W]ritten sometime after 1594" (Hyland 2005). "[M]ust have been written after *1 Henry IV* had become popular" (Nelson 1973); "probably written in late 1598 or early 1599" (Lancashire 1969b); acted 1598–99 (Hirsch 1980). "Lately played by" the Lord Admiral's Men, according to the TP, at the Rose, but the title is not "verifiable by Henslowe's" *Diary* (Knutson 2009a); the play's title "appears nowhere in Henslowe's record" (Gurr 2009c). "The play must belong to the series of King John and Robin Hood plays which Wilson, Chettle, Munday, and others were writing for the Admiral's men in late 1590s" (McMillin 1992). Henslowe may call *Look About You* "Desgysses" (Gurr).

SR none. Q 1600 *A Pleasant Comedy Called Look About You*; no author named; pantomimic SDs but "[n]o dumb shows in the stricter sense of the term" (Mehl 1965); not divided. Q was "probably a delayed printing since it announced itself as a play of the Lord Admiral's Men and makes no mention of Howard's elevation in 1597 to Nottingham" (Gurr). Elaborate pageantry: "*Sound trumpets, enter with a harrald on the one side,* Henry *the second crowned, after him* Lancaster, Chester, *Sir* Richard Faukenbridge: *on the other part, K.* Henry *the sonne crowned, herrald after him; after him* Prince Rich[ard], John, Leyster, *being set, enters fantasticall* Robert of Gloster *in a gowne girt: walkes up and downe.*" Staging seems to indicate the location of a "cave" underground: "Prince John asks the disguised

Skink whether there are not caves thereabouts, and [he] gets the reply, 'Yes, sir; tread the ground, sir, and you shall hear their hollowness'" (Lawrence 1927). The SDs "indicate that the fight between Richard and Gloster is drawn out for the sake of the spectacle" (Wright 1968). "[I]n its time the popularity of *Look About You* and plays like it could not have depended upon their poetry or the complexity or acuteness of their historical analysis, but rather upon a kind of spectacular performance dependent on specific kinds of acting skills that offered not depth and concentration, but hectic versatility and complex staging" (Hyland). "[O]nly three of its scenes are concerned with something akin to history; the remaining 16 deal with games played with history, and all those games are theatrical. The play is not primarily an analysis of history, but a celebration of theatre; disguise is what it is all about" (Hyland 2011).

This may be the same play that Henslowe calls *The Honorable Life of the Humorous Earl of Gloucester with His Conquest of Portugal* (Greg 1913d). *Look About You*, "though basically a multiple-disguise comedy, is very much an English history play in every sense of that term"; the play "deserves this label in that its author deals with events of the reign of Henry II, using these not as a mere frame for the comic multiple-disguise action but as a solid foundation for the plot" (Lancashire 1969b).

A Looking Glass for London and England. Robert Greene and Thomas Lodge. Influenced by the success of *Tamburlaine* and acted September 1587-spring 1588 (Clugston 1980) at undetermined venue. Probably first performed by the Queen's Men (Harbage 1952), "but it is not absolutely certain" that the play belonged to this company (Schoone-Jongen 2008); the Clown's name is Adam, possibly referring to John Adams, an actor with the Queen's Men in 1588 (Greg 1932); but this name "hardly points to John Adams of the Queen's Men" (McMillin & MacLean 1998). Performed also by Strange's Men at the Rose 8 and 27 March, 19 April, and 7 June 1592, according to Henslowe; this is the "earliest performance of a biblical play recorded by Henslowe" (Connolly 2007). "Revived by Prince Charles's company about 1620" (Astington 2006). The name of the actor Gilbert Reason appears "in a theatrically marked up copy" of the play, "perhaps played on tour between" 1617 and 1625 (Astington 2010).

SR 5 March 1594; transferred 14 August 1600. Q1 1594 unique copy at Huntington; "several pantomimic" SDs (Mehl 1965); not divided. The play is "remarkably spectacular" (Lawrence 1927). Staging calls for the prophet Oseas to be "*set downe over the stage in a throne*"; from this position above he observes the dramatic action and comments. But perhaps this SD means that the angel leads Oseas "across the stage to a throne that is already there and empty, and seats him in it" (Wickham 1979). Special (unexplained) effects include: sages enter "*with the miters on their heads, carrying fire in their hands*"; "*Magi with their rods beate the grounde, and from under the same riseth a brave arbour*" (this would have been a prop arbor [Rhodes 1976]); Jonah "*cast out of the whales belly upon the stage*"; "*a flame of fire appeareth from beneath* [the stage], *and Radagon is swallowed*"; "*a hand from out a cloud, threatneth a burning sword.*" This last effect "could easily be achieved by raising into view a wooden cut-out with the device painted on it, or by lowering it on a string" (Wickham 1979). "In one of the most spectacular thunderclaps in drama" (Drew-Bear 1994) the King, seeing lightning, asks that curtains be opened to reveal the beautiful Remelia: "*He drawes the curtaines and finds her stroken with thunder, blacke.*" Q2 1598. Q3 1602 unique copy at Bodleian. Q4 ND ?1604–05 (Maguire 1999b): "At some time between 1603 and 1606, an exemplar of a quarto . . . was marked up for use as a prompt-book, at least in part for London performances" (Taylor 1993a); it contains "theatrical cuts and annotations" (Astington 2006); located at the University of Chicago Library, it lacks a TP (Baskervill 1932). Q5 1617. The publication history suggests that the play was "much more popular in [its] own day than in ours" (Bruster 2004).

"The play may be the first written for the public theaters that dramatizes a biblical narrative [about Jonah and the fall of Nineveh], but it also represents the apex of Protestant attempts to achieve an effective and popular biblical theater" (O'Connell 2000b). *A Looking Glass* "adapts the loose form and didacticism of homiletic drama to secular comedy" (Newcomb 2004).

The Lost Lady, A Tragicomedy. William Berkeley. Acted late 1637-January 1638 (*JCS*) by the King's Men at the second Blackfriars (Williamson 2009). Performed also at court, soon after commercial-playhouse performance, "perhaps during the Christmas season" (Rowan et al. 1987). Performed at the Whitehall Cockpit, before the king and queen, 26 March 1638 (Adams 1917). There was apparently an amateur performance at the home of Thomas Peyton in Knowlton, Kent, 10 July 1654; Dorothy Osborne, somewhat unwillingly, acted the role of the heroine (Clare 2004).

Washington, Folger, MS J.b.4; ed. Rowan et al.; prepared for presentation to Queen Henrietta Maria; no separate TP; no author named; corrections made by the author and by another hand; damaged; one leaf is almost entirely torn away; incomplete (ending is missing); list of characters; prologue to king; five acts. SDs "in the Folger manuscript . . . clearly originate in the theatre" (Rowan et al.). SR 5 March 1638; transferred 24 September 1638; 5 September 1640. F1 1638, colophon has 1637; unique copy at Folger; no author named; no prologue. "One interesting feature of both the manuscript and F1 is the fact that they contain a number of directions which must have originated with a prompter or stage-manager" (Bald 1937b). F2 1638–39 the two issues have different dates.

Berkeley's notion of female sacrifice must have found a sympathetic audience in Queen Henrietta Maria: "the main characters connect the religious themes of sacrifice, suffering, and martyrdom with virtuous love and its eventual triumph" (Veevers 1989).

Love (*A Play of Love*). John Heywood. Acted 1528–33 (*DTRB* 1984). Perhaps intended for Lincoln's Inn (Axton & Happé 1991); the play consists of "a series of disputations" (Bevington 1962), "particularly well suited for performance before an audience of lawyers" (Walker 1998). "*Love* uses the device familiar in *Weather* and *Four PP* of ingenious debate about nothing" (Bevington 1968). Requires four actors (Lancashire 2002); "[t]here is no indication of doubling" (Happé 1994b). Despite "the fact that only two out of eight stage directions do more than indicate entrances and exits, the play is rich in visual incident" (Axton & Happé).

SR no original; transferred 15 January 1582. F 1534 (colophon); *A Play of Love, A New and A Merry Interlude Concerning Pleasure and Pain in Love*; unique copy in Pepys Library at Magdalene College, Cambridge; list of characters on the TP; "scant" SDs (Massai 2007); not divided. The play "begins with the arresting dramatic novelty of a young man walking about in moody silence. He is the melancholy Lover-Not-Loved" (Craik 1958). SD names No-Lover-Nor-Loved as the Vice, and spectacular staging involves this character: "*Here the Vyse cometh in ronnyng sodenly aboute the place among the audyens with a hye copyn tank on his hed full of squybs fyred, cryeng Water, water, fyre, fyre, fyre, water, water, fyre, tyll the fyre in the squybs be spent.*" A squib was a firework "that squirmed erratically to produce a fizzing shower of sparks that sometimes ended in a small report" (Butterworth 1998). "This eye-catching, heart-stopping display of fireworks brilliantly enlivens a play which, in most respects, resembles a formal debate" (Axton 1994). The Vice's "headdress is spectacular, probably in the shape of a tall sugar loaf and a parody of contemporary fashion" (Happé 2010). Q ND ?1550–57 (Somerset 1977); unique copy at Bodleian; lacks a TP.

Love contains "the first character in English drama designated as the Vice" (Creeth 1966). This, "the most divergent and theatrically potent character, 'No Lover nor Loved,' . . . comes to acquiescence only at the very last moment, leaving us reflecting upon his vigorous mockery of love at the centre of this play" (Happé 2007b). "The proper translation of 'Vice,' as Heywood uses it, would be 'jester'" (Potter 1980).

Love and Fortune. See *The Rare Triumphs of Love and Fortune.*

Love and Friendship. See *The Combat of Love and Friendship.*

Love and Honor. William Davenant. Licensed for acting 20 November 1634 (Bordinat & Blaydes 1981). Malone records that the play was originally entitled *The Courage of Love*: "it was afterwards named by Sir Henry Herbert, at D'Avenant's request, *The Nonpareilles, or the Matchless Maids*" (Adams 1917). Acted by the King's Men at the [second] Blackfriars, according to the Q TP. Performed at the same theater, 12 December 1634 (diary of Humphrey Mildmay); at Hampton Court, the night of 1 January 1637 (bill of King's Men for performances at court).

The play was "prompted by the queen's liking for romantic comedy and interest in Neoplatonism" (Edmond 2004b). In playlist of the King's Men 7 August 1641.

SR 4 September 1646; transferred 19 August 1667; 30 January 1673. Q 1649 dramatis personae (on an extra page at the end); prologue and epilogue; five acts and first scenes. A SD, "*Descends the cave*," seems to call for use of the trap in the stage floor. When Prospero enters, he says, "Evandra, speak, ascend to us." Then "*The stage opens, Prospero lifts Evand[ra] up*." Subsequently, "*They put Evandra downe in the cave*." F 1673 *The Works*; "now published out of the authors originall copies."

The Q epilogue, also printed in Davenant's *Madagascar, with Other Poems* (1638), describes the playwright as waiting in the theater to overhear comments made by playgoers: "Our poet waits below to heare his destiny; / Just in the entry as you passe, the place / Where first you mention your dislike or grace: / Pray whisper softly that he may not heare, / Or else such words as shall not blast his eare."

Love and War, A Tragedy. Thomas Meriton. ?Acted 1650s at undetermined venue.

Q 1658 dramatis personae; prologue; choral songs at end of each act; five acts and separate scenes. Wonderfully detailed SDs: "*The funeral of Burgargo passeth over the stage, with his scutcheon, armour, heralds, with flags, torches, and mourners*"; "*Fal's as if he were dead, & while he lies, eats up his pottage*"; "*He kicks* Quer[mero] *to see whether he be alive or no, and* Quer[mero] *answereth nothing, but makes a face.*"

The play "is an instance of well-intended amateurism, now interesting largely as a means of suggesting how a lay writer responded to the achievements of his professional predecessors" (Randall 1995).

Love at First Sight. See *The Parson's Wedding.*

Love Crowns the End, A Pastoral. John Tatham. Acted 1632 by students of the School of Bingham in the county of Nottingham, according to the separate 1640 TP (Wiseman 1998a); presumably Tatham was a schoolmaster there. He "subsequently at least, had professional connections, writing for the lord mayoral shows" (Sanders & Atherton 2006).

SR 15 October 1640 *The ffancies Theater*. O 1640 *The Fancies'* [?*Fancy's*] *Theater*; separate TP but continuous register; prologue; not divided. SDs specify a locality board and perhaps painted scenery: "*A place discover'd all greene mirtles, adorn'd with roses, a title written over 't thus.* LOVERS' VALLEY." Reissued 1657 with a new general TP: *The Mirror of Fancies, with a Tragicomedy entitled, "Love Crowns the End"*; omits prologue.

The O prologue, like that of many another play, adopts a gustatory metaphor: "Accept the choicest dish our wits prepare, / As a third course to please your eye, which still / Covets to have of novelties its fill. / We have not bundled up some kickshawes here / To bid you welcome; wee do hate such geere. / Our braine's the kitchin, and our wit's the meat, / Preparative to which, wee bid you eat, / If lik't, if not refrain't; you judges sit / To damne or save our not yet ripen'd wit."

A note on the final page acknowledges errors in printing and invites the reader to correct them: "there are some faults which (through the obscurity of the coppie, and absence of the author) have passed the presse; to particularize them were needlesse; but favourably looke o're them, and with thy pen courteously correct such defects as thou shalt finde, not condemning the presse or injuring the author."

Love in Its Ecstasy, or The Large Prerogative, A Kind of Royal Pastoral. William Peaps (identified in Kirkman's 1661 catalogue). Acted ?1634 (*JCS*). Probably performed by students at Eton; the TP indicates that this pastoral play was "written long since by a gentleman, student at Æton."

SR none. Q 1649 no author named on the TP; list of characters; five acts and separate scenes. The play's descriptive subtitle, *A Kind of Royal Pastoral*, points to its political stance: "That kings absolutely control the lives of their subjects, and, as God's representatives on earth, must not be questioned, are lessons piously emphasized in the play" (Wright 1934).

The epistle to the reader connects publication with the closing of the theaters: "The torrent of the presse that now sweepes all, amongst other pamphlets has laid this before you. Did the stage enjoy its former lustre, this would have lien still neglected and forgotten: but since those pastimes are denied us wherein we saw the soule and genius of all the world lye contracted in the litle compasse of an English theatre, I have thought fit amidst a number of more serious pieces to venture this in publike. You may be confident there lyes no treason in it nor state invective, (the common issues of this pregnant age). It is inoffensive all, soft as the milkie dayes it was written in, for although it appeares now so late before you like a winter blossome in the middle of a boysterous and ill-boding season, yet this interlude was long since the early recreation of a gentleman not fully seventeene, and those times admitted but of small distempers, or those yeares but little judgement to discerne them."

Love in Travail, A Comedy. Cosmo Manuche. Written after 9 December 1641 but "not later than 1655–56" (Williams 1980). "Very likely" intended for performance (Nelles 1990): it is "a lively, plot-packed comedy capable of holding its own with many plays that made their way into print" (Randall 1995). The play "could have been acted at Castle Ashby," the home of James Compton, third earl of Northampton, to whom the play is dedicated (Potter 1981), or it may have been acted at Northampton's London residence, Canonbury House, Islington (Wolf 1983).

London, BL, Additional MS 60275, fols. 3–46; a "presentation copy" (Nelles); no TP but Manuche signs the dedications to Northampton; list of characters;

prologue "intended for the stage" and epilogue (by Allworth); five acts. HT *Love in Travell: A Comedy*. "To call the work *Love in Travell* . . . is to opt for a pun. With sufficient emphasis in the text on travel . . . Manuche very likely wants to call our attention also to the lovers' travail" (Randall). The play contains "over two hundred" SDs (Nelles): "*Bolster brings in a boye in an antick dress: bearing a pastboard shield: with a golden halfe moone for the crest. The scutchion: 3 silver jewes harpes in a field sable.* . . ." The MS formerly belonged to the library at Castle Ashby.

In the dedication Manuche writes: "few there be / Is crittick-prooffe, in comic poetry. / And for the buskin stage, that's (quite) lay'd by. / There's terror in 't, where kings: are forc'd to dye." This remark "appears to be an acknowledgement that the execution of Charles I had made all stage tragedies impossible" (Potter 1987b).

The Love of King David and Fair Bethsabe. See *David and Bethsabe.*

Love Tricks. See *The School of Compliment.*

Love Will Find Out the Way. See *The Constant Maid.*

The Lover's Hospital. See *Love's Hospital.*

The Lover's Melancholy. John Ford. Licensed for acting 24 November 1628 (Adams 1917, Hill 1985). Acted by the King's Men "at the private house in the Blacke Friers" and "publikely" at the [second] Globe, according to the TP. Principal actors were John Lowin, Joseph Taylor, Robert Benfield, John Shank, Eilert Swanston, Antony Smith, Richard Sharp, Thomas Pollard, William Penn, Curtis Greville, George Vernon, Richard Baxter, John Thompson, John Honeyman, James Horn, William Trigg, and Alexander Gough, according to Q. "This list has some puzzling aspects: it is longer than most; it names seventeen players, though there are only sixteen named roles in the play; in the usual separation of men and boys, it names five players for the four female roles, including the waiting maid; James Horne was not a boy but a hired man who had received livery for King James's funeral procession four years before and had taken an adult role in *The Roman Actor* two years before" (Bentley 1984).

SR 2 June 1629. Q 1629 two issues; no author named on the TP but Ford signs the dedicatory epistle, and his name appears in the SR; list of actors; prologue and epilogue; five acts. SDs carefully describe makeup and costumes: e.g., "*Enter Rhetias, his face whited, blacke shag haire, long nailes, a piece of raw meate*"; "*Enter Pelias. A crowne of feathers on, antickly rich*"; "*Enter Grilla in a rich gowne, great vardingale, great ruffe, muffe, fan, and coxcombe on her head.*" Staging may involve a staircase in view of the playgoers: "Walk up these stairs" (Lawrence 1927). To cure Prince Palador of his depression, "Corax stages a masque of melancholy with illustrative types drawn from [Robert] Burton. Only the melancholic lover is left out: that role is assumed by Palador himself, who is, in a sense, drawn into the masque, the spectacle moving him to exorcise his own affliction" (Bulman 2003). The play's treatment of sexuality is especially interesting: a "disguised woman becomes embroiled in a love intrigue with a fellow female"; Eroclea, "disguised as a male, is accosted by not one woman, but two—both Thamasta and her maid Kala"; Kala declares "herself desperate to lose her virginity to a boy who, the audience knows, is meant to be representing another woman in disguise"; Thamasta "continues to declare herself in love with Eroclea, even when she knows that the latter is female" (Lomax 1995). Also issued in *Comedies, Tragicomedies, and Tragedies* (1652), a made-up book no longer extant.

Prologue announces the playwright's purpose: "To tell yee (gentlemen) in what true sense / The writer, actors, or the audience / Should mold their judgements for a play, might draw / Truth into rules, but we have no such law. / Our writer, for himselfe would have yee know, / That in his following sceanes, he doth not owe / To others fancies, nor hath layne in wait / For any stolne invention, from whose height / He might commend his owne, more then the right / A scholer claimes, may warrant for delight." Here Ford "assumes two artistic principles common to the Caroline professionals: an author imitates models, and an author makes the imitation his own" (Clark 1992). In achieving the latter, Ford may allude to the relationship of King Charles and his wife: "Published in 1629 and celebrating the loving reunion of a young, virtuous prince and his partner after the removal of a powerful blocking figure, it looks very like a gratulation on the renewed amity of Charles I and Henrietta Maria in the wake of the assassination of the duke of Buckingham" (Hopkins 2005b).

The Lover's Pilgrimage. See *Love's Pilgrimage.*

The Lovers' Progress. John Fletcher; revised by Philip Massinger (Hoy 1957). Lost original version licensed as *The Wandering Lovers*, 6 December 1623 (Adams 1917), ascribed to Fletcher, and performed by the King's Men at the [second] Blackfriars; and at Whitehall, before the prince, 1 January 1624 (Bawcutt 1996). Revised version licensed for acting 7 May 1634 as *The Tragedy of Cleander* (Adams) and performed by the King's Men at the Blackfriars, 21 May 1634 (diary of Humphrey Mildmay). Performed also at the same playhouse before Queen Henrietta Maria, 13 May 1634 (Bawcutt). Principal actors were Joseph Taylor, John Lowin, Robert Benfield, John Underwood, Thomas Pollard, Richard Sharp, John Thompson, and George Birch, according to F2. In playlist of the King's Men 7 August 1641.

SR 4 September 1646 *The Lovers progresse*; 9 September 1653 *The Wandring Lovers*; 30 January 1673. B&F F1 1647 *Comedies and Tragedies*; "never printed before, and now published by the authours originall copies"; *The Lovers' Progress*; list of characters; prologue and epilogue; five acts and first scenes. The SDs provide richly descriptive entries: "*Enter Dorilaus, his arme in a scarffe*"; "*Enter*

Lancelot like a Fortune-teller, with a purse, and two letters in it"; "*Enter Clarinda, with a key*"; "*Enter Clarinda with a taper, and Lisander with a pistole, two chaires set out.*" Offstage sound effects: "*Noise within*"; "*A pistoll shot within.*" B&F F2 1679 *Fifty Comedies and Tragedies*; "published by the authors original copies, the songs to each play being added"; *The Lovers' Progress, A Tragedy*; list of characters; actors' names.

The F prologue, written after Fletcher's death (in 1625) and alluding to Massinger's revision, considers the question, Why "present an old piece to us for a new?" and answers, "He vowes, and deeply, that he did not spare / The utmost of his strengths, and his best care / In the reviving it, and though his powers / Could not as he desired, in three short howers / Contract the subject, and much lesse expresse / The changes, and the various passages / That will be look'd for, you may heare this day / Some scænes that will confirme it is a play, / He being ambitious that it should be known / What's good was *Fletchers*, and what ill his owne." Epilogue alludes to the revision by Massinger, saying, "Still doubtfull, and perplex'd too, whether he / Hath done *Fletcher* right in this historie, / The poet sits within."

Love's Changelings' Change. Anonymous. ?Acted *c.* 1630–40 (Greg 1931) at undetermined venue; "no evidence of . . . use in a playhouse" (Davidson 1978). Of the plays inspired by *The Arcadia* (Harbage 1936), this one "comes closest to presenting the homoerotic intrigue in Sidney's prose romance" (Walen 2005).

London, BL, Egerton MS 1994, fols. 293–316, ed. Cutts 1974; slightly damaged; no author named; list of characters; prologue (on TP) and epilogue; five acts and separate scenes. The SDs are consistent with preparation for performance. "Both entrances and independent directions tend to be very elaborate, and the latter are pretty frequent" (Greg): e.g., "*Enter Amphialus dressed wth a messenger at one doore and Cecropia at an other[;] hee drawes the messengers sword[,] Cecropia runs backward & falls dead, messenger carries her out and comes in againe.*"

First edited by Rota 1966, then Cutts 1974.

Love's Cruelty, A Tragedy. James Shirley. Licensed for acting 14 November 1631 (Adams 1917, Nims 1980). "Presented by" Queen Henrietta Maria's Men at the Phoenix, according to the TP. Nicholas Burt played Clariana (*Historia Histrionica*). Michael Mohun played Bellamente (Astington 2010). Performed also by Ogilby's Men at the Werburgh Street theater, Dublin, *c.* 1638. In playlist of Beeston's Boys 10 August 1639.

SR 25 April 1639; 29 November 1639. Q 1640 five acts. In act 2 Hippolito gives a most elaborate description of a courtly masque in progress, involving Arion and the tritons. This account emphasizes verisimilitude and emotional effect: "a tempest so artificiall and suddaine in the clouds, with a generall darkenes and thunder so seeming made to threaten, that you would cry out with the marriners in the worke, you cannot scape drowning, in the turning of an eye, these waters ravish into a heaven, glorious and angelicall shapes presented, the starres distinctly with their motion and musick so inchanting you, that you would wish to be drowned indeed, to dwell in such a happinesse." The description alludes "to features found in several" of Jonson's masques and "is largely an account of Inigo Jones's stage pyrotechnics" (Wertheim 1973).

Love's Cure, or The Martial Maid. Francis Beaumont and John Fletcher; revised by Philip Massinger. Original version acted 1605–13 (Hoy 1961); *c.* 1606 (McDonald 2003). (This lost version may have been performed by Paul's Boys, 1605–6, or by the King's Men, 1609–13.) Revised version acted ?1625 (Clark 1993) by the King's Men at the second Blackfriars/second Globe. In playlist of King's Men 7 August 1641 as "The martiall maide."

SR 4 September 1646 *Martiall Maid*; 30 January 1673. B&F F1 1647 *Comedies and Tragedies*; "never printed before, and now published by the authours originall copies"; *Love's Cure, or The Martial Maid*; "prologue at the reviving of this play" and epilogue (a later addition that also appears in Lodowick Carlell's *The Deserving Favorite* [1629]); "a song is slightly misplaced within the text by the printer" (Stern 2004a); "either the playhouse had chosen to apply the same epilogue to both plays (a possibility), or a free-floating epilogue from elsewhere had simply made its way into the bundle handed the printers of *Comedies and Tragedies* by mistake" (Stern 2009c); five acts and separate scenes. B&F F2 1679 *Fifty Comedies and Tragedies*; "published by the authors original copies, the songs to each play being added"; *Love's Cure, or The Martial Maid, A Comedy*; list of characters.

The F1 prologue addresses the theatrical revival, arguing that the passage of time since first production does not diminish the play's appeal: "Poets and painters hold a sympathy; / Yet their workes may decay and lose their grace, / Receiving blemish in their limbs or face. / When the minds art has this preheminence, / She still retaineth her first excellence. / Then why should not this deere peece be esteem'd / Child to the richest fancies that ere teem'd?" The play's appeal must have owed much to its treatment of gender: a brother and sister have been raised separately, each in the guise of the opposite sex; "they are now mature and must resume their true identities"; their problem involves the difficulties they "encounter in casting off the sexual roles to which they have become accustomed" (Clark 1994). "Lucio has been brought up as a girl, which he wants to remain, despite the fact that society is now demanding that both return to their normal gender ascriptions" (Dollimore 1986). Especially interesting is Clara, the "martial maid," who is "presented as the only 'real man' in the play. When she 'becomes' a woman, she performs equally well in that role, revealing that gender (and not just masculinity) is only a performance, and furthermore, in a reversal of English Renaissance stage practice, that a woman can perform a man best" (Duncan 2000).

Love's Dominion. Richard Flecknoe. Written in the early 1650s when Flecknoe "was treading very warily, in the hope of getting permission to produce the play in England, and he took the precaution of dedicating it to Cromwell's daughter, Lady Claypole" (Potter 1987b): "I dare not interest you in its more publique representation, not knowing how the palat of the time may relish such things yet, which, till it was disgusted with them, was formerly numbred amongst its chiefest dainties, and is so much longed for still, by all the nobler and better sort." Performed "before a court audience in Flanders" (Potter 1981) and then, in Davenant's production of 1664, a revised version, entitled *Love's Kingdom*, at the Duke's Theater.

SR none. O1 1654 *Love's Dominion, A Dramatic Piece, Full of Excellent Morality, Written as a Pattern for the Reformed Stage*; two issues; no author named on the TP but Flecknoe signs the dedicatory epistle; list of characters with brief descriptions of each and of costumes; chorus; five acts and separate scenes. The first SD anticipates the use of painted scenery: "*The scene, a boscage, with the adjacent prospect of a delightfull valley, here and there inhabited, with a magnificent temple afar off discovered.*" Dialogue suggests the importance of spectacle: "what means this deadly tragick spectacle, / This funeral livery & those bloody ensigns of cruel / And abhorred death!" The play contains a wealth of SDs, including an elaborate dance of personified figures. O2 1664; "revised and retitled" (Potter 1987b) as *Love's Kingdom, A Pastoral Tragicomedy*; "not as it was acted at the theatre near Lincolns-Inn, but as it was written, and since corrected"; the TP names the author; list of characters; chorus; prologue "spoken by Venus from the clouds"; no epilogue but an addition: "Filena's song, of the commutation of Love's and Death's darts. In the narrative style." Appended to the 1664 edition is *"A Short Discourse [Treatise* on the general TP] *of the English Stage."*

The postscript anticipates production: "That this piece may receive no disadvantage . . . by the publishing it, I let thee understand (gentle reader) if ever it be acted, I intitle to my right in it, . . . Mr. *Will. Beeston*, who by reason of his long practice and experience in this way, as also for having brought up most of the actors extant, I think the fittest man for this charge and imployment." Alluding to the closed theaters, Flecknoe in his preface writes, "Devotion, (like gilding to matter) cleaving not, nor sticking to rough and unpolish'd minds, unlesse they be first prepared with politeness of manners, and the tincture of good education, for the receiving it; which is best taught on the *theater*, by how much those precepts move the mind more forcibly and efficaciously, which besides the allowance of the ear, have a powerfull recommendation of the *eye*."

Love's Hospital. George Wilde. Acted the afternoon of 30 August 1636 (Elliott & Buttrey 1985) though the MS TP and SR have August 29. By students of St. John's College, Oxford, before King Charles and Queen Henrietta Maria, according to the MS TP; performance took place in the refectory. Jasper Mayne's *The City Match* was originally scheduled for performance, but Wilde's play was substituted for it. The play was staged "to celebrate the opening of Laud's new quadrangle and was paid for privately by the archbishop himself" (Elliott 1997). Archbishop Laud, then Chancellor of Oxford, recorded the event: "I caused the windows of the hall to be shut, the candles lighted, and all things made ready for the play to begin"; "In the middle of the play, I ordered a short banquet for the king, the queen, and the lords. And the college was at that time so well furnished, as that they did not borrow any one actor from any college in town" (*JCS*). Laud deemed the play a success: "The plot was very good, and the action. It was merry, and without offence, and so gave a great deal of content" (Smyth 2006). No license for acting extant.

London, BL, Additional MS 14047, fols. 7–39; dramatis personae; five acts and separate scenes. The elaborate masque of the final scenes furnishes "numerous parts for students of St. John's and provid[es] a grand finale for the royal entertainment" (Shaw 1979). Washington, Folger, MS J.b.7, a fragment entitled *Lovers' Hospital*; it consists of two leaves (four pages) and twenty-two stubs containing some writing; no separate TP; no author named. SR 17 November 1655 a comedy entituled *Lovers hospitall*. If printed, no copy survives. First edited by Funston 1973.

Love's Kingdom. See *Love's Dominion.*

Love's Labor's Lost. William Shakespeare. Acted c. ?1591 (Gurr 2009d), or *c.* 1594 (Woudhuysen 1998), or 1595 (Carroll 2009) by the Lord Chamberlain's Men at the Cross Keys or Theater. Also "presented before her highnes this last Christmas" by this company, according to the Q1 TP, which "probably means, given early modern dating, Christmas 1597 or even Christmas 1598" (Carroll). The play is "the earliest instance of any Shakespeare play that we *know* to have been performed at court" (Dutton 2009a). Possibly acted by the Chamberlain's Men at the Curtain (Astington 2009), and later by the King's Men at the first Globe. The role of Costard may have been played by Will Kemp (Howard 2006b, Butler 2004d, Bate 2008). The play was "booked . . . by the Earl of Southampton at his house in London at Christmas 1604," but perhaps not performed there (Gurr 2004c). Performed at the Great Hall of Whitehall before the king and queen, Christmas season [between 1 and 6 January (Dutton 2011)] 1605. The Q2 TP claims performance at both the Globe and [second] Blackfriars. Francis Meres in *Palladis Tamia* (SR 7 September 1598) praises several Shakespearean comedies, including this play and the lost *Love's Labor's Won*.

SR no original; transferred 22 January 1607; 19 November 1607; ?4 August 1626 Paviers right in Shakesperes *plaies*; ?19 June 1627 widow of Isaac Jaggard . . . her parte in Shackspheere *playes*; 1 July 1637 Shakespeare *workes* their Part; 24 August 1642; 14 September 1642; 6 August 1674; 21 August 1683. Q1 1598 *A Pleasant Conceited Comedy called Love's Labor's Lost*; "newly corrected and augmented by W. Shakespere"; "an earlier edition has been lost" (Wells & Taylor

1987); not divided. Q1 is "the first play whose first edition includes Shakespeare's name on the title page" (Berger & Lander 1999). Unusual staging involves four love letters read aloud seriatim by their authors. The men's plan to forgo the company of women founders when they fall in love; although each seeks to conceal the truth from his friends, each recites a love poem, which is overheard by the others: "Shakespeare here (characteristically) pushes the eavesdropping gambit to its limits by stacking the eavesdroppers three deep" (David 1978). In the scene, "a third hiding place is required. Its position is indicated by Berowne's line, 'Like a demigod here sit I in the sky.' Evidently he has slipped out and reappeared in the stage gallery" (Harbage 1955), i.e., in a space corresponding to one of the compartments shown in De Witt's drawing of the Swan. "The eavesdropping episode . . . illustrates as well as any scene he wrote Shakespeare's flair for inventing and deploying props" (Kiefer 2004). The sonnet-reading scene is "metadramatic," as are the masque of Muscovites (*"Enter Black-moores with musicke . . . and the rest of the Lordes disguised"*) and pageant of the Nine Worthies (Carroll). Such theatrical inventiveness is made necessary by the virtual absence of a plot. The entry of Marcade, probably attired in black, with news of the King's demise may evoke personified Death. At the close Spring (the actor playing Jaquenetta) enters as a nubile woman, Winter (the actor playing Dull) as a bearded old man; they sing the songs that conclude the play (Kiefer 1995). F1 1623 *Comedies, Histories, & Tragedies*; three issues; "published according to the true originall copies"; five acts, but these are "of monstrously disproportionate lengths" (Greg 1955). Q2 1631 *Love's Labor's Lost, A Witty and Pleasant Comedy*. F2 1632 "the second impression"; three issues. F3 1663 "the third impression"; reissued 1664 with seven additional plays. F4 1685 "the fourth edition"; two issues.

In this play "we have a fascinating palimpsest of Continental female performance to consider: women of the French court, known for their skilled discourse in academic and salon settings, their literary activities, their performances in court entertainments, and their risqué reputations, are portrayed, or written over, in roles that look suspiciously like those created for commedia dell'arte actresses" (Campbell 2005). Simultaneously, the play places friendship among men at the center of the action: "The idealisation of male friendship as higher and stronger than heterosexual desire reflects, from one point of view, a fantasy of denial, a justification of a paralysis or blockage in 'normal' psychosexual development: the movement from same-sex to other-sex erotic relations" (Carroll).

Love's Loadstone. See *Pathomachia.*

Love's Metamorphosis, A Witty and Courtly Pastoral. John Lyly. Written "(though not necessarily performed) before the demise of the first Blackfriars in 1584" (Scragg 2008). "First playd by" Paul's Boys, according to the SR and TP, at Paul's playhouse; performance would have taken place before suppression of the company *c.* 1590. Subsequently revived by the Children of the Chapel, according to the SR and TP, at the second Blackfriars, in 1600 and revived "by Paul's in 1601" (Lamb 2009). "The revival of such plays was greeted with scorn by new dramatists like Marston, Jonson, and Chapman who were taking over the boys' companies for their own satiric purposes. These new men derided plays like Lyly's as 'musty fopperies'" (Hunter 2004). Possibly performed at court (Jankowski 2000), as the word *Courtly* in the title may suggest.

SR 25 November 1600. Q 1601 SDs "show that the texts of four songs are missing" (Greg 1939); five acts and separate scenes. Special effects include a tree that bleeds and groans; the man who fells the tree "is transformed through Famine, invoked by the wrath of Ceres, into the living skeleton of a man"; Protea is transformed from a young woman to an old man and then back into a woman (Scragg 2005). "A Siren is disclosed on (or rises from)" a rock; this Siren then "appears to 'shrink'" back into the rock (Scragg 2008). Also "Proserpine sends 'a thick mist,' under cover of which the transformation of the three nymphs takes place"; later Venus sends "what is vaguely termed 'a showre' to hide them again while they resumed their original shape" (Lawrence 1927). "Cupid's temple stands at the center of the stage" (Scragg 1987).

This comedy was not included in the first collected edition of Lyly's plays (1632).

Love's Mistress, or The Queen's Masque. Thomas Heywood. Acted November 1634 (*JCS*) by Queen Henrietta Maria's Men at the Phoenix. "Three times presented before" King Charles and Queen Henrietta Maria and various foreign ambassadors "within the space of eight dayes," according to the Q1 TP: first, between 13 and 18 November at the Phoenix without changeable scenery; second, on 19 November at Somerset [Denmark] House with changeable scenery; and third, between 20 and 26 November again at Somerset House with changeable scenery, which was designed by Inigo Jones, whom the playwright praises in his address to the reader. The royal performance at the Phoenix was possibly the first of the play: this "was obviously a private occasion, perhaps to see a dress rehearsal before the production at Denmark House" (Edwards 1981). The alternative title, *Queen's Masque,* "illustrates how, by 1634, dramatic productions, particularly at the queen's court, were being infiltrated by masque elements to the point of generic confusion" (Britland 2006b). In playlist of Beeston's Boys 10 August 1639.

SR 30 September 1635 *The Queenes Maske or Loves Mistresse.* Q1 1636 "publikely acted by the queens comoedians"; dramatis personae; prologue "the first time it was presented on the stage," which means "The Phoenix playhouse rather than court" (Stern 2009c); prologue for performance before the king (November 19); prologue to king and queen "the second time it was acted, the same weeke"; Cupid speaks all of the prologues as well as the epilogue; five acts. (Prologues for the first presentation at Somerset House and "To the king and queene, the second time it was acted the same weeke" and the epilogue were subsequently published in Heywood's *Pleasant Dialogues and Dramas* [1637].) Staging calls for descent and ascent (by Cupid "*in a cloude,*") employing machinery (Orrell 1985).

Special effects include *"A Storme"* and *"A great storme."* "The play is notable "for its employment of music to create atmospheric and mystical effects" (Britland). "In combining the dances, shows and classical material with allegory, Heywood was taking the dramatic form which he had used in the Age plays a stage further. The overall effect combined the pleasures and, indeed, the ideology of the court masque with those of the professional theatre" (McLuskie 1994). Q2 1640 "the second impression, corrected by the author." Q3 ?1662 (Rowland 2010); the TP bears a 1640 date, which is fraudulent. Despite the word "masque" in the play's title, this work is a drama: "What links the play with the masque is the use during its actual production of changeable scenery" (Limon 1990).

In his address to the Q1 reader Heywood discusses the visual delight of the second and third performances: "for the rare decorements which new apparell'd it when it came the second time to the royall viewe, (her gracious majestie then entertaining his highnesse at Denmarke-house, upon his birth-day), I cannot pretermit to give a due charractar to that admirable artist, Mr. *Inego Jones* . . . who to every act, nay almost to every sceane, by his excellent inventions, gave such an extraordinary luster; upon every occasion changing the stage, to the admiration of all the spectators: that, as I must ingeniously confesse, it was above my apprehension to conceive, so to their sacred majesties, and the rest of the auditory; it gave so generall a content, that I presume they never parted from any object, presented in that kind, better pleased, or more plentifully satisfied." Although a compliment, "there is a sense here that Heywood, Midas-like, is having some fun with the idea that his iconoclastic play should have been presented with all the elaborate iconography of Jones's designs" (Rowland).

Love's Pilgrimage. John Fletcher; revised by an unidentified author. Lost original version presumably acted by the King's Men at the [second] Blackfriars, c. 1616 (McMullan 2004). Revised version licensed 16 September 1635 (Adams 1917, Beaurline 1970); "who undertook the revision and which parts were revised is not known" (Whitlock 2005). F1 SDs mention "Rowl," who has been interpreted as Rowland Ashton, "a hired player for the King's Men" (Beaurline) and as Rowland Dowle (Powell 1941, Gurr 2004c); SDs also name John Bacon, a hired man; they may have performed in the 1635 revival (Gurr). Revived by the King's Men at Hampton Court, 16 December 1636 (bill of King's Men for performance at court). The revised version inserts passages from Ben Jonson's *The New Inn*, acted 1629. In playlist of the King's Men 7 August 1641 as "The Lovers Pilgrimage."

SR 4 September 1646 *The Lovers pilgrimage*; 30 January 1673. B&F F1 1647 *Comedies and Tragedies*; "never printed before, and now published by the authours originall copies"; prologue; five acts and separate scenes. Unusual SD: *"Enter Theodosia, and Phillippo on several beds"*; each bed would probably have been pushed onstage. B&F F2 1679 *Fifty Comedies and Tragedies*; "published by the authors original copies, the songs to each play being added"; *Love's Pilgrimage, A Comedy*; list of characters.

The F1 prologue, which appeals to women playgoers, expresses the view "that women spectators are more easily pleased than the men and will help to win the men's approval of the play" (Levin 1989b): "Ten to one / We please the women; and I would know that man / Follows not their example."

Love's Riddle, A Pastoral Comedy. Abraham Cowley. Acted 1633–36 (*JCS*). Probably performed by students at Westminster School: the TP reports, "written at the time of his being kings scholler in Westminster schoole." Dedicatory verses "allude to the popularity of 'Robinson, whom they at schoole, account essential to a play.' Richard Robinson was a member of the King's company who made his name as a boy actor as early as 1619 and lived till 1648" (Greg 1939).

SR 14 March 1638. O 1638 list of characters; epilogue (by Alupis); five acts and first scenes. Few SDs apart from entrances and exits and the climactic sword fight between brother and sister: *"[Florellus] drawes two swords from under his garment and offers one to Call[idora]"*; *"[they] fight."* "No doubt [the play] was revised . . . before its publication" (Harbage 1936).

The O dedication contrasts the contents of the play with fashionable fare and relates the play's subject and style to the time and place of its composition: "each line of it / Betray's the time and place wherein t'was writ, / And I could wish, that I might safely say / To th'reader, that t'was done but th' other day. / Yet 'tis not stuff'd with names of gods, hard words, / Such as the Metamorphosis affords. / Nor has't a part for Robinson, whom they / At schoole, account essentiall to a play. / The stile is low, such as you'le easily take / For what a swaine might speake, and a boy make."

Love's Sacrifice, A Tragedy. John Ford. Acted 1626–31 (Moore 2002), perhaps 1631 (Gurr 1988a). By Queen Henrietta Maria's Men at the Phoenix, according to the TP, which describes the play as "a tragedie received generally well." Richard Perkins, who "appears to have been the leading actor in Queen Henrietta's company" (Moore), probably played the Duke. The Queen's company "performed at the Phoenix Theatre from late 1625 or early 1626 until 1637." In playlist of Beeston's Boys 10 August 1639.

SR 21 January 1633. Q 1633 no author named on the TP but James Shirley addresses a poem to Ford, who signs the dedicatory epistle, and Ford is named in the SR; list of characters; dumb show; five acts. Highly detailed SDs: *"A curtaine drawne, below are discovered Biancha in her night attire, leaning on a cushion at a table, holding Fernando by the hand."* "Ford may here be evoking the contemporary symbolic association of cushions with lust" (Madelaine 1988). The plot involves three courtly women who perform an antic masque and stab to death the courtier who impregnated them; "the drama was beginning to register and respond to the topic of female acting in England" (Tomlinson 1992b). Staging includes a *coup de théâtre*: *"A sad sound of soft musicke. The tombe is discovered. Enter foure with torches, after them two fryars, after the Duke in mourning manner, after him the*

Abbot, Fiormonda, Colona, Julia, Roseilli, Petruchio, Nibrassa, and a guard. D'avolos following behinde. Comming neere the tombe they all kneele, making shew of ceremony. The Duke goes to the tombe, layes his hand on it. Musicke cease." Then *"One goes to open the tombe, out of which ariseth Fernando in his winding sheet, onely his face discovered."* This scene may have used a property tomb, but "the Duke and guards are able to walk into the tomb, which indicates that it was represented—or imagined—as a vault" (Moore). In any event the action "seems calculated to give the audience the gratuitous thrill of apparently seeing a walking corpse" (Madelaine 1988), though Fernando is actually alive. In other action a "fool plans to send his mistress a half-length portrait of himself with a mirror over his heart, so that she can gaze at herself and ultimately come to love him" (Rochester 2010). The play is "disconcertingly replete with echoes of Shakespeare and other dramatists of the period" (Moore), especially *Othello*. Also issued in *Comedies, Tragicomedies, and Tragedies* (1652), a made-up book.

Ford's Q dedication, referring apparently to William Prynne's attack on the stage, adopts an aggrieved stance: "The contempt throwne on studies of this kinde, by such as dote on their owne singularity, hath almost so out-fac'd invention, and prescrib'd judgement; that it is more safe, more wise, to be suspectedly silent, then modestly confident of opinion, herein."

Love's Trial. See *The Hollander.*

Love's Victory, A Tragicomedy. William Chamberlain. Probably written after the closing of the theaters and not acted, but the playwright hoped that his play would be performed. In his dedication he refers to "this rigid age," which "hath silenced" the stage.

SR none. Q 1658 list of characters; five acts. Detailed SDs: *"The song ended, the priests prepare to strike. A clap of thunder, groans, and shrieks throughout the temple, the priests robes dropt over with bloud, the images of the gods reverst."*

The address to the reader complains of the government edict that closed the theaters and precluded production: "Since by this active age 't hath been thought best / With their grave earnest to crush plots in jest; / The mourning stage being silent, justly I / May change a prologue to apologie; / That so in private each spectator may / Singly receive his welcome to a play." "This epistle is particularly interesting because it performs the invitational function of a stage prologue while transforming that function into the terms of a different social practice" (Straznicky 2004).

Love's Victory. Mary Wroth; authorship established by Roberts 1983. Written *c.* 1615–18 (Findlay 2006) or in the ?early 1620s, possibly for private performance (Van Elk 2004), perhaps "at one of the Sidney houses" (Findlay 1999). "The play would have been best suited to an amateur performance by some of the author's friends, with household servants or estate-workers perhaps taking the non-speaking pastoral parts and those of Venus's priests" (Brennan 1988), possibly at "the Sidney home of Penshurst" (Findlay 2006). No evidence of production but the SDs in the Penshurst MS "suggest that Wroth thought of the work in terms of an actual performance"; it is even "possible that *Love's Victory* was one of the plays staged by Sir Edward Dering, who was involved in amateur dramatics during the early 1620s" (Cerasano & Wynne-Davies 1996).

(1) San Marino, CA, Huntington, MS HM 600; fols. 1–21; no separate TP; no author named; in the hand of the author (Roberts); corrections by author; contains "the only known copy of the initial prologue . . . and the final prologue" (Swift 1989); incomplete—lacks opening interlude, breaks off after the beginning of act 5; Venus and Cupid function as chorus; five acts. Few SDs, only the names of characters at the beginning of act 2. But action culminates in a *deus ex machina*: "Silvestra comes upon the lovers at the moment when they are about to stab themselves, and offers them a lethal potion instead so that their blood will not be spilt"; "Upon discovering the collapsed lovers, the remaining characters place their corpses upon the altar in Venus's temple"; "The lovers' bodies become literally objectified as revered monuments in death"; finally "the lovers miraculously revive" (Bennett 2003). Extracts of MS (1) were edited by Halliwell [-Phillips] 1853; "it is virtually certain" that the MS Halliwell worked from is now Huntington, MS HM 600 (Brennan); Halliwell writes that it had belonged to Edward Dering, but there is no evidence for the claim. (2) Tonbridge, UK, Penshurst Place Library, fols. 1–49; published in facsimile by Brennan 1988, who writes: this "remains the most authoritative version of the play to have survived. It was first identified as being in the hand of Lady Mary Wroth by the late Peter J. Croft." "A list of dramatis personae is provided at the end of the manuscript, but it appears to be in a hand other than Lady Mary's" (Brennan). Some SDs: "*Venus and Cupid apeering in the clowds*"; "*The temple, and the dead bodys on the aulter, the sheapherds, and sheapherdesses casting flowers on them, while Venus apeers in glory they sing.*"

"The first original pastoral comedy by a woman writer, meant to be read or acted in a small family circle" (Rubik 1998), "Wroth's pastoral drama subverts the patriarchal ideology of the Jacobean court" (Lewalski 1991). "But the strict limitations imposed upon articulations of actual female desire are essential and unwavering" (Bennett). The dramaturgy "reflect[s] the special experience of a woman writing in Jacobean England" (McLaren 1990). "*Love's Victory* presents powerful female figures whose elevated viewing position allows them to direct the plot, offering female spectators on and offstage a controlling perspective over the garden of love" (Findlay 2006). The play "demonstrates values conversant with the *préciosité* and Platonism popular in the salon culture of early seventeenth-century France" (Hodgson-Wright 2000a).

The Lovesick Court, or the Ambitious Politique, A Comedy. Richard Brome. Acted 1638 (Shaw 1980), probably by Queen Henrietta Maria's Men at the Salisbury

Court playhouse (Steggle 2004b). Herbert's office-book records a 1638 date for *The Lovesick Courtier* at Salisbury Court, possibly the same play.

SR 4 August 1640. O 1658–59 two issues; *Five New Plays* (with *The English Moor*, *The New Academy*, *The Queen and Concubine*, *The Weeding of the Covent Garden*); separate TP dated 1658; separately paginated; dramatis personae; prologue and epilogue (also appears in *The Weeding of the Covent Garden*); two dumb shows enacted during songs; "[p]arts of the plot are presented as pantomimes" (Mehl 1965); five acts and separate scenes. The play features "elaborate emblematic spectacle" (McLuskie 1981): "*Recorders. Ent[er]* Disanius *before a herse.* Philocles *after.* Varillus *manacled, and led by* Tersulus. Euputhus *supports* Philocles, *as ready to sink with grief. . . . The herse set down,* Eudina *kneels to it.* Philo[cles] *kneels on the other side.*" In the most unusual SD, "Eudina, lulled by a song, falls asleep in the presence of two ladies, and has a dream which is shown to the audience in a dumb show. Meanwhile, the people on the stage are blissfully ignorant that a moving picture is in operation" (Lawrence 1927). "[A] full-scale parody of the absurdities of courtier drama" (Butler 1984b). "One might wonder whether *The Love-Sick Court* should be construed as an extended resignation letter from Queen Henrietta's Men" (Steggle).

The address to the readers of this collection expresses the wish that they would "be spectators, if the Fates so pleas'd, these comedies exactly being dressed for the stage"; the playwright "understood the proportions and beauties of a scene [i.e., the play in performance]." The address goes on to note that "The *Love-sick Court* and *Ambitious Politick* are but one play, though strange those two should dwell together." The double title equates "sexual drive and political hunger" (Steggle).

The Lovesick King. Anthony Brewer. Acted April-May 1617 (Martin 1991). Presumably first performed before King James in Newcastle (Dodds 1924, Martin 1991); the company may have been Palsgrave's Men, successor to Prince Henry's Men. "[T]he interest of the play is so local that one cannot help thinking that it must have been written for a Newcastle audience" (Swaen 1907).

SR 20 June 1655; transferred 16 July 1662. Q 1655 *The Lovesick King, an English Tragical History, with the Life and Death of Cartesmunda, the Fair Nun of Winchester*; list of characters; five acts. Scenes of extraordinary violence, as, e.g., the English pitted against the Danes: "*Alarm. Enter* Osbert, Erkinwald, Harold, *and the Danes crying Kill, kill, the wounded souldiers rise and fight, to them the King,* Alured, *and the English, who are driven out and the King slain.*" The playwright specifies what playgoers hear and see: "*A great cry within. Enter Abbot bearing a cross,* Cartesmunda *[the fair nun of Winchester] with two tapers burning, which she placeth on the altar, two or three nuns following.*" "The play's surprisingly positive attitude toward the nuns and their altar is the result of a dramatic strategy that valorizes religious chastity by emphasizing the threats made against it" (Williamson 2009).

The play "is a cocktail of patriotic assertions linking the British union to native liberty and thence to localism and the triumph of English merchants. Mercantile expansion is an alternative form of imperialism, one conceptualized . . . as a rising tide that lifts all boats" (Perry 2009).

The Loyal Citizens. A droll based upon a scene in B&F's *Cupid's Revenge* and performed in the 1640s and 50s. "This short, vivacious scene among the Citizens, requiring but four or five actors, is well adapted to performance as a droll" (Elson 1932).

Published in *1 The Wits, or Sport upon Sport* (O 1662 [two issues] and 1672), which mistakenly locates the source in *Philaster*; RT *The Humors of the Loyal Citizens*; argument; list of characters.

The Loyal Lovers, A Tragicomedy. Cosmo Manuche. ?Acted *c.* 1652. "Manuche's works may well have been performed at Castle Ashby, [the third earl of] Northampton's home" (Clare 2002) or at Northampton's London residence, Canonbury House, Islington (Wolf 1983). The play "contains an episode in which royalists stage a farce, in the vein of the pamphlet play, about the army preacher Hugh Peters. That the performance takes place in a private room of a tavern is some indication of one venue for the staging of political satire" (Clare 2004). "When the theatres closed in 1642 and it became clear that they were to remain closed for some time, household-style performance may have reappeared, with audience members rubbing shoulders more closely with performers in tavern rooms and private houses as Cosmo Maunuche's *Loyal Lovers* (1652) implies" (Milling 2004).

SR none. Q 1652 "the author to his honorable friends" [prologue to the reader]; "the author to his honorable friends" [epilogue]; list of characters; five acts and first scenes. Scores of detailed SDs: *"[Adrastus] looks in his watch"*; *"Enter Mettle with a black gown, and pen, ink, paper, and books"*; *"Symphronio standing behinde the hangings till his cue to enter, personating Fly-blow a butcher."*

"Though set in Amsterdam, [the play] offers a daring commentary upon England under the Commonwealth" (Phelps 1979), with "savagely funny satire involving Puritan caricatures" (Aggeler 1978). The play presents "a lively struggle between witty young cavaliers and elderly, narrow-minded Puritans" (Potter 1987b). "The play is a farcical pre-empting of *The Three Musketeers*, the Cavalier beaux making off with the daughters of Roundhead bores" (Smith 1994). The title is included in Kirkman's 1661 catalogue.

The Loyal Subject. John Fletcher. "Stylistic evidence suggests Fletcher's sole authorship, and this is confirmed by Sir Henry Herbert's note of 1633" (Finkelpearl 1990). Licensed for acting 16 November 1618 by Sir George Buc (Adams 1917) "in time for a court performance that day" (McMullan 2004). Acted by the King's Men at the second Blackfriars. Principal actors were Richard Burbage,

Henry Condell, John Lowin, Richard Sharp, Nathan Field, John Underwood, Nicholas Tooley, and William Eccleston, according to F2. License for acting renewed by Henry Herbert, "with some reformations allowed," 23 November 1633; Herbert calls this "an ould booke of Fletchers" (Adams). Performed by the King's Men at Whitehall before the king and queen, the night of 10 December 1633; Herbert records the king's judgment: "very well likt." Revived at Hampton Court, 6 December 1636 (bill of King's Men for performances at court). In play-list of the King's Men 7 August 1641.

SR 4 September 1646 by m^r Beamont & m^r fflesher; transferred 30 January 1673. B&F F1 1647 *Comedies and Tragedies*; "never printed before, and now published by the authours originall copies"; prologue and epilogue; five acts and separate scenes. B&F F2 1679 *Fifty Comedies and Tragedies*; "published by the authors original copies, the songs to each play being added"; *The Loyal Subject, A Tragicomedy*; list of characters; actors' names.

The F1 prologue was written for a revival after Fletcher's death (in 1625): "I could adde, so far / Behind him the most moderne writers are, / That when they would commend him, their best praise / Ruins the buildings which they strive to raise, / To his best memory." This prologue falls into the category of prologues and epilogues "not written by the authors of this volume," according to Humphrey Moseley, the publisher. The F1 epilogue alludes to the running time of the play in performance, which is longer than the "two hours traffic" alluded to in (the much earlier) *Romeo and Juliet*: "few here repent / Three hours of pretious time, or money spent / On our endeavours."

Lust's Dominion, or The Lascivious Queen, A Tragedy. Thomas Dekker, William Haughton, John Day, and John Marston (Cross 1958). D and the second issue of O and subsequent printings erroneously attribute the play to Marlowe. Kirkman, who signs the dedication, also ascribes the play to Marlowe in his catalogues of 1661 and 1671. Collier 1825 challenged the attribution and identified the play with *The Spanish Moor's Tragedy* as did Fleay 1891; Knutson 2006b is skeptical, and Gurr 2009c notes that "Dekker, Haughton and Day were not recorded as receiving 'full payment' to mark its completion"; Henslowe paid £3 to Dekker, Haughton, and Day on 13 February 1600, a sum "well below the figure that a new play could be expected at this time to command" (Ayres 1970), but perhaps indicating the revision of an extant play (Cathcart 2001b). Possibly written in the 1590s and revised by John Marston in September 1599 (Hoy 1980). But Cathcart 2001a argues that *Lust's Dominion* is indebted to *Hamlet* "independently of Marston's claims for authorship" and that *Hamlet* was probably written in 1599. Acted early in 1600 by the Lord Admiral's Men at the Rose. Possibly revised further by an unknown hand and revived *c.* 1606–08 (Cathcart 2001b), perhaps at the Whitefriars (Cathcart 2008). However, Simmons 1972 finds an allusion to the Globe in the last act; if true, this would mean that the play was first acted at the Globe by the Lord Chamberlain's Men. This play "may have been acquired from the Fortune company after 1625 by Beeston for the Cockpit or the Red Bull" (Gurr 2009c). Inspired by *The Jew of Malta*, *Lust's Dominion* dramatizes with glee "the intrigues of an ambitious villain" (Bowers 1940) and seems to have been popular. "The sheer proliferation of revenge schemes and their very complexity must be responsible for the appeal of this play in production" (Kiefer 2002).

SR none. O and D 1657 two issues; the "title most likely dates from the 1650s" (Steggle 2007); list of characters; five acts and separate scenes. The SDs "are frequent and usually quite elaborate" (Jewkes 1958): *"Alarum. They fight a combate, the Moor is struck down, which his side seeing, step all in and rescue him; the rest joine and drive in the Moors. Alarum continuing, Spaniards and Moors with drums and colours flye over the stage, persued by Philip, Cardinall, King Port[ugal]. And others. Enter Zarack Christofero, and Eleazar at severall doors."* Reissued 1658 and 1661.

The publication of the play in 1657 arose from "political ends, and its backers were advancing a critique of Cromwell's regime by analogy with the play" (Cathcart 1999).

Lusty Juventus. R[?Richard] Wever. Acted *c.* 1544 (Thomas 1982) at undetermined venue. "Foure [with doubling] maye playe it easely, taking such partes as they thinke best: so that any one take of those partes that be not in place at once," according to the Q TPs, but there is no chart explaining the doubling of the nine roles. "Clearly addressed to youth but . . . neither a 'school' play nor one composed for the privileged classes" (White 1993b). "Probably the property of a touring troupe of players, and therefore could have reached a geographically and socially wide audience" (King 1993). "No elaborate staging requirements" (Lancashire 2002). In *Sir Thomas More* (*c.* 1600 [Jowett 2011]) a company of actors visits More's home for the purpose of performing a play, which proves to be an adaptation of *Lusty Juventus*; this may suggest that the interlude had a long stage history.

SR 14 August 1560 *a playe called Juventus.* Q1 ND ?1550 *An Interlude Called Lusty Juventus, Lively Describing the Frailty of Youth, of Nature, Prone to Vice, by Grace and Good Counsel, Trainable to Virtue*; no author named on the TP, which lists the characters, but R. Wever's name appears on the last page; prologue by Messenger; "ends with a prayer to King Edward that was not changed for the publication of the play" (Schneider 2011); not divided but the play has a tripartite structure of "conversion, degeneration and recovery" (Sessions 2002). Q2 ND 1562–68 (Nosworthy 1966). Q3 ND 1569–75 (Nosworthy).

The play, which has an "aggressive anti-Catholic tone" (Dillon 1998) and which was "written under the influence" of John Bale (Thompson 1910), addresses "matters specific to the reign of a boy-king reformer" (Westfall 2002) and argues a Protestant agenda: "the devil, who has been established as a Catholic, complains that the young people no longer adhere to his laws and the traditions of men but insist on living according to the truth of the Scriptures" (Pineas

1962). "Juventus is a Reformation Everyman who must decide in his youth between the competing claims of traditional religion, on the one hand, and the plain gospel faith and stringent ethical demands of the reformers" (King 1982).

M

Macbeth. William Shakespeare. Acted the second half of 1606 (Brooke 1990) by the King's Men at the first Globe. Possibly performed at Hampton Court before Queen Anne and King Christian of Denmark, the evening of 7 August 1606 (Paul 1950), soon after commercial-playhouse performance; this "may explain why Norway is made Scotland's enemy in the opening battle, where it was Denmark in the *Chronicles*" (Bate 2009); "it seems inconceivable that King James would not have been interested in the play"; "King James surely must have wanted to see a play that included both witches and his ancestors" (Orgel 2002). "Of Shakespeare's great tragedies, *Macbeth* has always seemed the most topical, cannily alert not only to contemporary events but to King James's political beliefs and personal obsessions" (Greenblatt 1997). The acquisition of the Blackfriars theater would have allowed the King's Men to simulate the darkness that is "a central preoccupation of the play" (Brooke); but the company would not begin using the Blackfriars until 1610 (Barroll 2005). Richard Burbage probably played Macbeth; Robert Armin, the Porter (Butler 2004a). Lady Macbeth was played by a young male who "appeared feminine" (Kliman 2004); John Rice, the boy-actor, probably played the role in the performance that Simon Forman witnessed in 1611 (Bartholomeusz 1969).

SR 8 November 1623; transferred ?4 August 1626 Paviers right in Shakes-peres *plaies*; ?19 June 1627 widow of Isaac Jaggard . . . her parte in Shackspheere *playes*; 16 November 1630; 1 July 1637 Shakespeares *workes* their Part; 6 August 1674; 21 August 1683. F1 1623 *Comedies, Histories, & Tragedies*; three issues; "published according to the true originall copies"; *The Tragedy of Macbeth*; "as it is the shortest play in the Shakespeare canon it may have been cut at some point" (Ioppolo 2006); some evidence of revision (Braunmuller 2008); Old Man and Ross provide "choral commentary" (Kliman); witches "act as choric presenters" (Ewbank 2007); five acts and separate scenes. A copy of F1 at the University of Padua preserves the text "marked up, no later than the 1630s, for performance" (Orgel 2006). F2 1632 "the second impression"; three issues. F3 1663 "the third impression"; reissued 1664 with seven additional plays. Q 1673. F4 1685 "the fourth edition"; two issues.

"The actor playing Macbeth appears to have made his first entrance at the Globe on horseback" (Bartholomeusz); Simon Forman's eyewitness account of a performance at the Globe on 20 April 1611 (Oxford, Bodleian, MS Ashmole 208,

X, fol. 207) reports that Macbeth and Banquo were "riding through a wood." Or was Forman remembering the account in Holinshed describing how the two men "journeyed towarde Fores" and the 1577 *Chronicles* woodcut illustrating the two on horseback, rather than what he saw onstage? Scragg 1973 doubts the use of horses, but "Forman must either have thought riding the ordinary way for gentlemen to travel overland . . . or he refers to the scene on stage" (Benecke 2010).

Forman describes the creatures whom Macbeth and Banquo meet as "three women fairies or nymphes," who "are more fair than foul in Holinshed" (Bate 2009) and who appear as stately ladies in the 1577 *Chronicles* woodcut; they "are not witches" (McLuskie 2009). But "Scotland and witchcraft had long been associated" (Kinney 2001), and King James was the author of *Daemonologie* (1597). The three figures in F1 have been "transformed" into "ambiguously gendered women-with-beards" (Taylor 2002b) and enigmatically costumed (Kiefer 2003): "What are these, / So wither'd, and so wilde in their attyre, / That look not like th'inhabitants o'th'earth?" F1 SDs call them witches. These creatures were played by adult males. *Macbeth* had apparently been revised by Thomas Middleton, who was "as far as we know, the only dramatist whom the King's Men entrusted to revise a Shakespeare play" (Jowett 2002). Middleton's intervention may have come about because the play seems not to have been especially popular (Orgel). "The most likely date for the adaptation would . . . seem to be the summer or autumn of 1616" (Taylor 2007a). The original production featured three figures called "weyward" (or "weyard") in F; "the idea that they were witches seems to have come in with Middleton's additions to the play" (Cooper 2010). None of the weird sisters in the original production flew (Wickham 1973). Middleton's revision added Hecate (not mentioned by Forman) and other witches and, inspired by Jonson's *Masque of Queens*, used suspension gear for flight by Hecate and perhaps the other witches (Wickham). "The King's Men could have used snakes in the costuming of Hecate, either by having her handle the reptiles or by giving her a Medusa-like wig"; she may also have carried torches, "a visual allusion to Hecate's abode in the underworld" (Kiefer 2003). In F1 Macbeth suggests that the witches ride horses: "Infected be the ayre whereon they ride"; he adds, "I did heare / The gallopping of horse." "The witches are quintessential theatrical devices: they dance and sing, perform wonders, appear and disappear, fly, produce visions—do, in short, all the things that, historically, we have gone to the theater to see" (Orgel 2002). Two songs referred to in the F1 SDs have been lifted from Middleton's *The Witch*, acted 1616 (Taylor 2004b); "the Hecate passages are inextricably connected with the songs" (Ewbank 2007).

Middleton "was first identified as the adapter of *Macbeth* in 1869 (by W. G. Clark and W. A. Wright)" (Taylor 2004b). But despite this longstanding claim, the recent work of Taylor and Jowett, and the inclusion of *Macbeth* in the Oxford *Collected Works of Thomas Middleton* (2007), the issue of Middleton's involvement seems not entirely settled. Vickers 2010 finds "absolutely no trace of Middleton's hand" in the Hecate scenes, usually attributed to Middleton. And Miola 2004 apparently detects no evidence of Middleton in the play.

Macbeth is "perhaps the most visual of Shakespeare's tragedies" (Diehl 1983). The witches' cauldron (suggestive of hellmouth [Doebler 1974]), along with the three apparitions (armed [helmeted] head, bloody child, child crowned) that Macbeth sees, arise through a trap to the sound of thunder (Hodges 1999); Banquo's ghost may also have entered and exited through a trap (King 1971). Lady Macbeth's sleepwalking and handwashing represent some of the most memorable stage business in Shakespearean drama; less obvious is the meaning of her writing (apparently merely narrated) something that no one reads, a literalization of the book of conscience (Kiefer 1996b). Simon Forman's account contains a detail of staging: as Macbeth at a banquet stood "to drink a carouse" to the missing Banquo, "the ghost of Banquo came and sat down in his chair behind him. And he turning about to sit down again saw the ghost of Banquo, which fronted him so, that he fell into a great passion of fear and fury" (Salgādo 1975); playgoers saw the ghost before the king did. "Forman reacted strongly to moments when the Macbeths are confronted through supernatural agency with the guilt of their crimes" (Whitney 2006). The figures of the dumb show/pantomime "*of eight kings, and Banquo last, with a glasse [mirror] in his hand*" probably "entered through the central opening, marched around, and then departed by the centre, though it is also possible that the show crossed the stage from one flanking door to the other" (Ichikawa 2002); Fitzpatrick 2011, however, maintains that there were only two entry-points onto the stage. The last figure in the procession of kings, says Macbeth, "beares a glasse, / Which shewes me many more: and some I see / That two-fold balles and trebble scepters carry." "The 'twofold balls' probably refer to the ceremonial orbs used at James's two coronations at Scone and Westminster as King of Scotland and England respectively"; the scepters seem "to allude to James's title as King of Great Britain, France, and Ireland" (Bevington & Smith 1999).

An extraordinary array of sound effects contributes to the eerie atmosphere: "*thunder*" when the witches enter; hoboys/hautboys when Duncan arrives at Macbeth's castle; the "scream" of an owl and the sound of crickets; the cry of a raven; "*knocking within*," following the murder and answered by the porter; an alarm bell ringing in the stillness of the night; "lamentings heard i'th'ayre"; "*music and a song*" when Hecate chastises the other witches, and again when she "*commend[s]*" their work; the noise of horses' hooves before Banquo is killed; a "cry within of women" when Lady Macbeth dies; the sound of drums when Malcolm and Macduff march against Macbeth. "A drum played to march time was the stage convention to indicate the approach of an army" (Ogilvie 1927). The conversation of the witches in the opening scene "would have been prompted by the meow of a cat and the croak of a toad"; "[u]sed judiciously, the animal noises add to the supernatural quality of the meeting" (Shirley 1961). Following the show of kings, Hecate (or one of the other witches) says, "Ile charme the ayre to give a sound," and the witches dance an "antique [antic] round," requiring (unspecified) *"musicke"*; they would probably have moved "in an anticlockwise direction" (Brissenden 1981).

The performance of *Macbeth* at court in 1606 may have celebrated "James's triumph over the Gunpowder Plot traitors" the previous year; the speeches of the Porter allude to Father Henry Garnet, one of the conspirators (Lemon 2006), who became identified with the practice of equivocation.

Macrinus. See *Caracalla.*

A Mad Couple Well Matched. Richard Brome. Acted 1639 (Spove 1979) by Beeston's Boys (King and Queen's Young Company) at the Phoenix. *A Mad Couple* "probably started life as a play being written for Salisbury Court, before being transferred to Beeston" (Steggle 2004b). The number of boys in the company "probably enabled a play such as *A Madd Couple*, which features multiple leads for female characters" (Poulsen 2008). In playlist of Beeston's Boys 10 August 1639.

SR no original; transferred 11 June 1659 *The mad couple well matcht.* O 1653–54 *Five New Plays* (with *The City Wit, The Court Beggar, The Damoiselle, The Novella*); continuous register through *Court Beggar*; two issues; no separate TP; list of characters; prologue and epilogue; five acts and separate scenes. Considerable attention to hand props: *"Enter Carelesse, with two letters in his hand, and Wat with a candle, and wax."* Staging may call for a temporary structure: *"The shop discover'd."*

Prologue is striking in his unconventionality: "I'm sent a wo[o]ing to you, but how to do 't, / I han't the skill; tis true I've a new suite, / And ribbons fashionable, yclipt fancies, / But for the complements, the trips, and dances, / Our poet can't abide um, and he swears, / They're all but cheats; and sugred words but jeeres." This prologue "acknowledges the desire for a 'set' speech, at the same time questioning and undermining that same desire by apparently refusing to 'court' the audience" (Schneider 2011). The cheeky epilogue echoes the tone of the prologue: "Well! Had you mirth enough? Much good may't doe you, / If not, 'tis more than I did promise to you."

The play "brings significant innovations to scenarios of female homoerotic desire"; *A Mad Couple* places "the cross-dressed heroine in erotic relations with three different women" (Walen 2005). "In the world of the play, where sex equals money and all relationships are mercenary, female homoeroticism simply represents the homosocial flow of cash" (Poulsen 2008). Brome's play "is one of the period's most radical re-examinations of sexual relations within the gentry household" (Butler 2004b).

The Mad Lover. John Fletcher. Acted late 1616 by the King's Men at the second Blackfriars/second Globe. Performed at court "after supper," 5 January 1617 (diary of Lady Anne Clifford [Turner 1982]). Principal actors were Richard Burbage, Robert Benfield, Nathan Field, Henry Condell, John Lowin, William

Eccleston, and Richard Sharp, according to F2. A SD mentions Ed[ward] Hor[ton]; another mentions Richard Baxter, who acted in revivals. Revived at the Whitehall Cockpit, 5 November 1630, probably for the opening of this renovated theater (Bentley 1971); also performed 21 May 1639 (account book of Humphrey Mildmay). In playlist of the King's Men 7 August 1641.

SR 4 September 1646; 30 January 1673. B&F F1 1647 *Comedies and Tragedies*; "never printed before, and now published by the authours originall copies"; prologue and epilogue (of unknown authorship [Turner]); five acts and first scenes. "In *The Mad Lover*, the homoerotic aspects of the Orpheus myth are strongly implied by the context and content of the masque presented to cure Memnon of mad love" (DiGangi 1997): *"Enter the maske of beasts"* in which "a lion, a dog, an ape, a pied bird, and some trees danced" (Lawrence 1927). "Each beast is identified as a transformed lover" (Gossett 1988). The climactic SD involves the descent (to the sound of thunder and music), apparently by machinery, of a character impersonating Venus: *"Venus descends"* and then *"ascends."* "Such spectacle would have called for special structural preparations at court in 1617, whereas the Cockpit theatre had been planned to accommodate it" (Astington 1999a). B&F F2 1679 *Fifty Comedies and Tragedies*; "published by the authors original copies, the songs to each play being added"; *The Mad Lover, A Tragicomedy*; list of characters; actors' names.

The F1 prologue alludes to the admission price at the Blackfriars: "Remember ye'ar all venturers; and in this play / How many twelve-pences ye have 'stow'd this day."

A Mad World My Masters. Thomas Middleton (named in Archer's 1656 catalogue). Acted August 1605-June 1606 (Henning 1965). "Lately in action" by Paul's Boys, according to the Q1 TP, at Paul's playhouse. Later "often acted" by Queen Henrietta Maria's Men at the Salisbury Court playhouse, according to the Q2 TP. This company "has a history extending from 1625 to 1642; it was a reorganized group, however, that played at Salisbury Court between 1637 and 1642, and it is to this group that the revival belongs" (Henning), probably "by 1640" (Saccio 2007).

SR 4 October 1608; transferred 19 April 1613; 3 July 1630. Q1 1608 author's initials on the TP; within the act 5 play-within-the-play, Folly-Wit presents a prologue; five acts. SDs describe costumes and props: *"Enter in a masking sute with a vizard in his hand, Folly-wit"*; *"Viols, gallipots, plate, and an houre-glasse by her. The Curtizan on a bed, for her counterfeit fitt."* "[W]ith the help of the courtesan who feigns an illness, Mrs. Harebrain convinces [her husband] to allow her to visit the sickbed behind which she has arranged an assignation with her lover, Penitent Brothel" (Collington 1999). The play features a Succubus "in the form of Mistress Harebrain" (Cox 2000): *"Enter the divell in her shape."* She visits Penitent Brothel and "dances provocatively before him in an attempt to coax an erection — 'Once so firm, and now so hollow?'" (Collington). Staging seems to call for a trap when the Succubus stamps her foot and exits (Lawrence 1927). Q2 1640 *A Mad World My Masters, A Comedy*; list of characters; some SDs added; a single song is added at the end, "sung by Sir Bounteous Progresse to his guests."

The Q2 address of the printer and stationer to the reader treats changes in theatrical taste: "here & there you shall find some lines that doe answer in meetre, which I hope will not prove so disdainefull, whereby the booke may be so much slighted, as not to be read; or the authors judgement undervalued as of no worth. Consider (gentle reader) it is full twenty yeares since it was written, at which time meetre was most in use, and shewed well upon the conclusion of every act & scene." This address by John Spencer "functions as a rare moment of literary criticism, certainly some of the earliest of Middleton" (Bergeron 2006).

The Magnetic Lady, or Humors Reconciled, A Comedy. Ben Jonson. Licensed for acting 12 October 1632 as *Humors Reconciled, or the Magnetic Lady* (Adams 1917). Acted by the King's Men at the second Blackfriars: "There were at least three performances at the Blackfriars in 1632" (Happé 2000). A contemporary poem by Alexander Gill names two actors, John Lowin and Joseph Taylor; Lowin may have played Ironside; Taylor, Compass (Happé). The King's Men were summoned before the High Commission at Lambeth to answer charges "for uttring some prophane speaches in abuse of Scripture and wholly thinges"; "[p]ossibly they failed to observe deletion-marks Sir Henry [Herbert] had made in the text" (Bawcutt 1996). Initially the players tried to blame Jonson and Herbert, but on 24 October 1633 the actors admitted their responsibility. The play seems not to have been popular: "[T]his medley of satire, romance, and sentimental melodrama failed to please those who saw the King's Men perform it" (Riggs 1989). "The 'failure' of *The Magnetic Lady* on its original appearance at the Blackfriars in 1632 seems to have been quite arbitrary, and not really related to the play's apparent strengths and weaknesses. It may have been largely occasioned by the mockery at the performance by Inigo Jones and his companions, and this may have been compounded by politico-religious considerations in Laudian circles" (Happé 2001).

SR no original; 17 September 1658; transferred 20 November 1658; 19 August 1667. F2 1640–41 *The Works* vol. 3; separate TP dated 1640, an "erroneous date" (Giddens 2003); list of characters; "chorus by way of induction"; induction "includes a refusal to produce a prologue" but "Jonson has repeatedly included information regarding the play that is usually the province of prologues to provide" (Schneider 2011); chorus at end of each act; "chorus changed into an epilogue to the king"; five acts and separate scenes. The transformation of the final chorus in F2 suggests "that there may have been at least an intention to present the play at Court" (Happé), "but there is no record of a court performance" (Donaldson 2011). "The contents of Volume Three appeared with different sequences of page-numbering and bound in variously differing orders. Sometimes *The Magnetic Lady* is first, as though to continue the sequence of plays from Volume Two;

sometimes the masques begin the volume. Commonly copies of Volumes Two and Three are bound together with the [Richard] Meighen title-page which lists only the three 1631 plays: a practice which has proved misleading to cataloguers ever since" (Happé).

"The play's title suggests an explicit return to the humour theory of his early works, a move elucidated in the Induction" (Loxley 2002).

Magnificence. John Skelton. Acted *c.* 1520–22 (Neuss 1980) at undetermined venue. "Intended for performance in one of the Tudor halls as an entertainment to accompany some special banquet" (Neuss). "A clue for performance comes in the reference to the Taylors' Hall . . . which may suggest the Merchant Tailors' Hall" (Happé 1999). "*Magnificence* was probably staged in the presence of the Norfolk family, wherever else it may also have been put on" (Bevington 2002a); the Duke of Norfolk was opposed to Wolsey's policies and so might have found congenial the play's implicit criticism of the prelate. But Harris 1965 and Heiserman 1961 doubt that the play was chiefly a political satire directed against Wolsey. The eighteen roles may have been acted by four men and a boy (Walker 2000). "One of the five actors is a professional fool" (Bevington 1968). But McCarthy 2010 proposes that "*Magnificence* was written for chapel children or a song-school and staged originally in the exquisite monastic abbey of Westminster *c.* 1519, when Skelton resided there."

F ND *c.* 1530–33 (Norland 1995); *Magnificence, A Goodly Interlude and a Merry*; surviving copies at Cambridge University and BL; "a folio in fours" (Neuss); names of players at end of printed text; the opening speech by Felicity may be construed as a prologue; next-to-last speech of Magnificence may be construed as an epilogue; not divided. The SDs are "unusually detailed" (Southern 1973).

"[T]he finest contribution of the moralities to literary art" (Houle 1972), *Magnificence* "is a morality that has undergone a degree of secular transformation" (Bevington 1962). Skelton's drama "uses the format of the moral play to present the fall and redemption of a ruler" (Twycross 2007). "This is a moral play with a classic *psychomachia* scheme and a single fall and redemption, but with the specific theme of the use of moderation in the handling of wealth" (Grantley 2004). The play "was probably prompted by contemporary events at court — the Expulsion of the Minions of 1519" (Walker 2008). "Its secular, political intent is clear from the character of its Vices, who are not the Seven Deadly Sins but rather more specific and satirical personifictions of Courtly Abusyon, Clokyd Colusyon, and so on" (Dutton 2010).

Mahomet and His Heaven. See *Arabia Sitiens.*

The Maid in the Mill. John Fletcher and William Rowley; Henry Herbert records authorship (Hoy 1960). Licensed for acting as "a new Comedy, called, *The Maid in the Mill,*" 29 August 1623 (Adams 1917). Acted by the King's

Men at the second Globe. Performed also at Hampton Court the evening of 29 September 1623 (Adams); at St. James's Palace, "with reformations," probably in the Council Chamber, before the prince, 1 November 1623 (Astington 1986). "Revision of a play only two months old . . . is an odd phenomenon" (*JCS*). Performed as *The Maid of the Mill* at Whitehall, 26 December 1623, before the king and prince (Bawcutt 1996). Principal actors were Joseph Taylor, John Lowin, John Underwood, William Rowley, John Thompson, Robert Benfield, and Thomas Pollard, according to F2. "Rowley's characteristic fat-clown role [Bustofa] . . . appears in the play, and he probably wrote it for himself" (*JCS*). In playlist of King's Men 7 August 1641 as "The maid of the Mill."

SR 4 September 1646 *Maid of the Mill*; 30 January 1673. B&F F1 1647 *Comedies and Tragedies*; "never printed before, and now published by the authours originall copies"; *The Maid in the Mill*; attributed to B&F; pagination begins anew with this play though the register is continuous; five acts and separate scenes. Characters enact the Judgment of Paris: "*Enter Shepherd singing, with Ismena, Aminta, Florimell, (as Juno, Pallas, Venus).*" "[The clown] Bustopha instructs the shepherds to 'sing with dancing feet'" (Gossett 1988). B&F F2 1679 *Fifty Comedies and Tragedies*; "published by the authors original copies, the songs to each play being added"; *The Maid in the Mill, A Comedy*; list of characters; actors' names.

The play must have had a political resonance. When it was first performed, "Prince Charles was in Madrid, wooing the Spanish Infanta; concern about the Spanish Match was at its peak and, predictably enough, *The Maid in the Mill* is set in Spain" (Darby 2009).

Between the closing of the theaters and the Restoration three scenes were adapted for a droll entitled *The Surprise*, later published in *1 The Wits, or Sport upon Sport* (O 1662 [two issues] and 1672).

The Maid of Honor. Philip Massinger. No license for acting exists. Acted 1621–22 (E&G 1976). In 1621 "Massinger is known to have been writing for Christopher Beeston's actors at [the Phoenix], and *The Maid of Honour* may well be one of these efforts" (McDonald 1985). Perhaps first performed by either Prince Charles's Men or Lady Elizabeth's Men (Neill 2010), depending on the date; Lady Elizabeth's Men replaced Charles's in 1622. "Often presented with good allowance" by Queen Henrietta Maria's Men at the Phoenix, according to the TP. The recently discovered prologue (Beal 1980), written for a revival, suggests that the play was performed early in 1630 at the Phoenix (Rowland 2010). In playlist of Beeston's Boys 10 August 1639.

SR 16 January 1632. Q 1632 two issues; HT *The Maid of Honor, A Tragicomedy*; list of characters; "there was apparently a prologue, written for a revival of the play, which appears among a selection of unpublished handwritten verses in the Berkshire Record Office, Reading" (Schneider 2011); five acts and separate scenes. Massinger's "dramatic style is extremely sensitive to non-verbal theatrical effects and his unusually explicit stage directions show a precise awareness of the actor's craft" (McLuskie 1981): "[Signior] Sylli *walking by, and practicing his postures*"; "Adorni *starts and seems troubl'd*." "About 1633 Massinger had eight of his previously published plays bound together in a single volume [including *Maid of Honor*]. Possibly he was thinking of publishing a collection of his works; possibly he wanted the volume as a gift to a patron" (Edwards 1987).

Massinger "establishes parallels that enable his audiences to recognize similarities to historical persons and events. But instead of maintaining the parallels he dissolves them in the fictions of the play" (Loftis 1987). "The action is placed in Sicily, whose island setting was conventionally intended to remind audiences of England" (Worden 1987). Especially relevant is the intersection of sex and politics: the play "provides a particularly clear illustration of how the abusive sexual mediation of a favorite could be rendered as a symptom of misgoverned royal will" (DiGangi 2006).

The Maid's Metamorphosis. Anonymous. Acted *c.* September 1599-July 1600 (Chambers 1923). "Sundrie times acted" by Paul's Boys, according to the TP, at Paul's playhouse. Perhaps presented as an entertainment for the marriage of Henry, Lord Herbert, and Anne Russell, 16 June 1600 (Lawrence 1922), but "accounts of the wedding say nothing of a play" (Chambers 1923).

SR 24 July 1600; transferred 6 November 1615; 18 October 1617; 29 May 1638; 25 January 1639. Q 1600 no author named; prologue; ends with a song; five acts. Although various deities (Juno, Iris, Apollo) appear as characters, there is no indication that they arrive from above. SDs provide for a triple entrance: "*Enter Joculo, Frisco, and Mopso, at three severall doores.*" Fitzpatrick 2011, however, argues that there were ordinarily only two entry-points onto the stage. Gurr 2009d observes that a "central opening had a positive function as the '*locus*,' the site of authority, in contrast to the '*platea*,' the street area round the margins of the stage."

The title "suggests a conscious link to Lyly's *Love's Metamorphosis*" (Shapiro 1994). The author "may have drawn a hint for his plot from Lyly's *Gallathea*" (Greg 1906).

The Maid's Revenge, A Tragedy. James Shirley. Licensed for acting 9 February 1626 (Adams 1917, Carter 1980). "Acted with good applause" by Queen Henrietta Maria's Men at the Phoenix, according to the TP. In playlist of Beeston's Boys 10 August 1639.

SR 12 April 1639. Q 1639 two issues, one of which was probably printed in 1640; list of characters; five acts. Some detailed SDs: "*Enter Signior Sharkino in his study furnished with glasses, viols, pictures of wax characters, wands, conjuring habit, powders, paintings.*"

In his dedication Shirley writes, "It is a tragedy which received encouragement and grace on the English stage; and though it come late to the impression [i.e., printing], it was the second birth in this kinde." "The first was probably the lost *Tragedy of St. Albans*" (*JCS*).

The Maid's Tragedy. Francis Beaumont and John Fletcher; "Fletcher seems to have contributed only four of the eleven scenes" (Turner 1970). Acted winter 1610–11 (Craik 1988). "Divers times acted" by the King's Men at the [second] Blackfriars, according to the Q1–2 TPs. ("The first play printed with an exclusive advertisement of the King's Men at Blackfriars" [Knutson 2002b].) Performed also at court, 1612–13, during the celebration of Princess Elizabeth's wedding to the Elector Palatine (payment to John Heminges dated 20 May 1613); ?also performed 1619–20 (King 1971); by the King's Men at the Whitehall Cockpit-in-Court, 9 December 1630 (Astington 1999a); and at Hampton Court, 29 November 1636. In a copy at the Folger "there appears to have been at some time a manuscript cast," but cropping has mostly destroyed it (Bentley 1984). In the original production Richard Burbage "is likely to have taken" the part of Amintor (Astington 2010). John Lowin first played Melantius (Astington); he performed "with mighty applause" (*Historia Histrionica*). Joseph Taylor, having joined the King's Men in 1619, played Amintor in revivals (Gurr 2004c). Eilert Swanston, having joined the company in 1624, played Melantius (Gurr 2004c). Stephen Hammerton, "who was at first a most noted and beautiful woman actor" and who later played Amintor (*Historia Histrionica*), joined the company in 1632. The play "remained popular right up to the closing of the theatres" (McMullan 2004).

SR 28 April 1619; transferred 27 October 1629; 29 May 1638; 25 January 1639. Q1 1619 two issues; no author named; list of characters; five acts. Cynthia as moon goddess presides over a masque-like scene. The masque provides most interesting staging: a trap door is used when "*Neptune rises*"; "*Night rises in mists*," which would have been suggested by smoke (Gurr 2009d); but Dessen & Thomson 1999 are uncertain whether a mist was actually simulated. Also "*Enter Eolus out of a rock*." "The company may have been able to use sea-gods' costumes originally designed for Samuel Daniel's court masque, *Tethys' Festival*," performed 5 June 1610 (Wiggins 1998). Considerable onstage violence: in act 5 Evadne "*Ties his [the King's] arme to the bed*" "in what he takes at first to be sexual playfulness" (McMullan) and then "*Stabs him*." Amintor wounds Aspatia, and "Evadne rushes in, '*her hands bloudy with a knife*'"; "Aspatia, a woman dressed as a man, lies bleeding to death on the ground, while two people, both with blood-stained weapons, stand over her. All three of the characters have transgressed against the rules of gender, the women by bearing and using weapons and the man by fighting with a woman" (Guy-Bray 2002); finally Evadne "*Kills herselfe*," and Amintor, in turn, "*Kills himselfe*." Q2 1622 no author named; "newly perused, augmented, and inlarged, this second impression"; contains eighty additional lines, which "were not in fact additions, but lines which had originally been censored by [George] Buc *c*. 1610, and finally restored" (Clare 1999); Q2 "appears to have been based upon a different manuscript from the first quarto of three years earlier, and it is reasonable to infer from this that the new lines in the 1622 quarto were originally lines which had been excised at Buc's request back in 1610" (McMullan 1994). Q3 1630 "the third impression, revised and refined"; names B&F; a note from the printer in lieu of a prologue: "Good wine requires no bush, they say, / And I, no prologue such a play: / The makers therefore did forbeare / To have that grace prefixed here. / But cease here (censure) lest the buyer / Hold thee in this a vaine supplyer. / My office is to set it forth / Where Fame applauds it's reall worth." A Folger copy of Q3 contains the initials of actors who performed in a revival *c.* 1630 (George 1977). Q4 1638 "the fourth impression, revised and refined"; "King Charles himself annotated a copy" of Q4 (Massai 2007). Q5 1641 "the fifth impression, revised and refined." Q6 two issues; dated 1650 but probably printed 1660 (Norland 1968); "the sixth impression, revised and corrected exactly by the original." Despite this TP claim, Q6 "does not differ from the two preceding editions" (Bentley 1971). Q7 1661 this "is perhaps one of [Francis] Kirkman's fraudulent reprints" (Turner 1970); new TP (minus the woodcut). The Q TPs feature a woodcut "which must have been made for the play" (Foakes 1985). "Two figures are shown in poses that clearly indicate that they have just been dueling; indeed, one has wounded the other who has blood gushing from the breast. Both figures are wearing doublet and hose, and thus appear to be men, though only one has a moustache. However, one is labeled 'Amintor' and the other 'Aspatia.' The image thus hints at the interchangeability between men and women, a difficulty of distinguishing the boundaries between the sexes" (Hopkins 1999a). "[R]eaders are drawn to speculate on the obvious defloration-based symbolism of Aspatia's blood, which spurts from her body as she is penetrated by her troth-plight husband's sword" (Billing 2008). B&F F2 1679 *Fifty Comedies and Tragedies*; "published by the authors original copies, the songs to each play being added"; list of characters. During the 1640s and 50s, parts of the play were adapted for a droll entitled *The Testy Lord*, later published in *1 The Wits, or Sport upon Sport* (O 1662 [two issues] and 1672).

The play identifies sexual violation with political collapse. Evadne "challenges female stereotypes by refusing to regard herself as a victim; she is strong and aggressive, forcing Amintor into the victim's role in their wedding night confrontation. He is so horrified by her revelation that she is not a virgin that he foresees a total breakdown in the conventional structure of sexual relationships if it should be known" (Clark 1994). "Refusing to play the meek, subservient wife to Amintor, [Evadne] not only claims a right to her body but seeks to declare herself an autonomous subject" (Alfar 1995). "She radiates a sexual authority which she refuses to curb or shame" (Shullenberger 1982).

The Maiden's Tragedy. See *The Second Maiden's Tragedy* (Middleton).

A Maidenhead Well Lost. Thomas Heywood. Acted ?1625–34 (Taylor 2002a). "Publickly acted . . . with much applause" by Queen Henrietta Maria's Men at the Phoenix, according to the TP.

SR 25 June 1634. Q 1634 *A Pleasant Comedy called A Maidenhead Well Lost*; dramatis personae; prologue and epilogue; detailed description of dumb shows "summarizing important parts of the plot" (Mehl 1965); five acts. The TP features a woodcut depicting, on the left, a group of men at table and, in a separate panel on the right, a man and woman embracing: "the woodcut does not show any moment in the action, but is composite" (Foakes 1985). The woodcut appears again in the text of the last act. Although the play's title seems to suggest that a maidenhood will be lost, it is actually "lost prior to the play's beginning", for Julia and the Prince of Parma have already had a sexual encounter leading to pregnancy when the action begins; "we first see the baby when Stroza brings it onstage only to immediately abandon it in an elaborate dumbshow" (Love 2010). Later the baby becomes the focus of the play's most astonishing moment when Parma "sends the baby to the [wedding] celebration [of Julia and the Prince of Florence] in a feasting-dish" (Love); Parma wants to marry Julia himself: "*Enter a Serving-man with a child in a covered dish*"; on the breast of the child is written "'Tis fit, if Justice bee not quite exil'd / That he that wedds the mother, keepe the child." The unexpected appearance of the baby helps precipitate the marriage of Julia and Parma.

Heywood's address to the reader treats the connection between performance and print; the play has been "frequently and publickly acted without exception, and I presume may be freely read without distaste." Epilogue comments on theatrical fashion: "New playes are like new fashions; if they take? / Followed and worne: and happy's hee can make / First into 'th garbe: but when they once have past / Censure, and prove not well, they seldome last. / Our play is new, but whether shaped well / In act or s[c]eane, judge you, you best can tell."

The Malcontent. John Marston. Acted 1603 (Lamb 2009) by Children of the Chapel Royal/Children of the Queen's Revels at the second Blackfriars. "The boys' company acting at Blackfriars after 1600 was known by the old title of Children of the Chapel Royal, but when they received a new patent dated 4 February 1604 they were taken under the protection of the Queen and renamed the Children of the Queen's Revels" (Hunter 1975). "The boy company that originally played *The Malcontent* would have performed music before the play started and during the act intervals" (Carnegie 2007); in contrast to his plays acted at Paul's playhouse, where he makes considerable use of song, Marston relies "on orchestral performance" at the Blackfriars (Gair 2000). Nathan Field played Malevole (Astington 2010). Evidently this company stole either *1 Hieronimo* or *The Spanish Tragedy* or another (lost) play related to Kyd's: in the induction Condell says that the company of boys had performed "Jeronimo." In retaliation, the King's Men began performing Marston's play (in revised form) at the first Globe,

April-December 1604; Richard Burbage "certainly" played Malevole (Taylor 2002b). But this production "must have been unsatisfactory. The cramped, claustrophobic setting of a private theater is absolutely essential to Marston's purposes" (Finkelpearl 1969). When the King's Men adapted the play, "they introduced a new comic character, Passarello, a major role probably specifically intended to display the talents of Robert Armin" (White 1998); "Armin's enormous popularity had necessitated the addition of the artificial fool's part" (Hornback 2009b). And because the play had been written for a private theater, "in which a musical interlude was performed between each act, the play needed to be expanded to provide a proper afternoon's entertainment for the public theatre audience" (Kay 1998). John Sincler probably played Bilioso (Carnegie 2007). Revived February 1635, probably at the Blackfriars (diary of John Greene). "*The Malcontent* was one of the outstanding theatrical successes of its time" (Wiggins 2000).

SR 5 July 1604 an Enterlude called *the Malecontent, Tragiecomedia*; "the earliest self-styled English tragicomedy" (Lawrence 2007). Q1 1604 *The Malcontent*; the word *Tragiecomedia* "was ignored when the printer set the play's title page" (Gurr 2006); dramatis personae; "the second act begins with a pantomime" (Mehl 1965); five acts and separate scenes. "In the play Giovanni Altofronto, deposed Duke of Genoa, haunts his own court in the disguise of the bitter fool Malevole, offering satirical commentary on the corruptions of the time, but also plotting to regain his dukedom and in so doing taking over the plot of the play"; Marston's play led the King's men to commission "their own response to it in 1604, Shakespeare's *Measure for Measure*" (Hyland 2011). Other "disguised duke" plays include *Parasitaster, or The Fawn*, and *The Phoenix*. Q2 1604 adds prologue and epilogue, presumably for the Blackfriars. Q3 1604 "augmented by Marston. With the additions played by the kings majesties servants. Written by John Webster"; contains induction by Webster and additions to the text proper by Webster and Marston; there are eleven interpolations, a total of 450 lines; Hunter 1975 identifies six passages as Marston's and suggests that the other five "might have been written by him, or by Webster (since he is named) or by another dramatist of the period." [The following entry treats the added material in Q3 independently.] "*The Malcontent* is the only early modern play that was written for one company, appropriated by another, and rewritten to highlight the theft" (Munro 2010a). Reissued in a made-up book entitled *Comedies, Tragi-Comedies, and Tragedies* (1652), no longer extant (Wine 1964). "The texts of *The Malcontent* show obvious signs of censorship; but it is far from clear when this took place or who was responsible" (Clare 1999).

Marston's address to the Q2 reader underscores the primacy of theatrical performance over print: he laments "that scenes invented meerely to be spoken should be inforcively published to be read." Yet he approves publication; he "keeps negotiating the space for the author's voice, acknowledging the apparent cultural pressure to have the play printed, thus expanding its circulation and cultural exchange and participating in textual patronage by seeking readers" (Bergeron 2006).

The Malcontent, The Induction to. John Webster. Acted April–December 1604 (Hunter 1975). By the King's Men, according to the TP, at the first Globe. This company "hired Webster to adapt [the play] for the adult stage" (Wiggins 2000). Two kinds of text first appear in Q3 (1604): Webster's induction of about 135 lines wherein "three actors (Richard Burbage, Henry Condell, and John Lowin) appear on stage in their real-life characters as King's Men" (Hosley 1961); eleven sporadic additions to the text proper, some 450 lines, by Marston and by Webster. The additions "do not add in any significant way to the plot, characterization, or the message of *The Malcontent*; rather, they provide new comic and satiric segments" (Carnegie 2007). Much of the added material involves the character of Passarello, probably played by Robert Armin of the King's Men (Hunter); "Passarello's role, with the other lines added to support him, runs to 257 lines, almost as many as the Fool has in the nearly contemporary *King Lear*" (Bentley 1984). In the induction Richard Burbage, along with Henry Condell, John Lowin, William Sly, and John Sinklo [Sincler], makes an appearance; Burbage plays the role of Malevole.

HT *The Induction to the Malecontent, and the additions acted by the Kings Majesties servants. Written by John Webster.* On the basis of the HT and the Q3 TP, as well as the style of the additions, Lake 1981b confirms Hunter's earlier findings about authorship and further argues that Webster wrote not only the Induction but also much of the material added by the King's Men to the "main text." Although Jackson & Neill 1986 find that Marston's "augmentations" "are entirely compatible with the Blackfriars version," Cathcart 2006 argues that Marston's new material has "a special compatibility, not with the shorter version of the play, but with the version for the King's Men to which Webster contributed."

The induction calls attention to the play's origin at the Blackfriars when Will Sly replies to a criticism that he is seated on the stage: "Why? We may sit upon the stage at the private house." This remark alludes to "Blackfriars dandies insisting on following their usual practice of sitting on the stage" (Orrell 1988). Thomson 2010 suggests that "playgoers did sometimes sit on the Globe stage, [and] it is possible to understand the Sly-Tireman exchange as an attempt to *discourage* the practice." Later in the induction Burbage refers to the custom of playing music between acts at private theaters, when he says that the additions to the play are intended "to entertaine a little more time, and to abridge the not-received custome of musicke in our theater." "The boy company that originally played *The Malcontent* would have performed music before the play started and during the act intervals" (Carnegie 2007). The new induction "emphasises how much more important was the music in its original staging by the boys' company at the Blackfriars" (Thomson 1992b).

Malvolio. See *Twelfth Night.*

Marcus Tullius Cicero. Possibly written by Fulke Greville, Lord Brooke (Morrill 1991); Kirkman's 1661 catalogue ascribes the play to "Lord Brooks." "[P]robably written for school performance: it contains a large number of roles for children and gives detailed stage directions for achieving the illusion of violence" (Potter 1981). Q "could, with very little revision, be acted" (Aggeler 1978). "Several of the scenes make dramatic sense only if staged and there is a liveliness of movement not present in closet drama" (Clare 2002).

SR none. Q 1651 *The Tragedy of That Famous Roman Orator Marcus Tullius Cicero*; no author named; prologue by Caesar's ghost; chorus at end of each act except last; five acts. Some SDs describe the characters' appearance: "*Enter* Antony *in a morning gown; the haire of his head and beard very long and unkembed*"; "*Enter* Clodius *and* Laelius *in womens attire*"; "*Enter* Centurion *with* Salvius *head*"; "*Enter* Soldiers *with* Minutius *head*"; "*Enter* Popilius Lænas *with* Marcus Tullius Cicero's *head and hands.*"

"The theme-setting opening speech by the ghost of 'butcher'd *Julius*' . . . is likely to call to mind that more recently 'butcher'd' monarch, Charles I" (Randall 1991). "The orgy of decapitation at the end of the play suggests a crude attempt to hint ominously at the regicide, but the speeches of Cicero impart a hope for the benefits of the republic" (Smith 1994). Yet the work has also been seen as "a fully fledged anti-republican play" (Smith). "Whatever elements we call to mind from the English world of 1650–51, clearly some amalgam of them is seething in the interior of *Marcus Tullius Cicero*" (Randall 1995). "In its figuring and prefiguring of events from 1649 to 1653—the regicide to Cromwell's rise to power, leading to his forcible dissolution of the Long Parliament in April 1653—the play is remarkably prescient" (Clare).

Mariam. See *The Tragedy of Mariam.*

Mariamne, The Wife of Herod. James Compton (Kelliher 1980). Although the SDs are scanty, the play may have been written for performance at one of Compton's homes, Castle Ashby or Canonbury House, Islington (Wolf 1983).

London, BL, Additional MS 60280, fols. 2–32; no TP; no author named; damaged—the tops of the leaves in act 1 are torn off; chorus at end of each act; five acts and separate scenes. This MS, described by Wagonheim (*AED 3*) as a "rough draft," formerly belonged to the library at Castle Ashby.

"Deriving ultimately from the Jewish historian Flavius Josephus, the story of Herod and Mariamne had a compelling and understandable appeal for medieval and Renaissance storytellers and dramatists of various nationalities" (Randall 1995). But *Mariamne* appears to be "an original work, for it does not seem to be an adaptation of any of the half-dozen plays on this subject, written in no fewer than five modern European languages, that evidently preceded it in date of composition" (Kelliher).

Marie Magdalene. See *Mary Magdalene.*

The Marriage between Wit and Wisdom. Francis Merbury. Acted *c.* 1571–79 (Lennam 1966); possibly first performed at Christ's College, Cambridge. The MS TP contains a chart showing how the nineteen parts of "this interlude" may be played by six actors. "[A]dapts the school play action for performance by a professional troupe" (Norland 1995). "The text is rich in stage directions, many of them concerning the farcical activities of the Vice" (Happé 1999). *The Marriage of Wit and Wisdom* is one of the titles named in *Sir Thomas More* (written *c.* 1600 [Jowett 2011]) when a company of actors visits More's home for the purpose of entertaining the household; the naming of Merbury's play may suggest that it had a long stage history. However, the drama performed in *Sir Thomas More* does not seem related to Merbury's play, at least as it exists today; instead the fragment borrows from *Lusty Juventus, The Disobedient Child,* and *The Trial of Treasure.*

    London, BL, Additional MS 26782, fols. 1–32; no full title; the date 1579 is written on the TP, which is damaged; nineteen roles divided for six actors on the TP; "never before imprinteth" (the main scribe "copied the play to resemble a printed playbook" [Atkin 2009]); prologue and epilogue; although the words "the second act" appear, "the author never conceived of his play as formally structured in acts, but only as ten scenes grouped into two parts, which would provide the actors with an interval, if required" (Wickham 1976). The MS "reads like a prompt-copy for theatrical performance" (Bevington 1962), but Atkin argues that the MS is "entirely devoid of prompt-copy characteristics." Some detailed SDs: "*Here they fight a while and Ircksomnis [a giant] must run in a dores and Wit shall followe taking his visor of his hed and shall bring it in upon his sworde*" (Twycross & Carpenter 2002). Wantonness sings Wit asleep and blackens his face, identifying him with folly (Hornback 2009b). Edward Dering's collection of playbooks in the early seventeenth century apparently once contained the manuscript of the play (Lennam 1965). The SR entry "for around August 1569 licenses Thomas Marshe to print 'a play intituled the maryage of Wytt and Scyence,' and a play of that title was printed by him in the following year" (Atkin), but all copies have disappeared; transferred 23 June 1591 *The mariage of wyt & wi[s]dome.*

    This play "is lightly based upon John Redford's play, *Wit and Science*" (Lennam). "Merbury takes Redford's educational action out of the educational context with its boy-performers and rescripts it for the resources of a troupe of professional performers, adding a series of independent scenes that involve the comic figure of the Vice, in this case Idleness" (Mills 2007). The changes "provide public audiences (who demanded amusement rather than instruction in return for their money) with a much more light-hearted entertainment" (Wickham). First edited by Halliwell[-Phillipps] 1846; modern edition by Lennam 1966.

The Marriage Broker, or The Pander. M. W. Acted late 1630s (Baillie 1984) at un-determined venue, possibly a university. The prologue seems designed for perfor-mance: "You, who are seated, and for entrance pay, / I bid you hearty *Well-come* to our play."

SR none. D 1662 *Gratiae Theatrales* (with *Grim the Collier of Croydon* and *Thorney Abbey*); *A Comedy Called The Marriage Broker, or The Pander*; separate pagination for each play but continuous register; "never before published," ac-cording to the general TP; *A Comedy called The Marriage Broker, or The Pander*; author's initials (possibly spurious) on the TP; list of characters; prologue and epilogue (by Hymen); five acts and separate scenes (acts 1–2). The epilogue is au-thorial, but the prologue was written for the 1662 printing.

"*The Marriage Broker* resembles in many respects of plotting and language the late Caroline city comedies written for the various London theaters in the tradition of Middleton and Jonson" (Baillie). "*The Marriage Broker*, William Cartwright's *The Ordinary* (1635), Jasper Mayne's *The City Match* (1637), and Abraham Cowley's *The Guardian* (1642) all feature a London setting for com-plicated plots wherein multiple needy suitors seek prosperous marriages, that is, sizable dowries" (Clark 2003).

The Marriage of the Arts. See *Technogamia*.

The Marriage of Wit and Science. Anonymous. Acted *c.* 1567–69 (Brown et al. 1960) by a children's company (?Paul's Boys), perhaps at court; the play's "ac-tion and style are courtly" (Mills 2007). "The play is intended for performance by boys, and there is an unusual concentration on women characters which they would undertake" (Happé 1999). An adaptation of John Redford's *Wit and Sci-ence*, this play was "probably created by Sebastian Westcott, Redford's successor at St. Paul's" (Norland 1995). Probably performed also, under the title of *Wit and Will*, at Whitehall, Christmas 1567–68 (Walker 1998).

SR *c.* August 1569 or 1570 (Brown et al.). Q ND ?1570 *A New and Pleas-ant Interlude Entitled the Marriage of Wit and Science*; unique copy at Bodleian; the date 1570 is handwritten on the TP; no author named; list of characters; five acts and separate scenes. Few SDs. The play "features a 'house' of Lady Science with a functional 'gate' through which Wit and the others are invited" (Beving-ton 1973). "There is evidence to suggest that the house of Science was more solid and elaborate than the customary representational *domus* consisting of a lath and canvas façade framing a doorway"; another stage house belongs to the monster Tediousness; both abodes are "visually arresting" (Lennam 1975). The dramatic action aligns a black face with folly: "Following the scene in which 'Witte' is transformed into the likeness of the black fool Ignorance, Science and her fa-ther Reason mistake Witte for a fool and contemptuously refer to his blackness" (Hornback 2009b).

This play "is indebted to Redford's *Wit and Science,* which it follows closely even in small details" (Brown et al.). But *The Marriage of Wit and Science* "simplifies Redford's witty generic fusion into a courtly romance. Science is reconceived as a courtly lady, Wit as her faithful lover, and the final battle of Wit and Tediousness is presented as a tournament which Science watches, like a romance heroine, from her window above" (Mills).

The Marriage of Wit and Wisdom. See *The Marriage between Wit and Wisdom.*

The Martial Maid. See *Love's Cure.*

The Martyred Soldier. Henry Shirley. Acted *c.* 1618 (Kawachi 1986). "Sundry times acted with a generall applause" by "the queenes majesties servants" at the Phoenix "and at other publicke theaters," according to the TP. These words may designate Lady Elizabeth's company [the Queen of Bohemia's company] or Queen Anne's Men or Queen Henrietta Maria's Men. On 23 August 1623 Henry Herbert, who calls it "an olde playe," notes that he confiscated it: "formerlye allowed by Sir John Ashlye but called in & reallowed with reformations: which were not observed, for to every cross they added a stet of their owne & for this cause I have thought fitt to peruse itt & to keep the booke for a president to the office and to take my fee" (Bawcutt 1996). The company "blatantly reannotated [the MS] to return it to precensored form—as the outraged Henry Herbert realized when he called the text back" (Stern 2009c). On 28 August Herbert notes that Palsgrave's Men sought permission from Beeston to perform the play; the company needed scripts because they lost their playbooks when the Fortune theater burned the night of 9 December 1621.

SR 15 February 1638. Q 1638 list of characters; inserted following the play is the verse address "To the reader of this play now come in print" ("That this play's old, 'tis true") that had been previously published as the epilogue to Thomas Heywood's *The Royal King and the Loyal Subject* (1637); five acts. Unspecified staging accomplishes a disappearance: *"As he [Eugenius] is writing an Angel comes & stands before him: soft musick; he astonisht & dazel'd. . . . He falls flat on the earth, and whilst a song is heard, the Angel writes, and vanishes as it ends."* "Here the angel is unseen, seen, and vanished not only without leaving the stage but within a single line" (Dessen 1996). The threat of violence is palpable; the king orders a stoning: *"They binde him to a stake, and fetch stones in baskets."* A *cave* evidently designates a dungeon located beneath the stage: *"An angel ascends from the cave."* And *"Victoria rises out of the cave white."* In Shirley's play "a pagan tyrant attempts to rape a Christian martyr whose material body has been taken up to heaven, only to find that he is making love to a corpse" (Williamson 2009). Dramatic action includes torture; tormentors hang weights on the body of Bellizarius: *"They draw him up."* Special effects include repeated thunder, a customary sign of divine disapproval: *"A thunder-bolt strikes [the king]"*; Eugenius says, *"Thankes divine powers.*" "In outdoor playhouses . . . in addition to 'tempestuous' drums, a 'bullet,' i.e., a cannonball, was 'rolled' along a sheet of metal or a wooden trough [to simulate thunder]" (White 2007).

The address to the reader, probably written by the actor John Kirke (Bergeron 2008), reaffirms the TP claim about performance and cites that success as evidence of the printed play's appeal: "This worke not the meanest of his labours has much adorned not only one, but many stages, with such a generall applause; as it hath drawne even the rigid Stoickes of the time, who though not for pleasure, yet for profit, have gathered something out of his plentifull vineyard. My hopes are, it wil prove no lesse pleasing to the reader, then it has formerly beene to the spectators."

Mary Magdalene. Anonymous. Acted ?end of the 15th century-?1520s (Baker et al. 1982) at undetermined venue in East Anglia, perhaps Norwich or King's Lynn (Coletti 2004); "probably performed in Chelmsford in the 1560s" (Walker 1998). "[M]ay well have been played in a variety of circumstances, sometimes in an open field, or in a large square, on occasion as an arena-with-scaffolds play, at other times as a play with stages gathered in a semi-circle and separated by the platea from the audience" (Baker et al.). An instance of "place-and-scaffold staging" (Grantley 2007). "This required a single playing-space, which might be outdoors or indoors. Those outdoors might be fixed gameplaces recurrently used for performances and other entertainments too. East Anglia, which had a lively dramatic tradition of saints' plays and moralities that use this form of staging, had a number" (Cooper 2010). The play "has scaffolds for the Castle of Magdalen, Marcyll (Marseilles) and Jerusalem, though none of these shows any indication of visual specificity and the scaffolds are likely to have doubled, reducing the potential for individualization" (Grantley 2008b). "[F]rom the point of view of its staging, [*Magdalene* is] the most complex and interesting play in the whole repertoire of early English drama" (Grantley 2008b). The play calls for "castles, a tavern for Mary's seduction, a garden for her meeting with Christ after His resurrection, but also Marseilles, the Near East, a rock in the middle of the Mediterranean and a boat to traverse the latter" (Clopper 1999). The MS "is itself a production script, not a reader's copy" (Pentzell 1973); the play "has fifty-two characters" (Normington 2009).

Oxford, Bodleian, MS Digby 133, fols. 95–145; contains the initials of M[yles] B[lomefylde], a sixteenth-century collector of books; some lines are missing; some SDs inserted at the wrong places; prologue "is for travelling actors" (Chambers 1923); "the play divides naturally into two halves" (Grantley 2004). The play "requires very elaborate staging, involving some twenty-three actors and multiple doubling" (Grantley 1994). SDs "call for two major conflagrations" (Twycross 1994). One of these involves the descent of "a clowd from heven" and then the setting on fire of a temple; such a descent "would most probably have been managed by means of pulleys and ropes" (Grantley 1983). "Both Heaven and Hell are double-deckers, fitted with traps for mysterious and sud-

den appearances and disappearances and lifting machinery" (Twycross). The SD
"*Tunc descendet angelus*" may indicate "a descent by steps from a scaffold into the
place (*platea*)," but "*Asumpta est Maria in nubibus*" "suggests more than just a lifting from place to scaffold" (Dillon 2004a). Unusual staging involves "the expulsion of the seven devils from the body of Mary" (Grantley 1983); then "*the Bad
Angyll entyr into hell with thondyr*." "Other miracles which probably involved special design and construction of the scaffolds in which they took place . . . are the
quaking of the idols . . . and the 'sinking' of the heathen priest and boy" (Grantley
1983). The play "is especially significant for possessing most detailed references
to particularities of contemporary women's costume" (Southern 1973). "Master
Curiosity's seductive praise of Mary's 'sofreyn coloures set with synseryte' and
his praise of her as 'splendaunt of colour' . . . call attention to how her colored
face displays her corruption" (Drew-Bear 1994). First edited by Sharp 1835, then
Furnivall 1882; modern edition by Baker et al.

Although the MS "was probably copied in the first quarter of the sixteenth
century," the play may have been composed earlier (Coletti). "Saint plays became
an endangered species in England at the Reformation, and very few of such texts
from any pre-Reformation period have survived" (Lancashire 2002). "Perhaps
the most theologically ambitious and theatrically eclectic play in the entire corpus of Middle English drama" (Coletti). "[T]he only English mystery containing
a morality" (Houle 1972). The play "merges Biblical narrative with the familiar
pattern of the morality" (Bevington 1962); it combines "morality, biblical history
and saint legend" (Clopper 1999).

Mary Magdalene. Lewis Wager. Acted *c.* 1566 (Grantley 1994) at undetermined
venue; possibly "staged under parish auspices" (White 2008). This is "perhaps the
finest example of a Protestant biblical drama designed for professional touring"
(White 2004a); it uses "the motifs and conventions of medieval devotional theatre for irreproachably, even militantly, Protestant purposes" (Womack 1992).
The TP lists the names of the thirteen characters and indicates that "foure may
easily play this enterlude," but the doubling is not explained; five actors, not four,
are required (Craik 1958). Presumably the company consisted of four men and a
boy, who would have portrayed Mary. The seduction scene "makes it appear an
adult, professional play" (Southern 1973).

SR *c.* December 1566-January 1567. Q 1566–67 *A New Interlude, Never Before This Time Imprinted, Entreating of the Life and Repentance of Mary Magdalene*;
two issues; RT *An Interlude of the Repentance of Mary Magdalene*; list of characters on the TP; prologue the end of which speaks of "the preface"; not divided.
The SDs "are full and sometimes vivid" (Bevington 1962). The Vice Infidelity
"can exist in more shapes than one"; he boasts, "For every day I have a garment to
weare, / Accordyng to my worke and operation" (Craik 1958). He "flatters Mary
by praising her body and her face. He sets out to seduce her to vice by introducing her to Pride of Lyfe, Cupiditie, and Carnall Concupiscence, who, disguised

as men of honor, act as cosmetic seducers advising Mary on how to beautify her face and hair" (Drew-Bear 1994). A scaffold representing hell "appears to have been built on two levels" (Tydeman 1986). Thunder and lightning accompany the devils. Angels descend from heaven, "probably down a ramp" (Tydeman). "Wever mixes the personified abstractions of the moral interlude with realistic characters" (King 1982). The play has appeal for both readers and audiences: it is "very delectable for those which shall heare or reade the same." Q "begins a sequence of plays in which Roman type is commonly mixed with black letter on the title page and in the text" (Howard-Hill 1990a).

"Wager structures the drama as spectacular action, a strategy that makes him unusual, perhaps original, among mid-century playwrights. His transforming of the signs of iniquity into the signs of salvation, moreover, takes as its site a woman's body" (Cartwright 1999). "The piece comes close to being a Protestant saint play" (Grantley 1994); "this is the last surviving Protestant play that would attempt dramatic portrayal of Christ" (O'Connell 2000b). "[O]ffers the first known defense of the stage in a play by an English dramatist" (White 1993b). Prologue defends drama by arguing its didactic purpose: "Doth not our facultie learnedly extoll vertue? / Doth it not teach, God to be praised above al thing?" In keeping with this didactic purpose, personified abstractions share the stage with biblical figures.

The Massacre at Paris. Christopher Marlowe. "[T]he likely first performance" was "30 January 1592/3 by the Lord Strange's Men at the Rose theatre" (Esche 1998); "the entry in Henslowe's diary is difficult to interpret in detail" (Nicholl 2004a); 30 January [1593] is apparently an error for 26 Jan. "Plaide by" the Lord Admiral's Men, according to the O TP, at the Rose in 1594 (Gurr 2004a); the play was "probably written with the Rose's new [i.e. rebuilt] stage specifically in mind" (Gurr 2009c). Henslowe, who calls the play "the masacer," "the tragedey of the gvyes" [i.e., Guise], "the Gwies," or "the masaker of france," records performances in 1594: 30 January ("ne"); 19, 25 June; 3, 8, 16, 27 July; 8, 17 August; 7, 25 September. Entries for expenses, 19 and 27 November 1598, suggest revivals at the Rose by the Admiral's Men. Entries for expenses, 3, 8, 13, 26 November 1601, suggest revivals by Lord Admiral Nottingham's Men [first reference to this company 26 May 1599] at the first Fortune, which opened autumn 1600. Edward Alleyn played the Guise in early productions (Hopkins 2008a) and after 1600 when he emerged from retirement (McMillin 1989).

SR none. O ND ?1594 (Hillman 2002b) but estimates run to 1602 (Oliver 1968); *The Massacre of Paris, with the Death of the Duke of Guise*; "written by Christopher Marlow"; not divided. A single leaf of the play exists in Folger MS J.b.8. Because John Payne Collier first identified and reproduced the so-called "Collier leaf" (in 1825), it has sometimes been regarded as a forgery. Although not in Marlowe's hand, "the leaf is a genuine playhouse document" (Esche 1998). "Unfortunately *The Massacre at Paris* survives only in a pitifully mangled form" (Gill

1987); the "corrupt" text is "perhaps about half of its original length" (Loftis 1987). But Poole 1998 argues that "the material history of the text contradicts" such assumptions.

The play "is an appallingly savage catalogue of atrocities, committed by the Catholic Guises against the Huguenots" (Bevington 1968); Marlowe presents "some two dozen individual murders performed on-stage" (Styan 1996). "The old queen of Navarre accepts a pair of poisoned gloves too late to heed the warning of the Protestant Lord High Admiral. The admiral himself is shot down in the open streets, stabbed in bed, and mangled so that his head and hands may be sent 'for a present to the pope'" (Bevington). "The amputation of a corpse's hands, along with the head, is ordered" and the corpse "is returned to the stage at a later point . . . but the text does not indicate whether or not the mutilations have been carried out in the interim" (Owens 2005). At another point Mougeroun "slices off a cutpurse's ear and then, handing it to the victim, requests in exchange the return of the gold buttons stolen from his coat" (Owens). The Guise is stabbed to death onstage; two men strangle a Cardinal. "A man is murdered in the gallery and his body is thrown down onto the main stage"; "it seems that a dummy was used" (Rhodes 1976). The play is "perhaps best remembered for its depiction of the execution" of Peter Ramus, "one of the massacre's most famous victims" (Poole). A friar seeks to murder the king: *He stabs the king with a knife as he readeth the letter, and then the king getteth the knife and killes him.* At the close *"They march out with the body of the king, lying on, foure mens shoulders with a dead march, drawing weapons on the ground."*

"This lurid account of the St Bartholomew's day massacre in 1572 . . . is the most topical and overtly political of [Marlowe's] plays" (Nicholl 2004a). "[T]he reason that Marlowe's imagery of violence is simultaneously religious and modern is that, for Marlowe, religion, at least as he sees it practised in contemporary Europe, *is* violence" (Hopkins 2008a).

A Match at Midnight, A Comedy. W. R. [?William Rowley]; Archer's list credits the play to Rowley, but Jackson & Taylor 2007 find no evidence of Rowley's (or Middleton's) hand. Performed late 1622-May 1623 (Young 1980); 1621–23 (Gurr 2009d). "Acted by the Children of the Revells," according to the TP, at the Red Bull (Reynolds 1940).

SR 15 January 1633. Q 1633 *A Match at Midnight, a Pleasant Comedy*; author's initials on the TP; list of characters; five acts and first scenes. The SDs provide much domestic detail: *"Enter John with a rabbit in one hand, and a dish of egges in another, and the Mayd"*; *"Enter Sim, and John, passing over with a bason of rosemary, and a great flaggon with wine."*

Match Me in London. Thomas Dekker. "[P]erhaps originally written for Queen Anne's Men" *c.* 1611 (Dutton 1991). Acted 1620–21 (Hoy 1980). "Often presented; first, at the [Red] Bull in St. Johns-street; and lately, at the private-house in Drury-Lane, called the Phoenix," according to the TP, by the Red Bull Revels Company. Relicensed by Henry Herbert, 21 August 1623 (Adams 1917), and performed by Lady Elizabeth's Men at the Phoenix, 1623 (McLuskie 1994); Herbert calls this "an old playe."

SR 8 November 1630. Q 1631 *A Tragicomedy Called Match Me in London*; dramatis personae; detailed description of dumb show, which includes this special effect: "*it thunders and lightens*"; five acts. Unusual staging: "Either a bell or a clock struck twelve for the beginning" of the play (Reynolds 1940). Staging evidently calls for the representation of a tradesman's business: "*A shop opened*," with, presumably, appropriate props: "What is't you lacke gentlemen, rich garters, spangled roses, silke stockins, embrodered gloves or girdles."

"'Tragicomedy' is the most conspicuous word on the [title] page"; this drama "is Dekker's attempt to produce a play in the new style" (Hoy 1987b).

The Matchless Maids. See *Love and Honor.*

May Day, A Comedy. George Chapman. Acted 1601–02 (Spivack 1967). "Divers times acted" at the [second] Blackfriars, according to the TP, by the Children of the Chapel. "The use of music, dance, and masque elements . . . suggests that [Chapman] was taking full advantage of the choices available to him on the Blackfriars stage" (Burnett 2004). Revived "around 1610" by the Children of the Queen's Revels at the Whitefriars (Munro 2005).

A copy of Q at Worcester College, Oxford, catalogued as Plays 2.5, contains a "title-page, the head-title, and about sixty lines of the text at the beginning of the play, which were all lost [and] have been replaced by a manuscript version" (Yamada 1980). SR no original; transferred 11 June 1659. Q 1611 *May Day, A Witty Comedy*; "chorus juvenum cantantes & saltantes"; five acts and "further subdivided into unnumbered scenes, the divisions marked by full-width rules across the page" (Welsh 1970). A "sword dance seems to have been employed" by the miles gloriosus (Wright 1928).

"*May Day* was the first play to achieve a surprise ending by concealing the identity of the heroine from the audience beneath the first of her disguises" (Shapiro 1994). The character Lionell/Theagine is "a woman disguised as a boy disguised as a woman; complicating things further still, this character was originally, of course, played by a boy" (Munro).

The Mayor of Queenborough. See *Hengist King of Kent.*

Measure for Measure. William Shakespeare; ?revised by Thomas Middleton. Acted by the King's Men "at the Globe after 9 April [1604] when the theatres re-opened after closure caused" by the plague (Hadfield 2005) and then in the banqueting hall at Whitehall, St. Stephen's night, 26 December 1604 (Lever 1965), before the recently crowned king, who was "a mystery" to most people in Eng-

land despite his authorship of "two treatises on the theory and practice of kingship" (Kamps & Raber 2004). The play "almost certainly was in the King's Men
repertory for some years and performed both at the outdoor, public Globe theater
and the indoor, private Blackfriars theater" (Ioppolo 2010). "Robert Armin perhaps had the role of Pompey" (Astington 2010). Today the play exists "only in the
form of an adaptation by Thomas Middleton" (Egan 2010). "Middleton's apparent success with *Macbeth* may have prompted the King's Men to hire him again,
in 1621, to adapt *Measure for Measure*: he expanded the city comedy parts of Lucio, Overdone and Pompey, and transformed a play apparently originally set in
Italy into one located in Vienna at the outset of the Thirty Years' War" (Taylor
2002b). "Shakespeare's Vienna is a curious locale, a landscape of Italianate vice
(and with a cast of characters whose names are largely Italian) with its leader, the
Duke, bearing an Italian title" (Goldberg 1983). The revision also "reshaped the
play's structure, originally intended for uninterrupted performance, to accommodate act intervals" (Taylor). "The revision was concerned not only to make the
play topical, but also to intervene to make the play's structure, style, and fasci-
nations match the dramaturgy of an indoor hall theatre in the early 1620s. The
revision might have introduced all the act intervals" (Jowett 2007b). The case for
Middleton's intervention, while substantial, is not without controversy: "Taylor
and Jowett's arguments . . . depend upon too much unsupported speculation to
be conclusive" (Ioppolo 1996b); "no internal or external evidence exists to support Middleton's revision of this text" (Ioppolo 2010). What can be said is that
The Phoenix by Middleton probably antedates Shakespeare's comedy and that the
disguised duke in *Measure for Measure* "derives immediately from Middleton's"
(Pendleton 1987).

SR 8 November 1623; transferred ?4 August 1626 Paviers right in Shakesperes *plaies*; ?19 June 1627 widow of Isaac Jaggard . . . her parte in Shackspheere
playes; 16 November 1630; 1 July 1637 Shakespeares *workes* their Part; 6 August
1674; 21 August 1683. F1 1623 *Comedies, Histories, & Tragedies*; three issues;
"published according to the true originall copies"; list of characters at end; five
acts and separate scenes. The 1623 text may represent "a posthumous adaptation
of the play" (Jowett & Taylor 1993). "The Folio text is printed from an adapted
version of the play prepared by Middleton in 1621" (Jowett 2004a). An F1 copy
at the University of Padua preserves the text "marked up, no later than the 1630s,
for performance" (Orgel 2006). F2 1632 "the second impression"; three issues.
F3 1663 "the third impression"; three issues. The 1664 reissue adds seven plays,
apparently by other playwrights. F4 1685 "the fourth edition"; two issues. The
one-stanza song that appears at the beginning of 4.1 appears in a longer version
in Fletcher's *Rollo, Duke of Normandy, or The Bloody Brother* (Q 1639). Although
Fletcher may have added the second stanza for his play, it is also possible that
Shakespeare was not responsible for the song, that Fletcher wrote both stanzas,
and that the song was introduced into Shakespeare's play for a late Jacobean revival (Bawcutt 1996).

"A line of 'brothel plays' was staged at both public and private theatres, including *Measure for Measure* (1604), Dekker's *The Honest Whore* (1604), Marston's *The Dutch Courtesan* (1605), Sharpham's *Cupid's Whirligig* (1606–7) and Heywood's *The Royal King and the Loyal Subject*" (Gossett 2004b). Shakespeare's comedy "also seems to belong to a group of 'disguised ruler' plays associated with the start of the new reign (Marston's *The Malcontent* and *The Fawn*, Middleton's *The Phoenix*)" (Wells & Taylor 1987). "These plays evidently relate to a crisis in the perception of authority at the time Queen Elizabeth died and was replaced by the unknown King of Scotland" (Jowett 2001). In addition, *Measure for Measure* bears a resemblance to *A Woman Killed with Kindness*: "both plays are structured firmly on central brother/sister pairs, a relationship type which barely features in sixteenth-century drama but suddenly starts to come into focus around 1600"; "by 1604 *A Woman Killed with Kindness* and *Measure for Measure* were playing at the same time and to essentially the same audiences" (Smout 2010).

Meleager. Anonymous. Acted *c.* 1575 by Paul's Boys (Gair 1982) at Paul's playhouse.
Cambridge, MA, Harvard University, The Houghton Library, MS Eng. 1285. The MS, which likely represents the plot (argument) of a lost play, indicates that the play featured a dumb show and chorus and was divided into five acts. Staging calls for a flaming altar. Although it is not certain that the transcript represents a play that was performed or even written, it is possible that "between 1576 and 1584 the Children of Paul's shared access to the first Blackfriars theatre with Farrant's Children of the Chapel [and this arrangement] would allow for an elaborate production, fire and all" (Freeman 1971). First edited by Freeman.
This play cannot have been the Latin play of the same name written by William Gager, acted at Christ Church, Oxford, in 1582, and published in 1592 (Boas 1914).

The Merchant of Venice. William Shakespeare. Acted 1596–97 (Halio 1993). "Divers times acted by" the Lord Chamberlain's Men, according to the Q1 TP, at the Theater (Hosley 1979) or Curtain. Praised by Francis Meres in *Palladis Tamia* (SR 7 September 1598). Will Kemp probably played Lancelot (Butler 2004d). Performed also by the King's Men at Whitehall, 10 [Shrove Sunday] and 12 [Shrove Tuesday] February 1605 (Chambers 1930). "It has often been assumed that the repeat performance indicates that James particularly liked this play. . . . An alternative possibility is that James, out on one of his almost daily hunting trips, had missed the Sunday performance, but heard such enthusiastic reports from the Queen and Prince Henry that he decided to give it a try" (Duncan-Jones 2001).
SR 22 July 1598 *the Marchaunt of Venyce or otherwise called the Jewe of Venyce*; 28 October 1600; 8 July 1619; ?4 August 1626 Paviers right in Shakesperes *plaies*; ?19 June 1627 widow of Isaac Jaggard . . . her parte in Shackspheere *playes*; 1 July 1637 Shakespeares *workes* their Part; 17 October 1657; 6 August 1674;

21 August 1683. Q1 1600 *The Most Excellent History of the Merchant of Venice, with the Extreme Cruelty of Shylock the Jew towards the Said Merchant, in Cutting a Just Pound of His Flesh, and the Obtaining of Portia by the Choice of Three Chests*; RT *The Comical History of the Merchant of Venice*; "written by William Shakespeare"; not divided. In Venice and Belmont Shakespeare juxtaposes two worlds, a mercantile city and a country retreat, "an all-male world" and "an all-female world" (Smith 1991b). Bassanio wins Portia by choosing a casket that contains Portia's picture; this would have been a miniature portrait (Elam 2010). The casket scene may have been staged by placing the caskets behind a central discovery space (Tassi 2005) or behind a curtain stretching across a doorway onto the stage (Kiefer 2007); "Here musicke" and "a song" when Bassanio chooses the leaden casket; Portia had not ordered music for her other suitors (Lindley 2006); such music is "an element usually associated in Shakespeare's plays with semimagical, 'wonderful' transformation" (Garber 2004). In *Merchant* Shakespeare uses the word *music* "more often than anywhere else" (Levin 1989a). Portia's disguise as a lawyer carries symbolic meaning: "she becomes, in effect, a young Daniel, as if the robes allow her to express a part of her personality that would not so readily appear in the normal garments of the mistress of Belmont" (Mowat 1981). In the trial scene Shylock brings his scales to weigh Antonio's flesh, and Shylock whets his knife "earnestly"; "Antonio is about to give his body for Bassanio in a displaced act of sexual surrender" (Hammond 1996). Q2 1619 printed by William Jaggard for Thomas Pavier and falsely dated 1600. F1 1623 *Comedies, Histories, & Tragedies*; three issues; "published according to the true originall copies"; five acts. F2 1632 "the second impression"; three issues. Q3 1637 "printed from Q1" (Jowett 2007e); not divided. Q3 reissued with a new TP in 1652; the printing was "probably encouraged by mid-century hopes and fears regarding religious toleration and readmission of the Jews to England" (Randall 1995). F3 1663 "the third impression"; reissued 1664 with seven additional plays. F4 1685 "the fourth edition"; two issues. Scene divisions were introduced in the eighteenth century.

"The significant [social] critic-Jews (or Jew-like figures) in the drama of the 1590s include Gerontus in Robert Wilson, *The Three Ladies of London* (1581); Shylock; Pisaro in William Haughton, *Englishmen for my Money* (1598); and the English Mamon in Marston, *Jack Drum's Entertainment* (1600/01)" (Kermode 1995). Shakespeare's play "remembers and rewrites *The Jew of Malta*, for years one of the most popular plays in the repertory of a rival company" (Taylor 2002b). The immediate context for *The Merchant* was the trial and execution of Dr. Roderigo Lopez, Queen Elizabeth's personal physician, accused of conspiring to poison her. Although he was outwardly a Christian, his Jewish background made him suspect (Greenblatt 2004).

Mercurius Britanicus, or The English Intelligencer, A Tragicomedy. Richard Brathwaite, named in the 1656 catalogue of Rogers and Ley; the title also appears in

Kirkman's 1661 catalogue. A play-pamphlet originally written in Latin in the summer of 1641 (Butler 1984a) and published without the name of the author as *Mercurius Britanicus, Judicialis Censura, vel, Curialis Cura*; the play appeared in another Latin edition the same year. Subsequently translated into English and published three times in 1641. "Acted with great applause," according to the Q TPs. "It would have been an unwieldy but not impossible play to have staged. The cast is large, but many parts are short and could readily have been doubled; there are even rudimentary stage directions" (Butler 1984a). The play may have been staged in Paris, as the TP claims, under the auspices of Robert Sidney, second Earl of Leicester and "England's ambassador to France from 1636 to 1641" (Butler).

Q 1641 *Mercurius Britannicus, or The English Intelligencer, A Tragic-Comedy, at Paris*; HT *The Censure of the Judges: or, The Court Cure*; no author named; list of characters; chorus of parliamentarians; epilogue; four acts; "the first edition ends with an Epilogue explaining that '*the next day (by Joves permission) the fift act shall bee acted upon Tyber, I should say Tyburne, by a new Society of* Abalmites'" (Potter 1987b). The play has, then, been deliberately left incomplete. Ample SDs: "*Enter the Ghost of* Coriolanus *without an head*"; "Hortensius *Ghost with an amiable countenance appeareth & vanisheth*"; "*The Ghost of* Joachinus *appeares brusling with an horrid motion and so vanisheth.*" Q2 1641 no epilogue. Q3 1641 "reprinted with sundry additions"; prologue (printed at end) and epilogue.

"Its title associates it with the contemporary news-sheets, which were generally called Mercuries, and its title page also includes the phrase 'A Tragi-Comedy, at Paris,' suggesting that Braithwait may have been influenced by a French tradition of dramatic satire" (Potter 1987b). The author clearly intends a political meaning: "As Brathwaite's characters perceive, all society is upside down and parliament's reforming hand is needed everywhere" (Butler).

Meriasek. See *Saint Meriasek.*

The Merry Conceited Humors of Bottom the Weaver. See *Bottom the Weaver.*

The Merry Devil of Edmonton. Anonymous. Both Archer and Kirkman ascribe the play to Shakespeare, but such "external evidence is very weak" (Wells & Taylor 1987). "Probably in the playhouse as early as 1602" (Traister 2011); acted spring 1603 (Knutson 1991). "Sundry times acted by" the Lord Chamberlain's/King's Men at the [first] Globe "on the banke-side," according to the Q1 TP; this "is the only play to have been published in successive editions with an exclusive Globe attribution, and this throughout the period when it was standard practice for printers to advertise the Blackfriars auspices on the King's Men plays" (Straznicky 2006b). Richard Burbage was "presumably" in the first cast (Astington 2010). Henslowe records payment to Middleton for an epilogue "for the corte," 14 December 1602. Performed also by the King's Men at court, 1612–13 (payment to John Heminges dated 20 May 1613). "Perhaps its stage life was renewed by the successes of *The Alchemist* and *The Tempest*" (Knutson 1999). Revived at the Whitehall Cockpit, 3 May 1618, before the king; at the Cockpit-in-Court, 15 February 1631 (Teague 2009); at Richmond, 6 November 1638 (*JCS*) "to celebrate the birthday of one of Charles I's daughters" (Traister). Edmund Gayton mentions the play in *Pleasant Notes upon Don Quixot[e]* (1654).

SR 22 October 1607; transferred 21 June 1624; 9 September 1653 by Wm Shakespeare; 4 April 1655 *a comedie of the Merry Devill of Edmonton*; 18 April 1666. Q1 1608 no author named; induction (Hosley 1961); prologue; not divided. An auditory effect is called for as the prologue concludes: "*The chime goes.*" Peter Fabel has been "asleep in his bed at midnight, safeguarded from evil spirits by the warning chime at his head. But he is suddenly awakened by the ringing of the chime, and beholds Coreb drawing near to bear him off to Hell" (Lawrence 1927). Staging includes the entry of a spirit in "*sterne and horrid shape.*" Q2 1612. Q3 1617. Q4 1626. Q5 1631. Q6 1655. Q6 the TP features a woodcut depicting two men beside an inn-sign of a horse and rider; "the woodcut had been used earlier to illustrate a prose pamphlet, *The Life and Death of the Merry Devil of Edmonton*, entered in the Stationers' Register in 1608, the year in which the play was published" (Foakes 1985). The woodcut "depicts an episode that is not in the play text" (Levin 1999).

The Merry Devil became "one of the most popular plays in the seventeenth century and therefore one of the company's most reliable alternatives to *Dr. Faustus*, which it both imitates and corrects" (Cox 2000). *Merry Devil* may have been "written and staged partly with the expectation that its opening effect would be magnified by its audiences's knowledge of *Faustus*"; "subsequent acts may have been designed to recall the magical comedy *Friar Bacon and Friar Bungay*" (Traister).

A Merry Dialogue of Band, Cuff, and Ruff. See *Band, Cuff, and Ruff.*

Merry Humor of a Rogue. See *Pleasant and Merry Humor of a Rogue.*

A Merry Knack to Know a Knave. See *A Knack to Know a Knave.*

The Merry Milkmaids. See *The Two Merry Milkmaids.*

The Merry Wives of Windsor. William Shakespeare. Acted 23 April 1597 (Crane 2010) or perhaps February 1598 (Wells & Taylor 1987). "Divers times acted by" the Lord Chamberlain's Men, "both before her majestie, and else-where," according to the Q1 TP, which "seems to imply that the Queen saw the same *Merry Wives* as did the patrons of the Globe, but [the performances] . . . were unlikely to have been absolutely identical" (Dutton 2009a). Possibly first performed in the Great Chamber of Whitehall, in connection with the Garter Feast on St. George's Day, 23 April 1597 (Craik 1989); on 24 May George Carey, Lord

Hunsdon, was invested with the Order of the Garter at Windsor Castle (Hotson 1931); George Carey, the second Lord Hunsdon, became a patron of Shakespeare's company after the death of his father, Henry Carey, in July 1596; Henry had been the first patron of the company. Despite the probable attendance of the Chamberlain's Men at the Windsor Garter ceremony, however, the "occasionalist" argument for the play's origin at court is dubious; the play was more likely written for a popular audience (Freedman 1994); indeed, the comedy is "clearly intended, more than any other play in the canon, to reflect the life, to meet the expectations, and to endorse the values of the Elizabethan bourgeoisie" (Hibbard 1973). Performed at the Curtain (Gurr & Ichikawa 2000). Will Kemp probably played Falstaff in the earliest production (Gray 1930, Wiles 1987); John Lowin, after joining the King's Men in 1603, played the role. The character of Master Ford was originally called Brooke until 1601–02, but the name change was forced by Sir Henry Brooke, Lord Cobham, who was being caricatured (Taylor 1987). Performed by the King's Men in the Banqueting House at Whitehall on Sunday 4 November 1604 before King James (Crane 2010); possibly at Whitehall as *Sir John Falstaff*, 1612–13 (Chambers); possibly as *Sir John Falstaff*, 1 January 1625; and possibly at the second Blackfriars, April 1635 (John Greene records seeing "Falstaff" ([Gurr 2004c]). Performed at the Whitehall Cockpit, 15 November 1638 (Adams 1917). The notion that Queen Elizabeth suggested the play to Shakespeare seems to have originated with John Dennis in the early eighteenth century.

SR 18 January 1602; transferred the same day; ?4 August 1626 Paviers right in Shakesperes *plaies*; ?19 June 1627 widow of Isaac Jaggard . . . her parte in Shackspheere *playes*; 29 January 1630; 1 July 1637 Shakespeares *workes* their Part; 7 November 1646; 6 August 1674; 21 August 1683. Q1 1602 *A Most Pleasant and Excellent Conceited Comedy of Sir John Falstaff and the Merry Wives of Windsor, Intermixed with Sundry Variable and Pleasing Humors, of Sir Hugh the Welsh Knight, Justice Shallow, and His Wise Cousin Master Slender, with the Swaggering Vein of Ancient Pistol and Corporal Nym*; "by William Shakespeare"; not divided. Q1 possibly represents a much amplified adaptation of a Shakespearean masquelike entertainment, originally performed at the Garter Feast in April 1597 (Melchiori 2000). "The quarto is self-evidently a botched reconstruction of the play in performance" (Clare 1999). As the full title suggests, *Merry Wives* participates in the new vogue for humors comedy: "Falstaff's associate Nim enthusiastically throws about the fashionable new buzz-word, 'humours'" (Wiggins 2000). "Reflecting the craze for humors . . . the play offers many roles that can be created almost entirely by costume, appearance, and accent" (Potter 2012). The lecherous Falstaff makes no fewer than "three attempts at seduction (of the same woman!)" and suffers humiliation each time (Garber 2004). He escapes a jealous husband by hiding in a buck-basket of dirty clothes; he escapes another time by donning the disguise of an old woman; later he wanders the woods with horns on his head: "*Enter sir John with a bucks head upon him.*" Whether this SD designates "just the horns" or "a horned mask, in the form of a deer's head to cover the face as well, is not clear" (Crane). Falstaff impersonates Herne the Hunter and evokes the myth of Actaeon, becoming "an emblematic expression of lust and its chastisement" (Steadman 1963). There follows "*a noise of hornes*" and another entry: "*Enter sir Hugh like a satyre, and boyes drest like fayries, mistresse Quickly, like the queene of fayries: they sing a song about him.*" This SD is not entirely clear: "Are we meant to notice that the boy-actor who has been playing Mistress Quickly is now playing one of Sir Hugh's schoolboys dressing up as the Queen of Fairies? Or are we to assume that (the boy-actor playing Mistress Quickly) is now dressing up as the Queen of Fairies?" (Somogyi 2007). In any event the besieged Falstaff is subject to indignity: "*They put the tapers to his fingers, and he starts*"; then "*they pinch him, and sing about him.*" The fairies "dance in a ring around him, recumbent like the defeated stag he is, performing their rite of purification" (Brissenden 1981). This scene's SDs "count among the lengthiest given in any original text of a Shakespeare play" (Somogyi). Q2 1619. F1 1623 *Comedies, Histories, & Tragedies*; three issues; "published according to the true originall copies"; three issues; possibly revised by Shakespeare (Irace 1994); "unusual stage directions in that each scene is headed by the names of all the characters that appear in it" (King 1992a); five acts and separate scenes. The F1 text is nearly twice the length of Q1. It may represent Shakespeare's (incomplete) revision, probably made in 1604, of his earlier version (Dutton 2011). Q3 1630 "newly corrected"; "an alternative and more expansive version" of Q1–2 (Murphy 2003). F2 1632 "the second impression"; three issues. F3 1663 "the third impression"; reissued 1664 with seven additional plays. F4 1685 "the fourth edition"; two issues.

"With its location in an actual town situated not far from London, its characters taken from the middle ranks of society, and its representation of the homely details of everyday life, [*The Merry Wives*] comes closest in characterization and setting to the actual world that Shakespeare and his audiences inhabited" (Rackin 2005). "As its title may lead us to predict, the play offers a female fantasy in which household labor insures pleasure, profit, and social order" (Wall 2002). "Margaret Cavendish, the author of the first critical essay published on Shakespeare, regarded Shakespeare's representations of female characters as one of his greatest strengths. Among the eight characters she cited as examples, four are from *The Merry Wives of Windsor*" (Rackin 2006).

Messalina. Nathanael Richards. First performed between the date of Thomas Crosfield's diary entry for 18 July 1634 (*JCS*) and "before 12 May 1636, when the theatres were closed because of the plague" (King 1992a). "Acted with generall applause divers times" by the King's Revels Company, according to the TP. "Appear[s] to have been staged at the Salisbury Court theatre" (Astington 1991). Evidence of revision before printing (Stevens 1979). William Cartwright Sr. played the Emperor Claudius; Christopher Goad, Silius; John Robinson, Saufellus; Sam Tomson, Menester; Richard Johnson, Montanus; William Hall, Mela;

John Barrett, Messalina; Thomas Jordan, Lepida; Mathias Morris, Sylana, according to "The Actors Names." The cast list is "presumably the one for the first performance of the play" (Bentley 1984). "Nine men are needed to play nine small speaking parts and seven mutes; eleven boys are needed to play five small speaking parts and twenty mutes" (King 1992a). Because of the size of the company, "it is not unlikely that . . . parts of the play were cut for the performance" (Bentley). In his dedicatory epistle, Richards reports: "This play upon the stage, passed the generall applause as well of honorable personages as others. Two passages are past, the *stage* and the *presse*; nothing is absent now but the gentle approbation of your lordships clemency."

SR 3 October 1639. O 1640 *The Tragedy of Messalina, The Roman Empress*; list of characters; prologue and epilogue; detailed description of a masque ("*Eight Furies dance and anticke and depart*"); five acts. A note explains of a song that it "was left out of the play [in performance] in regard there was none could sing in parts." Richards displays "considerable feeling for stage-effect": "Of the twenty-eight persons of the play, eleven are slain on the stage, one dies broken hearted on the stage, and four are slain off the stage" (Skemp 1910). Staging calls for Furies to enter through a trap: "*Enter three Furies with the arrowes of Pride, Lust, and Murder.*" A trap is also used when "*Earth gapes and swallowes the three murders by degrees.*" When ghosts appear, they evoke terror in those who behold them: "*Enter angell, three murdered dames with revenge threatning.*" Special effects include "*thunder and lightning*"; a character is "*Shot with a thunderbolt.*" Staging includes torture: "*They put him on the rack.*" Staging also calls for the use of a scaffold for Messalina's execution, but the victim cheats the executioner: "*Shee mounts the scaffold, submits her head to the blocke, and soddainly rising up leaps downe, snatcheth* Evodius *sword and wounds her selfe*," thus dying by her own hand. Numerous sound effects: "*A bell rings as far off, three Roman dames knocke within*"; "*solemne musicke plays during his speech*"; "*Horrid musicke*"; "*Two spirits dreadfully enter and (to the treble violin and lute) sing a song of despaire.*" The engraved TP by Thomas Rawlins contains a picture of a contemporary stage, which has a low railing and is tapered slightly toward the front; behind the stage a curtain hangs on the tiring-house wall. But the engraving "has no independent authority as a depiction of a theatre, real or imagined. Like so many other title pages, it copies existing visual models" (Astington 1991).

Robert Davenport's prefatory poem comments on the power of the printed word to sustain drama: "Friend, y'ave so well limn'd Messallina's lust / T'were pitty that the peece should kisse the dust / Of darke oblivion; you have (I confesse) / Apply'd a due preservative the presse." "The play underscores the complicity of theatrical performance in Messallina's depravity. The Empress becomes infatuated with the actor Menester by watching him act Troilus" (Tomlinson 2005). She is "an insatiable whore" and when the actor playing Troilus resists her advances, "she has him racked out of his scruples" (Butler 1985). *Messalina* "has much to say on decadent courts and the perils of performance that is relevant to the contemporary situation in Caroline England" (Sanders 2004c).

Michaelmas Term. Thomas Middleton. The play was first assigned to Middleton in Archer's catalogue of plays, appended to *The Old Law* in 1656; also ascribed to Middleton in Kirkman's catalogues of 1661 and 1671; but the 1656 list by Rogers and Ley erroneously ascribes the play to George Chapman. Performed 1605 or early 1606 (Paster 2000). "Sundry times acted by" Paul's Boys, according to the Q1 TP, at Paul's playhouse.

SR 15 May 1607 no author named; transferred 29 January 1630; 7 November 1646. Q1 1607 no author named; induction, "an unusual feature in Middleton's city comedies" (Hutchings & Bromham 2008); "act divisions beginning with Act Two" (Leinwand 2007). Q1 "includes numerous, detailed" SDs (Leinwand). "Michaelmas Term symbolically removes his '*whitish cloak*' representing his 'conscience' and puts on his 'civil black' cloak reflecting 'civil' 'evil'" (Drew-Bear 1994). "What could be a more iconographic exposé of corruption than this black-robed figure, hands outstretched, receiving fees from both 'wronger and from wronged'?" (Collington 1999). "While there are no stage directions for [Quomodo's] shop, the dialogue places the action there and merchandise is shown, so probably this is an instance of Middleton's typically minimalist directions" (Thomson 2003). Q2 1630 no author named; "newly corrected" (an inaccurate claim [Levin 1966]).

Michaelmas Term, "the first play Middleton set in contemporary London, was—if not the first—among the earliest English plays explicitly and systematically to represent the present to itself" (Taylor 2004b). The play "alludes to an extraordinary legal battle between a Doctor of Divinity, John Milward, and a bookbinder, John Flaskett, over the legitimacy of their respective marital contracts with a young heiress, Agnes Howe" (Kok 2012).

Microcosmus, A Moral Masque. Thomas Nabbes. A "playhouse masque" acted either the week of 24 February-1 March 1637, when the theaters were open, or *c.* October 1637 when they reopened following closure; with the exception of that week in late February 1637, plague closed the theaters for seventeen months, from 12 May 1636 to 2 October 1637 (*JCS*). "There may . . . have been hopes of a private performance at court while the theatres were closed" (Richards 1968). "Presented with generall liking" at the Salisbury Court playhouse, according to the TP, by Queen Henrietta Maria's Men, possibly with changeable painted scenery (Freehafer 1973).

SR 6 August 1636 *A morrall Maske.* Q 1637 "set down according to the intention of the authour"; list of characters with a brief description of each and of costume; epilogue (by Love); five acts and separate scenes. "The text requires a special proscenium, or 'Front'" (Wickham et al. 2000), which has *"the title in an escocheon."* "*Microcosmus* reads like the offspring of a morality play and a Jonsonian court masque" (*JCS*). "The staging must . . . have been spectacular with its fixed setting of 'a perspective of ruins' within an arch 'adorn'd with brasse figures of Angels and Divels,' and the five moveable 'scenes' which revealed to the audience by means of screens an appropriate tableau at the main points of psychological change in each act" (Sanders 1987). The SDs pay special attention to how actors are arranged in space: "*The second scene is here discover'd, being a perspective of clouds, the inmost glorious, where* Bellamina *sits betwixt* Love *and* Nature*; behind her the* Bonus *and* Malus Genius." "Nabbes seems to have had some version of movable scenery in mind" (McLuskie 1981). "Perhaps Nabbes was the first playwright consciously to write with scenery in view" (Nicoll 1937). Some SDs suggest the use of machinery: e.g., "*While the following song is singing, they descend from the scene.*" Complementing the spectacle are directions for music appropriate to the action: "*After a confused noyse and musicke out of tune,* Nature *enters as amaz'd at it*"; "*The 4 Elements and their creatures dance a confused dance to their own antique musicke: in which they seeme to fight with one another: and so goe forth confusedly.*" Music reconciles the Elements, whose second dance is harmonious; "throughout the play dances are so used" (Vince 1972); the play's "central motif is the revelation of harmony through dance" (Bitot 1995). Also issued in *Plays, Masques, Epigrams, Elegies, and Epithalamiums*, a made-up book containing plays bearing publication dates between 1637 and 1640; general TP dated 1639.

"A morality play with songs and dances on man's creation and fall, a throwback to an otherwise extinct form" (Butler 1984b). "Where the court masque was moving to much more pointed political material, Nabbes was content to create a moral work" (McLuskie 1981).

Midas. John Lyly. Acted late 1589 (Bevington 2000a) by Paul's Boys at Paul's playhouse. "Plaied" also by the same company, before the queen, the night of 6 January (Twelfth Night) 1590, according to the Q TP, at Richmond Palace. Lyly's plays were "often presented and acted" before Queen Elizabeth, according to the D general TP, but "all of his works for the stage seem to have been produced in the commercial theater" (Levin 2001).

SR 4 October 1591; transferred 23 August 1601; 9 January 1628. Q 1592 no author named; prologue at Paul's; no epilogue but the play ends in song; "*Midas* is alone among Lyly's comedies in presenting a terminal song" (Lawrence 1922); five acts and separate scenes. "[O]ne side of the stage holds a palace-'mansion' to be Midas' palace and the temple at Delphi, and the other side is a pastoral scene to represent Mount Tmolus and the 'reedy place'" (Smith 1977). "*Midas's coup de théâtre* . . . is to provide talking reeds on stage"; the production may have used "a specially devised location that could be curtained off from view and periodically discovered to the spectators" (Bevington). Lancashire 1969a speculates that "possibly *periaktoi* (three-sided, revolving prisms) were used, one at each side of the stage, for actual scene changes." Unusual staging includes Midas's head being "crowned with ass's ears" and, later, "*the eares fall off*" (Scragg 2005). D 1632

Six Court Comedies (with *Campaspe, Endymion, Gallathea, Mother Bombie, Sappho and Phao*); two issues; by "John Lilly"; five songs added.

Midas must have had a specific political relevance in 1589–90: "the portrait of Midas is clearly and unequivocally intended to resemble King Philip II of Spain, whose famed Armada had been defeated by England just eighteen months earlier" (Daniel 1988). "Midas' expedition against Lesbos (England) has ended in failure and humiliating counterattack by the enemy (Drake's raid)" (Bevington 1968).

A Midsummer Night's Dream. William Shakespeare. Acted 1595 (Wells & Taylor 1987). "Sundry times publickely acted by" the Lord Chamberlain's Men, according to the Q1 TP, at the Theater (Hosley 1979). Possibly performed subsequently at a wedding (Brooks 1979): ?Thomas Berkeley and Elizabeth Carey, 19 February 1596 (May 1983); or ?William Stanley and Elizabeth Vere, 26 January 1595; if so, the play may have been revised for the occasion (Lawrence 1922). Or perhaps the play was written for a wedding and "then transferred to the public theatre" (Halio 1994b). But "there is neither proof nor likelihood that *A Midsummer Night's Dream* was written for and performed at an aristocratic wedding" (Holland 2004a). "[I]t is highly likely that [Queen Elizabeth] saw the play when the Lord Chamberlain's Men . . . performed at court, at Richmond Palace, on 22 February 1596" (Duncan-Jones 2011). Will Kemp probably played Bottom (Butler 2004d). Praised by Francis Meres in *Palladis Tamia* (SR 7 September 1598). Revived 1603 (Gurr 2004c). The play, apparently referred to as "Robin goode-fellow" in a letter by Dudley Carleton to John Chamberlain, was probably performed by the King's Men at Hampton Court, the evening of 1 January 1604 (Astington 1999a). F1 preserves the name of [William] Tawyer, an actor or attendant. Performed at Hampton Court, 17 October 1630 (*JCS*); perhaps revised for revival (Halio). Possibly performed before John Williams, Bishop of London, at Buckden Palace, Huntingdonshire, 27 September 1629 or 25 September 1631 (Chambers) by amateur players (Edwards 1981).

SR 8 October 1600; transferred ?4 August 1626 Paviers right in Shakesperes *plaies*; ?19 June 1627 widow of Isaac Jaggard . . . her parte in Shackspheere *playes*; 1 July 1637 Shakespeares *workes* their Part; 6 August 1674; 21 August 1683. Q1 1600 "written by William Shakespeare"; "the play performed by the craftsmen was to be preceded by a brief dumb show" (Mehl 1965); although no prologue for the play proper survives, a prologue precedes the play-within-the-play; the closing lines by Puck are "not classified in early editions as an epilogue," but he "directly addresses the audience and makes the spectators rethink their understanding of, and attitude to, the play they have just seen" (Schneider 2011); not divided. Q1's SDs "are both incomplete and inconsistent" (Holland 1994). Staging calls for a "'bank' or flower-covered bench" (Gurr & Ichikawa) on which Titania sleeps. Sound effects include birdsong: Puck says, "I do heare the morning larke." Theseus implies the sound of offstage hunting dogs: "Wee will . . . marke the musicall confusion / Of hounds and echo in conjunction"; a

SD specifies the sound *"Winde horne,"* which "signals a return from the erotically charged enchantment of the forest to the 'real' world of Athens" (Lindley
2006). A mist seems called for: Oberon directs Puck, "The starrie welkin cover
thou anon / With drooping fogge as blacke as Acheron." But is the fog literal or
"is the playgoer to see two actors who act as if they do not see each other and are
therefore understood to be in a fog?" (Dessen 2010). A play-within-the-play by
the "rude mechanicals" probably "used the central opening" in the tiring-house
wall (Gurr & Ichikawa 2000). Duke Theseus "leads his court in a lively critique
of the play, interrupting it so thoroughly that at points the amateur players themselves break the illusion of the play to respond to the noble audience" (Westfall
1990). Oberon calls for music and invites Titania to dance; later a Bergomask
[rustic dance] by the mechanicals follows their play of Pyramus and Thisbe; here
Shakespeare "used [dance] more abundantly than he was ever to do again"; dancing in this play "may have been connected with an unknown occasion for which
the play was perhaps written" (Brissenden 1981). Titania's dancing is identified
with "the rounds and hays associated with popular festivity, traditional dances
of the May Game and Midsummer Eve," while Oberon's dancing is identified
with the "gendered comportment" of the court (Howard 1998). A remark by
Theseus suggests the striking of a clock, "The iron tongue of midnight hath tolde
twelve," a signal for the couples to retire. "After the newly married couples depart
to consummate their marriages, fairies enter to make the finale spectacular. It is
likely that the lovers, or at least Theseus and Hippolyta, used the central opening
for their exit. Puck, the forerunner, would then enter from one of the side doors,
and Oberon and Titania and their train would enter from the same door. Oberon
and Titania would exit from the central opening, because they intend to bless the
bed of Theseus and Hippolyta" (Ichikawa 2002). Q2 1619 "a piratical edition"
(King 1992a) falsely dated 1600. F1 1623 *Comedies, Histories, & Tragedies*; three
issues; "published according to the true originall copies"; five acts, "and an extra
stage direction is added at 3.2.460.1, just before the beginning of act 4, specifying that '*They [the four lovers] sleep all the Act,*' (meaning, through the act interval)" (Taylor 2002b); "that is to say, during an interval for music between Acts
III and IV," a practice that evidently began when the King's Men began using
the Blackfriars *c.* 1610 (Hosley 1960). Most of the F1 "alterations and additions
affect stage directions" (Holland): e.g., this SD added to act 4: *"Musicke, tongs,
rurall musicke"* when Titania is enamored of Bottom. "Tongs struck by a piece of
metal were used in burlesques of music, and the bones, as their name implies,
were pieces of bone struck or rattled to make a sort of rude music" (Shirley 1961).
F2 1632 "the second impression." F3 1663 "the third impression"; the 1664 reissue adds seven additional plays by various hands. F4 1685 "the fourth edition";
two issues. After the closing of the theaters, parts of the play were adapted for
an unusually long droll entitled *The Merry Conceited Humors of Bottom the Weaver,*
"publikely acted by some of his majesties comedians, and, lately, privately, presented, by several apprentices for their harmless recreation, with great applause,"

printed by Kirkman and Marsh, Q 1661; included in *2 The Wits, or Sport upon Sport* (Q and O 1673).

"Shakespeare revised the opening of Act 5 twice. The mislined speeches in Q1 suggest that he revised the passage during composition; the variants between Q1 and F suggest a second stage of his thinking about this crucial passage" (Holland 1994).

Mind, Will, and Understanding. See *Wisdom.*

Mirza, A Tragedy. Robert Baron. Written between *c.* 1647 (Chew 1937) and 1655 (*AED 3*). Probably never performed, but the SDs are extensive: *"Wearied with resistance, he fals, and faints, the other 4 executioners proceed to strangle him, when the king comes out, and takes them off."* And a commendatory poem "expresses an optimistic confidence that, had the play been acted, it would have moved the audience 'with such a Sympathy / As might extract a deluge from their eyes'" (Steggle 2007).

SR 16 August 1655 *A Tragedy with annotations* by Robert Baron. O1 ND ?1647, but Baron was "only seventeen" in 1647 (Randall 1995); author's initials on the TP and the prefatory poems name Baron, who signs the dedication; argument; list of characters; chorus; Berger 1998 calls the speech of Mirza's ghost "a prologue" but Schneider 2011 terms it "an opening soliloquy"; five acts. "Illustrated with historicall annotations" (i.e., very detailed treatment of sources), which follow the play; "really acted in Persia, in the last age," according to the TP. "The copious notes to the tragedy are in some respects the most fascinating section of the book. Ranging, as they do, from veritable treatises on eastern geography, history, politics, and social customs to long digressions on dreams, witches, and prophecies . . . they show Baron as an industrious young scholar who read omnivorously and liked to write down what he had learned" (Forker 1965). O2 ND ?1655 (Loloi 1998).

Prefatory poem by John Quarles: "whilst you tell / Your tale, wee'l easily find a parallell." "The final line of the poem indicates as straightforwardly as possible that this is something good readers are supposed to do" (Randall). Baron "modelled *Mirza* on [Jonson's] *Catiline*" (Wiseman 1998b), itself a critique of imperial politics. *Mirza* is "a reworking of an earlier play, John Denham's *The Sophy*" (Birchwood 2007), but Baron says "he had finished '*three compleat* Acts' of his own play before learning of" *The Sophy* (Randall). Both *The Sophy* and *Mirza* are based on Thomas Herbert's 1638 *A Relation of Some Years Travels* (McJannett 1999a).

The Miseries of Enforced Marriage. George Wilkins. Acted sometime between September 1605 and June 1606 (Blayney 1963). Possibly staged again in 1607 (Gossett 2004b). "Now playd by" the King's Men, according to the Q TPs, at the first Globe; the production was "a popular success" (Wells & Taylor 1987). Robert Armin probably played the clown: "He is addressed as 'Robin' because that is Armin's own name, and he arrives in Yorkshire after a long journey from

London singing in terms that allude to [Will] Kemp's famous journey to Norwich" (Wiles 1987).

SR 31 July 1607 A tragedie called *the Miserye of inforced Marriage*; transferred 28 April 1637. Q1 1607 probably printed by William Jaggard (Greg 1939); not divided. A character "is required to ascend a tree at the beginning of Act Four. He may, of course, have used one of the stage pillars, but a free-standing climbable tree was not beyond the ingenuity of the Chamberlain's Men" (Thomson 1992b). Q2 1611 "contains quite extensive corrections and additions" (Blayney 1963). Q3 1629. Q4 1637.

"The only play known to have been written independently by the obscure person who . . . collaborated with Shakespeare in *Pericles*" (Brooke 1911). In *Miseries* "Wilkins constructs from *A Yorkshire Tragedy* and its source pamphlet, as well as bits of *Twelfth Night*, *Othello*, and *Henry IV*, a domestic tragicomedy built around the social and religious complications of private betrothals and the abuses of wardship" (Gossett 2004b). Both *Miseries* and *Yorkshire Tragedy* draw their plots from the same 1605 pamphlet about "the life of Walter Calverley and his crimes" (Blayney 1957).

The Misfortunes of Arthur. Thomas Hughes, with contributions by William Fulbecke, Francis Flower, Christopher Yelverton, Francis Bacon, John Lancaster, John Penruddock, and Nicholas Trotte (Ramel 1967). Acted 28 February 1588 by the gentlemen of Gray's Inn before the Queen at Greenwich Palace, according to the TP, "in the Hall" (Astington 1999a), but the O TP is dated 1587; "the whole question [of dating] may simply be a matter of noting where the year begins and ends during this period" (Schneider 2011). Flower, Penruddock, and Lancaster "directed these proceedings at court." A printed note in O indicates that Fulbecke contributed speeches for the character of Gorlois, and, at Greenwich, these were substituted for lines written earlier by Hughes. Flower wrote the choruses for acts 1 and 2. The dumb shows were "partly devised" by Yelverton, Bacon, Lancaster, and Flower. Nicholas Trotte wrote the introduction wherein three Muses bring five gentlemen students onstage "as captives" and present them to Elizabeth as reluctant authors of the drama to follow: Trotte's speech achieves a "delicate balance of apology, self-promotion, and loyalty required in a public address to the queen" (Perry 2011). A prefatory note says that the text is printed "as it was presented, excepting certaine wordes, and lines, where some of the actors either helped their memories by brief omission: or fitted their acting by some alteration." The play was performed "probably also at Gray's Inn Hall" (Astington 2010).

O 1587 *Certain Devices and Shows*; "argument of the tragedie"; list of characters; argument and symbolic dumb show precede each act; the first speech of Gorlois, a vengeful ghost, functions as a prologue; epilogue; chorus at end of each act except last; five acts and separate scenes. Although the play consists largely of argumentation, surviving records of expenditure suggest "lavish spectacle"

(Corrigan 1992). A scaffold was built for performance in the Hall at Greenwich: "Possibly the stage was placed before the screen . . . but the published text of the play makes clear that the performance featured stage houses: even if the screens end was the place of the stage the screen doors were not used as stage entries" (Astington 1999a). Staging includes the ghost of Gorlois entering from below; following his last appearance "*Descendit*." Three Furies arise "*from under the stage*." Stage houses were likely used for the second dumb show: "*there came out of* Mordred's *house a man*"; "*out of the house appointed for* Arthur, *there came three nymphes*." The dumb shows at the beginning of each act "are just as important a part of the whole tragedy as the formal dialogue" (Mehl 1969). Spectacle culminates in the last dumb show: four gentlemen dressed in funereal black enter, each bearing a symbolic object in one hand and a shield decorated with an *impresa* in the other (Kiefer 2011). By presenting enigmatic action and symbolism, the pantomimes create suspense and intensify the play's overall impact (Norland 2009). The shows "seem to have constituted the most important dramatic effects of the play" (Clemen 1961).

This tragedy and such other plays performed at the Inns of Court as *Gorboduc*, *Jocasta*, and *Gismond of Salerne*, "can all be read on one level as contributions to the debates on the succession" (Butler 2003a); *Misfortunes* has also been seen as commenting on "circumstances involved in Mary Stuart's death" (Reese 1945) and the soundness of "imperialist ambitions" (Spradlin 2005). Gamble 1991 believes that Queen Elizabeth is being presented with a model of action, "an Arthur who conquered Rome, whose death was never witnessed, and who is expected to return as the savior of his nation." But Crosbie 1999 finds an "emphasis on the associations between sexual corruption and the state of the body politic"; Hughes "furthers this image of sexual inversion of the natural order to his final artistic effect by positing the nation as wounded and sterile."

Misogonus. ?Lawrence Bariȯna [the spelling on the MS TP] (Tannenbaum 1933) or ?Anthony Rudd (also listed on the TP). Acted *c.* 1571 (Barber 1979b). Probably first performed at Cambridge University, perhaps Trinity College, ?1577 (Nelson 1989).

San Marino, CA, Huntington, MS HM 452, fols. 1–24; *A Merry and Pleasant Comedy called Misogonus*; dated 20 November 1577; Anthony Rudd, whose name appears between the title and the list of characters, may have played Misogonus (Tannenbaum); revisions by Laurentius Bariȯna whose name appears on the TP and who may have been Laurence Johnson (Kittredge 1901), a schoolmaster at Kettering, Northhamptonshire; damaged (many words and lines are missing) and incomplete; list of characters with instructions for doubling; prologue; the epilogue "has been lost" (Schneider 2011); four acts and separate scenes ("[a]t least one leaf is lost at the end of the manuscript, and it is theoretically possible that a fifth act was marked on one of the missing pages" [Barber]). The SDs "are sparse and are in

Latin" (Bevington 1962). First published by Brandl 1898. First edited in English by Farmer 1906, then Bond 1911; modern edition by Barber 1979b.

In keeping with his didactic intent, the playwright presents Misogonus as a son "gone wrong through parental indulgence" (Thompson 1910); in this prodigal-son play, "a wealthy but ignorant father shows nothing but disdain for academic learning" (Potter 2008). The playwright provides "one of the liveliest tavern-scenes in English drama prior to Shakespeare's 'Boar's Head,' with a very elaborate dicing sequence followed by a riotous country dance" (Wickham 1981).

Mistress Parliament Brought to Bed of a Monstrous Child of Reformation. Mercurius Melancholicus. Written and published 29 April 1648 (Raymond 1996). A quasi-dramatic dialogue, which lacks a generic title (tragedy, comedy, etc.), list of characters, and SDs. "The play-pamphlets authored by royalist mercuries were an unstable composite genre, mixing elements of drama, reportage, satire, and prose polemic" (Raymond).

SR none. Q1 1648 *Mistress Parliament Brought to Bed of a Monstrous Child of Reformation. With Her Seven Years Teeming, Bitter Pangs, and Hard Travail that She Hath Undergone in Bringing Forth Her First-Born, (Being a Precious Babe of Grace). With the Cruelty of Mistress London Her Midwife, and Great Affection of Mrs. Synod Her Nurse, Mrs. Schism, Mrs. Priviledge, Mrs. Ordinance, Mrs. Universal Toleration, and Mrs. Leveller Her Gossips*; "quasi-prologue" (Greg 1939); not divided. Q2 1648. Q3 1648 unique copy at Union Theological Seminary (New York). Q3 "formed the basis of at least two of the 'Mistress Rump' satires of 1660" (Potter 1987a): *Mistress Rump Brought to Bed of a Monster* and *The Life and Death of Mistress Rump*. The latter "reprints *Mistress Parliament Brought to Bed* word for word until after the birth of the monster, putting the image of the political monster back into circulation for the Restoration" (Purkiss 2005).

The play-pamphlet expresses royalist hostility toward puritan and parliamentary forces.

Mistress Parliament Her Gossiping, Full of Mirth, Merry Tales, Chat, and Other Pleasant Discourse. Mercurius Melancholicus [?Marchamont Nedham]. Written and published 22 May 1648 (Potter 1987a). A quasi-dramatic play-pamphlet, expressing royalist hostility toward puritan and parliamentary forces.

SR none. Q 1648 list of characters on the TP; prologue (though not so labeled); divided into two parts by the entry of Truth. The SDs suggest attention to what is seen: "*Enter Mrs. Parliament in a scarlet coloured robe, riding on a beast of many heads, and a cup of red wine in her hand* [Rev. 17:3–4]."

This and *Mistress Parliament Presented in Her Bed* are "*alternative* sequels: the disorder in the *Melancholicus* camp meant that Mistress Parliament's gossiping could not be got to the press in time, and the author of *Mistress Parliament Presented* stepped in with his own offering" (Potter).

Mistress Parliament Her Invitation of Mistress London to a Thanksgiving Dinner for the Great and Mighty Victory which Mr. Horton Obtained over Major Powell in Wales. Mercurius Melancholicus [?Marchamont Nedham]. A quasi-dramatic dialogue expressing royalist hostility toward puritan and parliamentary forces. "The play-pamphlets authored by royalist mercuries were an unstable composite genre, mixing elements of drama, reportage, satire, and prose polemic" (Raymond 1996).

SR none. Written and published 29 May 1648 (Potter 1987a). Q 1648 last lines constitute a kind of epilogue; not divided.

This play-pamphlet "makes more use of rhyming couplets than its predecessors, and also shows a predilection for blank verse (printed as prose) on its final pages" (Potter).

Mistress Parliament Presented in Her Bed, after the Sore Travail and Hard Labor which She Endured Last Week in the Birth of Her Monstrous Offspring, the Child of Deformation. Mercurius Melancholicus [?Marchamont Nedham]. Written and published 10 May 1648 (Potter 1987a). A play-pamphlet, expressing royalist hostility toward puritan and parliamentary forces, in the form of a dialogue; it lacks generic title (tragedy, comedy, etc.) and list of characters. However, this is "the only of the *Mistress Parliament* pamphlets with any real theatrical quality" (Potter).

SR none. Q 1648 "quasi-prologue" (Greg 1939); final couplet functions as epilogue; unique copy in BL; not divided. Brief SDs: e.g., "*Enter Mrs.* Say-and-Seal *in haste, after her Mrs.* Jealousie *and the rest of the gossips shreeking and screeming with Mrs.* Suburbs *the Deputy.*"

This is a sequel to *Mistress Parliament Brought to Bed* and adopts the same royalist tone: "Rowze up your valiant hearts brave English men / And put in Charles his hand his sword again."

The Mock Testator. See *The Sexton.*

Money Is an Ass, A Comedy. Thomas Jordan. The dedicatory epistle in the second issue reports, "This play was writ by me & pleas'd the stage, / When I was not full fifteen years of age"; "if his claim in the epistle is correct, this would mean that the play was performed in about 1631–2" (Kathman 2005), "seemingly for production by" the Children of the Revels (Munro 2006c). "Acted with good applause," according to the TP, by the King's Revels Company at the Salisbury Court playhouse. Prologue suggests that the actors are boys and specifies the size of the company: "we are but eight in number." Thomas Jordan played Captain Penniless; Walter Williams, Mr. Featherbrain; Thomas Loveday, Clutch; Thomas Lovell, Money; Nicholas Lowe, Credit; Thomas Sandes, Calumny; Amb[rose] Matchit, Felixina; William Charington, Femina, according to "the actors names." Several of these actors "became professional actors of the Restoration" (Harbage 1936).

SR none. "Licenced November the 16. 1667" (*JCS*). Q 1668 two issues, one entitled *Money Is an Ass, A Comedy*, the other *Wealth Outwitted, or Money's an Ass*; list of characters with names of the actors; prologue (by Night); five acts and separate scenes. A SD alludes to the music room, which corresponds to one of the "boxes" above the tiring-house in the drawing of the Swan by Johannes De Witt: *"Enter Callumney in the musique room."*

Monsieur Galliard. See *Monsieur, The French Dancing Master*.

Monsieur, The French Dancing Master. A droll based upon several scenes in William Cavendish's *The Variety* and performed in the 1640s and 50s. "Galliard, the French dancing-master, is a mildly amusing stock character, like the average stage Frenchman or Welshman of his time, and might well have pleased a droll-audience" (Elson 1932). Requires six actors.

Published in *1 The Wits, or Sport upon Sport* (O 1662 [two issues] and 1672); RT *The Humors of Monsieur Galliard*; argument; list of characters; "the fun is derived from his capers and broken English" (Foakes 1985). The frontispiece of *The Wits* pictures the French dancing-master, who dances and plays a fiddle.

Monsieur D'Olive, A Comedy. George Chapman. Acted summer 1605 (Tricomi 1977). "Sundrie times acted" by Her Majesty's Children at the [second] Blackfriars, according to the TP.

SR none. Q 1606 two issues; list of characters at the end in most copies; five acts. Also issued in *Comedies, Tragi-comedies, & Tragedies* (1652), a made-up book no longer extant.

One of the "bold and provocative satires on James's court" performed by the Children: "an open lampoon on the Earl of Nottingham's showy peace embassy to Spain [in April 1605]" (Heinemann 1993b). "Chapman takes to task . . . the cost of embassies, the abuse of monopolies, the Jacobean breed of knight, and the king's notorious dislike of tobacco" (Burnett 2004).

Monsieur Thomas, A Comedy. John Fletcher. Acted "1611 or thereabouts" (McMullan 1994); "about 1610–16" (Cox 2000); 1612–15 (Gurr 2009d). First performed by the Queen's Revels Children or Lady Elizabeth's Men (Collins 2007), or their combined company, at Whitefriars, Swan, or Rosseter's Blackfriars. Performed also at the Phoenix, 1621–39. "To judge from Richard Brome's dedication and commendatory verses, *Monsieur Thomas* did not enjoy either an initial or a lasting theatrical success" (Gabler 1979). In playlist of Beeston's Boys as *Father's Own Son* 10 August 1639. The TP "printed at the time of the revival by the King's men of the Restoration enables us to identify *Monsieur Thomas* with the *Father's Own Son* of the Cockpit repertory in 1639" (Chambers 1923).

SR 22 January 1639; transferred 31 October 1646. Q 1639 the TP ascribes the play to Fletcher alone; specifies performance at Blackfriars; five acts and separate scenes. The SDs "are few and unusually brief" (Jewkes 1958). A character "arranges for a maid to disguise herself briefly with a devil's vizard to scare Tom as he is climbing to Mary's bedroom, making him fall and break his leg. Later, when Tom believes he has found Mary in bed and proceeds to join her, it turns out she has tricked him again, this time having conveyed a 'blackamoor' in her place, whom Tom mistakes for a devil" (Cox): "*a bed discovered with a black Mo[o]re in it.*" Richard Brome, who signs the Q dedication, may have revised the play for publication (Steggle 2004b). Reissued with a different TP in an undated copy: *Father's Own Son, A Comedy.* B&F F2 1679 *Fifty Comedies and Tragedies*; "published by the authors original copies, the songs to each play being added." After the closing of the theaters, parts of the play were adapted for a droll entitled *The Doctors of Dullhead College*, later published in *1 The Wits, or Sport upon Sport* (O 1662 [two issues] and 1672); "the title presumably puns on the name of Dulwich College, founded by Edward Alleyn" (Elson 1932).

In a Q prefatory poem Brome praises John Fletcher, suggesting the playwright's appeal: "'Tis both the life of action and of wit, / When actors so the fanci'd humours hit, / As if 'twixt them and th'authour there were strife / How each to other should give mutuall life. / The last this wanted not. Invention strayes / Here in full many pleasant turning wayes, / That like Meanders their curld circles bend, / Yet in a smooth streame runne to crowne the end." Brome's Q dedication to Charles Cotton also celebrates Fletcher's accomplishment: "You will finde him in this poem [i.e., the play] as active as in others, to many of which, the dull apprehensions of former times gave but slender allowance, from malitious custome more than reason: yet they have since by your candid selfe and others, beene cleerely vindicated."

The Moor of Venice. See *Othello.*

A Moral and Pitiful Comedy Entitled All for Money. See *All for Money.*

More Dissemblers Besides Women, A Comedy. Thomas Middleton. Probably acted 1614 (Jowett 2007c) or May–June 1619 (Lake 1976) by the King's Men at the second Blackfriars/second Globe. Originally licensed by George Buc. Relicensed for acting 17 October 1623 by Henry Herbert, who calls it "an old play" (Adams 1917). Performed at Whitehall, before the prince, 6 January 1624, according to Herbert's office-book; he calls it "the worst play that ere I saw" (Adams). In playlist of the King's Men 7 August 1641.

SR 9 September 1653. O 1657 *Two New Plays* (with *Women Beware Women*); continuous register and pagination but each play has a separate TP; list of characters; five acts and separate scenes. The SD, "*Cupid descending,*" suggests the use of machinery. Another SD calls for a small menagerie: "*Enter a company of gipseys, men and women, with booties of hens, and ducks, &c. singing*"; at the close of the scene: "*Exit with a strange and wilde fashion'd dance to the hoboys or cornets.*"

"Sinquapace, who comes to teach Lactantio's page . . . stages an elaborate performance, with both song and dance" (Wright 1928). This dancing master complains "about the loss of his fiddle. Since 'fiddle' denoted both a musical instrument and the action of playing with 'the woman's part,' the dancing master's loss has sexual overtones"; in Sinquapace, whose name denotes a sprightly dance, "courtly dancing is defined as superannuated: he is not only an exhausted satiric convention, he is a relic" (Howard 1998). The frontispiece of *The Wits* (1662) depicts a French Dancing Master playing a fiddle (Foakes 1985).

Middleton's portrait of the Cardinal of Milan may have been inspired by "Marco Antonio de Dominis, Archbishop of Spalatro (Split), who appears again in Middleton's work as the Fat Bishop in *A Game at Chess* (1624)"; "De Dominis had left the Catholic Church and had come to England in December 1616, where he had been well recived by the King as a great convert to Protestantism"; later he "returned to the Catholic fold" (Bromham 1980).

Mortimer His Fall, A Tragedy. Ben Jonson. "The 'Arguments' of all five acts and two beginning scenes of a tragedy on *Mortimer His Fall* . . . survive" (Kay 1995), but the drama itself was never completed. With this play Jonson "took up a subject that had been treated in Marlowe's *Edward II* and set out to dramatize it, as his self-consciously archaic title would suggest, in the manner of a late medieval *de casibus* tragedy. Yet he also planned to satisfy the formal requirements of classical tragedy" (Riggs 1989). Included in Kirkman's 1661 catalogue.

SR 19 August 1667 Ben: Johnsons W*orkes* 3ᵈ Vol. F2 1640–41 *The Works* vol. 3; this fragment dated 1641 (Happé 2007); "printed MDCXL"; list of characters; arguments; chorus; act 1 (two pages of text); planned as a play of 5 acts. At the conclusion appears this note, probably by Kenelm Digby, Jonson's literary executor: "Hee dy'd, and left it unfinished."

Henslowe records the title *Mortimer,* 20 November 1601 and 10 September 1602, but there is presumably no connection with Jonson's play.

The Most Excellent History of the Merchant of Venice. See *The Merchant of Venice.*

The Most Lamentable Roman Tragedy of Titus Andronicus. See *Titus Andronicus.*

A Most Pleasant and Excellent Conceited Comedy of Sir John Falstaff and the Merry Wives of Windsor. See *The Merry Wives of Windsor.*

The Most Virtuous and Godly Susanna. See *Susanna.*

Mother Bombie. John Lyly. Acted 1590-September 1591 (Andreadis 1975); *c.* 1589 (Gurr 2009d). "Sundrie times plaied" by Paul's Boys, according to the Q1 TP, at Paul's playhouse. Lyly's plays were "often presented and acted" before Queen Elizabeth, according to the D general TP, but *Mother Bombie* is probably the only play of Lyly's not intended for court performance (Daniel 1988); "Lyly seems to have given up the courtly vein of classical allegory and returned to an earlier mode of classically organized scholastic comedy" (Hunter 2004).

SR 18 June 1594; 9 January 1628. Q1 1594 HT *A Pleasant Conceited Comedy Called Mother Bombie*; no author named; five acts and separate scenes. Q2 1598. D 1632 *Six Court Comedies* (with *Campaspe, Endymion, Gallathea, Midas, Sappho and Phao*); two issues; by "John Lilly"; adds four songs absent from the quartos; whether Lyly wrote the songs is uncertain (Lea & Smith 1939).

"The play is ideally suited to the boys for whom it was written; for though it might seem in terms of subject matter to be 'low comedy,' set against the 'high comedy' of Lyly's other plays, it is in fact far more a graceful and witty descant on low life than a raw slice of it" (Hunter 1968).

Mucedorus and Amadine. Anonymous; Archer in 1656 attributes the play to Shakespeare, who may have been "asked sometime between 1606 and 1610 to patch up the old *Mucedorus* for a court performance," leading to the additions in Q3 (Jackson 1964); Kirkman's 1661 catalogue also ascribes the play to Shakespeare. The original version, represented by Q1, may have been first performed by the Queen's Men (Chambers 1923) or Pembroke's and Sussex's Men (Harbage 1952), *c.* 1590 (Jupin 1987), then by the Lord Chamberlain's Men, 1594–98, at the Theater. "Eight persons may easily play it," according to Q1, which provides a chart showing the assignment of roles. Q1 also reports, "Newly set foorth as it hath bin sundrie times plaide in the honorable Cittie of London"; these words "do not imply the existence of an earlier edition" (Greg 1939). The Q1 epilogue, addressed to Elizabeth, suggests performance before the queen. The play, "an old relic of early 1590s theatrical taste, was revived by the King's Men in about 1605" in revised form (Wiggins 2000), as the 1606 Q2 TP indicates: changes in the epilogue and the suspension of acting during Elizabeth's last days and after her death suggest "that *Mucedorus* was revived in London between 9 April 1604 and the date the second edition was printed" (Thornberry 1977); the King's Men "usually playing at the Globe," according to Q3, performed the play (Pitcher 1994); this company also revived it at Whitehall, before the king, Shrove Sunday night, "either 18 February 1610 or 3 February 1611" (Chambers 1923). Richard Burbage may have acted in the performance before King James (Astington 2006). Ten actors instead of eight would be required for the Q3 version because of newly written additions (Hosley 1961). Also performed (illegally) "by a group of amateur actors who took it on tour in Oxfordshire, playing, as far as can be guessed, to a socially mixed audience" on a Sunday night at the White Hart Inn, Witney, 3 February 1653 (Potter 1989). This performance is recorded because the floor collapsed, killing several playgoers and injuring others. "[T]he reason the play was being given at an inn was that the local authorities had refused the actors permission to use the town hall" (Potter 1987b). According to the account in John Rowe's *Tragi-Comoedia* (1653), "The actors of the play were countreymen;

most of them, and for any thing I can heare, all of *Stanton-Harcourt* parish";
"they had been learning it ever since *Michaelmas*, and had been acting privately
every week" (Johnston 2001). *Mucedorus* may have been "the most popular [play
of its time], having been staged repeatedly at the Globe, performed before James
I at court, and alluded to in other works of the period" (White 2008); *The Jew of
Malta* and *The Spanish Tragedy*, however, were also hugely popular.

SR no original; transferred 17 September 1618; 27 June 1646; 4 April 1655;
17 June 1656. Q1 1598 *A Most Pleasant Comedy of Mucedorus, the King's Son of
Valentia, and Amadine, the King's Daughter of Aragon, with the Merry Conceits of
Mouse* [a rustic clown]; no author named; no prologue; list of parts divided for
eight actors; induction consists of a colloquy between Comedy, "*with a garland
of baies on her head*," and Envy, "*his armes naked besmeared with bloud*"; epilogue
consists of Comedy triumphing over Envy and inducing "him to join in prayer
for the Queen" (Cameron 1982); not divided. Unusual SD: "*Enter Mucedorus like
a shepheard with a sworde drawne and a beares head in his hande*"; later, "*Enter Amadine and a boie with a beares head.*" Q2 1606 "contains substantive textual changes"
(Thornberry); unique copy at V&A. Q2 contains "the most outrageous stage direction in all of drama: *Enter Segasto runing and Amadine after him, being persued
with a beare*" (Rooney 2007). Q3 1610 "amplified with new additions" — four additions and two revised passages; the 4.1 addition and the epilogue seem "characteristically Shakespearian" (Jackson 1964); acted by the King's Men "usually
playing at the Globe"; "ten persons may e[a]sily play it"; the (increased) list of
eighteen characters arranged for ten actors; SDs of the new material "are longer and more elaborate than those of the first edition" (Jewkes 1958). A new
speech labeled "The Prologue," before the colloquy between Comedy and Envy,
addresses James I: "Most sacred majestie, whose great desertes, / Thy subject
England; nay, the world admires: / Which, heaven graunt still increase; O may
your prayse / Multiplying with your houses, your fame still rayse"; epilogue for
Comedy and Envy extended. Q3 contains a new SD, with a larger role for the
bear, who encounters Mouse the clown: "*the Beare comes in, and he tumbles over
her, and runnes away . . .*' This scene was not in the second edition of the play,
published in 1606, and it is reasonable to suppose that the reference to '*some Divell in a Beares Doublet*' was added between 1606 and 1610" (Pitcher). Q4 1611.
Q5 1613. Publication of Q3–5 "suggest that it was revived at this time" (Knutson
1999). Q6 1615 [octavo-in-fours]. (There exists at the Folger evidence of a lost
edition: the fragment was "printed between 1615 and 1618 and surviv[es] only in
the form of five leaves used to make up deficiencies in a copy of a later quarto"
[Proudfoot 2002].) Q7 1618. Q8 1619. Q9 1621 unique copy at Stadtbibliothek,
Danzig/Gdansk. Q10 1626 "amplified with new additions, as it was acted," referring to "the most recent production on the stage" (Murray 1983). Q11 ND ?1629
no TP. Q12 1631. Q13 1634 [octavo-in-fours]. Q14 1639. Q15 ND ?1650–56.
Q16 1663. Q17 1668. None of these editions names the author.

This play has "a claim to be the most popular play of the period, having been reprinted thirteen times before 1639" (Hunter 1997). "The best-selling play of the early modern era was (by a substantial margin) *Mucedorus*" (Blayney 2005). It was "the most popular and durable of all the lower-class plays" (Gurr 2009d). This popularity was owing to "its sheer durability in amateur performance and popular taste" (Preiss 2007). "The effect of performances must have derived as much from music and spectacle as from the working out of plot and the creation of character. A contemporary noted that a performance of *Mucedorus* (including intervals?) lasted three hours" (Hattaway 1982). "*Mucedorus* contains one of the earliest appearances of a bear on the English Renaissance stage" (Aaron 2005); this creature was possibly a real bear, not a man in a bear costume (Wright 1927a, Reynolds 1959, Grant 2001), though Lawrence 1935, Coghill 1958, Pitcher 1994, Orgel 1996, and Rooney 2007 are skeptical. Barton 1994 speculates that the Jacobean production replaced the earlier man in a bear's costume with the real thing: "The Jacobean bear has a significantly larger part, and it is tempting to believe that this is so because the King's Men, arrestingly, had found it possible to replace the fake bear of the original *Mucedorus* with a live animal, presumably better trained and more biddable than most, which had become temporarily available." "The presence of a polar bear in the 1610 revival of *Mucedorus* offers the best explanation for the lasting popularity of this play" (Ravelhofer 2002).

Much Ado about Nothing. William Shakespeare. Acted at the end of 1598 (Zitner 1993); "prior to early 1599" (McEachern 2006). "Sundrie times publikely acted by" the Lord Chamberlain's Men, according to the Q TP, at the Curtain (Gurr & Ichikawa 2000). Probably performed at court, Christmas season 1598 (Shapiro 2005). Presumably played at the Globe after its opening in 1599. Richard Burbage was "presumably" the original Benedick (Astington 2010). Speech-prefixes in Q indicate that Will Kemp played the role of Dogberry; Richard Cowley played Verges. When Kemp left the Chamberlain's Men, Robert Armin apparently took over the role of Dogberry (Gurr 2004c, Sutcliffe 1996), though this part would not seem to have called upon Armin's talent as a wit and mimic. Nevertheless, Armin played Dogberry "successfully enough to erase memories of Kemp's performance" (Potter 2012). Armin may also have doubled as Balthasar, "the first adult character to sing in Shakespeare's canon, being assigned both the complete songs in the play" (Sutcliffe). A SD in F1 names Jack [?John] Wilson, a lutenist who probably played Balthasar in "a post-1611 revival of the play" (Kathman 2009). Performed also by the King's Men at Whitehall during the celebration of the betrothal and marriage of Princess Elizabeth, 1612–13 (payment to John Heminges dated 20 May 1613); Heminges was also paid on the same day for performance of "Benedicte and Betteris," perhaps the same play (Chambers 1930). A performance was planned to entertain visiting commissioners in Coleraine, Ireland, before 28 May 1628, but not carried out (Fletcher 2000).

SR 4 August 1600 *The comedie of muche A doo about nothinge*. A booke to be staied [not published without permission]; this was "perhaps an attempt to protect" the play from "unauthorized publication" (McEachern); 23 August 1600 Wrytten by master Shakespere — "Shakespeare's name appears for the first time in the SR" (Erne 2003a); transferred ?4 August 1626 Paviers right in Shakesperes *plaies*; ?19 June 1627 widow of Isaac Jaggard . . . her parte in Shackspheere *playes*; 1 July 1637 Shakespeares *workes* their Part; 6 August 1674; 21 August 1683. Q 1600 "written by William Shakespeare"; not divided. The festive atmosphere is expressed by the dancing masquers at the party, a precursor to the celebratory "*dance*" that ends the play (Brissenden 1981). F1 1623 *Comedies, Histories, & Tragedies*; three issues; "published according to the true originall copies"; five acts (and first scene of act 1). *Much Ado* is Shakespeare's "most accomplished attempt at a 'humours' comedy, especially if we call Dogberry's "persistent malapropism" a humor (Wiggins 2000). Staging involves a "penthouse": "Stand thee close then under this penthouse, for it drissels raine." "The interior of a Booth or Mansion, or some other enclosure, may have served as a shelter from the rain for Borachio and Conrade" (Saunders 1968). "Borachio stages a dumb show with Don John" when he tricks Claudio into believing that Hero is unchaste (Kinney 2003). When Claudio at the monument laments the (apparent) death of Hero, "we are simply being asked to imagine that the tiring-house wall, or some part thereof, is the tomb itself" (Meagher 2003). F2 1632 "the second impression"; three issues. F3 1663 "the third impression"; reissued 1664 with seven additional plays. F4 1685 "the fourth edition"; two issues. Division into separate scenes not made until eighteenth century.

"There is little doubt that [*Much Ado*] was a popular play, at least until the closing of the theaters. In the verse eulogy provided for the edition of Shakespeare's *Poems* in 1640 Leonard Digges wrote: 'let but Beatrice / And Benedick be seen, lo in a trice / The Cockpit, galleries, boxes, all are full'" (Mares 1988).

Muleasses the Turk. See *The Turk*.

Muly Mollocco [alternative name for Abdelmelec]. See *The Battle of Alcazar*.

Mundus et Infans. See *The World and the Child*.

The Muses' Looking Glass, or The Entertainment. Thomas Randolph. "First performed apparently in a Cambridge venue" (Levenson 1987), perhaps by students at Trinity College, in the college hall. "According to notes taken by Malone from a lost office-book of Henry Herbert, the King's Revels Company produced" the play "in the provinces," summer of 1630 (Kelliher 2004b). Acted that summer by the Children of the Revels "probably at the reopening of the Salisbury Court theatre" (Kelliher). "There is no plot, but a series of short, self-contained episodes that depict contrasting virtues and vices. Altogether thirty-four speaking parts are called for, plus an unspecified number of female virtues who dance the concluding masque. Such cast requirements are quite unlike the construction of plays for adult troupes" (Butler 2006). "Some remarks by William Prynne . . . suggest that Randolph's *The Muses' Looking Glass* was the first play" staged at the Salisbury Court playhouse (Wickham et al. 2000). Licensed for acting as *The Entertainment*, 25 November 1630 (Cutts 1985). "Had Randolph lived beyond thirty, through him the academic drama might have again significantly influenced the professional stage" (Butler 2003a).

London, BL, Additional MS 37425, fols. 54–55, contains the "Praeludium," which is probably in Randolph's hand and consists of about two hundred lines of dialogue between Histrio [i.e., a professional entertainer] and a Gentleman, chiefly concerned with the difficulties of actors during a plague closing; the Praeludium may have been specifically written for the opening of the Salisbury Court theater (Bentley 1948). "We have no external evidence of the occasion for which the *Praeludium* was written," but "we may assume" that Randolph intended it for *The Muses' Looking Glass* (Borias 1986).

SR 5 April 1642. O1 1638 *The Muses' Looking Glass*; also issued in *Poems* (with *Amyntas*); author's initials on the TP; separate pagination and register; epilogue spoken by Roscius, a player; five acts and separate scenes. "The first act is a kind of prologue in which Roscius attempts to convince two Puritan hawkers that the theatre can serve a moral function" (McLuskie 1981). Throughout the play Roscius functions as presenter: e.g., "This is *Agroicus*, a rustique, clownish fellow, whose discourse is all country, an extreame of urbanity, whereby you may observe there is a virtue in jesting." In one scene Comedy, Tragedy, Satire, and Mime argue their respective merits, and they allude to a crown of gold, wreath of laurel, whip of steel, and "apish imitation," respectively. Q2 and O2 1640 *Poems* (with *Amyntas*); "the 2ᵈ edition much enlarged," according to the engraved TP; general and separate TPs dated 1640; separate TP gives the author's initials; new register and new pagination for this play. O3 1643 *Poems* (with *Amyntas*, *The Jealous Lovers*); "the third edition inlarged"; both separate and general TPs dated 1643. O3 reissued 1646. O4 1652 *Poems* "the fourth edition inlarged" (with *Amyntas*, *Aristippus*, *The Conceited Peddler*, *The Jealous Lovers*); two issues; new register and new pagination for this play; author's initials on separate TP. O5 1664 *Poems* (*with Amyntas*, *Aristippus*, *The Conceited Peddler*, *The Jealous Lovers*); "the fifth edition, with several additions, corrected and amended"; separate TP dated 1662.

A SD points to the fusing of the allegorical and the social: "*The masque, wherein all the Vertues dance together.*" "This adaptation of morality form to masque, or moral absolutes to social virtues, seems entirely characteristic of the ideological trend in Stuart drama" (McLuskie 1981).

Musophilus. See *The Wisest Have Their Fools About Them.*

N

Narcissus. See *A Twelfth-Night Merriment.*

Narcissus, The Fountain of Self Love. See *Cynthia's Revels.*

Nature. Henry Medwall. Acted *c.* 1496 (Moeslein 1981) or *c.* 1500 (Alford 1995) or "around 1495–1500" (Milling 2004). "Probably performed within the household of Cardinal Morton, Medwall's patron, at Lambeth or at Knole, Kent, to a courtly audience" (Lancashire 2002). "The performance of *Nature* seems to have taken place on two separate evenings, possibly three days apart" (Potter 1975). Presented in a great hall (Southern 1973). The play requires "nothing more than the hall itself as a setting and the furniture of the hall—chairs and stools—as props" (Nelson 1980). "Doubtless performed by choir-boys" (Brooke 1911). "Professional actors may have performed the major roles," but "some of the actors were boys, perhaps choristers from Morton's chapel" (Nelson).

F ND ?1530–34 (Lennam 1975); *A Goodly Interlude of Nature*; list of characters at conclusion; ends with song; divided into two "partes" for performance at different times during a festivity. "*Nature* adheres to the pedagogical structure of moral *exempla*. The parade of the seven Sins and the seven Virtues, for example, teaches a spectator how to discern between good and evil" (Kitch 2005).

"In *Nature* conventional morality elements are strongly present . . . and there is much in the construction of the mankind figure which defines him in formal allegorical terms too. However, the process of historicization puts an emphasis on social trappings and, though the central figure is still just called 'Man,' he is fixed in an elite position with all its obligations and privileges" (Grantley 2000). Medwall is adapting "the morality form to the political and cultural climate of the first Tudor court" (Kitch). "[R]ealism appears in a breezy sketch of London's houses of prostitution, gaming-tables, and the fashions of the gentleman" (Thompson 1910). When the protagonist succumbs to temptation, the change is "reflected in his clothing in the 'new guyse' (a gown sewn with lace, a doublet open at the back, a silken shirt, and striped hose)" (Westfall 1990).

The Nature of the Four Elements. See *The Four Elements.*

Necromantes, or The Two Supposed Heads, A Comical Invention. William Percy. No evidence of production but, according to a note in MSS Huntington HM 4 and Alnwick 509, the author intended that his plays be staged either by Paul's Boys or by the Children of the Revels. Percy's "plays suggest private performance"; "the accession of his nephew Algernon [becoming earl of Northumberland in 1632], who enjoyed high favor with Charles I and under whom the family prospects greatly brightened, aroused him" to write this play (Hillebrand 1938). *Necromantes* "is designated 'For actors onely'" (Gair 2004).

(1) San Marino, CA, Huntington, MS HM 4 [later of the Percy MSS of this play], fols. 152–91; *Comedies and Pastorals*; the general TP, which gives the author's initials, is dated 1647; this play "finis 1632"; *Necromantes, or The Two Supposed Heads, A Comical Invention*; list of characters; list of properties; prologue (by Arcturus) and epilogue (by Tribunus Plebis); chorus; signs of revision; five acts and separate scenes. SDs call for the use of flat "scenic properties" on the tiring-house façade: "*Sundry hollow rocks over the stage and about. An altar of Neptune sited under two of the rocks and under the two heds drawn to. Written over the altar* Ara Neptuni, *being of red marble with a scutcheon of black marble. On the fore syde, painted on him a stone horse dapple graye, the armes of the god. Highest of the stage the title* Necromantes." Percy's plays "show a use of locality boards which is nowhere else so completely illustrated in Elizabethan drama; that such signboards existed is adequately proved by considerable other evidence, but Percy's plays furnish a unique statement as to how they were employed" (Reynolds 1914). Percy has a note addressed to "the Master of Children of Powles" and appended to the play, explaining that the running time of the performance may be shortened by reducing the musical interludes between the acts: "if any of the fine and formost of these pastoralls and comoedyes . . . shall but overreach in length . . . let passe some of the songs, and maketh consort the shorter." Percy integrates two songs within the dramatic action: "he uses a roundel dance-song for a witches dance, and a hymeneal song, both within, rather than at the end of, scenes" (Long 1980). In addition, Percy uses instrumental music: he "calls for a dance by 'Three bare-foot Maydes, in Red peticoates' to the rhythm of a copper kettle beaten with iron pestles by each of the dancers to the tune of 'Dowland's Cock'" (Long). (2) Alnwick, UK, Alnwick Castle, MS 509 *Necromantes, or The Two Supposed Heads, A Comical Invention*; damaged — the lower corners of some leaves have been torn away; the general TP, which gives author's initials, dated 1646; this play "finis 1632." At the end of the MS are a number of songs "composed by mee WP Esquier Anno 1636."

Nero. Possibly written by Thomas May (Fleay 1891, Morley 2006). Acted 1619–23 (Hill 1979) at undetermined venue.

London, BL, Egerton MS 1994, fols. 245–67; *The Tragedy of Nero*; no separate TP; no author named; slightly damaged, some words missing; "[t]wo leaves of the manuscript have been lost, and others have been bound in the wrong order" (*JCS*); five acts and some first scenes. The SDs "are rather scanty throughout" (Greg 1931), but Nero plays "his timbrel over burning Rome while a mother enters with her dead child and a son with his dead father; and as the two victims mourn in alternate strophes, Nero sings and congratulates himself on the symmetry and excellence of his pageant" (Spinrad 1987). The MS was first partially collated in Bullen's *Collection of Old English Plays*, vol. 1 (1882), which reprints Q1.

SR Herbert records that the play was allowed to be printed 15 May 1624 (Adams 1917); transferred 24 October 1633; 28 July 1641. Q1 1624 the words "newly written" on the TP are meant to distinguish this play from Matthew Gwinne's Latin *Nero* (1602–03 [Elliott et al.]) and from the anonymous *Claudius Tiberius Nero*; no author named; five acts. Q2 1633. Q3 1676 *Piso's Conspiracy, A Tragedy*; a shortened and revised version, with prologue and epilogue; list of characters; five acts and separate scenes.

In *Nero* the author "respond[s] imaginatively to the unique political pressures of the turbulent 1620s"; *Nero*, "like other depictions of Roman absolutism, offers us Nero and his court as a kind of carnival mirror in which perceived aspects of contemporary English politics—expanding prerogatives and the dominion of the favorite—appear in grotesquely exaggerated form" (Perry 2006a). The tyrant "is plunging his people into moral, social and political bankruptcy just as James and Charles seemed to their puritan critics to be doing to England" (Butler 1985).

Nero's Life and Death. See *Claudius Tiberius Nero.*

A New and Merry Interlude called The Trial of Treasure. See *The Trial of Treasure.*

A New and Merry Interlude Concerning Pleasure and Pain in Love. See *Love (A Play of Love).*

A New and Very Merry Interlude of All Manner Weathers. See *The Weather.*

A New Interlude . . . Entreating of the Life and Repentance of Mary Magdalene. See *Mary Magdalene.*

A New, Merry, and Witty Comedy or Interlude . . . Treating upon the History of Jacob and Esau. See *Jacob and Esau.*

The New Academy, or The New Exchange. Richard Brome. Acted "just before the substantial plague closure of 12 May 1636" (Steggle 2004b). Probably performed by the King's Revels Men at the Salisbury Court playhouse (Saeger & Fassler 1995).

SR 4 August 1640. O 1658–59 *Five New Plays* (with *The English Moor, The Lovesick Court, The Queen and Concubine, The Weeding of the Covent Garden*); two issues; separate TP dated 1658; separately paginated; dramatis personae; five acts and separate scenes. The address to the reader of the collection notes: "This *New Academy* concerns not that which eight years since peep'd up in White Friers; and this *New Exchange* knows nothing of that which now is cleaving to the Great Church wall." The play "takes devastating aim" at the academy established by Francis Kynaston, Museum Minervae, which sought to "train up the nobility and gentry of England in arms and arts" (Howard 2007).

"*The New Academy* extends the range of the 'place-realism' genre: it is set partly in the London location mentioned in the title, not for mere incidental colour but as a dynamic interaction with that place and the ideas it represents" (Steggle 2004b).

The New Brawl, or Turnmill Street against Rosemary Lane, being a Mock Comedy by Two Actors, viz. John Hold My-staff, Rope-maker, and Doll Do-Little, Rag Woman. A play-pamphlet possibly staged *c.* 1654.

Q 1654 prologue and epilogue (by Jack); not divided. One of several "misogynistic dramatizations of alehouse quarrels" (Potter 1981).

The prologue outlines the author's stance: "Jack being jealous of Doll his bozzy wife, / Like Dogge and catt, they always live at strife, / Jack he begins, and Doll doth open after, / Would break ones twatling strings with laughter. / All you that troubled are with scolding wives, / Learn by this book how to lead quiet lives."

A New Bull-baiting, or A Match Played at the Town-Bull of Ely by Twelve Mongrels, viz. 4 English, 4 Irish, 4 Scotch Dogs. Anonymous. A play-pamphlet possibly performed. Oliver Crum-Well's epitaph makes clear the author's political stance: "Here lies (the Devil take his soul) / One, for whom no bell would towl: / He liv'd a murderer, dy'd a knave; / Deserv'd a halter, not a grave."

SR none. Q 1649 list of characters; not divided. Some SDs: "*Enter* Noll, *drawn to the stake by the four bear-wards; his horns all bloudy, and a garland on his head; with carnation, scarlet, and other changable colours.*"

The address to the reader warns: "It is desired, that all gentlemen, citizens and others that shall come to see this bull-bayting, come not within the compasse of his roape for fear of a mischief, for this beast is so bloody and dangerous; that he hath with his powrfull hornes goared divers to death; therefore if they presume to come within his reach, (and have a faire warning before hand;) the bear-wards are blameless." "While being reminded of real political dangers outside the fictional space of the text, the reader is actually sheltered from those dangers by the very places in which they are anatomized—the public text and the private chamber, both of which secure anonymity" (Straznicky 1995).

"Those who are 'present' at the bull-baiting, literally the readers of the play, are potentially endangered, but the danger (although quite real in the political arena to which the play alludes) is muted by the irony resulting from the transfer of public to private space" (Straznicky 2004).

A New Comedy in English in Manner of an Interlude Right Elegant and Full of Craft of Rhetoric. See *Calisto and Melebea.*

A New Comedy or Interlude concerning Three Laws of Nature, Moses, and Christ. See *Three Laws of Nature, Moses, and Christ.*

***New Custom*.** Anonymous. Acted 1570–73 (*AED 3*) at undetermined venue. "Of professional auspices" and possibly performed at some point by Leicester's Men (White 1993a). The TP lists the names of the characters and divides the eleven roles for four (professional) actors: "fower may play this enterlude." However, the play "contains Latin tags and allusions suggesting a school or college play" (Walker 1998). The play probably "underwent considerable revision" between the time it was originally written and its printing (White 1991).

SR none. Q 1573 *A New Interlude No Less Witty Than Pleasant entitled New Custom*; "devised of late, and for diverse causes nowe set forthe, never before this tyme imprinted"; list of characters on the TP; prologue; ends with a prayer and song; three acts and separate scenes (further divisions may have been intended).

Prologue explains the play's title and sets forth its pro-Reformation agenda: "For the primitive constitution whiche was fyrst appointed / Even by God him self, and by Christ his annoynted: / Confirmed by thappostles, and of great antiquitie: / See howe it is perverted by mannes wicked iniquitie, / To be called newe custome, or new constitucion, / Surely a name of to[o] muche ungodly abusion." In *New Custom* "sectarian controversy makes up the bulk of the play" (Thompson 1910): e.g., "the Catholic Ignorance is so overcome by the virtue of the Protestant Light-of-the-Gospell that he is forced to describe him as 'A good personable fellowe, and in countenance so bright: / That I coulde not beholde him in visage aright'" (Pineas 1962). *New Custom* "presents a variety of allegorical characters who contrast the simplicity and soundness of Protestant doctrine with the bullying corruption of Catholicism" (Grantley 2007).

A New Disputation between the Two Lordly Bishops, York and Canterbury. L. P. [Laurence Price]. A pamphlet in the form of a dialogue.

SR none. Q dated 2 February 1642 on the TP, which gives the author's initials; not divided. A woodcut shows a family at table in the background, musicians in the foreground. Q2 dated 15 February 1642; "the second edition, corrected and enlarged."

The New Inn, or The Light Heart, A Comedy. Ben Jonson. Licensed for performance 19 January 1629 (Adams 1917). Acted by the King's Men, according to the O TP, at the second Blackfriars, where the play "received a disastrous reception" (Kay 1995). The second epilogue to O "shows that Jonson was expecting an early performance at court, but since it remained unspoken the play must already have flopped at the Blackfriars and must have disappeared from the repertory before the 1628–29 Whitehall season had finished" (Butler 2003b). Anticipating court performance, Jonson had sought to "reflect [Queen] Henrietta's preferences," especially her interest in "feminized etiquette and Platonic ideals of the *précieuses*" (Riggs 1989). "[A]lthough *The New Inn* was written before the neoplatonic cult had fully blossomed, it none the less demonstrates that in ethical commitment, if not in theatrical taste, Jonson was at one with the court" (Bulman

2003). "[D]espite being a sensational flop at the Blackfriars, the play reads like a seminal text for the court culture of the next generation" (Butler 1992). Charles's court was "notable for the emergence of a feminocentric culture associated with his wife, Henrietta Maria, who brought with her from France codes of polite manners, moral renewal and neoplatonic woman-worship" (Butler 2010). The play enacts "the increasing cultural visibility of women, specifically in the domain of theatrical performance" (Tomlinson 1999). "By 1629 and the composition of *The New Inn* Blackfriars was at the forefront of the debate over women and theatricals" (Sanders 1999c).

SR 17 April 1631. O 1631 "never acted but most negligently play'd"; an "excessively detailed, act-by-act" argument (Cannan 2002); prologue and two epilogues, one "made for the play in the poets defence"; elaborate descriptions of each character; five acts and separate scenes. "'The Light Heart,' the sign and signification of which the Host draws our attentions to in the opening speech of the play, conjures up all the *préciosité* associations of light and movement that Henrietta Maria was so fond of including in her masques at court" (Sanders 2000). "Jonson embraces female theatricality as a fertile source of dramatic complication and emotional affect. His engagement with shifting women in this play is apparent in its stunning array of five female roles, all of which involve literal or figurative disguise" (Tomlinson 2005). During the play "Prudence assumes the guise of Carnival Queen or Mistress of the Revels for the day, eliciting numerous jokes and metatheatrical references" (Sanders 1999c). "That Jonson elects as his figure of misrule a woman [Prudence], and a working-class one at that, is significant as part of a wider expansion of roles for women in his later drama, or at least of female roles for boy actors" (Sanders 1998b). The play dramatizes "a clandestine marriage in the shape of the partnership of Lord Beaufort and Laetitia. That Laetitia has been disguised at the commencement of the play as the Host's adopted orphan son, the boy Frank, only to be 'dressed up' as a young woman by Prudence and Lady Frances (and conveniently called 'Laetitia') in order to play the Carnival Queen's lady-in-waiting, evidences the complex and layered role that cross-dressing plays in *The New Inn*" (Sanders 1999c). *The New Inn* is only play of Jonson's to appear in octavo. Not included in F1 or F2. F3 1692 *The Works*; "with new additions never before published," according to the general TP; *A Comedy called The New Inn*; argument; list of characters with descriptions; prologue.

The O TP, maligning audience and actors alike, alludes to the play's unfortunate reception at the Blackfriars: "as it was never acted, but most negligently play'd, by some, the kings servants. And more squeamishly beheld, and censured by others, the kings subjects." Jonson's "dedication to the reader" complains of the original audience: "What did they come for, then? thou wil't aske me. I will as punctually answer: to see, and to bee seene. To make a generall muster of themselves in their clothes of credit: and possesse the stage, against the play. To dislike all, but marke nothing. And by their confidence of rising between the actes, in oblique lines, make *affidavit* to the whole house, of their not understanding one scene." After the prologue Jonson writes, "The just indignation the author tooke at the vulgar censure of his play, by some malicious spectators, beget this following Ode to himselfe." Jonson "explains in a second Epilogue [to O] appended to the printed text, apparently never performed on stage, that there was some controversy about the original name of Lady Frampul's chambermaid, Cis [changed to Pru]" (Kidnie 2000a). "The real truth about the squabble over 'Cis,' which is what Jonson originally called this character, why it created such animosity, will probably never be recovered" (Barton 1984).

A New Interlude and a Merry of the Nature of the Four Elements. See *The Four Elements.*

A New Interlude called Thersites. See *Thersites.*

A New Interlude drawn out of the Holy Scripture of Godly Queen Hester. See *Godly Queen Hester.*

A New Interlude . . . Entreating of the Life and Repentance of Mary Magdalene. See *Mary Magdalene.*

A New Interlude for Children to Play named Jack Juggler. See *Jack Juggler.*

A New Interlude, never before this time imprinted, entreating of the Life and Repentance of Mary Magdalene. See *Mary Magdalene.*

A New Interlude of Impatient Poverty. See *Impatient Poverty.*

A New Interlude of Vice. See *Horestes.*

A New Interlude No Less Witty Than Pleasant Entitled New Custom. See *New Custom.*

A New and Merry Interlude Called The Trial of Treasure. See *The Trial of Treasure.*

A New and Pleasant Interlude entitled the Marriage of Wit and Science. See *The Marriage of Wit and Science.*

A New Tragical Comedy of Appius and Virginia. See *Appius and Virginia* by R. B.

A New Trick to Cheat the Devil, A Comedy. Robert Davenport (but Lake 1975a, on stylistic grounds, doubts the attribution). Acted 1624–39 (*AED 3*) by an unidentified company at the Phoenix; "often acted, and so well approved," accord-

ing to the address to the reader. In playlist of Beeston's Boys 10 August 1639 as
A Trick to Beat the Devil.

SR 28 March 1639 by m^r Damport. Q 1639 *A Pleasant and Witty Comedy
Called A New Trick to Cheat the Devil*; two issues; author's initials on the TP;
dramatis personae; a symbolic dance functions as a dumb show; five acts and
separate scenes. Elaborate SDs: *"Enter an Anticke habited in parchment indentures,
bills, bonds, waxe seales, and pen, and inkhornes, on his breast writ,* I am a scrivener. *Dances a straine, and stands right before him"*; *"Enter the divell like a gentleman,
with glasse eyes"*; *"Ent[er] divells dauncing, with fire workes, and crackers."* "Master
Changeable disguises himself as a devil to perform an act of charity for his prospective son-in-law" (Cox 2000). Special effects include *"Thundering and howl-
ing, Ent[er] Chan[geable] like the divell."* "In outdoor playhouses . . . in addition
to 'tempestuous' drums, a 'bullet,' i.e., a cannonball, was 'rolled' along a sheet of
metal or a wooden trough [to simulate thunder]" (White 2007). "The dialogue
suggests that there is a 'staircase' backstage on which to make the move between
the area above and the main playing area" (King 1965).

A prefatory epistle expresses the wish that readers enjoy the play as much as
spectators did: "It is a comedy which hath bin often acted, and so well approved;
that I hope none will dislike of it now in the reading . . . my hopes are, it will
prove no lesse pleasing to the reader, than it hath formerly beene to the spectators." Here "the printer wants to underscore a connection between performance
and printing" (Bergeron 2006).

A New Way to Pay Old Debts, A Comedy. Philip Massinger. No license for acting
exists. Acted December 1625 or early 1626 (E&G 1976) by Prince Charles's Men
at the Phoenix (Gurr 2009d). The play was possibly "staged in the provinces, as its
unusual country setting might suggest" (Gibson 1978); the London theaters were
closed for a time by plague in 1625. "Often acted" by [the newly formed] Queen
Henrietta Maria's Men at the Phoenix, according to the TP, *c.* 1633 (Gurr). The
play "seems to have remained in the repertory of successive companies managed
[at the Phoenix] and at the Salisbury Court Theatre by William Beeston and
William Davenant, until the closing of the theatres" (Gibson). Performed also by
an unidentified company at Skipton Castle, Yorkshire, the home of Henry Clifford, February 1636 (Greenfield 2009); "the hall is 28 feet wide by 50 feet long"
(Palmer 2009b). In playlist of Beeston's Boys 10 August 1639.

SR 10 November 1632. Q 1633 dramatis personae; epilogue, possibly by
Welborne (Schneider 2011); five acts and separate scenes. Numerous offstage
sound effects: *"Loud musicke"*; *"Noise within as of a co[a]ch"*; *"A cry within."* A prefatory poem by Thomas Jay compliments the playwright on "The craftie mazes of
the cunning plot; / The polish'd phrase; the sweet expressions; got / Neither by
theft, nor violence; the conceipt / Fresh, and unsullied."

Massinger's plot borrows from Middleton's *A Trick to Catch the Old One,*
"though his adaptation of the city comedy mode in that play indicates the shift in

sensibility which took place in the satiric comedy of the 1620s" (McLuskie 1981). Massinger also "rewrites *The Merchant of Venice* for a new age, taking over character relationships and plot elements" (Clark 2007), but "in place of a villainous Jew . . . Massinger offers the instantly recognizable figure of Sir Giles Overreach, whom critics unanimously identify as Sir Giles Mompesson" (Corns 2007), "impeached in 1621 over his monopolies and patents" (Heinemann 1993a). "What is presented with disturbing force in *A New Way* is nothing less than the threatened disintegration of the existing social and administrative system" (Heinemann).

A New Wonder, A Woman Never Vexed, A Comedy. William Rowley; possibly revised by Thomas Heywood (Darby 1988). Acted *c.* 1611 (Grantley 2008a) or 1614–15 (Cheatham 1993). "Sundry times acted," according to the TP, perhaps by Prince Charles's Men (Nicol 2006a) at undetermined venue. "The minimum cast required is 16, including three for the female roles" (Darby). Rowley probably played the role of Roger (Nicol 2008b).

SR 24 November 1631; transferred 17 February 1648. Q 1632 *A New Wonder, A Woman Never Vexed, A Pleasant Conceited Comedy*; "never before printed"; the TP identifies Rowley as "one of his majesties servants"; five acts but "the act-divisions do not arise organically from the text" (Darby). Few SDs "and they are not elaborate" (Jewkes 1958), but offstage sound creates atmosphere: *"A noyse below in the bowling alley, betting, rubbing and wrangling"*; *"A noyse above at cards."* Unusual staging: "Old Foster, a newly arrived prisoner at Ludgate, is first instructed to beg at the iron grate above and then is to enter *'above at the grate, a box hanging downe,'* so that the main stage temporarily becomes the street where passers-by can put their contributions in the box" (Dessen 1980).

"A generically hybrid work, it mixes monarchical history with several 'unhistorical' scenes . . . set in the city of London and depicting characters drawn from 'ordinary' London life such as the London watch and members of London's criminal underworld" (Howard 2007).

1 Newmarket Fair, or a Parliament Outcry of State Commodities Set to Sale. The Man in the Moon (probably John Crouch [Raymond 1996] or John Overton [Wolfe 1958]). Written during the period 28 May-13 June 1649 (Werstine 1982a) and probably acted soon afterward. The Q1 prologue anticipates production: "Come Tom and Noll, Jane, Cisse, Sue and Doll, / and wise aldermen of the City. / See but this play, and before you goe away / you'l say 'tis wondrous pritty."

SR none. Q1 1649 *A Tragicomedy called Newmarket Fair*; no author named; list of characters; prologue (by the Cryer); divided into two scenes. A very short entertainment with adequate SDs. "Both the bitterest and the funniest of the royalist plays, it went through several editions in 1649" (Potter 1981). This play-pamphlet is an "attack on Cromwell, Fairfax, and other prominent members of the government, all of whom at the end of the play hear of Charles II's triumphs and commit suicide" (Rollins 1921); Scotland's Parliament proclaimed

Charles II King of Great Britain and Ireland in Edinburgh on 6 February 1649. Q2 1649 *A Tragicomedy called Newmarket Fair*; "the second edition, corrected and amended by the author." Q3 1649 "the third edition, corrected and amended." Q4 1661 unique copy at Bodleian; "advertised that it was 'reprinted at the request of some young gentlemen, to *Act in Christmas Holy-dayes*'" (Raymond). As this new edition suggests, *Part 1* "achieved a new popularity" in the Restoration (Potter 1987b).

The play's title "could mean a 'new market-fair,' that is, yet another sale of lands and goods, this time the King's, following upon the sale of the lands of the bishops and the lands of the deans and chapters. Or it could be read 'Newmarket fair,' with Newmarket, one of the King's estates, standing, through metonymy, for all the King's goods and lands" (Werstine). "The comical piece attempts to present the immediate aftermath of the King's execution as a period of gross confusion and rivalry amongst the regicides" (Clare 2002).

2 Newmarket Fair, or Mrs. Parliament's New Figaries. "Written by the Man in the Moon" [John Crouch]. Written July 1649 and acted soon afterward (Werstine 1982b). "Both the rhetoric and, particularly, the dynamics of the plot are very much geared to performance" (Clare 2002). *Part 2* "is longer, more ambitious, and more stage-oriented in its wording" than *Part 1* (Randall 1995). The prologue recommends "that the reader live 'to see this plaid another day,' projecting performance as something that would happen in an improved future" (Raymond 1996). The prologue establishes a royalist stance: Miles Corbet (a Jesuit) "will teach you in his part to paint / The devil in the likeness of a saint, / Which cannot chuse but make proud rebels rage, / To see themselves thus acted on the stage."

SR none. Q1 1649 *The Second Part of the Tragicomedy Called Newmarket Fair, or Mrs. Parliament's New Figaries*; list of characters; prologue and epilogue; "the text of the play resists the imposition of act or scene divisions: in the play itself Crouch has mocked such divisions" (Werstine). Ample SDs: *"Enter three or four Furies, and anticks dancing about him [Fairfax] with their hands all bloudy"*; *"Ghost appears from beneath the stage in fetters and flames of sulphire."* Q2 1649; "the second edition, corrected . . . by the author"; unique copy at Worcester College, Oxford.

The Q1 prologue reports the playwright's political intention: "His scenes (he vows) do only aime to please / The publique; and cure each foul disease / Of manners in the government." "The play ends with a second rebellion, the murder of Mrs. Cromwell by Lady Fairfax, and the crowd's decision to petition Charles II to return" (Potter 1987b): *"Lady Fairfax snatcht up Gorges sword, and runs Mrs Cromwell thorow"*; the people apprehend her for murder, and carry her to prison. They cry, "Lets petition our king home."

News from Plymouth. William Davenant. Licensed for acting as *News of Plymouth* 1 August 1635 (Adams 1917, Edmond 1987). Acted by the King's Men at the second Globe in the summer. "The only one of his early plays known to have been performed" at the Globe and "certainly the only one expressly written for it" (Edmond). In playlist of the King's Men 7 August 1641.

SR 4 September 1646; transferred 14 October 1672; 30 January 1673. F 1673 *The Works*; "now published out of the authors originall copies"; list of characters; prologue and epilogue by Sir Furious ("also printed in Davenant's *Madagascar; with other Poems* in 1638" [Schneider 2011]); five acts and a separate scene. The play "appeals to its audience in its salute to the English navy, its commitment to interclass marriage, and its satire on both foreigners and the gentry. But it is interesting today for the unintended conflict between these values and the author's ill-concealed hostility toward the very citizen classes for whom the play was meant" (Cohen 1985).

Prologue addresses the nature of the Globe audience: "each spectator knows / This house, and season, does more promise shewes, / Dancing, and buckler fights, then art, or witt; / Yet so much taxt of both, as will befit / Our humble theame, you shall receive, and such / As may please those, who not expect too much." In short, the play is staged "for a vacation audience at the Globe" (Bordinat & Blaydes 1981).

The Nice Valor, or The Passionate Madman. Thomas Middleton (Hoy 1960), ?with John Fletcher; "the play may originally have been a Fletcherian original that Middleton has revised" (Hoy 1987a). Acted autumn 1622 (Taylor 2004a) at undetermined venue. Probably "not written for the King's company" (*JCS*). Possibly included in the King's Men 1641 playlist as *The Bridegroom and the Madman* (Chambers 1911).

SR not included in the entry of 4 September 1646; 29 June 1660; 30 January 1673. B&F F1 1647 *Comedies and Tragedies*; "never printed before, and now published by the authours originall copies"; *The Nice Valor, or The Passionate Madman*; "prologue at the reviving of this play" and epilogue; five acts and separate scenes. The "Nice Valor" of the title "refers to Shamont, the Duke's favorite"; he is distinguished "from a character known only as the Passionate Lord ('the Passionate Madman' of the title)"; "Shamont's hypermasculine egotism sharply contrasts to the effeminate antics of the Passionate Lord" (DiGangi 1997). *Nice Valor* "is most musical, having in all at least two dance numbers and six songs" (Williams 1989); it "contains the period's most popular theatrical song (the beautifully melancholy 'Hence all ye vain delights')," which is sung by the madman (Taylor 2004b). Detailed directions for a masque: *"Enter againe the same Cupid, two brothers, 6 women maskers, Cupids bow bent all the way towards them, the first woman singing and playing . . . A dance, Cupid leading."* Descriptive entrances: *"The passionate man enters in furie, with a truncheon."* F2 1679 *Fifty Comedies and Tragedies*; "published by the authors original copies, the songs to each play being added"; *Nice Valor, A Comedy*; RT *The Nice Valor, or The Passionate Madman*; list of characters.

The F1 prologue pays tribute to the (unnamed) author: "He made the the-atre so soveraigne / With his rare scænes, he scorn'd this crowching veine: / We stabb'd him with keene daggers when we pray'd / Him write a preface to a play well made. / He could not write these toyes; 'twas easier farre, / To bring a fel-on to appeare at th' barre, / So much he hated basenesse; which this day, / His scænes will best convince you of in's play." Beaumont's letter to Ben Jonson, "written before he and master Fletcher came to London, with two of the prec-edent comedies then not finisht," follows the epilogue in F1.

Nice Wanton. ?Thomas Ingelend. Acted 1547–53 (Tennenhouse 1984) at unde-termined venue. Although the play was written during the reign of Edward VI, it must "have been revived for performance before Queen Elizabeth before it was printed" (Wickham 1976). "The concentration upon education and the upbring-ing of children, added to the address in the epilogue to 'ye children,' suggests a school play" (Walker 1998). "It was certainly composed for a company of child-actors" (Hillebrand 1926). "[P]layed by Paul's Boys before Queen Elizabeth in August of 1560" (Bevington 2002a). Probably performed "by pupils of provincial grammar schools rather than by the London schoolboy and chorister troupes, who brought plays to court each Christmas" (Shapiro 1977).

SR 10 June 1560. Q1 1560 *A Pretty Interlude Called Nice Wanton*; no author named; list of characters on the TP; prologue (by Messenger); epilogue by Barn-abas followed by a song; the epilogue "was apparently clumsily altered for Eliza-beth with the word 'King' changed to 'Queen'" (Schneider 2011); divided into two parts (the division is indicated by the need to change the costume and make-up of Dalilah, the "nice wanton" of the title). "The convention of representing moral corruption by facial alteration or disfigurement is evident" in a SD: "*Dalila cometh in ragged, her face hid, or disfigured, halting on a staff*" (Drew-Bear 1994). In keeping with the didactic nature of the play and the prevailing dramaturgy, per-sonified abstractions share the stage with biblical figures. Q2 ND ?1565.

The play addresses "matter specific to the reign of a boy-king reformer" (Westfall 2002); the play "supports in quite precise detail the mythography sur-rounding Edward VI, the young king Solomon with a wise head on young shoul-ders" (King 1993). Ingelend's drama represents "a morality well on the way to the concreteness and particularity of secular drama, because the central problem of the play, the upbringing of children, is given a firm location in a family and in society" (Margeson 1967). The play adapts "the older form of the Prodigal Son plays to the changed circumstances of the Reformation" (King 1982). *Nice Wan-ton* "includes the earliest dramatisation of incidents of a trial by jury according to the criminal law of England" (Dean 1991).

The Night Walker, or The Little Thief, A Comedy. John Fletcher; "corrected" by James Shirley, according to the entry in Henry Herbert's office-book for 11 May 1633, and confirmed by stylistic analysis (Hoy 1959). "Probably first acted ca. 1611" (Wertheim 1978) by the Queen's Revels Children or Lady Elizabeth's Men (Collins 2007) at the Whitefriars; these companies "merged in March 1613" (Hoy 1989). Revised version licensed for acting 11 May 1633 (Adams 1917); "[t]his revision must have been an extensive one" (Bentley 1971); "presented by" Queen Henrietta Maria's Men at the Phoenix, according to the Q1 TP (Bawcutt 1996). Performed also by the same company at court, before the king and queen, the night of 30 January 1634 (Hoy 1959) and "likt as a merry play." In playlist of Beeston's Boys 10 August 1639.

SR 25 April 1639. Q1 1640 "by John Fletcher"; list of characters; five acts. Special effects include a bell-ringing competition. "The scene being laid outside the church, the ringing is not seen, but betweenwhiles the ringers come out and discuss matters with the sexton, who is acting as judge" (Lawrence 1927). Henslowe's 1598 inventory of properties lists "j chyme of belles" (Lawrence 1935). Costume must create a shocking effect: "*Enter two Furies with blacke tapers.*" This prompts Lurcher's penitence: "What dreadfull apparitions!" Then "*Enter boy like an angell*" and he says, "Malicious Furies hence." In one scene Lurcher, "thieving, scares off detection by putting his boy, who wears a false beard, on his shoulders, and pretending to be the ghost of a giant. The comedy calls for this kind of simple, physical foolery" (Gossett 1988). Q2 1661. B&F F2 1679 *Fifty Comedies and Tragedies*; "the songs to each play being added"; actors' names.

No Wit, No Help, Like a Woman's, A Comedy. Thomas Middleton. Acted summer or early autumn 1611 (Johnson 1976) or 1612 (Gurr 2009d) at undetermined venue but "probably performed outdoors" (White 1998). If this play is identical to *The Almanac*, (as it "almost certainly" is [Gurr 2009c]), then it was initially staged at the first Fortune by Prince Henry's Men (the renamed Admiral's Men) and, later, on 29 December 1611, restaged at Whitehall (Jowett 1991b) by Lady Elizabeth's Men (Saeger & Fassler 1995) "for Prince Henry and his sister," 11 April 1612 (Gurr). Revived at court 1616 and retitled *The Almanac* "after its most 'humorous' character' (Gurr 2009c). Revived by Ogilby's Men at the Werburgh Street theater, Dublin, 1638 (Taylor 2004b). James Shirley may have revised the original script for the revival in Ireland (Johnson); "Shirley gave the play a new prologue" (Jowett 2007d).

SR 9 September 1653. O 1657 list of characters; prologue and epilogue; five-act structure probably introduced in the 1638 revival "unless [the act intervals] derive from the 1611 court performance or an unrecorded revival" (Jowett 2007d). "Shirley's *Poems* (London: 1646) contains 'A Prologue to a Play there [in Ireland]; call'd No wit to a Woman's'" (Schneider 2011). Extraordinary staging, enlisting descent machinery and special effects: "*A thing like a globe opens of one side o'th' stage, and flashes out fire, then Sir* Gilbert, *that presents the part, issues forth with yellow-hair and beard, intermingled with stroaks like wilde flames, a three forked fire in's hand; and at the same time Air comes down, hanging by a cloud, with a coat made like an almanack, all the twelve moons set in it, and the Four Quarters, Winter,*

Spring, Summer, and Autumn, with change of weathers, rain, lightning, and tempest, &c. And from under the stage at both ends, arises Water and Earth, two persons." "This kind of staging was traditionally associated with the repertoire of the Red Bull and the Fortune in London, outdoor amphitheaters rather than the Phoenix-style indoor theaters, as the St. Werburgh theater clearly was" (Dutton 2006). The play "shows ample signs of revision. It has act breaks inserted, an indoor playhouse practice the Fortune never adopted" (Gurr 2009c).

No Wit "might be described as a female-oriented continuation of male-oriented city comedy" (Jowett 2007d). The subplot "is a farcical reworking of the Viola-Olivia relationship in *Twelfth Night*" (Shapiro 1994). Dressed like a man, "Kate makes such an appealing but somewhat ambiguous figure that she attracts both men and women" (Walen 2005). "As part of a witty plot to defeat the rich widow Lady Goldenfleece, whose husband financially ruined her own, Kate Low-water poses as a young gallant, then woos and marries the widow" (Di-Gangi 1997).

The Noble Bondman. See *The Bondman.*

The Noble Enemy. See *The Humorous Lieutenant.*

The Noble Friend. See *The Faithful Friends.*

The Noble Gentleman. Francis Beaumont; revised by John Fletcher. Uncertain stage history. A lost original version may have been performed by Paul's Boys at Paul's playhouse 1605–06 (Hoy 1958). Perhaps first performed 1609 (Maxwell 1939) or 1611–15 (Finkelpearl 1990). Revised version licensed for acting 3 February 1626 as Fletcher's and "acted at the Blackfriars" (Adams 1917, Hoy 1958) by the King's Men. Or perhaps there was no version of 1605–06 or 1609 or 1611–15 and thus no revision; rather the play may not have been written until 1624–25 (Beaurline 1976). In playlist of King's Men 7 August 1641.

SR 4 September 1646; transferred 30 January 1673. B&F F1 1647 *Comedies and Tragedies*; "never printed before, and now published by the authours originall copies"; prologue and epilogue; five acts. Substantially the same prologue appears in the second issue of *Thierry and Theodoret* Q2 1649; "the prologue was written for *The Noble Gentleman*" (Beaurline). Epilogue "was published as the epilogue to Beaumont's *Woman Hater* in 1649" (Stern 2009c). B&F F2 1679 *Fifty Comedies and Tragedies*; "published by the authors original copies, the songs to each play being added"; *The Noble Gentleman, A Comedy*; list of characters.

The F1 prologue, written after Fletcher's death in 1625, comments on changes in theatrical fashion: "Wit is become an anticke, and puts on / As many shapes of variation, / To court the times applause, as the times dare, / Change severall fashions, nothing is thought rare / Which is not new and follow'd, yet we know, / That what was worne some twenty yeare agoe, / Comes into grace againe, and we pursue / That custome, by presenting to your view / A play in fashion then, not doubting now / But 'twill appear the same, if you allow / Worth to their noble memory, whose name, / Beyond all power of death live in their fame." This prologue "could have been written at any time from the period of the licensing date of 1625/6 to the printing date of 1647" (Finkelpearl 1990). The F1 epilogue comments on the gap between performance and publication: "The monuments of vertue, and desert, / Appeare more goodly, when the glosse of art / Is eaten off by time, then when at first / They were set up, not censur'd at the worst. / We have done our best, for your contents to fit / With new paines, this old monument of wit."

The Noble Ingratitude, A Pastoral Tragicomedy. William Lower. Possibly not performed (Gates 1932), but the SDs are ample and the prologue anticipates production: "every one that sits / Spectatour here usurps a priviledge, / Which is unjust, before he hears, to judge."

D1 1659 published in The Hague; HT *The Noble Ingratitude, A Tragicomedy*; list of characters; prologue and epilogue; five acts and separate scenes. A Folger copy contains "about fifteen manuscript corrections, all in Lower's hand" (Kathman 2004b). Ample SDs: *"Zaida feigning her self in a dream"*; *"He kisseth her hands"*; *"[Zaida] feigning to awake."* D2 1661 published in London: *Three New Plays*, a made-up book (with *The Amorous Phantasm* and *The Enchanted Lovers*); two issues; separate and general TPs dated 1661; each play has separate register and pagination; "whether separate publication of the three pieces was also intended is uncertain" (Greg 1939).

The prologue is intended for an audience rather than readers: "suspend / Your judgments till you see us at the end / Of the fifth act; three hours will soon be pass'd, / In sceans and songs the minutes fly too fast; / Then if we don't maintain our paradox, / Let me be sham'd, and sit three hours i' th' stocks / For punishing your patience." The epilogue, similarly, is addressed to playgoers: "Yours are the leading voices, in your looks / We read our fortune better then in books."

The Noble Soldier, or A Contract Broken, Justly Revenged, A Tragedy. Thomas Dekker (the MS "evidently bore Dekker's name" [Greg 1939]). Dekker may have revised an earlier play, perhaps with John Day; or they collaborated on a new play (Hoy 1980). Samuel Rowley may also have collaborated (Cerasano 2004c). Revised by Dekker in the early 1620s and acted *c.* 1622 (Hoy) at undetermined venue. Probably intended for Lady Elizabeth's Men at the Phoenix, but possibly not performed. Later reworked as *The Welsh Ambassador* (Lloyd 1927); but Lesser 2006a judges that "[w]hich play revises which" is unclear. What makes *Noble Soldier* unusual is that it "is one of the very few English plays of the period to depict a wholly virtuous Roman Catholic priest" (Lesser).

SR 16 May 1631 *The noble Spanish Souldier* by Tho. Deckar; re-entered 9 December 1633 (same title); both SR entries name Dekker. Q 1634 *The Noble*

Soldier, or A Contract Broken, Justly Revenged, A Tragedy; RT *The Noble Spanish Soldier*; the TP attributes the play, perhaps in error, to S. R. (?Samuel Rowley); dramatis personae; detailed description of entries read like dumb shows; five acts. Elaborate SDs, with attention to furnishings: *"A table set out cover'd with blacke: two waxen tapers: the kings picture at one end, a crucifix at the other, Onaelia walking discontentedly weeping to the crucifix, her mayd with her."* The King complains that his picture has been "defac'd" by Onaelia: she "has stabbed the portrait to satisfy her frustrated rage" (Bowers 1932). "Onaelia is driven to violence beause she believes the image possesses the king's *presence*—destroying his picture, therefore, expresses her desire to hurt the king" (Tassi 2005).

In his address to the reader, Nicholas Vavasour asserts the value of printing plays: "The poet [i.e., playwright] might conceive a compleat satisfaction upon the stages approbation: but the printer rests not there, knowing that that which was acted and approved upon the stage, might bee no lesse acceptable in print. It is now communicated to you whose leisure and knowledge admits of reading and reason."

The Noble Spanish Soldier. See *The Noble Soldier.*

The Noble Stranger. Lewis Sharpe. Acted 1638–40 (Kawachi 1986) by Queen Henrietta Maria's Men at the Salisbury Court playhouse, according to the TP. The author's Q dedication reports that "this play . . . was receiv'd generally well upon the stage." The prefatory poem by Richard Woolfall says the play "With pleasing strains has smooth'd the rugged fate / Of oft cram'd theatres, and prov'd fortunate."

SR none. Q 1640 author's initials on the TP and Sharpe signs the dedication; list of characters; prologue and epilogue; five acts. Ample SDs: "[Pupillus] *Takes out a booke and holds it in his hand, and looks on it at the breaches*"; "*Enter* Plod *with a boxe, in which are little pieces of paper rold up: a table set forth.*"

A remark in the prologue — "Blest fate protect me! what a lustre's here? / How many starres deck this our little spheare?"— probably refers to the "'circular' or rounded auditorium" of the Salisbury Court theater (Orrell 1988).

Nobody and Somebody, with the True Chronicle History of Elydure, Who Was Fortunately Three Several Times Crowned King of England. Anonymous, but there are "signs of [Robert] Wilson in the play" (Knutson 2009b). Possibly staged as early as "the 1590s" (Bosman 2004). *Nobody* may be "the same as the play 'albere galles,' for which Henslowe paid Thomas Heywood and Wentworth Smith in September 1602"; these two playwrights may have "revised an old play" of the 1590s; the play "must have been updated again before its publication" (Foakes 1985). Acted 1603–06 (Hay 1980) by the Queen's Men, according to the TP, at undetermined venue; although this is usually taken to mean Queen Anne's Men (Archdeacon 2012), it may designate Queen Elizabeth's Men (Knutson 2009b). A character's comment that "*somebody* once pickt a pocket in this play-house yard, / Was hoysted on the stage, and shamd about it," probably alludes to the Boar's Head (Berry 1986). The role of Nobody may have been played by Will Kemp, who in August 1602 was given five shillings by Philip Henslowe to buy "gyente hosse"; the TP woodcut shows the character wearing "a balloon-like pair of 'giant hose' that stretched from his knees up to his chin" (Bourke 2009).

SR 12 March 1606. Q ND ?1606 no author named; "the true coppy"; prologue and epilogue (by Nobody); not divided. "What is original here is to set Nobody not against some universal Everybody but against a particular, if still anonymous, Somebody; the effect is to organize the drama into a strict polarity of positive and negative pronouns, and hence . . . of positive and negative bodies as well" (Bosman 2004). The TP features a woodcut of Nobody apparently holding a roll of papers; following the last page of the text is a woodcut of Somebody holding a stave and armed with a sword. Also surviving is a watercolor portrait of 1608 perhaps depicting John Green as Nobody (Orgel 2003, Foakes 1985, Astington 2010); he holds "a book (?a bible or missal) in one hand, and a rosary with a cross attached to it in the other" (Foakes). But the identification of the figure in the picture with Green "may be wrong in every respect" (Bosman 2006). Although the picture "most likely depicts an English actor it does so in a German manuscript commemorating an Austrian performance and is titled in Latin" (Bosman 2006).

The play dramatizes "a story about repeatedly becoming and unbecoming king—put another way, about fluctuating between being somebody and being nobody" (Bosman 2004); Elydure regards "monarchy as an unwelcome assault upon the integrity" of his private life (Barton 1977); he "succeeds as king (three times)" (Henry 2007). There are notable similarities between *Nobody* and *King Lear*: "Both rely on Geoffrey of Monmouth and Holinshed for their British pseudo history; thematically, both plays manifest a preoccupation with nothing . . . and in both a king's unwillingness to rule creates a political problem with extensive social consequences" (Wilson 2000). *Nobody and Somebody* "might be read as an advice-to-princes style intervention, counselling fair and just rule, attacking sycophancy and the immoderate pursuit of power, and stressing the need for stable government"; at the same time it suggests that the wealthy and powerful "have a duty to take responsibility for the nobodies, or at least not to exploit them" (Archdeacon).

The Nonpareilles. See *Love and Honor.*

The Northern Lass, A Comedy. Richard Brome. Licensed for acting 29 July 1629 (Adams 1917, Fried 1980). "Often acted with good applause" by the King's Men at the [second] Globe and [second] Blackfriars, according to the Q1 TP; performance at the Globe probably occurred first since the company occupied that theater in the summer. Performed also at Whitehall Cockpit, 29 November 1638 (bill for plays before the king and queen); and at Richmond Palace, probably in the Great Chamber, 28 December 1638 (Adams).

SR 24 March 1632; transferred 9 July 1653. Q1 1632 list of characters; prologue; five acts and separate scenes. SDs "are unusually detailed" (Fried): "*The masquers enter. All in willow garlands. Foure men. Foure women. The two first payres are* Tridewell, *and* Constance, Anvile *and* Trainewell." Jonson, Dekker, and Ford, among others, contribute commendatory poems. Dedicatory epistle alludes to the play's "late long silence, and discontinuance," "a phrase vague enough to describe the previous year's plague closure, but perhaps alluding to some now-unknown legal trouble with the play" (Steggle 2004b). Q2 1663.

Ben Jonson's Q1 prefatory poem salutes Brome: "Now, you are got into a nearer roome, / Of fellowship, professing my old arts. / And you doe doe them well, with good applause, / Which you have justly gained from the stage, / By observation of those comick lawes, / Which I, your master, first did teach the age. / You learn'd it well; and for it, serv'd your time / A prentise-ship: which few doe now a dayes." "Brome himself, however, defended the comedy rather than the 'lawes'" (McLuskie 1981). "Jonson's commendation of this son on his first publication . . . is so important that it was reprinted in 1659 at the head of the second posthumous collection of Brome, *Five New Plays*" (Clark 1992).

Northward Ho! Thomas Dekker and John Webster. Acted 1605 (Hoy 1980). "Sundry times acted" by Paul's Boys, according to the TP, at Paul's playhouse. "Highly popular and frequently performed" (Gunby 2004).

SR 6 August 1607. Q 1607 five acts. Publication of Q followed the breakup of Paul's Boys in 1607. The play was written after the production of *Eastward Ho!* by Chapman, Jonson, and Marston: *Northward Ho!* "features a character named Bellamont whose resemblance to George Chapman is far from coincidental" (Steggle 1998); "Bellamont bears many comic similarities with the dramatist. The character is garrulous, vain, pedantic, fond of learning, and a shade myopic" (Burnett 2004).

"Though not strictly a sequel to *Westward Ho* (no characters are carried over from the first play to the later one), *Northward Ho* does dramatize a further stage in the comedy of attempted cuckoldry that is the common theme of both plays" (Hoy). With their two plays Dekker and Webster "introduce joint authorship into the private theaters, paving the way for the advent of the indoor playhouses' most important collaborators, Beaumont and Fletcher" (Hirschfeld 2004).

Norwich Grocers' Play: The Story of the Creation of Eve, with the Expelling of Adam and Eve out of Paradise. Anonymous. *The Creation of Eve* was acted in 1533, and *The Expelling* acted in 1565, and presumably in other years, as a pageant, one of a number prepared by various guilds and performed by amateurs in the city of Norwich. "The plays may have been, in their early history, performed on Corpus Christi, but by 1527 . . . they were shown on Whit Monday. The shift from

Corpus Christi to Pentecost week could have occurred as late as 1524" (Dutka 1984). "[T]here is no reason to seriously doubt that they shared the same general locale of the Pentecost Fair, that is to say, in Tombland, an open area between the walls of the Cathedral precinct and the city. . . . Processional staging cannot be ruled out, however, since the pageants were mounted on horse-drawn pageant wagons" (White 2008). "Pageant wagons were limited in size by the size of the streets, but they were substantial structures"; "they were often elaborate, with a heaven painted with sunbeams and stars, an upper balcony for God and the angels and selected action, and sometimes a hell-mouth" (Cooper 2010). "The last entry in the [Grocers'] book concerns the sad fate of the pageant wagon, a two-level 'Howsse of Waynskott' with a 'nether parte' built on a cart or wagon. By 1570 it was so badly deteriorated from having been left outdoors that it was scrapped" (Coldewey 1993). "Protestant England found the mystery plays too Catholic to allow their continuance" (Harty 1981).

"The *Grocers' Book* from which some extracts were taken was begun on June 16, 1533" (Davis 1970); one of those excerpts is the text of *The Story of the Creation*, which is incomplete, consists of 92 lines, and known as Text A; the other excerpt, from the 1565 *Grocers' Book*, consists of another version (revised) of the play, *The Expelling of Adam and Eve*; it is mostly complete, consists of 161 lines, and known as Text B; dating from 1565, "strictly speaking, it is an Elizabethan play" (Coldewey). *The Expelling* contains a prologue (28 lines) and an alternative prologue (21 lines), "the former to be used when the Grocers' pageant was the first one to be performed, and the latter when one or more pageants preceded the Grocers' play" (Davis); the prologues are intended to be spoken by the "Prolocutor," a rare term also used in John Bale's plays and in *King Darius* (Butler 2004f). "Satan's appearance in the form of an angel is treated in Text A with dramatic skill" (Dutka). Text B "shows an extensive Protestant revision" (White); Dolor and Misery confront Adam and Eve after the fall but they also find consolation. "The final scene in the [Text B] Norwich Grocers' Play is unique among the English mystery cycles in that it introduces the Holy Ghost on stage as an actual character in his role as intercessor for and comforter of man"; "the Norwich playwright has added a number of details, some also biblically inspired, not found in the other mystery plays of the Fall. These details heighten the dramatic effect of the Norwich play and attest the playwright's artistry and skill" (Harty). The Prolocutor in Text B "talks almost exclusively about the visual aspects of what is to be presented" (Schneider 2011).

The original MS is lost. However, in 1856 Robert Fitch prepared a transcript of an eighteenth-century transcript that is now also lost; Manly reproduced this version in 1897, and Waterhouse produced an edition in 1909. "It has generally been assumed that Fitch and Waterhouse used the same eighteenth-century transcript of the play from the long-lost Grocers' Book but they could equally well have been using different ones despite Waterhouse's assumption" (Dunn 1972). Newly edited (from Waterhouse's text) by Davis 1970. A MS discovered in the early 1970s "is clearly not the one used either by Fitch or Waterhouse. It is in the hand of [John] Kirkpatrick . . . and was done, presumably, some time in the 1720s" (Dunn 1972). "The transcripts are preserved among the Kirkpatrick Papers in the Norfolk Record Office," Norwich (Coldewey 2008).

The Novella, A Comedy. Richard Brome. Acted "Anno 1632" by the King's Men at the [second] Blackfriars, according to the O TP. In playlist of the King's Men 7 August 1641.

SR no original; transferred 11 June 1659. O 1653–54 *Five New Plays* (with *The City Wit*, *The Court Beggar*, *The Damoiselle*, *The Mad Couple Well Matched*); two issues; separate TP dated 1653; list of characters; prologue and epilogue; dumb show performed during a song; five acts and separate scenes.

Prologue reveals the conventional appearance of an actor who speaks at the start of a play: "Should I not speake a prologue, and appeare / In a starch'd for-mall beard and cloake, I feare, / Some of this auditory would be vext, / And say this is a sermon without a text. / Some thinke it so essentiall, that they say / Nor foole, nor prologue, there can be no play. / Our author's unprovided, and doth vow, / What e're I say must stand for prologue now." This speech attests to the "enhanced popularity of the prologue as a display in its own right of the author's wit and judgment" (Neill 1978).

O

The Obstinate Lady, A Comedy. Aston Cokain. Written 1629–31 (Shaw 1986). Although there is no record of performance, the play was written for production, probably at the Blackfriars or the Salisbury Court playhouse; Prologue addresses "gallants" and alludes to the price of admission at private theaters.

SR 29 September 1656; 4 May 1657 [*Poems of Divers Sorts*]. Q 1657 *The Obstinate Lady, A New Comedy*; "never formerly published"; dramatis personae; prologue and two-line epilogue; five acts and separate scenes. O 1658 *Small Poems of Divers Sorts* (with *Trappolin creduto Principe* [continuous register and pagination]); five issues: another in 1658–59 entitled *A Chain of Golden Poems* (with epilogue by Lucora and Cleanthe); two more in 1662 entitled *Poems*; and another in 1669 entitled *Choice Poems of Several Sorts*. The 1657 Q was apparently unauthorized: "Much of the verse was set as prose and someone else's conclusion substituted for Cokayne's missing last leaf" (Garrett 2004). In the author's apology to the 1658 edition, Cokain complains about the earlier botched printing: "Mr. William Godbid [a stationer] got my *Obstinate Lady*, and though he found it with the last leaf torn out, wherein my conclusion to the play with the epilogue were; he procured some acquaintance of his to supply the defect at the end, and so printed it. And though that comedy be very much of it writ in number [i.e., in verse], he put it forth as if the most part of it were prose. Here you have that defect much amended, and my own conclusion and epilogue added." In the 1658 O Cokain "restored the original ending and the Epilogue in which he made numerous revisions" (Shaw).

The Q prologue addresses playgoers who attend the theater for the wrong reasons: "'Troth gentlemen, we know that now adayes / Some come to take up wenches at our playes; / It is not in our power to please their sence, / We wish they may go discontented hence. / And many gallants do come hither, we think / To sleep and to digest there too much drink: / We may please them; for we will not molest / With drums and trumpets any of their rest."

Oedipus. Seneca; translated by Alexander Neville. Acted in English translation *c.* 1563 "either at Cambridge or the Inns of Court" (Winston 2006). In his dedication the translator uses the expression "upon stage" to describe Seneca's purpose and his own. "Neville's observation that the play was 'upon stage' is intriguing, providing the only concrete evidence of a performance of Seneca in English in the 1560s" (Winston). The title appears in Kirkman's 1661 catalogue of plays.

SR *c.* March 1563 (Greg 1939). O 1563 *The Lamentable Tragedy of Oedipus, the Son of Laius, King of Thebes*; argument; list of characters; chorus for each act except 2; five acts and separate scenes. Q [octavo-in-fours] 1581 *Seneca His Ten Tragedies, Translated into English*, edited by Thomas Newton; *Oedipus the Fifth Tragedy of Seneca Englished*; Neville's translation of *Oedipus* was revised between 1563 and 1581 (Kiefer 1978).

In the O dedicatory epistle, Neville explains his purpose as "onely to satisfye the instant requestes of a fewe my familiar frendes, who thought to have put it to the very same use, that *Seneca* hymself in his invention pretended: whiche was by the tragicall and pompous showe upon stage, to admonish all men of theyr fickle estates, to declare the unconstant head of wavering Fortune, her sodaine interchaunged and soone altered face, and lyvely to expresse the just revenge, & fearful punishments of horrible crimes, wherewith the wretched worlde in these our myserable daies pyteously swarmeth." "By allying 'tragicall' and 'pompous,' Neville shows that he thinks of tragedy not just as a certain kind of narrative but as a theatrical experience" (Smith 1988a). Neville's characterization of tragedy is among the most important of the Elizabethan era (Kiefer 1983). Seneca "had a far greater influence upon learned ideas of tragedy than any of the Greek dramatists or any of the critics; his influence also worked through to popular audiences by translations and a number of imitations on the popular stage" (Margeson 1967).

Oenone (Hobbinal). A droll performed in the 1650s and ascribed to Robert Cox in its first published form. Probably written in the sixteenth century. "Acted at the Red Bull," according to the Q2 TP of *Actaeon*. Requires six or seven actors.

Published along with *Actaeon and Diana* (Q1 ?1655, Q2 1656 ["the second edition"]) and entitled on the Q2 TP *A Pastoral Story of the Nymph Oenone*; HT *Here follow the Rurall Sports on the birth-day of the Nymph Oenone*; list of characters; "argument is needless"; not divided. Ample SDs: *"Enter the huntsmen, with three country wenches, as they come in, they sing this song"*; *"A dance of Diana and her Nymphs, in the later end of which Acteon and his huntsmen joyn with them."* The Q1–2 TPs list *Hobbinal the Shepherd*, but this "title is misleading" (Greg 1939) since Hobbinal is simply one of six or seven characters in *Oenone*. But the "humor" of the character was "extracted to form [an] independent" droll (Greg 1939) and published in *1 The Wits, or Sport upon Sport* (O 1662 [two issues] and 1672), entitled *The Humor of Hobbinal*; "argument is needless"; list of characters. And so *Hobbinal* is "a droll abridged from a droll" (Elson 1932). *Oenone, A Pastoral*, was also published in *2 The Wits* (Q and O 1673) in slightly expanded form. On the TP of *2 The Wits* Kirkman says that the drolls were "written I know not when, by several persons, I know not who"; however, his preface reports that Robert Cox "was not only the principal actor, but also the contriver and author of most of these farces." Kirkman's attribution is "probable" (Holland 2007).

"Striking parallels to features of *Oenone* are found . . . in Glapthorne's *Argalus and Parthenia*, 1639. They are the more significant because of the unquestionable indebtedness to this play of the non-comic droll, *Philetis and Constantia*" (Elson).

Of Gentleness and Nobility. See *Gentleness and Nobility*.

The Old Couple, A Comedy. Thomas May. Licensed and acted 1636 (Bawcutt 1996), according to Henry Herbert's office-book. Possibly performed at the second Blackfriars. "[R]ecord of a court performance in 1636" (Norbrook 2004).

SR 7 January 1658. Q 1658 list of characters; five acts. Unusual SDs: *"Enter Lady Covet on crutches"*; *"Sir Argent Scrape, Lady Covet, brought in chaires"* ["Here comes the lovely bride and bridegroom"].

At the end of Q the publisher includes "an advertisement of books worth buying to be sold by S. Speed at the printing-press in Paul's church-yard." In addition to the specific works named are "several romanes, poems and playes." Although the theaters had been closed since 1642, the appetite for drama led to the publication of numerous plays, some of which—like *The Old Couple*—had not previously been printed.

Old Fortunatus. Thomas Dekker. Acted November 1599 (Hoy 1980) by Lord Admiral Nottingham's Men at the Rose. Also "plaied before the queenes majestie," according to the TP, by the same company at Richmond Palace, 27 December 1599 (McLuskie 1994). Possibly performed at the Fortune "in the autumn of 1600 . . . to herald the new venue's name" (Gurr 2009c). Entries by Henslowe suggest the revision of an Admiral's play, perhaps by another playwright, performed

3, 10, and 20 February 1596; also 14 April, 11 and 24 May 1596. Dekker may have combined two earlier plays into one; Henslowe records payment to Dekker, 9 November 1599, for "the hole hystory of ffortunatus." Or Dekker may have revised an extant play and added a second part (Chambers 1923). But McInnis 2011 argues that "there is no evidence of a second part having been written or performed, despite Henslowe's designation of this play as 'the j p of fortewnatus.'" Henslowe records additional payments, 24 and 30 November 1599, as well as a payment of ten pounds to the actor Thomas Downton 12 December, "for the eande of fortewnatus for the corte." The size of this last payment suggests that the play was expanded (Bowers 1953); "[n]o expense was to be spared in making an impression at court" (Dutton 2011); presented at court on 27 December (Bednarz 2012). Court additions include a prologue, epilogue, and "a specially designed ending to the play, wherein the Queen is complimented" (Hoy 1987b). "Here we have what amounts to the creation of a play especially—possibly even solely—for court performance (since Henslowe records no subsequent performances)" (Dutton 2000). In the 1600 Q "we indisputably have the finished product of at least some of these revisions" (Dutton 2009a).

SR 20 February 1600 A commedie called *old Fortunatus in his newe lyverie*; this entry "suggests that this play was either a reworking of *The First Part of Fortunatus . . .* or a new adaptation of the legend" (Haldane 2006). *First Part* "implies a second part" but we "know of no *Second Part*" (Price 1969). The playbook seems a version of the play "specifically rewritten and elongated with music for court performance" (Stern 2009c). The contest among Fortune, Vice, and Virtue may have been added for court performance in order "to add moral gravity to the fantastic story" (Price). Q 1600 *The Pleasant Comedy of Old Fortunatus*; no author named on the TP but Dekker's name appears in the "explicit"; regular prologue; prologue and epilogue (between two old men) at court; detailed description of dumb shows; chorus (two entries); not divided. The chorus resembles in some respects that of *Henry V*, priority uncertain (Walsh 2009b); Bednarz 2012 believes that the choruses in *Henry V* precede those in Dekker's play. The play begins with an echo scene: "When the play was acted at the enlarged Rose . . . the actor playing the echo would have occupied the central space behind the stage hangings for better audibility" (Ichikawa 2005). An "extraneous dance" occurs when a Spanish prisoner "is brought on the stage and made to dance. Evidently there was a good dancer in the company for whom Dekker made the place in the performance without regard for dramatic propriety" (Wright 1928).

The play's opening scene, with its depiction of Fortune triumphing over four kings (Kiefer 2000), typifies Dekker's capacity to offer "a variety of theatrical pleasures in the visual display" of those kings (McLuskie). When "*Fortune takes her chaire, the kings lying at her feete, shee treading on them as she goes up,*" Dekker seems to recall Tamburlaine treading on Bajazeth. Representative of Dekker's attention to the visual is this dumb show: "*Vice with a gilded face, and hornes on her head: her garments long, painted before with silver halfe moones, increasing by little and little, till they come to the full . . . after her comes Vertue a coxecombe on her head, all in white before.*" "As in metaphoric discourse, it is Vice who wears a visor, a gold face demonstrating the false allure of sin. Virtue, who 'abhors to wear a borrowed face' is conversely unmasked, but a fool's coxcomb demonstrates the scorn in which she is held" (Twycross & Carpenter 2002). The planting of trees by Virtue and Vice "offers a startling visual spectacle, drawn from the traditions of Elizabethan courtly pageants" (McLuskie); when actors "*bring out a faire tree of gold with apples on it,*" they "clearly" carry a prop tree (Rhodes 1976); Henslowe's inventory includes a "tree of gowlden apelles."

The Old Law, or A New Way to Please You. Thomas Middleton, William Rowley, and Thomas Heywood (Taylor 2002a). Acted late spring or early summer 1618 (Shaw 1982) probably by Prince Charles's Men (Bentley 1971), most likely at the Red Bull; Rowley "likely" played Gnotho (Hutchings & Bromham 2008). Performed also at Salisbury House, perhaps designating the home of Edward Sackville, Earl of Dorset (*JCS*); however, "'House' could mean 'playhouse,' and it is perhaps more likely that the 1656 title-page refers to the Salisbury Court theatre, which did not open until *c.* November 1630" (Taylor). Whichever venue is meant, performance took place "before the king and queene," according to the Q TP: "This statement almost certainly refers to performances during the reign of Charles I. The 'Queen' who witnessed a performance must have been either Queen Henrietta Maria (who could have done so between 1625 and 1642) or Queen Anne (who died in March 1619). The more likely reference, for any reader in 1656, was Henrietta Maria" (Taylor). When revived in the 1630s, the play was "possibly revised . . . by Heywood, if he was not part of the initial collaboration" (Masten 2007a). The TP also indicates performance "at severall other places, with great applause," possibly by Prince Charles's Men (Nicol 2006a).

SR none. Q 1656 *The Excellent Comedy called The Old Law, or A New Way to Please You*; the TP attributes the play to Massinger, Middleton, and Rowley, "but recent linguistic investigations by Lake and Jackson [1979] can find no evidence of Massinger's participation" (Howard-Hill 1987a); "the prominence given to Massinger's name may be due to its having greater prestige at the date of publication or to the fact that the MS acquired by [Edward] Archer was in Massinger's handwriting" (Price 1953); list of characters; five acts and first scenes. Q may contain "revisions and alterations made at the time of the Caroline revival" (Taylor). The play features the "illusion of sound which was also an illusion of distance . . . blasts of the horn gradually get nearer and nearer" (Lawrence 1927). In this play about terminating life when people reach a certain age, "a whole scene is devoted to manly exercises . . . when Lysander gives an exhibition of his feats in dancing, fencing, and drinking to show that he is still young" (Wright 1928); "the dancing duel that [Lysander] foolishly provokes ridicules the deadly competitiveness of courtly self-fashioning"; courtly dancing "is mocked as the expended practice of a degenerate elite" (Howard 1998).

"In the second decade of the seventeenth century the absolutist tendencies of the monarchy were becoming apparent, and conflicts over the exercise and extent of royal authority were beginning to occur. These matters received particular emphasis, just before *The Old Law* was probably written, with the publication in 1615, by royal command, of a book entitled *God and the King*, and with the dismissal of Sir Edward Coke from the King's Bench in 1616 in the controversy over the Common Law and the royal prerogative. There are strong reasons for believing that in *The Old Law* Middleton intended his audience to think of both these matters, and to relate the play and its viewpoint to developments in the world outside the theater" (Bromham 1984).

The Q TP, which both records performance at the Salisbury House playhouse and advertises a catalogue of printed plays, "announces itself as the product of a culture in which plays were increasingly read as well as watched" (Masten 2007b). Appended to the Q in many copies, compiled by Archer, is "An exact and perfect catalogue of all the playes, with the authors names, and what are comedies, tragedies, histories, pastorals, masks, interludes, more exactly printed than ever before." More than 650 titles are listed.

Old News Newly Revived, or the Discovery of All Occurrences Happened Since the Beginning of the Parliament. ?John Taylor or ?Richard Overton (Wolfe 1958). This play-pamphlet, "printed in the yeare 1641," according to the TP, takes the form of a short dialogue between Inquisitive and Intelligencer.

Published June 1641; no author named; not divided. This "is an informative and didactic dialogue with a satirical edge: it celebrates the fact that Davenant, 'the Queenes Poet,' has not, like Sir Francis Windebank and Sir John Suckling, fled the country; he will be eligible for employment writing elegies for the parliament's enemies, including Strafford, Aldermen Abel and Kilvert, and even himself" (Raymond 1996). "Finch is described on the run, in terms that suggest a comic actor playing the part: 'a brother of the blade, with a tilting feather, a flaunting periwig, buff doublet, scarlet hose, and sword as broad as a lath, he looked as like a Dammee newly come out of the North as could be imagined'" (Heinemann 1978).

The TP features an elaborate woodcut depicting Intelligencer and Inquisitive. The latter is described on the TP as "a countrey gentleman," Intelligencer as "a news monger."

The Old Wives Tale, A Comedy. George Peele. Acted "not earlier than 1591 or later than 1594" (McMillin & MacLean 1998) at undetermined venue. "Played by" the Queen's Men, according to the TP. Despite this claim, "because it draws upon a range of narratives, some of a type associated with folk stories, and because it is rather shorter than usual, it seems likely that the play was meant to be performed by boys, perhaps at court" (Happé 1999). "The masque-like qualities of the play, with music, dancing, monsters (Furies) and some use of spectacle and machinery, suggest that it was designed for a court or some other private occasion, whatever may have been its subsequent fortunes in the hands of the Queen's Men" (Whitworth 1984). Yet the Queen's Men "were the most courtly of companies, if the number of performances actually given at court can be taken as a sign of 'courtliness'" (McMillin & MacLean). And the Queen's Men could have performed the play when they "toured the country, playing on trestle stages set up in innyards or in town halls" (Whitworth 1996). Possibly written as a marriage entertainment (Binnie 1980), "a possibility that is strengthened by the play's extreme brevity, its emphatically nocturnal setting and its pointed allusion to 'our young master' being led by Cupid to 'the fair lady' in the frame-prologue" (Whitworth 1996). Perhaps the disparity between performance by the Queen's Men and by children may be explained by positing initial playing by children, likely in a private setting, and then a scaling down "with some roles reduced to allow for doubling and for performance by a smaller cast" of adults (Whitworth).

SR 16 April 1595. Q 1595 *The Old Wives Tale, A Pleasant Conceited Comedy*; author's initials on the TP; the induction "introduces three pages called Antic, Frolic, and Fantastic, whose names herald the blatant improbabilities, the spirit of revelry, and the deliberate use of the stereotyped characters and situations that are the marks" of this comedy (Hattaway 1982); not divided. The play presents "at least two separate 'pavilions' with curtains (the old wife's cottage and Sacrapant's study); a wood with a cross-roads and a 'well of life' from which an enchanted head arose; a piece of 'enchanted ground,' with a hillock, where some characters dug and others were blasted with flames of fire" (Bradbrook 1962a). "Since the printed text is an author's version rather than a theatrical version, it represents what the author thought might be or should be done at certain points, rather than what was actually done" (Hook 1970). Nevertheless, Q calls for a variety of special effects: "*A voice and flame of fire*"; the entry of "*two Furies out of the conjurers cell*"; thunder and lightning; a head, "*full of golde*," rises from a well; a ghost "makes its final exit by jumping down a trap" (Lawrence 1927); a character enters "*invisible*," presumably wearing a special robe. A play of "often mesmerizing spectacle" (Braunmuller 1983a); Peele "employs a whole range of techniques that the new theatre largely rejected" (Cooper 2010). "*The Old Wives Tale* is the company's [Queen's Men] most scenic play" (McMillin & MacLean); it is also "a highly musical play" (Hook). Somewhat unusual is the staging of the induction, for "Madge and two of the jesters remain on stage observing and commenting on the action which follows as well as concluding the play. They neither vanish nor take up roles. They become instead an audience within an audience" (Free 1983). They are "frame characters," providing continuity and serving "as a kind of neutral ground for characters and styles" (Marx 1981).

Isaac Reed in *Biographia Dramatica* (1782) was the first in print to attribute the play to Peele.

Oldcastle. See *1 Henry IV*.

The Opportunity, A Comedy. James Shirley. Licensed for acting 29 November 1634 (Adams 1917, Mekemson 1991). "Presented by" Queen Henrietta Maria's Men at the Phoenix, according to the TP. "We have no evidence that it was ever performed in Dublin at all. But . . . it is a fair inference that it might well have been" (Dutton 2006). In playlist of Beeston's Boys 10 August 1639.

SR 25 April 1639. Q 1640 three issues; published in both London and Dublin as the different TPs indicate; list of characters; five acts. After the closing of the theaters, parts of the play were adapted for a droll entitled *A Prince in Conceit*, later published in *1 The Wits, or Sport upon Sport* (O 1662 [two issues] and 1672).

The Ordinary, A Comedy. William Cartwright. Acted spring 1635 "before an academic audience" (Evans 1951). Possibly first performed at Christ Church, Oxford (Elliott et al. 2004), in the great hall.

SR 4 May 1648 *The Citty Cozener, or, The Ordinary*. O 1651 *The Ordinary, A Comedy*; in *Comedies, Tragi-Comedies, with Other Poems* (with *The Lady Errant, The Royal Slave, The Siege, or Love's Convert*); separate register and pagination for *The Ordinary*; dramatis personae; prologue and epilogue; five acts and separate scenes.

"During the Commonwealth . . . certain portions [of the play] were lifted out of their context and, with a few changes and additions, turned into drolls, or more properly speaking, dialogues" (Evans). Three of these were subsequently printed in John Cotgrave's *Wits Interpreter, or the English Parnassus* (1655).

Orestes. Thomas Goffe. Acted *c*. 1613–18 (Elliott 1997). By students of Christ Church, Oxford, according to the Q TP, probably in the great hall. Although an academic play, it is manifestly influenced by "the popular tragedies of London's public theaters"; "Goffe's Orestes is nothing else but a Jacobean revenger" (Smith 1988a).

SR no original; transferred 7 November 1646. Q 1633 *The Tragedy of Orestes*; list of characters; prologue; dumb show; five acts and separate scenes. O 1656 *Three Excellent Tragedies* (with *The Courageous Turk* and *The Raging Turk*); "the second edition, carefully corrected by a friend of the authors," according to the general TP; continuous register and pagination. Grotesque spectacle: three witches petition Pluto to "send us out of hand, / The shapes of those that kild the king [Agamemnon]," and a pantomime, to the sound of "infernal musique," ensues: "*Enter in a dumbe shew Ægystheus, and Clytem[nestra] with their bloody daggers, looke upon the bed, goe to it, and stab, and then make a shew of gladnes*." A vengeful ghost subsequently appears: "*Enter Agamemnons ghost passing o're the stage all wounded*"; the ghost speaks of "these horrid wounds, which make me grone." Confronting his father's spirit, Orestes vows, "I'll thinke on thee, and then agine revenge, / And stab and wound." An orgy of bloodletting follows: "*Pylades binds Clytemnestra to the chaire: Orestes, Ægystheus: Pylades brings in the child [of Clytemnestra]*." When Orestes stabs the child, "*the blood spirts*" in the father's face, and Orestes "*Pulls [his father's] bones from his pocket*." Orestes "*fills two cups with the childs blood: gives it them [Clytemnestra and Aegystheus]*," then stabs the pair. Later Orestes and Pylades kill one another with rapiers.

The Q prologue, "spoken by the authour himselfe," addresses the writing of a modern play based on an ancient work by Euripides: "We here as builders which doe oft take stones, / From out old buildings, then must hew and cut, / To make them square, and fitting for a new, / So from an old foundation we have ta'n, / Stones ready squar'd for our new ædifice, / Which if in pleasing our weake skill offends / In making corners disporportionate, / Some roome too narrow or some loft too high; / Yet we will hope, if the whole structure fall, / Your hands like props will serve to beare up all."

Orestes (Pickering). See *Horestes*.

Orgula, or The Fatal Error, A Tragedy. Leonard Willan. No record of production, but the play has an obvious political application for the 1650s: it "has as its most important character a tyrannical ruler, Sinevero, described as 'Lord Protector.' Throughout the play unfavorable comment is made about the Lord Protector, and there is a large amount of rant about despots" (Wright 1934). "Though Willan claims in his essay that *Orgula* is an old work, his presentation of a lecherous, treacherous, tyrannical Lord Protector is unlikely to antedate December 1653 by very much, for it was then that [Oliver] Cromwell accepted that title" (Randall 1995).

SR 24 April 1657. Q 1658 author's initials on the TP; list of characters; five acts and separate scenes. "[C]ontains lengthy, solemnly prescriptive stage directions which tell of the printing of texts never to be produced in the theatre" (Pritchard 2004b): "*In great solemnity the judge with the court of justice, officers goes before the hearse, whom* Nefarius *busily entertains, as also two advocates, the one as plaintiffe being atturney generall for the state, the other as defendant for* Castrophilus. *Next the hearse,* Ludaster, Ambigamor, Gratianus, Fidelius *and others.*"

The long dedicatory epistle discusses the nature of poetry and argues for the moral and social importance of drama at a time when the theaters had been closed: "Nor is the action of a theatre lesse usefull in the education of our youth (a frequent exercise in forreign seminaries, societies and schools), to inanimate their spirits, render them plyant and susceptible to every form, might either frame them more agreeable in their society, or more successefull in their private commerce; as also, to lend a more assured gracefull unconstrain'd demeanour to their persons and in such habits, to indue them with undaunted confidence, facility, and readinesse to communicate in discourse the image of their thoughts to an attentive multitude, an acquisition of no little moment, in publique consultations, conferences and pleas: in managing whereof, who hath not gained this dexterity, shall finde the weightiest reasons in his argument silenc'd, smothered, o'resway'd by the lesse pertinent clamor of an insisting impudence." "Willan defends not only writing and reading dramas but also seeing them and playing in them" (Randall).

Orlando Furioso, One of the Twelve Peers of France. Robert Greene (identified by *The Defence of Conny-Catching* [1592]). Acted between 26 December 1588 and 1591 (Hayashi 1973) by the Queen's Men (Pinciss 1970) at undetermined venue, "but it is not absolutely certain" that the play belonged to the Queen's Men (Schoone-Jongen 2008). "Formed by royal decree in 1583, the company was set up with the best two or three players from each of the companies of the great lords, Leicester's, Warwick's, Oxford's, and Sussex's. They took Richard Tarlton, the most famous clown, and the most famous tragedians, [William] Knell and [John] Bentley" (Gurr 2004a). Performed also by that company before the queen, according to the Q1 TP, at Whitehall, 26 December 1591. Henslowe records a performance by Lord Strange's Men at the Rose, 21 February 1592; Edward Alleyn played Orlando (Cerasano 1994). Also performed by the Admiral's Men at some point (McMillin & MacLean 1998).

Dulwich, UK, Dulwich College, MS I, item 138; an incomplete player's part (531 lines) for Orlando, annotated by Edward Alleyn; no author named; "no scene divisions, has two-word or three-word cues (sometimes only one), short stage directions in Latin (longer ones in English)" (Thomson 1992b). The MS, consisting of "slips of paper six inches wide and pasted together" (Lawrence 1927), represents "the earliest surviving British professional theatre part" (Stern 2004a); the strips of paper were "pasted together to form a continuous roll (the French metonym *rôle* gives us our modern 'role' or part" (Hattaway 1982). "Alleyn's script abbreviates or omits many directions found in the Quarto of the play, and adds some not in this printed version" (Foakes 2004). "In this manuscript a horizontal line separates one speech from another and gives the actor his cue" (Smith 2006). "Unfortunately . . . the printed text records a revised and perhaps mutilated form of the play that does not compare directly to the text provided in the part" (Stern 2009a). The MS was edited "first and rather incorrectly by Collier as an appendix to his *Memoirs of Edward Alleyn* (1841)"; "again more incorrectly by Churton Collins in his edition of Greene's plays (1905)"; "next in [Greg's] *Henslowe Papers* (1907) . . . still with some errors, and lastly in [Greg's] *Alcazar and Orlando* (1923)" (Greg 1931). Modern edition by Hayashi 1973. SR 7 December 1593; transferred 28 May 1594; 16 October 1609; 2 March 1618; 23 February 1626; 4 March 1639. Q1 1594 *The History of Orlando Furioso, One of the Twelve Peers of France*; no author named; not divided. "With its spectacle, music, dances, kitchen humour, and feigned combats the play derives from folk games and tales and is the precursor of modern pantomime" (Hattaway). Q2 1599.

In *The Defence of Conny-Catching* (1592), Greene is accused of double-dealing: "Aske the Queens Players, if you sold them not *Orlando Furioso* for twenty nobles, and when they were in the country, sold the same play to the Lord Admirals Men for as much more." This may account for the differences between Orlando's part and the text of Q1 (Palfrey & Stern 2007).

Osmond the Great Turk, or The Noble Servant. Lodowick Carlell. "Often acted
. . . with great applause," "by the Queen's Majesty's Servants," according to the
general TP of *Two New Plays*, in 1637 (Birchwood 2007) at unspecified venue.
Although Bentley (*JCS*) believes that the TP is inaccurate, that Carlell's play is
the same as a play entitled *Osmond the Great Turk*, licensed for acting 6 September 1622, Duncan-Jones 1961 finds that "the earlier play was one wholly distinct
from Carlell's, dealing with the tragic events of May, 1622 [the deposition and
murder of Osman II]; that the difficulties which it encountered before being licensed [by John Astley, Master of the Revels], were perhaps due to its dealing
with very recent history; and that the mistake on the title page of Carlell's play
lies not, as Professor Bentley suggests, in the statement that it had been acted
by the Queen's servants, but in the inclusion in the title of the words 'the Great
Turk'"; Carlell's Osmund "is not a Turk at all but a Tartar" (Duncan-Jones). "Osmond is *not* the 'Great Turk' but the 'Noble Servant'" (Hutchings 2008).

    SR 9 September 1653. O 1657 *The Famous Tragedy of Osmond the Great Turk,
Otherwise Called The Noble Servant*; dramatis personae; five acts. Some copies
were issued with *The Fool Would Be a Favorite* in 1657 as *Two New Plays* (separate
register and pagination).

    When Carlell wrote *Osmond*, "Spain was feared and James's court distrusted
and ridiculed. This play may be regarded as an allegory of such discontent, and
the play may have met with problems from the censor" (Hutchings).

Othello, The Moor of Venice. William Shakespeare. Acted possibly as early as 1602
(Honigmann 1997); however, the play "may have been written with an eye to the
tastes of the company's new royal patron," King James I, and so acted after the
death of Elizabeth (Neill 2006b). "Divers times acted" by the King's Men at the
[first] Globe and, [later], the [second] Blackfriars, according to the Q1 TP; this
"is the only title-page that extols both the King's Men's open-air theater on the
South Bank and its more private space with the Blackfriars. It also marks the virtual end of Shakespeare's plays in quarto, with no new plays appearing after the
Folio 'established' the canon in 1623" (Berger 2007). Richard Burbage "almost
certainly" played the lead (Gurr 2004c); John Lowin probably played Iago (Potter 2002a); "when Lowin joined the company, the King's Men began to perform
plays which contained not one but two long and complex parts, of a kind hitherto limited to Burbage" (Taylor 2002b). Performed also as *The Moor of Venice*
in the first Whitehall Banqueting House, 1 November 1604, recorded by Edmund Tilney, Master of the Revels (Chambers 1930); at the Globe, with Ludwig
Friedrich, Prince of Württemburg, in attendance, 30 April 1610; in the city of
Oxford, 5 September 1610 (Elliott et al.). Henry Jackson of Corpus Christi College wrote of this Oxford performance: "the celebrated Desdemona, slain in our
presence by her husband, although she pleaded her case very effectively throughout, yet moved (us) more after she was dead, when, lying on her bed, she entreat-
ed the pity of the spectators by her very countenance" (Evans & Tobin 1997).

Jackson does not specify the venue; performance may have taken place at an inn or at a college hall (Keenan 2002). Revived at court, winter 1612–13, for the celebration of Princess Elizabeth's wedding to the Elector Palatine, Prince Frederick of Heidelberg (payment to John Heminges dated 20 May 1613). When Joseph Taylor joined the King's Men in 1619, he played Iago (*Historia Histrionica*). Later revived at the Blackfriars, 22 November 1629 [*The Moor of Venice*], a benefit for Henry Herbert (Chambers 1930); at Blackfriars, 6 May 1635, as *The Moor of Venice* (Chambers); and in the hall at Hampton Court, 8 December 1636, as *The Moor of Venice* (Adams 1917) "for Charles I and Henrietta Maria" (Neill 2006b). Following the death of Burbage in 1619, Eilert Swanston, who joined the King's Men in 1624, played Othello (*Historia Histrionica*). In a tribute published in 1640 Leonard Digges cites the play as having been a huge success: playgoers "priz'de . . . Honest Iago, or the jealous Moore" (Chambers).

SR 6 October 1621; transferred ?4 August 1626 Master Paviers right in Shakesperes *plaies*; ?19 June 1627 widow of Isaac Jaggard . . . her parte in Shackspheere *playes*; 1 March 1628; 1 July 1637 Shakespeares *workes* their Part; 29 May 1638; 25 January 1639; 6 August 1674; 21 August 1683. Q1 1622 *The Tragedy of Othello, the Moor of Venice*; "written by William Shakespeare"; in the first Cyprus scene "Desdemona and Cassio are seen in dumb show while their actions are 'read' by Iago" (McLuskie 1989); five acts (though no indication at beginning of play or act 3). Q1 is "the first [Shakespearean] quarto that is divided into acts" (Hirsh 2002). "[I]n the earliest performances of *Othello* the professional actor Burbage appeared in blackface"; he also "wore some kind of long black gloves and a 'corled hed Sculles of blacke Laune' or like Aaron a 'fleece of woolen hair,' prompting Iago's slur that Othello is 'an old black ram'" (Hornback 2001). Q1's SDs "are fuller and more descriptive than F's and give a welcome sense of the play's theatrical quality" (McMillin 2001). Desdemona's father appears "*at a window*," apparently corresponding to one of the boxes, or compartments seen in the De Witt drawing of the Swan (Hosley 1957), and he enters "*in his night gown* [i.e., dressing gown]." The most important hand prop is the handkerchief given by Othello to his wife; it is decorated with strawberries, "the fruit sometimes used in emblem books to signal treachery, because serpents hide beneath the attractive leaves" (Teague 1991). Staging requires a property bed (with curtains) in which Desdemona is murdered; the bed, like those in most other plays, was "brought on stage through a tiring-house door"; the bed, with Desdemona lying in it, is 'thrust out' of the tiring-house by stagekeepers or attendant players" (Hosley 1963). Othello "*fals on the bed*" when Emilia calls Iago a villain. Iago then "*kils his wife*" and Othello subsequently "*stabs himself*." Q1 is one of only two Shakespearean quartos to contain a preface (the other being the second issue of *Troilus and Cressida*) by a publisher (Thomas Walkley), who begins, "To set forth a booke without an epistle, were like to the old English proverbe, *A blew coat without a badge*." In other words, "the text would be incomplete without some kind of epistle, lacking the 'badge' that makes a blue coat significant" (Bergeron

2006). F1 1623 *Comedies, Histories, & Tragedies*; three issues; "published according to the true originall copies"; *The Tragedy of Othello, the Moor of Venice*; list of characters at end; five acts and separate scenes. "Musically speaking, [*Othello*] is probably best known for the 'willow song' assigned to Desdemona in Act 4, scene 3, whose oldest complete version has become one of the most performed extant pieces of early modern English music" (Austern 2006); "the 'Willow song' is absent" from Q1, "though the surrounding text still suggests the expectation that it should be sung" (Stern 2004a). "F contains approximately 160 lines that are absent from Q" (Neill 2006b); F1 represents "Shakespeare's revision of his tragedy" (Jones 1995). Q2 1630 conflates the editions of Q 1622 and F 1623 (Berger 2007); Q2 "offers a carefully corrected version of Q, produced by an editor who made extensive use of F" (Neill). F2 1632 "the second impression"; three issues. Q3 1655 "the fourth edition." F3 1663 "the third impression"; reissued 1664 with seven additional plays. Q4 1681 dramatis personae. F4 1685 "the fourth edition"; two issues.

Othello "belongs to a period when the London theatres were competing to produce plays of an apparently new genre, domestic drama. Longsuffering wives are central to" Dekker's *Patient Grissil*, the anonymous *Fair Maid of Bristol*, and *The London Prodigal* (Potter 2002a). Heywood's *Woman Killed with Kindness* (1603) "may be a subtext for *Othello*" (Rudnytsky 1983).

Ovid. Aston Cokain. Written ?late 1620s-early 1630s (Shaw 1986). Although there is no record of production, the play was written with performance in mind. The general TP of *Poems* says that *Ovid* "is intended to be acted shortly." Prologue addresses "gallants" and invites disappointed playgoers "To take your mony again; And to go hence." Epilogue begins, "Noble and generous spectators, stay! / A word at parting, and then go your way."

O1 1662 *Poems* (with *The Obstinate Lady, Trappolin Supposed a Prince*); *The Tragedy of Ovid*; two issues; new pagination with this play, which was attached to the earlier material; both separate and general TPs are dated 1662; dramatis personae; prologue and epilogue; five acts and separate scenes. *Ovid* "was also sold independently" (Shaw). SDs are sufficient for production: e.g., "*He opens the door, turns back and falls down, as in a swound.*" Reissued in *Choice Poems of Several Sorts*, 1669.

P

Palamon and Arcyte. Richard Edwards. Acted Monday night 2 September (part 1) and Wednesday night 4 September 1566 (part 2) by students of Christ Church, Oxford, before Queen Elizabeth (Wallace 1912), in the college hall; the size of the stage "is not known, but in 1566 it was large enough to accommodate a canopied choir for the Queen in full view of the audience" (Robertson 1969). "The first night was made memorable by the fall of a staircase wall, by which three persons were killed. The queen was sorry, but the play went on" (Chambers 1923). According to surviving accounts, the queen was highly pleased by the play and congratulated the playwright (Boas 1914). She "had appointed Edwards, an Oxford alumnus, as her Master of the Children of the Chapel Royal in 1561" (Shenk 2008). On each of the two nights, Elizabeth sent for the playwright to "express her great thanks for his pains and her high appreciation of his achievement" (Wallace).

SR none. No evidence of publication. Although the play is lost, plot summaries survive. One is an eyewitness account by Miles Windsor, an undergraduate, who played the role of Perithous (Theseus' cousin): two MSS, a draft and a fair copy, survive at Corpus Christi College, Oxford; they are bound together in MS 257, fols. 104–14 and 115–23. The fair copy was "transcribed by [Brian] Twyne in 1636 [Oxford, Bodleian, MS Twyne 17, pp. 157–67] and later published (without acknowledgment) by [Anthony à] Wood" (Elliott 1988). The fair copy contains a list of the actors. There also exists an account (in Latin) by John Bereblock, a playgoer and don, which survives at Oxford, Bodleian, MS Additional a. 63, fols. 1–22; Bodleian, MS Rawlinson D. 1071, fols. 1–25; and Washington, Folger, MS V.a.109, fols. 1–24. "Bereblock is careful to emphasise not just the beauty of the ceiling, but also the way that it signifies. For him (and, by extension, for the rest of the university) it is clearly representative of a desire to connect sixteenth century Oxford with the ancient Greek and Roman world" (Marlow 2008). A third (and much shorter) account by Nicholas Robinson survives in Washington, Folger, MS V.a.176, fol. 159. The dramatized action must have been spectacular: "The first part ended with a much admired hunting scene in which boys, standing in the windows, shouted at the cry of hounds in the quadrangle below" (Bevington 1962); Theseus has discovered Palamon and Arcyte fighting in the wood (Boas 1914). Part 2, "completing the story, with the tournament, the victory of Arcyte, his sudden death, and the happy union of Palaemon and Emilia, surpassed even the first" (Wallace). "On the second day a noble display was made in the lists. Other features included three altars [to Diana, Mars, and Venus] and a splendid funeral" (Bevington). The play "required a trapdoor and infernal sound effects coming from below" as well as "subterranean fire shooting out of the ground" (King 2001), which struck Arcyte (Axton 1977). After his death "Emilia was betrothed to Palamon, amid the applause of the spectators" (Cunliffe 1912). Emilia "was played by a schoolboy rather than an undergraduate" (Astington 2010). Two songs from the play survive at London, BL, Additional MS 26737, fols. 106–08.

"It was the first English dramatization of one of Chaucer's *Canterbury Tales*, the same tale [*The Knight's Tale*] which Shakespeare and Fletcher were to adopt in *The Two Noble Kinsmen* in 1613. This was the first play to be presented before visiting royalty by Oxford University. It marked the stage debut, and almost certainly the finale as well, of John Rainolds, who played the part of Queen Hippolyta, some thirty years before he was to take on his better-known role as the chief Puritan castigator of the stage" (Elliott). Henslowe records a play named *Palamon and Arcite* in 1594, "but this dramatisation of Chaucer's tale is unlikely to have been Richard Edwards's play of that name" (Gurr 2009c).

Pallantus and Eudora. See *The Conspiracy.*

The Palsgrave. See *The Hector of Germany.*

Parasitaster, or The Fawn. John Marston. Acted April–December 1604 (Blostein 1978); "1604–5" (Munro 2005); "probably in 1605" (Perry 1997). "Divers times presented" by the Children of the Queen's Revels at the [second] Blackfriars, according to the Q TPs. Later performed by Paul's Boys, according to the Q2 TP, at Paul's playhouse, "from early 1606" (Munro).

SR 12 March 1606 A playe called *the ffaune*; 16 February 1617; transferred 3 April 1626; 4 September 1638. Q1 1606 HT and RT *The Fawn*, a name that suggests both "sycophant" and "satyr" (Morris 1987); list of characters; prologue and epilogue; dumb show, a "short scene (part of the plot) before the last act" (Mehl 1965); five acts and separate scenes. SDs "are long and descriptive" (Jewkes 1958): "*Exit as Puttotta goes out she flinges away the letter, the page puts it up, and as he is talking Hercules steales it out of his pocket.*" SDs at the beginning of act 5 indicate performance during the inter-act music: "*Whilst the act is a playing, Hercules and Tiberio enter; Tiberio climbs the tree, and is received above by Dulcimel, Philocalia and a Priest: Hercules stayes beneath.*" Such music was customary at private playhouses and, after the King's Men began using the Blackfriars *c.* 1610, at other theaters too. In contrast to his plays acted at Paul's playhouse, Marston relies "on orchestral performance" at Blackfriars (Gair 2000). Staging includes a miniature portrait sent "to the beloved in the hopes of stimulating their desire" (Rochester 2010): the picture "purports to be a true likeness of Tiberio's father who is courting the fifteen-year-old Dulcimel but is a fake" (Gair). "These small, alluring pictures, frequently set in jewels, drew attention to the smallness and effeminacy of the boy actors" (Tassi 2005); Elizabethan, Jacobean, and Caroline painters raised the status of miniatures to a high art (Fumerton 1991). Q2 1606 "now corrected of many faults, which by reason of the authors absence, were let slip in the first edition"; "considerable portions of the type . . . reappear, altered but not reset" (Greg 1939) O 1633 *The Works of Mr. John Marston, Being Tragedies and Comedies, Collected into One Volume* (with *Antonio and Mellida, Antonio's Revenge, The Dutch Courtesan, What You Will, The Wonder of Women*); two issues. The reissue, entitled *Tragedies and Comedies Collected into One Volume*, removes Marston's name from the general and separate TPs; William Sheares had published the collection without Marston's consent; the type in the address "to my equall reader" has been reset. Also issued in a made-up Q entitled *Comedies,*

Tragicomedies and Tragedies (1652), no longer extant. In the first scenes of Q2 and O, the title reads *The Fawn*, which is also the RT.

The character of Duke Gonzago resembles in many respects King James, as Bullen 1887 and Upton 1929 observe. "If the Duke is a caricature of James, this would be the only full-length portrait of the ruling sovereign in Elizabethan drama" (Finkelpearl 1969).

In the address to the Q1 reader, Marston writes about the primacy of theatrical production and his own intention as a playwright: "If any shall wonder why I print a comedie, whose life rests much in the actors voice: let such know, that it cannot avoide publishing: let it therefore stand with good excuse, that I have been my owne setter out. If any desire to understand the scope of my comedie, know it hath the same limits, which *Juvenal* gives to his satyres." In a note to the Q2 reader about the earlier "first faulty impression," Marston says that "Comedies are writ to be spoken, not read: Remember the life of these things consists in action."

The Parator and the Proctor. See *The Proctor and Parator.*

The Pardoner and the Friar. John Heywood; identified by Francis Kirkman. Acted "in 1529" (Betteridge 2009) or "after 1529" (Walker 1998) at undetermined venue. Among the "prime candidates for livery company hall performances" (Lancashire 2002). But McCarthy 2008 argues for a chapel setting. "Though it is written for four actors, this is a virtuoso piece for two" (Axton & Happé 1991).

SR 5 April 1533. F 1533 no separate TP; HT *A Merry Play between the Pardoner and the Friar, the Curate and Neighbor Prat*; no author named; not divided. The Friar begins by addressing the audience in a sort of prologue. F contains "detailed directions as to how the desired effects are to be created" (Walker).

The play "is a microcosm of conflict, most of the action being the encounter of the two church protagonists who are rivals for the attention of the audience, and who both, in their different ways, present the power and the danger of heresy and folly" (Happé 2007b).

In *Historia Histrionica* (1699) a speaker, saying that he has a copy of *The Pardoner and the Friar*, comments, "The design of this play was to redicule friers and pardoners"; he then offers a plot summary and quotes several speeches. He concludes that the play is typical of "the plays of that age, acted in gentlemens halls at Christmas, or such like festival times, by the servants of the family, or strowlers who went about and made it a trade." The play, "though farcical, combines an attack on religious abuses with a positive belief in the Church and a defence of the Catholic faith" (Caputo 2008).

The Parliament of Bees, or a Beehive Furnished with Twelve Honeycombs. John Day. Written 1625–34 (Cocke 1979). Although there is no evidence of production, this entertainment, ordinarily termed a dialogue, among twelve characters

is "inextricably bound up with" Dekker's *The Noble Spanish Soldier* and *The Wonder of a Kingdom* (Golding 1927). The connection of Day's work with the two other plays prevents the characters' words from being "dismissed as dialogues rather than dramatic" (Greg 1939).

London, BL, Lansdowne MS 725, fols. 1–37; contains address "To the Impartiall Reader," missing from Q; "the author to his book"; "argument of the 12 colloquies"; list of speakers precedes each colloquy; twelve scenes. SR 23 March 1641. Q 1641 *The Parliament of Bees, with Their Proper Characters, or A Beehive Furnished with Twelve Honeycombs*; "the authors commission to his bees"; "the booke to the reader"; divided into twelve parts (i.e., "colloquies"). Q contains a woodcut depicting an assembly of bees (one of them crowned) and a hive; according to the caption, "The Parliament is held, bil[l]s and complaints / Heard and reform'd, with severall restraints / Of usurpt freedome; instituted law / To keepe the common wealth of bees in awe." "The quarto text is a revision of the manuscript" (Parr 2004a).

The Q TP points to a political motive: "an allegoricall description of the actions of good and bad men in these our daies." The play "demonstrates clearly how the social attitudes of the popular theatre survived in other forms right down to the Civil War" (Butler 1984b).

The Parliament of Love. Philip Massinger (Herbert's office-book supplies the attribution). Licensed for acting 3 November 1624 (Adams 1917, E&G 1976). Acted by Lady Elizabeth's Men at the Phoenix (Vaughan 2006). The play "was almost certainly a failure" (Edwards 1987).

London, V&A, Dyce MS 39 (D25.F33), fols. 1–38; no TP; the title appears on the verso of the last leaf and in a different hand; no author named; "probably the first two leaves have been lost" (Long 1999); some lines and speeches crossed out; theatrical provenance (Long 1989); extensively damaged (two or three scenes at the beginning are missing); "malicious damage" to the MS (Lea 1928), the bottoms of pages torn away; "regular division into [five] acts" (Greg 1931) "but not scenes" (Long 1999). Staging includes "*the image [i.e. statue] of Cupid*," which represents not a superstitious idol but "an allegory of 'pure Love, that had his birth in heaven'" and thus a symbol of virtue (Rochester 2010). This MS "may be the copy of the play submitted to Sir Henry Herbert, Master of the Revels, for licensing in 1624" (Edwards). "This copy once bore the censor's licence at the end, but it was later neatly cut out" (Ioppolo 2006). SR 29 June 1660; no trace of a printed edition exists from this time. First edited by Gifford 1805 in *The Plays of Philip Massinger*, vol. 2, then by Lea 1928.

This play "might well have influenced later versions of the disguised Moor plot device in plays performed at court" (Vaughan 2005). Such plays include William Berkeley's *The Lost Lady* and Richard Brome's *The English Moor*.

The Parnassus Plays. See *The Pilgrimage to Parnassus* and *1* and *2 The Return from Parnassus.*

The Parricide. See *Revenge for Honor.*

The Parson's Wedding, A Comedy. Thomas Killigrew. Probably written in 1640 or 1641 (Bulman 1987). Intended for production probably at the Blackfriars (Hosley 1961) by the King's Men (Greg 1939), and "there is reason to suppose that *The Parson's Wedding* was acted before the closing of the theatres" (Greg). But Bulman 2003 thinks that it "was probably not performed until after the Restoration." The play, an example of Cavalier drama (Bulman), was timely, containing "many satirical thrusts at the Presbyterian divines, political agitators, and the Parliament" (Harbage 1936). Killigrew's drama also treats "Platonic love as the subject of bawdy humour and derision" (Sharpe 1987). Stephen Hammerton, mentioned in the epilogue, was in the cast (Gurr 2004c). The play was staged in 1664.

SR 24 October 1663. F 1663–64 *Comedies and Tragedies*; two issues; the general TP is dated 1664, separate 1663; "written at Basil in Switzerland"; dramatis personae; the play's final speech (by Captain) functions as an epilogue; five acts and separate scenes. Prologue and epilogue are "printed in A. B.'s *Covent Garden Drollery,* 1672" (Greg 1939). F apparently represents a revision of the 1640 play. There are an exceptional number of SDs, many printed in the margins: "*The fidlers play in the tyring room, and the stage curtains are drawn, and discover a chamber, as it was, with two beds and the ladies asleep in them; Master* Wild *being at Mistris* Pleasant's *bed-side, and Master* Careless *at the* Widow's*; the musick awakes the* Widow." A SD indicates the use of the music room for action above: "*Enter Mistress* Pleasant, *Widow* Wild *her aunt, and* Secret, *her woman, above in the musick room, as dressing her, a glass, a table, and she in her night cloathes.*" Killigrew dramatizes a character's sexual advances: "*Still as he [Jolly] offers to touch her, she [Lady Love-all] starts as if he pluckt up her coats*"; "*He pulls her bodkin, that is tied in a piece of black bobbin. He pulls her,*" and says, "you shall be merciful." When she replies, "I will not," the SD reads, "*He pulls still.*"

"As Killigrew's annotated copy of his *Comedies and Tragedies* (1664) preserved in the library of Worcester College, Oxford, demonstrates, he was ambitious enough to prepare his own plays for production on the new, scenic [Restoration] stage" (Vander Motten 2004). This copy "has been heavily cut by the author, apparently in anticipation of the performance by a female cast" (*JCS*). According to *Historia Histrionica,* after the Restoration "some plays (in particular *The Parson's Wedding*) have been presented all by women, as formerly all by men."

The Part of "Poor." Anonymous. Now lost, the play was probably performed by students at Christ Church, Oxford, presumably in the Great Hall, in the early seventeenth century (Carnegie 1982); acted 1617–19 (Elliott 2004 et al.).

Cambridge, MA, Harvard University, Harvard Theatre Collection, MS Thr 10.1, fols. 21–46, ed. Carnegie et al. 1993; the player's side, or part, for the role of Poor in the lost play; no play title. Ample SDs. "The action of the play generally suits what we know of the extremely versatile Elizabethan and Jacobean open stage conventions" (Carnegie 1982). First edited by Carnegie et al. 1993.

The "part was the unit in which all texts were disseminated" (Stern 2009a).

The Partial Law, A Tragicomedy. Anonymous. Bullen 1882–85 suggests authorship by Glapthorne; Dobell 1908 disagrees, suggesting, "The writer to whom one would be most inclined to attribute [the play], were it only of a higher order of merit, is Massinger." Parrott 1948 speculates: "internal evidence seems to show that [the playwright] was a gentleman of the Court." Acted 1615–30 (Dobell) at undetermined venue. Despite Bentley's characterization of this play as closet drama, the SDs seem entirely practical, calling with confidence for staging that would presumably have caught and held the playgoers' interest.

Washington, Folger, MS V.a.165; list of characters; some evidence of correction; five acts and separate scenes. The staging includes pageantry: "*Trumpets sound, the* Challenger *passeth by, his* Page *bearing his shield, and his* Squire *his lance, the* King *&* Ladyes *are above in the window, the* Page *passing by presents the* King *with his Maister's scutshion.*" The King proceeds to interpret the symbolic painting on the shield in the manner of Marlowe's Edward II, who also interprets *imprese* on shields, and in the manner of Thaisa in the tournament scene of *Pericles* (Kiefer 2011). First edited by Dobell 1908.

1 The Passionate Lovers, A Tragicomedy. Lodowick Carlell. Acted 10 July 1638 (Wood 1987b). "Twice presented" by the King's Men, before the king and queen, at Somerset [Denmark] House, according to the TP, with changeable scenery, including a wooded landscape, designed by Inigo Jones (Orrell 1985) and "a proscenium stage built within the Hall" (Astington 1999a), 26 July (Gurr 2004c). Performed also at the Whitehall Cockpit, 18 December 1638 (*JCS*); this revival lacked the "benefit of scenery" (Orrell). Later performed at the [second] Blackfriars "with great applause," according to the TP. In playlist of King's Men 7 August 1641.

SR 4 September 1646; transferred 30 January 1673. O and Q 1655 two issues; HT *The Passionate Lover, First Part*; list of characters; epilogue to king; five acts. In Q the type has been impressed on Q leaves with new signatures.

Parts 1 and *2* were printed together as one book with continuous register and pagination; the two parts constitute a "ten-act romance" (Harbage 1936). Epilogue of *Part 1* anticipates *Part 2*: "Stay! Even in policie your grant is fit; / Hope quickens, what despair makes dull, the wit: / Nay, could our author some new arts display, / Yet this condemn'd, you'l slight the second play."

2 The Passionate Lovers, A Tragicomedy. Lodowick Carlell. Probably acted summer of 1638 in the hall of Somerset House, with changeable scenery designed by Inigo Jones (Orrell 1985), 28 July (Gurr 2004c). Also acted 20 December and 27 December 1638 by the King's Men at the Whitehall Cockpit (*JCS*); this revival lacked the "benefit of scenery" (Orrell). Performed also at the [second] Blackfriars "with great applause." "One set design for this play, by Inigo Jones, is inscribed 'The wood 6 sceane . . . a shutter in ye 2d part of Mr. Lodowicks play'" (Richards 1968). In playlist of the King's Men 7 August 1641.

SR 4 September 1646; transferred 30 January 1673. O and Q 1655 two issues; HT *The Passionate Lover, Second Part*; prologue and epilogue; five acts. *Parts 1* and *2* were printed together as one book with continuous register and pagination.

"Carlell prominently displays female homoerotic desire in a dialogue that is seen and heard rather than imagined"; he "constructs female homoeroticism as a component of romantic love commensurate with heterosexuality" (Walen 2005).

The Passions Calmed, or The Settling of the Floating Island. See *The Floating Island.*

A Pastoral. Jane Cavendish and Elizabeth Brackley. Written 1644–45 (Findlay 2006). A household entertainment "intended for a limited coterie audience" (Findlay 2000), perhaps at Welbeck Abbey where the authors were sequestered. "The Cavendish sisters clearly recognized that their own imprisonment within the confines of Welbeck Abbey reflected the destabilization of the whole Royalist hierarchy, upon which their noble identity and the security of their country house had depended" (Wynne-Davies 1998). Perhaps enacted at Bolsover Castle, another Cavendish property (Findlay 2006). No actual evidence of production, but "[u]nlike other Early Modern women dramatists, Wroth, Brackley and Cavendish all include sufficient stage directions and internal narrative evidence to prove that the plays were written with performance envisaged, if not intended" (Wynne-Davies). "In Cavendish's plays speech, particularly women's speech, takes precedence over action or characterisation" (Williams 2000).

Oxford, Bodleian, MS Rawlinson poet. 16, fols. 49–84; *Poems, Songs, a Pastoral, and a Play*; both authors named on the general TP; no separate TP for this play; two prologues (one by each author) addressed to their father William Cavendish; two epilogues; not divided into acts. "The author of each scene is designated by the initials 'JC' or 'EB' in the upper left-hand corner" (Ezell 1988).

"The authors rewrite the conventional masque form to enact their sense of loss at the absence of their exiled father and brothers" (Findlay). The "three shepherdesses, representing Jane, Elizabeth and their sister Frances, sing of their sadness now 'He,' their father William Cavendish, is no longer with them" (Wynne-Davies).

A Pastoral called The Arcadia. See *The Arcadia* by ?James Shirley.

Pathomachia, or The Battle of Affections (*Love's Loadstone*). Anonymous. Smith 1908 and Smith 1942 conjecture authorship by Thomas Tomkis, author of *Lingua*. Acted ?1617 by students of Trinity College, Cambridge (Nelson 1989).

(1) London, BL, Harley MS 6869; fols. 3–22; *Pathomachia or, Love's Loadstone*; no author named; five acts and separate scenes. (2) Oxford, Bodleian, MS Eng. misc. e.5, fols. 1–44; *Pathomachia, or Love's Loadstone*; no separate TP; no author named; the ending is missing. SR 16 April 1630 *The Battell of The affections or loves Loadstone*. Q 1630 *Pathomachia, or The Battle of Affections, Shadowed by a Feigned Siege of the City Pathopolis*; "written some yeeres since, and now first published by a friend of the deceassed author"; HT *Pathomachia, or Love's Loadstone*; RT *Love's Loadstone;* list of characters all of whom are personifications; five acts and separate scenes.

The Q dedication, explaining how the play came to be printed, views the medium of print as preserving the life of the author: "As tombes be the monuments of the body; so bookes, of the mind; leaving testimonie, that though a man live not long, yet that he once lived. This coppy therefore comming to my hands, I durst not but publish it, as holding the suppressing therof a kind of sacriledge. The author (being dead) neither affects fame, nor feares censure."

Patient and Meek Grissell. John Phillip. Acted 1558–61 (Grantley 2004) at undetermined venue, possibly before the queen (Southern 1973); production at court is suggested by "the prayerful epilogue, the songs, and the correspondences to related interludes" (Winkelman 2005). "[T]he large cast and use of music and song suggest a play for children" (Walker 1998); the child actors were possibly choristers (Lennam 1975). The TP claims that "eight persons maye easely play this commody," and it divides the roles for eight actors, "but the arrangement is faulty" (McKerrow & Greg 1909); the doubling plan requires "one actor to be in two places at once" (Walker 1998); the claim "is an example of a false advertisement, presumably by the publisher, who wishes to sell the play to a company smaller than that for which the author has inconsiderately designed it" (Craik 1958). The "hopelessly tangled casting chart, perhaps a publisher's fraud, is prefixed to a play that bears weighty evidence of having been acted by boys instead of an adult troupe" (Bevington 1962).

SR *c.* April 1565–66 and *c.* February 1568–69 (Grantley); "[t]he double entry in SR suggests that the earlier was not acted on" (Greg 1939). "The play is, no doubt, to be identified with the 'Old' *Patient Grissell*, recorded in the catalogues of Archer (1656) and Kirkman (1661 and 1671)" (McKerrow & Greg). Q ND ?1566 *The Comedy of Patient and Meek Grissell, Wherein Is Declared the Good Example of Her Patience towards Her Husband, and Likewise the Due Obedience of Children toward Their Parents*; RT *The Play of Patient Grissell*; "compiled by" John Phillip; list of characters on the TP, which includes "the first extant designation in print of a *dramatic* epilogue" (Schneider 2011); prologue called "The Preface"; speech by "The last speaker" identified in the margin as "Postemus Actor," who speaks the epilogue of 28 lines; Vulgus serves a choral function (Dessen 1977); not divided.

"At least five of the eight actors are obliged to undertake feminine or juvenile parts" (Bevington). "Phillip creates a world of women who speak for Grissell and who come to represent values alternative to those of the male world and without which the kingdom is politically unstable" (Cartwright 1999).

Patient Grissell. Thomas Dekker, Henry Chettle, and William Haughton. Acted January–March 1600 (Hoy 1980). "Sundrie times lately plaid" by Lord Admiral Nottingham's Men, according to the TP, at the Rose (Rhodes 1976) and Fortune, which opened autumn 1600. Henslowe records payment to the playwrights 16 October; 19, 26, 28, 29 December 1599; also payment for Grissell's gown, 26 January 1600. "Without the evidence of Henslowe's papers, we would not know that a dramatist named William Haughton existed, let alone be in a position to connect him with specific plays"; those papers identify the authors of *Patient Grissell* (Cathcart 2010).

SR 28 March 1600. Q 1603 *The Pleasant Comedy of Patient Grissell*; no author named; not divided. Detailed SDs with particular attention to hand props: "*Enter Babulo with a bundle of osiers in one arme and a childe in another, Grissill after him with another childe*"; "*Enter Janicola with an angling rod, Grissill with a reele*"; "*Enter Janicola and Babulo carrying coales, Laureo with wood, Grissill with wood.*"

"The character Emulo with his 'gallimaufry of language' is thought to be a caricature of Jonson" (Grantley 2000).

The Patient Man and The Honest Whore. See *The Honest Whore.*

The Peddler's Prophecy. Possibly written by Robert Wilson (Grantley 2004), *c.* 1579–80 (Cameron 1982), and acted at undetermined venue. A play "for the popular theater" (Jewkes 1958). Probably performed by the Queen's Men (Pinciss 1970), "but it is not absolutely certain" that the play belonged to this company (Schoone-Jongen 2008).

SR 13 May 1594. Q 1595 no author named; prologue and epilogue (by Peddler), though not so named; not divided.

The play has much in common with *The Cobbler's Prophecy*: "Both plays centre on a simple but wise artisan (the cobbler and pedlar, respectively) who has the gift of prophecy and warns his social superiors about the dangers facing the country (nominally Boeotia and Troy, but clearly meant to represent England)" (Kathman 2004f). *The Peddler's Prophecy* addresses contemporary issues: "an uninterrupted flow of immigrants, shortage of renting space, inflated prices, and a mongrelized population" (Bevington 1968).

Pelopidarum Secunda. Anonymous. Acted sometime between November 1558 and March 1603, possibly by students of Winchester School (*JCS*). "In smaller schoolrooms a stage was possibly unnecessary or impractical. It is perhaps more likely that platforms were used if and when troupes performed in larger school-rooms or halls of the kind found at the major Renaissance grammar schools such as Winchester" (Keenan 2002).

London, BL, Harley MS 5110, fols. 27–81; no separate TP; no author named; epilogue; chorus; five acts and separate scenes. Some SDs and speech headings written in red ink.

Pelopoea and Alope. See *Amphrisa, the Forsaken Shepherdess.*

Periander. John San[d]sbury. Acted 13 February 1608 (Richards 1982) by stu-dents of St. John's College, Oxford, in the college hall, at night, "at a Christmas entertainment" (Bowers 1959). Thomas Tucker acted in this production.

(1) Oxford, St. John's College, MS 52, pp. 209–58; in a collection of enter-tainments known as *The Christmas Prince: An Account of the St. John's College Revels Held at Oxford in 1607–8*; list of characters on the TP; chorus; induction (involv-ing the Master of the Revels and Boy, Resolution and Detraction) and epilogue; five acts and separate scenes. Appended to the text is a description of the play's reception: "All were so pleased att the whole course of this play that there were at least eight generall plaudites given in the mid'st of it in divers places and to div-ers persons." First edited in full by Boas & Greg 1922; Bliss 1816 had published excerpts. Reproduced in photographic facsimile by Richards 1982. (2) Washing-ton, Folger, MS J.a.1(11), fols. 134–57; "made bye Mr John Sansburye"; list of characters; prologue and epilogue; chorus; five acts and separate scenes. This MS "omits many stage directions, and abbreviates most of the others. It contains only a rudimentary dramatis personae, and no induction" (Harbage 1935a). "[I]t is possible that both manuscripts derive from a common source" (Gossett & Berger 1988). The Folger MS of *Periander* is the only part of *The Christmas Prince* that survives separately from the Oxford MS (Richards). Boas & Greg observe: "It has the interest of being one of the few plays of the period based at first hand on Greek originals."

Pericles, Prince of Tyre. William Shakespeare, probably with George Wilkins (Sykes 1919, Schrickx 1976, Wells & Taylor 1987, Vickers 2002, Jackson 2003), though Hoeniger 1963, Edwards 1976, and DelVecchio & Hammond 1998 are skeptical. Acted early 1608 (Delvecchio & Hammond) or April-June (Barroll 1991). "Divers and sundry times acted by" the King's Men at the [first] Globe, according to the Q1 TP. "[W]ritten before the company acquired the Blackfri-ars but at a time when they knew they would do so" (Stern 2006). "The Venetian Ambassador to England, Zorzi Giustinian, paid more than twenty crowns for the admission of a party of four to a performance of *Per[icles]* some time between 5 January 1606 and 23 November 1608 at a playhouse not identified" (King 1992a); in the party were the French ambassador and "the Secretary of Florence."

The play's "immediate popularity may be indicated by the presence of the French and Venetian ambassadors at a performance in 1608" (Holland 2004a). Performed also by Richard Cholmeley's players at the home of John Yorke, Gowthwaite Hall in the North Riding of Yorkshire, at Candlemas, 2 February 1610 (Sisson 1942, Hoeniger 1963); the players were known as the Simpsons and the "audience was almost exclusively Catholic" (Jensen 2003). *Pericles* seems related to *The Travails of the Three English Brothers* (by Wilkins, Day, and Rowley): "the two plays may be connected . . . by their popularity with Catholic private audiences" (Parr 2004b). For the performance at Gowthwaite Hall the actors used the recently published Q1 as their script (Mowat 1997). Revived by the King's Men in the Great Chamber at Whitehall, after supper, 20 May 1619 (recorded in a letter from Gerrard Herbert to Dudley Carleton); the French ambassador, Antoine Lefèvre de la Boderie, attended. Henry Herbert on 10 June 1631 records payment from the King's Men who played *Pericles* at the Globe; this represented a "gratuity for ther liberty gaind unto them of playinge, upon the cessation of the plague" (Chambers 1930). In early performances the role of Gower was "perhaps acted by Shakespeare himself" (Duncan-Jones 2001); Richard Burbage "was probably the eponymous lead" (White 1998). The play was "exceptionally popular" with early seventeenth-century audiences (Jackson 2003); "the continuing production of quarto editions suggests that it remained popular" (DelVecchio & Hammond). Ben Jonson in an "Ode to Himself," written 1629, laments that audiences are drawn to "some mouldy tale / Like *Pericles*."

SR 20 May 1608 *Pericles prynce of Tyre*; no author recorded; possibly refers to *The Painful Adventures of Pericles Prince of Tyre* by George Wilkins (King 1992a); transferred ?4 August 1626 Paviers right in Shakesperes *plaies*; ?19 June 1627 widow of Isaac Jaggard . . . her parte in Shackspheere *playes*; 8 November 1630; 1 July 1637 Shakespeares *workes* their Part; 6 August 1674; 21 August 1683. Wilkins' prose narrative "contains passages which read as if they were originally verse lines in a play, either the play reported in the Quarto text [of Shakespeare's *Pericles*] or something very close to it" (Warren 2003). Q1 1609 *The Late and Much Admired Play called Pericles, Prince of Tyre, with the True Relation of the Whole History, Adventures, and Fortunes of the Said Prince, as Also the No Less Strange and Worthy Accidents in the Birth and Life of His Daughter Mariana*; "by William Shakespeare"; Gower's first speech may be construed as a prologue, his last speech, an epilogue; three dumb shows, explained by Gower, who plays a choral role/presenter (Braunmuller 2003); not divided: "That Shakespeare and his company did not regard a Chorus speech as necessarily marking one of five act divisions is confirmed by *Pericles*, in which Gower has *eight* choral monologues" (Hirsh 2002), but Greg 1939 contends that some of these entries correspond to act divisions; Gossett 2004b finds that the play falls into "seven sections."

Death and the threat of death haunt the play: "the first thing that the audience sees is an empty stage lined with the heads of unsuccessful suitors" for the king's daughter (Teague 1991). And if Pericles in that scene "discloses what he knows [of the king's incest], he risks death at the hands of a man who sees him not as a future son-in-law but rather as a sexual rival" (Kiefer 1996). Staging calls for storms at sea, with appropriate visual and sound effects: in one Pericles says, "The god of this great vast, rebuke these surges, / Which wash both heaven and hell." Fisherman haul up "rusty armour," apparently using a trap in the stage floor: Pericles recognizes the armor as his own, a gift bequeathed by his dead father, and wears it at the tournament in Pentapolis (Harlan 2008). Staging requires a property coffin for Thaisa's body, which is consigned to the sea, and a tomb for Marina: the latter "may be a property, the tiring-house façade, or a tiring-house door" (Hosley 1975). Viols aid "in reviving Thaisa after the shipwreck" (Shirley 1961); "the moment must be slow, and the props elaborate and beautiful" (Mosely 2009): "*Shee moves.*" Staging also involves a vision of Diana, who may descend from the heavens by machinery. An auditory effect may be called for when Pericles hears "*the musicke of the spheres,*" but Helicanus claims not to hear it; "the absence of stage directions here from the quarto text of 1609 suggests that *Pericles* may have no audible music at all at this point, merely silence" (Dillon 2010). Knights at a tournament carry shields painted with symbolic pictures, which are described and interpreted (Kiefer 2011); "this parade of knights would probably have been a high point of the play's spectacle" (Brissenden 1981). "Since this is a ceremonial scene, it is very likely that King Simonedes and Thaisa would sit on thrones centre-stage. Each knight would walk in a curve in front of these observers" (Ichikawa 2002). "*Pericles* is especially full of dumb-shows, the effect of which is cumulative" (Dillon). Q2 1609 reprinting the play in the same year suggests "an exceptional public demand" (Warren). Q3 [octavo-in-fours] 1611. Q4 1619 printed for Thomas Pavier; "Pavier apparently intended to bring out a collection of Shakespeare's plays, but was stopped just at this point by order of the Lord Chamberlain" (Gossett 2004a). *Pericles* does not appear in Shakespeare F1 "perhaps because no alternative to the apparently defective text provided in the 1609 and 1611 editions was available, or perhaps because it was not considered to be substantially a product of Shakespeare's pen" (Murphy 2003). Q5 1630 two issues. Q6 1635 [octavo-in-fours] "probably printed from Q4" (Jowett 2007e). Shakespeare F3 1664 second issue; "the third impression. And unto this impression is added seven playes, never before printed in folio"; list of characters at end of play; "inept act divisions" (Wells & Taylor). *Pericles* "is the only one of the seven plays first added in a supplement to the Third Folio (1664) that has been accepted into the canon" (Gossett). F4 1685 "the fourth edition."

"Wilkins' influence [is] most evident in the early part of the play" (Hope 1994). "On internal evidence it seems that Wilkins wrote most of the first two acts and Shakespeare most of the last three" (Greenblatt 2010), a suggestion first made by Delius 1868; the use of rhyme, in particular, points to Wilkins' authorship of acts 1 and 2 (Jackson 2011). But Klause 2012 doubts that "rhyming practice by itself can distinguish and identify authors in *Pericles*." Vickers 2008 assigns 1,013 lines to Wilkins. "The intertwining of Wilkins's work with Shakespeare's makes it difficult to determine the direction of influence" (Gossett). "*Pericles* was written by the two men in co-ordinated collaboration" (Duncan-Jones); *Pericles* "was either a collaborative project from the outset, or one that Shakespeare took over after Wilkins had roughed out a plot and written the opening scenes" (Parr 2004b). Kirkman's 1661 catalogue ascribes the play to Shakespeare.

Perkin Warbeck. John Ford. Probably acted 1632 (Gurr 1988a) or 1633 (Clark 2007). By Queen Henrietta Maria's Men at the Phoenix, according to the TP. That page includes an unusual expression — "acted some-times." These words "must refer to other performances given prior to the date of publication, but their number and the date of the very first performances remain unknown" (Gibson 1986).

SR 24 February 1634 a Tragedy called *Perkin Warbecke*. The SR entry contains an odd phrase: "observing the caution in the license," which may constitute a warning to the actors not to play certain speeches in the script or perhaps a warning not to depart from the script as licensed. "It is also possible that the play came disconcertingly close to particular recent events, and that Herbert attempted to provide himself with some cover" (Pinciss 2000). Q 1634 *The Chronicle History of Perkin Warbeck, A Strange Truth*; no author named on the TP, which gives Ford's anagram, "Fide Honor," but Ford signs the dedication to William Cavendish; list of characters; prologue and epilogue; a highly detailed SD describing a ceremony that reads like a dumb show; five acts. Staging calls for "*A payre of stocks*," and Warbeck is placed in them, the fate of virtuous characters in the moral interludes. Some SDs are tantalizing: "*Enter at one dore foure Scotch antickes, accordingly habited; enter at another foure wilde Irish in trowse[r]s, long hayred, and accordingly habited*." Ford's contemporaries presumably knew what "accordingly" meant. Less mysterious are the descriptions of King Henry, "*his gorget on, his sword, plume of feathers*"; Katherine and Jane "*in riding suits*"; and Katherine "*in her richest attire*." Unusual staging includes the condemned Stanly making "*a crosse on Cliffords face with his finger*"; this action seems a "strange application of the baptismal sign" (Madelaine 1988). Also issued in *Comedies, Tragicomedies, and Tragedies* (1652), a made-up book no longer extant.

The play "tells the story of the last of the major challenges to the legitimacy of the Tudor line, the appearance of the Yorkist pretender Perkin Warbeck, who claimed to be the younger of Edward IV's two sons (the princes Richard III was supposed to have murdered in the Tower of London)" (Cantor 1987b). Although the historical sources indicate that Perkin was an impostor, "Ford's Perkin maintains his claims to the end despite Henry's hints of clemency should he renounce them" (Monta 1997). Even though historians are "now unanimous on the falsehood of Perkin Warbeck's claim to be the Duke of York, this was by no means the case when Ford wrote the play" (Hopkins 1995b). And "nothing in the play indicates conclusively that [Warbeck] is either Richard, Duke of York, or an impostor" (Kamps 1996). Prologue signals the combination of history and drama, remarking of the author, "Hee show's a historie, couch't in a play." By the time

Ford wrote *Perkin Warbeck*, the vogue for history plays had crested, and this play "is sometimes called the last English history play" (Corns 2007); Ford "was conscious of reviving an old-fashioned form" (McLuskie 1981). But "the traditional history play received an invigorating gift of new subject matter as the immediate effect of the accession of James I" (Barton 1977); "there is one contemporary context into which *Perkin Warbeck* fits very well indeed, and that relates to its insistent concern with questions of imposture, legitimacy, and identity, and most particularly as they affect those of royal blood" (Hopkins 1995a). Moreover, the historical characters had connections with the playwright and his circle: "Almost every major character in *Perkin Warbeck* is in fact a direct ancestor of a Ford dedicatee or of a member of their family" (Hopkins 1994). The play's "dramatization of Henry VII's reign serves as a sequel of sorts to Shakespeare's *Richard III*" (Di-Gangi 2002), but Ford "turns many of Shakespeare's assumptions on their head" (Neill 2004).

The Persian Slave. See *The Royal Slave.*

Philander, King of Thrace. Edward Dering (Folger catalogue, Yeandle 1986). No evidence of production. Written after 1627 (Davidson 1978). Apparently the plan for a play that was never completed. "It is clear that the play was intended to be a tragi-comedy rather than a tragedy" (Adams 1945–46).

   Washington, Folger, MS X.d.206, fols. 1–3; no separate TP; the title, "evidently apocryphal," was supplied by a dealer's catalogue (Davidson); no author named; list of characters; indication of locales (Thrace for act 1, Macedon for 2 and 3); three acts (incomplete) and separate scenes; "[s]ome use of red ink was made to distinguish act divisions" (Adams). MS gives a synopsis of acts 1, 2, and 3. Typical is scene 10 of act 3: *"Ascania [queen of Pseudonax, King of Macedon] meditating in the private walkes of her garden, Phonops [a begging courtier] . . . and Philocles enter: cast a hood over her and carry her away. Phonops bidds him gagge her and bind her: he warrants her and leades her by the two thumbes, leads her of[f] the stage and brings her on againe . . . then uncovers her, discovereth himself and placeth her with the sibyll."* The reference to the stage and to entries and exits indicates a sensitivity to theatrical dynamics. First reproduced by Adams.

   "[I]t may be that this is the plot for a collaborative play in which only acts 1–3 were of interest to this particular author; alternatively the plotter may have given up before completing the document" (Stern 2009c).

Philaster, or Love Lies a-Bleeding. Francis Beaumont and John Fletcher. Written "between late 1608 and early 1610" (Gurr 1969); it is "likely" that the play "was composed in 1609 during the theatre closure and acted for the first time in early 1610" (Gossett 2009a). "Acted at the Globe" by the King's Men, according to the Q1 TP. "Diverse times acted" at the Globe and Blackfriars, according to the Q2 TP, which implies "an indoor revival around 1621" (Graves 1978). *Philaster* is "the first play Beaumont and Fletcher wrote for the King's Men at Blackfriars" (Gurr 1987b). The initial production "was very successful" (Finkelpearl 1990). Elkanah Settle's epilogue ("spoken by a girle") for his revision of the play in 1695 suggests the importance of women playgoers: "Once our *Philaster* was a lady's play: / And if in the last age so warm a ray / From that high sphear the glittering boxes shin'd, / Shall beauties bright succession be less kind!" Revived at court, celebrating the betrothal and marriage of Princess Elizabeth to Frederick, Elector Palatine, 1612–13 (payment to John Heminges dated 20 May 1613); at court, 1619–20 (Gurr). An indoor revival is suggested by the Q2 TP, "around 1621" (Graves 1978). Revived at Whitehall Cockpit-in-Court, 14 December 1630 (Teague 2009); and at St. James's Palace, 21 February 1637 (Adams 1917), in the Presence Chamber (Astington 1986). "Presumably these performances followed or were accompanied by revivals in the theatres" (Gossett). Nathan Field, who joined the King's Men in 1615–16, performed in the play (Schoenbaum 1964b). Halliwell[-Phillipps] had a scrapbook page from Q4 featuring a handwritten list of actors' names; apparently Robert Benfield played the King; Hugh Clark, Philaster; Thomas Pollard, Pharamond; John Lowin, Dion; William Penn, Claremont; Theophilus Bird, Thrasaline; Charles Hart, Euphrasia; Walter Clun, Arethusa; William Patrick, an Old Captain and a Country Fellow (George 1974). "[T]his cast seems a likely one for a performance by the King's company in 1641, 1642, or 1643, but its authenticity cannot be assumed" (Bentley 1984).

London, BL, Harley MS 6918, fol. 99r-v; a fragment containing a prologue ["wonders of the age wherein they liv'd"] and epilogue ["The play is done, yet something we must say"] written for a revival. SR 10 January 1620; transferred 1 March 1628; 29 May 1638; 25 January 1639. Q1 1620 "a botched text throughout" (Gurr 1969); the TP names B&F; list of characters; five acts. The Q1 TP features a woodcut depicting Arethusa, Philaster, and "A Cuntrie Gentellman"; this illustration perhaps "conflates two incidents" in the play (Foakes 1985). "It signals action with Philaster sneaking off into the bushes on the right; at left, it conveys violence in the dark gash of blood staining the Princess' breast; it suggests sex in the illustration of her exposed nipples and also, perhaps, in the central figure of the 'Cuntrie Gentellman' with his upright sword"; "it is a remarkably concise rendering of the climactic scene of the play—Arethusa's survival of a chest wound from her murderous lover because of the melodramatic intervention of a bewildered countryman" (Collier 1998). Q2 1622 "the second impression, corrected, and amended"; "thorough revisions of the opening and the ending" (Bentley 1971); "the more authoritative" of the first two quartos (McMullan 2004); no list of characters; preface from publisher appended, which claims that "some dangerous and gaping wounds" suffered in Q1 have been remedied. Differences between Q1 and Q2 "are suggestive of censorship" (Clare 1990). No woodcut in Q2. Q3 1628 "the third impression"; the publisher says that the play "was affectionatly taken, and approved by the seeing auditors, or hearing spectators, (of which sort, I take, or conceive you to bee the greatest part)"; replaces the old preface with a new one; list of characters. Q4 1634 "the fourth impression"; "in more than twenty places" this reprint "had its oaths toned down or omitted" (Bawcutt 1996). Q4 provides "a list of characters . . . annotated in a contemporary hand by the names of actors who were with the King's Men in the early 1640s. 'Clarke' and 'Bird' are listed as playing Philaster and Thrasaline, but Hugh Clarke and Theophilus Bird were with other companies until at least 1635–7, and do not certainly appear with the King's Men until 1641" (Kathman 2005). Q5 1639 two issues; "the fourth impression [*sic*]." Q6 1652 "the fifth impression [*sic*]." Q7 dated 1652 but "actually printed about 1661" (Turner 1966); "the sixth impression [*sic*]." Q8 ND. Prologue and epilogue, written for a revival, were "printed in A. B.'s *Covent Garden Drollery*, 1672" (Greg 1939). B&F F2 1679 *Fifty Comedies and Tragedies*; "published by the authors original copies, the songs to each play being added"; list of characters; drops the Q3 preface. Q9 1687. (*Philaster* was not included in B&F F1, "which omitted plays previously printed" [Gossett].)

Philaster "seems to have initiated the fashion for what became the most significant dramatic genre of the century, romantic tragicomedy" (McMullan 2004). Whereas Shakespeare's tragicomedies "characteristically evoke wonder," Beaumont and Fletcher's "tragicomedies are defined by surprise" (Foster 2004): e.g. at the end of *Philaster* Bellario is revealed as a girl. Here "the page Bellario decides to remain permanently in drag and serve her lord and lady as an epicene youth, equally attractive to men and women" (Orgel 2010).

The printer's note to the Q3 reader reports that "the first impression swarm'd with errors" and compares the play to gold ore, which has been "refined" by subsequent publication. Sometime between the closing of the theaters and the Restoration, act 5, scene 4, was adapted for a droll entitled *The Club Men*, later published in *The Wits, or Sport upon Sport* (O 1662 [two issues] and 1672) and identified erroneously in *The Wits* as originating in *Cupid's Revenge* (Bowers 1970). "This brief and lively riot scene is excellently adapted to droll-performance" (Elson 1932).

Philetis and Constantia. A droll performed in the 1640s and 50s. Based on Abraham Cowley's narrative poem, *Constantia and Philetus*, in *Poetical Blossoms* (1633, 1636, and 1637). Possibly written by "a schoolfellow of Cowley's at Westminster, or some schoolboy elsewhere" (Elson 1932). But Kirkman, on the TP of *2 The Wits*, says that the drolls were "written I know not when, by several persons, I know not who"; however, his preface says that Robert Cox "was not only the principal actor, but also the contriver and author of most of these farces." Kirkman's attribution is "probable" (Holland 2007).

Published in *2 The Wits, or Sport upon Sport* (Q and O 1673), which gives as venues of performance fairs, halls, taverns, and "mountebancks stages at Charing Cross, Lincolns-Inn-Fields, and other places"; list of characters. Some detailed

SDs: "*Running over the stage a hunting,* Philetis *lyes in ambush and catcheth* Constantia; Giscardo, Philetis *his rival, finding him, runs him through the body.*"

This droll is "unique in having a composite origin; it contains a couplet from Cowley's *Pyramus and Thisbe*, an Ovidian romance (not indebted to Shakespeare) composed in 1628, and a couplet and a lengthy speech adapted from Henry Glapthorne's play, *Argalus and Parthenia*, published in 1639" (Elson).

Philotas. Samuel Daniel. "A closet tragedy revised for the commercial stage"; this is "the only known example in the Jacobean period of a play with closet origins that was performed before a paying audience" (Munro 2005). Acted autumn 1604 (Barroll 2001). "Possibly acted by the Children of the Queen's Revels" (McJannet 1999a) at the Blackfriars. Performed before the king by the same company "some time during the winter season at court, between November 1604 and February 1604/5, with 3 January as a probable date" (Gazzard 2000). "In 1607 Daniel extensively revised the work" (Harner 1987).

SR 29 November 1604; 19 August 1635. The play's printing history is unusually complicated. O1 1605 *The Tragedy of Philotas*; two issues; *Certain Small Poems Lately Printed* (with *Cleopatra*); argument; list of characters; chorus at close of acts 1–3 and beginning and end of act 5; play concludes with dialogue between the chorus and nuntius; scanty stage directions; five acts and separate scenes. The "use of the chorus makes it reminiscent of closet drama, seemingly designed for a specialised audience" (Clare 1999). "No copy of *Certaine Small Poems* is known to want *Philotas*" (Bland 1996). At the heart of Daniel's play lies ambivalence: "*Philotas* is a play that pulls us in two directions. It presents a character fully capable of treason but never allows us to believe entirely that he commits it. It offers a confession in its last moments, but makes that confession at least partially unreliable by having it issued under torture" (Curran 2012). O2 1607 *Certain Small Works* (with *Cleopatra*, *The Queen's Arcadia*); "now againe by him [Daniel] corrected and augmented"; list of characters omitted. D 1607 appended are a number of other works by Daniel; "the volume has no general title" (Munro 2005). D2 1611 *Certain Small Works* (with *Cleopatra*, *The Queen's Arcadia*); two issues. In the 1607 and 1611 editions, Daniel "made a number of revisions, but none that augment the play's fundamental indecisiveness on the subject of Philotas' guilt" (Curran). Q [octavo-in-fours] 1623 *The Whole Works* (with *Cleopatra*, *Hymen's Triumph*, *The Queen's Arcadia*); continuous register and pagination; begins with a dedication to Prince Charles by John Daniel; addition of an "apology" by the author. In 1635 "some copies of this drama portion of the *Whole Works* were reissued, with a new title page, as a set of 'Dramaticke poems'" (Pitcher 2005). *Philotas* "became one of the best-selling printed plays of the early seventeenth century" (Straznicky 2004).

Writing this play put Daniel in danger, for *Philotas* "is in large part an attack on [Robert] Cecil" and "it also voices more general complaints about the direction of the early Jacobean state" (Perry 1997). The playwright's "apology," first printed at the end of 1623 Q (Michel 1949), alludes to the play's evocation of the Essex conspiracy, which led to Daniel being called before the Privy Council early in 1605; he explained that he intended "to have had it [the play] presented in Bath by certaine gentlemens sonnes, as a private recreation for the Christmas, before the Shrovetide of that unhappy disorder [the Essex rebellion in February 1601]. But by reason of some occasion then falling out, and being called upon by my printer for a new impression of my workes, with some additions to the civ-ill warres, I intermitted this other subject. Which now lying by mee, and driven by necessity to make use of my pen, and the stage to bee the mouth of my lines, which before were never heard to speake but in silence, I thought the representing so true a history, in the ancient forme of a tragedy, could not but have had an un-reproveable passage with the time, and the better sort of men; seeing with what idle fictions, and grosse follies, the stage at this day abused mens recreations." In short, the play "was written for private performance some years before the fall of Essex, but then staged by the Queen's Revels after the fall, and misconstrued an as allegory of the Essex plot" (Bate 2008). But Daniel's claim was false (Stirling 1942, Michel 1949, Seronsy 1967, De Luna 1967, Gazzard 2000), as the authori-ties surmised. *Philotas* "was perceived to refer too closely to the Essex rebellion and he was sacked" (White 2004c); Daniel had seemed to imply approval of Es-sex. "After 1605 Daniel's prospects quickly faded, substantially if not entirely, because of the disgrace *Philotas* brought upon him" (Tricomi 1989).

Philotus. ?Alexander Montgomerie or ?George Buchanan. Acted 1583–86 (Mc-Diarmid 1967). Possibly performed at the court of King James VI of Scotland in Edinburgh. "Described internally as a 'ferse' and on the title page as a 'Treatise,' this play is built upon set-piece speeches between 'interloquitors' in 'rime couée,' but contains within a comic structure more than enough disguise, misapprehen-sion of gender, mistaken identity and satire to work well on stage" (McGavin 2004). Despite the word *Treatise* in the Q1 title, this comedy displays "exemplary theatricality" (Reid-Baxter 2002). All the speeches are numbered sequentially.

  Q1 1603 *A Very Excellent and Delectable Treatise Entitled Philotus Wherein We May Perceive the Great Inconveniences that Fall Out in the Marriage between Age and Youth*; printed in Edinburgh; no author named; list of characters; epilogue by Messenger; not divided. "The few stage-directions are as much expositions of the story or interpretations of the situation as instructions to the actors; entrances and exits are never indicated" (Craigie 1979). Q2 1612 the word *Old* is inserted before *Age* in the title, and the word *Treatise* is changed to *Comedy*; argument; omits the song printed at the end of Q1.

  Although the play is usually assigned to the court of King James, after 1581, it may have been intended for his mother: "*Philotus*, with its marked feminine focus, may well be designed to carry a carefully coded plea to Mary, Queen of Scots, for a reconciliation with her errant husband" (Reid-Baxter).

Phoenissae. See *Jocasta*.

The Phoenix. Thomas Middleton (identified in Kirkman's 1661 catalogue). Probably written "in the first year of James's reign" (Danson & Kamps 2007). Acted 20 February 1604 (Brooks 1980). "Sundry times acted" by Paul's Boys, according to the Q1 TP, at Paul's playhouse. Performed also by that company before the king, according to the Q1 TP, at Whitehall. Because of the plague closing of June 1603-March 1604, the court performance may have antedated the performance at Paul's.

SR 9 May 1607; transferred 29 January 1630; 7 November 1646. Q1 1607 no author named; prologue and epilogue (both added on a separate leaf at end and lifted from *The Turk* [1610]); not formally divided but a SD apparently refers to a musical interlude: "*Toward the close of the musick, the Justices three men prepare for a robberie.*" Few SDs apart from the entrances of characters. Q2 1630 no author named; lacks prologue and epilogue.

"Middleton's episodic panorama belongs to a group of disguised duke plays (including Marston's *The Fawn* and Shakespeare's *Measure for Measure*) written for rival companies in 1603–4, which adopt the conventions of the new Italian genre of tragicomedy to comment on English social and political life at a moment of profound but uncertain transition" (Taylor 2004b). *The Phoenix* and *Measure* "have much in common: both were written in the year of the accession to the throne of James I, and both present a disguised ruler (in the case of *The Phoenix* one just about to inherit his dukedom) who goes in disguise or in a series of disguises to observe his state" (Hyland 2011).

The Phoenix in Her Flames, A Tragedy. William Lower. "Although there is no evidence that *The Phoenix* was ever produced, there is every reason for thinking that Lower had the stage in mind as he wrote. Stage directions, matters of entrance and exit, and the words of the prologue and epilogue point to the author's conception of the piece as an acting play" (Gates 1932). Moreover, in its appeal to the senses, the prologue anticipates production: "This aire shall be perfum'd and every sence / Delighted . . . for please you know, / Gentle spectators, from our sceane doth grow / Abundance of such fragrant stuffe, you'll see / A play that breathes *Arabian* spicerie." And the epilogue speaks of "wrongs presented on the stage."

Q 1639 "there may have been two issues" (*JCS*); dramatis personae; prologue and epilogue; four acts and first scenes (five acts were undoubtedly intended); division into acts is "quite haphazard" (Gates). Ample SDs: when Rapinus "*Offers to ravish her* [Lucinda]," Amandus interposes himself: "[Rapinus] *draws his sword and assaults him,* Amand[us] *defends himself with a stoole, and at last closing with him, hath him at his mercy.*"

Prologue defends tragedy at a time when comedy was the preferred genre: "Our poet feares none but the common wits, / Who think a sceane's not good unles it fits / Their merry humours with some apish toyes." Epilogue points to performance: "Come, and be welcome still, and let your friends, / Who have not seene as yet our tragicke end, / Come here and weepe with you, untill together, / You make up this a full press'd theater: / Then it shall please our ghosts to think the age / Pitties our wrongs presented on the stage." This is one of several plays in the half dozen years before the closing of the theaters, in which, "after a twenty-five year hiatus, the matter of Persia reappears" (McJannet 1999a).

The Picture, A Tragicomedy. Philip Massinger. Licensed for acting 8 June 1629 (Adams 1917). "Often presented with good allowance" by the King's Men at the [second] Globe and [second] Blackfriars, according to the Q TP. Possibly also performed at the Inner Temple, acknowledged in Massinger's dedication of Q. Robert Benfield played King Ladislaus; John Lowin, Eubulus; Richard Sharp, Ferdinand; Joseph Taylor, Mathias; Thomas Pollard, Ubaldo; Eilert Swanston, Ricardo; John Shank, Hilario; William Penn, Julio Baptista; John Thompson, Honoria; Alexander Gough, Acanthe; John Honeyman, Sophia; William Trigg, Corsica, according to the Q cast list. "[T]he unassigned roles [6 masquers, 6 servants to the queen] indicate that at least six more [actors], even assuming extensive doubling, were required" (Bentley 1984).

SR no original; transferred 8 August 1634. Q 1630 two issues; HT *The Picture, A True Hungarian History*; dramatis personae; five acts and separate scenes. The picture of the play's title "is a miniature" (Rochester 2010), a highly accomplished art form in Elizabethan, Jacobean, and Caroline England (Fumerton 1991). "Massinger ignores or reworks the typical functions of the portrait miniature as love token. The portrait is given as an instrument of control" (Obermueller 2007): "Mathias' picture is an enchanted image of his wife Sophia, which will turn black if she cuckolds him: he acquires it from a magician as a tool to police her chastity while he is away at war" (Rochester). SDs "are numerous and often very full" (E&G 1976); a trap door is suggested by *"Ricardo entering with a great noyse above, as fallen"*; he says, "Zoones have you trap doores? . . . Whither am I falne into hell?" "About 1633 Massinger had eight of his previously published plays bound together [including *The Picture*] in a single volume. Possibly he was thinking of publishing a collection of his works; possibly he wanted the volume as a gift to a patron" (Edwards 1987). The Folger owns the collection, which contains corrections/revisions in Massinger's hand.

Massinger dedicates his play to gentlemen of the Inner Temple, who enjoyed *The Picture*: "The play in the presentment found such a generall approbation, that it gave mee assurance of their favour to whose protection it is now sacred, and they have profes'd they so sincerely allow of it, and the maker, that they would have freely granted that in the publication, which for some reasons, I denide my selfe." However, the play may have been "a failure in the [commercial] theatre" (Bentley 1971).

The Pilgrim. John Fletcher. Acted October–December 1621 (Maxwell 1939) by the King's Men at the second Blackfriars. Performed also at court, 1 January 1622 (Hoy 1987a); and at Whitehall, 29 December 1622 (Adams 1917). The play "seems to have been successful" (McMullan 2004). Principal actors were Joseph Taylor, John Lowin, Nicholas Tooley, John Underwood, Robert Benfield, John Thompson, George Birch, and James Horn, according to F2. "The longest role in the play was prepared for a boy player" (Bentley 1984). In playlist of the King's Men 7 August 1641.

SR 4 September 1646 "by m^r Beamont & m^r fflesher"; 30 January 1673. B&F F1 1647 *Comedies and Tragedies*; "never printed before, and now published by the authours originall copies"; five acts and separate scenes. Prologue "to the Pilgrim" printed in "A. B.'s *Covent Garden Drollery*, 1672" (Greg 1939). Auditory effects include birdsong: "The birds sing softly," says a character; then "*Musick & birds*"; finally "*Musick afar off. Pot birds.*" "[A] prompter's note makes it clear that bird song of different kinds was procured by blowing into water through whistles of various sorts and sizes" (Ogilvie 1927). "Players could easily become adroit at imitating bird-calls themselves" (Gurr 2009d). Other sound effects include the shaking of madmen's irons: "*Shake irons within.*" Sound figures importantly in the ceremony at the altar in the final scene; there are no fewer than six SDs for music in last scene. B&F F2 1679 *Fifty Comedies and Tragedies*; "published by the authors original copies, the songs to each play being added"; *The Pilgrim, A Comedy*; list of characters; actors' names.

The Pilgrim, A Tragedy. Thomas Killigrew. Written in Paris *c.* 1645–46 (Bulman 1987) or 1647 (Randall 1995), possibly for a company of English actors serving Prince Charles there (Harbage 1930); "may have been written for the Prince of Wales's Company in Paris" (Vander Motten 2004). Although there is no evidence of production, the SDs are highly detailed. "While *The Pilgrim* deserves to be placed among Killigrew's most playable dramas . . . , it is difficult nowadays to imagine an actual production that might include the overextended comic subplot or even the persistently word-heavy discourse of the major characters" (Randall).

SR 24 October 1663. F 1663–64 *Comedies and Tragedies*; two issues; the general TP is dated 1664, separate 1663; "written in Paris . . . 1651" (but Killigrew was in Italy in 1651 [Harbage]); list of characters; five acts and separate scenes. Extensive SDs signal violence: "*Enter* Baptista *and his party, four in all;* Cosmo *runs to them, and beats down* Baptista's *sword pursuing* Sforza *and* Richardo; *who after two or three passes,* Richardo *and one of the souldiers fall, with their wounds;* Cosmo *pulls off the head, and discovers a sword-blade in his staff; they fight and are all wounded:* Baptista *falls under* Sforza, *and the souldiers are kill'd by* Cosmo." Unusual SDs include: "*The scene must present a chimney, in which she throws the letter.*"

The Pilgrimage to Parnassus. Anonymous; presumably written by a scholar at St. John's College, Cambridge. Acted at the Christmas revels 1598–99 (Leishman 1949) by students of the college (Nelson 1989). The pilgrimage "is presented as a process of gaining a social identity through learning" (Grantley 2000). "[T]wo young men determined to follow the Muses travel a route laid out by an academic map through the lands of Logic, Rhetoric, and Philosophy" (Astington 2010).

Oxford, Bodleian, MS Rawlinson D.398, fols. 20–26; no author named; list of characters on the TP; prologue and, at the close, a bid for "*plaudite*" by Studioso; five acts. SR none. First edited by Macray 1886; modern edition by Leishman 1949.

The Pilgrimage would be followed by two sequels, *1 and 2 Return to Parnassus*. "The *Parnassus Plays* . . . offer a fascinating snapshot of contemporary literary taste" (Rhodes 2004). "The Parnassus Plays tell us more about writers and their concerns than all the rest of Elizabethan drama" (Glatzer 1977). *Pilgrimage* contains a reference to Will Kemp, one of the most accomplished comic actors of the time, who would become a character in *2 The Return to Parnassus*. "The Clown scene in *Pilgrimage to Parnassus* is a premeditated attempt to give the impression of spontaneous clowning, with its dangers and embarrassments. The Clown is thrust against his will onto the stage, with nothing prepared, and is merely given a catalogue of gross antics to perform, said to be the clown's stock-in-trade, and told to improvise" (Mann 1991).

The Pinner of Wakefield. See *George a Greene*.

A Piscatory. See *Sicelides*.

Piso's Conspiracy. See *Nero*.

The Platonic Lovers, A Tragicomedy. William Davenant. Licensed for acting 16 November 1635 (Adams 1917, Edmond 1987). Commissioned by Queen Henrietta Maria (Sturgess 1987). "Presented" by the King's Men at the [second] Blackfriars, according to the Q and O TPs. Performed also at court, probably during the Christmas season, 1635–36 (*JCS*). John Lowin delivered the prologue in the 1635 revival (Gurr 2004c). "*The Platonic Lovers* failed at court, perhaps because, as Davenant has one of his 'Platonic' characters say, it was 'too masculine'" (Veevers 1989). The play "is no less than an exposé of the hypocrisy of what some called Platonic love, but what was the pretence of men of little understanding or, worse, the disguise of vicious men who concealed their evil purposes under the name of morality" (Sharpe 1987).

SR 4 February 1636; transferred 7 November 1646; 31 October 1672. Q 1636 list of characters; prologue and epilogue; five acts. O 1665 *Two Excellent Plays* (with *The Wits*). F 1673 *The Works*; "now published out of the authors originall copies." SDs enumerate stage furnishings: "*Enter . . . Rosella with tapers. A tale and night-linnen set out*"; "*Enter Theander, Eurithea, a table, stooles, and lights set out.*"

Q Prologue speaks of changing theatrical taste: "Well, I (your servant) who have labour'd heere / In buskins, and in socks, this thirty yeare, / I'th truth of my experience, could not chuse / But say, these shifts would not secure his muse: / Then straight presented to his willing feare, / How you are growne of late, harsh, and severe. / (Excuse mee that I'm bold to speake my mind / I'th darke, of what so publickly I find.) / But this hath made him mourne; I've left him now / With's limber hat, o'reshadowing his brow, / His cloke cast thus — to hinder from his eare, / The scornes and censures hee may shortly heare: / Such as shall teach, dispaire, lead him the way, / Unto a grove of cypresse, not of bay." The play "openly pandered to Henrietta Maria's *précieuse* taste for love purified from sex, though on the evidence of [Davenant's] other sex-driven plays for the Blackfriars the new concept must have been distasteful to the tongue in his cheek" (Gurr 2004c).

The Play called the Four PP. See *The Four PP.*

A Play of Love. See *Love.*

The Play of Patient Grissell. See *Patient Grissell.*

The Play of Queen Elizabeth. See *1 If You Know Not Me.*

The Play of Robin Hood. See *Robin Hood.*

The Play of the Weather. See *The Weather.*

The Play of Wit and Science. See *Wit and Science.*

The Playhouse To Be Let. William Davenant. Acted summer 1663 (Edmond 1987). "There was humorous topicality in its title, seeing that in the May previous the King's Players had abandoned their Vere Street house, on opening the new Theatre Royal in Bridges Street" (Lawrence 1927).

SR 31 October 1672. F 1683 *The Works*; "now published out of the authors originall copies"; prologue and epilogue; act 1 opens with the housekeeper and player in conversation, along with others (tire-woman and charwoman); act 2 consists of a French farce by Molière; act 3 consists of Davenant's *The History of Sir Francis Drake*; act 4 consists of *The Cruelty of the Spaniards in Peru*; act 5 features the house-keeper and player again and goes on to present "a travesty of Mrs. Katherine Philips's *La mort de Pompée*" (Bordinat & Blaydes 1981). Philips had translated Corneille's classical tragedy in 1663; it was "brilliantly staged the same season in Dublin's new Theatre Royal" (Mulvihill 1991).

The play "is an anthology of scenic possibilities, and other than rhetoric might be the substance of drama. This is the heritage of [Inigo] Jones's theater, though it is not a theater he ever knew or contemplated, and it derives from the adaptation of masque stages to the production of plays" (Orgel 2002).

A Pleasant and Merry Humor of a Rogue. William Cavendish. Written probably between *c.* 1655 and 1660 (Needham 1933); 1658 (*AED 3*). It "appears to have been written in the last years of the Commonwealth" (Potter 1981).

Nottingham, UK, University of Nottingham, Portland Collection, Hallward Library, MS PwV 24, fols. 18–31 (formerly at Welbeck Abbey); written in the author's hand; epilogue (by the Rogue) followed by a song; eleven numbered scenes. Ample SDs: *"Enter the Roge agen, peepinge & goinge softlye, lookinge aboute him wether the Citisen bee ther"*; *"Enter the Roge alone In his perfumers habitt."* SR 12 February 1677. First transcribed by Needham; edited by Hulse 1996.

The entertainment "may perhaps be considered as a set of variations on the theme of Autolycus [in Shakespeare's *Winter's Tale*]" (Needham). The play "is little more than a series of drolls linked by the figure of the rogue himself" (Potter).

A Pleasant Comedy of Love and Fortune. See *The Rare Triumphs of Love and Fortune.*

A Pleasant Comedy of the Gentle Craft. See *The Shoemaker's Holiday.*

A Pleasant Comedy Showing the Contention between Liberality and Prodigality. See *Liberality and Prodigality.*

A Pleasant Conceited Comedy called Love's Labor's Lost. See *Love's Labor's Lost.*

The Pleasant History of The Two Angry Women of Abingdon. See *The Two Angry Women.*

Ploutophthalmia Ploutogamia. See *Hey for Honesty.*

Poëtaster, or The Arraignment. Ben Jonson. Acted September-October 1601 (Cain 1995) or "in the winter of 1601" (Donaldson 2011). "Sundry times privately acted" by the Children of the Queen's Chapel at the [second] Blackfriars, according to the Q TP. Possibly also performed at the Middle Temple, Christmas 1601–02. Principal actors were Nathan Field, John Underwood, Salomon Pavy, Thomas Day, Thomas Marton, and William Ostler, according to F1.

SR 21 December 1601; transferred 10 April 1627; 30 May 1627; 6 November 1628; 6 December 1630; 4 March 1639; 22 July 1644. Q 1602 *Poetaster, or The Arraignment*; *poetaster* "means 'second-rate poet'" (Duncan-Jones 2011); list of characters; prologue; five acts and separate scenes. Contrary to theatrical custom, the play begins with a personified (female) figure, Livor (Envy), arising through a trap door and addressing the audience before Prologue arrives; this constitutes "a pre-prologue prologue" (Schneider 2011); armed Prologue "wears a 'forc't defense' against his potentially inimical audience" (Stern 2009c). In lieu of an epilogue, Jonson presents an address to the reader: "Here (reader) in place of the epilogue was meant to thee an apology from the author, with his reasons for the publishing of this booke: but (since he is no lesse restrain'd, then thou depriv'd of it, by authoritie) hee praies thee to thinke charitably of what thou hast read, till thou maist heare him speake what hee hath written." *Poetaster*, "Jonson's first play set in the reign of Tiberius . . . anticipate[s] *Sejanus* (published 1605) in using annotations in the printed text" (Jowett 1993). Staging may have used a locality board: Envy "exclaims as she enters: 'The scene is, ha! / Rome? Rome? And Rome?' This seems clearly provoked by her reading separate locality boards above the two stage doors and the curtains concealing the middle door, and so discovering that the scene is not London, where she had expected it to be" (Reynolds 1967). F1 1616 *The Works*; *Poëtaster, or His Arraignment, A Comical Satire*; "acted in the yeere 1601"; prologue. The *apologeticall dialogue* (of Nasutus, Polyposus, and Author), "which was only once spoken upon the stage, and all the answere I ever gave, to sundry impotent libells then cast out (and some yet remayning) against me, and this play," was "added some time after the first performance, and was not originally part of the play" (Cain); Jonson himself may have played the Author (Barton 1984). F1 includes "four lengthy passages of dialogue not previously printed" (Kidnie 2000a). F2 1640 vol. 1. "The play is significantly different in each printed version" (Kidnie).

Jonson's Q prologue, spoken by an actor wearing a distinctive costume as "armed," strikes a defensive posture: "If any muse why I salute the stage, / An armed Prologue; know, 't is a dangerous age: / Wherein, who writes, had neede present his scenes / Fortie fold proofe against the conjuring meanes / Of base detractors, and illiterate apes, / That fill up roomes in faire and formall shapes. / 'Gainst these, have we put on this forc't defense: / Whereof the allegorie and hid sense / Is, that a well erected confidence / Can fright their pride, and laugh their follie hence." In F1 Jonson dedicates his work to Richard Martin, "who prevented the complete suppression of the play" (Clare 1999); the play was apparently "taken as defamatory" (Jowett 1993), but Martin "saved Jonson from any legal proceedings" (Sanders 1998b). *Poetaster*, originally entitled *The Arraignment*, contributes to the poetomachia, or "Poet's Quarrel" (Riggs 1989): in the characters of Crispinus and Demetrius, Jonson lampoons Marston and Dekker "and furthermore makes personal and specific insults against the players they are involved with" (Steggle 1998); "the idiotic, effeminate Crispinus is forced to vomit up his Marstonian fustian" (Knowles 2004). Demetrius represents Dekker, "a hack writer, 'a dresser of plays about the town,' one who will slander any man for money" (Twyning 2004).

The Politic Father. See *The Brothers.*

The Politician, A Tragedy. James Shirley. No license for acting exists. Possibly performed by Ogilby's Men at the Werburgh Street theater, Dublin. "Presented at Salisbury Court" by Queen Henrietta Maria's Men, according to the Q TP, 1639–40 (Fehrenbach 1980).

SR 9 September 1653. Q and O 1655 list of characters with "small characters [i.e., descriptions] of the persons"; five acts. Publication in O format permits buyers to bind this play with the 1652–53 collection *Six New Plays. The Politician* and *The Gentleman of Venice* "were issued at the same time by Humphrey Moseley . . . and the two octavo editions are frequently found together" (*JCS*). Ample SDs describe onstage violence: "*As the Prince is going forth, a pistoll is discharged within, he falls*"; "*He [Gotharus] bloodies himself with* Suenos *blood, and falls down as dead.*"

Shirley's dedication defends the stage: "Though the severity of the times took away those dramatique recreations (whose language so much glorified the English scene) and perhaps looking at some abuses of the common theaters, which were not so happily purg'd from scurrility, and under-wit, (the onely entertainment of vulgar capacities) they have outed the more noble and ingenious actions of the eminent stages; the rage yet hath not been epidemicall, there are left many lovers of this exiled posie, who are great masters of reason, and that dare conscientiously own this musicall part of humane learning, when it is presented without the staines of impudence and profanation."

The Poor Man's Comfort, A Tragicomedy. Robert Daborne [spelled Dauborne on the QTP]. "Daborne may have composed the play by 1614 or 1615, if not as early as 1610, but at least before 1618" (Ioppolo 2006). Acted at the Red Bull "by Queen Anne's company some time between 1615 and 1617 and, perhaps, after 1617 at Beeston's Cockpit in Drury Lane" (Vitkus 2000). "Divers times acted . . . with great applause" at the Phoenix, according to the Q TP, by an unidentified company, after 1620. The names of two actors are recorded in Q: Sands and Ellis (probably Thomas Sands and Ellis Bedowe).

London, BL, Egerton MS 1994, fols. 268–92, ed. Palmer 1954; "not a playhouse copy" (Palmer); although unnamed on the TP, the author's identity is recorded on the last folio; slightly damaged; one dumb show; "preserves a few lines not in the quarto" (Greg 1931); five acts. The name "P. Massam" is written on the last leaf, perhaps the scribe. SDs "are fairly full and of a rather theatrical type" (Greg). MS collated by Swaen in his 1899 edition of Q. SR 20 June 1655; transferred 16 July 1662. Q 1655 list of characters; prologue by E. M., perhaps Edward May (Greg 1939, Kingsley-Smith 2005).

Not published until 1655, the play involves "Lucius, a Thessalian nobleman clad as a shepherd, who fled into Arcadia 'when the King was overthrowne'"; the "poor man of the title proves to be Gisbert, a kindly old shepherd who has provided Lucius, 'a poor souldier in these wars' . . . with both a refuge and the opportunity to woo and wed his beautiful daughter"; eventually "the restored and virtuous King makes the old shepherd his Chief Justice. One surely may see here an aristocracy that has strayed and a strikingly renewed and comforting coalition of a good king and the humblest of his subjects" (Randall 1995).

Preist the Barber, Sweetball his Man. Anonymous. Acted at Cambridge University, 1611 (Gossett & Berger 1988), presumably by students of a college. Probably performed "soon after 6–7 February 1611" in Trinity College (Nelson 1989). "The play is short, has no female roles and few if any requirements for production: everything about it indicates that it is an entertainment for members of a Cambridge College" (Gossett & Berger).

Washington, Folger, MS J.a.2, fols. 48–49; no separate TP; no author named; conventional bid for applause at end; not divided. Minimal SDs. First edited by Gossett & Berger.

A *sweetball* is "a pomander worn to ward off infection" (Bowers 1959).

A Pretty and Merry Interlude called The Disobedient Child. See *The Disobedient Child*.

A Pretty Interlude called Nice Wanton. See *Nice Wanton*.

A Pretty New Interlude both Pithy and Pleasant of the Story of King Darius. See *King Darius*.

A Prince in Conceit. A droll based upon several scenes in James Shirley's *The Opportunity* and performed in the 1640s and 50s. "This droll is one of a group, including also *Invisible Smirk*, *The Bubble*, and perhaps *The Imperick*, which is notable for free and effective rehandling of dialogue and dramatic structure. It is quite possible that these pieces were abridged by a single distinct droll-maker, whose wit, ingenuity, and dramatic sense are not discernible in the other drolls" (Elson 1932).

Published in *1 The Wits, or Sport upon Sport* (O 1662 [two issues] and 1672); RT *The Humors of A Prince in Conceit*; argument; list of characters.

The Prince of Prig's Revels. J. S. A play-pamphlet written between 3 September and 11 November 1651 (*JCS*). Possibly acted *c.* autumn 1651 (Randall 1995). "[O]ne of a number of pamphlets inspired by the highwayman James Hind" (Potter 1981). The *OED* defines "prig" as meaning a thief.

SR none. Q 1651 *An Excellent Comedy called The Prince of Prig's Revels, or The Practices of That Grand Thief Captain James Hind, Relating Divers of His Pranks and Exploits*; "repleat with various conceits, and Tarltonian mirth, suitable to the subject"; "never heretofore published by any"; RT *Hind's Pranks*; author's initials on TP; each act begins with an argument (i.e. précis); list of characters; prologue and epilogue; five acts, each of which enacts "an anecdote from the hero's life" (Potter). Ample SDs: "*Enter* Hind *in rich apparel,* Furbo, Latro, Spolario *in costly liveries, bare-headed, attending him.*" The argument of act 3 gives the flavor of this entertainment: "Hind and his comrades disguising themselves in devil's habits, terrifie the country people, and rob an alderman of the City of York."

The address to the reader affirms the salutary nature of drama: the purpose of "tragedians and commedians of old was to magnifie virtue, and to depress vice; and you may observe throughout the *Works* of incomparable Johnson, excellent Shakespear, and elegant Fletcher, &c. they (however vituperated by some streight-laced brethren not capable of their sublimity) aim at no other end: my drift is the same in the composure of this comedy."

The Princess, or Love at First Sight, A Tragicomedy. Thomas Killigrew. "Most likely performed after the theaters reopened on 2 October 1637, possibly by the King's Men" (Bulman 1987) at the second Blackfriars.

SR 4 September 1646; 24 October 1663; 30 January 1673. F 1663–64 *Comedies and Tragedies*; two issues; the general TP is dated 1664, separate 1663; "written in Naples"; dramatis personae; five acts and separate scenes. Extraordinary onstage violence: "Bragadine *shoots*, Virgil *puts his hand to his eye, with a bloody spunge and the blood runs down.* Facertes *draws his sword, and takes him in his arms*"; "Virgilius . . . *runs his sword into the* Baud, *and kills her, she squeekes.*"

"As Killigrew's annotated copy of his *Comedies and Tragedies* (1664) preserved in the library of Worcester College, Oxford, demonstrates, he was ambitious enough to prepare his own plays for production on the new, scenic [Restoration] stage" (Vander Motten 2004).

The Prisoners, A Tragicomedy. Thomas Killigrew. Probably acted 1635 (Bulman 1987) by Queen Henrietta Maria's Men at the Phoenix, according to the D TP. The play "may have been a successful bid for royal favour" (Vander Motten 2004).

SR 2 April 1640 *a tragedy called The Prisoner*; 29 June 1660. D 1640–41 *The Prisoners and Claracilla, Two Tragicomedies*; general TP dated 1641, separate 1640; dramatis personae; five acts and separate scenes. F 1663–64 *Comedies and Tragedies*; two issues; the separate TP dated 1663 in some copies, 1664 in others; "written . . . in London." Extensive SDs. Special effects include "*The storm begins in the scene*"; in next scene "*Storm*" and "*Storm blows high.*" Unusual staging involves a character making a fire "*on the stage*" so that "any wretch unfortunate" may see the fire and find comfort.

A prefatory poem by William Cartwright in D pays tribute to the playwright: "Manners, and men, transcrib'd, customes express'd, / The rules, and lawes dramatique not transgress'd; / The points of place, and time, observ'd, and hit; / The words to things, and things to persons fit; / The persons constant to themselves throughout; / The machin[e] turning free, not forc'd about; / As wheeles by wheeles, part mov'd, and urg'd by part; / And choyce materials workt with choycer art; / Those, though at last begg'd from long sweate & toyle, / Fruits of the forge, the anvil, and the file, / Snatch reverence from our judgements; and we doe / Admire those raptures with new raptures too."

The Proctor and Parator, Their Mourning, or The Lamentation of the Doctors Commons for Their Downfall, Being a True Dialogue Relating the Fearful Abuses and Exorbitancies of Those Spiritual Courts, under the Names of Sponge the Proctor and Hunter the Parator. Richard Overton (Wolfe 1958). ?Acted 1639. A "satirical dialogue between Sponge the proctor and Hunter the parator" (Wolfe). This "sounds very close to the actual play staged by the King's Company at the Red Bull in 1639, and suppressed by the Privy Council as 'a scandalous and libellous [play]'" (Heinemann 1980).

Q 1641 HT *The Parator and the Proctor*; no author named; not divided. The TP woodcut shows a man seated at table, a standing man facing him, and a standing woman.

This belongs to a group of play-pamphlets "in which ecclesiastical officials, lazy priests and monopolists lament the decay of their fortunes" (Butler 1984a).

1 Promos and Cassandra. George Whetstone. Written 1578 (Chambers 1923). The play "was certainly written with performance in mind, perhaps at one of the Inns" (Potter 2012), but the playwright in 1582 describes it as "yet never presented upon stage." "The allusions to metropolitan mayoral ceremonials and the dedication of the text to William Fleetwood, Recorder of London, suggest civic auspices in the capital" (Walker 1998). Richard Jones, the publisher, writes of the difference between performance and print: "if by chaunce, thou light of some speache that seemeth dark, consider of it with judgement, before thou condemne the worke: for in many places he is driven, both to praise, and blame, with one breath, which in readinge wil seeme hard, & in action, appeare plaine."

SR 31 July 1578. Q 1578 *The Right Excellent and Famous History of Promos and Cassandra*; *Parts 1* and *2* printed as one book (continuous register); "devided into two commicall discourses"; argument; "no dumb shows proper, but various pantomimic scenes" (Mehl 1965); concludes with Cassandra's song; five acts and separate scenes. Pragmatic SDs include "*Promos, Mayor, Shirife, sword bearer: one with a bunche of keyes*"; "Phallax *readeth the Kinges letters patents, which must be fayre written in parchment, with some great counterfeat zeale*"; "*The* Hangman, *with a greate many ropes abought his necke.*" A SD "*Boy in the house*" may refer to a stage structure. Grotesque staging includes "Gaylar, *with a dead mans head in a charger.*"

In his dedication Whetstone contrasts his drama with that of contemporaries, abroad and at home, and he complains of English dramatic conventions: "at this daye, the *Italian* is so lascivious in his commedies, that honest hearers are greeved at his actions: the *Frenchman* and *Spaniarde* folowes the Italians humor: the *Germaine* is too holye: for he presentes on everye common stage, what preachers should pronounce in pulpets. The *Englishman* in this quallitie, is most vaine, indiscreete, and out of order: he fyrst groundes his worke, on impossibilities: then in three howers ronnes he throwe the worlde: marryes, gets children, makes children men, men to conquer kingdomes, murder monsters, and bringeth gods from heaven, and fetcheth divels from hel. And (that which is worst) their ground is not so unperfect, as their workinge indiscreete: not waying, so the people laugh, though they laugh them (for theyr follyes) to scorne: many tymes (to make mirthe) they make a clowne companion with a kinge: in theyr grave counsels, they allow the advice of fooles: yea they use one order of speach for all persons: a grose *indecorum*, for a crowe, wyll yll counterfet the nightingales sweete voice: even so, affected speeche doth misbecome a clowne." "Whetstone attacks dramatists who allow 'a clown' to use 'affected speech,' and (like a Vice) to offer counsel to a king. Decorum requires that characters must conform to type, and that 'clowns should speak disorderly'" (Wiles 1987).

2 Promos and Cassandra. Data as for *Part 1*. Entitled *The Second Part of the Famous History of Promos and Cassandra*. Printed with *Part 1* as a single book, "devided into two commicall discourses," according to the general TP. "The necessity for making a two-part play of this story was possibly occasioned by Whetstone's very expansive and minutely episodic narrative style. He uses a very large number of characters, many of whom appear only briefly and several only once" (Grantley 2004).

The SDs call for a temporary structure: "*Five or sixe, the one halfe men, the other women, neare unto the musick, singing on some stage, erected from the ground.*" Unusual staging includes: "*Two men, apparrelled lyke greene men at the mayors feast, with clubbes of fyre worke.*"

Promos and Cassandra is "the first tragical comedy in England to show a strong Italian influence" (Herrick 1955). "The midcentury play that perhaps best adumbrates later tragicomedy (though it does not use this title) while retaining an explicitly Christian orientation" is *Promos and Cassandra* (Foster 2004).

The Prophetess. John Fletcher and Philip Massinger. Licensed for acting 14 May 1622 (Adams 1917). Acted by the King's Men at the second Globe. Revived 21 July 1629, a benefit for Henry Herbert (Bawcutt 1996). Principal actors were John Lowin, Joseph Taylor, Robert Benfield, Nicholas Tooley, John Shank, Richard Sharp, George Birch, and Thomas Holcomb, according to F2. This is the only play by Beaumont and Fletcher that mentions John Shank, who joined the company after Robert Armin's retirement, as a principal actor; he "likely" played Geta, the clown (Hornback 2009b). In playlist of King's Men 7 August 1641.

SR 4 September 1646; 30 January 1673. B&F F1 1647 *Comedies and Tragedies*; "never printed before, and now published by the authours originall copies"; elaborate description of a dumb show explained by chorus; chorus reappears later in 4 and 5 to summarize offstage action; five acts and separate scenes. "The spectator at a performance of *The Prophetess* would no doubt have left the theatre talking about the special effects" (McDonald 1985); these include the entry of "*a spirit from the well*" (presumably through a trap); "*thunder and lightning*"; "*a hand with a [thunder]bolt appears above*"; "*Enter Delphia and Drusilla in a throne drawn by dragons.*" In the dumb show "Delphia *raises a mist*," which would be "[e]ffected by a cloud of smoke emerging from a stage trap" (Lawrence 1912a), though Dessen & Thomson 1999 are uncertain whether a mist was actually simulated.

Sound effects include *"Soft musick"*; *"Loud musick"*; *"Musick from the spheres"* [i.e., above]; *"Musicke belowe"*; music accompanying the dance of a She-devil, and a *"dance of shepherds and shepherdesses."* B&F F2 1679 *Fifty Comedies and Tragedies*; "published by the authors original copies, the songs to each play being added"; *The Prophetess, A Tragical History*; list of characters; actors' names.

Pugna Animi. See *De Pugna Animi.*

The Puritan, or The Widow of Watling Street. Thomas Middleton (Lake 1973). Acted January-June 1606 (Lake 1975a); 1607 (Gurr 2009d). By Paul's Boys, according to the Q TP, at Paul's playhouse.

SR 6 August 1607 the comedie of *the Puritan Widowe.* Q 1607 *The Puritan, or The Widow of Watling Street*; RT *The Puritan Widow*; "written by W. S." [?Wentworth Smith or ?William Shakespeare]; ascribed to Shakespeare in Archer's 1656 catalogue and in Kirkman's; five acts. Wonderfully detailed SDs: *"Enter at one doore Corporall* Oth, *a vaine-glorious fellow, and at the other, three of the Widow Puritaines servingmen,* Nicholas Saint-Tantlings, Simon Saint-Mary-Overies, *and* Frailtie *in black scurvie mourning coates, and bookes at their girdles, as coming from church."* In one scene "a Puritan widow lavish[es] kisses and tears upon her dead husband's portrait": *"Drawing out her husbands picture."* The playwright "makes a sly commentary on Puritan hypocrisy: not only does the widow betray a histrionic tendency rather than constancy or restrained emotion, but also an iconophilia, which the Puritans, among other religious radicals, opposed" (Tassi 2005). Action includes "a fake conjuration of demons" by con men, a "satire of Puritan fascination with uncanny effects by exposing them as nothing more than theatrical illusion" (Cox 2000). Shakespeare F3 1664 second issue; "the third impression. And unto this impression is added seven playes never before printed in folio"; list of characters (at end). The RT in Q and F3 is *The Puritan Widow*, which also appears on the F3 general TP. F4 1685 "the fourth edition"; two issues. The attribution to Shakespeare is now "universally rejected"; Lake 1975a argues for Middleton's authorship; and Jackson 1979 maintains that the resemblance of "linguistic features between *The Puritan* and Middleton's plays becomes obvious," but Hope 1994 finds Middleton's authorship doubtful.

The performance of this play about hypocritical puritans may have brought about the closure of Paul's playhouse (Gair 1982). The publication of Q "became the pretext for a blistering sermon from William Crashawe, preached at Paul's Cross on St. Valentine's Day, 1608" (Thomson 1992a). What Middleton had done was to invent "a plot that associated Catholic practices with Puritan practices. This technique for demonizing both groups had been popular with the conformist church establishment and had been adopted by James I, who disliked the challenges that Puritan reform interests posed to hierarchy" (Hamilton 2007).

The Puritan Widow. See *The Puritan, or The Widow of Watling Street.*

Q

The Queen and Concubine, A Comedy. Richard Brome. Probably acted summer 1635 (Steggle 2004b) by the King's Revels Company at the Salisbury Court playhouse. Possibly also performed "at court early in 1636" (Butler 1984b). Henry Herbert's office-book lists *A Queen and No Queen*, licensed 1639, possibly the same play (*JCS*).

SR none. O 1658–59 *Five New Plays* (with *The English Moor, The Lovesick Court, The New Academy, The Weeding of the Covent Garden*); two issues; separate TP dated 1659; separately paginated; "meant to be issued separately in advance of the collection," but was actually printed later (Greg 1939); dramatis personae; detailed descriptions of two dumb shows; epilogue; five acts and separate scenes. Sound effects include fowl: "*Birds chirp.*" A character's question suggests the importance of music: "What musick had the court compar'd to this?"

Brome's address to the reader of *Five New Plays* denies a connection between the matter of the play and political turmoil in England: "This *Queen* is a meer stranger to our island; her scene is Sicily, the persons and action taste nothing of England." But the play "obliquely but pointedly evoke[s] some of the constitutional anxieties posed by King Charles's personal rule" (Butler 2004b).

Queen Elizabeth's Troubles. See *2 If You Know Not Me, You Know Nobody.*

The Queen of Aragon, A Tragicomedy. William Habington. Acted 9 April 1640 (Burner 1988), according to Herbert, by the Earl of Pembroke's "servants out of his own family, and [at] his charge in the cloathes and sceanes [i.e., scenery], which were very riche and curious," according to the Master of the Revels, in the Great Hall at Whitehall; the actors were apparently amateurs (Orrell 1985); the scenery was designed "evidently by [William] Webb as well as by [Inigo] Jones" (Orrell). "The king and queene commended the generall entertaynment, as very well acted, and well set out" (Adams 1917). (Revels documents refer to the play as *Cleodora, Queen of Aragon*.) Performed at court with painted scenery; three set designs, including a fortified town and a courtyard, survive (Southern 1952, Freehafer 1971). "Allowed" to the King's Men 1640, according to Revels documents (Bawcutt 1996) and performed also by that company at the second Blackfriars, 11 April 1640. "It is not coincidental that plays like *The Royal Slave* and *The Queen of Aragon* . . . had stage sets by Inigo Jones, whose spectacular scenes were designed to evoke just the sense of wonder that is suggested by the text" (Veevers 1989).

SR 2 April 1640. F 1640 two issues; no author named but Kirkman's 1661 catalogue identifies Habington as the playwright; list of characters; prologue and epilogue at court; prologue and epilogue "at the Fryers"; two songs printed before the epilogues; five acts. Prologue at Blackfriars seems to anticipate a complaint by playgoers: "Ere we begin, that no man may repent / Two shillings and his time; the author sent / The prologue, with the errors of his play, / That who will, may take his money and away." "The implied joke of this address separates the actual audience from those who would be so crass as actually to calculate the value of money and time" (McLuskie 2005). SDs suggest the use of painted scenery: *"first sceane a shutter of a fortified towne & a campe a farr off"* (Southern 1952).

Habington argues "a radically new, and potentially revolutionary, understanding of the basis of government which anticipates (astonishingly) that distinction between *power* and *authority* which would enter the literature of political controversy only for the first time in the 1640s" (Butler 1984b). Habington manages to conflate the "love dilemmas" fashionable in courtly drama and "dilemmas of State" (Veevers).

The Queen of Corinth. John Fletcher (who "probably contributed only act II" [McMullan 2004]), Philip Massinger, and Nathan Field (Hoy 1959), who "composed Acts 3 and 4" (Turner 1987). Acted 1616–17 (E&G 1976) by the King's Men at the second Blackfriars/second Globe. Principal actors were Richard Burbage, Henry Condell, Nathan Field, John Lowin, John Underwood, Thomas Pollard, Nicholas Tooley, and Thomas Holcomb, according to F2. In playlist of King's Men 7 August 1641.

SR 4 September 1646 "by m^r Beamont & m^r fflesher"; 30 January 1673. B&F F1 1647 *Comedies and Tragedies*; "never printed before, and now published by the authours originall copies"; detailed description of a dumb show, "summarizing an important part of the plot" (Mehl 1965); five acts and separate scenes. Auditory effects include the sound of horses: "Horses, we are discry'd." The most shocking staging involves the rape of Merione by Theanor in Vesta's temple. "She begs marriage of her vizored assailant" (Gossett 1988): then *"Enter six disguis'd, singing and dancing to a horrid musick, and sprinkling water on her face."* This stage action suggests "a ritual sacrifice of virginity, a demonic parody of a religious ceremony" (Bamford 1999). The disguised figures "look like furies" (Gossett). Later Theanor rapes Merione a second time, though he does't know the true identity of his victim. In the tragicomic denouement Theanor marries the twice-raped Merione. "Here, more clearly than in any other Jacobean play, rape emerges starkly as a function of male relationships, female chastity is a function of male property, and the victim of rape absorbs the guilt" (Bamford). B&F F2 1679 *Fifty Comedies and Tragedies*; "published by the authors original copies, the songs to each play being added"; *The Queen of Corinth, A Tragicomedy*; list of characters; actors' names.

This play, "best known today for its appalling sexual politics and its treatment of rape" (Perry 2006a), "has one of the most sensational plots in all English tragicomedy" (Herrick 1955).

The Queen of Corsica, A Tragedy. Francis Jaques; the play "conveys the feeling of alert amateur work" (Randall 1995). "Anno Dom[ini]: 1642," according to the MS

TP. No record of production, but very detailed SDs: *"On a sodayne in a kinde of noyse like a wynde, the dores clattering, the tombstone flies open, and a great light appears."*

London, BL, Lansdowne MS 807, fols. 2–28; in the author's hand (Janzen & Woudhuysen 1989); some fols. illegible because of ink bleeding through; evidence of revision; dramatis personae; no prologue; an inserted slip contains eighteen lines of poetry—"it notably improves the text" (Leech 1947); the word "epilogue" appears at end but the text is missing; five acts and separate scenes. The MS was "written up by a scribe, perhaps for private performance, perhaps for reading" (Stern 2009c). The most interesting (and unexplained) SD is this: when Archaea and Florimond arrive at a temple and "are presented to the image of Hymen, it sweats blood" (Leech). SR none. First edited by Janzen & Woudhuysen 1989.

The MS is dated in the year that the theaters closed, and the dialogue considers such matters as the qualities that befit a king.

The Queen, or The Excellency of Her Sex. John Ford (Bang 1906, Sherman 1908). Probably acted in the 1620s at undetermined venue, perhaps "between 1618 and 1625" (Dawson 2007) or 1624–33 (Orbison 1968). "There are no substantive indications as to the probable date of *The Queen*"; "The record is equally blank about its place of performance (if any) and the company that owned it" (Neill 2004).

SR none. Q 1653 "an excellent old play found out by a person of honour, and given to the publisher [Alexander Gough]"; no author named; list of characters; five acts. Ford's play "is based" on an earlier work by Gervase Markham and Lewis Machin; "Ford reconfigures the assumptions about gender, power, and identity evident in Markham's *The Dumbe Knight*, transforming a highly sexist play into one that, as its subtitle suggests, contains a defence of women"; "[r]ather than supporting a critique of female government, misogyny is thus depicted by Ford as a destructive and delusional mental illness, grounded on fears of sexuality and requiring the aid of a good doctor" (Dawson).

A prefatory poem by Edmond Rookwood evokes the hostility toward drama that issued in the closing of the theaters in 1642; he defends the stage against detractors: "Are stages hurtful for the ill they teach, / And needless for the good? Which pulpits preach: / Then sports are hurtful, for the time they lose, / And needless to the good, which labour does. / Permit 'm both; or if you will allow / The minde no hawke, leave yours, and go to plough." Another prefatory poem, by R. C., compliments Alexander Gough and bitterly laments the loss of the theaters: "Is it unlawfull since the stage is down / To make the press act: where no ladies swoune / At the red coates intrusion: none are strip't; / No Hystriomastix has the copy whip't / No man d'on women's cloth's: the guiltles presse / Weares its own innocent garments: its owne dresse, / Such as free nature made it: Let it come / Forth Midwife *Goughe* [the publisher], securely; and if some / Like not the make or beautie of the play / Bear witnes to 't and confidently say / Such a relict as once the stage did own, / Ingenuous reader, merits to be known." A third poem, by T. C., asks: "How in the next age will our youth lament / The loss of wit, condem'd to banishment. / Wit that the duller rout despise, 'cause they / Miss it in what their zealous priests display: / For priests in melancholy zeal admit / Onely a grave formality for wit; / And would have those that govern us comply / And cherish their fallacious tyranny." "Such prefatory materials constitute a kind of interface between the private act of play-reading and the political exigencies which have forced previously performed drama into the closet. In this context, play-reading continues to be an activity imbued with the significance of civic engagement" (Straznicky 1995).

The Queen's Arcadia, A Pastoral Tragicomedy. Samuel Daniel. "Presented to her majesty and her ladies, by the University [students] of Oxford in Christe Church, in [30 (Rees 1964)] August 1605," according to Q2, before Queen Anne and Prince Henry, probably in the great hall; "the auditorium set up in the hall in Christ Church was designed by Inigo Jones" (Pitcher 2004). John Chamberlain called this pastoral "very excellent." An anonymous writer reports of the original performance: "I was not there present, but by report it was well acted and greatly applauded" (Greg 1906). Originally entitled *Arcadia Reformed*; published as *The Queen's Arcadia*. "Daniel seems to have considered [Queen] Anne to be its most important audience, prefacing the published version with a dedication to her and renaming it accordingly" (Perry 1997).

SR 26 November 1605; transferred 19 August 1635. Q1 1606 no author named; dedicated to the queen; list of characters; five acts and separate scenes. O 1607 *Certain Small Works* (with *Cleopatra, Philotas*); "corrected and augmented"; dedication omitted. D 1611 *Certain Small Works* (with *Cleopatra, Philotas*); "corrected and augmented" but this third edition "ignores the revisions of the 1607 edition" (Donno 1993); two issues; list of characters; dedication to the queen restored. Q2 1623 *The Whole Works* (with *Cleopatra, Hymen's Triumph, Philotas*); "lacks the revisions" of the 1607 edition (Donno). 1623 *Whole Works* begins with dedication to Prince Charles by John Daniel (brother of Samuel). In 1635 "some copies of this drama portion of the *Whole Works* were reissued, with a new title page, as a set of 'Dramaticke poems'" (Pitcher 2005).

"The first attempt in English to imitate the Italian pastoral drama" (Harner 1987), the play makes "extensive use of Tasso and Guarini" (Pigman 2010). Daniel's drama explores "female subjectivity, and the ways women express, or are inhibited from expressing, their feelings. This feature aligns Daniel's drama with the Jacobean pastoral tragicomedy of Lady Mary Wroth, *Love's Victory* (c. 1620), and with Walter Montagu's Caroline pastoral, *The Shepherds' Paradise*" (Tomlinson 2005). But the play culminates "on a note of moral severity worlds away from the romantic episodes culled from the Italians" (Rees 1964).

The Queen's Exchange, A Comedy. Richard Brome. "Acted with generall applause" by the King's Men at the [second] Blackfriars, according to the TP; "usually dated *c.* 1631, though conceivably later" (Butler 2004b). Like many another TP, this one cannot be trusted; the stationer's address to the reader seems to contradict it: "when [the play] 'twas written, or where acted, I know not." The play "could well have belonged to some other company" when it was first performed (Butler 2004b). "It is known that eighteen months before July 1635, that is, around January 1634, Brome was working for [Prince] Charles's men at the Red Bull Theatre" (Steggle 2004b).

SR 20 November 1656. Q 1657 list of characters; prologue; five acts and separate scenes. The play "opens with confused sounds of shouting, mingled with strains of music and the pealing of bells, all signs and tokens of the rejoicing over the King's nuptials" (Lawrence 1935). A SD indicates that an "engine" is used "to lower and then to lift one of the characters through the trap door to and from the space under the stage" (Astington 1985). Staging involves the impersonation of devils. "When devil costumes are used as a disguise . . . those who use them are comic tradesmen, and only a servant is taken in by the disguise; a noble lady who also sees the 'devils' knows at once that they are fake" (Cox 2000). Paintings figure onstage when "both Queen Bertha and Osric fall in love via portraits" (Rochester 2010). Reissued 1661 with a new title, *The Royal Exchange*, "a fraudulent attempt to sell the remaining sheets of the 1657 edition" (*JCS*).

The play, which "draws on the period of history between the end of Celtic Britain and before the arrival of the Normans, a period relatively little represented on the English stage," seems to "invite application to contemporary politics" (Steggle); considered "from a national perspective, it is clear that the proposed union of the two kingdoms in this play is at one level at least open to reading as an allegorical representation of the 'union of the crowns' of England and Scotland thirty years before the play was written" (Steggle).

The Queen's Masque. See *Love's Mistress.*

R

The Raging Turk, or Bajazet the Second, A Tragedy. Thomas Goffe. Acted "probably in the early 1620s" (White 1998) or *c.* 1613–18 (Elliott 1997). By students of Christ Church, Oxford, according to the Q TP, probably in the great hall.

Nuneaton, UK, Arbury Hall, MS A415; microfilm in Warwick, UK, Warwickshire County Record Office, M.I. 351/5/A.415/item 22; entitled *Bajazet*; written in ten hands one of which is John Newdigate's (Howard-Hill 1988); no separate TP; evidence of correction; much of the MS is difficult to read because of ink bleeding through the pages; epilogue; dumb shows; five acts and separate scenes. SR 7 September 1631 *The Tragedy of Bajazet the second or the rageing Turke*; transferred 7 November 1646 *Bajazett the Rageing Turke.* Q 1631 *The Raging Turk, or Bajazet the Second, A Tragedy*; two issues; list of characters; description of dumb shows; five acts and separate scenes. Staging includes a procession of ghosts "*with each a sword and burning taper, led in by* Nemesis, *with a sword*"; they "*encompasse Bajazet in his bed.*" After his death, the ghosts "*beare him out.*" Considerable onstage violence, with appropriate sound effects: "*Drums sounding, a confused noyse, with clashing of armour.*" O 1656 *Three Excellent Tragedies* (with *The Courageous Turk* and *Orestes*); "the second edition, carefully corrected by a friend of the authors," according to the general TP; continuous register and pagination.

The publisher's Q dedication explains that the MS of this play and of *The Courageous Turk* "came lately to my hands; he that gave them birth, because they were his *nugae*, or rather recreations to his more serious and divine studies, out of a nice modesty (as I have learnt) allowed them scarce private fostering. But I, by the consent of his especiall friend, in that they shew him rather *omnium scenarum homo* to his glory then disparagement: have published them, and doe tender this to your most safe protection."

Raguaillo D'Oceano [The Judgment of Oceanus]. Mildmay Fane. "Written & prepared to be acted in An[no] 1640" according to the MS TP. "The words 'prepared to be acted' are characteristic phraseology of the day, and do not signify that the performance failed to take place" (Harbage 1936). Probably acted at Fane's estate, Apethorpe, Northamptonshire, by members of the family and household.

London, BL, Additional MS 34221, fols. 107–23; no author named on the TP; chorus; three epilogues; divided into fifteen "entries." The SDs are extensive, costumes carefully described: "Three pages of the manuscript are given up to descriptions of the costumes worn by the fourteen nations and their rivers. These are quite detailed, and could have been written only by an author visualising production" (Leech 1938). Fane anticipates the use of painted scenery: "*A draweinge traverse waved like the sea & some sharpe heads of rockes peepeing through the waves.*" Above the entryways leading onto the stage are painted designations of locale: "*Over the doore he comes out att Gibralter written.*" First edited by Leech 1938.

"Fane [second earl of Westmorland] must have given considerable attention to preparing an area in his home for the production of his plays. In this regard, he was a more innovative and daring producer of dramas than were his counterparts in the professional theatre" (Morton 1988).

Ralph Roister Doister (Roister Doister). Nicholas Udall; authorship established by the third edition of Thomas Wilson's *Rule of Reason* (1553). "Performed either by schoolboys of Eton between 1536 and 1541 or those of Westminster between 1535 and 1556, probably at court" (Shapiro 1989); Wilson 1969 suggests "written 1545–53"; Norland 1995 favors a somewhat later date of composition, 1551–53; Hornback 2010 suggests *c.* 1552. "The presence of four songs, a 'psalmodie,' a burlesque of the requiem mass, and a peal of bells suggest that Udall wrote the play for choir boys" (King 1982). "The actors may have been the boys of Bishop

Gardiner's school at Southwark, engaging in a full ecclesiastical revels celebrating the Lord of Misrule"; "Udall's acute perceptivity about feminine psychology seems more apt for Mary's court than for the juvenile monasticism of Eton" (Bevington 1968). Possibly performed for Edward VI at Windsor Castle, September 1552 (Edgerton 1965). "[P]robably a Christmas comedy" (Scheurweghs 1939). Possibly revived for Queen Elizabeth (Norland).

SR 22 July 1566. Q 1566–67 unique copy, discovered at Eton College in 1818, lacks a TP and colophon; no author named; prologue; ends with prayer for the monarch, delivered by six characters, and a song; five acts and separate scenes. Stage houses may have been used for Custance and Roister Doister (Hornback 2009a).

The play has sometimes been called "the first English comedy" (Creeth 1966), and it anticipates "the comedies of the next eighty years in England by fusing the old allegorical morality with a sharp realism introduced by new humanist methods of literary analysis and new Protestant forms of psychological reflection" (Sessions 2002). Despite Terentian features in both performance and print, the "the style and content are self-consciously low" (Hornback). The prologue envisions both this comedy and Plautus and Terence as having didactic purpose: "The wyse poets long time heretofore, / Under merrie comedies secretes did declare, / Wherein was contained very virtuous lore, / With mysteries and forewarnings very rare." But "[m]odern audiences may not find as much 'virtuous lore' as Udall says he finds 'secretly' declared" in ancient Roman comedies (Danson 2000).

Ram Alley, or Merry Tricks, A Comedy. Lording Barry; Kirkman's 1661 catalogue attributes the play to "Lo. Barrey" (as does the Q1 TP), and this was expanded into Lord Barry in the 1671 catalogue; subsequently the author was misidentified as an Irishman named Lord Barry and as Lodowick Barry; only in 1912 did Adams properly identify the playwright (Lopez 2010). *Ram Alley* may not have been written by Barry alone: "its remarkably theft-ridden prose (including some sixteen echoes of *The Fleire*, a play written by the Whitefriars author Edward Sharpham) suggests that several hands joined in its production" (Bly 1998). Acted 1607–08 (Bly, Munro 2005); "probably first produced between March 10 and July 28, 1608" (Jones 1952); acted 1610, before the plague closing of July 12 (Holdsworth 1985). "Divers times here-to-fore acted" by Children of the King's Revels, according to the Q1 TP, at the Whitefriars (Munro 2010c); the Children were "tenants of the Whitefriars theater in 1607 and 1608" (Cathcart 2005).

SR 9 November 1610. Q1 1611 RT *Merry-Tricks*, a play on words: "i.e. meretrix: prostitute" (Bly 2009); "Ram Alley was a notorious London site of prostitution" (Sanders 1998b); list of characters; prologue and epilogue; five acts and first scenes. "Constantia, disguised as a page, tells a story of a city woman who went to see the baboons and tried to imitate their tricks. The actor who took Constantia's part illustrated the story by putting his leg behind his head, and probably doing other contortions not indicated in the text, for the play is filled with vaudeville matter" (Wright 1928). The woman, naked, falls out of bed, and calls out to her maid, "who proceeds to call the woman's husband and her neighbours. Once the neighbours arrive, their presence as onlookers turns the dame's chamber into the stage of a freak show" (Griffin 2006). Descriptive SDs: "*Enter Throte the lawyer from his study, bookes and bags of money on a table, a chaire and cushion*." "[W]e find Boutcher, in the last act . . ., hanging himself outside Will Smalshanke's door, but precisely where he hanged himself, with what, and how he was got down, are all equally unapparent" (Lawrence 1927). *Ram Alley* would later be adapted by John Cooke as *Greene's Tu Quoque*, acted 1611 (Bly 1998). Q2 1611 "a separate edition," not another issue (Corbin & Sedge 1981). Q3 [octavo-in-fours] 1636. "Ram Alley, running between the Temple and Fleet Street, was outside the jurisdiction of the city of London, and a known bolthole for those fleeing arrest" (Dillon 2000).

The Q1 prologue addresses Puritan opposition to the theater: "A vowes by paper, pen and inke, / And by the learned sisters drinke, / To spend his time, his lamps, his oyle, / And never cease his braine to toyle, / Till from the silent houres of night, / Hee doth produce for your delight, / Conceits so new, so harmlesse free, / That Puritanes them-selves may see / A play, yet not in publike preach, / That players such lewd doctrine teach / That their pure joynts do quake and tremble, / When they doe see a man resemble, / The picture of a villaine." The prologue also distinguishes this play from fashionable fare: "Home-bred mirth our muse doth sing, / The satyr's tooth and waspish sting, / Which most do hurt when least suspected, / By this play are not affected."

The Rape of Lucrece, A True Roman Tragedy. Thomas Heywood. Acted "around 1607" (Rowland 2010) or "*c*. 1608" (Gurr 2009d), or "*c*. 1609" (Hadfield 2005). By Queen Anne's Men at the Red Bull, according to the Q1 TP. *Lucrece* was "perhaps the first play ever staged at the [Red Bull] theater" (Bayer 2009). Performed also by the combined Queen Anne's and King's Men at Greenwich, before Queen Anne and Prince Henry, 13 January 1612 (Chambers 1930). Revived by Queen Henrietta Maria's Men at the Phoenix, before the Duke of Buckingham, 6 August 1628. In playlist of Beeston's Boys 10 August 1639.

SR 3 June 1608; transferred 21 May 1639. Q1 1608 *The Rape of Lucrece, A True Roman Tragedy, with the Several Songs in Their Apt Places, by Valerius, the Merry Lord amongst the Roman Peers*; dramatis personae; not divided. Despite the TP claim about the (eleven) songs, "someone aside from the printing house, probably Heywood himself, had the additional [two] songs instead collected together at the back of the playbook" (Stern 2009c). Staging calls for a property bed, the site of the rape: "*Lucr[ece] discovered in her bed*," which would have been thrust onto stage. Following the rape, Lucrece "*kil[l]s herself*," unleashing revenge: "*Alarum, enter in the fight Tarquin and Tullia flying, pursude by Brutus*"; "*Alarum, fight, Arnus slaine, Porsenna expulst. Alarum, enter Tarquin with an arrow in his brest*." Auditory effects include "*A great shout and a florish with drums and trumpetts,*" "*Alarum, battell within,*" "*A noise of knocking downe the bridge within.*" Staging calls for a property tent: "*A table and lights in the tent*"; "the tent recurs pretty much throughout the play" (Reynolds 1940). Amid the tumult there is action aloft: "*Enter in severall places, Sextus and Valerius above.*" Several places "are indeed necessary, for Sextus is supposed to be on a hill outside the city, Valerius on the city wall, and one of the stage doors to lead to the bridgehead which Horatius is protecting" (Reynolds). Q2 1609 unique copy at V&A; at the end appears an explanation of the songs that follow: "Because we would not that any mans expectation should be deceived in the ample printing of this booke, lo, (gentle reader) we have inserted these few songs, which were added by the stranger that lately acted *Valerius* his part." Holaday 1950 speculates that "the stranger" was the actor Robert Browne; Bentley 1984 finds the suggestion "unconvincing," adding, "this use of a player from outside the company was unusual." "[I]t appears that the part was written specifically with this unnamed entertainer in mind; thus, one of *Lucrece's* most distinctive features seems to derive in part from a temporary addition to its company's personnel" (Rutter 2009). Q3 1614 "the third impression." Q4 1630 "the fourth impression"; addition of four new songs. Q5 1638 "the fifth impression"; "the copy revised, and sundry [five] songs before omitted, now inserted in their right places"; "[j]ust when these new songs had been written is not apparent, but they are not in earlier editions of the play" (Bentley 1971); "except for the songs, there are no significant revisions in the dialogue or stage directions" (King 1965).

In an address to the Q1 reader, the playwright addresses a favorite topic, his reluctance to publish his plays: "It hath beene no custome in mee of all other men (curteous readers) to commit my plaies to the presse: the reason, though some may attribute to my own insufficiencie, I had rather subscribe in that to their seveare censure, then by seeking to avoide the imputation of weakenes, to incurre a greater suspition of honestie: for though some have used a double sale of their labours, first to the stage, and after to the presse, for my owne part I heere proclaime my selfe ever faithfull in the first, and never guiltie of the last: yet since some of my plaies have (unknown to me, and without any of my direction) accidentally come into the printers handes, and therfore so corrupt and mangled, (coppied onely by the eare) that I have bene as unable to know them, as ashamde to cha[l]lenge them. This therefore I was the willinger to furnish out in his native habit."

The play "adapts the conventions of late Elizabethan history plays—broad chronological span and frequent changes of locale, loose structure, large cast of characters, drum and trumpet—to address the preoccupations of the early Stuart era" (Kewes 2002).

The Rape Revenged, or The Spanish Revolution, A Tragedy. W. C. No evidence of staging but the prologue anticipates performance: "Ambition, love, revenge, rebellion, rage, / And death, are brought to-night upon the stage." Similarly, the SDs suggest that the play was intended for the theater: "*Between the two acts an assault is represented by the warlike sounds of drums, trumpets, &c, and shouts of soldiers at a distance.*" However, an "advertisement" in the MS speaks of printing rather than performance: "This dramatick poem of the tragick kind, if it should not be thought fit to be acted, by reason of the long descriptions and speeches in the dialogue-part, which would make it tedious, or for any other reason; may yet perhaps deserve to be printed."

London, BL, Additional MS 28807, fols. 1–54; author's initials on the TP; many lines and words crossed out; list of characters; "prologue by a friend"; five acts and separate scenes, the latter indicated by horizontal lines. Ample SDs, some of which may anticipate the use of painted scenery: "*Scene opening discovers the inside of a publick hall.*" Staging requires a front curtain: "*The curtain rising discovers Rinaldo as upon guard in the great hall of the palace.*" Sound effects include "*Between the two acts an assault is represented by the warlike sounds of drums, trumpets, &c, and shouts of soldiers at a distance.*"

Although *AED 3* conjectures composition *c.* 1690, the SDs and dialogue are consistent with a much earlier date. The preface indicates that the play was written in the author's youth and, much later, revised, but the MS itself is not dated: "The beginning of this dramatick poem was the amusement of my younger days. And now, after it hath lain-by neglected and almost forgotten for many years, I have revis'd and corrected it. Though it may never be thought good enough to make a figure upon the stage, yet I cannot but think it capable of giving some entertainment to the reader, who will look upon it, not with the severity of a critick, but with the candor of a friend."

Rape's Revenge. See *Valentinian.*

The Rare Triumphs of Love and Fortune. Anonymous. Acted summer-autumn 1582 (Owen 1979) by the Earl of Derby's Men (Harbage 1952) at undetermined venue. Or did the play belong to the Queen's Men (Knutson 2009b)? The Q TP reports performance before the queen. This is probably the play called *A History of Love and Fortune*, staged at Windsor, 30 December 1582. The conclusion involves the queen, who was apparently present at performance: "Love and Fortune reconcile their claims of supreme influence over the affairs of men by acknowledging Queen Elizabeth's ascendancy over them both. She is explicitly a corrective to the violence and ingratitude of the story just ended" (Bevington 1968). The costumes "could have been quite elaborate . . . and at court the actors are likely to have drawn on the resources of the Revels Office wardrobe store" (Astington 1999a).

SR none. Q 1589 no author named; RT *A Pleasant Comedy of Love and Fortune*; five "shows," akin to dumb shows, represent the power of Love and Fortune; "[p]antomimic stage directions throughout the play" (Mehl 1965); Fortune's final speech constitutes, in effect, an epilogue; five acts. The first act is essentially an induction (Hosley 1961). The play "was calculated to be confined within the limits of a platform stage, and is entirely suited for playing elsewhere, on playhouse or temporary stages" (Astington 1999a). Staging evidently involved the use of a trap (for a Fury's entrance and exit) and "houses" "(timber-framed structures covered with canvas and painted) of a city and a battlement" (Streitberger 2009). Spectacle and auditory effects accompany the entry of the personified characters: e.g., *"Fortunes triumph. Sound trumpets, drummes, cornets, and gunnes"* (Kiefer 1983, Dillon 2004a).

"Despite their popularity—they comprise one-third of all plays recorded 1570–1585—only three 'romances' have survived: *Clyomon and Clamydes, Common Conditions, The Rare Triumphs of Love and Fortune"* (Lunney 2002). The "combination of mythological morality and romance points the way for later drama in coordinating an overplot (a 'contest' of the pagan gods), a romantic plot, and an underplot with clownish actions" (Bruster 2005). "Similarities between this work and Shakespeare's late plays, in particular *Cymbeline* and *The Tempest*, have suggested that the *Rare Triumphs* may have been revived on the Jacobean stage" (Dobson 2001).

Read and Wonder: A War between Two Entire Friends, The Pope and the Devil. A short satirical dialogue possibly intended for performance *c.* 1641. Pasted into the BL copy is a notice: "probably written by George Wither," an attribution made in *The Dictionary of Anonymous and Pseudonymous Literature*, vol. 5 (1929) (Davidson 1978). Harbage 1936 suggests a similarity to *Canterbury His Change of Diet* (1641): both are "pamphlets in dialogue satirizing Archbishop Laud."

Q 1641 no author named; not divided. Some informative SDs: *"Enter the Divell, with him Pride, Lust, Covetousnesse, Treachery, Idolatry, Envy, Idlenesse."*

The Rebellion, A Tragedy. Thomas Rawlins. Acted October 1637–October 1639 (*JCS*); "probably performed around 1636" (Steggle 2004b). By the King's Revels Company "nine dayes together, and divers times since with good applause," according to the TP. Q refers to the acting company under one of its alternative names, "his Majesties Company of Revells." "[A]ppear[s] to have been staged at the Salisbury Court theatre" (Astington 1991). The Q dedication claims that "this tragedy had at the presentment a generall applause." There are eleven commendatory poems in Q, including one by the playwright John Tatham.

SR 20 November 1639. Q 1640 list of characters; five acts. "A play-within-a-play to be performed by 'The Taylers' is discussed and there is a stage direction: 'Enter Vermine in a Cloake for the Prologue.' In the event, no prologue is spoken and no play is performed" (Schneider 2011). Staging involves the partial descent of Love (i.e., Cupid), probably by machinery: *"Soft musicke, Love descends halfe way, then speakes."* Immediately after Love's speech, *"Enter from one side Death, and from the other side* Aurelia, *Death strikes three times at* Antonio, *and* Aurelia *diverts it.*" A trap opens when Aurelia "*takes a dogge and tyes it to the chaire, shee stampes: The chaire and dogge descends, a pistol shot within: a noise of a mill.*" A Captain bent on rape "*takes his dagger and windes it about her [Evadne's] haire, and sticks it in the ground: Thunder and lightning.*" Reissued 1652 with a new TP; author's initials on TP.

"Rawlins was an engraver who later became chief engraver at the Royal Mint; like so many amateur writers of plays he was insistent that he was not a professional dramatist" (Bentley 1971).

The Rebellion of Naples, or The Tragedy of Massenello. Anonymous. ?Acted 1649 at undetermined venue. Although there is no record of performance, SDs are ample and sometimes highly detailed.

O 1649 no author named; "T. B." signs the dedication; prologue and epilogue; five acts and separate scenes. Prologue addresses playgoers: "Court'ous spectators, you must know that he / Who is the writer of this tragedy, / Was actor and spectator in't: who means, / Here to present it into acts and scænes." The frontispiece pictures the tyrant who murders all who oppose him and who kills his own wife. "In the last act the mob is shown thirsting for Masaniello's gore. They demand his head, and he tells them curtly to 'take it.' Then comes the direction: 'He thrusts out his head, and they cut off a false head made of a bladder filled with blood'" (Lawrence 1927). "This suggests an author who had some sense of theatre" (Foakes 1985). "Since the play was written during the closure of the theatres the odds are that this was fanciful, but it might explain how the decapitations in plays like *Faustus, The Insatiate Countess* and *Sir John Van Olden Barnavelt* were done" (Gurr 2009d). The fold-out plate facing the TP "shows the General, Tomaso di Malfa, or Massenello as he was known, standing on a net, wielding a marshal's staff"; behind him is "a net being pulled by diminutive figures around the city of Naples" (Foakes).

The TP language hints at a connection between historical incident and theater: "written by a gentleman who was an eye-witnes where this was really acted upon that bloudy stage, the streets of Naples." T. B.'s address to the reader denies, rather unconvincingly, political implications: "if there be any thing in my booke which points at the present condition of our affairs, I assure you the times are busie with me, and not I with the times." "Published in the year of the King's execution, the play exposes the fundamental causes of rebellion, while also relaying apprehension about its consequences" (Clare 2002). Although the action takes place in Naples, the playwright "is clearly aware that his book points . . . to current English conditions, and he knows that English readers accustomed to 'paralogism' will know it too" (Randall 1995). The play "parallels Cromwell's career in a tragedy of Italian demagoguery" (Butler 2002). "[T]he play as a whole dramatizes T. B.'s sense of the utter futility of all revolutionary endeavor" (Aggeler 1978).

The Reign of King Edward III. See *Edward III*.

The Reign of the Emperor Caracalla. See *Caracalla.*

The Renegado, A Tragicomedy. Philip Massinger. Licensed for acting as *The Renegado, or The Gentleman of Venice*, 17 April 1624 (Adams 1917). "Often acted by the queenes majesties servants" [i.e., Lady Elizabeth's Men—the former Lady Elizabeth, who married 14 February 1613 and became Queen of Bohemia on 7 November 1619], at the Phoenix, according to the Q TP. John Blayney played Asambeg; John Sumner, Mustapha; Michael Bowyer, Vitelli; William Reignalds, Francisco; William Allen, Anthonio Grimaldi, the Renegado; William Robbins, Carazie; Edward Shakerley, Gazet; Edward Rogers, Donusa; Theophilus Bird/Bourne, Paulina, according to "The Actors names" in Q. The cast list "dates from 1625 or 1626" (Bentley 1984). Revived by Queen Henrietta Maria's Men at the Phoenix *c.* 1630 (Gurr 2009d). "Massinger designed his play for performance by a company of at least eighteen actors"; "the play's structure allows for no doubling" (Neill 2010). When "Queen Henrietta's Men were in turn replaced by the King and Queen's Young Company (sometimes known as Beeston's Boys) in 1637, *The Renegado* duly became their property" (Neill); in playlist of Beeston's Boys 10 August 1639. Massinger's play represents a "rewriting of Daborne's *A Christian Turn'd Turk*" (Parker 2002).

Oxford, Bodleian, MS Rawlinson poet. 20, fols. 1–45; no TP; dramatis personae (but no actors named); some words and lines crossed out; apparently adapted from the 1630 Q; this revision of the play "was evidently prepared for a Restoration performance" (Neill). SR 22 March 1630. Q 1630 *The Renegado, A Tragicomedy* ("first use of 'tragicomedy' as a title page description of a play belonging to the Chamberlain's/King's Men" [Gurr 2006]); dramatis personae together with the names of the actors who played the major roles; the Jesuit Francisco functions as "a choric moralizer" (Neill); five acts and separate scenes. SDs suggest a possible structure or a discovery space: *"A shop discovered, Gazet in it."* A scaffold becomes the site for Donusa's baptism: "[Vitelli] *throwes [water] on her face,"* prompting Donusa to say: "till this minute / I never liv'de, nor durst thinke how to dye. / How long have I beene blinde?" Staging calls for a character to be jailed, i.e., located below: "Vitelli *under the stage."* Staging also involves paintings, apparently of nudes, which "serve to initiate the hero Vitelli's affair with the Moorish princess Donusa, and to mark the erotically charged space of the playworld" (Rochester 2010). Massinger's "dramatic style is extremely sensitive to non-verbal theatrical effects and his unusually explicit stage directions show a precise awareness of the actor's craft" (McLuskie 1981): *"Gives him her hand to kisse"; "Unvailes her selfe"; "Whispers and uses vehement actions."* A variety of music complements the action: *"loude musicque"; "A solemne musicque"; "A dreadfull musicke."* "About 1633 Massinger had eight of his previously published plays bound together in a single volume. Possibly he was thinking of publishing a collection of his works; possibly he wanted the volume as a gift to a patron. He made extensive ink corrections in a number of plays [including *The Renegado*]" (Edwards 1987). The Folger owns this collection.

The "representation of the sexual intrigues and religious crises of the Tunisian court needs to be seen in the context of the fears about the Stuart monarchy articulated so powerfully in *A Game at Chess*" (Jowitt 2003). "Unlike *A Game at Chesse*—which was suppressed after its nine days' run—*The Renegado* remained in repertory for some time" (Robinson 2007). Shortly before the play was licensed, "Prince Charles and Buckingham traveled in disguise to Madrid in what seems to have been an effort to spur the negotiations [for a marriage between the son of King James and the Spanish Infanta]." Disappointed, the English travelers returned home, "convinced that the Spanish had no intention of finalizing the marriage, and set out to engineer one of the most rapid reversals in early seventeenth-century politics, forming a coalition with the forward Protestants in Parliament who were dedicated to maneuvering James into a war he did not want" (Robinson 2006).

The Repentance of Mary Magdalene. See *Mary Magdalene* (Wager).

Respublica. ?Nicholas Udall. Acted Christmas 1553–54 (Greg 1952); "made in the yeare of oure Lorde 1553," according to the MS TP. Probably first performed by the Chapel Children at court; "[a]ppears to have been designed for an aristocratic audience in London" (Norland 1995); possibly intended to celebrate the accession of Queen Mary; prologue alludes to the queen and to the Christmas season. Whether or not the play was intended for performance around the coronation, *Respublica* is "a play that dramatizes and comments on the accession of a new monarch, who is identified as Mary"; as such the play "constitutes an intriguing example of how an interlude engages with politics" (Hunt 2007). "The playwright's specific delicate task is to reconcile Mary's courtiers to her program of restitution, and at the same time to caution the queen gently about extremism in punishing or disenfranchising minor offenders" (Bevington 1968). "The probability that this play has school auspices, even if it were performed at court, is enhanced by the division into five acts, a feature which marries classical to morality-play methods" (Happé 1999).

Austin, University of Texas, Carl H. Pforzheimer Library, MS 40A; *A Merry Interlude entitled Respublica*; list of characters; People serves a choral function (Dessen 1977); prologue (by "a poet"); ends with a prayer for Queen Mary; five acts but the play observes a "tripartite morality structure" (Potter 1975). "In the main action of the play, the commonwealth is personified as a desolate widow, Respublica, besieged by Avarice, Oppression, Insolence, and Adulation. Disguised as Policy, Reformation, Authority, and Honesty, respectively, the vices merrily carry out their fiendish plans to deprive Respublica of her material wealth and natural resources as well as to impoverish her subjects" (Massey 1998). At last the vices "are exposed by the Four Daughters of God, who put things to rights and punish the evildoers" (Happé 2010). First edited by John Payne Collier (*Illustrations of Old English Literature*, vol. 1 [1866]), who called the play "one of the most remarkable early dramatic relics in our language." Modern edition by Greg 1952.

"The sole extant interlude to represent the Catholic perspective is *Respublica*" (Grantley 2007). As a political morality *Respublica* resembles *Magnificence* and *A Satire of the Three Estates*; the central character, however, differs from both "in being female" (Walker 1998). Although the play operates as an anti-Reformation tract, Respublica's own story has the texture of a woman's morality play" (Cartwright 1999). *Respublica* represents "an essentially feminine poetics, the establishment of a godly order in the care of matchless women" (Winkelman 2005).

The Resurrection of Christ. See *Christ's Burial and Christ's Resurrection.*

The Resurrection of Our Lord. Anonymous. "[W]ritten and printed sometime between 1526 and 1570"; "designed for performance over two, perhaps three, days" (White 1999). This is a "Protestantized mystery play" (O'Connell 2000b), which "reminds us that Protestant writers, especially in the early days of the Reformation in England, used the drama as a vehicle for disseminating their interpretations of the Gospel message" (Johnston 1998). However, "the reformist pronouncements" probably "represent revisions to an older resurrection play" (Marsalek 2004).

Washington, Folger, MS V.b.192; fragmentary MS of eighteen leaves, which originally probably "contained a prologue and epilogue at the extreme ends of each of the two days of the play" (Ritch 2007); no TP; no author named. Some SDs: "*here they fall downe as deade in hearing the gonnes shott of[f] & thunder Jesus riseth throwynge of Death [& the Angell].*" First edited by Wilson & Dobell 1912.

1 The Return from Parnassus. Anonymous; presumably written by a scholar at St. John's College, Cambridge, but "almost certainly" not the author of *Pilgrimage to Parnassus* (Glatzer 1977). Owen Gwyn may have contributed to the play (*AED 3*). Acted Christmas, 1599–1600 (Leishman 1949) by students of the college (Nelson 1989). "The lively dialogue . . . sustains the rather *ad hoc* continuity of the scenes, and demands a range of witty comic playing which, however subtle it may have been in every respect, was undoubtedly fun to undertake, and to watch" (Astington 2010).

Oxford, Bodleian, MS Rawlinson D.398, fols. 200–20; *The Return from Parnassus*; no author named; list of characters on TP; prologue and epilogue (consisting of "give us a plaudite"); five acts and separate scenes. A sequel to *The Pilgrimage to Parnassus*, *1 The Return* is called a "Christmas toy." First edited by Macray 1886, who gives as title *The First Part of the Return from Parnassus*. Modern edition by Leishman 1949.

In the play "the foolishly love-sick gentleman Gullio is teased for his uncritical devotion to 'pure Shakespeare and shreds of poetry that he hath gathered at the theatres.' It seems that the amorous young men who adored Shakespeare's 'sugared' writings also adored his person" (Duncan-Jones 2001). The Parnassus plays "sympathize with Jonson, not with Shakespeare, and the references to Shakespeare that cluster in *The First Part of the Returne* are to him as a popular writer of romantic poetry, appealing to undiscriminating followers of fashion" (Clark 2007).

2 The Return from Parnassus, or The Scourge of Simony. Anonymous; presumably written by a scholar at St. John's College; possibly written "by the satirist Joseph Hall" (Butler 2003a). "Acted in St. Johns Colledge in Cambridge, An[no] 1601," according to the first leaf of the MS. Performed at the Christmas revels, 1601–02 (Leishman 1949) by students of the college. Performed a second time at the Christmas revels, 1602–03.

Washington, Folger, MS V.a.355; no TP; no author named; "a later and revised version [by another]" of Q1–2 (Leishman); "the names of the actors [i.e., characters]"; induction (conversation among the Boy, Stagekeeper, Momus, and Defensor) includes beginning of a prologue; no epilogue as such but three characters say: "All give us a *plaudite*"; five acts. SR 16 October 1605 An Enterlude called *The Return from Parnassus*. Q1 1606 *The Return from Parnassus, or The Scourge of Simony*; no author named; prologues (one in prose "added for a second performance" [Leishman], another in verse) and epilogue ("give us a plaudite"); list of characters; five acts and separate scenes. Q2 1606. *2 Return* is the third play of a trilogy. The play may have been known as *The Progress from Parnassus* until it was printed (Leishman). "This play's superiority [over the other *Parnassus* plays] was immediately recognized"; "alone of the three plays it reached print" (Duncan-Jones 2011). First edited by Hawkins 1773; modern edition by Leishman 1949.

Both parts of *Return* "display considerable familiarity with recent developments in the literary world, specifically in relation to such personalities as Marston, Hall, Nashe, Gabriel Harvey and Shakespeare" (Hoy 1980). The play creates characters named [Richard] Burbage and [Will] Kemp, two of the preeminent actors in the Lord Chamberlain's Men, who "are brought on-stage to audition a pair of students for their acting company"; "the actors are mocked for their ignorance" (Keenan 2002). Kemp observes, "Few of the university [men] pen plaies well, they smell too much of that writer Ovid, and that writer Metamorphoses, and talke too much of Proserpina & Juppiter. Why heres our fellow Shakespeare puts them all downe, I and Ben Jonson too" (lines 1766–70). "The satirical comedy in this passage is based on 'Kempe's' ignorance and misunderstanding of the classics, while Shakespeare and Jonson, not university educated and writers for the despised public stage, are implicitly included in the satire by his promotion of them" (Grantley 2000). "In their backhanded tribute, the

Parnassus authors make plain that Shakespeare was a household name even at the universities" (Bevington 2004). The author Ingenioso is probably based on Thomas Nashe; the play contains an epitaph for Nashe (Nicholl 2004b).

Revenge for Honor, A Tragedy. ?Henry Glapthorne (Thomas 1908, Walter 1937, Braunmuller & Hattaway 2003). Acted ?1640 (*JCS*) at undetermined venue; the play's "prologue and epilogue suggest that it was indeed performed" (Nunn 2005); Prologue says: "I / Am a main actor in this tragedie: / You've grac'd me sometimes in another sphear, / And I do hope you'l not dislike me here"; the actor "has recently transferred from another theatre" (*JCS*). A play called *The Parricide* was licensed for acting 27 May 1624 by Prince Charles's Men at the Red Bull, and attributed to Glapthorne by the SR entry of 29 [December] 1653: *The Paraside, or, Revenge for honor* by Henry Glapthorne. Fleay 1891 suggests that this entry designates *Revenge for Honor, A Tragedy*, published in 1654. The SR title may signify a different play (Walter 1937, Shaver 1938). However, Thomas believes the two titles probably represent the same play, and Greg 1939 argues, "the two titles in the [SR] entry must be taken as alternative."

SR probably no original entry; transferred 11 June 1659 "by Geo. Chapman." Q 1654 two issues; erroneously ascribed to Chapman on the TP ("the attribution . . . was probably a sales device" [Squier 1987]); list of characters; prologue and epilogue; five acts and separate scenes. The climax involves dramatic legerdemain: Abilqualit appears to be blinded and then strangled in view of the playgoers. Actually, he has staged the blinding and killing as a ruse "to test those around him" (Nunn). Reissued 1659.

The Revenge of Bussy D'Ambois, A Tragedy. George Chapman. Acted 1610–11 (Lordi 1977). "Often presented at" the Whitefriars, according to the TP, by the Children of the Queen's Revels (Burnett 2004). Performed there in 1609–13 "in tandem with" the original *Bussy D'Ambois* after the 1604 play had been revised (Munro 2005); *The Revenge* "was presumably written to partner revivals of *Bussy d'Ambois*" (Dutton 2002). Chapman's *Revenge* belongs to a "two-part play that conforms to the pattern established by Kyd and followed by Marston and possibly Chettle" (Erne 2001a). Nathan Field may have played Clermont (Munro).

SR 17 April 1612; transferred 17 February 1623; 3 May 1651; 12 [December] 1653. Q 1613 list of characters; five acts and first scenes. In this sequel to *Bussy D'Ambois* "it is Bussy's fictional brother, Clermont D'Ambois, who is cast in the role of revenger" (Clark 2007). Building the play around the Stoic Clermont, who shrinks from exacting revenge, the playwright declines "to exploit the dramatic possibilities of his material" (Maus 1995). But Chapman uses the resources of his theater: staging includes the ascent of Bussy's ghost through a trap door: "*Ascendit umbra Bussi*"; the Countess enters from a vault (i.e., a trap): "He helps the Countess up"; Clermont too enters from below: "*The gulfe opens, Clermont ascends*." *Revenge* "is the only Queen's Revels play that calls for more than one fencing display"; although the play "is full of military displays and even a stage battle, most of this involves sound effects, marching, and some running about the stage waving weapons" (MacIntyre 1996). A grotesque masquelike scene is enacted near the end: "*Musicke, and the Ghost of Bussy enters, leading the Ghost of the Guise; Monsieur, Cardinall Guise, and Shattilion, they dance about the dead body [of Montsurry], and exit.*" Parrott 1910 calls the dance "an attempt on the part of the Whitefriars Theatre to add a little spectacular divertisement." The play "calls for offstage sound effects that seem not very feasible for an indoor theatre in a closely built-up neighborhood" (MacIntyre).

Chapman's Q dedication to Thomas Howard, Earl of Arundel, suggesting that the production was unsuccessful, sets forth his definition of tragedy: "materiall instruction, elegant and sententious excitation to vertue, and deflection from her contrary." In this formulation Chapman "outlines an aesthetic justification for his work, much as Jonson had in the address in *Sejanus*" (Bergeron 2006). The playwright also comments on the relationship between historical truth and dramatized history: "And for the autenticall truth of eyther person or action, who (worth the respecting) will expect it in a poeme, whose subject is not truth, but things like truth?" Here "Chapman divides the duty of the poet from that of the historian" (Munro). As a practical matter Chapman fuses foreign history with English politics: he uses "French settings to cloak an insistent critique of court culture and its corruptions as well as exploring the dilemma of survival in such a world" (Knowles 2001b). The "concentration of power in the sovereign" that characterized France as a nation-state "attracted those in England who welcomed such concentration of power and dismayed those who did not" (Maus). The play "points towards Chapman's self-conscious role of cautionary counseller to Prince Henry. It is notable that, whereas the play's Quarto publication may well have followed the Prince's death (in 1612), its composition may definitively be dated prior to that event" (Hillman 2005).

The Revenge of Hamlet. See *Hamlet.*

The Revenger's Tragedy. ?Thomas Middleton. The "most likely date of composition" is 1606 (Jackson 2007d). "Sundry times acted by" the King's Men, according to the TP, at the first Globe/second Blackfriars; the role of Vindice was "almost certainly played by Richard Burbage" (Taylor 2004b). However, "[i]t is possible that the author of *The Revenger's Tragedy* had an indoor playhouse and a boys' company in mind when writing his play" (White 1998). This revenge play, "probably the most accomplished and purest example of the genre in the early Jacobean period" (Corns 2007), was first attributed to Cyril Tourneur in Archer's 1656 catalogue; Archer "remains the closest to a contemporary witness for documenting who wrote *The Revenger's Tragedy*, and one must wonder why he would have gone out of his way to attribute the play to an obscure figure like Tourneur if he did not have some evidence for doing so" (Cantor 1987a). Archer's list, moreover, has a "tendency to award authorship to noted figures, not minor ones like Tourneur" (Ross 1966). Kirkman in 1661 and 1671 also credits the play to Tourneur, as does Winstanley 1687, but "the Rogers and Ley catalogue of 1656 lists it as anonymous" (Parfitt 1978). Fleay 1891 found Tourneur's authorship unlikely and proposed Webster instead. In 1911 and 1926 Oliphant noted stylistic resemblances to Middleton's plays. Barker 1958 found the play "almost certainly" Middleton's. Subsequent stylistic analyses by Lake 1975a, Jackson 1979, 1981, and Smith 1987c, 1991 strengthen the case for Middleton, as do the conclusions of Taylor 2004b, who calls the play Middleton's "reply to *Hamlet*." But "[t]here is no contemporary evidence for attribution to Middleton" (Gibbons 2008).

SR 7 October 1607 no author named. Q 1607–08 two issues; no author named; a dumb show consisting of the new Duke's installation; "Vindice's opening speech functions as a kind of prologue" (Gibbons 2008); four acts and first scenes; a division into five acts was probably intended. Dead bodies and body parts haunt a play characterized by extraordinary onstage violence. "Its shocks are pictorial" (Thomson 1983), and they begin with the first scene, which "inaugurates an experimental sequence of extraordinary gruesomeness—even by Jacobean standards" (Collington 1999). "The play opens, as it were, in the graveyard scene of *Hamlet*: a long-delayed revenger stands onstage, musing on mortality and his own grief, a skull in his hand" (Mullaney 1994); that skull belongs to a woman poisoned by the Duke for spurning his advances. "[T]wo violated female bodies" become central to the action: "the corpse of the raped wife of Antonio, who has killed herself; and the skull of the poisoned virgin Gloriana, grotesquely 'at-tired' in the scene of the Duke's murder" (Zimmerman 2005): "*Enter* Vindice, *with the skull of his love drest up in tires.*" Vindice applies paint to the skull and poisons its mouth, making it "a man trap" (Karim-Cooper 2006); although the skull "lacks a body, it does not . . . lack a sexuality" (Coddon 1994); the Duke later suffers a sensational death when he mistakes Gloriana's poisoned skull for a live woman and kisses it. Meanwhile Antonio finds the body of his wife and uses the corpse to motivate the vengefulness of his friends: "*Enter the discontented Lord* Antonio, *whose wife the Duchesses yongest sonne ravisht; he discovering the body of her dead to certaine lords.*" Having engineered the Duke's killing, Hippolito stamps on the dying Duke: "[w]hen villains are mercilessly trampled to death by angry characters who remind them of hell, the horrifying act may also suggest the infernal punishment of such sinners, much as artists depict lost souls being trampled underfoot by demons of hell" (Diehl 1980). Grotesque staging calls for "a single severed head" (the Duke's son executed by mistake) that drips blood (Owens 2005). "Dwindling late-afternoon daylight would certainly have assisted the play's most spectacular lighting effect" (Holdsworth 1990): "*A blasing-star appeareth*"; Lussurioso interprets it as a bad omen: "I am not pleasd at that ill-knotted fire." Blazing stars, "which consisted either of a firework on a line or flaming material suspended in an iron cage or cresset, and burned for up to a minute," "traditionally spelled the fall of rulers or disruptions of the state" (Holdsworth). "*It thunders*" when Vindice and the other revengers, attired as masquers, "*kill the foure at the table, in their chaires*" (Gibbons 2008); ordinarily thunder signals divine disapproval but here "the roll of thunder is handled so as to make the possible intervention of a deity seem a mere stage device" (Maus 1995). The "ritualised killing [is] carried out in the guise of a masque to celebrate" a marriage (Gibbons). As the revengers dance, they evoke the Dance of Death, often represented in the pictorial arts (Schoenbaum 1954). The masque stands "as an emblem of, or a metonymy for, the court world and its corruption" (Lindley 2009). For contemporaries that corruption would evoke the court of King James I, known for its profligacy, despotism, and sexual anxiety.

The Revenger's Tragedy may originally have been entitled *The Viper and Her Brood* (mentioned in a lawsuit of 1606) and "delivered to the Children of the Queen's Revels in May 1606"; perhaps the play was "pirated" by the King's Men (Holdsworth). But Corrigan 1998 doubts that the two titles represent the same play.

Rhodon and Iris, A Pastoral. Ralph Knevet. "Presented" 3 May 1631 at the Florists' Feast in Norwich, according to the TP, by the Society of Florists. "The characters in Knevet's play, probably dressed in costumes representing the flowers whose names they bore, must have presented a pretty spectacle on a May day in 1631" (Charles 1966).

SR 12 November 1631. Q 1631 two issues; no author named on the TP but Knevet signs the dedication; dramatis personae; prologue and epilogue; five acts and separate scenes.

Prefatory poem by Ri. Pert. [?Richard Peart] hints that the performance was not a popular success: "Disperse and vindicate thy makers merits, / Late disesteem'd by lynx ey'd censuring spirits: / Whose captivated judgements now may see, / In this cleere glasse their owne deformitie; / Whose malice found no cause to disrespect / Thy worth, but 'cause it past their intellect." Similarly, a prefatory poem by William Denny concludes, "Scorne blast their dwellings, in simplicity / That spit their poyson; none shall venome thee."

Richard II. William Shakespeare. Acted June-November 1595 (Gurr 1984). "Publikely acted by" the Lord Chamberlain's Men, according to the Q1 TP, at the Theater (Hosley 1979). Almost certainly the lead was played by Richard Burbage (Taylor 2002b), arguably "the first Shakespearean star" (Henderson 2007). Probably performed for Edward Hoby, 9 December 1595, at his house in the Strand (Gurr 2004c); Robert Cecil was a guest; Hoby's letter to Cecil, inviting him to supper and the play, survives. Praised by Francis Meres in *Palladis Tamia* (SR 7 September 1598): Meres "named *Richard II* first among the tragedies by Shakespeare that demonstrated his and the nation's theatrical excellence" (Worden 2006). Perhaps performed at the Curtain or Swan after the Chamberlain's Men were forced to leave the Theater because of a dispute over the lease (Forker 2002). Shakespeare's *Richard II* was probably the play performed by the

Chamberlain's Men at the first Globe on the afternoon of 7 February 1601, the eve of the Earl of Essex's rebellion (though the performance may have been of another dramatist's play that is now lost [Worden]); the revival was requested by Essex's supporters, who "apparently believed that the drama would serve as effective propaganda for their treasonable enterprise" (Forker). The rebels thereby "revealed some of the misconceptions which made their rebellion such a sickly miscalculation of London's mood at the time" (Gurr 1987b). But Hammer 2008 finds "no evidence that the play itself was intended to rouse the London commons to action. This performance was first and foremost about aristocrats — those portrayed on the stage and those who had arranged the play's staging." According to many scholars, in August 1601 Queen Elizabeth told William Lambarde that "this tragedy [about Richard II] was played 40^{tie} times in open streets and houses" (Chambers 1930) and that "I am Richard II. know ye not that?" "The trouble is, we do not know for sure that the encounter ever took place. And even if it did, there are good grounds for doubting the veracity of the dialogue"; the account of Lambarde's meeting with Elizabeth "first surfaced in print in the 1780s"; and the original MS on which the printed version is ostensibly based does not exist (Bate 2008). In any event "there is no evidence that the company [Chamberlain's Men] was ever interfered with, punished, or reprimanded in any way" (Aaron 2005). Questioned in the wake of the Essex rebellion, Augustine Phillips, a member of the company, said that the play "was so old and so long out of use as that they should have small or no company at it" (Barroll 1988). Probably performed by amateur actors aboard the *Red Dragon*, a ship of the East India Company, off the coast of Sierra Leone, 29 September 1607 (Taylor 2001a, Barbour 2009, Marino 2011), though this may have been another dramatist's play about King Richard (Shewring 1996); Kliman 2011, however, believes that there was no shipboard performance, that the account represents a forgery, probably by John Payne Collier. Possibly revived in 1615, around the time that Q5 was printed (Forker). Performed by the King's Men at the Globe, 12 June 1631, a benefit for Henry Herbert (Bawcutt 1996). Simon Forman reports seeing a play about Richard II in April 1611, but his plot summary makes clear that this was not Shakespeare's play (Whitney 2006).

SR 29 August 1597; transferred 25 June 1603; ?4 August 1626 Paviers right in Shakesperes *plaies*; ?19 June 1627 widow of Isaac Jaggard . . . her parte in Shackspheere playes; 1 July 1637 Shakespeares *workes* their Part; 6 August 1674; 21 August 1683. Q1 1597 *The Tragedy of King Richard the Second*; no author named; not divided. "On the bare stage of the Elizabethan popular theatre the opening scene allowed the visual establishment of all the spectacle and pageantry of a strongly hierarchical court, a pageantry shortly to be reinforced by the tournament" (Shewring). Richard is likely to have entered "from the central opening," a manifestation of "power and authority" (Ichikawa 2002), though Fitzpatrick maintains that there were only two entry-points (left and right) onto the stage. The ailing John of Gaunt would have "sat in a sick chair" (Gurr &

Ichikawa 2000): "*Enter John of Gaunt sicke*." As in many other history plays, the upper stage is used for confrontation: at Flint Castle "*The trumpets sound, Richard appeareth on the walls*" while Bolingbroke stands below. "Richard and his men . . . are situated in the gallery of the tiring-house wall"; their descent "is the turning point of the play" (Dillon 2012). Stage business is kept to a minimum, but the murder of the king is staged: "*Here Exton strikes him downe*." The most important sound effect is that which Richard hears during his last soliloquy, just before his murder: "*the musicke plaies*"; "the most likely kind of music would be wind (recorders) and strings" (Gurr 1984); the music may have been played on a bass viol (Lindley 2006). Following Richard's death the assassin presents his handiwork to Bolingbroke: "*Enter Exton with the coffin*." Q2 1598 "by William Shake-speare." Q3 1598. *Richard II* "was the first play-text to prove so popular as to warrant three printings in the space of two years" (Gurr 1984). Q4 1608 two issues, the second of which reports, "with new additions of the Parliament sceane, and the deposing of King Richard. As it hath been lately acted by the kinges majesties servantes, at the Globe." The deposition scene (164 lines) was not printed until this edition either because it was censored during Elizabeth's lifetime (Clegg 1997, Clare 1999) or because it did not previously exist (Bergeron 1974); Bate 2008 speculates: "Shakespeare may have written [the scene] as an addition after the real-life drama of February 1601, in order to give the impression of a formal, stately handing over of power, as opposed to the presumption and hugger-mugger of the original version that was now tarred by association with the trial of Essex and his accomplices." But Jones 1995 maintains that the deposition scene of Q4 represents "not a revision but a restoration."

The most important theatrical property would have been the throne, which stands "empty while Bullingbrook and Richard argue in front of it, disputing whose right it is to occupy it" (Gurr & Ichikawa 2000). The most important hand prop is the mirror requested by Richard, symbolic of both prudence and pride (Kiefer 1983, 2003). Q5 1615 "lately acted" by the King's Men. F1 1623 *Comedies, Histories, & Tragedies*; three issues; "published according to the true originall copies"; *The Life and Death of King Richard the Second*; five acts and separate scenes. F2 1632 "the second impression"; three issues. Q6 1634 "printed from F2" (Jowett 2007e). F3 1663 "the third impression"; reissued 1664 with seven additional plays. F4 1685 "the fourth edition"; two issues.

Richard II initiates Shakespeare's second tetralogy of history plays, written in the mid- to late 1590s, the others being *1* and *2 Henry IV*, and *Henry V*. The four plays, dramatizing the career of the man who became Henry V, are sometimes known as *The Henriad*, a term "coined by analogy with Virgil's *Aeneid*" (Dobson 2001). But *Richard II* "may not have been written with any view of a sequel" (Potter 2012).

1 Richard II (anonymous). See *Woodstock*.

Richard III. William Shakespeare. Acted *c.* 1592 (Jowett 2000) or ?1593 (Gurr 2009d), but Potter 2012 speculates that "it might have been as late as 1595 before London audiences saw Shakespeare's first great success." Probably first performed by "the Admiral's/Strange's conglomerate" (Hammond 1981) at the Theater. Possibly performed subsequently by Lord Pembroke's Men (Wentersdorf 1977) "in the provinces," then in London (Hammond). "Lately acted by" the Lord Chamberlain's Men, according to the Q1 TP, at the Theater. The play "probably relied heavily on the skills of a single actor, [Richard] Burbage" (Jowett 2000), arguably "the first Shakespearean star" (Henderson 2007); the play gave this actor "his first rich, complex Shakespearean role" (Honan 1998). Burbage was "unavoidably reminiscent of [Richard] Tarlton's jiz [combination of outline, bearing and voice identifying a performer]: two Richards in one body, the future King of England as Vice/clown. It is an extraordinarily bold trope" (Thomson 2000). Praised by Francis Meres in *Palladis Tamia* (SR 7 September 1598) where the play is termed a tragedy. An entry in John Manningham's diary (1602) alludes to an earlier performance by Burbage as the king. "A *Richard the Third* was performed at the Red Bull theatre, as a prologue and epilogue by [Thomas] Heywood reveal. This could have been another play" (Hammond); the two speeches were printed in Heywood's *Pleasant Dialogues and Dramas* (1637). Revived by the King's Men at St. James's Palace, before the king and queen, 16 November 1633, on the occasion of Queen Henrietta Maria's birthday (Bawcutt 1996), in the Presence Chamber (Astington 1986); this production "might well have served as a warning to the English queen not to become embroiled in her family's problems" (Britland 2006b). According to *Historia Histrionica*, Eilert Swanston, a member of the King's Men from 1624 to 1642, played the lead. The play "appears to have been the longest single stage play ever written in English, and remained so until Q 1604 *Hamlet*. Either it was abbreviated for staging, or its performance took more time than the Elizabethan average" (Siemon 2009).

SR 20 October 1597; transferred 25 June 1603; ?4 August 1626 Paviers right in Shakesperes *plaies*; ?19 June 1627 widow of Isaac Jaggard . . . her parte in Shackspheere *playes*; 1 July 1637 Shakespeares *workes* their Part; 6 August 1674; 21 August 1683. Q1 1597 *The Tragedy of King Richard the Third, Containing His Treacherous Plots against His Brother Clarence, the Pitiful Murder of His Innocent Nephews, His Tyrannical Usurpation, with the Whole Course of His Detested Life and Most Deserved Death*; no author named; "the three citizens who discuss the political situation" in 2.3 function as a chorus (Wiggins 2000); not divided. Whoever wrote the full title for Q1 "had seen the play in performance and registered the emotions appropriate to the main incidents in the plot" (Gurr 1987b). "Q1 is the later [than F1] and more performance-oriented text" (Jowett 1998b). Staging calls for a property coffin: "*Enter Lady Anne with the hearse of Harry the 6*"; Richard proceeds to woo Anne, prompting her response: "*Shee spitteth at him.*" Richard makes "the violation of ceremony into a new and opportunistic ceremony centred on the prop of sword and ring"; he offers Anne his sword, inviting her to kill him, but "*she lets fall the sword*"; "this is the turning point, and within a few lines Anne has accepted Richard's ring" (Dillon 2012). Costume points to Richard's nature: "*Enter Richard, and Buckingham, in rotten armour, marvellous ill-favoured*"; "Richard's 'rotten' armour emblematizes his moral and political corruption" (Harlan 2008). A SD in the same scene reveals Richard's hypocrisy: "*Enter Rich[ard] with [i.e., between] two bishops,*" a book in his hand. (Personified Hypocrisy carries a book in the hand [Kiefer 1996a].) Richard also equivocates verbally in the manner of a Vice (Spivack 1958): "Thus like the formall vice iniquity, / I moralize two meanings in one word." Moments later Richard's nephew asks for a dagger, and Richard answers "My dagger little cousen, withall my heart"; a dagger of lath was equipment belonging to a Vice (Dessen 1986). Grotesque staging includes "*Enter Catesby with Hast[ing's] head.*" Staging calls for the use of a "tent" into which Richard withdraws before the climactic battle, remaining in view of the audience; when he falls asleep, he has a vision of his victims' ghosts, then he "*starteth up out of a dreame.*" In the same scene the Earl of Richmond appears, sitting in his tent. "The tents appear to be movable structures, erected like real tents" (Jowett 2000), but Dessen & Thomson 1999 observe that there are no "signals for the pitching of *tents* onstage," and Meagher 2003 argues that "an actual enclosure would . . . be dramaturgically awkward as well as superfluous." The ghosts of Richard's victims may enter either from under the stage (Styan 1967) or through "the entrance doors" (Hammond). Sound effects include "*The clocke striketh,*" prompting Richard to call for a calendar in the final scene. "Shakespeare's most often quoted line, in early modern England, was . . . Richard III's passionate, desperate 'A horse, a horse, my kingdom for a horse'" (Taylor 2002b). Q2 1598 "by William Shake-speare." Q3 1602 "newly augmented, by William Shake-speare"; this false claim was made "in the hope of attracting new readers" (Bentley 1971). The printing of Q3 perhaps signals a theatrical revival (Knutson 2006a). Q4 1605. Q5 1612 "as it hath beene lately acted by the Kings majesties servants." Q6 1622. F1 1623 *Comedies, Histories, & Tragedies*; three issues; "published according to the true originall copies"; *The Tragedy of Richard the Third, with the Landing of Earl Richmond, and the Battle of Bosworth Field*; RT *The Life and Death of Richard the Third*; "divided imperfectly into acts and scenes" (King 1992a). The differences between Q1 and F1 "are legion" (Davison 1996); in F1 "a passage which appeared in all six earlier quartos is lost from the text," possibly the result of censorship (Clare 1999). The differences between Q1 and F1 "probably point to successive additions and revisions, perhaps designed for different audiences" (Potter 2012). Q7 1629. F2 1632 "the second impression"; three issues. Q8 1634. F3 1663 "the third impression"; reissued 1664 with seven additional plays. Undated prologue "printed in A. B.'s *Covent Garden Drollery*, 1672" (Greg 1939). F4 1685 "the fourth edition"; two issues.

Richard III is the culmination of Shakespeare's tetralogy of history plays written in the early 1590s, the others being *1, 2,* and *3 Henry VI.* However, "[w]hile we might think of the play as the last in Shakespeare's second tetralogy of history plays, it was nothing of the sort to the play's first readers. The genre [tragedy] begins the title-page in large upper-case letters" (Berger 2007). "In the histories section of the First Folio, only *Richard III* is called a 'tragedy'" (Lull 2009). Moreover, the "four plays in the sequence, the three parts of *Henry VI* and *Richard III*, had originally belonged to three distinct playing companies"; therefore, it is "remarkable that any coherence appears at all in a 'series' cobbled together from elements of three different repertories" (Marino 2011).

Richard III. Anonymous. See *The True Tragedy of Richard III.*

Richard, Duke of York. See *3 Henry VI.*

A Right Pithy, Pleasant and Meaty Comedy Entitled Gammer Gurton's Needle. See *Gammer Gurton's Needle.*

The Rival Friends, A Comedy. Peter Hausted. Acted 19 March 1632, according to the TP (Mills 1951), by students of Queens' College, Cambridge, before King Charles and Queen Henrietta Maria (Marlow 2009). "[P]erformed in Trinity College hall"; "prepared for 8 March 1632, but postponed on word of an accident befallen the chancellor, Lord Holland" (Nelson 1989). The TP recounts the contentious reception of the play: "cryed downe by boyes, Faction, Envie, and confident Ignorance, approv'd by the judicious, and now exposed to the publique censure"; the largely student audience behaved boisterously. The author's dedicatory epistle also reports, "'Twas made to please, and had the vicious age / Beene good enough, it had not left the stage / Without its due applause." Hausted's preface to the reader, complaining of playgoers who "came with starch'd faces and resolutions to dislike whatsoever they saw or heard," is "probably the longest such address in any dramatic text" (Bergeron 2006).

SR 13 June 1632; 30 January 1673. Q 1632 dramatis personae; prologue "upon occasion of their majesties comming being deferr'd" and epilogue; a song concludes each act but the last; five acts and separate scenes. An induction, "being a dialogue betwixt Venus, Thetis, and Phoebus, sung by two trebles, and a base," precedes the prologue. "Five songs composed for this play by George Jeffreys survive in a British Library manuscript" (Nelson).

A prefatory poem by John Rogers, an actor in the production, adopts a judicial metaphor to defend the play against detractors: "The court once set, straightwayes a jurie went / Upon thy comœdie, was fully bent / To finde it guiltie, though the king did sit / As judge himselfe that day, and cleared it. / If so, then let the foule-mouth'd world condemne / Thy innocent piece, shew that thou canst contemne / And slight the false inditements which they bring / To cast it, since tis quitted by the king, / And all the comicke lawes." The playwright himself acted in the play.

The Roaring Girl, or Moll Cutpurse. Thomas Middleton and Thomas Dekker. Acted April-May 1611 (Mulholland 1987). "Lately . . . acted" by Prince Henry's Men at the [first] Fortune, according to the TP; this is one of only two plays "identified on their title pages as having been performed at the Fortune" (Straznicky 2006b). The prologue speaks of "a play (expected long)," suggesting perhaps that the play was overdue in reaching the stage.

SR no original; 18 February 1612; transferred 10 February 1631. Q 1611 dramatis personae; prologue and epilogue; not divided despite the designation of act 1, scene 1. Epilogue predicts the visit of Moll Cutpurse to the Fortune, and Mary Frith did in fact appear there, "perhaps becoming the first Englishwoman to perform on the commercial stage" (Taylor 2004b). Dressed in masculine attire, she "sat there uppon the stage in the publique viewe of all the people there present" (*The Consistory of London Correction Book*, 27 January 1612). The Q TP features the woodcut of a woman: she smokes a pipe, holds a sword, and wears masculine attire. This may represent the historical Mary Frith or the boy actor who played the role of Moll. "[B]y basing the story of the play on the real-life character who had worn men's clothes, Dekker and Middleton could capitalize on fashion, give a truth to the popular theatre emphasis on real life and at the same time play with the theatrical convention of cross-dressing" (McLuskie 1994). "Moll in breeches picks up and makes literal the pamphleteers' insistence that masculine dress in women is equivalent to role transgression" (Jardine 1983). But Mary/Moll "is not in disguise"; she "seeks not to conceal her sexual identity, but rather to display it" (Rose 1988). The playwrights turn Moll "into a popular heroine, challenging a comparison with the 'roaring boys,' a phrase in use from about 1590 until well into the eighteenth century to describe young hooligans who were given to quarrelsome and riotous behaviour in order to show off their virility" (Foakes 1985). Alongside the TP woodcut of Moll is the caption: "My case is alter'd, I must worke for my living." "'Case' meant 'clothing' . . . but it was also slang for 'vagina,' the fantasised alteration to which is perhaps emblematised here by Moll's strategically positioned phallic sword. The merging of these two meanings in one word suggests their inseparability in this play" (Barker & Hinds 2003). "'[A]ltered case' aptly describes the blurring of gender and sexual boundaries produced by Moll's cross-dressing and 'masculine' behavior" (DiGangi 2011).

Middleton's epistle to the reader compares play-making to clothes: "our plaies followe the nicenes of our garments, single plots, quaint conceits, letcherous jests, drest up in hanging sleeves, and those are fit for the times, and the tearmers: Such a kind of light-colour summer stuffe, mingled with diverse colours, you shall finde this published comedy." Middleton's "stress on the impermanence of the work, its cultural relativity in the shifting world of fashion, runs right against Sidney's (and Jonson's) insistence on the permanence and imperishability of art" (Steggle 1998). The address to the reader suggests that the play is equally at home in the study or the theater: "[it] may bee allowed both gallery roome at the play-house, and chamber-roome at your lodging." Middleton's suggestion of the two locales "as alternative spaces for his play suggests a continuity between the watching and reading of plays" (Hackel 1997). "[W]e should not rule out the possibility of a spectator going to the theater with text in hand, a wonderful conjunction of publication and performance" (Bergeron 2006).

"This proto-feminist classic" (Taylor 2004b) "uses the image of the cross-dressed woman to defy expectations about woman's nature and to protest the injustices caused by the sex-gender system" (Howard 1988). In Moll "the contemporary sexual metaphysic was turned inside out: gender division was recognized as central not to a divinely sanctioned natural order but to a contingent and oppressive social order" (Dollimore 1986). "*The Roaring Girl* occupies a position in the Elizabethan-Jacobean canon quite analogous to the position occupied by Moll within the play. Like her it is marginal, a kind of outsider, hard to contextualize and integrate into the old rules (in this case the conventional rules of comedy)" (Garber 1991).

Robin Hood and the Friar. Anonymous. Acted ?1550s-60s. The Q1 publisher, William Copland, indicates that *Robin Hood* is "verye proper to be played in Maye games," presumably at an outdoor venue. "There is good reason . . . for believing that the Robin Hood game is a version of the king game, and that Robin Hood is a variant of the May King or Summer Lord" (Wiles 1987). "Robin Hood is frequently associated with May games and summer games, and the distinctions between Robin Hood and king games and summer lords are often blurred" (Greenfield 2004). "Short and simple enough to have been performed in the course of a money-gathering perambulation" (Pettitt 2000), the play is "typical of the numerous Robin Hood plays sponsored by parishes and civic organizations all across Britain throughout the Tudor era" (Knight & Ohlgren 1997). This play "recounts the now familiar tale of Robin's encounter with the truculent mendicant Friar Tuck"; "the characterization of Friar Tuck . . . reflects the anti-Catholicism of the sixteenth century" (Ohlgren 2007).

SR 30 November 1560 [mistakenly given as October] "the title was omitted" (Greg 1939). Q1 ND *c.* 1550 (Chambers 1903) or *c.* 1560 (Knight 1994); appended to *A Merry Gest of Robin Hood and of His Life*; Manly 1897 suggests the title used in this entry; Q1 calls the entertainment *The Play of Robin Hood* and describes it as "a newe playe"; list of characters on the TP; no SDs; not divided. Q1 "shows that the [Robin Hood] material was becoming part of a written or print culture, and also suggests that performance might be a matter of interest to the growing links between print and performance" (Happé 1999). The Q1 TP contains two woodcuts purporting to depict Robin Hood and "Lytel John," but the former's "garments are reminiscent of the earlier part of the century," and the latter "is repeated from de Worde's edition of *Hick Scorner*" (Davidson 1991). Q2 ND ?1565 fragment in All Souls College, Oxford. Q2's TP uses the same woodcut of Robin Hood holding a bow and arrow but a different representation of Little John. Q3 1590.

This play and *Robin Hood and the Potter* "foreground the carnivalesque elements associated with the medieval folk play: slapstick violence, disguisings, social inversion, anticlericalism, and sexual double-entendre" (White 2004b).

Robin Hood and the Potter. Anonymous. Acted ?1550s-60s. The Q1 publisher, William Copland, indicates that this is "verye proper to be played in Maye Games," presumably at an outdoor venue. Copland prints this play and *Robin Hood and the Friar* "as one play" (Chambers 1903). "Short and simple enough to have been performed in the course of a money-gathering perambulation" (Pettitt 2000). "Archival evidence suggests that Robin Hood performances were primarily regional games and plays performed in the south and west of England" (Sponsler 1997). "There is good reason . . . for believing that the Robin Hood game is a version of the king game, and that Robin Hood is a variant of the May King or Summer Lord" (Wiles 1987).

SR 30 November 1560 [mistakenly given as October]. Q1 ND *c.* 1550 (Chambers) or *c.* 1560 (Knight 1994); appended to *A Merry Gest of Robin Hood and of His Life*; no SDs; not divided. This play "is a shortened version of the poem by the same name" (Ohlgren 2007). Q2 ND ?1565. Editors have called the play "apparently incomplete" (Wiles 1981), "but they have in mind the quite different action of the ballad 'Robin Hood and the Potter.' The length and style of this short dramatic combat with the Potter match the three other Robin Hood sequences that survive in the early plays. They are brisk and depend heavily on action" (Knight). "The second piece similarly pits Robin against the potter (after a preliminary, largely verbal, encounter with the latter's comic servant) in a sword-and-buckler fight which Robin loses. There follows a confrontation between the potter and Little John whose outcome is not clear" (Pettitt 2000).

Later plays featuring a character named Robin Hood include *George a Green, The Pinner of Wakefield, Edward I, The Downfall of Robert, Earl of Huntingdon, The Death of Robert, Earl of Huntingdon, Look About You,* and *The Sad Shepherd.*

1 Robin Hood. See *The Downfall of Robert Earl of Huntingdon.*

2 Robin Hood. See *The Death of Robert Earl of Huntingdon.*

A Rogue. See *Pleasant and Merry Humor of a Rogue.*

Roister Doister. See *Ralph Roister Doister.*

Rollo, Duke of Normandy. See *The Bloody Brother.*

The Roman Actor, A Tragedy. Philip Massinger. Licensed for acting 11 October 1626 (Adams 1917). "Divers times . . . with good allowance acted" by the King's Men at the [second] Blackfriars, according to the TP; this is "the first play Massinger wrote for the King's Men as their attached playwright" (Rochester 2010). "[P]ossibly also performed at the Globe" but "the play is clearly designed for indoors" (White 2007). Principal actors and their roles: John Lowin played Domitian Caesar; Joseph Taylor, Paris; Richard Sharp, Parthenius; Thomas Pollard, Aelius Lamia and Stephanos; Robert Benfield, Junius Rusticus; Eilert Swanston, Aretinus Clemens; Richard Robinson, Aesopus; Anthony Smith, Philargus; William Patrick, Palphurius Sura; Curtis Greville, Latinus; George Vernon, a Tribune and a Lictor; James Horn, a Tribune and a Lictor; John Thompson (the company's "leading boy player" [White 1998]), Domitia; John Honeyman, Domitilla; William Trigg, Julia; Alexander Gough, Caenis, according to the cast list printed on the verso of TP. Taylor, the leading actor, contributes commendatory verses.

SR no original; transferred 1 July 1637. Q 1629 an extant copy contains corrections/revisions in Massinger's hand; list of characters together with the names of the actors; pantomimic elements but "[n]o dumb shows proper" (Mehl 1965); five acts and separate scenes. Unusual staging includes three inset plays. The SDs "are often elaborate and literary" (E&G 1976): *"Enter at one doore captaines with lawrels, Domitian, in his triumphant chariot."* Caesar's death is treated with considerable spectacle: *"A dreadfull musicke sounding, enter Junius Rusticus, and Palphurius Sura [spirits], with bloudie swords, they wave them over his head. Caesar in his sleepe troubled, seemes to pray to the image* [i.e., the statue of Minerva], *they [the spirits] scornefully take it away."* Caesar *"rises distractedly"* and interprets his dream to the sound and sight of *"thunder and lightning."* "In the indoor playhouses thunder would most likely have been simulated by drums"; "[l]ightning—provided by throwing powdered rosin at a burning torch, lighting rosin as it was blown out of a tube or setting off firecrackers—was a risky effect outdoors, and even more so indoors" (White). Finally, Caesar is murdered: *"These severally stab him."*

The Roman Actor is "the only play of the period to have a professional player at its centre" (Mann 1991). That player becomes a victim of "political tyranny" and of "cruel and arbitrary absolutism"; through the player Massinger "stresses the cathartic power of theatre" (Sanders 1999a). However, Butler 1985 sees the play as something very different from a defense of theater: "if [the theater] has power to improve it may also corrupt, and the effects of play-acting as Massinger shows them are disruptive, mischievous and downright subversive"; "Massinger is deliberately writing the most anti-theatrical play of the English Renaissance." The play "voices the absolute continuity . . . between politics and theater" (Goldberg 1983). *"The Roman Actor* criticizes the Caroline court's tendency to dramatize itself, to use theatrical self-fashioning as an instrument of power and persuasion" (Bulman 2003). "About 1633 Massinger had eight of his previously published plays bound together in a single volume. Possibly he was thinking of publishing a collection of his works; possibly he wanted the volume as a gift to a patron. He made extensive ink corrections in a number of the plays [including *The Roman Actor*]" (Edwards 1987). The Folger owns the collection.

In his dedicatory epistle Massinger distinguishes his intended (Blackfriars) audience from less sophisticated denizens of other theaters: "It hath beene happie in the suffrage of some learned, and judicious gentlemen when it was presented, nor shall they find cause I hope in the perusall, to repent them of their good opinion of it. If the gravity and height of the subject distaste such as are onely affected with jigges, and ribaldrie (as I presume it will,) their condemnation of me, and my poem, can no way offend me: my reason teaching me such malicious, and ignorant detractors deserve rather contempt, then satisfaction." Massinger "evidently took it for granted that both kinds of playgoer would be at his play, whether it was at the Blackfriars or the Globe, but that in his own ambition the play was designed only for the more refined playgoers" (Gurr 2004c).

Romeo and Juliet. William Shakespeare. Acted 1595 (Wells & Taylor 1987) or 1596 (Potter 2012). "Often (with great applause) plaid publiquely by" Lord Hunsdon's Men, according to the Q1 TP, at the Theater (Hosley 1979). (The Lord Chamberlain's Men were known as Hunsdon's Men from 23 July 1596, when Henry Cary died and George Cary succeeded to the title, to 14 April 1597 when Hunsdon became Lord Chamberlain; the play was probably produced before the Chamberlain's Men changed their name during that period.) "Sundry times publiquely acted" by the Lord Chamberlain's Men, according to the Q2 TP, at the Curtain, 1597–98, when the company had lost their lease on the land beneath the Theater. Almost certainly Will Kemp, whose name appears in a SD of Q2, played the role of Peter, the Nurse's servant (Bate 2008, Ford 2010), and Balthasar. "Kemp's contribution . . . may be a borderline case between embroidering a script, and being given a free hand to invent at will" (Mann 1991). Henry Condell probably played Mercutio (Potter 2012). Richard Burbage played Romeo. Praised by Francis Meres in *Palladis Tamia* (SR 7 September 1598).

SR none prior to Q1 or Q2; transferred 22 January 1607; 19 November 1607; ?4 August 1626 Paviers right in Shakesperes *plaies*; ?19 June 1627 widow of Isaac Jaggard . . . her parte in Shackspheere *playes*; 1 July 1637 Shakespeares *workes* their Part; 24 August 1642; 14 September 1642; 6 August 1674; 21 August 1683. Q1 1597 *An Excellent Conceited Tragedy of Romeo and Juliet*; no author named; prologue; lacks chorus at end of act 1; not divided, but "rows of printer's ornaments occasionally mark new scenes in Edward Allde's section of Q1" (Proudfoot et al. 2005). Q1 "probably takes us as close as we can get to the play as it would have been performed by Shakespeare and his fellow players in London and elsewhere" (Erne 2007); Q1 represents a shorter and revised version of the play that Shakespeare had written; it "became the acting version of the play" (Halio 2008). Q1 "adds stage directions to the dialogue at more than twenty points. A dozen times or so it supplements what the characters say and in the process makes the timing more precise" (Levenson & Gaines 2000). The SDs "may partly have been com-posed by Henry Chettle, serving as assistant to the printer John Danter" (Erne); these SDs are "strikingly elaborate, 'literary,' and even poetical" (Jowett 1998a). When the lovers meet, "Romeo does not dance" but Juliet "comes to him out of the dance . . . which probably continues behind them" (Brissenden 1981). In the so-called balcony scene, the actor playing Juliet at her window would have oc-cupied one of the boxes, or compartments, seen above the tiring-house in the De Witt drawing of the Swan (Hosley 1954, 1957); the word *balcony* does not appear in the play. A similar space is used for the couple's wedding night: "*En-ter Romeo and Juliet at the window.*" Sound effects may include birdsong after their night together ("It was the nightingale and not the larke / That pierst the fearfull hollow of thine eare"). "[O]ne scene in particular" in Q1 (2.6) "seems to have been composed by another hand entirely, it is so different from the style elsewhere in the play"; "[w]hether Chettle or someone else composed the scene, it seems clear that Shakespeare did not" (Halio). A crucial SD signals the kill-ing of Mercutio: "*Tibalt under Romeos arme thrusts Mercutio, in and flyes.*" Romeo feels compelled to avenge his friend: "*[Romeo and Tybalt] Fight, Tibalt falls*," pre-cipitating Romeo's banishment. Subsequently, Juliet takes a potion that counter-feits death: "*She fals upon her bed within the curtaines*"; when her apparently lifeless body is discovered, "*All at once cry out and wring their hands.*" "Juliet's bed must have been thrust out at some point in the previous scene" (Meagher 2003). In action of unusual rapidity, Romeo returns from Mantua and forces open Juliet's tomb with "*a crow of yron*," fights and slays Paris, and drinks poison, mistakenly believing his wife dead; when she awakes to find her husband slain, "*She stabs herselfe and falles.*" Romeo had bought the poison from an apothecary whose thin body evokes "a walking skeleton," a visual allusion "to the allegorical figure of Death" (Wiggins 2000). At the close all the actors would have exited "in proces-sion through the locus of harmony, the central opening" onto the stage from the tiring-house (Gurr 2009d). Q2 1599 *The Most Excellent and Lamentable Tragedy of Romeo and Juliet*; "newly corrected, augmented, and amended"; prologue spoken by "c[h]orus"; following the masked ball, the chorus reappears, saying, "passion lends them power." Q1 and Q2 "represent two different and legitimate kinds of witnesses to two different stages of an ongoing theatrical event. In Q2, the du-plication of several passages indicates authorial revision and therefore authorial working papers rather than a manuscript used in the theatre" (Levenson 1998). Q3 1609 acted by "Kings majesties servants" at the Globe. Q4 ND *c.* 1621–22 (Jowett 2007e); a variant title-page declares, "written by W. Shake-speare"; this is the first edition of *Romeo* "which attributes the play to Shakespeare" (Wells & Taylor). "Given the attention to theatrical detail in Q4, including some decisions that indicate direct experience of knowledge of production . . . it seems likely that the Q4 was edited by someone who had at least seen the play" (Hunter 2001?). F1 1623 *Comedies, Histories, & Tragedies*; three issues; "published according to the true originall copies"; *The Tragedy of Romeo and Juliet*; lacks prologue about "starre-crost lovers" but contains a choral speech, "passion lends them power"; not divided despite the designation of act 1, scene 1. F1 "adds eleven stage directions, edits and regularizes another eleven, and attempts to correct two" (Massai 2007). F2 1632 "the second impression"; not divided; three issues. Q5 1637 prologue by chorus. F3 1663 "the third impression"; reissued 1664 with seven additional plays. F4 1685 "the fourth edition"; two issues. Act and scene divisions were first marked by Nicholas Rowe in 1709.

"Today the death of young lovers seems a natural . . . choice for tragedy, but in 1594–6, when the play was probably written, tragedy typically focused upon the fall of political figures such as kings, princes, or generals. . . . Shakespeare effectively invites the audience to consider adolescent passion and parent-child relations as the stuff of serious drama" (Roberts 1998). "In its time *Romeo and Juliet* was distinctive and even radical for the way it favoured young love over family authority" (Gurr 2009c).

Rosania. See *The Doubtful Heir*.

The Royal Exchange. See *The Queen's Exchange*.

The Royal King and The Loyal Subject. Thomas Heywood. Acted *c.* 1600 (Baines 1984) or 1602 (Gurr 2009d) by Worcester's Men at the Boar's Head or Rose or Curtain. Later "acted with great applause" by the Queen's Men, according to the TP. This refers "no doubt to Queen Henrietta's men and indicates that the play had been recently revived" (Jewkes 1958). Queen Henrietta's Men was "apparently assembled during the long plague closing of 1625" (Bentley 1981).

SR 25 March 1637 a Comedy called *the Royall king and the Loyall Subjects*. Q 1637 dramatis personae; prologue to the stage, perhaps newly written for revival (Griffin 2001); epilogue to the reader; five acts.

Epilogue, with an eye to theatrical fashion, comments on the length of time separating production and printing: "That this play's old, 'tis true, but now if any / Should for that cause despise it, we have many / Reasons, both just and pregnant to maintaine / Antiquity, and those too, not al vaine. / We know (and not long since) there was a time, / Strong lines were not lookt after, but if rime, / O then 'twas excellent: who but beleeves, / But doublets with stuft bellies and bigge sleeves, / And those trunke-hose, which now the age doth scorn, / Were all in fashion, and with frequence worne; / And what's now out of date, who is't can tell, / But it may come in fashion, and sute well? / With rigour therefore judge not, but with reason, / Since what you read was fitted to that season." This verse address also appears immediately before the epilogue in Henry Shirley's *The Martyred Soldier* (1638).

The Royal Master. James Shirley. "Acted in the new theater [Werburgh Street] in Dublin," according to the TP, by Ogilby's Men, very late in 1637 or very early in 1638 (Fletcher 2000); "this was probably the opening play at the Werburgh Street Theatre" (Burner 1988). The play's "first datable performance took place before [Lord Deputy Thomas] Wentworth in Dublin Castle in 1638, on New Year's Day in the evening" (Fletcher). "*The Royal Master* is one of the few plays unequivocally performed in Dublin before it was performed anywhere else" (Dutton 2006). Licensed for acting in London 23 April 1638 (Adams 1917) and performed by an unidentified company.

SR 13 March 1638. Q 1638 published in both Dublin and London as the alternate TPs indicate; two epilogues, one written for the command performance before Lord Deputy Wentworth; five acts. Shirley's epistle describes the play as "unacted"; this "must must have been written some time before publication and presumably before he added the epilogue" (Greg 1939). The epilogue, with a slight change, was reprinted in Shirley's *Poems* (1646). The play dramatizes the intersection of sex and politics in Caroline drama: "the kings in Killigrew's *Claricilla* and Shirley's *The Royal Master* inadvertently provoke disorder by obstructing the marital (and hence political) ambitions of the favorites they nonetheless immoderately love and reward" (DiGangi 2006).

In his dedication, the playwright anticipates the time "when the English stage shall bee recovered from her long silence, and her now languishing scene changed into a welcome returne of wits and men." Shirley refers to the lengthy closing necessitated by the plague.

The Royal Slave, A Tragicomedy. William Cartwright. "Presented" the evening of 30 August 1636, by students of Christ Church, Oxford, before King Charles and Queen Henrietta Maria, according to the Q TP (Elliott & Buttrey 1985), in the great hall, with changeable scenery probably designed by Inigo Jones: "a Temple of the Sun," "a City in the front, and a Prison on the side," "a stately Palace"; "it would seem that sliding wings, in addition to shutters, were a feature" of the production (Richards 1968). "Jones seems to have concentrated most of his scenic invention in the area of the relieves" (Orrell 1985). "Though they had seen two other plays within two days (Strode's *The Floating Island* and Wilde's *Love's Hospital*), the royal visitors were delighted by *The Royal Slave*" (Aaron 2005), which dramatizes the "Platonic ideal" favored by the queen (Veevers 1989). But Sharpe 1987 argues: "Whilst Neo-Platonic philosophy and Platonic love pervade the plot, the play by no means echoes the court's fashionable cult, nor its political values." Performed also for the university community "and strangers" by students of Christ Church, the afternoon of 2 September 1636. Anthony à Wood records an account of the staging at Oxford; Archbishop Laud, Chancellor of Oxford, who reports that "the strangeness of the Persian habits gave great content," said, "It was very well penned and acted" (Smyth 2006). In a letter George Evelyn notes that the actors wore "a Persian habit" and that the "play much delighted his Majesty and all the nobles, commending it for the best that ever was acted" (*JCS*). The queen, having decided to stage the play at the royal court, asked that

Laud send the costumes that had been worn at Oxford, along with the "perspectives of the stage [painted scenery]"; Laud "stipulated that neither the play nor the costumes should appear on the public stage" (Bawcutt 1996). The play was performed by the King's Men at Hampton Court, 12 January 1637 (Adams 1917). For this presentation "a proscenium stage would have been set up, to accommodate the scenery" (Astington 1999a), and Cartwright "wrote a new prologue and epilogue" (Harbage 1936). No license for acting extant. A letter by George Garrard to Viscount Conway, 4 September 1636, refers to the play as *The Persian Slave*.

(1) London, BL, Additional MS 41616, fols. 1–24 (from the Petworth collection); *The Royal Slave, A Tragicomedy*; a later hand has recorded Cartwright's name and the date of performance on the TP; "acted before the king at Oxford"; also written in a later hand on the TP: "the songs were set by Henry Lawes"; list of characters; prologue (by "one of the Persian magi") to king and queen at Oxford and epilogue (by Cratander) to king and queen; five acts and separate scenes. (2) Washington, Folger, MS V.b.212; *The Royal Slave, A Tragicomedy*; no author named; list of characters; prologue by "one of the Persian magi" to king and queen; prologue by "a priest discover'd at his devotions" to the university; epilogue to king and queen, by Cratander, the royal slave; epilogue to university, by Arsamnes, king of Persia. (3) Oxford, Bodleian, MS Arch. Seld. B26; list of characters; prologue to king and queen; prologue to university; epilogue to king and queen; epilogue to university. MS (4) library of the Duke of Bedford; of the four MSS "this one, on the whole, is the least trustworthy" (Evans). "None of the four manuscripts [MSS 1–4 here] . . . is directly derived from any of the others" (Evans 1951). "A lost fifth MS—Heber: 1043—contained a cast list" (Elliott et al.). (5) New York Public Library, Drexel 4041 contains three songs. (6) London, BL, Egerton MS 2725, fols. 115–17; prologue and epilogue ("spoken by the slave") addressed to king and queen, as well as prologue and epilogue to university.

SR none. Q1 1639 two issues, one of which corrects the preliminary matter; no author named; list of characters; prologue to king and queen by one of the Persian magi; prologue to university (by same); prologue to their majesties at Hampton Court by Cratander; epilogue to king and queen; epilogue to university by Arsamnes; epilogue "to their majesties at Hampton-Court"; five acts and separate scenes. Extraordinarily detailed SDs: "*8th appearance, the sun eclipsed, and a showre of raine dashing out the fire. Whilse the last chorus is singing, the sunne appears eclipsed, &c. After the song Arsamnes [King of Persia] prepares to give the stroke, but is interrupted by the priest.*" Q2 1640 "the second edition." O 1651 *Comedies, Tragi-Comedies, with Other Poems* (with *The Lady Errant, The Ordinary, The Siege, or Love's Convert*); "the third edition." A droll based on 3.4 appeared during the Interregnum: it was entitled "*A Complemental Contestation . . . A Dialogue,*" and published in *The Marrow of Complements* (1655).

Ruff, Band, and Cuff. See **Band, Ruff, and Cuff.**

Rule a Wife and Have a Wife, A Comedy. John Fletcher. Licensed for performance 19 October 1624 (Adams 1917). Acted by the King's Men, according to the Q TP, at the second Blackfriars. Performed also at court "for the ladys," 2 November 1624, and again at Whitehall, before the prince, the evening of 26 December 1624 (Bawcutt 1996); revived at the Blackfriars, February 1635 (Adams). Epilogue, especially the words, "Good night our worthy friends," suggests evening performance. "The clown part of Cacafogo in the play seems very like the known roles of William Rowley, and it appears not unlikely that Fletcher wrote it for Rowley, who was a member of the King's company" (*JCS*).

SR no original; transferred 8 August 1661. Q 1640 "written by John Fletcher"; prologue ("presumably added for a court performance" [Corns 2007]) and epilogue; five acts and first scenes. Dialogue indicates offstage auditory effects: "What noise is this, what dismall cry"; printed in the margin is this SD: "*Clashing swords. A cry within, downe with their swords.*" At another point "*Cacafogo makes a noise below*"; he is "*i'th celler*"; the Duke thinks he's a devil. "Fletcher shaped the play so as to utilize intervals in staging at the Blackfriars Theatre and at Court, probably with inter-act music" (Williams 1985). B&F F2 1679 *Fifty Comedies and Tragedies*; "published by the authors original copies, the songs to each play being added"; *Rule a Wife and Have a Wife.* Sometime after the closing of the theaters parts of the play were adapted for a droll entitled *An Equal Match*, later published in *1 The Wits, or Sport upon Sport* (O 1662 [two issues] and 1672).

The November 1624 performance "for the ladys" suggests playgoers who were chiefly female: "An audience entirely composed of the leading noblewomen and their attendants is one possible kind of gathering at court entertainments . . .; if it were not entirely so composed, this particular occasion yet demonstrates the influence of female taste and patronage on court culture" (Astington 1999a).

The Rump, or The Mirror of the Late Times, A Comedy. John Tatham. Written between 11 February and mid-March 1660 and probably performed in March (Scott 1945) by Beeston's Company (*AED 3*). "Acted many times with great applause at the private house in Dorset-Court," according to the Q1 TP, and "then moved on to the Red Bull" (Randall 1995). "[P]erformed, and with great success, in 1660–1" (Potter 1981). "First staged in June 1660, a month after the king's return, and repeated at Oxford in July 1661" (Salmon 2004). What the play offers is "a remarkable picture of the approaching Restoration as seen through the eyes of the Londoners themselves" (Potter).

SR 23 August 1660. Q1 1660 *The Rump, or The Mirror of the Late Times, A New Comedy*; dramatis personae; prologue and epilogue; five acts and first scenes. Some very detailed SDs: "*Enter Duckingfield and Cobbet, they pass a complement to the rest,* Cobbet *takes* Stoneware *by the hand,* Duckinfield *and they walk together whispering,* Bertlam Woodfleet *and* Lockwhit *do the like, after a turn or two* Bertlam *speaks.*" Unusual SD calls for simulation of a bonfire: "*A piece of wood is set forth painted like a pile of faggots and fire, and faggots lying by to supply it*"; then

"*Racks are set out, one turns the spit with Rumps on't.*" Later, musicians "*dance about the bonfire.*" Q2 1661 "the second impression, corrected, with many additions"; two issues; argument. The Q2 dramatis personae differs from that of Q1: perhaps "the author was doubtful how far he was safe in bringing the mighty lords of the Commonwealth *personally* before the citizens of London" (Maidment & Logan 1879).

The Q1 prologue begins by seeking to adjust the expectations of playgoers: "Expect not here language three stories high; / Star-tearing strains fit not a comedy. / Here's no elaborate scenes, for he confesses / He took no pains in't, truth doth need no dresses. / No amorous puling passions, here the lord / And lady rather differ then accord. / What can be in't, youl say, if none of these? / It is all one; he's sure the thing will please / The truly loyal party; but what then? / Why, truly he thinks them the better men." "Appearing some months after the final expelling of the Purged Parliament (that is, the Rump Parliament) in October 1659, this play . . . grew out of (and has many affinities with) the pamphlet satires, particularly those in dialogue form, that burgeoned during the previous two decades" (Randall). This play belongs to a group of plays "dealing directly with the political crises of the 1640s and 1650s" (Wiseman 1990). Included in Kirkman's 1661 catalogue.

S

The Sad One, A Tragedy. John Suckling. Written between 1632 and 1637 (Beaurline 1971) and intended for performance but not finished or acted. The play contains a character who seems to caricature Ben Jonson (Steggle 2004b).

SR 29 June 1660. O3 1659 *The Last Remains of Sir John Suckling*, Part 2 of *Fragmenta Aurea* 1658–59, the general TP of which reports, "the third edition with some new additionals"; argument; list of characters; five acts and separate scenes; "the play breaks off in the midst of V.2" (*JCS*). Ample SDs: "*The King calls out Treason! Old* Cleonax *rising to go out at the door to call for help, is met by his son, who took him for the king and kill'd him:* Lorenzo *is presently of set purpose run through by* Parmenio."

In his address to the reader, Humphrey Moseley explains the inclusion of this play: "I hope I shall not need to crave your pardon for publishing this dramatick piece of Sir John Suckling, (imperfect I cannot say, but rather unfinish'd) there being a kind of perfection even in the most deficient fragments of this incomparable author. To evince that this copy was a faithful transcript from his own handwriting, I have said enough in my former epistle, and I thought it much better to send it into the world in the same state I found it, without the least addition, then procure it supplied by any other pen."

The Sad Shepherd, or A Tale of Robin Hood. Ben Jonson. Probably written 1635–36 (Barton 1984) or *c.* 1637 (Sanders 2003). In all likelihood this draft "was a late work left unfinished at its author's death" in 1637 (Greg 1905). Included in Kirkman's 1661 catalogue. "The concept is that Robin Hood, who is the lord of Sherwood, . . . has invited a group of genteel shepherds from the Vale of Belvoir to a feast" (Knight 1994). Jonson's play may "be a response to two recent pastorals by his 'sons' — Thomas Randolph's *Amyntas* and Joseph Rutter's *The Shepherds' Holiday* (both written before 1635)" (Kay 1995). "As one of the finest examples of pastoral drama in English, it is far from Jonson's customary dramatic mode and astonishing evidence of the range of his powers" (*JCS*). "Jonson evidently intended that *The Sad Shepherd* should be acted with scenery and effects" (*JCS*). In shaping his pastoral, Jonson "revitalizes the over-stylized rhetoric of the Caroline masque"; the description of the set design "owes much to the sets of the masques from *Oberon* on" (Chan 1980). "Probably Jonson began writing *The Sad Shepherd* because of the vogue of pastoral plays with scenery at the Caroline court" (Freehafer 1973).

"The play was not entered on the SR before publication. But [Thomas] Walkley included it in his belated entry of the contents of the 'third volume' on 17 September, 1658, before he transferred it to Humphrey Moseley on 20 November" (H&S). F2 1640–41 *The Works* vol. 3; "[v]ery rarely *The Sad Shepherd* is missing from the volume altogether" (Giddens 2003); separate TP dated 1641; list of characters; detailed argument before each act; prologue "obviously intended for the stage" (Greg 1905); divided into three acts and separate scenes (incomplete); the play breaks off after act 3, scene 5. Some detailed SDs are suggested in the argument: e.g., "*there ariseth a mist sodainly, which, darkning all the place,* Clarion *looseth himselfe.*"

"Jonson undertook this project at a moment when pastoral drama . . . was enjoying a remarkable revival" (Riggs 1989). In the prologue "Jonson declares firmly that his pastoral play is native, rather than classically inspired"; despite "the presence of Theocritus and Virgil, and of Tasso and Guarini," the play "is English through and through" (Barton); Jonson chooses for his setting Sherwood Forest and its inhabitants, "Robin Hood and his merry men amongst the greensward" (Sanders 1998b). *The Sad Shepherd* mixes "pastoral with folk traditions" (Hayes 1992). "At the heart of the play . . . is a trenchant investigation of rural community as against the hierarchical quasi-aristocratic structures of dominant society" (Sanders 1999a). *Sad Shepherd* "acknowledges the ways in which an ethos of loyal social amity (most conspicuously announced in the 'Book of Sports' promulgated by Charles in 1632) was struggling to contain social and economic forces that were working to reshape the wider political culture" (Butler 2010).

Saint Hermenigildus. Cosmo Manuche or James Compton (Williams 1980). Written in mid- to late 1640s, "probably not earlier than 1642" (Williams).

Possibly written for performance at Castle Ashby, Compton's home. Perhaps performed at his London residence, Canonbury House, Islington (Wolf 1983).

MS BL Additional 60276, fols. 2–34; no TP; no author named; damaged by a dark stain; MS is a "draft" (Williams) and possibly never finished; list of characters; chorus; five acts. MS formerly belonged to the library at Castle Ashby.

Saint Hermenigild was "son of the Visigothic King of Spain, Leovigild. This saint's life provides the proper mixture of religion and warfare for a royalist play of the 1640s" (Williams).

Saint John the Evangelist. See *John the Evangelist.*

Saint Meriasek (*Beunans Meriasek, The Life of Saint Meriasek*). Anonymous. Acted 1495–1504 (Harris 1977) in or near Camborne, Cornwall, "since the only dedication in Cornwell to St Meriasek occurs at Camborne parish church" (Joyce & Newlyn 1999). Although the MS is dated 1504, "the play may have been composed in the latter part of the previous century" (Joyce & Newlyn). This is a "saint's play intended for performance over two days"; enactment took place "in an open-air amphitheatre called in Middle Cornish a plain-an-gwary, from the Cornish words 'plen,' meaning 'arena' or 'field,' and 'guary,' meaning 'play'" (Joyce & Newlyn). An instance of "place-and-scaffold staging" (Grantley 2007). The MS "suggests a circular acting area enclosed in a raised bank which is punctuated with scaffolds" (Twycross 1994). The MS provides for "thirteen scaffolds placed in a circular arrangement, with a central chapel for the first day" (Grantley 2008b).

Aberystwyth, UK, National Library of Wales, MS Peniarth 105; ed. and trans. Harris; written in Cornish; dated 1504; partly damaged; diagram for the first day's performance; divided in two parts for performance on separate days (Grantley 2008b). The MS contains name of the scribe, Dom[inus] Hadton, who may also have been the author. Although the play is written in Cornish, it "is particularly interesting in having primary stage directions in Latin, with later secondary comments sometimes in Latin, more often in English" (Murdoch 1994). "*Trompe l'oeil* technology" is required for "the appearance and taming of the dragon and the summoning of the fountain" (Grantley 2008b); the fiery dragon must be "of some size since some of the soldiers are swallowed by it"; the dragon "may have been mounted on wheels and had a hinged mouth to open and close" (Grantley 1983). "Four outlaws are the target of a stage direction which states: 'Hic ignis venit super illos' (Here fire comes upon them)" (Butterworth 1998). During an execution scene "bodies are cut down from the gallows" and mutilated (Butterworth 2005). "The stage trick of producing springs of water from the earth is required in a number of plays," including this one (Butterworth 2005). First edited by Stokes 1872.

"One of the few survivals of the Saint plays which were undoubtedly very common in England and in France" (Happé 1999), "the play of Saint Meriasek is unique in British medieval drama" (Murdoch).

1 Saint Patrick for Ireland. James Shirley. Acted 1639–40 (Turner 1979) by Ogil-by's Men at the Werburgh Street theater, Dublin (Wertheim 1967). No record of licensing for performance in London. "It seems reasonable to infer that *Saint Patrick for Ireland* was a deliberate attempt on Shirley's part . . . to write a play calculated to attract a local audience, possibly without regard for any further per-formances in London" (Dutton 2006).

SR 28 April 1640. Q 1640 *Saint Patrick for Ireland, The First Part*; list of characters; prologue and epilogue; five acts. "The play is staged almost as a pag-eant, and Shirley ambitiously applies the techniques of an elaborate masque, in-cluding spectacles, chanting, and processions" (Burner 1988). The play "opens with the entrance of three druid magicians no doubt dressed in fantastic and elaborate costume," followed by "three spirits that serve the druid magicians" (Wertheim). When these figures exit, "*Enter Angell Victor, bearing a banner with a crosse, St. Patrick and other priests in procession singing.*" A coup de théâtre occurs with the entry of the King, Queen, and others; then "*A flame beside the altar*"; "*After the song the Queen offers, and her daughters, garlands, which are placed upon the heads of the idols*"; "*The song being ended, the idol that presented* Jupiter *moveth.*" Then "Jupiter addresses his startled worshippers" (Wertheim). In another scene "Emeria is raped by the brother of her fiancé, disguised as the pagan god" (Ker-rigan 2008): "*The Devils rejoycing in a dance conclude the act.*" A man who has sought to burn St. Patrick alive leaps into a fire and "*burnes himselfe,*" presumably by jumping into the space beneath the (opened) trap in the stage floor. In the play's final scene St. Patrick drives the serpents out of Ireland: the "entrance and exit of the serpents must have been created through the use of the trap doors" (Wertheim). Also issued in made-up book of 1657 entitled *Two Plays* (with *The Constant Maid*).

Saint Patrick is the first part of a projected two-play sequence; according to the prologue, "if ye / First welcome this, you'll grace our poets art, / And give him courage for a second part." *Part 1* "may well have been a piece of special pleading on behalf of Shirley's former patron, Queen Henrietta Maria, who had requested Wentworth to reopen St Patrick's Purgatory, an Irish site of Catholic pilgrimage demolished in 1632 by zealous reformers" (Morash 2002). "On the whole, one can find little in Shirley's version of Ireland in this play which would reveal the development of any insight into the situation of the colonized in that country" (Coughlan 1990). Indeed, the play represents "the locals as sullen, bar-baric and needing acculturation" (Butler 2002). Almost certainly the play failed to find an enthusiastic audience, and *Part 2* was therefore never written. Shirley returned to England.

Salisbury Plain. See *The Converted Robber*.

Sappho and Phao. John Lyly. Acted late 1583 (Pincombe 1996) by Paul's Boys or by the combined Queen's Children and Paul's Boys at the first Blackfriars.

Performed soon after at court before the queen by the combined companies, according to the Q1 TP, on Shrove Tuesday, 3 March 1584. The combined troupe "functioned under the patronage of the Earl of Oxford" (Scragg 2002). Lyly's plays were "often presented and acted" before Queen Elizabeth, according to the D general TP. "The praise of Sapho throughout the play is clearly intended for Queen Elizabeth" (Morris 1987).

SR 6 April 1584 the commedie of *Sappho*; transferred 12 April 1597; 23 August 1601; 9 January 1628. Q1 1584 [the chief character's name is spelled *Sapho*]; no author named; prologue at Blackfriars and prologue at court; epilogue ("seems to have doubled for both" court performance and private theater [Dutton 1991]); five acts and separate scenes. Stage "houses," made of canvas, "were readily available for the play's fixed locations," the cave of Sibylla and the bedchamber of Sappho (Bevington 1991). A *periaktos* may also have been used for Vulcan's workplace (Best 1968b). Sappho's bed "is a free-standing structure denoting the Queen's preoccupation with amatory affairs" (Scragg 2008). Q2 1584. Q3 1591. D 1632 *Six Court Comedies* (with *Campaspe, Endymion, Gallathea, Midas, Mother Bombie*); two issues; by "John Lilly"; adds "songs to the plays where in quarto they had only been indicated by stage directions" (Bevington).

The Q1 prologue for the Blackfriars distinguishes Lyly's comedic purpose from that of other playwrights: "Our intent was at this time to move inward delight, not outward lightnesse, and to breede, (if it might bee) soft smiling, not loude laughing: knowing it to the wise to be as great pleasure to heare counsell mixed with witte, as to the foolish to have sporte mingled with rudenesse." (This prologue would later turn up "without explanation" [Steggle 2007] in Q2 of *The Knight of the Burning Pestle* [1635].) Lyly's purpose and achievement would have a profound effect on Shakespeare: Lyly's "works suggested more dramatic possibilities to Shakespeare than those of any other comic playwright" (Honan 1998). The play "reveals the secret world of women's sexuality in complex and perhaps contradictory ways" (Pincombe 1996); "the 'lesbian desire' which is enigmatically hinted at in *Sappho and Phao* is not as readily assimilable to modern notions of lesbianism as that so frankly delineated in *Galatea*" (Pincombe 1998). "Venus makes Phao both overpoweringly attractive to women and uninterested in them" (Wiggins 2000).

A Satire of the Three Estates. David Lindsay. Lost original version known from a contemporary description by William Eure to Thomas Cromwell in a letter dated 26 January 1540 (London, BL, Royal MS 7.C.xvi, fols. 137–39). Acted indoors before King James V and Marie of Lorraine at Linlithgow Palace on the feast of the Epiphany. Revised version, in place-and-scaffold performances, acted on Castle Hill at Cupar, Fife, 7 June 1552, and at the Greenside playfield, Calton Hill, Edinburgh, 12 August 1554, before Mary of Guise, the queen regent (Mace 1998). Probably performed also in the amphitheatre at Perth, 1540–42 (Mill 1932). "The actors number at least forty" (Brooke 1911). Lindsay may himself have played the role of the herald Diligence (Edington 1994). "The staging requirements for the outdoor productions were clearly spectacular and expensive" (Walker 2000). "The *Satire* requires a Place (referred to as *the field*), a scaffold (with chair and ladder), perhaps additional scaffolds referred to as '*seats*,' a hill ('*Here shall the Boy cry off the hill*'), and a body of water" (Hosley 1971).

Edinburgh, National Library of Scotland, Advocates Library, MS Bannatyne 19.1.1, fols. 164–210, dated 1568; probably represents the Cupar performance (Norland 1995); list of characters; speeches by messenger function as prologue and epilogue; divided into two "parts" for performance before and after a "collatioun." The MS is reproduced in facsimile by Fox & Ringler 1980. The original version of the play "did not include the character of Divyne Correctioun. He seems to have entered the play as it was being developed for the Cupar and then Edinburgh performances" (McGavin 2007b). The play "foregrounds the spectacular events of royal *adventus*, burghal procession, supplication to the monarch, the calling of Parliament, punishment and execution which made up the public theatre of the real world" (McGavin 2007a). "Dance is called for" after the play (Baskervill 1929). First edited by Ritchie 1928, then Hamer 1931–36. Q 1602 *A Satire of the Three Estates in Commendation of Virtue and Vituperation of Vice*; "there are seven surviving copies of this edition, at least one and probably two of which were supplied with a new title page and published in London in 1604" (Lyall 1989). The two extant texts, MS and Q, represent essentially the same long version of the play, MS reflecting the performance at Cupar, Q reflecting the performance at Edinburgh and the presumed performance at Perth, but Q is about 1200 lines longer. "Notable are the large number of stage directions, several quite complex, and some substantial structures including a body of water" (Grantley 2007). Staging calls for Verity to be "imprisoned by the wicked clergy" (Craik 1958), a conventional fate of virtuous characters in the moral interludes. The "vices' assumption of false identities includes elaborate physical disguise" (Griffiths 2008). Reissued 1604 with a new TP, *The Works*; "newly corrected and vindicate from the former errors, wherewith they were before corrupted, and augmented with sundrie workes never before imprinted."

"The only Scottish morality play whose text has survived" (Kantrowitz 1972); Lindsay's work and *Philotus* together constitute "the whole surviving corpus of Middle Scots drama" (Craigie 1979). "As the play moves from allegory and personal morality to politics and religion, we increasingly view it through the representation of Scotland the nation rather than the person of the prince" (Walker 2007). "In moving from the relatively secure genre of a hall-based interlude to the multiple staging, extravagant theatricality and generic instability of the play as we have it, Lindsay also developed a strongly metatheatrical strain" (McGavin 2004). "Lindsay peppers his drama with extremely coarse elements of low comedy, dramatizing the materiality of the body in all its appetites and excretions. This obsession with the grotesque body provides a connecting thread between the play's carnival elements and the more serious subversions of authority" (Goldstein 1999). "Tudor playwrights were discovering . . . that the carnival represents a healthy release from the tensions produced by the constant effort of imposing an arbitrary order" (Westfall 1990).

Satiromastix, or The Untrussing of the Humorous Poet. Thomas Dekker. Acted autumn 1601 (Hoy 1980). By Paul's Boys, according to the TP, at Paul's playhouse. Also "presented publikely by" the Lord Chamberlain's Men, according to the TP, at the first Globe. "Staged first at Paul's" (Gurr 1996). "Perhaps written originally for the Chamberlain's Men, at the Globe" (Knutson 2001b). "Giving a play staged in one company's repertoire to another was a unique action. It might have been done to redouble the publicity about the play, or it might have been handed over to the adults to release Paul's from its involvement in the notorious quarrel" (Gurr). Collins 2007 suggests that *Satiromastix* was "performed jointly" by Paul's Boys and the Chamberlain's Men. John Sincler may have played Asinius Bubo at the Globe (Gurr 2004c); this "malicious portrait" probably represents John Weever (Honigmann 1987). Shakespeare may have acted in the play (Potter 2012).

SR 11 November 1601 *the untrussinge of the humorous poetes.* Q 1602 dramatis personae ("the very first appearance of 'Dramatis Personae' in a printed English play" [Taylor et al. 2007]); dumb show; epilogue (by Tucca) written for the Globe; not divided. Prefatory address to the reader specifies the sound effect that heralded dramatic performances: "In steed of the trumpets sounding thrice, before the play begin: it shall not be amisse . . . first to beholde this short comedy of errors, and where the greatest enter, to give them in stead of a hisse, a gentle correction."

In his address "To the world," Dekker refers to "that terrible *Poetomachia*," a conflict involving himself, Jonson, and Marston, "which seems to have begun in *Every Man out of His Humour*" (Twyning 2004). Dekker uses "a mock portrait of Ben Jonson . . . in order to 'untruss' or undo this rival dramatist" (Tassi 2005). In the character of Horace, *Satiromastix* satirizes Jonson, who had recently written *Cynthia's Revels* (Steggle 1998); Dekker presents Horace, "alias Jonson, as a self-promoting, self-creating figure, shooting his quills like a porcupine and flicking 'inke in everie mans face'" (Donaldson 2004). "At the heart of the disagreement lies the struggle for supremacy between city comedy and romantic comedy" (Moore 1999). "After *Satiromastix* was staged, Jonson withdrew from the battlefield, conceding the quarrel" (Knutson 1997).

The School of Compliment. James Shirley. Licensed for acting as *Love-Tricks with Compliments*, 11 February 1625 (Adams 1917, Burner 1988). Acted by Lady Elizabeth's Men at the Phoenix; later by Queen Henrietta Maria's Men, according to the TP; this troupe was "apparently assembled during the long plague closing of 1625" (Bentley 1981). In playlist of Beeston's Boys as *Love Tricks with Compliments* 10 August 1639.

SR 25 February 1631 *The Schoole of Compliment*. Q1 1631 *The School of Compliment*; author's initials on TP but Shirley signs the dedication; dramatis personae; prologue; conclusion by Bubulcus, Gorgon, and Jenkins, including epilogue by the latter; five acts and first scenes. Q2 1637. Q3 1667 *Love Tricks, or The School of Compliments*; new prologue. After the closing of the theaters, parts of the play involving a comic Welshman were adapted for a droll entitled *Jenkin's Love-Course and Perambulation*, later published in *1 The Wits, or Sport upon Sport* (O 1662 [two issues] and 1672).

"The company performing at the Cockpit or Phoenix theatre in Drury Lane at the time of this [acting] license was the Lady Elizabeth's men . . . though their existence as a London company was soon ended by the great plague of 1625"; Beeston kept the script, and "most of the performances of the play were given by the successors of the Lady Elizabeth's company, Queen Henrietta's men" (*JCS*).

The Scornful Lady, A Comedy. John Fletcher and Francis Beaumont; Philip Massinger was likely a collaborator (Clark 1994). "Acted (with great applause)" by the Children of the Queen's Revels at the [second] Blackfriars, according to the Q1 TP, 1610 (Munro 2005) or "mid-1613" (McMullan 1994). Subsequently performed at Whitefriars (Munro). Performed by the combined Lady Elizabeth's and Prince Charles's Men at Rosseter's Blackfriars, January–March 1616; by the King's Men at the Blackfriars, between April 1616 and March 1625; at the Whitehall Cockpit-in-Court, 27 December 1630 (Teague 2009); at the Blackfriars, 18 October 1633. (The actors had planned to present *The Tamer Tamed* but replaced it with *Scornful Lady* for the 1633 performance [Bawcutt 1996].) Revived at Thornton House, Buckinghamshire, the seat of Edward Tyrrell, 12 January 1638 (Randall 1995). Revived at the Whitehall Cockpit, before Prince Charles, 6 January (Twelfth Night) 1642; this was the last King's Men play "to be performed before the outbreak of the Civil War" (Munro); Henry Herbert writes, "the kinge and queene were not there; and it was the only play acted at courte in the whole Christmas" (Adams 1917). "Court drama was about to disappear altogether, since Charles abandoned Whitehall in January, not to return for another seven years" (Butler 2004c). For the King's Men John Shank played Sir Roger (*Historia Histrionica*). *The Scornful Lady* was revived at the second Fortune in the summer of 1647 in defiance of the ban on play production (Wickham et al. 2000).

SR 19 March 1616; transferred 8 May 1617; 24 October 1633; 28 July 1641; 4 March 1647. Q1 1616 the TP names B&F; five acts and first scenes. The SDs are generally "long and descriptive" (Jewkes 1958): "*Musicke. Enter young Lovelesse and Widdow, going to be married: with them his comrades.*" The play "may have been altered either for the Queen's Revels-Lady Elizabeth's amalgamation or the King's Men" (MacIntyre 1996). Q2 1625 "now lately acted (with great applause)" by the King's Men at the [second] Blackfriars, according to the TP; "I find no indication of Blackfriars provenance for a play by the King's Servants until the 1625 quarto" of *The Scornful Lady* (Barroll 2005); list of characters. Q3 1630 "the third edition." Q4 1635 "the fourth edition." Q5 1639 "the fift[h] edition." Q6 1651 "the sixt[h] edition, corrected and amended"; two later "pirated editions" also bear a 1651 imprint (Hoy 1970). Q7 1677 "the seventh edition corrected and amended"; two issues. B&F F2 1679 *Fifty Comedies and Tragedies*; "published by the authors original copies, the songs to each play being added"; list of characters. "On the evidence of the ten quartos published in the seventeenth century, perhaps the most objective measure of such matters, *The Scornful Lady* was the most successful play in the canon" (Finkelpearl 1990), partly because of its appeal to women playgoers; Thomas Stanley's poem in F2 reports of the original performance: "then the *Scornfull Lady* did beguile / Their easie griefs and teach them all to smile." After the closing of the theaters, parts of the play were adapted for a droll entitled *The False Heir and Formal Curate*, later published in *1 The Wits, or Sport upon Sport* (O 1662 [two issues] and 1672).

The Scornful Lady "is the most popular example of a kind of play, in fact the largest single group of private theater plays, that has come to be called 'city comedies'" (Finkelpearl 1990).

The Scot's Figaries, or A Knot of Knaves, A Comedy. John Tatham. Possibly performed (Potter 1981) in the 1640s and 50s.

SR none. Q 1652 no author named on the TP but Tatham signs the dedication and Winstanley 1687 ascribes the play to him as does Langbaine 1680; list of characters; five acts. Ample SDs: "*He begins to be drunk*"; "*He takes* Townshifts *cloake up*"; "*He snatcheth up the money.*" Q2 1652–53 "some copies dated 1652, some 1653" (*JCS*).

As the title suggests, the play satirizes the Scots: "A 'fegary' or 'figary' is a prank or freak, a whim or eccentricity, and 'to fig' is to pick pockets" (Randall 1995). This play belongs to a group of plays "dealing directly with the political crises of the 1640s and 1650s" (Wiseman 1990). Tatham depicts "two comic Scotsmen (the Scottish accent mercilessly satirized) trying to gull the English in London, and ending up being fooled themselves" (Bancroft 2013). "The author heaps venom upon a race that many another loyal Englishman hated for their Presbyterianism, their opposition to the Laudian liturgy, and their alliance with Parliament in the first Civil War" (Wright 1934). "The Scots beggars who come south to prey on the English offer a universal remedy for the country's problems, which turns out to be the pill of sedition. In a trial scene at the end, this remedy is shown to be lethal" (Potter).

The Scottish History of James IV. See *James IV.*

The Scottish Politick Presbyter, Slain by an English Independent, or The Independents' Victory over the Presbyterian Party, . . . A Tragicomedy. Anonymous. A play-pamphlet. ?Acted 1640s at undetermined venue.

SR none. Q 17 September 1647 no author named; list of characters; prologue; description of dumb show; five short acts and separate scenes. Ample SDs: "*The stoole of Repentance brought forth, contrived in the fashion of a pulpit covered ore* [over] *with blacke.*"

The play-pamphlet "represents Anarchy (an Independent) as a friend to the royalist Moneyless, and ends with Anarchy's murder of the Presbyterian who has been cuckolding him" (Potter 1981).

The Sea Voyage. John Fletcher and Philip Massinger (Hoy 1957). Licensed for acting 22 June 1622 (Adams 1917). Acted by the King's Men at the [second] Globe, according to Henry Herbert. Principal actors were Joseph Taylor, John Lowin, William Eccleston, Nicholas Tooley, and John Underwood, according to F2. Taylor "presumably played Albert [a French pirate] here"; Lowin "probably took the part of Tibalt [a merry gentleman and friend to Albert]" (Parr 1995).

SR 4 September 1646; 30 January 1673. B&F F1 1647 *Comedies and Tragedies*; "never printed before, and now published by the authours originall copies"; five acts and first scenes. Special effects include "*A tempest, thunder and lightning*" at the outset, staging probably inspired by the opening scene of *The Tempest* (Parr 1995). Auditory effects are suggested by a SD, "*horrid musicke,*" and by this question, "What dreadfull sounds are these?"; a character replies, "Infernall musick, / Fit for a bloody feast." B&F F2 1679 *Fifty Comedies and Tragedies*; "the songs to each play being added"; *The Sea Voyage, A Comedy*; list of characters; actors' names.

While mindful of *The Tempest*, "Fletcher has the confidence to incorporate the Shakespearian material and move beyond it, while also remaining genial and deferent in relation to his predecessor" (Lyne 2007). "Both plays are set on islands distant from Europe, and likewise both plays avoid precisely identifying the geography of their setting" (Feerick 2006). *The Sea Voyage* "draws on colonial narratives for its tale of islands, shipwreck, Amazons, and the threat of cannibalism" (McMullan 2004). Specifically, the play "satirizes the unpreparedness—in terms of human and material resources, expectations and skills—that characterized the early Jamestown experience" (Walters 2002).

The Second Maiden's Tragedy (*The Lady's Tragedy; The Ladies' Tragedy; The Maiden's Tragedy*). ?Thomas Middleton; first attributed to Middleton by Swinburne 1875, then by Oliphant 1926, and Schoenbaum 1955; linguistic analysis by Lake 1975a and Jackson 1979 supports the attribution. Licensed for acting 31 October 1611, according to the last folio of the MS. Acted by the King's Men at, presumably, the second Blackfriars, the winter home of the company. "By its title . . . *The Second Maiden's Tragedy* sounds like the second part of *The Maid's Tragedy*, a pairing that might have enabled the two plays to be scheduled on successive afternoons"; "the two 'maiden' tragedies are not literally sequels, but they share a lurid theatricality and a hysterical morality that is expressed in attempted rape and revenge" (Knutson 1999). Possibly performed at court, 1611–12 (Lancashire 1978).

George Buc calls the play "This second Maydens tragedy (for it hath no name inscribed)." The play "has come to be known as *The Second Maiden's Tragedy* . . . through a misunderstanding: Buc meant to call it *The Maiden's Tragedy*" (Wiggins 1998); "Buc gave the manuscript this provisional title because its theme of tyrannicide and its anti-court satire reminded him of Beaumont and Fletcher's *The Maid's Tragedy*, submitted by the same company in the previous year" (Briggs 2007).

MS BL Lansdowne 807, fols. 29–56; anonymous scribe employed by the King's Men (Briggs 1998); no TP; theatrical provenance (Long 1989); includes license for acting signed by Buc, Master of the Revels, which allows performance "wth the reformations"; the last leaf of the MS says, "By Thomas Goff"; this name is cancelled and replaced by George Chapman; in turn, Chapman's name is cancelled and replaced by "Will Shakspear" (each name written in a different hand); John Warburton, who owned the MS that narrowly escaped the hands of his cook, assigned the play to Chapman; contains corrections by someone other than the author (Jackson 1979); SDs preserve the names of two actors, Rich[ard] Robinson, who played the Lady, and R[obert] Gough, who probably played Memphonius (Gurr 2004c); description of dumb show involving the Lady's corpse; five acts. Revisions written on five pieces of paper are pasted into the MS; Rasmussen 1989 and 1990 believes it "possible" that Shakespeare wrote the revisions "during the early stages of production"; Jackson 1990 thinks the additions were made by Middleton himself. "[T]he purpose of the additional passages seems to have been to tighten up the plot" (Briggs 2007). The MS bears signs of considerable censorship: "The 'reformations' delete references to the absolute power claimed by the monarch; corruption at court; exploitation of the poor to finance court luxury; and praying in Latin" (Heinemann 1980). The MS is "the only extant playbook of a play performed by the King's Men when Shakespeare was an active member of the company" (Rasmussen 1997). Of the plays surviving from Shakespeare's time, "only three 'allowed books' have come down to us. Two are play manuscripts"; one is *The Second Maiden's Tragedy*, and the other is *Believe As You List* (Gurr 2009d).

"Costuming references in the stage directions and dialogue . . . make clear the playwright's concern with visual detail" (Lancashire 1978). Staging calls for a property tomb, that of the Lady who kills herself to escape the Tyrant: "*Enter the Tirant agen at a farder dore, which opened, bringes hym to the toombe wher the Lady lies buried; the toombe here discovered ritchly set forthe.*" The Tyrant, "refusing to accept the Lady's death and vowing to reverse it, violates her tomb, steals her corpse and threatens to make love to it" (Zimmerman 2005): "ile claspe the bodie for the spirit that dwelt in't." Govianus, the "rightful heir," subsequently "kneeles at the toomb wondrous passionatly." The second tomb scene is even more spectacular: "*On a sodayne in a kinde of noyse like a wynde, the dores clattering, the toombstone flies open, and a great light appeares in the midst of the toombe; his Lady as went owt, standing just before hym all in white, stuck with jewells and a great crucifex on her brest."* The audience is "encouraged to attend to the skill of the boy actor who plays a Lady in black, then her corpse in white, then her identical Spirit in quick succession" (Neely 2011). The Lady's Ghost tells Govianus that her body has been stolen: "behold, I'me gon / my bodie taken up." The Tyrant arranges the corpse in a chair: "*They bring the body in a chaire drest up in black velvet which setts out the pailenes of the handes and face, and a faire chayne of pearle crosse her brest and the crucyfex above it; he standes silent awile letting the musique play, becknynge the soldiers that bringe her in to make obeisaunce to her, and he hymself makes a lowe honour to the body and kisses the hande."* He "at least touches her, holds her, and kisses her" (Crawford 2003). Govianus disguised as "an artist is commissioned to paint a dead Lady for the Tyrant's erotic pleasure" (Karim-Cooper 2007): "let but thy arte hide death upon her face." In the Tyrant's chamber, the Lady's spirit visits her body: "*Enter the Ghost in the same form as the the lady is drest in the chayre."* It is not clear whether two actors enact the Ghost and dead body "or whether the painted body has been a dummy all along" (Nunn 2005). In any event the Tyrant is doomed by kissing the corpse's lips (poisoned by Govianus), and "*The Spirit [of the Lady] enters agen and stayes to goe out with the body as it were attendinge it."*

SR 9 September 1653 *The Maids Tragedie*, 2ᵈ part; this is listed among "some forty plays or so" that Humphrey Moseley intended to print, an indication that the play was "already identified only by Buc's provisional title" (Briggs 1998). First edited by Baldwyn 1824 in *The Old English Drama: A Selection of Plays from the Old English Dramatists* (vol. 1), which divides the play into five acts and separate scenes. Modern editions by Greg 1909 and Lancashire 1978 (annotated).

"The role of Helvetius in pandering his daughter to the Tyrant's lusts has been associated with the Earl of Northampton's enthusiastic encouragement of a liaison between his niece Frances Howard and the King's favorite, Robert Carr. The censor, George Buc, would have had extra reason to show caution on this issue, as the Earl of Northampton was responsible for having obtained Buc his position" (Auchter 2001).

The Second Part of Antonio and Mellida. See *Antonio's Revenge.*

The Second Part of Arviragus and Philicia. See *2 Arviragus and Philicia.*

The Second Part of Bellamira Her Dream. See *2 Bellamira Her Dream.*

The Second Part of Cicilia and Clorinda. See *2 Cicilia and Clorinda.*

The Second Part of Crafty Cromwell. See *2 Crafty Cromwell.*

The Second Part of Friar Bacon. See *John of Bordeaux.*

The Second Part of Henry IV. See *2 Henry IV.*

The Second Part of If You Know Not Me. See *2 If You Know Not Me.*

The Second Part of King Edward the Fourth. See *2 Edward IV.*

The Second Part of King Henry the Fourth. See *2 Henry IV.*

The Second Part of King Henry the Sixth. See *2 Henry VI.*

The Second Part of Love's Adventures. See *2 Love's Adventures.*

The Second Part of Queen Elizabeth's Troubles. See *If You Know Not Me.*

The Second Part of Tamburlaine. See *2 Tamburlaine.*

The Second Part of the Bloody Conquests of Mighty Tamburlaine. See *2 Tamburlaine.*

The Second Part of the Cid. See *2 The Cid.*

The Second Part of the Contention. See *3 Henry VI.*

The Second Part of the Converted Courtesan. See *2 Honest Whore.*

The Second Part of the Famous History of Promos and Cassandra. See *2 Promos and Cassandra.*

The Second Part of the History of Antonio and Mellida. See *Antonio's Revenge.*

The Second Part of the Honest Whore. See *2 Honest Whore.*

The Second Part of the Iron Age. See *2 Iron Age.*

The Second Part of the Siege of Rhodes. See *2 Siege of Rhodes.*

The Second Part of the Tragicomedy called Newmarket Fair. See *2 Newmarket Fair.*

The Second Part of the Troublesome Reign. See *2 Troublesome Reign.*

The Second Part of the Valiant Cid. See *2 The Cid.*

The Second Part of Thomaso. See *2 Thomaso.*

See Me and See Me Not. See *Hans Beer-Pot.*

Sejanus His Fall. Ben Jonson. Acted ?March 1603-January 1604 (Ayres 1990). By the King's Men, according to the F1 TP, at undetermined venue. This TP gives as the year of first performance 1603 during much of which the theaters were closed because of Elizabeth's death and because of the plague. "The first performances cannot have taken place before Queen Elizabeth died (24 March), for the folio says that the actors were 'the King's Men'" (Butler 2003b). First performance may have taken place at court, perhaps in the "autumn or winter of 1603" (Chambers 1923), "the most likely dates being 26, 27, 28 and 30 December 1603, 1 January 1604, and 2 and 19 February 1604" (Ayres). First performance at the Globe probably occurred after 9 April 1604, when the theaters reopened following a plague closure. Principal actors were Richard Burbage, William Shakespeare (his "last recorded acting assignment" [Dutton 1996]), Augustine Phillips, John Heminges, William Sly, Henry Condell, John Lowin, Alexander Cooke, according to F1. Shakespeare probably played the role of Tiberius (Duncan-Jones 2001); Cooke may have played Agrippina (Forse 1993). Later, in 1626, "the typology of Sejanus became firmly attached to Charles's unpopular favorite Buckingham. During the parliamentary procedures for Buckingham's impeachment, Sir John Eliot offered the resemblance in a speech to the Commons" (Patterson 1982).

SR 2 November 1604 *the tragedie of Sejanus*; transferred 6 August 1605; 3 October 1610; 4 July 1635; 4 March 1639. Q 1605 *Sejanus His Fall*; argument ("*Sejanus* was the first professional playbook, or one of the first, to contain an 'Argument' summarizing the play and situating it in a larger historical context" [Farmer 2010]); list of characters; five acts. Few SDs, only the names of speakers. Staging calls for a property altar and a statue of Fortune. Special effects include the statue coming to life: "See, see, the image stirres"; another character reports, "And turns away" (Kiefer 1983). Grotesque staging includes the dismembering of Sejanus' "already beheaded body" (Nunn 2005) by the mob. Marginal references in Latin give the sources of Jonson's historical knowledge: these notes "came near to overwhelming Jonson's own text, all this to bolster his claim to 'integrity in the story'" (Levy 1995). This material "creates a fissure between the playscript and the reading text, one that Jonson exploits to recreate himself as author and the viewer as reader" (Miola 1999). "In selecting the reign of Tiberius, and particularly the career of Sejanus, for his play, Jonson seized on the section of Tacitus's writings that made the deepest impression on readers of the late Renaissance. Jonson's generation became ever more troubled by the growing ostentation and corruption and duplicity of courts, and by the mounting influence and vaulting ambition of upstart favourites at the expense of ancient noblemen and ancient virtue" (Worden 1994). "In no Renaissance play are sodomy and parasitism so constitutive of national politics as in Jonson's *Sejanus*" (DiGangi 1997). The "dissolution of sexual roles portends social chaos" (Smith 1991b). F1 1616 *The Works*; *Sejanus His Fall, A Tragedy*; "first acted in the yeere 1603"; argument;

list of characters; "chorus — of musicians" at end of acts 1–4, though they cannot have been part of the original performance at the Globe since inter-act music was not yet heard at the public theater (Hosley 1975). "Absent [in F1] are Q's epistle '*To the Readers*,' its coda to the Argument, and six out of eight commendatory verses. . . . As some compensation, F offers a new Dedication. The marginal annotations have all but disappeared" (Jowett 1988). SDs incorporated in F1 (Kidnie 2000a). F2 1640 vol. 1.

Jonson's F1 dedication reports, "It is a poeme [i.e., play], that . . . suffer'd no lesse violence from our people here, then the subject of it did from the rage of the people of Rome; but, with a different fate, as (I hope) merit: for this hath outliv'd their malice, and begot it selfe a greater favour then he lost, the love of good men." In verses published in 1640 Leonard Digges contrasts "irkesome" *Sejanus* with Shakespeare's *Julius Caesar* (Chambers 1930); both plays were performed by the same company, and Richard Burbage probably acted in both (Donaldson 2000). Both plays, moreover, offered "images of the nature of political power, its inherent theatricalization, displaying a sphere in which the body of the ruler, opaque and transparent, extends to the body politic" (Goldberg 1983). But "[a]udiences at the Globe missed the intimate engagement with character of Shakespeare's *Julius Caesar*" (Lever 1971b). *Sejanus* also landed Jonson in trouble with the authorities: this "would seem to be the first occasion on which any dramatist was made to answer *by the government* for his text" (Dutton 1991), and Jonson was "possibly imprisoned" (Dollimore 2004). William Drummond reports that the playwright was "called before ye [Privy] Councell for his *Sejanus* & accused both of popperie and treason." "[T]he play was seen as politically charged" (Perry 1997). Henry Howard, earl of Northampton, who had had some kind of altercation with Jonson, seems to have caused trouble for the playwright, though it is not clear whether the offensive material appeared in the staged or the published play (Dutton 1993). In the Q epistle to the reader, Jonson says that the version staged at the Globe for an unreceptive audience was in part written by "a second pen," often assumed to be George Chapman (Corballis 1979), who contributes a prefatory poem to Q, though Jonson may refer to Shakespeare (Barton 1984). For unspecified reasons Jonson purged the printed play of his collaborator's contributions: "this booke, in all numbers, is not the same with that which was acted on the publicke stage, wherein a second pen had good share." (F1 omits acknowledgment of a "second pen.") Perhaps this purging was undertaken to render the play less offensive to the authorities and thus able to be printed. The Q epistle (missing from F1) also sets forth Jonson's definition of tragedy: "truth of argument, dignity of persons, gravity and height of elocution, fulnesse and frequencie of sentence [i.e., sententious aphorism]." Affirming that his play fulfills these criteria, Jonson defends the work "on aesthetic grounds" (Bergeron 2006).

In his preface Jonson as classicist acknowledges "the want of a proper chorus, whose habits and moods are such and so difficult as not any whom I have seen since the ancients — no, not they who have most presently affected laws — have yet come in the way of." "And yet most of his characters function just as a Chorus would" (Smith 1988a).

1 Selimus. Anonymous. Acted 1591–94 (Chambers 1923); 1592 (Demiralp 2012). "Playd by the" Queen's Men, according to the Q TP, at undetermined venue. "Formed by royal decree in 1583, the company was set up with the best two or three players from each of the companies of the great lords, Leicester's, Warwick's, Oxford's, and Sussex's. They took Richard Tarlton, the most famous clown, and the most famous tragedians, Knell and Bentley" (Gurr 2004a). The 1638 TP ascribes the play to T. G., "supposed to refer to Thomas Goffe, whose Turkish tragedies were then fairly recent" (Bang 1908), but Goffe "was at most four years old" at publication (McMillin & MacLean 1998). The play has also been attributed to Thomas Greene, "and this has never been convincingly refuted" (Vitkus 2000); Murphy 2009 believes that Thomas Lodge was "co-author."

    SR none. Q 1594 *The First Part of the Tragical Reign of Selimus, Sometime Emperor of the Turks and Grandfather to Him that Now Reigneth, Wherein Is Shown How He Most Unnaturally Raised Wars against His Own Father Bajazet, and Prevailing Therein, in the End Caused Him to be Poisoned. Also with the Murdering of His Two Brethren, Corcut and Acomat*; two issues; no author named; prologue and "conclusion" [epilogue]; not divided. Shocking onstage violence includes one character putting out the eyes of another, then amputating the victim's hands. Acomat *"Puls out his [Aga's] eyes."* Aga reports to Bajazet what has happened: "with remorcelesse heart, / [Acomat] Puld out mine eyes, and cut off my weake hands"; *"Mustaffa opens his bosome and takes out his [Aga's] hands."* "Alleged Turkish cruelty was proverbial and stories of fratricide among Turks common knowledge" (Erne 2001a). The blinding of Aga "seems a contributing influence upon" the blinding of Gloucester in *King Lear* (Ronan 1986), a connection observed by Ekeblad 1957. Reissued 1638 with a new TP and without a prologue; author's initials on the TP: "written T. G." Printed at the end of Q is a "conclusion," anticipating *2 Selimus*: "Thus have we brought victorious Selimus, / Unto the crowne of great Arabia: / Next shall you see him with triumphant sword, / Dividing kingdomes into equall shares, / And give them to their warlike followers. / If this first part gentles, do like you well, / The second part, shall greater murthers tell." There is no evidence that *Part 2* was ever written.

    The first part of a projected two-play sequence, *Selimus* is an "attempt to rival *Tamburlaine*" (McMillin & MacLean). Closely related to *Locrine* (Berek 1980, 1987), *Selimus* "is the earliest play extant to be based entirely within the bounds of the Ottoman empire and to be primarily concerned with Ottoman dynastic history" (Dimmock 2005). There are also "some intriguing parallels between" *Selimus* and *Jack Straw* (Demiralp 2012): both plays define rebellion as "unnatural."

The Settling of The Floating Island. See *The Floating Island*.

The Seven Champions of Christendom. ?Wentworth Smith (Freehafer 1969b) and ?Thomas Heywood (Merchant 1978). Acted "with a generall liking" at the Red Bull, according to the TP, by Queen Anne's Men 1613–14; revived at the Phoenix, according to the TP, 1617–19 (Freehafer); performance at the Phoenix may have been by Lady Elizabeth's company, or Queen Henrietta Maria's Men, or Beeston's Boys, all of whom inherited plays formerly acted at the Red Bull.

SR 13 July 1638. Q 1638 initials on the TP (J. K.); dedicatory epistle signed by John Kirke, probably not the playwright; "never printed till this yeare 1638"; list of characters; chorus; five acts. The play may originally have been entitled *St. George for England* (Freehafer); Kirkman 1661 calls it *Champions of Christendom*. The playwright "calls on an array of devices associated with stage devils: thunder and lightning, fireworks, stage smoke, elaborate costumes, enchanters, rocks that open and close, ascending thrones, and magically transformed maidens (three swans turn into women before the spectators' eyes)" (Cox 2000). Staging includes the entry of spirits with a throne, apparently from above, and later *"the throne ascends into the air."* Special effects include repeated *"thunder and lightning"*; the descent of Tarpax, a winged devil, who apparently exits at stage level; the entry of spirits wielding *"fiery clubs"*; a *"rock cleaves"* and a witch *"sinkes"* to hell (through a trap); *"divels run laughing over the stage."* This play contains "the most directions for thunder and lightning" of any in this era (Thomson 1999). *Champions* "closely recalls many of the ambitiously panoramic plays by Heywood staged at the same venue a decade earlier, and explicitly advertises its eclectic inclusion of elements drawn from several generic and dramatic traditions from years past, the same kind of 'mingling of kings and clowns' that had gone out of favor with more fashionable playgoers" (Bayer 2009).

The dedicatory epistle refers to the play's reception when first performed: "it received the rights of a good play, when it was acted, which were applauses & commendations, whether it merited them or not, I leave to your judgement." The epistle also comments on genre: "the nature of the worke being history; it consists of many parts, not walking in one direct path, of *comedy*, or *tragedy*, but having a larger field to trace, which me thinks should yeeld more pleasure to the reader, novelty and variety being the only objects these our times are taken with: the tragedy may be too dull and solid, the comedy too sharpe and bitter; but a well mixt portion of either, doubtlesse would make the sweetest harmony." "To supply the comic element [the playwright] has introduced the conventional clown of the period, talking in puns and malapropisms, brave and boastful in speech but cowardly in deed" (Dawson 1929).

The Seven Days of the Week. Anonymous. Acted "privately in the lodging" of the college president by "divers youths whose voices or personages would not suffer them to act any thing in publicke" at St. John's College, Oxford, 10 January 1608 (Elliott et al. 2004); performed again for the vice-chancellor and Lord Clifford, 17 January. "Nothing throughout the whole yeare was better liked and more pleasaunt then this shewe insomuch that, allthough it were more privately done before our selves onely or some few friends, yet the report of it went about all the towne till it came to the Vicechauncellours and my L: Cliffords eares, who were very desyrous to see it acted againe and so it was," according to the MS.

The MS containing *Seven Days* has come to be known as *The Christmas Prince*; the other English plays are *Periander* and *Time's Complaint*. Oxford, St. John's College, MS 52, pp. 119–28; evidence of revision; list of characters on the TP; prologue and epilogue (both by Clerk of St. Giles); chorus ("Act I ends with a chorus by a woman because 'A play without a woman in't / Is like a face without a nose'" (Richards 1982); seven short acts. Ample SDs. First edited by Bliss 1816. Modern edition by Boas & Greg 1922. Reproduced in photographic facsimile by Richards.

The "mock play" was apparently written by the author of *A Twelfth Night Merriment*: "In both shows each of the actors on his first appearance gives a ridiculously naïve description of the part that he is playing, much after the fashion of Bottom and his fellows in *Pyramus and Thisbe*" (Boas & Greg).

2 Seven Deadly Sins. The "platt" (plot, or "backstage storyboard" [Bate 2008]) of a play that has disappeared but that appears "to belong to the years 1590–91" (Beckerman 1989). "The plot probably related to the play *Four Plays in One*, performed by Strange's Men on 6 March 1592. . . . This appears to have been a survival of Richard Tarlton's play on The Seven Deadly Sins, written for the Queen's Men about 1585" (Foakes 2002). However, although "the extant 'plot' . . . is often taken to be related to Tarlton's play [*The Seven Deadly Sins*], . . . there is no convincing evidence for this connection" (McMillin & MacLean 1998). The date may be later than Beckerman and Foakes assumed: acted 1597–98 by the Lord Chamberlain's Men at the Theater or Curtain (Kathman 2004d, 2005, 2011). The plot "is apparently derived from a performance by an amalgamation of Lord Strange's Men and the Admiral's Men at the Theatre about 1590" (King 1992a). "[I]t is unlikely that the company that performed *2 Seven Deadly Sins* can have been much smaller than thirty" (Carson 1988). The "twenty-two actors . . . handle approximately sixty roles (in all three parts of the play)" (Bevington 1962). "Richard Burbage plays two principal roles, Gorboduc in the first sequence (about Envy) and Tereus in the third sequence (about Lechery), while Richard Cowley plays six minor parts, five of which are identified by function: Lieutenant, Soldier, Lord, Captain, and Musician"; "John Sincler (or Sincklo) plays four small parts [Keeper/Warder, Soldier, Captain, Musician]"; "John Holland [plays] four small parts [Attendant, Soldier, Captain, Warder]" (King). Others in the cast include: George Bryan (Damascus, Lord, Councillor, Warwick); Thomas Pope (Arbactus); Augustine Phillips (Sardanapalus); William Sly (Porrex, Lord); John Duke (Pursuivant, Attendant and Soldier, Will Fool, Lord); Robert Pallant (Warder, Attendant, Soldier, Dordan, Nicanor, Julio); Thomas Goodale (Lucius, Councillor, Phronesius, Messenger, Lord). Also in the cast are

Edward Alleyn, William Sly, John Duke, Robert Pallant, T[homas] Belt (Servant, Panthea), Thomas Goodale, and actors known only by the abbreviations V and W. Henry Condell, who played Ferrex and Lord, was "possibly" the actor named Harry (Gurr 2004c). "Kit," who played Attendant, Soldier, and Captain, may have been Christopher Beeston (Potter 2012); "Vincent," who played a Musician, may have been Thomas Vincent; R. Go., who played Aspatia and Philomela, may have been Robert Gough; Ned, who played ?Rodope, may have been Edmund Shakespeare (Potter); Will, who played Itis, may have been William Ostler or William Eccleston (Kathman 2004d). Other female roles were played by Saunder (Queen Videna and Procne), who may have been Alexander Cooke; Nick (Lady, Pompeia) may have been Nicholas Tooley (King). The actors named were "connected with Strange's Men in the 1590s" (McMillin & MacLean).

Dulwich, UK, Dulwich College MS XIX; ed. Greg 1931; "[t]wo or possibly three dumb shows" explained by Lydgate (Mehl 1965); epilogue; chorus; "divided into three playlets on the subjects of Envy, Sloth, and Lechery, surrounded by an Induction" (Kathman 2004d), but no "formal division into acts" (Greg). SR none. Perhaps the same as *Three Plays in One* or *Five Plays in One* (?parts of *Seven*), performed by the Queen's Men in 1585 (Fleay 1890). But this speculation "depends on arithmetic that does not add up" (McMillin & MacLean). "It is possible that the Plot represents a performance of *Four Plays in One* by Strange's company at the Rose on 6 March 1592" (Bradley 1992).

This "is the second part of a two-part play. Together the parts must have treated seven historical or mythic incidents, each of which exemplified one of the sins"; "[f]raming the action of these individual playlets is the drama of an imprisoned Henry VI visited by the poet Lydgate" (Beckerman 1989). *Seven Deadly Sins* represents "an experimental blending of history play and allegory" (McMillin 2005). Edmond Malone discovered the platt (plot) and printed it in 1780.

The Sexton, or the Mock Testator. A droll based upon a scene in B&F's *The Spanish Curate* and performed in the 1640s and 50s. "The droll presents a single well-developed episode, with an amusing situation and an unexpected ending" (Elson 1932). Performance requires five actors.

Published in *1 The Wits, or Sport upon Sport* (O 1662 [two issues] and 1672); RT *The Humors of The Sexton, or the Mock Testator*; argument; list of characters.

The Shepherds' Holiday, A Pastoral Tragicomedy. Joseph Rutter. Acted 1633–35 (*AED 3*). By Queen Henrietta Maria's Men, according to the TP, at the Phoenix. Performed also at Whitehall, before the king and queen, according to the TP, before 1635.

SR 19 January 1635 a TragiComedy called *the Sheaperdes holliday*. O 1635 author's initials on the TP; Rutter signs the dedication, and he is named in the SR; list of characters; chorus of shepherds and shepherdesses; prologue for the stage; epilogue to the king and queen; five acts and separate scenes.

Rutter "was closely associated with people in the Queen's circle. He was living in Sir Kenelm Digby's house when he wrote his play, and was also tutor to the sons of the Earl of Dorset, the Queen's Lord Chamberlain, who was responsible for arranging her entertainments" (Veevers 1989). Ben Jonson, who regarded Rutter as a "deare sonne," warmly praised the play in a poem prefixed to O (Townsend 1947). Epilogue to the king and queen identifies the stage with virtue: "To you most royall paire, whose lives have brought / Vertue in fashion, and the world have taught, / That chast innocuous sports become the stage / No lesse then civill manners do the age / We dedicate this piece." Here Rutter "flatteringly attributes both the much-proclaimed purity of the new drama and its social refinement to the influence of their majesties" (Neill 1978).

The Shepherds' Paradise, A Pastoral. Walter Montagu and, possibly, Thomas Killigrew (Poynting 1997). Apparently intended for performance in November 1632 at the Paved Court theater, Denmark House, "to celebrate the King's birthday" (Ravelhofer 1999). Acted 9 January 1633; additional performance planned for Candlemas, 2 February, but probably not given until 3 February (Poynting), though Revels accounts do not specifically name the play presented on that date (Orrell 1976). "Privately acted before the late king Charles by the queen's majesty [Queen Henrietta Maria], and ladies of honour," according to the O TP, in the theater at Somerset [Denmark] House, with changeable scenery designed by Inigo Jones: "In addition to the backcloth, the plan shows grooves for back shutters, four pairs of flat wings, and the proscenium and standing scene" (Poynting). This venue was "covered with a pine roof to protect the performance from bad weather, as the French ambassador reported" (Findlay 2006). Possibly revived Shrove Tuesday, March 5 (Orgel & Strong 1973), but Orrell and Poynting are skeptical. The play had been rehearsed for about six months before production (Gough 2005). "Joseph Taylor, one of the leading actors in the King's Company at the Globe, had been brought in as an acting coach for the ladies" (Elliott & Buttrey 1985); he "conducted rehearsals at court from 15 September 1632 until [the play] was finally performed" in January 1633 (Potter 1992). The play is "one of the first to have an all-female cast made up entirely of aristocrats and royalty" (Aaron 2005); Queen Henrietta Maria "took the chief part" (Cotton 1980), the role of Bellessa (White 2006), "the newly elected queen of the Shepherds' Paradise, an order devoted to the ideals of beauty and chastity" (Tomlinson 2005). By staging the play, "Henrietta Maria was breaking every rule in the book" (Findlay 2002). "Nine out of the thirteen actresses played masculine roles" (Tomlinson). Candelabra were brought to Somerset House from Whitehall for the performance (*Calendar of State Papers Venetian*). The Paved Court theater, designed by William Webb and Inigo Jones, seems to have been specially constructed in late 1632 for the performance of Montagu's play (Orrell 1985). John Pory records in October

1632 that the play, originally intended for production on the king's birthday, 19 November, was extremely long (Aaron); performance lasted nearly eight hours.

(1) Washington, Folger, MS V.b.203 [Tixall MS], fols. 1–63, ed. Poynting 1997; no TP; no author named; evidence of corrections; prologue/induction consists of colloquy between Diana and Apollo; songs between the acts; five acts and separate scenes. (2) Folger, MS V.b.204; no TP, no author named; list of characters. (3) London, BL, Stowe MS 976, fols. 1–68; no TP; list of characters. (4) BL Sloane 3649, fols. 1–87; no TP; no author named; list of characters; prologue (Apollo-Diana colloquy); extensive SDs. (5) BL, Additional MS 41617, fols. 1–112; *The Shepherds' Paradise, A Pastoral*; author named; list of characters on the TP; no prologue or epilogue. The play "circulated in manuscript" (Harbage 1936). SR 27 September 1658 written by a person of honour. O 1659 *The Shepherds' Paradise, A Comedy*; some copies are misdated 1629 on the TP; list of characters with names of actors; no prologue; no songs between the acts; five acts.

"The rules of Platonic discipline [an interest of Queen Henrietta Maria] are illustrated with painful fullness of detail" (Lynch 1926). The play dramatizes "ideas on love encouraged by the Queen, and a pattern for the kind of conduct acceptable amongst her group at court" (Veevers 1989). "The play introduced *préciosité* to the English stage, made courtier playwrights respectable" (Franceschina 1997). "[T]he first English play written specifically for women" (Tomlinson 1999), "*Shepherds' Paradise* struggles with women's expression of sexual feeling with a fastidiousness which suggests the novelty of the theatrical situation for the original audience" (Tomlinson 2005). "Despite the fact that *The Shepherd's Paradise* was penned by a man, it nevertheless accorded its female participants the means of investigating alternative ways of expressing themselves, not least because they were members of a female acting troupe whose interaction upon the stage produced a specific cultural artifact" (Britland 2006b). William Prynne, who attacked women actors in *Histrio-Mastix* (1633) around the time that the queen acted in Montagu's play, was called before the Star Chamber and sentenced to have his cheeks branded and his ears cut off.

A Shoemaker, A Gentleman. William Rowley. Acted 1617–18 (Darby 2002); acted "before 1620" (Nicol 2003) by Prince Charles's Men, "who performed at the Bull from 1616–19 and from 1624–6" (Nicol). "Sundry times acted at the Red Bull and other theaters, with a generall and good applause," according to the TP. Possibly revived in the late 1620s or 30s. Rowley's play "celebrates the hybrid and devolved make-up of British religion": Rowley "has changed his sources to emphasize the Welshness of the British saints, and thus how much Protestant England owes to the principality" (Kerrigan 2008).

SR 28 November 1637 *A Shoomaker is a gentleman.* Q 1638 *A Merry and Pleasant Comedy Never before Printed, Called A Shoemaker, A Gentleman*; author's initials on the TP; list of characters; five acts. Staging calls for use of a trapdoor: "Musicke . . . *Enter, an* Angell *ascends out of the well, and after descends againe* . . . .

Musicke heere descends." These last words may indicate that the musicians leave the music room above and enter the main stage. A discovery scene may involve a temporary structure: *"Enter discover'd in a shop, a shoo-maker, his wife spinning,"* though it is more likely that the shop constituted the discovery space, covered by a curtain (Kiefer 2007). Staging involves elaborate entrances: *"Enter* Dioclesian, *the eagle borne before him at one doore, at the other,* Huldrick *and* Rodrick, *Kings of the* Goths, *and* Vandalls, *with their army."*

In an address borrowed in part from Heywood's *Four Prentices,* the printer John Okes comments on the gap between performance and publication, acknowledging a change in theatrical fashion: "I know it may come short of that accuratenes both in plot and style that this witty age doth with greater curiosity acquire, I may thus excuse; that as plaies were then, some twenty yeares agone, it was in the fashion. Nor could it have found a fitter or more seasonable publication than at this time; when the glory of our nation is so much admired, and the valour of our English so much esteemd, that it is sought for by forraigne natives, as you may reade in this subject we have in hand." "In other words, these [earlier] plays are not merely *older than* but significantly *different from* Caroline plays, and while they may fall short of contemporary drama in the nicety of form and language (together with the scurrility and ribaldry) favored by a 'witty age' of 'greater curiosity,' they surpass them in a direct and unrefined style appreciated by numerous playgoers and readers" (Farmer & Lesser 2006).

The Shoemakers' Holiday, or The Gentle Craft, with the Humorous Life of Simon Eyre, Shoemaker and Lord Mayor of London. Thomas Dekker. Acted late summer-autumn 1599 (Smallwood & Wells 1979). By Lord Admiral Nottingham's Men, according to the Q1 TP, at the Rose. (Henslowe records payment for "A Boocke of Thomas dickers Called the gentle Craft," 15 July 1599.) Also "acted before the queenes most excellent majestie" by the same company, the night of 1 January 1600, according to the Q1 TP, at Richmond Palace (Harris 2008). "The play was reprinted several times before the closing of the theatres in 1642, and this suggests that it probably enjoyed a number of revivals" (Parr 1990).

SR no original; transferred 19 April 1610; 27 June 1646; 4 April 1655. Q1 1600 no author named; RT *A Pleasant Comedy of the Gentle Craft;* prologue at court; not divided. The words "Humorous Life" in the title suggests the connection between Dekker's play and recently popular "humors" comedy (Gurr 2009c). Q1 prints two songs at the beginning, but "the text affords no indications of their placing" (Knowles 2001a). "Removed from their location in the performance, the songs take on the conventional appearance of a broadside ballad" (Lesser 2006b). The songs "seem to date from a revision of the play" (Stern 2009c). In this drama of high spirits and celebration, the most affecting moment involves the shoemaker Rafe, who returns from the war wounded: *"Enter Rafe being lame."* His "safe return, after he has been reported dead, is a welcome fantasy of wish-fulfillment for a nation wearied and worried by war" (Kastan 1991). He is reunited with his wife, who has left Simon Eyre's business, when a servant brings Rafe a shoe and asks him to craft a duplicate. Rafe instantly recognizes the footwear as his own earlier gift to Jane: "This is the verie shoe I gave my wife." At one point Simon Eyre commands, "Open my shop windowes!" "One possibility . . . is that one or more of the stage doors was itself outfitted with shutters" (Smallwood & Wells 1990). "The most eye-catching stage properties" are "sartorial items": footwear, clothes, and ceremonial robes (Harris). "A morris dance is one of the diversions furnished" in the play (Wright 1928). Unusual sound effects include the ringing of a "pancake-bell" (Lawrence 1935). Q2 1610. Q3 1618. Q4 1624. Q5 1631. Q6 1657 the songs have been dropped. The publication history suggests that the play was "much more popular in [its] own day than in ours" (Bruster 2004).

The play "is defined by the lively invocation of its urban setting. This is not surprising considering Dekker's lifelong, intimate fascination with London" (Walsh 2006). Dekker "subtly dramatizes the change from an old code of communal fellowship to a new capitalist one, in which commercial venturing in luxury commodities has become the individual's means to wealth and social status" (Harris). "Although the play concludes with a feast and the eponymous holiday, it carefully depicts some of the cultural tensions of contemporary London society"; the play includes "a compassionate and sensitive presentation of lower-class characters and an intimate depiction of London" (Twyning 2004).

Shore's Wife. See *1 Edward IV.*

Sicelides, A Piscatory. Phineas Fletcher. "[P]repared by students of King's College [Cambridge] for performance before the king (?in Trinity College hall) in case he stayed the night of Saturday 11 March [1615]; although not performed then because of his departure, it was performed at King's College (probably in the hall) on Monday, 13 March [1615]" (Nelson 1989). Prologue refers to the youthful actors: "they will all agree, / Gently to beare their actors infancy."

(1) London, BL, Additional MS 4453, fols. 1–34; "a Piscatorie made by Phinees Fletcher and acted in Kings Colledge in Cambridge"; list of characters on the TP; prologue and epilogue; chorus at close of the first four acts; five acts and separate scenes. Unusual staging includes the entry of two characters "*with their boate from fishing.*" Special effects include: "*The rocke opens.*" This MS is also catalogued as BL Sloane 4453. (2) Oxford, Bodleian, MS Rawlinson poet. 214, fols. 1–65; no separate TP; no author named; dramatis personae; prologue and epilogue. SR 25 April 1631. Q 1631 no author named; dramatis personae; prologue (by Chamus) and epilogue; chorus at close of first four acts; five acts and separate scenes. Epilogue speaks of the "playwright's duty to provide delight" to both hearing and sight (Schneider 2011): "As in a feast, so in a comedy, / Two sences must be pleasd in both the eye, / In feasts, the eye and taste must be invited, / In comedies, the eye and eare delighted."

"Fletcher called his piscatory *Sicelides* . . . a 'comedy' [in the epilogue]; but the play has virtually all the characteristics of a pastoral tragicomedy. Its main action was indebted to the Italian pastoral and to pastoral romance as well as to classical mythology" (Herrick 1955).

Sicily and Naples, or The Fatal Union, A Tragedy. Samuel Harding. Circumstances of production, if any, are unclear: apparently intended for performance at Exeter College, Oxford, but not performed there. "Possibly there was an abortive attempt at staging the play" (Roberts 1986). A prefatory poem by Richard Doddridge says mysteriously, "As soone as shee had life, she was wish't dead, / Or under her owne ashes buried; / But now a glorious phoenix rais'd is shee / From this and her supposed tragedie." The playwright clearly anticipates production; the epilogue begins: "After these ruines, thus your poët stands, / Expecting his owne destiny from your hands." And the play shows "a distinct awareness of variations offered by the physical make-up of the stage" (Shaw 1979).

SR none. Q 1640 author's initials on the TP; dramatis personae; epilogue; five acts and separate scenes. Very detailed SDs: "*Calantha discovered lying upon a banke of flowers, with a chaplet upon her head, enter severall wayes sixe furies, in anticke postures: at the sound of the musicke they dance, which ended, enter Mercury conducting in a chorus of ghosts: the Furies runne severall wayes: Mercury goes to Calantha, touches her with his rod, whereupon she rises, and he speakes.*"

In his address to the reader, Philip Papillon alludes to criticism of the play: "Those that have dar'd dislike it already, would grow proud, if by presenting it to the common view, I did not shew for what a nothing I esteeme their censures; whatsoever syllables there be, that they ever cavill'd at, is therefore not omitted that thou may'st have wherein, or to laugh at their vaine criticizing, or to shew thine own candour." This statement suggests that "pressure had been put on him to alter his play in the light of criticism" (Stern 2004b). Samuel Hall of Exeter College, alluding to a play by John Suckling renowned for its expensive costumes, writes of Harding's work, "She'le out-blaze bright *Aglaura's* shining robe: / Her scene shall never change, the world's her Globe." *Sicily and Naples* illustrates "the carrying power of the new dramatic fashion initiated by the Caroline courtiers" (Harbage 1936).

The Siege. William Davenant. Licensed for acting, possibly, as *The Colonel*, 22 July 1629 (Adams 1917, Harbage 1935, Edmond 1987). Acted by the King's Men at the second Globe.

SR ?1 January 1630 A play called *The Collonell*; 9 September 1653; transferred 14 October 1672. F 1673 *The Works*; "now published out of the authors originall copies"; *The Siege*; list of characters; five acts. The F version of *The Siege* evidently represents a revision of the play licensed in 1629.

"This piece has been thought to be the same as 'The Colonel' by Davenant licensed for acting by Sir Henry Herbert on 22 July 1629 and entered in SR on

1 Jan. 1630 . . . but the identification is very uncertain since the colonel in *The Siege* as printed is hardly of sufficient importance to have supplied the title of the play" (Greg 1939).

1 *The Siege of Rhodes*. William Davenant. Acted probably September 1656 at Rutland House in Aldersgate Street; the venue proved unsatisfactory to Davenant because of "the cramped conditions under which performances had to be given" (Lawrence 1913b); "its sets, though adapted to the tiny dimensions of the Rutland House stage, were the work of John Webb, a pupil of Inigo Jones" (Potter 1981). "[W]e possess [Webb's] measured scene designs" for this play; "we also have, collected in the Lansdowne MS folio of Webb drawings at the British Library, a plan and section—clearly in Webb's hand—of a stage which appears to be related to them" (Orrell 1985). Davenant "moved his production of *The Siege of Rhodes* from Rutland House to the Phoenix in 1658" (King 1965): "Made a representation by the art of prospective [i.e., perspective] in scenes, and the story sung in recitative musick," according to the Q1 TP. (The Cockpit [Phoenix] "had been dismantled in 1649," but William Beeston "had refitted it, at the high cost of £200, in 1651" [Edmond 1987].) "Davenant uses the inverse of what was to be normal Restoration practice, by changing the scenery before the Act begins"; the "effect of Davenant's method is to allow the audience to interpret the set before the action commences" (Holland 1979). "It can be assumed that" the "indistinct generic identity, part debate, part opera, part masque, and part play" of this and other such works by Davenant "enabled them to circumvent the prohibition of 1642, subsequently reinforced, on the presentation of plays" (Clare 1994). The production featured "the presence in the play of the first Englishwoman, Mrs. [Catherine] Coleman, to act on an English public stage" (Cauthen 1987b). "In 1661 both parts of *The Siege of Rhodes* were staged alternately at the Lisle's Tennis Court theatre" (Wiseman 1990). Also performed at the Duke of York's theater: "lately represented at his highness the Duke of York's theatre in Lincoln's-Inn Fields," according to Q3 1663 and F 1673. The revised version of the play, contained in Q3, may have been performed before the Restoration (Hedbäck 1973). "When *The Siege of Rhodes* was revised for the opening of the more spacious Duke's playhouse in 1661 Davenant, because he now had more than one actress, added the character Roxolana . . . [who] was played by Hester Davenport, the first well-known English actress" (Cauthen).

SR 27 August 1656 a maske called *The siege of Rhodes*; 30 May 1659; the play "resembled the court masque in its division into entries rather than acts and scenes, in its librettist and musical personnel, and in the perspective scenery designed by John Webb" (Tomlinson 2005). Q1 1656 two issues; no author named on the TP but Davenant signs the address to the reader; list of characters and, at the end, names of the actors who played the roles; several choruses; divided into five "entries," the entries "closely resembling acts" (Clare 2004); "presumably *entries* was a safer term than *acts*" (Randall). "Twice reissued with different title pages" (Holland 1979). Q2 1659 the TP records a change of venue from Rutland House to the Phoenix. Reissued 1663, *The Siege of Rhodes, The First and Second Part*, with additions: "the first part being lately enlarg'd," "in anticipation of a more commodious stage than that described in the preface of the 1656 play" (Birchwood 2007); Davenant named on the TP; new list of characters; this revision includes "Roxolana (Solyman's wife and empress) and various female attendants" (Randall); the new material is "added on three new half-sheets and one single leaf"; four leaves have been replaced (Holland). Q3 1663; "in spite of Greg, the second part of the play was not printed at the same time as Q3 but instead as the running-titles show, was printed with the additions to Q2" (Holland). Q4 1670. F 1673 *The Works*; "now published out of the authors originall copies"; the general TP dated 1673, separate 1672.

"One of the most important dramatic creations of the century," *The Siege of Rhodes* "is nowadays generally held to be both the first English opera and a forerunner of the Restoration heroic play" (Randall). In 1661 Davenant "opened the new theatre at Lincoln's Inn Fields with a revised and expanded version of *The Siege of Rhodes*, probably offering both parts on alternating days" (Winn 1998). The description of the first scene suggests how detailed were the set designs: "*The ornament which encompass'd the scene, consisted of several columns, of gross rustick work, which bore up a large freese. In the middle of the freese was a compartiment, wherein was written RHODES. The compartiment was supported by divers habiliments of war; intermix'd with the military ensignes of those several nations who were famous for defence of that island.*" "We have a full set of wing and backscene designs" for the play (Orrell 1988). This production employed "a proscenium arch for the first time on a public English stage" (Randall 1995). The music, now lost, was provided by Henry Lawes, Henry Cook, Matthew Locke, Charles Coleman, and George Hudson, according to the second issue of Q1.

2 The Siege of Rhodes. William Davenant. Probably staged June 1659 (Edmond 1987), at the Phoenix (Lawrence 1913b). Later staged at the Duke's Playhouse in Lincoln's Inn Fields, 2 July 1661 (diary of Samuel Pepys).

SR 30 May 1659. Q1 1663 *The Siege of Rhodes, The First and Second Part*; two issues; no author named on the TP; "lately represented at his highness the Duke of York's theatre in Lincoln's-Inn Fields"; prologue and epilogue; "choruses have been omitted in this part" (Hedbäck 1973); five acts. Q1 prints *Part 1* and *Part 2* as one book but with separate register and pagination. The SDs indicate painted scenery and attention to perspective: "*The scene is chang'd to the camp of Solyman, the tents and guards seem near, and part of Rhodes at a distance.*" However, "we have no plans or designs as we have for the First Part" (Southern 1952). The second issue of Q1 reports, "The First Part being lately enlarg'd." Q2 1670 printed together with *Part 1*; continuous register and pagination; prologue and epilogue. F 1673 *The Works*; "now published out of the authors originall copies"; the general TP is dated 1673, the separate 1672.

Part 2 "was conceived by Davenant along more traditional dramatic lines [than *Part 1*]" (Hedbäck).

The Siege, or Love's Convert, A Tragicomedy. William Cartwright. Although no evidence exists that this play was produced, Evans 1951 notes that William Towers' commendatory poem "suggest[s] an actual performance of the play," perhaps in the 1630s; acted 1628–38 (*AED 3*). Bentley is dubious about performance (*JCS*).

SR 4 May 1648. O 1651 *Comedies, Tragi-Comedies, with Other Poems* (with *The Lady Errant, The Ordinary, The Royal Slave*); list of characters; five acts and separate scenes. Staging involves a nuptial masque, which begins with the display of five generals standing like statues: "*The statues by the stealth of a slow motion, do by little and little as it were assume life; and descending from their pedestals walk about the stage in a grave sad march to trumpets, with their severall weapons in their hands, the curtain in the mean time shutting: but making at last toward their former station, the curtain flies aside, and they find five ladies on their pedestalls, in the posture of amorous statues; at whose feet they having laid their weapons, conduct them down, and fall into a sprightly dance to violins.*"

"Cartwright planned to destroy the manuscript of *The Siege*, but upon Charles' intervention it was revised and published" (Harbage 1936). This is "the only play before the Restoration dedicated directly to the reigning sovereign" (Evans).

Sight and Search. See *Time's Distractions*.

The Silent Woman. See *Epicene*.

The Silver Age. Thomas Heywood. Acted 1609–11 (Taylor 1993a) by Queen Anne's Men at the Red Bull (Harbage 1952). Performed also by the combined Queen Anne's and King's Men at Greenwich, before Queen Anne and Prince Henry, 12 January 1612 (Chambers 1930). Dramatis personae in Q lists thirty-two named parts plus another twenty characters, necessitating the collaboration of two companies. "Such amalgamations were extremely rare" (Gurr 2009d).

SR no original; transferred 2 August 1630. Q 1613 *The Silver Age, Including The Love of Jupiter to Alcmena, The Birth of Hercules, and The Rape of Proserpine, Concluding with The Arraignment of the Moon*; dramatis personae; first and last speeches by Homer serve functions of prologue and epilogue; chorus altered for court performance (Griffin 2001); elaborate descriptions of five dumb shows explained by Homer; "imperfectly divided into acts, with the entries of Homer as chorus . . . and some dumb shows" (Greg 1939). Staging involves considerable use of machinery: the descent of Jupiter "*in a cloude*"; "*Juno and* Iris *descend from the heavens*"; "Mercury *flies from above.*" "*Earth riseth from under the stage*"; then "*Earth sinkes.*" Staging calls for liberal use of fireworks: "Hercules *sinkes himselfe: flashes of fire; the divels appear at every corner of the stage with severall fire-workes. The judges of hell and the three sisters [Fates] run over the stage, Hercules after them:*

fire-workes all over the house"; the SDs suggest no fewer than four trap doors from which devils emerge (Hodges 1999), but the devils may come "from under the platform, with a clambering up at each corner" (Nicoll 1959); they emerge directly into the yard from beneath the stage (Bowsher 1998). Spectacular action: "*Thunder and lightning. All the servants run out of the house affrighted, the two Captains and* Blepharo, Amphitrio *and* Socia *amazedly awake:* Jupiter *appeares in his glory under a raine-bow, to whom they all kneele*"; entry of Pluto "*his chariot drawne in by divels*"; at another point Pluto enters "*with a club of fire, a burning crowne,* Proserpine, *the Judges, the Fates, and a guard of divels, all with burning weapons.*" Also the entries of Triton "*as from the sea.*" "*Thunder, lightnings,* Jupiter *descends in his majesty, his thunderbolt burning*"; "*As he touches the bed it fires, and all flyes up*"; this represents "an unexampled and unexplainable effect" (Lawrence 1913a). At the close "Pluto, *hels judges, the Fates and Furies downe to hell:* Jupiter, *the gods and planets ascend to heaven.*"

Acts 2 and 4, dealing with the stories of Alcmena and Semele, were revised by Heywood as acts 4–5 and 3 of *The Escapes of Jupiter, c.* 1625. The epistle to the reader suggests the order of composition of the *Ages* plays: "wee begunne with *Gold*, follow with *Silver*, proceede with *Brasse*, and purpose by Gods grace, to end with *Iron.*" Part of the play was adapted as a droll entitled *The Conceited Humors of Simpleton the Smith* and later printed in *The Wits, or Sport upon Sport* (O 1662 [two issues] and 1672).

Simpkin. See *Singing Simpkin.*

Simpleton the Smith. An entertainment possibly written by Robert Cox and apparently starring this actor, according to *2 The Wits.* Written *c.* 1647 (Halliwell[-Phillipps] 1860a). "Acted at the Red Bull," according to the Q2 TP of *Actaeon.* This is a "genuine short farce" and therefore different from drolls adapted from plays and printed in *The Wits* (Elson 1932).

Q 1656 *Actaeon and Diana*; "second edition"; *Simpleton* is appended to this book; "not before extant," perhaps meaning that it had not yet been printed. Published in "very slightly abridged" form (Elson) in *1 The Wits, or Sport upon Sport* (O 1662 [two issues] — RT *The Conceited Humors of Simpleton the Smith* — and O 1672 [*The Humor of Simpleton*]); "argument needless, it being a thorow farce, and very well known"; list of characters; not divided. "In Kirkman's *Wits* there is a frontispiece where Cox is represented in the role of Simpleton" (Rollins 1921). He is represented "entering 'with a great piece of Bread and Butter.' The droll concerns the trick by which the whore he marries, Doll, prevents him from catching her gentlemen with her"; according to Kirkman, "Cox was celebrated for his appearance in this droll eating bread and butter" (Foakes 1985).

"*Simpleton* is reminiscent of jestbooks from both the sixteenth and seventeenth centuries and carries forward a strain of broad humor something like that in *John John, Gammer Gurton's Needle,* and probably many a now-lost jig" (Randall 1995).

Singing Simpkin. Originally a jig, which "is almost certainly Elizabethan, indicating the continuity of jig, interlude and droll" (Clare 2004); "[n]ot only was there overlap between the genres of droll and jig; sometimes there was identity" (Randall 1995). "'Singing Simpkin' (1595), [was] originally danced by Will Kemp" (Smith 1999); the SR entry lists "a ballad called Kemp's new jig betwixt a soldier and a miser and Sim the clown" (Wiles 1987). "[I]n *Singing Simpkin*, Simpkin uses a contrivance involving concealment in a chest to enable him to cuckold an old man and outwit a blustering soldier who is trying to seduce the same woman" (Butler 2004d). This jig, or "short song-play" (Elson 1932), was apparently revised by Robert Cox, taking the form of a droll. Cox was a "Commonwealth comedian, who, in the days of Puritanical ascendancy, strolled about the country with a little troupe of three or four players, giving these drolls at fairs and wakes. In this way the vogue of the jig survived the silencing of the theatres" (Lawrence 1927). Cox was apparently not the originator of this jig: "At least two of his drolls, *Singing Simpkin* and *The Black Man*, are nothing but revivals of popular old jigs, now lost, of which translations, earlier in date than his own work, survive in German, Dutch, and Scandinavian versions" (Rollins 1921). Subsequently performed in the 1650s. "Acted at the Red Bull," according to the Q2 TP of *Actaeon*. "*Singing Simpkin* may be pithily described as a salacious operetta of intrigue, written to be sung to a variety of well-worn tunes by five characters" (Lawrence). Performance requires four or five actors.

Published in *Actaeon and Diana* (Q1 ?1655 and Q2 1656 ["the second edition"]); TP *Singing Simkin*; list of characters; not divided. Adequate SDs: "*Knock within*"; "*The tune alters*"; "*A chest set out.*" Later published by Kirkman in *The Wits, or Sport upon Sport* (O 1662 [two issues] and 1672); RT *The Humors of Simpkin*; in place of an argument are the words "a continued farce," which "may hint that the publisher knew the piece to be older than Cox" (Elson); list of characters.

Singing Simpkin "perhaps provides a hint for *The Merry Wives of Windsor*" (Bate 2008).

Sir Clyomon and Clamydes. See *Clyomon and Clamydes.*

1 Sir Francis Drake. William Davenant. Acted at the rebuilt Cockpit in Drury Lane, the winter of 1658–59 (Randall 1995). "It can be assumed that" the "indistinct generic identity, part debate, part opera, part masque, and part play, enabled" this and other such works by Davenant "to circumvent the prohibition of 1642, subsequently reinforced, on the presentation of plays" (Clare 1994). Although "operatic, it had more of the elements of a play than its predecessors—dialogue, more action, and conflict" (Bentley 1981).

SR 20 January 1659. Q 1659 *The History of Sir Francis Drake, Expressed by Instrumental and Vocal Music and by Art of Perspective in Scenes, The First Part*; no author named; chorus; divided into six "entries." Extensive SDs, which explain what playgoers see: "*The preparation of the opening of the scene is by a prelude and corante. Afterwards the curtain rises by degrees to an ascending ayre, and a harbour is discern'd . . . where two ships are moor'd, and sea-carpenters are erecting a pinnace, whilst others are felling trees to build a fort. The narrowness to the entrance of the harbour may be observ'd, with rocks on either side; and out at sea a ship towing a prize."* Staging calls for a front curtain; at the close *"The curtain falls."* F1 1673 *Works*; "now published out of the authors originall copies"; conjoined with *The Cruelty of the Spaniards in Peru* and entitled *The Playhouse to be Let* [*Sir Francis Drake* constitutes the third act]; prologue and epilogue; divided into five acts with separate "entries." In *Playhouse to Be Let*, "first performed in the late summer of 1663, Davenant revived *The Cruelty of the Spaniards in Peru* and *Sir Francis Drake*, but framed them ironically, thus economically recycling his own materials while indicating his awareness of the tastes of the Restoration audience" (Winn 1998).

"The drama helps to promote the idea of a continuity of British sea domination and colonization from the 1580s to the 1650s" (Clare 2002).

Sir Giles Goosecap, Knight, A Comedy. George Chapman. Acted between autumn 1601 and spring 1603 (Parrott 1910); *c.* 1602 (Braden 1987a). By the Children of the Chapel, according to the Q1 TP, at the second Blackfriars; "reference to Children of the Chapel places it in Blackfriars repertory of 1600–3" (Munro 2005). Possibly performed 18 September 1602 (Tricomi 1982). "Lately acted with great applause" at the Salisbury Court playhouse, according to the Q2 TP, by an unidentified boys' company (Butler 2006).

SR 10 January 1606. Q1 1606 no author named; list of characters; evidence of revision (Hennedy 1987); play ends in "song and dance" (Baskervill 1929); five acts and separate scenes. "Lord Momford gives an uncalled for exhibition of his dancing ability. The direction is simply, 'He daunceth speaking'" (Wright 1928). "*Sir Giles* presents an array of humours characters" (Cathcart 2012); it capitalized on the success of Chapman's *Blind Beggar of Alexandria* and *Humorous Day's Mirth*, as well as Jonson's *Every Man In His Humor* and *Every Man Out*. Q2 1636 no author named; new dedicatory epistle by the publisher Hugh Perry.

By studying stylistic details, Parrott 1906 was influential in making the case for Chapman's authorship, which is accepted today, though there is a "continuing sense that the play stands on the margins of Chapman's dramatic canon" (Cathcart 2012). The play is attributed to Chapman "in part because of the similarity of its character Clarence to Dowsecer in *A Humorous Day's Mirth* and to Chapman himself" (Braden).

Sir John Falstaff. See *The Merry Wives of Windsor*.

1 Sir John Oldcastle, the Good Lord Cobham. Michael Drayton, Anthony Munday, Robert Wilson, and Richard Hathway. Acted between 1 and 8 November 1599 (Rittenhouse 1984), according to Henslowe's *Diary*. "Lately acted by" Lord Admiral Nottingham's Men, according to the Q1 TP, at the Rose (Rhodes 1976).

Performed 6 March 1600 at the home of Lord Hunsdon, according to a letter from Rowland Whyte to Robert Sidney. "*Oldcastle* was thoroughly refurbished for its revival by Worcester's Men [which had absorbed Oxford's Men]" (Rutter 1984), 1602–03 (Taylor 2002b). ["A second part of the play (now lost) followed in 1600 and was apparently revived in 1602" (O'Connell 2000b).] Henslowe records payment to the playwrights, apparently for *Part 1*, 16 October 1599; he records payment for *Part 2*, "between 19 and 26 Dec. 1599" (Simpson 1908). Henslowe records payment to Dekker "for new A dicyons in owldcastelle" 17 August 1602, and to Dekker "for his adicions in owld castell," 7 September 1602. Henslowe also records payment "to bye a sewt for owld castell" 21 August 1602; this was apparently a costume worn by Will Kemp, "probably to play Sir John of Wrotham, a parodic version of Falstaff" (Gurr 2004c). There is "regular reference to Shakespeare's play in the *Oldcastle* text" (Gurr 2000). Possibly revived at the Whitehall Cockpit, 6 January 1631, but more likely the performance was of Shakespeare's *1 Henry IV*.

SR 11 August 1600; transferred 4 August 1626; 8 November 1630; 6 August 1674; 21 August 1683. Q1 1600 *The First Part of the True and Honorable History of the Life of Sir John Oldcastle, the Good Lord Cobham*; "Lord Cobham [was] his title through marriage" (Gurr 2000); no author named; Kirkman's 1661 catalogue ascribes "Old Castles life and death" to Shakespeare; prologue (possibly "written for the play's publication" [Corbin & Sedge 1991]); not divided. "Wilson probably wrote the comic scenes, which bear definite similarities to his earlier work" (Kathman 2004f). Q2 1619 published by Thomas Pavier and falsely dated 1600; "printed by William Jaggard" (Greg 1939); "written by William Shakespeare"; "presumably attributed to Shakespeare because 'Oldcastle' was the original name of 'Falstaff' in *1 Henry IV*" (Wells & Taylor 1987); "clearly based on Q1 and there are no signs of authorial intervention or playhouse practice in the revisions that characterise Q2" (Corbin & Sedge). Shakespeare F3 1664 second issue; "the third impression. And unto this impression is added seven playes, never before printed in folio"; not divided. Shakespeare F4 1685 "the fourth edition"; two issues. The attribution to Shakespeare is not credited today.

Oldcastle was apparently written to capitalize on the popularity of Shakespeare's *Henry IV* plays. The Q1 prologue alludes disparagingly to Shakespeare's Falstaff, who was originally named Sir John Oldcastle: "It is no pamperd glutton we present, / Nor aged councellour to youthfull sinne, / But one, whose vertue shone above the rest, / A valiant martyr, and a vertuous peere." "Criticism of Shakespeare's disrespectful portrait of Oldcastle as well as of his ill-served replacement, the historical figure Sir John Fastolf, continued through the Interregnum, but actual intervention was probably quick. As early as the 1596–97 holiday season William Brooke, Lord Cobham and Lord Chamberlain overseeing dramatic production at court, may have reacted against Shakespeare's satirical representation of Oldcastle, a predecessor of Lord Cobham related to Brooke by marriage" (Whitney 2006). The original Oldcastle was a Lollard martyr, and the living Lord Cobham was a "Puritan descendant of Oldcastle" (Bevington 1968); the Oldcastle of the play, loyal to his king, shares "Puritan sympathies"; the "contemporary significance" of the play "seems, therefore, unquestionable" (Adkins 1942). Oldcastle "is presented as an exemplum of private Puritan values" (Corbin & Sedge); "*Oldcastle* is the moderate Puritans' warning to extremists of their own party" (Bevington). "While the historical Oldcastle is being scrupulously whitewashed as 'the good Lord Cobham,' the fat knight creeps in through the back door, thinly disguised as Sir John the Parson of Wrotham, accompanied by his deplorable concubine Doll, and sweeps everything before him" (Barton 1984).

Sir John Oldcastle (Shakespeare). See *1 Henry IV.*

Sir John van Olden Barnavelt. John Fletcher and Philip Massinger (Hoy 1957). Scheduled for performance 14 August 1619 but blocked, for the play criticized Spanish power in the Low Countries; "its political and religious tone offended the Bishop of London, or someone who moved the Bishop of London to act, and the play was prohibited" (Edwards 1981). George Buc, "Master of the Revels demanded extensive revisions" (Butler 2002). "One wonders if the Jacobean audience was expected to see analogies between the affairs of Barnavelt and those of Sir Walter Raleigh, who had been executed the previous year" (*JCS*). Acted by 16 August 1619 (Long 1999); acted 27 August 1619 (Howard-Hill 1979) by the King's Men at the second Globe; "it played for some days to packed houses" (Heinemann 1980), despite the rewritten ending, confusing "the final political effect of the play" (Heinemann 2003). Joseph Taylor probably played Orange; John Lowin, Barnavelt; Robert Benfield, Bredero; Henry Condell, Leidenberch; John Underwood, Vandort; William Eccleston, Modesbargen; R[obert] Gough, an Attendant; Richard Sharp, Mrs. Barnavelt; T[homas] Holc[omb], the Provost's Wife and a Dutch Woman; G. Lowin, Barnavelt's daughter; Tho[mas] Po[llard], Holderus and a Servant; [Richard] Rob[inson], Boisise and a Captain of the Guard; George Birch, a Servant and an Officer; Jo[hn] Rice, a Captain and a Servant; other actors' names are known only by abbreviations: e.g., R. T., who played five minor roles (King 1988). After he joined the King's Men in 1618, [George] Bir[ch] probably played Morier (Gurr 2004c). Nicholas Underhill is "very likely the 'Nick' noted in *Barnavelt* as Barnavelt's wife" (Gurr 2004c); but Kathman 2005 believes "the 'Nick' of *Barnaveldt* is most likely Nicholas Crosse."

    London, BL, Additional MS 18653, fols. 1–31; *The Tragedy of Sir John van Olden Barnavelt*; no author named; copied by Ralph Crane; signs of extensive censorship by George Buc; theatrical provenance (Long 1989); additions on pieces of paper glued into the MS; "full division into acts and scenes all duly numbered" (Greg 1931). "*Barnavelt* is one of the more heavily marked dramatic manuscripts of the period" (Howard-Hill 1979). The MS "shows every sign of *preparation* for performance" (Hammond & DelVecchio 1995). The annotator of the MS "calls for a bar for the major trial scene and a scaffold for the execution scene, two significant properties that recur in the stage directions of printed texts; clearly, at appropriate moments, large properties . . . could be introduced and could bring with them some sense of locale" (Dessen 1980). "There has . . . been an extensive playhouse revision; and many additional directions, including a number of actors' names, have been supplied in a much rougher hand" (Greg). "No printed edition of the play was ever published [in the time of its performance]. It is possible that the controversial nature of the play made printers unwilling to risk investing in the project" (Auchter 2001). First edited by Bullen 1883, *A Collection of Old English Plays*, vol. 2, then by Frijlinck 1922, then Howard-Hill 1979.

The play has been called "a brilliant piece of theatrical journalism" (Lawrence 1927) and "a staged newsbook" (Levy 2000). "[P]olitically the most scandalous play in the [Fletcher and Massinger] canon" (McMullan 2004), *Barnavelt* "makes no bones about depicting recent events" (Dutton 1991). "The struggle for political domination in the Netherlands was viewed with interest in England because it also represented a clash of doctrinal interests which impinged on the beliefs and practices of the Anglican Church" (Clare 1999). "Barnavelt's story was highly topical (he had only recently been executed). A leader of the Dutch rebellion against Spanish rule, and an Arminian in religion (Protestantism's liberal wing, at odds with Calvinist orthodoxy), his career raised explosive issues" (Butler 2002). *Barnavelt* may also have implicitly commented on the demise of Walter Ralegh: "the play's *foreign* topicality conveniently disguised its *English* application, an over-layering which would be doubly taxing for any censor" (Dutton 1998). And if King James "had been able to presage the fateful events that were to take place outside the Banqueting House in Whitehall on 30 January 1649, he would never have allowed Barnavelt to march across the Globe stage" (Kamps 1996).

Sir Thomas More (The Book of Sir Thomas More). Anthony Munday, with additions by Henry Chettle, Thomas Dekker, William Shakespeare, and Thomas Heywood. "It seems likely that Anthony Munday wrote the lion's share of the original play" (Twyning 2004), which may have been written *c.* 1593 (Hamilton 2005); likely intended for performance by Lord Strange's Men at the Rose (McMillin 1987) but "probably never staged" (Heinemann 2003). Additions by various playwrights were possibly written 1593–94 (Hoy 1987b). But Jowett 2011, who believes that Munday was the first author, "perhaps working in collaboration with Henry Chettle," contends that the play was not written until *c.* 1600 and that the additions by various hands were made after the intervention of Edmund Tilney, Master of the Revels; the playwrights "were assisted and guided by a playhouse annotator and scribe, unknown by name and so identified simply as 'Hand C.'" Those additions "make no serious attempt to respond to Tilney's objections" (Wells & Taylor). An addition of 147 lines and often ascribed to Shakespeare may not have been written till *c.* 1603 (Wells & Taylor 1987). "Shakespeare was a politically acceptable figure added to a potentially scandalous team of Henry Chettle, Thomas Dekker and Antony Munday, to deflect attention from a project that was attracting unwelcome interest from the authorities" (Hadfield 2005): the play tells the story of "More the Catholic martyr in his rise to power and death on the scaffold" (Jones 1995), a sensitive subject for Protestant England. Heywood "almost certainly worked as a type of 'script-doctor'" for this play (Ioppolo 2006). Lord Admiral Nottingham's Men probably revised the play, intending to perform it *c*. 1603 at the first Fortune (Gabrieli & Melchiori 1990); the role of Thomas More was probably "originally written" for Edward Alleyn (McMillin 1989). But Jowett proposes that if the play was written *c*. 1600, it might have been commissioned by Derby's Men; the Lord Chamberlain's Men or Worcester's/Queen Anne's Men may have intended to stage the play in its revised form, which dates from *c*. 1603–04. "The original text of the play was designed for an unusually large company of actors" (McMillin 1987). The name T[homas] Goodale appears in the section of the MS ascribed to Hand C; he would have played a messenger (Nungezer 1929). "[C]ontains a play within a play acted by the fictional Lord Cardinal's players" (Streitberger 2009); the play is an adaptation of *Lusty Juventus* and *The Trial of Treasure*. "More's guests . . . believe they are in fact being entertained by *The Marriage of Wit and Wisdom*" (Schneider 2011).

London, BL, Harley MS 7368, fols. 3–22, *The Book of Sir Thomas More*; no title; *book* "means theatrical manuscript" (Jones); no author named; no date; prologue to play-within-the-play; some leaves of original MS are missing, others damaged; a "mixed foul- and fair-copy" MS (Ioppolo 2002b); "no trace of any division into acts or scenes" (Greg 1931). The MS "is written in six hands by men who worked on either the original or revised version of the play" (Knutson 2004); a seventh hand is that of Edmund Tilney, Master of the Revels. Three leaves of a revision, Hand D, are possibly in Shakespeare's hand (Simpson 1871, Spedding 1872), a view that continues to find support (Thompson 1916, Greg 1955, Blayney 1972, Schoenbaum 1977, Howard-Hill 1989, Taylor 1989, Dawson 1990, Jones 1995, Evans 1997, Holland 2004a, Jackson 2006b, 2007c, Watt 2009a, Jowett 2011), though some scholars remain doubtful (Chillington 1980, Kinney 1999, Werstine 2007, Elliott & Valenza 2010). "The text gives the impression of being in a confused state, leading some scholars to conclude that the play as we have it may be unfinished" (Metz 1989). "[T]he earliest extant manuscript to demonstrate state interference with secular drama" (Clare 1999); Tilney suppressed "displays of xenophobic disorder in the anti-alien riots and More's role in opposing Henry VIII's break with Rome." "The play was written during (and I believe conceived for) a time (1592–3) of intense domestic political turmoil—indeed, of the threat of civil riot" (Long 1999). Tilney's annotations in the MS express the fear that "objectionable scenes might stimulate new attacks on the foreigners whom the government allowed to work in London" (Bentley 1971). "It appears that Munday recognized that *Sir Thomas More* could not be rewritten in a manner that would suit the censor and still be a play that would appeal to an audience" (Auchter 2001). First edited by Dyce 1844, then Hopkinson

1902, Brooke 1908, Farmer 1910 (photofacsimile), Greg 1911a, Jowett 2011. The play is included in the second edition of the Oxford Shakespeare *Complete Works*; the additions ascribed to Shakespeare are included in the second edition of *The Riverside Shakespeare*.

Staging calls for a scaffold for an execution: the playwrights may have "found it necessary to refrain from showing any visual signs of the beheading in order to suppress suggestions of martyrdom. And yet the scaffold scene itself could not be omitted altogether, as More's words and behavior in confronting execution held an almost legendary status" (Owens 2005). The play's "ambiguous characterization of More seems to praise him for his wisdom and sense of humor while reserving judgment on whether More's refusal to submit to his king was admirable or foolish" (Monta 2005).

Sir Thomas Wyatt. Thomas Dekker, John Webster, Thomas Heywood, Henry Chettle, and Wentworth Smith. Acted 1602 (Hoy 1980) by the Earl of Worcester's Men at the Boar's Head or Rose. "Plaied by" Queen Anne's Men [successor to Worcester's Men], according to the Q1 TP, probably at the Red Bull (Reynolds 1940). The role of the clown "must have been written for [Will] Kemp," who had left Shakespeare's company several years earlier (Wiles 1987).

SR none. Q1 1607 *The Famous History of Sir Thomas Wyatt, with the Coronation of Queen Mary, and the Coming in of King Philip*; the TP names only Dekker and Webster; not divided. "Some stage tricks that are not strictly juggling tricks are those concerning strangulation and hanging"; in *Sir Thomas Wyatt* a SD "determines that Homes enter with 'a Halter about his necke,' and the Clowne speaking of Homes' state of mind suggests that 'in this moode hee would hang himselfe!' An explicit stage direction confirms this mood by stating that 'He strangles himselfe'" (Butterworth 2005). Although the execution of Lady Jane Grey happens offstage, an ensuing SD conveys the horror of what has transpired: "*Enter the heades-man with Janes head.*" In a bizarre response to the head, her husband "praises it for retaining its beauty, noting 'a ruddie lippe, / A cleere reflecting eye, / Cheekes purer then the maiden oreant pearle'" (Williamson 2009). The play presents Lady Jane as a Protestant martyr "cruelly persecuted by Stephen Gardiner, Bishop of Winchester, who loomed in the Elizabethan imagination as a monstrous figure of Catholic perfidy" (Owens 2005). Q2 1612.

The play may be an abridged version of the projected two-play sequence recorded by Henslowe as *Lady Jane* (Hammond 1987a), a collaboration with Dekker, Chettle, Heywood, and Wentworth Smith; Henslowe's *Diary* records payments for the lost version on 15, 21, and 27 October 1602, as well as 6 November. Henslowe calls the play "either 'lady Jane' or 'The overthrow of the rebels'" (McLuskie 1993). Dyce, in his *Works of John Webster* (1830), vol. 2, made the connection between *Lady Jane* and *Sir Thomas Wyatt*. There may also be "some connection" between *Sir Thomas Wyatt* and Thomas Heywood's *If You Know Not Me, You Know Nobody*, for "Heywood's [play] begins at the historical point at which *Sir Thomas Wyatt* leaves off, and refers to events in that play; while Mary's coronation and Philip's landing, advertised on the title-page of the latter, are incidents not of that piece but of *If You Know Not Me*" (Doran 1934a).

The play "deals, daringly, with more recent events than any English history play so far, the uprising by Sir Thomas Wyatt against Mary Tudor in 1554, which constituted a huge crisis in the history of the Tudor regime and came close to unseating the monarch" (Clark 2007). The play makes "ingenious use of the coincidental similarities between the rebellion of Sir Thomas Wyatt in 1554 and the Essex rebellion of 1601" (Gasper 1993). In 1602 the play's "subject of a disputed succession and aristocratic manipulation of the resistance to it had obvious immediate resonances" (McLuskie).

The Sisters, A Comedy. James Shirley. Licensed for acting 26 April 1642 (Adams 1917). Acted "with great applause" at the [second] Blackfriars, according to the general TP, by the King's Men. *The Sisters* belongs to a cluster of plays in the early 1640s dealing with stage beggars or outlaws who are "deployed in a symbolic manner"; others include Suckling's *The Goblins* and Brome's *A Jovial Crew* (Sanders 2002). Shirley's comedy "brings the techniques of Jonsonian satire out of the city and into the forest" (Gaby 1994).

SR 4 September 1646. O 1652–53 *Six New Plays* (with *The Brothers, The Cardinal, The Court Secret, The Doubtful Heir, The Imposture*); "never printed before"; general TP dated 1653, separate 1652; separate register and pagination; list of characters; prologue and epilogue (by Frapolo); five acts. Unusual auditory effect: "*He whistles.*" Other sounds: "*A noise within*"; "*Whooting within*"; "*Loud musick.*"

In his 1646 *Poems* Shirley prints the prologue but identifies it as "Prologue to his tragedy call'd *the Cardinall.*" "Probably Shirley revised his *Sisters* prologue with the addition of eight new lines for some revival of *The Cardinal* early in the summer of 1642" (*JCS*). The prologue voices apprehension about the dearth of playgoers in the spring of 1642 and comments on the nation's political troubles, especially the king's departure from London in January: "Our poet thinks the whole town is not well, / Has took some physick lately, and for fear / Of catching cold dares not salute this ayr. / But ther's another reason, I hear say / London is gone to York, 'tis a great way." "Shirley was drawing attention to Charles's absence from the capital, and his decision to make a temporary home in the north" (Butler 2004c). The dedication also expresses concern over the diminished stature of drama: "Compositions of this nature, have heretofore been graced by the acceptance, and protection of the greatest nobility (I may say princes) but in this age, when the scene of drammatick poetry is changed into a wilderness, it is hard to find a patron to a legitimate muse. Many that were wont to encourage poems [plays], are faln beneath the proverbiall want of the composers, and by their ruins are only at leasure to take measure with their eye, of what they have been. Some extinguished with their fortune, have this happiness, to be out of capacity of further shipwrack, while their sad remaynes peep out of the sea, and may serve naked marks, and caution to other navigators, malignant stars the while!"

The Soddered Citizen. John Clavell (Pafford & Greg 1935, Gurr 2004c) or Shackerley Marmion (Schlueter 2011). "Acted between 1631 and 25 January 1632" (Drakakis 2004) by the King's Men at the second Blackfriars/second Globe. Richard Sharp played Witworth as well as Prologue and Epilogue; Robert Benfield, Makewell; John Lowin, Undermine; John Thompson, Miniona; William Trigg, Modestina; John Honeyman, Sly; Curtis Greville, Mountain; Thomas Pollard, Brainsick; Alexander Gough, Fewtricks; Anthony Smith, Clutch; Nicholas Underhill, Shackle; John Shank, Hodge; John Shank's boy, a Maid, according to "The Persons (and) Actours," which probably dates from *c.* 1630 (King 1971). The MS lists six sharers of the King's Men and four apprentices; "at least seven other roles are cited plus an unspecified number of servants and Mutes" (Bentley 1984). "[T]he players had probably cajoled the piece out of Clavell . . . in order to exploit the sensation of the sentencing and later pardoning of this gentleman-turned-highwayman" (Bentley 1971).

The MS was formerly in the library of E. G. Troyte-Bullock "when edited for the Malone Society in 1936" (Gurr 2004c) by Pafford & Greg; now in Chippenham, UK, Wiltshire and Swindon Archives, MS 865 502/2; the name "John Clavell," though mutilated, is written on fol. 2; "Clavell's authorship is evident from a reference in the prologue to his having been a highwayman, a crime for which Clavell was given a royal pardon" (Gurr); dated 1633; theatrical provenance (Long 1989); damaged; signs of censorship; evidence of revision; list of characters; prologue; epilogue missing on account of damage; five acts and separate scenes. "In 2,826 lines of text," the playwright "supplied eighty playwright's advisory directions" (Long 1999). SR 9 September 1653 *The crafty merchant, or the souldred citizen* [actually two different titles] and attributed to Shackerley Marmion; transferred 29 June 1660 *The Sodered Citizen*, a Comedy. The word *soddered* [*soldered*] in the title means *mended*; the term evidently refers to a bankrupt who has been "redeemed" (Schlueter). First edited by Pafford & Greg 1935.

The play "owes much to the work of Massinger, especially to *A New Way to Pay Old Debts*"; "if we seek for someone who might have suggested the *Soddered Citizen* or who was even a collaborator or guiding hand in its composition—and collaboration in play-writing was a feature of the age and a practice of Massinger's—it is much more likely to have been Massinger, the chief dramatist to the King's Men, and Clavell's friend, rather than Marmion or anyone else" (Pafford 1993).

Soliman and Perseda. Thomas Kyd (Erne 2001a); authorship first suggested by Hawkins 1773. "This play is assigned fairly conclusively to Kyd on grounds of style and the fact of its being an elaboration of the play-within-the-play in *The Spanish Tragedy*" (Jewkes 1958). Vickers 2008b concurs. Acted in 1588 or 1589 (Erne) or 1591 (Dimmock 2005) at undetermined venue; perhaps intended for an audience at court. "If *Soliman and Perseda* was performed at court, it may well have been one of the two plays acted by Lord Pembroke's Men on 26 December (St. Stephen's Day) 1592 and 6 January (the Feast of the Epiphany) 1593" (Erne).

SR 20 November 1592. Q1 [octavo-in-fours] ND ?1592 *The Tragedy of Soliman and Perseda, Wherein is Laid Open Love's Constancy, Fortune's Inconstancy, and Death's Triumphs*; no author named; induction with Love, Fortune, and Death serving as chorus; they find inspiration in "the topos which, since the Middle Ages, linked" these three figures (Kiefer 1983); divided into five parts by the appearance of the choral trio. The play revels "in gratuitous cruelty and murder"; there are "twenty-eight killings" (Riggs 2004). Q2 [octavo-in-fours] 1599; two issues, one of which claims to be "newly corrected and amended." The BL possesses a spurious edition meant to resemble the 1599 Q2 but actually printed *c.* 1810 (Murray 1991).

Soliman contains the "first dramatic presentation of the Christian convert to Islam" (Matar 1998).

The Sophister, A Comedy. Richard Zouch. Acted 1610–31 (Kawachi 1986) at Oxford, presumably by students.

London, BL, Harley MS 6869, fols. 24–56; *Fallacy, or The Troubles of Great Hermenia*; written at the end is 13 August 1631, possibly the date of transcription; no separate TP; author identified by initials; list of characters (i.e. "Personae"); prologue (by Vox) and "conclusion," which serves as an epilogue; five acts and separate scenes. Ample SDs: "*Enter ffallacye's followers madde, dauncing, singing, & at last fall together by the eares; hee entering they disperse & fly.*" SR 7 November 1638. Q 1639 *The Sophister, A Comedy*; no author named; dramatis personae; prologue (by Mercury to "the academicall auditors") and epilogue (by Invention). Q is an abridged version of the MS. The connection between *Fallacy* and *The Sophister* was first noticed by Morgan 1911.

The Q epilogue, different from the MS, contrasts academic playgoers with those at popular theaters: "Should this our play on common stage appeare, / Some of the ignorant multitude would sweare / That we chopt logick; for such strains of wit / They still like worse, the better they are writ. / But you, that fill this orbe, whose ears have hung / Attentively upon each actors tongue, / Who ken where the least string of art is crackt, / Where the conceit is proper, and where rackt, / From whence a work is spun, out of what fleece, / And know the woof and warp of the whole piece; / The SOPHISTER doth on your suffrage stand, / That for his grace, you would put to your hand."

Sophonisba. See *The Wonder of Women.*

The Sophy. John Denham. Licensed for acting 1642, according to Revels documents (Bawcutt 1996). "Acted" by the King's Men at the [second] Blackfriars, according to the F and O TPs, and "apparently . . . at court as well" in 1641

(McJannet 1999a). Winstanley 1687 claims that the play "is equal to any of the chiefest authors" and "will make his name famous to all posterity."

SR 6 August 1642 A Tragedy called *The Sophy*; transferred 4 February 1650 *The Sophy*, A tragedy; 19 August 1667; 9 February 1668. F 1642 no author named; list of characters; prologue and epilogue; five acts. O1 1668 *Poems and Translations, with The Sophy*; separate TP, dated 1667, lacks the author's name; the play, which has separate pagination, has been "somewhat cut and slightly rewritten from the 1642 edition" (O Hehir 1968). "*The Sophy* may perhaps have been sold separately [in 1668], but it was never registered by [Henry] Herringman as a distinct book in the Stationers' Register" (O Hehir). O2 1671 "the second impression."

Written and performed shortly before the closing of the theaters, "the tragedy depicts a world that offers a frightening paradigm of a realm where mutual distrust has become so entrenched that appeals to reason fall on deaf ears" (Wilcher 2001). *The Sophy*, "one of the most original plays of the Caroline era" (Harbage 1936), dramatizes in its protagonist a state of fear so intense that it leads the king to kill his own son (Feinberg 1980). In its treatment of a tyrannical king, the play seems to comment on the authoritarian Charles I.

The Spanish Comedy of Don Horatio. See *1 Hieronimo*.

The Spanish Curate. John Fletcher and Philip Massinger (Hoy 1957); the play "is essentially Fletcherian in spirit" (Hoy 1985). Licensed for acting 24 October 1622 (Adams 1917). Acted by the King's Men at the [second] Blackfriars, according to Herbert. Performed also at Whitehall, the night of 26 December 1622 (Adams). Probably performed at the home of Edward Dering, Surrenden Hall, Kent, before 1624 (Roberts 1983); a "list of actors for a private production of John Fletcher's *The Spanish Curate* appears on the obverse of a torn scrap of paper attached to the first page of Edward Dering's conflation of Shakespeare's *I Henry IV* and *II Henry IV*"; performance took place *c.* 1622 (Gibson 2002). Revived at the Whitehall Cockpit, 6 December 1638 (bill of King's Men for performances before the king and queen); and at Richmond Palace, probably in the Great Chamber, 7 January 1639 (Astington 1999a). The play "was popular before the closing of the theatres" (Turner 1996). Principal actors were Joseph Taylor, John Lowin, Nicholas Tooley, William Eccleston, Thomas Pollard, and Robert Benfield, according to F2. In playlist of King's Men 7 August 1641.

SR 4 September 1646; transferred 30 January 1673. B&F F1 1647 *Comedies and Tragedies*; "never printed before, and now published by the authours originall copies"; prologue and epilogue; five acts and separate scenes. Anticipatory SDs: "*Chess-board and men set ready*"; in the next scene "*Enter Moore with chesse-board.*" "*Diego ready in bed, wine cup*"; then later in the scene "*Enter Diego (in a bed) Millanes, Arsenio, and parishoners.*" Offstage sound effects include: "*Pewter ready for noyse*"; in next scene, "*A great noyse within*"; then "*Noyse still.*" B&F F2

1679 *Fifty Comedies and Tragedies*; "published by the authors original copies, the songs to each play being added"; *The Spanish Curate, A Comedy*; list of characters.

Following the closing of the theaters, part of the play was adapted for a droll entitled *The Sexton, or The Mock Testator*, later published in *1 The Wits, or Sport upon Sport* (O 1662 [two issues] and 1672).

The Spanish Gypsy. "[William] Rowley has often been assigned a share" in the play, but Sykes 1924 argues for John Ford, and "David J. Lake [1975] finds it a Ford-Dekker collaboration, while MacDonald P. Jackson [1979] says it is 'probably the work of Ford and another dramatist—Dekker, Rowley, or Brome'" (Howard-Hill 1987b). Taylor 2004a argues for Middleton's authorship chiefly, although Ford contributed to the play and although they probably collaborated with Rowley and Dekker. Darby 2009 sees the hand of Rowley. Licensed for acting 9 July 1623, according to Herbert's office-book. "[P]robably written for the Red Bull" (Gurr 1988a). "Acted (with great applause)" at the Phoenix and at the Salisbury Court playhouse, according to the Q1 TP, by Lady Elizabeth's Men (Schoenbaum 1966b). Performed by "the Cockpitt company" [i.e., Lady Elizabeth's Men] at Whitehall, 5 November 1623, "the prince [Charles] being there only" (Adams 1917). Revival at Salisbury Court must have taken place in the 1630s. "Bentley [*JCS*] concludes that performance at the Salisbury Court must have been by Queen Henrietta's men, for no other company occupied both houses . . ., but the Queen Henrietta's at Salisbury Court was the remnants of the earlier company, forced out of the Cockpit by Beeston in the plague closing of 1636–7" (Gossett 2007). In playlist of Beeston's Boys 10 August 1639.

SR 28 June 1624 *the Spanish Jepsye*; if this entry designates the play, no publication ensued; transferred 11 June 1659. Q1 1653 the TP attributes the play to Thomas Middleton and William Rowley, whose names are bracketed; "never before printed"; dramatis personae; prologue precedes play-within-the-play; five acts. On the last page Kirkman offers for sale "all the playes that were ever yet printed." Q2 1661 "the second impression."

"*Gypsy* is the last of three Jacobean plays—the others are *The Queen of Corinth* and *Women, Beware Women*—in which the heroine, in a striking rejection of the Lucrece and Philomel models that had previously determined the course and aftermath of rape on the English stage, survives and marries the rapist" (Gossett). "A crucifix property allows Clara, a young woman who has been raped, to recognize and claim her right to marry the young nobleman who ravished her"; "the recovery of the crucifix successfully preserves the family honor of both the rapist and his victim" (Williamson 2009).

The Spanish Lovers. See *The Distresses.*

The Spanish Moor's Tragedy. See *Lust's Dominion.*

The Spanish Tragedy. Thomas Kyd, whose authorship is known only because Thomas Heywood records it in *An Apology for Actors* (1612); Francis Meres in *Palladis Tamia* (1598) praises Kyd as among "our best for tragedie."

Acted 1587 (Erne 2001a, Honigmann 1998) at undetermined venue. The play "seems not to have been written for the Queen's Men but for one of its competitors that played in London towards the end" of the 1580s (Gurr 2009a). Performed by Lord Strange's Men at the Rose, according to Henslowe, in 1592: 14, 20, 31 March; 7, 10, 14, 24 April; 2, 9, 13, 22, 27 May; 9, 18 June; 30 December. Also 8, 22 January 1593. "As a property of Strange's Men it could have been acted as well at the Cross Keys Inn, The Theater and at Newington Butts" (Rowan 1975). Will Kemp "would have acted in" Kyd's play when Strange's Men performed it at the Rose (Butler 2004d). Acted by Lord Pembroke's Men at the Rose. Also acted by the Lord Admiral's Men at the Rose, according to Henslowe, in 1597: 7, 11, 17, 22, 31 January; 9 February; 8 March; 21 April; 4, 25 May; 19 July; 11 October; Edward Alleyn presumably played Hieronimo (Styan 1996). "As an Admiral's play it was certainly acted at the Fortune, and again possibly at The Theatre and Newington Butts" (Rowan). Early in his career Ben Jonson may have played Hieronimo in revivals, perhaps for Pembroke's Men, "who were on the road in 1595–6" (Donaldson 2004). (The play that Henslowe calls "Jeronymo," "Geronymo," "Joronymo," or "Jeronemo" in the 1590s is probably Kyd's; there is some confusion, however, because Henslowe may also refer to *1 Hieronimo* by this title.) The Admiral's Men revived the play in 1601, perhaps in response to Edward Alleyn's emerging from retirement and performing roles "he had made famous" (Knutson 1985), perhaps "as part of a themed 'Spanish' season" (Wiggins 2000). Acted by the Chamberlain's/King's Men, before 1604; depending on the date, performance would have occurred at the Theater, Curtain, or first Globe. Richard Burbage played Hieronimo at some point in his career (Kahan 1998), which is revealed in a 1619 elegy. Possibly performed also by Children of the Queen's Revels at the second Blackfriars, before 1604: the induction to Marston's *Malcontent* indicates that the boys' company had played "Jeronimo," though this title may designate *1 Hieronimo*. "[I]n revival at the Fortune" theater in 1615 (Lesser 1999). During the 1630s Richard Fowler played the lead at the Fortune (Astington 2006). Kyd's play "was probably acted more times during the sixteenth century than any other English play" (Bevington 2004). And it "remained popular at the Fortune all the way until the theatres were closed" (Gurr 2009d).

SR 6 October 1592 *the Spanishe tragedie of Don Horatio and Bellimpera*; 18 December 1592; transferred 13 August 1599; 14 August 1600; 4 August 1626. Q1 was probably first published by Abell Jeffes, apparently in 1592; all copies have disappeared. Q2 [octavo-in-fours] *The Spanish Tragedy, Containing the Lamentable End of Don Horatio and Bel-imperia, with the Pitiful Death of Old Hieronimo*; ND ?1592; unique copy at BL; published by Edward White; "newly corrected and amended of such grosse faults as passed in the first impression"; no author named; induction consisting of Revenge and Ghost of Andrea, who remain on-stage and serve as chorus, speaking at the close of each act; at one point Revenge falls asleep, leaving the anguished Andrea apoplectic; Revenge describes a dumb show wherein Hymen, clothed in black, blows out nuptial torches and quenches them with blood; another dumb show "is a historical pageant, presented by Hieronimo to entertain the Court" (Mehl 1965); four acts—a division into five was probably intended, for "the third [act] is longer than any two of the other acts together, suggesting that an act break went lost in the original printing" (Erne 2001b), but "the extant text lacks any interlude to mark a fourth act break" (Gurr 2009a); "it seems likely that the absence or loss of a chorus has led to a wrong division and numbering" (Greg 1939). Andrea's Ghost and Revenge may have entered through a trap at the opening of the play, "perhaps accompanied by smoke and fireworks" (White 2004c), but Gurr finds no warrant for such an entry from below and observes that "Kyd most likely meant them to sit at the edge of the stage as visible witnesses." Hieronimo's entertainment for the court takes the form of a pantomime in which knights carry shields painted with symbolic pictures; Calvo & Tronch 2013 call this a "play within the play"; "Hieronimo's masque of English conquests is the first surviving instance of a character playing the role of Master of the Revels" (Bate 1992); "the specifics of Hieronimo's masque are a puzzle" (Smith 1998). Sound effects probably include birdsong: Bel-imperia, in her love scene with Horatio, says, "Cupid counterfeits the nightingale / To frame sweet musick to Horatio's tale," and "all textual references to the hearing of bird song were accompanied by imitative warbling" (Lawrence 1927). Shocking onstage violence begins when, in a garden, murderers kill and mutilate Horatio: "*They hang him in the arbor . . . They stab him.*" Horatio may have been hanged from a stage-property tree; Henslowe's list of props includes "j baye tree" and "j tree of gowlden Apelles" (Gurr 2009c). "There was a property arbour on stage" (Rowan); later the mad Isabella "*cuts downe the arbour.*" "When the murderers enter, surprising Horatio and Bel-Imperia, the direction reads, 'Enter *Lorenzo, Balthazar, Serberin, Pedringano*, disguised.' . . . This could mean 'muffled' like the conspirators in *Julius Caesar*, but the 1615 [TP] illustration shows Lorenzo wearing a black mask" (MacIntyre 1992). Such an appearance "would probably recall to an audience the Vice of the interludes, who sometimes blackened his face" (Kiefer 1983). The murderer Serberine is subsequently shot onstage by Pedringano, who is arrested and hanged, "a direct contrast to Horatio's base and treacherous murder" by hanging (Smith 1992); Pedringano's trial and execution resemble "the spectacle of public execution with which Londoners would have been familiar" (Shapiro 1991); similarly evocative of Elizabethan practice is tying Alexandro to a stake in preparation for a fiery execution that is narrowly averted. When he finds his son's body, Hieronimo dips a scarf (earlier Bel-imperia's gift to Don Andrea and retrieved on the battlefield by Horatio) into his son's blood "and presents [it] onstage several times as a reminder of his unavenged death" (Smith 1992); this represents "[p]erhaps the first bloody napkin on the commercial Elizabethan stage" (Sofer 2003). When Hieronimo meditates on suicide, he carries a rope and dagger, conventional symbols of despair (Craik 1958). Hieronimo's revenge finds direction when he receives a letter written in blood ("*red ink*") from the sequestered Bel-imperia, who names the murderers; the letter "*falleth*," presumably from above the tiring house. Another letter, written by Pedringano and delivered by the Hangman to Hieronimo, confirms the information; the letter is found on Pedringano's body; he consents "to mount the scaffold for his execution, falsely believing that his associates will halt his execution at the last minute" (Steggle 2007); but the box that ostensibly contains his pardon proves empty. When Hieronimo "moves to exact his revenge, he enters with a book in his hand" (Tweedie 1976), presumably a copy of Seneca's tragedies (McMillin 1974), though he begins his speech with a biblical citation (Romans 12:19). "The protagonist finds in writing of various kinds the information that motivates him to action, the justification for his vengefulness, and even the vehicle of revenge" (Kiefer 1996). The play-within-the-play, written by Hieronimo in his student days, employs a title-board: "Hang up the title. / Our scene is Rhodes." Before performance of the playlet Castile asks for a copy of the script; then he and the other royal spectators move to the "gallery" whence they will behold the drama. Hieronimo asks Castile "to throwe me downe the key": his request implies "that the stage audience will be above" (Craik 1975). "It seems most likely that Kyd wanted the king and his party to '*enter*' on the main stage, and then re-enter the tiring house to climb to the balcony after Hieronimo gives him the book" (Gurr 2009a). The most unusual staging involves the actors in the playlet speaking in four different languages, an evocation of Babel/Babylon (Barrie 1995, Dillon 1995); when the play was printed, the languages were translated into English. During the playlet, the stage fills with corpses as Hieronimo avenges his son. The courtly audience "sit isolated above the tiring-house wall" (Rowan) and fail to realize that they are witnessing actual murders not the simulation of death. As explanation for his action Hieronimo displays the unburied body of the murdered Horatio (presumably hidden by a curtain in the discovery space) and, at the close, bites out his tongue and "apparently spits it onto the stage" (Hughes 2006); it seems "as if the audience must be shown the detached tongue" (Butterworth 2005). This violent act symbolizes "his — and all revengers' — renunciation of language for the tongueless 'speech' of murder" (Diehl 1980). When the King and Viceroy demand further explanation, Hieronimo signals for a knife to sharpen his quill pen; with it he stabs Castile. Hieronimo conflates revenge and theater: he "uses his power over his enemies to force them, or their surviving kin, to see things from his perspective. 'See here my show, look on this spectacle!'" (Maus 1995).

Q3 [octavo-in-fours] 1594; "printed and published by Jeffes, [Edward] White accepting the subordinate position of bookseller" (Greg & Smith 1948); unique copy at the University of Göttingen. Q4 1599. Q5 1602; "newly corrected, amended, and enlarged with new additions of the painters part, and others, as it hath of late been divers times acted"; "four stage-directions are added" (Edwards 1959). The Q5 additions, probably incorporated by Thomas Pavier (Mulryne 1989), are five in number, totaling about 330 lines, apparently by Ben Jonson (H&S, Barton 1984, Riggs 1989), who was paid by Henslowe on 25 September 1601 and 22 June 1602; these two entries may indicate "more than one stage in the alterations" (Bentley 1971). However, Knutson 1985 argues, largely on the basis of entries in Henslowe's *Diary*, that "there is evidence that the playbook was revised for revival in 1597"; she also maintains that "the additions [of Q5] have no obvious marks of Jonson's style." If she is right, then the 1602 payments to Jonson represent "a second set of revisions" (Knutson). The additions expand upon "the mental processes of the protagonist Hieronimo" (Hillman 2002a). Whereas Kyd "lets the protagonist's insanity develop gradually," the third addition "has him go stark raving mad the moment he discovers his son's body" (Riggs 1989). Although Jonson's responsibility for the additions is disputed (Lidh 2010), "since he had ridiculed Kyd's play for its melodrama and out-dated rhetoric, he might not have wished to acknowledge them as his own" (Kay 1995). Stevenson 1968, 2008 finds the claims for Jonson's authorship dubious and, inspired by Coleridge's 1833 proposal, suggests Shakespeare instead; similarly Craig 2009 believes that the additions may have been written by Shakespeare in the mid- to late 1590s. In any event, whether the additions replaced scenes by Kyd or were simply added to the extant script is a "matter for speculation"; the most acclaimed new scene is the Painter's, wherein the artist visits the mad Hieronimo to seek redress for a murdered son (Tassi 2005). The painter is named Bazardo, which may be "a misspelling of Kyd's original character Buzalto," the name of the old man in Q2 (Kahan 2003). Q6 1602, 1603 colophon. Q7 1610 TP, 1611 colophon. Q8 1615 two issues; this is the first edition to give the alternate title, *or Hieronimo is Mad Again*; the TP woodcut depicts Hieronimo's discovery of his murdered son and "most likely" shows what playgoers saw (Gurr 2009a): "Hieronimo's entrance in his nightshirt carrying a torch imprinted itself on the Elizabethan imagination" (Hattaway 1982). The woodcut actually conflates three moments (the murder itself, the sequestration of Bel-imperia, and the discovery of Horatio's body). The woodcut "shows the picture of an arbor, presumably that used in the play" (Reynolds 1940); it is "a vine-covered, arched lattice work" (Reynolds 1967). The place where Horatio and Bel-imperia have their assignation is called an *arbor*, "which could mean a bower of which the sides and roof are formed by the branches of trees, or a lattice-work frame" (Foakes 1985). "Considering that the first edition to which the woodcut was attached was printed in 1615, some thirteen years after the Painter's scene was added, the artist who drew the scene for the title-page illustration may have incorporated Hieronimo's description of his actions from the Fourth Addition into the action of the woodcut" (Jakacki 2010). Q9 1618. Q10 1623 two issues. Q11 1633. None of these editions names Kyd.

A "'first' for *The Spanish Tragedy* is Kyd's use of a play-within-play" and "this innovation proved most popular" (Freeman 1967). "If the play precedes *The Jew of Malta* and *The Massacre at Paris* it contains the first Machiavellian villain"; "if it precedes *Titus Andronicus* it may also be styled the first modern revenge tragedy" (Freeman). "An important dramatic device is the justifiable hesitation of the revenger" as well as his madness (Bowers 1940). A disparaging allusion in the induction to Jonson's *Bartholomew Fair* (1614) suggests the enduring popularity of *The Spanish Tragedy*, "the most influential play of the early modern English theater" (Smith 1999). Kyd's play, which "invented revenge drama for the English public stage" (Bate 1997), was "the third most popular play of the period" (Hodgdon 2010).

The Sparagus Garden, A Comedy. Richard Brome. "Acted in the yeare 1635" by the King's Revels Company at the Salisbury Court playhouse, according to the TP (McClure 1980); "it seems likely that [the King's Revels] were a mixed company of child and adult actors" (Steggle 2004b). The play must have been written after January 1635 and before the middle of July (Steggle). The production was "the big Salisbury Court hit of 1635" (Butler 2006).

SR 19 March 1640; transferred 17 February 1648. Q 1640 list of characters; prologue and epilogue; five acts and separate scenes. "Some issues contain the epilogue directly below the prologue before the play starts, but others have it accurately placed at the conclusion of the playbook" (Stern 2009c). The SDs provide domestic detail: *"Enter two boyes, they cover a table, two bottles of wine, dishes of sugar, and a dish of asparagus."* In a deposition Brome claimed that the play "earned the company more than £1,000 in income"; "that figure is surely legal hyperbole" (Steggle). But the play was "an astounding success in its own day" (Corns 2007). "Its spectacular popularity may have been due to its synthesis of so many elements of contemporary theatre within easily accepted ideological limits" (McLuskie 1981).

Prologue relates the play's language to its subject: "the subject is so low, / That to expect high language, or much cost, / Were a sure way, now, to make all be lost. / Pray looke for none: he'le promise such hereafter, / To take your graver judgments, now your laughter / Is all he aymes to move." The play's "title is based on the rather wonderful premise that asparagus is a new exotic variety of vegetable that has just been introduced into the country, and such is the desire to taste it that a hotel has been established solely for the purpose. All kinds of powers, not least aphrodisiac, are ascribed to the plant in question, but of course in practice the hotel becomes little more than a high-class brothel" (Sanders 1999a).

The Stallion. A droll based upon scenes in B&F's *The Custom of the Country* and performed in the 1640s and 50s. "The piece requires four or five actors" (Elson 1932).

Published in *1 The Wits, or Sport upon Sport* (O 1662 [two issues] and 1672); RT *The Humors of the Stallion*; argument; list of characters. The title derives from a line in the play: "this base stallion trade."

The Staple of News, A Comedy. Ben Jonson. Acted February 1626 (Parr 1988). By the King's Men, according to the TP, at the second Blackfriars. Apparently performed also at court, *c.* 19–21 February 1626 (Parr); this performance may have preceded that at the Blackfriars (Corns 2007). The play responds to the growing print culture of the 1620s: "That decade witnessed the circulation of *corantos*, news-sheets [single sheets in folio size] deriving from the Continent and relating the progress of the European wars; it also saw the transition towards domestically printed newsbooks," which were "between 16 and 24 pages in size" (Sanders 1998b). "Ostensibly a satire on news-mongering, *The Staple of News* also boldly touches on questions of filial inheritance and succession that might well have seemed relevant to the political moment" (Donaldson 2004).

SR 14 April 1626; transferred 7 September 1631; 1 July 1637. "By 1631 [Jonson] had prepared and partially supervised what he must have thought of as Volume Two of his *Works*, comprising *Bartholomew Fair*, *The Staple of News* and *The Devil is an Ass*. His quarrel with John Beale, the printer, and John Allot, the bookseller or publisher, caused the suspension of the project even though Jonson may have intended to add other works to it. Though these plays were undoubtedly printed by 1631, they were not released, and they became part of a complex trade dispute" (Happé 2000). *The Staple of News*, *Bartholomew Fair*, and *The Devil Is an Ass* "were meant to be bound together in a single volume" (Riggs 1989). Printed in 1631 for the abortive Folio and later included as "The Second Volume" of F2 1640–41 *The Works*; two issues; separate TP dated 1631; "acted in the yeare, 1625"; list of characters; induction; prologue for the Blackfriars and prologue for court; epilogue; five acts and separate scenes. *The Staple of News* was "issued probably no fewer than four times: in 1631 at the time of printing, in 1640 with Meighen's title-page, in the following year without the title-page but with a 1641 reprint of *The Devil is an Ass*, and finally in 1641 again in the combined volume" (Parr). Jonson creates an "onstage audience of the four Gossips—Mirth, Tattle, Expectation, and Censure"; they "speak and converse in the Intermeans following each act—they are a Grex or Chorus in the Ancient Greek tradition" (Sanders 1999c); these four "compare the play they are watching to their experience of other drama" (Steggle 2007). Unusual staging calls for Pennyboy senior to put "his two dogs Block and Lollard on trial by due process of law for certain offences" (Lawrence 1935).

The F2 prologue for the Blackfriars announces Jonson's distaste for spectacle: "Would you were come to heare, not see a play." Jonson "derides the audience for its weak critical faculties and readiness to be distracted from the high moral purposes of the play" (Fleck 2005). The induction indicates that women characters, presumably played by boys in costume, were present onstage as playgoers. Mirth says, "Pray you help us to some stooles here," and continues: "Wee are persons of quality, I assure you, and women of fashion, and come to see, and to be seene." Jonson had little use for the custom of accommodating wealthy playgoers by giving them seats on the Blackfriars stage. Staging may have included onstage structures for the staple and the house of Pennyboy Senior; these could have been placed at the left and right doorways leading from the tiring-house (Waith 1974).

Jonson's address "to the readers" between acts 2 and 3 suggests that the play was not well received in the theater: "In this following act, the office is open'd, and shew'n to the prodigall, and his princesse Pecunia, wherein the allegory, and purpose of the author hath hitherto beene wholly mistaken, and so sinister an interpretation beene made, as if the soules of most of the spectators had liv'd in the eyes and eares of these ridiculous gossips that tattle betweene the acts. But hee prayes you thus to mend it. To consider the newes here vented, to be none of his newes, or any reasonable mans; but newes made like the times newes, (a weekly cheat to draw mony) and could not be fitter reprehended, then in raising this ridiculous office of the Staple, wherin the age may see her owne folly, or hunger and thirst after publish'd pamphlets of newes, set out every Saturday, but made all at home, & no syllable of truth in them: then which there cannot be a greater disease in nature, or a fouler scorne put upon the times." "The spectators who made 'so sinister an interpretation' of Jonson's allegory were advising him to avoid political satire altogether; and despite his vexation with them, he would follow their advice in the future" (Riggs 1989).

The Stately Tragedy of Claudius Tiberius Nero. See *Claudius Tiberius Nero, Rome's Greatest Tyrant.*

Stonehenge. See *The Converted Robber.*

The Story of King Darius. See *King Darius.*

The Strange Discovery, A Tragicomedy. John Gough. ?Acted 1624–40 (*AED 3*); January 1640 (*JCS*) at undetermined venue. "A number of stage directions . . . are in the past tense, which might suggest a remembered academic performance" (*JCS*).

SR 31 January 1640. Q 1640 two issues the earlier of which identifies the author by initials; list of characters; prologue; detailed description of dumb show; five acts and separate scenes. Elaborate SDs: *"Aura mistaks and gives the poison'd cupp to Cibile, she drinks, but powres halfe of it on the ground when she tasted what it was, looking cruellie upon Aura, the poison sudenlie workes and she begins to fall, Cariclea supportes her."* Staging calls for a trap: *"Aristippus drags her along, but she [Thisbe] pulling herselfe out of the old mans hands, fell suddenlie of purpose into a pit made in the stage, and so ended her life."* Also a property tomb: *"the tombe of Pirrhus in the manner of a hecatombe."*

Stukeley. See *Captain Thomas Stukeley.*

Summer's Last Will and Testament. Thomas Nashe. Acted late summer 1592 (Wells 1964) or "early autumn of 1592" (Geller 1995), probably by an unidentified children's troupe in the household of John Whitgift, Archbishop of Canterbury, at his palace in Croydon, apparently in the Great Hall; the "likeliest date for a first performance is St Michael's day 1592, or shortly thereafter" (Axton 1995). "The actors were most likely members of Whitgift's household; the exception is Toy, the professional who played the role of pseudo-extempore commentator" (Geller). "The boys may have been those of St. Paul's, though their opening remark . . . suggests otherwise" (Wickham et al. 2000). In addition, "local people, neighbors and tenants" took part (Barber 1959). In fact, "[t]he text itself repeatedly indicates that these entertainers were local, country folk" (White 2008). "Written not for the public theaters but for a special and private occasion" (Wells). Dick Huntley was "apparently the book-holder (prompter) or an actor" (Nungezer 1929).

SR 28 October 1600; transferred 16 October 1609; 2 March 1618; 23 February 1626. Q 1600 *A Pleasant Comedy Called Summer's Last Will and Testament*; induction, including prologue, and epilogue; "Will Summer acts as chorus or commentator" (Greg 1939), and he speaks before the prologue and following the epilogue; not divided. "Songs and musical entries predominate, linked by dialogue exchanged in either blank verse or prose" (Axton). The SDs offer considerable detail about costumes and props: "*Enter Solstitium like an aged Hermit, carrying a payre of ballances, with an houre-glasse in eyther of them; one houre-glasse white, the other blacke.*" SDs "indicate that actors enter from a concealed space"; "the large processions of players and dancers who accompany Summer, Ver, Harvest, and the other major figures in scene after scene suggest they entered and exited through the kitchen and buttery doors" (White 2008).

The play's "conventional format, a masque-like presentation of seasonal themes, is enlivened by the unruly chorus, Will Summers (based on the historical Tudor jester Will Sommers (*d.* 1569), who remains on stage to 'flout the actors' and to act as mouthpiece for Nashe's comic prose" (Nicholl 2004b).

The Summoning of Everyman. See *Everyman.*

The Sun's Darling, A Moral Masque. John Ford and Thomas Dekker (Pierce 1912a). Licensed for acting at the Phoenix by Lady Elizabeth's Men, 3 March 1624 (Adams 1917). A playhouse masque, i.e., "a masque written for the public theater in emulation of the elaborate masques that by the 1620s had come to be such a notable feature of Stuart court entertainment" (Hoy 1987b). The "combination of allegory and shows offered a curious hybrid of spectacle and narration, described by Henry Herbert in his licence for the Phoenix as being 'in the nature of a masque'" (McLuskie 1994). "Presented . . . with great applause" by Beeston's Boys at the Phoenix, according to the TP, winter 1638–39 (Hoy 1980). Possibly performed with painted scenery (Freehafer 1973), but the play "makes no scenic demands that could not have been satisfied by the resources of the Jacobean public theatre" (Hoy 1980). Performed also at Whitehall, according to the TP, Christmas, 1638–39, when revisions were made (*JCS*). In playlist of Beeston's Boys 10 August 1639.

SR none. Q 1656–57 three issues; "written by" Ford and Dekker, whose names are bracketed on the TP; list of characters; five acts. Most of the characters are personifications: "*Enter* Time *with a whip, whipping* Follie *before him*." "Perhaps the most striking visual effect called for in the text" is a SD "which reports that '*The* Sun *by degrees is clowded*'" (Hoy); then a character says, "Oh! What strange light appears," and this SD follows: "*The sun above*." Masque-like effects of the kind seen at court "had something of a vogue in the 1620s and 1630s" (Hoy); playwrights were "democratizing this most aristocratic of genres" (Kiefer 2003).

Certain anomalies of the play may be explained by positing "that either the authors wrote a bad, inconsistent play, or—which seems more likely—that the original text was altered, or rewritten, either by the authors, or by (an)other poet(s), and this altered version reached the press and is the only one extant" (Limon 1986).

A character says: "We must descend, and leav[e] a while our sphere / To greet the world—ha, there does now appear / A circle in this round, of beams that shine, / As if their friendly lights would darken mine." "The circle is located 'in this round,' a phrase that must refer to the architectural form of the auditorium [i.e., the Phoenix]" (Orrell 1988).

Supposes, A Comedy. George Gascoigne. Acted during the Christmas to Lent revels, 1565–66 or 1566–67, by the Gentlemen of Gray's Inn (Pigman 2000). Probably revived at Trinity College, Oxford, 8 January 1582 (Chambers 1923). "[T]hough comedies of Italian origin were frequently acted at Cambridge, this is the only one known to have been played at Oxford during Elizabeth's reign" (Boas 1914). "*Supposes* provided a new model for neoclassical comedy and was to become . . . a source for Shakespeare's *The Taming of the Shrew*" (Bevington 2004).

SR no original; 6 November 1598 Gascoynes *woorkes*. Q1 1573 [TP is undated but the epistle to the reader indicates the publication date] *A Hundreth Sundry Flowers* (with *Jocasta*); list of characters; "prologue or argument"; conventional bid for applause at close; these constitute "the first extant prologue and epilogue in a non-verse form" (Schneider 2011); five acts and separate scenes. Costume functions symbolically: "the hero puts off the scholar's robe and dallies with pleasure; he is dressed in garments that signify a fall in estate; he suffers humiliation and danger; he is saved and is returned to his original robes and to a marriage" (Mowat 1981). Q2 1575 *The Posies*; two issues; "corrected, perfected, and augmented by the authour," according to the general TP. Q3 [octavo-in-fours] 1587 *The Whole Works*, actually an enlarged edition of *A Hundreth Sundry Flowers*; two issues.

An adaptation of Ariosto's *I Suppositi*, *Supposes* is "the first vernacular prose comedy" in English (Grantley 2000) and "the first comedy produced in England with a modern Italian setting" (Creeth 1966). It is also "the first comedy in English turning on 'rediscoveries'" (Salingar 1974).

The Surprise. A droll based upon several scenes in B&F's *The Maid in the Mill* and performed in the 1640s and 50s. For one scene "at least nine and probably ten actors are required. For the concluding scene only seven speaking parts are essential, but more persons should be present" (Elson 1932).

Published in *1 The Wits, or Sport upon Sport* (O 1662 [two issues] and 1672); argument; list of characters.

Susanna. Thomas Garter. Acted *c.* 1562 (*DTRB* 1984) in a great hall (Walker 1998). "The play's treatment of . . . legal themes suggests that its auspices might well have been the Inns of Court or a gathering of magistrates" (O'Connell 2000b). "Eyght persons may easyly play it"; a chart on the Q TP shows how the seventeen roles are assigned.

SR *c.* April-May 1563; *c.* January 1569 (Greg 1939). Q 1578 *The Comedy of the Most Virtuous and Godly Susanna*; "never before this tyme printed"; RT *The Comedy of Susanna*; list of characters on the TP; prologue and epilogue; not divided. The dramatic action "is intelligible only if we imagine an acting area bisected by a partition which runs from the front to the back. This is the orchard wall" (Craik 1958). "The text is notably rich in" SDs (Happé 1999): "*Sensuality and Voluptas sitteth downe at a table turning of b[o]okes*"; "*Note that from the entrance of Susanna, the Judges eyes shall never be of[f] her, till her departure, whispering betweene themselves, as though they talked of her*"; "*Here shall the Cryer, the Bayly, and the rest go stand before the Judge and tell him the crie is made.*" When evil judges victimize Susanna, a problematic SD appears: "*Susanna is led to execution, and God rayseth the sprite of Danyell.*" This SD, "paraphrasing the Scriptures, is baffling as a guide to production . . . and as a definition of legal and political authority"; "[f]ollowing legal rules of evidence, Daniel shows how the trial should have been conducted" (Bevington 1968). Another SD says a character "*goeth up*": "Up to what? Presumably up on to a dais" (Southern 1961).

"The earliest version of a miracle play clearly intended for professional actors, with sixteen parts to be doubled by eight actors" (Wasson 1986b), *Susanna* "is, in effect, a Protestant saint's play" (Cox 2000).

The Swaggering Damsel, A Comedy. Robert Chamberlain. Acted before April 1640, perhaps at the Phoenix (*JCS*). Possibly performed by Beeston's Boys (Saeger & Fassler 1995), who in 1637 "began performing there [at the Phoenix] and continued to do so until the closing of the theaters" (Dezur 2009).

SR 2 April 1640. Q 1640 two issues; initials on the TP and prefatory poems indicate the author, who signs the dedication; list of characters; prologue; Dezur calls Fairefaith's final speech an epilogue; five acts.

This play "makes a female character its emotional centre" (Dezur). The prefatory poem by E. B. compliments the play's treatment of women: "Your pen hath taught all women to begin, / A new: yet civill way to swagger in; / Our natures you have chang'd, and men adore, / The self-same thing which they did hate before: / A woman cavellier, nor is your Muse, / In forfeiting her modesty profuse; / No debaucht scenes, nor such base mirth as we / Place in the scenes, of obscene ribaldry, / Pollutes thy pen, thy happy influence, / Virgins may read with a safe innocence: / And shall applaud thee as one borne to be, / The sole restorer of their liberty." "The repeated references to the ladies in the prologue would be more appropriate for a private theatre like the Phoenix than for a public theatre" (*JCS*).

Swetnam the Woman-Hater, Arraigned by Women, A Comedy. Anonymous. Baines 1984 conjectures Thomas Heywood's authorship, as do Miller & Forse 2011; Woodbridge 1984 conjectures Webster's. Acted 1617–18 (Gurr 2009d) or late 1618–October 1619 (Crandall 1969). By Queen Anne's Men at the Red Bull, according to the TP. Possibly performed *c.* 1633 at the Salisbury Court playhouse (*JCS*).

SR 17 October 1619. Q 1620 *Swetnam the Woman-Hater, Arraigned by Women, A New Comedy*; no author named; list of characters; prologue (by Loretta) and epilogue (dialogue of Swetnam, "muzzled," and two women, Loretta and Leonida); dumb show; five acts and separate scenes (indication of act 5, scene 1, omitted). The TP woodcut portrays a man standing at a bar before the queen; the queen probably sits in a chair of state, raised "two or three steps above the level of the stage" (King 1965). This depiction "probably is not a reproduction of the stage performance" (Gurr 1987b), but Foakes 1985 believes that the "woodcut evidently was made to illustrate" Swetnam, whose name appears next to the figure.

"This play takes the real person Joseph Swetnam, author of the anti-woman tract *The Arraignment of Lewd, idle, froward, and unconstant women* (1615) and a book on fencing (1619), and turns him into a fictional character, on the lam from female animosity in England and living incognito in Sicily" (Fortier 2005). The prologue, addressed to "The Women," "explicitly dismisses the men ('our care's not for them')" (Levin 1989b). *Swetnam* "is a mold-breaking play. Its use of prose polemic to rework dramatic conventions and its legitimizing representation of women as a unified group in protest jolt its eponymous 'hero' into a newly typical and therefore politically significant status" (Jones 1998). However, the play's treatment of the Swetnam controversy proves ambiguous: "Ostensibly joining the chorus of voices prompted to speak out against *The Arraignment*, the play in fact adopts a compromise stance which reinforces, rather than challenges, the patriarchal status quo" (Kidnie 2002).

The Swisser. Arthur Wilson. "Acted at the Blackfriers 1631," according to the MS TP, by the King's Men. Richard Sharp played the King of the Lombards; Joseph Taylor, Arioldus; John Lowin, Andrucho; Thomas Pollard, Timentes; Robert Benfield, Antharis; William Penn, Clephis; Eilert Swanston, Alcidonus; Anthony Smith, Asprandus; Curtis Greville, Iseas; John Thompson, Panopia; Alexander Gough, Eurinia; William Trigg, Selina, according to the MS. "[P]resumably originally written for" performance at a great house (Bentley 1971). In playlist of the King's Men 7 August 1641.

London, BL, Additional MS 36759, fols. 1–64; no author named; in Wilson's hand; list of characters and the actors who played the parts at the Blackfriars; prologue and epilogue; five acts and separate scenes. SR 4 September 1646 [with *The Corporal*, a play by Wilson that survives only as fragmentary MSS] but "not subsequently printed" (Itzoe 1984); transferred 30 January 1673. "The piece was never printed in its own time, though listed more than once in the Stationers Register" (Bentley 1984). The appearance of a ravished woman is indicated in a SD: Eurinia enters "*with her hair about her ears.*" First edited by Feuillerat 1904, then Itzoe 1984.

T

A Tale of a Tub, A Comedy. Ben Jonson. Licensed for acting 7 May 1633 as *The Tale of the Tub* (Adams 1917), though possibly acted earlier (in a different form) *c.* 1596 (Barton 1984); Teague 1979 argues: "It uses some of the same material as two of Shakespeare's comedies, *A Midsummer Night's Dream* and *As You Like It*, a circumstance strongly suggesting an early production of the play, which was then revised in the 1630s to serve as a vehicle for Jonson's satire on Inigo Jones." Analysis of the play's language suggests "old material included and unevenly revised, together with altogether new scenes which may well constitute Jonson's last writing for the stage" (Craig 1999). Unlike most of Jonson's late plays, *Tale of a Tub* was acted by Queen Henrietta Maria's Men at the Phoenix; "Jonson, possibly disturbed by the trouble with the players [i.e., the King's Men] over *The Magnetic Lady*, chose Queen Henrietta's Men" (Happé 2000). Performed at Whitehall, the night of 14 January 1634 (Dutton 1996). Censored for an attack on Inigo Jones in the form of a character named Vitruvius Hoop, Jonson was required to remove the character before licensing. But Jonson still manages to satirize Jones in the character of In-and-In Medlay. "Could [Henry] Herbert have missed the new satire because it was assigned to a character inoffensive in the original version he had read? Even if he did, the theatre audience surely noticed it, and Jones must have heard of it" (King 1971). Jonson's hostility toward Jones, "rather than [the play's] political implications," may have caused the play to be "not likte" (Adams), as Herbert reports (Butler 1992).

SR no original; 17 September 1658; 20 November 1658; 19 August 1667. F2 1640–41 *The Works* vol. 3; *A Tale of a Tub*; separate TP dated 1640; two issues; list of characters; prologue ("written for the performance at court" in 1634 [Barton 1984]) and epilogue (by Squire Tub); five acts and separate scenes. The prologue disingenuously "takes pains to stress that the playtext does *not* engage with state affairs" but the play suggests otherwise: "In 1629, Charles I had dissolved Parliament" and "he did not summon another until 1640"; "[t]his is the context for Jonson's composition of *A Tale of a Tub*" (Sanders 1998b). *A Tale of a Tub* is "unusually precise in its depiction of the workings of provincial administration and in this respect Jonson seems to be acknowledging two of the most striking social developments of the Tudor and Stuart period, the proliferation of the responsibiliites of parish officials and the tendency of central authority to put increasing demands onto local government" (Butler 1990).

The "somewhat tongue-in-cheek" prologue (McLuskie 1981) seeks to shape the expectations of playgoers: "No state-affaires, nor any politique club, / Pretend wee in our tale, here, of a tub. / But acts of clownes and constables, to day / Stuffe out the scenes of our ridiculous play." The play "gave the Caroline audience a picture of rural sports that mirrored the ideas of King Charles and Bishop William Laud" (Riggs 1989). However, "[i]t is entirely possible that village life north of London offered him an opportunity for criticizing the remoteness of Caroline Whitehall from everyday concerns, but the country communities he depicts are not exactly ideal. His villagers have a certain charm, but much of that derives from their stupidity, and they are not regarded quite without condescension" (Butler).

1 Tamar Cam [Cham]. Anonymous. Inspired by the success of *Tamburlaine* and thus written after 1587. Acted ?1592 (Bradley 1992) at undetermined venue. "[O]riginally in the repertory of Lord Strange's Men" and transferred to the Admiral's Men by Edward Alleyn "when the reorganized troop began playing again in London in the spring of 1594" (Greg 1931). Although the play itself is lost, the plot, or "backstage storyboard" (Bate 2008), edited by Greg and "datable to 1602–3" (Kathman 2005), survives. Henslowe records the following performances of *Part 1* ("we should take the entries marked 'second pte' as accurate, and treat all entries not so named as entries of the first part of the play" [Knutson 1983]): 26 May; 8, 21 June 1592; 19 January 1593. In 1596: 6, 12, 17, 25 May; 5, 10, 19, 26 June; 8 July; 13 November. *Part 2* performed in 1592: 28 April; 10 May; 11, 20, 27 June; 8 July. "Apparently revived by the Admiral's Men some time in 1602" (Bruster & Weimann 2004).

The plot was "transcribed by George Steevens and published in 1803 [by Isaac Reed for the Variorum Shakespeare] but [is] now lost" (Stern 2009c). What survives is a synopsis of the lost play, "an outline of entrances, exits, and casting assignments" (Knutson 1997); divided by a chorus into five acts ("these are not numbered" [Greg]).

Twenty-nine actors are named: Edward Alleyn played Tamar Cam (Cerasano 1994). The cast also included William Bird/Bourne (Colmogra, a Persian Nobleman, Artabisus), Charles Massey (Artaxes/Attaxes), Dick Juby (Chorus, Trebassus, Diaphines, Messenger, Trumpet), Edward Juby (the satyr Pitho and a Moor), George Somerset, Jack Gregory (one of Tarmia's sons, the nymph Heron), John Singer (Assinico, the clown), Edward Browne (a Crim), Samuel Rowley (Ascalon), Thomas Downton (Mango Cham, a Tartar), Thomas Parsons (Spirit, Nurse), Thomas Rowley (a "Nagar"), Thomas Towne (Shah, the Oracle, a Tartar), William Cartwright (Nobleman), Anthony Jeffes (the satyr Linus), Humphrey Jeffes (Otanes), Will Barne, William Parr (Nobleman), Thomas Marbeck (Pontus, Nobleman), Jack Jones ("appears to have played Palmeda" [Kathman 2005]), Giles's boy, and [Thomas] Doughton's little boy. "The Admiral's Men bought the *Book of Tambercam* [whether the first or the second part is not known] from Edward Alleyn on 2 October 1602" (Bradley); performance would presumably have been at the Fortune, which opened autumn 1600.

1 Tamburlaine the Great. Christopher Marlowe. Acted summer 1587 (Fuller 1998) at undetermined venue, possibly "the newly built Rose Theatre" (Dawson 1997) or the Theater (Gurr 2009c). "The existence of a stage post shows that it was an open amphitheater, not a city inn" (Gurr 1996). Performed by the Lord Admiral's Men "before 1590" (Carson 1988), perhaps on tour during the performance restraint of May–August 1587. The O1 TP attributes performance to the Admiral's Men: "sundrie times shewed upon stages in the Citie of London," probably the Theater, Rose, and Red Bull (Roberts 2002), though Geckle 1988 interprets the wording as designating an "inn-yard performance"; the O2 TP adds the words "most stately [shewed]." "Edward Alleyn, the leading player of the Admiral's Men in the late 1580s, made [Tamburlaine] his most famous role" (Gurr 2004a). "Tamburlaine's stalking gait and grand style, portrayed by the towering, magnetic Edward Alleyn, emerged as the most sensational and challenging play yet performed" (Whitney 2006). Henslowe records performances at the Rose by the Admiral's Men in 1594: 28 August; 12, 28 September; 15, 17 October; 4, 27 November; 17, 30 December. In 1595: 27 January; 17 February; 11 March; 21 May; 15 September; 12 November. Probably revived by Lord Admiral Nottingham's Men at the first Fortune (Gurr 2009c), which opened autumn 1600. Later acted by Prince Henry's Men, successors of the Admiral's Men, at the Fortune. By the 1630s the part of Tamburlaine was being played by Richard Fowler (Astington 2006). "There are allusions to performances during the reign of Charles I, including one in 1641" (Dawson).

SR 14 August 1590 *The twooe commicall discourses of Tomberlein the Cithian shepparde*; the O1 TP refers to "two Tragicall Discourses"; but the two plays "make up an epic biography rather than a tragedy" (Margeson 1967). O1 1590

Tamburlaine the Great, Who, from a Scythian Shepherd, by His Rare and Wonderful Conquests, Became a Most Puissant and Mighty Monarch, and (for His Tyranny and Terror in War) Was Termed The Scourge of God; "now first, and newlie published"; published with *Part 2*; copies at Bodleian and Huntington; HT *The Tragical Conquests of Tamburlaine the Scythian Shepherd*; no author named; prologue; five acts and separate scenes. The printer Richard Jones, addressing the O1 reader, reveals that he has "(purposely) omitted and left out some fond and frivolous jestures, digressing, (and in my poore opinion) far unmeet for the matter." Jones "might mean either comic subplots or . . . irrelevant episodes" (Potter 2012). "[T]o include such material in the printed text, Jones argues, would 'proove a great disgrace to so honorable & stately a historie'" (Bergeron 2006). "Whatever the nature of the deleted material, the *Tamburlaine* plays which London audiences knew in the late 1580s contained a comic counterweight to tyranny that is lacking in the printed text" (Keefer 2002). Costume has symbolic force: "When Tamburlaine removes his shepherd's robe to reveal the armour beneath . . . we seem very close to morality costuming" (Mowat 1981). The staging is "highly pictorial" (McMillin & MacLean 1998): "*Bajazeth, the Kings of Fess, Morocco, and Argier, with others in great pompe.*" Later the captive Bajazeth is humiliated when he is forced to become Tamburlaine's "foot-stoole." Bajazeth is also confined to a "cage," drawn onto the stage by "*two Moores*"; eventually he "braines himselfe against the cage," and his wife "brains her selfe." Much of the combat occurs offstage: "*Sound trumpets to the battell, and he runs in*"; "*Enter to the battel, & and after the battle, enter Cosroe wounded.*" Spectacle includes the entry of Tamburlaine, attired completely in white, before the city of Damascus; having threatened the city, he subsequently enters "*al in scarlet*" on the second day; finally, "*all in blacke.*" Tamburlaine's evocation of Death, spoken to the Virgins of Damascus, "recalls the coming of death in homiletic morality plays like *Everyman*" (Riggs 2004): on his sword "sits imperious death, keeping his circuit by the slicing edge." The play "is a good deal closer to the English popular morality play than to classical drama. Each of the play's two parts consists of a linear sequence of conquests by the humbly born but seemingly invincible Tamburlaine" (Bevington 2004). A SD records one of the rare moments of silence in a Renaissance play: "*Tamburlaine goes to her, & takes her away lovingly by the hand, looking wrathfully on Agidas, and sayes nothing.*" "There are only three such eloquent silences in all Shakespeare" (Gurr 2009d). O2 1592 or 1593; one possibility is that a 1593 date on the TP of the unique BL copy has been tampered with and can be read as 1592; another is that the date was actually 1592 (Gill 1973). O3 1597. (*Parts 1* and *2* were printed together as one book in O1, O2, and O3. A woodcut depicting Tamburlaine in armor follows *Part 1* in these three editions. The picture probably "represents a typical military figure, and has no immediate connection with the play"; similarly, the woodcut of a woman in O3, perhaps meant to represent Zenocrate, "has no immediate bearing on the play" [Foakes 1985].) Q [octavo-in-fours] 1605 *Part 1* published as a separate volume; no author named.

The O1 prologue alludes disparagingly to the rhymed verse common in contemporary plays: "jygging vaines of ryming mother wits." Marlowe, by contrast, adopts unrhymed iambic pentameter and becomes "the first great author of blank verse" (Wootton 2005). And in *Tamburlaine* "language at last becomes a genuinely dramatic medium of expression and of character-portrayal" (Clemen 1961).

2 Tamburlaine the Great. Christopher Marlowe. Acted autumn 1587 (Fuller 1998) at undetermined venue. The O1 general TP attributes performance to the Lord Admiral's Men; Henslowe records performance 19 December 1594. Then staged in 1595: 1, 29 January; 18 February; 12 March; 22 May; 13 November. Ordinarily, *Part 2* was played "a day or two after" *Part 1* (Cunningham 1981); "the two parts of *Tamburlaine* were repertorial partners, each drawing playgoers into the playhouse for the other" (Knutson 2002a). "Part Two makes a significantly greater call on the physical resources of the playing area than Part One, and this may reflect a transition to a public playhouse from whatever stage the first Part was meant for—inn or game house or outdoor space of some kind" (Cunningham). Probably revived at the Fortune, which opened autumn 1600.

SR 14 August 1590. O1 1590 no author named; *The Second Part of the Bloody Conquests of Mighty Tamburlaine, with His Impassionate Fury for the Death of His Lady and Love, Fair Zenocrate: His Form of Exhortation and Discipline to His Three Sons, and the Manner of His Own Death,* on separate TP; continuous register with *Part 1*; prologue; five acts and separate scenes. Some entries read like dumb shows: "*Enter the Kings of Trebizond and Soria, one bringing a sword, and another a scepter, next Natolia and Jerusalem with the emperiall crowne, after Callapine, and after him other Lords: Orcanes and Jerusalem crowne him, and the other give him the scepter.*" Staging requires a chariot: "*Tamburlaine drawn in his chariot by Trebizon and Soria with bittes in their mouthes, reines in their left hand, in his right hand a whip, with which he scourgeth them*"; a March 1598 inventory in Henslowe's *Diary* records "Tamberlyne brydell"; the *Diary* also lists "tamberlynes cotte with coper lace" and "Tamberlanes breeches of crymson vellvet." The chariot's entry may have evoked triumphal Fortune, who appears similarly ensconced in *Jocasta* and *Liberality and Prodigality* (Kiefer 1983); the significance of the dramatic action is that Tamburlaine "is usurping Fortune's attributes" (Craik 1958). Entry of the chariot, which also evokes "memories of the Triumph of Death" (Spinrad 1987), must have used a central opening onto the stage, for the action "demanded a wider opening than either of the more normal doors in the flanking bays provided" (Gurr 2009c). Upon the death of Tamburlaine's wife, "a procession enters with '*foure bearing the hearse of Zenocrate,*' which seems to be her coffin or bier, provided with a framework supporting a rich cloth—probably black or purple" (Rhodes 1976); this funeral procession probably issued "from one flanking stage door to the other, possibly with fire and smoke belching out at balcony level, all figures marching in time to a doleful drum with the usual four carrying the coffin" (Gurr 2009d). At her funeral Tamburlaine directs, "burne the turrets of this cursed towne"; the accompanying SD has "*the towne burning*"; Harris and Korda 2002 interpret this as signifying "the simulated burning of an entire town"; but "not in this or any subsequent play have we any slightest clue to the nature of the effect" (Lawrence 1927). A trap may have been used "for the cremation of Olympia's husband and son . . . and perhaps for the burning of the Koran" (Dawson 1997). "The Qur'an in this play serves both as an example of the kind of sacred text that could be burned on stage without exciting controversy and, ironically, as proof of how much theatrical and symbolic meaning the theater was able to attach to an otherwise ordinary property" (Williamson 2009). The Governor of Babylon first appears "*upon the walles*," i.e., perhaps in one of the compartments above the tiring house; Tamburlaine's men proceed to "scale the walles" and capture the Governor, who hangs "in chaines upon the citie walles" and is shot, "presumably . . . with muskets" (Dawson). It may have been this stage action that led to a theatrical mishap recorded on 16 November 1587: the Admiral's Men "'having a devyse in ther play to tye one of their fellows to a poste and so to shoote him to death,' one of the 'callyvers' (muskets) proved to be loaded; the player 'swerved his peece being charged with bullet, missed the fellowe he aymed at, and killed a chyld and a woman great with chyld forthwith'" (Nicholl 2004a). Staging requires a discovery space ("*The arras is drawen and Zenocrate lies in her bedde of state*") and a tent ("*Amyras & Celebinus issues from the tent*"). O2 1593 unique copy at BL. O3 1597. (Parts 1 and 2 printed together as one book in O1, O2, and O3.) Q [octavo-in-fours] 1606 *Part 2* published as a separate volume. "No author is given in any of the four early texts" (Fuller).

The O1 prologue begins by referring to *Part 1*: "The generall welcomes Tamburlain receiv'd, / When he arrived last upon our stage: / Hath made our poet pen his second part." Marlowe "constructed his Part Two in such a way that he has produced a two-part play which is unified in structure if not always in effect" (Hunter 1978). Tamburlaine's two-part play "had a pervasive influence on the early modern stage and in particular on those plays grouped under the flexible generic label 'Turk plays,'" including *Selimus, Alphonsus, King of Aragon, The Battle of Alcazar, Soliman and Perseda, Othello, A Christian Turned Turk, The Renegado, Guy, Earl of Warwick,* and *The Four Prentices of London* (Connolly 2009).

The Tamer Tamed. See *The Woman's Prize.*

The Taming of A Shrew. Anonymous. Acted between mid-1592 and spring 1594 (Miller 1998a) at undetermined venue. "Sundry times acted by" Pembroke's Men, according to the Q1 TP. Henslowe records a performance of "tamyng of A shrowe" at Newington Butts, 11 June 1594, where the Lord Admiral's Men and Chamberlain's Men performed (they "took turns playing their own plays" [Wickham et al. 2000]), but it is uncertain whether Henslowe refers to *A Shrew* or to Shakespeare's *The Shrew*; "Henslowe was notoriously casual with titles" (Potter 2012).

SR 2 May 1594 *A plesant conceyted historie called "the Tayminge of a Shrowe"*; re-entered 22 January 1607 [*a Shrewe*]; 19 November 1607 *The tameing of A Shrew*; 14 September 1642 [*a shrew*]. Q1 1594 *A Pleasant Conceited History called The Taming of a Shrew*; unique copy at Huntington; no author named; induction; not divided. "The fact that [Shakespeare's] *The Taming of the Shrew* did not appear in print until the First Folio suggests that it may have been less popular than the other version [i.e., *A Shrew*]" (Rackin 2005). Q2 1596. Q3 1607.

The play may be an adaptation of Shakespeare's *Taming of The Shrew* (Hickson 1850, Hosley 1964a, Wells & Taylor 1987, Miller 1998a), possibly in a form different from that of Shakespeare F1 (Oliver 1984), or it may be a source, written by another playwright, of *The Shrew* (Boas 1908, Chambers 1930, Duthie 1943, Schroeder 1958), or an earlier version by Shakespeare of *The Taming of the Shrew*. *The Shrew* may have preceded the writing of *A Shrew* (Alexander 1926, Quiller-Couch & Wilson 1928). Marcus 2010 believes that *A Shrew* was "an earlier play that Shakespeare either wrote, helped write, or mined." Potter 2012 believes that "*The Shrew* is a version of *A Shrew* designed for a somewhat smaller company, with a star actor and a star clown." It is possible that *A Shrew* and *The Shrew* "derive from a common source," a lost play (Houk 1942).

"Although *A Shrew* is only about sixty per cent the length of *The Shrew*, the plays share three plot strands" (Miller 1998b), one of these being the induction presented to the drunken Sly. "The Sly material forms a complete frame for *A Shrew*, rather than an induction only, with matter for Sly at both the beginning and end as well as interruptions during the whole course of the shrew play-within-a-play" (Miller 1998b). "*A Shrew* is the first *printed* play where the induction material is neither set apart nor labelled" (Hodgdon 2010). "*A Shrew* is both more solidly within the category of farce than *The Shrew*, and considerably less misogynist" (Marcus 1996).

"In 1594 the play might well have been performed in the self-reflexive, metadramatic and alienatory manner of Brecht's epic theatre, delivering its patriarchal message with appropriate detachment, distancing and irony to an audience highly skeptical of such propagandist rhetoric" (Holderness & Loughrey 1992).

The Taming of the Shrew. William Shakespeare. Acted *c.* 1590–92 (Thompson 1984), but the F1 text "likely dates from the early seventeenth century, and . . . *The Shrew* may well have been composed quite a bit later than we have tended to date it" (Marcus 2010). Possibly written for the Queen's Men (Thompson). Probably first performed by the Earl of Pembroke's Men (Bevington 2007c), "a company with which Shakespeare may have been associated" (Hodgdon 2010). Possibly performed by the Admiral's and Chamberlain's Men at Newington Butts, 11 June 1594; Henslowe's entry for the date lists "the tamynge of A shrowe," but this might designate Shakespeare's version. The production "was dominated by the farcical style of Will Kemp and Thomas Pope" (Haring-Smith 1985). Kemp may have played Christopher Sly (Gray 1930). The Q TP specifies performance by the King's Men at both the Blackfriars and Globe. Revived by the King's Men at St. James's Palace, before the king and queen, the evening of 26 November 1633 in the Presence Chamber (Astington 1986); Herbert describes the court performance as "likt" (Adams 1917). (Fletcher's *The Woman's Prize, or The Tamer Tamed* was staged at court two days later.) The induction names "Sincklo" as one of the players in F; "this is probably John Sincler" (King 1992a). A line in F also mentions "Soto," a name that "evidently refers to a character in Fletcher's *Women Pleased*"; the name seems to suggest that the (revised) F version of *Shrew* dates from 1619 to 1623 (Marino 2011). Despite having been acted in the early 1590s, the play "does not appear among the titles cited in 1598 in Francis Meres's *Palladis Tamia* as examples of Shakespeare's excellence as a playwright"; "another indication that the play may not have been much admired — or even noticed — in Shakespeare's time is the fact that there are only three recorded references to it before 1649" (Rackin 2006).

SR "not entered separately" (Hodgdon 2010); transferred ?4 August 1626 Paviers right in Shakesperes *plaies*; ?19 June 1627 widow of Isaac Jaggard . . . her parte in Shackspheere *playes*; ?24 August 1642 [*a shrew*]; ?14 September 1642 [*a shrew*]. F1 1623 *Comedies, Histories, & Tragedies*; three issues; "published according to the true originall copies"; induction ("Pope was the first editor to call the two Sly scenes an 'Induction'" [Thompson]); incomplete division into five acts and first scenes; such divisions "almost certainly represent printing-house additions" (Hodgdon). Although a conclusion seems lacking, the play "did not originally have a dramatic epilogue, the folio text being substantially complete as we have it" (Hosley 1961). However, Wells & Taylor 1987 argue that it "is perfectly possible that the play as acted by Shakespeare's company included a continuation and rounding-off of the Sly framework written by Shakespeare himself at a later stage of composition than that represented by the Folio text, and that the corresponding episodes in *A Shrew* derive from these." "Perhaps [Sly] was removed from the play when frame scenes went out of fashion, and the survival of the Induction is an anomaly" (Potter 2012). The induction "enacts a scene in which travelling players enter a noble household"; "the Lord is familiar with their expertise, so the players are welcomed, given food and lodging for the night, and warned to behave themselves" (Westfall 1990). "[T]he text included in the First Folio was printed by virtue of a copyright which appears to have related to the earlier published text [i.e., *A Shrew*]" (Holderness & Loughrey 1992). The SDs are "adequate, even generous" (Hodgdon). The "wanton pictures" shown to Christopher Sly in the induction "are not necessarily — or indeed usually, in production — physically present in performance" (Elam 2010). Sound effects probably include birdsong: a Lord says, "Harke Apollo plaies, / And twentie caged nightingales do sing." Another kind of sound figures in the use of "a lute session as cover for amatory exchange" between Bianca and Hortensio (Lindley 2006). Q 1631 *A Witty and Pleasant Comedy called The Taming of the Shrew*; "by Will. Shakespeare." F2 1632 "the second impression"; three issues. F3 1663 "the third impression"; reissued 1664 with seven additional plays. F4 1685 "the fourth edition"; two issues. The play may be a source of the anonymous *Taming of a Shrew*, or *A Shrew* may be a redaction of Shakespeare's play, or *A Shrew* may be entirely independent of Shakespeare's *The Shrew*, or both plays may be adaptations of a lost *Shrew* play.

"Alone among Shakespeare's plays, *The Shrew* provoked a theatrical 'reply' in his lifetime in the form of Fletcher's *The Woman's Prize, or The Tamer Tamed*, written and performed around 1611, a sequel in which Petruchio, now a widower, marries again and is himself tamed by his second wife" (Thompson).

Tancred and Gismund. Robert Wilmot, reviser. Probably acted 1591 (Greg 1914a). The Q TP records performance by gentlemen of the Inner Temple, presumably in their hall, though this may refer to the original performance of the earlier *Gismond of Salerne*. Wilmot's dedication, which refers to "wearie winter," expresses the hope that the play "may serve ye also for a solemne revell against this festivall time." Wilmot also "suggests that the play might be performed at the private house of either Mary Petre or Anne Grey" (Kingsley-Smith 2008). *Tancred* is a very substantial reworking of *Gismond of Salerne*: the TP indicates that the earlier play has been "newly revived and polished according to the decorum of these daies." "What prompted Robert Wilmot's extensive revision of the tragedy and its subsequent publication is not clear" (Norland 2009). Wilmot's changes render this revision more stageworthy: he substitutes blank verse for rhyme, makes more use of dialogue in place of set speeches, adds more extensive stage directions, and introduces four dumb shows (Kiefer 1977).

SR none. Q 1591–92 *The Tragedy of Tancred and Gismund*; two issues; argument (one version in verse, the other in prose) and epilogue (by Julio); chorus at ends of acts 1–4; five acts, the last four of which are preceded by carefully described dumb shows (specially written for this recasting of *Gismond of Salerne*). Guil. Webbe's prefatory epistle, addressed to Wilmot, is dated 8 August 1591. Preceding the play is "A Preface to the Queenes Maidens of Honor," intended "apparently for reading"; "Another to the same" is intended "apparently for acting" (Greg 1939). Cupid *"commeth out of the heavens in a cradle of flowers"* and later ascends, apparently by means of machinery. Megaera with the other Furies *"riseth out of hell"* through a trap; a prisoner is kept in a dungeon, *"under the stage."* In a dumb show when Tancred discovers that his daughter has a secret lover, he *"ariseth enraged, then was heard & seen a storm of thunder & lightning, in which the furies rise up."* Another dumb show describes a stunning theatrical effect: Renuchio *"bringeth foorth a standing cup of gold, with a bloudy hart reeking"*; this represents the heart of Gismunda's lover, killed by her jealous father. Sound effects, described in dumb shows, include: *"a sweete noice of stil pipes"*; *"the hobaies sounded a lofty Almain"*; *"a consort of sweet musick"*; *"a dead march plaid."* This use of music represents "a significant advance on the principle of the purely symbolical dumb show. The intercalated pantomime was performed to . . . appropriate music" (Lawrence 1912a). In this revised version of *Gismond*, Gismunda's death scene is considerably enlarged, and Tancred puts out his eyes and kills himself on the stage" (Cunliffe 1893). The name of the playwright responsible for each act in the original *Gismond* is appended to that act in *Tancred*: Roderick Stafford, Henry Noel, G. Al., Christopher Hatton, and Robert Wilmot, respectively.

TEXNOΓAMIA. See *Technogamia*.

Technogamia, or The Marriages of the Arts, A Comedy. Barten Holyday. "[F]irst performed at Christ Church in 1617" (Knight 2008); acted 13 February by students of Christ Church, Oxford, in the hall at Shrovetide, according to the Q1 TP. Performed also before King James at Woodstock, the evening of 26 August 1621, a Sunday (Elliott et al. 2004). Anthony à Wood records the King's reaction to the performance at Woodstock: "it being too grave for the king, & too scholarlike for the auditory (or as some say that the actors had taken too much wine before) his majesty after [2] acts offered severall times to withdraw but being perswaded by some of those that were neare him, to have patience till it was ended, least the yong men should be disencouraged, adventured it, though much against his will" (Elliott et al.).

SR 20 April 1618; transferred 4 September 1638. Q1 1618 list of characters; prologue and epilogue; five acts and separate scenes. A SD during the prologue suggests the complexity of the staging: "*Here the upper part of the scene open'd; when straight appear'd an heaven, and all the* Pure Arts *sitting on two semicircular benches, one above another: who sate thus till the rest of the prologue was spoken, which being ended, they descended in order within the scene, whiles the musicke plaid.*" The SDs also describe in elaborate detail the costumes of personified characters: e.g., "Physica *with a coronet on her head, bearing on the front a woman with two children sucking at her brests, and a* Ceres *horne passing up betweene her armes; round about on the border of her coronet were beasts and trees; in a loose-bodied gowne of greene branch'd taffata, in gloves and white pumps.*" In his characterizations and attention to spectacle, "Holyday relies on masque conventions" (Knight). Q2 1630. A copy in the Folger "carries MS corrections, apparently in the hand of the author" (Elliott).

The Telltale. Anonymous; possibly William Rowley (Bullen 1883, Harbage 1935) or ?John Nichols (*JCS*) or Thomas Dekker (Freeman 1963, Price 1969); Lake 1975b doubts the attribution to Dekker and concludes, "this is one play that must remain anonymous." Acted after 1605 (Foakes & Gibson 1959), 1630–40 (Greg 1931, Ioppolo 2006) at undetermined venue.

Dulwich, UK, Dulwich College, MS XX; fols. 1–25; no separate TP; no author named; five acts (but no heading for act 1). It "seems relatively certain that Dulwich MS. XX was made as a reading copy for further purposes or for persons unknown by a playhouse scribe sometime between 1630 and 1640 copying a theatrical playbook of unknown date which (most likely) was written in the playwright's holograph" (Long 2005). "[T]here are an atypically large number of" advisory directions, "thirty to be exact" (Long). The play concludes with a masque (Shaw 1979).

First edited by Foakes & Gibson 1959. Although the play's title shows up in an advertisement of 1658, "[t]here is no evidence that it was ever in fact published" (Davidson 1978).

The Tempest. William Shakespeare. Acted 1610 to mid-1611 (Orgel 1987) by the King's Men at the second Blackfriars and first Globe. The King's Men began using the Blackfriars at "some point after January 1610" (Barroll 2005). "*The Tempest* is the first of Shakespeare's plays definitely written for the Blackfriars" (Gurr 1996). Performed also at the Whitehall Banqueting House, before the king, 1 November 1611 (Revels Account); "Shakespeare might well have written [*The Tempest*] specifically with an eye to the royal favor that the play was to gain" (Jowett 2003b). Acted at court during the winter revels of 1612–13 (payment to John Heminges dated 20 May 1613), celebrating Princess Elizabeth's betrothal to Frederick, the Elector Palatine. The F text requires "thirteen men and four boys" for performance (Vaughan & Vaughan 1999).

SR 8 November 1623; transferred ?4 August 1626 Paviers right in Shakesperes *plaies*; ?19 June 1627 widow of Isaac Jaggard . . . her parte in Shackspheere *playes*; 16 November 1630; 1 July 1637 Shakespeares *workes* their Part; 6 August 1674; 21 August 1683. F1 1623 *Comedies, Histories, & Tragedies*; three issues; "published according to the true originall copies"; the play was chosen to open F1 "as a showpiece for the book" (Jowett 2003b); list of characters at end; epilogue (by Prospero); the dumb show of a disappearing banquet functions as a "demonstration of Prospero's power" (Mehl 1965); five acts and separate scenes. The SDs, unusually detailed for a Shakespearean play, may have been supplied by the copyist Ralph Crane and may have "come after" performance (Jowett 2007e, 1983a). The storm scene "employs powerfully realistic strategies" and specifies "the components of an offstage noise," a "highly unusual" feature (Lyne 2007). "There are no real precedents anywhere in earlier plays for mounting a storm complete with a shipwreck on stage" (Gurr 1988b). When the Boatswain tells the mariners to "Tend to th'master's whistle," he refers to "the ship captain's whistle" (Shirley 1961). Caliban's "complaint about being kept 'In this hard Rocke' . . . seems to suggest the entry-point which is fitter to represent a recessed place, i.e., either the central opening or the trap" (Gurr & Ichikawa). Cues for music are many: "*The Tempest* with its off-stage mood music was the only play Shakespeare wrote for the Blackfriars using the newly acquired consort and planned act breaks" (Gurr 2004c). *The Tempest* is "exceptional because music is more fundamental to its action and its symbolism than it is in any other Shakespearean play" (Lindley 2002). Auditory effects include "*A tempestuous noise of thunder and lightning heard*"; Ariel enters "*invisible playing & singing*"; "*Enter Stephano singing*"; "*Caliban sings drunkenly*"; "*Ariell plaies the tune on a tabor and pipe*"; "*a noyse of thunder heard.*" "Antonio claims to hear the roaring of bulls or lions in II,i, but Gonzalo, wakened by Ariel's song, remembers confusedly 'a humming, And that a strange one too'" (Sturgess 1987). Other sounds are suggested by Caliban: "the isle is full of noyses." Staging combines auditory and visual effects: "*Solemne and strange musicke: and Prosper[o] on the top (invisible) Enter severall strange shapes, bringing in a banket; and dance about it with gentle actions of salutations, and inviting the king, &c. to eate, they depart*"; "*Thunder and lightning. Enter Ariell (like a harpey) claps his wings upon the table, and with a quient device the banquet vanishes.*" This last SD points to the use of a trick table "flipped over by a stage assistant" (Sturgess); Ariel "*vanishes in thunder* [perhaps through a trap (Dessen & Thomson 1999)]: *then (to soft musicke) Enter the shapes againe, and daunce (with mockes and mowes) and carrying out the table.*" When, at different points, Ariel and Prospero enter "invisible," they probably wear a black garment, though it "need not be plain" (Palmer 2008).

Prospero conjures a kind of betrothal masque with Iris, Ceres, and Juno; descent machinery is presumably used for Juno: "*Juno descends,*" though Meagher 2003 asks: "from what place does she descend and how?" He speculates "that she walks in rather than being winched down." During the masque "*Enter certain reapers (properly habited) they joyne with the nimphes, in a gracefull dance, towards the end whereof,* Prospero *starts sodainly and speakes, after which to a strange hollow and confused noyse, they heavily vanish*"; the dance "should be particularly attractive and orderly so that the interruption and departure of the performers will be the more noticeable" (Brissenden 1981). The masque requested by Prospero "does not seem to be the one presented": it "appears to replace a different and more relevant masque, having perhaps been added into the text for performance at the court celebrations of the wedding of Princess Elizabeth and the Elector Palatine" (Stern 2010b). The malefactors who plan to kill Prospero are pursued by his magic: "*A noyse of hunters heard. Enter divers spirits in shape of dogs and hounds, hunting them about.*" When Prospero confronts his adversaries, "*They all enter the circle which* Prospero *had made, and there stand charm'd.*" The scene wherein Prospero "*discovers*" Miranda and Ferdinand "*playing at chess*" may have used the central opening in the tiring-house wall (Gurr & Ichikawa 2000); Prospero "may be pulling back a curtain in front of the discovery space at the rear centre of the stage, so that the framing of a stage within a stage works in conjunction with the still bodies of Ferdinand and Miranda to construct the lovers as an emblematic tableau" (Dillon 2010). "The moment has an almost sacramental quality for the onlookers onstage" (Sturgess). The central opening in the tiring-house wall was likely used for the ending, "appropriate for an exit signifying reunion and reconciliation" (Ichikawa 2002). Prospero's final act is to renounce his magic, but the nature of that magic is beside the point: "The model for what he practices is theater. His resources and repertoire include a troupe of actors, flying machines, thunder and lighting, disappearing banquets, mysterious music, ascents and descents, a masque of goddesses, even a closet full of costumes, the glittering apparel that proves so fatally attractive to Stephano and Trinculo" (Orgel 2011). F2 1632 "the second impression"; two issues. F3 1663 "the third impression"; re-issued 1664 with seven additional plays. F4 1685 "the fourth edition"; two issues. "*The Tempest* seems to have meant something special to the Folio compilers, since they gave it pride of place as the first play in the volume, against all interests of chronology and dramatic development" (McMullan 1994).

"*The Tempest* seems . . . to be the most revealingly personal of all Shakespeare's plays — the one in which commentary on his lifelong craft is most deeply woven into the text" (Duncan-Jones 2001).

The Temptation of Our Lord and Savior Jesus Christ. John Bale. Acted *c.* 1538 (White 1993b). Possibly first performed by Bale's "fellows" at St. Stephens [Hackington] near Canterbury, 8 September 1538; Thomas Cromwell sponsored the production. However, the performance "need not have taken place in the church building" (Gibson 2002). Performed also by Bale's "young men" at the market cross in Kilkenny, Ireland, 20 August 1553, the day Mary was proclaimed monarch. The play was performed "by a local group of players, perhaps [Bale's] cathedral choristers" (White 2004a). Requires a minimum of four actors in addition to Bale (Fletcher 2000). Performance took place in the afternoon (Happé 2004). The play "may have been performed with nothing more in mind than a bare acting space, leaving it to the characters to identify the location for the audience through dialogue"; however, "raised stages were constructed for church performances and the architectural setting of the sanctuary itself provided further possibilities for dramatizing particular scenes" (White 1993b).

Q ND ?1547 *A Brief Comedy or Interlude Concerning the Temptation of Our Lord and Savior Jesus Christ by Satan in the Desert*; unique copy at Bodleian; "compyled" by Bale in 1538; list of characters on the TP; Bale speaks as Prolocutor ("In vernacular plays before 1585, 'prolocutor' occurs only in Bale's plays," in *King Darius*, and in the Norwich Grocers' play [Butler 2004f]); Bale also gives the final speech; not divided. *The Temptation* "was apparently printed" with *John Baptist's Preaching* "and was separated from it at the distribution of the Harleian Library" (Happé 1986). "This play was intended by its author to form a self-contained part of a sequence of four interrelated religious plays [the others being *God's Promises, John Baptist's Preaching,* and *Three Laws*]" (Wickham 1976). The plays "adopt themes, conventions, and devices from the medieval mystery and morality plays to protestant purposes" (King 2004).

This is the "only non-saint play drawing on the New Testament" (Grantley 2007). "Bale rejects the liturgical basis for the mystery plays and returns to scripture for his biblical dramas" (Shrank 2007).

The Testy Lord. A droll based on several scenes in B&F's *The Maid's Tragedy* and performed in the 1640s and 50s. "The first scene requires six actors. The banquet scene in the play presents at least five of the characters who appear in the droll, and a larger company is supposed to be present" (Elson 1932).

Published in *1 The Wits, or Sport upon Sport* (O 1662 [two issues] and 1672); argument; list of characters.

Thersites. ?Nicholas Udall (Axton 1982, Hornback 2007). Acted 1537 (*DTRB* 1984). "[T]he references to Oxford and the Proctor and his men suggest a college play" (Walker 1998), performed by students. Acted at court between 12 and 24 October 1537 (Axton) by students of Eton College.

SR none. Q ND ?1562 *A New Interlude called Thersites, This Interlude Following Doth Declare How that the Greatest Boasters Are Not the Greatest Doers*; list of characters on the TP; epilogue by Miles; not divided. A SD specifies: "*Mulciber must have a shop made in the place*," apparently a freestanding structure, perhaps a curtained booth or "a full, four-sided, framed canvas erection with a door" (Southern 1973). Another structure was probably used for the home of Thersites' mother: "*Then the mother goeth in the place which is prepareth for her.*"

"Early evangelical comedy, particularly in Udall's more than capable hands, could be simultaneously crude and complex, low and learned, iconoclastically antipapal and Latinate, shockingly offensive, even bigoted, but undeniably witty" (Hornback).

Thierry and Theodoret. John Fletcher and Philip Massinger; Francis Beaumont "is responsible for Act III" (Hoy 1985). Acted 1613–21 (E&G 1976). "Divers times acted" by the King's Men at the [second] Blackfriars, according to the Q TPs. While working for this company, Nathan Field acted in the play (Williams 2004a).

SR no original; transferred 22 February 1648 a play by Mr Bea[u]mont & Fletcher. Q1 1621 *The Tragedy of Thierry, King of France, and His Brother Theodoret*; no author named; five acts and separate scenes. Q2 1648–49 two issues: the earlier attributes play to Fletcher, the other to both Fletcher and Massinger, and adds dramatis personae. The 1649 reissue contains a prologue and epilogue not originally written for this play; the same prologue appears in *The Noble Gentleman*, published in B&F F1 1647 *Comedies and Tragedies*; the epilogue appears in *The Changes* (1632) by James Shirley. B&F F2 1679 *Fifty Comedies and Tragedies*; "published by the authors original copies, the songs to each play being added"; *The Tragedy of Thierry and Theodoret*; no dramatis personae; no prologue or epilogue.

The Q2 prologue acknowledges the play's age and complains of trendiness in the theater: "Wit is become an antick; and puts on / As many shapes of variation, / To court the times applause, as the times dare / Change severall fashions; nothing is thought rare / Which is not new and follow'd; yet we know / That what was worne some twenty yeares agoe / Comes into grace againe, and we pursue / That custome, by presenting to your view / A play in fashion then, not doubting now / But 'twill appeare the same, if you allow / Worth to their noble memories, whose names / Beyond all power of death live in their fames." The epilogue, printed on the verso of the prologue, takes note of the closure of the theaters and looks forward to their re-opening: "If not for what we are, (for alas, here / No *Roscius* moves to charme your eyes or ear) / Yet as you hope hereafter to see playes, / Incourage us, and give our poet bayes."

In this "misogynistic" drama women are polarized "as supremely virtuous or supremely vicious"; "the play makes the orthodox link between regal and masculine supremacy both of which are endorsed in its conclusion. Women are valued when submissive and chaste" (Clark 1994).

The Third Part of King Henry the Sixth. See *3 Henry VI.*

Thomas Lord Cromwell. Anonymous. Acted 1600 (Heinemann 2003) or 1601 (Gurr 2009d). "Sundrie times publikely acted" by the Lord Chamberlain's Men, according to the Q1 TP, at the Curtain or first Globe. Perhaps written "in response to the Admiral's *Oldcastle* plays" (Bevington 1968). Both plays are "built round idealized heroes who stood out for religious reform in the name of conscience and were martyred for it" (Heinemann).

SR 11 August 1602; transferred 16 December 1611; 16 February 1617; 3 April 1626; 4 September 1638. Q1 1602 *The True Chronicle History of the Whole Life and Death of Thomas Lord Cromwell*; RT *The Life and Death of Thomas Lord Cromwell*; "written by W. S."; Archer's 1656 catalogue ascribes the play to Shakespeare as does Kirkman's; chorus (3 entries) functions "as a device to summarize sections of the longer version" (Jewkes 1958); not divided. Although this history play is generally free of violence, staging at the end calls for the executioner to carry onstage Cromwell's severed head. Q2 1613 specifies performance by King's Men; attributes the play to "W. S.," sometimes interpreted as Wentworth Smith (Brooke 1908), but "the possibility that Shakespeare had a hand in the plotting or revising of this undistinguished piece cannot be utterly discounted" (Thomson 1983). Shakespeare F3 1664 second issue; "the third impression. And unto this impression is added seven playes, never before printed in folio"; not divided. Shakespeare F4 1685 "the fourth edition." The attribution to Shakespeare, made by F3, is not usually credited today.

This is a "martyrdom play, its source being Foxe's *Book of Martyrs*" (Wasson 1986b). The play "dramatizes for us a strain of support for favoritism that has deep roots in Protestant court culture but was greatly encouraged by the popularity of Elizabeth's volatile favorite, Robert Devereaux, Earl of Essex" (Perry 2006a).

Thomas of Woodstock. See *Woodstock.*

Thomas Stukeley. See *Captain Thomas Stukeley.*

1 Thamaso, or The Wanderer, A Comedy. Thomas Killigrew. Written in Paris *c.* 1654 (Harbage 1930, Bulman 1987); perhaps begun even earlier in Venice *c.* 1650 and then "revised or completed in 1654" (Wertheim 1971). Although there is no record of performance, the SDs anticipate production, especially the use of painted scenery: e.g., "*The scene changes, and discovers a* piazza *and* balcony-windows *in which* Angellica *and her woman appear, other windows, and other women in them; neer the door of* Angellica *stands a pillar, upon which hanges her picture, and by it stand two* Bravoes *to protect it from affronts; and to give answer to such questions as are ask'd.*" "As Killigrew's annotated copy of his *Comedies and Tragedies* (1664) preserved in the library of Worcester College, Oxford, demonstrates, he was ambitious enough to prepare his own plays for production on the new, scenic [Restoration] stage" (Vander Motten 2004).

SR 24 October 1663. F 1663–64 *Comedies and Tragedies*; two issues; general TP dated 1664, separate TP 1663; *The First Part of Thomaso, or The Wanderer*; "written in Madrid"; dramatis personae; five acts and separate scenes. Extensive SDs specify onstage violence: "Edwardo *strikes him* [Mathias] *and they cuff in the bed;* Edwardo *throws him down, there they cuff and struggle upon the floore, and are both bloody, occasion'd by little spunges ty'd of purpose to their middle fingers in the palmes of their hands.*" Sound effects include "*The noyse is heard into* Philippo's *chamber, where* Lucetta, Philippo, *and* Sancro *are undressing her; they open the curtain window and listen to the noyse.*" "*He falls down by her, she starts and would rise, but he holds her. Then he offers to force a kiss.*" A woman is "*carried by two* Bravo's *to the Mountebanks stage, where she is lifted up.*"

Thomaso "shows intimate familiarity with the life of a rootless, debt-ridden Englishman abroad" (Raber 2000). This autobiographical play ("'Thomaso' is a continentalized version of Killigrew's own name" [Randall 1995]) was later adapted by Aphra Behn as *The Rover, or The Banished Cavaliers*, and performed in 1677.

2 Thomaso, or The Wanderer, A Comedy. Thomas Killigrew. Data as for *Part 1*. *The Second Part of Thomaso, or The Wanderer*. Detailed SDs: "*She stands still with her eyes fix'd on the ground, then walks a little, looks after him, shrugs and shakes her head, till* Calis *pulls her by the slieve.*"

Thorney Abbey, or The London Maid, A Tragedy. T. W. Acted *c.* 1615 (Baillie 1984) at undetermined venue. "The play was intended for performance by a popular troupe in a London theater," perhaps the Red Bull (Baillie). "Some parts of this play have been thought from the style to be Elizabethan: others are considerably later, but not necessarily after the closing of the theatres" (Greg 1939). The address to the reader, signed by R. D., makes a claim for the play's appeal in both the theater and the study: "A play's commended, if the stage be full, / And what book sells well, 's never counted dull. / Thus do the actor's and bookseller's gains / Give the best judgement of the poet's brains."

SR none. D 1662 *Gratiae Theatrales* (with *Grim the Collier of Croydon*, *The Marriage Broker*); separate pagination for each play but continuous register; "never before published," according to the general TP; author's initials (possibly spurious) on the TP; list of characters; "prelude" (the Fool enters "with a pa-per in his hand for a prologue" and together with the Prompter enacts the pro-logue); epilogue; chorus; elaborate description of two dumb shows; not divided. Both prelude and epilogue were "almost certainly" commissioned by the pub-lisher (Baillie). Special effects include "*Thunder loud*"; "*A blasing star appears*" and "hangs directly o're this fatall house." A blazing star "consisted either of a firework on a line or flaming material suspended in an iron cage or cresset, and burned for up to a minute" (Holdsworth 1990). Staging calls for a property tomb: "*Ent[er] Old Thorney in his tombe.*"

The subplot, based on *Macbeth*, is the "earliest known adaptation of a Shake-spearian tragedy" (Baillie). An anonymous prefatory poem at the beginning of the collection predicts rather too confidently the fate of T. W.'s play: "This I'le dare to foretell, although no seer, / That *Thorney Abbey* will out-date *King Lear*."

The Thracian Wonder, A Comical History. ?William Rowley and ?Thomas Hey-wood (Nolan 1997). Performed ?1599 (Butler 2005) or 1611-early 1612 (Nolan) or "late 1610s or early 1620s" (Nicol 2008a). "Several times acted with great ap-plause," according to the TP, possibly at the Red Bull.

SR 29 [December] 1653. Q 1661 the TP attributes the play to Webster and Rowley; Francis Kirkman "would have no commercial reason for falsely attach-ing Rowley's or even Webster's name to the play" (Nolan); dramatis personae; dumb show explained by chorus; five acts (and scene divisions in act 3). Some copies of Q were issued in 1661 with *A Cure for a Cuckold* (already published) and entitled *Two New Plays* by Webster and Rowley. Staging calls for thunder, light-ning, and storm. Unusual SD: "Pythia *speaks in the musick-room behinde the cur-tains.*" This apparently means that the actor playing Pythia, a goddess, occupies a box, or compartment, above the tiring-house, like those depicted in De Witt's drawing of the Swan, the box ordinarily occupied by musicians (Hosley 1960). A curtain seems to have blocked the spectators' view of the musicians. Offstage sound includes "*Groans of dying men heard within.*" SDs specify costumes: "*Enter Pallemon frantickly habited, dancing over the stage, old Antimon, antick-like, clown-like maid Marian.*" When shepherds enter with decorated shields and a character asks, "What meanes that strange device upon their shields?" the symbolic design is interpreted; other such instances of imprese appear in *The Misfortunes of Arthur*, *Edward II*, *The Insatiate Countess*, and *Pericles* (Kiefer 2011).

Kirkman, in the stationer's address to the reader, recalls the closing of the theaters: "We have had the private stage for some years clouded, and under a tyrannical command, though the publick stage of England has produc'd many monstrous villains, some of which have deservedly made their *exit*. I believe fu-ture ages will not credit the transactions of our late times to be other than a *play*, or a *romance*: I am sure in most romantick plays there hath been more probability, then in our true (though sad) stories."

The Three Ladies of London. Robert Wilson. Written "at the beginning of the 1580s" (Kermode 1999); performed *c*. 1581 (Mithal 1988). "*The Three Ladies* is very much a professional and stageable play, giving the impression of being confidently in touch with its audience" (Lunney 2002). "Publiquely plaied," according to the Q1–2 TPs, perhaps first by Leicester's Men (McMillin & MacLean 1998), at undetermined venue, and, later, by the Queen's Men (Walen 2005), but "the evidence is just too tenuous to allow of definite conclusions" (Dutton 1991). A "late morality play" (Geckle 1980), *Three Ladies* "may represent the old travelling Interlude tradition, especially if it is remembered that at the time of its writing, only five years after the opening of The Theatre, the public playhouse was still a new thing" (Southern 1973). "[R]evived with *The Three Lords* in 1590"; possibly revived in 1592 at the time of Q2 (Kermode 2009a). Richard Tarlton, the acclaimed comic actor, performed (Bradbrook 1962b, Heinemann 2003, Henderson 2004) the role of Simplicity. "Tarlton, who most likely honed his skills at insults and jigging while working as a tavern host, became the biggest star of the Queen's Men in the 1580s" (Henderson 2007). He "was not only a stage clown but a man of many parts, a maker of plays and ballads, a drummer, tumbler and qualified Master of Fencing" (Gurr 2009d).

SR none. Q1 1584 *A Right Excellent and Famous Comedy Called The Three Ladies of London, wherein is Notably Declared and Set Forth, How by the Means of Lucre, Love and Conscience is so Corrupted that the One is Married to Dissimulation, the Other Fraught with All Abomination*; author's initials on the TP; prologue; not divided but the designations "the firste acte" and "the second acte" appear on first page following the prologue; these divisions probably "came into the text at a later date" (Jewkes 1958). "Q1 was probably a lightly cut version of the original play" (Kermode). Detailed and symbolic SDs: "*Enter Userie with a paynted boxe of incke in hys hand.*" Then "*Here let Lucar open the boxe [of ink] and dip her finger in it, and spotte Conscience face.*" "The stage action of face-painting visually symbolizes the corrupting of Conscience, who is persuaded by Lucre to accept a five-thousand-pound bribe in return for opening her house to all manner of sweet delight and, in effect, turning it into a bawdy house" (Drew-Bear 1994). "Love, Conscience, and Lucre have 'a dainty face,' 'a lovely face,' 'a face angelical'"; "the concept of the mask is alien to the supposedly pure and unmediated nature of virtue" (Twycross & Carpenter 2002). Q2 1592 designation of "the second acte" omitted; the number of alterations in Q2 "bespeak the author's hand" (Mithal), but Kermode 2009b notes that it's unclear whether "the revisions were made by Wilson or by members of the Queen's Men's company"; perhaps those revisions were made "during a revival of *Three Ladies* to play in repertory with *Three Lords*" (Kermode); this printing was "timed to comment on the building tension in the capital" (Kermode 2009a).

Three Ladies is a play of "lively social criticism" (Cameron 1982), especially of "certain economic evils that England was then burdened with" (Thompson 1910); it "combines its detestation of all foreigners with hysterical anxiety about the Catholic league, showing another way in which Reformation religious propaganda could express itself in economic and social terms" (Bevington 2007b). *Three Ladies* is "the earliest extant play to include London in its title" (Dillon 2000). "[T]his is very much in the mould of the allegorical interlude drama, and blends something of that genre's conceptual representation of London with some contemporary realities of the rapidly developing city" (Grantley 2008a). "One of the earliest dramas to represent a 'turke' on the stage" (Dimmock 2005), it is "the earliest Elizabethan play to bring the figures of the Muslim and Jew into strategic conjunction" (Burton 2005). "Alongside the allegorical plot is the story of Gerontus the Jew. Gerontus is a sympathetic figure who probably influenced Shakespeare's Shylock" (Kathman 2004f). "Wilson's play was one of the first representations of female homoeroticism in the commercial theatre of early modern England" (Walen 2005).

Three Laws of Nature, Moses, and Christ. John Bale. Acted *c.* 1536 (White 1993b). Presumably performed by Bale's "fellows" in or near St. Stephen's Church, near Canterbury, *c.* September 1538-January 1539. Some evidence of rehearsal in Bishopstoke, Hampshire, 1551 (O'Connell 2000b). Perhaps performed at George May's home in Canterbury, 1559 (White). Possibly performed at Magdalen College, Oxford, 1560–61 (Elliott et al. 2004). Evidence of doubling suggests that Bale worked with professional actors (Happé 1985–86). *Three Laws* "was certainly designed for touring" (White 2004a). This play and Bale's *King John* "are uncomplicated in their staging demands in such a way as to render them adaptable to itinerant stages or the great hall" (Bevington 2002a). "*Three Laws* is the earliest extant text to publish a full casting chart" (Bevington 1962); "into fyve personages maye the partes of this comedy be devyded." Bale also describes the costumes to be worn by the six vices: e.g., Hypocrisy ahould be attired "*lyke a graye fryre*," Idolatry "*lyke an old wytche*." Revised by Bale after initial publication (Happé).

 SR no original; *c.* August 1562. O ND ?1548–50 *A Comedy Concerning Three Laws of Nature, Moses, and Christ, Corrupted by the Sodomites, Pharisees and Papists*; "compyled" by Bale in 1538; list of characters at end; divided for five actors; Bale speaks as Prolocutor [prologue]; play ends with song and prayer; five acts. Bale's staging manages a *coup de théâtre*: "Natural Law's reappearance at the close of the first act is calculated to shock. Utterly transformed from his former glory through the black magic of Infidelity's evil, he enters as a leper. His disease is the consequence of man's attempt to accommodate divine truth to his own conceits" (Kendall 1986). O features "the first unified decorative border on a title page in an English playbook" (Davidson 1991): the design represents the story of Adam and Eve. "Unfortunately, the woodcut not only fails to depict anything of the action of the play, but also is of foreign manufacture" (Davidson). Q 1562 *A New Comedy or Interlude Concerning Three Laws*; "nowe newly imprynted"; names of characters on the TP. The "three laws" of the title are Natural, Mosaic, and Christian.

Although Bale's dramaturgy is shaped by tradition, he uses the stage "for a new purpose — not primarily as a sermon on holiness, but as a weapon in religious controversy. His play is a coarse and bitter attack upon the Papacy" (Thompson 1910). Bale's drama "clearly toe[s] the royal and Cromwellian party-line" (Westfall 2004). "The very structure of the play is made to serve Bale's anti-Catholic purpose, since the Law of Nature is corrupted by the unnatural acts of idolatry and sodomy, which prepares the way for the parallel corruption of the Law of Christ, with the implication that Catholicism is also unnatural" (Pineas 1989). "This play contains the earliest extant dramatic treatment of homosexuality" in English drama (Grantley 2004).

The Three Lords and Three Ladies of London. Robert Wilson. Acted "early 1580s" (Munro 2009), or *c.* 1588 (Mithal 1988), or "*c.* late 1588–89" (Kermode 2009a). The play, "a continuation of the *Three Ladies of London*" (Houle 1972), "may have originally belonged to Leicester's Men" (Munro). Either first performed by the Queen's Men (McMillin & MacLean 1998) or revived by this company, at undetermined venue. "Unmistakably devised for direct public playhouse presentation" (Southern 1973). The play incorporates "a lament for the death of their star player, Richard Tarlton, who died in 1588" (Dillon 2000); "this was a catastrophe from which the company never recovered" (George 1981). The lament was delivered by a character named Simplicity, "who may have been played by Wilson himself" (Kathman 2004f), but Tarlton was so well known that "such a reference need hardly be confined to the company both men had once graced" (Dutton 1991).

SR 31 July 1590. Q 1590 *The Pleasant and Stately Moral of the Three Lords and Three Ladies of London, with the Great Joy and Pomp Solemnized at Their Marriages, Comically Interlaced with Much Honest Mirth for Pleasure and Recreation;* author's initials on the TP; list of characters; "preface" [i.e., prologue] consisting of speech by personified London, "a lady very richly attyred"; processions and battle scenes "must have been very much like dumb shows in performance" (Mehl 1965); not divided. "The style of performance is predominantly visual" (McMillin & MacLean). The play "is ritualistic and celebratory, close to civic street pageantry in its elaborately ornate spectacle" (Bevington 1968); it "is openly jubilant and anti-Spanish in celebration of the Armada victory of 1588" (Bevington 2007b). "What playgoers see onstage has the air of an elaborate quadrille. The chief weapons of the Spaniards are not fire and steel but splendor and elegance. As the title of the play in its printed form indicates, the action is 'stately,' meaning that it is stylized and deliberate rather than sudden and naturalistic" (Kiefer 2011). Characters are personified abstractions, whose symbolism is described in the SDs: Enter "Pride, *bearing his shield himself, his ympreze, a* peacocke: *the worde, Non parilli, his Page* Shame *after him with a launce, having appendent gilt, with this word in it, Sur le Ciel,* Ambition *his ympreze, a blacke horse salliant, with one hinder foote upon the globe of the earth.*" "The famous victory is presented not naturalistically but symbolically, the London lords defying the Spanish lords and capturing their shields in scenes of elaborate pageantry" (Cameron 1982). "This sequel to *The Three Ladies of London* was a resolutely up-to-date play, utilizing the newly fashionable blank verse and exploiting popular taste for the spectacular" (Lunney 2002). By contrast, the earlier *Three Ladies* had been written "in fourteeners and doggerel" (Cameron).

The TP features a woodcut that depicts Understanding showing the author a number of Virtues in the house of Reason; the picture previously appeared in Stephen Batman's *The Travailed Pilgrim* (1569). "It therefore has no reference to Wilson's play" (Foakes 1985).

The Three Merry Boys. A droll based upon two scenes in *Rollo, Duke of Normandy*, and performed in the 1640s and 50s. "An audience accustomed to enjoy public executions would relish it, and the only obstacle to performance would be the droll-troupe's inadequacy for a crowd scene" (Elson 1932). At least eight actors are needed.

Published in *1 The Wits, or Sport upon Sport* (O 1662 [two issues] and 1672); RT *The Humors of the Three Merry Boys*; argument; list of characters. The title of the droll "comes from the chorus of the condemned men" (Elson).

Three New Plays. See *The Bashful Lover, The Guardian, A Very Woman.*

Tiberius. See *Claudius Tiberius Nero.*

The Tide Tarrieth No Man. George Wapull. Acted 1571–75 (*DTRB* 1984). "[R]eferences to London and the stress on the wealthy citizenry as the receptacles of godliness suggest a merchants' hall" (Walker 1998) in London. The TP claims that "fowre persons may easily play it" and assigns the eighteen roles. Probably played by a professional company (White 1993b).

SR 22 October 1576. Q 1576 *The Tide Tarrieth No Man, A Most Pleasant and Merry Comedy, Right Pithy and Full of Delight*; list of characters on the TP; prologue; Christianity speaks what amounts to an epilogue, but not so named; not divided. Costumes are symbolic: "Greed is represented iconographically as a rich merchant, Pride as a courtier" (Mowat 1981). Courage wields a dagger, familiar implement of the Vice (Dessen 1977). Christianity "should be wearing the well known Pauline armor but, owing to the wicked nature of the world, is instead 'deformed' in appearance" (Dessen 1986): *"Christianity must enter with a sword, with a title of pollicy, but on the other syde of the tytle, must be written gods word, also a shield, wheron must be written riches, but on the other syde of the shield must be Fayth."* "At one point, Faithful Few turns the titles so that Faith and God's Word take their proper place" (Dessen). A SD "specifies that Despair, later called a 'monster,' should 'enter in some ugly shape,' suggesting a shape-changing costume including a mask or head" (Twycross & Carpenter 2002); "the entrance of such a loathsome figure could produce a striking effect in both theatrical and psychological terms" (Dessen 1977).

Wapull's play dramatizes a critique of civic misdoing: "Christianity is represented as dishonored and enervated by the abuses of the citizens; she complains against the wrongdoers; and eventually is rescued by the intervention of Faithful Few, who represents middle-class citizenship and authority" (Thompson 1910). The play's "preoccupations are overwhelmingly with economic problems" (Grantley 2007).

Time's Alteration, A Dialogue between my Lord Finch and Secretary Windebank, at Their Meeting in France, the Eighth of January 1641, Brought Up to Billingsgate the Next Spring Tide Following. Anonymous. A short play-pamphlet.

F 1642 no author named; not divided. *Time's Alteration* "belongs to a group of play-pamphlets "in which public figures are brought forward confessing their crimes or making their wills" (Butler 1984a).

The work contains two pictures with accompanying verses. Under the portrait of Finch is this caption: "That I have wrong'd the land, I now repent, / But who the divell thought o'th Parliament?" Under the portrait of Windebank is written: "Beware you false traytors that are left behind / T'is best for you to sayle by Windebanck's wind."

Time's Complaint. Anonymous. Acted before the university by students at St. John's College, Oxford, in the college hall, 1 January 1608 (Richards 1982). Thomas Tucker acted in this production. The performance was a "disastrous failure" (Bradbrook 1962b). According to the MS, "To make up the messe of absurdityes the company had so fild the stage that there was no ro[o]me to doe any thing well to bee sure many thinges were mistaken and therefore could not but bee very distastfull."

Oxford, St. John's College, MS 52, pp. 86–112; no author named; list of characters on the TP; prologue; "epilogue not designated, but speech by Time" (Schneider 2011); five acts and separate scenes. Ample SDs.

The MS, a miscellaneous collection of entertainments known as *The Christmas Prince*, also contains other English plays: *Periander* and *The Seven Days of the Week*. But most of the entertainments are written in Latin. *Time's Complaint* was first edited in full by Boas & Greg 1922; Bliss 1816 had provided a summary. Reproduced in photographic facsimile by Richards 1982.

Time's Distractions. Anonymous. Possibly written in whole or part by Richard Brome (Cutts 1967–68, Steggle 2004b), or Mildmay Fane (Harbage 1936), or George Chapman (Jump 1935). "[T]he drama is datable to between the outbreak of the Civil War and the date on the manuscript [5 August 1643]" (Steggle). "In its clearly stated or implicit production requirements and in its attention to the details of stage business, the play consistently attests that its author expected performance" (Strommer 1976). Extensive SDs, which describe masquelike staging.

Possibly acted ?1641–43 (*AED 3*); at Oxford August 1643 before the queen and court (Cutts 1967–68). "Perhaps a relic of one of the surreptitious post-closure performances by professional companies in London" (Steggle).

London, BL, Egerton MS 1994, fols. 212–23; dated 5 August 1643; damaged; no TP; no author named; list of characters all of whom are personifications; five acts. The play has been variously called *Time's Triumph, Juno in Arcadia, Sight and Search, Juno's Pastoral*, and *The Bonds of Peace*. Strommer coined the title adopted in this entry, which Randall 1995 finds the "most helpful." First edited by Ralph Cecil Elsley, M.A. thesis, University of Birmingham (1950), who favored the title *Juno in Arcadia*, then by Strommer 1976.

Despite the pastoral setting, Arcadia "is configured to remind one of certain aspects of England" (Randall). "*Time's Distractions* reflects a pacifist, conservative, Royalist view of England's crisis" (Strommer).

Time's Trick upon the Cards. Mildmay Fane. "Prepared to be represented at Apethorpe by the youth and servants their [*sic*]," 22 February 1642, according to the MS.

London, BL, Additional MS 34221, fols. 19–49; no author named on the TP; list of characters; prologue ("comitragicall") and epilogue; Fame as chorus; "[t]he play is divided into twelve scenes, but the occasional numbering of these begins afresh after the sixth" (Leech 1938). Ample SDs.

Time's Trick "is an essay in dramatic allegory in which personification is all and incident nothing. Fane was still busily preoccupied with the actualities of his day, but he was expressing them in a remote and impersonal form" (Leech). At the end of the play Fane includes "a key which conveniently gives us the moral significations of nearly all the persons and places mentioned in the text" (Leech). The play is "characteristically packed with social and political allusion and allegory" (Randall 1995). "Fane indicates not that Parliament or sovereign is responsible for the stability of the state, but rather a unity of the two" (Morton 1991).

Time's Triumph. See *Time's Distractions*.

Timon (The Comedy of Timon). Anonymous; possibly written by Marlowe (Baker 1998). Acted 1602–03 (Bulman et al. 1978). The play may have been revised *c.* 1606 (Baker) and subsequently revived (Hattaway 1983). An Inner Temple play for one of its festivals: "a law students' burlesque of Shakespeare's *Timon*, presented probably at the Christmas revels" (Bradbrook 1966); but Goldsmith 1958 and Bulman 1976 argue that Shakespeare made extensive use of the anonymous play. Wells & Taylor 1987 are equivocal: Shakespeare's play "may or may not draw upon the anonymous play *Timon*." Jowett 2004c seems persuaded by Bulman.

London, V&A, Dyce MS 52 (D25.F48), fols. 1–24; no TP; no author named; list of characters; epilogue (by Timon); five acts and separate scenes. No "actual evidence of playhouse use. At the same time the addition and alteration of certain stage-directions suggest that the play was prepared for production" (Greg 1931). First edited by Dyce 1842, then by Bulman et al. 1978.

Timon of Athens. William Shakespeare with interpolations by or in collaboration with Thomas Middleton (Wells 1920, Sykes 1924, Lake 1973, 1975a, Jackson 1979, Holdsworth 1982, Wells & Taylor 1987, Vickers 2002, Jowett 2004c). Bevington & Smith 1999 observe that "the Folio editors, Heminges and Condell, appear to regard the play as essentially Shakespeare's." But "the evidence for Middleton's hand in *Timon of Athens* is as strong as that for Fletcher's hand in *Henry VIII*" (Jowett 2003b). "Middleton worked on the play after Shakespeare drafted his contribution"; "[i]n most of the scenes of mixed authorship it seems clear that Shakespeare supplied the core and Middleton added passages to it" (Jowett 2004b); but there are passages "in which Shakespeare's and Middleton's writing seems so closely intertwined that it is difficult, if not impossible, to understand how they were produced" (Bednarz 2011). Middleton wrote "about a third" of the play (Taylor 2004b); Vickers 2008a assigns him 894 lines. The two playwrights "seem to have left [the play] unfinished" (Potter 2012). Possibly acted *c.* 1605 (Wells & Taylor) by the King's Men at the first Globe. "[S]pring 1606 offers the most plausible date of composition" (Jowett 2004c), but Dawson & Minton 2008 suggest 1607. Possibly not performed at all: "There is no evidence that *Timon of Athens* was ever performed at the time it was written or shortly afterwards" (Klein 2001). "The absence of any record of performance is a reminder of our precarious understanding of early staging" (Jowett 2006).

SR 8 November 1623; transferred ?4 August 1626 Paviers right in Shakesperes *plaies*; ?19 June 1627 widow of Isaac Jaggard . . . her parte in Shackspheere *playes*; 16 November 1630; 1 July 1637 Shakespeares *workes* their Part; 6 August 1674; 21 August 1683. F1 1623 *Comedies, Histories, & Tragedies*; three issues; "published according to the true originall copies"; *The Life of Timon of Athens*; list of characters (incomplete) at end; not divided despite the designation of act 1, scene 1; *Timon* has a two-part structure, he "is first inside the city walls, and then out in the wilderness" (Jones 1971); act and scene divisions were introduced by Edward Capell. *Timon* was not originally to have been part of F1; "it was inserted into a space early in F that had been originally designated for the longer *Troilus and Cressida*, a play for which the printer initially had trouble obtaining copyright" (Maus 1997). "*Timon* is the only play in the Tragedies section of F not described as a tragedy" (Wells & Taylor 1987); the F title is "enigmatic": "not *The Tragedy of Timon of Athens*, on the model of every other play in the Folio tragedies, nor even *The Life and Death of Timon of Athens*, on the model of history plays such as *King John* and *Richard III*" (Jowett 2004c).

"Despite the virtual absence of actual women, allegorical representations of female power play an important rhetorical role in *Timon of Athens*. The first half of the play is dominated by the allegorical figure of Dame Fortune" (Maus); in the opening dialogue the Poet says, "I have upon a high and pleasant hill / Feign'd

Fortune to be throned." Timon "takes Fortuna's place and nurses his many worshippers, who 'through him drink the free air'" (Kahn 1987). Female power is on display at Timon's banquet: "*Enter the maskers of Amazons, with lutes in their hands, dauncing and playing.*" When Cupid enters "*with the maske of ladies,*" the audience apparently sees the Five Senses, all female, dancing (Kiefer 2003). "The effect of the episode depends largely on costume, and one would guess that a Jacobean production would have been as lavish as possible in this respect" (Jowett 2004c). In the subsequent mock banquet, a disgruntled Timon invites friends to a feast and serves covered dishes: "*The banket brought in*"; with the covers removed, the platters prove empty of food; "stones painted to look like artichokes are thrown along with Timon's insults" (Meads 2001). "The two scenes [banquets] are structurally a pair; the first being a statement of the accepted Athenian hierarchy and the second depicting the breaking down of that order. Without the first banquet scene, the second would lose a good deal of its dramatic impact and relevance" (Meads). When at the second banquet Timon splashes water on the faces of friends who have disappointed him, he is "symbolically washing off their false deceptive veneers and revealing their true ugliness" (Drew-Bear 1994). The play's most important prop may be "the empty box that Timon's servant Flaminius takes to Lucullus in search of silver"; the box is "pungently emblematic" of Timon's collapsed creditworthiness (Jowett 2003a). Timon's "cave" may have been represented by a trap, but a central opening in the tiring-house wall may have served as the cave entrance (Gurr & Ichikawa 2000). Timon's discovery and burial of gold in 4.3 may have employed a trap. Timon describes the gold "as a means of putting on a false gloss to hide women's ulcerous sores—a verbal image then realized visually by the appearance of Phrynia and Timandra, Alcibiades' painted whores"; "[l]ike the painted whore Fortuna, the painted Phrynia and Timandra betray men recklessly" (Drew-Bear). Timon's tomb, discovered by a soldier, is represented by "either a door or the tiring-house façade" (Hosley 1975) or perhaps by a property tomb; a "soldier claims to be taking a wax impression, so it appears that there must be *something* there to imprint his wax—but appearance may be all that Shakespeare requires here" (Meagher 2003). F2 1632 "the second impression"; three issues. F3 1663 "the third impression"; reissued 1664 with seven additional plays. F4 1685 "the fourth edition"; two issues.

Staging "requires a picture for the Painter to give Timon, yet no stage direction appears in the playscript" (most Shakespeareans assume that the painting is a portrait of Timon); other plays "that employ painter characters or a painter disguise" include *Arden of Faversham*, *Antonio and Mellida*, *The Wisdom of Doctor Dodypoll*, the Painter Addition to *The Spanish Tragedy*, *The Wit of a Woman*, and *The Trial of Chivalry* (Tassi 2005).

'Tis Pity She's a Whore. John Ford. Acted 1630–31 (Gurr 1988a) by Queen Henrietta Maria's Men at the Phoenix, according to the TP. "There is a good chance" that the play was performed at court between 1629 and 1633 (Wiggins 2003).

Richard Perkins, leading man of the company, probably played the role of Vasques or Florio (Wiggins). In playlist of Beeston's Boys 10 August 1639.

SR none. Q 1633 two issues; no author named on the TP but Ford signs the dedication; list of characters; five acts. "The title *'Tis Pity She's A Whore* puts Annabella rather than Giovanni centre stage, and indicates that the play's primary concern is with woman's position in religious discourse" (Findlay 1999). Annabella rejects a suitor while, above, her brother eavesdrops: the "arrangement, with its asides on two levels, enables the audience to share three individual points of view" (Styan 1996). Later, Annabella *above* watches as two suitors fight over her below: "Suddenly she sees 'some celestial creature' over whose 'blessed shape' she exclaims—only to be told by Putana, her confidante, that the object of her adoration is her brother" (Lancaster 1977). The play "contains the most compelling dramatization of brother-sister incest in the canon of English Renaissance drama" (Bergeron 1986). Staging calls for a property bed, the site of incest: "*Enter* Giovanni *and* Anabella *lying on a bed*." Detailed SDs resemble a dumb show: "*Enter the Fryar in his study, sitting in a chayre,* Annabella *kneeling and whispering to him, a table before them and wax-lights, she weepes, and wrings her hands*." At a banquet the villainous Vasques tells Florio: "O sir, I had forgot to tell you; certain you[n]g maidens of Parma in honour to Madam Annabella's marriage have sent their loves to her in a masque . . . *Enter Hippolita and ladies in white roabes with garlands of willowes. Musicke and a daunce*"; Vasques gives Hippolita "*a poysoned cup*"; she drinks and dies a terrible death; the cup, intended for Soranzo, has been switched by the servant Vasques. Further grotesque action includes the blinding of Putana, a nurse, by Vasques: "Gag her instantly, and put out her eyes." Although this incident apparently occurs offstage, it "carries the power to shock and disturb playhouse spectators" (Nunn 2005), a shock sustained as the Cardinal orders her to be burned alive. Grotesque staging involves Giovanni, who "*stabs*" his sister while she lies on a bed in a wedding dress; Giovanni later enters with her "*heart upon his dagger*." With Giovanni's entry, "the hideousness of the stage picture reinforces the conventional meanings of the heart—passion, desire, love—by startling the viewer" (Diehl 1980); the heart on the dagger "encapsulates both the sexual energy and also the image of the heart as the bearer of truth and selfhood which have powered much of the play" (Hopkins 1995b). The brutality of Giovanni and Soranzo, Annabella's suitor, "is quite literally marked out on her body, by her broken hymen, her pregnancy, Soranzo's physical assaults, and Giovanni's ultimate decision to cut out her heart, thus killing both her and her unborn child" (Sanders 1999a). Also issued in *Comedies, Tragicomedies, and Tragedies* (1652), a made-up book no longer extant.

At the end of the play appears a statement combining praise of the actors with an apology for flaws in the printing: "The generall commendation deserved by the actors, in their presentment of this tragedy, may easily excuse such few faults, as are escaped in the printing: a common charity may allow him the ability of spelling, whom a secure confidence assures that hee cannot ignorantly erre in the application of sence." "This apology for misprints was probably added by Ford himself after most of the play had passed through the press" (Roper 1975).

'*Tis Pity* repeatedly evokes the precedent of *Romeo and Juliet*; Ford "liked to invoke and build upon his audience's memory of earlier plays, in particular those of Shakespeare" (Barton 1977). Ford "relocated the entire romantic action in the corrupt bourgeois world of Middletonian satire, and reinvented the lovers as a mutually infatuated brother and sister . . . whose fatally intense passion is protected from the audience's instinctive condemnation by its contrast with the cynical opportunism and thoroughgoing Italianate viciousness that characterize the society whose norms they defy" (Neill 2004). The parallels between the two plays "create a shock effect, tantalizingly suggesting similarity but exposing difference" (Clark 2007).

Titus Andronicus. William Shakespeare and George Peele (Jackson 1996, Vickers 2002), though Price 1943 maintains Shakespeare's sole authorship as do Bate 1995 and Hughes 2006. Parrott 1919 and subsequent scholars argue for Peele's authorship of act 1, act 2, scenes 1 and 2, and act 4, scene 1; Vickers 2008a assigns 775 lines to Peele. Adams 1964 believes that Shakespeare revised an old play. The Q1 TP indicates performance "by the Right Honourable the Earle of Darbie, Earle of Pembrooke, and Earle of Sussex their Servants"; "the *Titus* title page must . . . indicate the sequence of Shakespeare's own company membership" (Gurr 2004a). Perhaps "Shakespeare wrote a crude draft of *Titus Andronicus* before he turned dramatist—even as early as 1588, when he may still have been living in Stratford"; he later "revised it and offered it either to Strange's or Pembroke's Men. They may have played it in the provinces" (Hughes 2006), presumably in the early 1590s. (Lord Strange "became Earl of Derby in September 1593"; Pembroke's Men, also known as Derby's, may have been "a touring offshoot of Strange's" [Bate 1995].) *Titus* "must be a work of early 1594" (Tobin 2002). Performed by Sussex's Men, probably at the Rose, 23 and 28 January, and 6 February 1594 (Henslowe records performance of "titus & ondronicus," in receipts from the period beginning 27 December 1593); the gate receipts "were among the highest that season" (Keenan 2002); some scholars believe that these receipts represent the first performances of *Titus*, in part because of a speculation that the Q1 TP means that Pembroke's Men joined forces with Sussex's Men, at least for the 1594 season (George 1981), in part because Henslowe writes the term "ne" [?new] next to the entries (Bate). But "it is more likely that 'ne' means 'newly revised,' 'newly (re-)licensed,' or 'newly entered in the repertoire'" (Berger & Mowat 2003). Performed at Newington Butts, occupied by the Admiral's and Chamberlain's Men, 5 and 12 June 1594; the two companies "took turns playing their own plays" (Wickham et al. 2000); but King 1992a believes that performance was by "probably an amalgamation" of the companies. Performed by a professional London company, presumably the Chamberlain's Men, for John Harington of Exton at Burley-on-the-Hill, Rutland, the evening of

1 January 1596 (recorded in a letter by Jacques Petit to Anthony Bacon); Petit writes that "'la monstre a plus valeu que le suiect' (the spectacle was worth more than the subject matter)" (Potter 2012). But Marino 2011 demurs: "it is barely possible for [the Chamberlain's Men] to have made the trip for the performance." Presumably played at the Theater by the Chamberlain's Men in the 1590s. Richard Burbage almost certainly played the role of Titus (Potter). Will Kemp "likely played" the unnamed clown (Kinney 2003, Ford 2010). Praised by Francis Meres in *Palladis Tamia* (SR 7 September 1598).

Henry Peacham possibly saw the play in performance and may have drawn a sketch, now at Longleat House, of what he saw; the date on the sketch has been variously interpreted "as either 1595 or (more persuasively) 1614/15" (Orgel 2007); in any event the date may be a forgery by John Payne Collier; "[t]here is no evidence that [Peacham] ever saw *Titus* on stage" (Bate); in the sketch (a conflation of two scenes) the costumes are a mixture of the classical, "vaguely medieval" (Orgel), and contemporary: it is possible that the sketch "was drawn from recollection"; the artist may have brought "together into a group separate sketches of individual actors made when watching a performance" (Foakes 1985); it is also possible that the sketch represents a different drama about Titus, "a play performed in Germany by English actors" (Schlueter 1999). "A German *Tragoedia von Tito Andronico* was published in *Engelische Comedien und Tragedien* (1620), which suggests that it was played on the Continent in some form, possibly by some of the English actors who are known to have worked there, and that it was successful enough for German actors to want a translation (however garbled) for their own use" (Hughes); this version may preserve SDs that were originally part of Shakespeare's play (Keenan). Levin 2002 argues convincingly that "the artist of the Longleat drawing did see a performance of the play . . . and that his drawing was influenced by what he saw on the stage—or rather, by what he remembered"; Duncan-Jones 2011 concurs.

SR 6 February 1594 *a Noble Roman Historye of Tytus Andronicus*; transferred 19 April 1602; 8 November 1623; "possibly transferred 4 August 1626 from widow of [Thomas] Pavier to Edward Brewster and Robert Bird" (Jowett 2007e); ?19 June 1627 widow of Isaac Jaggard . . . her parte in Shackspheere *playes*; 8 November 1630; 1 July 1637 Shakespeares *workes* their Part; 6 August 1674; 21 August 1683. Q1 1594 *The Most Lamentable Roman Tragedy of Titus Andronicus*; unique copy at Folger (minor damage); no author named; not divided. Q1 is the "first play of Shakespeare's to be published" (Murphy 2003). Q1 "contains more explicit stage directions . . . than most subsequent works, possibly because Shakespeare was not a leading member of a company of players" (Hughes 2006). The "pageant-like entry" of Titus in a funeral procession has the "quality" of a dumb show (Wells 1997). Staging calls for a property coffin in that procession; perhaps more than one coffin was used, for Titus buries two sons (Wells 1984). A *"tombe"* is needed to receive the coffin(s); the tomb "cannot be visually fictitious" and may be located in "the *frons* of the tiring house" (Meagher 2003), though Fitzpatrick

2011 doubts a central entry-point onto the stage. Stairs figure in the staging: "Saturninus and Bassianus clamor at the gates for admission to the *'Senate house,'* that is, the gallery, and are admitted: *'They goe up into the Senate house'*" (Rhodes 1976). Martius and Quintus fall into a "pit," presumably represented by a trap in floor of the stage. Offstage sound signals a hunt: *"Here a crie of hounds, and windhornes in a peale,"* followed by entry of the characters. Titus' frustrated quest for justice takes a unique form: he writes messages to the gods, attaches them to arrows, and shoots them skyward; this staging is inspired by emblem literature (Haaker 1970–71). Although arrows could have been shot "through the open top of the playhouse," it seems "more likely that the shooting was mimed and that the lines spoken referred directly to the signs of the zodiac, if indeed the underside of the roof was so decorated" (White 1998). The play "features spectacular scenes of amputation, both off stage and in one case" onstage (Duncan-Jones 2001); "dismemberment is so multiplied as to defy summary" (Owens 2005). At one point Aaron the Moor *"cuts off* Titus *hand"*; a little later Titus' sons are beheaded: *"Enter a messenger with two heads and a hand."* Dismemberment "expresses, in an immediate, physical way the horror and impotency of a divided state" (Diehl 1980). A SD captures the horrific nature of sexual violation: *"Enter the Empresse sonnes with* Lavinia, *her handes cut off, and her tongue cut out, & ravisht."* Subsequently Lavinia finds a way to reveal the identities of her tormentors: *"Shee takes the staffe in her mouth, and guides it with her stumps and writes."* Later she is slain by her father onstage. Unusual costuming is implied when Tamora arrives with her sons at Titus's home *"disguised"*; Tamora tells Titus that she is Revenge and that her two sons are Rape and Murder (Kiefer 2003). Titus binds the sons and *"cuts their throats"*; later he enters *"like a cooke"* and serves their flesh to Tamora at a feast; after this grotesque meal Titus kills her.

Q2 1600 "playde by . . . the Lorde Chamberlaine theyr servants." Q3 1611 [octavo-in-fours]; "plaide by the king's majesties servants" (i.e., the King's Men). F1 1623 *Comedies, Histories, & Tragedies*; three issues; "published according to the true originall copies"; three issues; *The Lamentable Tragedy of Titus Andronicus*; five acts; however, the act division "is certainly not original, and may have been introduced at the time of printing" (Greg 1955). Scene 3.2, the fly-scene, an addition of some 85 lines and difficult to date, first appears at the end of act 3 in F1, which also provides "more extensive stage directions" (Dobson 2001); the scene "could have been added on the occasion of a revival in the 1590s" (Wells & Taylor 1987); it was "possibly not performed in Shakespeare's lifetime" (Scott 2008). "When Shakespeare's foul papers were given to the printer in 1594 it may be that no copy of the added scene was made to accompany them. Thus the added scene would not have reached the printer" (Waith 1984). The scene may have been written by someone else (Hughes), but Jones 1995 believes that it "reads like early Shakespeare." F2 1632 "the second impression"; three issues. F3 1663 "the third impression"; reissued 1664 with seven additional plays. F4 1685 "the fourth edition"; two issues.

Titus is "Shakespeare's first experiment with revenge tragedy" (Andrews 1987) and the first play of Shakespeare's to be printed. *Titus* is "Shakespeare's answer to Kyd, his demonstration to the public that he can match, even outdo, the most successful play of the age [i.e., *The Spanish Tragedy*]" (Bate 1992). Both Kyd and Shakespeare "link political revolution to sexual violation" (Gossett 2000). Jonson's disparaging reference in *Bartholomew Fair* (1614) testifies to the enduring popularity of *Titus* in performance.

Tom a Lincoln. ?Thomas Heywood. Acted *c.* 1611–16 (Proudfoot et al. 1992) by the gentlemen of Gray's Inn, perhaps at the Christmas revels. The play may have belonged to a professional company, which adapted it for Christmas performance at Gray's Inn, or the play may have been written expressly for Gray's Inn. "Suggestive of professionalism are the stage directions, which use the formulae of the professional playhouses; many are extended and circumstantial" (Proudfoot 1993).

London, BL, Additional MS 61745, fols. 1–46, ed. Proudfoot et al. 1992; no author named; lacks TP and three or four leaves at the beginning, also another leaf in the middle; Time functions as chorus/presenter, introducing four dumb shows, which are carefully described; epilogue; not divided. The MS was "prepared by a series of copyists, possibly professionals" (Stern 2009c). SDs ample for production. A complicated dumb show begins when "*Time drawes a curtaine & discovers Angellica in her bed a sleep, the infant lyinge by her.*"

The name Morganus Evans, apparently the scribe, appears at the end of the MS, which was discovered at Melbourne Hall, Derbyshire, the home of John Coke's son Thomas, in 1973. The play is "perhaps the work of a prominent and prolific professional dramatist, but it has survived only in an amateur transcript, made . . . with a considerable degree of efficiency, but made in what would seem to have been unpropitious circumstances and for uncertain purposes" (Proudfoot 1993).

Tom Strowd. See *The Blind Beggar of Bednal Green.*

Tom Tyler and His Wife. Anonymous. Acted *c.* 1563 (*DTRB* 1984) at undetermined venue. In his 1656 catalogue Archer lists *Tom tyler, C[omedy]* without naming the author. The play "borrows from morality elements, especially in the play's Vice figure named Desire, but the play is essentially a comic treatment of domestic discord played by boy actors" (Bevington 2002a); Prologue calls this "a play set out by prettie boyes." The play "has characteristics of a chorister presentation" (Lennam 1975).

SR *c.* April-May 1563. Q 1661 *Tom Tyler and His Wife, An Excellent Old Play*; two issues; no author named; described on the TP as "printed and acted about a hundred years ago"; "the second impression," but no earlier edition survives; list of characters; prologue; "an epilogue in the form of a song" (Lennam); "replete with the popular songs of its day" (Houle 1972); not divided.

There may have been earlier editions *c.* 1551, 1578, and 1598 (Farmer 1912). Appended to some copies of 1661 Q is *A True, Perfect, and Exact Catalogue of All the Comedies, Tragedies, Tragi-Comedies, Pastorals, Masques and Interludes, that Were Ever Yet Printed and Published, Till this Present Year 1661* by Francis Kirkman. The TP of some copies of Q announce Kirkman's catalogue.

Tottenham Court, A Comedy. Thomas Nabbes. Possibly first acted by the King's Revels or Prince Charles's company (*JCS*). "Acted at" the Salisbury Court playhouse in 1633, according to the TP, by Queen Henrietta Maria's Men.

SR 5 April 1638. Q 1638–39 *Tottenham Court, A Pleasant Comedy*; two issues; list of characters; prologue and epilogue (by the Hostess); five acts and separate scenes. Also issued in *Plays, Masques, Epigrams, Elegies, and Epithalamiums*, a made-up book containing plays published between 1637 and 1640; the general TP is dated 1639; in some copies the separate TP is dated 1638, others 1639. Several characters enter "breathless after a footrace . . . and do some jumping exercises"; later they "do some sort of dance" (Wright 1928).

The first-issue dedication disparages playgoers who disliked the play and suggests that the reader will find merit where the original audience did not: "If you vouchsafe the reading of it, you will find (after the light title) a light subject, more gravely drest then the vulgar perhaps expected: who please their senses oftner with showes, then their intellects with the true morall end of playes, instruction."

Tottenham Court participates in the "brief vogue for city comedies centred around specific locations in London" (Kathman 2004c). Other such plays include *Holland's Leaguer, Hyde Park, The Weeding of the Covent Garden, The Sparagus Garden*, and *Covent Garden* (Miles 1942).

A Tragedy Called All's Lost by Lust. See *All's Lost by Lust.*

A Tragedy Called The Jew of Malta. See *The Jew of Malta.*

A Tragedy Called The Valiant Scot. See *The Valiant Scot.*

A Tragedy of Cola's Fury, or Lirenda's Misery. See *Cola's Fury.*

A Tragedy of Herod and Antipater. See *Herod and Antipater.*

The Tragedy of Albovine. See *Albovine, King of the Lombards.*

The Tragedy of Alexander the Sixth. See *The Devil's Charter.*

The Tragedy of Andromana. See *Andromana.*

The Tragedy of Antipoe. See *Antipoe.*

The Tragedy of Bajazet the Second. See *The Raging Turk.*

The Tragedy of Bonduca. See *Bonduca.*

The Tragedy of Brennoralt. See *Brennoralt.*

The Tragedy of Caesar and Pompey, or Caesar's Revenge. See *Caesar and Pompey.*

The Tragedy of Charles Duke of Byron. See *2 Charles Duke of Byron.*

The Tragedy of Claudius Tiberius Nero. See *Claudius Tiberius Nero, Rome's Greatest Tyrant.*

The Tragedy of Cleander. See *The Lovers' Progress.*

The Tragedy of Cleopatra (Samuel Daniel). See *Cleopatra.*

The Tragedy of Cleopatra, Queen of Egypt (Thomas May). See *Cleopatra, Queen of Egypt.*

The Tragedy of Coriolanus. See *Coriolanus.*

The Tragedy of Cymbeline. See *Cymbeline.*

The Tragedy of Dido, Queen of Carthage. See *Dido, Queen of Carthage.*

The Tragedy of Edward II. See *Edward II.*

The Tragedy of Gismond of Salerne. See *Gismond of Salerne.*

The Tragedy of Gorboduc. See *Gorboduc.*

The Tragedy of Hamlet. See *Hamlet.*

The Tragedy of Heildebrand. See *The Unfortunate Lovers.*

The Tragedy of Hoffman. See *Hoffman.*

The Tragedy of Jocasta. See *Jocasta.*

The Tragedy of Julia Agrippina. See *Julia Agrippina.*

The Tragedy of Julius Caesar. See *Julius Caesar*.

The Tragedy of King Charles I Basely Butchered. See *The Famous Tragedy of Charles I*.

The Tragedy of King Richard the Second. See *Richard II*.

The Tragedy of King Richard the Third. See *Richard III*.

The Tragedy of Locrine. See *Locrine*.

The Tragedy of Lodovick Sforza. See *Lodovick Sforza*.

The Tragedy of Macbeth. See *Macbeth*.

The Tragedy of Mariam, The Fair Queen of Jewry. Elizabeth Cary, wife of Henry Cary, Viscount Falkland, and "the first Englishwoman to write a tragedy" (Cerasano & Wynne-Davies 1996). Written "after 1602" (Britland 2010), perhaps 1606–08 (Hodgson-Wright 2000b). No evidence of production and virtually no SDs, only the names of speakers: "Action is discussed rather than dramatized" (Cotton 1980). However, "the dramatic energy of *Mariam* makes the play seem more consonant with the popular stage than most 'closet dramas' are," and it "seems indebted" to Daniel's *Cleopatra* (Weller & Ferguson 1994). And "*Mariam* reveals a knowledge of stagecraft that suggests Cary's familiarity with popular as well as closet drama" (Roberts 2009). The play "must have circulated in manuscript" among Cary's friends (Dunstan & Greg 1914, Straznicky 1994). "*Mariam*'s implied audience would likely be a circumscribed group of readers capable of seeing in the tragic example of Mariam their culture's tyrannical silencing of dissenting, perhaps especially female, voices" (Valbuena 2003). However, "*Mariam* itself is not a very encouraging feminist fable. It concerns itself with competition between women for the favour of a tyrannical male; in typical patriarchal fashion, it damns most women in order to celebrate one singularly chaste paragon; it contrasts its 'fair' (pale-skinned) heroine with vicious women whose bodies are 'brown' and 'black'" (Daileader & Taylor 2006).

SR 17 December 1612; transferred 29 May 1638; 25 January 1639. The title appears in Archer's 1656 catalogue and in Kirkman's 1661 catalogue. Q 1613 two issues; author identified on the TP as "that learned, vertuous, and truly noble ladie, E. C."; "dedicatory sonnet and list of characters appear only in the Huntington Library and Houghton Library copies" (Purkiss 1998); list of characters "printed on the verso of the dedicatory sonnet . . . was removed from most copies of the play" (Straznicky 2004); the Eton copy contains a handwritten list divided into male and female characters (Purkiss); argument; chorus, "who remain on stage throughout the play" (Cerasano & Wynne-Davies) and who comment at the conclusion of each act; five acts and separate scenes.

"The first original play written by an Englishwoman" (Clarke 2006). "The first original play by a woman to be published in England" (Weller & Ferguson). "[T]he only extant play written by a woman in this era that was not a translation" (Bergeron 2006). "The earliest known English play on the popular subject of Herod's turbulent family affairs, and it is the first to concentrate on the private relationship of Herod and Mariam" (Straznicky & Rowland 1992); "Mariam's conflict between obedience to and rebellion against Herod's authority [is] the central concern" (Beilin 1987). "We encounter a range of female characters that manage to step outside the parameters for womanhood dictated by early modern culture" (Clarke). *Mariam* "features at least seven would-be revengers, four of whom are women" (Roberts 2003). "The play's production of femininity, alternatively vilified as wanton and valorized as virtuous, is crucially dependent upon 'race.' That is, the cultural polarization of the category 'woman' is constructed via racial marking" (Callaghan 1994). "In *Mariam*, race is something at once hidden and physically there: hard to see, but nonetheless dangerous" (Ferguson 2003). The play "presents a bleak vision of female self-determination within the confines of Renaissance society" (Findlay 1999).

The Tragedy of Messalina. See *Messalina.*

The Tragedy of Nero. See *Nero* (*Piso's Conspiracy*).

The Tragedy of Orestes. See *Orestes.*

The Tragedy of Ovid. See *Ovid.*

The Tragedy of Paulo Giordano Orsini. See *The White Devil.*

The Tragedy of Philotas. See *Philotas.*

The Tragedy of Rollo. See *The Bloody Brother.*

The Tragedy of Sejanus. See *Sejanus.*

The Tragedy of Sir John van Olden Barnavelt. See *Sir John van Olden Barnavelt.*

The Tragedy of Soliman and Perseda. See *Soliman and Perseda.*

The Tragedy of Sophonisba. See *The Wonder of Women.*

The Tragedy of Tancred and Gismund. See *Tancred and Gismund.*

The Tragedy of That Famous Roman Orator Marcus Tullius Cicero. See *Marcus Tullius Cicero.*

The Tragedy of the Duchess of Malfi. See *The Duchess of Malfi.*

The Tragedy of the Guise. See *The Massacre at Paris.*

The Tragedy of The Unhappy Fair Irene. See *The Unhappy Fair Irene.*

The Tragedy of Thierry and Theodoret. See *Thierry and Theodoret.*

The Tragedy of Tiberius. See *Claudius Tiberius Nero.*

The Tragedy of Troilus and Cressida. See *Troilus and Cressida* (Shakespeare).

The Tragedy of Valentinian. See *Valentinian.*

A Tragedy or Interlude Manifesting the Chief Promises of God. See *The Chief Promises.*

The Tragical Actors. Anonymous. A play-pamphlet. The play "could only have been staged in private locations, or in inns on an ad hoc basis" (Ravelhofer 2008).
    Q_ND ?1660 *The Tragical Actors or the Martyrdom of the Late King Charles wherein Oliver's Late Falsehood, with the Rest of His Gang Are Described in Their Several Actions and Stations*; no author named; not divided.
    "The action is confined to January 1649; the protagonists discuss how the law must be bent so as to legitimize the verdict on Charles I" (Ravelhofer).

A Tragical Comedy of Alexander and Campaspe. See *Campaspe.*

The Tragical Comedy of Damon and Pithias. See *Damon and Pithias.*

The Tragical Conquests of Tamburlaine. See *Tamburlaine.*

The Tragical History of Doctor Faustus. See *Doctor Faustus.*

The Tragical History of Hamlet. See *Hamlet.*

The Tragical Life and Death of Claudius Tiberius Nero. See *Claudius Tiberius Nero.*

A Tragicomedy Called Match Me in London. See *Match Me in London.*

A Tragicomedy Called Newmarket Fair. See *Newmarket Fair.*

A Tragicomedy Called the Witch. See *The Witch.*

The Traitor, A Tragedy. James Shirley. Licensed for acting 4 May 1631 (Adams 1917). "Acted by" Queen Henrietta Maria's Men, according to the TP, at the Phoenix. In playlist of Beeston's Boys 10 August 1639. The play dramatizes the intersection of sex and politics in Caroline culture: the prince "indulge[s] in passion for women, thus making [himself] vulnerable" to a favorite's "treacherous manipulations of erotic and political alliances" (DiGangi 2006).

SR 3 November 1634. Q 1635 list of characters; five acts. Lively staging includes a masquelike scene: "*Enter Lust richly apparreld, the pleasures attending*"; then "*Enter a young man in rich habit and crownd*"; "*The Furies joyne in the dance, and in the end carries the young man away.*" The play seems a pastiche of familiar characters and dramatic situations: e.g., "The final episode of Amidea's body 'discover'd in a bed prepar'd by two Gentlewomen' is reminiscent of 'Vendice, with the skull of his betrothed dressed up in tires,' in *The Revenger's Tragedy,* or the painted (and poisoned) corpse of the Duchess Marcelia in Massinger's *The Duke of Milan*" (Carter 1965). In response to the Duke's importuning, Amidea "*wounds her arme.*" Then Sciarrha "*wounds*" Amidea and "*She dyes.*" The Duke finds her dead body: "Amidea *discovered in a bed, prepar'd by two gentlewomen.*" Unusual staging includes Lorenzo revealing "*the dukes picture, a ponyard sticking in it.*" Here "the portrait substitutes for its sitter, the Duke of Florence, as object of violent action" (Elam 2010). "The portrait's wounds constitute an artistic representation of the Duke's future" (Nunn 2005).

Shirley dedicates the play to William Cavendish, hoping that he will "read these 'cold papers' and smile on them, thereby giving them new life beyond 'what scene exactly gave them, in the presentment, rewarded with frequent applause'" (Bergeron 2006).

Trappolin creduto Principe, or Trappolin Supposed a Prince, An Italian Tragicomedy. Aston Cokain. Written in 1633 when the author was returning from a trip to the continent (*JCS*). Although the play was intended for the stage, there is no record of performance. But *Trappolin* had immediate application to political events, especially to the hypocrisy of the Puritans (Wright 1934).

SR 4 May 1657. O 1658 *Small Poems of Divers Sorts;* list of characters; prologue and epilogue (mislabeled "prologue"); five acts and separate scenes. Printed with *The Obstinate Lady;* continuous register and pagination. Staging includes dances by maskers named Hymen, Luna, Mars, Mercury, Jupiter, Venus, Saturn, and Sol. Reissued 1658–59 *A Chain of Golden Poems* (with *The Obstinate Lady*). Reissued twice in 1662 *Poems* (with *Tragedy of Ovid* added); TP of *Trappolin* dated 1658. Reissued 1669 *Choice Poems of Several Sorts* (with *Obstinate Lady, Ovid*).

The O epilogue addresses playgoers: "Ther's nothing now remains, / Saving the guerdon of our poets pains: / He for himself is careless, only wo'd, / That for the actors sakes you'd say 'tis good." The author's address to the reader of the 1662 O reports a difficulty in securing the scripts of his plays for publication: "[I] made a diligent enquiry after them and when I had found them out could not get them delivered without parting with some money, and promising my honest friend Mr. W. Godbid, (after I had afforded them some small correction) I would bestow them on him, (with my consent) for the press: for indeed without his (assistance) I should not have recovered them out of a gentlemans hands whom I will forbear to name."

The Travails of the Three English Brothers. John Day, William Rowley, and George Wilkins. Acted April (Gossett 2004b) or summer 1607 (Parr 1995). "Now play'd by" Queen Anne's Men, according to the TP, at the Curtain (SR). "But it was labelled a Red Bull play in Beaumont's *The Knight of the Burning Pestle*, written for the Blackfriars Boys in the same year" (Gurr 1996). "The play could have been written for the Curtain and later performed at the Red Bull" (Wickham et al. 2000) by Queen Anne's Men in 1607. *Travails* was performed at both theaters (Parr). Probably revived by Richard Cholmeley's players at Gowthwaite Hall, the North Riding of Yorkshire, home of John Yorke, Christmas season 1609–10, as "The three shirleyes" [Sir Thomas, Sir Antony, and Sir Robert Shirley] (Sisson 1942); the players were known as the Simpsons, and the "audience was almost exclusively Catholic" (Jensen 2003).

SR 29 June 1607 as yt was played at the Curten; transferred 19 April 1613. Q 1607 two issues, one entitled *The Three English Brothers*; no author named on the TP but Day, Rowley, and Wilkins sign the dedication in the second issue; prologue ("attired like Fame") and epilogue (also Fame); during the play Fame as chorus appears three times to summarize offstage action; her garment would have been decorated with eyes and ears (Kiefer 2003); expansive SDs describe what are essentially dumb shows; not divided. The play "would have been elongated in performance by its numerous dumb shows, processions and battle-scenes" (Parr 1995): e.g., *"A battell presented, excursion, the one halfe drive out the other, then enter with heads on their swords."* *"Chambers go off"* during a chorus. "Chambers were small pieces of ordnance which stood on their breeching, without other support" (Lawrence 1927). "The play is virtually obsessed with decapitation" (Owens 2005): *"Enter an officer with a counterfeit head like Sherleys."* But in this instance Sherley is actually alive. Sir Thomas is consigned to the stocks, the fate of virtuous characters in the moral interludes. "The presence of a rack is assumed, the text reading 'Hoist him up,' 'Wrinch him againe'" (Reynolds 1940). The play's final action brings together the three principal characters, who are located in Spain, England, and Persia: Fame *"gives to each a prospective glasse, they seeme to see one another, and offer to embrace, at which Fame parts them."* Although Fitzpatrick 2011 argues that there were only two entrances onto the stage, SDs here specify the use of three doorways: "*Enter three severall waies the three brothers.*" Although most scholars, though not Jewkes 1958, Gossett 2004b, or Egan 2006a, render the play's title as *Travels*, the word on the Q TP, in the RT, and in the SR is *Travailes*, which ambiguously suggests both *travels* and *travails* (Gossett); Kirkman entitles the play *The travailes of the three English brothers, Shirleys*.

Prologue affirms the essential truth of the dramatization while conceding that history has been adapted to suit the requirements of the stage: "Our sceane is mantled in the robe of truth, / Yet must we crave (by law of poesie) / To give our history an ornament. / But equalling this definition, thus, / Who gives a foule unto his cooke to dresse: / Likewise expects to have a foule againe, / Though in the cookes laborious workmanship / Much may be deminisht, som-what added, / The losse of fethers and the gaine of sauce: / Yet in the back surrender of this dish, / It is (and may be truelie cald) the same: / Such are our acts." Prologue's speech, together with the ensuing chorus, suggests a resemblance to *Henry V*: "Like Shakespeare, the dramatists present the unabashedly patriotic main action of their chronicle within the framework of a recurring chorus, apologizing for the limitations of the theatre and the inevitable discrepancy between narrated time and narrative time, guiding the action with its multiple location shifts, and inviting the audience to use its imagination to make good any imperfections" (Hoenselaars 1995).

The Traveler. See *The English Traveler.*

The Trial of Chivalry. Anonymous; possibly written by Henry Chettle and Thomas Heywood "in the late 1590s" (Woods 2007) or *c.* 1600 (Cahill 2008). "Lately acted by" the Earl of Derby's Men, according to the 1605 TP, at undetermined venue. "This must be the company led by Robert Browne 'of the Boar's Head,' a company which came to prominence in London around 1598–9 and seems to have become provincial again after Browne's death in 1603" (Lloyd 2005).

SR 4 December 1604 *The life and Deathe of Cavaliero Dick Boyer.* Q 1605 *The History of the Trial of Chivalry, with the Life and Death of Cavaliero Dick Bowyer*; two issues; no author named; not divided. The second issue is entitled *This Gallant Cavaliero Dick Bowyer* and claims to be "newly acted" but "omits the reference to Derby's Men" (Woods). The SDs "are literary and descriptive, quite elaborately so in the battle scenes" (Jewkes 1958); in the climactic scene "two of the heroes who epitomize the chivalric values of the play (Ferdinand and Pembroke) take on two armies, while the third hero (Philip) disposes of the arch villain (Roderick) in single combat" (Dessen 1984): "*They fight, Bowyer hath the wench, rescued by France, recovered by Navar: Philip meetes Rodorick, rescued by Peter: retreat is sounded, the enemies begin to retire, Rodorick chas'd by Philip: Enter at severall doores, after retreate sounded, Pembrooke and Ferdinand.*" Staging includes an "orgy of fighting beyond all dramatic needs" (Wright 1968). Perhaps the most appalling violence is that enacted against Bellamira: out of frustrated love, the Duke of

Burbon "rubd [her] face with an infectious herbe," and she is "[m]ade a loathsome leper." "Despite her disfigured face her beloved Prince Philip proclaims his love for her and his intention to marry her" (Drew-Bear 1994).

A different kind of SD suggests the latitude exercised by comic actors: "*Enter Forrester, missing the other taken away, speake any thing, and Exit.*" "Here the player is given complete freedom to please the audience by any sort of business, stock routine or improvisation the player can provide" (Sutcliffe 1996).

The Trial of Treasure. ?William Wager; the author may also have written *Enough Is as Good as a Feast* (Happé 2008). Acted ?1565 (Craik 1958). "[R]eferences to filling all the pots in the house suggest a hall or inn setting; the frequent classical allusions point towards a school or college play" (Walker 1998); "throughout the play the testimony of the ancient philosophers is freely adduced" (Thompson 1910). The play "may have been intended for one of the Gracechurch Street inns across from Wager's parish" (White 2009). The TP divides the fifteen roles for five actors.

SR none. Q 1567 *A New and Merry Interlude Called The Trial of Treasure*; "newly set foorth, and never before this tyme imprinted"; two issues; list of characters on the TP; eight-stanza preface functions as prologue; ends with exhortation to "learne of the just" and "subdue thy beastly luste"; not divided. "The text is exceptionally valuable for its fifty or so stage directions" (Happé). "A "strong visual presentation . . . characterizes" *The Trial* (Grantley 2007): "*Enter Lust like a gallaunt.*" The playwright "enforces an ascetic moral by denouncing Treasure ('a woman, finely appareled') through a visual contrast with Trust ('a woman playnly' [appareled])" (Craik 1958). This is the only interlude that brings Time as character to the stage: "Time's costume here is not indicated, probably because his forelock, hourglass, and scythe were too familiar to need mention" (Craik). Moral interludes such as this "are undeniably a visually emblematic drama. They tend to present ideas in emblematic action . . . [as in] the comic bridling of the recalcitrant Lust" (Twycross & Carpenter 2002).

When a visiting troupe of players enact a play in *Sir Thomas More*, written c. 1600 (Jowett 2011), their entertainment borrows from *Trial of Treasure*, perhaps suggesting that it had a long stage history.

A Trick to Catch the Old One. Thomas Middleton, named in Kirkman's catalogues of 1661 and 1671. Acted 1604 (Lamb 2009). "Lately acted by the Children of Paules," according to first issue of Q1, at Paul's playhouse. After the closure of that company the play "was transferred to the other boys' company at the Blackfriars" (Wayne 2007). "Often in action, both at Paules, and the Black-fryers [by the Children of the Queen's Revels (Munro 2005)]," according to the revised TPs of Q1, which also report that the play was "presented before his majestie on New-yeares night last": this performance took place "most likely in 1607 or

1608" (Wayne). In playlist of Beeston's Boys 10 August 1639 as *A Trick to Cheat the Devil*.

SR 7 October 1607. Q1 1608 three TPs survive; the first records Paul's Boys but fails to record the author; the other two preserve the reference to Paul's Boys but mention performance at Blackfriars and court; these latter two also add, "composed by T. M."; five acts but no designation of act 1. Q2 1616 [octavo-in-fours]; "by T. Midleton."

"Combining figures from Roman comedy with the prodigal son of morality plays and English literature's first accurate portrayal of a terminal alcoholic, [the play] dramatizes the pursuit of credit, financial and sexual" (Taylor 2004b). Here "human relationships are dominated by money; love and marriage are a matter of hard cash" (Barber 1968). The play "illustrates the tendency of Jacobean comedy to move away both from Shakespeare's romantic vein and Jonson's morally satirical vein toward a more lighthearted comedy of manners, anticipating the style of Restoration comedy" (Bevington 2004).

Tricks of Youth. See *The Walks of Islington and Hogsdon*.

The Triumph of Death. See *Four Plays in One*.

The Triumph of Honor. See *Four Plays in One*.

The Triumph of Love. See *Four Plays in One*.

The Triumph of Time. See *Four Plays in One*.

Troilus and Cressida. ?Thomas Dekker and ?Henry Chettle. Acted *c*. April 1599 (Foakes & Rickert 1961) at undetermined venue. The fragmentary "plot," or "backstage storyboard" (Bate 2008) of a play. "[T]here is every reason to suppose that the fragmentary Plot belongs to Chettle and Dekker's *Troilus and Cressida*, and no reason to doubt that it was prepared for the original performance" (Greg 1931). The play "belonged to the Admiral's Men some time about the turn of the century" (Bradley 1992) and so was presumably staged at the Rose (Rhodes 1976). Actors included Thomas Hunt, Richard Jones as Priam, Stephen [?Maget] (a Beggar), John Pig/Pyk, and "Mr. Jones his boy." Henslowe records payments to Dekker and Chettle, 7 and 16 April 1599.

London, BL, Additional MS 10449, fol. 5 [fragment], ed. Greg 1931. The MS "is badly mutilated" (Beckerman 1989). "There is no indication whatever of any division into acts" (Greg).

Troilus and Cressida. William Shakespeare. Acted the second half of 1601 (Dawson 2003) by the Lord Chamberlain's Men, according to the SR entry, at the first Globe; 1609 Qa states that the play "was acted by the kings majesties servants at the Globe" (i.e., the King's Men), but the play's "bitter spirit" and philosophical discourse "are not the sort to hold the attention of an Elizabethan popular audience" (Campbell 1938). Possibly first performed at an Inn of Court (Alexander 1928), which could explain the play's "arcane vocabulary" (Jones 1995), "yet no compelling historical evidence exists to connect *Troilus* with the Inns of Court, and Shakespeare is not known ever to have written a play on commission for a private audience" (Bevington 1998). "The suggestion that *Troilus* is somehow too intellectual for the public playhouse, that it was written for elite 'private' taste, is mere condescension" (Bate 2008). Although the Qa TP indicates performance at the Globe, Qb omits this information and claims in a newly added (anonymous) preface: "you have heere a new play, never stal'd with the stage, never clapper-clawd with the palmes of the vulger" ("A never writer to an ever Reader. Newes"); "the phrase may refer to performance in a space other than the Globe" (Holland 2004a). "[T]he point of the epistle is that it announces a *reading version* of the play, new to a print readership and superior to what had doubtless been performed in a cut text by the King's Men at the Globe" (Dutton 2000). "Thoroughgoing authorial revision of the play, deliberately transformed from an acting text to one designed above all to be read, would explain the discrepancy" between the Qa and Qb TPs (Duncan-Jones 2001). Possibly revived at court 1609 (Gurr). The play "does not seem to have made a hit when it was first written" (Dawson); Shakespeare employs "a variety of devices that purposely alienate the audience and prohibit sustained sympathy" (Rose 1988). Robert Armin, renowned for his wit, "presumably" played the bitter Thersites (Butler 2004a).

SR 7 February 1603 entry by James Roberts to print *Troilus and Cressida* "when he hath gotten sufficient aucthority for yt" (apparently he never did) — this is perhaps a blocking entry (King 1992a); the abortive attempt at publication may suggest "a certain notoriety" (Love 1993); re-entered 28 January 1609; transferred ?4 August 1626 Paviers right in Shakesperes *plaies*; ?19 June 1627 widow of Isaac Jaggard . . . her parte in Shackspheere *playes*; 1 July 1637 Shakespeares *workes* their Part; 6 August 1674; 21 August 1683. Qa [first state] 1609 *The History of Troilus and Cressida*; "written by William Shakespeare"; epilogue (by Pandarus); not divided. Qb [second state] 1609 *The Famous History of Troilus and Cressida, Excellently Expressing the Beginning of Their Loves, with the Conceited Wooing of Pandarus, Prince of Licia*; "written by William Shakespeare"; preface, possibly written by John Marston (Elton 1975) or by "one of the two publishers, Henry Walley or Richard Boniam" (Bergeron 2006); no prologue; not divided. (Qb is one of only two Shakespearean Quartos to contain a preface.) F1 1623 *Comedies, Histories, & Tragedies*; three issues; "published according to the true originall copies"; *The Tragedy of Troilus and Cressida*; prologue spoken by an actor wearing a distinctive costume as "arm'd" (Stern 2004b); the actor "may well have been clad as a soldier primarily to introduce this Trojan war play" (Bruster & Weimann 2004); the costume "alludes to the armed epilogue of Marston's *Antonio and Mellida* (1599) and Jonson's armed prologue to *Poetaster*" (Potter 2012);

although the prologue "appears only in F, [it] was probably written for an early performance" (Dawson); the prologue "was almost accidentally acquired for the Folio late in the publication process to fill what had, for other reasons, become a spare recto before the start of the play" (Stern 2004b); Pandarus' speech at the close may be construed as an epilogue (Schneider 2011); not divided despite designation of act 1, scene 1. *Troilus* is not included in the F1 "catalogue" of plays [i.e., table of contents]. "It is generally agreed that the Folio editors must have run into a problem with copyright" (Jowett 2007e). "The Folio printers planned to bind [the play] after *Romeo and Juliet*, but inserted *Timon of Athens* there and moved *Troilus and Cressida* to an unpaginated place between the Histories and Tragedies, with an added Prologue filling the blank page before the title and Act I" (Shirley 2005). The various generic designations in the titles of Q and F1 suggest uncertainty on the part of actors, editors, and/or printers. Although today the play is often grouped with *All's Well* and *Measure for Measure* "as a 'dark' or 'problem' comedy, it differs markedly from these later plays in a number of ways" (Foakes 1987). F2 1632 "the second impression"; three issues. F3 1663 "the third impression"; reissued 1664 with seven additional plays. F4 1685 "the fourth edition"; two issues. "The traditional act division was introduced by [Nicholas] Rowe" (Wells & Taylor 1987).

The disparity of the two Q TPs may be owing to apprehension over the play's political implications: "The play was written shortly after the Essex crisis, and . . . its dangerous resemblance to recent events was not appreciated, or not fully appreciated, until it was ready for performance — at which point . . . it was deemed prudent not to proceed" (Honigmann 1989). Designed to capitalize on the poetomachia, the F1 version apparently represents a reworked version of the original (Ioppolo 1991); Shakespeare "jokingly included a few of Jonson's traits in the Ajax of *Troilus*" (Honan 1998).

The Troublesome Reign . . . of Edward the Second. See *Edward II*.

1 The Troublesome Reign of King John. ?George Peele (Vickers 2004, Forker 2011), a suggestion made originally by Sykes 1919. Both Sams 1995 and Everitt 1954 believe that the young Shakespeare wrote this play. Acted "not earlier than 1587 or later than 1591" (McMillin & MacLean 1998); "probably composed in 1589–90" (Forker). "Sundry times publikely acted . . . in the honourable Citie of London" by the Queen's Men, according to the Q1 TP, at undetermined venue, possibly an inn-yard (Lawrence 1927), though "when actors performed at inns they usually occupied a large room rather than a yard and performed by candlelight" (Orrell 1997).

SR none. Q1 1591 *The Troublesome Reign of John, King of England, with the Discovery of King Richard Cordelion's Base Son (Vulgarly Named the Bastard Falconbridge), also the Death of King John at Swinstead Abbey*; no author named; prints *Part 1* and *Part 2* as one book with continuous register; "What is possibly a stage-prologue, but which in the printed edition is addressed to 'the Gentle-men Readers,' serves as a paratext setting forth the outlines of the play" (Grif-fin 2001); not divided. The play features "spectacular elements — of King John's second coronation, of the battle scenes, and of royal parleys" (Oberer 2009). The most striking visual effect accompanies John's crowning: "*There the five moones appeare*," a sign to Pembroke that "The heavens frowne upon the sinfull earth." "Here we undoubtedly encounter some sort of mechanical illuminant" (Law-rence 1927). Q2 1611 *The First and Second Part of the Troublesome Reign of John, King of England*; "lately acted by the queens majesties players," but the Queen's Men were defunct in 1611; "written by W. Sh." — "the publisher intended to deceive unwary buyers looking for Shakespeare's *King John*" (Sider 1979). The printing of Q2 is "a possible sign that *King John* was revived" (Knutson 1999). Q3 1622 "written by W. Shakespeare." Q3 prints *Part 1* and *Part 2* as one book. The attribution to Shakespeare is not usually accepted today: "no one has been able to show conclusively that this play was composed by the author of [Shake-speare's] *King John*" (Mayer 2006). But *Troublesome Reign* "is, scene-for-scene, almost identical to *King John*, although stylistically the two plays are distinct" (Schoone-Jongen 2008).

The play may antedate Shakespeare's *King John* (Everitt 1965, Vickers 2004, Forker 2010); however, Honigmann 1954, 1998 argues that Shakespeare's *King John* precedes *Troublesome Reign*. Another possibility is that both plays derive from an earlier text (Braunmuller 1989). Whichever play came first, the two "parts" of *Troublesome Reign*, though bibliographically independent, constitute a single play rather than a two-play sequence, and they were published together. *Troublesome Reign* "was obviously intended to do battle with *Tamburlaine* on the bookstalls" (McMillin & MacLean); the two-part division was made "in an at-tempt to profit from the popularity of the two parts" of the earlier play (Erne 2003a). The address to the reader of *Part 1* evokes Marlowe's protagonist: "You that with friendly grace of smoothed brow / Have entertained the *Scythian Tam-burlaine*, / And given applause unto an infidel: / Vouchsafe to welcome (with like curtesie) / A warlike Christian and your countreyman."

2 The Troublesome Reign of King John. ?George Peele (Vickers 2004, Forker 2011). Acted 1591 (Sider 1979). "Sundry times publikely acted . . . in the honourable Citie of London" by the Queen's Men, according to the Q1 TP, at undetermined venue, possibly an inn-yard (Lawrence 1927), though "when actors performed at inns they usually occupied a large room rather than a yard and performed by candlelight" (Orrell 1997).

SR none. Q1 1591 *The Second Part of the Troublesome Reign of King John, Con-taining the Death of Arthur Plantagenet, the Landing of Lewis, and the Poisoning of King John at Swinstead Abbey*; no author named; prints *Part 1* and *Part 2* as one book with continuous register; address to "the Gentlemen Readers" reads like a prologue; not divided. Few SDs apart from entrances and exits. Staging includes elaborate pageantry: "*Drums and trumpets, enter* Lewes, Melun, Salisbury, Essex, Pembrooke, *and all the nobles from Fraunce and England.*" Q2 1611 *The First and Second Parts of the Troublesome Reign of John, King of England*; "written by W. Sh." Q3 1622 "written by W. Shakespeare." The attribution to Shakespeare is not generally credited today except for Sams 1995.

The address to the Q1–2 readers recapitulates the plot of *Part 1* and summarizes *Part 2*: "Arthur himselfe begins our latter act, / Our act of outrage, desperate furie, death; / Wherein fond rashness murdreth first a prince, / And monkish falsnes poysneth last a king." "Very roughly, the two parts of the play deal respectively with the claims of Arthur Plantagenet and of Lewis of France in right of his wife Blanche of Castile" (Axton 1977).

The True and Honorable History of the Life of Sir John Oldcastle. See *Sir John Oldcastle.*

True and Strange. See *The Four Prentices of London.*

A True Chronicle History Called War Hath Made All Friends. See *Edmond Ironside.*

The True Chronicle History of the Life and Death of King Lear. See *King Lear; King Leir.*

The True Chronicle History of the Whole Life and Death of Thomas Lord Cromwell. See *Thomas Lord Cromwell.*

The True Tragedy of Herod and Antipater. See *Herod and Antipater.*

The True Tragedy of Richard III. Anonymous. Possibly acted before 1588 (Knutson 2009b), perhaps at an inn-yard (Lawrence 1927), though "when actors performed at inns they usually occupied a large room rather than a yard and performed by candlelight" (Orrell 1997). Performed 1588–92 (Munro 2005). "Playd by" the Queen's Men, according to the TP, at undetermined venue: possibly performed at New Park or Knowsley, estates owned by the Stanley family, 1587–90 (Manley 2009). If the Chamberlain's Men performed Shakespeare's *Richard III* in 1594–95, the Queen's Men might then have been tempted to revive their *True Tragedy of Richard III* at the Swan in 1595" (Knutson 2001b). The play "has 48 speaking roles and . . . 68 roles in all" (McMillin & MacLean 1998). Probably antedates Shakespeare's *Richard III* (Lull 2009).

SR 19 June 1594 an enterlude intituled *The Tragedie of Richard the Third, wherein is showen the Death of Edward the Ffourthe, with the smotheringe of the twoo princes in the Tower, with a lamentable end of Shores wife, and the Conjunction of the twoo houses of Lancaster and Yorke.* Q 1594 *The True Tragedy of Richard the Third,*

Wherein Is Shown the Death of Edward the Fourth, with the Smothering of the Two Young Princes in the Tower, with a Lamentable End of Shore's Wife, an Example for All Wicked Women, and Lastly, the Conjunction and Joining of the Two Noble Houses, Lancaster and York; no author named; induction consisting of dialogue between Truth and Poetry (the ghost of George, Duke of Clarence, is present as the induction begins); at the end "the text offers speech prefixes for two undifferentiated messengers (both given as '*Mess.*'), and the Queen Mother and Princess Elizabeth" (Walsh 2009b); not divided. The climactic moment bears an uncanny resemblance to the similar scene in Shakespeare's *Richard III*: "*The battell enters, Richard wounded, with his Page*"; the king says, "A horse, a horse, a fresh horse." "It is possible that the anonymous playwright borrowed from Shakespeare rather than the other way around" (Lull 2009); Sams 1995 believes that Shakespeare was the author of *True Tragedy*. "Its style is lost to us today unless we picture the visual literalism of the dramaturgy. One scene is pure pantomime: '*Enters mother Queen and her daughter, and her son, to sanctuary*'" (McMillin & MacLean 1998).

   "As a response to the challenges posed by performing the past, the Queen's Men worked toward a conception of history wherein the past is a fictive construct to which audiences gain access through flamboyantly theatrical gestures rather than through carefully crafted similitude" (Walsh).

The True Tragedy of Richard Duke of York. See *3 Henry VI*.

The True Tragicomedy. ?Francis Osborne. Written *c.* 1654 (Randall 1995) and ?acted mid- to late 1650s. "Formerly acted at court & now revived by ane eie witnes," according to the MS. Epilogue seems intended for recitation in a theater: "Yet could our acting reach the writer's pegg / We'd claime applause—which now wee humbly begg." "Osborne's model is popular rather than closet drama"; and he "may have seen some of the curious miniature plays that were published in the 1640s" (Potter 1983).

   London, BL, Additional MS 25348, fols. 1–46; *The True Tragicomedy Formerly Acted at Court and Now Revived by an Eyewitness*; transcribed by Potter and John Pitcher; no author named on the TP; preceding the play are "lively pictures," i.e., lengthy accounts of the (historical) characters; prologue and epilogue (by Poetry); adequate SDs; five acts and separate scenes. The play is based on the annulment of the marriage of the Earl of Essex and Lady Frances Howard in 1613. First edited by Potter 1983.

   The play "is unique for turning back to the time of King James and offering a direct representation of actual persons at the Jacobean court. In particular, it treats events leading up to the Overbury scandal" (Randall). "There are prophecies about the future career of the Earl of Essex, the events of the Civil War, and the role of Cromwell" (Potter 1987b).

The True Trojans. See *Fuimus Troes*.

Tu Quoque. See *Greene's Tu Quoque*.

The Turk, a Tragedy. John Mason. Acted 1607–08 (Jowitt 2002–03). "Divers times acted by the Children of" the King's Revels, according to the Q1 TP, at the Whitefriars; the Children were "tenants of the Whitefriars theater in 1607 and 1608" (Cathcart 2005).

SR 10 March 1609 *The tragedy of the Turke with the death of Borgias*; transferred 22 June 1631. Q1 1610 *The Turk, a Worthy Tragedy*; RT *Muleasses the Turk*; Kirkman's 1661 catalogue calls it *Muleasses the Turk*; list of characters ("scænarum personae"); prologue and epilogue; five acts and separate scenes. There are "multitudes of marginal directions, many of them descriptive" (Jewkes 1958): "*Enter a frier, after him a funerall in white, and bearers in white, after them Borgias, then the two dukes, after them the senate, &c.*" Unusual staging includes: "*He* [Borgias] *strangles her* [his wife Timoclea] *with her owne haire*"; "*Enter Timoclea like a ghost.*" The ensuing speech gives a clue about the ghost's appearance: "Blush not thou chast and modest queene of night, / Nor hide thy silver crescent in a clowde, / To see me thus *Rhamnusia* like attir'd." Timoclea is later identified as "the ghost of the murdred Julia." Q2 1632 *An Excellent Tragedy of Muleasses the Turk*; "divers times acted (with generall applause)"; "full of interchangeable variety, beyond expectation"; (new) argument; omits prologue and epilogue.

The Q1 printer "leaves an apology for the reader (or, perhaps, author) together with the epilogue at the front of the play" (Stern 2009c): "This Epilogue should have bene printed at the end of the booke, but there was no spare place for it."

Twelfth Night, or What You Will. William Shakespeare. Performed by the Lord Chamberlain's Men, "presumably" (Nelson 2009a) at the Globe, "around 1600–1" (Schafer 2009). (The play's subtitle evokes the title of Marston's *What You Will*, played about the same time as Shakespeare's comedy; the two dramatists "wrote their plays simultaneously and in friendly emulation" [Duncan-Jones 2011].) John Manningham's diary entry of 2 February 1602, Candlemas feast, records a performance at the Middle Temple, one of the Inns of Court (Elam 2008); this is "the only play by Shakespeare known to have had such an audience" (Riggs 1989); staging took place in the Great Hall (George 1983). This "was probably a revival" (Thomson 1983), but "it seems certain . . . that *Twelfth Night* was written with a Temple performance in mind" (Gras 1989). Will Kemp's leaving the company and his replacement by Robert Armin resulted in the creation of a different kind of comic character (Thomson 1983). Armin was "less athletic than Kemp but more sharp-witted, ruminative, and self-conscious about his artifice" (Butler 2004a). In what amounts to a "concealed allusion" (Thomson 2000), the characterization of Malvolio may evoke Richard Tarlton, the inventive comic actor. "Feste's prominence in the play (appearing in all the acts) may owe something to its having been conceived for performance in the Middle Temple" (Grantley 2000). "If the play's title refers . . . to the occasion of its first performance, it was presumably staged on 6 January of the same year [1602], or possibly the year before" (Elam), by the Chamberlain's Men. The character of Orsino may have been intended as a compliment to Don Virginio Orsino, Duke of Bracciano, who was entertained by Queen Elizabeth at Whitehall, 6 January 1601 (Hotson 1954), but the name of the play staged by the Chamberlain's Men on that occasion is not recorded. Moreover, "the portrayal of a lovesick Orsino would be an affront both to the queen and to her noble visitor" (Donno 1985), and "all plays were tested in the public playhouse before a commissioned performance" (Clare 2005). "[P]robably revised by 1606" (Ioppolo 2006). "The play's imagined world is represented by the semiotic use of stage space. The Globe had a deep and wide thrust stage, with its two doors of entrance in the tiring-house wall upstage; the same configuration could easily be re-created in Middle Temple Hall or the halls of royal palaces" (Gay 2004). Revived by the King's Men at court before King James, Easter Monday night, 6 April 1618 (payment to John Heminges dated 20 April), probably in the Banqueting House (Wickham 1972); and at Whitehall under the title *Malvolio*, Candlemas, 2 February 1623 (diary of Henry Herbert). In a work published in 1640 Leonard Digges cites the play as a huge success: "loe in a trice / The Cockpit galleries, boxes, all are full / To heare Malvoglio that cross garter'd gull" (Chambers 1930). "Charles I, in annotating his Shakespeare Folio, wrote 'Malvolio' by the title of the play" (Schafer).

SR 8 November 1623; transferred ?4 August 1626 Paviers right in Shakesperes *plaies*; ?19 June 1627 widow of Isaac Jaggard . . . her parte in Shackspheere *playes*; 16 November 1630; 1 July 1637 Shakespeares *workes* their Part; 6 August 1674; 21 August 1683. F1 1623 *Comedies, Histories, & Tragedies*; three issues; "published according to the true originall copies"; Feste's song at the close has been construed as an epilogue but "there is little to suggest that this is a final framing text" (Schneider 2011); five acts and separate scenes. "*Twelfth Night* begins and ends with music: it is the only play in the Shakespearean canon to do so explicitly" (Gay). "Music is not a decorative addition to *Twelfth Night* but an essential part of the play's dramatic economy" (Elam). This play "is almost unique among Shakespeare's plays in having . . . a song [sung by Robert Armin] as its ending" (Gurr 2004c). "The songs in *Twelfth Night* . . . seem to have been taken from Viola and given to Feste" (Stern 2004a), "a professional singer, the most developed representation of such a figure in the whole canon" (Lindley 2006). Another auditory effect, "*Clocke strikes*," prompts Olivia "to realize how long and fruitlessly she has tried to win the disguised Viola's love" (Shirley 1961). When Olivia gives her portrait to Cesario, calling it a "jewel," she hands over a miniature painting (Elam 2010). "Olivia coyly unveils *herself* as a picture to be gazed upon by the disguised Viola" (Tassi 2005). Malvolio's costume, when he is gulled, is symbolically significant: his yellow hose and "crossed garters signify his new role [as lover], in contrast to the customary black of his steward's office. When he says he is 'not black in my mind, though yellow in my legs' he means that his yellow stockings show him to be a lover, but that he is not a melancholy (black-minded) one" (Gurr 2009d). "Yellow in hose or footwear had three meanings in drama: love, marriage, and jealousy after marriage" (Linthicum 1936). A trap may be used when Malvolio is confined (Astington 1988): "they have layde mee heere in hideous darknesse." But "[a] door including a grating could have been used. It is even possible that Feste reveals Malvolio *within* by opening the curtains" in a doorway onto the stage (Ichikawa 2005). Also, the SD "that Malvolio be '*within*' . . . suggests that the supposed madman is either offstage (with a stage door representing his prison) or within some discovery space at the rear of the stage or within some temporary boxlike structure carried on stage or thrust up through a trap door" (Dessen 1977). The play's title may refer to "contemporary social custom and religious practice, particularly to the feast's associations with madness and disorder" (Teague 1991). Malvolio, perhaps a representation of Ben Jonson, is the only character who refuses to join in the celebratory music at the close. F2 1632 "the second impression"; three issues. F3 1663 "the third impression"; reissued 1664 with seven additional plays. F4 1685 "the fourth edition"; two issues.

John Manningham's account likens *Twelfth Night* to earlier comedies: [it was] "much like the commedy of errores, or Menechmi in Plautus, but most like and neere to that in Italian called Inganni" (Sorlien 1976). "In likening *Twelfth Night* to the Italian play *Gl'Inganni*, Manningham may have been referring to the play of that title by Nicolò Secchi (1562) . . . or to an imitation of it by Curzio Gonzaga (1592)" (Donno 1985). "Manningham's knowledge of Italian drama seems to have been less solid than his study of Plautus at school. The play closest to *Twelfth Night* is the *Ingannati*, not any of the group known as the *Inganni*" (Gurr 1987b). Manningham also "records and registers admiration for the elaborate gulling of Malvolio, Olivia's steward" (Whitney 2006). What Manningham and the other lawyers "responded to in the play was not its portrayal of romantic love and erotic desire, but the baiting and gulling of the would-be social climber" (Clare 2005).

"While cross-dressing does allow the expression of female desire, it also threatens to eclipse it under the overbearing shadow of homoerotic attraction" (Findlay 1999). Shakespeare's play constructs "a homoerotic scenario between his two heroines" (Walen 2005); "a woman (Olivia) woos a woman (Viola), and a social superior (Olivia) woos a social inferior (Caesario), and a boy actor playing a woman woos a boy actor playing a woman playing a boy" (Danson 2000). "Viola's disguise as the page Caesario is underscored by the interpretations of her apparently male body by the other characters" (Lamb 2009). Orsino, moreover, "figures as the repressed homoerotic analogue to Antonio" (Traub 1992). "*Twelfth Night* includes the only overtly homosexual couple in Shakespeare [Antonio and Sebastian] except for Achilles and Patroclus" (Orgel 1989).

A Twelfth Night Merriment. ?Francis Clarke (Chambers 1923). Acted 5 January 1603 (Elliott et al. 2004) by "youths of the parish" at St. John's College, Oxford.

"A Christmas piece, an imitation of the Yule-tide mummeries acted by disguised villagers or townsfolk at the houses of such wealthier persons as would afford them hospitality" (Lee 1893). But the play "is evidently the work of a scholar humanist" (Boas 1914), and the student performers appear "in the guise of gauche town lads, who come into the Hall wassailing" (Mann 1991). The play, "very similar in general tone to the 'Pyramus and Thisbe' burlesque in *A Midsummer Night's Dream*" (Mann), was apparently written by the author of *The Seven Days of the Week*, contained in *The Christmas Prince* (Boas & Greg 1922).

Oxford, Bodleian, MS Rawlinson poet. 212, fols. 67–82; no author named; list of characters on the TP; "anno 1602"; prologue and epilogue both spoken by Porter; not divided. Some detailed SDs. *Narcissus* is the title proposed by Lee for her edition, the first printed version.

In the play "the Narcissus myth is mined for the comic potential of scenes of disorderly homoerotic and heteroerotic courtship"; the play "generates 'merriment' from incongruous and inept seductions, culminating in Narcissus's futile wooing of the 'delicate pretty youth' he spies in the water" (DiGangi 2011).

The Twice Changed Friar, A Comedy. John Newdigate III (Howard-Hill 1988). "Reasonably dated 1624–27" (*AED 3*). This and the other MS plays from Arbury Hall "were written by an author attuned to live performance" (Kidnie 2007). In the epilogue "the playwright expresses concern for the physical discomfort his audience might experience after sitting through a play. 'If your vneasie seats haue tyr'd you so,' he surmises, 'You're glad to leave 'em'" (Scott 2011).

Nuneaton, UK, Arbury Hall, MS A414, fols. 196–229; microfilm in Warwickshire County Record Office, M.I. 351/3, Item 20; no author named; list of characters; prologue and epilogue; evidence of revision; much of the MS is difficult to read because of ink bleeding through the pages; five acts.

The plot, based in part on a story in the *Decameron*, concerns Friar Albert's attraction to a married woman, Lisetta. He claims that Cupid has appeared to him in a vision and is resolved to visit her. She agrees and, ostensibly, Cupid disguises himself as the Friar for the assignation! When his perfidy is discovered, the Friar is forced to disguise himself in a bearskin to effect his escape from Lisetta's brothers.

The Twins, A Tragicomedy. W. [?William] Rider. Acted December 1630-August 1642 (*JCS*). "With general applause" at the Salisbury Court playhouse, according to the TP, by an unidentified company, perhaps the King's Revels (Saeger & Fassler 1995).

SR 20 June 1655 "by W. Rider"; transferred 16 July 1662 "by Wᵐ Rider." Q 1655 "written by W. Rider"; list of characters; five acts. SDs "are elaborately descriptive" (*JCS*): "*Enter a wood-nimph and sings to him, waving a silver rod, o'r his head, and departs: after that enters* Corbo, *in* Alphonso's *clothes, with* Alphonso's *sword, and* Carolo's *dagger naked by his side, trying several waies to wear his cloak and hat, conguing to the post as to a gentlewoman, kissing her, and offering to lead her in gentle manner."*

This play has been confused with *The Twins' Tragedy*, performed at court 1 January 1612 and entered in the SR 15 February 1612.

The Two Angry Women of Abingdon. Henry Porter. Probably "first performed in 1598" (Cathcart 2010); acted *c.* 1598–99 (Evett 1980); possibly staged *c.* 1590 (Gurr 1987a). "Lately playde by" Lord Admiral Nottingham's Men, according to the TP, at the Rose (Rhodes 1976). "From December 1598 to February 1599, Henry Porter was paid for what seems to be a second part of this play. The published text . . . offers no indication of whether it is the first or second part. Quite possibly it presents both parts together" (McMillin 1992). Henslowe records expenditures, 22 December 1598, 31 January 1599, and 12 February 1599.

SR none. Q1 1599 *The Pleasant History of the Two Angry Women of Abingdon, with the Humorous Mirth of Dick Coomes and Nicholas Proverbs, Two Servingmen*; unique copy at BL; "lately played"; prologue and epilogue ("which may have been added for the 1599 performance" [Nosworthy 1940]); not divided. The words "Humorous Mirth" in the title suggest the connection between Porter's play and recently fashionable comedies of humors. Q2 1599 list of characters.

The play, "distinctly a parodic jab at *Romeo and Juliet*" (Bly 2000), is "the first extant example of sustained realistic treatment of country life" (Wood 1987a). The play contains "a skit of the 'balcony scene' in *Romeo*" (Stern 2009b). "*The Merry Wives of Windsor* bears a number of tempting similarities to Porter's play other than the one implicit in its title" (Nosworthy).

Two Excellent Plays. See *The Platonic Lovers, The Wits*

The Two Gentlemen of Verona. William Shakespeare. Possibly written in Stratford before September 1588 in the expectation that it might be performed by the Queen's Men, with Richard Tarlton, on tour (Warren 2008). Acted 1590–91 (Wells & Taylor 1987) at undetermined venue. Possibly first performed by Lord Strange's Men. Will Kemp probably played the role of Launce when the Lord Chamberlain's Men performed the play (Wiles 1987, Ford 2010), "though Kemp is not otherwise known for a double act with a dog" (Butler 2004d). Praised by Francis Meres in *Palladis Tamia* (SR 7 September 1598): "for comedy, witness his *Gentlemen of Verona*." *Two Gentlemen* is probably "Shakespeare's earliest surviving play" (Warren); it is also "quite short and has the smallest cast of any Shakespearean play" (Ringler 1968).

SR 8 November 1623; transferred ?4 August 1626 Paviers right in Shakesperes *plaies*; ?19 June 1627 widow of Isaac Jaggard . . . her parte in Shackspheere *playes*; 16 November 1630; 1 July 1637 Shakespeares *workes* their Part; 6 August 1674; 21 August 1683. F1 1623 *Comedies, Histories, & Tragedies*; three issues; "published according to the true originall copies"; list of characters at end; five acts and separate scenes. Despite the "absence of all stage directions" (Schlueter 1990), staging requires the handling of a painting when Julia "exclaims as she holds up a portrait [Silvia's] onstage" (Tassi 2005). Although Proteus implies that it is a wall portrait, "[t]he passing of the picture from hand to hand . . . and the ease with which it is put aside and picked up . . . seems instead to suggest a small and manageable prop" (Elam 2010). Staging also calls for an extraordinary number of love letters: "as hand properties, they command attention: in full view of the audience, the characters give and receive, hide and destroy, write and read those letters" (Kiefer 1986). Staging calls for a dog named Crab to accompany Launce onstage; together they so engage the audience that they "have often tended to monopolise the stage" (Schlueter). F2 1632 "the second impression"; three issues. F3 1663 "the third impression"; reissued 1664 with seven additional plays. F4 1685 "the fourth edition"; two issues.

This comedy "is one of the earliest English plays to bring the motif" of the heroine in male disguise onstage (Shapiro 1994). Although *Clyomon and Clamydes* earlier adopted the device, "Shakespeare is among the first playwrights to introduce this romance motif into the theatre, and he is certainly the first to develop the idea to the sophisticated levels we see in *Two Gentlemen*" (Carroll 2004). The play also dramatizes a "tension between male-female love and male friendship" (Howard 1997). In the outlaws, "who establish a new society in the forest," Shakespeare represents "a recurring dream that men might be able to inhabit an all-male world" (Hammond 1996).

Two Italian Gentlemen. See *Fedele and Fortunio*.

Two Lamentable Tragedies. Traditionally ascribed to Robert Yarington (Chambers 1923), but his "signature at the end" of the play "marked his role as transcriber for the press, not his authorship" (Gurr 2009c); Henslowe's *Diary*, 27 November 1599, "identifies the writers who were paid for the play as [William] Haughton and [John] Day" (Gurr). Acted *c.* 1598 (Lake 1983) at undetermined venue.

SR none. Q 1601 *Two Lamentable Tragedies, the One of the Murder of Master Beech a Chandler in Thames Street, and His Boy, Done by Thomas Merry, the Other of a Young Child Murdered in a Wood by Two Ruffians, with the Consent of His Uncle*; HT *Two Tragedies in One*; induction in which personified characters, Homicide, Avarice, and Truth, have a choral function; the "induction ends with what is in effect a prologue by Truth" (Greg 1939); the play closes with a colloquy of Truth, Homicide, and Covetousness; not divided. "Long, descriptive" SDs (Jewkes 1958): "*When the boy goeth into the shoppe* Merrie *striketh six blowes on his head & with the seventh leaves the hammer sticking in his head, the boy groaning must be heard by a maide who must crye to her maister.*" Grotesque staging calls for the butchering of a corpse and the subsequent discovery of the remains: "One of two watermen" in the play "trips over a bag lying on the floor. A stage direction states:

'Taking the sack by the end, one of the legs and head drops out'" (Butterworth 2005). Two characters are hanged onstage.

As the title stipulates, the play features two distinct plots. "A plausible pretext for their dramatic juxtaposition is given in the induction, in which Homicide and Avarice conspire and Truth takes upon herself the duties of expositor, appearing afterwards as Chorus" (Lawrence 1927). The plots "are structurally counterpointed with episodes of each alternating with the other, the only thematic link being that the tragedies are bourgeois and domestic, and the murders are committed by people who were known to and trusted by the victims, thus heightening their poignancy and horror" (Grantley 2008a). The topical events that are dramatized powerfully move the playgoers: "A series of addresses to the audience by Truth through the play insist that they will weep, that they are weeping, and that they have wept" (Steggle 2007).

The Two Maids of Moreclack. Robert Armin. First acted 1597–99 (Foakes 1985), in a shortened version by an unidentified company "in the Citty [of London]," "perhaps in an inn" (Bly 2000). Later "played by the Children of" the King's Revels, according to the TP, at the Whitefriars, *c.* 1607–July 1608 (Chambers 1923); the Children were "tenants of the Whitefriars theater in 1607 and 1608" (Cathcart 2005). But Armin's "epistle in the quarto suggests that he had not written *Two Maids* for them" (MacIntyre 1996). Liddie 1979 suggests that Armin began writing the play *c.* 1598–99 and continued revising it for years afterward. Johnson 2003 suggests that Armin wrote the play before 1603 and substantially revised it after 1606. The original play was "perhaps [written] for Chandos's Men" (Thomson 2004a). "Armin acted with the boys at the private Whitefriars' theatre, in a cut version of the text" (Wiles 1987). "Almost certainly, the difference in length [between the two versions] results from dialogue added to the language of Armin's two bawdy virgins, not to the portions featuring a 'natural' clown, played by Armin himself" (Bly). Armin "specialized in Celtic cameos like the Welsh Knight" in this play (Wilson 2010).

SR none. Q 1609 *The History of the Two Maids of Moreclack, with the Life and Simple Manner of John in the Hospital*; epilogue (by Earl); not divided. SDs are "long and descriptive, and quite frequent" (Jewkes 1958): "*Enter a maide strowing flowers, and a serving man perfuming the doore.*" Considerable panoply: "*Enter the solemne shewe of the marriage*"; "*Enter the solemne order of the bride-groomes returne from church.*" A trap is used for the scene in which two sailors bring a trunk onstage, and others bear pickaxe and spades: "Dig ho"; others come along and "*They lift it out*"; when the trunk is opened, "she [Mary] sits up." The Q TP features a woodcut of Robert Armin, chief player of fools and clowns for Shakespeare's company from 1599, in the role of Blue John, "the contemporary adult idiot-protégé of Christ's Hospital" (Hotson 1952): Armin as John "is marked out as a fool by the objects which hang from his belt: a handkerchief to mop his dribble, and a pen and inkhorn which signify that this adult has yet to complete his schooling"

(Wiles 1987). Armin also played the role of Tutch, a witty fool (Johnson 2003), who "sheds his tattered livery-coat for disguises, first as a Welsh knight, and second as Blue John. In his final scene, Armin/Tutch the artificial fool thus becomes John/Armin the natural fool" (Wiles). *The Two Maids* is "built around contrasting clown roles that Armin wrote for himself to double" (Butler 2004a). The word "More" puns on fool in this play; "according to the *OED*, More-clacke, or Mortlake, a town in Surrey, is also 'Fool-chatter' or 'Fool-clatter,' since 'clacke' could mean 'Din of speech, noise or clatter of human tongues; contemptuously, loquacious talk, chatter sensless or continuous.' More-clacke is a fitting pun for a play with both an artificial and a natural fool, a play written, moreover, by Shakespeare's company's punning author-fool, Armin, who specialized in writing fool literature such as *Fool Upon Fool* (1600)" (Hornback 2001). Q "was printed for a revival in which [Armin] could not perform" (Preiss 2006).

Armin's address to the reader reports: "I have boldly put into your hands, a historical discourse, acted by the boyes of the Revels, which perchaunce in part was sometime acted more naturally in the Citty, if not in the [w]hole." What Armin does not say is that the play "echoes phrases strewn about the Shakespeare canon, and a whole plot is devoted to parodying *Hamlet*" (Preiss).

The Two Merry Milkmaids, or The Best Words Wear the Garland. J. C. [?John Cumber or ?John Cooke or ?John Cart (Lawrence 1927)]. Acted September-December 1619 (Metz 1979). By the Company of the Revels, according to the Q1 TP, at the Red Bull (Cox 2000). "[D]uring the time the play was first performed, the Company of the Revels and its predecessor, Queen Anne's Servants, were using both the Red Bull and Phoenix theaters—perhaps explaining why the generally informative title page gives no venue"; the play was perhaps originally intended for the indoor venue (Thomson 1996). Performed also at court, "before the king, with generall approbation," according to the Q1 TP, probably 2 January 1620 (entry in Chamber Accounts). A passage in Edmund Gayton's *Pleasant Notes upon Don Quixot[e]* (1654) may refer to this play; if so, the play must have remained popular in the 1630s and 1640s (Thomson). Anthony à Wood records that he saw the play at Oxford, 5 July 1661.

SR 22 May 1620; transferred 13 September 1623; 29 June 1674. Q1 1620 *A Pleasant Comedy Called The Two Merry Milkmaids*; two issues; author's initials on the TP; list of characters; prologue, probably "added to the play for performance at the Red Bull because, as it implies, *Milkmaids* was not the usual fare for that theater" (Thomson); five acts and separate scenes. The play's title "is not particularly well chosen. It merely refers to a disguise taken by Dorigene and Julia, the two heroines" (Shaw 1979). The Folger owns a quarto that "seems to have been marked for use as a promptbook some time after it was first published" (Gurr 2009c); in July 1992 "Leslie Thomson and William Long came across the catalogue entry" for this book (Dessen 1996), marked up by two hands. "Quite probably, and surprisingly from a modern point of view, the markings on the pages of this quarto would have been sufficient for performance" (Thomson). A Folger copy "makes clear that whoever prepared the play for the stage realized that the long printed text needed to undergo substantial abridgement" (Erne 2003a). The play contains "[p]erhaps the most complex treatment of devils in a self-consciously theatrical context" (Cox). Q2 1661. After the closing of the theaters, act 5 was adapted for a droll entitled *Invisible Smirk, or The Pen Combatants*, performed in the 1640s and 50s and later published in *1 The Wits, or Sport upon Sport* (O 1662 [two issues] and 1672).

The Q1 printer's address relates that "the play would not have been published at all 'had not false Copies trauail'd abroad (even to surbating [i.e., excess]).' Because no manuscripts of the play have survived, we can only speculate as to their source and nature. My guess is that . . . the copies were made by the author for his friends" (Howard-Hill 1999).

The Q1 prologue, like many another, seeks to adjust the expectations of playgoers by explaining what the play is *not*: "This day we entreat all that are hither come, / To expect no noyse of guns, trumpets, nor drum, / Nor sword and targuet; but to heare sence and words, / Fitting the matter that the scene affords. / So that the stage being reform'd, and free / From the lowd clamors it was wont to bee, / Turmoyl'd with battailes; you I hope will cease / Your dayly tumults, and with us wish peace." Such prologues "frequently attempted to manipulate audience expectations of the generic and theatrical content of the afternoon" (Milling 2004). The Company of the Revels (from remnants of the Queen's Men) had recently moved to the Red Bull, a theater that had a reputation for attracting rowdy crowds; this prologue announces the intention "to raise the standard of plays, acting and the taste of audiences there" (Wickham et al. 2000). The printer's address to the reader notes a connection between the playwright, on the one hand, and the theater, actor, and playgoer on the other: "Every writer must governe his penne according to the capacitie of the stage he writes too, both in the actor and the auditor."

Two New Plays. See *The Fool Would Be a Favorite, Osmond the Great Turk.*

Two New Plays. See *A Cure for a Cuckold, The Thracian Wonder.*

The Two Noble Kinsmen. William Shakespeare and John Fletcher (Mincoff 1952, Hoy 1962), with ?Nathan Field (Potter 1997). Vickers 2008a assigns 1,477 lines to Fletcher. Acted winter 1613–14 (Potter). "Presented . . . with great applause" by the King's Men at the [second] Blackfriars, according to the Q TP. *Kinsmen* "must have been one of the few King's Men plays to be written specifically for Blackfriars" (Potter). The Morris dance in 3.5 originated in Beaumont's *Masque of the Inner Temple and Gray's Inn*, performed 20 February 1613 and printed in an undated quarto *c.* 1613. The King's Men may have acquired costumes that had been used in this masque (Potter). *Kinsmen* may have been the first play staged at the Globe after its catastrophic fire and reconstruction (Wells & Taylor 1987). "Perhaps some of the discontinuities in the play are the result of revisions necessitated by the company's reduced circumstances. The scene in which the combatants are described by Pirithous and an anonymous messenger . . . might have replaced a more elaborate pageant-like entry, like those of the knights in *Pericles*, whose shields are described by Thaisa" (Potter 1992). Possibly performed at court *c.* 1619 (Chambers 1930) and again "soon after November, 1625" (Proudfoot 1970). Q preserves the names of two actors: T. Tucke, who was "probably Thomas Tuckfeild," and Curtis, who was "probably Curtis Greville" (King 1992a).

SR 8 April 1634 a TragiComedy called *the two noble kinsmen*, by John Ffletcher and William Shakespeare; transferred 31 October 1646; Kirkman's catalogue names only Fletcher. Q 1634 the TP names Shakespeare and Fletcher; prologue, "probably by Fletcher" (Cooper 2010), possibly for a revival (Masten 1997), and epilogue; five acts and separate scenes; "[n]o other first quarto edition of a Shakespeare play is divided into acts and scenes" (Proudfoot et al. 2005). *Kinsmen* was "the first play published with the names of Shakespeare and another author on the title page, that is, advertising the collaboration" (Gossett 2009b). Staging combines visual splendor with small moments like Emilia's quandary about the attentions of Palamon and Arcite; Emilia handles miniature paintings (Potter 1997) of the men: "*Enter Emilia alone, with 2 pictures.*" "This is the only original stage direction in Shakespeare (unless it is John Fletcher's) specifying the introduction of a picture or pictures on stage" (Elam 2010). Sound effects include: "*Cornets in sundry places. Noise and hallowing as people a Maying*"; "*Cornets. A great cry and noice within.*" Rustic entertainment takes the form of a morris dance by villagers and the Jailer's Daughter. The SDs are unusually detailed for a Shakespearean play, especially descriptions of the opening procession with Hymen, as well as the scene wherein characters propitiate the gods; in performance the processions "possibly assumed the character of dumb shows" (Mehl 1965). Staging calls for one or more property altars. Special effects include "*clanging of armor, with a short thunder*" as Arcite propitiates Mars; "*musicke is heard, doves are seene to flutter*" as Palamon propitiates Venus; "*a silver hynde, in which is conveyed incense and sweet odours, which being set upon the altar . . . she sets fire to it,*" as Emilia propitiates Diana; this object "*vanishes under the altar*" and "*in the place ascends a rose tree, having one rose upon it*"; then "*is heard a sodaine twang of instruments, and the rose fals from the tree.*" In this adaptation of Chaucer's *Knight's Tale*, the playwrights imagine a "momentary all-male world of mutual love" between Palamon and Arcite, until they are separated by a woman (Hammond 1996). "The scenario of two male friends set at odds by a woman clearly fascinated Shakespeare" (Smith 1991b).

The play "may have been left out of the First Folio simply because Fletcher, who was still alive in 1623, did not consider . . . [the] play a finished product" (Potter 1997) or because authorship was collaborative (Wells & Taylor). "Perhaps the 1634 quarto was intended as a supplementary volume to be sold in association with the Shakespeare Second Folio," published in 1632 (Proudfoot et al.). B&F F2 1679 *Fifty Comedies and Tragedies*; "published by the authors original copies, the songs to each play being added"; no "reference to Shakespeare as part-author" (Proudfoot 1970); list of characters. The play did not appear "in any edition of Shakespeare until [Charles] Knight included it in the 'Doubtful Plays' volume of his *Pictorial Shakespeare* in 1841; [Alexander] Dyce admitted it into the Shakespeare canon in his second edition in 1866" (Rasmussen 2008).

The Two Noble Ladies and The Converted Conjurer. Anonymous. "Often tymes acted with approbation" by the Company of the Revels at the Red Bull, according to the MS, "a print-ready attribution" (Straznicky 2006b). "We can date the play to 1620 because the Queen Anne's Men at the Red Bull became known as the Revels Company after Anne died in 1619" (Gurr 2004b). Marginal notation in the MS records the names of [Thomas] Bond, who played a Triton; Anthony Brew[er], a Lord of Babylon and a Soldier; [H.] Gibs[on], a Soldier, a Nobleman; G[eorge] Stutfield, a Spirit and a Triton; Tay[lor], a Nobleman and Soldier. These actors "may or may not have taken part in the Red Bull performance" (Greg 1931). No license for acting exists.

London, BL, Egerton MS 1994, fols. 224–44; the verso of the TP calls the play *The two noble Ladies: A Trage-comicall Historie*; no author named; theatrical provenance (Long 1989); evidence of revision; "two leaves are missing from the end section, along with the first half of one containing a section from Act I" (Gurr 2004b); list of characters with short descriptions; carefully described dumb show; "an original division throughout into acts and scenes, duly numbered" (Greg 1931). "The manuscript is remarkable for the elaboration of the stage-directions supplied by the author in the right-hand margin" (Greg). MS is "a theatrically annotated manuscript with signals for music and other sounds, including thunder linked to supernatural events" (Thomson 1999). Unusual staging: two soldiers are drowned in a river when, after they would drown Justina in the Euphrates, they are seized by Tritons, who "*dragge them in.*" "The bookkeeper's accompanying stage directions show how the players managed to drown themselves"; "If the play had gone to the press it is unlikely that the book-keeper's informative notes would have been printed" (Gurr 2009d). At another point characters "bite" one another. Spectacle includes the appearance of "*a spirit, like a souldier in armour, on his breast a sable shield written on with [golden] letters*"; also "*an angell shaped like a patriarch, upon his breast a blew table full of silver letters, in his right hand a red croissier staffe, on his shoulders large wings*"; "*The devills sinck roaring* [presumably through a trap]: *a flame of fier riseth after them.*" A character's words, "A mist is rising," designate a special effect, probably achieved by smoke. In one scene Cantharides, "a familiar," is invisible except to Barebones. First edited by Bullen, *A Collection of Old English Plays*, vol. 4 (1885). Modern edition by Rhoads 1930.

"*The Two Noble Ladies* is nearly unique among early modern play texts in that it seems to call for a copy of the scriptures to be brought on stage. The Bible appears in only three other surviving play scripts; the vast majority of religious book properties mentioned are ordinary prayer books used as tokens of personal devotion" (Williamson 2009).

Two Tragedies. See *Cleopatra, Julia Agrippina* by Thomas May.

Two Tragedies in One. See *Two Lamentable Tragedies.*

Two Wise Men and All the Rest Fools, A Comical Moral. Anonymous; Kirkman's 1661 catalogue attributes the play to Chapman, but the ascription is not accepted today. "Diverse times acted," according to the Q TP, 1613–19 (*JCS*), at undetermined venue. Probably a university play.

SR none. "Since there is no entry of the piece in the SR and no imprint on the title-page of the first edition, Dr. Greg suggests . . . that it may have been privately printed. It may also have been privately acted" (*JCS*). Q ND ?1619 *Two Wise Men and All the Rest Fools: A Comical Moral, Censuring the Follies of This Age*; no author named; list of characters; prologue and epilogue (by Probertio); "very oddly divided" (Greg 1939) into seven acts and separate scenes. Ample SDs: "*She openeth her Bible, and makes shew to reade, and many times turnes her eyes with the white upward.*"

The prologue makes a case for the utility of drama: "It hath beene a very auncient and laudable custome, in the best governed common-wealthes, to admit and favourably to allow interludes and discourses upon the stage for divers reasons; but especially two. The one, to entertaine the wel-conditioned people with some delightfull and fruitfull conceits, thereby as it were to deceive idleness of that time which it had allotted for worse purposes. The other, for the just reprehension of such as with serious and more grave advisings cannot or will not be so freely admonished and corrected."

U

The Unfortunate Lovers, A Tragedy. William Davenant. Licensed for acting 16 April 1638 (Adams 1917, Edmond 1987). "Lately acted with great applause" by the King's Men at the [second] Blackfriars, according to the Q TP. Performed also at that playhouse before Queen Henrietta Maria, 23 April 1638, probably at night (*JCS*); at the Whitehall Cockpit 31 May 1638 (bill of the King's Men for performances at court); and at Hampton Court 30 September 1638. "Few dramatists enjoyed greater favour at the court of Charles I" (Sharpe 1987). In playlist of the King's Men 7 August 1641.

SR no original; 7 March 1646; 19 August 1667. Q two issues 1643 and 1649; list of characters; prologue and epilogue; five acts. F 1673 *The Works*; "now published out of the authors originall copies." The play may be identical with *The Tragedy of Heildebrand*, a title recorded by Malone in 1821 (Jackson 1973); the name of the King in *The Unfortunate Lovers* is Heildebrand.

The Q prologue at Blackfriars mockingly describes theatrical conditions that had prevailed at public playhouses: playgoers "to th'theatre would come, / Ere they had din'd, to take up the best roome; / There sit on benches, not adorn'd with mats, / And graciously did vaile their high-crown'd hats / To every halfe dress'd player, as he still / Through th'hangings peep'd to see how th'house did fill. / Good easie judging soules, with what delight / They would expect a jigge or target fight, / A furious tale of Troy, which they ne're thought / Was weekly written, so 'twere strongly fought. / Laught at a clinch, the shadow of a jest, / And cry *A passing good one I protest*. / Such dull and humble-witted people were / Even your fore-fathers, whom wee govern'd here; / And such had you been too hee sweares, had not / The poets taught you how t'unweave a plot, / And tract the winding scenes, taught you to admit / What was true sense, not what did sound like wit." Here Davenant, "casting a nostalgic though patronizing look back at Jacobean and Elizabethan audiences," sees the stage as "itself instrumental in developing educated judgement" (Grantley 2000).

The Unfortunate Mother, A Tragedy. Thomas Nabbes. Written ?1639 (*JCS*). Intended for performance by an unidentified company, possibly Beeston's Boys, at the Phoenix, but rejected by the players: "never acted; but set downe according to the intention of the author," according to the Q TP. Prefatory poem by R. W. asks of the play: "Well writ; well plotted: why not acted then?"

SR 4 November 1639. Q 1640 list of characters; five acts [indication of scene divisions in the margins, but these seem unrelated to a cleared stage]. Nabbes describes the locale of each act: "The scene being the Dutchesse chamber"; "The scene being the gallery"; "The scene the grove." "Perhaps Nabbes was the first playwright consciously to write with scenery in view" (Nicoll 1937). Also issued in *Plays, Masques, Epigrams, Elegies, and Epithalamiums*, a made-up book containing plays published between 1637 and 1640; general TP dated 1639, separate TP 1640.

In the "Proeme to the Reader" Nabbes describes the play's contents: "Ile tell thee what shalt not, and what shalt find. / Here are no bumbast raptures swelling high, / To plucke Jove and the rest downe from the sky. / Here is no sence that must by thee be scann'd, / Before thou canst the meaning understand. / Here is not any glorious scene of state; / Nor Christning set out with the lottery plate. / There's no disguise in't; no false beard, that can / Discover severall persons in one man. / No politician tells his plots unto / Those in the pit, and what he meanes to doe. / But now me thinkes I heare some criticke say, / *All these left out there's nothing in the play.* / Yes: Thou shalt find plaine words, and language cleane; / That *Cockram* needs not tell thee what they meane. / Shalt fine strict method in't, and every part / Severely order'd by the rules of art. / A constant scene: the businesse it intends / The two houres time of action comprehends. / Read it with observation then, and be / My judge from reason; not from tyranny." "Though his drift is Jonsonian, Nabbes's comments contrast sharply even with the Prologue to *Epicoene*, which promises different fare for each type of playgoer. The earlier theatre more directly accommodated separate constituencies" (Whitney 2006).

The Unhappy Fair Irene. Gilbert Swinhoe. ?Acted 1650s at undetermined venue. A prefatory poem by F. S. suggests that the author is a young man (perhaps a student) from Northumbria and that the play was staged: "So young! And yet so good a tragedy, / If I'de not seen't, I'de sworn 'tad been a lye: / But since I see't, sir, give me leave to tell / Northumberland can boast a miracle / Of wit and worth."

SR none. Q 1658 *The Tragedy of the Unhappy Fair Irene*; two issues; prologue; not divided despite the designation "Actus primi, scena prima" and a few early numbered scenes. Ample SDs: *"Enter Mahomet the Turk with drum and colours, as into Hadrianople: then enter Citizens, as to meet the Emperour."* The play "is the first extant English drama to treat of Mahomet the Great's violently passionate, fatal love for Irene, a Greek woman of incomparable beauty" (Pritchard 2004a).

The play's closing couplet, "separated from the text by a space as if to form a sort of epilogue" (Greg 1939), evokes Shakespearean tragedy: "This is a spectacle of like woe / To that of Juliet, and her Romeo."

The Unnatural Combat, A Tragedy. Philip Massinger. "There is a strong case for a late 1624 or early 1625 date for the play"; "Massinger's picture of a depraved 'unnatural' Admiral and his daughter was clearly targeted at England's Lord Admiral and the choice of Henrietta Maria for Queen" (Jowitt 2006a). The "representation of political corruption and the influence of sensual counsel resonates with English political debates of the mid 1620s" (Jowitt 2005). "Presented by" the King's Men at the [second] Globe, according to the TP; this is one of "[o]nly seven non-Shakespearean plays . . . advertised on title pages as exclusively Globe productions" (Straznicky 2006b). William Rowley probably played the role of Belgarde (Nicol 2008b).

SR 14 February 1639. Q 1639 list of characters; five acts and separate scenes. The SDs "are frequently long and 'literary,' describing gestures, appearance, actions, and dress" (E&G 1976). Staging includes a shocking entry: *"Enter the Ghost of young* Malefort, *naked from the wast, full of wounds, leading in the shadow of a ladie, her face leprous."* Witnessing the spectacle Malefort Senior asks, "Are your aeriall forms depriv'd of language?" In response *"The Ghosts use severall gestures."* When the ghosts exit, *"He's [Malefort] kill'd with a flash of lightning."* Unusual staging includes Montrevile on the upper stage, partially concealed so that he may eavesdrop: "Montrevile *above the curtaine, suddenly drawn*." A SD indicates the conventional appearance of a ravished woman: Theocrine, the protagonist's daughter, is thrust forth, "*her garments loose, her hair disheveled*."

Massinger's dedication comments on the unusual absence of a prologue and epilogue: "I present you with this old tragedie, without prologue, or epilogue, it being composed in a time (and that too, peradventure, as knowing as this) when such by ornaments, were not advanced above the fabricque of the whole worke." In other words the prologue and epilogue "have now disappeared" (Stern 2004b).

Untitled pastoral play. Anonymous. No information about production, but the SDs suggest preparation for performance.

London, BL, Additional MS 29496; no TP; no author named; list of characters; prologue; "written in a seventeenth-century hand" (*JCS*); five acts and separate scenes.

The SDs "are of a literary type, and they assume the use of scenery" (*JCS*): "*The scene draws, & the prospect of a temple is discover'd': upon a large pedestal, one representing the statue of Mars, whom, as Ortelius & other historians and geographers report, the T[h]racians worshipt. Several of the priests all bloody & busy at the altar, as having newly ended their sacrifice.*"

"According to a manuscript note in the *Catalogue of the Additions to the Manuscripts in the British Museum* (24027–29909), the play seems to have been adapted from Jonathan Sidnam's 1655 translation of the *Filli di Sciro* of Bonarelli" (*JCS*).

Untitled play. ?John Tatham; prologues from his other plays "suggest that Tatham was attached to a troupe of Red Bull players" (*JCS*). Written "certainly after 23 December 1641 and probably within the following twelvemonth" (Murphy 1971).

Chelmsford, UK, Essex Record Office, MS D/DW Z5; no TP; no author named; list of characters; the beginning of play is missing; seven consecutive scenes; not divided into acts. Adequate SDs: "*Enter to him Clowter staring about*"; "*ffetherfue runnes to her and holds her hands.*" First edited by Murphy 1971.

The Untrussing of the Humorous Poet. See *Satiromastix*. *Satiromastix* "would appear to be the literary title and 'The Untrussing of the Humorous Poet' the theatrical" (Bowers 1953).

V

Valentinian. John Fletcher; "ascription to Fletcher alone is based on stylistic grounds" (Finkelpearl 1990). Acted 1610–11 (Knutson 1991) by the King's Men at the first Globe/second Blackfriars; acted between 1610 and 1614, probably 1613 (Finkelpearl). Principal actors were Richard Burbage, Henry Condell, John Lowin, William Ostler, and John Underwood, according to F2. In playlist of King's Men 7 August 1641 as "The Emperour Valentinian."

SR 4 September 1646 *The Emperor Valentinian*; 30 January 1673. B&F F1 1647 *Comedies and Tragedies*; "never printed before, and now published by the authours originall copies"; *The Tragedy of Valentinian*; the epilogue is, "in a collection of poems by Beaumont [1653], more convincingly ascribed to *The Fair Maid of the Inn*" (Stern 2009c); five acts and separate scenes. Descriptive SDs: "*Enter Phidias with his dagger in him, and Aretius poysond*"; "*Enter Emperor sicke in a chaire.*" "This deliberate exhibition of the tyrant's mortal punishment demystifies the sacredness of royal power, and may have been especially significant to the original audiences after 1610. In that year Henry IV of France was assassinated, an event which caused alarm to the timorous King James" (Clark 2007). B&F F2 1679 *Fifty Comedies and Tragedies*; "published by the authors original copies, the songs to each play being added"; list of characters; actors' names. "Seventeenth-century musical settings survive for three of the songs" (Wiggins 1998). The title is given as *Valentinian or Rape's Revenge* in the undated notebook of Abraham Hill (*JCS*).

In *Valentinian* Fletcher "presents a Rome whose instabilities can all too easily be equated with those of Jacobean England"; the central problem of the play "is the level of loyalty owed by virtuous courtiers to a corrupt king and court" (McMullan 1994). The issue finds dramatic shape when the emperor rapes Lucina. Before this point she "respects the concept of imperial authority"; afterward "her initial determination to force him to a recognition of its meaning is worn down by his cold assertion of absolutist principle" (Clark 1994).

The Valiant Cid. See *The Cid.*

The Valiant Scot. J. W. Probably acted *c.* 1626 (Byers 1980) at undetermined venue. Also performed by the Red Bull/King's Company (Bentley 1981) at the second Fortune, 1639. A Puritan observer, writing in *Vox Borealis, or The Northern Discovery* (1641), notes that the revival of the play in 1639 "played five dayes with great applause, which vext the bishops" (*JCS*). This new staging followed "Charles's unsuccessful attempt to force a new prayer book upon the Scots" (Tricomi 1989).

SR 26 April 1637 a Tragedy called *the Valiant Scott*. Q 1637 the author's initials on the TP; five acts. The play dramatizes the most appalling violence: Wallace, the Scotsman, directs that one captive English ambassador be decapitated, another suffer the cutting out of his tongue, and still another be blinded. Although these atrocities happen offstage, we witness the result: e.g., "*Sebastian's head is carried in a wallet*," while the blind Glascot is led onto stage along with the mutilated Mountford. Later the English and Scottish armies meet in battle. The victorious English king orders that Wallace be put to death: "hang, draw, and quarter him." "The play is an old-fashioned chronicle history in the late form of Ford's *Perkin Warbeck* and Glapthorne's *Albertus Wallenstein*" (Davidson 1978). "Scotland is here portrayed as a romantic, turbulent country where old ideals of chivalry and personal valour linger on as they do not in England" (Barton 1977).

In his edition Byers discounts the theory that the initials J. W. stand for John Webster.

The Valiant Welshman, or The True Chronicle History of the Life and Valiant Deeds of Caradoc the Great, King of Cambria, now called Wales. R. A. The playwright may be Robert Alleyne (Marshall 2000), or Robert Anton (Lloyd 1952), or possibly Robert Armin (Johnson 2003, Butler 2005), but "everything about this [Q1] title-page, except the initials, points away from Robert Armin" (Lake 1977). "Sundry times acted" by the Prince's Men, according to the Q1 TP, 1610–15 (Chambers 1923), at undetermined venue. Depending upon the date of first performance, the company could be either Prince Henry's Men or Prince Charles's Men. Prince Charles "became Prince of Wales in 1616, the year after *The Valiant Welshman* was published (Prince Henry, who died in 1612, had been created Prince of Wales in 1610)" (Foakes 1985). The Q1 TP "more likely refers to a performance by Prince Henry's Men" than Prince Charles's Men (Nicol 2006a).

SR 21 February 1615. Q1 1615 the author's initials on the TP; list of characters; two entries by Bardh who serves as chorus/presenter, in one instance to describe a dumb show; "[p]antomimic elements throughout the play" (Mehl 1965); epilogue by Bardh; five acts and separate scenes. SDs "are fairly elaborate" (Jewkes 1958). Staging involves a descent perhaps by machinery: "*Fortune descends downe from heaven to the stage.*" Special effects include the entry of a witch from her cave, perhaps through a trap; also a trap door when "*Shee* [the fairy queen] *fals downe under the stage, and he* [Sir Thomas] *follows her, and fals into the ditch.*" A bard "*riseth from his tombe*," perhaps through the trap. Unusual staging includes "*enter the serpent*," created by the witch and described as a "*hellish fiend*"; then "*the serpent flies into the temple.*" More conventional staging includes "*thunder and lightning.*" "[A] witch is flung into the flames of a burning castle" (Lawrence 1927). Opposite the Q1 TP is the woodcut of a knight, facing left, on horseback; it "seems to have no connection with the play, and to be merely ornamental" (Foakes 1985). Q2 1663. A woodcut opposite the Q2 TP depicts a knight on horseback, facing right, holding his lance in the left hand, the reins of his horse in the right.

The author's address to the Q1 reader justifies the choice of subject: "As it hath been a custome of long continuance, as well in Rome the capitall city, as in divers other renowned cities of the world, to have the lives of princes and worthy men, acted in their theatres, and especially the conquests & victories which their owne princes and captains had obtained, thereby to incourage their youths to follow the steps of their ancestors; which custome even for the same purpose, is tolerated in our age, although some peevish people seeme to dislike of it: amongst so many valiant princes of our English nation, whose lives have already even cloyed the stage, I searched the chronicles of elder ages, wherein I found amongst divers renowned persons, one Brittish prince, who of his enemies, received the title of *Valiant Brittaine*, his name was *Caradoc.*" "The play tracks the successful military exploits that eventually lead Caradoc to his position as King of Wales, a kingdom he will ultimately defend against Roman invasion" (Cull 2010). "[L]ike King James ending the Elizabethan wars against continental Catholicism, Caradoc agrees to live in peace with Rome without losing his freedom" (Kerrigan 2008).

The Variety, A Comedy. In his 1661 catalogue Kirkman identifies the author as William Cavendish. Licensed for acting 1641 (Bawcutt 1996). "Lately presented by" the King's Men at the [second] Blackfriars, according to the D TP, "between 1639 and 1642" (Ravelhofer 2006). Revels documents indicate that James Shirley made "several reformations" of the play.

Nottingham, UK, University of Nottingham, Hallward Library, MS PwV 25, fols. 70a, 71a, 76a, contains three songs from the play, ed. Hulse 1996; they "were set to music by the theatre composer John Wilson (1595–1674) and published in his *Cheerful Airs or Ballads*" (Hulse). SR 4 September 1646 *Varieties*, by my Lord of Newcastle. D 1649 printed in The Hague and published in London with *The Country Captain* and entitled *Two Comedies* (separate pagination for each); no author named on the separate TP, but the general TP says, "written by a person of honor"; dramatis personae; five acts. Staging involves the descent of a throne, presumably by machinery: "*Musick, throne descends.*" Following the closing of the theaters, two scenes were made into a droll entitled *The Humors of Monsieur Galliard* or *Monsieur, The French Dancing Master*, performed in the 1640s and 50s and later published in *1 The Wits, or Sport upon Sport* (O 1662 [two issues] and 1672). Engraved frontispiece of *The Wits* depicts "The French Dancing Master": "Fiddling as he dances and poised on one toe, beribboned and befeathered, long hair flowing down his shoulders, the French dancing master cuts a ridiculous figure, which is just as Cavendish would have wanted" (Howard 2007).

The Variety "depicts a female academy where a company of young gentlewomen under the guidance of some matrons live and study together until a group of enraged men conquer the premises" (Pohl 2006). "*The Variety* . . . is in parts deliberately modeled on [Jonson's] *The Magnetic Lady*" (Happé 2000). Although a courtier's play, the language is characterized by a "plain and satirical style" (Butler 1984b).

Venus and Adonis, or the Maid's Philosophy. Anonymous. A playlet/droll perhaps acted in the 16th century. "The play is exceedingly brief, compressing four episodes into forty-nine lines"; it "bears only slight resemblance to the classic myth" (Elson 1932). Kirkman, on the TP of *2 The Wits*, says that drolls were "written I know not when, by several persons, I know not who." "This perhaps suggests the folk humor of some of the pieces as well as the contemporary need for anonymity" (Randall 1995). Kirkman's preface reports that Robert Cox "was not only the principal actor, but also the contriver and author of most of these farces." Kirkman's attribution is "probable" (Holland 2007).

Published in *2 The Wits, or Sport upon Sport* (Q and O 1673), which gives as venues of performance fairs, halls, taverns, and "mountebancks stages at Charing Cross, Lincolns-Inn-Fields, and other places"; list of characters.

A Very Merry and Pithy Comedy called The Longer Thou Livest. See *The Longer Thou Livest.*

A Very Woman, or The Prince of Tarent, A Tragicomedy. John Fletcher and Philip Massinger; revised by Massinger. The lost original version was acted 1613–25, presumably by the King's Men. The revised version, attributed to Massinger, was licensed for acting 6 June 1634 (Adams 1917). "Often acted . . . with great applause" by the King's Men at the [second] Blackfriars, according to the separate TP.

SR 9 September 1653 *A very woman, or, the woman's plot* ("presumably, two distinct pieces" [Greg 1939]). O 1655 *Three New Plays* (with *The Bashful Lover, The Guardian*); "never printed before," according to the general TP; Massinger's name alone appears on the separate TP; separate pagination and TP but continuous register; list of characters; prologue ("presumably written for the 1634 performance" [Gill 1967]) and epilogue; five acts and first scenes. Although the SDs "are for the most part very curt" (E&G 1976), a few concern what playgoers see: "*Enter* Almira *in black, carelessly habited*"; "*A bed drawn forth,* Martino *upon it, a book in's hand.*" Unusual sound effect: "*[Boatswain] whistles within.*"

The prologue looks back to the earlier version of the play and claims that the present (revised) version is superior: "To such (and some there are, no question here,) / Who happy in their memories do bear / This subject long since acted, and can say / *Truly, we have seen something like this play.* / Our author with becoming modesty / (For in this kinde he ne'er was bold) by me, / In his defence, thus answers, By command / He undertook this task, nor could it stand / With his low Fortune to refuse to do; / What by his patron he was call'd unto. / For whose delight and yours, we hope, with care / He hath review'd it; and with him we dare / Maintain to any man, that did allow / 'Twas good before, it is much better'd now."

Vice, The Interlude of. See *Horestes.*

The Virgin Martyr, A Tragedy. Philip Massinger and Thomas Dekker. Licensed for acting 6 October 1620 (Hoy 1980). "Divers times publickely acted with great applause" by the King's Revels Company, according to the Q1 TP, at the Red Bull (Monta 2005). Herbert licensed an additional scene 7 July 1624 "probably because the play was being performed again by a new company" (Monta), "but this [scene] was never printed" (Hoy 1987b).

SR 7 December 1621; transferred 24 October 1633; 28 July 1641. Q1 1622 two issues; list of characters; five acts and first scenes. "The fact that the play was written for the Red Bull theatre may account for such large-scale effects as the procession of Jupiter" (McLuskie 1981): *"Enter Priest with the image [i.e. statue] of Jupiter, incense and censers"*; then *"They [Caliste and Christeta] both spit at the image, throw it downe, and spurne it."* At one point Angelo enters *"in the angels habit,"* which "makes him invisible except to Dorothea" (Reynolds 1940). The action converges on the suffering and death of Dorothea: *"Enter Sapritius dragging in Dorothea by the haire, Angelo attending."* Unusual staging includes *"Enter Dorothea lead prisoner, a guard attending, a hangman with cords in some ugly shape, sets up a pillar in the middle of the stage,"* where they *"strike at her."* Staging also calls for *"a scaffold thrust forth"* for her execution. "Dorothea is decapitated by the Roman authorities. This execution takes place on stage" (Myhill 2004): *"Her head strucke off."* This "beheading of a canonized saint" is the only such instance "from the period 1570 to 1642" (Owens 2005). "After Dorothea's death, she sends a basket of flowers and fruit from heaven to convert her former tormentor, Theophilus" (Williamson 2009). Special effects include the entry of Harpax, an evil spirit, *"in a fearefull shape, fire flashing out of the study"* (probably a discovery space); later, *"the divell sinkes with lightning,"* presumably through a trap. Sound effects include "heavenly music" at the martyrdom of Dorothea, who appears resplendent following her execution: *"Enter Dorothea in a white robe, crownes upon her robe, a crowne upon her head, lead in by the Angell."* Q2 1631. Q3 1651. Q4 1661.

"This play could . . . have been written in 1520 as easily as in 1620" (Wasson 1986b); it is "the last saint's play staged in early modern England" (Monta), "the sole post-Reformation saint's play on the London stage" (Cohen 1985). "*The Virgin Martyr* revives the Tudor genre of the protestant saint's play, such as Thomas Garter's *Virtuous and Godly Susanna* . . . or Elizabeth Cary's *Tragedy of Mariam*" (Cox 2002). "In its portrayal of the torture and martyrdom of St. Dorothea of Caesarea, [the play] seems strikingly Catholic in its baroque dramaturgy. If nothing else, *The Virgin Martyr* suggests that the genre of the saint's life had not been erased from consciousness, but remained a possibility for dramatic exploitation" (O'Connell 2000a). "*The Virgin Martyr* has affinities with the Baroque idealism of Counter Reformation *tragedia sacra* on the continent" (Cox 2000).

The Virgin Widow, A Comedy. Francis Quarles. Acted *c.* 1640 (Jankowski 2000) at undetermined venue; "privately acted, 1641" (Stern 2009c). The stationer describes the auspices of production: "This enterlude, to sweeten the brackish distempers of a deluded age, is here . . . to thy judicious view freely offered: having been sometimes at Chelsie privately acted (by a company of young gentlemen) with good approvement."

SR none. Q1 1649 list of characters; five acts and first scenes. Ample SDs. A theatrical property is suggested by a SD: *"[Quibble] Drawes a curtaine, and discovers his shop furnisht"*; he says, "Here's physic of all kinds for all diseases," and he *"Takes a box and reads [aloud]."* Spectacular staging includes *"A flash of fire from the oracle; a cloud of smoak; which being vanisht,* Augusta *is found dead in her chair of state, her crown struck off."* Q2 1656 "the second edition."

Virtue's Triumph. Mildmay Fane. "Writ in ann—1644," according to the MS, and possibly performed at Fane's estate, Apethorpe, in Northamptonshire (Morton 1988). "The play provides evidence that Parliament's 1642 ban on public theatricals did not stop writers interested in the drama from producing scripts which could receive private performance. It is, in addition, an example of the type of material which Royalists produced to present their political ideology and register their condemnation of Parliament's attacks on the crown" (Morton). The play's continuity with dramatic tradition is expressed in a structure that seems shaped by the Tudor interlude and in dramaturgy indebted to Jacobean and Caroline masques.

London, BL, Additional MS 34221, fols. 69–106; no author named; the TP describes play as "this comedy"; revisions in Fane's hand; argument; dramatis personae; prologue; five acts and separate scenes. Extensive SDs. First edited by Morton 1988.

By the time Fane wrote this play, "his perspective was entirely Royalist, for he found with the security of the king rested that of the nobility and thus himself" (Morton 1991).

Virtuous and Godly Susanna. See *Susanna*.

Vittoria Corombona. See *The White Devil*.

Volpone, or The Fox. Ben Jonson. Acted January–June 1606, "probably about mid-March" (Donaldson 2004), despite the F1 TP claim, "first acted in the yeere 1605," "a dating that in the old-style legal calendar could extend to 25 March 1606" (Parker 1983). By the King's Men, according to the F1 TP, at the first Globe. Performed also at Oxford and Cambridge (1606–07), according to Jonson's Q dedication. *Volpone* "was certainly performed [in Oxford] on 7 September 1607 during a period of plague in London" (Donaldson 2011). Despite the skepticism of Nelson 1989 about performance at Cambridge, Bednarz 2010b argues that *Volpone* was indeed performed in that city. "Where *Volpone* was presented is not specified but as Jonson alludes to it being well received by the universities there is a slim possibility that it was acted within a university space in both towns" (Keenan 2002). Possibly performed "at one of the city inns" (Boas 1922). Principal actors were Richard Burbage, John Heminges, Henry Condell, William Sly, John Lowin, and Alexander Cooke, according to F1. Burbage "possibly" played Volpone (Donaldson); later John Lowin played the role (Butler 2004e). "Condell, it seems, was the original Mosca" (Potter 2012); Joseph Taylor later played Mosca when he joined the King's Men (*Historia Histrionica*). John Underwood played Bonario (Astington 2010). Robert Armin may have played Nano the dwarf (Wiles 1987). "John Heminges played Corbaccio" (Potter). Cooke may have played Madam Would-Be (Forse 1993). As an adult Nicholas Tooley played Corvino (Potter). Lowin "is assigned the part of Sir Pol in the manuscript cast list for *Volpone* relating to the period 1615–19" (Astington 2010). Nathan Field played Voltore upon joining the company *c.* 1616 (Williams 2004); George Birch probably played Lady Would-Be in revivals (Astington 2010). Subsequently revived at Whitehall, before the prince and the Duke of Brunswick, the evening of 27 December 1624 (Adams 1917)—the title on this occasion given as *The Fox*; at Whitehall Cockpit 19 November 1630 (Dutton 1996); at second Blackfriars 27 October 1638; and at the Whitehall Cockpit 8 November 1638 (*The Fox*). Leonard Digges, in a work published in 1640, compliments "the Fox and subtill Alchemist" (Chambers 1930). The popularity of the play may have been occasioned, in part, by its evocation of the recent (1605) Gunpowder Plot (De Luna 1967, Dutton 2008). "Sir Politic Would-be is generally understood to be a parody of the English ambassador to Venice, Sir Henry Wotton" (Sanders 1998b). Since 1921 "*Volpone* has been produced more than any other non-Shakespearean play of the period" (Watson 2003).

SR none prior to Q, but George Buc "almost certainly licensed *Volpone* for the press in 1607" (Dutton 2008); transferred 3 October 1610; 10 June 1621; 4 July 1635. Q 1607 two issues; RT *The Fox*; list of characters; argument; prologue and epilogue (by Volpone); five acts and separate scenes. Staging calls for use of a property bed from which Volpone entertains his visitors. Jonson "stages a theatrical homoeroticism that becomes inseparable from sodomy. A homoerotic cooperation in theatrical role-playing allows Volpone and Mosca to overmaster the foolish legacy hunters"; "it is Mosca who receives Volpone's kisses, embraces, and ecstatic praises" (DiGangi 1997). "Volpone instructs Mosca on how he should deal with the interested visitors who are coming to monitor Volpone's state of health; meanwhile he will get up 'Behind the curtain, on a stool, and hearken; Sometime peep over, see how they do look'. . . . This connotes a curtain with enough space behind it for someone to stand on a stool and peep over, and probably refers to an upstage centre concealment space" (Fitzpatrick 2011). The issue is complicated, however, by this enigmatic direction: "*Volpone peeps from behind a traverse.*" Although this SD is usually interpreted as a curtain, "it is possible that the 'traverse' is some sort of screen, for the *OED* defines the term as 'a curtain or screen placed crosswise, or drawn across a room, hall, or theatre,'" and the *OED* lists the SD in *Volpone* as one of its examples (Kiefer 2007). Staging requires "a raised platform" for "the mountebank speeches" when Volpone is in disguise (Gurr 2009d). At the denouement staging includes "fake demonic possession and dispossession," which serve "the purposes of political and religious satire" (Cox 2000). F1 1616 *The Works*; *Volpone, or The Fox, A Comedy*; "acted in the yeere 1605"; "Jonson's '1605' almost certainly means '1606'" (Butler 2003b). In F1 Jonson adds "twenty-nine extra stage directions" in the margins (Parker & Bevington 1999). F2 1640–41.

Jonson dedicates the Q "To the most noble and most æquall sisters the two famous universities, for their love and acceptance shew'n to his poeme in the presentation," an allusion apparently to the university performances. In his prefatory epistle, Jonson describes "the offices and function of a poët," asserting "the impossibility of any mans being the good poët, without first being a good man." As for the "imputation of sharpnesse," Jonson asks: "Where have I beene particular? Where personall?"

The Vow Breaker, or The Fair Maid of Clifton. William Sampson. Acted ?1625–36 (*JCS*). Apparently first performed in the neighborhood of Nottingham and Derby: "In Notinghamshire as it hath beene divers times acted by severall companies with great applause," according to the TP.

SR none. Q 1636 prologue; five acts. Staging calls for either a property tree or one of the stage posts to represent a tree from which a man hangs himself: "*Young Bateman in's shirt, a halter about his necke*"; "Behold a tree"; then he "*falls, hangs*"; later he reappears as a ghost. A painting figures onstage when "a father obsessively mourns over the portrait of his son, who has been driven to suicide by love" (Rochester 2010). Unusual SD: "*Enter* Joshua *his cat in a string*"; Joshua says, "I adjudge thee to be hanged this munday for killing a mouse yesterday." Q contains a single woodcut depicting four scenes in the play. The illustration "is based closely on the action of the play, and cites lines of dialogue from it" (Foakes 1985). Opposite the picture is printed a description.

Prologue addresses "censurers": "Bring not the author then, in your mislikes, / If on the ages vice, quaintly he strikes / And hits your guilt! . . . If in his scenes, he any vice have hit / To you farre better knowne then to his wit, / Tak't to your selves alone: for him, his penn / Strikes at the vices, and not mindes the men."

W

The Walks of Islington and Hogsdon, with the Humors of Woodstreet Counter, A Comedy. Thomas Jordan. Licensed for acting 2 August 1641, according to Herbert's license, which is printed in Q following the epilogue; this is the only printed playbook that contains "the Master's license at the end" (Gurr 2009d). "Pub-

likely acted . . . with extraordinary applause" for run of nineteen days, according
to the Q TP. By the Red Bull[-King's] Company, according to the SR entry, at
the Red Bull. In the dedicatory epistle Jordan writes that "this comedy gained
the success of a good censure, and received more acceptation then I thought it
merited." "[I]t is not implausible that this play was as popular as the dramatist
claimed" (Munro 2006c).

SR 21 April 1657. Q 1657 "never printed before"; dramatis personae; prologue and epilogue; five acts and separate scenes. "Fittingly for a play with so
many tavern scenes, there is much singing, on-stage music and dancing" (Munro).
The most detailed SDs involve dancing: "*They all dance to a sprightly ayr, but in the
fourth change they all dance off from the stage into the tyring-house, where they remain
till the tune is plaid once over; then they dance all in again, and come to their severall
figures, and continue dancing the tune once more over; then they dance in and out again
as before.*" An unusual SD has Splendora stand "*within the arras*"; "[i]t is most
likely that '*within the Arras*' is equivalent to '*behind the Arras*'" (Ichikawa 2005).
While there Splendora finds pen and paper and writes a note; "the offstage character shows herself through the gap between the hangings" (Ichikawa). Reissued ND ?1663; *Tricks of Youth, or The Walks of Islington and Hogsdon*; prologue in
theater and prologue to king. "The prologue is also printed in *A Royal Arbour of
Loyal Poesie*, where it is titled 'A Prologue to the King, August 16. 1660'" (Munro
2006c). This play may be identical with Jordan's *Youth's Figaries*, usually considered lost (Bancroft 2013).

The Q prefatory poem by R. C. speaks of the unusual interval between performance and publication: "Now by the bounty of the press we be / Possess'd of
that which we before did see, / Not pleasing onely nineteen times read o're, / But
nineteen ages, or till time's no more." The new dedicatory epistle in the reissue
looks back to a time when the theaters were closed: "The time is come again,
in which we may / Use *Tricks of Youth*, and safely see a play; / Hear tavern-
musick, and such harmless things / As neither wrong Gods precept, nor the
kings: / For all those recreations are set free / In sixty one, were damn'd in forty
three, / By those trienial traytors, who agreed / To make the publick faith weigh
down the creed." Similarly, the new prologue to the king in the ?1663 reissue recalls the prohibition forbidding playing before the Restoration: "We have been
so perplext with gun and drum, / Look to your hats and clokes, the red-coats
come. / D'amboys is routed, Hotspur quits the field, / Falstaff's out-filch'd, all in
confusion yield, / Even auditor and actor, what before / Did make the Red Bull
laugh, now makes him roar." The new king has put to rout those who left the theaters dark: "your presence / Hath nullified their power."

The Wandering Lover, A Tragicomedy. Thomas Meriton. Performed 1650s at undetermined venue. "Acted severall times privately at sundry places by the author
and his friends with great applause," according to the TP. Reading Meriton's

work "is one way to inform oneself about some midcentury tastes, perceptions, presumptions, attitudes, and aspirations" (Randall 1995).

SR none. Q 1658 author's initials on the TP and the prefatory poem by R. B. spells out the author's name; dramatis personae; prologue and epilogue; five acts and separate scenes. The SDs are confined chiefly to entrances and exits.

Prologue anticipates production: "But why should I thus trifle time away? / For 'tis full season that our comick play / Should be now acted in our solemn doom; / Lo here the player's come, and I will give in room."

The Wandering Lovers. See *The Lovers' Progress.*

War Hath Made All Friends. See *Edmond Ironside.*

The Ward, A Tragicomedy. Thomas Neale. No evidence of production but possibly "aimed at professional performance" (Mitchell 1937).

Oxford, Bodleian, MS Rawlinson poet. 79, fols. 1–52; dated 16 September 1637; prologue and epilogue (by Thomaso); five acts and separate scenes. Some SDs indicative of preparation for performance: "*Sir Wary Wastefull thrust forth on the stage in a couche sicke*"; enter various characters "*in buffe, souldier like, with a flourish.*" First edited by Mitchell 1937.

"The author of *The Warde* belongs to that miscellaneous group of writers who experimented with the drama following the fad for dramatic authorship set by those at court after 1633. He was one of those among the gentry who no doubt would never have written but for the prevailing fashion" (Mitchell). *The Ward* is "inspired by the author's indignation at the vagaries of the law, and presents as its central character a pathetic little orphan who has been victimized by a bad will" (Harbage 1936).

A Warning for Fair Women. Anonymous. Performed *c.* 1589 at the Curtain (Grantley 2008a). "Probably revived in the late 1590s" (Munro 2005). "Lately divers times acted by" the Lord Chamberlain's Men, according to the TP, at undetermined venue. "This is the first play centered on contemporary London in the extant repertory of the Chamberlain's Men" (McMillin 2005).

SR 17 November 1599. Q 1599 *A Warning for Fair Women, Containing The Most Tragical and Lamentable Murder of Master George Sanders of London*; no author named; induction in which History, "with drum and ensigne," contends with Comedy and Tragedy, "in one hand a whip, in the other hand a knife"; epilogue, though not identified as such, spoken by Tragedy; "'history' and 'comedy' were starting to overtake tragedy in popularity in the 1590s" (Stern 2009c); divided into four parts by three dumb shows, explained by Tragedy, who "acts as a kind of chorus" (Jewkes 1958). Personified History says, "The stage is hung with blacke; and I perceive / The auditors preparde for Tragedie"; this remark suggests that black hangings were a customary accoutrement for tragedies (Kiefer 2007).

The custom "appears to have stopped by the end of the first decade of the seventeenth century" (Gurr 2006). "History's claim to be a genre equal to Comedy and Tragedy was of recent and very local origin: History gets onto the stage of *A Warning for Fair Women* because Shakespeare's success put her there" (Danson 2000). The character Comedy characterizes the dramatic action typical of tragedy: "a filthie whining ghost . . . cries Vindicta, revenge, revenge: / With that a little rosen flashes forth, / Like smoke out of a tabacco pipe, or a boyes squib." In a dumb show *"suddenly riseth up a great tree,"* evidently through a trap door (Habicht 1971); a character then *"hewes downe the tree."* Characters in dumb shows interact with abstractions; the play "fuses the virtual choreography of the allegorical dumb show with a type of plot normally treated realistically" (McMillin). The play's "pivotal event, the seduction of Mistress Sanders, is presented not by a realistic temptation sequence but by an allegorical dumb show" (Dessen 1977): *"next comes* Lust *before* Browne, *leading mistris* Sanders *covered with a black vaile:* Chastitie *all in white, pulling her backe softly by the arme: then* Drewry, *thrusting away* Chastitie, Roger *following: they march about, and then sit to the table: the* Furies *fill wine,* Lust *drinckes to* Brown, *he to* Mistris Sanders, *shee pledgeth him:* Lust *imbraceth her."* "By alternating the dumb shows, which stylize the events, with depictions of the careful planning and hard work needed to commit a murder, the playwright comments on both modes of representation, exposing the inadequacies of each to explain the crime" (Dolan 1989). "After the corruption of Anne Sanders has been acted out in dumb show, Chastity enters *'with her hair disheveled'"* (Dessen 1984). She then takes Mistress Sanders by the hand and *"brings her to her husbands picture hanging on the wall"*; unlike many other portraits onstage, this one is not a miniature but a wall portrait (Elam 2010). Sound effects include offstage music: *"Here some strange solemne musike, like belles is heard within."* This SD indicates that the musicians are located in the tiring-house (Hosley 1960).

The induction "is an extended argument for a remarkable and noteworthy innovation on the Elizabethan stage as the company conceived it: a new form, domestic tragedy set in London, telling a true tale" (Gurr 2004c). Like the story of Jane Shore in the two parts of *Heywood's History of Edward IV* and that of Alice Arden in *Arden of Faversham*, the story of Anne Sanders in *Warning* offers the "theatrical pleasures of pathos and a focus on women's suffering" (McLuskie 2002).

The Wars of Caesar and Pompey. See *Caesar and Pompey.*

The Wars of Cyrus, King of Persia, against Antiochus, King of Assyria, with the Tragical End of Panthea. ?Richard Farrant (Brawner 1942). Acted *c.* 1577–80 (Wilson 1969). "Played by the Children of" the Queen's Chapel, according to the TP, probably at the first Blackfriars (Shapiro 2009). "[I]t was probably the unnamed play mentioned in the Revels Accounts as having been given by Farrant's boys before the Queen at Richmond on December 27, 1578" (Lawrence 1921). "*Cyrus* is our first extant blank-verse play written for and produced by child actors" (Brawner).

SR none. Q 1594 no author named; address "to the audience" (i.e., prologue) appears after some 600 lines of dialogue; "the prologue links itself to a no-longer-extant singing 'chorus'" (Stern 2009c); five acts. "Act divisions are confused, the prologue is misplaced, choruses are removed. The songs too have been left out" (Wilson). "The typography and printing of" Q "are of a poor order" (Brawner). Q may be a revision of the play performed in the 1570s (Shapiro 1977). Onstage violence: "the king of Susa's hand is cut off by his Egyptian foes after he has fallen in battle" (Owens 2005).

Prologue distinguishes this play from others: "our muse / That seemes to trouble you, againe with toies / Or needlesse antickes imitations, / Or shewes, or new devises sprung a late, / We have exilde them from our tragicke stage, / As trash of their tradition, that can bring / Nor instance, nor excuse. For what they do / In stead of mournefull plaints our chorus sings, / Although it be against the upstart guise, / Yet warranted by grave antiquitie, / We will revive the which hath long beene done." This address "shuns the predilections of both the vulgar and the 'virtuous'—that is, those inclining to Puritanism" (Bevington 1968). "*The Wars of Cyrus*, like *Tamburlaine*, deals with the problem of political obedience, and it offers a doctrine which differs from both Marlowe's and from the Tudor orthodoxy of men like William Tyndale and Thomas Cranmer. The play holds that a tyrant is not entitled to the unquestioning obedience which must be given to a just and lawful king" (Ribner 1954).

The Wars of Pompey and Caesar. See *Caesar and Pompey* (Chapman).

The Wasp, or Subject's Precedent. Anonymous. Acted 1636–39 by the King's Revels Company at the Salisbury Court playhouse (Lever 1974b). MS contains six names of actors: [Thomas] Jordan, [John] Barrett, Mathias Morris, "Noble," "Ellis," and "Ambrose"; Bentley 1984 suggests that the last name of Ellis is either Bedowe or Worth, and that of Ambrose is either Matchit or Beeland/Byland; Lever 1974a suggests that the former's last name of Ellis is either Worth or Guest, and that of Ambrose is likely to be Matchit.

Alnwick, UK, Alnwick Castle, MS 507, fols. 1–22; no author named; "used in the playhouse for performance" (Greg 1931); the edges of some leaves have been damaged; the end seems to be missing; some additions, some speeches crossed out; top corners of some leaves torn away; signs of revision; the bookkeeper "regularised or added stage directions for actor entrances, stage properties and music" (Ioppolo 2006); five acts. Fols. 1 and 2 have these titles: "A Comicall History Calld The waspe" and "The Waspe or subjects President." Unusual staging includes "*A table ffurnisht*"; subsequently "*the table turns & such things ap[p]eare.*" "The 'such things' that suddenly appear are 'snakes toads & newts.' It seems, therefore, that the table-top, or part of it, that contains the items for the banquet, is turned over to reveal the reptiles. Items on either side must be fastened in position" (Butterworth 2005). Near the end, the usurping Gerald claims to see a sword hanging over his head and a Fury "armd / w[th] sheeres to cut it"; it is not clear how this would have been staged. "[F]requent use of sound effects" (Lever): e.g., "*Sollempne musick*" for a funeral procession; "*Soft musi[k]e*" for a banquet. First edited by Lever 1974b.

"A shrewd comment on Stuart politics," the play attacks George Villiers, first Duke of Buckingham (Lever 1974a). "*The Wasp*, with its vigorous action, violent clashes of character and racy language, is an extraordinary demonstration of the tenacity of older forms, and of the pointedness of their perspectives on recent politics" (Butler 1984b).

The Weakest Goeth to the Wall. Anonymous; Thomas Dekker may be responsible for the comic scenes (Levenson 1980). Acted 1595–1600 (Levenson). "Sundry times plaide by" Oxford's Men, according to the Q1 TP, at undetermined venue, possibly a London inn-yard (Lawrence 1927), though "when actors performed at inns they usually occupied a large room rather than a yard and performed by candlelight" (Orrell 1997). "A company playing under Oxford's patronage was occupying the Boar's Head in 1602, and that year merged with Worcester's Men" (Jewkes 1958).

SR 23 October 1600; transferred 6 November 1615; 18 October 1617; 29 May 1638; 25 January 1639. Q1 1600 "pantomime" (Mehl 1965) explained by the prologue; not divided. The staging of the opening pantomime may call for a property concealing a trap when the Duchess of Burgundy leaps into a river (Lawrence); Dessen & Thomson 1999 call *river* in the SD "a rare fictional term" for the trap. Q2 1618.

Wealth and Health. Anonymous. Acted 1554–55 (Craik 1958) or 1557 (Kermode 2009a). Probably performed at court before Queen Mary (Craik 1953), possibly by children (Walker 1998) in the Christmas season; "probably written for Queen Mary's interluders early in her reign" (Milling 2004). The TP lists the names of seven characters and indicates that "foure may easely play this playe," but the roles are not assigned and the play actually requires six actors (Lancashire 2002). The TP "seems a clear case of printer's fraud, added to attract buyers among the troupes" (Bevington 1962).

SR year beginning 19 July 1557 (Greg 1907c). Q ND ?1565 *An Interlude of Wealth and Health, Very Merry and Full of Pastime*; possibly the reprint of a book published near the date in the SR—"newly at this tyme imprinted"; "very mery and full of pastyme"; the epilogue addressed to Queen Mary may be "a publisher's addition" (Craik 1958); not divided. Copies of the play must have been available long after its initial run onstage: Rogers and Ley include it in their 1656 catalogue, as does Archer; Kirkman includes it in his catalogues of 1661 and 1671.

Although originally Catholic in its moralizing, the play has taken a new form in Q. This drama, bristling with hostility to Queen Mary and her politics, "amounts to a post-Marian rewriting of *Respublica*" (Winkelman 2005); the play has been revised to turn it "into a polemical Protestant morality" (Pineas 1965). The playwright provides "three figures, Wealth, Health, and Liberty, whose fortunes enact the recent history of England"; they "are corrupted . . . by two figures, Ill Will and Shrewd Wit," and "ultimately are restored to health by Remedy (proper authority)" (Dessen 1986). "Unlike many mid-Tudor plays, *Wealth and Health* provides a curious blend of allegory and realistic narrative drama. As an allegory about the social and economic troubles facing England, the play features the virtues Good Remedy, Health, Wealth, and Liberty and the vices Ill Will and Shrewd Wit. These characters supply the main action" (Oldenburg 2009).

Wealth Outwitted. See ***Money Is an Ass***.

The Weather (***The Play of the Weather***). John Heywood. Acted Christmas 1527 (Robinson 1987), or after 1529 (Walker 2000, Happé 2010), or Shrovetide 1533 (Forest-Hill 1996). "[T]here is a high probability that the cast consisted wholly or largely of boys" (Happé 1994b); a SD, "*The boy comyth in, the lest that can play*," implies "that all the rest of the actors are boys also" (Fox 1989). The boy actors were "drawn from among the choristers of the Chapel Royal or St Paul's" (Walker 2005). "The cast required, ten actors with no doubling possible . . . , strongly suggests that Heywood could call upon the resources of the royal court to furnish his actors" (Walker 2000). "[I]ntended for an evening performance in a dining hall" (Walker 1991a), "possibly for Henry VIII" (Milling 2004). But McCarthy 2008 argues for performance in a chapel rather than a hall. Heywood himself may have played the part of Merry Report, the Vice (Happé 1999); the term Vice is "used here for the first time in English drama" (Bevington 1975).

SR no original; transferred 15 January 1582. F 1533 *The Play of the Weather, A New and Very Merry Interlude of All Manner Weathers*; names of characters on the TP; "scant" SDs (Massai 2007); not divided. The play "requires only one major property, the curtained and canopied throne (similar to that used in *Godly Queene Hester*) which Jupiter occupies for most of the play, and which must conceal the musicians who play a song" (Walker 2000). A scaffold may have been used for Jupiter's throne. Q1 ND ?1544 (Greg 1930); unique copy at Cambridge. Q2 ND ?1554–60 (Lennam 1971); unique copy at Bodleian. Q3 ?1565 (Lennam) at BL.

"The function Heywood intends for the play is . . . to laugh men out of folly, and persuade them of the need for tolerance, charity, and commitment to the common good" (Fox). There is, however, also a political implication, for the play "purports to advise the King on the 'weather' of religious dispute around 1530. A metatheatrical gesture situates the play in the Great Hall or Presence Chamber of Jupiter, where the true Father of Heaven appoints a courtier-servant, Merry

Report, to hear complaints about the weather and report back. Merry Report, an updated Vice, receives complaints across a social spectrum—water-miller, laundress and little boy, none of whom will compromise on a definition of the right weather" (Sessions 2002). The actor playing Jupiter "might have looked like [King] Henry," and the "Gentlewoman whom Merry Report offers to Henry as a new wife, might have resembled Anne Boleyn" (Happé 2007b).

The Weather Woman. See *Arabia Sitiens.*

The Wedding. James Shirley. No license for acting survives. Probably performed May 1626 (Flavin 1980). "Lately acted by" Queen Henrietta Maria's Men at the Phoenix, according to the Q1 TP. The dedication speaks of "this comedy coming forth to take the ayre in summer." Richard Perkins played Sir John Belfare; Michael Bowyer, Beauford; John Sumner, Marwood; William Robbins, Rawbone; William Sherlock, Lodam; Anthony Turner, Justice Landby; William Allen, Captain Landby; William Wilbraham, Isaac; John Young, Haver; John Dobson, Cameleon; Hugh Clark, Gratiana; John Page, Jane; Edward Rogers, Millicent; Timothy Reade, Cardona, according to "The Actors Names" in Q1. In playlist of Beeston's Boys 10 August 1639.

SR no original; transferred 25 September 1637. Q1 1629 epilogue by William Robbins as Rawbone; five acts and first scenes. A *coup de théâtre* is achieved when Millicent arrives with a coffin supposedly containing the body of Marwood, slain for slandering Gratiana, who has herself died; the guilt-ridden Beauford opens the coffin "to drop one funerall teare upon his wound," and Gratiana arises (Stevens 1977). Q2 1633. Q3 1660.

The Weeding of the Covent Garden, or the Middlesex Justice of Peace, A Facetious Comedy. Richard Brome. Acted 1632–33 (Kaufmann 1961). Possibly performed by the King's Men (*JCS*) at the Blackfriars (Grantley 2008a). Possibly performed by Prince Charles's Men; revived summer 1641, perhaps by Beeston's Boys (Steggle 2004b). Brome's play has "some sort of relationship" with Thomas Nabbes's *Covent Garden*, "which has the same subject," though perhaps "the two plays were developed simultaneously and independently" (Steggle). Brome's play "concerns the settling of country gentry into the newly fashionable Covent Garden district" (Bulman 2003).

SR 4 August 1640 *The Covent Garden*. O 1658–59 *Five New Plays* (with *The English Moor, The Lovesick Court, The New Academy, The Queen and Concubine*); two issues; *Covent Garden Weeded* on the general TP and HT; *The Weeding of the Covent Garden* on the separate TP, dated 1658 in some copies, 1659 in others; separately paginated; list of characters; two prologues, one of which "seems to be for the original first performance of *Weeding* and is likely to have been written by Brome" (Stern 2009c); an additional prologue, "for the play in revival" (Stern), explains that the playwright wrote the play "some ten years since"; two epilogues, the first of which is also appended to *Lovesick Court*; five acts and separate scenes.

Brome's prefatory poem sharply attacks John Suckling's *Aglaura*, which had been printed in grandiose (folio) format: "When I saw so much white, I did begin / To think *Aglaura* either did lie in, / Or else took pennance. Never did I see / (Unless in bills dasht in the chancerie) / So little in so much; as if the feet / Of poetry, like law, were sold by th'sheet. / If this new fashion should but last one yeare, / Poets, as clerks, would make our paper dear."

The Welsh Ambassador, or A Comedy in Disguises. "[A]ttributed to Thomas Dekker" (Tudeau-Clayton 2010); with ?John Ford (Lloyd 1945, Vickers 2002, Neill 2004). Acted 1623 (Hoy 1980) by Lady Elizabeth's Men at the Phoenix (Long 1999).

Cardiff, UK, Cardiff Public Library, MS 4.12, fols. 1–22; no author named but "considered Dekker's since Abraham Hill's attribution of it to him ca. 1678" (Anderson 1978); theatrical provenance (Long 1989); severely damaged by mice at the foot of leaves; list of characters; some speeches deleted; "a regular division into [five] acts only" (Greg 1931). "The text carries frequent marginal notations for music cues and properties, along with warnings for actors to 'bee redy' ten to thirty lines before almost every entrance. A number of crucial stage directions are inserted at the edge of the text" (King 1965). The SDs "call for '*Enter Carintha at a table readinge*' . . . and '*Enter Clowne in his study writinge*'"; "but the text does not specify how these properties are brought into view" (King 1971); perhaps the actors parted a curtain covering a discovery space. In action aloft Carintha "*shews Penda with a leadinge staff voltimar at his back; his sword in him.*" "She explains to the King that she has hired a workman to carve this 'statue' of Penda" (King 1971). "'The Welsh Ambassador' is a proverbial phrase for the cuckoo" and so "it generally carries implications of cuckoldry" (Hoy). First edited by Littledale & Greg 1920.

"Dekker rewrote some scenes from his *Noble Spanish Soldier*, a revenge tragedy of 1604, to create a fashionable tragicomedy" (Rasmussen 1997).

Westward Ho! Thomas Dekker and John Webster. Acted "late autumn or early winter of 1604" (Van Fossen 1979). "Divers times acted by" Paul's Boys, according to the TP, at Paul's playhouse. "Highly popular and frequently performed" (Gunby 2004).

SR 2 March 1605 [entry crossed out]. Q 1607 song printed at end; five acts and a single additional scene. The SDs are "long and descriptive" (Jewkes 1958): "*Whilst the song is heard. The earle drawes a curten, and sets forth a banquet: he then exit[s], and enters presently with Parenthesis attird like his wife maskt: leads him to the table, places him in a chaire, and in dumb signes, courts him, til the song be done.*" A "distinguishing custom of the early private theatre began with the child-players and may have been confined to them. This was the valedictory song at the close of the comedy. In *Westward Ho* . . . this was sung off the stage after the actors had departed" (Lawrence 1912a).

The success of this play prompted "the rival Children of her Majesty's Revels at the Blackfriars to produce a city comedy of their own," *Eastward Ho!* (Hoy 1980). In turn, Dekker and Webster in *Northward Ho!* would reply to *Eastward Ho!* With their two plays Dekker and Webster "introduce joint authorship into the private theaters, paving the way for the advent of the indoor playhouses' most important collaborators, Beaumont and Fletcher" (Hirschfeld 2004).

The Wether. See *The Weather.*

What You Will. John Marston. Acted spring/summer 1601 (Cain 1995) by Paul's Boys at Paul's playhouse (Geckle 1987). Possibly written for performance at the Middle Temple as well (Duncan-Jones 2001). Perhaps played at the Blackfriars (Hunter 1975). "Between 1600 and 1602" both Marston and Shakespeare "wrote comedies called *What You Will*" (Gossett 2004b). The play "appears to have been known to at least one writer for the King's Revels prior to its publication" (Cathcart 2008).

SR 6 August 1607. Q 1607 induction; prologue; pantomimes ("Marston does not normally use the term dumb show for all his mimes" [Mehl 1965]); five acts. The play "gives great prominence to music"; there are "a number of songs and dances within the play, as well as music between the acts" (Steggle 2000): "Quadratus remarks to Laverdure: 'Come, let's see thy vein— / Dances, scenes, and songs, royal entertain'" (Wright 1928). The printing of Q followed the breakup of Paul's Boys in 1607. O 1633 *The Works of Mr. John Marston, Being Tragedies and Comedies, Collected into One Volume* (with *Antonio and Mellida, Antonio's Revenge, The Dutch Courtesan, Parasitaster, The Wonder of Women*); two issues. The reissue, entitled *Tragedies and Comedies Collected into One Volume*, removes Marston's name from the separate TPs and general TP; William Sheares had published the collection without Marston's consent. Also issued in *Comedies, Tragicomedies, and Tragedies* (1652), a made-up Q no longer extant.

The induction begins "with what appears to be simply a non-dramatic illusion, but it is also a new method of opening a scene": the conversation of three gallants who attack critics of Paul's playhouse and allude to plays performed at this theater (Gair 1978b). This induction refers to two features of the so-called private (indoor) theaters, instrumental music preceding each act and the lighting of candles for illumination: "*Before the musicke sounds for the acte: enter* Atticus, Doricus, *&* Phylomuse, *they sit a good while on the stage before the candles are lighted, talking together.*" As this direction suggests, Marston introduces dramatic action during the inter-act music as, for example, at the start of act 3: "*Enter* Francisco *halfe drest, in his black doublet and round cap, the rest riche,* Jacomo *bearing his hatte and feather,* Adrean *his doublet and band,* Randolfo *his cloake and staffe: they cloath* Francisco, *whilst* Bydet *creepes in and observes them. Much of this done whilst the acte is playing.*"

What You Will contributes to the poetomachia: "in the character of Lampatho Doria," Marston satirizes Jonson's *Cynthia's Revels* (Steggle 1998). Moreover, "Marston wrote his metatheatrical Induction fundamentally to distinguish his theoretical position on the nature of drama and its relationship to its audience from Jonson's" (Bednarz 2010a). Marston's was "the first play to lampoon Jonson in public" (Riggs 1989).

When You See Me, You Know Me, or The Famous Chronicle History of King Henry VIII. Samuel Rowley. Acted April-December 1604 (Wilson & Crow 1952); "played by" Prince Henry's Men, according to the TP, at the first Fortune (Gurr 2009c); the Admiral's Men were renamed Prince Henry's Men after James I's accession. ("[O]ver the Christmas period 1603/4, the Lord Admiral, Charles Howard, Earl of Nottingham, transferred his patronage of the Alleyn/Henslowe-run theatre company based at the Fortune Theatre in Golding Lane to Prince Henry" [Grant 2008].) The TP description of Rowley as "servant to the prince" implies that he "was a member of Prince Henry's company" (Greg 1939); "he no doubt played" a role (Astington 2010). "The most probable date of a first court performance" is late 1604; "the company played in front of the queen on 23 November and the prince on the 24th" (Grant). Edward Alleyn may have played King Henry. On 6 May 1632 nine men were apprehended in a Warrington [Lancashire] alehouse for acting a play called *Henry VIII*. . . . The play performed was presumably either Shakespeare's *Henry VIII* . . . or, more likely, Samuel Rowley's *When You See Me, You Know Me*" (George 1991).

SR 12 February 1605; transferred 21 May 1639. Q1 1605 *When You See Me, You Know Me, or The Famous Chronicle History of King Henry VIII, with the Birth and Virtuous Life of Edward, Prince of Wales*; not divided. The SDs are limited chiefly to entrances and exits but some SDs describe costume: "*Enter Will Sommers booted and spurred, blowing a horne*"; "*Enter the Cardinall reading a letter, Bonner in his Bishops roabes.*" Q2 1613 the TP features a woodcut, based on Holbein's famous painting, of a standing Henry VIII. Q3 1621. Q4 1632.

"The play resembles other generically hybrid plays produced around 1600 such as Heywood's *Edward IV, Parts I and II*, which intertwine material from chronicle history regarding the reign of Edward with an urban plot involving citizens of London, especially Matthew and Jane Shore" (Howard 2007). "Yet *When You See Me You Know Me* is primarily about diplomacy and display rather than wars, street brawls, or even pranks of wise fools, and in its focus on court politics it breaks from Elizabethan conventions to share the masque-like qualities identified with Shakespeare's Jacobean *Henry VIII*" (Nostbakken 1995).

The White Devil, or The Tragedy of Paolo Giordano Ursini, Duke of Brachiano, with the Life and Death of Vittoria Corombona, the Famous Venetian Courtesan. John Webster. Acted January-March 1612 (Gunby et al. 1995). By Queen Anne's Men, according to the Q1 TP, "almost certainly [at] the Red Bull" (Dollimore

& Sinfield 1983). Revived by Queen Henrietta Maria's Men at the Phoenix, according to the Q2 TP, 1630–31 (Williamson 2009). In a note on the last page, Q1 singles out for praise the performance of Richard Perkins, presumably as Flamineo, the first time an individual actor was so honored by specific mention (Brown 1966); this "singling out of Richard Perkins makes it tempting to think that Flamineo must have been seen as the central role" (Carnegie 1995b).

SR no original; transferred 10 February 1631; 15 September 1634; 15 February 1665; 8 April 1667. Q1 1612 HT *The Tragedy of Paulo Giordano Ursini, Duke of Brachiano, and Vittoria Corombona*; two dumb shows "produced by a magician" (Mehl 1965); a Latin verse by Martial "in stead of an epilogue"; not divided. Marginal stage directions were added to the text "perhaps while the first part was already being set by the printer" (Luckyj 2008). Dumb shows, which "make moments memorable, and lend events a particular emotional colour" (Carnegie 1995b), dramatize murder by ingenious means; characters kill Isabella by using a poisoned painting: "*Enter suspiciously,* Julio *and* Christophero, *they draw a curtaine wher* Brachian's *picture is, they put on spectacles of glasse, which cover their eyes and noses, and then burne perfumnes afore the picture*"; Isabella enters, "*kneeles downe as to prayers, then drawes the curtaine of the picture, doe's three reverences to it, and kisses it thrice, shee faints and will not suffer them to come nere it, dies.*" In a second show, Flamineo kills Camillo by staging what looks like an accident at a vaulting horse: "Flamineo *pitcheth him upon his necke.*" Similarly clever is the murder of Brachiano: "Lodovico *sprinckles* Brachiano's *bever* [faceguard of helmet] *with a poison*"; then, incapacitated, "Brachiano *is strangled.*" Later Brachiano's ghost enters "*in his leather cassock & breeches, bootes, a coule* [cowl], *a pot of lily-flowers with a scull in't.*" Flamineo is shot and his murderers "*tread upon him*"; "when villains are mercilessly trampled to death by angry characters who remind them of hell, the horrifying act may also suggest the infernal punishment of sinners, much as artists depict lost souls being trampled underfoot by demons of hell" (Diehl 1980). Webster's play contains a rare reference to a traverse, which is moved to reveal a disconcerting sight: "Cornelia, [Zanche] *the Moore and 3 other ladies discovered, winding* Marcello's *coar[p]se.*" Another unusual reference involves "*a cardinal on the tarras,*" "one of the few mentions in Elizabethan drama" (Reynolds 1940) of "a gallery or a series of windows or rooms that may have served . . . as private viewing rooms for the wealthy" (McDonald 2001); these correspond to the compartments above the stage in the De Witt drawing of the Swan. "[O]ne of the most spectacular sequences in the play" involves the barriers in the final act where various contestants fight (Carnegie 1995b); "for entertainment and display of prowess, duels were fought on foot across a waist-high barrier; the usual weapons were pike and sword" (Brown 1966). Q2 1631 "divers times acted, by the Queenes majesties servants, at the Phœnix." Q3 1665 *The White Devil, or Vittoria Corombona, A Lady of Venice, A Tragedy*; list of characters but "omits some minor characters and extras" (Dollimore & Sinfield); omits the closing paragraph, with its praise of Richard Perkins; five acts. Q4 1672 *Vittoria Corombona, or The White Devil, A Tragedy*; five acts and separate scenes.

The playwright attributes the failure of the original production to circumstance. In his Q1 address to the reader, Webster complains: "[the play] was acted, in so dull a time of winter, presented in so open and blacke a theater, that it wanted . . . a full and understanding auditory." Webster also criticizes unsophisticated playgoers at the Red Bull: "since that time I have noted, most of the people that come to that play-house, resemble those ignorant asses (who visiting stationers shoppes their use is not to inquire for good bookes, but new bookes)." But Webster "also acknowledges the skill of the actors whose performance of the play was 'the best that ever became them'"; "[t]his is important evidence for the potential disjunction of theatres and repertories in the period" (Straznicky 2006b). Of course, contributing to the failure of the first production may have been "Webster's radical experimentation with gender and genre, as well as his unorthodox moral complexities" (Luckyj).

Webster's address to the reader salutes his fellow playwrights: "I have ever truly cherisht my good opinion of other mens worthy labours, especially of that full and haightned stile of Maister *Chapman*: the labor'd and understanding workes of Maister *Johnson*: the no lesse worthy composures of the both worthily excellent Maister *Bea[u]mont*, & Maister *Fletcher*: and lastly . . . the right happy and copious industrie of M. *Shake-speare*, M. *Decker*, & M. *Heywood*, wishing what I write may be read by their light."

The White Ethiopian. Anonymous. Written *c.* 1650 (Randall 1995). The prologue, with reference to things heard, and the epilogue, with a bid for applause, suggest a play written for performance. But "the text is over 5,000 lines" (Schneider 2011).

London, BL, Harley MS 7313, fols. 1–139; no author named; list of characters; prologue and epilogue; chorus at end of each act; signs of considerable revision; four acts and separate scenes (incomplete). Ample SDs: *"Enter Thiamis solus, with his sword drawne & bloody"*; *"Enter old woman witch, weeping, and wringing her hands"*; *"Excursions, frightings, pursuits."*

The Whole Contention between the Two Famous Houses, York and Lancaster. See *2 Henry VI* and *3 Henry VI*.

The Whore of Babylon. Thomas Dekker. Acted January-June 1606 (Hoy 1980, Krantz 1995). "Acted by" Prince Henry's Men, according to the TP, at the first Fortune (Gurr 2009c). "Not a dramatic success" (Twyning 2004); "the audience may have found its dramaturgy too old-fashioned" (Price 1969). The play is "an allegorical response to the Gunpowder Plot figuring Elizabeth as 'Titania' and representing the Catholic threats to her life during her long reign" (Grant 2008). "*The Whore of Babylon* stands out as the most unstinting celebration of Elizabethan Protestant imperialism produced during the first decade of James's reign" (Perry 1997).

SR 20 April 1607. Q 1607 dramatis personae; prologue; five elaborate dumb shows; "signs of revision" undertaken during production (Hoy); not divided. "*The Whore of Babylon* is a highly artificial and 'theatrical' play, mirroring in its elaborate spectacles and speaking pageants its characters' preoccupations with artifice and shapeshifting" (Howard 1994b). Time initiates the first dumb show when he "*drawes a curtaine, discovering Truth in sad abiliments; uncrownd: her haire disheveld, & sleeping on a rock.*" "While Truth slumbers, a royal funeral procession [Queen Mary's], passing across the stage, causes Truth at last to awaken"; Truth is then "instantaneously transformed, Times somber mourning attire '*being shifted into light Cullors*'" (Massey 1998). Here symbolic staging gives "the drama an extra dimension by adding to the scenes of ordinary dialogue something in the nature of a morality play" (Mehl 1965). "A simple but forceful paradigm of the mask of moral corruption is found in *The Whore of Babylon* (1607) which opposes figures of Truth and Falsehood, distinguishing them solely by their faces: the directions for the dumbshow specify '*Falsehood* (attir'd as *Truth* is) her face spotted'" (Twycross & Carpenter 2002). Falsehood emerges from a "cave," possibly represented by a central opening in the tiring-house wall (Gurr & Ichikawa 2000), though Fitzpatrick 2011 argues that there were only two entry-points onto the stage. The staging represents a conflation of the symbolic and the realistic: "The action of this strange play takes us into an allegorical fairy world . . . among personifications and fairy-tale characters, but the spectator soon realizes that behind this allegorical guise a patriotic history play is being acted in which contemporary events are described and interpreted in terms of moral conflict" (Mehl 1969). Staging calls for the use of a trap when Campeius, a Friar, a Gentleman, and another enter in succession from below. And Falsehood, "*with her foot in severall places strikes the earth, and upriseth* Campeius, *a Frier with a boxe, a gentleman with a drawn sword, another with rich gloves in a boxe, another with a bridle*"; this SD may suggest multiple traps (Lawrence 1927). In a dumb show various prelates enter "*with images,*" presumably Catholic statuary. The play "concludes with a two-act re-creation of the Armada victory as a foreshadowing of James's triumph over the Gunpowder conspirators" (Watkins 2002): "*The seafight.*"

In his address to the reader, Dekker attacks the production at the Fortune by criticizing actors who subvert the intention of the playwright through poor acting: "let the poet set the note of his nombers, even to *Apolloes* own lyre, the player will have his owne crochets, and sing false notes, in despite of all the rules of musick. It fares with these two, as it does with good stuffe and a badde tayler: it is not mard in the wearing, but in the cutting out." In addition, Dekker, perhaps bristling from criticism that his chronology of events is faulty (Riely 1980), defends his right to reimagine history: "know that I write as a poet, not as an historian, and that these two doe not live under one law." "In using Spenser's distinction between poets and historians, Dekker is also echoing Sidney's *Defence*.

At the same time he is problematizing the relationship between himself and the players who perform his work" (Steggle 1998).

The Widow, A Comedy. Thomas Middleton (Lake 1975a); Archer makes the attribution. Acted *c.* 1616 (Levine 1975), "with great applause" by the King's Men at the [second] Blackfriars, according to the TP. "[A]pparently revived in the 1630s" (Taylor 2007b). The title "appears in a list of performances of plays by 'the Kings Companie at the Red Bull and the new house in Gibbon's Tennis Court near Clare Market'" (Adams 1918). In playlist of the King's Men 7 August 1641.

SR 12 April 1652 "by John Fletcher & Tho: Middleton." Q 1652 "printed by the originall copy"; the TP attributes the play to Jonson, Fletcher, and Middleton, whose names are bracketed (TP adds "the names of Fletcher and Jonson in order to make the play saleable" [Taylor 2004a]); list of characters; prologue and epilogue (both printed on same page at end); five acts and separate scenes. "The title-page ascription of Q 1652 is probably the responsibility not so much of the publisher, Humphrey Moseley, as of the actor Alexander Gough, the author of the preface 'To the Reader'" (Lake 1975a).

Middleton "expands the convention of the cross-dressed heroine in romantic comedy and evokes both female and male homoerotic imagery" (Walen 2005).

The Widow's Tears, A Comedy. George Chapman. Acted 1604 (Tricomi 1982). "Often presented" at the [second] Blackfriars and Whitefriars, according to the TP, by the Children of the Chapel, who moved from one venue to the other "toward the end of 1609" (Smeak 1966); "Chapman was exploiting the possibilities of a variety of playing spaces" (Burnett 2004). Revived at the Whitefriars, *c.* 1611 (Munro 2005); and at court, before Prince Charles, 27 February 1613, during the celebration of Princess Elizabeth's marriage to the Elector Palatine. The play "may later have been property of King's Men" (Munro).

SR 17 April 1612; transferred 11 June 1659. Q 1612 list of characters; five acts. "*The Widow's Tears* is profuse in stage directions. Some of them are extremely elaborate and mainly concerned with the outward appearance and behaviour of the characters, and several suggest that they may have been penned by the dramatist with his readers in mind" (Yamada 1975): "*Enter Lysander like a souldier disguisde at all parts, a halfe pike, gorget, &c. he discovers the tombe, lookes in and wonders, &c.*" The most interesting staging involves "the permanent presence of the door of the tomb" during the last scenes; this could have been accomplished either "by the use of a 'booth' structure set up against the tiring-house façade" or by "a space behind the open middle doorway" in that façade (Yamada). There are no fewer than six discoveries involving the tomb (Hosley 1975): e.g., "*Tomb opens, and Lysander within lies along, Cynthia and Ero*"; the direction indicates that the character "positioned within should be made visible to the audience" (Ichikawa 2005). Staging involves the descent of Hylus impersonating Hymen, probably by suspension gear: "*Musique: Hymen descends: and sixe Sylvanes enter beneath, with torches.*"

The play "makes mocking allusions to Scottish lords, new knights, monopolies, and jurisprudence, giving it a specific context in a wider Jamesian satiric polemic" (Burnett 2004).

A Wife for a Month. John Fletcher. Licensed for acting 27 May 1624 (Adams 1917). The date and "the attribution to Fletcher alone are based on Sir Henry Herbert's license" (Finkelpearl 1990). Acted by the King's Men at the second Globe. William Rowley probably played the role of Tony (Nicol 2008b). Revived at St. James's Palace, 9 February 1637 (bill of the King's Men for plays performed at court), in the Presence Chamber (Astington 1986). Principal actors were Joseph Taylor, Richard Robinson, Robert Benfield, John Underwood, Nicholas Tooley, and George Birch, according to F2. "The list is wrong in including Tooley, who had died almost a year before *A Wife for a Month* was licensed" (Turner 1985). In playlist of King's Men 7 August 1641.

SR 4 September 1646; transferred 30 January 1673. B&F F1 1647 *Comedies and Tragedies*; "never printed before, and now published by the authours originall copies"; prologue and epilogue; five acts and first scenes. Considerable evidence of revision (Turner). Spectacular staging includes "*Cupid descends, the Graces sitting by him, Cupid being bound the Graces unbinde him*"; "*Enter the maskers Fancy, Desire, Delight, Hope, Feare, Distrust, Jealousie, Care, Ire, Despaire, they dance, after which Cupid speakes*"; then "*Cupid and the Graces ascend in the chariot.*" "The low ceilings in the St James's chambers . . . would have prevented the use of descent machinery, so that the scenes were probably restaged as entries from the tiring house" (Astington 1999a); "a triumphal car" may have replaced the flying chariot (Astington 1986). The wedding masque scene "is quite extraordinary in its demands, since it appears to call for ten dancers in addition to sixteen actors, stretching the company beyond its usual limits" (Astington 1986). B&F F2 1679 *Fifty Comedies and Tragedies*; "published by the authors original copies, the songs to each play being added"; *A Wife for a Month, A Tragicomedy*; list of characters; actors' names.

The principal action involves a lecherous tyrant, who desires the virtuous Evanthe, a lady in waiting to the queen. She "flouts King Frederick by refusing his advances and insisting on marrying Valerio whom she loves." In turn, the king issues an ultimatum: if Evanthe and Valerio consummate their marriage, "Evanthe will instantly be put to death"; if Valerio "reveals his reason for abstention he too will die and be blamed as her murderer" (Clark 1994).

The Wild-Goose Chase, A Comedy. John Fletcher. Acted December–January 1621–22 (Lister 1980) during the Christmas revels at court; payment for performance recorded 24 January 1622 (*JCS*). This production "may well be a revival" (Bly 2000); "it is likely that Fletcher's play was performed publicly earlier that season"

(Chalmers et al. 2006). "Acted with singular applause" by the King's Men at the [second] Blackfriars, according to the 1652 TP. Revived 6 November 1632, at the Blackfriars, a benefit for Herbert: the play's "sustained popularity is indicated by Sir Henry Herbert's choosing it in 1632 as one of the two plays in a given year for which he received the proceeds of the second day after revival (the substantial sum of £15, in this case)" (McMullan 2004). Robert Benfield played DeGard; Richard Robinson, La Castre; Joseph Taylor, Mirabell; Thomas Pollard, Pinac; John Lowin, Belleur; William Penn, Nantolet; Eilert Swanston, Lugier; Stephen Hammerton, Oriana [the heroine]; William Trigg, Rosalura; Alexander Gough, Lillia-Bianca; John Shank, Servant to Lilia-Biancha (Bowers 1985); and John Honeyman, the Young Factor, according to dramatis personae of 1652. "[T]he cast list printed in the 1652 edition is impossible for 1621; Swanston and Penn had not yet joined the company in that year, and Stephen Hammerton had not yet been apprenticed as a boy actor"; "[t]he cast is probably that for a revival in the winter of 1632" (Bentley 1984). In playlist of King's Men 7 August 1641.

SR 4 September 1646 "by m^r Beamont & m^r fflesher"; 12 April 1652 "by Fra: Beaumont & John Fletcher"; 30 January 1673. Intended for publication in the B&F F1 1647 but not published therein. Humphrey Moseley explains, "[it] hath beene long lost, and I feare irrecoverable; for a person of quality borrowed it from the actours many yeares since, and (by the negligence of a servant) it was never return'd." F 1652 *The Wild-Goose Chase, A Comedy*; the TP attributes play to B&F, though the dedication by Lowin and Taylor names only Fletcher; "retriv'd for the publick delight of all the ingenious; and private benefit of John Lowin and Joseph Taylor . . . by a person of honour"; dramatis personae with descriptions of the characters; five acts and separate scenes. "This publication is one of the most handsome and elaborate issues of a single play in the time" (*JCS*); the F format allows this play to be bound with B&F F1. B&F F2 1679 *Fifty Comedies and Tragedies*; "published by the authors original copies, the songs to each play being added."

The 1652 dedication "to the honour'd few, lovers of drammatick poesie," by Lowin and Taylor alludes to the traumatic closing of the theaters in 1642: "'Tis not unknown unto you all, how by a cruell destinie we have a long time been mutes and bound, although our miseries have been sufficiently clamorous and expanded." The two former actors of the King's Men also salute the late Fletcher as "pride and life o'th'stage!"

Wiltshire Tom, An Entertainment at Court. A droll based on a court masque entitled *The King and Queen's Entertainment at Richmond* (1636), and acted in the 1640s and 50s at undetermined venue. "Mainly an excuse for some dancing and singing, *Wiltshire Tom* is of particular interest for its stage directions. . . . Unlike most drolls, this one calls for a painted backdrop" (Randall 1995). The reference to a backdrop suggests that "this piece was printed from the original edition and not from a droll-troupe's acting text" (Elson 1932). Eight or ten actors required.

Published in *2 The Wits, or Sport upon Sport* (Q and O 1673), which gives as venues of performance fairs, halls, taverns, and "mountebancks stages at Charing Cross, Lincolns-Inn-Fields, and other places"; list of characters. The title may have been inspired by a dance tune, "Wiltshire Tom's Delight" (Elson). In his preface to *2 The Wits*, Kirkman reports that Robert Cox "was not only the principal actor, but also the contriver and author of most of these farces." Kirkman's attribution is "probable" (Holland 2007).

Wily Beguiled. Anonymous. Acted late 1601–early 1602 (Maxwell 1922). Probably a revision of the lost *Wily-Beguily* (Cox 2000), performed at Merton College, Oxford, 3 January 1567 (Elliott et al. 2004). Possibly "the play was in its origin at least a Cambridge piece of the circle of Parnassus" (Greg 1912), but Bentley finds the play not "markedly academic" (*JCS*). Probably a university play adapted for a London audience. "[B]ased on *Grim the Collier*" (Gurr 2009c). The suggestion has been made that the play was "part-written by Samuel Rowley, which would have made it an Admiral's or Prince's play, but its epilogue specifies performance in 'a circled round,' which indicates that it was not composed for the Fortune. Other signs suggest that it was probably not for the Rose either" (Gurr 2009c).

SR 12 November 1606; transferred 12 October 1629; 8 March 1636; 23 March 1639. Q1 1606 *A Pleasant Comedy Called Wily Beguiled, The Chief Actors Are These: A Poor Scholar, A Rich Fool, and A Knave at a Shift*; no author named; list of characters; induction including two prologues; epilogue; not divided. "[A]n ingenious surprise is sprung upon the spectator at the outset. The Prologue and the Player enter simultaneously, and the former asks the latter, 'How now my honest rogue; what play shall we have here to-night?' He gets as reply, 'Sir, you may look upon the title.' He glances at the [title] board, and, more in the role of spectator than of Prologue, says, with some petulance, 'What *Spectrum* once again?'" (Lawrence 1912b). Later "'*Spectrum* is conveied away: and *Wily beguiled*, stands in the place of it'" (*JCS*). "The text of the play is liberally supplied with directions for stage business" (Jewkes 1958): *"Enter Lelia* and Nurse *gathering of flowers"*; *"Enter . . . a boy with wine and a napkin . . . He fills the wine & gives them napkins.*" Characters include the con man Robin Goodfellow, "a devil only in disguise, which he uses to frighten the gullible" (Cox 2000). Staging recalls the traditional association of the devil with a prominent nose: "Ile put me on my great carnation nose" (Craik 1958). Q2 1614 omits epilogue. Q3 1623. Q4 1630. Q5 1635. Q6 1638 two issues. Q7 ND ?1653. The publication history suggests that the play was "much more popular in [its] own day than in ours" (Bruster 2004).

The Q1 prologue begins by complaining of actors unready for performance: "What hoe, where are these paltrie plaiers? Stil poaring in their papers and never perfect? for shame come forth, your audience stay so long, their eies waxe dim with expectation."

Wine, Beer, and Ale, Together by the Ears, A Dialogue. Anonymous. Probably acted 1624–26, perhaps by students at Cambridge University (Hanford 1915). "*JCS* makes an argument for Cambridge, though the evidence is admittedly slim" (Nelson 1989). "The many scraps of Latin quotation . . . and other bits of humorous pedantry, like the derivation of Ale from *alo*, are indicative of academic origin" (Hanford 1913). "It appears to have been designed for representation, and its allusions in the text to London, and its lively setting as if in a tavern, suggest that it may have been revised for the London stage" (Foakes 1985).

Edinburgh, UK, University of Edinburgh, MS Laing iii.493, fols. 57–66; no TP. SR no original; transferred 15 July 1662 *Wyne, Beere, Ale, & Tobacco, contending for superiority*. O1 1629 "written first in Dutch by Gallobelgicus, and faithfully translated out of the originall copie, by Mercurius Brittanicus" ("the play is no translation from the Dutch but an original product of English wit" [Hanford 1915]); list of characters; not divided. O1 ends with a tantalizing SD: "*A daunce, wherein the severall natures of them all is figured and represented.*" Q2 1630 *Wine, Beer, Ale, and Tobacco, Contending for Superiority, A Dialogue*; "the second edition, much enlarged"; the pseudonyms are omitted from the TP; this edition adds an episode about tobacco. Q3 1658 same title as Q2; list of characters. Facing the Q3 TP is a woodcut showing a man and three women playing dice at an inn; "it clearly has nothing to do with the text of the dialogue, and was presumably added by the printer to suggest a tavern atmosphere" (Foakes).

Included in Kirkman's 1661 catalogue. The entertainment seems related to *Band, Cuff, and Ruff* as well as to *Work for Cutlers* (Hanford 1915).

The Winter's Tale. William Shakespeare. Acted 1609 (Wells & Taylor 1987, Butler 2005), or 1611 (Orgel 1996), or "by May 1611" (Pitcher 2010) by the King's Men at the first Globe/second Blackfriars. "Probably the first of his plays performed at the Blackfriars" (McMullan 2000), though the Globe is equally likely as a venue; the King's Men began playing at the Blackfriars at "some point after January 1610" (Barroll 2005). Simon Forman records seeing a performance at the Globe, 15 May 1611 (Oxford, Bodleian, MS Ashmole 208, fols. 201–2); "Forman probably found Autolycus more intriguing and amusing than any other aspect of the play" (Whitney 2006); the role was probably played by Robert Armin (Butler 2004a). Forman was concerned "not at all with the great reawakening and reconciliation scene at the play's end" (Traister 2001). "The boy actor who played Hermione's young son Mamillius could also have played, in the second half of the play, Hermione's daughter Perdita—thus reuniting, in the harmonies of the play's ending, mother and lost child" (Taylor 2002b). John Rice may have played Hermione (Astington 2010). Possibly revised after Forman saw the play (Bergeron 1978, Snyder 2002); such revision may have included the revival of Hermione, which is not mentioned by Forman, who also fails to mention a bear onstage; but "Forman is not a reliable witness" (Pitcher). Performed also at court, probably in the Banqueting House, on 5 November 1611 (Revels Account); at court as "part of the nuptial festivities surrounding the marriage of Princess Elizabeth to the Elector Palatine on 14 February 1613" (Snyder & Curren-Aquino 2007), payment to John Heminges dated 20 May 1613; at court, before the king, Easter Tuesday, 7 April 1618 (payment to Heminges dated 20 April), probably in the Banqueting House (Wickham 1972); ?at court, "probably in the season 1619–20 (King 1992a). Relicensed by Herbert, 19 August 1623 (Adams 1917). Performed at Whitehall, 18 January 1624, "in the kings absence"; and at Whitehall, the night of 16 January 1634; Herbert reports the play was "likt" (Adams). When he relicensed the play, Herbert wrote: "An olde playe called *Winter's Tale*, formerly allowed of by Sir George Bucke, and likewyse by mee on Mr. Hemmings his worde that there was nothing profane added or reformed, thogh the allowed booke was missinge" (Bawcutt 1996). The original MS with Buc's license attached was "possibly lost in the Globe fire of 1613" (Dutton 1991).

SR 8 November 1623; transferred ?4 August 1626 Paviers right in Shakesperes *plaies*; ?19 June 1627 widow of Isaac Jaggard . . . her parte in Shackspheere *playes*; 16 November 1630; 1 July 1637 Shakespeares *workes* their Part; 6 August 1674; 21 August 1683. F1 1623 *Comedies, Histories, & Tragedies*; three issues; "published according to the true originall copies"; list of characters at end; five acts and separate scenes; however, the play "has an obvious and daring two-part structure" (Hirsh 2002). The hinge on which the play turns is the appearance of Time as chorus: he wears wings, carries an hourglass, possibly even a scythe, and may be bald and bearded (Kiefer 1999); when he upends his hourglass, he calls attention to the play's structural division. If Time has the legs of an animal, they are those of a deer not a goat (Kiefer 2003). F1 contains what is perhaps the most celebrated SD in Shakespeare: "*Exit pursued by a beare.*" This was perhaps a real bear, not a man in a bear costume (Reynolds 1959, Callaghan 2000, Grant 2001), though Lawrence 1935, Pitcher 1994, and Orgel 1996 are skeptical. Possibly "for at least the first few performances of the play" the bear was real (Barton 1994). "Shakespeare's bear remains an enigma" (Ravelhofer 2002). "What did that moment really feel like for early modern audiences at the Globe or Blackfriars?" (Dillon 2010); we simply don't know. Staging of the sheepshearing festival, presided over by Perdita dressed as Flora, involves "*a daunce of shepheards and shephearddesses,*" as well as a "*dance of twelve satyres.*" The shepherds' dance belongs to Bohemia, "a place where dance and song go naturally with celebrations" (Brissenden 1981). (An anomaly of the play is that "Bohemia, famously, and in defiance of ordinary geography, is given a 'seacoast'" [Garber 2004].) The satyrs' dance "seems to have been borrowed from Ben Jonson's *Masque of Oberon*, acted at court on 1 January 1611, but its irrelevance there and the awkwardness with which it it is introduced by the surrounding dialogue suggests that this may be a late interpolation, indicating that the play was written before Jonson's masque rather than after it" (Dobson 2001); the satyrs' dance "was one of acrobatics" (Wright 1928), a symbol of "unruled passions" (Brissenden).

A stunning stage effect is the "statue" of Hermione coming to life, an incident not found in the playwright's source. "In the 'discovery space' at Globe or Blackfriars, Hermione's curtained environs would resemble the Easter sepulcher structure in church architecture" (Marsalek 2007). Shakespeare "went out of his way to make the audience believe in the Queen's death so that we might share fully in Leontes's sense of wonder at the miracle of the statue that comes to life" (Foster 2004). "The actor counterfeiting the statue presumably stands either in a doorway of the tiring-house or in a central alcove, a curtain drawn across the opening" (Kiefer 2007). Sound effects accompany the transformation: "Musick; awake her"; "the music is essential to the explicitly theatrical magic that the scene enacts" (Lindley 2006). Hermione's transformation is "masque-like" (Gossett 1988). F2 1632 "the second impression"; three issues. F3 1663 "the third impression"; reissued 1664 with seven additional plays. F4 1685 "the fourth edition"; two issues.

"In the late nineteenth century Edward Dowden became the first to classify *The Winter's Tale* and those final plays usually grouped with it (*Pericles*, *Cymbeline*, and *The Tempest*) as romances" (Snyder & Curren-Aquino). Dowden 1877 explains: "winter's tales were strange and fanciful oral narratives intended to while away the long, cold hours of the dark nights of winter and, therefore, not meant to be taken seriously or to withstand the rigours of logical interrogation." But the play "is a far cry from winter folk tales imagined by Mamillius or told by old women at the fireside. As this instance exemplifies, Shakespeare's dramaturgy can be seen as either a transformed tribute to popular culture and folk wisdom, or a sophisticated displacement of them" (Henderson 2007).

Wisdom (*Mind, Will, and Understanding*). Anonymous; possibly written by a monk of Bury St. Edmund's, Norfolk, named [?Thomas] Hyngham, who once owned the MS (Coldewey 2008), though there is no record of performance there. Acted *c.* 1490–1500 and earlier (Baker et al. 1982) at undetermined venue. Perhaps performed as early as 1460–70 (Grantley 2007). May have been "intended for school performance" (Chambers 1945). May "have been written for St. Edmundsbury Abbey"; "seems intended both for monastic and more general audiences" (Bevington 1962). Possibly "commissioned from the abbey by some local magnate" (Johnston 1986). "*Wisdom* is a banquet play; it is masque-like; and it was probably played before an aristocratic audience which included some religious" (Riggio 1986). The audience would also have included lawyers (Klausner 2007). This "is very much the sort of play we should expect to be staged in a great household" (Westfall 2004). Possibly performed by a professional troupe (Baker 1986). "The play does not have a great deal of narrative action, but there is much ceremony and dance" (Grantley). "There is much opportunity in *Wisdom* for elaborate costumes and stately processions" (Houle 1972); the costumes "are meticulously described because it is a morality with masque-like qualities, where the costume is meant to speak emblematically" (Twycross 1983). *Wisdom* "is one of the most theatrically interesting of the morality plays, simply in terms of stage directions and display" (Coldewey 1993). The play "derives its theatrical form from the visualizing of metaphor, from the concretizing of homiletic and scriptural proposition" (Bevington 1986). "Christ (or Wisdom) wears purple, cloth of gold and ermine, and has a crown, orb, and sceptre. This costume . . . represents absolute worth and majesty" (Craik 1958). "Unusually among the morality plays, *Wisdom* raises significant issues of gender" (Klausner 2009). This play "differs from the other Macro plays in several respects, but none more startling than the portrayal of the 'every*man*' character as an aristocratic woman, the queen of heaven and consort of Christ" (Riggio 1998).

(1) Oxford, Bodleian, MS Digby 133, fols. 158–69; a fragment containing 755 lines (Coldewey 2008); no title; not divided. "Though there are no scene-divisions marked in either manuscript, the play falls into four distinct phases" (Davenport 1982). The Digby MS is probably the older of the two MSS (Riggio 1998). (2) Washington, Folger, MS V.a.354, fols. 14–37; no title; not divided. The Folger MS, formerly called the Macro MS, named for Cox Macro of Bury St. Edmunds, seems to have been written *c.* 1465–70; the SDs in this MS are especially detailed and the text is complete; "at the center of the play . . . lies an elaborate dumbshow demonstrating how debauchery of the world has personal, political, and social consequences" (Coldewey 1993). "Anima's change of appearance" signals "her fall into sin"; "small boys dressed as devils run in and out from under her foul mantle" (Grantley 2007). The dramatic action is characterized by three symbolic dances: they are "the most striking representations of vice in the early drama. The tradition from which they stem is that of court pageants and entertainments, which, like the 'subtleties' of court banquets, were often allegorical" (Davenport). "The masked dances, although wholly detachable from the rest of the play, vividly express its themes with the elaborate masks flamboyantly presenting moral ideas" (Twycross & Carpenter 2002). At the play's conclusion "Wisdom appears as a figure like the devotional images illustrating Christ in the late Middle Ages" (Davidson 1989).

The Digby MS version was first published by Sharp 1835, and the Macro version was, in part, published by Turnbull 1837; Furnivall 1896 edited the Digby version [reprinted 1930]; Furnivall & Pollard 1904, the Macro version; Eccles 1969, the Macro MS; Baker et al. 1982 edited the Digby MS. The play has been variously named. "Sharp in 1835 called the play *Mind, Will, and Understanding*; Furnivall in 1882 called it *A Morality of Wisdom, Who is Christ* and referred to it as *Wisdom*" (Eccles). Bevington 1972 prepared an edition with facsimiles and transcriptions on facing pages. Riggio 1998 published "an eclectic text rather than a faithful transcription of either the Digby or the Macro" MS; it is essentially a version of of the Macro MS, collated with Digby, and with a modern translation on facing pages.

The Wisdom of Doctor Dodypoll. Anonymous. Acted 1599 (Gurr 2009d) or early 1600 (Matson 1964). "Sundrie times acted" by Paul's Boys, according to the SR and TP, at Paul's playhouse. "Appears to call for a cast of twenty-one players" (Knutson 2001).

SR 7 October 1600; transferred 5 January 1616; 4 September 1638. Q 1600 no author named; five acts (but the heading for act 3 is missing). "The play's most alluring stage image is that of the artist painting a woman. This is *Dodypoll's* central image — a kind of romantic fantasy — that achieves its power through the complementary union of stage picture and painting tropes" (Tassi 2005); at the play's opening the disguised Earl Lassingbergh "*is discovered (like a painter) painting* Lucilia, *who sits working on a piece of cushion worke.*" Another SD indicates the presence of a miniature portrait: "*Enter* Cornelia *sola, looking upon the picture of Alberdure in a little jewell*"; "Alberdure [is] a composite of Albrecht Dürer's name" (Tassi). In this and other plays "unrequited lovers take the beloved's pictures to bed with them" (Rochester 2010).

"The brevity of the play combined with the fullness of incident may suggest condensation of a longer work" (Matson).

The Wise Man of West Chester. See *John a Kent and John a Cumber.*

The Wise Woman of Hogsdon, A Comedy. Thomas Heywood. Acted *c.* 1603–05 (Leonard 1980). "Sundry times acted with great applause," according to the TP, by Worcester's/Queen Anne's Men, probably at the Curtain (Reynolds 1940) or Red Bull (Bentley 1981). Possibly written for performance at court in December 1604 (Merchant 1996).

SR 12 March 1638. Q 1638 dramatis personae; five acts and separate scenes. "The title character in Heywood's comedy, although denounced as a witch by dissolute young gallants, turns out to be the agent for effecting their reform and bringing about the desired resolution of the plot" (Rackin 2006).

The last page prints Samuel King's poem "To his chosen friend, the learned author Mr Thomas Heywood": "So thy works will show. / The debt, I pay 's no more but what I owe."

The Wisest Have Their Fools about Them. Anonymous. Acted late 1620s, possibly at the Inns of Court, or a university, or a civic banquet; the play "was intended, and even prepared," for performance (Baldwin 2001).

Chelmsford, UK, Cheshire and Chester Archives, MS DCR/27/8; damaged; no TP; some missing and/or incomplete lines; five acts and separate scenes. Ample SDs. First edited by Baldwin, who provides the conjectural title; the play was previously known as *Musophilus* (the name of a major character).

Wit and Folly. See *Witty and Witless.*

Wit and Science (Anonymous). See *The Marriage of Wit and Science*.

Wit and Science. John Redford. Written between 1535 and 1547 (Pettigrew 2004). "[D]esigned to be performed before Henry VIII and his court" and staged at an undetermined time and place (Norland 1995), or perhaps "a school drama for boys" (Pettigrew); written "presumably" for performance by the boys of Redford's choir-school (Mills 2007). The number of female characters "suggests a choir-school boys' play" (Southern 1973). "Possibly written for the Paul's choristers when Redford was their master" (Lancashire 2002). The play is "innocently and totally involved in a boys' world of education, tedium, and the need for relaxation" (Bevington 1968). "The play requires a minimum of eleven actors, even with doubling" (Grantley 2004); Redford creates "four significant female roles" (Norland). Later adapted and performed by Paul's Boys, perhaps at court, 1567–68, with the title *The Marriage of Wit and Science*.

London, BL, Additional MS 15233; no TP but the colophon reads, "Thus endyth the Play of Wit and Science"; "[t]he beginning of the play is missing" (Scherb 2005); ends with a prayer and song; not divided. The text provides "no stage directions" (Vaughan 2005), but two properties help Wit in his pursuit of Science: a portrait of Wit and the mirror of Reason (Tassi 2005). The play "may require a den for Tediousness (perhaps a decorated doorway) and some representation of Mount Parnassus" (Bevington 1973). While Wit sleeps, the Vice Idleness blackens his face (Hornback 2009b). "Face-blackening and face-spotting are . . . used to symbolically transform the face to indicate sin" (Drew-Bear 1994). "Wit boasts of his ability to dance; the minstrels pipe up, and Wit gives a galliard" (Wright 1928). Redford "makes extensive and subtle use of musical effects" (Westfall 1990). Costumes have an important symbolic function: when Wit removes his scholar's garment, "we are to understand this as self-betrayal. He soon falls asleep in the arms of Idleness and is there dressed in a Fool's robe. After he is beaten by Shame he repents, and Reason takes away the Fool's robe and gives him back his gown" (Mowat 1981). "Tediousness is called 'the feend' and has a 'vyser over hys hed,' this false head being brought in (like Macbeth's) by his triumphant slayer" (Craik 1958).

Possibly published in the sixteenth century, though no copy survives; the SR records a play entitled *the maryage of Wytt and Scyence, c.* 1569–70. "[I]ts plot was well enough known to be borrowed by at least two later dramatists," the authors of *The Marriage of Wit and Science* and *The Marriage between Wit and Wisdom* (Potter 1980). First edited by Halliwell[-Phillipps] 1848b. Modern edition by Brown, Greg & Wilson 1951.

Wit and Wisdom. See *The Marriage between Wit and Wisdom*.

Wit at Several Weapons. Perhaps originally written by John Fletcher and then revised by Thomas Middleton and William Rowley (Hoy 1960). Acted 1613 (Lake

1975a) or later (Jackson 1979), probably by Prince Charles's Men (Nicol 2006a), perhaps at the Curtain (Gurr 2009d). Possibly John Fletcher "wrote the original version for the Queen's Revels; in 1613 the playbook shifted to Lady Elizabeth's Men; and around 1614 or so, following the merger of Lady Elizabeth's Men with the Prince's Men, Middleton and Rowley undertook a revision of the play" (Nicol). "If the play is based on an earlier one by Fletcher, the clown role [Pompey Doodle, played by William Rowley] is probably a product of the revisers" (Nicol 2008b). The F1 prologue, written for a revival, speaks of the play's original reception: "'Twas well receiv'd before, and we dare say, / You now are welcome to no vulgar play." "It was certainly popular enough to be still in the live repertory some six or seven years after its première, when its title . . . appears at the top of a fragmentary list of plays jotted down on scrap paper by the Master of the Revels" (Dobson 2007).

SR not included in the entry for 4 September 1646; 29 June 1660; 30 January 1673. B&F F1 1647 *Comedies and Tragedies*; "never printed before, and now published by the authours originall copies"; epilogue "at the reviving of this play" (but the speech "is in fact a prologue" [Schneider 2011]); five acts and first scenes. Unusually, the play employs a masque as "a trick: by means of its cover, marriages are quickly huddled up under the very noses of the disapproving elders" (Gossett 1988). B&F F2 1679 *Fifty Comedies and Tragedies*; "published by the authors original copies, the songs to each play being added"; *Wit at Several Weapons, A Comedy*; list of characters.

The play "marked Middleton's collaborative début with William Rowley, the fat and jolly leading comic actor of Prince Charles's Men (who merged with Lady Elizabeth's company at about this time)" (Taylor 2004b).

Wit in a Constable, A Comedy. Henry Glapthorne. The lost original version may have been performed at the Phoenix by Queen Henrietta Maria's Men before May 1636, or by Beeston's Boys after October 1637. The revised version, 1639 (Hosley 1961), was "lately acted . . . with good allowance" by Beeston's Boys at the Phoenix, according to the TP. The revision was apparently responsible for such anomalies as characters' change of names.

SR 27 April 1640; transferred 17 February 1648 (Greg has 27 February). Q 1640 "printed as it was lately acted"; "written 1639"; list of characters; prologue and epilogue; five acts. The prologue was spoken by an actor wearing a distinctive costume as "armed" (Stern 2004b): "You need not feare me gentlemen, although / I come thus arm'd."

The Wit of a Woman. ?Anthony Munday (Morgan 1966). Possibly "written for Pembroke's Men to play while on a foreign tour in 1598" (Tassi 2005). Acted before 1604 (Chambers 1923) at undetermined venue. "It may have been a children's play, since it is a light comedy, based upon puns and name reversals, and there is dancing at several points; however, there is no proof that it was ever acted by one of the regular children's companies" (Jewkes 1958). The play "is in prose throughout, like almost all the plays written for the boy companies after Lyly, and has parts for thirteen men, six of them young and seven old, and seven women, two old and five young" (Gurr 2009c).

SR none. Q 1604 [octavo-in-fours] *A Pleasant Comedy, Wherein Is Merrily Shown, The Wit of a Woman*; no author named; list of characters; prologue and epilogue; not divided, despite the designation of act 1, scene 1. Ample SDs: e.g., "*Enter servants with nose-gaies, cakes and wine*"; "*Enter Bizardo with the Vintners boy, Gero, halfe dronke, and the wine.*" A painter "is discovered exhibiting several of his works," probably "visible wall paintings" (Elam 2010). When Isabella says, "You are a painter of the new fashion," she "most likely refers to the perspective art practiced by continental masters" (Tassi 2005).

Wit without Money, A Comedy. John Fletcher. Written 1611 (McMullan 1994). Acted by Lady Elizabeth's Men (McMullan 2004) at undetermined venue. "The play seems to have been revised in 1620" (Hoy 1987a) or perhaps *c.* 1625 (Gabler 1985). "Presented with good applause" by Queen Henrietta Maria's Men at the Phoenix, according to the Q1 TP, 10 June 1635; and by Beeston's Boys at St. James's Palace, 14 February 1637 (Adams 1917), in the Presence Chamber (Astington 1986). In playlist of Beeston's Boys 10 August 1639. Performed at the Red Bull, 3 February 1648, in defiance of the act forbidding playing (Clare 2002), possibly by a group of actors headed by John Lowin (Butler 2004e). During performance on 30 December 1654, the theater was raided: "The players at the Red Bull were on the last Saturday despoiled of their acting cl[o]ths by some of the soldiery, they having not so ful a liberty as they pretended" (*Kingdom's Weekly Intelligencer,* 26 December–2 January).

SR 25 April 1639. Q1 1639 TP names Beaumont and Fletcher; list of characters; five acts and first scenes. Q2 1661 "the second impression, corrected"; TP names B&F. The final page of Q2 provides a list of seventeen plays by B&F "printed in Quarto." B&F F2 1679 *Fifty Comedies and Tragedies*; "published by the authors original copies, the songs to each play being added"; list of characters. Few SDs apart from entrances and exits.

The Witch. Thomas Middleton. "Written between 1610 and 1615" (Orgel 2002); "likely written in late 1613 or early 1614" (Yachnin 1999); "1615–16" (Schafer 1994); "the middle of 1616" (O'Connor 2007). Acted early 1616 (Esche 1993). By the King's Men at the [second] Blackfriars, according to the first folio of the MS, which reports, "long since acted by his majesties servants at the Black-Friers"; *The Witch* "may have opened the Blackfriars Theater in 1610" (Kinney 2001). The production "was a failure" (Greg & Wilson 1948). The play was "perhaps suppressed (because of its allusions to the Overbury trials)" (Taylor 2004b). Hecate may have been played by Robert Armin or by Richard Robinson, who replaced him (Wickham 1973).

Oxford, Bodleian, MS Malone 12, fols. 1–95; *A Tragicomedy called The Witch*; "by Tho. Middleton"; a presentation MS (Briggs 1998) copied by Ralph Crane 1624–25 (Jowett 2007e); list of characters on the TP; five acts and separate scenes. Two songs from *The Witch* also appear in a Shakespearean tragedy originally written several years earlier: they "were inserted into a pre-Folio revival of *Macbeth* to catch the prevailing fashion for theatrical spectacle" (Corbin & Sedge 1986). Staging seems to call for flying machinery (for the witches); SDs indicate the descent of a spirit in the form of "*a catt* [Malkin] *(playing on a fidle)*"; "the noise of the machinery facilitating this descent is covered in its turn by the off-stage choir" (Wickham 1973); later the spirit reascends with Hecate. Another SD stipulates the exit of the witches: "*Here they daunce ye witches dance, & exit.*" Intriguing SDs: "*Enter Heccat: & other witches: (with properties, and habitts fitting)*"; the properties and costumes are not described and must be inferred (Kiefer 2003), though O'Connor 2002, finding "implicit stage directions," suggests that in Hecate's first scene she has an infant corpse, snakeskins, "and a brass dish or cauldron into which Hecate is seen to squeeze venom from the snakes." *The Witch* is "the most informative play of the period on the topic of contemporary witchcraft" (Reed 1965). The play was "printed in 1778 by John Nichols at the expense of Isaac Reed" (O'Connor 2007); George Steevens edited this edition (Esche). Edited by Dyce 1840. Modern editions by Corbin & Sedge 1986, O'Connor 2007.

In his dedicatory epistle, Middleton calls the play "this (ignorantly ill-fated) labour of mine. Witches are (ipso facto) by the law condemn'd, & that onely (I thinck) hath made her lie so-long in an imprison'd-obscuritie." This may allude to the divorce case involving Frances Howard and Robert Devereux, Earl of Essex, who claimed that his impotence with his wife was due to *maleficium* (witchcraft). If so, the neglect of Middleton's play may have been due to censorship (Lancashire 1983).

The Witch of Edmonton: A Known True Story, A Tragicomedy. William Rowley, Thomas Dekker, and John Ford (Pierce 1912b). The Q TP adds "&c" to the names of the three "well-esteemed poets," suggesting the possibility of other authors; the TP "might well refer to Middleton, or Webster, or both" (Jackson & Taylor 2007). Acted April-December 1621 (Onat 1980). Acted "with singular applause," by Prince Charles's Men, according to the TP, at the Phoenix; performed also by that company at Whitehall, 29 December 1621, according to the Inner Temple Library MS 515, no. 7 (Nicol 2006a), during the Christmas revels. Revived by Queen Henrietta Maria's Men at the Phoenix before 1638 (Kathman 2005). Rowley acted "the exuberantly infectious, endearing, dog-loving rustic ass Cuddy Banks, one of the funnier clown roles of the English Renaissance" (Hornback 2009b). The TP specifies performance "once at court" and "often at the Cock-Pit in Drury-Lane [i.e., the Phoenix]."

SR 21 May 1658 *The witch of Edmonton*, A Tragi-comedy. Q 1658 *The Witch of Edmonton: A Known True Story, Composed into a Tragicomedy*; "never printed till now"; list of characters; brief argument (a couplet); prologue "written for a revival" by Theophilus Bird at the Phoenix (Gurr 1988a) c. 1635 (*JCS*); epilogue by "Phen.," apparently Ezekiel Fenn (Greg 1939), possibly "a late addition" (Wiggins 2008); five acts and separate scenes. Special effects include "*thunder and lightning*." Staging seems to call for a trap when Mother Sawyer stamps on the ground and a dog appears; "the usual cue for the opening of a trap was a stamp of the foot" (Lawrence 1927). Q is characterized by "irregular and often omitted" SDs (Kinney 1998) but a few are detailed: "*She gone, he searches first one, then the other pocket. Knife found. Dog runs off. He lies on one side: the spirit of Susan his second wife comes to the beds side. He stares at it; and turning to the other side, it's there too.*" Staging includes a Morris dance "invaded by Dog who strips Sawgut the fiddler from his sweet music and ends the dance in chaos" (Kinney). "This is the stuff of popular drama both in its representation of actual popular festivity and in its vivid theatrical effects" (McLuskie 1994); a group of clowns "dance, posture, and engage in buffoonery" (Wright 1928). "The 1658 quarto would appear to derive not from the original production but from a revival of the play in the mid 1630s as is evidenced by the prologue and references to the actors, [Theophilus] Bird, [W.] Hamluc and [Ezekiel] Fenn" (Corbin & Sedge 1986). The Q TP features a woodcut depicting three figures: the devil in the form of a black dog; Mother Sawyer, the witch; and Cuddy Banks, the clown. "There is no reason to think the woodcut made for the title-page has any reference to the theater" (Foakes 1985).

The play "was based on the story of Elizabeth Sawyer who was tried and condemned as a witch and executed at Tyburn only weeks before the play took to the stage" (McLuskie 1994). "*The Witch of Edmonton* comes as close as any English Renaissance drama to social protest" (Cantor 1987b). The play "is unusual in that the dramatists deliberately discredit supernatural causation by treating witchcraft as a complex social construction" (Comensoli 1996). "Elizabeth is presented more as a victim than a criminal; she effectively turns the accusation of witchcraft back onto those who have injured her" (Findlay 1999). The play may have been occasioned by "a spectacular, contemporary political crisis that went to the heart of James's court—the Frances Carr scandal," which involved a claim that her previous marriage to the Earl of Essex had been unconsummated because her husband had been bewitched (Hutchings & Bromham 2008).

The Witches of Lancashire. See *The Late Lancashire Witches.*

Wit's Triumvirate, or The Philosopher. Probably written by William Cavendish (Kelliher 1993). "[N]o record of its being staged either in the public theatre or at court" (Hulse 1996). Possibly acted *c.* late 1634-March 1636 (Nelson 1975). "Acted, or intended to be acted, before Charles and Henrietta Maria at some time during the winter of 1635–6" (Kelliher). The wording of both prologues, "the second of which is addressed to Charles I and Henrietta Maria in 1635, suggests that the play was written with performance in mind" (Hulse 1996), possibly by a professional company (Nelson). However, all the characters are male, and "this masculine casting would be unique in a play produced in the London theater"; an audience that would find such "casting acceptable would be a University or school audience" (Nelson). The author was probably "a young gentleman recently down from the University," who, like other young gentlemen, "invaded the professional theatre in the 1630's" (Schoenbaum 1964b).

London, BL, Additional MS 45865, fols. 1–96; no author named; list of characters; two prologues and two epilogues, one set for the king and queen; marginal revisions in Cavendish's hand (Kelliher); five acts and separate scenes. The MS TP, containing the prologue addressed to the royal couple, is dated 1635; this may be the date of composition or the date of transcription. SR 12 February 1677. The play "is modeled on *The Alchemist*" (Davidson 1978). First edited by Nelson 1975.

The Wits, A Comedy. William Davenant. Initially, the play was not licensed for performance by Henry Herbert, who objected to some of the language, but the king interceded. On 10 January 1634, Herbert returned to Davenant the playbook, which had been "corrected by the kinge." King Charles was apparently more indulgent than Herbert on the matter of oaths in drama, for he determined that "faith" and "slight" were "asseravations only, and no oathes" (Adams). Licensed for acting 19 January 1634 (Adams 1917, Edmond 1987). "Presented by" the King's Men at the [second] Blackfriars, according to the Q and O TPs. Performed at the Blackfriars, 22 January 1634 (diary of Humphrey Mildmay). Performed also at court, before the king and queen, the night of 28 January 1634 (Adams); Herbert reports that it was "well likt" and adds, "It had a various fate on the stage, and at court, though the kinge commended the language, but dislikt the plott and characters" (Adams).

SR 4 February 1636; transferred 7 November 1646. Q 1636 two issues; list of characters; prologue and epilogue; five acts. The play, which anticipates "key elements of Restoration theatre" (Corns 2007), was again published in the 1660s and 1670s. O 1665 *Two Excellent Plays* (with *The Platonic Lovers*). Davenant "dramatizes the consequences of the movement of country gentry to the town"; "[t]he country, portrayed in pastoral terms, is England's backbone, the seat of traditional values, and in it those gentry who have estates to manage—men of substance—rightly belong. In town, on the other hand, good sense can make a living and even thrive" (Bulman 2003). F 1673 *The Works*; "now published out of the authors originall copies"; prologue and epilogue at Blackfriars; prologue and epilogue at the Duke's Theater.

The Q prologue alludes to the shape of the Blackfriars: "Conceave now too, how much, how oft each eare / Hath surfeited in this our hemispheare." This remark "indicates that the Blackfriars auditorium was semicircular in plan, even though polygonal rather than actually rounded in detail" (Orrell 1988).

Witty and Witless (Wit and Folly). John Heywood (authorship suggested by the play's stylistic features). Acted 1525-*c.* 1530s (Happé 1991); "Heywood envisaged a performance at court" (Walker 1998). "[P]robably written or revived for a performance before the King in 1533" (Walker 2005). Requires three actors (Lancashire 2002).

London, BL, Harley MS 367, fols. 110–19; lacks title and beginning; ends with prayers; not divided. The play "has a detachable epilogue preceded by the direction that *'thes thre stave next folowyng in the Kyngs absens are voyde'* (675), demonstrating that the king's presence is a possible but not a necessary condition of performance" (Dillon 1996). The MS is not in Heywood's hand, "but many of its verbal and rhetorical characteristics link it with the other plays, and make the attribution to him in the colophon plausible" (Happé 2007b). "[T]here is only one stage direction" (Axton & Happé 1991).

The play was named by Humfrey Wanley, who catalogued the MS. First printed "in a shortened version" (Happé) by Fairholt 1846 and entitled *A Dialogue on Wit and Folly*. Modern edition by Happé 1991.

The Witty Fair One, A Comedy. James Shirley. Licensed for acting 3 October 1628 (Adams 1917). "Presented" by Queen Henrietta Maria's Men at the Phoenix, according to the TP. In playlist of Beeston's Boys 10 August 1639.

SR 15 January 1633. Q 1633 dramatis personae; five acts and first scenes. License for printing, dated 14 January 1633, published in Q. Some descriptive SDs: "*The hearse brought in, tapers*"; "*While the musicke is playing enter Breynes without his shooes with a letter in his hand.*"

In his dedicatory epistle Shirley reflects on the difference between a staged and a printed play: "It wanted no grace on the stage, if it appeare acceptable to you in this new trimme of the presse, it will improove abroad, and you oblige the author to acknowledge a favour beyond the first applause."

The Wizard. Simon Baylie. Acted 1620–40 (*JCS*) at undetermined venue. "[P]robably it was devised for some private amateur performance in some family, possibly for some society, or a body of professional men" (Vocht 1930).

(1) Durham, UK, Durham Cathedral Library, MS Hunter 77, fols. 1–45; "the first 15 leaves have been considerably damaged on the side and at foot" (Vocht); signs of revision; dramatis personae; five acts and separate scenes. Detailed SDs: "*Enter Antonio in the habit of his father, Clerimont, a Parson, Hog disguis'd, with a dark lanthorne in his hand, and some habits in his arms.*" Unusual staging includes "*Enter Mr. Shallow eating paper.*" (2) London, BL, Additional MS 10306, fols. 1–55; formerly at Dulwich College; no author named; dramatis personae. "There are extensive corrections and alterations, in part by a reviser who might be the

original author, but in part apparently of later date" (Greg 1931). First edited by Vocht 1930.

The Woman Hater. Francis Beaumont and John Fletcher (Finkelpearl 1990). "Though the play is substantially the work of Beaumont, Fletcher's hand can be traced in at least five scenes" (Hoy 1987a). "Lately acted by" Paul's Boys, according to the SR and the Q1 TP, at Paul's playhouse, 1606 (Finkelpearl). "The play is the only work Beaumont and Fletcher seem to have done for the Children of Paul's" (McMullan 1994). During a journey to London on 16 March 1624, Edward Dering "bought three copies of Francis Beaumont's *The Woman Hater*, . . . possibly for a proposed performance at Surrenden [Hall, Kent]" (Gibson 2002). The play "was revived about 1638" (Levin 1989b).

SR 20 May 1607; transferred 19 April 1613. Q1 1607 *The Woman Hater*; two issues; no author named; prologue; five acts and separate scenes. Q2 1648–49 two issues; "acted by his majesties servants with great applause"; the TP of the first issue names Fletcher. The 1649 reissue names Beaumont and Fletcher on the TP, gives an alternate title (*or, The Hungry Courtier*), gives "a prologue in verse written by Sir William Davenant, presumably for a revival of the play in or before 1638" (Williams 1966b), prints an epilogue that had appeared in *The Noble Gentleman* (1647), and provides dramatis personae. Although Q1 "is in prose and begins 'Gentlemen'" Q2 "is in verse and begins 'Ladies.' The total change of address from the male to the female in the intervening 40 or so years reveals tellingly the increasing presence, relevance and influence of the female spectator" (Schneider 2011). B&F F2 1679 *Fifty Comedies and Tragedies*; "published by the authors original copies, the songs to each play being added."

The unusually long Q1 prologue is written in prose, contrary to customary practice. It indicates the typical appearance of an actor delivering a prologue and suggests the nature of the ensuing play: "Inductions are out of date, and a prologue in verse is as stale as a blacke velvet cloake, and a bay garland: therefore you shall have it plaine prose thus: If there be any amongst you, that come to heare lascivious scenes, let them depart: for I doe pronounce this, to the utter discomfort of all two peny gallerie men, you shall have no bawdrie in it: or if there bee any lurking amongst you in corners, with table bookes, who have some hope to finde fitt matter to feede his — — mallice on, let them claspe them up, and slinke away, or stay and be converted. For he that made this play, meanes to please auditors so, as hee may bee an auditor himselfe hereafter, and not purchase them with the deare losse of his eares: I dare not call it comedie, or tragedie; 'tis perfectly neyther: A play it is, which was meant to make you laugh, how it will please you, is not written in my part: For though you should like it today, perhaps your selves know not how you should digest it tomorrow: Some thinges in it you may meete with, which are out of the common roade: a duke there is, and the scene lyes in Italy, as those two thinges lightly wee never misse. But you shall not finde in it the ordinarie and over-worne trade of jeasting at lords and courtiers, and citizens, without taxation of any particular or new vice by them found out, but at the persons of them: such, he that made this, thinkes vile; and for his owne part vowes, that hee did never thinke, but that a lord borne might bee a wise man, and a courtier an honest man." Davenant's prologue (written "probably in or before 1638" [Clark 1994]) in the second issue of Q2 asks women playgoers "to excuse Fletcher for this play because of his sympathetic treatment of women characters in his other works" (Levin).

The Woman in the Moon. John Lyly. Acted 1591–95 (Saccio 1969) at undetermined venue. Performed at court ("presented before her Highnesse"), according to the Q TP, before publication in 1597, but the TP "gives no indication of the acting company" (Hunter 2004). Probably performed by an adult company of actors (Saccio), but "[o]f the twenty named parts only four are for adult men" (Scragg 2006).

SR 22 September 1595. Q 1597 "the first play by Lyly to carry his name on the title-page" (Scragg 2006); prologue; five acts and an additional scene in act 3. "Costuming and staging are detailed more fully . . . than in any previously published Lylian play" (Scragg 2006). The most interesting SD appears when "*They draw the curtins from before Natures shop, where stands an image* [statue] *clad and some unclad, they bring forth the cloathed image*," and then "*The image walkes about fearefully.*" Subsequently the statue "speakes." Entry of planetary gods may employ machinery: e.g., "Saturne *descendeth on the stage*"; "*Venus* ascendeth." But "no indication is given how or where they ascend to or descend from" (Wickham 1979). Lyly's "use of individual gods to direct each act" of the play "bears a striking resemblance" to "the dramaturgical use of the gods in *The Rare Triumphs of Love and Fortune*"; "one might even conjecture that Lyly actually drew from either *Love and Fortune* or very similar plays" (Cartwright 1998). Lyly's play has much to offer onstage: "Theatrically, *The Woman in the Moone* employs audience asides, staged playacting, deceptions, near-frantic entrances and exits, and considerable physical comedy" (Cartwright). But it "may well have been a failure" (Scragg 2003), and it is not included in Lyly's *Six Court Comedies*.

Prologue implies that this is the first of Lyly's plays: "If many faults escape in her discourse, / Remember all is but a poets dreame / The first he had in Phœbus holy bowre." "No one knows quite what to make of the prologue's assertion: perhaps it means that this play is the first Lyly wrote for performance by a specific men's company during the 1590s, a guess that gains some support from the fact that only this one among Lyly's plays does not seem to have been intended for child actors" (Daniel 1988). "The title-page (uniquely) fails to name the actors, and the text strongly suggests that this play was not designed for the boys at all. They were prevented from acting in the decade 1590 to 1600. . . . [The play] may be regarded as an attempt to straddle the gap between the public theater with its adult actors, and its mixed audiences, and the court" (Hunter 1968). If the dramatist wrote the play for adult actors, "[t]his may explain its use of a rather rigid blank verse instead of the flexible dramatic prose which Lyly had developed in his earlier works" (Best 1968a). Lyly's decision to write in blank verse, however, may be due to the impact of Marlowe's *Tamburlaine* and Kyd's *Spanish Tragedy*: "The sound of drama had changed forever" (Wiggins 2000).

A Woman Is a Weathercock, A Comedy. Nathan Field. Acted 1609–10 (MacIntyre 1996); *c.* 1610 (Lamb 2009). "Acted before the King in White-Hall, and divers times privately at the White-friers," by the Children of the Queen's Revels, according to the TP. "Court performance probably took place either Christmas 1609–10, or 13 December 1610/2 February 1611" (Munro 2005). Possibly performed later by Prince Charles's Men (Nicol 2006a).

SR 23 November 1611; transferred 4 September 1626; 1 July 1637. Q 1612 *A Woman is a Weathercock, A New Comedy*; dramatis personae; one dumb show; five acts. Unusually full SDs: Scudmore *"passeth one door and entereth the other, where* Bellafront *sits in a chaire, under a taffata canopie"*; "her canopied chair sounds like a 'state,' not readily movable by the attendants who bring on furniture in other scenes, but set up in the discovery space to be revealed once Scudmore has passed from *'one door'* to *'the other'"* (MacIntyre). "A devil costume is used briefly . . . and though it does not signify a 'real' devil, it is designated as an 'emblem' that has the same effect as a 'real' devil" (Cox 2000). A "distinguishing custom of the early private theatre began with the child-players and may have been confined to them. This was the valedictory song at the close of the comedy"; in Field's play "the song is bound to the action by Sir John Worldly's closing speech beginning, 'On parson on; and boy, outvoice the music'" (Lawrence 1912a).

In his dedication Field alludes to the customary payment offered playwrights for such flattery: "I did determine, not to have dedicated my play to any body, because forty shillings I care not for, and above, few or none will bestowe on these matters, especially falling from so famelesse a pen as mine is yet." Field's address "To the Reader" points to the conventionality of such an epistle and couples this with an assertion of the play's value: "Reader, the sale-man sweares, youle take it very ill, if I say not somewhat to you too, In troth you are a stranger to me; why should I write to you? You never writ to mee, nor I thinke will not answere my epistle. I send a comedie to you heer, as good as I could then make; nor sleight my presentation, because it is a play: For I tell thee reader, if thou bee'st ignoraunt, a play is not so ydle a thing as thou art, but a mirrour of mens lives and actions now, be it perfect or imperfect, true or false, is the vice or virtue of the maker." Field also looks forward to the enhanced reputation he will enjoy when "my next play be printed," "that is, his *Amends for Ladies*" (Lamb 2009).

A Woman Killed with Kindness. Thomas Heywood. Acted early March 1603 (Van Fossen 1961). By the Earl of Worcester's Men at the Rose (Chambers 1923). Henslowe records payment to the playwright, 12 February and 6 March 1603. "The troupe appears to have left London for a provincial tour in March 1603, and [John]

Lowin's name is mentioned in this connection" (Bowers 1987). Also "oftentimes acted by" Queen Anne's Men (formerly Worcester's Men), according to the Q3 TP, at other public playhouses, 1603–17, probably the Red Bull (Reynolds 1940) and the Curtain (Gurr 2009d). The play "appears to have been an instant and memorable success. The original production was lavish, even by the standards of Worcester's Men" (Smout 2010); the costume for the actor playing Anne Frankford cost more than the playbook. The servant Jenkin may have been played by Will Kemp (Wiles 1987); this was one of "Kemp's most important roles with Worcester's Men" (Butler 2004d). But Rowland 2010 thinks that Kemp played Nicholas, while Potter 2012 assigns the role of Nick either to Kemp or to John Lowin. Heywood, an actor himself, may have "appeared in the first production" (Cardullo 2011). "Whether Heywood's work preceded or followed *Othello*, the two dramas were similar enough in kind to compete" (Honan 1998); "*Othello* might almost be a paradoxical and ironic coment on the action" of Heywood's play (Farley-Hills 1990). Heywood's tragedy "may be a subtext for *Othello*" (Rudnytsky 1983). Although it is common to deprecate Heywood's play today, the RSC's 1991–92 production, directed by Katie Mitchell, was absolutely stunning.

SR none. Q1 1607 unique copy at BL; prologue and epilogue; not divided. A rustic atmosphere is created at the wedding reception when the servants dance "*after the country fashion*." SDs offer domestic details: "*Enter Franckeford as it were brushing the crums from his cloths with a napkin, and newly risen from supper*"; "*Enter Butler, and Jenkin with a table-cloath, bread, trenchers, and salt*." This last direction indicates "that this is a household too rustic to use plate or china for meals" (McLuskie 1999). When servants prepare a table for card-playing, they bring "*cards, carpet, stooles, and other necessaries*"; carpets, too valuable to use on the floor, were placed on tables following a meal. A SD when Frankford discovers his wife and her lover together is tantamount to a dumb show (McLuskie 1994): "*Enter Wendol, running over the stage in a night-gowne, he [Frankford] after him with his sword drawn, the maid in her smocke staies his hand, and clasps hold on him, he pauses a while*." Similarly, "*Enter Sir Charles in prison, with yrons, his feet bare, his garments al ragged and torne*." "Each entry is a speaking picture, stylized and unsubtle" (Sturgess 1969). Q2 not extant. Q3 1617 "the third edition."

The Q1 prologue seeks to adjust the expectations of playgoers to domestic tragedy: "Looke for no glorious state, our muse is bent / Upon a barrein subject: a bare sceane." "Dramatic representations of disorder in the non-elite household flourished on the London stage between 1590 and 1610, seen in such plays as *Arden of Faversham*, *A Warning for Fair Women*, *Two Lamentable Tragedies*, and *A Yorkshire Tragedy*. Challenging standard definitions of tragedy as espoused by Donatus, Diomedes, and Sidney, these plays located protagonists of the middling sort and comic situations in tragic frameworks" (Wall 2002).

Although Heywood's play has been seen chiefly as domestic tragedy, "we can see a later genealogy of heterosexuality"; *Woman Killed with Kindness* and *Arden of Faversham* "are as much tragedies of relations between husband and guests as they are marital tragedies" (Bach 2007). "Frankford chooses to take a bosom friend the way that most men choose a mate" (Panek 1994). "Wendoll's adultery with Anne Frankford is all the more heinous for his homoerotic relation to John Frankford, his patron and host" (DiGangi 1997).

A Woman Will Have Her Will. See *Englishmen for My Money.*

The Woman's Prize, or The Tamer Tamed. John Fletcher. "Probably first performed between December 1609 and April 1610 in the Whitefriars Theatre by the Children of the Queen's Revels" (Daileader & Taylor 2006). Belonged to the King's Men in the 1630s; intended for playing at St. James's Palace, the afternoon of 18 October 1633, but Herbert ordered the company to cancel the performance because of "complaints of foule and offensive matters conteyned therein" (Bawcutt 1996). (*The Scornful Lady* was acted in its place.) Herbert returned the play, "purgd of oaths, prophaness, and ribaldrye," on 21 October 1633. Subsequently performed at St. James's Palace before the king and queen, the night of 28 November 1633 in the Presence Chamber (Astington 1986); Herbert describes the play as "very well likt" (Adams 1917). (*The Taming of the Shrew* had been performed at court two days earlier and "likt.") In playlist of King's Men 7 August 1641.

Washington, Folger, MS J.b.3, fols. 1–52, ed. Livingston 2007; no TP; no author named; evidence of correction; minor damage; five acts and some separate scenes. A later hand has written: "This is a transcript of Beaumont and Fletcher's comedy entitled *The Woman's Prize, or The Tamer Tamed*"; it "contains eleven passages . . . not found in F1" (Livingston). SR 4 September 1646; 30 January 1673; 21 August 1683. B&F F1 1647 *Comedies and Tragedies*; "never printed before, and now published by the authours originall copies"; prologue ("perhaps composed for the court performance of 1633" [Clark 1994]) and epilogue, which are missing from the MS; five acts and separate scenes. In keeping with the play's focus on gender, "both prologue and epilogue to the revival after 1630 . . . address themselves primarily to female spectators, and only the epilogue attempts to placate the men, by asserting the play's purpose: 'To teach both sexes due *equality*'" (Schneider 2011). B&F F2 1679 *Fifty Comedies and Tragedies*; "published by the authors original copies, the songs to each play being added"; *The Woman's Prize, or The Tamer Tamed, A Comedy*; list of characters. "F and F2 include two short scenes and some shorter sections omitted in MS" (Munro 2010c).

"John Fletcher's companion/response play to Shakespeare's *The Taming of the Shrew*" (Henderson 1997); McLuskie 1992 calls it "an updated sequel and contrasting response." "Alone among Shakespeare's plays, *The Shrew* provoked a theatrical 'reply' in his lifetime in the form of Fletcher's *The Woman's Prize*" (Thompson 1984): Fletcher produced "an imagined history of the marriage of Petruchio and Katherine, which rejected the success of the taming by the end of Shakespeare's play as a sham" (Bayman & Southcombe 2010). "In this play Petruchio's second wife, Maria, turns the tables on him, enlisting the support of other women to baffle and torment her husband" (Clark 2007). Fletcher's comedy "suggests a sustained popularity both for *Shrew* and for plays focusing on negotiations of gender" (Aspinall 2002). "For a sequel . . . [*The Woman's Prize*] pays scant regard to the details of the Shakespearian play which it purports to extend" (Wiggins 1996); "Fletcher's starting point was a rejection of Shakespeare's ending" (Bayman & Southcombe). However, "we cannot expect Fletcher simply to 'continue' Shakespeare's play" (Bergeron 1996). Daileader & Taylor reject the term "sequel" and prefer to call the play "a 'counter-part,' as Gerard Langbaine called it in 1691."

The F1 prologue seeks to adjust the expectations of playgoers: "We do intreat the angry men would not / Expect the mazes of a subtle plot, / Set speeches, high expressions; and what's worse, / In a true comedy, politique discourse. / The end we ayme at, is to make you sport; / Yet neither gall the City, nor the Court." This prologue is "typical of its form in disingenuously alerting the audience to find exactly what it tells them they should not expect—in this case the 'politique discourse' of sexual comedy" (Dutton 1998).

The Woman's Prize "is one of a number of plays written around this time which debate the nature and status of women, including Ben Jonson's *Epicoene, or The Silent Woman*, Nathan Field's *A Woman is a Weathercock* and *Amends for Ladies*, Thomas Dekker and Thomas Middleton's *The Roaring Girl*, John Marston, William Barksted and Lewis Machin's *The Insatiate Countess*, and Fletcher's own *Bonduca* . . . and the plays he wrote collaboratively with Francis Beaumont, *The Maid's Tragedy* and *The Scornful Lady*" (Munro 2010c).

Women Beware Women, A Tragedy. Thomas Middleton. Acted 1621 (Mulryne 1975b) or 1622 (Gill 1968) at undetermined venue. Possibly acted by a combination of Lady Elizabeth's Men and the Queen's Revels Children 1613–14 (Dutton 1999). The play requires an unusually large cast, and there are numerous important roles for female characters; the final scene alone "calls for at least 23 parts" (Dutton). No license for acting exists.

SR 9 September 1653 *A right woman, or women beware of women* ['*A Right Woman* must be a separate piece" (Greg 1939)]. O 1657 *Two New Plays* (with *More Dissemblers Besides Women*); continuous register and pagination; list of characters; pantomimes used throughout the play merge "completely into the dialogue" (Mehl 1965); five acts and separate scenes. Elaborate ceremony: "*Enter in great solemnity six Knights bare-headed, then two Cardinals, and then the Lord Cardinal, then the Duke; after him the states of* Florence *by two and two, with vari[e]ty of musick and song.*" A game of chess figures in the best-known scene, wherein "the play's scheming villainess, Livia, entices a neighboring mother and daughter to an afternoon game. As the older women play, the daughter Bianca is ushered to the upper stage where she is shown 'naked pictures' and then raped by the Duke of Florence" (Collington 1999); at the same time "a game of chess is played out on the main stage below and mirrors what is happening above" (Darby 2006).

The "chess game serves to distract the widow's attention from her daughter-in-law's seduction, and the ingenuous conversation between the players is in ironic counterpoint to the scene of seduction itself" (McLuskie 1988). The "effect of the chess match on the main level renders the seduction a gamelike play-within, Livia's domination of the match mirroring clearly and cynically the defeat of Bianca's small honor above" (Shand 1985). This scene, with "its lower-stage chess game and upper-stage and off-stage rape of Biancha [is] one of the most brilliantly managed pieces of stagecraft in all of Jacobean drama" (Carroll 1994). Another instance of "split-level" staging occurs when "[t]he royal train are stationed on the upper stage while the masque is played below"; "an actual audience watches an audience on the stage watching the play-within-the-play" (Lancaster 1977). The masque "remains somewhat obscure, as the scene is famously bereft of stage directions to guide a director" (Carroll). The masquelike ending begins with a symbolic entrance: "*Enter* Hymen *in yellow*, Ganymed *in a blue robe powdered with stars, and* Hebe *in a white robe with golden stars, with covered cups in their hands: they dance a short dance.*" Perhaps the wedding party "should begin the scene on the upper stage and descend [by the tiring-house stairs] to the main stage before the play ends" (Thomson 1986). Staging involves the descent of Livia costumed "*like* Juno"; as she descends "Livia breathes in poisoned incense prepared by Isabella" (Carroll). An annotation in a Yale copy of O indicates that Livia then "*Throw's flameing gold upon Isabella who falls: dead*"; the annotator "is simply describing what he had seen on stage" (Mulryne 1975a); the "lapful of burning treasure' . . . is the image of violent phallic penetration" (Carroll). The masque, "which considerably reduces the dancing of the court masque, and replaces it with a revels of death" (Howard 1998), stands "as an emblem of, or a metonymy for, the court world and its corruptions" (Lindley 2009). The denouement includes a plethora of theatrical effects: "Here we have elaborate contraptions with poisonous darts, caltrops, cupids shooting arrows with envenomed arrows, and conspirators falling through the wrong trap doors, while the Duke complains that something has gone wrong with the programme notes and dies still trying to understand the allegory" (Heinemann 1980). Unusually, "the deaths of the two protagonists, the Duke and Bianca, occur on the upper stage, and the principal survivor, the Cardinal, speaks the final moralizing words from the same location" (Thomson).

Nathaniel Richards contributes a commendatory poem, reporting of Middleton and the success of the play onstage, "he knew the rage, / Madness of women crost; and for the stage / Fitted their humors, hell-bred malice, strife / Acted in state, presented to the life. / I that have seen't can say, having just cause, / Never came tragedy off with more applause." "Richards provides the only seventeenth-century evidence that *Women Beware Women* was actually staged, and was a success" (Carroll 1994). The theatrical appeal of the drama may be located in Livia, "perhaps the most powerful of Middleton's characters and, with Tamora [from *Titus Andronicus*], arguably among the most powerful female characters in early modern English drama" (Bruster 2003). "One of the great schemers of early modern tragedy, Livia exerts her social, economic, and rhetorical powers to maneuver other women into sexual relationships that serve her own ambitions and pleasures" (DiGangi 2011). The play's title signals that the play "is a study of the moral, spiritual, and sexual disintegration of women at various life stages" (Gossett 2011).

Women Pleased. John Fletcher. In its original form acted 1603–04 (Sams 1985b), but Wells & Taylor 1987 favor "a much earlier period of composition." Possibly revised by Fletcher (?revision of an earlier play by a different hand) and acted 1619–23 (*JCS*) by the King's Men at the second Blackfriars/second Globe. "Yet no very convincing traces of a supposed revision have been isolated" (Gabler 1982). Principal actors were Joseph Taylor, John Lowin, John Underwood, Robert Benfield, William Eccleston, Nicholas Tooley, Richard Sharp, and Thomas Holcomb, according to F2; the cast list represents a revival, "which cannot belong to a performance earlier than *c.* 1620" (Wells & Taylor).

SR 4 September 1646; 30 January 1673. B&F F1 1647 *Comedies and Tragedies*; "never printed before, and now published by the authours originall copies"; five acts and separate scenes. The most intriguing SD occurs after Silvio learns that the princess who was to have been his bride has disappeared; a "hag claims him in marriage for her assistance, the marriage takes place, and at this point the masque proper is introduced" (Gossett 1988): *"Enter a masquerado of severall shapes and daunces, after which enter Belvidere and disperses them."* The shapes are not described but Gossett believes "that they looked like hags." B&F F2 1679 *Fifty Comedies and Tragedies*; "published by the authors original copies, the songs to each play being added"; *Women Pleased, A Tragicomedy*; list of characters; actors' names.

Women Will Have Their Will, or Give Christmas His Due. Anonymous. ?Acted at undetermined venue *c.* summer 1648.

Thomason records this date: printed 12 December 1648. D 1649 [1648]; no author named; epilogue; not divided. A dialogue between Mistress Custom, a victualler's wife, and Mistress New-Come, a captain's wife; both are depicted in the TP woodcuts.

The play contains an attack on the Parliamentary/Puritan forces. Mistress New-Come says approvingly: "the two houses of Parliament . . . have jumped together in one opinion, for the putting downe and destroying of this Romish beast Christmas; for which they are to be commended." Mistress Custom sharply attacks this view: "I doe not know this Parliament, 'tis no kin to me; if this is the authoritie you talked of, God deliver me from such authoritie; this is worser authoritie then my husbands." Mistress Custom also takes aim at the effort to ban a traditional Christmas: "You say that the Parliament hath power to pull down Christmas; I pray then what will they put up in the roome on't, stage-playes, dancing upon the ropes, & *hocus pocus?*"

The Wonder of a Kingdom. Thomas Dekker. Acted 1619–31 (Hoy 1980). Possibly intended for the Phoenix, though Herbert's diary entry of 18 September 1623 for *Come See a Wonder* ("written by John Daye for a company of strangers") has been interpreted as referring to *Wonder of a Kingdom* and meaning that the play "was acted at the Red Bull, and licensed without his hand to it, because they [the company of actors] were none of the four companys" (Adams 1917).

SR 16 May 1631; 24 February 1636. Q 1636 dramatis personae; prologue (nearly the same as that published in William Rowley's *All's Lost by Lust* [1633]); three dumb shows "like festive processions" (Mehl 1965); five acts and first scenes. Typical of the play's spectacle is this SD: "*Enter Torrenti very brave, betweene the two Dukes, attended by all the courtiers, wondring at his costly habit. Enter a mask, women in strang[e] habitts, dance. Exit. He gives jewells, and ropes of pearle to the Duke; and a chaine of gold to every courtier.*" John Day's *Parliament of Bees* (1641) lifts four scenes from *Wonder of a Kingdom* (*JCS*).

Somewhat defensively the prologue, arguing that the playwright has known success in the theater, seeks to forestall the potential criticism of readers: "'Tis not a gay sute, or distorted face, / Can beate his merit off, —, which has won grace / In the full theater; — nor can now feare / The teeth of any snaky whisperer; / But to the white, and sweete unclowded brow, / (The heaven where true worth moves) our poet do's bow."

The Wonder of Women, or The Tragedy of Sophonisba. John Marston. Acted 1605 (White 1998). "Sundry times acted" at the [second] Blackfriars, according to the TPs, by the Children of the Blackfriars. The TP fails to call the actors "The Children of the Queen's Revels"; this may mean that the queen's patronage had been withdrawn at time of performance (Chambers 1923). "One of the very few plays containing major battle scenes written for the boy company while it occupied the Blackfriars" (Gurr 2004c).

SR 17 March 1606; transferred 19 April 1613. Q 1606 two issues, one of which is entitled *The Tragedy of Sophonisba*; RT *The Tragedy of Sophonisba*; list of characters; argument; prologue and epilogue (by Massinissa); chorus of singers; dumb shows precede two acts; five acts and separate scenes. (The writing of the play had been announced in a note to the second edition of *Parasitaster, or The Fawn*.) "'The Wonder of Women' appears in substantially larger print than 'The Tragedy of Sophonisba.' Notably, 'wonder' is by far the most prominent word in the 1606 title-page: of both the titles, it is the only word which appears in capital letters, the only word to be given a line of print to itself, and its lettering is about twice as large as that of the next complete, largest word" (Rist 2007). "One of the richest plays in [stage] directions of value" (Reynolds 1905a). "The prologue is an elaborate stage spectacle which includes music and which has the Prologist delivering his speech standing between two groups of actors, who play the opposing forces in the drama" (Schneider 2011). Staging includes a descent into a vault, employing a trap in the stage floor; later "*the ghost of Asdruball ariseth*" out of an altar. "The altar was near the trap, probably in front of it, so the ghost could seem to rise from the altar" (Reynolds 1905b). Marston "frequently inserts a shocking, unexpected event" (Finkelpearl 1969), as on Sophonisba's wedding night: "*Enter* Carthalon *his sword drawne, his body wounded, his shield strucke full of darts:* Massin[issa] *being reddy for bedde*"; "Syphax *with his dagger twon about her haire drags in* Sophonisba *in hir nightgowne petticoate.*" When Syphax discovers that he has had sex with a witch/succubus, he would strike her with his sword, but "she slips '*into the ground*' (presumably through the trap door)" (Vaughan 2005). In his staging "Marston reponds to the new demands of the contemporary audience and provides masque and anti-masque elements combined with the methods of a dumb show" (Gair 2000): "*Enter foure boyes antiquely attiered with bows and quivers, dauncing to the cornets a phantastique measure;* Massinissa *in his night gowne, led by* Asdruball *and* Hanno, *followed by* Bytheas *and* Jugurth. *The boyes draw the curtaines, discovering* Sophonisba." A note following the Q epilogue alludes to the extraordinary attention to music: "let me intreat my reader not to taxe me, for the fashion of the entrances and musique of this tragidy, for know it is printed onely as it was presented by youths, & after the fashion of the private stage." (This note is omitted in the 1633 O.) In contrast to his plays acted at Paul's playhouse, where he makes considerable use of song, Marston relies "on orchestral performance" at the Blackfriars (Gair 2000). The SD "*Infernall musicke plaies softly whilst Erictho enters*" "indicates that certain strains of music were conventionally associated with the appearance of evil spirits" (Lawrence 1927); the infernal music comes "from beneath the stage" (Corbin & Sedge 1986). Another SD stipulates, "*A treble violl and a bass lute play softly within the canopy*"; this apparently designates "the curtained 'discovery' space in the centre of the tiring-house façade" (Jackson & Neill 1986), where Syphax has sex with a demon. By contrast, "*A short song to soft musique above*" signals "a music-room over the stage" (Hosley 1960). The SDs "are notable in specifying not the brass instruments used to convey orders to cavalry on the battlefield and to summon latecomers to the amphitheatres but cornets, a woodwind which gave out a similar but quieter sound compared with a trumpet" (Gurr 2009d). Marston's play "is a unique record of the most powerful dramatic and erotic use of music in the period" (Mann 2012). O 1633 *The Works of Mr. John Marston, Being Tragedies and Comedies, Collected into One Volume* (with *Antonio and Mellida, Antonio's Revenge, The Dutch Courtesan, Parasitaster, What You Will*); two issues. The reissue, entitled *Tragedies and Comedies Collected into One Volume*, removes Marston's name from the general and separate TPs; William Sheares had published the collection without Marston's consent. Also issued in *Comedies, Tragicomedies, and Tragedies* (1652), a made-up Q no longer extant.

Marston's address to the Q reader, probably alluding to Jonson's *Sejanus* (Geckle 1980), distinguishes between the dramatist as historian and the dramatist as poet: "Know, that I have not labored in this poeme [i.e., play], to tie my selfe to relate any thing as an historian, but to inlarge every thing as a poet. To transcribe authors, quote authorities, & translate Latin prose orations into English blank-verse, hath in this subject beene the least aime of my studies." This address leads to the speculation that the play was "written in deliberate competition with Jonson's *Sejanus* (performed 1603, printed 1605)" (Jackson & Neill 1986).

Woodstock (*Thomas of Woodstock*; *1 Richard II*). Anonymous; probably a work of collaboration (Long 1999). Possibly written by Shakespeare (Egan 2006b) or by Samuel Rowley (Jackson 2001c, 2007a). Acted early 1590s at undetermined venue (Corbin & Sedge 2002); probably first performed "in the season of 1594–95" (Long 1985a). Or perhaps not written till 1598–1609 (Jackson) when it might have been intended for the first Fortune (Gurr 2009c). Probably revised by Samuel Rowley *c*. 1604–10 (Lake 1983). Probably revived *c*. 1602–04 and *c*. 1633 (Long 1989). On 30 April 1611 Simon Forman saw the performance of a play about Richard II at the Globe, but *Woodstock* is not that play. The MS "may well have been transcribed for the purposes of a Jacobean revival" (Corbin & Sedge). Possibly revived at the Salisbury Court playhouse (Butler 1984b).

London, BL, Egerton MS 1994, fols. 161–85; no TP; no author named; damaged; some speeches and lines crossed out; no conclusion—last leaf is missing; theatrical provenance (Long 1989); five acts but "divisions were supplied only by a later hand" (Taylor 1993a). *Woodstock* is a more appropriate title than *1 Richard II* (Rossiter 1946); "the play should be considered as *Jack Straw II* rather than *The First Part of Richard the Second*" (Longstaffe 2006). Staging calls for the entry of "*a spruce courtier a horseback*"; he mistakes Woodstock for a groom "owing to his customary plainness of garb" (Lawrence 1935). "It is most likely that the horseman entered into the playhouse yard thus providing the actor playing Woodstock with the opportunity for a close actor/audience engagement as he walked the horse" (Corbin & Sedge 2002). "[P]erhaps the most powerful visual effect is one which immediately precedes Woodstock's imprisonment. King Richard appears in a masque of the goddess Cynthia and her attendants" (Axton 1977): "*Antic dance and music; then a great shout and winding o' horns. Then enters* Cynthia"; "*Music. Enter King Richard, Green, Bushy [and] Bagot, like Diana's knights, led in by four other knights in green, with horns about their necks and boar-spears in their hands.*" "The most likely performer of the role of Cynthia is the boy actor playing Queen Anne" (Corbin & Sedge). A SD calling for "*Thunder and lightning*" later accompanies the Ghost of the Black Prince; upon his exit thunder sounds again and Edward III's Ghost enters. Woodstock rises from his bed immediately before his death; a murderer strikes him with a hammer and the two murderers strangle him in view of playgoers; the killers are, in turn, killed. The MS shows "signs that scenes or characters have been omitted in transcription or performance" (Carson 1988). SR none. First edited by Halliwell[-Phillipps] 1870 (*A Tragedy of King Richard the Second*), then Keller 1899 (*Richard II. Erster Teil*), then Frijlinck 1929 (*The First Part of the Reign of King Richard the Second, or Thomas of Woodstock*), then Rossiter 1946 (*Woodstock: A Moral History*). Recent editions by Corbin & Sedge 2002, Egan 2006b.

"*Woodstock* is closely related conceptually and verbally to both [Shakespeare's] *2 Henry VI* and [Marlowe's] *Edward II*" (Forker 2002). Somewhat less clear is the connection between *Richard II* and *Woodstock*: *Woodstock* "may well have influenced" Shakespeare's *Richard II* (Dutton 1991); "*Woodstock* was written after *Richard II*" (Jackson 2001c) and thus "a deliberate prequel to Shakespeare's *Richard II* and not a source" (Holland 2006). *Woodstock* is "in some ways the boldest and most subversive of all Elizabethan historical plays" (Heinemann 2003).

Work for Cutlers, or A Merry Dialogue between Sword, Rapier, and Dagger. "Acted in a shew in the famous Universitie of Cambridge," according to the TP, possibly at Trinity College in ?1615. Perhaps written by Thomas Heywood (Sieveking 1904). The entertainment bears a resemblance to *Band, Cuff, and Ruff* (Smith 1908) and *Wine, Beer, and Ale* (Hanford 1915). Epilogue points to an academic venue: "At last hee dares not stand ins owne defence; / But this hee hopes, with you it will suffize, / To crave a pardon for a schollers prize."

SR 4 July 1615. Q 1615 no author named; epilogue by Dagger; not divided.

Work for Jupiter. See *Gigantomachia*.

The World and the Child, Otherwise Called Mundus & Infans. Anonymous. "[M]ust have been performed in a noble or well-off household celebrating Christmas ca. 1506–09," probably at Ampthill, Bedfordshire, the seat of Richard Grey, thirteenth earl of Kent (Lancashire 1976). Presented indoors (Davidson & Happé 1999), probably in "an evening or night-time setting" (Lester 1981). The play was intended for performance in "a great hall" (Twycross 2008). Requires "only two actors for its five roles" (Bevington 1962).

SR none. The play "had been inventoried on 5 November 1520" by an Oxford bookseller (Lancashire). Printed as Q in 1522, *Here beginneth a proper new Interlude of The World and the Child, Otherwise Called Mundus & Infans, & It Showeth of the Estate of Childhood and Manhood*; not divided. No SDs but costumes are elaborate: "Wisdom (Christ) is dressed in regal purple and ermine, while Anima (Soul) appears as a maid in rich attire, and Lucifer enters 'in a dewylls array wythout and withyn as a prowde galonte'" (Norland 1995). Q features an illustrated TP, depicting a king on his throne, covered with a canopy: "The king in the illustration is Mundus, who is shown at the beginning of the drama bragging to the audience" (Davidson 1991).

"This is the best example of an 'ages of man' play among the English interludes" (Grantley 2004). From this play onwards, "printers frequently referred to the novelty of their playbooks in title pages and prefaces, in what looks like a conscious attempt to advertise them to acting companies" (Walker 1998).

The World in a Maze, or Oliver's Ghost. Anonymous. A pamphlet in the form of a dialogue between Richard and Oliver Cromwell, who "talk, not like figures in a

Menippean satire, but in the semi-doggerel of the Fool and Old Man of a mummers' play" (Potter 1981).

Q 1659 no author named; concludes with a song; not divided. The TP features the woodcut of a ghost holding a torch. The dialogue "hints at the royalist identification of Charles I with Christ, but offers no political analysis" (Potter).

The World Runs on Wheels. See *All Fools.*

The World Tossed at Tennis. Thomas Middleton and William Rowley. In its lost original form it was intended for performance as a masque at Somerset [Denmark] House, according to the HT, for Prince Charles during the winter of 1619–20 but was not performed there "for reasons that remain obscure" (Hoy 1980). King James "may have scuttled the entertainment at Denmark House, planned by Prince Charles," because the king "wanted to restore peace and order in Europe by negotiation" whereas his son favored a more militant Protestantism, expressed in the masque (McGee 2007). Prologue explains that the play "was intended for a royall night," apparently in celebration of the 22 April 1620 wedding of Charles, Lord Howard, Baron of Effingham, and Mary Cokayne; the play is dedicated to the bride and her husband: "Imagine this (mixt with delight and state, / Being then an entertainment for the best) / Your noble nuptials comes to celebrate," according to Middleton's dedicatory epistle. The play was later revised: it "was probably altered and expanded from its original form in order to make it more suitable for presentation on the public stage" (Foakes 1985); it thereby became a "playhouse masque" and was "acted at the Princes Arms" (i.e., the Swan [Greg 1939]), according to the SR; "divers times presented to the contentment of many noble and worthy spectators" by Prince Charles's Men, according to the Q TPs. This was "the first time" a courtly masque was brought "into commercial playhouses for popular audiences" (Taylor 2004b). But the play was "modified by the elimination of much of the spectacle and of the elaborate presentation of masquers, though it still includes more songs and dances than were usual in commercial theatres" (Bentley 1981). "[William] Rowley may have acted the part of Simplicity" (Howard-Hill 1987b); Rowley, who "specialized in the part of the fat clown" (Bentley 1971), signs the preface to the reader. The playlist of Beeston's Boys, 10 August 1639, may represent this play as *The World* (Lawrence 1927).

SR 4 July 1620. Q1 1620 *A Courtly Masque: The Device Called The World Tossed at Tennis*; two issues; list of characters; induction; prologue ("written for presentation on a public stage" [Foakes 1985]) and epilogue; not divided. Staging involves descents to the sound of music and, presumably, by machinery: "*Musique and this song as an invocation to the nine Muses; (who in the time) are discover'd on the upper stage, plac'd by the nine Worthies, and toward the conclusion descend, each one led by a Muse, the most proper and pertinent to the person of the Worthy.*" The TP of the second issue features a woodcut depicting an orb, representing the world, handled by six symbolic figures, while the Devil and Deceit try to seize the orb. This woodcut "seems to be a stage illustration" (Orgel 2006). "The figure in the centre of the group on the left is probably the King (or Majesty), the large feathered hat and general appearance perhaps being designed to suggest King James I" (Foakes). "[T]he images of the characters may be intended as portraits of the actors who performed them"; "two of these actors can now be identified": William Rowley and Hugh Attwell (Nicol 2006b).

Prologue alludes to the original purpose of the entertainment and calls attention to its difference from conventional plays: "This our device, wee doe not call a play, / Because we breake the stages lawes today / Of acts & sceanes."

The Wounds of Civil War Lively Set Forth in The True Tragedies of Marius and Scilla. Thomas Lodge. Acted either 1586–87 or 1589 (Houppert 1969). "Publiquely plaide in London" by the Lord Admiral's Men, according to the TP, at undetermined venue, possibly an inn-yard (Lawrence 1927), though "when actors performed at inns they usually occupied a large room rather than a yard and performed by candlelight" (Orrell 1997). The play "must have been acted by the Admiral's company before its reorganization with [Edward] Alleyn in 1594" (Jewkes 1958). The play may have been inspired by the huge success of *Tamburlaine*, if Marlowe's play, also staged by the Admiral's Men, preceded Lodge's.

SR 24 May 1594. Q 1594 five acts "but the divisions are not always accurately marked" (Wilson & Greg 1910); divisions are "irregular and confused" (Jewkes 1958). SDs "are frequent, very long and descriptive" (Jewkes). Spectacular staging includes the entry of Scilla: *"Enter Scilla in triumph in his cha[i]re triumphant of gold, drawen by foure Moores before the chariot: his colours, his crest, his captaines, his prisoners."* Scilla's "forcing captive kings to draw him in a chariot and his treading on the neck of the Consul Carbo are not to be found in Lodge's Roman sources and appear instead to be echoes of *Tamburlaine*" (Bevington 1968), though two decades earlier, Gascoigne and Kinwelmarshe's *Jocasta* had brought Fortune onstage in her chariot (Kiefer 1983). At the close, staging calls for *"The funeralls of Scilla in greate pompe."* The Genius, who warns Scilla of his impending fate, must have entered and exited through a trap (Lawrence 1927): a SD reads, *"Evanescit subitò."* Scilla's response suggests that the Genius's appearance was striking: "What apparitions fantasies are these?" The sound of thunder, in other plays a sign of divine disapproval, prompts this conclusion by Anthonius: "Harke how the heavens our follies hath contrould." Scilla "makes a good death, and the play ends with '*The funerals of* Scilla *in great pomp*'" (Waith 1988).

"If Lodge's play was written between 1586 and 1589 it is the oldest extant example of a play based on classical history" (Houppert). Clemen 1961 calls it the "earliest Roman play in English literature."

Wyatt's History [title recorded in Kirkman's 1661 catalogue]. See *Sir Thomas Wyatt*.

Y

A Yorkshire Tragedy. ?Thomas Middleton (Lake 1973, Jackson 1979, Holdsworth 1994, Taylor 2004b, Wells 2007), but others have speculated that George Wilkins was the playwright (Sturgess 1969). Acted mid 1605 (Cawley & Gaines 1986). By the King's Men at the [first] Globe, according to the Q1 TP.

SR 2 May 1608 "by Wylliam Shakespere"; transferred 4 August 1626; 8 November 1630; 6 August 1674; 21 August 1683. Q1 1608 *A Yorkshire Tragedy, Not so New as Lamentable and True*; "written by W. Shakspeare" and published by Thomas Pavier; "attribution to Shakespeare is probably, in this instance, deliberately dishonest" (Wells & Taylor 1987); ascribed to Shakespeare in Archer's 1656 catalogue and Kirkman's; not divided. This is a very short play, only about 700 lines, and both quartos have as HT *All's One, or One of the Four Plays in One, called a Yorkshire Tragedy*. "Obviously it was one item in a four-item program at the Globe" (Lake 1975a), "but none of the others in the set have been identified" (Braden 1987c); "the subject, genre, and authorship of the other parts remain unknown" (Taylor 2004b). It is possible that one of the other plays was by Shakespeare, thus giving rise to the attribution [to him]" (Hope 1994). *Timon of Athens* was possibly "at one time short enough to be part of *All's One*" (Potter 2012). "If *A Yorkshire Tragedy* was only one of four plays, Shakespeare, as chief dramatist of the King's Men, with duties that seem to have included occasionally touching up the work of others, may have had something to do with the overall production" (Gossett 2004b). "The positive evidence for Shakespeare's authorship of the piece has been seriously understated by twentieth-century scholars" (Duncan-Jones 2001). Q2 1619 "written by W. Shakespeare" and published by Pavier; the TP does not mention the King's Men or the Globe. "There may have been an attempt to suggest that some copies of the 1619 edition were printed in 1608" (Feldman & Proudfoot 1969). Shakespeare F3 1664 second issue; "the third impression. And unto this impression is added seven playes never before printed in folio"; not divided. Shakespeare F4 1685 "the fourth edition"; two issues. The ascription to Shakespeare is not generally credited today: "The omission of the play from the First Folio argues strongly against the attribution" (Feldman & Proudfoot).

The play "is first cousin to Protestant homiletic tragedies of the type of *Enough is as Good as a Feast*. It may also be related to damnation plays in the biblical cycles" (Cawley 1989).

The Young Admiral. James Shirley. Licensed for acting 3 July 1633 (Adams 1917, Ericksen 1979). "Presented by" Queen Henrietta Maria's Men at the Phoenix, according to the TP. Performed also at St. James's Palace, before the king and queen, on the occasion of the king's birthday, 19 November 1633 in the Presence Chamber (Astington 1986); Herbert says the play was "likt" by the royal couple (Adams). Shirley's dedication states that the play "hath beene gratefull to the stage, and graciously entertain'd at court by their majesties." In playlist of Beeston's Boys 10 August 1639.

SR 13 April 1637. Q 1637 list of characters; five acts. Herbert praised the play: "being free from oaths, prophaness, or obsceanes, [it] hath given mee much delight and satisfaction in the readinge, and may serve for a patterne to other poetts, not only for the bettring of maners and language, but for the improvement of the quality [i.e., the profession of playwriting and acting], which hath received some brushings of late" (Bawcutt 1996). The meaning of "some brushings" is unclear: it may refer to Prynne's *Histriomastix* (Bawcutt); or perhaps Herbert "was thinking of his own dressing down of Shirley and the Queen's Men for *The Ball*, and indeed the intervention of the High Commission over *The Magnetic Lady*, which was still unresolved business at this time" (Dutton 1998).

The play "was both a birthday present to Charles from his wife and a declaration of her household's complicity in his reformatory projects, demonstrating the cultural and religious values he wished to promote at court and throughout his country" (Britland 2006b). *Young Admiral* may have been performed "because of its oblique dramatization of politico-religious concerns" (Britland 2008).

Your Five Gallants. Thomas Middleton. Acted "1606 or 1607" (Cohen & Jowett 2007). "Often in action at the Black-friers," according to the TP, "by the Children of the Chappell" [Blackfriars Children], according to the SR entry.

SR 22 March 1608 *the ffyve Wittie Gallantes*. Q ND ?1608 (Jackson 2007b); "no prologue is designated, but the play begins with a Dumb Show and the stage direction: 'Presenter or prologue, passing over the stage'" (Schneider 2011); the pantomime performs the function of exposition (Mehl 1965); five acts. "[T]wo comic interludes are printed out of play sequence" (Stern 2009c). "The characters are not so much human beings as illustrations . . . of various underworld tricks and swindles" (Barker 1958). The SDs "are seriously inadequate, even though this is a play whose intelligibility depends on small actions, many of them requiring props that go from hand to hand" (Cohen & Jowett). The play ends with an elaborate dance in which five villains, "seeking the hand of Katherine, a wealthy orphan . . . present themselves to her in a masque as knights, each preceded by a boy holding an emblazoned shield. The mottoes have been devised by the play's hero, Fitsgrave, so that they are ambiguous and can be interpreted as good by the suitors while in reality describing their particular vices" (Brissenden 1981). Middleton's dumb shows are "deliberately used as old-fashioned devices" (Gurr 2009d).

Youth. Anonymous. Acted Christmas 1513 or Shrovetide 1514 (Lancashire 1980). Probably written "for indoor performance at a hall banquet" and performed at the Yorkshire seat of Henry Algernon Percy, fifth earl of Northumberland (Lancashire). Presumably performed by five actors (Grantley 2004). Possibly performed in the chapel of a private household (Westfall 2004). Robert Langham [Laneham] in a letter written at Coventry in August 1575 mentions the play's title when he describes the contents of a private library (Ingram 1981, Kuin 1983).

SR between 19 July 1557 and 9 July 1558; transferred 15 January 1582. Q1 ND ?1530 *The Interlude of Youth*; fragment in Lambeth Palace Library; "almost certainly older than" the BL editions (Bang & McKerrow 1905); not divided. This Lambeth fragment contains three woodcuts (two men and a woman), with scrolls above each, but identifying labels are missing. The woodcuts "are derived from" those in a French book printed *c.* 1500 (Bang & McKerrow). "The imprisonment of a virtue is the principal piece of physical action"; staging calls for Charity to be fettered by Riot and Pride; Riot threatens Charity, "We shall set him in the stockes"; "like Pity in *Hickscorner*, Charity is not only fettered about the ankles but also bound at the wrists" (Craik 1958). The consigning of virtuous characters to the stocks became conventional, witness the fate of Kent in *King Lear*. Q2 ND ?1557. Q2 "has a woodcut representing 'Charitie' and 'Youth' that in spite of its decorative quality might reflect stage possibilities" (Davidson 1991). Q3 ND ?1565; features different woodcuts of three figures, two of whom are identified as Charity and Youth.

Plays such as *Youth* "furnished an exemplary model that could be used simultaneously to suggest the behaviour desired from a political figure, such as the king, and the dire consequences that might befall him should he fail to adopt it. . . . in its warning against dissoluteness and pride, [the play] is probably directed both at Henry VIII and his ardent supporter, Henry Percy, heir to the fifth Earl of Northumberland" (Fox 1989). The penitential theme and prodigal son motif "would have been well suited to a Shrovetide occasion and to a household that included Lord Percy's romantic son and heir, Henry, who had been recently called to court" (McCarthy 2008).

BIBLIOGRAPHY

Aaron
Melissa D. Aaron. *Global Economics: A History of the Theater Business, The Chamberlain's/King's Men, and Their Plays, 1599–1642*. Newark, DE: University of Delaware Press, 2005.

ACMRS
Arizona Center for Medieval and Renaissance Studies

Adams 1908
Joseph Quincy Adams. "*The Cyprian Conqueror, or The Faithless Relict.*" *Modern Language Notes* 23.3 (1908): 65–67.

Adams 1912
Joseph Quincy Adams. "Lordinge (*alias* 'Lodowick') Barry." *Modern Philology* 9.4 (1912): 567–70.

Adams 1913
Joseph Quincy Adams. "*Every Woman In Her Humor* and *The Dumb Knight.*" *Modern Philology* 10.3 (1913): 413–32.

Adams 1914
Joseph Quincy Adams. "William Heminge and Shakespeare." *Modern Philology* 12.1 (1914): 51–64.

Adams 1917
Joseph Quincy Adams. *The Dramatic Records of Sir Henry Herbert, Master of the Revels, 1623–1673*. New Haven: Yale University Press; London: Oxford University Press, 1917. Repr. New York: Benjamin Blom, [?1964]).

Adams 1943
Henry Hitch Adams. *English Domestic or, Homiletic Tragedy, 1575 to 1642*. New York: Columbia University Press, 1943.

Adams 1945–46
Joseph Quincy Adams. "The Author-Plot of an Early Seventeenth Century Play." *Library*, 4th series, 26 (1945–46): 17–27.

Adams 1964
John Cranford Adams. "Shakespeare's Revisions in *Titus Andronicus.*" *Shakespeare Quarterly* 15.2 (1964): 177–90.

Adkins

Mary Grace Muse Adkins. "Sixteenth-Century Religious and Political Implications in *Sir John Oldcastle*." *University of Texas Studies in English* 22 (1942): 86–104.

Adler

Doris Adler. *Philip Massinger*. TEAS 435. Boston: Twayne, 1987.

AED 1

Alfred Harbage. *Annals of English Drama, 975–1700: An Analytical Record of All Plays, Extant or Lost, Chronologically Arranged and Indexed by Authors, Titles, Dramatic Companies, &c.* Philadelphia: University of Pennsylvania Press, 1940.

AED 2

Alfred Harbage. *Annals of English Drama, 975–1700*. 2nd ed. Rev. S. Schoenbaum. London: Methuen, 1964.

AED 3

Alfred Harbage. *Annals of English Drama, 975–1700*. 3rd ed. Rev. Sylvia Stoler Wagonheim. London and New York: Routledge, 1989.

Aggeler

Geoffrey Aggeler. "The Rebellion in Cavalier Drama." *Western Humanities Review* 32 (1978): 53–75.

Alexander 1926

Peter Alexander. "The Taming of a Shrew." *TLS* 16 September 1926: 614.

Alexander 1928

Peter Alexander. "*Troilus and Cressida*, 1609." *Library* 9 (1928): 267–86.

Alfar

Cristina León Alfar. "Staging the Feminine Performance of Desire: Masochism in *The Maid's Tragedy*." *Papers on Language and Literature* 31.3 (1995): 313–33.

Alford

John A. Alford. "'My Name is Worship': Masquerading Vice in Medwall's *Nature*." In *From Page to Performance: Essays in Early English Drama*, ed. idem, 151–77. East Lansing: Michigan State University Press, 1995.

Allen & Muir

Shakespeare's Plays in Quarto: A Facsimile Edition of Copies Primarily from the Henry E. Huntington Library, ed. Michael J. B. Allen and Kenneth Muir. Berkeley: University of California Press, 1981.

Anderson 1978

Donald K. Anderson Jr. "John Ford." In *The Later Jacobean and Caroline Dramatists: A Survey and Bibliography of Recent Studies in English Renaissance*

Drama, ed. Terence P. Logan and Denzell S. Smith, 120–51. Lincoln and London: University of Nebraska Press, 1978.

Anderson 1986
Donald K. Anderson Jr. "Sequentiality and Manipulation of Response in Ford's *The Fancies Chaste and Noble*." In *"Concord in Discord": The Plays of John Ford, 1586–1986*, ed. idem, 241–64. New York: AMS Press, 1986.

Andreadis
John Lyly. *Mother Bombie*. Ed. A. Harriette Andreadis. Salzburg: Institut für Englische Sprache und Literatur, Universität Salzburg, 1975.

Andrews 1913
Clarence Edward Andrews. *Richard Brome: A Study of His Life and Works*. Yale Studies in English 46. New York: Henry Holt, 1913.

Andrews 1971
Michael C. Andrews. "*Jack Drum's Entertainment* as Burlesque." *Renaissance Quarterly* 24.2 (1971): 226–31.

Andrews 1987
John F. Andrews. "William Shakespeare." In *Dictionary of Literary Biography* 62: *Elizabethan Dramatists*, ed. Fredson Bowers, 267–353. Detroit: Gale, 1987.

Arber
Edward Arber, ed. *A Transcript of the Registers of the Company of Stationers of London, 1554–1640 A.D.* 5 vols. London: privately printed, 1875–1877, and Birmingham, 1894. Repr. New York: Peter Smith, 1950.

Archdeacon
Anthony Archdeacon. "The Publication of *No-body and Some-body*: Humanism, History and Economics in the Early Jacobean Public Theatre." *Early Modern Literary Studies* 16.1 (2012). http://purl.org.emls/16–1/archnobo.htm.

Archer 1656
Edward Archer. *An Exact and Perfect Catalogue of All the Plays that Were Ever Printed*. London, 1656.

Archer 2011
John Michael Archer. "Citizens and Aliens as Working Subjects in Dekker's *The Shoemaker's Holiday*." In *Working Subjects in Early Modern English Drama*, ed. Michelle Dowd and Natasha Korda, 37–52. Farnham, UK, and Burlington, VT: Ashgate, 2011.

Arden
The Arden Edition of the Works of William Shakespeare

Armstrong
R. L. Armstrong, ed. *Edward III*. In *Six Early Plays Related to the Shakespeare Canon*, ed. Ephraim B. Everitt. Anglistica 14. Copenhagen: Rosenkilde and Bagger, 1965.

Arrell

Douglas H. Arrell. *"King Leir* at Gowthwaite Hall." *Medieval and Renaissance Drama in England* 25 (2012): 83–93.

Ashe

Dora Jean Ashe. "The Text of Peele's *Edward I." Studies in Bibliography* 7 (1955): 153–70.

Ashton

J. W. Ashton. "Revision in Munday's *John a Kent and John a Cumber." Modern Language Notes* 48.8 (1933): 531–37.

ASMAR

Arizona Studies in the Middle Ages and the Renaissance.

Aspinall

Dana E. Aspinall. "The Play and Its Critics." In *"The Taming of the Shrew": Critical Essays*, ed. idem, 3–38. New York and London: Routledge, 2002.

Astington 1979

John H. Astington. "The Popularity of *Cupid's Revenge." Studies in English Literature, 1500–1900* 19.2 (1979): 215–27.

Astington 1985

John H. Astington. "Descent Machinery in the Playhouse." *Medieval and Renaissance Drama in England* 2 (1985): 119–33.

Astington 1986

John H. Astington. "Staging at St James's Palace in the Seventeenth Century." *Theatre Research International* 11.3 (1986): 199–213.

Astington 1988

John H. Astington. "Malvolio and the Dark House." *Shakespeare Survey* 41 (1988): 55–62.

Astington 1991

John H. Astington. "The Origins of the *Roxana* and *Messallina* Illustrations." *Shakespeare Survey* 43 (1990 [1991]): 149–69.

Astington 1992

John H. Astington, ed. *The Development of Shakespeare's Theater*. New York: AMS Press, 1992.

Astington 1999a

John H. Astington. *English Court Theatre, 1558–1642*. Cambridge: Cambridge University Press, 1999.

Astington 1999b

John H. Astington. "Tarlton and the Sanguine Temperament." *Theatre Notebook* 53.1 (1999): 2–7.

Astington 2006

John H. Astington. "Playing the Man: Acting at the Red Bull and the Fortune." *Early Theatre* 9.2 (2006): 130–43.

Astington 2009

John H. Astington. "Court Theatre." In *The Oxford Handbook of Early Modern Theatre*, ed. Richard Dutton, 307–22. Oxford: Oxford University Press, 2009.

Astington 2010

John H. Astington. *Actors and Acting in Shakespeare's Time: The Art of Stage Playing*. Cambridge: Cambridge University Press, 2010.

Aston

Margaret Aston. *The King's Bedpost: Art, Reformation and Iconography in a Tudor Group Portrait*. Cambridge: Cambridge University Press, 1993.

Atkin

Tamara Atkin. "Manuscript, Print, and the Circulation of Dramatic Texts: A Reconsideration of the Manuscript of *The Marriage of Wit and Wisdom*." *English Manuscript Studies 1100–1700* 15 (2009): 152–65.

Auchter

Dorothy Auchter. *Dictionary of Literary and Dramatic Censorship in Tudor and Stuart England*. Westport, CT, and London: Greenwood Press, 2001.

Austern

Linda Phyllis Austern. "The Music in the Play [*Othello*]." In William Shakespeare, *Othello, The Moor of Venice*, ed. Michael Neill, 445–54. Oxford: Clarendon Press, 2006.

Axton 1977

Marie Axton. *The Queen's Two Bodies: Drama and the Elizabethan Succession*. London: Royal Historical Society, 1977.

Axton 1979

Three Rastell Plays: "Four Elements," "Calisto and Melebea," "Gentleness and Nobility." Ed. Richard Axton. Cambridge: Brewer, 1979.

Axton 1982

Three Tudor Classical Interludes: "Thersites," "Jacke Jugeler," "Horestes." Ed. Marie Axton. Cambridge: Brewer; Totowa, NJ: Rowman and Littlefield, 1982.

Axton 1994

Richard Axton. "Royal Throne, Royal Bed: John Heywood and Spectacle." *Medieval English Theatre* 16 (1994): 66–75.

Axton 1995

Marie Axton. "*Summer's Last Will and Testament*: Revels' End." In *The Reign of Elizabeth I: Court and Culture in the Last Decade*, ed. John Guy, 258–73.

Cambridge: Cambridge University Press in association with the Folger Institute, 1995.

Axton & Happé

The Plays of John Heywood. Ed. Richard Axton and Peter Happé. Cambridge: Brewer, 1991.

Ayres 1970

Philip J. Ayres. "The Revision of 'Lust's Dominion'." *Notes and Queries* 17.6 (1970): 212–13.

Ayres 1972

Philip J. Ayres. "Marston's *Antonio's Revenge*: The Morality of the Revenging Hero." *Studies in English Literature, 1500–1900* 12.2 (1972): 359–74.

Ayres 1990

Ben Jonson. *Sejanus His Fall.* Ed. Philip J. Ayres. Revels Plays. Manchester: Manchester University Press; New York: St. Martin's Press, 1990.

Bach

Rebecca Ann Bach. *Shakespeare and Renaissance Literature before Heterosexuality.* Basingstoke, UK, and New York: Palgrave Macmillan, 2007.

Bailey

Amanda Bailey. "Custom, Debt, and the Valuation of Service Within and Without Early Modern England." In *Working Subjects in Early Modern English Drama*, ed. Michelle M. Dowd and Natasha Korda, 193–208. Farnham, UK, and Burlington, VT: Ashgate, 2011.

Baillie

A Choice Ternary of English Plays: Gratiae Theatrales (1662). Ed. William M. Baillie. MRTS 26. Binghamton, NY: Center for Medieval and Early Renaissance Studies, State University of New York at Binghamton, 1984.

Baines

Barbara J. Baines. *Thomas Heywood.* TEAS 388. Boston: Twayne, 1984.

Baker 1986

Donald C. Baker. "Is *Wisdom* a 'Professional' Play?" In *The Wisdom Symposium: Papers from the Trinity College Medieval Festival*, ed. Milla Cozart Riggio, 67–86. New York: AMS Press, 1986.

Baker 1998

John C. Baker. "Towards a New Date and Suggested Authorship Attribution for the *Timon* MS." *Notes and Queries* 45.3 (1998): 300–02.

Baker et al.

The Late Medieval Religious Plays of Bodleian MSS Digby 133 and e Museo 160. Ed. Donald C. Baker, John L. Murphy, and Louis B. Hall Jr. EETS 283. Oxford: Oxford University Press, 1982.

Baker & Murphy
Donald C. Baker and J. L. Murphy. "The Late Medieval Plays of MS. Digby 133: Scribes, Dates, and Early History." *Research Opportunities in Renaissance Drama* 10 (1967): 153–56.

Bald 1929
Thomas Middleton. *A Game at Chesse*. Ed. R. C. Bald. Cambridge: Cambridge University Press, 1929.

Bald 1937a
R. C. Bald. "The Chronology of Middleton's Plays." *Modern Language Review* 32.1 (1937): 33–43.

Bald 1937b
R. C. Bald. "Sir William Berkeley's *The Lost Lady*." *Library*, 4th ser., 17 (1937): 395–426.

Bald 1938a
R. C. Bald. *Bibliographical Studies in the Beaumont and Fletcher Folio of 1647*. Oxford: Oxford University Press for the Bibliographical Society, 1937 [1938].

Bald 1938b
Thomas Middleton. *Hengist, King of Kent; or The Mayor of Queenborough*. Ed. R. C. Bald. New York and London: Charles Scribner's, 1938.

Bald & Brown
The Knave in Grain. Ed. R. C. Bald and Arthur Brown. MSR. Oxford: Oxford University Press, 1960 [1961].

Baldwin 1927
Thomas Whitfield Baldwin. *The Organization and Personnel of the Shakespearean Company*. Princeton: Princeton University Press, 1927.

Baldwin 2001
The Wisest Have Their Fools about Them. Ed. Elizabeth Baldwin. MSR. Oxford: Oxford University Press, 2001.

Baldwyn
The Old English Drama: A Selection of Plays from the Old English Dramatists. Ed. Charles Baldwyn. 2 vols. London: Hurst, Robinson, 1824–1825.

Bale
John Bale. *A brefe Comedy or Enterlude of Johan Baptystes preachynge in the wyldernesse*. In *The Harleian Miscellany: or, a Collection of Scarce, Curious, and Entertaining Pamphlets and Tracts, as well in Manuscript as in Print, Found in the late Earl of Oxford's Library*, 1: 97–110. London: printed for T. Osborne in Gray's Inn, 1744.

Ballaster

Ros Ballaster. "The First Female Dramatists." In *Women and Literature in Britain, 1500–1700*, ed. Helen Wilcox, 267–90. Cambridge: Cambridge University Press, 1996.

Bamford

Karen Bamford. "Sexual Violence in *The Queen of Corinth*." In *Other Voices, Other Views: Expanding the Canon in English Renaissance Studies*, ed. Helen Ostovich, Mary V. Silcox, and Graham Roebuck, 234–52. Newark, DE: University of Delaware Press; London: Associated University Presses, 1999.

Bancroft

Victoria Bancroft. "A 'Lost' Play Found: Thomas Jordan's *The Walks of Islington and Hogsdon*." *Notes and Queries* 60.1 (2013): 45–47.

Bang 1906

Willy Bang, ed. *The Queen, or The Excellency of Her Sex*. Materialien zur Kunde des älteren Englischen Dramas 13. Louvain: Uystpruyst, 1906.

Bang 1908

"*The Tragical Reign of Selimus*," *1594*. Ed. Willy Bang. MSR. Oxford: Oxford University Press, 1908 [1909].

Bang & McKerrow

"*The Enterlude of Youth*" nebst Fragmenten des "*Playe of Lucres*" und von "*Nature*." Ed. Willy Bang and R. B. McKerrow. Materialien zur Kunde des älteren Englischen Dramas 12. Louvain: Uystpruyst, 1905.

Barber 1959

C. L. Barber. *Shakespeare's Festive Comedy: A Study of Dramatic Form and Its Relation to Social Custom*. Princeton: Princeton University Press, 1959.

Barber 1968

Thomas Middleton. *A Trick to Catch the Old One*. Ed. Charles Barber. Fountainwell Drama Texts. Berkeley and Los Angeles: University of California Press, 1968.

Barber 1979a

Thomas Heywood and Richard Brome. *An Edition of "The Late Lancashire Witches*." Ed. Laird H. Barber. New York and London: Garland, 1979.

Barber 1979b

Misogonus. Ed. Lester E. Barber. New York and London: Garland, 1979.

Barbour

Richard Barbour. *The Third Voyage Journals: Writing and Performance in the London East India Company, 1607–10*. New York: Palgrave Macmillan, 2009.

Barish

Jonas Barish. *The Antitheatrical Prejudice*. Berkeley: University of California Press, 1981.

Barker 1958
Richard Hindry Barker. *Thomas Middleton*. New York: Columbia University Press, 1958.

Barker 2004
"Common Conditions" [?1576]. Ed. Roberta Barker. MSR. Oxford: Oxford University Press, 2004.

Barker 2011
Roberta Barker. "The Duchess High and Low: A Performance History of *The Duchess of Malfi*." In *The Duchess of Malfi: A Critical Guide*, ed. Christina Luckyj, 42–65. Continuum Renaissance Drama. London and New York: Continuum, 2011.

Barker & Hinds
The Routledge Anthology of Renaissance Drama. Ed. Simon Barker and Hilary Hinds. London and New York: Routledge, 2003. Repr. 2005.

Barrie
Robert Barrie. "'Unknown Languages' and Subversive Play in *The Spanish Tragedy*." *Explorations in Renaissance Culture* 21 (1995): 63–80.

Barroll 1988
Leeds Barroll. "A New History for Shakespeare and His Time." *Shakespeare Quarterly* 39.4 (1988): 441–64.

Barroll 1991
Leeds Barroll. *Politics, Plague, and Shakespeare's Theater: The Stuart Years*. Ithaca, NY, and London: Cornell University Press, 1991.

Barroll 2001
Leeds Barroll. *Anna of Denmark, Queen of England: A Cultural Biography*. Philadelphia: University of Pennsylvania Press, 2001.

Barroll 2002
Leeds Barroll. "Shakespeare, Noble Patrons, and the Pleasures of 'Common' Playing." In *Shakespeare and Theatrical Patronage in Early Modern England*, ed. Paul Whitfield White and Suzanne R. Westfall, 90–121. Cambridge: Cambridge University Press, 2002.

Barroll 2005
Leeds Barroll. "Shakespeare and the Second Blackfriars Theater." *Shakespeare Studies* 33 (2005): 156–70.

Barroll 2007
Leeds Barroll. "Mythologizing the Ottoman: *The Jew of Malta* and *The Battle of Alcazar*." In *Remapping the Mediterranean World in Early Modern English Writings*, ed. Goran V. Stanivukovic, 117–30. Basingstoke, UK, and New York: Palgrave Macmillan, 2007.

Bartels 1993

Emily C. Bartels. *Spectacles of Strangeness: Imperialism, Alienation, and Marlowe.* Philadelphia: University of Pennsylvania Press, 1993.

Bartels 2007

Emily C. Bartels. *"The Battle of Alcazar,* the Mediterranean, and the Moor." In *Remapping the Mediterranean World in Early Modern English Writings,* ed. Goran V. Stanivukovic, 97–116. Basingstoke, UK, and New York: Palgrave Macmillan, 2007.

Bartels 2008

Emily C. Bartels. *Speaking of the Moor: From "Alcazar" to "Othello."* Philadelphia: University of Pennsylvania Press, 2008.

Bartholomeusz

Dennis Bartholomeusz. *"Macbeth" and the Players.* Cambridge: Cambridge University Press, 1969.

Bartolovich

Crystal Bartolovich. "London's the Thing: Alienation, the Market, and *Englishmen for My Money." Huntington Library Quarterly* 71.1 (2008): 137–56.

Barton 1973

Anne Barton. "'Nature's piece 'gainst fancy': The Divided Catastrophe in *Antony and Cleopatra.*" An Inaugural Lecture. London: Bedford College (University of London), 1973.

Barton 1977

Anne Barton. "'He that plays the king': Ford's *Perkin Warbeck* and the Stuart History Play." In *English Drama: Forms and Development: Essays in Honour of Muriel Clara Bradbrook,* ed. Marie Axton and Raymond Williams, 69–93. Cambridge: Cambridge University Press, 1977.

Barton 1984

Anne Barton. *Ben Jonson, Dramatist.* Cambridge: Cambridge University Press, 1984.

Barton 1994

Anne Barton. "'Enter Mariners Wet': Realism in Shakespeare's Last Plays." In *Essays, Mainly Shakespearean,* 182–203. Cambridge: Cambridge University Press, 1994.

Baskervill 1929

Charles Read Baskervill. *The Elizabethan Jig and Related Song Drama.* Chicago: University of Chicago Press, 1929.

Baskervill 1932

Charles Read Baskervill. "A Prompt Copy of *A Looking Glass for London and England." Modern Philology* 30.1 (1932): 29–51.

Bate 1992
Jonathan Bate. "The Performance of Revenge: *Titus Andronicus* and *The Spanish Tragedy*." In *The Show Within: Dramatic and Other Insets. English Renaissance Drama (1550–1642)*, ed. François Laroque, 1:267–83. 2 vols. Montpellier: Publications de l'Université Paul-Valéry, 1992.

Bate 1995
William Shakespeare. *Titus Andronicus*. Ed. Jonathan Bate. Arden 3. London and New York: Routledge, 1995.

Bate 1997
Jonathan Bate. *The Genius of Shakespeare*. London: Picador, 1997.

Bate 2008
Jonathan Bate. *Soul of the Age: The Life, Mind and World of William Shakespeare*. London and New York: Viking, 2008.

Bate & Rasmussen 2009
Jonathan Bate. Introduction to *Macbeth*. Ed. idem and Eric Rasmussen. RSC Shakespeare. Basingstoke, UK: Macmillan, 2009.

Bate & Rasmussen 2010
William Shakespeare. *Henry V*. Ed. Jonathan Bate and Eric Rasmussen. RSC Shakespeare. Basingstoke, UK: Macmillan, 2010.

Baumann
"Claudius Tiberius Nero": A Critical Edition of the Play Published Anonymously in 1607. Ed. Uwe Baumann. Frankfurt-am-Main: Lang, 1990.

Bawcutt 1958
Thomas Middleton and William Rowley. *The Changeling*. Ed. Nigel W. Bawcutt. Revels Plays. London: Methuen, 1958.

Bawcutt 1978
Christopher Marlowe. *The Jew of Malta*. Ed. N. W. Bawcutt. Revels Plays. Manchester: Manchester University Press; Baltimore: Johns Hopkins University Press, 1978.

Bawcutt 1991
William Shakespeare. *Measure for Measure*. Ed. N. W. Bawcutt. Oxford: Clarendon Press, 1991.

Bawcutt 1996
N. W. Bawcutt. *The Control and Censorship of Caroline Drama: The Records of Sir Henry Herbert, Master of the Revels 1623–73*. Oxford: Clarendon Press, 1996.

Bawcutt & Duncan-Jones
Ralph Crane's Transcript of "A Game at Chess," Bodleian Manuscript Malone 25. Ed. N. W. Bawcutt and Katherine Duncan-Jones. Malone Society *Collections XV*, 1–93. Oxford: Oxford University Press, 1993.

Bayer

Mark Bayer. "The Red Bull Playhouse." In *The Oxford Handbook of the Early Modern Theatre*, ed. Richard Dutton, 225–39. Oxford: Oxford University Press, 2009.

Bayman & Southcombe

Anna Bayman and George Southcombe. "Shrews in Pamphlets and Plays." In *Gender and Power in Shrew-Taming Narratives, 1500–1700*, 11–28. Basingstoke, UK, and New York: Palgrave Macmillan, 2010.

Beadle

Richard Beadle. "Ingelend, Thomas (*fl.* 1550–1560)." In *ODNB*, 29: 243.

Beal

Peter Beal. "Massinger at Bay: Unpublished Verses in a War of the Theatres." *Yearbook of English Studies* 10 (1980): 190–203.

Beaurline 1966a

L. A. Beaurline, ed. *The Captain*. In *The Dramatic Works in the Beaumont and Fletcher Canon*, vol. 1. Cambridge: Cambridge University Press, 1966.

Beaurline 1966b

Ben Jonson. *Epicoene or The Silent Woman*. Ed. L. A. Beaurline. RRDS. Lincoln: University of Nebraska Press, 1966.

Beaurline 1970

L. A. Beaurline, ed. *Love's Pilgrimage*. In *The Dramatic Works in the Beaumont and Fletcher Canon*, vol. 2. Cambridge: Cambridge University Press, 1970.

Beaurline 1971

The Works of Sir John Suckling. Ed. L. A. Beaurline. Vol. 2: *The Plays*. Oxford: Clarendon Press, 1971.

Beaurline 1976

L. A. Beaurline, ed. *The Noble Gentleman*. In *The Dramatic Works in the Beaumont and Fletcher Canon*, vol. 3. Cambridge: Cambridge University Press, 1976.

Beaurline 1990

William Shakespeare. *King John*. Ed. L. A. Beaurline. New Cambridge Shakespeare. Cambridge: Cambridge University Press, 1990.

Beckerman 1962

Bernard Beckerman. *Shakespeare at the Globe, 1599–1609*. New York: Macmillan, 1962.

Beckerman 1980

Bernard Beckerman. "The Persons Personated: Character Lists in English Renaissance Play Texts." In *Poetry and Drama in the English Renaissance*, ed. Koshi Nakanori and Yasuo Tamaizumi, 61–69. Tokyo: Kinokuniya, 1980.

Beckerman 1989

Bernard Beckerman. "Theatrical Plots and Elizabethan Stage Practice." In *Shakespeare and Dramatic Tradition: Essays in Honor of S. F. Johnson*, ed. W. R. Elton and William B. Long, 109–24. Newark, DE: University of Delaware Press; London and Toronto: Associated University Presses, 1989.

Bednarz 1991

James P. Bednarz. "Representing Jonson: *Histriomastix* and the Origin of the Poets' War." *Huntington Library Quarterly* 54.1 (1991): 1–30.

Bednarz 2001

James P. Bednarz. *Shakespeare and the Poets' War*. New York: Columbia University Press, 2001.

Bednarz 2002

James P. Bednarz. "Writing and Revenge: John Marston's *Histriomastix*." *Comparative Drama* 36.1–2 (2002): 21–51.

Bednarz 2010a

James P. Bednarz. "John Marston's Induction to *What You Will*: A Re-examination." *Ben Jonson Journal* 17.2 (2010): 293–308.

Bednarz 2010b

James P. Bednarz. "Was *Volpone* Acted at Cambridge in 1606?" *Ben Jonson Journal* 17.2 (2010): 183–96.

Bednarz 2011

James P. Bednarz. "Collaboration: The Shadow of Shakespeare." In *Thomas Middleton in Context*, ed. Suzanne Gossett, 211–18. Cambridge: Cambridge University Press, 2011.

Bednarz 2012

James P. Bednarz. "Dekker's Response to the Chorus of *Henry V* in 1599." *Notes and Queries* 59.1 (2012): 63–68.

Beecher

Donald Beecher. Introduction to *Supposes (I suppositi)*, by Lodovico Ariosto. Translated by George Gascoigne. Ottawa: Dovehouse Editions, 1999.

Beilin

Elaine V. Beilin. *Redeeming Eve: Women Writers of the English Renaissance*. Princeton: Princeton University Press, 1987.

Belsey

Catherine Belsey. "Emblem and Antithesis in *The Duchess of Malfi*." *Renaissance Drama* n.s. 11 (1980): 115–34.

Benbow

R. Mark Benbow, ed. *The Arraignment of Paris*. In *The Dramatic Works of George Peele*, vol. 3. New Haven and London: Yale University Press, 1970.

Benecke

Ingrid Benecke. "Simon Forman's Notes on *Macbeth*—The Alternative Reading." *Notes and Queries* 57.3 (2010): 389–93.

Bennett 1965

A. L. Bennett. "The Early Editions of Philip Massinger's Plays." *Papers on Language and Literature* 1.2 (1965): 177–81.

Bennett 2000

Alexandra G. Bennett. "Female Performativity in *The Tragedy of Mariam*." *Studies in English Literature, 1500–1900* 40.2 (2000): 293–309.

Bennett 2003

Alexandra G. Bennett. "Playing by and with the Rules: Genre, Politics, and Perception in Mary Wroth's *Love's Victorie*." In *Women and Culture at the Courts of the Stuart Queens*, ed. Clare McManus, 122–39. Basingstoke, UK, and New York: Palgrave Macmillan, 2003.

Bentley

Gerald Eades Bentley. *The Jacobean and Caroline Stage*. 7 vols. Oxford: Clarendon Press, 1941–68.

Bentley 1948

Gerald Eades Bentley. "Randolph's *Praeludium* and the Salisbury Court Theatre." In *Joseph Quincy Adams Memorial Studies*, ed. James G. McManaway, Giles E. Dawson, and Edwin E. Willoughby, 775–83. Washington, DC: Folger Shakespeare Library, 1948.

Bentley 1971

Gerald Eades Bentley. *The Profession of Dramatist in Shakespeare's Time, 1590–1642*. Princeton: Princeton University Press, 1971.

Bentley 1981

Gerald Eades Bentley. "The Theatres and the Actors." In *The Revels History of Drama in English*, vol. 4, *1613–1660*, ed. Philip Edwards, idem, Kathleen McLuskie, and Lois Potter, 69–124. London and New York: Methuen, 1981.

Bentley 1984

Gerald Eades Bentley. *The Profession of Player in Shakespeare's Time, 1590–1642*. Princeton: Princeton University Press, 1984.

Berek 1980

Peter Berek. "*Locrine* Revised, *Selimus*, and Early Responses to *Tamburlaine*." *Research Opportunities in Renaissance Drama* 23 (1980): 33–54.

Berek 1987

Peter Berek. "*Locrine* and *Selimus*." In *Dictionary of Literary Biography* 62: *Elizabethan Dramatists*, ed. Fredson Bowers, 369–72. Detroit: Gale, 1987.

Berger 1979
Thomas Leland Berger, ed. *A Critical Old-Spelling Edition of Thomas Dekker's "Blurt, Master Constable" (1602).* Salzburg: Institut für Anglistik und Amerikanistik, Universität Salzburg, 1979.

Berger 1996
Thomas L. Berger. "Looking for Shakespeare in Caroline England." *Viator* 27 (1996): 323–59.

Berger 1998
Thomas L. Berger, William C. Bradford, and Sidney L. Sondergard. *An Index of Characters in Early Modern English Drama: Printed Plays, 1500–1660.* Rev. ed. Cambridge: Cambridge University Press, 1998.

Berger 2007
Thomas L. Berger. "Shakespeare Writ Small: Early Single Editions of Shakespeare's Plays." In *A Concise Companion to Shakespeare and the Text*, ed. Andrew Murphy, 57–70. Oxford: Blackwell, 2007.

Berger & Donovan
Thomas L. Berger and Dennis G. Donovan, eds. *Caesar and Pompey.* In *The Plays of George Chapman: The Tragedies with "Sir Gyles Goosecappe."* Cambridge: Brewer, 1987.

Berger & Lander
Thomas L. Berger and Jesse M. Lander. "Shakespeare in Print, 1593–1640." In *A Companion to Shakespeare*, ed. David Scott Kastan, 395–413. Oxford: Blackwell, 1999.

Berger & Mowat
William Shakespeare. *"Titus Andronicus," 1594.* Ed. Thomas L. Berger and Barbara Mowat. MSR. Oxford: Oxford University Press, 2003.

Bergeron 1974
David M. Bergeron. "The Deposition Scene in *Richard II.*" *Renaissance Papers* 1974: 31–37.

Bergeron 1978
David Bergeron. "The Restoration of Hermione." In *Shakespeare's Romances Reconsidered*, ed. Carol McGinnis Kay and Henry E. Jacobs, 125–33. Lincoln: University of Nebraska Press, 1978.

Bergeron 1986
David M. Bergeron. "Brother-Sister Relationships in Ford's 1633 Plays." In *"Concord in Discord": The Plays of John Ford, 1586–1986*, ed. Donald K. Anderson Jr., 195–219. New York: AMS Press, 1986.

Bergeron 1996
David M. Bergeron. "Fletcher's *The Woman's Prize*, Transgression, and *Querelle des Femmes.*" *Medieval and Renaissance Drama in England* 8 (1996): 146–64.

Bergeron 2006

David M. Bergeron. *Textual Patronage in English Drama, 1570–1640*. Aldershot, UK, and Burlington, VT: Ashgate, 2006.

Bergeron 2008

David M. Bergeron. "A Murdered Playwright, a Presumptuous Actor, and *The Martyred Soldier*." *Research Opportunities in Medieval and Renaissance Drama* 47 (2008): 72–81.

Berman

Alan J. Berman, ed. *"Greene's Tu Quoque or, The Cittie Gallant," by J. Cooke: A Critical Edition*. New York and London: Garland, 1984.

Berry 1984

Herbert Berry. "The Globe Bewitched and *El Hombre Fiel*." *Medieval and Renaissance Drama in England* 1 (1984): 211–30.

Berry 1986

Herbert Berry. *The Boar's Head Playhouse*. Washington, DC: Folger Shakespeare Library; London and Toronto: Associated University Presses, 1986.

Best 1968a

Michael R. Best. "Lyly's Static Drama." *Renaissance Drama* n.s. 1 (1968): 75–86.

Best 1968b

Michael R. Best. "The Staging and Production of the Plays of John Lyly." *Theatre Research* 9.2 (1968): 104–17.

Betteridge

Thomas Betteridge. "John Heywood and Court Drama." In *The Oxford Handbook of Tudor Literature, 1485–1603*, ed. Mike Pincombe and Cathy Shrank, 170–86. Oxford: Oxford University Press, 2009.

Bevington 1962

David M. Bevington. *From "Mankind" to Marlowe: Growth of Structure in the Popular Drama of Tudor England*. Cambridge, MA: Harvard University Press, 1962. Repr. 1968.

Bevington 1968

David M. Bevington. *Tudor Drama and Politics: A Critical Approach to Topical Meaning*. Cambridge, MA: Harvard University Press, 1968.

Bevington 1972

The Macro Plays: "The Castle of Perseverance," "Wisdom," "Mankind." A Facsimile Edition with Facing Transcriptions, ed. David Bevington. Folger Facsimiles, Manuscript Series 1. New York: Johnson Reprint, 1972.

Bevington 1973
David M. Bevington. "Popular and Courtly Traditions on the Early Tudor Stage." In *Medieval Drama*, ed. Neville Denny, 91–107. Stratford-upon-Avon Studies 16. London: Edward Arnold, 1973.

Bevington 1975
Medieval Drama. Ed. David Bevington. Boston: Houghton Mifflin, 1975.

Bevington 1986
David M. Bevington. "'Blake and wyght, fowll and fayer': Stage Picture in *Wisdom*." In *The Wisdom Symposium: Papers from the Trinity College Medieval Festival*, ed. Milla Cozart Riggio, 18–38. New York: AMS Press, 1986.

Bevington 1987
William Shakespeare. *Henry IV, Part 1*. Ed. David Bevington. Oxford: Clarendon Press, 1987.

Bevington 1990
William Shakespeare. *Antony and Cleopatra*. Ed. David Bevington. New Cambridge Shakespeare. Cambridge: Cambridge University Press, 1990.

Bevington 1991
John Lyly. *Campaspe*. Ed. G. K. Hunter; *Sappho and Phao*. Ed. David Bevington. Revels Plays. Manchester: Manchester University Press; New York: St. Martin's Press, 1991.

Bevington 1996
John Lyly. *Endymion*. Ed. David Bevington. Revels Plays. Manchester: Manchester University Press; New York: St. Martin's Press, 1996.

Bevington 1998
William Shakespeare. *Troilus and Cressida*. Ed. David Bevington. Arden 3. Walton-on-Thames, UK: Thomas Nelson, 1998.

Bevington 2000a
John Lyly. *Midas*. Ed. David Bevington. Revels Plays. Manchester: Manchester University Press; New York: St. Martin's Press, 2000.

Bevington 2000b
David Bevington. "The Major Comedies." In *The Cambridge Companion to Ben Jonson*, ed. Richard Harp and Stanley Stewart, 72–89. Cambridge: Cambridge University Press, 2000.

Bevington 2002a
David Bevington. "Literature and the Theatre." In *The Cambridge History of Early Modern English Literature*, ed. David Loewenstein and Janel Mueller, 428–56. Cambridge: Cambridge University Press, 2002.

Bevington 2002b
David Bevington. "Staging the A- and B-Texts of *Doctor Faustus*." In *Marlowe's Empery: Expanding His Critical Contexts*, ed. Sara Munson Deats and Robert

A. Logan, 43–60. Newark, DE: University of Delaware Press; London: Associated University Presses, 2002.

Bevington 2004
David Bevington, ed. *The Complete Works of Shakespeare*. 5th ed. New York: Pearson, 2004.

Bevington 2007a
David Bevington. "One Hell of an Ending: Staging Last Judgment in the Towneley Plays and in *Doctor Faustus* A and B." In *"Bring furth the pagants": Essays in Early English Drama Presented to Alexandra F. Johnston*, ed. David N. Klausner and Karen Sawyer Marsalek, 292–310. Toronto, Buffalo, and London: University of Toronto Press, 2007.

Bevington 2007b
David Bevington. "Staging the Reformation: Power and Theatricality in the Plays of William Wager." In *Interludes and Early Modern Society: Studies in Gender, Power and Theatricality*, ed. Peter Happé and Wim Hüsken, 353–80. Amsterdam and New York: Rodopi, 2007.

Bevington 2007c
David Bevington. *This Wide and Universal Theater: Shakespeare in Performance, Then and Now*. Chicago and London: University of Chicago Press, 2007.

Bevington 2009
David Bevington. "Christopher Marlowe's *Doctor Faustus* and Nathaniel Woodes's *The Conflict of Conscience*." In *The Oxford Handbook of Tudor Literature, 1485–1603*, ed. Mike Pincombe and Cathy Shrank, 704–17. Oxford: Oxford University Press, 2009.

Bevington 2010
David Bevington. "The Performance History." In *Doctor Faustus: A Critical Guide*, ed. Sara Munson Deats, 41–71. London and New York: Continuum, 2010.

Bevington & Rasmussen
Christopher Marlowe. *Doctor Faustus: A- and B-texts (1604, 1616)*. Ed. David Bevington and Eric Rasmussen. Revels Plays. Manchester: Manchester University Press; New York: St Martin's Press, 1993.

Bevington & Shapiro
David Bevington and James Shapiro. "'What are kings, when regiment is gone?': The Decay of Ceremony in *Edward II*." In *"A Poet and a filthy Play-maker": New Essays on Christopher Marlowe*, ed. Kenneth Friedenreich, Roma Gill, and Constance B. Kuriyama, 263–78. New York: AMS Press, 1988.

Bevington & Smith
David Bevington and David L. Smith. "James I and *Timon of Athens*." *Comparative Drama* 33.1 (1999): 56–87.

Billing
Christian M. Billing. *Masculinity, Corporality and the English Stage, 1580–1635.* Farnham, UK, and Burlington, VT: Ashgate, 2008.

Binnie
George Peele. *The Old Wives Tale.* Ed. Patricia Binnie. Revels Plays. Manchester: Manchester University Press; Baltimore: Johns Hopkins University Press, 1980.

Birchwood
Matthew Birchwood. "Turning to the Turk: Collaboration and Conversion in William Davenant's *The Siege of Rhodes.*" In *Remapping the Mediterranean World in Early Modern English Writings*, ed. Goran V. Stanivukovic, 207–26. Basingstoke, UK, and New York: Palgrave Macmillan, 2007.

Bitot
Michel Bitot. "'Alteration in a Commonwealth': Disturbing Voices in Caroline Drama." *Cahiers Elisabéthains* 47 (1995): 79–86.

BL
The British Library, London

Bland 1996
Mark Bland. "'Invisible Dangers': Censorship and the Subversion of Authority in Early Modern England." *Papers of the Bibliographical Society of America* 90.2 (1996): 151–93.

Bland 1998
Mark Bland. "The Appearance of the Text in Early Modern England." *TEXT* 11 (1998): 91–154.

Bland 1999
Mark Bland. "The London Book-Trade in 1600." In *A Companion to Shakespeare*, ed. David Scott Kastan, 450–63. Oxford: Blackwell, 1999.

Blatt
Thora Balslev Blatt. *The Plays of John Bale: A Study of Ideas, Technique and Style.* Copenhagen: Gad, 1968.

Blayney 1957
Glenn H. Blayney. "Wilkins's Revisions in *The Miseries of Inforst Mariage.*" *JEGP* 56.1 (1957): 23–41.

Blayney 1963
George Wilkins. *The Miseries of Enforced Marriage.* Ed. Glenn H. Blayney. MSR. Oxford: Oxford University Press, 1963 [1964].

Blayney 1972
Peter W. M. Blayney. "*The Booke of Sir Thomas Moore* Re-Examined." *Studies in Philology* 69.2 (1972): 167–91.

Blayney 1982

Peter W. M. Blayney. *The Texts of "King Lear" and Their Origins*, vol. 1: *Nicholas Okes and the First Quarto*. Cambridge: Cambridge University Press, 1982.

Blayney 1991

Peter W. M. Blayney. *The First Folio of Shakespeare*. Washington, DC: Folger Shakespeare Library, 1991.

Blayney 1997

Peter W. M. Blayney. "The Publication of Playbooks." In *A New History of Early English Drama*, ed. John D. Cox and David Scott Kastan, 383–422. New York: Columbia University Press, 1997.

Blayney 2005

Peter W. M. Blayney. "The Alleged Popularity of Playbooks." *Shakespeare Quarterly* 56.1 (2005): 33–50.

Blayney 2007

Peter W. M. Blayney. "STC Publication Statistics: Some Caveats." *Library*, 7th ser., 8.4 (2007): 348–54.

Bliss 1814

Arthur Wilson. *The Inconstant Lady*. Ed. Philip Bliss. Oxford: Samuel Collingwood, 1814.

Bliss 1816

The Seven Dayes of the Weeke. Ed. Philip Bliss. *An Account of "The Christmas Prince," as it was exhibited in the University of Oxford, in the year 1607, now first published from the original manuscript*. In *Miscellanea Antiqua Anglicana; or A Select Collection of Curious Tracts, Illustrative of the History, Literature, Manners, and Biography of the English Nation*, vol. 1, no. 7: 39–55. London: Robert Triphook, 1816.

Bliss 1987

Lee Bliss. *Francis Beaumont*. TEAS 458. Boston: Twayne, 1987.

Bliss 1997

Lee Bliss. "Scribes, Compositors, and Annotators: The Nature of the Copy for the First Folio Text of *Coriolanus*." *Studies in Bibliography* 50 (1997): 224–61.

Bliss 2004

Francis Beaumont and John Fletcher. *A King and No King*. Ed. Lee Bliss. Revels Plays. Manchester: Manchester University Press; New York: Palgrave, 2004.

Bliss 2010

William Shakespeare. *Coriolanus: Updated Edition*. Ed. Lee Bliss. New Cambridge Shakespeare. Cambridge: Cambridge University Press, 2010.

Blissett

William Blissett. "Roman Ben Jonson." In *Ben Jonson's 1616 Folio*, ed. Jennifer Brady and W. H. Herendeen, 90–110. Newark, DE: University of Delaware Press; London and Toronto: Associated University Presses, 1991.

Blistein

David and Bethsabe. Ed. Elmer Blistein. In *The Dramatic Works of George Peele*, vol. 3. New Haven, and London: Yale University Press, 1970.

Blostein

John Marston. *Parasitaster or The Fawn*. Ed. David A. Blostein. Revels Plays. Manchester: Manchester University Press; Baltimore: Johns Hopkins University Press, 1978.

Bly 1998

Mary Bly. "John Cooke: A Playwright Connected to the Whitefriars." *Notes and Queries* 45.3 (1998): 360–61.

Bly 2000

Mary Bly. *Queer Virgins and Virgin Queans on the Early Modern Stage*. Oxford: Oxford University Press, 2000.

Bly 2009

Mary Bly. "The Boy Companies, 1599–1613." In *The Oxford Handbook of Early Modern Theatre*, ed. Richard Dutton, 136–50. Oxford: Oxford University Press, 2009.

Boas 1896

Frederick S. Boas. *Shakespeare and His Predecessors*. London: Murray, 1896. Repr. New York: Haskell House, 1968.

Boas 1901

The Works of Thomas Kyd. Ed. Frederick S. Boas. Oxford: Clarendon Press, 1901. Repr. with corrections, Oxford: Clarendon Press, 1955.

Boas 1908

William Shakespeare. *The Taming of a Shrew*. Ed. Frederick S. Boas. London: Chatto & Windus, 1908.

Boas 1914

Frederick S. Boas. *University Drama in the Tudor Age*. Oxford: Clarendon Press, 1914. Repr. New York: Benjamin Blom, 1966.

Boas 1923

Frederick S. Boas. *Shakespeare & the Universities, and Other Studies in Elizabethan Drama*. New York: Appleton; Oxford: Blackwell, 1923. Repr. Folcroft, PA: Folcroft Library Editions, 1969.

Boas 1950a

Frederick S. Boas. *Queen Elizabeth in Drama and Related Studies*. London: George Allen & Unwin, 1950.

Boas 1950b
Frederick S. Boas. *Thomas Heywood*. London: Williams & Norgate, 1950.

Boas & Greg 1911
The Tragedy of Caesar's Revenge. Ed. Frederick S. Boas and W. W. Greg. MSR. Oxford: Oxford University Press, 1911.

Boas & Greg 1922
The Christmas Prince. Ed. Frederick S. Boas and W. W. Greg. MSR. Oxford: Oxford University Press, 1922 [1923].

Boas & Reed
"Fulgens & Lucres": A Fifteenth-Century Secular Play. Ed. Frederick S. Boas and A. W. Reed. Oxford: Clarendon Press, 1926.

Bodleian
The Bodleian Library, Oxford

Bolton & Gardner
Ben Jonson. *Catiline*. Ed. W. F. Bolton and Jane F. Gardner. RRDS. Lincoln: University of Nebraska Press, 1973.

Bond
Early Plays from the Italian. Ed. R. Warwick Bond. Oxford: Oxford University Press, 1911. Repr. New York: Benjamin Blom, 1967.

Bond & Greg
The Birth of Hercules. Ed. R. Warwick Bond and W. W. Greg. MSR. Oxford: Oxford University Press, 1911.

Booth
Roy Booth. "Witchcraft, Flight and the Early Modern English Stage." *Early Modern Literary Studies* 13.1 (2007). http://purl.oclc.org/emls/13–1/boot-witc.htm.

Borden
Ian Borden. "The Blackfriars Gladiators: Masters of Fence, Playing a Prize, and the Elizabethan and Stuart Theater." In *Inside Shakespeare: Essays on the Blackfriars Stage*, ed. Paul Menzer, 132–46. Selinsgrove, PA: Susquehanna University Press, 2006.

Bordinat & Blaydes
Philip Bordinat and Sophia B. Blaydes. *Sir William Davenant*. TEAS 303. Boston: Twayne, 1981.

Borias
Georges Borias. "Randolph's *Praeludium*: An Edited Transcription, Comprising a Short Introductory Note." *Cahiers Elisabéthains* 29 (1986): 53–76.

Born 1971
Hanspeter Born. *The Rare Wit and the Rude Groom: The Authorship of "A Knack to Know a Knave" in Relation to Greene, Nashe & Shakespeare*. Swiss Studies in English 64. Bern: Francke, n.d. [?1971].

Born 1974
Hanspeter Born. "The Date of *2, 3 Henry VI*." *Shakespeare Quarterly* 25.3 (1974): 323–34.

Borot
Luc Borot. "Richard Overton and Radicalism: The New Intertext of the Civic Ethos in Mid-Seventeenth-Century England." In *English Radicalism, 1550–1850*, ed. Glenn Burgess and Matthew Festenstein, 37–61. Cambridge: Cambridge University Press, 2007.

Bosman 2004
Anston Bosman. "Renaissance Intertheater and the Staging of *Nobody*." *ELH* 71.3 (2004): 559–85.

Bosman 2006
Anston Bosman. "History between Theaters." In *From Performance to Print in Shakespeare's England*, ed. Peter Holland and Stephen Orgel, 191–207. Basingstoke, UK, and New York: Palgrave Macmillan, 2006.

Bosonnet
Felix Bosonnet. *The Function of Stage Properties in Christopher Marlowe's Plays*. Bern: Francke, 1978.

Boswell
Edmond Ironside or War Hath Made All Friends. Ed. Eleanore Boswell. MSR. Oxford: Oxford University Press, 1927 [1928].

Bourke
Roger Bourke. "Falstaff, Nobody, and Will Kemp's 'Giant Hose'." *Notes and Queries* 55.2 (2008): 183–85.

Bowers 1932
Fredson Bowers. "The Stabbing of a Portrait in Elizabethan Tragedy." *Modern Language Notes* 47.6 (1932): 378–85.

Bowers 1937–38
Fredson Bowers. "Problems in Thomas Randolph's *Drinking Academy* and Its Manuscript." *Huntington Library Quarterly* 1.2 (1937–38): 189–98.

Bowers 1939
Fredson Bowers. "Marriot's Two Editions of Randolph's *Aristippus*." *Library*, 4th ser., 20.2 (1939): 163–66.

Bowers 1940
Fredson Bowers. *Elizabethan Revenge Tragedy, 1587–1642*. Princeton: Princeton University Press, 1940.

Bowers 1942

"*The Fa[i]ry Knight or Oberon the Second*": *A Manuscript Play Attributed to Thomas Randolph*. Ed. Fredson Bowers. Chapel Hill: University of North Carolina Press, 1942.

Bowers 1953

Fredson Bowers, ed. *The Dramatic Works of Thomas Dekker*. 4 vols. Cambridge: Cambridge University Press, 1953–61.

Bowers 1959

R. H. Bowers. "Some Folger Academic Drama Manuscripts." *Studies in Bibliography* 12 (1959): 117–30.

Bowers 1970

Fredson Bowers, ed. *Cupid's Revenge*. In *The Dramatic Works in the Beaumont and Fletcher Canon*, vol. 2. Cambridge: Cambridge University Press, 1970.

Bowers 1976

Fredson Bowers, ed. *Beggars' Bush*. In *The Dramatic Works in the Beaumont and Fletcher Canon*, vol. 3. Cambridge: Cambridge University Press, 1976.

Bowers 1979

Fredson Bowers, ed. *The Woman's Prize*. In *The Dramatic Works in the Beaumont and Fletcher Canon*, vol. 4. Cambridge: Cambridge University Press, 1979.

Bowers 1985

Fredson Bowers, ed. *The Wild-Goose Chase*. In *The Dramatic Works in the Beaumont and Fletcher Canon*, vol. 6. Cambridge: Cambridge University Press, 1985.

Bowers 1987

Rick Bowers. "John Lowin: Actor-Manager of the King's Company." *Theatre Survey* 28.1 (1987): 15–35.

Bowers 1996

Fredson Bowers, ed. *The Fair Maid of the Inn*. In *The Dramatic Works in the Beaumont and Fletcher Canon*, vol. 10. Cambridge: Cambridge University Press, 1996.

Bowers 2002

Rick Bowers. "Hysterics, High Camp, and *Dido Queene of Carthage*." In *Marlowe's Empery: Expanding His Critical Contexts*, ed. Sara Munson Deats and Robert A. Logan, 95–106. Newark, DE: University of Delaware Press; London: Associated University Presses, 2002.

Bowsher

Julian Bowsher. *The Rose Theatre: An Archaeological Discovery*. London: Museum of London, 1998.

Boyd
Brian Boyd. "*King John* and *The Troublesome Raigne*: Sources, Structure, Sequence." *Philological Quarterly* 74.1 (1995): 37–56.

Bradbrook 1955
M. C. Bradbrook. *The Growth and Structure of Elizabethan Comedy.* London: Chatto and Windus, 1955.

Bradbrook 1962a
M. C. Bradbrook. "Peele's *Old Wives' Tale*: A Play of Enchantment." *English Studies* 43.1–6 (1962): 323–30.

Bradbrook 1962b
M. C. Bradbrook. *The Rise of the Common Player: A Study of Actor and Society in Shakespeare's England.* London: Chatto and Windus, 1962.

Bradbrook 1966
M. C. Bradbrook. "*The Comedy of Timon*: A Reveling Play of the Inner Temple." *Renaissance Drama* 9 (1966): 83–103.

Bradbrook 1991
Muriel C. Bradbrook. "The Rose Theatre." In *The Arts of Performance in Elizabethan and Early Stuart Drama: Essays for G. K. Hunter,* ed. Murray Briggs, Philip Edwards, Inga-Stina Ewbank, and Eugene M. Waith, 200–10. Edinburgh: Edinburgh University Press, 1991.

Braden 1987a
Gordon Braden. "George Chapman." In *Dictionary of Literary Biography* 62: *Elizabethan Dramatists,* ed. Fredson Bowers, 3–29. Detroit: Gale, 1987.

Braden 1987b
Gordon Braden. "James Shirley." In *Dictionary of Literary Biography* 58: *Jacobean and Caroline Dramatists,* ed. Fredson Bowers, 249–66. Detroit: Gale, 1987.

Braden 1987c
Gordon Braden. "*A Yorkshire Tragedy*." In *Dictionary of Literary Biography* 58: *Jacobean and Caroline Dramatists,* ed. Fredson Bowers, 309–12. Detroit: Gale, 1987.

Braden 2010
Gordon Braden. "Comedy." In *The Oxford History of Literary Translation in English,* vol. 2: *1550–1660,* ed. idem, Robert Cummings, and Stuart Gillespie, 280–92. Oxford: Oxford University Press, 2010.

Bradley 1903
Gammer Gurton's Needle. Ed. Henry Bradley. In *Representative English Comedies with Introductory Essays and Notes,* vol. 1: *From the Beginnings to Shakespeare,* ed. Charles Mills Gayley, 195–261. New York: Macmillan, 1903.

Bradley 1992

David Bradley. *From Text to Performance in the Elizabethan Theatre: Preparing the Play for the Stage*. Cambridge: Cambridge University Press, 1992.

Brandl

Alois Brandl, ed. *Quellen der weltlichen Dramas in England vor Shakespeare*. Strassburg: Trübner, 1898.

Braunmuller 1975

A. R. Braunmuller. "'A Greater Wound': Corruption and Human Frailty in Chapman's 'Chabot, Admiral of France'." *Modern Language Review* 70.2 (1975): 241–59.

Braunmuller 1979

A. R. Braunmuller. "Chapman's 'Bussy D'Ambois' and Field's 'Amends for Ladies'." *Notes and Queries* 26.5 (1979): 401–03.

Braunmuller 1982

The Captive Lady. Ed. A. R. Braunmuller. MSR. Oxford: Oxford University Press, 1982.

Braunmuller 1983a

A. R. Braunmuller. *George Peele*. TEAS 356. Boston: Twayne, 1983.

Braunmuller 1983b

A. R. Braunmuller. "How to Do Things with the Dekker Commentary." *Research Opportunities in Renaissance Drama* 26 (1983): 13–21.

Braunmuller 1984

A. R. Braunmuller. "Early Shakespearian Tragedy and Its Contemporary Context: Cause and Emotion in *Titus Andronicus*, *Richard III*, and *The Rape of Lucrece*." In *Shakespearian Tragedy*, ed. David Palmer and Malcolm Bradbury, 97–128. Stratford-upon-Avon Studies 20. London: Edward Arnold, 1984.

Braunmuller 1989

William Shakespeare. *The Life and Death of King John*. Ed. A. R. Braunmuller. Oxford: Clarendon Press, 1989.

Braunmuller 1990

A. R. Braunmuller. "'To the Globe I rowed': John Holles Sees *A Game at Chess*." *English Literary Renaissance* 20.2 (1990): 340–56.

Braunmuller 1992

A. R. Braunmuller. *Natural Fictions: George Chapman's Major Tragedies*. Newark, DE: University of Delaware Press; London: Associated University Presses, 1992.

Braunmuller 2003
A. R. Braunmuller. "The Arts of the Dramatist." In *The Cambridge Companion to English Renaissance Drama*, ed. idem and Michael Hattaway, 53–92. 2nd ed. Cambridge: Cambridge University Press, 2003.

Braunmuller 2008
William Shakespeare. *Macbeth: Updated Edition*. Ed. A. R. Braunmuller. Cambridge: Cambridge University Press, 2008.

Braunmuller & Hattaway
A. R. Braunmuller and Michael Hattaway, eds. *The Cambridge Companion to English Renaissance Drama*. 2nd ed. Cambridge: Cambridge University Press, 2003.

Brawner
"The Wars of Cyprus," An Early Classical Narrative Drama of the Child Actors: Critical Edition with Introduction and Notes. Ed. James Paul Brawner. Illinois Studies in Language and Literature 28.3–4. Urbana: University of Illinois Press, 1942.

Bray 1988
Alan Bray. *Homosexuality in Renaissance England*. 2nd ed. Boston: GMP, 1988.

Bray 1990
Alan Bray. "Homosexuality and the Signs of Male Friendship in Elizabethan England." *History Workshop* 29 (1990): 1–19.

Brayne
Charles Brayne. "Mead, Robert (1615/16–1653)." In *ODNB* 37: 641–42.

Brennan
Lady Mary Wroth's "Love's Victory": The Penshurst Manuscript. Ed. Michael G. Brennan. London: Roxburghe Club, 1988.

Briggs 1998
Julia Briggs. "'The Lady Vanishes': Problems of Authorship and Editing in the Middleton Canon." In *New Ways of Looking at Old Texts, II: Papers of the Renaissance English Text Society, 1992–1996*, ed. W. Speed Hill, 109–20. Tempe, AZ: Medieval & Renaissance Texts & Studies in conjunction with Renaissance English Text Society, 1998.

Briggs 2007
"The Lady's Tragedy": Parallel Texts. Ed. Julia Briggs. In *Thomas Middleton: The Collected Works*, gen. eds. Gary Taylor and John Lavagnino. Oxford: Clarendon Press, 2007.

Brissenden 1981
Alan Brissenden. *Shakespeare and the Dance*. London: Macmillan, 1981.

Brissenden 2002
Thomas Middleton. *A Chaste Maid in Cheapside*. Ed. Alan Brissenden. 2nd ed. New Mermaids. London: Black; New York: Norton, 2002.

Britland 2006a
Karen Britland. "Buried Alive: Thomas May's 1631 *Antigone*." In *The 1630s: Interdisciplinary Essays on Culture and Politics in the Caroline Era*, ed. Ian Atherton and Julie Sanders, 138–53. Manchester: Manchester University Press; New York: Palgrave, 2006.

Britland 2006b
Karen Britland. *Drama at the Courts of Queen Henrietta Maria*. Cambridge: Cambridge University Press, 2006.

Britland 2007
Karen Britland. "'Tyred in her banish'd dress': Henrietta Maria in Exile." *Early Modern Literary Studies*, special issue 15 (August 2007). http://purl.oclc.org/ emls/si-15/brithenr.htm.

Britland 2008
Karen Britland. "Queen Henrietta Maria's Theatrical Patronage." In *Henrietta Maria: Piety, Politics and Patronage*, ed. Erin Griffey, 57–72. Aldershot, UK, and Burlington, VT: Ashgate, 2008.

Britland 2010
Elizabeth Cary. *The Tragedy of Mariam*. Ed. Karen Britland. New Mermaids. London: Methuen, 2010.

Brockbank
William Shakespeare. *Coriolanus*. Ed. Philip Brockbank. Arden 2. London: Methuen, 1976.

Bromham 1980
A. A. Bromham. "Middleton's Cardinal of Milan." *Notes and Queries* 27.2 (1980): 155–57.

Bromham 1984
A. A. Bromham. "The Contemporary Significance of *The Old Law*." *Studies in English Literature, 1500–1900* 24.2 (1984): 327–39.

Bromham & Bruzzi
A. A. Bromham and Zara Bruzzi. *"The Changeling" and the Years of Crisis, 1619–1624: A Hieroglyph of Britain*. London and New York: Pinter, 1990.

Brooke 1908
C. F. Tucker Brooke, ed. *The Shakespeare Apocrypha, Being a Collection of Fourteen Plays Which Have Been Ascribed to Shakespeare*. Oxford: Clarendon Press, 1908. Repr. Oxford: Clarendon Press, 1967.

Brooke 1911
C. F. Tucker Brooke. *The Tudor Drama: A History of English National Drama to the Retirement of Shakespeare.* Boston and New York: Houghton Mifflin, 1911.

Brooke 1964
George Chapman. *Bussy D'Ambois.* Ed. Nicholas Brooke. Revels Plays. Manchester: Manchester University Press, 1964.

Brooke 1967
C. F. Tucker Brooke. "The Renaissance." In *A Literary History of England,* ed. Albert C. Baugh, 313–696. 2nd ed. New York: Appleton-Century-Crofts, 1967.

Brooke 1990
William Shakespeare. *The Tragedy of Macbeth.* Ed. Nicholas Brooke. Oxford: Clarendon, 1990.

Brooks 1979
William Shakespeare. *A Midsummer Night's Dream.* Ed. Harold F. Brooks. Arden 2. London: Methuen, 1979.

Brooks 1980
"The Phoenix" by Thomas Middleton: A Critical Modernized Edition. Ed. John Bradbury Brooks. New York and London: Garland, 1980.

Brown 1953
Thomas Heywood. *The Captives.* Ed. Arthur Brown. MSR. Oxford: Oxford University Press, 1953.

Brown 1954a
John Russell Brown. "Chapman's 'Caesar and Pompey': An Unperformed Play?" *Modern Language Review* 49.4 (1954): 466–69.

Brown 1954b
Arthur Brown. "An Edition of the Plays of Thomas Heywood: A Preliminary Survey of Problems." *Renaissance Papers* 1954: 71–77.

Brown 1958
The Lady Mother. Ed. Arthur Brown. MSR. Oxford: Oxford University Press, 1958 [1959].

Brown 1960
John Webster. *The White Devil.* Ed. John Russell Brown. Revels Plays. London: Methuen, 1960.

Brown 1962
The Fair Maid of the Exchange. Ed. Arthur Brown. MSR. Oxford: Oxford University Press, 1962 [1963].

Brown 1964a
John Webster. *The Duchess of Malfi.* Ed. John Russell Brown. Revels Plays. London: Methuen, 1964.

Brown 1964b
John Russell Brown. "Marlowe and the Actors." *Tulane Drama Review* 8.4 (1964): 155–73.

Brown 1966
John Webster. *The White Devil*. Ed. John Russell Brown. 2nd ed. London: Methuen, 1966. Repr. 1968.

Brown 1967
Arthur Brown. *Thomas Kyd: Facts and Problems*. Oxford: Clarendon, 1967.

Brown 1999
Dorothy H. Brown. *Christian Humanism in the Late English Morality Plays*. Gainesville: University Press of Florida, 1999.

Brown 2009
John Webster. *The Duchess of Malfi*. Ed. John Russell Brown. Revels Plays. 2nd ed. Manchester: Manchester University Press, 2009.

Brown et al. 1951
John Redford. *Wit and Science*. Ed. Arthur Brown, W. W. Greg, and F. P. Wilson. MSR. Oxford: Oxford University Press, 1951.

Brown et al. 1960
The Marriage of Wit and Science. Ed. Arthur Brown, John Crow, and F. P. Wilson. MSR. Oxford: Oxford University Press, 1960 [1961].

Brown & Wilson
Damon and Pythias. Ed. Arthur Brown and F. P. Wilson. MSR. Oxford: Oxford University Press, 1957.

Browne
Paul Browne. "A Source for the 'Burning Crown' in Henry Chettle's *The Tragedy of Hoffman*." *Notes and Queries* 51.3 (2004): 297–99.

Brucher
Richard Brucher. "Piracy and Parody in Chettle's *Hoffman*." *Ben Jonson Journal* 6 (1999): 209–22.

Bruster 1992
Douglas Bruster. *Drama and the Market in the Age of Shakespeare*. Cambridge: Cambridge University Press, 1992.

Bruster 2003
Douglas Bruster. *Shakespeare and the Question of Culture: Early Modern Literature and the Cultural Turn*. Basingstoke, UK, and New York: Palgrave Macmillan, 2003.

Bruster 2004
Douglas Bruster. "The Birth of an Industry." In *The Cambridge History of British Theatre*, vol. 1: *Origins to 1660*, ed. Jane Milling and Peter Thomson, 224–41. Cambridge: Cambridge University Press, 2004.

Bruster 2005
Douglas Bruster. "The Politics of Shakespeare's Prose." In *Rematerializing Shakespeare: Authority and Representation on the Early Modern English Stage*, ed. Bryan Reynolds and William N. West, 95–114. Basingstoke, UK, and New York: Palgrave Macmillan, 2005.

Bruster 2007
The Changeling. Ed. Douglas Bruster. In *Thomas Middleton: The Collected Works*, gen. eds. Gary Taylor and John Lavagnino. Oxford: Clarendon Press, 2007.

Bruster & Rasmussen
"Everyman" and "Mankind." Ed. Douglas Bruster and Eric Rasmussen. Arden Early Modern Drama. London: Black, 2009.

Bruster & Weimann
Douglas Bruster and Robert Weimann. *Prologues to Shakespeare's Theatre: Performance and Liminality in Early Modern Drama*. London and New York: Routledge, 2004.

Bruzzi 1990
Zara Bruzzi. "Postscript: *The Changeling* and Political Myths." In *"The Changeling" and the Years of Crisis, 1619–1624: A Hieroglyph of Britain*, ed. A. A. Bromham and eadem, 184–98. London and New York: Pinter, 1990.

Buc
Sir George Buc, Master of the Revels, 1597–1622

Buckridge
Patrick Buckridge. "Safety in Fiction: Marston's Recreational Poetics." In *The Drama of John Marston: Critical Re-Visions*, ed. T. F. Wharton, 60–81. Cambridge: Cambridge University Press, 2000.

Bullen 1882–85
A Collection of Old English Plays. Ed. A. H. Bullen. 4 vols. London: privately printed by Wyman & Sons, 1882–85. Repr. New York: Benjamin Blom, [?1964], in 7 vols.

Bullen 1887
The Works of John Marston. Ed. A. H. Bullen. 3 vols. London: Nimmo, 1887.

Bulman 1976
James C. Bulman Jr. "Shakespeare's Use of the 'Timon' Comedy." *Shakespeare Survey* 29 (1976): 107–16.

Bulman 1987
James C. Bulman. "Thomas Killigrew." In *Dictionary of Literary Biography* 58: *Jacobean and Caroline Dramatists*, ed. Fredson Bowers, 123–31. Detroit: Gale, 1987.

Bulman 2003

James Bulman. "Caroline Drama." In *The Cambridge Companion to English Renaissance Drama*, ed. A. R. Braunmuller and Michael Hattaway, 344–71. 2nd ed. Cambridge: Cambridge University Press, 2003.

Bulman et al.

Timon. Ed. J. C. Bulman, J. M. Nosworthy, and G. R. Proudfoot. MSR. Oxford: Oxford University Press, 1978 [1980].

Burks

Deborah G. Burks. *Horrid Spectacle: Violation in the Theater of Early Modern England*. Pittsburgh: Duquesne University Press, 2003.

Burner

Sandra A. Burner. *James Shirley: A Study of Literary Coteries and Patronage in Seventeenth-Century England*. Stony Brook, NY; Lanham, MD; and London: University Press of America, 1988.

Burnett

Mark Thornton Burnett. "Chapman, George (1559/60–1634)." In *ODNB* 11: 46–52.

Burns 1980

John Day's "The Isle of Guls": A Critical Edition. Ed. Raymond S. Burns. New York and London: Garland, 1980.

Burns 1987

Raymond S. Burns. "John Day." In *Dictionary of Literary Biography* 62: *Elizabethan Dramatists*, ed. Fredson Bowers, 40–44. Detroit: Gale, 1987.

Burns 2000

William Shakespeare. *King Henry VI, Part 1*. Ed. Edward Burns. Arden 3. London: Thomson Learning, 2000.

Burt

Richard Burt. *Licensed by Authority: Ben Jonson and the Discourses of Censorship*. Ithaca, NY, and London: Cornell University Press, 1993.

Burton

Jonathan Burton. *Traffic and Turning: Islam and English Drama, 1579–1624*. Newark, DE: University of Delaware Press, 2005.

Butler 1983

Martin Butler. "Entertaining the Palatine Prince: Plays on Foreign Affairs 1635–1637." *English Literary Renaissance* 13.3 (1983): 319–44.

Butler 1984a

Martin Butler. "A Case Study in Caroline Political Theatre: Brathwaite's 'Mercurius Britannicus'." *Historical Journal* 27.4 (1984): 947–53.

Butler 1984b
Martin Butler. *Theatre and Crisis 1632–1642*. Cambridge: Cambridge University Press, 1984.

Butler 1985
Martin Butler. "Romans in Britain: *The Roman Actor* and the Early Stuart Classical Play." In *Philip Massinger: A Critical Reassessment*, ed. Douglas Howard, 139–70. Cambridge: Cambridge University Press, 1985.

Butler 1988
Martin Butler. "The Auspices of Thomas Randolph's *Hey for Honesty, Down with Knavery.*" *Notes and Queries* n.s. 35.4 (1988): 491–92.

Butler 1990
Martin Butler. "Stuart Politics in Jonson's *Tale of a Tub.*" *Modern Language Review* 85.1 (1990): 12–28.

Butler 1992
Martin Butler. "Late Jonson." In *The Politics of Tragicomedy*, ed. Gordon McMullan and Jonathan Hope, 166–88. London and New York: Routledge, 1992.

Butler 2002
Martin Butler. "Literature and the Theatre to 1660." In *The Cambridge History of Early Modern Literature*, ed. David Loewenstein and Janel Mueller, 565–602. Cambridge: Cambridge University Press, 2002.

Butler 2003a
Martin Butler. "Private and Occasional Drama." In *The Cambridge Companion to English Renaissance Drama*, ed. A. R. Braunmuller and Michael Hattaway, 131–63. 2nd ed. Cambridge: Cambridge University Press, 2003.

Butler 2003b
Martin Butler. "The Riddle of Jonson's Chronology Revisited." *Library*, 7th ser., 4.1 (2003): 49–63.

Butler 2004a
Martin Butler. "Armin, Robert (1563–1615)." In *ODNB* 2: 395–96.

Butler 2004b
Martin Butler. "Brome, Richard (c. 1590–1652)." In *ODNB* 7: 811–16.

Butler 2004c
Martin Butler. "The Condition of the Theatres in 1642." In *The Cambridge History of British Theatre*, vol. 1: *Origins to 1660*, ed. Jane Milling and Peter Thomson, 439–57. Cambridge: Cambridge University Press, 2004.

Butler 2004d
Martin Butler. "Kemp, William (*d.* in or after 1610?)." In *ODNB* 31: 182–85.

Butler 2004e
Martin Butler. "Lowin, John (*bap.* 1576, *d.* 1653)." In *ODNB* 34: 591–93.

Butler 2004f

Michelle M. Butler. "Baleus Prolocutor and the Establishment of the Prologue in Sixteenth-Century Drama." In *Tudor Drama before Shakespeare, 1485–1590: New Directions for Research, Criticism, and Pedagogy*, ed. Lloyd Edward Kermode, Jason Scott-Warren, and Martine van Elk, 93–109. Basingstoke, UK, and New York: Palgrave Macmillan, 2004.

Butler 2005

William Shakespeare. *Cymbeline*. Ed. Martin Butler. New Cambridge Shakespeare. Cambridge: Cambridge University Press, 2005.

Butler 2006

Martin Butler. "Exeunt Fighting: Poets, Players, and Impresarios at the Caroline Hall Theaters." In *Localizing Caroline Drama: Politics and Economics of the Early Modern English Stage, 1625–1642*, ed. Adam Zucker and Alan B. Farmer, 97–128. Basingstoke, UK, and New York: Palgrave Macmillan, 2006.

Butler 2009

Martin Butler. "Adult and Boy Playing Companies 1625–1642." In *The Oxford Handbook to Early Modern Theatre*, ed. Richard Dutton, 104–19. Oxford: Oxford University Press, 2009.

Butler 2010

Martin Butler. "Jonson in the Caroline Period." In *Ben Jonson in Context*, ed. Julie Sanders, 31–38. Cambridge: Cambridge University Press, 2010.

Butterworth 1998

Philip Butterworth. *Theatre of Fire: Special Effects in Early English and Scottish Theatre*. London: Society for Theatre Research, 1998.

Butterworth 2005

Philip Butterworth. *Magic on the Early English Stage*. Cambridge: Cambridge University Press, 2005.

Byers

George F. Byers, ed. *"The Valiant Scot" by J. W.: A Critical Edition*. New York and London: Garland, 1980.

Byrne

Muriel St. Clare Byrne, ed. *John a Kent & John a Cumber*. MSR. Oxford: Oxford University Press, 1923.

Cahill

Patricia A. Cahill. *Unto the Breach: Martial Formations, Historical Trauma, and the Early Modern Stage*. Oxford: Oxford University Press, 2008.

Cain 1995

Ben Jonson. *Poetaster*. Ed. Tom Cain. Revels Plays. Manchester: Manchester University Press; New York: St. Martin's Press, 1995.

Cain 1999
Tom Cain. "'A Sad Intestine War': Mildmay Fane and the Poetry of Civil Strife." In *The English Civil Wars in the Literary Imagination*, ed. Claude J. Summers and Ted-Larry Pebworth, 27–51. Columbia and London: University of Missouri Press, 1999.

Cain 2009
Tom Cain. "Jonson's Humanist Tragedies." In *Ben Jonson and the Politics of Genre*, ed. A. D. Cousins and Alison V. Scott, 162–89. Cambridge: Cambridge University Press, 2009.

Cairncross 1957
William Shakespeare. *The Second Part of King Henry VI*. Ed. Andrew S. Cairncross. Arden. Cambridge, MA: Harvard University Press, 1957. Repr. London and New York: Methuen, 1980.

Cairncross 1967
"[The Spanish Comedy, or] The First Part of Hieronimo" and "The Spanish Tragedy [or Hieronimo is Mad Again]." Ed. Andrew S. Cairncross. RRDS. Lincoln: University of Nebraska Press, 1967.

Callaghan 1994
Dympna Callaghan. "Re-Reading Elizabeth Cary's *The Tragedie of Mariam, Faire Queene of Jewry*." In *Women, "Race," and Writing in the Early Modern Period*, ed. Margo Hendricks and Patricia Parker, 163–77. London and New York: Routledge, 1994.

Callaghan 2000
Dympna Callaghan. *Shakespeare without Women: Representing Gender and Race on the Renaissance Stage*. London and New York: Routledge, 2000.

Calvo & Tronch
Thomas Kyd. *The Spanish Tragedy*. Ed. Clara Calvo and Jesús Tronch. Arden Early Modern Drama. London: Bloomsbury, 2013.

Cameron 1941
Kenneth Walter Cameron. *Authorship and Sources of "Gentleness and Nobility": A Study in Early Tudor Drama, Together with a Text of the Play Based on the Black-Letter Original*. Raleigh, NC: Thistle, 1941.

Cameron 1982
George Macgregor Cameron. *Robert Wilson and the Plays of Shakespeare*. Riverton, New Zealand: G. M. Cameron, 1982.

Campbell 1938
Oscar James Campbell. *Comicall Satyre and Shakespeare's "Troilus and Cressida."* San Marino, CA: Huntington Library, 1938.

Campbell 2005

Julie D. Campbell. "'Merry, nimble, stirring spirit[s]': Academic, Salon, and Commedia dell'arte Influence on the *Innamorate* of *Love's Labour's Lost*." In *Women Players in England, 1500–1660: Beyond the All-Male Stage*, ed. Pamela Allen Brown and Peter Parolin, 145–70. Aldershot, UK, and Burlington, VT: Ashgate, 2005.

Cannan

Paul D. Cannan. "Ben Jonson, Authorship, and the Rhetoric of English Dramatic Prefatory Criticism." *Studies in Philology* 99.2 (2002): 178–201.

Cannon

"A Warning for Fair Women": A Critical Edition. Ed. Charles Dale Cannon. The Hague and Paris: Mouton, 1975.

Cantor 1987a

Paul A. Cantor. "Cyril Tourneur." In *Dictionary of Literary Biography* 58: *Jacobean and Caroline Dramatists*, ed. Fredson Bowers, 277–83. Detroit: Gale, 1987.

Cantor 1987b

Paul A. Cantor. "John Ford." In *Dictionary of Literary Biography* 58: *Jacobean and Caroline Dramatists*, ed. Fredson Bowers, 91–106. Detroit: Gale, 1987.

Cantor 2006

Paul A. Cantor. "Shakespeare's *Henry V*: From the Medieval to the Modern World." In *Perspectives on Politics in Shakespeare*, ed. John A. Murley and Sean D. Sutton, 11–31. Lanham, MD: Rowman & Littlefield, 2006.

Caputi

Anthony Caputi. *John Marston, Satirist*. Ithaca, NY: Cornell University Press, 1961.

Caputo

Nicoletta Caputo. "The Defence of Religious Orthodoxy in John Heywood's *The Pardoner and the Frere*." *Yearbook of English Studies* 38 (2008): 34–48.

Cardullo

Robert Cardullo. "The First Production of Thomas Heywood's *A Woman Killed with Kindness*." *Studia Neophilologica* 83.2 (2011): 199–210.

Carnegie 1971

David Carnegie. "The Identification of the Hand of Thomas Goffe, Academic Dramatist and Actor." *Library*, 5th series, 26.2 (1971): 161–65.

Carnegie 1982

David Carnegie. "Actors' Parts and the 'Play of Poore'." *Harvard Library Bulletin* 30.1 (1982): 5–24.

Carnegie 1995a

David Carnegie. "Theatrical Introduction" [to *The Duchess of Malfi*]. In *The Works of John Webster: An Old-Spelling Critical Edition*, ed. David Gunby, idem,

Antony Hammond, and Doreen DelVecchio, 1: 411–49. Cambridge: Cambridge University Press, 1995.

Carnegie 1995b
David Carnegie. "Theatrical Introduction" [to *The White Devil*]. In *The Works of John Webster: An Old-Spelling Critical Edition*, ed. David Gunby, idem, Antony Hammond, and Doreen DelVecchio, 1: 84–120. Cambridge: Cambridge University Press, 1995.

Carnegie 2003a
David Carnegie. "Theatrical Introduction" [to *The Devil's Law-Case*]. In *The Works of John Webster: An Old-Spelling Critical Edition*, ed. David Gunby, idem, and MacDonald P. Jackson, 2: 36–58. Cambridge: Cambridge University Press, 2003.

Carnegie 2003b
David Carnegie. "Theatrical Introduction" [to *A Cure for a Cuckold*]. In *The Works of John Webster: An Old-Spelling Critical Edition*, ed. David Gunby, idem, and MacDonald P. Jackson, 2: 282–93. Cambridge: Cambridge University Press, 2003.

Carnegie 2003c
David Carnegie. "Theatrical Introduction" [to *Appius and Virginia*]. In *The Works of John Webster: An Old-Spelling Critical Edition*, ed. David Gunby, idem, and MacDonald P. Jackson, 2: 476–93. Cambridge: Cambridge University Press, 2003.

Carnegie 2007
David Carnegie. "Introduction" to "Webster's Induction and Additions to *The Malcontent*." In *The Works of John Webster. An Old-Spelling Critical Edition*, ed. David Gunby, idem, and MacDonald P. Jackson, 3: 297–308. Cambridge: Cambridge University Press, 2007.

Carnegie et al.
The Part of "Poore." Ed. David Carnegie, G. Blakemore Evans, and John Creaser. Malone Society *Collections XV*, 111–69. Oxford: Oxford University Press, 1993.

Carnegie & Davison
Thomas Goffe. *The Courageous Turk*. Ed. David Carnegie and Peter Davison. MSR. Oxford: Oxford University Press, 1968 [1974].

Carpenter
Sarah Carpenter. "'My Lady Tongue': Thomas Tomkis's *Lingua*." *Medieval English Theatre* 24 (2002): 3–14.

Carroll 1994
Thomas Middleton. *Women Beware Women*. Ed. William C. Carroll. 2nd ed. New Mermaids. London: Black; New York: Norton, 1994.

Carroll 2004
William Shakespeare. *The Two Gentlemen of Verona*. Ed. William C. Carroll. Arden 3. London: Thomson Learning, 2004.

Carroll 2009
William Shakespeare. *Love's Labour's Lost*. Ed. William C. Carroll. New Cambridge Shakespeare. Cambridge: Cambridge University Press, 2009.

Carson 1988
Neil Carson. *A Companion to Henslowe's Diary*. Cambridge: Cambridge University Press, 1988.

Carson 1989
Neil Carson. "Collaborative Playwriting: The Chettle, Dekker, Heywood Syndicate." *Theatre Research International* 14.1 (1989): 13–23.

Carter 1965
James Shirley. *The Traitor*. Ed. John Stewart Carter. RRDS. Lincoln: University of Nebraska Press, 1965.

Carter 1980
James Shirley's "The Maid's Revenge": A Critical Edition. Ed. Albert Howard Carter. New York and London: Garland, 1980.

Cartwright 1998
Kent Cartwright. "The Confusions of *Gallathea*: John Lyly as Popular Dramatist." *Comparative Drama* 32.2 (1998): 207–39.

Cartwright 1999
Kent Cartwright. *Theatre and Humanism: English Drama in the Sixteenth Century*. Cambridge: Cambridge University Press, 1999.

Cathcart 1999
Charles Cathcart. "'You will crown him King that slew your King': *Lust's Dominion* and Oliver Cromwell." *Medieval and Renaissance Drama in England* 11 (1999): 264–74.

Cathcart 2001a
Charles Cathcart. "*Hamlet*: Date and Early Afterlife." *Review of English Studies* 52 (2001): 341–59.

Cathcart 2001b
Charles Cathcart. "*Lust's Dominion; or, The Lascivious Queen*: Authorship, Date, and Revision." *Review of English Studies* 52 (2001): 360–75.

Cathcart 2003a
Charles Cathcart. "*Club Law, The Family of Love*, and the Familist Sect." *Notes and Queries* 50.1 (2003): 65–68.

Cathcart 2003b
Charles Cathcart. "*The Insatiate Countess*: Date, Topicality, and Company Appropriation." *Medieval and Renaissance Drama in England* 16 (2003): 81–100.

Cathcart 2005
Charles Cathcart. "Authorship, Indebtedness, and the Children of the King's Revels." *Studies in English Literature, 1500–1900* 45.2 (2005): 357–74.

Cathcart 2006
Charles Cathcart. "John Marston, *The Malcontent*, and the King's Men." *Review of English Studies* 57 (2006): 43–63.

Cathcart 2008
Charles Cathcart. *Marston, Rivalry, Rapprochement, and Jonson*. Aldershot, UK, and Burlington, VT: Ashgate, 2008.

Cathcart 2009
Charles Cathcart. "*How a Man May Choose a Good Wife from a Bad* and *The Taming of the Shrew*." *Notes and Queries* 56.4 (2009): 612–15.

Cathcart 2010
Charles Cathcart. "*Romeo* at the Rose in 1598." *Early Theatre* 13.2 (2010): 149–62.

Cathcart 2012
Charles Cathcart. "*Sir Giles Goosecap, Knight*: George Chapman; *Poetaster*; and the Children of the Chapel." *Medieval and Renaissance Drama in England* 25 (2012): 42–61.

Cauthen 1966
Irby B. Cauthen Jr., ed. *The Coxcomb*. In *The Dramatic Works in the Beaumont and Fletcher Canon*, gen. ed. Fredson Bowers, vol. 1. Cambridge: Cambridge University Press, 1966.

Cauthen 1970
Thomas Sackville and Thomas Norton. *Gorboduc, or Ferrex and Porrex*. Ed. Irby B. Cauthen Jr. RRDS. Lincoln: University of Nebraska Press, 1970.

Cauthen 1987a
Irby B. Cauthen Jr. "Nathan Field." In *Dictionary of Literary Biography* 58: *Jacobean and Caroline Dramatists*, ed. Fredson Bowers, 86–90. Detroit: Gale, 1987.

Cauthen 1987b
Irby B. Cauthen Jr. "Sir William Davenant." In *Dictionary of Literary Biography* 58: *Jacobean and Caroline Dramatists*, ed. Fredson Bowers, 59–72. Detroit: Gale, 1987.

Cavanaugh 1942
Sister M. Jean Carmel Cavanaugh, ed. "*Technogamia*" by Barten Holyday: A Critical Edition. Washington, DC: Catholic University of America Press, 1942.

Cave

Richard Cave. "Visualising Jonson's Text." In *Ben Jonson and Theatre: Performance, Practice and Theory*, ed. idem, Elizabeth Schafer, and Brian Woolland, 33–44. London and New York: Routledge, 1999.

Cawley

A. C. Cawley. "*A Yorkshire Tragedy* Considered in Relation to Biblical and Moral Plays." In *"Everyman" & Company: Essays on the Theme and Structure of the European Moral Play*, ed. Donald Gilman, 155–68. New York: AMS Press, 1989.

Cawley & Gaines

A Yorkshire Tragedy. Ed. A. C. Cawley and Barry Gaines. Revels Plays. Manchester: Manchester University Press, 1986.

Cerasano 1994

S. P. Cerasano. "Edward Alleyn: 1566–1626." In *Edward Alleyn: Elizabethan Actor, Jacobean Gentleman*, ed. Aileen Reed and Robert Maniura, 11–31. London: Dulwich Picture Gallery, 1994.

Cerasano 2004a

S. P. Cerasano. "Alleyn, Edward (1566–1626*)."* In *ODNB* 1: 846–49.

Cerasano 2004b

S. P. Cerasano. "Fermedo, Sir Cornelius (*c.* 1600–1638)." In *ODNB* 19: 395–96.

Cerasano 2004c

S. P. Cerasano. "Rowley, Samuel (*d.* 1624)." In *ODNB* 48: 24–25.

Cerasano 2004d

S. P. Cerasano. "Tomkis, Thomas (*b. c.* 1580, *d.* in or after 1615)." In *ODNB* 54: 931–32.

Cerasano 2005

S. P. Cerasano. "Edward Alleyn, the New Model Actor, and the Rise of the Celebrity in the 1590s." *Medieval and Renaissance Drama in England* 18 (2005): 47–58.

Cerasano 2012

William Shakespeare. *Julius Caesar: A Norton Critical Edition*. Ed. S. P. Cerasano. New York and London: W. W. Norton, 2012.

Cerasano & Wynne-Davies

S. P. Cerasano and Marion Wynne-Davies. *Renaissance Drama by Women: Texts and Documents*. London and New York: Routledge, 1996. Repr. 1997.

Cetin

Iclal Cetin. "Tyrant, Thy Name is King: *The Tragedy of Tiberius* and Neo-Stoic Taciteanism." *Early Modern Literary Studies* 15.1 (2009–10). http://purl.oclc.org/emls/15–1/tibetrag.htm.

Chalmers

Hero Chalmers. *Royalist Women Writers, 1650–1689*. Oxford: Clarendon Press, 2004.

Chalmers et al.

Three Seventeenth-Century Plays on Women and Performance. Ed. Hero Chalmers, Julie Sanders, and Sophie Tomlinson. Revels Plays Companion Library. Manchester and New York: Manchester University Press, 2006.

Chamberlain

Letters Written by John Chamberlain during the Reign of Queen Elizabeth. Ed. Sarah Williams. Works of the Camden Society 79. [Westminster]: Camden Society, 1861.

Chambers 1903

E. K. Chambers. *The Mediaeval Stage*. 2 vols. Oxford: Oxford University Press, 1903. Repr. 1925, 1948.

Chambers 1911

E. K. Chambers. "Plays of the King's Men in 1641." Malone Society *Collections* [Vol.1], *Parts IV & V*, 364–69. Oxford: Oxford University Press, 1911.

Chambers 1923

E. K. Chambers. *The Elizabethan Stage*. 4 vols. Oxford: Clarendon Press, 1923. Repr., with corrections, Oxford: Oxford University Press, 2009.

Chambers 1930

E. K. Chambers. *William Shakespeare: A Study of Facts and Problems*. 2 vols. Oxford: Clarendon Press, 1930. Repr. 1951, 1963, 1966. Reissued 1988.

Chambers 1945

E. K. Chambers. *English Literature at the Close of the Middle Ages*. Oxford History of English Literature. New York and Oxford: Oxford University Press, 1945.

Chan

Mary Chan. *Music in the Theatre of Ben Jonson*. Oxford: Clarendon Press, 1980.

Charles

Amy M. Charles, ed. *The Shorter Poems of Ralph Knevet: A Critical Edition*. Columbus: Ohio State University Press, 1966.

Cheatham

William Rowley. *"A New Wonder, A Woman Never Vext": An Old-Spelling, Critical Edition*. Ed. George Cheatham. New York: Peter Lang, 1993.

Chetwood

William Rufus Chetwood. *A General History of the Stage, from Its Origin in Greece down to the Present Time*. London: W. Owen, 1749.

Chew

Samuel C. Chew. *The Crescent and the Rose: Islam and England during the Renaissance*. New York: Oxford University Press, 1937. Repr. New York: Octagon Books, 1965.

Chillington

Carol A. Chillington. "Playwrights at Work: Henslowe's, not Shakespeare's, *Book of Sir Thomas More*." *English Literary Renaissance* 10.3 (1980): 423–79.

Cioni

Fernando Cioni. "Stages at the University of Cambridge in Tudor England." In *English Renaissance Stages: From Canon to Margins*, ed. Paola Pugliatti and Alessandro Serpieri, 127–54. Bern: Lang, 2008.

Clare 1990

Janet Clare. "The Censorship of the Deposition Scene in *Richard II*." *Review of English Studies* 41 (1990): 89–94.

Clare 1994

Janet Clare. "The Production and Reception of Davenant's *Cruelty of the Spaniards in Peru*." *Modern Language Review* 89.4 (1994): 832–41.

Clare 1998

Janet Clare. "Jonson's 'Comical Satires' and the Art of Courtly Compliment." In *Refashioning Ben Jonson: Gender, Politics and the Jonsonian Canon*, ed. Julie Sanders with Kate Chedgzoy and Susan Wiseman, 28–47. Basingstoke, UK: Macmillan; New York: St. Martin's Press, 1998.

Clare 1999

Janet Clare. *"Art made tongue-tied by authority": Elizabethan and Jacobean Dramatic Censorship*. 2nd ed. Revels Plays Companion Library. Manchester: Manchester University Press; New York: St. Martin's Press, 1999.

Clare 2002

Drama of the English Republic, 1649–60. Ed. Janet Clare. Revels Plays Companion Library. Manchester: Manchester University Press; New York: Palgrave, 2002.

Clare 2004

Janet Clare. "Theatre and Commonwealth." In *The Cambridge History of British Theatre*, vol. 1: *Origins to 1660*, ed. Jane Milling and Peter Thomson, 458–76. Cambridge: Cambridge University Press, 2004.

Clare 2005

Janet Clare. "The 'Complexion' of *Twelfth Night*." *Shakespeare Survey* 58 (2005): 199–207.

Clark 1931

Arthur Melville Clark. *Thomas Heywood: Playwright and Miscellanist*. Oxford: Blackwell, 1931.

Clark 1952
Arthur Melville Clark. Review of Allan Holaday, *Thomas Heywood's "The Rape of Lucrece"* (Urbana: University of Illinois Press, 1950). *Review of English Studies* n.s. 3.11 (1952): 285–89.

Clark 1955
William Smith Clark. *The Early Irish Stage: The Beginnings to 1720*. Oxford: Clarendon Press, 1955.

Clark 1979
"The Bugbears": A Modernized Edition. Ed. James D. Clark. New York and London: Garland, 1979.

Clark 1992
Ira Clark. *Professional Playwrights: Massinger, Ford, Shirley, and Brome*. Lexington: University Press of Kentucky, 1992.

Clark 1993
Ira Clark. *The Moral Art of Philip Massinger*. Lewisburg, PA: Bucknell University Press; London and Toronto: Associated University Presses, 1993.

Clark 1994
Sandra Clark. *The Plays of Beaumont and Fletcher: Sexual Themes and Dramatic Representation*. New York and London: Harvester Wheatsheaf, 1994.

Clark 2003
Ira Clark. *Comedy, Youth, Manhood in Early Modern England*. Newark, DE: University of Delaware Press; London: Associated University Presses, 2003.

Clark 2004
Ira Clark. "Shirley, James (*bap.* 1596, *d.* 1666)." In *ODNB* 50: 391–96.

Clark 2007
Sandra Clark. *Renaissance Drama*. Cambridge: Polity Press, 2007.

Clarke 1911
"The Comedy of George a Green," 1599. Ed. F. W. Clarke. MSR. Oxford: Oxford University Press, 1911.

Clarke 2006
Danielle Clarke. "*The Tragedy of Mariam* and the Politics of Marriage." In *Early Modern English Drama: A Critical Companion*, ed. Garrett A. Sullivan Jr., Patrick Cheney, and Andrew Hadfield, 248–59. New York and Oxford: Oxford University Press, 2006.

Clayton
Thomas Clayton, ed. *The Works of Sir John Suckling*, vol. 1: *The Non-Dramatic Works*. Oxford: Clarendon Press, 1971.

Clegg 1997
Cyndia Susan Clegg. "'By the choise and inuitation of al the realme': *Richard II* and Elizabethan Press Censorship." *Shakespeare Quarterly* 48.4 (1997): 432–48.

Clegg 1999
Cyndia Susan Clegg. "Liberty, License, and Authority: Press Censorship and Shakespeare." In *A Companion to Shakespeare*, ed. David Scott Kastan, 464–85. Oxford: Blackwell, 1999.

Clemen
Wolfgang Clemen. *English Tragedy before Shakespeare: The Development of Dramatic Speech*. Trans. T. S. Dorsch. London: Methuen, 1961.

Clinch
A Critical Edition of John Fletcher's Comedy "Monsieur Thomas or Father's Own Son." Ed. Nanette Cleri Clinch. New York and London: Garland, 1987.

Clopper 1979
Lawrence M. Clopper, ed. *Chester*. REED. Toronto and Buffalo: University of Toronto Press, 1979.

Clopper 1999
Lawrence M. Clopper. "English Drama: From Ungodly *Ludi* to Sacred Play." In *The Cambridge History of Medieval English Literature*, ed. David Wallace, 739–66. Cambridge: Cambridge University Press, 1999.

Clopper 2001
Lawrence M. Clopper. *Drama, Play, and Game: English Festive Culture in the Medieval and Early Modern Period*. Chicago and London: University of Chicago Press, 2001.

Clough
Cecil H. Clough. "Rastell, John (*c.* 1475–1536)." In *ODNB* 46: 80–82.

Clugston
Thomas Lodge and Robert Greene. *"A Looking Glasse for London and England": A Critical Edition*. Ed. George Alan Clugston. New York and London: Garland, 1980.

Cocke
A Critical Edition of John Day's "The Parliament of Bees." Ed. William T. Cocke III. New York and London: Garland, 1979.

Coddon
Karin S. Coddon. "'For Show or Useless Property': Necrophilia and *The Revenger's Tragedy*." *ELH* 61.1 (1994): 71–88.

Coghill
Nevill Coghill. "Six Points of Stage-craft in *The Winter's Tale*." *Shakespeare Survey* 11 (1958): 31–41.

Cohen 1985

Walter Cohen. *Drama of a Nation: Public Theater in Renaissance England and Spain*. Ithaca, NY, and London: Cornell University Press, 1985.

Cohen 1997

Walter Cohen. Introduction to *The Life and Death of King John*. In *The Norton Shakespeare based on the Oxford Edition*, ed. Stephen Greenblatt, idem, Jean E. Howard, and Katharine Eisaman Maus, 1015–21. New York and London: Norton, 1997.

Cohen 2009

Ralph Alan Cohen. "The Most Convenient Place: The Second Blackfriars Theater and Its Appeal." In *The Oxford Handbook of the Early Modern Theatre*, ed. Richard Dutton, 209–24. Oxford: Oxford University Press, 2009.

Cohen & Jowett

Your Five Gallants. Ed. Ralph Alan Cohen with John Jowett. In *Thomas Middleton: The Collected Works*, gen. eds. Gary Taylor and John Lavagnino. Oxford: Clarendon Press, 2007.

Coldewey 1993

John C. Coldewey, ed. *Early English Drama: An Anthology*. New York and London: Garland, 1993.

Coldewey 2004

John C. Coldewey. "From Roman to Renaissance in Drama and Theatre." In *The Cambridge History of British Theatre*, vol. 1: *Origins to 1660*, ed. Jane Milling and Peter Thomson, 3–69. Cambridge: Cambridge University Press, 2004.

Coldewey 2008

John C. Coldewey. "The Non-Cycle Plays and the East Anglian Tradition." In *The Cambridge Companion to Medieval English Theatre*, ed. Richard Beadle and Alan J. Fletcher, 211–34. 2nd ed. Cambridge: Cambridge University Press, 2008.

Colegrove

A Critical Edition of Thomas Middleton's "Your Five Gallants." Ed. Clare Lee Colegrove. New York and London: Garland, 1979.

Coletti

Theresa Coletti. *Mary Magdalene and the Drama of Saints: Theater, Gender, and Religion in Late Medieval England*. Philadelphia: University of Pennsylvania Press, 2004.

Collier 1825

Robert Dodsley. *A Select Collection of Old Plays*. Ed. John Payne Collier. 12 vols. London: Prowett, 1825–27.

Collier 1831

John Payne Collier. *The History of English Dramatic Poetry to the Time of Shakespeare*. 3 vols. London: John Murray, 1831.

Collier 1838

John Bale. *Kynge Johan: A Play in Two Parts*. Ed. John Payne Collier. London: Camden Society, 1838.

Collier 1851

Anthony Munday. *John a Kent and John a Cumber; A Comedy . . . Printed from the Original Manuscript*. Ed. John Payne Collier. London: Shakespeare Society, 1851.

Collier 1866

Illustrations of Old English Literature. Ed. John Payne Collier. 3 vols. London: privately printed, 1866.

Collier 1998

Susanne Collier. "Cutting to the Heart of the Matter: Stabbing the Woman in *Philaster* and *Cymbeline*." In *Shakespearean Power and Punishment: A Volume of Essays*, ed. Gillian Murray Kendall, 39–58. Madison and Teaneck, NJ: Fairleigh Dickinson University Press, 1998.

Collington

Philip Collington. "'A Puppet-Play in Pictures': Thomas Middleton's Emblematic Drama." In *Other Voices, Other Views: Expanding the Canon in English Renaissance Studies*, ed. Helen Ostovich, Mary V. Silcox, and Graham Roebuck, 91–131. Newark, DE: University of Delaware Press; London: Associated University Presses, 1999.

Collins

Eleanor Collins. "Richard Brome's Contract and the Relationship of Dramatist to Company in the Early Modern Period." *Early Theatre* 10.2 (2007): 116–28.

Comensoli

Viviana Comensoli. *"Household Business": Domestic Plays of Early Modern England*. Toronto, Buffalo, and London: University of Toronto Press, 1996.

Connolly 2007

Annaliese Connolly. "Peele's *David and Bethsabe*: Reconsidering Biblical Drama of the Long 1590s." *Early Modern Literary Studies*, special issue 16 (October 2007). http://purl.oclc.org/emls/si-16/connpeel.htm.

Connolly 2009

Annaliese Connolly. "Guy of Warwick, Godfrey of Bouillon, and Elizabethan Repertory." *Early Theatre* 12.2 (2009): 207–22.

Cook 1991
Ben Jonson. *The Alchemist*. Ed. Elizabeth Cook. 2nd ed. New Mermaids. London: Black; New York: Norton, 1991.

Cook 1997
Thomas Middleton and Thomas Dekker. *The Roaring Girl*. Ed. Elizabeth Cook. 2nd ed. New Mermaids. London: Black; New York: Norton, 1997.

Cook & Wilson
John Fletcher. *Demetrius and Enanthe [The Humorous Lieutenant]*. Ed. Margaret McLaren Cook and F. P. Wilson. MSR. Oxford: Oxford University Press, 1950 [1951].

Cooper 2006
Helen Cooper. "Guy of Warwick, Upstart Crows and Mounting Sparrows." In *Shakespeare, Marlowe, Jonson: New Directions in Biography*, ed. Takashi Kozuka and J. R. Mulryne, 119–38. Aldershot, UK, and Burlington, VT: Ashgate, 2006.

Cooper 2010
Helen Cooper. *Shakespeare and the Medieval World*. Arden Critical Companions. London: Black, 2010.

Cooper & Wortham
The Summoning of Everyman. Ed. Geoffrey Cooper and Christopher Wortham. Nedlands: University of Western Australia Press, 1980.

Cope 1984
Jackson I. Cope. *Dramaturgy of the Daemonic: Studies in Antigeneric Theater from Ruzante to Grimaldi*. Baltimore and London: Johns Hopkins University Press, 1984.

Cope 1999
Kevin L. Cope. "The Glory That Was Rome — and Grenada, and Rhodes, and Tenochtitlan: Pleasurable Conquests, Supernatural Liaisons, and Apparitional Drama in Interregnum Entertainments." *Studies in the Literary Imagination* 32.2 (1999): 1–17.

Corballis
R. P. Corballis. "The 'Second Pen' in the Stage Version of *Sejanus*." *Modern Philology* 76.3 (1979): 273–77.

Corbin & Sedge 1981
Lording Barry. *Ram Alley*. Ed. Peter Corbin and Douglas Sedge. Nottingham Drama Texts. Nottingham: Nottingham University Press, 1981.

Corbin & Sedge 1986
Three Jacobean Witchcraft Plays: "The Tragedy of Sophonisba," "The Witch," "The Witch of Edmonton." Ed. Peter Corbin and Douglas Sedge. Revels Plays Companion Library. Manchester: Manchester University Press, 1986.

Corbin & Sedge 1991
The Oldcastle Controversy: "Sir John Oldcastle, Part I" and "The Famous Victories of Henry V." Ed. Peter Corbin and Douglas Sedge. Revels Plays Companion Library. Manchester: Manchester University Press; New York: St. Martin's Press, 1991.

Corbin & Sedge 2002
Thomas of Woodstock or Richard the Second, Part One. Ed. Peter Corbin and Douglas Sedge. Revels Plays. Manchester: Manchester University Press; New York: Palgrave, 2002.

Corns
Thomas N. Corns. *A History of Seventeenth-Century English Literature.* Oxford: Blackwell, 2007.

Corrigan 1992
"The Misfortunes of Arthur": A Critical, Old-Spelling Edition. Ed. Brian Jay Corrigan. New York and London: Garland, 1992.

Corrigan 1998
Brian Jay Corrigan. "Middleton, *The Revenger's Tragedy*, and Crisis Literature." *Studies in English Literature, 1500–1900* 38.2 (1998): 281–95.

Cotton
Nancy Cotton. *Women Playwrights in England, c. 1363–1750.* Lewisburg, PA: Bucknell University Press; London and Toronto: Associated University Presses, 1980.

Coughlan 1990
Patricia Coughlan. "'Cheap and common animals': The English Anatomy of Ireland in the Seventeenth Century." In *Literature and the English Civil War*, ed. Thomas Healy and Jonathan Sawday, 205–23. Cambridge: Cambridge University Press, 1990.

Coughlan 2004
Patricia Coughlan. "Burkhead, Henry (*fl.* 1645–1646)." In *ODNB* 8: 858–59.

Coughlan 2009
Patricia Coughlan. Introduction to *Cola's Fury*, by Henry Burkhead. Ed. Angelina Lynch. Dublin: Four Courts Press, 2009.

Cousin
Geraldine Cousin. *King John.* Shakespeare in Performance. Manchester: Manchester University Press; New York: St. Martin's Press, 1994.

Cox 2000
John D. Cox. *The Devil and the Sacred in English Drama, 1350–1642.* Cambridge: Cambridge University Press, 2000.

Cox 2002

John D. Cox. "'To obtain his soul': Demonic Desire for the Soul in Marlowe and Others." *Early Theatre* 5.2 (2002): 29–46.

Cox & Rasmussen

William Shakespeare. *King Henry VI, Part 3*. Ed. John D. Cox and Eric Rasmussen. Arden 3. London: Thomson Learning, 2001.

Craig 1999

Hugh Craig. "Jonsonian Chronology and the Styles of *A Tale of a Tub*." In *Re-Presenting Ben Jonson: Text, History, Performance*, ed. Martin Butler, 210–32. Basingstoke, UK, and London: Macmillan, 1999.

Craig 2009

Hugh Craig. "The 1602 Additions to *The Spanish Tragedy*." In *Shakespeare, Computers, and the Mystery of Authorship*, ed. idem and Arthur F. Kinney, 162–80. Cambridge: Cambridge University Press, 2009.

Craigie

James Craigie. "*Philotus*: A Late Middle Scots Comedy." *Scottish Literary Journal* 6.1 (1979): 19–33.

Craik 1953

T. W. Craik. "The Political Interpretation of Two Tudor Interludes: *Temperance and Humility* and *Wealth and Health*." *Review of English Studies* 4.14 (1953): 98–108.

Craik 1958

T. W. Craik. *The Tudor Interlude: Stage, Costume, and Acting*. Leicester: Leicester University Press, 1958. Repr. 1962.

Craik 1966

T. W. Craik. "The Tudor Interlude and Later Elizabethan Drama." In *Elizabethan Theatre*, ed. John Russell Brown and Bernard Harris, 36–57. Stratford-upon-Avon Studies 9. London: Edward Arnold, 1966.

Craik 1975

T. W. Craik. "The Reconstruction of Stage Action from Early Dramatic Texts." *The Elizabethan Theatre* 5 (1975): 76–91.

Craik 1988

Francis Beaumont and John Fletcher. *The Maid's Tragedy*. Ed. T. W. Craik. Revels Plays. Manchester: Manchester University Press; New York: St Martin's Press, 1988.

Craik 1989

William Shakespeare. *The Merry Wives of Windsor*. Ed. T. W. Craik. Oxford: Clarendon Press, 1989.

Craik 1995
William Shakespeare. *King Henry V.* Ed. T. W. Craik. Arden 3. London and New York: Routledge, 1995.

Crandall
"Swetnam the Woman-hater": The Controversy and the Play, A Critical Introduction and Notes. Ed. Coryl Crandall. West Lafayette, IN: Purdue University Studies, 1969.

Crane
William Shakespeare. *The Merry Wives of Windsor: Updated Edition.* Ed. David Crane. Cambridge: Cambridge University Press, 2010.

Crawford 1906
Charles Crawford. "The Authorship of 'Arden of Feversham'." In *Collectanea*, 1st ser., 101–30. Stratford-upon-Avon: Shakespeare Head, 1906.

Crawford 1999
Julie Crawford. "Fletcher's *The Tragedie of Bonduca* and the Anxieties of the Masculine Government of James I." *Studies in English Literature, 1500–1900* 39.2 (1999): 357–81.

Crawford 2003
Kevin Crawford. "'All His Intents Are Contrary to Man': Softened Masculinity and Staging in Middleton's *The Lady's Tragedy*." *Medieval and Renaissance Drama in England* 16 (2003): 101–29.

Crawford 2005
Julie Crawford. "'Pleaders, Atturneys, Petitioners and the like': Margaret Cavendish and the Dramatic Petition." In *Women Players in England, 1500–1660: Beyond the All-Male Stage*, ed. Pamela Allen Brown and Peter Parolin, 241–60. Aldershot, UK, and Burlington, VT: Ashgate, 2005.

Creeth
Edmund Creeth, ed. *Tudor Plays: An Anthology of Early English Drama.* Garden City, NY: Anchor, 1966. Repr. 1972.

Croker
Philip Massinger. *Believe as You List.* Ed. Thomas Crofton Croker. London: Percy Society, 1849.

Crosbie
Christopher J. Crosbie. "Sexuality, Corruption, and the Body Politic: The Paradoxical Tribute of *The Misfortunes of Arthur* to Elizabeth I." *Arthuriana* 9.3 (1999): 68–80.

Cross
K. Gustav Cross. "The Authorship of 'Lust's Dominion'." *Studies in Philology* 55.1 (1958): 39–61.

Crow
"Law Tricks" by John Day, 1608. Ed. John Crow. Oxford: Oxford University Press, 1949 [1950].

Crumley
J. Clinton Crumley. "Anachronism and Historical Romance in Renaissance Drama: *James IV*." *Explorations in Renaissance Culture* 24 (1998): 75–90.

Crupi 1995
Charles W. Crupi. "Ideological Contradiction in Part I of Heywood's *Edward IV*: 'Our Musicke Runs . . . Much upon Discords'." *Medieval and Renaissance Drama in England* 7 (1995): 224–56.

Crupi 1998
Charles W. Crupi. "Subduing Bess Bridges: Ideological Shift in the Two Parts of *The Fair Maid of the West*." *Cahiers Elisabéthains* 54 (1998): 75–87.

Crupi 2004
Charles W. Crupi. "Reading Nascent Capitalism in Part II of Thomas Heywood's *If You Know Not Me, You Know Nobody*." *Texas Studies in Literature and Language* 46.3 (2004): 296–323.

Culhane
Peter Culhane. "The Date of Heywood and Webster's *Appius and Virginia*." *Notes and Queries* 51.3 (2004): 300–01.

Cull
Marisa R. Cull. "Contextualizing 1610: *Cymbeline*, *The Valiant Welshman*, and the Princes of Wales." In *Shakespeare and Wales: From the Marches to the Assembly*, ed. Willy Maley and Philip Schwyzer, 127–42. Farnham, UK, and Burlington, VT: Ashgate, 2010.

Cunliffe 1893
John W. Cunliffe. *The Influence of Seneca on Elizabethan Tragedy*. London: Macmillan, 1893.

Cunliffe 1912
Early English Classical Tragedies. Ed. John W. Cunliffe. Oxford: Clarendon Press, 1912.

Cunningham
Christopher Marlowe. *Tamburlaine the Great*. Ed. J. S. Cunningham. Revels Plays. Manchester: Manchester University Press; Baltimore: Johns Hopkins University Press, 1981.

Curran 2007
Kevin Curran. "Shakespeare and Daniel Revisited: *Antony and Cleopatra* II.v.50–4 and *The Tragedy of Philotas* V.ii.2013–15." *Notes and Queries* 54.3 (2007): 318–20.

Curran 2012

Kevin Curran. "Treasonous Silence: *The Tragedy of Philotas* and Legal Epistemology [with illustrations]." *English Literary Renaissance* 42.1 (2012): 58–89.

Cutts 1963

John P. Cutts. "Thomas Nabbes's 'Hannibal and Scipio'." *English Miscellany* 14 (1963): 73–81.

Cutts 1965

John P. Cutts. "*Everie Woman in Her Humor.*" *Renaissance News* 18.3 (1965): 209–13.

Cutts 1967–68

John P. Cutts. "The Anonymous Masque-like Entertainment in Egerton MS. 1994, and Richard Brome." *Comparative Drama* 1.4 (1967–68): 277–87.

Cutts 1974

Love's Changelinges Change. Ed. John P. Cutts. North American Mentor Texts and Studies 2. Fenimore, WI: John Westburg, 1974.

Cutts 1985

John Cutts. "Thomas Randolph's *The Muses' Looking-Glass* and *The Battle of the Vices against the Virtues.*" *Notes and Queries* 32.2 (1985): 161–62.

Daileader & Taylor

John Fletcher. *The Tamer Tamed; or, The Woman's Prize.* Ed. Celia R. Daileader and Gary Taylor. Revels Student Editions. Manchester: Manchester University Press; New York: Palgrave, 2006.

D'Amico

Jack D'Amico. *The Moor in English Renaissance Drama.* Tampa: University of South Florida Press, 1991.

Daniel

The Plays of John Lyly. Ed. Carter A. Daniel. Lewisburg, PA: Bucknell University Press; London and Toronto: Associated University Presses, 1988.

Daniell

William Shakespeare. *Julius Caesar.* Ed. David Daniell. Arden. London: Thomas Nelson, 1998.

Danson

Lawrence Danson. *Shakespeare's Dramatic Genres.* Oxford Shakespeare Topics. Oxford: Oxford University Press, 2000.

Danson & Kamps

The Phoenix. Ed. Lawrence Danson and Ivo Kamps. In *Thomas Middleton: The Collected Works*, gen eds. Gary Taylor and John Lavagnino. Oxford: Clarendon Press, 2007.

Darby 1988
Trudi Laura Darby. *A Critical Old-Spelling Edition of William Rowley's "A New Wonder, A Woman Never Vexed."* New York and London: Garland, 1988.

Darby 2002
William Rowley. *A Shoemaker, A Gentleman.* Ed. Trudi L. Darby. Globe Quartos. London: Nick Hern Books, 2002. Repr. London: Routledge, 2003.

Darby 2006
Trudi L. Darby. "The Black Knight's Festival Book? Thomas Middleton's *A Game at Chess.*" In *The Spanish Match: Prince Charles's Journey to Madrid, 1623*, ed. Alexander Samson, 173–87. Aldershot, UK, and Burlington, VT: Ashgate, 2006.

Darby 2009
Trudi L. Darby. "William Rowley: A Case Study in Influence." In *The Cervantean Heritage: Reception and Influence of Cervantes in Britain*, ed. J. A. G. Ardila, 249–57. London: Modern Humanities Research Association and Maney Publishing, 2009.

Darby 2011
Trudi L. Darby. "The Obsession with Spain." In *Thomas Middleton in Context*, ed. Suzanne Gossett, 144–50. Cambridge: Cambridge University Press, 2011.

Davenport 1982
W. A. Davenport. *Fifteenth-Century English Drama: The Early Moral Plays and Their Literary Relations.* Cambridge: Brewer; Totowa, NJ: Rowman and Littlefield, 1982.

Davenport 1998
Edwin Davenport. "The Representation of Robin Hood in Elizabethan Drama: *George a Greene* and *Edward I.*" In *Playing Robin Hood: The Legend as Performance in Five Centuries*, ed. Lois Potter, 45–62. Newark, DE: University of Delaware Press; London: Associated University Presses, 1998.

David
Richard David. *Shakespeare in the Theatre.* Cambridge: Cambridge University Press, 1978.

Davidson 1978
Richard B. Davidson. "Anonymous Plays." In *The Later Jacobean and Caroline Dramatists: A Survey and Bibliography of Recent Studies in English Renaissance Drama*, ed. Terence P. Logan and Denzell S. Smith, 210–27. Lincoln and London: University of Nebraska Press, 1978.

Davidson 1989
Clifford Davidson. *Visualizing the Moral Life: Medieval Iconography and the Macro Morality Plays.* New York: AMS Press, 1989.

Davidson 1991
Clifford Davidson. *Illustrations of the Stage and Acting in England to 1580.* Early Drama, Art, and Music Monograph Series 16. Kalamazoo: Medieval Institute, Western Michigan University, 1991.

Davidson & Happé
The Worlde and the Chylde. Ed. Clifford Davidson and Peter Happé. Early Drama, Art, and Music Monograph Series 26. Kalamazoo: Medieval Institute, Western Michigan University, 1999.

Davidson et al.
Clifford Davidson, Martin W. Walsh, and Ton J. Broos, eds. *"Everyman" and Its Dutch Original "Elckerlijc."* Middle English Texts Series. Kalamazoo: Medieval Institute, Western Michigan University, 2007.

Davis 1967
Joe Lee Davis. *The Sons of Ben: Jonsonian Comedy in Caroline England.* Detroit: Wayne State University Press, 1967.

Davis 1970
Norman Davis, ed. *Non-Cycle Plays and Fragments.* EETS, Supplementary Text 1. London, New York, and Toronto: Oxford University Press, 1970.

Davis 1980
Robert Davenport's "King John and Matilda": A Critical Edition. Ed. Joyce O. Davis. New York and London: Garland, 1980.

Davis & Wilson
Nathaniel Woodes. *The Conflict of Conscience.* Ed. Herbert Davis and F. P. Wilson. MSR. Oxford: Oxford University Press, 1952.

Davison 1987
Peter Davison. "Thomas Heywood." In *Dictionary of Literary Biography* 62: *Elizabethan Dramatists*, ed. Fredson Bowers, 101–35. Detroit: Gale, 1987.

Davison 1996
William Shakespeare. *The First Quarto of "King Richard III."* Ed. Peter Davison. Cambridge: Cambridge University Press, 1996.

Dawson 1929
Giles Edwin Dawson, ed. *"The Seven Champions of Christendome* by John Kirke." *Western Reserve University Bulletin* n.s. 32 (1929): 1–82.

Dawson 1990
Giles E. Dawson. "Shakespeare's Handwriting." *Shakespeare Survey* 42 (1990): 119–28.

Dawson 1997
Christopher Marlowe. *Tamburlaine, Parts One and Two.* Ed. Anthony B. Dawson. 2nd ed. New Mermaids. London: Black; New York: Norton, 1997.

Dawson 2003
William Shakespeare. *Troilus and Cressida*. Ed. Anthony B. Dawson. New Cambridge Shakespeare. Cambridge: Cambridge University Press, 2003.

Dawson 2007
Lesel Dawson. "Dangerous Misogyny: John Ford's *The Queen* and the Earl of Essex's 1601 Uprising." *Explorations in Renaissance Culture* 33.1 (2007): 64–82.

Dawson & Brown
July and Julian. Ed. Giles Dawson and Arthur Brown. MSR. Oxford: Oxford University Press, 1955.

Dawson & Minton
William Shakespeare and Thomas Middleton. *Timon of Athens*. Ed. Anthony B. Dawson and Gretchen E. Minton. Arden 3. London: Cengage Learning, 2008.

Day 1926
Cyrus L. Day. "Thomas Randolph's Part in the Authorship of *Hey for Honesty*." *PMLA* 41.2 (1926): 325–34.

Day 1928
Cyrus L. Day. "Thomas Randolph and *The Drinking Academy*." *PMLA* 43.3 (1928): 800–09.

Dean 1981
Paul Dean. "'Friar Bacon and Friar Bungay' and 'John of Bordeaux': A Dramatic Diptych." *English Language Notes* 18.4 (1981): 262–66.

Dean 1991
William Dean. "The Trial of Ismael in *Nice Wanton*." *Medieval English Theatre* 13 (1991): 27–38.

Delius
Nicolaus Delius. "Üeber Shakespeare's *Pericles, Prince of Tyre*." *Shakespeare Jahrbuch* 3 (1868): 175–204.

De Luna
B. N. De Luna. *Jonson's Romish Plot: A Study of "Catiline" and Its Historical Context*. Oxford: Clarendon Press, 1967.

DelVecchio & Hammond
William Shakespeare. *Pericles, Prince of Tyre*. Ed. Doreen DelVecchio and Antony Hammond. Cambridge: Cambridge University Press, 1998.

Demiralp
Ayse Nur Demiralp. "*The Life and Death of Jack Straw* and *The Tragical Reign of Selimus*: A Note on Some Verbal and Thematic Parallels." *Notes and Queries* 59.1 (2012): 45–48.

DePorte
Michael V. DePorte. "William Davenant." In *The Later Jacobean and Caroline Dramatists: A Survey and Bibliography of Recent Studies in English Renaissance Drama*, ed. Terence P. Logan and Denzell S. Smith, 192–209. Lincoln and London: University of Nebraska Press, 1978.

De Ricci 1920a
Henry Medwall. *Fulgens and Lucres*. Ed. Seymour de Ricci. Henry E. Huntington Facsimile Reprints 1. New York: George D. Smith, 1920.

De Ricci 1920b
W. Wager. *Enough Is As Good As a Feast*. Ed. Seymour de Ricci. Henry E. Huntington Facsimile Reprints 2. New York: George D. Smith, 1920.

Dering
George Walton Williams and Gwynne Blakemore Evans, eds. *William Shakespeare, "The History of King Henry the Fourth," As Revised by Sir Edward Dering, Bart*. Charlottesville: University of Virginia Press, 1974.

Dessen 1977
Alan C. Dessen. *Elizabethan Drama and the Viewer's Eye*. Chapel Hill: University of North Carolina Press, 1977.

Dessen 1980
Alan C. Dessen. "Elizabethan Audiences and the Open Stage: Recovering Lost Conventions." *Yearbook of English Studies* 10 (1980): 1–20.

Dessen 1984
Alan C. Dessen. *Elizabethan Stage Conventions and Modern Interpreters*. Cambridge: Cambridge University Press, 1984.

Dessen 1986
Alan C. Dessen. *Shakespeare and the Late Moral Plays*. Lincoln and London: University of Nebraska Press, 1986.

Dessen 1996
Alan C. Dessen. "Recovering Elizabethan Staging: A Reconsideration of the Evidence." In *Textual and Theatrical Shakespeare: Questions of Evidence*, ed. Edward Pechter, 44–65. Iowa City: University of Iowa Press, 1996.

Dessen 2006
Alan C. Dessen. "'The difference betwixt reporting and representing': Thomas Heywood and the Playgoer's Imagination." In *Acts of Criticism: Performance Matters in Shakespeare and His Contemporaries*, ed. Paul Nelsen and June Schlueter, 46–57. Madison and Teaneck, NJ: Fairleigh Dickinson University Press, 2006.

Dessen 2009
Alan C. Dessen. "On-Stage Allegory and Its Legacy: *The Three Ladies of London*." In *Locating the Queen's Men, 1583–1603: Material Practices and Conditions*

of Playing, ed. Helen Ostovich, Holger Schott Syme, and Andrew Griffin, 147–58. Farnham, UK: Ashgate, 2009.

Dessen 2010

Alan C. Dessen. "Mist and Fog on the Elizabethan and Jacobean Stage." In *Speaking Pictures: The Visual/Verbal Nexus of Dramatic Performance*, ed. Virginia Mason Vaughan, Fernando Cioni, and Jacquelyn Bessell, 106–18. Madison and Teaneck, NJ: Fairleigh Dickinson University Press, 2010.

Dessen & Thomson

Alan C. Dessen and Leslie Thomson. *A Dictionary of Stage Directions in English Drama, 1580–1642*. Cambridge: Cambridge University Press, 1999.

Dezur

Kathryn Dezur. "Prodigal Daughter, Usurer's Son: Sexual, Rhetorical, and Monetary Economies in Robert Chamberlain's *The Swaggering Damsel* (1640)." *Renaissance and Reformation* 32.4 (2009): 5–30.

Dick

Thomas Tomkis. *Albumazar: A Comedy*. Ed. Hugh G. Dick. University of California Publications in English 13. Berkeley and Los Angeles: University of California Press, 1944.

Diehl 1980

Huston Diehl. "The Iconography of Violence in English Renaissance Tragedy." *Renaissance Drama* n.s. 11 (1980): 27–44.

Diehl 1981

Huston Diehl. "'Reduce Thy Understanding to Thine Eye': Seeing and Interpreting in *The Atheist's Tragedy*." *Studies in Philology* 78.1 (1981): 47–60.

Diehl 1983

Huston Diehl. "Horrid Image, Sorry Sight, Fatal Vision: The Visual Rhetoric of *Macbeth*." *Shakespeare Studies* 16 (1983): 191–203.

Diehl 1986

Huston Diehl. "Iconography and Characterization in English Tragedy 1585–1642." In *Drama in the Renaissance: Comparative and Critical Essays*, ed. Clifford Davidson, C. J. Gianakaris, and John H. Stroupe, 11–20. New York: AMS Press, 1986.

Diehl 1991

Huston Diehl. "Observing the Lord's Supper and the Lord Chamberlain's Men: The Visual Rhetoric of Ritual and Play in Early Modern England." *Renaissance Drama* 22 (1991): 147–74.

Diehl 1997

Huston Diehl. *Staging Reform, Reforming the Stage: Protestantism and Popular Theater in Early Modern England*. Ithaca, NY, and London: Cornell University Press, 1997.

DiGangi 1997
Mario DiGangi. *The Homoerotics of Early Modern Drama*. Cambridge: Cambridge University Press, 1997.

DiGangi 2002
Mario DiGangi. "John Ford." In *A Companion to Renaissance Drama*, ed. Arthur F. Kinney, 567–83. Oxford: Blackwell, 2002.

DiGangi 2006
Mario DiGangi. "A Beast So Blurred: The Monstrous Favorite in Caroline Drama." In *Localizing Caroline Drama: Politics and Economics of the Early Modern English Stage, 1625–1642*, ed. Adam Zucker and Alan B. Farmer, 157–81. Basingstoke, UK, and New York: Palgrave Macmillan, 2006.

DiGangi 2011
Mario DiGangi. *Sexual Types: Embodiment, Agency, and Dramatic Character from Shakespeare to Shirley*. Philadelphia: University of Pennsylvania Press, 2011.

Dillon 1995
Janette Dillon. "*The Spanish Tragedy* and Staging Languages in Renaissance Drama." *Research Opportunities in Renaissance Drama* 34 (1995): 15–40.

Dillon 1996
Janette Dillon. "John Rastell's Stage." *Medieval English Theatre* 18 (1996): 15–45.

Dillon 1998
Janette Dillon. *Language and Stage in Medieval and Renaissance England*. Cambridge: Cambridge University Press, 1998.

Dillon 2000
Janette Dillon. *Theatre, Court and City, 1595–1610: Drama and Social Space in London*. Cambridge: Cambridge University Press, 2000.

Dillon 2002
Janette Dillon. "Elizabethan Comedy." In *The Cambridge Companion to Shakespearean Comedy*, ed. Alexander Leggatt, 47–63. Cambridge: Cambridge University Press, 2002.

Dillon 2004a
Janette Dillon. "Chariots and Cloud Machines: Gods and Goddesses on Early English Stages." In *Tudor Drama before Shakespeare, 1485–1590: New Directions for Research, Criticism, and Pedagogy*, ed. Lloyd Edward Kermode, Jason Scott-Warren, and Martine van Elk, 111–29. Basingstoke, UK, and New York: Palgrave Macmillan, 2004.

Dillon 2004b
Janette Dillon. "Theatre and Controversy, 1603–1642." In *The Cambridge History of British Theatre*, vol. 1: *Origins to 1660*, ed. Jane Milling and Peter Thomson, 364–82. Cambridge: Cambridge University Press, 2004.

Dillon 2007
Janette Dillon. "Powerful Obedience: *Godly Queen Hester* and Katherine of Aragon." In *Interludes and Early Modern Society: Studies in Gender, Power and Theatricality*, ed. Peter Happé and Wim Hüsken, 117–39. Amsterdam and New York: Rodopi, 2007.

Dillon 2008
Janette Dillon. "The Early Tudor History Play." In *English Historical Drama, 1500–1660: Forms Outside the Canon*, ed. Teresa Grant and Barbara Ravelhofer, 32–57. Basingstoke, UK, and New York: Palgrave Macmillan, 2008.

Dillon 2010
Janette Dillon. "Shakespeare's Tragicomedies." In *The New Cambridge Companion to Shakespeare*, ed. Margreta de Grazia and Stanley Wells, 169–84. Cambridge: Cambridge University Press, 2010.

Dillon 2012
Janette Dillon. *Shakespeare and the Staging of English History*. Oxford Shakespeare Topics. Oxford: Oxford University Press, 2012.

Dimmock 2005
Matthew Dimmock. *New Turkes: Dramatizing Islam and the Ottomans in Early Modern England*. Aldershot, UK, and Burlington, VT: Ashgate, 2005.

Dimmock 2006
William Percy's "Mahomet and His Heaven": A Critical Edition. Ed. Matthew Dimmock. Aldershot, UK, and Burlington, VT: Ashgate, 2006.

Dobell 1907
The Poetical Works of William Strode. Ed. Bertram Dobell. London: privately printed, 1907.

Dobell 1908
The Partiall Law, A Tragi-Comedy by an Unknown Author. Ed. Bertram Dobell. London: privately printed, 1908.

Dobson 2001
Michael Dobson. "*Cardenio*." In *The Oxford Companion to Shakespeare*, gen. ed. Michael Dobson, assoc. gen. ed. Stanley Wells, 66–67. Oxford: Oxford University Press, 2001.

Dobson 2007
Wit at Several Weapons. Ed. Michael Dobson. In *Thomas Middleton: The Collected Works*, gen. eds. Gary Taylor and John Lavagnino. Oxford: Clarendon, 2007.

Dobson 2011
Michael Dobson. *Shakespeare and Amateur Performance*. Cambridge: Cambridge University Press, 2011.

Dodds 1924

Madeleine Hope Dodds. "'Edmond Ironside' and 'The Love-sick King'." *Modern Language Review* 19.2 (1924): 158–68.

Dodds 1931a

Madeleine Hope Dodds. "William Percy and Charles Fitzjeffrey." *Notes and Queries* 160 (June 1931): 420–22.

Dodds 1931b

Madeleine Hope Dodds. "William Percy and James I." *Notes and Queries* 161 (July 1931): 13–14.

Dodds 1931c

Madeleine Hope Dodds. "William Percy's 'Aphrodysial'." *Notes and Queries* 161 (October 1931): 237–40 and 257–61.

Dodds 1933

Madeleine Hope Dodds. *"A Dreame of a Drye Yeare." JEGP* 32.2 (1933): 172–95.

Dodds 1945

Madeleine Hope Dodds. "'A Forrest Tragaedye in Vacunium'." *Modern Language Review* 40.4 (1945): 246–58.

Dodsley

Robert Dodsley, ed. *A Select Collection of Old English Plays.* Rev. and enlarged with notes by W. Carew Hazlitt. 15 vols. London: Reeves and Turner, 1874–76.

Doebler 1967

Francis Beaumont. *The Knight of the Burning Pestle.* Ed. John Doebler. RRDS. Lincoln: University of Nebraska Press, 1967.

Doebler 1974

John Doebler. *Shakespeare's Speaking Pictures: Studies in Iconic Imagery.* Albuquerque: University of New Mexico Press, 1974.

Doh

Thomas Heywood and William Rowley. *A Critical Edition of "Fortune by Land and Sea."* Ed. Herman Doh. New York and London: Garland, 1980.

Dolan 1989

Frances E. Dolan. "Gender, Moral Agency, and Dramatic Form in *A Warning for Fair Women." Studies in English Literature, 1500–1900* 29.2 (1989): 201–18.

Dolan 2007

Frances E. Dolan. "Hermione's Ghost: Catholicism, the Feminine, and the Undead." In *The Impact of Feminism in English Renaissance Studies,* ed. Dympna Callaghan, 213–37. Basingstoke, UK, and New York: Palgrave Macmillan, 2007.

Dollimore 1986
Jonathan Dollimore. "Subjectivity, Sexuality, and Transgression: The Jacobean Connection." *Renaissance Drama* n.s. 17 (1986): 53–81.

Dollimore 2004
Jonathan Dollimore. *Radical Tragedy: Religion, Ideology and Power in the Drama of Shakespeare and His Contemporaries.* 3rd ed. Basingstoke, UK, and New York: Palgrave Macmillan, 2004.

Dollimore & Sinfield
The Selected Plays of John Webster. Ed. Jonathan Dollimore and Alan Sinfield. Cambridge: Cambridge University Press, 1983.

Dominik
Mark Dominik. *William Shakespeare and "The Birth of Merlin."* New York: Philosophical Library, 1985.

Donaldson 1970
Ian Donaldson. "'Living Backward': *The Antipodes.*" In *The World Upside-Down: Comedy from Jonson to Fielding*, 78–99. Oxford: Clarendon Press, 1970.

Donaldson 2000
Ian Donaldson. "'Misconstruing Everything': *Julius Caesar* and *Sejanus.*" In *Shakespeare Performed: Essays in Honor of R. A. Foakes*, ed. Grace Ioppolo, 88–107. Newark, DE: University of Delaware Press; London: Associated University Presses, 2000.

Donaldson 2004
Ian Donaldson. "Jonson, Benjamin (1572–1637)." In *ODNB* 30: 681–94.

Donaldson 2010
Ian Donaldson. "Talking with Ghosts: Ben Jonson and the English Civil War." *Ben Jonson Journal* 17.1 (2010): 1–18.

Donaldson 2011
Ian Donaldson. *Ben Jonson: A Life.* Oxford: Oxford University Press, 2011.

Donno 1985
William Shakespeare. *Twelfth Night or What You Will.* Ed. Elizabeth Story Donno. New Cambridge Shakespeare. Cambridge: Cambridge University Press, 1985. Repr. 1987.

Donno 1993
Three Renaissance Pastorals: Tasso, Guarini, Daniel. Ed. Elizabeth Story Donno. MRTS 102. Binghamton, NY: Center for Medieval and Early Renaissance Studies, SUNY, 1993.

Donovan 1987
Kevin J. Donovan. "Ben Jonson." In *Dictionary of Literary Biography* 62: *Elizabethan Dramatists*, ed. Fredson Bowers, 136–82. Detroit: Gale, 1987.

Donovan 1999
Kevin Donovan. "Forms of Authority in the Early Texts of *Every Man Out of His Humour.*" In *Re-Presenting Ben Jonson: Text, History, Performance*, ed. Martin Butler, 59–75. Basingstoke, UK, and London: Macmillan, 1999.

Doran 1934a
Thomas Heywood. *If You Know Not Me You Know Nobody, Part I.* Ed. Madeleine Doran. MSR. Oxford: Oxford University Press, 1934 [1935].

Doran 1934b
Thomas Heywood. *If You Know Not Me You Know Nobody, Part II.* Ed. Madeleine Doran. MSR. Oxford: Oxford University Press, 1934 [1935].

Dorenkamp
John Fletcher and Philip Massinger. *Beggars Bush.* Ed. John H. Dorenkamp. The Hague and Paris: Mouton, 1967.

Dorsch & King
William Shakespeare. *The Comedy of Errors: Updated Edition.* Ed. T. S Dorsch. Rev. Ros King. Cambridge: Cambridge University Press, 2004.

Douglas & Greenfield
Audrey Douglas and Peter Greenfield, eds. *Cumberland, Westmorland, Gloucestershire.* REED. Toronto, Buffalo, and London: University of Toronto Press, 1986.

Dowden 1875
Edward Dowden. *Shakspere: A Critical Study of His Mind and Art.* London: Henry S. King, 1875.

Dowden 1877
Edward Dowden. *Shakspere.* London: Macmillan, 1877.

Drakakis 2004
John Drakakis. "Marmion, Shackerley (1603–1639)." In *ODNB* 36: 734–35.

Drakakis 2007
John Drakakis. "Afterword." In *A Concise Companion to Shakespeare and the Text*, ed. Andrew Murphy, 221–38. Oxford: Blackwell, 2007.

Drew-Bear
Annette Drew-Bear. *Painted Faces on the Renaissance Stage: The Moral Significance of Face-Painting Conventions.* Lewisburg, PA: Bucknell University Press; London and Toronto: Associated University Presses, 1994.

DTRB
Ian Lancashire. *Dramatic Texts and Records of Britain: A Chronological Topography to 1558.* Studies in Early English Drama 1. Toronto, Buffalo, and London: University of Toronto Press, 1984.

Duncan

Anne Duncan. "It Takes a Woman to Play a Real Man: Clara as Hero(ine) of Beaumont and Fletcher's *Love's Cure*." *English Literary Renaissance* 30.3 (2000): 396–407.

Duncan-Jones 1961

E. E. Duncan-Jones. "The Two 'Osmund' Plays." *Notes and Queries* 8.4 (1961): 128–29.

Duncan-Jones 2001

Katherine Duncan-Jones. *Ungentle Shakespeare: Scenes from His Life*. London: Arden Shakespeare, 2001.

Duncan-Jones 2011

Katherine Duncan-Jones. *Shakespeare: Upstart Crow to Sweet Swan, 1592–1623*. Arden Shakespeare Library. London: A. & C. Black, 2011.

Dunn 1969

Philip Massinger and Nathan Field. *The Fatal Dowry*. Ed. T. A. Dunn. Fountainwell Drama Texts. Berkeley and Los Angeles: University of California Press, 1969.

Dunn 1972

F. I. Dunn. "The Norwich Grocers' Play and the Kirkpatrick Papers at Norwich." *Notes and Queries* 19.6 (1972): 202–03.

Dunn 2003

Kevin Dunn. "Representing Counsel: *Gorboduc* and the Elizabethan Privy Council." *English Literary Renaissance* 33.3 (2003): 279–308.

Dunstan & Greg

Elizabeth Cary. *The Tragedy of Mariam*. Ed. A. C. Dunstan and W. W. Greg. MSR. Oxford: Oxford University Press, 1914. Reissued with supplement by Marta Straznicky and Richard Rowland, 1992.

Dusinberre

William Shakespeare. *As You Like It*. Ed. Juliet Dusinberre. Arden. London: Thomson Learning, 2006.

Dust

"*The Levellers Levelled*." Ed. Philip C. Dust. *AEB: Analytical & Enumerative Bibliography* 4.3–4 (1980): 183–240.

Duthie

G. I. Duthie. "*The Taming of a Shrew* and *The Taming of the Shrew*." *Review of English Studies* 19.76 (1943): 337–56.

Dutka

Joanna Dutka. "The Lost Dramatic Cycle of Norwich and the Grocers' Play of The Fall of Man." *Review of English Studies* 35 (1984): 1–13.

Dutton 1983
Richard Dutton. *Ben Jonson: To the First Folio*. Cambridge: Cambridge University Press, 1983.

Dutton 1991
Richard Dutton. *Mastering the Revels: The Regulation and Censorship of English Renaissance Drama*. Iowa City: University of Iowa Press, 1991.

Dutton 1993
Richard Dutton. "Ben Jonson and the Master of the Revels." In *Theatre and Government under the Early Stuarts*, ed. J. R. Mulryne and Margaret Shewring, 57–86. Cambridge: Cambridge University Press, 1993.

Dutton 1996
Richard Dutton. *Ben Jonson: Authority, Criticism*. London and New York: Macmillan, 1996.

Dutton 1998
Richard Dutton. "'Discourse in the players, though no disobedience': Sir Henry Herbert's Problems with the Players and Archbishop Laud, 1632–34." *Ben Jonson Journal* 5 (1998): 37–61.

Dutton 1999
"Women Beware Women" and Other Plays. Ed. Richard Dutton. Oxford World's Classics. Oxford and New York: Oxford University Press, 1999.

Dutton 2000
Richard Dutton. *Licensing, Censorship and Authorship in Early Modern England: Buggeswords*. Basingstoke, UK, and New York: Palgrave, 2000.

Dutton 2002
Richard Dutton. "The Revels Office and the Boy Companies, 1600–1613: New Perspectives." *English Literary Renaissance* 32.2 (2002): 324–51.

Dutton 2003
Ben Jonson. *Epicene, or The Silent Woman*. Ed. Richard Dutton. Revels Plays. Manchester: Manchester University Press; New York: Palgrave, 2003.

Dutton 2004
Richard Dutton. "Thomas Middleton's *A Game at Chess*: A Case Study." In *The Cambridge History of British Theatre*, vol. 1: *Origins to 1660*, ed. Jane Milling and Peter Thomson, 424–38. Cambridge: Cambridge University Press, 2004.

Dutton 2005
Richard Dutton. "'Methinks the truth should live from age to age': The Dating and Contexts of *Henry V*." *Huntington Library Quarterly* 68.1–2 (2005): 173–204.

Dutton 2006
Richard Dutton. "The St. Werburgh Street Theater, Dublin." In *Localizing Caroline Drama: Politics and Economics of the Early Modern English Stage, 1625–1642*, ed. Adam Zucker and Alan B. Farmer, 129–55. Basingstoke, UK, and New York: Palgrave Macmillan, 2006.

Dutton 2008
Richard Dutton. *Ben Jonson, "Volpone" and the Gunpowder Plot.* Cambridge: Cambridge University Press, 2008.

Dutton 2009a
Richard Dutton. "The Court, the Master of the Revels, and the Players." In *The Oxford Handbook of the Early Modern Theatre*, ed. idem, 362–79. Oxford: Oxford University Press, 2009.

Dutton 2009b
Richard Dutton. "*The Famous Histories* and the 1600 Quarto of *Henry V.*" In *Locating the Queen's Men, 1583–1603: Material Practices and Conditions of Playing*, ed. Helen Ostovich, Holger Schott Syme, and Andrew Griffin, 135–44. Farnham, UK, and Burlington, VT: Ashgate, 2009.

Dutton 2010
Elisabeth Dutton. "Medieval Secular Drama." In *The Oxford Handbook of Medieval Literature in English*, ed. Elaine Treharne and Greg Walker, 384–94. Oxford: Oxford University Press, 2010.

Dutton 2011
Richard Dutton. "A Jacobean *Merry Wives?*" *Ben Jonson Journal* 18.1 (2011): 1–26.

Duxfield 2004
Andrew Duxfield. "Fferrarae's Heire: A Note on the Date of *The Fatal Marriage; or A Second Lucretia.*" *Notes and Queries* 51.3 (2004): 296–97.

Duxfield 2007
Andrew Duxfield. "'That Horse that Runnes upon the Toppe of Powles': Middleton, Dekker and the Anonymous *The Fatal Marriage.*" *Notes and Queries* 54.3 (2007): 264–65.

Dyce 1830
Demetrius and Enanthe, being The Humorous Lieutenant . . . Published from a Manuscript Dated 1625, and Containing Passages Never Before Printed. Ed. Alexander Dyce. London: Thomas Rodd, 1830.

Dyce 1833
The Dramatic Works and Poems of James Shirley, Now First Collected. Ed. Alexander Dyce. 6 vols. London: John Murray, 1833.

Dyce 1840
The Works of Thomas Middleton. Ed. Alexander Dyce. 8 vols. London: E. Lumley, 1840.

Dyce 1842
Timon: A Play, Now First Printed. Ed. Alexander Dyce. London: Shakespere Society, 1842.

Dyce 1844
"Sir Thomas More," A Play. Ed. Alexander Dyce. London: Shakespere Society, 1844.

Eccles
The Macro Plays: "The Castle of Perseverance," "Wisdom," "Mankind." Ed. Mark Eccles. EETS o.s. 262. London, New York, and Toronto: Oxford University Press, 1969.

Edelman 2005
The Stukeley Plays [*Battle of Alcazar, Captain Thomas Stukeley*]. Ed. Charles Edelman. Revels Plays Companion Library. Manchester and New York: Manchester University Press, 2005.

Edelman 2012
Charles Edelman. "Knights, Pigeons, and Chapman's *All Fools.*" *Notes and Queries* 59.4 (2012): 553–57.

Edgerton
William L. Edgerton. *Nicholas Udall.* TEAS 30. New York: Twayne, 1965.

Edington
Carol Edington. *Court and Culture in Renaissance Scotland: Sir David Lindsay of the Mount.* Amherst: University of Massachusetts Press, 1994.

Edmond 1987
Mary Edmond. *Rare Sir William Davenant.* Revels Plays Companion Library. Manchester: Manchester University Press, 1987.

Edmond 2004a
Mary Edmond. "Burbage, Richard (1568–1619)." In *ODNB* 8: 716–19.

Edmond 2004b
Mary Edmond. "Davenant, Sir William (1606–1668)." In *ODNB* 15: 254–60.

Edmondson
Paul Edmondson. "'Beyond the Fringe'?: Receiving, Adapting, and Performing *The London Prodigal.*" *Shakespeare Yearbook* 16 (2007): 195–221.

Edwards 1959
Thomas Kyd. *The Spanish Tragedy.* Ed. Philip Edwards. Revels Plays. London: Methuen, 1959. Repr. 1965 and 1969.

Edwards 1976
William Shakespeare. *Pericles Prince of Tyre*. Ed. Philip Edwards. Harmondsworth, UK: Penguin, 1976.

Edwards 1981
Philip Edwards. "Society and the Theatre." In *The Revels History of Drama in
English*, vol. 4: *1613–1660*, 1–67. London and New York: Methuen, 1981.

Edwards 1987
Philip Edwards. "Philip Massinger." In *Dictionary of Literary Biography* 58: *Jacobean and Caroline Dramatists*, ed. Fredson Bowers, 169–89. Detroit: Gale,
1987.

EEBO
Early English Books Online

EETS
Early English Text Society

Egan 1998
Gabriel Egan. "The Use of Booths in the Original Staging of Jonson's *Bartholomew Fair*." *Cahiers Elisabéthains* 53 (1998): 43–52.

Egan 2001
Gabriel Egan. "Hearing or Seeing a Play? Evidence of Early Modern Theatrical
Terminology." *Ben Jonson Journal* 8 (2001): 327–47.

Egan 2006a
Gabriel Egan. "'As it was, is, or will be played': Title-pages and the Theatre
Industry to 1610." In *From Performance to Print in Shakespeare's England*,
ed. Peter Holland and Stephen Orgel, 92–110. Basingstoke, UK, and New
York: Palgrave Macmillan, 2006.

Egan 2006b
Michael Egan, ed. *"The Tragedy of Richard II, Part One": A Newly Authenticated
Play by William Shakespeare*. 3 vols. Lewiston, Queenston, Lampeter: Edwin
Mellen Press, 2006.

Egan 2010
Gabriel Egan. *The Struggle for Shakespeare's Text: Twentieth-Century Editorial
Theory and Practice*. Cambridge: Cambridge University Press, 2010.

Ekeblad
Inga-Stina Ekeblad. "'King Lear' and 'Selimus'." *Notes and Queries* 202 (1957):
193–94.

Elam 2008
William Shakespeare. *Twelfth Night, or What You Will*. Ed. Keir Elam. Arden.
London: Cengage Learning, 2008.

Elam 2010

Keir Elam. "'Most truly limned and living in your face': Looking at Pictures in Shakespeare." In *Speaking Pictures: The Visual/Verbal Nexus of Dramatic Performance*, ed. Virginia Mason Vaughan, Fernando Cioni, and Jacquelyn Bessell, 63–89. Madison and Teaneck, NJ: Fairleigh Dickinson University Press, 2010.

Ellerbeck

Erin Ellerbeck. "The Female Tongue as Translator in Thomas Tomkis's *Lingua, or The Combat of the Tongue and the Five Senses for Superiority*." *Renaissance and Reformation* 32.1 (2009): 27–45.

Elliott 1988

John R. Elliott Jr. "Queen Elizabeth at Oxford: New Light on the Royal Plays of 1566." *English Literary Renaissance* 18.2 (1988): 218–29.

Elliott 1995

John R. Elliott Jr. "Plays, Players and Playwrights in Renaissance Oxford." In *From Page to Performance: Essays in Early English Drama*, ed. John A. Alford, 179–94. East Lansing: Michigan State University Press, 1995.

Elliott 1997

John R. Elliott Jr. "Drama." In *The History of the University of Oxford*, vol. 4: *Seventeenth-Century Oxford*, ed. Nicholas Tyacke, 641–58. Oxford: Clarendon Press, 1997.

Elliott 2004

John R. Elliott Jr. "Edwards, Richard (1525–1566)." In *ODNB* 17: 958–59.

Elliott et al.

John R. Elliott Jr., Alan H. Nelson, Alexandra F. Johnston, and Diana Wyatt, eds. *Oxford*. 2 vols. REED. Toronto, Buffalo, and London: British Library and University of Toronto Press, 2004.

Elliott & Buttrey

John R. Elliott Jr. and John Buttrey. "The Royal Plays at Christ Church in 1636: A New Document." *Theatre Research International* 10.2 (1985): 93–106.

Elliott & Valenza

Ward E. Y. Elliott and Robert J. Valenza. "'Two Tough Nuts to Crack': Did Shakespeare Write the 'Shakespeare' Portions of *Sir Thomas More* and *Edward III*?" *Literary and Linguistic Computing* 25.1 (2010): 67–83; 25.2 (2010): 165–77.

Ellis-Fermor

Una Ellis-Fermor. *Jacobean Drama: An Interpretation*. 4th ed. Rev. London: Methuen, 1958.

Elson
John James Elson, ed. *The Wits or, Sport upon Sport*. Ithaca, NY: Cornell University Press; London: Humphrey Milford, 1932.

Elton
W. R. Elton. "Textual Transmission and Genre of Shakespeare's *Troilus*." In *Literatur als Kritik des Lebens: Festschrift zum 65. Geburtstag von Ludwig Borinski*, ed. Rudolf Haas, Heinz-Joachim Müllenbrock, and Claus Uhlig, 63–82. Heidelberg: Quelle & Meyer, 1975.

Engel
James Shirley. *The Gentleman of Venice*. Ed. Wilson F. Engel. Salzburg: Institut für Englische Sprache und Literatur, Universität Salzburg, 1976.

Ephraim 2001
Michelle Ephraim. "From Jewish Monarch to Virgin Queen: Elizabeth I and *The Godly Queen Hester*." *Women's Studies* 30.5 (2001): 605–22.

Ephraim 2003
Michelle Ephraim. "Jewish Matriarchs and the Staging of Elizabeth I in *The History of Jacob and Esau*." *Studies in English Literature, 1500–1900* 43.2 (2003): 301–21.

Ericksen
A Critical Old-Spelling Edition of "The Young Admiral" by James Shirley. Ed. Kenneth J. Ericksen. New York and London: Garland, 1979.

Erne 2001a
Lukas Erne. *Beyond "The Spanish Tragedy": A Study of the Works of Thomas Kyd*. Revels Plays Companion Library. Manchester: Manchester University Press, 2001.

Erne 2001b
Lukas Erne. "Thomas Kyd's Christian Tragedy." *Renaissance Papers* 2001: 17–34.

Erne 2003a
Lukas Erne. *Shakespeare as Literary Dramatist*. Cambridge: Cambridge University Press, 2003.

Erne 2003b
Lukas Erne. "'Throughly ransackt': Elizabethan Novella Collections and Henry Wotton's *Courtlie Controuersie of Cupid's Cautels* (1578)." *Cahiers Elisabéthains* 64 (2003): 1–8.

Erne 2007
William Shakespeare. *The First Quarto of "Romeo and Juliet."* Ed. Lukas Erne. Cambridge Early Quartos. Cambridge: Cambridge University Press, 2007.

Esche 1993
A Critical Edition of Thomas Middleton's "The Witch." Ed. Edward J. Esche. New York and London: Garland, 1993.

Esche 1998
The Massacre at Paris with the Death of the Duke of Guise. Ed. Edward J. Esche. In *The Complete Works of Christopher Marlowe*, vol. 5. Oxford: Clarendon Press, 1998.

ESTC
English Short-Title Catalogue

Evans 1942
G. Blakemore Evans. "Shakespeare's *Julius Caesar*: A Seventeenth-Century Manuscript." *JEGP* 41.4 (1942): 401–17.

Evans 1951
The Plays and Poems of William Cartwright. Ed. G. Blakemore Evans. Madison: University of Wisconsin Press, 1951.

Evans 1970
George Chapman. *All Fools.* Ed. G. Blakemore Evans. In *The Plays of George Chapman: The Comedies.* Urbana and London: University of Illinois Press, 1970.

Evans 1987
The Tragedie of Chabot Admirall of France. Ed. G. Blakemore Evans. In *The Plays of George Chapman: The Tragedies with "Sir Gyles Goosecappe," A Critical Edition.* Cambridge: Brewer, 1987.

Evans 1989
Robert C. Evans. *Ben Jonson and the Poetics of Patronage.* Lewisburg, PA: Bucknell University Press; London and Toronto: Associated University Presses, 1989.

Evans 1997
The Riverside Shakespeare. 2nd ed. Ed. G. Blakemore Evans, assisted by J. J. M. Tobin. Boston and New York: Houghton Mifflin, 1997.

Evans & Greg 1936a
Jack Juggler (Third Edition). Ed. B. Ifor Evans and W. W. Greg. MSR. Oxford: Oxford University Press, 1936 [1937].

Evans & Greg 1936b
Thomas Garter. *The Most Virtuous & Godly Susanna.* Ed. B. Ifor Evans and W. W. Greg. Oxford: Oxford University Press, 1936 [1937].

Evans & Tobin
G. Blakemore Evans and J. J. M. Tobin. "Appendix C: Records, Documents, and Allusions." In *The Riverside Shakespeare*, 1951–78. 2nd ed. Boston and New York: Houghton Mifflin, 1997.

Everitt 1954
Ephraim Everitt. *The Young Shakespeare: Studies in Documentary Evidence*. Anglistica 2. Copenhagen: Rosenkilde and Bagger, 1954.

Everitt 1965
Ephraim B. Everitt and R. L. Armstrong, eds. *Six Early Plays Related to the Shakespeare Canon*. Anglistica 14. Copenhagen: Rosenkilde and Bagger, 1965.

Evett
Henry Porter's "The Two Angry Women of Abington": A Critical Edition. Ed. Marianne Brish Evett. New York and London: Garland, 1980.

Ewbank 1975
Inga-Stina Ewbank. "'What words, what looks, what wonders?': Language and Spectacle in the Theatre of George Peele." *The Elizabethan Theatre* 5 (1975): 124–54.

Ewbank 2007
Inga-Stina Ewbank. Introduction to *The Tragedy of Macbeth*, ed. Gary Taylor, 1165–69. In *Thomas Middleton: The Collected Works*, gen. eds. Taylor and John Lavagnino. Oxford: Clarendon Press, 2007.

Eyre
George Edward Briscoe Eyre, Charles Robert Rivington, and Henry Robert Plomer, eds. *A Transcript of the Registers of the Worshipful Company of Stationers from 1640–1708 A.D.* 3 vols. London: privately printed, 1913–14. Repr. New York: Peter Smith, 1967.

Ezell
Margaret J. M. Ezell. "'To Be Your Daughter in Your Pen': The Social Functions of Literature in the Writings of Lady Elizabeth Brackley and Lady Jane Cavendish." *Huntington Library Quarterly* 51.4 (1988): 281–96.

E&G
Philip Edwards and Colin Gibson, eds. *The Plays and Poems of Philip Massinger*. 5 vols. Oxford: Clarendon Press, 1976.

Fairholt
John Heywood. *A Dialogue on Wit and Folly, Now First Printed from the Original Manuscript in the British Museum*. Ed. Frederick William Fairholt. London: Percy Society, 1846.

Farley-Hills 1990
David Farley-Hills. *Shakespeare and the Rival Playwrights, 1600–1606*. London and New York: Routledge, 1990.

Farley-Hills 2002
David Farley-Hills. "The Theatrical Provenance of *The Comedy of Errors*." *Notes and Queries* 49.2 (2002): 220–22.

Farmer 1906

John S. Farmer, ed. *Six Anonymous Plays (Second Series)*. London: Early English Drama Society, 1906. Repr. New York: Barnes & Noble, 1966.

Farmer 1910

John S. Farmer, ed. *The Book of Sir Thomas Moore (Harleian MSS. 7368, c. 1590–96)*. Tudor Facsimile Texts, Folio Series. London: Oxford University Press, 1910. Repr. New York: AMS Press, 1970.

Farmer 1912

John S. Farmer, ed. *Tom Tyler and His Wife*. Amershand, UK: Tudor Facsimile Texts, 1912.

Farmer 2010

Alan B. Farmer. "Print Culture and Reading Practices." In *Ben Jonson in Context*, ed. Julie Sanders, 192–200. Cambridge: Cambridge University Press, 2010.

Farmer & Lesser 2000

Alan B. Farmer and Zachary Lesser. "Vile Arts: The Marketing of English Printed Drama, 1512–1660." *Research Opportunities in Renaissance Drama* 39 (2000): 77–165.

Farmer & Lesser 2006

Alan B. Farmer and Zachary Lesser. "Canons and Classics: Publishing Drama in Caroline England." In *Localizing Caroline Drama: Politics and Economics of the Early Modern English Stage, 1625–1642*, ed. Adam Zucker and Alan B. Farmer, 17–41. Basingstoke, UK, and New York: Palgrave Macmillan, 2006.

Farnham

Willard Farnham. *The Medieval Heritage of Elizabethan Tragedy*. Oxford: Blackwell, 1936. Repr. 1970.

Farnsworth

Jane Farnsworth. "Defending the King in Cartwright's *The Lady-Errant* (1636–37)." *Studies in English Literature, 1500–1900* 42.2 (2002): 381–98.

Feather

John Feather. "Robert Armin and the Chamberlain's Men." *Notes and Queries* 19.12 (1972): 448–50.

Feerick

Jean Feerick. "'Divided in Soyle': Plantation and Degeneracy in *The Tempest* and *The Sea Voyage*." *Renaissance Drama* n.s. 35 (2006): 27–54.

Fehrenbach

A Critical Edition of "The Politician" by James Shirley. Ed. Robert J. Fehrenbach. New York and London: Garland, 1980.

Feinberg
Anat Feinberg. "The Perspective of Fear in Sir John Denham's *The Sophy.*" *Studia Neophilologica* 52.2 (1980): 311–22.

Feldman & Proudfoot
A Yorkshire Tragedy. Ed. Sylvia D. Feldman and G. R. Proudfoot. MSR. Oxford: Oxford University Press, 1969 [1973].

Ferguson 1966
John Fletcher. *The Woman's Prize; or, The Tamer Tamed: A Critical Edition.* Ed. George B. Ferguson. The Hague: Mouton, 1966.

Ferguson 2003
Margaret W. Ferguson. *Dido's Daughters: Literacy, Gender, and Empire in Early Modern England and France.* Chicago and London: University of Chicago Press, 2003.

Feuillerat 1904
Arthur Wilson. *The Swisser.* Ed. Albert Feuillerat. Paris: Fischbacher, 1904.

Feuillerat 1908
Albert Feuillerat. *Documents Relating to the Office of the Revels in the Time of Queen Elizabeth.* Ed. W. Bang. Materialen zur Kunde des älteren Englischen Dramas. Louvain: Uystpruyst, 1908.

Findlay 1994
Alison Findlay. *Illegitimate Power: Bastards in Renaissance Drama.* Manchester and New York: Manchester University Press, 1994.

Findlay 1998
Alison Findlay. "'She Gave You the Civility of the House': Household Performance in *The Concealed Fancies.*" In *Readings in Renaissance Women's Drama: Criticism, History, and Performance 1594–1998,* ed. S. P. Cerasano and Marion Wynne-Davies, 259–71. London and New York: Routledge, 1998.

Findlay 1999
Alison Findlay. *A Feminist Perspective on Renaissance Drama.* Oxford: Blackwell, 1999.

Findlay 2000
Alison Findlay. "'Upon the World's Stage': The Civil War and Interregnum." In *Women and Dramatic Production, 1550–1700,* ed. eadem and Stephanie Hodgson-Wright, with Gweno Williams, 68–94. Harlow, UK: Pearson Education; New York: Longman, 2000.

Findlay 2001
Alison Findlay. "Women and Drama." In *A Companion to English Renaissance Literature and Culture,* ed. Michael Hattaway, 499–512. Oxford: Blackwell, 2001.

Findlay 2002

Alison Findlay. "Gendering the Stage." In *A Companion to Renaissance Drama*, ed. Arthur Kinney, 399–415. Oxford and Malden, MA: Blackwell, 2002.

Findlay 2006

Alison Findlay. *Playing Spaces in Early Women's Drama*. Cambridge: Cambridge University Press, 2006.

Findlay et al.

Alison Findlay, Gweno Williams, and Stephanie J. Hodgson-Wright. "'The Play is ready to be Acted': Women and Dramatic Production, 1570–1670." *Women's Writing* 6.1 (1999): 129–48.

Finkelpearl 1966

Philip J. Finkelpearl. "John Marston's *Histrio-Mastix* as an Inns of Court Play: A Hypothesis." *Huntington Library Quarterly* 29.3 (1966): 223–34.

Finkelpearl 1969

Philip J. Finkelpearl. *John Marston of the Middle Temple*. Cambridge, MA: Harvard University Press, 1969.

Finkelpearl 1990

Philip J. Finkelpearl. *Court and Country Politics in the Plays of Beaumont and Fletcher*. Princeton: Princeton University Press, 1990.

Finkelpearl 2004

Philip J. Finkelpearl. "Beaumont, Francis (1584/5–1616)." In *ODNB* 4: 652–56.

Fishman

Burton J. Fishman. "Pride and Ire: Theatrical Iconography in Preston's *Cambises*." *Studies in English Literature, 1500–1900* 16.2 (1976): 201–11.

Fitch

Robert Fitch. "Norwich Pageants. The Grocers' Play. From a Manuscript in the Possession of Robert Fitch." Norwich: privately printed, 1856. Published also in *Norfolk Archaeology* 5 (1859): 8–31.

Fitzgibbons

Thomas May. *The Old Couple*. Ed. Sister M. Simplicia Fitzgibbons. Washington, DC: Catholic University of America Press, 1943.

Fitzmaurice

William Cavendish. *The Humorous Lovers: A Comedy*. Ed. James Fitzmaurice. Oxford: Seventeenth Century Press, 1997.

Fitzpatrick

Tim Fitzpatrick. *Playwright, Space and Place in Early Modern Performance: Shakespeare and Company*. Studies in Performance and Early Modern Drama. Farnham, UK, and Burlington, VT: Ashgate, 2011.

Flavin

A Critical, Modern-Spelling Edition of the 1629 Quarto of "The Wedding" by James Shirley. Ed. Sister Martin Flavin. New York and London: Garland, 1980.

Fleay 1890

Frederick Gard Fleay. *A Chronicle History of the London Stage, 1559–1642.* London: Reeves and Turner, 1890.

Fleay 1891

Frederick Gard Fleay. *A Biographical Chronicle of the English Drama, 1559–1642.* 2 vols. London: Reeves and Turner, 1891. Repr. New York: Burt Franklin, 1969.

Fleck

Andrew Fleck. "Vulgar Fingers of the Multitude: Shakespeare, Jonson, and the Transformation of News from the Low Countries." *Shakespeare Yearbook* 15: *Shakespeare and the Low Countries* (2005): 89–111.

Fleissner 1987

Robert F. Fleissner. *"Arden of Faversham."* In *Dictionary of Literary Biography* 62: *Elizabethan Dramatists*, ed. Fredson Bowers, 361–64. Detroit: Gale, 1987.

Fleissner 1996

Robert F. Fleissner. "The Likely Misascription of *Cardenio* (and Thereby *Double Falsehood*) in Part to Shakespeare." *Neuphilologische Mitteilungen* 97.2 (1996): 217–30.

Fletcher

Alan J. Fletcher. *Drama, Performance, and Polity in Pre-Cromwellian Ireland.* Cork: Cork University Press; Toronto: University of Toronto Press, 2000.

Florby

Gunilla Florby. *Echoing Texts: George Chapman's "Conspiracy and Tragedy of Charles Duke of Byron."* Lund: Department of English, Lund University, 2004.

Flynn

Dennis Flynn. "Mayne, Jasper (1604–1672)." In *ODNB* 37: 603–05.

Foakes 1985

R. A. Foakes. *Illustrations of the English Stage, 1580–1642.* Stanford: Stanford University Press, 1985.

Foakes 1987

William Shakespeare. *Troilus and Cressida.* Ed. R. A. Foakes. New Penguin. Harmondsworth, UK, and New York: Penguin, 1987.

Foakes 1997

William Shakespeare. *King Lear.* Ed. R. A. Foakes. Arden. Walton-on-Thames, UK: Thomas Nelson, 1997.

Foakes 2002

R. A. Foakes, ed. *Henslowe's Diary*. 2nd ed. Cambridge: Cambridge University Press, 2002.

Foakes 2003

R. A. Foakes. "Playhouses and Players." In *The Cambridge Companion to English Renaissance Drama*, ed. A. R. Braunmuller and Michael Hattaway, 1–52. 2nd ed. Cambridge: Cambridge University Press, 2003.

Foakes 2004

R. A. Foakes. "Henslowe's Rose/Shakespeare's Globe." In *From Script to Stage in Early Modern England*, ed. Peter Holland and Stephen Orgel, 11–31. Basingstoke, UK, and New York: Palgrave Macmillan, 2004.

Foakes & Gibson

The Telltale. Ed. R. A. Foakes and J. C. Gibson. MSR. Oxford: Oxford University Press, 1959 [1960].

Foakes & Rickert

Henslowe's Diary. Ed. R. A. Foakes and R. T. Rickert. Cambridge: Cambridge University Press, 1961. Repr. 1968.

Folger

The Folger Shakespeare Library, Washington, DC

Ford

Elizabeth Ford. "Will Kemp, Shakespeare, and the Composition of *Romeo and Juliet*." *Early Theatre* 13.2 (2010): 162–75.

Forest-Hill

Lynn Forest-Hill. "Lucian's Satire of Philosophers in Heywood's *Play of the Wether*." *Medieval English Theatre* 18 (1996): 142–60.

Forker 1964

James Shirley. *The Cardinal*. Ed. Charles R. Forker. Indiana University Humanities Series 56. Bloomington: Indiana University Press, 1964.

Forker 1965

Charles R. Forker. "Robert Baron's Use of Webster, Shakespeare, and Other Elizabethans." *Anglia* 83 (1965): 176–98.

Forker 1994

Christopher Marlowe. *Edward the Second*. Ed. Charles R. Forker. Revels Plays. Manchester: Manchester University Press; New York: St Martin's Press, 1994.

Forker 2002

William Shakespeare. *King Richard II*. Ed. Charles R. Forker. Arden. London: Thomson Learning, 2002.

Forker 2005
Charles R. Forker. "Royal Carnality and Illicit Desire in the English History Plays of the 1590s." *Medieval and Renaissance Drama in England* 17 (2005): 99–131.

Forker 2010
Charles R. Forker. "*The Troublesome Reign, Richard II*, and the Date of *King John*: A Study in Intertextuality." *Shakespeare Survey* 63 (2010): 127–48.

Forker 2011
George Peele. *The Troublesome Reign of John, King of England*. Ed. Charles R. Forker. Revels Plays. Manchester: Manchester University Press; New York: Palgrave Macmillan, 2011.

Forse
James D. Forse. *Art Imitates Business: Commercial and Political Influences in Elizabethan Theatre*. Bowling Green, OH: Bowling Green State University Popular Press, 1993.

Forsythe
Robert S. Forsythe. *The Relations of Shirley's Plays to the Elizabethan Drama*. Studies in English and Comparative Literature. New York: Columbia University Press, 1914.

Fortier
Mark Fortier. *The Culture of Equity in Early Modern England*. Aldershot, UK, and Burlington, VT: Ashgate, 2005.

Foster
Verna A. Foster. *The Name and Nature of Tragicomedy*. Studies in European Cultural Transition 18. Aldershot, UK, and Burlington, VT: Ashgate, 2004.

Fox 1989
Alistair Fox. *Politics and Literature in the Reigns of Henry VII and Henry VIII*. Oxford: Blackwell, 1989.

Fox & Ringler
The Bannatyne Manuscript: National Library of Scotland, Advocates' MS. 1.1.6. Introduction by Denton Fox and William A. Ringler. London: Scolar Press in association with the National Library of Scotland, 1980.

Franceschina
John Franceschina. *Homosexualities in the English Theatre, From Lyly to Wilde*. Contributions in Drama and Theatre Studies 79. Westport, CT, and London: Greenwood Press, 1997.

Free
Mary G. Free. "Audience within Audience in *The Old Wives Tale*." *Renaissance Papers* (1983): 53–61.

Freedman
Barbara Freedman. "Shakespearean Chronology, Ideological Complicity, and Floating Texts: Something Is Rotten in Windsor." *Shakespeare Quarterly* 45.2 (1994): 190–210.

Freehafer 1968
John Freehafer. "Brome, Suckling, and Davenant's Theater Project of 1639." *Texas Studies in Literature and Language* 10.3 (1968): 367–83.

Freehafer 1969a
John Freehafer. "*Cardenio,* by Shakespeare and Fletcher." *PMLA* 84.3 (1969): 501–13.

Freehafer 1969b
John Freehafer. "Shakespeare's *Tempest* and *The Seven Champions.*" *Studies in Philology* 66.1 (1969): 87–103.

Freehafer 1971
John Freehafer. "Inigo Jones's Scenery for *The Cid.*" *Theatre Notebook* 25.3 (1971): 84–92.

Freehafer 1973
John Freehafer. "Perspective Scenery and the Caroline Playhouses." *Theatre Notebook* 27.3 (1973): 98–113.

Freeman 1963
Arthur Freeman. "The Authorship of *The Tell-Tale.*" *JEGP* 62.2 (1963): 288–92.

Freeman 1967
Arthur Freeman. *Thomas Kyd: Facts and Problems.* Oxford: Clarendon Press, 1967.

Freeman 1971
Arthur Freeman. "The Argument of *Meleager.*" *English Literary Renaissance* 1 (1971): 122–31.

Fried
A Critical Edition of Brome's "The Northern Lasse." Ed. Harvey Fried. New York and London: Garland, 1980.

Frijlinck 1922
"The Tragedy of Sir John van Olden Barnavelt," Anonymous Elizabethan Play. Ed. Wilhelmina P. Frijlinck. Amsterdam: Van Dorssen, 1922.

Frijlinck 1929
The First Part of the Reign of King Richard the Second, or Thomas of Woodstock. Ed. Wilhelmina P. Frijlinck. MSR. Oxford: Oxford University Press, 1929.

Frost 1968
David L. Frost. *The School of Shakespeare: The Influence of Shakespeare on English Drama 1600–42.* Cambridge: Cambridge University Press, 1968.

Frost 1978
The Selected Plays of Thomas Middleton. Ed. David L. Frost. Cambridge: Cambridge University Press, 1978.

Frye
Susan Frye. "Anne of Denmark and the Historical Contextualisation of Shakespeare and Fletcher's *Henry VIII.*" In *Women and Politics in Early Modern England, 1450–1700,* ed. James Daybell, 181–93. Aldershot, UK, and Burlington, VT: Ashgate, 2004.

Fuller
Tamburlaine the Great, Parts 1 and 2. Ed. David Fuller. In *The Complete Works of Christopher Marlowe,* vol. 5. Oxford: Clarendon Press, 1998.

Fumerton
Patricia Fumerton. *Cultural Aesthetics: Renaissance Literature and the Practice of Social Ornament.* Chicago and London: University of Chicago Press, 1991.

Funston
George Wilde. *A Critical Edition of "Love's Hospital."* Ed. Jay Louis Funston. Salzburg Studies in English Literature, Jacobean Drama Series 13. Salzburg: Institut für Englische Sprache und Literatur, Universität Salzburg, 1973.

Furnivall 1882
Frederick J. Furnivall, ed. *The Digby Mysteries.* London: Trübner for the New Shakspere Society, 1882.

Furnivall 1896
Frederick J. Furnivall, ed. *The Digby Plays, with an Incomplete "Morality" of Wisdom Who Is Christ.* EETS e.s. 70. Oxford: Oxford University Press, 1896. Repr. Oxford: Clarendon Press, 1930.

Furnivall & Pollard
The Macro Plays: "Mankind," "Wisdom," "The Castle of Perseverance." Ed. Frederick J. Furnivall and Alfred W. Pollard. EETS e.s. 91. London: Kegan Paul, Trench, Trübner, 1904. Repr. 1924.

Gabler 1979
Hans Walter Gabler, ed. *Monsieur Thomas.* In *The Dramatic Works in the Beaumont and Fletcher Canon,* gen. ed. Fredson Bowers, vol. 4. Cambridge: Cambridge University Press, 1979.

Gabler 1982
Hans Walter Gabler, ed. *Women Pleased.* In *The Dramatic Works in the Beaumont and Fletcher Canon,* gen. ed. Fredson Bowers, vol. 5. Cambridge: Cambridge University Press, 1982.

Gabler 1985

Hans Walter Gabler, ed. _Wit without Money_. In _The Dramatic Works in the Beaumont and Fletcher Canon_, gen. ed. Fredson Bowers, vol. 6. Cambridge: Cambridge University Press, 1985.

Gabrieli & Melchiori

Anthony Munday and others. _Sir Thomas More_. Ed. Vittorio Gabrieli and Giorgio Melchiori. Revels Plays. Manchester: Manchester University Press; Baltimore: Johns Hopkins University Press, 1990.

Gaby

Rosemary Gaby. "Of Vagabonds and Commonwealths: _Beggars' Bush_, _A Jovial Crew_, and _The Sisters_." _Studies in English Literature, 1500–1900_ 34.2 (1994): 401–24.

Gaggero

Christopher Gaggero. "Pleasure Unreconciled to Virtue: George Gascoigne and Didactic Drama." In _Tudor Drama before Shakespeare, 1485–1590: New Directions for Research, Criticism, and Pedagogy_, ed. Lloyd Edward Kermode, Jason Scott-Warren, and Martine van Elk, 167–93. Basingstoke, UK, and New York: Palgrave Macmillan, 2004.

Gair 1978a

John Marston. _Antonio's Revenge_. Ed. W. Reavley Gair. Revels Plays. Manchester: Manchester University Press; Baltimore: Johns Hopkins University Press, 1978.

Gair 1978b

Reavley Gair. "The Presentation of Plays at Second Paul's: The Early Phase (1599–1602)." _The Elizabethan Theatre_ 6 (1978): 21–47.

Gair 1982

Reavley Gair. _The Children of Paul's: The Story of a Theatre Company, 1553–1608_. Cambridge: Cambridge University Press, 1982.

Gair 2000

W. Reavley Gair. "John Marston: A Theatrical Perspective." In _The Drama of John Marston: Critical Re-Visions_, ed. T. F. Wharton, 27–44. Cambridge: Cambridge University Press, 2000.

Gair 2004

Reavley Gair. "Percy, William (1574–1648)." In _ODNB_ 43: 752–53.

Galloway

David Galloway. _Norwich, 1540–1642_. REED. Toronto, Buffalo, London: University of Toronto Press, 1984.

Gamble

Giles Y. Gamble. "Power Play: Elizabeth I and _The Misfortunes of Arthur_." _Quondam et Futurus_ 1.2 (1991): 59–69.

Garber 1991

Marjorie Garber. "The Logic of the Transvestite: *The Roaring Girl* (1608)." In *Staging the Renaissance: Reinterpretations of Elizabethan and Jacobean Drama*, ed. David Scott Kastan and Peter Stallybrass, 221–34. New York and London: Routledge, 1991.

Garber 2004

Marjorie Garber. *Shakespeare After All*. New York: Pantheon, 2004.

Garrett

Martin Garrett. "Cokayne, Sir Aston, baronet (1608–1684)." In *ODNB* 12: 444–45.

Gasior

Thomas Heywood's "The Four Prentices of London": A Critical, Old-Spelling Edition. Ed. Mary Ann Weber Gasior. New York and London: Garland, 1980.

Gasper 1990

Julia Gasper. *The Dragon and the Dove: The Plays of Thomas Dekker*. Oxford: Clarendon Press, 1990.

Gasper 1993

Julia Gasper. "The Reformation Plays on the Public Stage." In *Theatre and Government under the Early Stuarts*, ed. J. R. Mulryne and Margaret Shewring, 190–216. Cambridge: Cambridge University Press, 1993.

Gasper 2007

The Bloody Banquet. Ed. Julia Gasper [with Gary Taylor]. In *Thomas Middleton: The Collected Works*, gen. eds. Gary Taylor and John Lavagnino. Oxford: Clarendon Press, 2007.

Gates

William Bryan Gates, ed. "The Dramatic Works and Translations of Sir William Lower with a Reprint of 'The Enchanted Lovers'." Ph.D. diss., University of Pennsylvania, Philadelphia: Westbrook, 1932.

Gay

Penny Gay. Inroduction to *Twelfth Night or What You Will: Updated Edition*, by William Shakespeare. Ed. Elizabeth Story Donno. New Cambridge Shakespeare. Cambridge: Cambridge University Press, 2004.

Gayton

Edmund Gayton. *Pleasant Notes upon Don Quixot[e]*. London: William Hunt, 1654.

Gazzard

Hugh Gazzard. "'Those Grave Presentments of Antiquitie': Samuel Daniel's *Philotas* and the Earl of Essex." *Review of English Studies* n.s. 51 (2000): 423–50.

Geckle 1980

George L. Geckle. *John Marston's Drama: Themes, Images, Sources.* Rutherford, Madison, and Teaneck, NJ: Fairleigh Dickinson University Press; London and Toronto: Associated University Presses, 1980.

Geckle 1987

George L. Geckle. "John Marston." In *Dictionary of Literary Biography* 58: *Jacobean and Caroline Dramatists*, ed. Fredson Bowers, 139–68. Detroit: Gale, 1987.

Geckle 1988

George L. Geckle. *"Tamburlaine" and "Edward II": Text and Performance.* London: Macmillan, 1988.

Geller

Sherri Geller. "Commentary as Cover-Up: Criticizing Illiberal Patronage in Thomas Nashe's *Summer's Last Will and Testament.*" *English Literary Renaissance* 25.2 (1995): 148–78.

George 1974

David George. "Early Cast-Lists for Two Beaumont and Fletcher Plays." *Theatre Notebook* 28.1 (1974): 9–11.

George 1977

David George. "Pre-1642 Cast-Lists and a New One for *The Maid's Tragedy.*" *Theatre Notebook* 31.3 (1977): 22–27.

George 1981

David George. "Shakespeare and Pembroke's Men." *Shakespeare Quarterly* 32.3 (1981): 305–23.

George 1983

David George. "Jacobean Actors and the Great Hall at Gawthorpe, Lancashire." *Theatre Notebook* 37.3 (1983): 109–21.

George 1991

David George, ed. *Lancashire.* REED. Toronto, Buffalo, and London: University of Toronto Press, 1991.

Gerritsen

"The Honest Man's Fortune": A Critical Edition of MS Dyce 9 (1625). Ed. Johan Gerritsen. Groningen Studies in English 3. Groningen and Djakarta: Wolters, 1952.

Gibbons 1980

William Shakespeare. *Romeo and Juliet.* Ed. Brian Gibbons. Arden. London and New York: Methuen, 1980.

Gibbons 2001

John Webster. *The Duchess of Malfi.* Ed. Brian Gibbons. 4th ed. New Mermaids. London: Black; New York: Norton, 2001.

Gibbons 2004

B. J. Gibbons. "Overton, Richard (*fl.* 1640–1663)." In *ODNB* 42: 166–71.

Gibbons 2008

Anon. *The Revenger's Tragedy*. Ed. Brian Gibbons. 3rd ed. New Mermaids. London: Black; New York: Norton, 2008.

Gibbs

Sir William Davenant. *The Shorter Poems, and Songs from the Plays and Masques.* Ed. A. M. Gibbs. Oxford: Clarendon Press, 1972.

Gibson 1947

Strickland Gibson. *A Bibliography of Francis Kirkman, with His Prefaces, Dedications, and Commendations (1652–80)*. Oxford Bibliographical Society Publications n.s. 1, fasc. 2. Oxford: Oxford University Press, 1947.

Gibson 1978

The Selected Plays of Philip Massinger. Ed. Colin Gibson. Cambridge: Cambridge University Press, 1978.

Gibson 1986

The Selected Plays of John Ford. Ed. Colin Gibson. Cambridge: Cambridge University Press, 1986.

Gibson 2002

James M. Gibson, ed. *Kent: Diocese of Canterbury*. 3 vols. REED. London, Buffalo, and Toronto: University of Toronto Press, 2002.

Giddens

Eugene Giddens. "The Final Stages of Printing Ben Jonson's *Works*, 1640–1." *Papers of the Bibliographical Society of America* 97.1 (2003): 57–68.

Gifford

The Plays of Philip Massinger. Ed. William Gifford. 4 vols. London: Nicol, 1805.

Gill 1967

Roma Gill. "Collaboration and Revision in Massinger's *A Very Woman*." *Review of English Studies* 18 (1967): 136–48.

Gill 1968

Thomas Middleton. *Women Beware Women*. Ed. Roma Gill. New Mermaids. London: Ernest Benn, 1968. Repr. New York: Norton, 1980.

Gill 1973

Christopher Marlowe. *Tamburlaine the Great*. Ed. Roma Gill. London: Scolar Press, 1973 [facsimile of 1593 edition in BL].

Gill 1987

Roma Gill. "Christopher Marlowe." In *Dictionary of Literary Biography* 62: *Elizabethan Dramatists*, ed. Fredson Bowers, 212–31. Detroit: Gale, 1987.

Gill 1990

Roma Gill, ed. *The Complete Works of Christopher Marlowe.* Vol. 2. Oxford: Clarendon Press, 1990.

Giordano-Orsini

G. N. Giordano-Orsini. "Thomas Heywood's Play on 'The Troubles of Queen Elizabeth'." *Library,* 4th ser., 14.3 (1933): 313–38.

Glatzer

Paula Glatzer. *The Complaint of the Poet: The Parnassus Plays.* Salzburg Studies in English Literature 60. Salzburg: Institut für Englische Sprache und Literatur, Universität Salzburg, 1977.

Godfrey

R. A. Godfrey. "Nervous Laughter in Henry Medwall's *Fulgens and Lucres.*" In *Tudor Theatre* 3: *Emotion in the Theatre,* 81–97. Tours Round Tables on Tudor Drama. Bern: Lang, 1996.

Goldberg 1983

Jonathan Goldberg. *James I and the Politics of Literature.* Baltimore and London: Johns Hopkins University Press, 1983.

Goldberg 1986

Dena Goldberg. "Appius and Virginia: A Story of Rape and Tyranny—Two Renaissance Versions." *Dalhousie Review* 66.1–2 (1986): 98–106.

Golding

S. R. Golding. "*The Parliament of Bees.*" *Review of English Studies* 3 (1927): 280–304.

Goldsmith

Robert Hillis Goldsmith. "Did Shakespeare Use the Old Timon Comedy?" *Shakespeare Quarterly* 9.1 (1958): 31–38.

Goldstein

R. James Goldstein. "Writing in Scotland, 1058–1560." In *The Cambridge History of Medieval English Literature,* ed. David Wallace, 229–54. Cambridge: Cambridge University Press, 1999.

Gooch

"The Lamentable Tragedy of Locrine": A Critical Edition. Ed. Jane Lytton Gooch. New York and London: Garland, 1981.

Gossett 1974

Suzanne Gossett. "The Term 'Masque' in Shakespeare and Fletcher, and *The Coxcomb.*" *Studies in English Literature, 1500–1900* 14.2 (1974): 285–95.

Gossett 1988

Suzanne Gossett. *The Influence of the Jacobean Masque on the Plays of Beaumont and Fletcher.* New York and London: Garland, 1988.

Gossett 2000
Suzanne Gossett. "Dramatic Achievements." In *The Cambridge Companion to English Literature, 1500–1600*, ed. Arthur F. Kinney, 153–77. Cambridge: Cambridge University Press, 2000.

Gossett 2004a
Suzanne Gossett. "Marston, Collaboration, and *Eastward Ho!*" *Renaissance Drama* 33 (2004): 181–200.

Gossett 2004b
William Shakespeare. *Pericles*. Ed. Suzanne Gossett. Arden. London: Thomson Learning, 2004.

Gossett 2007
Suzanne Gossett. Introduction to *The Spanish Gypsy*. In *Thomas Middleton: The Collected Works*, gen. eds. Gary Taylor and John Lavagnino, 1723–27. Oxford: Clarendon Press, 2007.

Gossett 2009a
Francis Beaumont and John Fletcher. *Philaster, or, Love Lies A-Bleeding*. Ed. Suzanne Gossett. Arden Early Modern Drama. London: Black, 2009.

Gossett 2009b
Suzanne Gossett. "*The Two Noble Kinsmen* and *King Henry VIII*: The Last Plays." In *The Cambridge Companion to Shakespeare's Last Plays*, ed. Catherine M. S. Alexander, 185–202. Cambridge: Cambridge University Press, 2009.

Gossett 2011
Suzanne Gossett. "Middleton and Dramatic Genre." In *Thomas Middleton in Context*, ed. eadem, 235–42. Cambridge: Cambridge University Press, 2011.

Gossett & Berger
Jacobean Academic Plays. Malone Society *Collections XIV*. Ed. Suzanne Gossett and Thomas L. Berger. Oxford: Oxford University Press, 1988.

Gough
Melinda J. Gough. "Courtly *Comédiantes*: Henrietta Maria and Amateur Women's Stage Plays in France and England." In *Women Players in England, 1500–1660: Beyond the All-Male Stage*, ed. Pamela Allen Brown and Peter Parolin, 193–215. Aldershot, UK, and Burlington, VT: Ashgate, 2005.

Grabau
Carl Grabau, ed. "*The Bugbears*: Komödie aus der Zeit kurz vor Shakspere." *Archiv für das Studium der neueren Sprachen und Litteraturen* 98 (1897): 301–22, 99 (1897): 25–58.

Graham
Elspeth Graham. "Reading, Writing, and Riding Horses in Early Modern England: James Shirley's *Hyde Park* (1632) and Gervase Markham's *Cavelarice* (1607)." In *Renaissance Beasts: Of Animals, Humans, and Other Wonderful*

Creatures, ed. Erica Fudge, 116–37. Urbana and Chicago: University of Illinois Press, 2004.

Grant 2001
Teresa Grant. "White Bears in *Mucedorus*, *The Winter's Tale*, and *Oberon*, *The Fairy Prince.*" *Notes and Queries* 48.3 (2001): 311–13.

Grant 2003
Teresa Grant. "Drama Queen: Staging Elizabeth in *If You Know Not Me You Know Nobody.*" In *The Myth of Elizabeth*, ed. Susan Doran and Thomas S. Freeman, 120–42. Basingstoke, UK, and New York: Palgrave Macmillan, 2003.

Grant 2008
Teresa Grant. "History in the Making: the Case of Samuel Rowley's *When You See Me You Know Me* (1604/5)." In *English Historical Drama, 1500–1660: Forms Outside the Canon*, ed. eadem and Barbara Ravelhofer, 125–57. Basingstoke, UK, and New York: Palgrave Macmillan, 2008.

Grantley 1983
Darryll Grantley. "Producing Miracles." In *Aspects of Early English Drama*, ed. Paula Neuss, 78–91. Cambridge: Brewer; Totowa, NJ: Barnes & Noble, 1983.

Grantley 2000
Darryll Grantley. *Wit's Pilgrimage: Drama and the Social Impact of Education in Early Modern England.* Aldershot, UK, and Burlington, VT: Ashgate, 2000.

Grantley 2004
Darryll Grantley. *English Dramatic Interludes 1300–1580: A Reference Guide.* Cambridge: Cambridge University Press, 2004.

Grantley 2007
Darryll Grantley. "Morality and Interlude Drama." In *A Companion to Medieval English Literature and Culture c. 1350–c. 1500*, ed. Peter Brown, 473–87. Oxford: Blackwell, 2007.

Grantley 2008a
Darryll Grantley. *London in Early Modern English Drama: Representing the Built Environment.* Basingstoke, UK, and New York: Palgrave Macmillan, 2008.

Grantley 2008b
Darryll Grantley. "Saints and Miracles." In *The Cambridge Companion to Medieval English Theatre*, ed. Richard Beadle and Alan J. Fletcher, 263–86. 2nd ed. Cambridge: Cambridge University Press, 2008.

Gras
Henk Gras. "*Twelfth Night*, *Every Man Out of His Humour*, and the Middle Temple Revels of 1597–98." *Modern Language Review* 84.3 (1989): 545–64.

Graves 1978

R. B. Graves. *"The Duchess of Malfi* at the Globe and Blackfriars." *Renaissance Drama* 9 (1978): 193–209.

Graves 1994

Michael A. R. Graves. *Thomas Norton: The Parliament Man.* Oxford and Cambridge, MA: Blackwell, 1994.

Graves 1999

R. B. Graves. *Lighting the Shakespearean Stage, 1567–1642.* Carbondale and Edwardsville: Southern Illinois University Press, 1999.

Gravett

Darlene Johnson Gravett, ed. *A Critical Edition of Abraham Cowley's "Cutter of Coleman Street."* The Renaissance Imagination 21. New York and London: Garland, 1987.

Gray

Henry David Gray. "The Rôles of William Kemp." *Modern Language Review* 25.3 (1930): 261–73.

Green

Allan P. Green. "Shakerley Marmion." In *Dictionary of Literary Biography* 58: *Jacobean and Caroline Dramatists*, ed. Fredson Bowers, 131–39. Detroit: Gale, 1987.

Greenberg

Marissa Greenberg. "Women and the Theatre in Thomas Heywood's London." In *The Idea of the City: Early-Modern, Modern and Post-Modern Locations and Communities*, ed. Joan Fitzpatrick, 79–89. Newcastle upon Tyne: Cambridge Scholars Publishing, 2009.

Greenblatt 1997

Stephen Greenblatt. Introduction to *Macbeth.* In *The Norton Shakespeare Based on the Oxford Edition*, ed. idem, Walter Cohen, Jean E. Howard, and Katharine Eisaman Maus, 2555–62. New York and London: Norton, 1997.

Greenblatt 2004

Stephen Greenblatt. *Will in the World: How Shakespeare Became Shakespeare.* New York and London: Norton, 2004.

Greenblatt 2010

Stephen Greenblatt. "The Traces of Shakespeare's Life." In *The New Cambridge Companion to Shakespeare*, ed. Margreta de Grazia and Stanley Wells, 1–13. 2nd ed. Cambridge: Cambridge University Press, 2010.

Greenfield 1969

Thelma N. Greenfield. *The Induction in Elizabethan Drama.* Eugene: University of Oregon Books, 1969.

Greenfield 2004

Peter H. Greenfield. "Drama outside London after 1540." In *The Cambridge History of British Theatre*, vol. 1: *Origins to 1660*, ed. Jane Milling and Peter Thomson, 178–99. Cambridge: Cambridge University Press, 2004.

Greenfield 2009

Peter Greenfield. "Touring." In *The Oxford Handbook of the Early Modern Theatre*, ed. Richard Dutton, 292–306. Oxford: Oxford University Press, 2009.

Greg 1904

"Everyman," Reprinted from the Edition by John Skot at Britwell Court. Ed. W. W. Greg. Materialen zur Kunde des älteren Englischen Dramas 4. Louvain: Uystpruyst, 1904.

Greg 1904–08

W. W. Greg, ed. *Henslowe's Diary*. 2 vols. London: Bullen, 1904–08.

Greg 1905

Ben Jonson's "Sad Shepherd" with Waldron's Continuation. Ed. W. W. Greg. Materialien zur Kunde des älteren Englischen Dramas 11. Louvain: Uystpruyst, 1905.

Greg 1906

W. W. Greg. *Pastoral Poetry and Pastoral Drama: A Literary Inquiry*. London: Bullen, 1906. Repr. New York: Russell & Russell, 1959.

Greg 1907a

"The History of King Leir," 1605. Ed. W. W. Greg. MSR. Oxford: Oxford University Press, 1907 [1908].

Greg 1907b

The Interlude of Johan the Evangelist. Ed. W. W. Greg. MSR. Oxford: Chiswick, 1907.

Greg 1907c

The Interlude of Wealth and Health. Ed. W. W. Greg. MSR. Oxford: Oxford University Press, 1907.

Greg 1908

The Interlude of Calisto and Melebea. Ed. W. W. Greg. MSR. Oxford: Oxford University Press, 1908.

Greg 1909

"The Second Maiden's Tragedy," 1611. Ed. W. W. Greg. MSR. Oxford: Oxford University Press, 1909 [1910].

Greg 1911a

The Book of Sir Thomas More. Ed. W. W. Greg. MSR. Oxford: Oxford University Press, 1911. Repr. with a supplement by Harold Jenkins, 1961.

Greg 1911b
George Peele. *King Edward the First.* Ed. W. W. Greg. MSR. Oxford: Oxford University Press, 1911.

Greg 1912
Wily Beguiled. Ed. W. W. Greg. MSR. Oxford: Oxford University Press, 1912 [1913].

Greg 1913a
"Clyomon and Clamydes," 1599. Ed. W. W. Greg. MSR. London: Oxford University Press, 1913. Repr. New York: AMS Press, 1985.

Greg 1913b
"The Contention between Liberality and Prodigality," 1602. Ed. W. W. Greg. MSR. Oxford: Oxford University Press, 1913.

Greg 1913c
A Larum for London. Ed. W. W. Greg. MSR. Oxford: Oxford University Press, 1913.

Greg 1913d
Look About You. Ed. W. W. Greg. MSR. Oxford: Oxford University Press, 1913.

Greg 1914a
Robert Wilmot. *"The Tragedy of Tancred and Gismund," 1591–2.* Ed. W. W. Greg. MSR. Oxford: Oxford University Press, 1914 [1915].

Greg 1914b
"The Tragedy of Tiberius," 1607. Ed. W. W. Greg. MSR. Oxford: Oxford University Press, 1914 [1915].

Greg 1923
W. W. Greg. *Two Elizabethan Stage Abridgements: "The Battle of Alcazar" and "Orlando Furioso."* Oxford: Clarendon Press, 1923.

Greg 1925
W. W. Greg. "'The Escapes of Jupiter': An Autograph Play of Thomas Heywood's." In *Anglica: Untersuchungen zur Englischen Philologie*, ed. Wilhelm Dibelius, Hans Hecht, and Wolfgang Keller, 2:211–43. 2 vols. Palaestra 148. Leipzig: Mayer and Müller, 1925.

Greg 1927
Fair Em. Ed. W. W. Greg. MSR. Oxford: Oxford University Press, 1927 [1928].

Greg 1928
Christopher Marlowe. *The Massacre at Paris.* Ed. W. W. Greg. MSR. Oxford: Oxford University Press, 1928 [1929].

Greg 1929

"*The True Tragedy of Richard the Third*," *1594*. Ed. W. W. Greg. MSR. Oxford: Oxford University Press, 1929.

Greg 1930

W. W. Greg. "Notes on Some Early Plays." *The Library*, 4th series, 11 (1930): 44–56.

Greg 1931

W. W. Greg. *Dramatic Documents from the Elizabethan Playhouses: Stage Plots, Actors' Parts, Prompt Books*. 2 vols. Oxford: Clarendon Press, 1931. Repr. Oxford: Oxford University Press, 1969.

Greg 1932

"*A Looking-Glass for London and England*" by *Thomas Lodge & Robert Greene 1594*. Ed. W. W. Greg. MSR. Oxford: Oxford University Press, 1932.

Greg 1933

"*Alexander and Campaspe*" by *John Lyly, 1584*. Ed. W. W. Greg. MSR. Oxford: Oxford University Press, 1933 [1934].

Greg 1934

Nicholas Udall. *Roister Doister*. Ed. W. W. Greg. MSR. Oxford: Oxford University Press, 1934 [1935].

Greg 1939

W. W. Greg. *A Bibliography of the English Printed Drama to the Restoration*. 4 vols. London: Oxford University Press for the Bibliographical Society, 1939–59. Repr. 1962. Repr. London: Scolar Press, 1970.

Greg 1945

W. W. Greg. "Shakespeare and *Arden of Feversham*." *Review of English Studies* 21 (1945): 134–36.

Greg 1951

John Fletcher. *Bonduca*. Ed. W. W. Greg. MSR. Oxford: Oxford University Press, 1951.

Greg 1952

Respublica. Ed. W. W. Greg. EETS o.s. 226. London: Oxford University Press, 1952.

Greg 1955

W. W. Greg. *The Shakespeare First Folio: Its Bibliographical and Textual History*. Oxford: Clarendon Press, 1955.

Greg 1967

W. W. Greg. *A Companion to Arber: Being a Calendar of Documents in Edward Arber's "Transcript of the Registers of the Company of Stationers of London, 1554–1640."* Oxford: Clarendon Press, 1967.

Greg & Smith 1937
George Chapman. *An Humorous Day's Mirth*. Ed. W. W. Greg and David Nichol Smith. MSR. Oxford: Oxford University Press, 1937 [1938].

Greg & Smith 1948
Thomas Kyd. *"The Spanish Tragedy" (1592)*. Ed. W. W. Greg and David Nichol Smith. MSR. Oxford: Oxford University Press, 1948 [1949].

Greg & Wilson
Thomas Middleton. *The Witch*. Ed. W. W. Greg and F. P. Wilson. MSR. Oxford: Oxford University Press, 1948 [1950].

Griffin 2001
Benjamin Griffin. *Playing the Past: Approaches to English Historical Drama, 1385–1600*. Woodbridge, UK; Rochester, NY: Brewer, 2001.

Griffin 2006
Andrew Griffin. *"Ram Alley* and Female Spectatorship." *Early Theatre* 9.2 (2006): 91–97.

Griffin 2009a
Eric J. Griffin. *English Renaissance Drama and the Specter of Spain: Ethnopoetics and Empire*. Philadelphia: University of Pennsylvania Press, 2009.

Griffin 2009b
Eric Griffin. "Nationalism, the Black Legend, and the Revised *Spanish Tragedy*." *English Literary Renaissance* 39.2 (2009): 336–70.

Griffiths 1996
Trevor R. Griffiths, ed. *A Midsummer Night's Dream*. Shakespeare in Production. Cambridge: Cambridge University Press, 1996.

Griffiths 2006
Jane Griffiths. *John Skelton and Poetic Authority: Defining the Liberty to Speak*. Oxford: Clarendon Press, 2006.

Griffiths 2008
Jane Griffiths. "Counterfet Countenaunce: (Mis)representation and the Challenge to Allegory in Sixteenth-Century Morality Plays." *Yearbook of English Studies* 38 (2008): 17–33.

Grivelet
Michel Grivelet. *Thomas Heywood et le drame domestique Elizabéthain*. Paris: Didier, 1957.

Groeneveld
Leanne Groeneveld. *"Christ's Burial* and *Christ's Resurrection*: Provenance and Performance." *Research Opportunities in Medieval and Renaissance Drama* 48 (2009): 48–72.

Grote
David Grote. *The Best Actors in the World: Shakespeare and His Acting Company.* Contributions in Drama and Theatre Studies 97. Westport, CT, and London: Greenwood Press, 2002.

Gruber
William E. Gruber. "Building a Scene: The Text and Its Representation in *The Atheist's Tragedy.*" *Comparative Drama* 19.3 (1985): 193–208.

Guinle
Francis Guinle. "The Songs in a 16th Century Manuscript Play: *The Bugbears*, by John Jeffere." *Cahiers Elisabéthains* 21 (1982): 13–26.

Gunby 2004
David Gunby. "Webster, John (1578×80–1638?)." In *ODNB* 57: 885–91.

Gunby & Lees-Jeffries
David Gunby and Hester Lees-Jeffries. "George Villiers, Duke of Buckingham, and the Dating of Webster and Heywood's *Appius and Virginia.*" *Notes and Queries* n.s. 49.3 (2002): 324–27.

Gunby et al.
The Works of John Webster: An Old-Spelling Critical Edition. Vol. 1, ed. David Gunby, David Carnegie, Antony Hammond, and Doreen DelVecchio. Vol. 2, ed. David Gunby, David Carnegie, and MacDonald P. Jackson. Cambridge: Cambridge University Press, 1995–2003.

Gurr 1969
Francis Beaumont and John Fletcher. *Philaster or Love Lies a-Bleeding.* Ed. Andrew Gurr. Revels Plays. London: Methuen, 1969.

Gurr 1984
William Shakespeare. *King Richard II.* Ed. Andrew Gurr. Cambridge: Cambridge University Press, 1984.

Gurr 1987a
Andrew Gurr. "Intertextuality at Windsor." *Shakespeare Quarterly* 38 (1987): 189–200.

Gurr 1987b
Andrew Gurr. *Playgoing in Shakespeare's London.* Cambridge: Cambridge University Press, 1987.

Gurr 1988a
Andrew Gurr. "Singing through the Chatter: Ford and Contemporary Theatrical Fashion." In *John Ford: Critical Re-Visions*, ed. Michael Neill, 81–96. Cambridge: Cambridge University Press, 1988.

Gurr 1988b
Andrew Gurr. "*The Tempest's* Tempest at Blackfriars." *Shakespeare Survey* 41 (1988): 91–102.

Gurr 1992

Andrew Gurr. *The Shakespearean Stage, 1574–1642.* 3rd ed. Cambridge: Cambridge University Press, 1992.

Gurr 1996

Andrew Gurr. *The Shakespearian Playing Companies.* Oxford: Clarendon, 1996.

Gurr 1997

Andrew Gurr. "Traps and Discoveries at the Globe." *PBA* 94 (1997): 85–101.

Gurr 2000

William Shakespeare. *The First Quarto of "King Henry V."* Ed. Andrew Gurr. Cambridge: Cambridge University Press, 2000.

Gurr 2004a

Andrew Gurr. "The Great Divide of 1594." In *Words That Count: Essays on Early Modern Authorship in Honor of MacDonald P. Jackson,* ed. Brian Boyd, 29–48. Newark, DE: University of Delaware Press, 2004.

Gurr 2004b

Andrew Gurr. "A New Theatre Historicism." In *From Script to Stage in Early Modern England,* ed. Peter Holland and Stephen Orgel, 71–88. Basingstoke, UK, and New York: Palgrave Macmillan, 2004.

Gurr 2004c

Andrew Gurr. *The Shakespeare Company, 1594–1642.* Cambridge: Cambridge University Press, 2004.

Gurr 2005

William Shakespeare. *"King Henry V": Updated Edition.* Ed. Andrew Gurr. Cambridge: Cambridge University Press, 2005.

Gurr 2006

Andrew Gurr. "'The Stage Is Hung with Black': When Did Melpomene Lose Her Identity?" In *Acts of Criticism: Performance Matters in Shakespeare and His Contemporaries: Essays in Honor of James P. Lusardi,* ed. Paul Nelsen and June Schlueter, 58–73. Madison and Teaneck, NJ: Fairleigh Dickinson University Press, 2006.

Gurr 2008

Andrew Gurr. Foreword to *Shakespeare's Globe: A Theatrical Experiment,* ed. Christie Carson and Farah Karim-Cooper, xvii–xx. Cambridge: Cambridge University Press, 2008.

Gurr 2009a

Andrew Gurr. Introduction to *The Spanish Tragedy,* by Thomas Kyd. Ed. J. R. Mulryne. 3rd ed. New Mermaids. London: Black, 2009.

Gurr 2009b

Andrew Gurr. "Professional Playing in London and Superior Cambridge Responses." *Shakespeare Studies* 37 (2009): 43–53.

Gurr 2009c
Andrew Gurr. *Shakespeare's Opposites: The Admiral's Company 1594–1625.* Cambridge: Cambridge University Press, 2009.

Gurr 2009d
Andrew Gurr. *The Shakespearean Stage, 1574–1642.* 4th ed. Cambridge: Cambridge University Press, 2009.

Gurr & Ichikawa
Andrew Gurr and Mariko Ichikawa. *Staging in Shakespeare's Theatres.* Oxford Shakespeare Topics. Oxford: Oxford University Press, 2000.

Guy-Bray
Stephen Guy-Bray. *Homoerotic Space: The Poetics of Loss in Renaissance Literature.* Toronto, Buffalo, and London: University of Toronto Press, 2002.

Haaker 1966
Richard Brome. *The Antipodes.* Ed. Ann Haaker. RRDS. Lincoln: University of Nebraska Press, 1966.

Haaker 1968
Richard Brome. *A Jovial Crew.* Ed. Ann Haaker. RRDS. Lincoln: University of Nebraska Press, 1968.

Haaker 1970–71
Ann Haaker. "*Non sine causa*: The Use of Emblematic Method and Iconology in the Thematic Structure of *Titus Andronicus*." *Research Opportunities in Renaissance Drama* 13–14 (1970–71): 143–68.

Habicht
Werner Habicht. "Tree Properties and Tree Scenes in Elizabethan Theater." *Renaissance Drama* n.s. 4 (1971): 69–92.

Hackel
Heidi Brayman Hackel. "'Rowme' of Its Own: Printed Drama in Early Libraries." In *A New History of Early English Drama*, ed. John D. Cox and David Scott Kastan, 113–30. New York: Columbia University Press, 1997.

Hadfield
Andrew Hadfield. *Shakespeare and Republicanism.* Cambridge: Cambridge University Press, 2005.

Haldane
Michael Haldane. "The Date of Thomas Combe's *Fortunatus* and Its Relation to Thomas Dekker's *Old Fortunatus*." *Modern Language Review* 101.2 (2006): 313–24.

Halio 1993
William Shakespeare. *The Merchant of Venice.* Ed. Jay L. Halio. Oxford: Clarendon Press, 1993.

Halio 1994a
William Shakespeare. *The First Quarto of "King Lear."* Ed. Jay L. Halio. New Cambridge Shakespeare: The Early Quartos. Cambridge: Cambridge University Press, 1994.

Halio 1994b
Jay L. Halio. *A Midsummer Night's Dream.* Shakespeare in Performance. Manchester: Manchester University Press; New York: St. Martin's Press, 1994.

Halio 1998
Jay L. Halio. *"Romeo and Juliet": A Guide to the Play.* Westport, CT, and London: Greenwood Press, 1998.

Halio 1999
William Shakespeare. *King Henry VIII, or All is True.* Ed. Jay L. Halio. Oxford: Oxford University Press, 1999.

Halio 2005
William Shakespeare. *The Tragedy of King Lear: Updated Edition.* Ed. Jay L. Halio. Cambridge: Cambridge University Press, 2005.

Halio 2008
"Romeo and Juliet": Parallel Texts of Quarto 1 (1597) and Quarto 2 (1599). Ed. Jay L. Halio. Newark, DE: University of Delaware Press, 2008.

Hall
Kim F. Hall. *Things of Darkness: Economies of Race and Gender in Early Modern England.* Ithaca, NY, and London: Cornell University Press, 1995.

Haller
William Haller, ed. *Tracts on Liberty in the Puritan Revolution, 1638–1647.* 3 vols. New York: Columbia University Press, 1934.

Halliwell 1846
The Marriage of Wit and Wisdom: An Ancient Interlude. Ed. James Orchard Halliwell[-Phillipps]. London: Shakespeare Society, 1846.

Halliwell 1848a
Thomas Ingelend. *The Interlude of the Disobedient Child.* Ed. James Orchard Halliwell[-Phillipps]. London: printed for the Percy Society, 1848.

Halliwell 1848b
James Orchard Halliwell[-Phillipps], ed. *The Moral Play of Wit and Science.* London: Shakespeare Society, 1848.

Halliwell 1853
James Orchard Halliwell[-Phillipps]. *A Brief Description of the Ancient and Modern Manuscripts Preserved in the Public Library, Plymouth.* London: privately printed, 1853 [includes an excerpt from Lady Mary Wroth's *Love's Victory* (212–36), a MS now at the Huntington Library].

Halliwell 1860a
The Conceited Humours of Simpleton the Smith, A Theatrical Droll. Ed. James Orchard Halliwell[-Phillipps]. London: privately printed, 1860.

Halliwell 1860b
James Orchard Halliwell[-Phillipps]. *A Dictionary of Old English Plays Existing either in Print or in Manuscript, from the Earliest Times to the Close of the Seventeenth Century.* London: John Russell Smith, 1860.

Halliwell 1860c
James Orchard Halliwell[-Phillipps]. Ed. *The Droll of the Bouncing Knight, or the Robbers Robbed.* London: privately printed, 1860.

Halliwell 1860d
James Orchard Halliwell[-Phillipps]. Ed. *The Merry Conceited Humours of Bottom the Weaver, A Droll.* London: privately printed, 1860.

Halliwell 1861
James Orchard Halliwell[-Phillipps]. Ed. *Jenkin of Wales; His Love-Course and Perambulation.* London: privately printed, 1861.

Halliwell 1870
A Tragedy of Richard the Second Concluding with the Murder of the Duke of Gloucester at Calais [*Woodstock*]. Ed. James Orchard Halliwell[-Phillipps]. London: privately printed, 1870.

Hallward
Hallward Library, University of Nottingham

Hamer
The Works of Sir David Lindsay of the Mount, 1490–1555. Ed. Douglas Hamer. 4 vols. Scottish Text Society. Edinburgh and London: Blackwood, 1931–36.

Hamilton 2005
Donna B. Hamilton. *Anthony Munday and the Catholics, 1560–1633.* Aldershot, UK, and Burlington, VT: Ashgate, 2005.

Hamilton 2007
The Puritan Widow or *The Puritan* or *The Widow of Watling Street.* Ed. Donna B. Hamilton. In *Thomas Middleton: The Collected Works,* gen. eds. Gary Taylor and John Lavagnino. Oxford: Clarendon Press, 2007.

Hammer
Paul E. J. Hammer. "Shakespeare's *Richard II*, the Play of 7 February 1601, and the Essex Rising." *Shakespeare Quarterly* 59.1 (2008): 1–35.

Hammond 1981
William Shakespeare. *King Richard III.* Ed. Antony Hammond. Arden. London: Methuen, 1981.

Hammond 1984
Brean S. Hammond. "The Performance History of a Pseudo-Shakespearean Play: Theobald's *Double Falsehood.*" *Journal for Eighteenth-Century Studies* 7.1 (1984): 49–60.

Hammond 1987a
Antony Hammond. "John Webster." In *Dictionary of Literary Biography* 58: *Jacobean and Caroline Dramatists*, ed. Fredson Bowers, 284–302. Detroit: Gale, 1987.

Hammond 1987b
Antony Hammond. "'It must be your imagination then': The Prologue and the Plural Text in *Henry V* and Elsewhere." In *"Fanned and Winnowed Opinions": Shakespearean Essays Presented to Harold Jenkins*, ed. John W. Mahon and Thomas A. Pendleton, 133–50. London and New York: Methuen, 1987.

Hammond 1996
Paul Hammond. *Love between Men in English Literature.* Basingstoke, UK, and London: Macmillan, 1996.

Hammond 2010
Lewis Theobald. *Double Falsehood or The Distressed Lovers.* Ed. Brean Hammond. Arden. London: Methuen, 2010.

Hammond & DelVecchio
Antony Hammond and Doreen DelVecchio. "Textual Introduction" [to *The Duchess of Malfi*]. In *The Works of John Webster: An Old-Spelling Critical Edition*, ed. David Gunby, David Carnegie, idem, and Doreen DelVecchio, 1: 450–66. Cambridge: Cambridge University Press, 1995.

Hampton-Reeves & Rutter
Stuart Hampton-Reeves and Carol Chillington Rutter. *The "Henry VI" Plays.* Shakespeare in Performance. Manchester: Manchester University Press; New York: Palgrave, 2006.

Hanabusa
"The Famous Victories of Henry the Fifth," 1598. Ed. Chiaki Hanabusa. MSR. Manchester: Manchester University Press, 2006 [2007].

Hanford 1913
James Holly Hanford. "The Debate Element in the Elizabethan Drama." In *Anniversary Papers by Colleagues and Pupils of George Lyman Kittredge*, 445–56. Boston: Ginn, 1913. Repr. New York: Russell & Russell, 1967.

Hanford 1915
"Wine, Beere, Ale, and Tobacco": A Seventeenth Century Interlude. Ed. James Holly Hanford. University of North Carolina Studies in Philology 12:1. Chapel Hill: University of North Carolina Press, 1915. [*Studies in Philology* 12 (1915): 1–54]

Happé 1985–86
The Complete Plays of John Bale. Ed. Peter Happé. 2 vols. Cambridge: Brewer, 1985–86.

Happé 1991
Two Moral Interludes [Witty and Witless, Like Will to Like]. Ed. Peter Happé. MSR. Oxford: Oxford University Press, 1991.

Happé 1994a
Ben Jonson. *The Devil is an Ass.* Ed. Peter Happé. Revels Plays. Manchester and New York: Manchester University Press, 1994.

Happé 1994b
Peter Happé. "Spectacle in Bale and Heywood." *Medieval English Theatre* 16 (1994): 51–64.

Happé 1999
Peter Happé. *English Drama before Shakespeare.* London and New York: Longman, 1999.

Happé 2000
Ben Jonson. *The Magnetic Lady.* Ed. Peter Happé. Revels Plays. Manchester: Manchester University Press; New York: St. Martin's Press, 2000.

Happé 2001
Peter Happé. "*The Magnetic Lady* Seen Again." *Ben Jonson Journal* 8 (2001): 369–74.

Happé 2004
Peter Happé. "Drama in 1553: Continuity and Change." In *The Cambridge History of British Theatre*, vol. 1: *Origins to 1660*, ed. Jane Milling and Peter Thomson, 116–36. Cambridge: Cambridge University Press, 2004.

Happé 2007a
Peter Happé. "Printing the Third Volume of Jonson's *Works*." *Ben Jonson Journal* 14.1 (2007): 20–42.

Happé 2007b
Peter Happé. "'Rejoice Ye in Us with Joy Most Joyfully': John Heywood's Plays and the Court." *Cahiers Elisabéthains* 72 (2007): 1–8.

Happé 2008
The Trial of Treasure. Ed. Peter Happé. MSR. Oxford: Oxford University Press, 2008 [2010].

Happé 2010
Peter Happé. "John Heywood and 'The Vice'." *Research Opportunities in Medieval and Renaissance Drama* 49 (2010): 60–79.

Harbage 1930
Alfred Harbage. *Thomas Killigrew: Cavalier Dramatist, 1612–83.* Philadelphia: University of Pennsylvania Press, 1930.

Harbage 1934
Alfred Harbage. "An Unnoted Caroline Dramatist." *Studies in Philology* 31.1 (1934): 28–36.

Harbage 1935a
Alfred Harbage. "The Authorship of *The Christmas Prince*." *Modern Language Notes* 50.8 (1935): 501–05.

Harbage 1935b
Alfred Harbage. *Sir William Davenant: Poet Venturer, 1606–1668*. Philadelphia: University of Pennsylvania Press, 1935.

Harbage 1936
Alfred Harbage. *Cavalier Drama: An Historical and Critical Supplement to the Study of the Elizabethan and Restoration Stage*. New York: Modern Language Association; London: Oxford University Press, 1936.

Harbage 1937
Alfred Harbage. "Shirley's *The Wedding* and the Marriage of Sir Kenelm Digby." *Philological Quarterly* 16.1 (1937): 35–40.

Harbage 1938
Alfred Harbage. "The Authorship of the Dramatic *Arcadia*." *Modern Philology* 35.3 (1938): 233–37.

Harbage 1939
Alfred Harbage. "Elizabethan Acting." *PMLA* 54.3 (1939): 685–708.

Harbage 1940
Alfred Harbage. *Annals of English Drama, 975–1700*. Philadelphia: University of Pennsylvania Press, 1940.

Harbage 1952
Alfred Harbage. *Shakespeare and the Rival Traditions*. New York: Macmillan, 1952.

Harbage 1955
Alfred Harbage. *Theatre for Shakespeare*. Toronto: University of Toronto Press, 1955.

Haring-Smith
Tori Haring-Smith. *From Farce to Metadrama: A Stage History of "The Taming of the Shrew," 1594–1983*. Westport, CT, and London: Greenwood Press, 1985.

Harlan
Susan Harlan. "'Certain condolements, certain vails': Staging Rusty Armour in Shakespeare's *Pericles*." *Early Theatre* 11.2 (2008): 129–40.

Harleian Misc

A brefe Comedy or Enterlude of Johan Baptystes preachynge in the wyldernesse. In *The Harleian Miscellany: or, A Collection of Scarce, Curious, and Entertaining Pamphlets and Tracts*, vol. 1: 97–110. London: T. Osborne, 1744.

Harner

James L. Harner. "Samuel Daniel." In *Dictionary of Literary Biography* 62: *Elizabethan Dramatists*, ed. Fredson Bowers, 30–39. Detroit: Gale, 1987.

Harris 1940

J. W. Harris. *John Bale: A Study in the Minor Literature of the Reformation.* Urbana: University of Illinois Press, 1940.

Harris 1965

William O. Harris. *Skelton's "Magnyfycence" and the Cardinal Virtue Tradition.* Chapel Hill: University of North Carolina Press, 1965.

Harris 1977

Life of Meriasek: A Medieval Cornish Miracle Play. Ed. Markham Harris. Washington, DC: Catholic University of America Press, 1977.

Harris 2008

Thomas Dekker. *The Shoemaker's Holiday.* Ed. Jonathan Gil Harris. 3rd ed. New Mermaids. London: Black, 2008.

Harris & Korda

Jonathan Gil Harris and Natasha Korda. Introduction to *Staged Properties in Early Modern English Drama*, ed. eidem, 1–33. Cambridge: Cambridge University Press, 2002.

Hart 1909

William Shakespeare. *The First Part of King Henry the Sixth.* Ed. H. C. Hart. Arden. London: Methuen, 1909.

Hart 1985

John Ford. *"The Fancies, Chast and Noble" by J. Ford: A Critical Edition.* Ed. Dominick J. Hart. The Renaissance Imagination 12. New York and London: Garland, 1985.

Hartwell

Abraham Hartwell. *Regina Literata.* London: G. Serres, 1565.

Harty

Kevin J. Harty. "The Norwich Grocers' Play and Its Three Cyclic Counterparts: Four English Mystery Plays on the Fall of Man." *Studia Neophilologica* 53.1 (1981): 77–89.

Harvey

A. D. Harvey. "Virginity and Honour in *Measure for Measure* and Davenant's *The Law Against Lovers.*" *English Studies* 75.2 (1994): 123–32.

Haslewood
William Percy. *The Cuck-Queanes and Cuckolds Errants or The Bearing Down the Inne; The Faery Pastorall or Forrest of Elves*. Ed. Joseph Haslewood. London: William Nicol for the Shakspeare Press, 1824.

Hattaway 1982
Michael Hattaway. *Elizabethan Popular Theatre: Plays in Performance*. London: Routledge and Kegan Paul, 1982.

Hattaway 1983
Michael Hattaway. Review of *Timon*, ed. J. C. Bulman and J. M. Nosworthy. *Review of English Studies* 34 (1983): 215–17.

Hattaway 1984
Ben Jonson. *The New Inn*. Ed. Michael Hattaway. Revels Plays. Manchester: Manchester University Press, 1984.

Hattaway 1990
William Shakespeare. *The First Part of King Henry VI*. Ed. Michael Hattaway. New Cambridge Shakespeare. Cambridge: Cambridge University Press, 1990.

Hattaway 1991
William Shakespeare. *The Second Part of King Henry VI*. Ed. Michael Hattaway. New Cambridge Shakespeare. Cambridge: Cambridge University Press, 1991.

Hattaway 1993
William Shakespeare. *The Third Part of King Henry VI*. Ed. Michael Hattaway. New Cambridge Shakespeare. Cambridge: Cambridge University Press, 1993.

Hattaway 1996
Michael Hattaway. "'Seeing things': Amazons and Cannibals." In *Travel and Drama in Shakespeare's Time*, ed. Jean-Pierre Maquerlot and Michèle Willems, 179–92. Cambridge: Cambridge University Press, 1996.

Hattaway 2000a
William Shakespeare. *As You Like It*. Ed. Michael Hattaway. New Cambridge Shakespeare. Cambridge: Cambridge University Press, 2000.

Hattaway 2000b
Michael Hattaway. "Playhouses and the Role of Drama." In *A Companion to English Renaissance Literature and Culture*, ed. idem, 133–47. Oxford: Blackwell, 2000.

Hattaway 2002
Francis Beaumont. *The Knight of the Burning Pestle*. Ed. Michael Hattaway. 2nd ed. New Mermaids. London: Black; New York: Norton, 2002.

Hattaway 2009
William Shakespeare. *As You Like It: Updated Edition*. Ed. Michael Hattaway. Cambridge: Cambridge University Press, 2009.

Hawkins
Thomas Hawkins. *The Origin of the English Drama, Illustrated in Its Various Species, viz. Mystery, Morality, Tragedy, and Comedy*. 3 vols. Oxford: Clarendon Press, 1773.

Hay
"Nobody and Somebody": An Introduction and Critical Edition. Ed. David L. Hay. New York and London: Garland, 1980.

Hayashi
Tetsumaro Hayashi. *A Textual Study of Robert Greene's "Orlando Furioso" with an Elizabethan Text*. Ball State Monographs 21. Muncie, IN: Ball State University Press, 1973.

Hayes
Tom Hayes. *The Birth of Popular Culture: Ben Jonson, Maid Marian and Robin Hood*. Pittsburgh: Duquesne University Press, 1992.

Hazlitt
A Select Collection of Old Plays. Ed. Robert Dodsley. Rev. W. C. Hazlitt. 4th ed. 15 vols. London: privately printed, 1874–76.

Hedbäck
Sir William Davenant. *"The Siege of Rhodes": A Critical Edition*. Ed. Ann-Mari Hedbäck. Acta Universitatis Upsaliensis, Studia Anglistica Upsaliensia 14. Uppsala: University of Uppsala, 1973.

Hedley
Judith Hedley, ed. *An Edition of R. B.'s "Appius and Virginia."* New York and London: Garland, 1988.

Heinemann 1978
Margot Heinemann. "Popular Drama and Leveller Style—Richard Overton and John Harris." In *Rebels and Their Causes: Essays in Honour of A. L. Morton*, ed. Maurice Cornforth, 69–92. London: Lawrence and Wishart, 1978.

Heinemann 1980
Margot Heinemann. *Puritanism and Theatre: Thomas Middleton and Opposition Drama under the Early Stuarts*. Cambridge: Cambridge University Press, 1980.

Heinemann 1992
Margot Heinemann. "'God Help the Poor: The Rich Can Shift': The World Upside-Down and the Popular Tradition in the Theatre." In *The Politics of Tragicomedy: Shakespeare and After*, ed. Gordon McMullan and Jonathan Hope, 151–65. London and New York: Routledge, 1992.

Heinemann 1993a
Margot Heinemann. "Drama and Opinion in the 1620s: Middleton and Massinger." In *Theatre and Government under the Early Stuarts*, ed. J. R. Mulryne and Margaret Shewring, 237–65. Cambridge: Cambridge University Press, 1993.

Heinemann 1993b
Margot Heinemann. "Rebel Lords, Popular Playwrights, and Political Culture: Notes on the Jacobean Patronage of the Earl of Southampton." In *Patronage, Politics, and Literary Traditions in England, 1558–1658*, ed. Cedric C. Brown, 135–58. Detroit: Wayne State University Press, 1993. [Orig. *Yearbook of English Studies* 21 (1991): 63–86.]

Heinemann 2003
Margot Heinemann. "Political Drama." In *The Cambridge Companion to English Renaissance Drama*, ed. A. R. Braunmuller and Michael Hattaway, 164–96. 2nd ed. Cambridge: Cambridge University Press, 2003.

Heiserman
Arthur Ray Heiserman. *Skelton and Satire*. Chicago: University of Chicago Press, 1961.

Henderson 1997
Diana E. Henderson. "The Theater and Domestic Culture." In *A New History of Early English Drama*, ed. John D. Cox and David Scott Kastan, 173–94. New York: Columbia University Press, 1997.

Henderson 2004
Diana E. Henderson. "Theatre and Controversy, 1572–1603." In *The Cambridge History of British Theatre*, vol. 1: *Origins to 1660*, ed. Jane Milling and Peter Thomson, 242–63. Cambridge: Cambridge University Press, 2004.

Henderson 2007
Diana E. Henderson. "From Popular Entertainment to Literature." In *The Cambridge Companion to Shakespeare and Popular Culture*, ed. Robert Shaughnessy, 6–25. Cambridge: Cambridge University Press, 2007.

Hennedy
John F. Hennedy, ed. *Sir Gyles Goosecappe, Knight*. In *The Plays of George Chapman: The Tragedies with "Sir Gyles Goosecappe": A Critical Edition*, gen. ed. Allan Holaday. Cambridge: Brewer, 1987.

Henning 1965
Thomas Middleton. *A Mad World, My Masters*. Ed. Standish Henning. RRDS. Lincoln: University of Nebraska Press, 1965.

Henning 1980
"Fair Em": A Critical Edition. Ed. Standish Henning. New York and London: Garland, 1980.

Henry

Anne C. Henry. "Tragedy and the Sign of the Eclipse." In *Tragedy in Transition*, ed. Sarah Annes Brown and Catherine Silverstone, 78–102. Oxford: Blackwell, 2007.

Henslowe

Henslowe's Diary. Ed. R. A. Foakes and R. T. Rickert. Cambridge: Cambridge University Press, 1961.

Herbert

Sir Henry Herbert, Master of the Revels, 1623–73

Herendeen

W. H. Herendeen. "A New Way to Pay Old Debts: Pretexts to the 1616 Folio." In *Ben Jonson's 1616 Folio*, ed. Jennifer Brady and idem, 38–63. Newark, DE: University of Delaware Press; London and Toronto: Associated University Presses, 1991.

Herford

Charles H. Herford. *Studies in the Literary Relations of England and Germany in the Sixteenth Century*. Cambridge: Cambridge University Press, 1886.

Herrick

Marvin T. Herrick. *Tragicomedy: Its Origin and Development in Italy, France, and England*. Illinois Studies in Language and Literature 39. Urbana: University of Illinois Press, 1955.

Hibbard 1973

William Shakespeare. *The Merry Wives of Windsor*. Ed. G. R. Hibbard. New Penguin Shakespeare. London: Penguin, 1973.

Hibbard 1987

William Shakespeare. *Hamlet*. Ed. G. R. Hibbard. Oxford: Oxford University Press, 1987.

Hibbard 1990

William Shakespeare. *Love's Labour's Lost*. Ed. G. R. Hibbard. Oxford: Clarendon, 1990.

Hibbard 2007

Ben Jonson. *Bartholomew Fair*. Ed. G. R. Hibbard. Introduction by Alexander Leggatt. 2nd ed. Rev. New Mermaids. London: Black, 2007.

Hickson 1847

S. Hickson. "The Shares of Shakespeare and Fletcher in *The Two Noble Kinsmen*." *Westminster and Foreign Quarterly Review* 47 (1847): 59–88.

Hickson 1850

Samuel Hickson. "The Taming of the Shrew." *Notes and Queries* 1.22 (1850): 345–47.

Hila

Marina Hila. "Dishonourable Peace: Fletcher and Massinger's *The False One* and Jacobean Foreign Policy." *Cahiers Elisabéthains* 72 (2007): 21–30.

Hill 1979

The Tragedy of Nero. Ed. Elliott M. Hill. New York and London: Garland, 1979.

Hill 1985

John Ford. *The Lover's Melancholy*. Ed. R. F. Hill. Revels Plays. Manchester: Manchester University Press, 1985.

Hill 1992

Eugene D. Hill. "The First Elizabethan Tragedy: A Contextual Reading of *Cambises*." *Studies in Philology* 89.4 (1992): 404–33.

Hill 2004

Tracey Hill. *Anthony Munday and Civic Culture: Theatre, History and Power in Early Modern London, 1580–1633*. Manchester and New York: Manchester University Press, 2004.

Hillebrand 1915

Harold Newcomb Hillebrand. "Sebastian Westcote, Dramatist and Master of the Children of Paul's." *JEGP* 14.4 (1915): 568–84.

Hillebrand 1926

Harold Newcomb Hillebrand. *The Child Actors: A Chapter in Elizabethan Stage History*. University of Illinois Studies in Language and Literature 11. Urbana: University of Illinois Press, 1926. Repr. New York: Russell and Russell, 1964.

Hillebrand 1938

Harold N. Hillebrand. "William Percy: An Elizabethan Amateur." *Huntington Library Quarterly* 1.4 (1938): 391–416.

Hillman 2002a

Richard Hillman. "Botching the Soliloquies in *The Spanish Tragedy*: Revisionist Collaboration and the 1602 Additions." *The Elizabethan Theatre* 15 (2002): 111–29.

Hillman 2002b

Richard Hillman. *Shakespeare, Marlowe and the Politics of France*. Basingstoke, UK, and New York: Palgrave, 2002.

Hillman 2005

Richard Hillman. "The Tragic Channel-Crossings of George Chapman, Part II: *The Revenge of Bussy d'Ambois, The Tragedy of Chabot*." *Cahiers Elisabéthains* 67 (2005): 23–31.

Hirsch

"A Pleasant Commodie Called Looke About You": A Critical Edition. Ed. Richard S. M. Hirsch. New York and London: Garland, 1980.

Hirschfeld
Heather Anne Hirschfeld. *Joint Enterprises: Collaborative Drama and the Institutionalization of the English Renaissance Theater.* Amherst and Boston: University of Massachusetts Press, 2004.

Hirsh
James Hirsh. "Act Divisions in the Shakespeare First Folio." *Papers of the Bibliographical Society of America* 96.2 (2002): 219–56.

Hirst
Derek Hirst. "The Politics of Literature in the English Republic." *Seventeenth Century* 5.2 (1990): 133–55.

Historia
James Wright. *Historia Histrionica: An Historical Account of the English Stage, Shewing the Ancient Use, Improvement, and Perfection, of Dramatick Representations, in This Nation. In a Dialogue, of Plays and Players.* London: G. Croom for William Haws, 1699.

Hodgdon 2007
Barbara Hodgdon. "Shakespearean Stars: Stagings of Desire." In *The Cambridge Companion to Shakespeare and Popular Culture*, ed. Robert Shaughnessy, 46–66. Cambridge: Cambridge University Press, 2007.

Hodgdon 2010
William Shakespeare. *The Taming of the Shrew.* Ed. Barbara Hodgdon. Arden 3. London: Black, 2010.

Hodges 1968
C. Walter Hodges. *The Globe Restored: A Study of the Elizabethan Theatre.* 2nd ed. New York: Coward-McCann, 1968. Repr. New York: Norton, 1973.

Hodges 1999
C. Walter Hodges. *Enter the Whole Army: A Pictorial Study of Shakespearean Staging, 1576–1616.* Cambridge: Cambridge University Press, 1999.

Hodgson-Wright 2000a
Stephanie Hodgson-Wright. "Beauty, Chastity and Wit: Feminising the Centrestage." In *Women and Dramatic Production, 1550–1700*, ed. Alison Findlay and eadem, with Gweno Williams, 42–67. Harlow, UK: Pearson Education; New York: Longman, 2000.

Hodgson-Wright 2000b
Elizabeth Cary. *The Tragedy of Mariam.* Ed. Stephanie Hodgson-Wright. Peterborough, Ontario: Broadview, 2000.

Hoeniger
William Shakespeare. *Pericles.* Ed. F. D. Hoeniger. Arden. London: Methuen, 1963.

Hoenselaars 1992a
A. J. Hoenselaars. *Images of Englishmen and Foreigners in the Drama of Shakespeare and His Contemporaries: A Study of Stage Characters and National Identity in English Renaissance Drama, 1558–1642.* Rutherford, Madison, and Teaneck, NJ: Fairleigh Dickinson University Press, 1992.

Hoenselaars 1992b
A. J. Hoenselaars. "Reconstructing Babel in English Renaissance Drama: William Haughton's *Englishmen for My Money* and John Marston's *Antonio and Mellida.*" *Neophilologus* 76.3 (1992): 464–79.

Hoenselaars 1995
A. J. Hoenselaars. "The Elizabethans and the Turk at Constantinople." *Cahiers Elisabéthains* 47 (1995): 29–42.

Holaday 1950
Thomas Heywood. *The Rape of Lucrece.* Ed. Allan Holaday. Illinois Studies in Language and Literature 34. Urbana: University of Illinois Press, 1950.

Holaday 1970
Allan Holaday, ed. *An Humorous Day's Mirth.* In *The Plays of George Chapman: The Comedies, A Critical Edition*, gen. ed. idem. Urbana, Chicago, and London: University of Illinois Press, 1970.

Holderness & Loughery
Graham Holderness and Bryan Loughrey, eds. *A Pleasant Conceited Historie, Called The Taming of a Shrewe.* Shakespearean Originals: First Editions. Hemel Hempstead, UK: Harvester Wheatsheaf, 1992.

Holdsworth 1974
Thomas Middleton and William Rowley. *A Fair Quarrel.* Ed. R. V. Holdsworth. New Mermaids. London: Ernest Benn, 1974.

Holdsworth 1982
R. V. Holdsworth. "Middleton and Shakespeare: The Case for Middleton's Hand in *Timon of Athens.*" Ph.D. diss., University of Manchester, 1982.

Holdsworth 1985
R. V. Holdsworth. "Ben Jonson and the Date of *Ram Alley.*" *Notes and Queries* n.s. 32 (1985): 482–86.

Holdsworth 1990
R. V. Holdsworth. "*The Revenger's Tragedy* on the Stage." In *Three Jacobean Revenge Tragedies: A Casebook*, ed. idem, 105–20. London: Macmillan, 1990.

Holdsworth 1994
R. V. Holdsworth. "Middleton's Authorship of *A Yorkshire Tragedy.*" *Review of English Studies* 45 (1994): 1–25.

Holland 1979
Peter Holland. *The Ornament of Action: Text and Performance in Restoration Comedy*. Cambridge: Cambridge University Press, 1979.

Holland 1994
William Shakespeare. *A Midsummer Night's Dream*. Ed. Peter Holland. Oxford: Clarendon Press, 1994.

Holland 2004a
Peter Holland. "Shakespeare, William (1564–1616)." In *ODNB* 49: 939–76.

Holland 2004b
Peter Holland. "Theatre without Drama: Reading *REED*." In *From Script to Stage in Early Modern England*, ed. idem and Stephen Orgel, 43–67. Basingstoke, UK, and New York: Palgrave Macmillan, 2004.

Holland 2006
Peter Holland. "Mapping Shakespeare's Britain." In *Spectacle and Public Performance in the Late Middle Ages and the Renaissance*, ed. Robert E. Stillman, 157–81. Leiden and Boston: Brill, 2004.

Holland 2007
Peter Holland. "Shakespeare Abbreviated." In *The Cambridge Companion to Shakespeare and Popular Culture*, ed. Robert Shaughnessy, 26–45. Cambridge: Cambridge University Press, 2007.

Holmes
David M. Holmes. "Thomas Middleton's 'Blurt Master-Constable, or The Spaniard's Night-Walk'." *Modern Language Review* 64.1 (1969): 1–10.

Honan
Park Honan. *Shakespeare: A Life*. Oxford: Oxford University Press, 1998.

Honigmann 1954
William Shakespeare. *King John*. Ed. E. A. J. Honigmann. Arden. London: Methuen, 1954.

Honigmann 1987
E. A. J. Honigmann. *John Weever: A Biography of a Literary Associate of Shakespeare and Jonson*. Revels Plays Companion Library. Manchester: Manchester University Press, 1987.

Honigmann 1989
E. A. J. Honigmann. "Shakespeare Suppressed: The Unfortunate History of *Troilus and Cressida*." In *Myriad-minded Shakespeare: Essays, Chiefly on the Tragedies and Problem Comedies*, 112–29. London: Macmillan, 1989.

Honigmann 1997
William Shakespeare. *Othello*. Ed. E. A. J. Honigmann. Arden. London: Thomas Nelson, 1997.

Honigmann 1998
E. A. J. Honigmann. *Shakespeare: The "Lost Years."* 2nd ed. Manchester and New York: Manchester University Press, 1998.

Hook 1961
Edward I. Ed. Frank S. Hook. In *The Life and Works of George Peele*, gen. ed. Charles Tyler Prouty, vol. 2. New Haven and London: Yale University Press, 1961.

Hook 1970
The Old Wives Tale. Ed. Frank S. Hook. In *The Dramatic Works of George Peele*, vol. 3. New Haven and London: Yale University Press, 1970.

Hope
Jonathan Hope. *The Authorship of Shakespeare's Plays: A Socio-linguistic Study.* Cambridge: Cambridge University Press, 1994.

Hopkins 1994
Lisa Hopkins. *John Ford's Political Theatre.* Revels Plays Companion Library. Manchester: Manchester University Press; New York: St. Martin's Press, 1994.

Hopkins 1995a
Lisa Hopkins. "Acting the Self: John Ford's *Perkin Warbeck* and the Politics of Imposture." *Cahiers Elisabéthains* 48 (1995): 31–36.

Hopkins 1995b
Lisa Hopkins. "Speaking Sweat: Emblems in the Plays of John Ford." *Comparative Drama* 29.1 (1995): 133–46.

Hopkins 1996
Lisa Hopkins. "Judith Shakespeare's Reading: Teaching *The Concealed Fancies.*" *Shakespeare Quarterly* 47.4 (1996): 396–406.

Hopkins 1999a
Lisa Hopkins. "'A place privileged to do men wrong': The Anxious Masculinity of *The Maid's Tragedy.*" In *The Image of Manhood in Early Modern Literature: Viewing the Male*, ed. Andrew P. Williams, 55–72. Westport, CT, and London: Greenwood Press, 1999.

Hopkins 1999b
Lisa Hopkins. "Play Houses: Drama at Bolsover and Welbeck." *Early Theatre* 2 (1999): 25–44.

Hopkins 2005a
Lisa Hopkins. *A Christopher Marlowe Chronology.* Author Chronologies Series. Basingstoke, UK, and New York: Palgrave Macmillan, 2005.

Hopkins 2005b
Lisa Hopkins. "Staging Passion in Ford's *The Lover's Melancholy.*" *Studies in English Literature, 1500–1900* 45.2 (2005): 443–59.

Hopkins 2008a

Lisa Hopkins. *Christopher Marlowe, Renaissance Dramatist.* Edinburgh: Edinburgh University Press, 2008.

Hopkins 2008b

Lisa Hopkins. *The Cultural Uses of the Caesars on the English Renaissance Stage.* Aldershot, UK, and Burlington, VT: Ashgate, 2008.

Hopkinson

A. F. Hopkinson, ed. *Sir Thomas More.* London: privately printed, 1902.

Hornback 2001

Robert Hornback. "Emblems of Folly in the First *Othello*: Renaissance Blackface, Moor's Coat, and 'Muckender'." *Comparative Drama* 35.1 (2001): 69–99.

Hornback 2007

Robert Hornback. "Lost Conventions of Godly Comedy in Udall's *Thersites*." *Studies in English Literature, 1500–1900* 47.2 (2007): 281–303.

Hornback 2009a

Robert Hornback. "A *Dirige* and Terence 'in the Briers': Mock-Ritual and Mock-Classicism as Iconoclastic Translation in Udall's *Ralph Roister Doister*." *Research Opportunities in Medieval and Renaissance Drama* 48 (2009): 22–47.

Hornback 2009b

Robert Hornback. *The English Clown Tradition from the Middle Ages to Shakespeare.* Cambridge: D. S. Brewer, 2009.

Hornback 2010

Robert Hornback. "'Holy Crap!': Scatological Iconoclasm in Tudor Evangelical Comedy." In *Thunder at a Playhouse: Essaying Shakespeare and the Early Modern Stage*, ed. Peter Kanelos and Matt Kozusko, 67–86. Selinsgrove, PA: Susquehanna University Press, 2010.

Horner

Olga Horner. "*Fulgens and Lucres*: An Historical Perspective." *Medieval English Theatre* 15 (1993): 49–86.

Horsman

Ben Jonson. *Bartholomew Fair.* Ed. E. A. Horsman. Revels Plays. Cambridge, MA: Harvard University Press, 1960.

Hoskins

John Ford's "Love's Sacrifice." Ed. Herbert W. Hoskins Jr. Washington, DC: University Press of America, 1978.

Hosley 1954

Richard Hosley. "The Use of the Upper Stage in *Romeo and Juliet*." *Shakespeare Quarterly* 5.4 (1954): 371–79.

Hosley 1957
Richard Hosley. "The Gallery over the Stage in the Public Playhouse of Shakespeare's Time." *Shakespeare Quarterly* 8.1 (1957): 15–31.

Hosley 1959
Richard Hosley. "The Discovery-Space in Shakespeare's Globe." *Shakespeare Survey* 12 (1959): 35–46.

Hosley 1960
Richard Hosley. "Was There a Music-Room in Shakespeare's Globe?" *Shakespeare Survey* 13 (1960): 113–23.

Hosley 1961
Richard Hosley. "Was There a 'Dramatic Epilogue' to *The Taming of the Shrew?*" *Studies in English Literature, 1500–1900* 1.2 (1961): 17–34.

Hosley 1963
Richard Hosley. "The Staging of Desdemona's Bed." *Shakespeare Quarterly* 14.1 (1963): 57–65.

Hosley 1964a
Richard Hosley. "Sources and Analogues of *The Taming of the Shrew.*" *Huntington Library Quarterly* 27.3 (1964): 289–308.

Hosley 1964b
Richard Hosley. "The Staging of the Monument Scenes in *Antony and Cleopatra.*" *Library Chronicle* 30.2 (1964): 62–71.

Hosley 1973
Richard Hosley. "Three Renaissance English Indoor Playhouses." *English Literary Renaissance* 3.1 (1973): 166–82.

Hosley 1975
Richard Hosley. "The Playhouses." In *The Revels History of Drama in English*, vol. 3: *1576–1613*, ed. J. Leeds Barroll, Alexander Leggatt, idem, and Alvin Kernan, 119–235. London: Methuen, 1975.

Hosley 1979
Richard Hosley. "The Theatre and the Tradition of Playhouse Design." In *The First Public Playhouse: The Theatre in Shoreditch, 1576–1598*, ed. Herbert Berry, 47–79. Montreal: McGill-Queen's University Press, 1979.

Hosley 1981
A Critical Edition of Anthony Munday's "Fedele and Fortunio." Ed. Richard Hosley. New York and London: Garland, 1981.

Hosley 1992
Richard Hosley. "The Stage Superstructures of the First Globe and the Swan." In *The Development of Shakespeare's Theater*, ed. John H. Astington, 119–83. New York: AMS Press, 1992.

Hotson 1928
Leslie Hotson. *The Commonwealth and Restoration Stage.* Cambridge, MA: Harvard University Press, 1928.

Hotson 1931
Leslie Hotson. *Shakespeare versus Shallow.* Boston: Little, Brown, 1931.

Hotson 1952
Leslie Hotson. *Shakespeare's Motley.* New York: Oxford University Press, 1952.

Hotson 1954
Leslie Hotson. *The First Night of "Twelfth Night."* New York: Macmillan, 1954. Repr. 1955.

Houghton
The Houghton Library Theater Collection at Harvard University

Houk
Raymond A. Houk. "The Evolution of *The Taming of the Shrew.*" *PMLA* 57.4 (1942): 1009–38.

Houle
Peter J. Houle. *The English Morality and Related Drama: A Bibliographical Survey.* Hamden, CT: Shoestring (Archon Books), 1972.

Houppert
Thomas Lodge. *The Wounds of Civil War.* Ed. Joseph W. Houppert. RRDS. Lincoln: University of Nebraska Press, 1969.

Howard 1984
Jean E. Howard. *Shakespeare's Art of Orchestration: Stage Technique and Audience Response.* Urbana and Chicago: University of Illinois Press, 1984.

Howard 1985
Douglas Howard. "Massinger's Political Tragedies." In *Philip Massinger: A Critical Reassessment*, ed. idem, 117–37. Cambridge: Cambridge University Press, 1985.

Howard 1988
Jean E. Howard. "Crossdressing, the Theatre, and Gender Struggle in Early Modern England." *Shakespeare Quarterly* 39.4 (1988): 418–40.

Howard 1994a
Jean E. Howard. "An English Lass among the Moors: Gender, Race, Sexuality, and National Identity in Heywood's *The Fair Maid of the West.*" In *Women, "Race," and Writing in the Early Modern Period*, ed. Margo Hendricks and Patricia Parker, 101–17. London and New York: Routledge, 1994.

Howard 1994b
Jean E. Howard. *The Stage and Social Struggle in Early Modern England.* London and New York: Routledge, 1994.

Howard 1997
Jean E. Howard. Introduction to *The Two Gentlemen of Verona*. In *The Norton Shakespeare*, ed. Stephen Greenblatt, Walter Cohen, eadem, and Katharine Eisaman Maus, 77–83. New York: W. W. Norton, 1997.

Howard 1998
Skiles Howard. *The Politics of Courtly Dancing in Early Modern England*. Amherst: University of Massachusetts Press, 1998.

Howard 2002
Jean E. Howard. "Prostitutes, Shopkeepers, and The Shaping of Urban Subjects in *The Honest Whore*." *The Elizabethan Theatre* 15 (2002): 161–79.

Howard 2005
Jean E. Howard. "Staging the Absent Woman: The Theatrical Evocation of Elizabeth Tudor in Heywood's *If You Know Not Me, You Know Nobody, Part 1*." In *Women Players in England, 1500–1660: Beyond the All-Male Stage*, ed. Pamela Allen Brown and Peter Parolin, 263–80. Aldershot, UK, and Burlington, VT: Ashgate, 2005.

Howard 2006a
Jean E. Howard. "Dancing Masters and the Production of Cosmopolitan Bodies in Caroline Town Comedy." In *Localizing Caroline Drama: Politics and Economics of the Early Modern English Stage, 1625–1642*, ed. Adam Zucker and Alan B. Farmer, 183–211. Basingstoke, UK, and New York: Palgrave Macmillan, 2006.

Howard 2006b
Jean E. Howard. "Stage Masculinities, National History, and the Making of London Theatrical Culture." In *Center or Margin: Revisions of the English Renaissance in Honor of Leeds Barroll*, ed. Lena Cowen Orlin, 199–214. Selinsgrove, PA: Susquehanna University Press, 2006.

Howard 2007
Jean E. Howard. *Theater of a City: The Places of London Comedy 1598–1642*. Philadelphia: University of Pennsylvania Press, 2007.

Howard-Hill 1979
John Fletcher and Philip Massinger. *Sir John van Olden Barnavelt*. Ed. T. H. Howard-Hill. MSR. Oxford: Oxford University Press, 1979 [1980].

Howard-Hill 1980
T. H. Howard-Hill. "Boccaccio, *Ghismonda*, and Its Foul Papers, *Glausamond*." *Renaissance Papers* 1980: 19–28.

Howard-Hill
1987a T. H. Howard-Hill. "Thomas Middleton." In *Dictionary of Literary Biography* 58: *Jacobean and Caroline Dramatists*, ed. Fredson Bowers, 196–222. Detroit: Gale, 1987.

Howard-Hill 1987b

T. H. Howard-Hill. "William Rowley." In *Dictionary of Literary Biography* 58: *Jacobean and Caroline Dramatists*, ed. Fredson Bowers, 241–48. Detroit: Gale, 1987.

Howard-Hill 1988

T. H. Howard-Hill. "Another Warwickshire Playwright: John Newdigate of Arbury." *Renaissance Papers* (1988): 51–62.

Howard-Hill 1989

T. H. Howard-Hill, ed. *Shakespeare and "Sir Thomas More": Essays on the Play and Its Shakespearian Interest*. Cambridge: Cambridge University Press, 1989.

Howard-Hill 1990a

T. H. Howard-Hill. "The Evolution of the Form of Plays in English during the Renaissance." *Renaissance Quarterly* 43.1 (1990): 112–45.

Howard-Hill 1990b

"A Game at Chess" by Thomas Middleton, 1624. Ed. T. H. Howard-Hill. MSR. Oxford: Oxford University Press, 1990.

Howard-Hill 1993

Thomas Middleton. *A Game at Chess*. Ed. T. H. Howard-Hill. Revels Plays. Manchester: Manchester University Press; New York: St. Martin's Press, 1993.

Howard-Hill 1999

T. H. Howard-Hill. "'Nor Stage, nor Stationers Stall Can Showe': The Circulation of Plays in Manuscript in the Early Seventeenth Century." *Book History* 2 (1999): 28–41.

Howlett

"Craftie Cromwell, Part 1." Ed. T. R. Howlett. *AEB: Analytical & Enumerative Bibliography* 2.3 (1978): 169–219.

Hoy 1956

Cyrus Hoy. "The Shares of Fletcher and His Collaborators in the Beaumont and Fletcher Canon (I)." *Studies in Bibliography* 8 (1956): 129–46.

Hoy 1957

Cyrus Hoy. "The Shares of Fletcher and His Collaborators in the Beaumont and Fletcher Canon (II)." *Studies in Bibliography* 9 (1957): 143–62.

Hoy 1958

Cyrus Hoy. "The Shares of Fletcher and His Collaborators in the Beaumont and Fletcher Canon (III)." *Studies in Bibliography* 11 (1958): 85–106.

Hoy 1959

Cyrus Hoy. "The Shares of Fletcher and His Collaborators in the Beaumont and Fletcher Canon (IV)." *Studies in Bibliography* 12 (1959): 91–116.

Hoy 1960

Cyrus Hoy. "The Shares of Fletcher and His Collaborators in the Beaumont and Fletcher Canon (V)." *Studies in Bibliography* 13 (1960): 77–108.

Hoy 1961

Cyrus Hoy. "The Shares of Fletcher and His Collaborators in the Beaumont and Fletcher Canon (VI)." *Studies in Bibliography* 14 (1961): 45–67.

Hoy 1962

Cyrus Hoy. "The Shares of Fletcher and His Collaborators in the Beaumont and Fletcher Canon (VII)." *Studies in Bibliography* 15 (1962): 71–90.

Hoy 1964

Philip Massinger. *The City Madam*. Ed. Cyrus Hoy. RRDS. Lincoln: University of Nebraska Press, 1964.

Hoy 1966

Cyrus Hoy, ed. *The Knight of the Burning Pestle*. In *The Dramatic Works in the Beaumont and Fletcher Canon*, gen. ed. Fredson Bowers, vol. 1. Cambridge: Cambridge University Press, 1966.

Hoy 1970

Cyrus Hoy, ed. *The Scornful Lady*. In *The Dramatic Works in the Beaumont and Fletcher Canon*, gen. ed. Fredson Bowers, vol. 2. Cambridge: Cambridge University Press, 1970.

Hoy 1976

Cyrus Hoy. "Critical and Aesthetic Problems of Collaboration." *Research Opportunities in Renaissance Drama* 19 (1976): 3–6.

Hoy 1979

Cyrus Hoy, ed. *Bonduca*. In *The Dramatic Works in the Beaumont and Fletcher Canon*, gen. ed. Fredson Bowers, vol. 4. Cambridge: Cambridge University Press, 1979.

Hoy 1980

Cyrus Hoy. *Introductions, Notes, and Commentaries to Texts in "The Dramatic Works of Thomas Dekker" Edited by Fredson Bowers*. 4 vols. Cambridge: Cambridge University Press, 1980.

Hoy 1985

Cyrus Hoy. "Massinger as Collaborator: The Plays with Fletcher and Others." In *Philip Massinger: A Critical Reassessment*, ed. Douglas Howard, 51–82. Cambridge: Cambridge University Press, 1985.

Hoy 1987a

Cyrus Hoy. "Francis Beaumont (circa 1584–1616) and John Fletcher." In *Dictionary of Literary Biography* 58: *Jacobean and Caroline Dramatists*, ed. Fredson Bowers, 3–26. Detroit: Gale, 1987.

Hoy 1987b

Cyrus Hoy. "Thomas Dekker." In *Dictionary of Literary Biography* 62: *Elizabethan Dramatists*, ed. Fredson Bowers, 45–70. Detroit: Gale, 1987.

Hoy 1989

Cyrus Hoy, ed. *The Night Walker.* In *The Dramatic Works in the Beaumont and Fletcher Canon*, gen. ed. Fredson Bowers, vol. 7. Cambridge: Cambridge University Press, 1989.

Hoy 1992a

Cyrus Hoy, ed. *The Custom of the Country.* In *The Dramatic Works in the Beaumont and Fletcher Canon*, gen. ed. Fredson Bowers, vol. 8. Cambridge: Cambridge University Press, 1992.

Hoy 1992b

Cyrus Hoy, ed. *Four Plays, or Moral Representations, in One.* In *The Dramatic Works in the Beaumont and Fletcher Canon*, gen. ed. Fredson Bowers, vol. 8. Cambridge: Cambridge University Press, 1992.

Hoy 1994

Cyrus Hoy, ed. *The Double Marriage.* In *The Dramatic Works in the Beaumont and Fletcher Canon*, gen. ed. Fredson Bowers, vol. 9. Cambridge: Cambridge University Press, 1994.

Hoy 1996

Cyrus Hoy, ed. *The Honest Man's Fortune.* In *The Dramatic Works in the Beaumont and Fletcher Canon*, gen. ed. Fredson Bowers, vol. 10. Cambridge: Cambridge University Press, 1996.

Huebert 1981

Ronald Huebert. "The Staging of Shirley's *The Lady of Pleasure.*" *The Elizabethan Theatre* 9 (1981): 41–59.

Huebert 1986

James Shirley. *The Lady of Pleasure.* Ed. Ronald Huebert. Revels Plays. Manchester: Manchester University Press, 1986.

Hughes

William Shakespeare. *Titus Andronicus: Updated Edition.* Ed. Alan Hughes. Cambridge: Cambridge University Press, 2006.

Hulse

Lynn Hulse, ed. *Dramatic Works by William Cavendish.* MSR. Oxford: Oxford University Press, 1996.

Humphreys

William Shakespeare. *Julius Caesar.* Ed. Arthur Humphreys. Arden. Oxford: Clarendon Press, 1984.

Hunt
Alice Hunt. "Legitimacy, Ceremony and Drama: Mary Tudor's Coronation and *Respublica.*" In *Interludes and Early Modern Society: Studies in Gender, Power and Theatricality*, ed. Peter Happé and Wim Hüsken, 331–51. Amsterdam and New York: Rodopi, 2007.

Hunter 1965
John Marston. *Antonio and Mellida.* Ed. G. K. Hunter. RRDS. Lincoln: University of Nebraska Press, 1965.

Hunter 1968
G. K. Hunter. *Lyly and Peele.* Writers and Their Work 206. London: Longmans, Green, for the British Council, 1968.

Hunter 1975
John Marston. *The Malcontent.* Ed. G. K. Hunter. Revels Plays. London: Methuen, 1975.

Hunter 1978
G. K. Hunter. "*Henry IV* and the Elizabethan Two-Part Play." In *Dramatic Identities and Cultural Tradition: Studies in Shakespeare and His Contemporaries*, 303–18. Liverpool: Liverpool University Press, 1978.

Hunter 1980
G. K. Hunter. "Flatcaps and Bluecoats: Visual Signals on the Elizabethan Stage." *Essays & Studies* 33 (1980): 16–47.

Hunter 1987
G. K. Hunter. "The Making of a Popular Repertory: Hollywood and the Elizabethans." In *Shakespearean Continuities: Essays in Honour of E. A. J. Honigmann*, ed. John Batchelor, Tom Cain, and Claire Lamont, 247–58. London: Macmillan; New York: St. Martin's Press, 1987.

Hunter 1991
John Lyly. *Campaspe.* Ed. G. K. Hunter. Revels Plays. Manchester: Manchester University Press; New York: St. Martin's Press, 1991.

Hunter 1997
G. K. Hunter. *English Drama, 1586–1642: The Age of Shakespeare.* Oxford: Clarendon Press, 1997.

Hunter 2000
John Lyly. *Galatea.* Ed. G. K. Hunter. Revels Plays. Manchester: Manchester University Press; New York: St. Martin's Press, 2000.

Hunter 2001
Lynette Hunter. "The Dating of Q4 *Romeo and Juliet* Revisited." *The Library*, 7th ser., 2.3 (2001): 281–85.

Hunter 2001?

Lynette Hunter. "Why Has Q4 *Romeo and Juliet* Such an Intelligent Editor?" In *Re-constructing the Book: Literary Texts in Transmission*, ed. Maureen Bell et al., 9–21. Aldershot, UK, and Burlington, VT: Ashgate, ND [?2001].

Hunter 2004

G. K. Hunter. "Lyly, John (1554–1606)." In *ODNB* 34: 867–72.

Huntington

The Henry E. Huntington Library, San Marino, California

Hurley

Ann Hollinshead Hurley. "Editing the Unknown: Writing the Introduction to Two Plays by Elizabeth Polwhele." In *Women Editing/Editing Women: Early Modern Women Writers and the New Textualism*, ed. eadem and Chanita Goodblatt, 189–201. Newcastle upon Tyne: Cambridge Scholars, 2009.

Hutchings

Mark Hutchings. "The Stage Historicizes the Turk: Convention and Contradiction in the Turkish History Play." In *English Historical Drama, 1500–1660: Forms Outside the Canon*, ed. Teresa Grant and Barbara Ravelhofer, 158–78. Basingstoke, UK, and New York: Palgrave Macmillan, 2008.

Hutchings & Bromham

Mark Hutchings and A. A. Bromham. *Middleton and His Collaborators*. Horndon, UK: Northcote House, 2008.

Hyland 2005

Peter Hyland. "*Look About You*, Anonymity, and the Value of Theatricality." *Research Opportunities in Medieval and Renaissance Drama* 44 (2005): 65–74.

Hyland 2011

Peter Hyland. *Disguise on the Early Modern English Stage*. Farnham, UK, and Burlington, VT: Ashgate, 2011.

H&S

Ben Jonson. Ed. C. H. Herford and Percy Simpson. 11 vols. Oxford: Clarendon Press, 1925–52.

Ichikawa 2002

Mariko Ichikawa. *Shakespearean Entrances*. Basingstoke, UK, and New York: Palgrave Macmillan, 2002.

Ichikawa 2005

Mariko Ichikawa. "'*Maluolio within*': Acting on the Threshold between Onstage and Offstage Spaces." *Medieval and Renaissance Drama in England* 18 (2005): 123–45.

Inglis & Johnstone

Kirsten Inglis and Boyda Johnstone. "'The Pen lookes to be canoniz'd': John Newdigate III, Author and Scribe." *Early Theatre* 14.2 (2011): 27–61.

Ingram 1978
R. W. Ingram. *John Marston*. TEAS 216. Boston: Twayne, 1978.

Ingram 1981
R. W. Ingram. *Coventry*. REED. Toronto and Buffalo: University of Toronto Press, 1981.

Ingram 1992
William Ingram. *The Business of Playing: The Beginnings of the Adult Professional Theater in Elizabethan London*. Ithaca, NY: Cornell University Press, 1992.

Ioppolo 1990
Grace Ioppolo. "'The Final Revision of *Bonduca*': An Unpublished Essay by W. W. Greg." *Studies in Bibliography* 43 (1990): 62–80.

Ioppolo 1991
Grace Ioppolo. *Revising Shakespeare*. Cambridge, MA: Harvard University Press, 1991.

Ioppolo 1995
Grace Ioppolo. "Revision, Manuscript Transmission and Scribal Practice in Middleton's *Hengist, King of Kent, or, The Mayor of Queenborough*." *Critical Survey* 7.3 (1995): 319–31.

Ioppolo 1996a
Grace Ioppolo. "Sexual Treason, Treasonous Sexuality, and the Eventful Politics of James I in Middleton's *Hengist, King of Kent*." *Ben Jonson Journal* 3 (1996): 87–107.

Ioppolo 1996b
William Shakespeare. *Measure for Measure*. Ed. Grace Ioppolo. Shakespearean Originals: First Editions. Hemel Hempstead, UK: Prentice Hall, 1996.

Ioppolo 2002a
Grace Ioppolo. "'The foule sheet and ye fayr': Henslowe, Daborne, Heywood and the Nature of Foul-Paper and Fair-Copy Dramatic Manuscripts." *English Manuscript Studies 1100–1700* 11 (2002): 132–53.

Ioppolo 2002b
Grace Ioppolo. "The Transmission of an English Renaissance Play-Text." In *A Companion to Renaissance Drama*, ed. Arthur F. Kinney, 163–79. Oxford: Blackwell, 2002.

Ioppolo 2003
Thomas Middleton. *Hengist, King of Kent, or The Mayor of Queenborough*. Ed. Grace Ioppolo, assisted by John Jowett, G. R. Proudfoot, and H. R. Woudhuysen. MSR. Oxford: Oxford University Press, 2003.

Ioppolo 2005
Grace Ioppolo. "'A Jointure more or less': Re-measuring *The True Chronicle History of King Leir and His Three Daughters.*" *Medieval and Renaissance Drama in England* 17 (2005): 165–79.

Ioppolo 2006
Grace Ioppolo. *Dramatists and Their Manuscripts in the Age of Shakespeare, Jonson, Middleton and Heywood: Authorship, Authority and the Playhouse.* Routledge Studies in Renaissance Literature and Culture 6. London and New York: Routledge, 2006.

Ioppolo 2007
Thomas Middleton. *Hengist, King of Kent.* Ed. Grace Ioppolo. In *Thomas Middleton and Early Modern Textual Culture: A Companion to the Collected Works*, gen. eds. Gary Taylor and John Lavagnino. Oxford: Clarendon Press, 2007.

Ioppolo 2010
William Shakespeare. *Measure for Measure: A Norton Critical Edition.* Ed. Grace Ioppolo. New York and London: Norton, 2010.

Irace 1994
Kathleen O. Irace. *Reforming the "Bad" Quartos: Performance and Provenance of Six Shakespearean First Editions.* Newark, DE: University of Delaware Press; London and Toronto: Associated University Presses, 1994.

Irace 1998
William Shakespeare. *The First Quarto of "Hamlet."* Ed. Kathleen O. Irace. Cambridge: Cambridge University Press, 1998.

Irish
Bradley J. Irish. "Vengeance, Variously: Revenge before Kyd in Early Elizabethan Drama." *Early Theatre* 12.2 (2009): 117–34.

Itzoe 1980
Arthur Wilson. *"The Inconstant Lady," A Critical Edition.* Ed. Linda V. Itzoe. New York and London: Garland, 1980.

Itzoe 1984
Arthur Wilson. *The Swisser.* Ed. Linda V. Itzoe. New York and London: Garland, 1984.

Jackson 1964
MacDonald P. Jackson. "Edward Archer's Ascription of 'Mucedorus' to Shakespeare." *AUMLA: Journal of the Australasian Universities Language and Literature Association* 22 (1964): 233–48.

Jackson 1971
MacDonald P. Jackson. "Three Old Ballads and the Date of 'Doctor Faustus'." *AUMLA: Journal of the Australasian Universities Language and Literature Association* 36 (1971): 187–200.

Jackson 1973
MacDonald P. Jackson. "Three Unidentified Play Titles of the Early Seventeenth Century." *Notes and Queries* n.s. 20.12 (1973): 465–66.

Jackson 1979
MacDonald P. Jackson. *Studies in Attribution: Middleton and Shakespeare.* Jacobean Drama Studies. Salzburg: Institut für Anglistik und Amerikanistik, Universität Salzburg, 1979.

Jackson 1981
MacDonald P. Jackson. "Compositorial Practices in *The Revenger's Tragedy*, 1607–08." *Papers of the Bibliographical Society of America* 75.2 (1981): 157–70.

Jackson 1983
MacDonald P. Jackson. *"The Revenger's Tragedy," Attributed to Thomas Middleton: A Facsimile of the 1607/8 Quarto.* Rutherford, Madison, and Teaneck, NJ: Fairleigh Dickinson University Press, 1983.

Jackson 1985
MacDonald P. Jackson. "John Webster and Thomas Heywood in *Appius and Virginia*: A Bibliographical Approach to the Problem." *Studies in Bibliography* 8 (1985): 217–35.

Jackson 1990
MacDonald P. Jackson. "The Additions to *The Second Maiden's Tragedy*: Shakespeare or Middleton?" *Shakespeare Quarterly* 41.3 (1990): 402–05.

Jackson 1993
MacDonald P. Jackson. "Shakespearean Features of the Poetic Style of *Arden of Faversham*." *Archiv für das Studium der neueren Sprachen und Literaturen* 230 (1993): 279–304.

Jackson 1996
MacDonald P. Jackson. "Stage Directions and Speech Headings in Act 1 of *Titus Andronicus* Q (1594): Shakespeare or Peele?" *Studies in Bibliography* 49 (1996): 134–48.

Jackson 1998
MacDonald P. Jackson. "The Compositors of *Appius and Virginia* (1654)." *Papers of the Bibliographical Society of America* 92.4 (1998): 535–40.

Jackson 2001a
MacDonald P. Jackson. "'But with just cause': *Julius Caesar*, III.i.47." *Notes and Queries* 48.3 (2001): 282–84.

Jackson 2001b
MacDonald P. Jackson. "Late Webster and His Collaborators: How Many Playwrights Wrote *A Cure for a Cuckold*?" *Papers of the Bibliographical Society of America* 95.3 (2001): 295–313.

Jackson 2001c
MacDonald P. Jackson. "Shakespeare's *Richard II* and the Anonymous *Thomas of Woodstock.*" *Medieval and Renaissance Drama in England* 14 (2001): 17–65.

Jackson 2001d
MacDonald P. Jackson. "Spurio and the Date of *All's Well That Ends Well.*" *Notes and Queries* 48.3 (2001): 298–99.

Jackson 2003
MacDonald P. Jackson. *Defining Shakespeare: "Pericles" as Test Case.* Oxford: Oxford University Press, 2003.

Jackson 2006a
MacDonald P. Jackson. "*Anything for a Quiet Life*, IV.ii.1–44: The Hazards of Collaboration." *Notes and Queries* 53.1 (2006): 87–90.

Jackson 2006b
MacDonald P. Jackson. "The Date and Authorship of Hand D's Contribution to *Sir Thomas More*: Evidence from 'Literature Online'." *Shakespeare Survey* 59 (2006): 69–78.

Jackson 2006c
MacDonald P. Jackson. "Shakespeare and the Quarrel Scene in *Arden of Faversham.*" *Shakespeare Quarterly* 57.3 (2006): 249–93.

Jackson 2007a
MacDonald P. Jackson. "The Date and Authorship of *Thomas of Woodstock*: Evidence and Its Interpretation." *Research Opportunities in Medieval and Renaissance Drama* 46 (2007): 67–100.

Jackson 2007b
MacDonald P. Jackson. "Early Modern Authorship: Canons and Chronologies." In *Thomas Middleton and Early Modern Textual Culture: A Companion to the Collected Works*, gen. eds. Gary Taylor and John Lavagnino, 80–97. Oxford: Clarendon Press, 2007.

Jackson 2007c
MacDonald P. Jackson. "Is 'Hand D' of *Sir Thomas More* Shakespeare's? Thomas Bayes and the Elliott-Valenza Authorship Tests." *Early Modern Literary Studies* 12.3 (2007). http://purl.oclc.org/emls/12–3/jackbaye.htm.

Jackson 2007d
The Revenger's Tragedy. Ed. MacDonald P. Jackson. In *Thomas Middleton: The Collected Works*, gen. eds. Gary Taylor and John Lavagnino. Oxford: Clarendon Press, 2007.

Jackson 2008
MacDonald P. Jackson. "New Research on the Dramatic Canon of Thomas Kyd." *Research Opportunities in Medieval and Renaissance Drama* 47 (2008): 107–27.

Jackson 2010
MacDonald P. Jackson. "Parallels and Poetry: Shakespeare, Kyd, and *Arden of Faversham*." *Medieval and Renaissance Drama in England* 23 (2010): 17–33.

Jackson 2011
MacDonald P. Jackson. "Rhymes and Authors: Shakespeare, Wilkins, and *Pericles*." *Notes and Queries* 58.2 (2011): 260–66.

Jackson & Neill
The Selected Plays of John Marston. Ed. MacDonald P. Jackson and Michael Neill. Cambridge: Cambridge University Press, 1986.

Jackson & Taylor
MacDonald P. Jackson and Gary Taylor. "Works Excluded from This Edition." In *Thomas Middleton and Early Modern Textual Culture: A Companion to the Collected Works*, gen. eds. Gary Taylor and John Lavagnino, 444–46. Oxford: Clarendon Press, 2007.

Jacob 1770
Edward Jacob, ed. *The Lamentable and True Tragedie of Master Arden of Feversham, in Kent*. Feversham, UK: Stephen Doorne, 1770.

Jacob 2002
Alexander Jacob. *The Roman Civil War in English Renaissance Tragedy: An Edition of "Catiline," "Caesar and Pompey," and "Julius Caesar."* Studies in Renaissance Literature 22. Lewiston, Queenston, and Lampeter: Edwin Mellen Press, 2002.

Jakacki 2010
Diane K. Jakacki. "'Canst paint a doleful cry?': Promotion and Performance in the *Spanish Tragedy* Title-Page Illustration." *Early Theatre* 13.1 (2010): 13–36.

Jakacki 2011
Diane Jakacki. "Title Page Engraving and Re-Ordering the Quartos of *A Game at Chess*." *ROMARD: Research on Medieval and Renaissance Drama* 50 (2011): 47–72.

James & Walker
Henry James and Greg Walker. "The Politics of *Gorboduc*." *English Historical Review* 110, no. 435 (1995): 109–21.

Jankowski
Theodora A. Jankowski. *Pure Resistance: Queer Virginity in Early Modern English Drama*. Philadelphia: University of Pennsylvania Press, 2000.

Janzen 1976
Thomas Heywood. *The Escapes of Jupiter*. Ed. Henry D. Janzen. MSR. Oxford: Oxford University Press, 1976 [1978].

Janzen 1993
Henry D. Janzen. "Recycling Sex and Texts: Heywood's *Escapes of Jupiter*." *Research Opportunities in Renaissance Drama* 32 (1993): 53–66.

Janzen & Woudhuysen
Francis Jaques. *The Queen of Corsica*. Ed. Henry D. Janzen and H. R. Woudhuysen. MSR. Oxford: Oxford University Press, 1989.

Jardine
Lisa Jardine. *Still Harping on Daughters: Women and Drama in the Age of Shakespeare*. Brighton, UK: Harvester; Totowa, NJ: Barnes & Noble, 1983.

JCS
Gerald Eades Bentley. *The Jacobean and Caroline Stage: Dramatic Companies and Players*. 7 vols. Oxford: Clarendon Press, 1941–68.

Jenkins 1934
Harold Jenkins. *The Life and Work of Henry Chettle*. London: Sidgwick & Jackson, 1934.

Jenkins 1950
Henry Chettle. *The Tragedy of Hoffman*. Ed. Harold Jenkins. MSR. Oxford: Oxford University Press, 1950 [1951].

Jenkins 1982
William Shakespeare. *Hamlet*. Ed. Harold Jenkins. Arden. London and New York: Methuen, 1982.

Jensen
Phebe Jensen. "Recusancy, Festivity and Community: The Simpsons at Gowthwaite Hall." In *Region, Religion and Patronage: Lancastrian Shakespeare*, ed. Richard Dutton, Alison Findlay, and Richard Wilson, 101–20. Manchester: Manchester University Press; New York: Palgrave, 2003.

Jewkes
Wilfred T. Jewkes. *Act Division in Elizabethan and Jacobean Plays, 1583–1616*. Hamden, CT: Shoe String, 1958.

Johnson 1968a
Robert Carl Johnson. "Antedatings from 'Cambises'." *Notes and Queries* 15.7 (1968): 246.

Johnson 1968b
Robert Carl Johnson. "Press Variants in 'Cambises'." *Notes and Queries* 15.7 (1968): 246–47.

Johnson 1968c
Robert Carl Johnson. "The Third Quarto of 'Cambises'." *Notes and Queries* 15.7 (1968): 247.

Johnson 1975
A Critical Edition of Thomas Preston's "Cambises." Ed. Robert Carl Johnson. Salzburg: Institut für Englische Sprache und Literatur, Universität Salzburg, 1975.

Johnson 1976
Thomas Middleton. *No Wit, No Help Like a Woman's.* Ed. Lowell E. Johnson. RRDS. Lincoln: University of Nebraska Press, 1976.

Johnson 2003
Nora Johnson. *The Actor as Playwright in Early Modern Drama.* Cambridge: Cambridge University Press, 2003.

Johnson 2006
Nora Johnson. "Spectacle and the Fantasy of Immateriality: Authorship and Magic in *John a Kent and John a Cumber.*" In *Spectacle and Public Performance in the Late Middle Ages and the Renaissance,* ed. Robert E. Stillman, 105–20. Leiden and Boston: Brill, 2006.

Johnson & Woudhuysen
William Cavendish. *The Country Captain.* Ed. Anthony Johnson. Rev. H. R. Woudhuysen. MSR. Oxford: Oxford University Press, 1999.

Johnston 1986
Alexandra F. Johnston. "*Wisdom* and the Records: Is There a Moral?" In *The Wisdom Symposium: Papers from the Trinity College Medieval Festival,* ed. Milla Cozart Riggio, 87–102. New York: AMS Press, 1986.

Johnston 1998
Alexandra F. Johnston. "The Emerging Pattern of the Easter Play in England." *Medieval English Theatre* 20 (1998): 3–23.

Johnston 2001
Alexandra F. Johnston. "'It pleased the Lord to discover his displeasure': The 1652 performance of *Mucedorus* in Witney." *Leeds Studies in English* n.s. 32 (2001): 195–209.

Johnston & Rogerson
Alexandra F. Johnston and Margaret Rogerson, eds. *York.* 2 vols. REED. Toronto, Buffalo, and London: University of Toronto Press, 1979.

Johnstone 2006
Nathan Johnstone. *The Devil and Demonism in Early Modern England.* Cambridge: Cambridge University Press, 2006.

Jones 1812
Stephen Jones. *Biographia Dramatica; or a Companion to the Playhouse, Containing Historical and Critical Memoirs, and Original Anecdotes, of British and Irish Dramatic Writers.* 3 vols. London: Longman, Hurst, Rees, Orme, and Brown, 1812.

Jones 1952

Lording Barry. *Ram-Alley or Merrie-Trickes*. Ed. Claude E. Jones. Materials for the Study of the Old English Drama 23. Louvain: Uystpruyst, 1952.

Jones 1971

Emrys Jones. *Scenic Form in Shakespeare*. Oxford: Clarendon Press, 1971.

Jones 1977

Emrys Jones. *The Origins of Shakespeare*. Oxford: Clarendon Press, 1977.

Jones 1983

Marion Jones. "Early Moral Plays and the Earliest Secular Drama." In *The Revels History of Drama in English* 1: *Medieval Drama*, ed. A. C. Cawley, idem, Peter F. McDonald, and David Mills, 211–91. London and New York: Methuen, 1983.

Jones 1987

William F. Jones, ed. *An Old-Spelling Critical Edition of James Shirley's "The Example."* New York and London: Garland, 1987.

Jones 1995

John Jones. *Shakespeare at Work*. Oxford: Clarendon Press, 1995.

Jones 1998

Ann Rosalind Jones. "Revenge Comedy: Writing, Law, and the Punishing Heroine in *Twelfth Night*, *The Merry Wives of Windsor*, and *Swetnam the Woman-Hater*." In *Shakespearean Power and Punishment: A Volume of Essays*, ed. Gillian Murray Kendall, 23–38. Madison and Teaneck, NJ: Fairleigh Dickinson University Press, 1998.

Jones & White

Norman Jones and Paul Whitfield White. "*Gorboduc* and Royal Marriage Politics: An Elizabethan Playgoer's Report of the Premiere Performance." *English Literary Renaissance* 26.1 (1996): 3–16.

Jowett 1983a

John Jowett. "New Created Creatures: Ralph Crane and the Stage Directions in 'The Tempest'." *Shakespeare Survey* 36 (1983): 107–20.

Jowett 1983b

Henry Chettle. *The Tragedy of Hoffman*. Ed. J. D. Jowett. Nottingham: Nottingham University Press, 1983.

Jowett 1988

John Jowett. "'Fall before this Booke': The 1605 Quarto of *Sejanus*." *TEXT* 4 (1988): 279–95.

Jowett 1991a

John Jowett. "Jonson's Authorization of Type in *Sejanus* and Other Early Quartos." *Studies in Bibliography* 44 (1991): 254–65.

Jowett 1991b
John Jowett. "Middleton's *No Wit* at the Fortune." *Renaissance Drama* n.s. 22 (1991): 191–208.

Jowett 1993
John Jowett. "Jonson's Authorization of Type in *Sejanus* and Other Early Quartos." In *New Ways of Looking at Old Texts: Papers of the Renaissance English Text Society, 1985–1991*, ed. W. Speed Hill, 175–86. MRTS 107. Binghamton, NY: Center for Medieval and Early Renaissance Studies, State University of New York at Binghamton, 1993.

Jowett 1994
John Jowett. "Notes on Henry Chettle (Concluded)." *Review of English Studies* 45 (1994): 517–22.

Jowett 1998a
John Jowett. "Henry Chettle and the First Quarto of *Romeo and Juliet*." *Papers of the Bibliographical Society of America* 92.1 (1998): 53–74.

Jowett 1998b
John Jowett. "*Richard III* and the Perplexities of Editing." *TEXT* 11 (1998): 224–45.

Jowett 2000
William Shakespeare. *The Tragedy of Richard III*. Ed. John Jowett. Oxford: Oxford University Press, 2000.

Jowett 2001
John Jowett. "The Audacity of *Measure for Measure* in 1621." *Ben Jonson Journal* 8 (2001): 229–47.

Jowett 2002
John Jowett. "Thomas Middleton." In *A Companion to Renaissance Drama*, ed. Arthur F. Kinney, 507–23. Oxford: Blackwell, 2002.

Jowett 2003a
John Jowett. "Middleton and Debt in *Timon of Athens*." In *Money and the Age of Shakespeare: Essays in New Economic Criticism*, ed. Linda Woodbridge, 219–35. New York and Basingstoke, UK: Palgrave Macmillan, 2003.

Jowett 2003b
John Jowett. "Varieties of Collaboration in Shakespeare's Problem Plays and Late Plays." In *A Companion to Shakespeare's Works*, 4: *The Poems, Problem Comedies, Late Plays*, ed. Richard Dutton and Jean E. Howard, 106–28. Malden, MA: Blackwell, 2003.

Jowett 2004a
John Jowett. "Addressing Adaptation: 'Measure for Measure' and 'Sir Thomas More'." In *Textual Performances: The Modern Reproduction of Shakespeare's*

Drama, ed. Lukas Erne and Margaret Jane Kidnie, 63–76. Cambridge: Cambridge University Press, 2004.

Jowett 2004b

John Jowett. "The Pattern of Collaboration in *Timon of Athens*." In *Words That Count: Essays on Early Modern Authorship in Honor of MacDonald P. Jackson*, ed. Brian Boyd, 181–205. Newark, DE: University of Delaware Press, 2004.

Jowett 2004c

William Shakespeare and Thomas Middleton. *The Life of Timon of Athens*. Ed. John Jowett. Oxford World's Classics. Oxford: Oxford University Press, 2004.

Jowett 2006

John Jowett. "From Print to Performance: Looking at the Masque in *Timon of Athens*." In *From Performance to Print in Shakespeare's England*, ed. Peter Holland and Stephen Orgel, 73–91. Basingstoke, UK, and New York: Palgrave Macmillan, 2006.

Jowett 2007a

John Jowett. "For Many of Your Companies: Middleton's Early Readers." In *Thomas Middleton and Early Modern Textual Culture: A Companion to the Collected Works*, gen. eds. Gary Taylor and John Lavagnino, 286–327. Oxford: Clarendon Press, 2007.

Jowett 2007b

Measure for Measure. Ed. John Jowett. In *Thomas Middleton: The Collected Works*, gen. eds. Gary Taylor and John Lavagnino. Oxford: Clarendon Press, 2007.

Jowett 2007c

More Dissemblers besides Women. Ed. John Jowett. In *Thomas Middleton: The Collected Works*, gen. eds. Gary Taylor and John Lavagnino. Oxford: Clarendon Press, 2007.

Jowett 2007d

No Wit, No Help, Like a Woman's; or, The Almanac. Ed. John Jowett. In *Thomas Middleton: The Collected Works*, gen. eds. Gary Taylor and John Lavagnino. Oxford: Clarendon Press, 2007.

Jowett 2007e

John Jowett. *Shakespeare and Text*. Oxford Shakespeare Topics. Oxford: Oxford University Press, 2007.

Jowett 2011

Anthony Munday, Henry Chettle, and Others. *Sir Thomas More*. Ed. John Jowett. Arden. London: A & C Black, 2011.

Jowett & Taylor
John Jowett and Gary Taylor. "'With New Additions': Theatrical Interpolation in *Measure for Measure*." In *Shakespeare Reshaped, 1606–1623*, 107–236. Oxford: Clarendon Press, 1993.

Jowitt 2002
Claire Jowitt. "'Antipodean Tricks': Travel, Gender and Monstrousness in Richard Brome's *The Antipodes*." In *Consuming Narratives: Gender and Monstrous Appetite in the Middle Ages and the Renaissance*, ed. Liz Herbert McAvoy and Teresa Walters, 81–93. Cardiff: University of Wales Press, 2002.

Jowitt 2002–3
Claire Jowitt. "Political Allegory in Late Elizabethan and Early Jacobean 'Turk' Plays: *Lust's Dominion* and *The Turke*." *Comparative Drama* 36 (2002–3): 411–43.

Jowitt 2003
Claire Jowitt. *Voyage Drama and Gender Politics, 1589–1642: Real and Imagined Worlds*. Manchester: Manchester University Press; New York: Palgrave, 2003.

Jowitt 2005
Claire Jowitt. "Piracy and Court Scandals in Massinger's *The Unnatural Combat* (1624–25?)." *Cahiers Elisabéthains* 67 (2005): 33–41.

Jowitt 2006a
Claire Jowitt. "'I Am Another Woman': The Spanish and French Matches in Massinger's *The Renegado* (1624) and *The Unnatural Combat*." In *The Spanish Match: Prince Charles's Journey to Madrid, 1623*, ed. Alexander Samson, 151–71. Aldershot, UK, and Burlington, VT: Ashgate, 2006.

Jowitt 2006b
Claire Jowitt. "*The Island Princess* and Race." In *Early Modern English Drama: A Critical Companion*, ed. Garrett A. Sullivan Jr., Patrick Cheney, and Andrew Hadfield, 287–97. New York and Oxford: Oxford University Press, 2006.

Joyce & Newlyn
Sally L. Joyce and Evelyn S. Newlyn, eds. *Cornwall*. In *Dorset, Cornwall*. REED. Toronto and Buffalo: Brepols and University of Toronto Press, 1999.

Judson
Thomas Heywood. *The Captives; or, The Lost Recovered*. Ed. Alexander Corbin Judson. New Haven: Yale University Press, 1921.

Jump 1935
J. D. Jump. "The Anonymous Masque in Ms. Egerton 1994." *Review of English Studies* 11 (1935): 186–91.

Jump 1948
Rollo Duke of Normandy or The Bloody Brother. Ed. J. D. Jump. Liverpool English
Texts and Studies. Liverpool: University Press of Liverpool; London: Hod-
der and Stoughton, 1948. Repr. 1969.

Jump 1962
Christopher Marlowe. *Doctor Faustus.* Ed. John D. Jump. Revels Plays. London:
Methuen, 1962.

Jupin
A Contextual Study and Modern-Spelling Edition of "Mucedorus." Ed. Arvin H.
Jupin. The Renaissance Imagination 29. New York and London: Garland,
1987.

Kahan 1998
Jeffrey Kahan. "Re-evaluating Philip Edwards's Argument: Could Burbage
Have Played Hieronimo?" *Ben Jonson Journal* 5 (1998): 253–55.

Kahan 2003
Jeffrey Kahan. "An Argument for Emending Bazardo to Buzalto in the 1602
Version of *The Spanish Tragedy.*" *English Language Notes* 40.3 (2003): 13–19.

Kahan 2007
Jeffrey Kahan. "Canonical Breaches and Apocryphal Patches." *Shakespeare Yearbook* 16: *The Shakespeare Apocrypha* (2007): 293–316.

Kahn
Coppélia Kahn. "'Magic of bounty': *Timon of Athens*, Jacobean Patronage, and
Maternal Power." *Shakespeare Quarterly* 38.1 (1987): 34–57.

Kamps
Ivo Kamps. *Historiography and Ideology in Stuart Drama.* Cambridge: Cambridge
University Press, 1996.

Kamps & Raber
William Shakespeare. *Measure for Measure: Texts and Contexts.* Ed. Ivo Kamps and
Karen Raber. Boston and New York: Bedford/St. Martin's Press, 2004.

Kantrowitz
Joanne Spencer Kantrowitz. "Encore: Lindsay's *Thrie Estaitis*, Date and New Evidence." *Studies in Scottish Literature* 10.1 (1972): 18–32.

Karim-Cooper 2006
Farah Karim-Cooper. *Cosmetics in Shakespearean and Renaissance Drama.* Edinburgh: Edinburgh University Press, 2006.

Karim-Cooper 2007
Farah Karim-Cooper. "'This alters not thy beauty': Face-paint, Gender and Race
in Richard Brome's *The English Moor.*" *Early Theatre* 10.2 (2007): 140–49.

Kastan 1991
David Scott Kastan. "Workshop and/as Playhouse: *The Shoemaker's Holiday* (1599)." In *Staging the Renaissance: Reinterpretations of Elizabethan and Jacobean Drama*, ed. idem and Peter Stallybrass, 151–63. New York and London: Routledge, 1991.

Kastan 2005
Christopher Marlowe. *Doctor Faustus*. Ed. David Scott Kastan. Norton Critical Edition. New York and London: Norton, 2005.

Kathman 2004a
David Kathman. "Haughton, William (*d.* 1605)." In *ODNB* 25: 838–39.

Kathman 2004b
David Kathman. "Lower, Sir William (*c.* 1610–1662)." In *ODNB* 34: 588–89.

Kathman 2004c
David Kathman. "Nabbes, Thomas (1604/5–1641)." In *ODNB* 40: 99–100.

Kathman 2004d
David Kathman. "Reconsidering *The Seven Deadly Sins*." *Early Theatre* 7.1 (2004): 13–44.

Kathman 2004e
David Kathman. "Sharpham, Edward (*bap.* 1576, *d.* 1608)." In *ODNB* 50: 60–61.

Kathman 2004f
David Kathman. "Wilson, Robert (*d.* 1600)." In *ODNB* 59: 626–28.

Kathman 2005
David Kathman. "How Old Were Shakespeare's Boy Actors?" *Shakespeare Survey* 58 (2005): 220–46.

Kathman 2009
David Kathman. "Actors' Names as Textual Evidence." *Theatre Notebook* 63.2 (2009): 70–79.

Kathman 2011
David Kathman. "*The Seven Deadly Sins* and Theatrical Apprenticeship." *Early Theatre* 14.1 (2011): 121–39.

Kaufmann
R. J. Kaufmann. *Richard Brome: Caroline Playwright*. New York and London: Columbia University Press, 1961.

Kawachi
Yoshiko Kawachi. *Calendar of English Renaissance Drama 1558–1642*. Garland Reference Library of the Humanities 661. New York and London: Garland, 1986.

Kay 1991

Dennis Kay. *Shakespeare: His Life, Work and Era.* London: Sidgwick & Jackson, 1991.

Kay 1995

W. David Kay. *Ben Jonson: A Literary Life.* Basingstoke, UK, and London: Macmillan, 1995.

Kay 1998

John Marston. *The Malcontent.* Ed. W. David Kay. 2nd ed. New Mermaids. London: Black, 1998.

Keefer 2002

Michael Keefer. "Text, Apparatus, History." *Elizabethan Theatre* 15 (2002): 131–57.

Keefer 2007

Christopher Marlowe. *"Doctor Faustus": A 1604-Version Edition.* Ed. Michael Keefer. 2nd ed. Plymouth, UK; Peterborough, Ontario; and Orchard Park, NY: Broadview, 2007.

Keenan 2002

Siobhan Keenan. *Travelling Players in Shakespeare's England.* Basingstoke, UK: Palgrave Macmillan; New York: St. Martin's Press, 2002.

Keenan 2010

John Newdigate. *The Emperor's Favourite.* Ed. Siobhan Keenan. MSR. Manchester: Manchester University Press; New York: Palgrave, 2010.

Keenan 2011

Siobhan Keenan. "Staging Roman History, Stuart Politics, and the Duke of Buckingham: The Example of *The Emperor's Favourite.*" *Early Theatre* 14.2 (2011): 63–103.

Keller

Wolfgang Keller, ed. *"Richard II. Erster Teil*: Ein Drama aus Shakespeares Zeit." *Jahrbuch der Deutschen Shakespeare-Gesellschaft* 35 (1899): 1–121.

Kelliher 1980

Hilton Kelliher. "A Hitherto Unrecognized Cavalier Dramatist: James Compton, Third Earl of Northampton." *British Library Journal* 6.2 (1980): 158–87.

Kelliher 1993

Hilton Kelliher. "Donne, Jonson, Richard Andrews and the Newcastle Manuscript." *English Manuscript Studies 1100–1700* 4 (1993): 134–73.

Kelliher 2004a

W. H. Kelliher. "Compton, James, third earl of Northampton (1622–1681)." In *ODNB* 12: 890–91.

Kelliher 2004b
W. H. Kelliher. "Randolph, Thomas (*bap.* 1605, *d.* 1635)." In *ODNB* 46: 2–22.

Kendall
Ritchie Kendall. *The Drama of Dissent: The Radical Poetics of Nonconformity, 1380–1590*. Chapel Hill and London: University of North Carolina Press, 1986.

Kennedy
Edward D. Kennedy. "James I and Chapman's Byron Plays." *JEGP* 64.4 (1965): 677–90.

Kermode 1995
Lloyd Edward Kermode. "'Marlowe's Second City': The Jew as Critic at the Rose in 1592." *Studies in English Literature, 1500–1900* 35.2 (1995): 215–29.

Kermode 1999
Lloyd Edward Kermode. "The Playwright's Prophecy: Robert Wilson's *The Three Ladies of London* and the 'Alienation' of the English." *Medieval and Renaissance Drama in England* 11 (1999): 60–87.

Kermode 2009a
Lloyd Edward Kermode. *Aliens and Englishness in Elizabethan Drama*. Cambridge: Cambridge University Press, 2009.

Kermode 2009b
Lloyd Edward Kermode, ed. *Three Renaissance Usury Plays*. Revels Plays Companion Library. Manchester: Manchester University Press; New York: Palgrave Macmillan, 2009.

Kernan 1958
Alvin Kernan. "John Marston's Play *Histriomastix*." *Modern Language Quarterly* 19.2 (1958): 134–40.

Kernan 1995
Alvin Kernan. *Shakespeare, the King's Playwright: Theater in the Stuart Court, 1603–1613*. New Haven, and London: Yale University Press, 1995.

Kerrigan 2006
John Kerrigan. "The Romans in Britain, 1603–1614." In *The Accession of James I: Historical and Cultural Consequences*, ed. Glenn Burgess, Rowland Wymer, and Jason Lawrence, 113–39. Basingstoke, UK, and New York: Palgrave Macmillan, 2006.

Kerrigan 2008
John Kerrigan. *Archipelagic English: Literature, History, and Politics, 1603–1707*. Oxford: Oxford University Press, 2008.

Kewes
Paulina Kewes. "Roman History and Early Stuart Drama: Thomas Heywood's *The Rape of Lucrece*." *English Literary Renaissance* 32.2 (2002): 239–67.

Kidnie 2000a
Margaret Jane Kidnie, ed. *Ben Jonson: "The Devil Is an Ass" and Other Plays*. Oxford World's Classics. Oxford: Oxford University Press, 2000.

Kidnie 2000b
Margaret Jane Kidnie. "Text, Performance, and the Editors: Staging Shakespeare's Drama." *Shakespeare Quarterly* 51.4 (2000): 456–73.

Kidnie 2002
Margaret Jane Kidnie. "'Enter [. . .] Lorenzo, disguised like an Amazon': Powerdressing in *Swetnam the Woman-hater, Arraigned by Women*." *Cahiers Elisabéthains* 62 (2002): 33–45.

Kidnie 2007
Margaret Jane Kidnie. "Near Neighbours: Another Early Seventeenth-Century Manuscript of *The Humorous Magistrate*." *English Manuscript Studies 1100–1700* 13 (2007): 187–211.

Kidnie 2011
Margaret Jane Kidnie. "Trying to be Diplomatic: Editing *The Humorous Magistrate*." *Early Theatre* 14.2 (2011): 245–56.

Kiefer 1977
Frederick Kiefer. "Love and Fortune in Boccaccio's Tancredi and Ghismonda Story and in Wilmot's *Gismond of Salerne*." *Renaissance and Reformation* n.s. 1.1 (1977): 36–45.

Kiefer 1978
Frederick Kiefer. "Seneca Speaks in English: What the Elizabethan Translators Wrought." *Comparative Literature Studies* 15.4 (1978): 372–87.

Kiefer 1983
Frederick Kiefer. *Fortune and Elizabethan Tragedy*. San Marino, CA: Huntington Library, 1983.

Kiefer 1986
"Love Letters in *The Two Gentlemen of Verona*." *Shakespeare Studies* 18 (1986): 65–85.

Kiefer 1987
Frederick Kiefer. "The Dance of the Madmen in *The Duchess of Malfi*." *Journal of Medieval and Renaissance Studies* 17.2 (1987): 211–33.

Kiefer 1995
Frederick Kiefer. "Spring and Winter in *Love's Labor's Lost*: An Iconographic Reconstruction." *Comparative Drama* 29 (1995): 91–107.

Kiefer 1996a
Frederick Kiefer. *Writing on the Renaissance Stage: Written Words, Printed Pages, Metaphoric Books*. Newark, DE: University of Delaware Press; London: Associated University Presses, 1996.

Kiefer 1996b
Frederick Kiefer. "'Written Troubles of the Brain': Lady Macbeth's Conscience." In *Reading and Writing in Shakespeare*, ed. David M. Bergeron, 64–81. Newark, DE: University of Delaware Press; London: Associated University Presses, 1996.

Kiefer 1999
Frederick Kiefer. "The Iconography of Time in *The Winter's Tale*." *Renaissance and Reformation* 32.3 (1999): 49–64.

Kiefer 2000
Frederick Kiefer. "Fortune on the Renaissance Stage: An Iconographic Reconstruction." In *Fortune: "All Is but Fortune*," ed. Leslie Thomson, 98–113. Seattle and London: University of Washington Press for the Folger Shakespeare Library, 2000.

Kiefer 2002
Frederick Kiefer. "Creating a Christian Revenger: *The Spanish Tragedy* and Its Progeny vs. *Hamlet*." *Shakespeare Yearbook* 13: *Shakespeare and Spain* (2002): 159–80.

Kiefer 2003
Frederick Kiefer. *Shakespeare's Visual Theatre: Staging the Personified Characters.* Cambridge: Cambridge University Press, 2003.

Kiefer 2004
Frederick Kiefer. "Poems as Props in *Love's Labor's Lost* and *Much Ado About Nothing*." In *Reading and Literacy in the Middle Ages and Renaissance*, ed. Ian Frederick Moulton, 127–41. ASMAR 8. Turnhout: Brepols, 2004.

Kiefer 2007
Frederick Kiefer. "Curtains on the Shakespearean Stage." *Medieval and Renaissance Drama in England* 20 (2007): 151–86.

Kiefer 2011
Frederick Kiefer. "The Visual and the Verbal: Blazons on the Renaissance Stage." *Allegorica* 27.1 (2011): 90–109.

Kiefer 2012
Frederick Kiefer. "Architecture." In *The Oxford Handbook of Shakespeare*, ed. Arthur F. Kinney, 680–701. Oxford: Oxford University Press, 2012.

Kincaid
Patrick Kincaid. "John Marston's *The Dutch Courtesan* and William Percy's *The Cuck-queanes and Cuckolds Errants*." *Notes and Queries* 48.3 (2001): 309–11.

King 1965
T. J. King. "Staging of Plays at the Phoenix in Drury Lane, 1617–42." *Theatre Notebook* 19.4 (1965): 146–66.

King 1971

T. J. King. *Shakespearean Staging, 1599–1642*. Cambridge, MA: Harvard University Press, 1971.

King 1975

T. J. King. *"Hannibal and Scipio* (1637): How 'The Places Sometimes Changed'." *Theatre Notebook* 29.1 (1975): 20–22.

King 1982

John N. King. *English Reformation Literature: The Tudor Origins of the Protestant Tradition*. Princeton: Princeton University Press, 1982.

King 1992a

T. J. King. *Casting Shakespeare's Plays: London Actors and Their Roles, 1590–1642*. Cambridge: Cambridge University Press, 1992.

King 1992b

T. J. King. "Thomas Nabbes's *Covent Garden* (1638) and Inigo Jones's Drawings for the Phoenix or Cockpit in Drury Lane." In *The Development of Shakespeare's Theater*, ed. John H. Astington, 185–202. New York: AMS Press, 1992.

King 1993

Pamela M. King. "Minority Plays: Two Interludes for Edward VI." *Medieval English Theatre* 15 (1993): 87–102.

King 2001

Ros King. *The Works of Richard Edwards: Politics, Poetry and Performance in Sixteenth-Century England*. Revels Plays Companion Library. Manchester: Manchester University Press; New York: Palgrave, 2001.

King 2004

John N. King. "Bale, John (1495–1563)." In *ODNB* 3: 482–86.

King 2008a

Pamela M. King. "Morality Plays." In *The Cambridge Companion to Medieval English Theatre*, ed. Richard Beadle and Alan J. Fletcher, 235–62. 2nd ed. Cambridge: Cambridge University Press, 2008.

King 2008b

Christopher Marlowe. *Doctor Faustus*. Ed. Roma Gill. Rev. Ros King. 3rd ed. New Mermaids. London: Black, 2008.

Kingsley-Smith 2005

Robert Daborne. *The Poor Man's Comfort*. Ed. Jane Kingsley-Smith. Globe Quartos. London: Globe Education; New York: Theatre Arts/Routledge, 2005.

Kingsley-Smith 2008

Jane Kingsley-Smith. *"Gismond of Salerne*: An Elizabethan and Cupidean Tragedy." *Yearbook of English Studies* 38 (2008): 199–215.

Kinney 1998
Thomas Dekker, John Ford, and William Rowley. *The Witch of Edmonton*. Ed. Arthur Kinney. New Mermaids. London: Black; New York: Norton, 1998.

Kinney 1999
Arthur F. Kinney. "Text, Context, and Authorship of *The Booke of Sir Thomas Moore*." In *Pilgrimage for Love: Essays in Early Modern Literature in Honor of Josephine A. Roberts*, ed. Sigrid King, 133–60. MRTS 213. Tempe: Arizona Center for Medieval and Renaissance Studies, 1999.

Kinney 2001
Arthur F. Kinney. *Lies Like Truth: Shakespeare, Macbeth, and the Cultural Moment*. Detroit: Wayne State University Press, 2001.

Kinney 2003
Arthur F. Kinney. *Shakespeare by Stages: An Historical Introduction*. Malden, MA, and Oxford: Blackwell, 2003.

Kinney 2009a
Arthur F. Kinney. "Authoring *Arden of Faversham*." In *Shakespeare, Computers, and the Mystery of Authorship*, ed. Hugh Craig and idem, 78–99. Cambridge: Cambridge University Press, 2009.

Kinney 2009b
Arthur F. Kinney. "Transforming *King Lear*." In *Shakespeare, Computers, and the Mystery of Authorship*, ed. Hugh Craig and idem, 181–201. Cambridge: Cambridge University Press, 2009.

Kirkman
Francis Kirkman. *A True, Perfect, and Exact Catalogue of All the Comedies, Tragedies, Pastorals, Masques and Interludes, That Were Ever yet Printed and Published, till This Present Year*. London: N. Brook et al., 1661.

Kitch 2005
Aaron Kitch. "Medwall's 'Condycion': *Fulgens and Lucrece* and the New Tudor Drama." *Cahiers Elisabéthains* 68 (2005): 1–8.

Kitch 2009
Aaron Kitch. *Political Economy and the States of Literature in Early Modern England*. Farnham, UK; Burlington, VT: Ashgate, 2009.

Kittredge
George Lyman Kittredge. "The *Misogonus* and Laurence Johnson." *JEGP* 3 (1901): 335–41.

Klause
John Klause. "A Controversy over Rhyme and Authorship in *Pericles*." *Notes and Queries* 59.4 (2012): 538–44.

Klausner 1990
David N. Klausner, ed. *Herefordshire, Worcestershire*. REED. Toronto and Buffalo: University of Toronto Press, 1990.

Klausner 2007
David N. Klausner. "The Modular Structure of *Wisdom*." In *"Bring furth the pagants": Essays in Early English Drama Presented to Alexandra F. Johnston*, ed. idem and Karen Sawyer Marsalek, 181–96. Toronto, Buffalo, and London: University of Toronto Press, 2007.

Klausner 2009
David N. Klausner, ed. *Two Moral Interludes: "The Pride of Life" and "Wisdom."* Middle English Texts Series. Kalamazoo, MI: Medieval Institute, Western Michigan University, 2009.

Klein
William Shakespeare. *Timon of Athens*. Ed. Karl Klein. Cambridge: Cambridge University Press, 2001.

Kliman 2004
Bernice W. Kliman. *Macbeth*. Shakespeare in Performance. 2nd ed. Manchester: Manchester University Press; New York: Palgrave, 2004.

Kliman 2011
Bernice W. Kliman. "At Sea about *Hamlet* at Sea: A Detective Story." *Shakespeare Quarterly* 62.2 (2011): 180–204.

Knapp & Kobialka
Margaret Knapp and Michal Kobialka. "Shakespeare and the Prince of Purpoole: The 1594 Production of *The Comedy of Errors* at Gray's Inn Hall." *Theatre History Studies* 4 (1984): 71–81.

Knight 1839
Charles Knight, ed. *The Pictorial Edition of the Works of Shakspere*. 8 vols. London: C. Knight, 1839–43.

Knight 1994
Stephen Knight. *Robin Hood: A Complete Study of the English Outlaw*. Oxford: Blackwell, 1994.

Knight 2008
Sarah Knight. "Fantastical Distempers: The Psychopathology of Early Modern Scholars." In *Early Modern Academic Drama*, ed. Jonathan Walker and Paul D. Streufert, 129–52. Farnham, UK, and Burlington, VT: Ashgate, 2008.

Knight & Ohlgren
Stephen Knight and Thomas Ohlgren, ed. *Robin Hood and Other Outlaw Tales*. Kalamazoo, MI: Medieval Institute, Western Michigan University, 1997.

Knoll
Robert E. Knoll. *Ben Jonson's Plays: An Introduction.* Lincoln: University of Nebraska Press, 1964.

Knowles 1999
William Shakespeare. *King Henry VI, Part 2.* Ed. Ronald Knowles. Arden. Walton-on-Thames, UK: Thomas Nelson, 1999.

Knowles 2001a
James Knowles, ed. *"The Roaring Girl" and Other City Comedies.* Oxford: Oxford University Press, 2001.

Knowles 2001b
James Knowles. "'Tied / To Rules of Flattery?': Court Drama and the Masque." In *A Companion to English Renaissance Literature and Culture*, ed. Michael Hattaway, 525–44. Oxford: Blackwell, 2001.

Knowles 2002
Richard Knowles. "How Shakespeare Knew *King Leir.*" *Shakespeare Survey* 55 (2002): 12–35.

Knowles 2004
James Knowles. "Marston, John (*bap.* 1576, *d.* 1634)." In *ODNB* 36: 894–97.

Knowles 2008
Richard Knowles. "The Evolution of the Texts of *Lear.*" In *"King Lear": New Critical Essays*, ed. Jeffrey Kahan, 124–54. New York: Routledge, 2008.

Knutson 1983
Roslyn L. Knutson. "Henslowe's Naming of Parts: Entries in the *Diary* for *Tamar Cham*, 1592–93, and *Godfrey of Bulloigne*, 1594–5." *Notes and Queries* n.s. 30.2 (1983): 157–60.

Knutson 1984
Roslyn L. Knutson. "Play Identifications: *The Wise Man of West Chester* and *John a Kent and John a Cumber*; *Longshanks* and *Edward I.*" *Huntington Library Quarterly* 47.1 (1984): 1–11.

Knutson 1985
Roslyn L. Knutson. "*Henslowe's Diary* and the Economics of Play Revision for Revival, 1592–1603." *Theatre Research International* 10.1 (1985): 1–18.

Knutson 1991
Roslyn Lander Knutson. *The Repertory of Shakespeare's Company, 1594–1613.* Fayetteville: University of Arkansas Press, 1991.

Knutson 1997
Roslyn L. Knutson. "The Repertory." In *A New History of Early English Drama*, ed. John D. Cox and David Scott Kastan, 461–80. New York: Columbia University Press, 1997.

Knutson 1999

Roslyn L. Knutson. "Shakespeare's Repertory." In *A Companion to Shakespeare*, ed. David Scott Kastan, 346–61. Oxford: Blackwell, 1999.

Knutson 2001a

Roslyn L. Knutson. "*Histrio-Mastix*: Not by John Marston." *Studies in Philology* 98.3 (2001): 359–77.

Knutson 2001b

Roslyn Lander Knutson. *Playing Companies and Commerce in Shakespeare's Time*. Cambridge: Cambridge University Press, 2001.

Knutson 2002a

Roslyn L. Knutson. "Filling Fare: The Appetite for Current Issues and Traditional Forms in the Repertory of the Chamberlain's Men." *Medieval and Renaissance Drama in England* 15 (2002): 57–76.

Knutson 2002b

Roslyn L. Knutson. "Two Playhouses, Both Alike in Dignity." *Shakespeare Studies* 30 (2002): 111–17.

Knutson 2004

Roslyn L. Knutson. "Working Playwrights, 1580–1642." In *The Cambridge History of British Theatre*, vol. 1: *Origins to 1660*, ed. Jane Milling and Peter Thomson, 341–63. Cambridge: Cambridge University Press, 2004.

Knutson 2006a

Roslyn L. Knutson. "Theater Companies and Stages." In *Early Modern English Drama: A Critical Companion*, ed. Garrett A. Sullivan Jr., Patrick Cheney, and Andrew Hadfield, 12–22. New York and Oxford: Oxford University Press, 2006.

Knutson 2006b

Roslyn L. Knutson. "Toe to Toe across Maid Lane: Repertorial Competition at the Rose and Globe, 1599–1600." In *Acts of Criticism: Performance Matters in Shakespeare and His Contemporaries: Essays in Honor of James P. Lusardi*, ed. Paul Nelsen and June Schlueter, 21–37. Madison and Teaneck, NJ: Fairleigh Dickinson University Press, 2006.

Knutson 2009a

Roslyn L. Knutson. "Adult Playing Companies, 1593–1603." In *The Oxford Handbook of Early Modern Theatre*, ed. Richard Dutton, 56–71. Oxford: Oxford University Press, 2009.

Knutson 2009b

Roslyn L. Knutson. "The Start of Something Big." In *Locating the Queen's Men, 1583–1603: Material Practices and Conditions of Playing*, ed. Helen Ostovich, Holger Schott Syme, and Andrew Griffin, 99–108. Farnham, UK, and Burlington, VT: Ashgate, 2009.

Kok

Su Mei Kok. "Contexts for Thomas Middleton's *Michaelmas Term* (1604)." *Notes and Queries* 59.1 (2012): 89–91.

Korhonen

Anu Korhonen. "Washing the Ethiopian White: Conceptualising Black Skin in Renaissance England." In *Black Africans in Renaissance Europe*, ed. T. F. Earle and K. J. P. Lowe, 94–112. Cambridge: Cambridge University Press, 2005.

Krantz

Susan E. Krantz. "Thomas Dekker's Political Commentary in *The Whore of Babylon*." *Studies in English Literature, 1500–1900* 35.2 (1995): 271–91.

Kreps

Barbara Kreps. "The Paradox of Women: The Legal Position of Early Modern Wives and Thomas Dekker's *The Honest Whore*." *ELH* 69.1 (2002): 83–102.

Kuin

R. J. P. Kuin. *Robert Langham: "A Letter."* Medieval and Renaissance Texts 2. Leiden: Brill, 1983.

LaGrandeur

Kevin LaGrandeur. "The Talking Brass Head as a Symbol of Dangerous Knowledge in *Friar Bacon* and in *Alphonsus, King of Aragon*." *English Studies* 80.5 (1999): 408–22.

Lake 1973

David J. Lake. "The Shares of Middleton and Others in 'A Yorkshire Tragedy'." *Notes and Queries* 20.12 (1973): 456–58.

Lake 1975a

David J. Lake. *The Canon of Thomas Middleton's Plays: Internal Evidence for the Major Problems of Authorship*. Cambridge: Cambridge University Press, 1975.

Lake 1975b

David J. Lake. "Dekker and 'The Telltale': Some Difficulties." *Notes and Queries* 22.6 (1975): 253–55.

Lake 1976

David J. Lake. "The Date of 'More Dissemblers besides Women'." *Notes and Queries* 221 (1976): 219–21.

Lake 1977

David J. Lake. "The Canon of Robert Armin's Works: Some Difficulties." *Notes and Queries* 222 (1977): 117–20.

Lake 1981a

David J. Lake. "*Histriomastix*: Linguistic Evidence for Authorship." *Notes and Queries* 226 (1981): 148–52.

Lake 1981b
David J. Lake. "Webster's Additions to *The Malcontent*: Linguistic Evidence."
Notes and Queries 28.2 (1981): 153–58.

Lake 1983
David J. Lake. "Three Seventeenth-Century Revisions: *Thomas of Woodstock*, *The
Jew of Malta*, and *Faustus B*." *Notes and Queries* 228 (1983): 133–43.

Lamb 1980
Margaret Lamb. *"Antony and Cleopatra" on the English Stage*. Rutherford, Madison, and Teaneck, NJ: Fairleigh Dickinson University Press, 1980.

Lamb 2009
Edel Lamb. *Performing Childhood in the Early Modern Theatre: The Children's
Playing Companies (1599–1613)*. Basingstoke, UK, and New York: Palgrave
Macmillan, 2009.

Lancashire 1969a
John Lyly. *"Gallathea" and "Midas."* Ed. Anne Begor Lancashire. RRDS. Lincoln: University of Nebraska Press, 1969.

Lancashire 1969b
Anne B. Lancashire. *"Look About You* as a History Play." *Studies in English Literature, 1500–1900* 9.2 (1969): 321–34.

Lancashire 1976
Ian Lancashire. "The Auspices of *The World and the Child*." *Renaissance and Reformation* 12 (1976): 96–105.

Lancashire 1978
The Second Maiden's Tragedy. Ed. Anne Lancashire. Revels Plays. Manchester:
Manchester University Press; Baltimore: Johns Hopkins University Press,
1978.

Lancashire 1980
Two Tudor Interludes: "The Interlude of Youth," "Hick Scorner." Ed. Ian Lancashire.
Revels Plays. Manchester: Manchester University Press; Baltimore: Johns
Hopkins University Press, 1980.

Lancashire 1983
Anne Lancashire. "*The Witch*: Stage Flop or Political Mistake?" In *"Accompaninge
the players": Essays Celebrating Thomas Middleton, 1580–1980*, ed. Kenneth
Friedenreich, 161–81. New York: AMS Press, 1983.

Lancashire 2002
Anne Lancashire. *London Civic Theatre: City Drama and Pageantry from Roman
Times to 1558*. Cambridge: Cambridge University Press, 2002.

Lancaster
Marjorie S. Lancaster. "Middleton's Use of the Upper Stage in *Women Beware
Women*." *Tulane Studies in English* 22 (1977): 69–85.

Langbaine 1680
Gerard Langbaine. *An Exact Catalogue of All the Comedies, Tragedies, Tragi-Comedies . . . that Were Ever yet Printed and Published, till This Present Year 1680.* Oxford: L. Lichfield for Nicholas Cox, 1680.

Langbaine 1691
Gerard Langbaine. *An Account of the English Dramatick Poets.* Oxford: L. L. for G. West and H. Clements, 1691.

Lannam
The Marriage between Wit and Wisdom. Ed. Trevor N. S. Lannam. MSR. Oxford: Oxford University Press, 1966 [1971].

Lapides
"The Raigne of King Edward the Third": A Critical, Old-Spelling Edition. Ed. Fred Lapides. New York and London: Garland, 1980.

Larkum
Eleri Larkum. "Goffe [Gough], Thomas (1590/91–1629)." In *ODNB* 22: 635–36.

Latham
William Shakespeare. *As You Like It.* Ed. Agnes Latham. Arden Shakespeare. London: Methuen, 1975.

Lawless & Pafford
Donald S. Lawless and J. H. P. Pafford. "John Clavell, 1603–42: Highwayman, Author, and Quack Doctor." *Notes and Queries* n.s. 4.1 (1957): 9.

Lawrence 1912a
William J. Lawrence. "Music and Song in the Elizabethan Theatre." In *The Elizabethan Playhouse and Other Studies*, 73–96. First Series. Stratford-upon-Avon: Shakespeare Head Press, 1912.

Lawrence 1912b
William J. Lawrence. "Title and Locality Boards on the Pre-Restoration Stage." In *The Elizabethan Playhouse and Other Studies*, 41–71. First Series. Stratford-upon-Avon: Shakespeare Head Press, 1912.

Lawrence 1913a
William J. Lawrence. "Light and Darkness in the Elizabethan Theatre." In *The Elizabethan Playhouse and Other Studies*, 1–22. Second Series. Stratford-upon-Avon: Shakespeare Head Press, 1913.

Lawrence 1913b
William J. Lawrence. "The Origin of the English Picture-Stage." In *The Elizabethan Playhouse and Other Studies*, 119–47. Second Series. Stratford-upon-Avon: Shakespeare Head Press, 1913.

Lawrence 1921

William J. Lawrence. "The Earliest Private-Theatre Play." *TLS* 11 August 1921: 514.

Lawrence 1922

William J. Lawrence. "A Plummet for Bottom's Dream." *Fortnightly Review*, n.s. 111 (1922): 833–44.

Lawrence 1927

William J. Lawrence. *Pre-Restoration Stage Studies.* Cambridge, MA: Harvard University Press, 1927. Repr. New York: Benjamin Blom, 1967.

Lawrence 1935

William J. Lawrence. *Those Nut-Cracking Elizabethans: Studies of the Early Theatre and Drama.* London: Argonaut Press, 1935.

Lawrence 2007

Jason Lawrence. "Re-make/re-model: Marston's *The Malcontent* and Guarinian Tragicomedy." In *Italian Culture in the Drama of Shakespeare & His Contemporaries: Rewriting, Remaking, Refashioning*, ed. Michele Marrapodi, 155–66. Aldershot, UK, and Burlington, VT: Ashgate, 2007.

Lea

The Parliament of Love. Ed. Kathleen Marguerite Lea. MSR. Oxford: Oxford University Press, 1928 [1929].

Lea & Smith

"Mother Bombie" by John Lyly, 1594. Ed. Kathleen M. Lea and D. Nichol Smith. MSR. Oxford: Oxford University Press, 1939 [1948].

Lee

Narcissus, A Twelfe Night Merriment. Ed. Margaret L. Lee. London: David Nutt, 1893.

Leech 1935

Clifford Leech. "The Plays of Edward Sharpham: Alterations Accomplished and Projected." *Review of English Studies* 11 (1935): 69–74.

Leech 1938

Mildmay Fane's "Raguaillo D'Oceano" 1640 and "Candy Restored" 1641. Ed. Clifford Leech. Materials for the Study of the Old English Drama n.s. 15. Louvain: Uystpruyst, 1938. Repr. 1963.

Leech 1947

Clifford Leech. "Francis Jaques, Author of *The Queene of Corsica.*" *Durham University Journal* 39 (1947): 111–19.

Leech 1959

Clifford Leech. "Marlowe's 'Edward II': Power and Suffering." *Critical Quarterly* 1.3 (1959): 181–96.

Leggatt 2003

Alexander Leggatt. Introduction to *All's Well That Ends Well* by William Shakespeare. Ed. Russell Fraser. New Cambridge Shakespeare. Updated Edition. Cambridge: Cambridge University Press, 2003.

Leggatt 2007

Ben Jonson. *Bartholomew Fair*. Intro. Alexander Leggatt. Ed. G. R. Hibbard. 2nd ed. Rev. New Mermaids. London: Black, 2007.

Leininger

Jeffrey Leininger. "The Dating of Bale's *King John*: A Re-Examination." *Medieval English Theatre* 24 (2002): 116–37.

Leinwand

Thomas Middleton. *Michaelmas Term*. Ed. Theodore B. Leinwand. In *Thomas Middleton and Early Modern Textual Culture: A Companion to the Collected Works*, gen. eds. Gary Taylor and John Lavagnino. Oxford: Clarendon, 2007.

Leishman 1944

J. B. Leishman. Review of Bowers' *The Fary Knight*. *Review of English Studies* 20 (1944): 321–22.

Leishman 1949

The Three Parnassus Plays (1598–1601). Ed. J. B. Leishman. London: Nicholson & Watson, 1949.

Lemon

Rebecca Lemon. *Treason by Words: Literature, Law, and Rebellion in Shakespeare's England*. Ithaca, NY, and London: Cornell University Press, 2006.

Lennam 1965

T. N. S. Lennam. "Sir Edward Dering's Collection of Playbooks, 1619–1624." *Shakespeare Quarterly* 16.2 (1965): 145–53.

Lennam 1966

The Marriage between Wit and Wisdom. Ed. Trevor N. S. Lennam; checked by Arthur Brown. MSR. Oxford: Oxford University Press, 1966 [1971].

Lennam 1971

John Heywood. *The Play of the Weather*. Ed. T. N. S. Lennam. MSR. Oxford: Oxford University Press, 1971 [1977].

Lennam 1975

Trevor Lennam. *Sebastian Westcott, the Children of Paul's, and "The Marriage of Wit and Science."* Toronto and Buffalo: University of Toronto Press, 1975.

Leonard

A Critical Edition of Thomas Heywood's "The Wise Woman of Hogsdon." Ed. Michael H. Leonard. New York and London: Garland, 1980.

Leonidas

Eric Leonidas. "Theatrical Experiment and the Production of Knowledge in the Gray's Inn Revels." In *Early Modern Academic Drama*, ed. Jonathan Walker and Paul D. Streufert, 115–28. Farnham, UK, and Burlington, VT: Ashgate, 2008.

Lesser 1999

Zachary Lesser. "Walter Burre's *The Knight of the Burning Pestle.*" *English Literary Renaissance* 29.1 (1999): 22–43.

Lesser 2002

Zachary Lesser. "Mixed Government and Mixed Marriage in *A King and No King*: Sir Henry Neville Reads Beaumont and Fletcher." *ELH* 69.4 (2002): 947–77.

Lesser 2004

Zachary Lesser. *Renaissance Drama and the Politics of Publication: Readings in the English Book Trade.* Cambridge: Cambridge University Press, 2004.

Lesser 2006a

Thomas Dekker. *The Noble Spanish Soldier.* Ed. Zachary Lesser. Globe Quartos. London: Nick Hern Books, 2006.

Lesser 2006b

Zachary Lesser. "Typographic Nostalgia: Play-Reading, Popularity, and the Meanings of Black Letter." In *The Book of the Play: Playwrights, Stationers, and Readers in Early Modern England*, ed. Marta Straznicky, 99–126. Amherst and Boston: University of Massachusetts Press, 2006. Repr. in *New Ways of Looking at Old Texts* 4: *Papers of the Renaissance English Text Society 2002–2006*, ed. Michael Denbo, 279–93. MRTS 345. Tempe: ACMRS, 2008.

Lester

G. A. Lester, ed. *Three Late Medieval Morality Plays.* New Mermaids. London: Benn; New York: Norton, 1981. Repr. London: Black; New York: Norton, 2006.

Levenson 1978

Jill Levenson. "Anonymous Plays." In *The Predecessors of Shakespeare: A Survey and Bibliography of Recent Studies in English Renaissance Drama*, ed. Terence P. Logan and Denzell S. Smith, 230–39. Lincoln: University of Nebraska Press, 1978.

Levenson 1980

A Critical Edition of the Anonymous Elizabethan Play "The Weakest Goeth to the Wall." Ed. Jill L. Levenson. New York and London: Garland, 1980.

Levenson 1987
Jill L. Levenson. "Thomas Randolph." In *Dictionary of Literary Biography* 58: *Jacobean and Caroline Dramatists*, ed. Fredson Bowers, 231–40. Detroit: Gale, 1987.

Levenson 1998
Jill L. Levenson. "Editing *Romeo and Juliet*: 'A challenge[,] on my life'." In *New Ways of Looking at Old Texts 2: Papers of the Renaissance English Text Society, 1992–1996*, ed. W. Speed Hill, 61–70. Tempe: MRTS in conjunction with Renaissance English Text Society, Arizona State University, 1998.

Levenson & Gaines
William Shakespeare. *"Romeo and Juliet"* 1597. Ed. Jill L. Levenson and Barry Gaines. MSR. Oxford: Oxford University Press, 2000.

Lever 1965
William Shakespeare. *Measure for Measure*. Ed. J. W. Lever. Arden. London: Methuen, 1965.

Lever 1971a
Ben Jonson. *Every Man in His Humour: A Parallel-Text Edition of the 1601 Quarto and the 1616 Folio*. Ed. J. W. Lever. RRDS. Lincoln: University of Nebraska Press, 1971.

Lever 1971b
J. W. Lever. *The Tragedy of State*. London: Methuen, 1971.

Lever 1974a
J. W. Lever. *"The Wasp*: A Trial Flight." *Elizabethan Theatre* 4 (1974): 57–79.

Lever 1974b
The Wasp. Ed. J. W. Lever and G. R. Proudfoot. MSR. Oxford: Oxford University Press, 1974 [1976].

Levin 1966
Thomas Middleton. *Michaelmas Term*. Ed. Richard Levin. RRDS. Lincoln: University of Nebraska Press, 1966.

Levin 1989a
Harry Levin. "A Garden in Belmont: *The Merchant of Venice*, 5.1." In *Shakespeare and Dramatic Tradition: Essays in Honor of S. F. Johnson*, ed. W. R. Elton and William B. Long, 13–31. Newark, DE: University of Delaware Press; London and Toronto: Associated University Presses, 1989.

Levin 1989b
Richard Levin. "Women in the Renaissance Theatre Audience." *Shakespeare Quarterly* 40.2 (1989): 165–74.

Levin 1999
Richard Levin. "Tarlton in *The Famous History of Friar Bacon and Friar Bungay*." *Medieval and Renaissance Drama in England* 12 (1999): 84–98.

Levin 2001

Kate D. Levin. "Playing with Lyly: Theatrical Criticism and Non-Shakespearean Drama." *Research Opportunities in Renaissance Drama* 40 (2001): 25–53.

Levin 2002

Richard Levin. "The Longleat Manuscript and *Titus Andronicus*." *Shakespeare Quarterly* 53.3 (2002): 323–40.

Levine

A Critical Edition of Thomas Middleton's "The Widow." Ed. Robert Trager Levine. Salzburg Studies in English Literature, Jacobean Drama Series 56. Salzburg: Institut für Englische Sprache, Universität Salzburg, 1975.

Levinson & Proudfoot

The Famous History of Captain Thomas Stukeley. Ed. Judith C. Levinson and Richard Proudfoot. MSR. Oxford: Oxford University Press, 1970 [1975].

Levy 1995

Fritz Levy. "The Theatre and the Court in the 1590s." In *The Reign of Elizabeth I: Court and Culture in the Last Decade*, ed. John Guy, 274–300. Cambridge: Cambridge University Press in association with the Folger Institute, 1995.

Levy 2000

F. J. Levy. "Staging the News." In *Print, Manuscript & Performance: The Changing Relations of the Media in Early Modern England*, ed. Arthur F. Marotti and Michael D. Bristol, 252–78. Columbus: Ohio State University Press, 2000.

Lewalski

Barbara K. Lewalski. "Mary Wroth's *Love's Victory* and Pastoral Tragicomedy." In *Reading Mary Wroth: Representing Alternatives in Early Modern England*, ed. Naomi J. Miller and Gary Waller, 88–108. Knoxville: University of Tennessee Press, 1991.

Liddie

An Old-Spelling, Critical Edition of "The History of the Two Maids of More-clack." Ed. Alexander S. Liddie. New York and London: Garland, 1979.

Lidh

Todd M. Lidh. "'To know the author were some ease of grief': Ben Jonson's Lost Play." *Ben Jonson Journal* 17.1 (2010): 60–75.

Limon 1986

Jerzy Limon. *Dangerous Matter: English Drama and Politics in 1623/24.* Cambridge: Cambridge University Press, 1986.

Limon 1990

Jerzy Limon. *The Masque of Stuart Culture.* Newark, DE: University of Delaware Press; London and Toronto: Associated University Presses, 1990.

Lindley 2002
William Shakespeare. *The Tempest.* Ed. David Lindley. New Cambridge Shakespeare. Cambridge: Cambridge University Press, 2002.

Lindley 2006
David Lindley. *Shakespeare and Music.* Arden Critical Companions. London: Thomson Learning, 2006.

Lindley 2009
David Lindley. "Blackfriars, Music and Masque: Theatrical Contexts of the Plays." In *The Cambridge Companion to Shakespeare's Last Plays*, ed. Catherine M. S. Alexander, 29–45. Cambridge: Cambridge University Press, 2009.

Linthicum
Marie Channing Linthicum. *Costume in the Drama of Shakespeare and His Contemporaries.* Oxford: Clarendon Press, 1936. Repr. New York: Russell and Russell, 1963.

Lister
A Critical Edition of John Fletcher's Comedy "The Wild-Goose Chase." Ed. Rota Herzberg Lister. New York and London: Garland, 1980.

Littledale & Greg
Thomas Dekker. *The Welsh Embassador.* Ed. H. Littledale and W. W. Greg. MSR. Oxford: Oxford University Press, 1920 [1921].

Littleton
"Sir Clyomon and Clamydes": A Critical Edition. Ed. Betty J. Littleton. The Hague and Paris: Mouton, 1968.

Livingston
"The Woman's Prize" by John Fletcher. Ed. Meg Powers Livingston. MSR. Manchester: Manchester University Press for the Malone Society; New York: Palgrave, 2007 [2008].

Lloyd 1927
Bertram Lloyd. "*The Noble Spanish Soldier* and *The Welsh Embassador.*" *Review of English Studies* 3 (1927): 304–07.

Lloyd 1945
Bertram Lloyd. "The Authorship of *The Welsh Embassador.*" *Review of English Studies* 21 (1945): 192–201.

Lloyd 1952
Bertram Lloyd. "The Authorship of *The Valiant Welshman.*" *Notes and Queries* 197.20 (1952): 425–27.

Lloyd 2005
William Lloyd. "John Webster and *The London Prodigal*: New Sources for *The Devil's Law-case.*" *Research Opportunities in Medieval and Renaissance Drama* 44 (2005): 75–102.

Lockwood
Tom Lockwood. Revised introduction to *Arden of Faversham*. Ed. Martin White. 2nd ed. New Mermaids. London: Black, 2007.

Loewenstein
Joseph Loewenstein. "The Script in the Marketplace." *Representations* 12 (1985): 101–14.

Loftis
John Loftis. *Renaissance Drama in England and Spain: Topical Allusion and History Plays*. Princeton: Princeton University Press, 1987.

Logan & Smith
Terence P. Logan and Denzell S. Smith. "Other Dramatists." In *The Later Jacobean and Caroline Dramatists: A Survey and Bibliography of Recent Studies in English Renaissance Drama*, ed. eidem, 228–59. Lincoln and London: University of Nebraska Press, 1978.

Loloi
Robert Baron. *Mirza, A Tragedy*. In *Two Seventeenth-Century Plays*. Ed. Parvin Loloi. Vol. 2. Salzburg, Oxford and Portland: Institut für Anglistik und Amerikanistik, Universität Salzburg, 1998.

Lomax 1987
Marion Lomax. *Stage Images and Traditions: Shakespeare to Ford*. Cambridge: Cambridge University Press, 1987.

Lomax 1995
John Ford. *The Lover's Melancholy, The Broken Heart, 'Tis Pity She's a Whore, Perkin Warbeck ['Tis Pity She's a Whore and Other Plays* printed on the book cover]. Ed. Marion Lomax. Oxford Drama Library. Oxford: Clarendon Press, 1995.

Long 1971
John H. Long. *Shakespeare's Use of Music: The Histories and Tragedies*. Gainesville: University of Florida Press, 1971.

Long 1980
John H. Long. "The Music in Percy's Play Manuscripts." *Renaissance Papers* (1980): 39–44.

Long 1985a
William B. Long. "'A bed / for woodstock': A Warning for the Unwary." *Medieval and Renaissance Drama in England* 2 (1985): 91–118.

Long 1985b
William B. Long. "Stage-Directions: A Misinterpreted Factor in Determining Textual Provenance." *TEXT* 2 (1985): 121–37.

Long 1989
William B. Long. "*John a Kent and John a Cumber*: An Elizabethan Playbook and Its Implications." In *Shakespeare and Dramatic Tradition: Essays in Honor of S. F. Johnson*, ed. W. R. Elton and idem, 125–43. Newark, DE: University of Delaware Press; London and Toronto: Associated University Presses, 1989.

Long 1999
William B. Long. "'Precious Few': English Manuscript Playbooks." In *A Companion to Shakespeare*, ed. David Scott Kastan, 414–33. Oxford: Blackwell, 1999.

Long 2005
William B. Long. "Dulwich MS. XX, *The Telltale*: Clues to Provenance." *Medieval and Renaissance Drama in England* 17 (2005): 180–204.

Longstaffe 2002
Stephen Longstaffe. *A Critical Edition of "The Life and Death of Jack Straw" 1594*. Mellen Critical Editions and Translations 9. Lewiston, Queenston, and Lampeter: Edwin Mellen Press, 2002.

Longstaffe 2006
Stephen Longstaffe. "The Commons Will Revolt: *Woodstock* after the Peasants' Revolt." In *Shakespeare's Histories and Counter-Histories*, ed. Dermot Cavanagh, Stuart Hampton-Reeves, and idem, 135–51. Manchester: Manchester University Press; New York: Palgrave, 2006.

Loomba 1989
Ania Loomba. *Gender, Race, Renaissance Drama*. Manchester: Manchester University Press; New York: St. Martin's Press, 1989.

Loomba 2002
Ania Loomba. *Shakespeare, Race and Colonialism*. Oxford: Oxford University Press, 2002.

Lopez 2003
Jeremy Lopez. *Theatrical Convention and Audience Response in Early Modern Drama*. Cambridge: Cambridge University Press, 2003.

Lopez 2010
Jeremy Lopez. "Success the Whitefriars Way: *Ram Alley* and the Negative Force of Acting." *Renaissance Drama* n.s. 38 (2010): 199–224.

Lordi 1964
George Chapman. *Bussy D'Ambois*. Ed. Robert J. Lordi. RRDS. Lincoln: University of Nebraska Press, 1964.

Lordi 1977
George Chapman. *The Revenge of Bussy D'Ambois*. Ed. Robert J. Lordi. Salzburg: Institut für Englische Sprache und Literatur, Universität Salzburg, 1977.

Louis

Cameron Louis, ed. *Sussex*. REED. Toronto and Buffalo: Brepols and the University of Toronto Press, 2000.

Love 1993

Harold Love. *Scribal Publication in Seventeenth-Century England*. Oxford: Clarendon Press, 1993.

Love 2010

Genevieve Love. "Performance Criticism Without Performance: The Study of Non-Shakespearean Drama." In *New Directions in Renaissance Drama and Performance Studies*, ed. Sarah Werner, 131–46. London and New York: Palgrave Macmillan, 2010.

Loxley

James Loxley. *The Complete Critical Guide to Ben Jonson*. London and New York: Routledge, 2002.

Luckyj 1996

John Webster. *The White Devil*. Ed. Christina Luckyj. 2nd ed. New Mermaids. London: Black, 1996.

Luckyj 2008

John Webster. *The White Devil*. Ed. Christina Luckyj. 3rd ed. New Mermaids. London: Black, 2008.

Lull 1999

William Shakespeare. *King Richard III*. Ed. Janis Lull. Cambridge: Cambridge University Press, 1999.

Lull 2009

William Shakespeare. *King Richard III: Updated Edition*. Ed. Janis Lull. Cambridge: Cambridge University Press, 2009.

Lunney

Ruth Lunney. *Marlowe and the Popular Tradition: Innovation in the English Drama before 1595*. Revels Plays Companion Library. Manchester: Manchester University Press; New York: Palgrave, 2002.

Lyall

David Lindsay. *Ane Satyre of the Thrie Estaitis*. Ed. Roderick Lyall. Edinburgh: Canongate, 1989. Repr. 1992.

Lynch 1926

Kathleen M. Lynch. *The Social Mode of Restoration Comedy*. New York: Macmillan, 1926.

Lynch 2009

Henry Burkhead. *A Tragedy of Cola's Furie, or Lirenda's Miserie*. Ed. Angelina Lynch. Dublin: Four Courts Press, 2009.

Lyne
Raphael Lyne. *Shakespeare's Late Work*. Oxford Shakespeare Topics. Oxford: Oxford University Press, 2007.

MacDonald 1940
"Arden of Feversham" 1592. Ed. Hugh MacDonald. MSR. Oxford: Oxford University Press, 1940 [1947].

MacDonald 1999
Joyce Green MacDonald. "Marlowe's Ganymede." In *Enacting Gender on the English Renaissance Stage*, ed. Viviana Comensoli and Anne Russell, 97–113. Urbana and Chicago: University of Illinois Press, 1999.

Mace
David Lindsay. *The Three Estates, in a New English Version by Nigel Mace*. Aldershot, UK, and Brookfield, VT: Ashgate, 1998.

MacIntyre 1992
Jean MacIntyre. *Costumes and Scripts in the Elizabethan Theatres*. Edmonton: University of Alberta Press, 1992.

MacIntyre 1996
Jean MacIntyre. "Production Resources at the Whitefriars Playhouse, 1609–1612." *Early Modern Literary Studies* 2.3 (1996). http://purl.oclc.org/emls/02–3/maciwhit.html.

MacLean
Gerald MacLean. *Looking East: English Writing and the Ottoman Empire before 1800*. Basingstoke, UK, and New York: Palgrave Macmillan, 2007.

Macray
"The Pilgrimage to Parnassus" with "The Two Parts of the Return from Parnassus": Three Comedies Performed in St. John's College Cambridge A.D. MDXCVII-MDCI. Ed. William Dunn Macray. Oxford: Clarendon Press, 1886.

Madelaine 1988
Richard Madelaine. "'Sensationalism' and 'Melodrama' in Ford's Plays." In *John Ford: Critical Re-Visions*, ed. Michael Neill, 29–53. Cambridge: Cambridge University Press, 1988.

Madelaine 1998
Richard Madelaine. *Antony and Cleopatra*. Shakespeare in Production. Cambridge: Cambridge University Press, 1998.

Maguire 1986
Laurie E. Maguire. "A Stage Property in *A Larum for London*." *Notes and Queries* 33.3 (1986): 371–73.

Maguire 1992
Nancy Klein Maguire. *Regicide and Restoration: English Tragicomedy, 1660–1671*. Cambridge: Cambridge University Press, 1992.

Maguire 1996
Laurie E. Maguire. *Shakespearean Suspect Texts: The "Bad" Quartos and Their Contexts.* Cambridge: Cambridge University Press, 1996.

Maguire 1999a
Laurie E. Maguire. "(Mis)diagnosing Memorial Reconstruction in *John of Bordeaux.*" *Medieval and Renaissance Drama in England* 11 (1999): 114–28.

Maguire 1999b
Laurie E. Maguire. "The Printer and Date of Q4 of *A Looking Glass for London and England.*" *Studies in Bibliography* 52 (1999): 155–60.

Maidment & Logan 1872
The Dramatic Works of Sir William D'Avenant. Ed. James Maidment and W. H. Logan. 5 vols. Edinburgh: William Patterson; London: H. Sotheran, 1872–74. Repr. New York: Benjamin Blom, 1968.

Maidment & Logan 1879
The Dramatic Works of John Tatham. Ed. James Maidment and W. H. Logan. Edinburgh: William Paterson; London: H. Sotheran, 1879. Repr. New York: Benjamin Blom, 1967.

Malcolmson
Cristina Malcolmson. "'As Tame as the Ladies': Politics and Gender in *The Changeling.*" *English Literary Renaissance* 20.2 (1990): 320–39.

Malone
Edmond Malone. *Supplement to the Edition of Shakespeare's Plays Published in 1778 by S. Johnson and G. Stevens . . . with Notes by the Editor [Edmond Malone] and Others.* 2 vols. London: C. Bathhurst, W. Strahan, 1780.

Mandel
George Mandel. "*Julius Caesar* and *Caesar's Revenge*, Yet Again." *Notes and Queries* 59.4 (2012): 534–36.

Manley 1968
George Chapman. *All Fools.* Ed. Frank Manley. RRDS. Lincoln: University of Nebraska Press, 1968.

Manley 2001
Lawrence Manley. "Playing with Fire: Immolation in the Repertory of Strange's Men." *Early Theatre* 4 (2001): 115–29.

Manley 2009
Lawrence Manley. "Motives for Patronage: The Queen's Men at New Park, October 1588." In *Locating the Queen's Men, 1583–1603: Material Practices and Conditions of Playing*, ed. Helen Ostovich, Holger Schott Syme, and Andrew Griffin, 51–64. Farnham, UK, and Burlington, VT: Ashgate, 2009.

Manly
John Matthews Manly. *Specimens of the Pre-Shaksperean Drama*. 2 vols. Boston: Ginn, 1897. Repr. New York: Dover, 1967.

Mann 1991
David Mann. *The Elizabethan Player: Contemporary Stage Representation*. London and New York: Routledge, 1991.

Mann 2008
David Mann. *Shakespeare's Women: Performance and Conception*. Cambridge: Cambridge University Press, 2008.

Mann 2010
David Mann. "Reinstating Shakespeare's Instrumental Music." *Early Theatre* 15.2 (2012): 67–91.

Manningham
The Diary of John Manningham of the Middle Temple, 1602–1603. Ed. Robert Parker Sorlien. Hanover, NH: University Press of New England for the University of Rhode Island, 1976.

Marcus 1986
Leah S. Marcus. *The Politics of Mirth: Jonson, Herrick, Milton, Marvell, and the Defense of Old Holiday Pastimes*. Chicago and London: University of Chicago Press, 1986.

Marcus 1996
Leah S. Marcus. *Unediting the Renaissance: Shakespeare, Marlowe, Milton*. London and New York: Routledge, 1996.

Marcus 2000
Leah S. Marcus. "Dramatic Experiments: Tudor Drama, 1490–1567." In *The Cambridge Companion to English Literature, 1500–1600*, ed. Arthur F. Kinney, 132–52. Cambridge: Cambridge University Press, 2000.

Marcus 2009
John Webster. *The Duchess of Malfi*. Ed. Leah S. Marcus. Arden Early Modern Drama. London: Black, 2009.

Marcus 2010
Leah S. Marcus. "The Shrew as Editor/Editing *Shrews*." In *Gender and Power in Shrew-Taming Narratives, 1500–1700*, ed. David Wootton and Graham Holderness, 84–100. Basingstoke, UK, and New York: Palgrave Macmillan, 2010.

Mares 1967
Ben Jonson. *The Alchemist*. Ed. F. H. Mares. Revels Plays. London: Methuen, 1967.

Mares 1988
William Shakespeare. *Much Ado about Nothing.* Ed. F. H. Mares. Cambridge: Cambridge University Press, 1988.

Margeson 1967
J. M. R. Margeson. *The Origins of English Tragedy.* Oxford: Clarendon Press, 1967.

Margeson 1988
George Chapman. *The Conspiracy and Tragedy of Charles Duke of Byron.* Ed. John Margeson. Revels Plays. Manchester: Manchester University Press; New York: St. Martin's Press, 1988.

Margeson 1990
William Shakespeare. *King Henry VIII.* Ed. John Margeson. Cambridge: Cambridge University Press, 1990.

Marino 2009
James J. Marino. "Adult Playing Companies 1613–1625." In *The Oxford Handbook of Early Modern Theatre*, ed. Richard Dutton, 88–103. Oxford: Oxford University Press, 2009.

Marino 2011
James J. Marino. *Owning William Shakespeare: The King's Men and Their Intellectual Property.* Philadelphia: University of Pennsylvania Press, 2011.

Marlow 2008
Christopher Marlow. "The Performance of Learning: University Drama at Oxford in 1566." *Cahiers Elisabéthains* 73 (2008): 1–7.

Marlow 2009
Christopher Marlow. "A Crisis of Friendship?: Representation and Experience in Two Late University Plays." *Shakespeare Studies* 37 (2009): 54–66.

Marotti
Arthur Marotti. *Manuscript, Print, and the English Renaissance Lyric.* Ithaca, NY and London: Cornell University Press, 1995.

Marsalek 2004
Karen Sawyer Marsalek. "'Doctrine Evangelicall' and Erasmus's *Paraphrases* in *The Resurrection of Our Lord.*" In *Tudor Drama before Shakespeare, 1485–1590: New Directions for Research, Criticism, and Pedagogy*, ed. Lloyd Edward Kermode, Jason Scott-Warren, and Martine van Elk, 35–66. Basingstoke, UK, and New York: Palgrave Macmillan, 2004.

Marsalek 2007
Karen Sawyer Marsalek. "'Awake your faith': English Resurrection Drama and *The Winter's Tale.*" In *"Bring furth the pagants": Essays in Early English Drama Presented to Alexandra F. Johnston*, ed. David N. Klausner and eadem, 271–91. Toronto, Buffalo, and London: University of Toronto Press, 2007.

Marshall
Tristan Marshall. *Theatre and Empire: Great Britain on the London Stages under James VI and I.* Manchester: Manchester University Press; New York: St. Martin's Press, 2000.

Martin 1991
"Edmond Ironside" and Anthony Brewer's "The Love-sick King." Ed. Randall Martin. New York and London: Garland, 1991.

Martin 2001
William Shakespeare. *Henry VI, Part Three.* Ed. Randall Martin. Oxford: Oxford University Press, 2001.

Marx
Joan C. Marx. "'Soft, Who Have We Here?': The Dramatic Technique of *The Old Wives Tale.*" *Renaissance Drama* n.s. 12 (1981): 117–43.

Massai
Sonia Massai. *Shakespeare and the Rise of the Editor.* Cambridge: Cambridge University Press, 2007.

Massey
Dawn Massey. *"Veritas filia Temporis*: Apocalyptic Polemics in the Drama of the English Reformation." *Comparative Drama* 32.1 (1998): 146–75.

Masten 1992
Jeffrey A. Masten. "Beaumont and/or Fletcher: Collaboration and the Interpretation of Renaissance Drama." *ELH* 59.2 (1992): 337–56.

Masten 1997
Jeffrey Masten. *Textual Intercourse: Collaboration, Authorship, and Sexualities in Renaissance Drama.* Cambridge: Cambridge University Press, 1997.

Masten 2002
Jeffrey Masten. "Living Arrangements, Writing Arrangements (Looking for Francis Beaumont)." *Elizabethan Theatre* 15 (2002): 39–64.

Masten 2006
Jeffrey Masten. "Editing Boys: The Performance of Genders in Print." In *From Performance to Print in Shakespeare's England*, ed. Peter Holland and Stephen Orgel, 113–34. Basingstoke, UK, and New York: Palgrave Macmillan, 2006.

Masten 2007a
Jeffrey Masten, ed. *An/The Old Law.* In *Thomas Middleton: The Collected Works*, gen. eds. Gary Taylor and John Lavagnino. Oxford: Clarendon Press, 2007.

Masten 2007b
Jeffrey Masten, ed. *An/The Old Law*. In *Thomas Middleton and Early Modern Textual Culture: A Companion to the Collected Works*, gen. eds. Gary Taylor and John Lavagnino. Oxford: Clarendon Press, 2007.

Matar
Nabil Matar. *Islam in Britain, 1558–1685*. Cambridge: Cambridge University Press, 1998.

Matson
The Wisdom of Doctor Dodypoll. Ed. M. N. Matson. MSR. Oxford: Oxford University Press, 1964 [1965].

Maus 1995
Katharine Eisaman Maus, ed. *Four Revenge Tragedies: The Spanish Tragedy, The Revenger's Tragedy, The Revenge of Bussy D'Ambois, The Atheist's Tragedy*. Oxford Drama Library. Oxford: Clarendon Press, 1995.

Maus 1997
Katharine Eisaman Maus. Introduction to *The Life of Timon of Athens*. In *The Norton Shakespeare*, ed. Stephen Greenblatt, Walter Cohen, Jean E. Howard, and eadem, 2245–51. New York and London: W. W. Norton, 1997.

Maxwell 1922
Baldwin Maxwell. "Wily Beguiled." *Studies in Philology* 19.2 (1922): 206–37.

Maxwell 1926
Baldwin Maxwell. "The Hungry Knave in the Beaumont and Fletcher Plays." *Philological Quarterly* 5 (1926): 299–305.

Maxwell 1939
Baldwin Maxwell. *Studies in Beaumont, Fletcher, and Massinger*. Chapel Hill: University of North Carolina Press, 1939.

Maxwell 1948
Baldwin Maxwell. "Middleton's *The Phoenix*." In *Joseph Quincy Adams Memorial Studies*, ed. James G. McManaway, Giles E. Dawson, and Edwin E. Willoughby, 743–53. Washington, DC: Folger Shakespeare Library, 1948.

Maxwell 1956
Baldwin Maxwell. *Studies in the Shakespeare Apocrypha*. New York: King's Crown Press of Columbia University, 1956.

May
Steven W. May. "*A Midsummer Night's Dream* and the Carey-Berkeley Wedding." *Renaissance Papers* (1983): 43–52.

Mayer
Jean-Christophe Mayer. *Shakespeare's Hybrid Faith: History, Religion and the Stage*. Basingstoke, UK, and New York: Palgrave Macmillan, 2006.

McCarthy 2008
Jeanne H. McCarthy. "'The Sanctuarie is become a plaiers stage': Chapel Stagings and Tudor 'Secular' Drama." *Medieval and Renaissance Drama in England* 21 (2008): 56–86.

McCarthy 2010
Jeanne H. McCarthy. "Skelton's *Magnificence* and the Monastic Playing Tradition: Implications for the First and Second Blackfriars." In *Thunder at a Playhouse: Essaying Shakespeare and the Early Modern Stage*, ed. Peter Kanelos and Matt Kozusko, 154–74. Selinsgrove, PA: Susquehanna University Press, 2010.

McClure
A Critical Edition of Richard Brome's "The Weeding of Covent Garden" and "The Sparagus Garden." Ed. Donald S. McClure. New York and London: Garland, 1980.

McDiarmid
M. P. McDiarmid. "*Philotus*: A Play of the Scottish Renaissance." *Forum for Modern Language Studies* 3.3 (1967): 223–35.

McDonald 1985
Russ McDonald. "High Seriousness and Popular Form: The Case of *The Maid of Honour.*" In *Philip Massinger: A Critical Reassessment*, ed. Douglas Howard, 83–116. Cambridge: Cambridge University Press, 1985.

McDonald 1988
Russ McDonald. *Shakespeare & Jonson, Jonson & Shakespeare.* Lincoln and London: University of Nebraska Press, 1988.

McDonald 2001
Russ McDonald. *The Bedford Companion to Shakespeare: An Introduction with Documents.* 2nd ed. Boston and New York: Bedford/St. Martin's, 2001.

McDonald 2003
Russ McDonald. "Fashion: Shakespeare and Beaumont and Fletcher." In *A Companion to Shakespeare's Works*, 4: *The Poems, Problem Comedies, Late Plays*, ed. Richard Dutton and Jean E. Howard, 150–74. Oxford and Malden, MA: Blackwell, 2003.

McEachern
William Shakespeare. *Much Ado about Nothing.* Ed. Claire McEachern. Arden 3. London: Thomson Learning, 2006.

McEvilla
Joshua J. McEvilla. "The Original Salisbury Court Players of Richard Brome's *The Antipodes.*" *Notes and Queries* 59.2 (2012): 168–71.

McGavin 2004
John J. McGavin. "Faith, Pastime, Performance and Drama in Scotland to 1603." In *The Cambridge History of British Theatre*, vol. 1: *Origins to 1660*, ed. Jane Milling and Peter Thomson, 70–86. Cambridge: Cambridge University Press, 2004.

McGavin 2007a
John J. McGavin. *Theatricality and Narrative in Medieval and Early Modern Scotland*. Aldershot, UK, and Burlington, VT: Ashgate, 2007.

McGavin 2007b
John J. McGavin. "Working Towards a Reformed Identity in Lindsay's *Satyre of the Thrie Estaitis*." In *Interludes and Early Modern Society: Studies in Gender, Power and Theatricality*, ed. Peter Happé and Wim Hüsken, 239–60. Amsterdam and New York: Rodopi, 2007.

McGee
C. E. McGee, ed. *The World Tossed at Tennis*. In *Thomas Middleton: The Collected Works*, gen. eds. Gary Taylor and John Lavagnino. Oxford: Clarendon Press, 2007.

McInnis
David McInnis. "Fortunatus and the 'Tree of Gowlden Apelles' in Henslowe's Inventory." *Notes and Queries* 58.2 (2011): 270–72.

McIntosh
Shona McIntosh. "Knighthoods, *Hamlet*, and the Date of George Chapman's *All Fools*." *Notes and Queries* 56.1 (2009): 64–67.

McJannet 1999a
Linda McJannet. "Bringing in a Persian." *Medieval and Renaissance Drama in England* 12 (1999): 236–67.

McJannet 1999b
Linda McJannet. *The Voice of Elizabethan Stage Directions: The Evolution of a Theatrical Code*. Newark, DE: University of Delaware Press; London: Associated University Presses, 1999.

McKenzie
Robert Tailor. *The Hogge Hath Lost His Pearl*. Ed. D. F. McKenzie. MSR. Oxford: Oxford University Press, 1967 [1972].

McKerrow 1908
"The Tragedy of Locrine," 1595. Ed. Ronald B. McKerrow. MSR. Oxford: Oxford University Press, 1908.

McKerrow 1911
"A Newe Interlude of Impacyente Poverte" from the Quarto of 1560. Ed. R. B. McKerrow. Materialien zur Kunde des älteren Englischen Dramas 33. Louvain: Uystpruyst, 1911.

McKerrow 1927
Ronald B. McKerrow. *An Introduction to Bibliography for Literary Students.* Oxford: Oxford University Press, 1927.

McKerrow & Greg
The Play of Patient Grissell. Ed. Ronald B. McKerrow and W. W. Greg. MSR. London: C. Whittingham, 1909.

McLaren
Margaret Anne McLaren. "An Unknown Continent: Lady Mary Wroth's Forgotten Pastoral Drama, 'Loves Victorie'." In *The Renaissance Englishwoman in Print: Counterbalancing the Canon*, ed. Anne M. Haselkorn and Betty S. Travitsky, 276–94. Amherst: University of Massachusetts Press, 1990.

McLuskie 1981
Kathleen McLuskie. "The Plays and the Playwrights: 1613–42." In *The Revels History of Drama in English*, vol. 4: *1613–1660*, ed. Philip Edwards, Gerald Eades Bentley, eadem, and Lois Potter, 127–258. London and New York: Methuen, 1981.

McLuskie 1988
Kathleen McLuskie. "'Language and Matter with a Fit of Mirth': Dramatic Construction in the Plays of John Ford." In *John Ford: Critical Re-Visions*, ed. Michael Neill, 97–127. Cambridge: Cambridge University Press, 1988.

McLuskie 1989
Kathleen McLuskie. *Renaissance Dramatists.* Feminist Readings Series. London: Harvester Wheatsheaf, 1989.

McLuskie 1992
Kathleen McLuskie. "'A Maidenhead, *Amintor*, at My Yeares': Chastity and Tragicomedy in the Fletcher Plays." In *The Politics of Tragicomedy: Shakespeare and After*, ed. Gordon McMullan and Jonathan Hope, 92–121. London and New York: Routledge, 1992.

McLuskie 1993
Kathleen McLuskie. "Politics and Dramatic Form in Early Modern Tragedy." In *Theatre and Government under the Early Stuarts*, ed. J. R. Mulryne and Margaret Shewring, 217–36. Cambridge: Cambridge University Press, 1993.

McLuskie 1994
Kathleen E. McLuskie. *Dekker and Heywood: Professional Dramatists.* New York: St. Martin's Press; Basingstoke, UK: Macmillan, 1994.

McLuskie 1999
Kathleen E. McLuskie. "Introduction" to *Plays on Women*, ed. eadem and David Bevington, 1–60. Revels Student Editions. Manchester: Manchester University Press; New York: St. Martin's Press, 1999.

McLuskie 2002
Kathleen McLuskie. "Dekker's Public and Private Theatre Collaborations." *Elizabethan Theatre* 15 (2002): 65–88.

McLuskie 2005
Kathleen McLuskie. "Figuring the Consumer for Early Modern Drama." In *Rematerializing Shakespeare: Authority and Representation on the Early Modern English Stage*, ed. Bryan Reynolds and William N. West, 186–206. Basingstoke, UK, and New York: Palgrave Macmillan, 2005.

McLuskie 2006
Kathleen E. McLuskie. "Politics and Aesthetic Pleasure in 1630s Theater." In *Localizing Caroline Drama: Politics and Economics of the Early Modern English Stage, 1625–1642*, ed. Adam Zucker and Alan B. Farmer, 43–68. Basingstoke, UK, and New York: Palgrave Macmillan, 2006.

McLuskie 2009
Kathleen E. McLuskie. *William Shakespeare: Macbeth*. Writers and Their Work. Horndon, UK: Northcote House, 2009.

McManaway 1945
James G. McManaway. "Latin Title-Page Mottoes as a Clue to Dramatic Authorship." *Library* 26.1 (1945): 28–36.

McManaway 1955
Dick of Devonshire. Ed. James G. and Mary R. McManaway. MSR. Oxford: Oxford University Press, 1955.

McMillin 1974
Scott McMillin. "The Book of Seneca in *The Spanish Tragedy*." *Studies in English Literature, 1500–1900* 14.2 (1974): 201–08.

McMillin 1987
Scott McMillin. *The Elizabethan Theatre and "The Book of Sir Thomas More."* Ithaca, NY, and London: Cornell University Press, 1987.

McMillin 1989
Scott McMillin. "*The Book of Sir Thomas More*: Dates and Acting Companies." In *Shakespeare and Sir Thomas More: Essays on the Play and Its Shakespearian Interest*, ed. T. H. Howard-Hill, 57–76. Cambridge: Cambridge University Press, 1989.

McMillin 1991
Scott McMillin. "Sussex's Men in 1594: The Evidence of *Titus Andronicus* and *The Jew of Malta*." *Theatre Survey* 32.2 (1991): 214–23.

McMillin 1992
Scott McMillin. "The Rose and the Swan." In *The Development of Shakespeare's Theater*, ed. John H. Astington, 159–83. New York: AMS Press, 1992.

McMillin 2001
William Shakespeare. *The First Quarto of "Othello."* Ed. Scott McMillin. Cambridge: Cambridge University Press, 2001.

McMillin 2005
Scott McMillin. "Shakespeare and the Chamberlain's Men in 1598." *Medieval and Renaissance Drama in England* 17 (2005): 205–15.

McMillin & MacLean
Scott McMillin and Sally-Beth MacLean. *The Queen's Men and Their Plays.* Cambridge: Cambridge University Press, 1998.

McMullan 1994
Gordon McMullan. *The Politics of Unease in the Plays of John Fletcher.* Amherst: University of Massachusetts Press, 1994.

McMullan 2000
William Shakespeare and John Fletcher. *King Henry VIII.* Ed. Gordon McMullan. Arden 3. London: Thomson Learning, 2000.

McMullan 2002
Gordon McMullan. Introduction to *The Island Princess* [by John Fletcher]*: This Edition Prepared for the Royal Shakespeare Company.* London: Nick Hern Books, 2002.

McMullan 2004
Gordon McMullan. "Fletcher, John (1579–1625)." In *ODNB* 20: 107–13.

McNeir
Waldo F. McNeir. "Robert Greene and *John of Bordeaux.*" *PMLA* 64.4 (1949): 781–801.

Meads
Chris Meads. *Banquets Set Forth: Banqueting in English Renaissance Drama.* Revels Plays Companion Library. Manchester: Manchester University Press; New York: Palgrave, 2001.

Meagher 1964
Anthony Munday. *The Downfall of Robert Earl of Huntingdon.* Ed. John C. Meagher. MSR. Oxford: Oxford University Press, 1964 [1965].

Meagher 1965
Anthony Munday. *The Death of Robert Earl of Huntingdon.* Ed. John C. Meagher. MSR. Oxford: Oxford University Press, 1965 [1967].

Meagher 1980
John Carney Meagher. *The Huntingdon Plays: A Critical Edition of "The Downfall and The Death of Robert, Earl of Huntingdon."* New York and London: Garland, 1980.

Meagher 2003
John C. Meagher. *Pursuing Shakespeare's Dramaturgy: Some Contexts, Resources, and Strategies in His Playmaking.* Madison and Teaneck, NJ: Fairleigh Dickinson University Press, 2003.

Mehl 1962
Dieter Mehl. "Beaumont und Fletchers *The Faithful Friends.*" *Anglia* 80.4 (1962): 417–24.

Mehl 1965
Dieter Mehl. *The Elizabethan Dumb Show: The History of a Dramatic Convention.* London: Methuen, 1965.

Mehl 1969
Dieter Mehl. "Emblems in English Renaissance Drama." *Renaissance Drama* 2 (1969): 39–57.

Mehl 2004
Dieter Mehl. "*The London Prodigal* as Jacobean City Comedy." In *Plotting Early Modern London: New Essays on Jacobean City Comedy*, ed. idem, Angela Stock, and Anne-Julia Zwierlein, 165–76. Aldershot, UK, and Burlington, VT: Ashgate, 2004.

Mekemson
A Critical, Modern-Spelling Edition of James Shirley's "The Opportunity." Ed. Mary J. Mekemson. New York and London: Garland, 1991.

Melchiori 1984
John Marston and others. *The Insatiate Countess.* Ed. Giorgio Melchiori. Revels Plays. Manchester: Manchester University Press, 1984.

Melchiori 1989
William Shakespeare. *The Second Part of King Henry IV.* Ed. Giorgio Melchiori. Cambridge: Cambridge University Press, 1989.

Melchiori 1998
King Edward III. Ed. Giorgio Melchiori. Cambridge: Cambridge University Press, 1998.

Melchiori 2000
William Shakespeare. *The Merry Wives of Windsor.* Ed. Giorgio Melchiori. Arden. Walton-on-Thames, UK: Thomas Nelson, 2000.

Melton
John Melton. *Astrologaster, or The Figure Caster.* [London, 1620]. Introduction by Hugh G. Dick. Los Angeles: William Andrews Clark Memorial Library, University of California, 1975.

Merchant 1978
Paul Merchant. "Thomas Heywood's Hand in *The Seven Champions of Christendom.*" *The Library*, 5th ser., 33.3 (1978): 226–30.

Merchant 1996
Thomas Heywood. *Three Marriage Plays: "The Wise-Woman of Hogsdon," "The English Traveller," "The Captives."* Ed. Paul Merchant. Revels Plays Companion Library. Manchester: Manchester University Press; New York: St. Martin's Press, 1996.

Meres
Francis Meres. *Palladis Tamia, Wit's Treasury, being the Second Part of Wit's Commonwealth.* London: P. Short for Cuthbert Burbie, 1598.

Merriam 2000
Thomas Merriam. "Marlowe and Nashe in *Dido Queen of Carthage.*" *Notes and Queries* 47.4 (2000): 425–28.

Merriam 2012
Thomas Merriam. "Unhouseled, Disappointed, Unaneled." *Notes and Queries* 59.1 (2012): 70–76.

Metz 1979
"The Two Merry Milkmaids" by J. C. (1620). Ed. G. Harold Metz. New York and London: Garland, 1979.

Metz 1989
Sources of Four Plays Ascribed to Shakespeare: "The Reign of King Edward III," "Sir Thomas More," "The History of Cardenio," "The Two Noble Kinsmen." Ed. G. Harold Metz. Columbia: University of Missouri Press, 1989.

Michel
Samuel Daniel. *The Tragedy of Philotas.* Ed. Laurence Michel. New Haven, Yale University Press, 1949.

Michie
Donald M. Michie, ed. *A Critical Edition of "The True Chronicle History of King Leir and His Three Daughters, Gonorill, Ragan and Cordella."* New York and London: Garland, 1991.

Miles 1942
Theodore Miles. "Place-Realism in a Group of Caroline Plays." *Review of English Studies* 18 (1942): 428–40.

Miles 1990
Rosalind Miles. *Ben Jonson: His Craft and Art.* Savage, MD: Barnes & Noble, 1990.

Milhous
Judith Milhous. "Polewheele, E. (1651?-1691?), playwright." *ODNB* 44: 741.

Milhous & Hume
Judith Milhous and Robert D. Hume. "New Light on English Acting Companies in 1646, 1648, and 1660." *Review of English Studies* 42.4 (1991): 487–509.

Mill

Anna J. Mill. "Representations of Lyndsay's *Satyre of the Thrie Estaitis*." *PMLA* 47.3 (1932): 636–51.

Miller 1998a

"*The Taming of A Shrew*": *The 1594 Quarto*. Ed. Stephen Roy Miller. New Cambridge Shakespeare. Cambridge: Cambridge University Press, 1998.

Miller 1998b

"*The Taming of A Shrew*" *1594*. Ed. Stephen Roy Miller. MSR. Oxford: Oxford University Press, 1998.

Miller 1988c

Stephen Miller. "*The Taming of a Shrew* and the Theories; or, 'Though this be badness, yet there is method in't'." In *Textual Formations and Reformations*, ed. Laurie E. Maguire and Thomas L. Berger, 251–63. Newark, DE: University of Delaware Press; London: Associated University Presses, 1988.

Miller & Forse

Erin Miller and James H. Forse. "The Failure to Be a 'Goode Husbande' in Thomas Heywood's *Edward IV* (*Parts I/II*) and *A Woman Killed with Kindness*." *Ben Jonson Journal* 18.2 (2011): 254–73.

Milling

Jane Milling. "The Development of a Professional Theatre, 1540–1660." In *The Cambridge History of British Theatre*, vol. 1: *Origins to 1660*, ed. eadem and Peter Thomson, 139–77. Cambridge: Cambridge University Press, 2004.

Mills 1951

Peter Hausted. *The Rival Friends*. Ed. Laurens J. Mills. Indiana University Publications, Humanities Series 23. Bloomington: Indiana University Press, 1951.

Mills 1959

L. J. Mills. "The Acting in University Comedy of Early Seventeenth-Century England." In *Studies in the English Renaissance Drama*, ed. Josephine W. Bennett, Oscar Cargill, and Vernon Hall Jr., 212–30. New York: New York University Press, 1959.

Mills 1983

David Mills. "Drama and Folk-Ritual." In *The Revels History of Drama in English*. 1: *Medieval Drama*, ed. A. C. Cawley, Marion Jones, Peter F. McDonald, and idem, 122–51. London and New York: Methuen, 1983.

Mills 1995

David Mills. "The Theaters of *Everyman*." In *From Page to Performance: Essays in Early English Drama*, ed. John A. Alford, 127–49. East Lansing: Michigan State University Press, 1995.

Mills 1996
David Mills. "Anglo-Dutch Theatres: Problems and Possibilities." *Medieval English Theatre* 18 (1996): 85–98.

Mills 2007
David Mills. "Wit to Woo: The Wit Interludes." In *Interludes and Early Modern Society: Studies in Gender, Power and Theatricality*, ed. Peter Happé and Wim Hüsken, 163–90. Amsterdam and New York: Rodopi, 2007.

Mincoff
Marco Mincoff. "The Authorship of *The Two Noble Kinsmen*." *English Studies* 33.1–6 (1952): 97–115.

Miola 1999
Robert S. Miola. "Creating the Author: Jonson's Latin Epigraphs." *Ben Jonson Journal* 6 (1999): 35–48.

Miola 2000
Ben Jonson. *Every Man in His Humor.* Ed. Robert S. Miola. Revels Plays. Manchester: Manchester University Press; New York: St. Martin's Press, 2000.

Miola 2002
Robert S. Miola. "Euripides at Gray's Inn: Gascoigne and Kinwelmersh's *Jocasta*." In *The Female Tragic Hero in English Renaissance Drama*, ed. Naomi Conn Liebler, 33–50. New York: Palgrave, 2002.

Miola 2004
William Shakespeare. *Macbeth: A Norton Critical Edition.* Ed. Robert S. Miola. New York and London: Norton, 2004.

Miscellanea
Miscellanea Antiqua Anglicana; or A Select Collection of Curious Tracts, Illustrative of the History, Literature, Manners, and Biography of the English Nation. Vol. 1. London: Robert Triphook, 1816.

Mitchell
Thomas Neale. *"The Warde" by Thomas Neale.* Ed. John Arthur Mitchell. Lancaster, PA: Lancaster Press, 1937.

Mithal 1960
H. S. D. Mithal. "The Authorship of 'Fair Em' and 'Martin Mar-Sixtus'." *Notes and Queries* 7.1 (1960): 8–10.

Mithal 1988
An Edition of Robert Wilson's "Three Ladies of London" and "Three Lords and Three Ladies of London." Ed. H. S. D. Mithal. New York and London: Garland, 1988.

Moeslein
M. E. Moeslein, ed. *The Plays of Henry Medwall: A Critical Edition.* New York and London: Garland, 1981.

Monie

A Critical Edition of Robert Davenport's "The City–Night-Cap." Ed. Willis J. Monie. New York and London: Garland, 1979.

Monta 1997

Susannah Brietz Monta. "Marital Discourse and Political Discord: Reconsidering *Perkin Warbeck.*" *Studies in English Literature, 1500–1900* 37.2 (1997): 391–413.

Monta 2005

Susannah Brietz Monta. *Martyrdom and Literature in Early Modern England.* Cambridge: Cambridge University Press, 2005.

Montgomery

William Montgomery. "The Original Staging of *The First Part of the Contention* (1594)." *Shakespeare Survey* 41 (1988): 13–22.

Montrose

Louis Adrian Montrose. *The Purpose of Playing: Shakespeare and the Cultural Politics of the Elizabethan Theatre.* Chicago and London: University of Chicago Press, 1996.

Mooney 1980

Michael E. Mooney. "'The Common Sight' and Dramatic Form: Rowley's Embedded Jig in *A Faire Quarrel.*" *Studies in English Literature, 1500–1900* 20.2 (1980): 305–23.

Mooney 1986

Michael E. Mooney. "'Framing' as Collaborative Technique: Two Middleton-Rowley Plays." In *Drama in the Renaissance: Comparative and Critical Essays,* ed. Clifford Davidson, C. J. Gianakaris, and John H. Stroupe, 300–14. New York: AMS Press, 1986.

Moore 1999

Helen Moore. "Jonson, Dekker, and the Discourse of Chivalry." *Medieval and Renaissance Drama in England* 12 (1999): 121–65.

Moore 2002

John Ford. *Love's Sacrifice.* Ed. A. T. Moore. Revels Plays. Manchester: Manchester University Press; New York: Palgrave, 2002.

Moore 2006

Helen Moore, ed. *"Guy of Warwick" 1661.* MSR. Manchester: Manchester University Press for the Malone Society, 2006 [2007].

Morash

Christopher Morash. *A History of Irish Theatre.* Cambridge: Cambridge University Press, 2002.

Morgan 1911
Louise B. Morgan. "The Latin University Drama." *Shakespeare Jahrbuch* 47 (1911): 69–91.

Morgan 1966
June J. Morgan. "Toward a Textual Study of *The Wit of a Woman*." *Emporia State Research Studies* 15.1 (1966): 8–17.

Morillo
James Shirley's "The Humorous Courtier." Ed. Marvin Morillo. New York and London: Garland, 1979.

Morley
Carol A. Morley, ed. *The Plays and Poems of William Heminge*. Madison and Teaneck, NJ: Fairleigh Dickinson University Press, 2006.

Morrill
John Morrill. "Charles I, Cromwell and Cicero (A Response to Dale B. J. Randall)." *Connotations* 1.1 (1991): 96–102.

Morris 1981
William Shakespeare. *The Taming of the Shrew*. Ed. Brian Morris. Arden 2. London: Methuen, 1981.

Morris 1987
Brian Morris. "Elizabethan and Jacobean Drama." In *The New History of English Literature*, vol. 3: *English Drama to 1710*, ed. Christopher Ricks, 55–102. New York: Peter Bedrick Books, 1987.

Morton 1988
A Critical Edition of Mildmay Fane's "Vertues Triumph" (1644). Ed. Gerald William Morton. New York: Peter Lang, 1988.

Morton 1991
Gerald W. Morton. *A Biography of Mildmay Fane, Second Earl of Westmorland, 1601–1666: The Unknown Cavalier*. Studies in British History 22. Lewiston, Queenston, and Lampeter: Edwin Mellen Press, 1991.

Moseley
Charles Moseley. "The Literary and Dramatic Contexts of the Last Plays." In *The Cambridge Companion to Shakespeare's Late Plays*, ed. Catherine M. S. Alexander, 47–69. Cambridge: Cambridge University Press, 2009.

Mowat 1981
Barbara A. Mowat. "'The Getting up of the Spectacle': The Role of the Visual on the Elizabethan Stage, 1576–1600." *The Elizabethan Theatre* 9 (1981): 60–76.

Mowat 1997
Barbara A. Mowat. "The Theater and Literary Culture." In *A New History of Early English Drama*, ed. John D. Cox and David Scott Kastan, 213–30. New York: Columbia University Press, 1997.

MRTS
Medieval & Renaissance Texts & Studies

MSR
Malone Society Reprints

Muir 1960
Kenneth Muir. *Shakespeare as Collaborator.* London: Methuen, 1960.

Muir 1982
William Shakespeare. *Troilus and Cressida.* Ed. Kenneth Muir. Oxford and New York: Oxford University Press, 1982.

Muir & Wilson
"The Life and Death of Jack Straw," 1594. Ed. Kenneth Muir and F. P. Wilson. MSR. Oxford: Oxford University Press, 1957.

Mulholland 1977
P. A. Mulholland. "The Date of *The Roaring Girl.*" *Review of English Studies* n.s. 28 (1977): 18–31.

Mulholland 1987
Thomas Middleton and Thomas Dekker. *The Roaring Girl.* Ed. Paul A. Mulholland. Revels Plays. Manchester: Manchester University Press, 1987.

Mulholland 2007
The Patient Man and the Honest Whore. Ed. Paul Mulholland. In *Thomas Middleton: The Collected Works,* gen. eds. Gary Taylor and John Lavagnino. Oxford: Clarendon Press, 2007.

Mullaney
Steven Mullaney. "Mourning and Misogyny: *Hamlet, The Revenger's Tragedy,* and the Final Progress of Elizabeth I, 1600–1607." *Shakespeare Quarterly* 45.2 (1994): 139–62.

Mullini
Roberta Mullini. *"Impatient Poverty*: The Intertextual Game of Satire." In *Interludes and Early Modern Society: Studies in Gender, Power and Theatricality,* ed. Peter Happé and Wim Hüsken, 291–314. Amsterdam and New York: Rodopi, 2007.

Mulryne 1975a
J. R. Mulryne. "Annotations in Some Copies of *Two New Playes by Thomas Middleton,* 1657." *The Library,* 5th ser., 30.3 (1975): 217–21.

Mulryne 1975b

Thomas Middleton. *Women Beware Women*. Ed. J. R. Mulryne. Revels Plays. Manchester: Manchester University Press, 1975.

Mulryne 1989

Thomas Kyd. *The Spanish Tragedy*. Ed. J. R. Mulryne. 2nd ed. New Mermaids. 1989; rpt. London: Black, 2003.

Mulryne 2009

Thomas Kyd. *The Spanish Tragedy*. Ed. J. R. Mulryne, intro. and notes Andrew Gurr. 3rd ed. New Mermaids. London: Black, 2009.

Mulvihill

Maureen E. Mulvihill. "A Feminist Link in the Old Boys' Network: The Cosseting of Katherine Philips." In *Curtain Calls: British and American Women and the Theater, 1660–1820*, ed. Mary Anne Schofield and Cecilia Macheski, 71–104. Athens, OH: Ohio University Press, 1991.

Munro 2005

Lucy Munro. *Children of the Queen's Revels: A Jacobean Theatre Repertory*. Cambridge: Cambridge University Press, 2005.

Munro 2006a

Edward Sharpham. *The Fleer*. Ed. Lucy Munro. Globe Quartos. London: Nick Hern Books, 2006.

Munro 2006b

Lucy Munro. "*The Knight of the Burning Pestle* and Generic Experimentation." In *Early Modern English Drama: A Critical Companion*, ed. Garrett A. Sullivan Jr., Patrick Cheney, and Andrew Hadfield, 189–99. New York and Oxford: Oxford University Press, 2006.

Munro 2006c

Lucy Munro. "Popular Theatre and the Red Bull." *Early Theatre* 9.2 (2006): 99–113.

Munro 2006d

Lucy Munro. "Reading Printed Comedy: Edward Sharpham's *The Fleer*." In *The Book of the Play: Playwrights, Stationers, and Readers in Early Modern England*, ed. Marta Straznicky, 39–58. Amherst and Boston: University of Massachusetts Press, 2006.

Munro 2009

Ian Munro. "Page Wit and Puppet-like Wealth: Orality and Print in *Three Lords and Three Ladies of London*." In *Locating the Queen's Men, 1583–1603: Material Practices and Conditions of Playing*, ed. Helen Ostovich, Holger Schott Syme, and Andrew Griffin, 109–22. Farnham, UK, and Burlington, VT: Ashgate, 2009.

Munro 2010a

Ian Munro. "Knightly Complements: *The Malcontent* and the Matter of Wit." *English Literary Renaissance* 40.2 (2010): 215–37.

Munro 2010b

John Fletcher. *The Tamer Tamed.* Ed. Lucy Munro. New Mermaids. London: Black, 2010.

Munro 2010c

Lucy Munro. "The Whitefriars Theatre and the Children's Companies." In *Ben Jonson in Context*, ed. Julie Sanders, 116–23. Cambridge: Cambridge University Press, 2010.

Murdoch

Brian O. Murdoch. "The Cornish Medieval Drama." In *The Cambridge Companion to Medieval English Theatre*, ed. Richard Beadle, 211–39. Cambridge: Cambridge University Press, 1994.

Murphy 1971

J. L. Murphy, ed. "A Seventeenth-Century Play from the Essex Record Office." Malone Society *Collections IX*, 30–51. Oxford: Oxford University Press, 1971 [1977].

Murphy 1984

John L. Murphy. *Darkness and Devils: Exorcism and "King Lear."* Athens, OH: Ohio University Press, 1984.

Murphy 2003

Andrew Murphy. *Shakespeare in Print: A History and Chronology of Shakespeare Publishing.* Cambridge: Cambridge University Press, 2003.

Murphy 2009

Donna N. Murphy. "*Locrine, Selimus*, Robert Greene, and Thomas Lodge." *Notes and Queries* 56.4 (2009): 559–63.

Murphy 2012a

Donna N. Murphy. "*George a Greene* and Robert Greene." *Notes and Queries* 59.1 (2012): 53–58.

Murphy 2012b

Donna N. Murphy. "*The Life and Death of Jack Straw* and George Peele." *Notes and Queries* 59.4 (2012): 513–18.

Murray 1983

Timothy Murray. "From Foul Sheets to Legitimate Model: Antitheater, Text, Ben Jonson." *New Literary History* 14.3 (1983): 641–64.

Murray 1991

"The Tragedye of Solyman and Perseda": Edited from the Original Texts with Introduction and Notes. Ed. John J. Murray. New York and London: Garland, 1991.

Myhill
Nova Myhill. "Making Death a Miracle: Audience and the Genres of Martyr-dom in Dekker and Massinger's *The Virgin Martyr.*" *Early Theatre* 7.2 (2004): 9–31.

Nason
Arthur Huntington Nason. *James Shirley, Dramatist: A Biographical and Criti-cal Study.* New York: A. H. Nason, 1915. Repr. New York: Benjamin Blom, 1967.

Needham
William Cavendish. *A Pleasante & Merrye Humor off a Roge.* Ed. Francis Need-ham. *Welbeck Miscellany* 1 (1933): 1–38.

Neely
Carol Thomas Neely. "Madness and Theatricality in Middleton." In *Thomas Mid-dleton in Context*, ed. Suzanne Gossett, 306–13. Cambridge: Cambridge University Press, 2011.

Neill 1978
Michael Neill. "'Wits Most Accomplished Senate': The Audience of the Caro-line Private Theaters." *Studies in English Literature, 1500–1900* 18.2 (1978): 341–60.

Neill 1985
Michael Neill. "'Exeunt with a Dead March': Funeral Pageantry on the Shake-spearean Stage." In *Pageantry in the Shakespearean Theater*, ed. David M. Bergeron, 153–93. Athens, GA: University of Georgia Press, 1985.

Neill 1988
Michael Neill. "'What Strange Riddle's This?': Deciphering *'Tis Pity She's a Whore.*" In *John Ford: Critical Re-Visions*, ed. idem, 153–79. Cambridge: Cambridge University Press, 1988.

Neill 1994
William Shakespeare. *The Tragedy of Antony and Cleopatra.* Ed. Michael Neill. Oxford: Clarendon, 1994.

Neill 2000a
Michael Neill. "Broken English and Broken Irish: Nation, Language, and the Optic of Power in Shakespeare's Histories." In *Putting History to the Ques-tion: Power, Politics, and Society in English Renaissance Drama*, 339–72. New York: Columbia University Press, 2000.

Neill 2000b
Michael Neill. "'Material Flames': Romance, Empire, and Mercantile Fantasy in John Fletcher's *Island Princess.*" In *Putting History to the Question: Power, Pol-itics, and Society in English Renaissance Drama*, 311–38. New York: Columbia University Press, 2000.

Neill 2004

Michael Neill. "Ford, John (*bap.* 1586, *d.* 1639x53?)." In *ODNB* 20: 331–36.

Neill 2006a

Thomas Middleton and William Rowley. *The Changeling.* Ed. Michael Neill. 3rd ed. New Mermaids. London: Black, 2006.

Neill 2006b

William Shakespeare. *Othello, The Moor of Venice.* Ed. Michael Neill. Oxford: Clarendon Press, 2006.

Neill 2010

Philip Massinger. *The Renegado.* Ed. Michael Neill. Arden Early Modern Drama. London: Methuen (Black), 2010.

Neill & Jackson

Michael Neill and MacDonald P. Jackson. "Morphew, Leprosy, and the Date of Marston's *Antonio and Mellida.*" *Notes and Queries* 45.3 (1998): 358–60.

Nelles

William Nelles. "Cosmo Manuche's Castle Ashby Plays as Theater Pieces." *English Language Notes* 27.4 (1990): 39–51.

Nelson 1973

Malcolm A. Nelson. *The Robin Hood Tradition in the English Renaissance.* Salzburg Studies in English Literature. Salzburg: Institut für Englische Sprache und Literatur, Universität Salzburg, 1973.

Nelson 1975

A Critical Edition of "Wit's Triumvirate, or The Philosopher." Ed. Cathryn Anne Nelson. 2 vols. Salzburg: Institut für Englische Sprache und Literatur, Universität Salzburg, 1975.

Nelson 1980

The Plays of Henry Medwall. Ed. Alan H. Nelson. Cambridge: Brewer; Totowa, NJ: Rowman and Littlefield, 1980.

Nelson 1989

Alan H. Nelson, ed. *Cambridge.* 2 vols. REED. Toronto, Buffalo, and London: University of Toronto Press, 1989.

Nelson 1992

Alan H. Nelson. "Hall Screens and Elizabethan Playhouses: Counter-Evidence from Cambridge." In *The Development of Shakespeare's Theater,* ed. John Astington, 57–76. New York: AMS Press, 1992.

Nelson 1994

Alan H. Nelson. *Early Cambridge Theatres: College, University, and Town Stages, 1464–1720.* Cambridge: Cambridge University Press, 1994.

Nelson 1998
Alan H. Nelson. "George Buc, William Shakespeare, and the Folger *George a Greene.*" *Shakespeare Quarterly* 49.1 (1998): 74–83.

Nelson 2006
Alan H. Nelson. "Calling All (Shakespeare) Biographers! Or, a Plea for Documentary Discipline." In *Shakespeare, Marlowe, Jonson: New Directions in Biography*, ed. Takashi Kozuka and J. R. Mulryne, 55–67. Aldershot, UK, and Burlington, VT: Ashgate, 2006.

Nelson 2009a
Alan H. Nelson. "Emulating Royalty: Cambridge, Oxford, and the Inns of Court." *Shakespeare Studies* 37 (2009): 67–76.

Nelson 2009b
Alan H. Nelson. "The Universities and the Inns of Court." In *The Oxford Handbook of the Early Modern Theatre*, ed. Richard Dutton, 280–91. Oxford: Oxford University Press, 2009.

Neuss
John Skelton. *Magnificence.* Ed. Paula Neuss. Revels Plays. Manchester: Manchester University Press; Baltimore: Johns Hopkins University Press, 1980.

Newberry
The Newberry Library, Chicago, Illinois

Newcomb
L. H. Newcomb. "Greene, Robert (*bap.* 1558, *d.* 1592)." In *ODNB* 23: 577–82.

Newman
Karen Newman. *Fashioning Femininity and English Renaissance Drama.* Chicago and London: University of Chicago Press, 1991.

Nicholl 2004a
Charles Nicholl. "Marlowe, Christopher (*bap.* 1564, *d.* 1593)." In *ODNB* 36: 721–31.

Nicholl 2004b
Charles Nicholl. "Nashe, Thomas (*bap.* 1567, *d. c.* 1601)." In *ODNB* 40: 237–43.

Nicol 2003
David Nicol. "*A Shoemaker A Gentleman*: Dates, Sources and Influence." *Notes and Queries* 50.4 (2003): 441–43.

Nicol 2006a
David Nicol. "The Repertory of Prince Charles's (I) Company, 1608–1625." *Early Theatre* 9.2 (2006): 57–72.

Nicol 2006b
David Nicol. "The Title-Page of *The World Tossed at Tennis*: A Portrait of a Jacobean Playing Company?" *Notes and Queries* 53.2 (2006): 158–59.

Nicol 2008a
David Nicol. "The Date of *The Thracian Wonder.*" *Notes and Queries* 55.2 (2008): 223–25.

Nicol 2008b
David Nicol. "The Stage Persona of William Rowley, Jacobean Clown." *Cahiers Elisabéthains* 74 (2008): 23–31.

Nicol 2009
David Nicol. "Middleton and Rowley's *A Fair Quarrel* at the Court of King James." *Notes and Queries* 56.2 (2009): 201–03.

Nicoll 1926
Edward Sharpham. *Cupid's Whirligig (1607).* Ed. Allardyce Nicoll. London: Golden Cockerel, 1926.

Nicoll 1937
Allardyce Nicoll. *Stuart Masques and the Renaissance Stage.* London: Harrap, 1937. Repr. New York: Harcourt, Brace, 1938; New York: Benjamin Blom, 1963.

Nicoll 1959
Allardyce Nicoll. "'Passing Over the Stage'." *Shakespeare Survey* 12 (1959): 47–55.

Nims
James Shirley's "Love's Cruelty": A Critical Edition. Ed. John Frederick Nims. New York and London: Garland, 1980.

Nolan
Wlliam Rowley and Thomas Heywood. *The Thracian Wonder.* Ed. Michael Nolan. Salzburg Studies in English Literature. Salzburg: Institüt für Anglistik und Amerikanistik, Universität Salzburg, 1997.

Norbrook
David Norbrook. "May, Thomas (*b.* in or after 1596, *d.* 1650)." In *ODNB* 37: 559–61.

Norland 1968
Francis Beaumont and John Fletcher. *The Maid's Tragedy.* Ed. Howard B. Norland. RRDS. Lincoln: University of Nebraska Press, 1968.

Norland 1992–93
Howard B. Norland. "'Lamentable tragedy mixed ful of pleasant mirth': The Enigma of *Cambises.*" *Comparative Drama* 26.4 (1992–93): 330–43.

Norland 1995
Howard B. Norland. *Drama in Early Tudor Britain, 1485–1558.* Lincoln and London: University of Nebraska Press, 1995.

Norland 2000

Howard Norland. "The Allegorizing of Revenge in *Horestes*." In *Tudor Theatre* 5: *Allegory in the Theatre*, 169–85. Tours Round Tables on Tudor Drama. Bern: Peter Lang, 2000.

Norland 2009

Howard B. Norland. *Neoclassical Tragedy in Elizabethan England*. Newark, DE: University of Delaware Press, 2009.

Norman

Arthur M. Z. Norman. "'The Tragedie of Cleopatra' and the Date of 'Antony and Cleopatra'." *Modern Language Review* 54.1 (1959): 1–9.

Normington

Katie Normington. *Medieval English Drama: Performance and Spectatorship*. Cultural History of Literature. Cambridge, UK, and Malden, MA: Polity Press, 2009.

Norton

The Norton Shakespeare Based on the Oxford Edition. Ed. Stephen Greenblatt, Walter Cohen, Jean E. Howard, and Katharine Eisaman Maus. New York and London: Norton, 1997.

Nostbakken

Faith M. Nostbakken. "Rowley's *When You See Me You Know Me*: Political Drama in Transition." *Cahiers Elisabéthains* 47 (1995): 71–78.

Nosworthy 1940

J. M. Nosworthy. "Notes on Henry Porter." *Modern Language Review* 35.4 (1940): 517–21.

Nosworthy 1955

William Shakespeare. *Cymbeline*. Ed. J. M. Nosworthy. Arden. Cambridge, MA: Harvard University Press, 1955.

Nosworthy 1966

Lusty Juventus. Ed. J. M. Nosworthy. MSR. Oxford: Oxford University Press, 1966 [1971].

Nungezer

Edwin Nungezer. *A Dictionary of Actors and of Other Persons Associated with the Public Representation of Plays in England before 1642*. New Haven: Yale University Press; London: Oxford University Press, 1929.

Nunn

Hillary M. Nunn. *Staging Anatomies: Dissection and Spectacle in Early Stuart Tragedy*. Literary and Scientific Cultures of Early Modernity. Aldershot, UK, and Burlington, VT: Ashgate, 2005.

Oberer

Karen Oberer. "Appropriations of the Popular Tradition in *The Famous Victories of Henry V* and *The Troublesome Raigne of King John*." In *Locating the Queen's Men, 1583–1603: Material Practices and Conditions of Playing*, ed. Helen Ostovich, Holger Schott Syme, and Andrew Griffin, 171–82. Farnham, UK, and Burlington, VT: Ashgate, 2009.

Obermueller

Erin V. Obermueller. "'On Cheating Pictures': Gender and Portrait Miniatures in Philip Massinger's *The Picture*." *Early Theatre* 10.2 (2007): 87–107.

O'Callaghan

James F. O'Callaghan. "Chapman's Caesar." *Studies in English Literature, 1500–1900* 16.2 (1976): 319–31.

O'Connell 2000a

Michael O'Connell. "Continuities between 'Medieval' and 'Early Modern' Drama." In *A Companion to English Renaissance Literature and Culture*, ed. Michael Hattaway, 477–85. Oxford: Blackwell, 2000.

O'Connell 2000b

Michael O'Connell. *The Idolatrous Eye: Iconoclasm and Theater in Early-Modern England*. New York and Oxford: Oxford University Press, 2000.

O'Connor 2002

Marion O'Connor. "Snakeskins, Mirrors & Torches: Theatrical Iconography & Middleton's *The Witch*." *Research Opportunities in Renaissance Drama* 41 (2002): 15–28.

O'Connor 2007

The Witch. Ed. Marion O'Connor. In *Thomas Middleton: The Collected Works*, gen. eds. Gary Taylor and John Lavagnino. Oxford: Clarendon Press, 2007.

ODNB

Oxford Dictionary of National Biography. Ed. H. C. G. Matthew and Brian Harrison. 60 vols. Oxford and New York: Oxford University Press, 2004.

O'Donnell

Norbert F. O'Donnell. "The Authorship of *The Careless Shepherdess*." *Philological Quarterly* 33 (1954): 43–47.

Ogilvie

Janet Ogilvie. "Heard 'Off': Stage Noises in the Elizabethan Theatre." *The English Review* 45 (1927): 67–77.

O Hehir

Brendan O Hehir. *Harmony from Discords: A Life of Sir John Denham*. Berkeley and Los Angeles: University of California Press, 1968.

Ohlgren

Thomas H. Ohlgren. *Robin Hood: The Early Poems, 1465–1560, Texts, Contexts, and Ideology.* Newark, DE: University of Delaware Press, 2007.

Oldenburg

Scott Oldenburg. "Toward a Multicultural Mid-Tudor England: The Queen's Royal Entry circa 1553, *The Interlude of Wealth and Health*, and the Question of Strangers in the Reign of Mary I." *ELH* 76.1 (2009): 99–129.

Oliphant 1911

E. H. Oliphant. "Problems of Authorship in Elizabethan Dramatic Literature." *Modern Philology* 8.3 (1911): 411–59.

Oliphant 1926

E. H. C. Oliphant. "The Authorship of *The Revenger's Tragedy*." *Studies in Philology* 23.2 (1926): 157–68.

Oliphant 1927

E. H. Oliphant. *The Plays of Beaumont and Fletcher: An Attempt to Determine Their Respective Shares and the Shares of Others.* New Haven: Yale University Press, 1927. Repr. New York: AMS Press, 1970.

Oliphant 1929

E. H. Oliphant. *Shakespeare and His Fellow Dramatists.* 2 vols. New York: Prentice-Hall, 1929.

Oliver 1959

William Shakespeare. *Timon of Athens.* Ed. H. J. Oliver. Arden Shakespeare. Cambridge, MA: Harvard University Press, 1959.

Oliver 1968

Christopher Marlowe. *"Dido Queen of Carthage" and "The Massacre at Paris."* Ed. H. J. Oliver. Revels Plays. London: Methuen, 1968.

Oliver 1984

William Shakespeare. *The Taming of the Shrew.* Ed. H. J. Oliver. Oxford and New York: Oxford University Press, 1984.

O'Malley

A Critical Old-Spelling Edition of Thomas Goffe's "The Courageous Turk." Ed. Susan Gushee O'Malley. New York and London: Garland, 1979.

Onat

"The Witch of Edmonton": A Critical Edition. Ed. Etta Soiref Onat. New York and London: Garland, 1980.

O'Neill

Stephen O'Neill. *Staging Ireland: Representations in Shakespeare and Renaissance Drama.* Dublin: Four Courts Press, 2007.

Orbison

Tucker Orbison. "The Date of *The Queen*." *Notes and Queries* 15.7 (1968): 255–56.

Orgel 1987
William Shakespeare. *The Tempest*. Ed. Stephen Orgel. Oxford: Clarendon Press, 1987.

Orgel 1989
Stephen Orgel. "Nobody's Perfect: Or, Why Did the English Stage Take Boys for Women?" *South Atlantic Quarterly* 88.1 (1989): 7–29.

Orgel 1996
William Shakespeare. *The Winter's Tale*. Ed. Stephen Orgel. Oxford: Clarendon Press, 1996.

Orgel 2002
Stephen Orgel. *The Authentic Shakespeare and Other Problems of the Early Modern Stage*. New York and London: Routledge, 2002.

Orgel 2003
Stephen Orgel. *Imagining Shakespeare: A History of Texts and Visions*. Basingstoke, UK, and New York: Palgrave Macmillan, 2003.

Orgel 2006
Stephen Orgel. "The Book of the Play." In *From Performance to Print in Shakespeare's England*, ed. Peter Holland and idem, 13–54. Basingstoke, UK, and New York: Palgrave Macmillan, 2006.

Orgel 2007
Stephen Orgel. "Shakespeare Illustrated." In *The Cambridge Companion to Shakespeare and Popular Culture*, ed. Robert Shaughnessy, 67–92. Cambridge: Cambridge University Press, 2007.

Orgel 2010
Stephen Orgel. "Shakespeare, Sexuality and Gender." In *The New Cambridge Companion to Shakespeare*, ed. Margreta de Grazia and Stanley Wells, 217–31. Cambridge: Cambridge University Press, 2010.

Orgel 2011
Stephen Orgel. "Open Secrets." In *Spectacular Performances: Essays on Theatre, Imagery, Books, and Selves in Early Modern England*, 143–59. Manchester: Manchester University Press; New York: Palgrave Macmillan, 2011.

Orgel & Strong
Stephen Orgel and Roy Strong. *The Theatre of the Stuart Court*. 2 vols. London: Sotheby Parke Bernet; Berkeley: University of California Press, 1973.

Orlin
Lena Cowen Orlin. "Domestic Tragedy: Private Life on the Public Stage." In *A Companion to Renaissance Drama*, ed. Arthur F. Kinney, 367–83. Oxford: Blackwell, 2002.

Ornstein 1970

George Chapman. *The Gentleman Usher*. Ed. Robert Ornstein. In *The Plays of George Chapman: The Comedies, A Critical Edition*. Gen. ed. Allan Holaday. Urbana, Chicago, and London: University of Illinois Press, 1970.

Ornstein 1972

Robert Ornstein. *A Kingdom for a Stage: The Achievement of Shakespeare's History Plays*. Cambridge, MA: Harvard University Press, 1972.

Orrell 1976

John Orrell. "Productions at the Paved Court Theatre, Somerset House, 1632/3." *Notes and Queries* 23.5–6 (1976): 223–25.

Orrell 1985

John Orrell. *The Theatres of Inigo Jones and John Webb*. Cambridge: Cambridge University Press, 1985.

Orrell 1988

John Orrell. *The Human Stage: English Theatre Design, 1567–1640*. Cambridge: Cambridge University Press, 1988.

Orrell 1997

John Orrell. "The Theaters." In *A New History of Early English Drama*, ed. John D. Cox and David Scott Kastan, 93–112. New York: Columbia University Press, 1997.

Ostovich

Ben Jonson. *Every Man Out of His Humour*. Ed. Helen Ostovich. Revels Plays. Manchester: Manchester University Press; New York: Palgrave, 2001.

Owen

An Edition of "The Rare Triumphs of Love and Fortune." Ed. John Isaac Owen. New York and London: Garland, 1979.

Owens 1996

Margaret E. Owens. "Desperate Juggling Knacks: The Rehearsal of the Grotesque in *Doctor Faustus*." *Medieval and Renaissance Drama in England* 8 (1996): 63–93.

Owens 2005

Margaret E. Owens. *Stages of Dismemberment: The Fragmented Body in Late Medieval and Early Modern Drama*. Newark, DE: University of Delaware Press, 2005.

Oxford

William Shakespeare: The Complete Works. Ed. Stanley Wells and Gary Taylor, with John Jowett and William Montgomery. The Oxford Shakespeare. Oxford: Clarendon Press, 1986. 2nd ed. 2005.

Oxley
A Critical Edition of John Fletcher's "The Humorous Lieutenant." Ed. Philip Oxley. New York and London: Garland, 1987.

Pacheco
Anita Pacheco. "'A mere cupboard of glasses': Female Sexuality and Male Honor in *A Fair Quarrel.*" *English Literary Renaissance* 28.3 (1998): 441–63.

Pafford 1963
William Shakespeare. *The Winter's Tale.* Ed. J. H. P. Pafford. Arden. London: Methuen, 1963. Repr. London: Thomson Learning, 2000.

Pafford 1993
J. H. P. Pafford. *John Clavell, 1601–43: Highwayman, Author, Lawyer, Doctor.* Oxford: Leopard's Head, 1993.

Pafford & Greg 1931
John Bale. *King Johan.* Ed. John Henry Pyle Pafford and W. W. Greg. MSR. Oxford: Oxford University Press, 1931.

Pafford & Greg 1935
John Clavell. *The Soddered Citizen.* Ed. John Henry Pyle Pafford and W. W. Greg. MSR. Oxford: Oxford University Press, 1935 [1936].

Pajuante
A. Luis Pajuante. "*Double Falsehood* and the Verbal Parallels with Shelton's *Don Quixote.*" *Shakespeare Survey* 51 (1998): 95–105.

Palfrey & Stern
Simon Palfrey and Tiffany Stern. *Shakespeare in Parts.* Oxford: Oxford University Press, 2007.

Palmer 1954
Robert Daborne. *The Poor Man's Comfort.* Ed. Kenneth Palmer. MSR. Oxford: Oxford University Press, 1954 [1955].

Palmer 2008
Barbara D. Palmer. "Staging Invisibility in English Early Modern Drama." *Early Theatre* 11.2 (2008): 113–28.

Palmer 2009a
Philip Palmer. "*Edmond Ironside* and the Question of Shakespearean Authorship." In *Shakespeare, Computers, and the Mystery of Authorship*, ed. Hugh Craig and Arthur F. Kinney, 100–15. Cambridge: Cambridge University Press, 2009.

Palmer 2009b
Barbara D. Palmer. "On the Road and on the Wagon." In *Locating the Queen's Men, 1583–1603: Material Practices and Conditions of Playing*, ed. Helen Ostovich, Holger Schott Syme, and Andrew Griffin, 27–39. Farnham, UK, and Burlington, VT: Ashgate, 2009.

Panek 1994
Jennifer Panek. "Punishing Adultery in *A Woman Killed with Kindness*." *Studies in English Literature, 1500–1900* 34.2 (1994): 357–78.

Panek 2011
Thomas Middleton and Thomas Dekker. *The Roaring Girl*. Ed. Jennifer Panek. Norton Critical Editions. New York and London: Norton, 2011.

Pantzer
Katharine F. Pantzer. See STC

Parfitt
The Plays of Cyril Tourneur. Ed. George Parfitt. Cambridge: Cambridge University Press, 1978.

Parker 1969
Thomas Middleton. *A Chaste Maid in Cheapside*. Ed. R. B. Parker. Revels Plays. London: Methuen, 1969.

Parker 1983
Ben Jonson. *Volpone*. Ed. R. B. Parker. Revels Plays. Manchester: Manchester University Press, 1983.

Parker 1994
William Shakespeare. *The Tragedy of Coriolanus*. Ed. R. B. Parker. Oxford: Clarendon Press, 1994.

Parker 2002
Patricia Parker. "Preposterous Conversions: Turning Turk and Its 'Pauline' Re-righting." *Journal for Early Modern Cultural Studies* 2.1 (2002): 1–34.

Parker 2008
John Parker. "Barabas and Charles I." In *Placing the Plays of Christopher Marlowe: Fresh Cultural Contexts*, ed. Sara Munson Deats and Robert A. Logan, 167–81. Aldershot, UK, and Burlington, VT: Ashgate, 2008.

Parker & Bevington
Ben Jonson. *Volpone*. Ed. Brian Parker and David Bevington. Revels Student Editions. Manchester: Manchester University Press; New York: St. Martin's Press, 1999.

Parr 1988
Ben Jonson. *The Staple of News*. Ed. Anthony Parr. Revels Plays. Manchester: Manchester University Press; New York: St. Martin's Press, 1988.

Parr 1990
Thomas Dekker. *The Shoemaker's Holiday*. Ed. Anthony Parr. 2nd ed. New Mermaids. London: Black; New York: Norton, 1990.

Parr 1995
Three Renaissance Travel Plays: "The Travels of the Three English Brothers," "The Sea Voyage," "The Antipodes." Ed. Anthony Parr. Revels Plays Companion

Library. Manchester: Manchester University Press; New York: St. Martin's Press, 1995.

Parr 2004a

Anthony Parr. "Day, John (1573/4–1638?)." In *ODNB* 15: 587–89.

Parr 2004b

Anthony Parr. "Wilkins, George (*d.* 1618)." In *ODNB* 58: 977–79.

Parrott 1906

Thomas Marc Parrott. "The Authorship of 'Sir Gyles Goosecappe'." *Modern Philology* 4.1 (1906): 25–37.

Parrott 1910

Thomas Marc Parrott, ed. *The Plays and Poems of George Chapman*. 2 vols. London: Routledge, 1910.

Parrott 1919

Thomas Marc Parrott. "Shakespeare's Revision of *Titus Andronicus*." *Modern Language Review* 14.1 (1919): 16–37.

Parrott 1948

Thomas Marc Parrott. "Two Late Dramatic Versions of the Slandered Bride Theme." In *Joseph Quincy Adams Memorial Studies*, ed. James G. McManaway, Giles E. Dawson, and Edwin E. Willoughby, 537–51. Washington, DC: The Folger Shakespeare Library, 1948.

Parry

Graham Parry. "Entertainments at Court." In *A New History of Early English Drama*, ed. John D. Cox and David Scott Kastan, 195–211. New York: Columbia University Press, 1997.

Partridge & Wilson

Gentleness and Nobility. Ed. A. C. Partridge and F. P. Wilson. MSR. Oxford: Oxford University Press 1949 [1950].

Paster

Thomas Middleton. *Michaelmas Term*. Ed. Gail Kern Paster. Revels Plays. Manchester: Manchester University Press; New York: St. Martin's Press, 2000.

Pasupathi

Vimala Pasupathi. "The King's Privates: Sex and the Soldier's Place in John Fletcher's *The Humorous Lieutenant* (ca. 1618)." *Research Opportunities in Medieval and Renaissance Drama* 47 (2008): 25–50.

Patterson 1982

Annabel Patterson. "'Roman-cast Similitude': Ben Jonson and the English Use of Roman History." In *Rome in the Renaissance: The City and the Myth*, ed. P. A. Ramsey, 381–94. MRTS 18. Binghamton, NY: Center for Medieval & Early Renaissance Studies, 1982.

Patterson 1984

Annabel Patterson. *Censorship and Interpretation: The Conditions of Writing and Reading in Early Modern England.* Madison: University of Wisconsin Press, 1984.

Paul

Henry N. Paul. *The Royal Play of Macbeth: When, Why, and How It Was Written by Shakespeare.* New York: Macmillan, 1950. Repr. New York: Octagon Books, 1971, 1978.

Payne 1906

Wentworth Smith. *The Hector of Germanie or the Palsgrave, Prime Elector.* Ed. Leonidas Warren Payne Jr. University of Pennsylvania Series in Philology and Literature 11. Philadelphia: University of Pennsylvania Press, 1906.

Payne 1993

Deborah C. Payne. "Patronage and the Dramatic Marketplace under Charles I and II." In *Patronage, Politics, and Literary Traditions in England, 1558–1658,* ed. Cedric C. Brown, 159–74. Detroit: Wayne State University Press, 1993.

PBA

Proceedings of the British Academy

Pearson 1981

Jacqueline Pearson. "Shakespeare and *Caesar's Revenge.*" *Shakespeare Quarterly* 32.1 (1981): 101–04.

Pearson 1985

Jacqueline Pearson. "'Women may discourse . . . as well as men': Speaking and Silent Women in the Plays of Margaret Cavendish, Duchess of Newcastle." *Tulsa Studies in Women's Literature* 4.1 (1985): 33–45.

Pearson 1988

Jacqueline Pearson. *The Prostituted Muse: Images of Women and Women Dramatists 1642–1737.* New York and London: Harvester Wheatsheaf, 1988.

Pechter

Edward Pechter. "The Year's Contribution to Shakespeare Studies." *Shakespeare Survey* 55 (2002): 336–66.

Peery

The Plays of Nathan Field. Ed. William Peery. Austin: University of Texas Press, 1950.

Peltonen

Markku Peltonen. *Classical Humanism and Republicanism in English Political Thought, 1570–1640.* Ideas in Context. Cambridge: Cambridge University Press, 1995.

Pendleton

Thomas A. Pendleton. "Shakespeare's Disguised Duke Play: Middleton, Marston, and the Sources of *Measure for Measure.*" In *"Fanned and Winnowed Opinions": Shakespearean Essays Presented to Harold Jenkins*, ed. John W. Mahon and idem, 79–98. London and New York: Methuen, 1987.

Pennell

An Edition of Anthony Munday's "John a Kent and John a Cumber." Ed. Arthur E. Pennell. New York and London: Garland, 1980.

Pentzell

Raymond J. Pentzell. "The Medieval Theatre in the Streets." *Theatre Survey* 14.1 (1973): 1–21.

Perry 1997

Curtis Perry. *The Making of Jacobean Culture: James I and the Renegotiation of Elizabethan Literary Practice.* Cambridge: Cambridge University Press, 1997.

Perry 2006a

Curtis Perry. *Literature and Favoritism in Early Modern England.* Cambridge: Cambridge University Press, 2006.

Perry 2006b

Curtis Perry. "1603 and the Discourse of Favouritism." In *The Accession of James I: Historical and Cultural Consequences*, ed. Glenn Burgess, Rowland Wymer, and Jason Lawrence, 155–76. Basingstoke, UK, and New York: Palgrave Macmillan, 2006.

Perry 2009

Curtis Perry. "'For They Are Englishmen': National Identities and the Early Modern Drama of Medieval Conquest." In *Shakespeare and the Middle Ages*, ed. idem and John Watkins, 172–95. Oxford: Oxford University Press, 2009.

Perry 2011

Curtis Perry. "British Empire on the Eve of the Armada: Revisiting *The Misfortunes of Arthur.*" *Studies in Philology* 108.4 (2011): 508–37.

Perry & Walter

Curtis Perry and Melissa Walter. "Staging Secret Interiors: *The Duchess of Malfi* as Inns of Court and Anticourt Drama." In *The Duchess of Malfi: A Critical Guide*, ed. Christina Luckyj, 87–105. Continuum Renaissance Drama. London and New York: Contiuum, 2011.

Pesta

Duke Pesta. "Articulating Skeletons: *Hamlet, Hoffman,* and the Anatomical Graveyard." *Cahiers Elisabéthains* 69 (2006): 21–39.

Peters

Julie Stone Peters. *Theatre of the Book, 1480–1880: Print, Text, and Performance in Europe*. Oxford: Oxford University Press, 2000.

Petter

A Critical Old Spelling Edition of The Works of Edward Sharpham. Ed. Christopher Gordon Petter. New York and London: Garland, 1986.

Pettigrew

Todd H. Pettigrew. "Sex, Sin, and Scarring: Syphilis in Redford's *Wit and Science*." In *Tudor Drama before Shakespeare, 1485–1590: New Directions for Research, Criticism, and Pedagogy*, ed. Lloyd Edward Kermode, Jason Scott-Warren, and Martine van Elk, 213–27. New York: Palgrave Macmillan, 2004.

Pettitt 1988

Thomas Pettitt. "Formulaic Dramaturgy in *Doctor Faustus*." In *"A Poet and a filthy Play-maker": New Essays on Christopher Marlowe*, ed. Kenneth Friedenreich, Roma Gill, and Constance B. Kuriyama, 167–91. New York: AMS Press, 1988.

Pettitt 2000

Thomas Pettitt. "Local and 'Customary' Drama." In *A Companion to English Renaissance Literature and Culture*, ed. Michael Hattaway, 464–76. Oxford: Blackwell, 2000.

Phelps

Wayne H. Phelps. "Cosmo Manuche, Royalist Playwright of the Commonwealth." *English Language Notes* 16.3 (1979): 207–11.

Pierce 1912a

Frederick E. Pierce. "The Collaboration of Dekker and Ford (I): The Authorship of *The Sun's Darling*." *Anglia* 34 (1912): 141–68.

Pierce 1912b

Frederick E. Pierce. "The Collaboration of Dekker and Ford (II): The Authorship of *The Witch of Edmonton*." *Anglia* 34 (1912): 289–312.

Pigman 2000

George Gascoigne. *A Hundreth Sundrie Flowres*. Ed. G. W. Pigman III. Oxford: Clarendon Press, 2000.

Pigman 2010

G. W. Pigman III. "Pastoral Drama." In *The Oxford History of Literary Translation in English*, vol. 2: *1550–1660*, ed. Gordon Braden, Robert Cummings, and Stuart Gillespie, 293–98. Oxford: Oxford University Press, 2010.

Pilkinton

Mark C. Pilkinton, ed. *Bristol*. REED. Toronto, Buffalo, and London: University of Toronto Press, 1997.

Pinciss 1970

Gerald M. Pinciss. "Thomas Creede and the Repertory of the Queen's Men 1583–1592." *Modern Philology* 67.4 (1970): 321–30.

Pinciss 2000

Gerald M. Pinciss. *Forbidden Matter: Religion in the Drama of Shakespeare and his Contemporaries*. Newark, DE: University of Delaware Press; London: Associated University Presses, 2000.

Pinciss & Proudfoot

The Faithful Friends. Ed. G. M. Pinciss and G. R. Proudfoot. MSR. Oxford: Oxford University Press, 1970 [1975].

Pincombe 1996

Michael Pincombe. *The Plays of John Lyly: Eros and Eliza*. Revels Plays Companion Library. Manchester: Manchester University Press; New York: St. Martin's Press, 1996.

Pincombe 1998

Michael Pincombe. "Lyly and Lesbianism: Mysteries of the Closet in *Sappho and Phao*." In *Renaissance Configurations: Voices/Bodies/Spaces, 1580–1690*, ed. Gordon McMullan, 89–107. London: Macmillan; New York: St. Martin's Press, 1998.

Pineas 1962

Rainer Pineas. "The English Morality Play as a Weapon of Religious Controversy." *Studies in English Literature, 1500–1900* 2.2 (1962): 157–80.

Pineas 1965

Rainer Pineas. "The Revision of *Wealth and Health*." *Philological Quarterly* 44.4 (1965): 560–62.

Pineas 1989

Rainer Pineas. "The Polemical Drama of John Bale." In *Shakespeare and Dramatic Tradition: Essays in Honor of S. F. Johnson*, ed. W. R. Elton and William B. Long, 194–210. Newark, DE: University of Delaware Press; London and Toronto: Associated University Presses, 1989.

Pitcher 1994

John Pitcher. "'Fronted with the sight of a Bear': Cox of Collumpton and *The Winter's Tale*." *Notes and Queries* 41.1 (1994): 47–53.

Pitcher 2004

John Pitcher. "Daniel, Samuel (1562/3–1619)." In *ODNB* 15: 71–78.

Pitcher 2005

John Pitcher. "Samuel Daniel's Gifts of Books to Lord Chancellor Egerton." *Medieval and Renaissance Drama in England* 17 (2005): 216–38.

Pitcher 2010
William Shakespeare. *The Winter's Tale*. Ed. John Pitcher. Arden 3. London: Black, 2010.

Pitcher & Woudhuysen
Samuel Daniel. *Hymen's Triumph*. Ed. John Pitcher and H. R. Woudhuysen. MSR. Oxford: Oxford University Press, 1994.

Plomer
H. R. Plomer. "Secret Printing during the Civil War." *The Library*, n.s. 5 (1904): 374–403.

Pogue
Barnabe Barnes. *"The Devil's Charter": A Critical Edition*. Ed. Jim C. Pogue. New York and London: Garland, 1980.

Pohl
Nicole Pohl. *Women, Space and Utopia, 1600–1800*. Aldershot, UK, and Burlington, VT: Ashgate, 2006.

Polito & Scott
Mary Polito and Amy Scott. "Circles and Circuits: Drama and Politics in the Midlands." *Early Theatre* 14.2 (2011): 15–26.

Polito & Windle
Mary Polito and Jean Sébastien Windle. "'You see the times are dangerous': The Political and Theatrical Situation of *The Humorous Magistrate*." *Early Theatre* 12.1 (2009): 93–118.

Pollard
Alfred W. Pollard. See STC

Poole 1998
Kristen Elizabeth Poole. "Garbled Martyrdom in Christopher Marlowe's *The Massacre at Paris*." *Comparative Drama* 32.1 (1998): 1–25.

Poole 2002
William Poole. "*Julius Caesar* and *Caesars Revenge* Again." *Notes and Queries* 49.2 (2002): 227–28.

Potter 1975
Robert Potter. *The English Morality Play: Origins, History and Influence of a Dramatic Tradition*. London and Boston: Routledge and Kegan Paul, 1975.

Potter 1980
Lois Potter. "The Plays and the Playwrights." In *The Revels History of Drama in English*, vol. 2: *1500–1576*, ed. Norman Sanders, Richard Southern, T. W. Craik, and eadem, 141–257. London and New York: Methuen, 1981.

Potter 1981
Lois Potter. "The Plays and the Playwrights: 1642–60." In *The Revels History of Drama in English*, vol. 4: *1613–1660*, ed. Philip Edwards, Gerald Eades

Bentley, Kathleen McKluskie, and eadem, 261–304. London and New York: Methuen, 1981.

Potter 1983

Francis Osborne. *The True Tragicomedy Formerly Acted at Court*. Ed. Lois Potter. The Renaissance Imagination 3. New York and London: Garland, 1983.

Potter 1987a

Lois Potter. "EPD: The *Mistress Parliament* Political Dialogues." *AEB: Analytical & Enumerative Bibliography* n.s. 1 (1987): 101–70.

Potter 1987b

Lois Potter. "'True Tragicomedies' of the Civil War and the Commonwealth." In *Renaissance Tragicomedy: Explorations in Genre and Politics*, ed. Nancy Klein Maguire, 196–217. AMS Studies in the Renaissance 20. New York: AMS Press, 1987.

Potter 1988

Lois Potter. "Marlowe in the Civil War and Commonwealth: Some Allusions and Parodies." In *"A Poet and a filthy Play-maker": New Essays on Christopher Marlowe*, ed. Kenneth Friedenreich, Roma Gill, and Constance B. Kuriyama, 73–82. New York: AMS Press, 1988.

Potter 1989

Lois Potter. *Secret Rites and Secret Writing: Royalist Literature, 1641–1660*. Cambridge: Cambridge University Press, 1989.

Potter 1992

Lois Potter. "Topicality or Politics? *The Two Noble Kinsmen*, 1613–34." In *The Politics of Tragicomedy: Shakespeare and After*, ed. Gordon McMullan and Jonathan Hope, 77–91. London and New York: Routledge, 1992.

Potter 1996

Lois Potter. "Pirates and 'Turning Turk' in Renaissance Drama." In *Travel and Drama in Shakespeare's Time*, ed. Jean-Pierre Maquerlot and Michèle Willems, 124–40. Cambridge: Cambridge University Press, 1996.

Potter 1997

John Fletcher and William Shakespeare. *The Two Noble Kinsmen*. Ed. Lois Potter. Arden 3. London: Thomas Nelson, 1997.

Potter 2002a

Lois Potter. *Othello*. Shakespeare in Performance. Manchester: Manchester University Press; New York: Palgrave, 2002.

Potter 2002b

Ursula Potter. "Cockering Mothers and Humanist Pedagogy in Two Tudor School Plays." In *Domestic Arrangements in Early Modern England*, ed. Kari Boyd McBride, 244–78. Pittsburgh: Duquesne University Press, 2002.

Potter 2008
Ursula Potter. "The Spectre of the Shrew and the Lash of the Rod: Gendering Pedagogy in *The Disobedient Child*." In *Early Modern Academic Drama*, ed. Jonathan Walker and Paul D. Streufert, 65–86. Farnham, UK, and Burlington, VT: Ashgate, 2008.

Potter 2012
Lois Potter. *The Life of William Shakespeare: A Critical Biography*. Oxford and Malden, MA: Wiley-Blackwell, 2012.

Poulsen
Rachel E. Poulsen. "The 'plentifull Lady-feast' in Brome's *A Madd Couple Well Matcht*." *Early Theatre* 11.1 (2008): 77–97.

Powell 1941
William C. Powell. "A Note on the Stage History of Beaumont and Fletcher's *Love's Pilgrimage* and *The Chances*." *Modern Language Notes* 56.2 (1941): 122–27.

Powell 1964
Jocelyn Powell. "Marlowe's Spectacle." *Tulane Drama Review* 8.4 (1964): 195–210.

Poynting
Walter Montagu. *The Shepherds' Paradise*. Ed. Sarah Poynting. MSR. Oxford: Oxford University Press, 1997 [1998].

Preiss 2006
Richard Preiss. "Robert Armin Do the Police in Different Voices." In *From Performance to Print in Shakespeare's England*, ed. Peter Holland and Stephen Orgel, 208–27. Basingstoke, UK, and New York: Palgrave Macmillan, 2006.

Preiss 2007
Richard Preiss. "A Play Finally Anonymous." *Shakespeare Yearbook* 16: *The Shakespeare Apocrypha* (2007): 117–33.

Price 1943
H. T. Price. "The Authorship of *Titus Andronicus*." *JEGP* 42 (1943): 55–81.

Price 1949
George R. Price. "The First Edition of *A Faire Quarrell*." *Library*, 5th ser., 4.2 (1949): 137–41.

Price 1953
George R. Price. "The Authorship and the Manuscript of *The Old Law*." *Huntington Library Quarterly* 16.2 (1953): 117–39.

Price 1969
George R. Price. *Thomas Dekker*. TEAS 71. New York: Twayne, 1969.

Price 1976a
Thomas Middleton and William Rowley. *A Fair Quarrel*. Ed. George R. Price. RRDS. Lincoln: University of Nebraska Press, 1976.

Price 1976b
Thomas Middleton. *"Michaelmas Term" and "A Trick to Catch the Old One": A Critical Edition*. Ed. George R. Price. The Hague and Paris: Mouton, 1976.

Pritchard 2004a
Jonathan Pritchard. "Swinhoe, Gilbert (*fl.* 1658–1671)." In *ODNB* 53: 505.

Pritchard 2004b
Jonathan Pritchard. "Willan, Leonard (*fl.* 1648–1670)." In *ODNB* 59: 8–9.

Procter
Johanna Procter. *"The Queenes Arcadia* (1606) and *Hymens Triumph* (1615): Samuel Daniel's Court Pastoral Plays." In *The Renaissance in Ferrara and its European Horizons*, ed. June Salmons and Walter Moretti, 83–109. Cardiff: University of Wales Press; Ravenna: Girasole, 1984.

Proudfoot 1963
A Knack to Know a Knave. Ed. G. R. Proudfoot. MSR. Oxford: Oxford University Press, 1963 [1964].

Proudfoot 1967
[John Heywood.] *Johan Johan the Husband*. Ed. G. R. Proudfoot. MSR. Oxford: Oxford University Press, 1967 [1972].

Proudfoot 1970
John Fletcher and William Shakespeare. *The Two Noble Kinsmen*. Ed. G. R. Proudfoot. RRDS. Lincoln: University of Nebraska Press, 1970.

Proudfoot 1993
Richard Proudfoot. "Richard Johnson's *Tom a' Lincoln* Dramatized: A Jacobean Play in British Library MS. Add. 61745." In *New Ways of Looking at Old Texts: Papers of the Renaissance English Text Society, 1985–1991*, ed. W. Speed Hill, 75–101. MRTS 107. Binghamton: Center for Medieval and Early Renaissance Studies, State University of New York at Binghamton, 1993.

Proudfoot 2002
Richard Proudfoot. "'Modernizing' the Printed Play-Text in Jacobean London: Some Early Reprints of *Mucedorus*." In *"A Certain Text": Close Readings and Textual Studies on Shakespeare and Others in Honor of Thomas Clayton*, ed. Linda Anderson and Janis Lull, 18–28. Newark, DE: University of Delaware Press; London: Associated University Presses, 2002.

Proudfoot et al. 1992
Tom a Lincoln. Ed. G. R. Proudfoot, H. R. Woudhuysen, and John Pitcher. MSR. Oxford: Oxford University Press, 1992.

Proudfoot et al. 2005
The Two Noble Kinsmen. Ed. G. R. Proudfoot, Eric Rasmussen, and H. R. Woudhuysen. MSR. Oxford: Oxford University Press, 2005.

Pujante
A. Luis Pujante. "*Double Falsehood* and the Verbal Parallels with Shelton's *Don
Quixote.*" *Shakespeare Survey* 51 (1998): 95–105.

Purkiss 1998
Diane Purkiss, ed. *Three Tragedies by Renaissance Women.* London: Penguin,
1998.

Purkiss 2005
Diane Purkiss. *Literature, Gender and Politics during the English Civil War.* Cambridge: Cambridge University Press, 2005.

Quiller-Couch & Wilson
William Shakespeare. *The Taming of the Shrew.* Ed. Arthur Wilson Quiller-
Couch and John Dover Wilson. The New Shakespeare. Cambridge: Cam-
bridge University Press, 1928.

Raber 2000
Karen Raber. "Warrior Women in the Plays of Cavendish and Killigrew." *Studies
in English Literature, 1500–1900* 40.3 (2000): 413–33.

Raber 2001
Karen Raber. *Dramatic Difference: Gender, Class, and Genre in the Early Modern
Closet Drama.* Newark, DE: University of Delaware Press; London: Associ-
ated University Presses, 2001.

Rackin 1987
Phyllis Rackin. "Androgyny, Mimesis, and the Marriage of the Boy Heroine on
the English Renaissance Stage." *PMLA* 102.1 (1987): 29–41.

Rackin 1990
Phyllis Rackin. *Stages of History: Shakespeare's English Chronicles.* Ithaca, NY:
Cornell University Press, 1990.

Rackin 2005
Phyllis Rackin. *Shakespeare and Women.* Oxford Shakespeare Topics. Oxford:
Oxford University Press, 2005.

Rackin 2006
Phyllis Rackin. "Our Canon, Ourselves." In *Center or Margin: Revisions of the
English Renaissance in Honor of Leeds Barroll*, ed. Lena Cowen Orlin, 91–113.
Selinsgrove, PA: Susquehanna University Press, 2006.

Raman
Shankar Raman. "Imaginary Islands: Staging the East." *Renaissance Drama* 26
(1995): 131–61.

Ramel
Jacques Ramel. "Biographical Notices on the Authors of 'The Misfortunes of Arthur' (1588)." *Notes and Queries* 14.12 (1967): 461–67.

Randall 1991
Dale B. J. Randall. "The Head and the Hands on the Rostra: *Marcus Tullius Cicero* as a Sign of Its Time." *Connotations* 1.1 (1991): 34–54.

Randall 1995
Dale B. J. Randall. *Winter Fruit: English Drama 1642–1660.* Lexington: University Press of Kentucky, 1995.

Rasmussen 1989
Eric Rasmussen. "Shakespeare's Hand in *The Second Maiden's Tragedy.*" *Shakespeare Quarterly* 40.1 (1989): 1–26.

Rasmussen 1990
Eric Rasmussen. "Reply to MacD. P. Jackson." *Shakespeare Quarterly* 41.3 (1990): 406–07.

Rasmussen 1993
Eric Rasmussen. *A Textual Companion to "Doctor Faustus."* Revels Plays Companion Library. Manchester: Manchester University Press; New York: St. Martin's Press, 1993.

Rasmussen 1997
Eric Rasmussen. "The Revision of Scripts." In *A New History of Early English Drama,* ed. John D. Cox and David Scott Kastan, 441–60. New York: Columbia University Press, 1997.

Rasmussen 2001
Eric Rasmussen. "The Date of Q4 *Hamlet.*" *Papers of the Bibliographical Society of America* 95.1 (2001): 21–29.

Rasmussen 2003
Eric Rasmussen. "Introduction: The Texts of Shakespeare's *Hamlet* and Their Origins." In *The Three Text Hamlet: Parallel Texts of the First and Second Quartos and First Folio,* ed. Bernice W. Kliman and Paul Bertram, ix-xxviii. 2nd ed., rev. and expanded. New York: AMS Press, 2003.

Rasmussen 2008
Eric Rasmussen. "Editions and Textual Studies." *Shakespeare Survey* 61 (2008): 388–94.

Rasmussen 2011
Eric Rasmussen. *The Shakespeare Thefts: In Search of the First Folios.* New York: Palgrave Macmillan, 2011.

Ravelhofer 1999

Barbara Ravelhofer. "Bureaucrats and Courtly Cross-Dressers in the *Shrovetide Masque* and *The Shepherd's Paradise.*" *English Literary Renaissance* 29.1 (1999): 75–96.

Ravelhofer 2002

Barbara Ravelhofer. "'Beasts of Recreacion': Henslowe's White Bears." *English Literary Renaissance* 32.2 (2002): 287–323.

Ravelhofer 2006

Barbara Ravelhofer. "Non-Verbal Meaning in Caroline Private Theatre: William Cavendish's and James Shirley's *The Varietie* (*c.* 1641)." *Seventeenth Century* 21.2 (2006): 195–214.

Ravelhofer 2008

Barbara Ravelhofer. "News Drama: The Tragic Subject of Charles I." In *English Historical Drama, 1500–1660: Forms Outside the Canon,* ed. Teresa Grant and eadem, 179–201. Basingstoke, UK, and New York: Palgrave Macmillan, 2008.

Ray

Chapman's "The Conspiracy and Tragedy of Charles, Duke of Byron." Ed. George Ray. 2 vols. New York and London: Garland, 1979.

Raymond

Joad Raymond. *The Invention of the Newspaper: English Newsbooks, 1641–1649.* Oxford: Clarendon Press, 1996.

Read

Leslie Du S. Read. "Edward Alleyn and the Rose Playhouse: Biography and Repertoire." *Theatre Survey* 14 (1994): 85–93.

Redgrave

G. R. Redgrave. See STC

Reed 1778

Thomas Middleton. *A Tragi-Coomodie called The Witch.* Ed. Isaac Reed. London: J. Nichols, 1778.

Reed 1782

Isaac Reed. *Biographia Dramatica, or, a Companion to the Playhouse. A New Edition: Carefully Corrected; Greatly Enlarged; and Continued from 1764 to 1782.* 2 vols. London: Rivingtons, 1782.

Reed 1965

Robert R. Reed Jr. *The Occult on the Tudor and Stuart Stage.* Boston: Christopher, 1965.

REED

Records of Early English Drama

Rees 1953
Joan Rees. "An Elizabethan Eyewitness of *Antony and Cleopatra?*" *Shakespeare Survey* 6 (1953): 91–93.

Rees 1954
Ennis Rees. *The Tragedies of George Chapman*. Cambridge, MA: Harvard University Press, 1954.

Rees 1964
Joan Rees. *Samuel Daniel: A Critical and Biographical Study*. Liverpool: Liverpool University Press, 1964.

Reese
Gertrude Reese. "Political Import of *The Misfortunes of Arthur*." *Review of English Studies* 21 (1945): 81–91.

Regina Literata
See Abraham Hartwell

Reibetanz
John Reibetanz. "Hieronimo in Decimosexto: A Private-Theater Burlesque." *Renaissance Drama* n.s. 5 (1972): 89–121.

Reich
"Claracilla" by Thomas Killigrew: A Critical Edition. Ed. William T. Reich. New York and London: Garland, 1980.

Reid-Baxter
Jamie Reid-Baxter. *"Philotus*: The Transmission of a Delectable Treatise." In *Literature, Letters and the Canonical in Early Modern Scotland*, ed. Theo van Heijnsbergen and Nicola Royan, 52–68. East Linton, UK: Tuckwell, 2002.

Renwick & Greg
John of Bordeaux or The Second Part of Friar Bacon. Ed. William Lindsay Renwick and W. W. Greg. MSR. Oxford: Oxford University Press, 1935 [1936].

Reynolds 1905a
George F. Reynolds. "Some Principles of Elizabethan Staging: Part I." *Modern Philology* 2.4 (1905): 581–614.

Reynolds 1905b
George F. Reynolds. "Some Principles of Elizabethan Staging: Part II." *Modern Philology* 3.1 (1905): 69–97.

Reynolds 1914
George F. Reynolds. "William Percy and His Plays, with a Summary of the Customs of Elizabethan Staging." *Modern Philology* 12.4 (1914): 241–60.

Reynolds 1940
George Fullmer Reynolds. *The Staging of Elizabethan Plays at the Red Bull Theater, 1605–1625*. New York: Modern Language Association of America; London: Oxford University Press, 1940.

Reynolds 1948
George F. Reynolds. "*Troilus and Cressida* on the Elizabethan Stage." In *Joseph Quincy Adams Memorial Studies*, ed. James G. McManaway, Giles E. Dawson, and Edwin E. Willoughby, 229–38. Washington, DC: Folger Shakespeare Library, 1948.

Reynolds 1959
George F. Reynolds. "*Mucedorus*, Most Popular Elizabethan Play?" In *Studies in the English Renaissance Drama*, ed. Josephine W. Bennett, Oscar Cargill, and Vernon Hall Jr., 248–68. New York: New York University Press, 1959.

Reynolds 1967
George F. Reynolds. *On Shakespeare's Stage*. Ed. Richard K. Knaub. Boulder: University of Colorado Press, 1967.

Rhoads 1930
The Two Noble Ladies. Ed. Rebecca G. Rhoads. MSR. Oxford: Oxford University Press, 1930.

Rhoads 1936
Howard Garrett Rhoads. *Wm. Hawkins' Apollo Shroving: An Edition*. Philadelphia: University of Pennsylvania Press, 1936.

Rhodes 1976
Ernest L. Rhodes. *Henslowe's Rose: The Stage & Staging*. Lexington: University Press of Kentucky, 1976.

Rhodes 2004
Neil Rhodes. *Shakespeare and the Origins of English*. Oxford: Oxford University Press, 2004.

Ribner 1954
Irving Ribner. "*Tamburlaine* and *The Wars of Cyprus*." *JEGP* 53.4 (1954): 569–73.

Ribner 1964
Cyril Tourneur. *The Atheist's Tragedy*. Ed. Irving Ribner. Revels Plays. London: Methuen, 1964.

Ribner 1965
Irving Ribner. *The English History Play in the Age of Shakespeare*. London: Methuen, 1965.

Richards 1968
Kenneth R. Richards. "Changeable Scenery for Plays on the Caroline Stage." *Theatre Notebook* 23.1 (1968): 6–20.

Richards 1982
The Christmas Prince. Ed. Earl Jeffrey Richards. Renaissance Latin Drama in England, 1st Series, 11. Hildesheim and New York: Olms, 1982.

Richmond 1994
Hugh M. Richmond. *King Henry VIII*. Shakespeare in Performance. Manchester: Manchester University Press; New York: St. Martin's Press, 1994.

Richmond 1996
Velma Bourgeois Richmond. *The Legend of Guy of Warwick*. New York and London: Garland, 1996.

Riddell 1969
James A. Riddell. "Some Actors in Ben Jonson's Plays." *Shakespeare Studies* 5 (1969): 285–98.

Riddell 1997
James A. Riddell. "Jonson and Stansby and the Revisions of *Every Man in His Humour*." *Medieval and Renaissance Drama in England* 9 (1997): 81–91.

Riely
Thomas Dekker. *The Whore of Babylon*. Ed. Marianne Gateson Riely. New York and London: Garland, 1980.

Riemer
A. P. Riemer. "Shirley's Revisions and the Date of *The Constant Maid*." *Review of English Studies* 17.66 (1966): 141–48.

Riggio 1986
Milla C. Riggio. "The Staging of *Wisdom*." In *The Wisdom Symposium: Papers from the Trinity College Medieval Festival*, ed. eadem, 1–17. New York: AMS Press, 1986.

Riggio 1998
Milla Cozart Riggio, ed. *"The Play of Wisdom": Its Texts and Contexts*. AMS Studies in the Middle Ages 14. New York: AMS Press, 1998.

Riggs 1989
David Riggs. *Ben Jonson: A Life*. Cambridge, MA: Harvard University Press, 1989.

Riggs 2004
David Riggs. *The World of Christopher Marlowe*. London: Faber, 2004.

Ringler 1968
William A. Ringler Jr. "The Number of Actors in Shakespeare's Early Plays." In *The Seventeenth-Century Stage: A Collection of Critical Essays*, ed. Gerald Eades Bentley, 110–34. Chicago and London: University of Chicago Press, 1968.

Ringler 1981
William A. Ringler Jr. "Shakespeare and His Actors: Some Remarks on *King Lear*." In *Shakespeare's Art from a Comparative Perspective*, ed. Wendell M. Aycock, 183–94. Lubbock: Texas Tech Press, 1981.

Ringler & May
William A. Ringler and Steven W. May. "An Epilogue Possibly by Shakespeare." *Modern Philology* 70.2 (1972): 138–39.

Ripley
John Ripley. *"Coriolanus" on Stage in England and America, 1609–1994.* Madison and Teaneck, NJ: Fairleigh Dickinson University Press; London: Associated University Presses, 1998.

Rist
Thomas Rist. "The Wonder of Women: Virginity, Sexuality and Religio-Politics in Marston's *The Tragedy of Sophonisba*." In *Marian Moments in Early Modern British Drama*, ed. Regina Buccola and Lisa Hopkins, 111–25. Aldershot, UK, and Burlington, VT: Ashgate, 2007.

Ritch
K. Janet Ritch. "The Role of the Presenter in Medieval Drama." In *"Bring furth the pagants": Essays in Early English Drama Presented to Alexandra F. Johnston*, ed. David N. Klausner and Karen Sawyer Marsalek, 230–68. Toronto, Buffalo, and London: University of Toronto Press, 2007.

Ritchie
David Lindsay. *The Bannatyne Manuscript Written in Tyme of Pest, 1568.* Ed. William Tod Ritchie. Scottish Text Society, 2nd ser., 23. 4 vols. Edinburgh and London: Blackwood, 1928–34. Repr. New York: Johnson Reprint, 1972.

Rittenhouse
A Critical Edition of "1 Sir John Oldcastle." Ed. Jonathan Rittenhouse. New York and London: Garland, 1984.

Riverside
The Riverside Shakespeare. Ed. G. Blakemore Evans with the assistance of J. J. M. Tobin. 2nd ed. Boston: Houghton Mifflin, 1997.

Roberts 1983
Josephine A. Roberts. "The Huntington Manuscript of Lady Mary Wroth's Play, *Loves Victorie*." *Huntington Library Quarterly* 46.2 (1983): 156–74.

Roberts 1986
Joan Warthling Roberts, ed. *"Sicily and Naples or, The Fatall Union," a Tragoedy by S. Harding.* The Renaissance Imagination 15. New York and London: Garland, 1986.

Roberts 1997
Jeanne Addison Roberts. "Margaret Cavendish Plays with Shakespeare." *Renaissance Papers* (1997): 113–24.

Roberts 1998
Sasha Roberts. *William Shakespeare: "Romeo and Juliet."* Writers and Their Work. Plymouth, UK: Northcote House, 1998.

Roberts 2002

Sasha Roberts. "'Let me the curtains draw': The Dramatic and Symbolic Properties of the Bed in Shakespearean Tragedy." In *Staged Properties in Early Modern English Drama*, ed. Jonathan Gil Harris and Natasha Korda, 153–74. Cambridge: Cambridge University Press, 2002.

Roberts 2003

Jeanne Addison Roberts. "Revenge Tragedy and Elizabeth Cary's *Mariam*." *Renaissance Papers* (2003): 149–66.

Roberts 2009

Josephine Roberts. "Editing the Women Writers of Early Modern England." In *Women Editing/Editing Women: Early Modern Women Writers and the New Textualism*, ed. Ann Hollinshead Hurley and Chanita Goodblatt, 17–23. Newcastle upon Tyne: Cambridge Scholars, 2009.

Robertson

Roderick Robertson. "Oxford Theatre in Tudor Times." *Educational Theatre Journal* 21.1 (1969): 41–50.

Robinson 1987

A Critical Edition of "The Play of the Wether." Ed. Vicki Knudsen Robinson. New York and London: Garland, 1987.

Robinson 2006

Benedict S. Robinson. "The 'Turks,' Caroline Politics, and Philip Massinger's *The Renegado*." In *Localizing Caroline Drama: Politics and Economics of the Early Modern English Stage, 1625–1642*, ed. Adam Zucker and Alan B. Farmer, 213–37. Basingstoke, UK, and New York: Palgrave Macmillan, 2006.

Robinson 2007

Benedict S. Robinson. *Islam and Early Modern English Literature: The Politics of Romance from Spenser to Milton*. Basingstoke, UK, and New York: Palgrave Macmillan, 2007.

Rochester

Joanne Rochester. *Staging Spectatorship in the Plays of Philip Massinger*. Farnham, UK, and Burlington, VT: Ashgate, 2010.

Rogers & Ley

Richard Rogers and William Ley. *An Exact and Perfect Catalogue of All Plays that are Printed*. Appended to Thomas Goffe, *The Careless Shepherdess*. London: William Ley, 1656.

Rollins 1921

Hyder E. Rollins. "A Contribution to the History of the English Commonwealth Drama." *Studies in Philology* 18.3 (1921): 267–333.

Rollins 1923a

Hyder E. Rollins. *Cavalier and Puritan: Ballads and Broadsides Illustrating the Period of the Great Rebellion, 1640–1660.* New York: New York University Press, 1923.

Rollins 1923b

Hyder E. Rollins. "The Commonwealth Drama: Miscellaneous Notes." *Studies in Philology* 20.1 (1923): 52–69.

Rollins 1924

Hyder E. Rollins. "*The Drinking Academy, or The Cheaters' Holiday.*" *PMLA* 39.4 (1924): 837–71.

Rollins 1928

Hyder E. Rollins. "A Note on Richard Edwards." *Review of English Studies* 4 (1928): 204–06.

Ronan 1986

Clifford J. Ronan. "*Selimus* and the Blinding of Gloster." *Notes and Queries* 33.3 (1986): 360–62.

Ronan 1987

Clifford J. Ronan. "*Caesar's Revenge* and the Roman Thoughts in *Antony and Cleopatra.*" *Shakespeare Studies* 19 (1987): 171–82.

Ronan 2005

Clifford Ronan. "Caesar On and Off the Renaissance English Stage." In *"Julius Caesar": New Critical Essays*, ed. Horst Zander, 71–89. New York and London: Routledge, 2005.

Rooney

Tom Rooney. "Who 'Plaid' the Bear in *Mucedorus?*" *Notes and Queries* 54.3 (2007): 259–62.

Roper

John Ford. '*Tis Pity She's a Whore.* Ed. Derek Roper. Revels Plays. London: Methuen, 1975.

Rose

Mary Beth Rose. *The Expense of Spirit: Love and Sexuality in English Renaissance Drama.* Ithaca, NY, and London: Cornell University Press, 1988.

Ross 1966

Cyril Tourneur. *The Revenger's Tragedy.* Ed. Lawrence J. Ross. Regents Renaissance Drama Series. Lincoln: University of Nebraska Press, 1966.

Ross 1979

Gervase Markham and William Sampson. *A Critical Edition of "The True Tragedy of Herod and Antipater."* Ed. Gordon Nicholas Ross. New York and London: Garland, 1979.

Rossiter 1946

Woodstock, A Moral History. Ed. A. P. Rossiter. London: Chatto and Windus, 1946.

Rossiter 1950

A. P. Rossiter. *English Drama from Early Times to the Elizabethans: Its Background, Origins and Developments.* London: Hutchinson, 1950. Repr. New York: Barnes & Noble, 1967.

Rota

Felicina Rota. *L'Arcadia di Sidney e il teatro, con un testo inedito.* Biblioteca di studi inglesi 6. Bari: Adriatica, 1966.

Rowan

D. F. Rowan. "The Staging of *The Spanish Tragedy.*" *Elizabethan Theatre* 5 (1975): 112–23.

Rowan et al.

William Berkeley. *The Lost Lady.* Ed. D. F. Rowan, G. R. Proudfoot, John Pitcher, and Lois Potter. MSR. Oxford: Oxford University Press, 1987.

Rowe

John Rowe. *Tragi-Comœdia, Being a Brief Relation of the Strange and Wonderfull Hand of God Discovered at Witny.* Oxford: L. Lichfield for Henry Cripps, 1653.

Rowland 1994

Richard Rowland. "'Thou teachest me humanitie': Thomas Heywood's *The English Traveller.*" In *English Comedy*, ed. Michael Cordner, Peter Holland, and John Kerrigan, 137–57. Cambridge: Cambridge University Press, 1994.

Rowland 1995

Richard Rowland. "*The Captives*: Thomas Heywood's 'Whole Monopoly off Mischeiff'." *Modern Language Review* 90.3 (1995): 585–602.

Rowland 2005a

Thomas Heywood. *The First and Second Parts of King Edward IV.* Ed. Richard Rowland. Revels Plays. Manchester: Manchester University Press; New York: Palgrave, 2005.

Rowland 2005b

Richard Rowland. "'Speaking some words, but of no importance'? Stage Directions, Thomas Heywood, and *Edward IV.*" *Medieval and Renaissance Drama in England* 18 (2005): 104–22.

Rowland 2010

Richard Rowland. *Thomas Heywood's Theatre, 1599–1639: Locations, Translations, and Conflict.* Farnham, UK, and Burlington, VT: Ashgate, 2010.

Rowse

A. L. Rowse. *Simon Forman: Sex and Society in Shakespeare's Age.* London: Weidenfeld and Nicolson, 1974.

RRDS
Regents Renaissance Drama Series

RSC
Royal Shakespeare Company

Rubik
Margarete Rubik. *Early Women Dramatists, 1550–1800.* Basingstoke, UK: Macmillan; New York: St. Martin's Press, 1998.

Rudnytsky
Peter L. Rudnytsky. *"A Woman Killed with Kindness* as a Subtext for *Othello."* *Renaissance Drama* 14 (1983): 103–24.

Rühl
Grobianus in England: Nebst Neudruck der ersten Übersetzung "The Schoole of Slovenrie" (1605) und erster Herausgabe des Schwankes "Grobiana's Nuptials" (c. 1640) aus Ms. 30. Bodl. Oxf. Ed. Ernst Rühl. Palaestra 38. Berlin: Mayer & Müller, 1904.

Ruoff 1955
James E. Ruoff. "A 'Lost' Manuscript of Lodowick Carlell's *Arviragus and Philicia."* *Notes and Queries* n.s. 2.1 (1955): 21–22.

Ruoff 1956
James E. Ruoff. "The Dating of Carlell's 'Passionate Lovers'." *Notes and Queries* n.s. 3.2 (1956): 68–70.

Russell
David L. Russell, ed. *Stuart Academic Drama: An Edition of Three University Plays.* New York and London: Garland, 1987.

Rutter 1984
Carol Chillington Rutter. *Documents of the Rose Playhouse.* Revels Plays Companion Library. Manchester: Manchester University Press, 1984.

Rutter 2006
Carol Chillington Rutter. "Of Tygers' Hearts and Players' Hides." In *Shakespeare's Histories and Counter-Histories*, ed. Dermot Cavanagh, Stuart Hampton-Reeves, and Stephen Longstaffe, 182–97. Manchester: Manchester University Press; New York: Palgrave, 2006.

Rutter 2009
Tom Rutter. "Adult Playing Companies 1603–1613." In *The Oxford Handbook of Early Modern Theatre*, ed. Richard Dutton, 72–87. Oxford: Oxford University Press, 2009.

Saccio 1969
Peter Saccio. *The Court Comedies of John Lyly: A Study in Allegorical Dramaturgy.* Princeton: Princeton University Press, 1969.

Saccio 1975

Peter Saccio. "The Oddity of Lyly's *Endimion.*" *Elizabethan Theatre* 5 (1975): 92–111.

Saccio 2007

A Mad World, My Masters. Ed. Peter Saccio. In *Thomas Middleton: The Collected Works,* gen. eds. Gary Taylor and John Lavagnino. Oxford: Clarendon Press, 2007.

Saeger & Fassler

James P. Saeger and Christopher J. Fassler. "The London Professional Theater, 1576–1642: A Catalogue and Analysis of the Extant Printed Plays." *Research Opportunities in Renaissance Drama* 34 (1995): 63–109.

Salgādo

Gāmini Salgādo. *Eyewitnesses of Shakespeare: First Hand Accounts of Performances 1590–1890.* London: Sussex University Press by Chatto & Windus, 1975.

Salingar

Leo Salingar. *Shakespeare and the Traditions of Comedy.* Cambridge: Cambridge University Press, 1974.

Salmon

Eric Salmon. "Tatham, John (*fl.* 1632–1664)." In *ODNB* 53: 823.

Sams 1985a

Shakespeare's Lost Play: "Edmund Ironside." Ed. Eric Sams. London: Fourth Estate; New York: St. Martin's Press, 1985.

Sams 1985b

Eric Sams. "The Timing of the *Shrews.*" *Notes and Queries* 32.1 (1985): 33–45.

Sams 1995

Eric Sams. *The Real Shakespeare: Retrieving the Early Years, 1564–1594.* New Haven, and London: Yale University Press, 1995.

Sams 1996

Shakespeare's "Edward III": An Early Play Restored to the Canon. Ed. Eric Sams. New Haven, and London: Yale University Press, 1996.

Sanders 1970

Robert Greene. *James the Fourth.* Ed. Norman Sanders. Revels Plays. London: Methuen, 1970.

Sanders 1987

Norman Sanders. "Thomas Nabbes." In *Dictionary of Literary Biography* 58: *Jacobean and Caroline Dramatists,* ed. Fredson Bowers, 223–30. Detroit: Gale, 1987.

Sanders 1998a

Eve Rachele Sanders. *Gender and Literacy on Stage in Early Modern England.* Cambridge: Cambridge University Press, 1998.

Sanders 1998b

Julie Sanders. *Ben Jonson's Theatrical Republics*. Basingstoke, UK, and London: Macmillan, 1998.

Sanders 1999a

Julie Sanders. *Caroline Drama: The Plays of Massinger, Ford, Shirley and Brome*. Writers and Their Work. Plymouth, UK: Northcote House, 1999.

Sanders 1999b

Julie Sanders. "The Politics of Escapism: Fantasies of Travel and Power in Richard Brome's *The Antipodes* and Ben Jonson's *The Alchemist*." In *Writing and Fantasy*, ed. Ceri Sullivan and Barbara White, 137–50. London and New York: Longman, 1999.

Sanders 1999c

Julie Sanders. "'Twill fit the players yet': Women and Theatre in Jonson's Late Plays." In *Ben Jonson and Theatre: Performance, Practice and Theory*, ed. Richard Cave, Elizabeth Schafer, and Brian Woolland, 179–90. London and New York: Routledge, 1999.

Sanders 2000

Julie Sanders. "Caroline Salon Culture and Female Agency: The Countess of Carlisle, Henrietta Maria, and Public Theatre." *Theatre Journal* 52.4 (2000): 449–64.

Sanders 2002

Julie Sanders. "Beggars' Commonwealths and the Pre-Civil War Stage: Suckling's *The Goblins*, Brome's *A Jovial Crew*, and Shirley's *The Sisters*." *Modern Language Review* 97.1 (2002): 1–14.

Sanders 2003

Julie Sanders. "*The New Inn* and *The Magnetic Lady*: Jonson's Dramaturgy in the Caroline Context." In *Jonsonians: Living Traditions*, ed. Brian Woolland, 51–66. Studies in Performance and Early Modern Drama. Aldershot, UK, and Burlington, VT: Ashgate, 2003.

Sanders 2004a

Julie Sanders. "Carlell [Carlile], Lodowick (1601/2–1675)." In *ODNB* 10: 103–04.

Sanders 2004b

Julie Sanders. "Glapthorne, Henry (*bap.* 1610)." In *ODNB* 22: 428–29.

Sanders 2004c

Julie Sanders. "Richards, Nathanael (*fl.* 1630–1660)." In *ODNB* 46: 787.

Sanders 2010

Julie Sanders, ed. *Ben Jonson in Context*. Cambridge: Cambridge University Press, 2010.

Sanders & Atherton

Julie Sanders and Ian Atherton. "Introducing *The 1630s*: Questions of Parliaments, Peace and Pressure Points." In *The 1630s: Interdisciplinary Essays on Culture and Politics in the Caroline Era*, ed. eidem, 1–27. Manchester: Manchester University Press; New York: Palgrave, 2006.

Saunders

J. W. Saunders. "Staging at the Globe, 1599–1613." In *The Seventeenth-Century Stage: A Collection of Critical Essays*, ed. Gerald Eades Bentley, 235–66. Chicago and London: University of Chicago Press, 1968.

Savage

James E. Savage. "The Date of Beaumont and Fletcher's *Cupid's Revenge.*" *ELH* 15.4 (1948): 286–94.

Scattergood

John Scattergood. "*The Contention between Liberality and Prodigality*—A Late Morality Play." *Acta* 13 (1987): 153–67.

Schafer 1994

Thomas Middleton. *The Witch*. Ed. Elizabeth Schafer. New Mermaids. London: Black; New York: Norton, 1994.

Schafer 2009

William Shakespeare. *Twelfth Night*. Ed. Elizabeth Schafer. Shakespeare in Production. Cambridge: Cambridge University Press, 2009.

Schell & Shuchter

English Morality Plays and Moral Interludes. Ed. Edgar T. Schell and J. D. Shuchter. New York: Holt, Rinehart and Winston, 1969.

Schelling

Felix E. Schelling. *Elizabethan Playwrights: A Short History of the English Drama from Mediæval Times to the Closing of the Theaters in 1642*. New York and London: Harper, 1925.

Scherb

Victor L. Scherb. "Playing at Maturity in John Redford's *Wit and Science.*" *Studies in English Literature, 1500–1900* 45.2 (2005): 271–97.

Scheurweghs

Nicholas Udall's "Roister Doister." Ed. G. Scheurweghs. Materials for the Study of the Old English Drama n.s. 16. Louvain: Uystpruyst, 1939.

Schillinger

Stephen Schillinger. "Begging at the Gate: *Jack Straw* and the Acting Out of Popular Rebellion." *Medieval and Renaissance Drama in England* 21 (2008): 87–127.

Schleiner
Louise Schleiner. *Tudor and Stuart Women Writers*. Bloomington and Indianapolis: Indiana University Press, 1994.

Schlueter 1990
William Shakespeare. *The Two Gentlemen of Verona*. Ed. Kurt Schlueter. New Cambridge Shakespeare. Cambridge: Cambridge University Press, 1990.

Schlueter 1999
June Schlueter. "Rereading the Peacham Drawing." *Shakespeare Quarterly* 50.2 (1999): 171–84.

Schlueter 2011
June Schlueter. "Shackerley Marmion *Redux*: A Second Look at *The Soddered Citizen*." *Ben Jonson Journal* 18.1 (2011): 101–12.

Schneider
Brian W. Schneider. *The Framing Text in Early Modern English Drama: "Whining" Prologues and "Armed" Epilogues*. Farnham, UK, and Burlington, VT: Ashgate, 2011.

Schoell
"*Charlemagne (The Distracted Emperor)*," *Drame Élisabéthain Anonyme: Edition Critique*. Ed. Franck L. Schoell. Princeton: Princeton University Press; London: Humphrey Milford, 1920.

Schoenbaum 1954
Samuel Schoenbaum. "*The Revenger's Tragedy*: Jacobean Dance of Death." *Modern Language Quarterly* 15.3 (1954): 201–07.

Schoenbaum 1955
Samuel Schoenbaum. *Middleton's Tragedies: A Critical Study*. New York: Columbia University Press, 1955.

Schoenbaum 1964a
Alfred Harbage. *Annals of English Drama, 975–1700*. Rev. S. Schoenbaum. London: Methuen, 1964.

Schoenbaum 1964b
S. Schoenbaum. "*Wit's Triumvirate*: A Caroline Comedy Recovered." *Studies in English Literature, 1500–1900* 4.2 (1964): 227–37.

Schoenbaum 1966a
S. Schoenbaum. *Annals of English Drama, 975–1700: Supplement to the Revised Edition*. Evanston, IL: Department of English, Northwestern University, 1966.

Schoenbaum 1966b
S. Schoenbaum. *Internal Evidence and Elizabethan Dramatic Authorship: An Essay in Literary History and Method*. Evanston, IL: Northwestern University Press, 1966.

Schoenbaum 1970

S. Schoenbaum. *Annals of English Drama, 975–1700: A Second Supplement to the Revised Edition.* Evanston, IL: Department of English, Northwestern University, 1970.

Schoenbaum 1977

S. Schoenbaum. *William Shakespeare: A Compact Documentary Life.* New York: Oxford University Press, 1977.

Schoenbaum & Brown

Thomas Drue. *The Bloody Banquet.* Ed. Samuel Schoenbaum and Arthur Brown. MSR. Oxford: Oxford University Press, 1961 [1962].

Schoone-Jongen

Terence G. Schoone-Jongen. *Shakespeare's Companies: William Shakespeare's Early Career and the Acting Companies, 1577–1594.* Farnham, UK, and Burlington, VT: Ashgate, 2008.

Schrickx

Willem Schrickx. "'Pericles' in a Book-List of 1619 from the English Jesuit Mission and Some of the Play's Special Problems." *Shakespeare Survey* 29 (1976): 21–32.

Schroeder

John W. Schroeder. "*The Taming of a Shrew* and *The Taming of the Shrew*: A Case Reopened." *JEGP* 57.3 (1958): 424–43.

Scott 1810

Walter Scott [BL catalogue]. *The Ancient British Drama.* 3 vols. London: William Miller, 1810.

Scott 1945

Virgil Joseph Scott. "A Reinterpretation of John Tatham's *The Rump: or The Mirrour of the Late Times.*" *Philological Quarterly* 24.2 (1945): 114–18.

Scott 2008

Charlotte Scott. "Still Life? Anthropocentrism and the Fly in *Titus Andronicus* and *Volpone.*" *Shakespeare Survey* 61 (2008): 256–68.

Scott 2011

Amy Scott. "Events and Texts: The Prologues and Epilogues of the Arbury Plays." *Early Theatre* 14.2 (2011): 227–44.

Scoville

Chester Scoville. "On Bombshells and Faulty Assumptions: What the Digby *Conversion of Saint Paul* Really Did with the Acts of the Apostles." In *"Bring furth the pagants": Essays in Early English Drama Presented to Alexandra F. Johnston,* ed. David N. Klausner and Karen Sawyer Marsalek, 197–211. Toronto, Buffalo, and London: University of Toronto Press, 2007.

Scragg 1973
Leah Scragg. "Macbeth on Horseback." *Shakespeare Survey* 26 (1973): 81–88.

Scragg 1987
Leah Scragg. "John Lyly." In *Dictionary of Literary Biography* 62: *Elizabethan Dramatists*, ed. Fredson Bowers, 196–211. Detroit: Gale, 1987.

Scragg 1997
John Lyly: Selected Prose and Dramatic Work. Ed. Leah Scragg. Manchester: Carcanet, 1997.

Scragg 1998
John Lyly. *"Gallathea," 1592*. Ed. Leah Scragg. MSR. Oxford: Oxford University Press, 1998.

Scragg 1999
Leah Scragg. "*Campaspe* and the Construction of Monarchical Power." *Medieval and Renaissance Drama in England* 12 (1999): 59–83.

Scragg 2002
John Lyly. *"Sapho and Phao," 1584*. Ed. Leah Scragg. MSR. Oxford: Oxford University Press, 2002.

Scragg 2003
John Lyly. *"Euphues: The Anatomy of Wit" and "Euphues and His England."* Ed. Leah Scragg. Revels Plays Companion Library. Manchester: Manchester University Press; New York: Palgrave, 2003.

Scragg 2005
Leah Scragg. "Speaking Pictures: Style and Spectacle in Lylian Comedy." *English Studies* 86.4 (2005): 298–311.

Scragg 2006
John Lyly. *The Woman in the Moon*. Ed. Leah Scragg. Revels Plays. Manchester and New York: Manchester University Press, 2006.

Scragg 2008
John Lyly. *Love's Metamorphosis*. Ed. Leah Scragg. Revels Plays. Manchester: Manchester University Press, 2008.

Seltzer 1962
The Interlude of Vice (Horestes). Ed. Daniel Seltzer. MSR. Oxford: Oxford University Press, 1962.

Seltzer 1963
Robert Greene. *Friar Bacon and Friar Bungay*. Ed. Daniel Seltzer. RRDS. Lincoln: University of Nebraska Press, 1963.

Senescu
James Shirley's "The Bird in a Cage": A Critical Edition. Ed. Frances Frazier Senescu. New York and London: Garland, 1980.

Seronsy
Cecil Seronsy. *Samuel Daniel*. TEAS 49. New York: Twayne, 1967.

Sessions
William A. Sessions. "Literature and the Court." In *The Cambridge History of Early Modern English Literature*, ed. David Loewenstein and Janel Mueller, 229–56. Cambridge: Cambridge University Press, 2002.

Shand
G. B. Shand. "The Stagecraft of *Women Beware Women*." *Research Opportunities in Renaissance Drama* 28 (1985): 29–36.

Shapiro 1955
I. A. Shapiro. "The Significance of a Date." *Shakespeare Survey* 8 (1955): 100–05.

Shapiro 1977
Michael Shapiro. *Children of the Revels: The Boy Companies of Shakespeare's Time and Their Plays*. New York: Columbia University Press, 1977.

Shapiro 1989
Michael Shapiro. "John Pikeryng's *Horestes*: Auspices and Theatricality." In *Shakespeare and Dramatic Tradition: Essays in Honor of S. F. Johnson*, ed. W. R. Elton and William B. Long, 211–26. Newark, DE: University of Delaware Press; London and Toronto: Associated University Presses, 1989.

Shapiro 1991
James Shapiro. "'Tragedies naturally performed': Kyd's Representation of Violence, *The Spanish Tragedy* (*c.* 1587)." In *Staging the Renaissance: Reinterpretations of Elizabethan and Jacobean Drama*, ed. David Scott Kastan and Peter Stallybrass, 99–113. New York and London: Routledge, 1991.

Shapiro 1994
Michael Shapiro. *Gender in Play on the Shakespearean Stage: Boy Heroines and Female Pages*. Ann Arbor: University of Michigan Press, 1994.

Shapiro 1998
Michael Shapiro. "Cross-dressing in Elizabethan Robin Hood Plays." In *Playing Robin Hood: The Legend as Performance in Five Centuries*, ed. Lois Potter, 77–90. Newark, DE: University of Delaware Press; London: Associated University Presses, 1998.

Shapiro 2002
Michael Shapiro. "Patronage and the Companies of Boy Actors." In *Shakespeare and Theatrical Patronage in Early Modern England*, ed. Paul Whitfield White and Suzanne R. Westfall, 272–94. Cambridge: Cambridge University Press, 2002.

Shapiro 2005
James Shapiro. *1599, A Year in the Life of William Shakespeare*. London: Faber, 2005.

Shapiro 2009
Michael Shapiro. "Early (Pre-1590) Boy Companies and Their Acting Venues." In *The Oxford Handbook of the Early Modern Theatre*, ed. Richard Dutton, 120–35. Oxford: Oxford University Press, 2009.

Sharp 1835
Thomas Sharp. *Ancient Mysteries from the Digby Manuscripts, Preserved in the Bodleian Library, Oxford*. Edinburgh: Abbotsford Club, 1835.

Sharpe 1987
Kevin Sharpe. *Criticism and Compliment: The Politics of Literature in the England of Charles I*. Cambridge: Cambridge University Press, 1987.

Shaver
Chester Linn Shaver. "The Date of *Revenge for Honour*." *Modern Language Notes* 53.2 (1938): 96–98.

Shaw 1979
Catherine M. Shaw. *"Some Vanity of Mine Art": The Masque in English Renaissance Drama*. 2 vols. Salzburg Studies in English Literature 81. Salzburg: Institut für Anglistik und Amerikanistik, Universität Salzburg, 1979.

Shaw 1980
Catherine M. Shaw. *Richard Brome*. TEAS 290. Boston: Twayne, 1980.

Shaw 1982
Thomas Middleton and William Rowley. *The Old Law*. Ed. Catherine M. Shaw. New York and London: Garland, 1982.

Shaw 1986
Aston Cokayne. *The Obstinate Lady*. Ed. Catherine Shaw. New York and London: Garland, 1986.

Shenk
Linda Shenk. "Gown before Crown: Scholarly Abjection and Academic Entertainment under Queen Elizabeth I." In *Early Modern Academic Drama*, ed. Jonathan Walker and Paul D. Streufert, 19–44. Farnham, UK, and Burlington, VT: Ashgate, 2008.

Shepherd & Womack
Simon Shepherd and Peter Womack. *English Drama: A Cultural History*. Oxford: Blackwell, 1996.

Sherman
Stuart P. Sherman. "A New Play by John Ford." *Modern Language Notes* 23.8 (1908): 245–49.

Shewring
Margaret Shewring. *King Richard II*. Shakespeare in Performance. Manchester: Manchester University Press; New York: St. Martin's Press, 1996.

Shirley 1961
Frances Ann Shirley. *Shakespeare's Use of Off-Stage Sounds*. Lincoln: University of
    Nebraska Press, 1963.

Shirley 1972
John Webster. *The Devil's Law-Case*. Ed. Frances A. Shirley. RRDS. Lincoln:
    University of Nebraska Press, 1972.

Shirley 2005
William Shakespeare. *Troilus and Cressida*. Ed. Frances A. Shirley. Shakespeare
    in Production. Cambridge: Cambridge University Press, 2005.

Shrank
Cathy Shrank. "John Bale and Reconfiguring the 'Medieval' in Reformation
    England." In *Reading the Medieval in Early Modern England*, ed. Gordon
    McMullan and David Matthews, 179–92. Cambridge: Cambridge Univer-
    sity Press, 2007.

Shroeder
John W. Shroeder. "*The Taming of a Shrew* and *The Taming of the Shrew*: A Case
    Reopened." *JEGP* 57.3 (1958): 424–43.

Shullenberger
William Shullenberger. "'This For the Most Wrong'd of Women': A Reappraisal
    of *The Maid's Tragedy*." *Renaissance Drama* n.s. 13 (1982): 131–56.

Sider
The Troublesome Raigne of John, King of England. Ed. J. W. Sider. New York and
    London: Garland, 1979.

Siemon 1994
Christopher Marlowe. *The Jew of Malta*. Ed. James R. Siemon. 2nd ed. New
    Mermaids. London: Black; New York: Norton, 1994. Repr. 2002.

Siemon 2009
William Shakespeare. *King Richard III*. Ed. James R. Siemon. Arden 3. London:
    Black, 2009.

Sieveking
Work for Cutlers or A Merry Dialogue between Sword, Rapier and Dagger. Ed. Al-
    bert Forbes Sieveking. London: Clay, 1904.

Simmons
J. L. Simmons. "*Lust's Dominion*: A Showpiece for the Globe?" *Tulane Studies in
    English* 20 (1972): 11–22.

Simpson 1871
Richard Simpson. "Are There Any Extant MSS. in Shakespeare's Handwriting?"
    Notes and Queries, 4th ser., 8 (1 July 1871): 1–3.

Simpson 1878
Richard Simpson, ed. *The School of Shakspere*. 2 vols. New York: Bouton, 1878.

Simpson 1908
The Life of Sir John Oldcastle, 1600. Ed. Percy Simpson. MSR. Oxford: Oxford University Press, 1908.

Singman
Jeffrey L. Singman. "Munday's Unruly Earl." In *Playing Robin Hood: The Legend as Performance in Five Centuries*, ed. Lois Potter, 63–76. Newark, DE: University of Delaware Press; London: Associated University Presses, 1998.

Sisson 1927
Philip Massinger. *Believe as You List.* Ed. Charles J. Sisson. MSR. Oxford: Oxford University Press, 1927 [1928].

Sisson 1942
Charles J. Sisson. "Shakespeare Quartos as Prompt-Copies, with Some Account of Cholmeley's Players and a New Shakespeare Allusion." *Review of English Studies* 18 (1942): 129–43.

Skantze
P. A. Skantze. *Stillness in Motion in the Seventeenth-Century Theatre.* London and New York: Routledge, 2003.

Skemp
Nathanael Richards' "Tragedy of Messallina, The Roman Emperesse." Ed. A. R. Skemp. Materialien zur Kunde des älteren Englischen Dramas 30. Louvain: Uystpruyst, 1910.

Skerpan
Elizabeth Skerpan. *The Rhetoric of Politics in the English Revolution, 1642–1660.* Columbia and London: University of Missouri Press, 1992.

Skura
Meredith Skura. "Anthony Munday's 'Gentrification' of Robin Hood." *English Literary Renaissance* 33.2 (2003): 155–80.

Smallwood & Wells
Thomas Dekker. *The Shoemaker's Holiday.* Ed. R. L. Smallwood and Stanley Wells. Revels Plays. Manchester: Manchester University Press; Baltimore: Johns Hopkins University Press, 1979.

Smart & Greg
Jack Juggler. Ed. Eunice Lilian Smart and W. W. Greg. MSR. Oxford: Oxford University Press, 1933.

Smeak
George Chapman. *The Widow's Tears.* Ed. Ethel M. Smeak. RRDS. Lincoln: University of Nebraska Press, 1966.

Smith 1872

The Female Rebellion, A Tragicomedy from a MS. in the Hunterian Museum, University of Glasgow. Ed. Alexander Smith. Glasgow: privately printed, 1872. Notes supplied by John Payne Collier.

Smith 1907a

"*Club Law*": *A Comedy Acted in Clare Hall, Cambridge about 1599–1600.* Ed. G. C. Moore Smith. Cambridge: Cambridge University Press, 1907.

Smith 1907b

Logan Pearsall Smith. *The Life and Letters of Sir Henry Wotton.* 2 vols. Oxford: Clarendon Press, 1907.

Smith 1908

G. C. Moore Smith. "Notes on Some English University Plays." *Modern Language Review* 3.2 (1908): 141–56.

Smith 1923

G. C. Moore Smith. *College Plays Performed in the University of Cambridge.* Cambridge: Cambridge University Press, 1923.

Smith 1927

G. C. Moore Smith. *Thomas Randolph.* Warton Lecture on English Poetry, British Academy. London: Oxford University Press, 1927.

Smith 1929

G. C. Moore Smith. "*The Drinking Academy* and Its Attribution to Thomas Randolph." *PMLA* 44.2 (1929): 631–33.

Smith 1942

Paul Edward Smith, ed. "*Pathomachia*": *An Edition.* Washington, DC: Catholic University of America Press, 1942.

Smith 1954

Warren D. Smith. "The *Henry V* Choruses in the First Folio." *JEGP* 53.1 (1954): 38–57.

Smith 1956

Irwin Smith. *Shakespeare's Globe Playhouse: A Modern Reconstruction in Text and Scale Drawings.* New York: Charles Scribner's Sons, 1956.

Smith 1965

John Marston. *The Fawn.* Ed. Gerald A. Smith. RRDS. Lincoln: University of Nebraska Press, 1965.

Smith 1970

George Chapman. *The Gentleman Usher.* Ed. John Hazel Smith. RRDS. Lincoln: University of Nebraska Press, 1970.

Smith 1977

Mary E. Smith. "Staging Marlowe's *Dido Queene of Carthage.*" *Studies in English Literature, 1500–1900* 17.2 (1977): 177–90.

Smith 1978

Denzell S. Smith. "Francis Beaumont and John Fletcher." In *The Later Jacobean and Caroline Dramatists: A Survey of Recent Studies in English Renaissance Drama*, ed. Terence P. Logan and idem, 3–89. Lincoln and London: University of Nebraska Press, 1978.

Smith 1979

Thomas May. *"The Tragoedy of Cleopatra, Queene of Aegypt": A Critical Edition*. Ed. Denzell S. Smith. New York and London: Garland, 1979.

Smith 1987a

John H. Smith, ed. *Bussy D'Ambois: A Tragedie*. In *The Plays of George Chapman: The Tragedies with "Sir Gyles Goosecappe": A Critical Edition*. Gen. ed. Allan Holaday. Cambridge: Brewer, 1987.

Smith 1987b

J. Smith. "The Authorship of *The Contention between Liberality and Prodigality*." *Notes and Queries* 34.2 (1987): 188–89.

Smith 1987c

M. W. A. Smith. "*The Revenger's Tragedy*: The Derivation and Interpretation of Statistical Results for Resolving Disputed Authorship." *Computers and the Humanities* 21.1 (1987): 21–55, 267.

Smith 1987d

Nigel Smith. "Richard Overton's Marpriest Tracts: Towards a History of Leveller Style." In *The Literature of Controversy: Polemical Strategy from Milton to Junius*, ed. Thomas N. Corns, 39–66. London: Frank Cass, 1987.

Smith 1988a

Bruce R. Smith. *Ancient Scripts and Modern Experience on the English Stage, 1500–1700*. Princeton: Princeton University Press, 1988.

Smith 1988b

A Critical Edition of Mildmay Fane's "Vertues Triumph" (1644). Ed. Gerald William Smith. New York: Lang, 1988.

Smith 1991a

M. W. A. Smith. "The Authorship of *The Revenger's Tragedy*." *Notes and Queries* 38.4 (1991): 508–13.

Smith 1991b

Bruce R. Smith. *Homosexual Desire in Shakespeare's England: A Cultural Poetics*. Chicago and London: University of Chicago Press, 1991.

Smith 1992

Molly Smith. "The Theater and the Scaffold: Death as Spectacle in *The Spanish Tragedy*." *Studies in English Literature, 1500–1900* 32.2 (1992): 217–32.

Smith 1994

Nigel Smith. *Literature and Revolution in England, 1640–1660.* New Haven and London: Yale University Press, 1994.

Smith 1998

Thomas Kyd: "The Spanish Tragedie" with Anonymous: "The First Part of Jeronimo." Ed. Emma Smith. London and New York: Penguin, 1998.

Smith 1999

Emma Smith. "Author v. Character in Early Modern Dramatic Authorship: The Example of Thomas Kyd and *The Spanish Tragedy.*" *Medieval and Renaissance Drama in England* 11 (1999): 129–42.

Smith 2000

Robert A. H. Smith. "Marlowe and Peele: A Further Note on the Final Scholar Scene in the *Doctor Faustus* B Text." *Notes and Queries* 47.1 (2000): 40–42.

Smith 2006

Bruce R. Smith. "Speaking What We Feel about *King Lear.*" In *Shakespeare, Memory and Performance*, ed. Peter Holland, 23–42. Cambridge: Cambridge University Press, 2006.

Smith 2012

Emma Smith, ed. *Five Revenge Tragedies: Kyd, Shakespeare, Marston, Chettle, Middleton.* London and New York: Penguin, 2012.

Smout

Clare Smout. "Actor, Poet, Playwright, Sharer . . . Rival? Shakespeare and Heywood, 1603–4." *Early Theatre* 13.2 (2010): 175–89.

Smyth 2006

Adam Smyth. "'Art Reflexive': The Poetry, Sermons, and Drama of William Strode (1601?-1645)." *Studies in Philology* 103.4 (2006): 436–64.

Snyder 1980

A Critical Edition of "The Faire Maide of the Exchange." Ed. Karl E. Snyder. New York and London: Garland, 1980.

Snyder 1993

William Shakespeare. *All's Well That Ends Well.* Ed. Susan Snyder. Oxford: Clarendon Press, 1993.

Snyder 2002

Susan Snyder. *Shakespeare: A Wayward Journey.* Newark, DE: University of Delaware Press; Cranbury, NJ: Associated University Presses, 2002.

Snyder & Curren-Aquino

William Shakespeare. *The Winter's Tale.* Ed. Susan Snyder and Deborah T. Curren-Aquino. New Cambridge Shakespeare. Cambridge: Cambridge University Press, 2007.

Soellner

Rolf Soellner. "Chapman's *Caesar and Pompey* and the Fortunes of Prince Henry." *Medieval and Renaissance Drama in England* 2 (1985): 135–51.

Sofer

Andrew Sofer. *The Stage Life of Props*. Ann Arbor: University of Michigan Press, 2003.

Sohmer

Steve Sohmer. *Shakespeare's Mystery Play: The Opening of the Globe Theatre 1599*. Manchester: Manchester University Press; New York: St. Martin's Press, 1999.

Solve

Norma Dobie Solve. *Stuart Politics in Chapman's "Tragedy of Chabot."* University of Michigan Publications: Language and Literature 4. Ann Arbor: University of Michigan Press, 1928.

Somerset 1974

J. A. B. Somerset, ed. *Four Tudor Interludes*. London: Athlone Press, 1974.

Somerset 1977

"A Play of Love," 1534. Ed. J. A. B. Somerset. MSR. Oxford: Oxford University Press, 1977 [1978].

Somerset 1985

J. A. B. Somerset. "Local Drama and Playing Places at Shrewsbury: New Findings from the Borough Records." *Medieval and Renaissance Drama in England* 2 (1985): 1–32.

Somerset 1994

J. Alan B. Somerset, ed. *Shropshire*. REED. 2 vols. Toronto, Buffalo, and London: University of Toronto Press, 1994.

Somogyi 1998

Nick de Somogyi. *Shakespeare's Theatre of War*. Aldershot, UK; Brookfield, VT: Ashgate, 1998.

Somogyi 2007

William Shakespeare. *The Merry Wives of Windsor*. Ed. Nick de Somogyi. The Shakespeare Folios. London: Nick Hern Books, 2007.

Sonnenshein

Shakerly Marmion. *"A Fine Companion," A Critical Edition*. Ed. Richard Sonnenshein. New York and London: Garland, 1979.

Sorlien

Robert Parker Sorlien, ed. *The Diary of John Manningham of the Middle Temple, 1602–1603*. Hanover, NH: University Press of New England for the University of Rhode Island, 1976.

Southern 1952
Richard Southern. *Changeable Scenery: Its Origin and Development in the British Theatre*. London: Faber, 1952.

Southern 1961
Richard Southern. *The Seven Ages of the Theatre*. New York: Hill and Wang, 1961.

Southern 1973
Richard Southern. *The Staging of Plays before Shakespeare*. London: Faber and Faber, 1973.

Spedding 1850
James Spedding. "Who Wrote Shakespeare's *Henry VIII*?" *Gentleman's Magazine* 178 (August and September 1850): 115–23, 381–82.

Spedding 1872
James Spedding. "Shakespeare's Handwriting." *Notes and Queries* 4.10 (1872): 227–28.

Spencer
John Ford. *The Broken Heart*. Ed. T. J. B. Spencer. Revels Plays. Manchester: Manchester University Press; Baltimore: Johns Hopkins University Press, 1980.

Spinrad
Phoebe S. Spinrad. *The Summons of Death on the Medieval and Renaissance English Stage*. Columbus: Ohio State University Press, 1987.

Spevack
William Shakespeare. *Julius Caesar*. Ed. Marvin Spevack. New Cambridge Shakespeare. Cambridge: Cambridge University Press, 1988.

Spivack 1958
Bernard Spivack. *Shakespeare and the Allegory of Evil: The History of a Metaphor in Relation to His Villains*. New York and London: Columbia University Press, 1958.

Spivack 1967
Charlotte Spivack. *George Chapman*. TEAS 60. New York: Twayne, 1967.

Sponsler
Claire Sponsler. *Drama and Resistance: Bodies, Goods, and Theatricality in Late Medieval England*. Medieval Cultures 10. Minneapolis and London: University of Minnesota Press, 1997.

Spove
A Critical Old-Spelling Edition of Richard Brome's "A Mad Couple Well Match'd." Ed. Steen H. Spove. New York and London: Garland, 1979.

Spradlin

Derrick Spradlin. "Imperial Anxiety in Thomas Hughes's *The Misfortunes of Arthur.*" *Early Modern Literary Studies* 10.3 (2005). http://purl.oclc.org/emls/10-3/spramisf.htm.

Squier

Charles L. Squier. "Henry Glapthorne." In *Dictionary of Literary Biography* 58: *Jacobean and Caroline Dramatists*, ed. Fredson Bowers, 107–14. Detroit: Gale, 1987.

SR

Stationers' Register; see entries for Arber as well as Eyre and Rivington

Stanton

Kamille Stone Stanton. "The Domestication of Royalist Themes in *The Concealed Fancies* by Jane Cavendish and Elizabeth Brackley." *Clio* 36.2 (2007): 177–97.

Star

L. R. Star. "A Note on the Use of Scenery at the Cockpit-in-Court." *Theatre Notebook* 26.3 (1972): 89–91.

Starr

Nathan Comfort Starr. "*The Concealed Fansyes*: A Play by Lady Jane Cavendish and Lady Elizabeth Brackley." *PMLA* 46.3 (1931): 802–38.

STC

A Short-Title Catalogue of Books Printed in England, Scotland, & Ireland and of English Books Printed Abroad, 1475–1640. Compiled by A. W. Pollard and G. R. Redgrave. 2nd ed. Revised and enlarged by W. A. Jackson, F. S. Ferguson, and Katharine F. Pantzer. 3 vols. London: Bibliographical Society, 1976–91.

Steadman

John M. Steadman. "Falstaff as Actaeon: A Dramatic Emblem." *Shakespeare Quarterly* 14.3 (1963): 231–44.

Steen

Richard Brome. *The English Moore; or The Mock-Marriage.* Ed. Sara Jayne Steen. Columbia: University of Missouri Press, 1983.

Steggle 1998

Matthew Steggle. *Wars of the Theatres: The Poetics of Personation in the Age of Jonson.* English Literary Studies Monograph Series 75. Victoria, British Columbia: University of Victoria Press, 1998.

Steggle 2000

Matthew Steggle. "Varieties of Fantasy in 'What You Will'." In *The Drama of John Marston: Critical Re-Visions*, ed. T. F. Wharton, 45–59. Cambridge: Cambridge University Press, 2000.

Steggle 2004a

Matthew Steggle. "*The Knave in Grain* Puts Holland's Leaguer On Stage." *Notes and Queries* 51.4 (2004): 355–56.

Steggle 2004b

Matthew Steggle. *Richard Brome: Place and Politics on the Caroline Stage.* Revels Plays Companion Library. Manchester: Manchester University Press; New York: Palgrave; Vancouver: UBC Press, 2004.

Steggle 2007

Matthew Steggle. *Laughing and Weeping in Early Modern Theatres.* Aldershot, UK, and Burlington, VT: Ashgate, 2007.

Steggle 2010

Matthew Steggle. "Jonson in the Elizabethan Period." In *Ben Jonson in Context*, ed. Julie Sanders, 15–22. Cambridge: Cambridge University Press, 2010.

Stern 1997

Tiffany Stern. "Was *Totus Mundus Agit Histrionem* Ever the Motto of the Globe Theatre?" *Theatre Notebook* 51.3 (1997): 122–27.

Stern 2002

Globe Quartos: "King Leir." Ed. Tiffany Stern. London: Nick Hern Books; New York: Routledge, 2002.

Stern 2004a

Tiffany Stern. "Re-patching the Play." In *From Script to Stage in Early Modern England*, ed. Peter Holland and Stephen Orgel, 151–77. Basingstoke, UK, and New York: Palgrave Macmillan, 2004.

Stern 2004b

Tiffany Stern. "'A small-beer health to his second day': Playwrights, Prologues, and First Performances in the Early Modern Theater." *Studies in Philology* 101.2 (2004): 172–99.

Stern 2006

Tiffany Stern. "Taking Part: Actors and Audience on the Stage at Blackfriars." In *Inside Shakespeare: Essays on the Blackfriars Stage*, ed. Paul Menzer, 35–53. Selinsgrove, PA: Susquehanna University Press, 2006.

Stern 2009a

Tiffany Stern. "Actors' Parts." In *The Oxford Handbook of the Early Modern Theatre*, ed. Richard Dutton, 496–512. Oxford: Oxford University Press, 2009.

Stern 2009b

Tiffany Stern. "'The Curtain Is Yours'." In *Locating the Queen's Men, 1583–1603: Material Practices and Conditions of Playing*, ed. Helen Ostovich, Holger Schott Syme, and Andrew Griffin, 77–96. Farnham, UK, and Burlington, VT: Ashgate, 2009.

Stern 2009c
Tiffany Stern. *Documents of Performance in Early Modern England*. Cambridge: Cambridge University Press, 2009.

Stern 2010a
Tiffany Stern. "Epilogues, Prayers after Plays, and Shakespeare's *2 Henry IV.*" *Theatre Notebook* 64.3 (2010): 122–29.

Stern 2010b
Tiffany Stern. "The Theatre of Shakespeare's London." In *The New Cambridge Companion to Shakespeare*, ed. Margreta de Grazia and Stanley Wells, 45–59. Cambridge: Cambridge University Press, 2010.

Stern 2011
Tiffany Stern. "'The Forgery of some modern Author'?: Theobald's Shakespeare and Cardenio's *Double Falsehood.*" *Shakespeare Quarterly* 62.4 (2011): 555–93.

Stevens 1977
David Stevens. "The Stagecraft of James Shirley." *Educational Theatre Journal* 29.4 (1977): 493–516.

Stevens 1979
David Stevens. "The Staging of Plays at the Salisbury Court Theatre, 1630–1642." *Theatre Journal* 31.4 (1979): 511–25.

Stevens 2009
Andrea Stevens. "Mastering Masques of Blackness: Jonson's *Masque of Blackness*, The Windsor Text of *The Gypsies Metamorphosed*, and Brome's *The English Moor.*" *English Literary Renaissance* 39.2 (2009): 396–426.

Stevens 2010
Andrea Stevens. "'*The Eunuch Much Sears Her Breast*': Remedying Adulteration in William Heminge's *The Fatal Contract.*" In *Thunder at a Playhouse: Essaying Shakespeare and the Early Modern Stage*, ed. Peter Kanelos and Matt Kozusko, 212–33. Selinsgrove, PA: Susquehanna University Press, 2010.

Stevenson 1968
Warren Stevenson. "Shakespeare's Hand in *The Spanish Tragedy* 1602." *Studies in English Literature, 1500–1900* 8.2 (1968): 307–21.

Stevenson 2008
Warren Stevenson. *Shakespeare's Additions to Thomas Kyd's "The Spanish Tragedy": A Fresh Look at the Evidence Regarding the 1602 Additions*. Lewiston, Queenston, and Lampeter: Edwin Mellen Press, 2008.

Stirling
Brents Stirling. "Daniel's *Philotas* and the Essex Case." *Modern Language Quarterly* 3.4 (1942): 583–94.

Stokes 1872
Beaunans Meriasek, The Life of Saint Meriasek, Bishop and Confessor, A Cornish Drama. Ed. and trans. by Whitley Stokes. London: Trübner, 1872.

Stokes 1996
James Stokes, with Robert J. Alexander. *Somerset including Bath.* REED. 2 vols. Toronto, Buffalo, and London: University of Toronto Press, 1996.

Straznicky 1994
Marta Straznicky. "'Profane Stoical Paradoxes': *The Tragedie of Mariam* and Sidneian Closet Drama." *English Literary Renaissance* 24.1 (1994): 104–34.

Straznicky 1995
Marta Straznicky. "Reading the Stage: Margaret Cavendish and Commonwealth Closet Drama." *Criticism* 37.3 (1995): 355–412.

Straznicky 2004
Marta Straznicky. *Privacy, Playreading, and Women's Closet Drama, 1550–1700.* Cambridge: Cambridge University Press, 2004.

Straznicky 2006a
Marta Straznicky. "Reading through the Body: Women and Printed Drama." In *The Book of the Play: Playwrights, Stationers, and Readers in Early Modern England,* ed. eadem, 59–79. Amherst and Boston: University of Massachusetts Press, 2006.

Straznicky 2006b
Marta Straznicky. "The Red Bull Repertory in Print, 1605–60." *Early Theatre* 9.2 (2006): 144–56.

Straznicky & Rowland
"The Tragedy of Mariam" 1613. Ed. A. C. Dunstan and W. W. Greg. Reprinted with a supplement by Marta Straznicky and Richard Rowland. MSR. Oxford: Oxford University Press, 1992.

Streitberger
W. R. Streitberger. "Adult Playing Companies to 1583." In *The Oxford Handbook of Early Modern Theatre,* ed. Richard Dutton, 19–38. Oxford: Oxford University Press, 2009.

Stretter
Robert Stretter. "Cicero on Stage: *Damon and Pithias* and the Fate of Classical Friendship in English Renaissance Drama." *Texas Studies in Literature and Language* 47.4 (2005): 345–65.

Strommer
Time's Distractions: A Play from the Time of Charles I. Ed. Diane Weltner Strommer. College Station: Texas A&M University Press, 1976.

Sturgess 1969
Keith Sturgess, ed. *Three Elizabethan Domestic Tragedies: "Arden of Faversham," "A Yorkshire Tragedy," "A Woman Killed with Kindness."* Baltimore: Penguin, 1969.

Sturgess 1987
Keith Sturgess. *Jacobean Private Theatre.* London and New York: Routledge, 1987.

Styan 1967
J. L. Styan. *Shakespeare's Stagecraft.* Cambridge: Cambridge University Press, 1967.

Styan 1996
J. L. Styan. *The English Stage: A History of Drama and Performance.* Cambridge: Cambridge University Press, 1996.

Sullivan 1998
Garrett A. Sullivan Jr. *The Drama of Landscape: Land, Property, and Social Relations on the Early Modern Stage.* Stanford: Stanford University Press, 1998.

Sullivan 2002
Ceri Sullivan. *The Rhetoric of Credit: Merchants in Early Modern Writing.* Madison and Teaneck, NJ: Fairleigh Dickinson University Press; London: Associated University Presses, 2002.

Sunesen
Bent Sunesen. "Marlowe and the Dumb Show." *English Studies* 35.1–6 (1954): 241–53.

Sutcliffe
Christopher Sutcliffe. "Kempe and Armin: The Management of Change." *Theatre Notebook* 50.3 (1996): 122–34.

Swaen 1899
A. E. H. Swaen. "Robert Daborne's Plays: *The Poor Man's Comfort.*" *Anglia* 21 (1899): 373–440.

Swaen 1907
Anthony Brewer's "The Love-sick King." Ed. A. E. H. Swaen. Materialien zur Kunde des älteren Englischen Dramas 18. Louvain: Uystpruyst, 1907.

Swaen 1912
How a Man May Chuse a Good Wife from a Bad. Ed. A. E. H. Swaen. Materialien zur Kunde des älteren Englischen Dramas 35. Louvain: Uystpruyst, 1912.

Swift
Carolyn Ruth Swift. "Feminine Self-Definition in Lady Mary Wroth's *Love's Victorie* (c. 1621)." *English Literary Renaissance* 19.2 (1989): 171–88.

Swinburne
Algernon Charles Swinburne. *A Study of Shakespeare*. London: Chatto and Windus, 1880.

Sykes 1919
H. Dugdale Sykes. *Sidelights on Shakespeare*. Stratford-upon-Avon: Shakespeare Head Press, 1919.

Sykes 1924
H. Dugdale Sykes. *Sidelights on Elizabethan Drama: A Series of Studies Dealing with the Authorship of Sixteenth and Seventeenth Century Plays*. London and New York: Oxford University Press, 1924. Repr. London: Cass, 1966.

Tannenbaum
Samuel A. Tannenbaum. "The Author of *Misogonus*." In *Shaksperian Scraps and Other Elizabethan Fragments*, 129–41. New York: Columbia University Press, 1933.

Tannenbaum & Rollins
Thomas Randolph. *The Drinking Academy*. Ed. Samuel A. Tannenbaum and Hyder E. Rollins. Cambridge, MA: Harvard University Press; London: Humphrey Milford, 1930.

Tassi
Marguerite A. Tassi. *The Scandal of Images: Iconoclasm, Eroticism, and Painting in Early Modern English Drama*. Selinsgrove, PA: Susquehanna University Press, 2005.

Tatzl
Dietmar Tatzl. *"Secret, Black, and Midnight Hags": The Conception, Presentation and Functions of Witches in English Renaissance Drama*. Vienna: Braumüller, 2005.

Taunton
Nina Taunton. "A Camp 'well planted': Encamped Bodies in 1590s Military Discourses and Chapman's *Caesar and Pompey*." In *The Body in Late Medieval and Early Modern Culture*, ed. Darryll Grantley and eadem, 83–95. Aldershot, UK; Burlington, VT: Ashgate, 2000.

Taylor 1979
Gary Taylor. *Three Studies in the Text of "Henry V."* Oxford: Clarendon Press, 1979. [published with Stanley Wells, *Modernizing Shakespeare's Spelling*]

Taylor 1982
William Shakespeare. *Henry V.* Ed. Gary Taylor. Oxford: Clarendon Press, 1982.

Taylor 1987
Gary Taylor. "William Shakespeare, Richard James and the House of Cobham." *Review of English Studies* 38 (1987): 334–54.

Taylor 1989
Gary Taylor. "The Date and Auspices of the Additions to *Sir Thomas More.*" In *Shakespeare and Sir Thomas More: Essays on the Play and Its Shakespearian Interest*, ed. T. H. Howard-Hill, 101–29. Cambridge: Cambridge University Press, 1989.

Taylor 1993a
Gary Taylor. "The Structure of Performance: Act-Intervals in the London Theatres, 1576–1642." In *Shakespeare Reshaped, 1606–1623*, ed. idem and John Jowett, 3–50. Oxford Shakespeare Studies. Oxford: Clarendon Press, 1993.

Taylor 1993b
Gary Taylor. "'Swounds Revisited: Theatrical, Editorial, and Literary Expurgation." In *Shakespeare Reshaped, 1606–1623*, ed. idem and John Jowett, 51–106. Oxford Shakespeare Studies. Oxford: Clarendon Press, 1993.

Taylor 1995
Gary Taylor. "Shakespeare and Others: The Authorship of *Henry the Sixth, Part One.*" *Medieval and Renaissance Drama in England* 7 (1995): 145–205.

Taylor 2000
Gary Taylor. "Thomas Middleton, Thomas Dekker, and *The Bloody Banquet.*" *Papers of the Bibliographical Society of America* 94.2 (2000): 197–233.

Taylor 2001a
Gary Taylor. "*Hamlet* in Africa 1607." In *Travel Knowledge: European "Discoveries" in the Early Modern Period*, ed. Ivo Kamps and Jyotsna G. Singh, 223–48. Basingstoke, UK, and New York: Palgrave, 2001.

Taylor 2001b
Gary Taylor. "'The Nice Valour' and the Court of James I." *The Court Historian* 6.1 (2001): 1–36.

Taylor 2002a
Gary Taylor. "Middleton and Rowley—and Heywood: *The Old Law* and New Attribution Technologies." *Papers of the Bibliographical Society of America* 96.2 (2002): 165–217.

Taylor 2002b
Gary Taylor. "Shakespeare Plays on Renaissance Stages." In *The Cambridge Companion to Shakespeare on Stage*, ed. Stanley Wells and Sarah Stanton, 1–20. Cambridge: Cambridge University Press, 2002.

Taylor 2004a
Gary Taylor. "Thomas Middleton, *The Spanish Gypsy*, and Collaborative Authorship." In *Words That Count: Essays on Early Modern Authorship in Honor of MacDonald P. Jackson*, ed. Brian Boyd, 241–73. Newark, DE: University of Delaware Press, 2004.

Taylor 2004b
Gary Taylor. "Middleton, Thomas (*bap.* 1580, *d.* 1627)." In *ODNB* 38: 79–85.

Taylor 2007a
Gary Taylor. "*Macbeth* (adaptation)." In *Thomas Middleton and Early Modern Textual Culture: A Companion to the Collected Works*, gen. eds. idem and John Lavagnino, 383–98. Oxford: Clarendon Press, 2007.

Taylor 2007b
The Widow. Ed. Gary Taylor with Michael Warren. In *Thomas Middleton: The Collected Works*, gen. eds. idem and John Lavagnino. Oxford: Clarendon Press, 2007.

Taylor 2008
Andrew W. Taylor. "The Reformation of History in John Bale's Biblical Dramas." In *English Historical Drama, 1500–1660: Forms outside the Canon*, ed. Teresa Grant and Barbara Ravelhofer, 58–97. Basingstoke, UK, and New York: Palgrave Macmillan, 2008.

Taylor 2011
Gary Taylor. Review of *Shakespeare, Computers, and the Mystery of Authorship*, ed. Hugh Craig and Arthur F. Kinney. *Medieval and Renaissance Drama in England* 24 (2011): 198–201.

Taylor & Jowett
Gary Taylor and John Jowett. *Shakespeare Reshaped, 1606–1623.* Oxford Shakespeare Studies. Oxford: Clarendon Press, 1993.

Taylor et al. 1999
Gary Taylor, Paul Mulholland, and MacD. P. Jackson. "Thomas Middleton, Lording Barry, and *The Family of Love*." *Papers of the Bibliographical Society of America* 93.2 (1999): 213–41.

Taylor et al. 2007
Gary Taylor, Celia R. Daileader, and Alexandra G. Bennett. "The Order of Persons." In *Thomas Middleton and Early Modern Textual Culture: A Companion to the Collected Works*, gen. eds. Gary Taylor and John Lavagnino, 31–79. Oxford: Clarendon Press, 2007.

Teague 1979
Frances Teague. "The Date of Ben Jonson's *A Tale of a Tub*." *Renaissance Papers* (1979): 49–57.

Teague 1985
Frances Teague. *The Curious History of "Bartholomew Fair."* Lewisburg, PA: Bucknell University Press; London and Toronto: Associated University Presses, 1985.

Teague 1991
Frances Teague. *Shakespeare's Speaking Properties*. Lewisburg, PA: Bucknell University Press; London and Toronto: Associated University Presses, 1991.

Teague 2009
Frances Teague. "The Phoenix and the Cockpit-in-Court Playhouses." In *The Oxford Handbook of Early Modern Theatre*, ed. Richard Dutton, 240–59. Oxford: Oxford University Press, 2009.

TEAS
Twayne's English Authors Series

Tennenhouse 1984
The Tudor Interludes "Nice Wanton" and "Impatient Poverty." Ed. Leonard Tennenhouse. New York and London: Garland, 1984.

Tennenhouse 1986
Leonard Tennenhouse. *Power on Display: The Politics of Shakespeare's Genres*. New York and London: Methuen, 1986.

Theobald
Lewis Theobald. *Double Falsehood, or The Distrest Lovers, A Play as it is acted at the Theatre-Royal in Drury Lane; Written originally by W. Shakespeare; and now revised and adapted to the stage by Mr. Theobald.* London: J. Watts, 1728.

Thomas 1908
D. L. Thomas. "Authorship of *Revenge for Honour.*" *Modern Philology* 5.4 (1908): 617–36.

Thomas 1982
R. Wever. *An Enterlude Called Lusty Juventus: An Old-Spelling Critical Edition.* Ed. Helen Scarborough Thomas. New York and London: Garland, 1982.

Thompson 1910
Elbert N. S. Thompson. *The English Moral Plays*. New Haven: Yale University Press, 1910. Repr. Folcroft, PA: Folcroft Press, 1969.

Thompson 1916
Edward Maunde Thompson. *Shakespeare's Handwriting*. Oxford: Oxford University Press, 1916.

Thompson 1984
William Shakespeare. *The Taming of the Shrew*. Ed. Ann Thompson. Cambridge: Cambridge University Press, 1984.

Thompson 2010
Ann Thompson. "'Why do you bend your eye on vacancy?': Visual Meaning and Its Absence in *Hamlet*." In *Speaking Pictures: The Visual/Verbal Nexus of Dramatic Performance*, ed. Virginia Mason Vaughan, Fernando Cioni, and Jacquelyn Bessell, 90–105. Madison and Teaneck, NJ: Fairleigh Dickinson University Press, 2010.

Thompson & Taylor
William Shakespeare. *Hamlet.* Ed. Ann Thompson and Neil Taylor. Arden. London: Arden, 2006. Repr. London: Thomson Learning, 2007.

Thomson 1983
Peter Thomson. *Shakespeare's Theatre.* London and Boston: Routledge, 1983.

Thomson 1986
Leslie Thomson. "'*Enter Above*': The Staging of *Women Beware Women.*" *Studies in English Literature, 1500–1900* 26.2 (1986): 331–43.

Thomson 1988a
R. S. Thomson. "*Boote and Spurre*: A Jacobean Quête from Folger MS J.a.1." *English Literary Renaissance* 18.2 (1988): 275–93.

Thomson 1988b
Leslie Thomson. "*Antony and Cleopatra*, Act 4 Scene 16: 'A Heavy Sight'." *Shakespeare Survey* 41 (1988): 77–90.

Thomson 1991
Leslie Thomson. "Window Scenes in Renaissance Plays: A Survey and Some Conclusions." *Medieval and Renaissance Drama in England* 5 (1991): 225–43.

Thomson 1992a
Peter Thomson. *Shakespeare's Professional Career.* Cambridge: Cambridge University Press, 1992.

Thomson 1992b
Peter Thomson. *Shakespeare's Theatre.* 2nd ed. London and New York: Routledge, 1992.

Thomson 1996
Leslie Thomson. "A Quarto 'Marked for Performance': Evidence of What?" *Medieval and Renaissance Drama in England* 8 (1996): 176–210.

Thomson 1999
Leslie Thomson. "The Meaning of *Thunder and Lightning*: Stage Directions and Audience Expectations." *Early Theatre* 2 (1999): 11–24.

Thomson 2000
Peter Thomson. "The True Physiognomy of a Man: Richard Tarlton and His Legend." In *Shakespeare and His Contemporaries in Performance*, ed. Edward J. Esche, 191–210. Aldershot, UK, and Burlington, VT: Ashgate, 2000.

Thomson 2002
Leslie Thomson. "The Theatrical Rhetoric of *Edward III.*" *Medieval and Renaissance Drama in England* 15 (2002): 43–56.

Thomson 2003

Leslie Thomson. "'As proper a woman as any in Cheap': Women in Shops on the Early Modern Stage." *Medieval and Renaissance Drama in England* 16 (2003): 145–61.

Thomson 2004a

Peter Thomson. "Clowns, Fools and Knaves: Stages in the Evolution of Acting." In *The Cambridge History of British Theatre*, vol. 1: *Origins to 1660*, ed. Jane Milling and idem, 407–23. Cambridge: Cambridge University Press, 2004.

Thomson 2004b

Peter Thomson. "Tarlton, Richard (*d.* 1588), Actor and Clown." In *ODNB* 53: 786–89.

Thomson 2005

Leslie Thomson. "Marlowe's Staging of Meaning." *Medieval and Renaissance Drama in England* 18 (2005): 19–36.

Thomson 2006

Leslie Thomson. "Who's In, Who's Out?: *The Knight of the Burning Pestle* on the Blackfriars Stage." In *Inside Shakespeare: Essays on the Blackfriars Stage*, ed. Paul Menzer, 61–71. Selinsgrove, PA: Susquehanna University Press, 2006.

Thomson 2007

Peter Thomson. "Sound City Jests and Country Pretty Jests: *Jack Juggler* and *Gammer Gurton's Needle*." In *Interludes and Early Modern Society: Studies in Gender, Power and Theatricality*, ed. Peter Happé and Wim Hüsken, 315–30. Amsterdam and New York: Rodopi, 2007.

Thomson 2010

Leslie Thomson. "Playgoers on the Outdoor Stages of Early Modern London." *Theatre Notebook* 64.1 (2010): 3–11.

Thornberry

Richard T. Thornberry. "A Seventeenth-Century Revival of *Mucedorus* in London before 1610." *Shakespeare Quarterly* 28.3 (1977): 362–64.

Thorssen

Marilyn J. Thorssen, ed. *A Critical Edition of James Shirley's "The Lady of Pleasure."* New York and London: Garland, 1980.

Tiffany

Grace Tiffany. *Erotic Beasts and Social Monsters: Shakespeare, Jonson, and Comic Androgyny*. Newark, DE: University of Delaware Press; London and Toronto: Associated University Presses, 1995.

TLS

Times Literary Supplement

Tobin 1997
J. J. M. Tobin. Introduction to *The Reign of King Edward the Third*. In *The Riverside Shakespeare*, ed. G. Blakemore Evans with the assistance of J. J. M. Tobin, 1732–34. 2nd ed. Boston and New York: Houghton Mifflin, 1997.

Tobin 2002
J. J. M. Tobin. "More Evidence for a 1594 *Titus*." *Notes and Queries* 49.2 (2002): 222–24.

Tomlinson 1992a
Sophie Tomlinson. "'My Brain the Stage': Margaret Cavendish and the Fantasy of Female Performance." In *Women, Texts and Histories, 1575–1760*, ed. Clare Brant and Diane Purkiss, 134–63. London and New York: Routledge, 1992.

Tomlinson 1992b
Sophie Tomlinson. "She That Plays the King: Henrietta Maria and the Threat of the Actress in Caroline Culture." In *The Politics of Tragicomedy: Shakespeare and After*, ed. Gordon McMullan and Jonathan Hope, 189–207. London and New York: Routledge, 1992.

Tomlinson 1999
Sophie Eliza Tomlinson. "Too Theatrical? Female Subjectivity in Caroline and Interregnum Drama." *Women's Writing* 6.1 (1999): 65–79.

Tomlinson 2003
Sophie Tomlinson. "Theatrical Vibrancy on the Caroline Court Stage: *Tempe Restored* and *The Shepherds' Paradise*." In *Women and Culture at the Courts of the Stuart Queens*, ed. Clare McManus, 186–203. Basingstoke, UK, and New York: Palgrave Macmillan, 2003.

Tomlinson 2005
Sophie Tomlinson. *Women on Stage in Stuart Drama*. Cambridge: Cambridge University Press, 2005.

Townsend
Freda L. Townsend. "Ben Jonson's 'Censure' of Rutter's *Shepheards Holy-Day*." *Modern Philology* 44.4 (1947): 238–47.

Traister 2001
Barbara Howard Traister. *The Notorious Astrological Physician of London: Works and Days of Simon Forman*. Chicago and London: University of Chicago Press, 2001.

Traister 2011
Barbara Howard Traister. "Dealing with Dramatic Anonymity: The Case of *The Merry Devil of Edmonton*." In *Anonymity in Early Modern England: "What's In A Name?"*, ed. Janet Wright Starner and eadem, 99–111. Farnham, UK, and Burlington, VT: Ashgate, 2011.

Traub 1992
Valerie Traub. *Desire and Anxiety: Circulations of Sexuality in Shakespearean Drama*. London and New York: Routledge, 1992.

Traub 2002
Valerie Traub. *The Renaissance of Lesbianism in Early Modern England*. Cambridge: Cambridge University Press, 2002.

Traub 2009
Valerie Traub. "The Joys of Martha Joyless: Queer Pedagogy and the (Early Modern) Production of Sexual Knowledge." In *The Forms of Renaissance Thought: New Essays in Literature and Culture*, ed. Leonard Barkan, Bradin Cormack, and Sean Keilen, 170–98. Basingstoke, UK, and New York: Palgrave Macmillan, 2009.

Tricomi 1972
Albert H. Tricomi. "The Revised *Bussy D'Ambois* and *The Revenge of Bussy D'Ambois*: Joint Performance in Thematic Counterpoint." *English Language Notes* 9.4 (1972): 253–62.

Tricomi 1977
Albert H. Tricomi. "The Focus of Satire and the Date of *Monsieur D'Olive*." *Studies in English Literature, 1500–1900* 17.2 (1977): 281–94.

Tricomi 1979
Albert H. Tricomi. "The Problem of Authorship in the Revised *Bussy D'Ambois*." *English Language Notes* 17.1 (1979): 22–29.

Tricomi 1982
Albert H. Tricomi. "The Dates of the Plays of George Chapman." *English Literary Renaissance* 12.2 (1982): 242–66.

Tricomi 1986
Albert H. Tricomi. "Philip, Earl of Pembroke, and the Analogical Way of Reading Political Tragedy." *JEGP* 85.3 (1986): 332–45.

Tricomi 1989
Albert H. Tricomi. *Anticourt Drama in England, 1603–1642*. Charlottesville: University Press of Virginia, 1989.

Tricomi 1991
Albert H. Tricomi. "*A Dialogue betweene Pollicy and Piety* by Robert Davenport." *English Literary Renaissance* 21.3 (1991): 190–216.

Tricomi 1993
Robert Knightley. "*Alfrede or Right Reinthron'd*": *A Translation of William Drury's "Aluredus sive Alfredus*." Ed. Albert H. Tricomi. MRTS 99. Binghamton, NY: Medieval & Renaissance Texts & Studies, 1993.

Tricomi 2001
Albert H. Tricomi. "Counting Insatiate Countesses: The Seventeenth-Century Annotations to Marston's *The Insatiate Countess*." *Huntington Library Quarterly* 64.1/2 (2001): 107–22.

Truchet
Sybil Truchet. "*Campaspe*: A Brave New World?" *Cahiers Elisabéthains* 15 (1979): 17–28.

Tudeau-Clayton
Margaret Tudeau-Clayton. "Shakespeare's 'welsch men' and the 'King's English'." In *Shakespeare and Wales: From the Marches to the Assembly*, ed. Willey Maley and Philip Schwyzer, 91–110. Farnham, UK, and Burlington, VT: 2010.

Turnbull
William B. D. D. Turnbull, ed. *"Mind, Will, and Understanding," A Morality*. Edinburgh: Abbotsford Club, 1837.

Turner 1963
Francis Beaumont and John Fletcher. *A King and No King*. Ed. Robert K. Turner. RRDS. Lincoln: University of Nebraska Press, 1963.

Turner 1966
Philaster. Ed. Robert K. Turner. In *The Dramatic Works in the Beaumont and Fletcher Canon*, gen. ed. Fredson Bowers, vol. 1. Cambridge: Cambridge University Press, 1966.

Turner 1967
Thomas Heywood. *The Fair Maid of the West, Parts I and II*. Ed. Robert K. Turner. RRDS. Lincoln: University of Nebraska Press, 1967.

Turner 1970
Robert K. Turner, ed. *The Maid's Tragedy*. In *The Dramatic Works in the Beaumont and Fletcher Canon*, gen. ed. Fredson Bowers, vol. 2. Cambridge: Cambridge University Press, 1970.

Turner 1979
A Critical Edition of James Shirley's "St. Patrick for Ireland." Ed. John P. Turner. New York and London: Garland, 1979.

Turner 1982
Robert K. Turner, ed. *The Mad Lover*. In *The Dramatic Works in the Beaumont and Fletcher Canon*, gen. ed. Fredson Bowers, vol. 5. Cambridge: Cambridge University Press, 1982.

Turner 1985
Robert K. Turner, ed. *A Wife for a Month*. In *The Dramatic Works in the Beaumont and Fletcher Canon*, gen. ed. Fredson Bowers, vol. 6. Cambridge: Cambridge University Press, 1985.

Turner 1987

Robert Kean Turner. "Collaborators at Work: *The Queen of Corinth* and *The Knight of Malta*." In *Shakespeare: Text, Language, Criticism: Essays in Honour of Marvin Spevack*, ed. Bernhard Fabian and Kurt Tetzeli von Rosador, 315–33. Hildesheim, Zurich, and New York: Olms-Weidmann, 1987.

Turner 1992

Robert K. Turner, ed. *The False One*. In *The Dramatic Works in the Beaumont and Fletcher Canon*, gen. ed. Fredson Bowers, vol. 8. Cambridge: Cambridge University Press, 1992.

Turner 1996

Robert K. Turner, ed. *The Spanish Curate*. In *The Dramatic Works in the Beaumont and Fletcher Canon*, gen. ed. Fredson Bowers, vol. 10. Cambridge: Cambridge University Press, 1996.

Tweedie

Eleanor M. Tweedie. "'Action is Eloquence': The Staging of Thomas Kyd's *Spanish Tragedy*." *Studies in English Literature, 1500–1900* 16.2 (1976): 223–39.

Twycross 1983

Meg Twycross. "'Apparell comly'." In *Aspects of Early English Drama*, ed. Paula Neuss, 30–49. Cambridge: Brewer; Totowa, NJ: Barnes & Noble, 1983.

Twycross 1994

Meg Twycross. "The Theatricality of Medieval English Plays." In *The Cambridge Companion to Medieval English Theatre*, ed. Richard Beadle, 37–84. Cambridge: Cambridge University Press, 1994.

Twycross 2007

Meg Twycross. "Medieval English Theatre: Codes and Genres." In *A Companion to Medieval English Literature and Culture c. 1350–c. 1500*, ed. Peter Brown, 454–72. Oxford: Blackwell, 2007.

Twycross 2008

Meg Twycross. "The Theatricality of Medieval English Plays." In *The Cambridge Companion to Medieval English Theatre*, ed. Richard Beadle and Alan J. Fletcher, 26–74. 2nd ed. Cambridge: Cambridge University Press, 2008.

Twycross & Carpenter

Meg Twycross and Sarah Carpenter. *Masks and Masking in Medieval and Early Tudor England*. Studies in Performance and Early Modern Drama. Aldershot, UK, and Burlington, VT: Ashgate, 2002.

Twyning

John Twyning. "Dekker, Thomas (*c.* 1572–1632)." In *ODNB* 15: 697–701.

Tydeman

William Tydeman. *English Medieval Theatre, 1400–1500*. London: Routledge, 1986.

Tyson
"Every Woman in Her Humor": A Critical Edition. Ed. Archie Mervin Tyson. New York and London: Garland, 1980.

Udall
A Critical, Old-Spelling Edition of "The Birth of Merlin" (Q 1662). Ed. Joanna Udall. London: Modern Humanities Research Association, 1991.

Ullyot
Michael Ullyot. "Seneca and the Early Elizabethan History Play." In *English Historical Drama, 1500–1660: Forms Outside the Canon,* ed. Teresa Grant and Barbara Ravelhofer, 98–124. Basingstoke, UK, and New York: Palgrave Macmillan, 2008.

Ungerer
Gustav Ungerer. *Anglo-Spanish Relations in Tudor Literature.* Swiss Studies in English 38. Bern: Francke, 1956.

Upton
Alexander W. Upton. "Allusions to James I and His Court in *The Fawne*." *PMLA* 44.4 (1929): 1048–65.

Ure 1952
Peter Ure. "The Date of the Revision of Chapman's 'The Tragedy of Bussy D'Ambois'." *Notes and Queries* 197.1 (1952): 1–2.

Ure 1968
John Ford. *The Chronicle History of Perkin Warbeck, A Strange Truth.* Ed. Peter Ure. Revels Plays. London: Methuen, 1968.

Urkowitz 1980
Steven Urkowitz. *Shakespeare's Revision of "King Lear."* Princeton: Princeton University Press, 1980.

Urkowitz 1986
Steven Urkowitz. "'Well-sayd olde Mole': Burying Three *Hamlets* in Modern Editions." In *Shakespeare Study Today: The Horace Howard Furness Memorial Lectures,* ed. Georgianna Ziegler, 37–70. New York: AMS Press, 1986.

Valbuena
Olga L. Valbuena. *Subjects to the King's Divorce: Equivocation, Infidelity, and Resistance in Early Modern England.* Bloomington and Indianapolis: Indiana University Press, 2003.

Vander Motten
J. P. Vander Motten. "Killigrew, Thomas (1612–1683)." In *ODNB* 31: 564–68.

Van Elk
Martine Van Elk. "Lady Mary (Sidney) Wroth, 'Love's Victorie' (c. 1622)." In *Reading Early Modern Women: An Anthology of Texts in Manuscript and Print,*

1550–1700, ed. Helen Ostovich and Elizabeth Sauer, 423–28. New York and London: Routledge, 2004.

Van Fossen 1961
Thomas Heywood. *A Woman Killed with Kindness*. Ed. R. W. Van Fossen. Revels Plays. London: Methuen, 1961.

Van Fossen 1979
George Chapman, Ben Jonson, and John Marston. *Eastward Ho*. Ed. R. W. Van Fossen. Revels Plays. Manchester: Manchester University Press; Baltimore: Johns Hopkins University Press, 1979.

Vaughan 2005
Virginia Mason Vaughan. *Performing Blackness on English Stages, 1500–1800*. Cambridge: Cambridge University Press, 2005.

Vaughan 2006
Virginia Mason Vaughan. "Blacking-up at the Blackfriars Theatre." In *Inside Shakespeare: Essays on the Blackfriars Stage*, ed. Paul Menzer, 123–31. Selinsgrove, PA: Susquehanna University Press, 2006.

Vaughan 2010
Virginia Mason Vaughan. "*Enter three Turks and a Moor*: Signifying the 'Other' in Early Modern English Drama." In *Speaking Pictures: The Visual/Verbal Nexus of Dramatic Performance*, ed. eadem, Fernando Cioni, and Jacquelyn Bessell, 119–38. Madison and Teaneck, NJ: Fairleigh Dickinson University Press, 2010.

Vaughan & Vaughan
William Shakespeare. *The Tempest*. Ed. Virginia Mason Vaughan and Alden T. Vaughan. Arden 3. Walton-on-Thames, UK: Nelson, 1999.

Veevers
Erica Veevers. *Images of Love and Religion: Queen Henrietta Maria and Court Entertainments*. Cambridge: Cambridge University Press, 1989.

Vickers 1997
Brian Vickers. "'Suppose you see': The Chorus in *Henry V* and *The Mirror for Magistrates*." In *Shakespearean Continuities: Essays in Honour of E. A. J. Honigmann*, ed. John Batchelor, Tom Cain, and Claire Lamont, 74–90. Basingstoke, UK: Macmillan; New York: St. Martin's Press, 1997.

Vickers 2002
Brian Vickers. *Shakespeare, Co-Author: A Historical Study of Five Collaborative Plays*. Oxford: Oxford University Press, 2002.

Vickers 2004
Brian Vickers. "*The Troublesome Raigne*, George Peele, and the Date of *King John*." In *Words That Count: Essays on Early Modern Authorship in Honor of*

MacDonald P. Jackson, ed. Brian Boyd, 78–116. Newark, DE: University of Delaware Press, 2004.

Vickers 2007
Brian Vickers. "Incomplete Shakespeare: Or, Denying Coauthorship in *1 Henry VI.*" *Shakespeare Quarterly* 58.3 (2007): 311–52.

Vickers 2008a
Brian Vickers. "Coauthors and Closed Minds." *Shakespeare Studies* 36 (2008): 101–13.

Vickers 2008b
Brian Vickers. "Thomas Kyd, Secret Sharer." *TLS* 18 April 2008: 13–15.

Vickers 2010
Brian Vickers. "Disintegrated: Did Middleton Adapt *Macbeth*?" *TLS* 28 May 2010: 14–15.

Vickers 2011
Brian Vickers. "Review Essay: Shakespeare and Authorship Studies in the Twenty-First Century." *Shakespeare Quarterly* 62.1 (2011): 106–42.

Vince 1971
R. W. Vince. "Thomas Nabbes's *Hannibal and Scipio*: Sources and Theme." *Studies in English Literature, 1500–1900* 11.2 (1971): 327–43.

Vince 1972
R. W. Vince. "Morality and Masque: The Context for Thomas Nabbes's *Microcosmus.*" *English Studies* 53.4 (1972): 328–34.

Vincent
Paul J. Vincent. "Structuring and Revision in *1 Henry VI.*" *Philological Quarterly* 84.4 (2005): 377–402.

Vitkus 2000
Three Turk Plays from Early Modern England: Selimus, A Christian Turned Turk, and The Renegado. Ed. Daniel J. Vitkus. New York: Columbia University Press, 2000.

Vitkus 2003
Daniel Vitkus. *Turning Turk: English Theater and the Multicultural Mediterranean, 1570–1630.* Basingstoke, UK, and New York: Palgrave Macmillan, 2003.

Vocht 1910
"A Knack to Know an Honest Man," 1596. Ed. Henry de Vocht. MSR. London: Oxford University Press, 1910. Repr. New York: AMS Press, 1985.

Vocht 1930
"The Wizard": A Play by Simon Baylie. Ed. Henry de Vocht. Materials for the Study of the Old English Drama 4. Louvain: Uystpruyst, 1930.

Wagner 1931
Bernard M. Wagner. "Thomas Randolph's *The Conceited Pedlar.*" *TLS* 9 April 1931: 288.

Wagner 2001
John A. Wagner. *Encyclopedia of the Wars of the Roses.* Santa Barbara, CA, Denver, CO, and Oxford: ABC-CLIO, 2001.

Wagonheim
See *AED 3*

Waith 1952
Eugene M. Waith. *The Pattern of Tragicomedy in Beaumont and Fletcher.* New Haven: Yale University Press, 1952. Repr. Hamden, CT: Archon Books, 1969.

Waith 1974
Eugene M. Waith. "Things as They Are and the World of Absolutes in Jonson's Masques and Plays." In *Elizabethan Theatre IV: Papers given . . . in July 1972*, 106–26. Hamden, CT: Archon Books, 1974.

Waith 1984
William Shakespeare. *Titus Andronicus.* Ed. Eugene M. Waith. Oxford: Clarendon Press, 1984.

Waith 1988
Eugene M. Waith. "The Wounds of Civil War in Plays by Shakespeare and His Predecessors." In *Patterns and Perspectives in English Renaissance Drama*, 127–37. Newark, DE: University of Delaware Press; London and Toronto: Associated University Presses, 1988.

Waith 1989
Eugene M. Waith. "The Death of Pompey: English Style, French Style." In *Shakespeare and Dramatic Tradition: Essays in Honor of S. F. Johnson*, ed. W. R. Elton and William B. Long, 276–85. Newark, DE: University of Delaware Press; London and Toronto: Associated University Presses, 1989.

Wakelin
Daniel Wakelin. *Humanism, Reading, and English Literature, 1430–1530.* Oxford: Oxford University Press, 2007.

Walen
Denise A. Walen. *Constructions of Female Homoeroticism in Early Modern Drama.* Early Modern Cultural Studies. New York: Palgrave Macmillan, 2005.

Walker 1989
Greg Walker. "Sir David Lindsay's *Ane Satire of the Thrie Estaitis* and the Politics of Reformation." *Scottish Literary Journal* 16.2 (1989): 5–17.

Walker 1991a
Greg Walker. *Plays of Persuasion: Drama and Politics at the Court of Henry VIII.* Cambridge: Cambridge University Press, 1991.

Walker 1991b
Kim Walker. *"New Prison*: Representing the Female Actor in Shirley's *The Bird in a Cage* (1633)." *English Literary Renaissance* 21.3 (1991): 385–400.

Walker 1998
Greg Walker. *The Politics of Performance in Early Renaissance Drama*. Cambridge: Cambridge University Press, 1998.

Walker 2000
Greg Walker, ed. *Medieval Drama: An Anthology*. Oxford: Blackwell, 2000.

Walker 2005
Greg Walker. *Writing under Tyranny: English Literature and the Henrician Reformation*. Oxford: Oxford University Press, 2005.

Walker 2006
Greg Walker. *"Fulgens and Lucres* and Early English Drama." In *Early Modern English Drama: A Critical Companion*, ed. Garrett A. Sullivan Jr., Patrick Cheney, and Andrew Hadfield, 23–34. New York and Oxford: Oxford University Press, 2006.

Walker 2007
Greg Walker. "Flytyng in the Face of Convention: Protest and Innovation in Lindsay's *Satyre of the Thrie Estaitis*." In *Interludes and Early Modern Society: Studies in Gender, Power and Theatricality*, ed. Peter Happé and Wim Hüsken, 211–38. Amsterdam and New York: Rodopi, 2007.

Walker 2008
Greg Walker. "John Skelton and the Royal Court." In *John Skelton and Early Modern Culture: Papers Honoring Robert S. Kinsman*, ed. David R. Carlson, 3–18. MRTS 300. Tempe: Arizona Center for Medieval and Renaissance Studies, 2008.

Wall 1993
Wendy Wall. *The Imprint of Gender: Authorship and Publication in the English Renaissance*. Ithaca, NY: Cornell University Press, 1993.

Wall 2002
Wendy Wall. *Staging Domesticity: Household Work and English Identity in Early Modern Drama*. Cambridge: Cambridge University Press, 2002.

Wallace 1903
The Birthe of Hercules. Ed. Malcolm William Wallace. Chicago: Scott, Foresman, 1903. Repr. Folcroft, PA: Folcroft Press, 1973.

Wallace 1912
Charles William Wallace. *The Evolution of the English Drama up to Shakespeare, with a History of the First Blackfriars Theatre*. Berlin: Reimer, 1912. Repr. Port Washington, NY: Kennikat Press, 1968.

Wallace 1960
John M. Wallace. "The Case for Internal Evidence (10): The Date of John Tatham's *The Distracted State*." *Bulletin of the New York Public Library* 64.1 (1960): 29–40.

Walsh 1973
Martin W. Walsh. "Thomas Randolph's *Aristippus* and the English Mummers' Play." *Folklore* 84.2 (1973): 157–59.

Walsh 2006
Brian Walsh. "Performing Historicity in Dekker's *The Shoemaker's Holiday*." *Studies in English Literature, 1500–1900* 46.2 (2006): 323–48.

Walsh 2009a
Brian Walsh. "Charismatic Authority and Political Subversion in *John of Bordeaux*." *Research Opportunities in Medieval and Renaissance Drama* 48 (2009): 1–21.

Walsh 2009b
Brian Walsh. *Shakespeare, the Queen's Men, and the Elizabethan Performance of History*. Cambridge: Cambridge University Press, 2009.

Walsh 2009c
Brian Walsh. "Truth, Poetry, and Report in *The True Tragedy of Richard III*." In *Locating the Queen's Men, 1583–1603: Material Practices and Conditions of Playing*, ed. Helen Ostovich, Holger Schott Syme, and Andrew Griffin, 123–33. Farnham, UK, and Burlington, VT: Ashgate, 2009.

Walter 1933
Walter Mountfort. *The Launching of the Mary*. Ed. John Henry Walter. MSR. Oxford: Oxford University Press, 1933.

Walter 1937
J. H. Walter. "*Revenge for Honour*: Date, Authorship and Sources." *Review of English Studies* 13 (1937): 425–37.

Walter & Greg
Charlemagne or The Distracted Emperor. Ed. John Henry Walter and W. W. Greg. MSR. Oxford: Oxford University Press, 1937 [1938].

Walters
Teresa Walters. "'Such Stowage as These Trinkets': Trading and Tasting Women in Fletcher and Massinger's *The Sea Voyage* (1622)." In *Consuming Narratives: Gender and Monstrous Appetite in the Middle Ages and the Renaissance*, ed. Liz Herbert McAvoy and eadem, 67–80. Cardiff: University of Wales Press, 2002.

Ward 2008a
Allyna E. Ward. "'If the head be evill the body cannot be good': Legitimate Rebellion in Gascoigne and Kinwelmershe's *Jocasta*." *Early Modern Literary*

Studies 14.1/Special Issue 18 (2008). http://purl.oclc.org/emls/14–1/article2. htm.

Ward 2008b

Allyna Ward. "'Whosoever Resisteth Shall Get to Themselfes Dampnacioun': Tyranny and Resistance in *Cambises* and *Horestes.*" *Yearbook of English Studies* 38.1/2 (2008): 150–67.

Warren 1978

Michael Warren. "Quarto and Folio *King Lear* and the Interpretation of Albany and Edgar." In *Shakespeare: Pattern of Excelling Nature*, ed. David Bevington and Jay L. Halio, 95–107. Newark, DE: University of Delaware Press; London: Associated University Presses, 1978.

Warren 1989a

Roger Warren, ed. *The Complete "King Lear," 1608–1623: Texts and Parallel Texts in Photographic Facsimile.* Berkeley, Los Angeles, and London: University of California Press, 1989.

Warren 1989b

Roger Warren. *Cymbeline.* Shakespeare in Performance. Manchester: Manchester University Press, 1989.

Warren 1998

William Shakespeare. *Cymbeline.* Ed. Roger Warren. Oxford: Clarendon Press, 1998.

Warren 2002

William Shakespeare. *Edward III.* Ed. Roger Warren. London: Nick Hern Books in association with the Royal Shakespeare Company, 2002.

Warren 2003

William Shakespeare and George Wilkins. *A Reconstructed Text of "Pericles, Prince of Tyre."* Ed. Roger Warren on the basis of the text prepared by Gary Taylor and MacD. P. Jackson for the Oxford edition. Oxford: Oxford University Press, 2003.

Warren 2008

William Shakespeare. *The Two Gentlemen of Verona.* Ed. Roger Warren. Oxford and New York: Oxford University Press, 2008.

Warren & Wells

William Shakespeare. *Twelfth Night, or What You Will.* Ed. Roger Warren and Stanley Wells. Oxford: Clarendon Press, 1994.

Wasson 1986a

John M. Wasson, ed. *Devon.* REED. Toronto, Buffalo, and London: University of Toronto Press, 1986.

Wasson 1986b
John Wasson. "The Secular Saint Plays of the Elizabethan Era." In *The Saint Play in Medieval Europe*, ed. Clifford Davidson, 241–60. Early Drama, Art, and Music Monograph Series 8. Kalamazoo: Medieval Institute, Western Michigan University, 1986.

Waterhouse
Osborn Waterhouse, ed. [*The Norwich Grocers' Play.*] *The Non-Cycle Mystery Plays, together with the Croxton Play of the Sacrament and The Pride of Life*. EETS e.s. 104. London: K. Paul, Trench, Trübner, 1909.

Watkins 1999
John Watkins. "The Allegorical Theatre: Moralities, Interludes, and Protestant Drama." In *The Cambridge History of Medieval English Literature*, ed. David Wallace, 767–92. Cambridge: Cambridge University Press, 1999.

Watkins 2002
John Watkins. *Representing Elizabeth in Stuart England: Literature, History, Sovereignty*. Cambridge: Cambridge University Press, 2002.

Watson
Ben Jonson. *Volpone*. Ed. Robert N. Watson. 2nd ed. New Mermaids. London: Black; New York: Norton, 2003.

Watt 2009a
Timothy Irish Watt. "The Authorship of the Hand-D Addition to *The Book of Sir Thomas More*." In *Shakespeare, Computers, and the Mystery of Authorship*, ed. Hugh Craig and Arthur F. Kinney, 134–61. Cambridge: Cambridge University Press, 2009.

Watt 2009b
Timothy Irish Watt. "The Authorship of *The Raigne of Edward the Third*." In *Shakespeare, Computers, and the Mystery of Authorship*, ed. Hugh Craig and Arthur F. Kinney, 116–33. Cambridge: Cambridge University Press, 2009.

Wayne
A Trick to Catch the Old One. Ed. Valerie Wayne. In *Thomas Middleton: The Collected Works*, gen. eds. Gary Taylor and John Lavagnino. Oxford: Clarendon Press, 2007.

Weil & Weil
William Shakespeare. *The First Part of King Henry IV: Updated Edition*. Ed. Herbert Weil and Judith Weil. New Cambridge Shakespeare. Cambridge: Cambridge University Press, 2007.

Weiner
Thomas Heywood's "The Iron Age." Ed. Arlene W. Weiner. New York and London: Garland, 1979.

Weis 1983

René J. A. Weis. *"Caesar's Revenge*: A Neglected Elizabethan Source of *Antony and Cleopatra." Shakespeare Jahrbuch* (1983): 178–86.

Weis 1998

William Shakespeare. *Henry IV, Part 2.* Ed. René Weis. Oxford: Clarendon Press, 1998.

Weis 2010

"King Lear": A Parallel Text Edition. Ed. René Weis. 2nd ed. London and New York: Longman, 2010.

Weller & Ferguson

Elizabeth Cary. *The Tragedy of Mariam, The Fair Queen of Jewry.* Ed. Barry Weller and Margaret W. Ferguson. Berkeley and Los Angeles: University of California Press, 1994.

Wells 1920

William Wells. "'Timon of Athens'." *Notes and Queries* 6 (1920): 266–69.

Wells 1928

William Wells. "'The Bloody Brother'." *Notes and Queries* 54 (1928): 6–9.

Wells 1964

Thomas Nashe. Ed. Stanley Wells. Stratford-upon-Avon Library 1. London: Edward Arnold, 1964.

Wells 1970

"Bottom the Weaver," A Facsimile. Ed. Stanley Wells. London: Cornmarket, 1970.

Wells 1984

Stanley Wells. *Re-Editing Shakespeare for the Modern Reader.* Oxford Shakespeare Studies. Oxford: Clarendon Press, 1984.

Wells 1997

Stanley Wells. "The Integration of Violent Action in *Titus Andronicus." In Shakespearean Continuities,* ed. John Batchelor, Tom Cain, and Claire Lamont, 206–20. Basingstoke, UK: Macmillan; New York: St. Martin's Press, 1997.

Wells 2006

Stanley Wells. *Shakespeare and Co.* London: Penguin, 2006.

Wells 2007

A Yorkshire Tragedy. Ed. Stanley Wells. In *Thomas Middleton: The Collected Works,* gen. eds. Gary Taylor and John Lavagnino. Oxford: Clarendon Press, 2007.

Wells & Taylor

Stanley Wells and Gary Taylor, with John Jowett and William Montgomery. *William Shakespeare: A Textual Companion.* Oxford: Clarendon Press, 1987.

Welsh
George Chapman. *May Day*. Ed. Robert F. Welsh. In *The Plays of George Chapman: The Comedies, A Critical Edition*. Gen. ed. Allan Holaday. Urbana, Chicago, and London: University of Illinois Press, 1970.

Wentersdorf
Karl P. Wentersdorf. "Repertory and Size of Pembroke's Company." *Theatre Annual* 33 (1977): 71–85.

Werner 1995
Hans Werner. "A Vindication of A. H. Bullen's Dating of *The Costlie Whore*." *Notes and Queries* 42.3 (1995): 352–57.

Werner 1996
Hans Werner. "*The Hector of Germanie, or The Palsgrave, Prime Elector* and Anglo-German Relations of Early Stuart England: The View from the Popular Stage." In *The Stuart Court and Europe: Essays in Politics and Political Culture*, ed. R. Malcolm Smuts, 113–32. Cambridge: Cambridge University Press, 1996.

Werstine 1982a
"*New-Market-Fayre*." Ed. Paul Werstine. *AEB: Analytical & Enumerative Bibliography* 6.2 (1982): 71–103.

Werstine 1982b
"*The Second Part of New-Market-Fayre*." Ed. Paul Werstine. *AEB: Analytical & Enumerative Bibliography* 6.4 (1982): 209–39.

Werstine 1990
Paul Werstine. "Narratives about Printed Shakespeare Texts: 'Foul Papers' and 'Bad Quartos'." *Shakespeare Quarterly* 41.1 (1990): 65–86.

Werstine 1997
Paul Werstine. "Plays in Manuscript." In *A New History of Early English Drama*, ed. John D. Cox and David Scott Kastan, 481–97. New York: Columbia University Press, 1997.

Werstine 2007
Paul Werstine. "The Science of Editing." In *A Concise Companion to Shakespeare and the Text*, ed. Andrew Murphy, 109–27. Oxford: Blackwell, 2007.

Wertheim 1967
Albert Wertheim. "The Presentation of James Shirley's 'St. Patrick for Ireland' at the First Irish Playhouse." *Notes and Queries* n.s. 14.6 (1967): 212–15.

Wertheim 1971
Albert Wertheim. "A New Light on the Dramatic Works of Thomas Killigrew." *Studies in Bibliography* 24 (1971): 149–52.

Wertheim 1973
Albert Wertheim. "James Shirley and the Caroline Masques of Ben Jonson." *Theatre Notebook* 27.4 (1973): 157–61.

Wertheim 1978
Albert Wertheim. "James Shirley." In *The Later Jacobean and Caroline Dramatists: A Survey and Bibliography of Recent Studies in English Renaissance Drama*, ed. Terence P. Logan and Denzell S. Smith, 152–71. Lincoln and London: University of Nebraska Press, 1978.

Westfall 1990
Suzanne R. Westfall. *Patrons and Performance: Early Tudor Household Revels.* Oxford: Clarendon Press, 1990.

Westfall 2002
Suzanne Westfall. "'What Revels Are in Hand?': Performances in the Great Households." In *A Companion to Renaissance Drama*, ed. Arthur F. Kinney, 266–80. Oxford: Blackwell, 2002.

Westfall 2004
Suzanne Westfall. "'An example of courtesy and liberality': Great Households and Performance." In *The Cambridge History of British Theatre*, vol. 1: *Origins to 1660*, ed. Jane Milling and Peter Thomson, 200–23. Cambridge: Cambridge University Press, 2004.

White 1980
Richard Edwards' "Damon and Pythias": A Critical Old-Spelling Edition. Ed. D. Jerry White. New York and London: Garland, 1980.

White 1982
Martin White, ed. *The Tragedy of Master Arden of Faversham.* New Mermaids. London: Ernest Benn; New York: Norton, 1982.

White 1987
D. Jerry White. "Richard Edwards." In *Dictionary of Literary Biography* 62: *Elizabethan Dramatists*, ed. Fredson Bowers, 71–76. Detroit: Gale, 1987.

White 1991
Paul Whitfield White. "Patronage, Protestantism, and Stage Propaganda in Early Elizabethan England." *Yearbook of English Studies* 21 (1991): 39–52.

White 1992
Reformation Biblical Drama in England: "The Life and Repentaunce of Mary Magdalene," "The History of Jacob and Esau," An Old-Spelling Critical Edition. Ed. Paul Whitfield White. New York and London: Garland, 1992.

White 1993a
Paul Whitfield White. "Patronage, Protestantism, and Stage Propaganda in Early Elizabethan England." In *Patronage, Politics, and Literary Traditions*

in England, 1558–1658, ed. Cedric C. Brown, 111–24. Detroit: Wayne State University Press, 1993.

White 1993b
Paul Whitfield White. *Theatre and Reformation: Protestantism, Patronage, and Playing in Tudor England*. Cambridge: Cambridge University Press, 1993.

White 1998
Martin White. *Renaissance Drama in Action: An Introduction to Aspects of Theatre Practice and Performance*. London and New York: Routledge, 1998.

White 1999
Paul Whitfield White. "Reforming Mysteries' End: A New Look at Protestant Intervention in English Provincial Drama." *Journal of Medieval and Early Modern Studies* 29.1 (1999): 121–47.

White 2000
Paul Whitfield White. "Playing Companies and the Drama of the 1580s: A New Direction for Elizabethan Theatre History?" *Shakespeare Studies* 28 (2000): 265–84.

White 2004a
Paul Whitfield White. "The Bible as Play in Reformation England." In *The Cambridge History of British Theatre*, vol. 1: *Origins to 1660*, ed. Jane Milling and Peter Thomson, 87–115. Cambridge: Cambridge University Press, 2004.

White 2004b
Paul Whitfield White. "Holy Robin Hood! Carnival, Parish Guilds, and the Outlaw Tradition." In *Tudor Drama before Shakespeare, 1485–1590*, ed. Lloyd Edward Kermode, Jason Scott-Warren, and Martine van Elk, 67–89. Basingstoke, UK, and New York: Palgrave Macmillan, 2004.

White 2004c
Martin White. "London Professional Playhouses and Performances." In *The Cambridge History of the British Theatre*, vol. 1: *Origins to 1660*, ed. Jane Milling and Peter Thomson, 298–338. Cambridge: Cambridge University Press, 2004.

White 2006
Michelle Anne White. *Henrietta Maria and the English Civil Wars*. Aldershot, UK, and Burlington, VT: Ashgate, 2006.

White 2007
Philip Massinger. *The Roman Actor*. Ed. Martin White. Revels Plays. Manchester: Manchester University Press; New York: Palgrave, 2007.

White 2008
Paul Whitfield White. *Drama and Religion in English Provincial Society, 1485–1660*. Cambridge: Cambridge University Press, 2008.

Whitlock
Keith Whitlock. "The Theatrical Construction of a Cavalier Mentality in Fletcher's Plays and a Jonsonian Riposte." In *Post/Imperial Encounters: Anglo-Hispanic Cultural Relations*, ed. Juan E. Tazón Salces and Isabel Carrera Suárez, 63–85. Amsterdam and New York: Rodopi, 2005.

Whitney
Charles Whitney. *Early Responses to Renaissance Drama*. Cambridge: Cambridge University Press, 2006.

Whitworth 1984
Three Sixteenth-Century Comedies. Ed. Charles Walters Whitworth. New Mermaids. London: Ernest Benn; New York: Norton, 1984.

Whitworth 1996
George Peele. *The Old Wife's Tale*. Ed. Charles Whitworth. 2nd ed. New Mermaids. London: Black; New York: Norton, 1996.

Wickham 1964
Glynne Wickham. "*Exeunt to the Cave*: Notes on the Staging of Marlowe's Plays." *Tulane Drama Review* 8.4 (1964): 184–94.

Wickham 1972
Glynne Wickham. *Early English Stages, 1300 to 1660*. Vol. 2: *1576 to 1660*, part 2. London: Routledge; New York: Columbia University Press, 1972.

Wickham 1973
Glynne Wickham. "To Fly or Not to Fly?: The Problem of Hecate in Shakespeare's *Macbeth*." In *Essays on Drama and Theatre: Liber Amicorum Benjamin Hunningher*, ed. P. Binnerts et al., 171–82. Amsterdam: Moussault's; Antwerp: Standaard, 1973.

Wickham 1976
English Moral Interludes. Ed. Glynne Wickham. London: Dent; Totowa, NJ: Rowman and Littlefield, 1976.

Wickham 1979
Glynne Wickham. "'Heavens,' Machinery, and Pillars in the Theatre and Other Early Playhouses." In *The First Public Playhouse: The Theatre in Shoreditch, 1576–1598*, ed. Herbert Berry, 1–15. Montreal: McGill-Queen's University Press, 1979.

Wickham 1981
Glynne Wickham. *Early English Stages, 1300 to 1660*, vol. 3: *Plays and Their Makers to 1576*. London and Henley: Routledge; New York: Columbia University Press, 1981. Repr. London: Routledge, 2002.

Wickham et al.
Glynne Wickham, Herbert Berry, and William Ingram. *English Professional Theatre, 1530–1660*. Cambridge: Cambridge University Press, 2000.

Wiggins 1995
Martin Wiggins. "The Date of *A Cure for a Cuckold*." *Notes and Queries* 42.3 (1995): 377–78.

Wiggins 1996
Martin Wiggins. "The King's Men and After." In *Shakespeare: An Illustrated Stage History*, ed. Jonathan Bate and Russell Jackson, 23–44. Oxford: Oxford University Press, 1996.

Wiggins 1998
Four Jacobean Sex Tragedies. Ed. Martin Wiggins. Oxford English Drama. Oxford and New York: Oxford University Press, 1998.

Wiggins 2000
Martin Wiggins. *Shakespeare and the Drama of His Time*. Oxford Shakespeare Topics. Oxford and New York: Oxford University Press, 2000.

Wiggins 2003
John Ford. *'Tis Pity She's a Whore*. Ed. Martin Wiggins. 2nd ed. New Mermaids. London: Black; New York: Norton, 2003.

Wiggins 2004
Martin Wiggins. "Things That Go Bump in the Text: *Captain Thomas Stukely*." *Papers of the Bibliographical Society of America* 98.1 (2004): 5–20.

Wiggins 2008
Martin Wiggins, ed. *"A Woman Killed with Kindness" and Other Domestic Plays*. Oxford World's Classics. Oxford: Oxford University Press, 2008.

Wiggins & Lindsey
Christopher Marlowe. *Edward the Second*. Ed. Martin Wiggins and Robert Lindsey. 2nd ed. New Mermaids. London: Black; New York: Norton, 1997.

Wilcher
Robert Wilcher. *The Writing of Royalism, 1628–1660*. Cambridge: Cambridge University Press, 2001.

Wilders
William Shakespeare. *Antony and Cleopatra*. Ed. John Wilders. Arden. London and New York: Routledge, 1995.

Wiles 1981
David Wiles. *The Early Plays of Robin Hood*. Cambridge: Brewer, 1981.

Wiles 1987
David Wiles. *Shakespeare's Clown: Actor and Text in the Elizabethan Playhouse*. Cambridge: Cambridge University Press, 1987.

Wiley
Autrey Nell Wiley. *Rare Prologues and Epilogues, 1642–1700*. London: George Allen and Unwin, 1940.

Williams 1914
Jacke Jugeler. Ed. William Henry Williams. Cambridge: Cambridge University Press, 1914.

Williams 1966a
Thomas Middleton and William Rowley. *The Changeling.* Ed. George Walton Williams. RRDS. Lincoln: University of Nebraska Press, 1966.

Williams 1966b
The Woman Hater. Ed. George Walton Williams. In *The Dramatic Works in the Beaumont and Fletcher Canon,* gen. ed. Fredson Bowers, vol. 1. Cambridge: Cambridge University Press, 1966.

Williams 1977
"*Canterbury His Change of Diet.*" Ed. William P. Williams. *AEB: Analytical & Enumerative Bibliography* 1.1 (1977): 37–65.

Williams 1979
John Fletcher. *The Chances.* Ed. George Walton Williams. In *The Dramatic Works in the Beaumont and Fletcher Canon,* gen. ed. Fredson Bowers, vol. 4. Cambridge: Cambridge University Press, 1979.

Williams 1980
William P. Williams. "The Castle Ashby Manuscripts: A Description of the Volumes in Bishop Percy's List." *Library,* 6th ser., 2.4 (1980): 391–412.

Williams 1985
George Walton Williams, ed. *Rule a Wife and Have a Wife.* In *The Dramatic Works in the Beaumont and Fletcher Canon,* gen. ed. Fredson Bowers, vol. 6. Cambridge: Cambridge University Press, 1985.

Williams 1989
George Walton Williams, ed. *The Nice Valour.* In *The Dramatic Works in the Beaumont and Fletcher Canon,* gen. ed. Fredson Bowers, vol. 7. Cambridge: Cambridge University Press, 1989.

Williams 1992
William Proctor Williams. "Evidence of Performance." *English Language Notes* 30.1 (1992): 11–16.

Williams 1996
George Walton Williams, ed. *Rollo, Duke of Normandy.* In *The Dramatic Works in the Beaumont and Fletcher Canon,* gen. ed. Fredson Bowers, vol. 10. Cambridge: Cambridge University Press, 1996.

Williams 2000
Gweno Williams. "'No *Silent Woman*': The Plays of Margaret Cavendish, Duchess of Newcastle." In *Women and Dramatic Production, 1550–1700,* ed. Alison Findlay and Stephanie Hodgson-Wright, with eadem, 95–122. Harlow, UK: Pearson Education; New York: Longman, 2000.

Williams 2004a
M. E. Williams. "Field, Nathan (*bap.* 1587, *d.* 1619/20)." In *ODNB* 19: 481–82.

Williams 2004b
William Proctor Williams. "Manuche, Cosmo (*bap.* 1613, *d.* 1673?)." In *ODNB* 36: 569–70.

Williams 2007
Deanne Williams. "*Friar Bacon and Friar Bungay* and the Rhetoric of Temporality." In *Reading the Medieval in Early Modern England*, ed. Gordon McMullan and David Matthews, 31–48. Cambridge: Cambridge University Press, 2007.

Williamson
Elizabeth Williamson. *The Materiality of Religion in Early Modern English Drama*. Farnham, UK, and Burlington, VT: Ashgate, 2009.

Willis
R[obert] W[illis]. *Mount Tabor, or Private Exercises of a Penitent Sinner*. London: R[ichard] B[adger] for P. Stephens and C. Meredith, 1639.

Wilson 1952
William Shakespeare. *The First Part of King Henry VI*. Ed. J. Dover Wilson. Cambridge: Cambridge University Press, 1952.

Wilson 1969
F. P. Wilson. *The English Drama, 1485–1585*. Ed. G. K. Hunter. Oxford History of English Literature. Oxford: Clarendon Press, 1969.

Wilson 2000
Luke Wilson. *Theaters of Intention: Drama and the Law in Early Modern England*. Stanford: Stanford University Press, 2000.

Wilson 2010
Richard Wilson. "Cackling Home to Camelot: Shakespeare's Welsh Roots." In *Shakespeare and Wales: From the Marches to the Assembly*, ed. Willy Maley and Philip Schwyzer, 191–210. Farnham, UK, and Burlington, VT: Ashgate, 2010.

Wilson & Crow
Samuel Rowley. *When You See Me, You Know Me*. Ed. F. P. Wilson and John Crow. MSR. Oxford: Oxford University Press, 1952.

Wilson & Dobell
The Resurrection of Our Lord. Ed. J. Dover Wilson and Bertram Dobell. MSR. Oxford: Oxford University Press, 1912 [1913].

Wilson & Greg 1910
Thomas Lodge. *The Wounds of Civil War*. Ed. J. Dover Wilson and W. W. Greg. MSR. Oxford: Oxford University Press, 1910.

Wilson & Greg 1920
Ben Jonson. *"Every Man Out of His Humour" 1600*. Ed. J. Dover Wilson and W. W. Greg. MSR. Oxford: Oxford University Press, 1920 [1921].

Wine 1935
Celesta Wine. "Nathaniel Wood's *Conflict of Conscience*." *PMLA* 50.3 (1935): 661–78.

Wine 1964
John Marston. *The Malcontent*. Ed. M. L. Wine. RRDS. Lincoln: University of Nebraska Press, 1964.

Wine 1965
John Marston. *The Dutch Courtesan*. Ed. M. L. Wine. RRDS. Lincoln: University of Nebraska Press, 1965.

Wine 1973
The Tragedy of Master Arden of Faversham. Ed. M. L. Wine. Revels Plays. London: Methuen, 1973.

Winkelman
Michael A. Winkelman. *Marriage Relationships in Tudor Political Drama*. Aldershot, UK, and Burlington, VT: Ashgate, 2005.

Winn
James A. Winn. "Theatrical Culture 2: Theatre and Music." In *The Cambridge Companion to English Literature, 1650–1740*, ed. Steven N. Zwicker, 104–19. Cambridge: Cambridge University Press, 1998.

Winstanley
William Winstanley. *The Lives of the Most Famous English Poets, or the Honour of Parnassus; in a Brief Essay of the Works and Writings of Above Two Hundred of Them, from the Time of King William the Conqueror, to the Reign of His Present Majesty King James II*. London: Samuel Manship, 1687.

Winston 2005
Jessica Winston. "Expanding the Political Nation: *Gorboduc* at the Inns of Court and Succession Revisited." *Early Theatre* 8.1 (2005): 11–34.

Winston 2006
Jessica Winston. "Seneca in Early Elizabethan England." *Renaissance Quarterly* 59.1 (2006): 29–58.

Wiseman 1990
Susan J. Wiseman. "History Digested: Opera and Colonialism in the 1650s." In *Literature and the English Civil War*, ed. Thomas Healy and Jonathan Sawday, 189–204. Cambridge: Cambridge University Press, 1990.

Wiseman 1998a
Susan Wiseman. *Drama and Politics in the English Civil War*. Cambridge: Cambridge University Press, 1998.

Wiseman 1998b
Susan Wiseman. "'The Eccho of Uncertaintie': Jonson, Classical Drama and the English Civil War." In *Refashioning Ben Jonson: Gender, Politics and the Jonsonian Canon*, ed. Julie Sanders with Kate Chedgzoy and eadem, 208–29. Basingstoke, UK, and London: Macmillan; New York: St. Martin's Press, 1998.

The Wits
The Wits, or Sport upon Sport. Ed. John James Elson. Ithaca, NY: Cornell University Press; London: Humphrey Milford, 1932.

2 The Wits
The Wits, or Sport upon Sport, being a Curious Collection of Several Drols and Farces, Presented and Shewn for the Merriment and Delight of Wise Men and the Ignorant, as they have been sundry times acted in publique and private. London: Francis Kirkman, 1673.

Wolf 1980
William D. Wolf. "The Authorship of *The Mandrake* and *Leontius, King of Cyprus*." *The Library*, 6th series, 2.4 (1980): 456–60.

Wolf 1983
William D. Wolf. "Lord and Lady Northampton and Queen Henrietta's Men: An Approach to the Castle Ashby Plays." *Theatre Research International* 8.1 (1983): 17–22.

Wolfe 1958
Don M. Wolfe. "Unsigned Pamphlets of Richard Overton: 1641–1649." *Huntington Library Quarterly* 21.2 (1958): 167–201.

Wolfe 2006
Heather Wolfe. "Manuscripts in Early Modern England." In *A Concise Companion to Early Renaissance Literature*, ed. Donna B. Hamilton, 114–35. Oxford and Malden, MA: Blackwell, 2006.

Womack
Peter Womack. "Imagining Communities: Theatres and the English Nation in the Sixteenth Century." In *Culture and History, 1350–1600: Essays on English Communities, Identities and Writing*, ed. David Aers, 91–145. Hemel Hempstead, UK: Harvester Wheatsheaf, 1992.

Wood 1954
James O. Wood. "Thomas Fuller's Oxford Interlude." *Huntington Library Quarterly* 17.3 (1954): 185–208.

Wood 1987a
Karen Wood. "Henry Porter." In *Dictionary of Literary Biography* 62: *Elizabethan Dramatists*, ed. Fredson Bowers, 254–57. Detroit: Gale, 1987.

Wood 1987b
Karen Wood. "Lodowick Carlell." In *Dictionary of Literary Biography* 58: *Jacobean and Caroline Dramatists*, ed. Fredson Bowers, 45–50. Detroit: Gale, 1987.

Woodbridge 1984
Linda Woodbridge. *Women and the English Renaissance: Literature and the Nature of Womankind, 1540–1620*. Urbana and Chicago: University of Illinois Press, 1984.

Woodbridge 2007
Thomas Middleton. *A Chaste Maid in Cheapside*. Ed. Linda Woodbridge. In *Thomas Middleton and Early Modern Textual Culture: A Companion to the Collected Works*, gen. eds. Gary Taylor and John Lavagnino. Oxford: Clarendon Press, 2007.

Woods
Gillian Woods. "The Contexts of *The Trial of Chivalry*." *Notes and Queries* 54.3 (2007): 313–18.

Woodson
William Charles Woodson. "English Political Dialogues: 1641–1651: *The Kentish Fair*." *AEB: Analytical & Enumerative Bibliography* 8.1 (1984): 3–17.

Wootton
Christopher Marlowe. *Doctor Faustus*. Ed. David Wootton. Indianapolis and Cambridge: Hackett, 2005.

Worden 1987
A. B. Worden. "Literature and Political Censorship in Early Modern England." In *Too Mighty to Be Free: Censorship and the Press in Britain and The Netherlands*, ed. A. C. Duke and C. A. Tamse, 45–62. Britain and The Netherlands 9. Zutphen: De Walburg, 1987.

Worden 1994
Blair Worden. "Ben Jonson among the Historians." In *Culture and Politics in Early Stuart England*, ed. Kevin Sharpe and Peter Lake, 67–89. Basingstoke, UK, and London: Macmillan, 1994.

Worden 1999
Blair Worden. "Politics in *Catiline*: Jonson and His Sources." In *Re-Presenting Ben Jonson: Text, History, Performance*, ed. Martin Butler, 152–73. Basingstoke, UK, and London: Macmillan, 1999.

Worden 2006
Blair Worden. "Shakespeare in Life and Art: Biography and *Richard II*." In *Shakespeare, Marlowe, Jonson: New Directions in Biography*, ed. Takashi Kozuka and J. R. Mulryne, 23–42. Aldershot, UK, and Burlington, VT: Ashgate, 2006.

Worthen
W. B. Worthen. *Shakespeare and the Authority of Performance*. Cambridge: Cambridge University Press, 1997.

Wotton
Sir Henry Wotton, 1568–1639

Woudhuysen 1998
William Shakespeare. *Love's Labour's Lost*. Ed. H. R. Woudhuysen. Arden 3. Walton-on-Thames, UK: Nelson, 1998.

Woudhuysen 2004
H. R. Woudhuysen. "The Foundations of Shakespeare's Text." *Proceedings of the British Academy* 125 (2004): 69–100.

Wright 1699
See *Historia Histrionica*

Wright 1927a
Louis B. Wright. "Animal Actors on the Elizabethan Stage before 1642." *PMLA* 42.3 (1927): 656–69.

Wright 1927b
Louis B. Wright. "Elizabethan Sea Drama and Its Staging." *Anglia* 51 (1927): 104–18.

Wright 1928
Louis B. Wright. "Vaudeville Dancing and Acrobatics in Elizabethan Plays." *Englische Studien* 63.1 (1928): 59–76.

Wright 1934
Louis B. Wright. "The Reading of Plays during the Puritan Revolution." *Huntington Library Bulletin* 6 (1934): 73–108.

Wright 1944
Ghismonda: A Seventeenth-Century Tragedy. Ed. Herbert G. Wright. Manchester: Manchester University Press, 1944.

Wright 1968
Louis B. Wright. "Stage Duelling in the Elizabethan Theater." In *The Seventeenth-Century Stage: A Collection of Critical Essays*, ed. Gerald Eades Bentley, 156–69. Chicago and London: University of Chicago Press, 1968.

Wright & Halliwell
Thomas Wright and James Orchard Halliwell[-Phillips], eds. *Reliquiae Antiquae, Scraps from Ancient Manuscripts*. 2 vols. London: William Pickering, 1841–43.

Wymer
Rowland Wymer. "Jacobean Tragedy." In *A Companion to English Renaissance Literature and Culture*, ed. Michael Hattaway, 545–55. Oxford: Blackwell, 2001.

Wynne-Davies 1998
Marion Wynne-Davies. "'My Seeled Chamber and Dark Parlour Room': The English Country House and Renaissance Women Dramatists." In *Readings in Renaissance Women's Drama: Criticism, History, and Performance 1594–1998*, ed. S. P. Cerasano and eadem, 60–68. London and New York: Routledge, 1998.

Wynne-Davies 2000
Marion Wynne-Davies. "'My Fine Delitive Tomb': Liberating 'Sisterly' Voices during the Civil War." In *Female Communities 1600–1800: Literary Visions and Cultural Realities*, ed. Rebecca D'Monté and Nicole Pohl, 111–28. Basingstoke, UK: Macmillan; New York: St. Martin's Press, 2000.

Yachnin
Paul Yachnin. "Scandalous Trades: Middleton's *The Witch*, the 'Populuxe' Market, and the Politics of the Theater." *Medieval and Renaissance Drama in England* 12 (1999): 218–35.

Yamada 1975
George Chapman. *The Widow's Tears*. Ed. Akihiro Yamada. Revels Plays. London: Methuen, 1975.

Yamada 1980
Akihiro Yamada. "The Seventeenth-Century Manuscript Leaves of Chapman's *May-Day*, 1611." *Library*, 6th series, 2.1 (1980): 61–69.

Yeandle
Laetitia Yeandle. "The Dating of Sir Edward Dering's Copy of 'The History of King Henry the Fourth.'" *Shakespeare Quarterly* 37.2 (1986): 224–26.

Yearling
James Shirley. *The Cardinal*. Ed. E. M. Yearling. Revels Plays. Manchester: Manchester University Press, 1986.

Yoklavich
John Yoklavich, ed. *The Battle of Alcazar*. In *The Life and Works of George Peele*. Vol. 2. Gen. ed. Charles Tyler Prouty. 3 vols. New Haven, CT, and London: Yale University Press, 1961.

Young
A Critical Old-Spelling Edition of "A Match at Midnight." Ed. Stephen Blase Young. New York and London: Garland, 1980.

Younghughes & Jenkins
The Fatal Marriage. Ed. S. Brigid Younghughes and Harold Jenkins. MSR. Oxford: Oxford University Press, 1958 [1959].

Zimmerman
Susan Zimmerman. *The Early Modern Corpse and Shakespeare's Theatre*. Edinburgh: Edinburgh University Press, 2005.

Zitner 1984

Francis Beaumont. *The Knight of the Burning Pestle*. Ed. Sheldon P. Zitner. Revels Plays. Manchester: Manchester University Press, 1984. Repr. 2004.

Zitner 1993

William Shakespeare. *Much Ado about Nothing*. Ed. Sheldon P. Zitner. Oxford: Clarendon Press, 1993.